PRENTICE HALL
Chemistry
Connections to Our Changing World

H. Eugene LeMay, Jr.
Professor of Chemistry
University of Nevada
Reno, Nevada

Karen M. Robblee
Chemistry Writer
Waltham, Massachusetts

Herbert Beall
Professor of Chemistry
Worcester Polytechnic Institute
Worcester, Massachusetts

Douglas C. Brower
Former Assistant Professor of Chemistry
Catawba College
Salisbury, North Carolina

PRENTICE HALL
Upper Saddle River, New Jersey
Glenview, Illinois
Needham, Massachusetts

PRENTICE HALL
Chemistry
Connections to Our Changing World

Student Edition
Teacher's Edition
Teaching Resources
Laboratory Manual
Laboratory Manual, ATE
Solutions Manual
Color Transparencies
Classroom Manager
Molecular Model Set

Assessment Resources and Dial-A-Test®
   (includes CD-ROM)
ChemGuide: Essentials of Chemistry
   with Math Refresher
Interactive Student Tutorial
Chemistry Field Trips Videotapes (two volumes)
CHEMedia ™ Videodiscs
CHEMedia ™ Simulation Software

The illustration on the cover, rendered by Sonja Lamet and Nenad Jakesevic, represents the variety of ways in which chemistry is connected to our changing world—a world in which plants and animals, hot-air balloons, and fireworks are all related to chemistry.

Photo Credits begin on page 970.

ISBN 0-13-434776-5

4 5 6 7 8 9 10   02 01 00

STAFF CREDITS

The people who made up the *Chemistry: Connections to Our Changing World* team—representing editorial, design services, field marketing, managing editor, manufacturing/inventory planning, marketing services, on-line services/multimedia development, product marketing, and production services—are listed below. Bold type denotes core team members.

Allison Aydelotte, Kristin Ball, Christine Caputo, Rhett Conklin, Libby Forsyth, **Annemarie Franklin, Maureen Grassi,** Katherine Kotik, **Paula Massenaro,** Cindy Noftle, Ann Shea, Gerry Schrenk, Annette Simmons, Kathleen Ventura, and **Jane Walker Neff.**

ACKNOWLEDGMENTS   Many people contributed their ideas and expertise in the preparation of *Chemistry: Connections to Our Changing World*. Among them are the chemistry teachers, writers, and consultants whose names are listed here. Their contributions are gratefully acknowledged.

Panel of Experts

Pamela Benford
Cedar Grove High School
DeKalb County, Georgia

Michael De Stio
Half Hollow Hills CSD
Dix Hills, New York

Sam Febba
Eastern High School
Lansing, Michigan

Robert Forsythe
Warren East High School
Bowling Green, Kentucky

Katherine Ladd
Naperville North High School
Naperville, Illinois

Daniel R. Morton
Roseville Area High School
Roseville, Minnesota

Rosalind Philips
New Century High School
Lacey, Washington

Paul D. Prather
White Station High School
Memphis, Tennessee

Jay Salon
Miami Palmetto Senior High School
Miami, Florida

Linda Sinclair
Lexington High School
Lexington, South Carolina

Joseph Trebella
Cañon City High School
Cañon City, Colorado

Costella Watson
Tennyson High School
Haywood, California

College Reviewers

Toby Block
Georgia Institute of Technology
Atlanta, Georgia

Cynthia M. Friend
Harvard University
Cambridge, Massachusetts

Mary Kay Gleicher
Oregon State University
Corvallis, Oregon

Thomas J. Greenbowe
Iowa State University
Ames, Iowa

Kenneth E. Hyde
State University of New York
Oswego, New York

Jeffrey Kovac
University of Tennessee
Knoxville, Tennessee

Zaida Morales-Martinez
Florida International University
Miami, Florida

Dr. David M. Whisnant
Wofford College
Spartanburg, South Carolina

Howard P. Williams
University of Southern Mississippi
Hattiesburg, Mississippi

Secondary Reviewers

Steve Bender
Austin Community College
Chicago, Illinois

Howard Bugdon (retired)
Cornerbrook, Newfoundland, Canada

Charles Carrington
Sisler High School
Winnipeg, Manitoba, Canada

Frank Chambers
Aragone High School
San Mateo, California

Dick Christensen
Glenforest Secondary School
Mississauga, Ontario, Canada

Keith Chu
Sir Winston Churchill Secondary School
Vancouver, British Columbia, Canada

Peter E. Demmin
Amherst Central Senior High School
Amherst, New York

Carol Elliott
Burnaby South Secondary School
Burnaby, British Columbia, Canada

Lloyd Esralson
Burnaby North Secondary School
Burnaby, British Columbia, Canada

John Fesperman
George Washington High School
Danville, Virginia

Loch Gibb
North Surrey Secondary School
Surrey, British Columbia, Canada

Leona Groot
Gimli High School
Gimli, Manitoba, Canada

Michelle Hicks
Fort Lee High School
Fort Lee, New Jersey

Denny Holm
Grant High School
Portland, Oregon

John Ivany
St. Paul's Central High School
Gander, Newfoundland, Canada

Julia Lee
Science Editor
Prentice Hall Canada, Inc.

Barry McGavin
Sir Charles Tupper Secondary School
Vancouver, British Columbia, Canada

Bruce Miller
Bear Creek High School
Lakewood, Colorado

Jim Morwick
Humberside Collegiate
Toronto, Ontario, Canada

Tim Pschigoda
St. Joseph High School
St. Joseph, Michigan

Harold Rideout
Grand Falls Academy
Grand Falls, Newfoundland, Canada

Kevin Toope
Booth Memorial High School
St. John's, Newfoundland, Canada

Wilton Wong
Capuchino High School
San Bruno, California

Shirley N. Wrinkle
Reidland High School
Paducah, Kentucky

Unit Reviewers

Anna Kaplan (retired)
Skokie, Illinois

Jim Sikkema
Unity Christian High School
Hudsonville, Michigan

F. Lee Slick
Morgan Park High School
Chicago, Illinois

Samuel Weiner
Ramaz Upper School
New York, New York

Laboratory Safety Expert

James A. Kaufman
Director, Laboratory Safety Workshop
Natick, Massachusetts

Contributing Writer

Heather Hirschfeld
Science Writer
Durham, North Carolina

Solutions to Problems

Joseph Denchi
City University of New York
New York, New York

Lloyd Esralson
Burnaby North Secondary School
Burnaby, British Columbia, Canada

Kenneth May
Camden Central School
Camden, New York

Performance-Based Assessment

Karen Fujii
American High School
Fremont, California

Clark C. Mason
Milpitas High School
Milpitas, California

CONTENTS

UNIT 3   *Interactions of Matter* **222**

MATH

CHEMedia™ The Writing on the Wall

FEATURES

Laboratory Investigation

Connection—Science, Technology, and Society

Problem Solving—Chemistry at Work

ChemActivity

Welcome to Chemistry!

You are about to embark on an amazingly exciting journey into a world of discoveries and surprises—the world of chemistry. Throughout the pages of this textbook, you will come to understand the nature of matter and energy and the interactions between them. You will also gain an appreciation of the scientific process that has resulted in the body of knowledge we have today.

There is a great deal to learn between the covers of this textbook. Much care has been taken to write and present the concepts of chemistry in a manner that makes your learning easier. But you have an important role to play in the process too! You must learn to use your textbook effectively in order to get the most out of it. The following pages illustrate some of the features that were designed with you, the student, in mind.

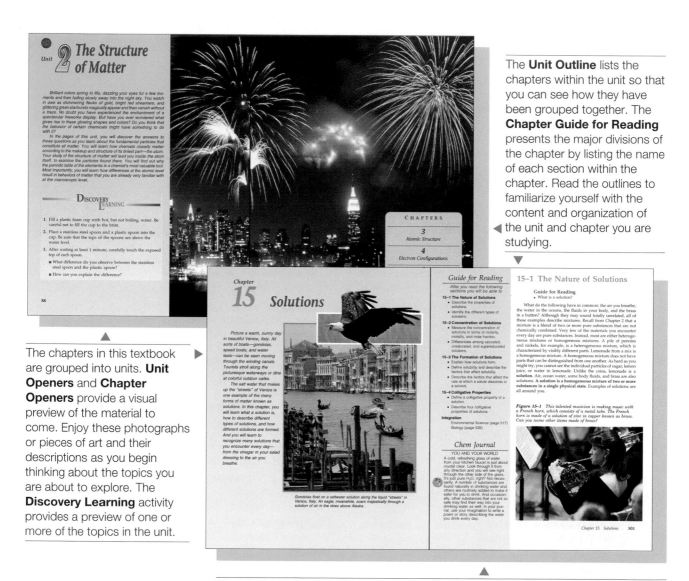

The **Unit Outline** lists the chapters within the unit so that you can see how they have been grouped together. The **Chapter Guide for Reading** presents the major divisions of the chapter by listing the name of each section within the chapter. Read the outlines to familiarize yourself with the content and organization of the unit and chapter you are studying.

The chapters in this textbook are grouped into units. **Unit Openers** and **Chapter Openers** provide a visual preview of the material to come. Enjoy these photographs or pieces of art and their descriptions as you begin thinking about the topics you are about to explore. The **Discovery Learning** activity provides a preview of one or more of the topics in the unit.

The **Chem Journal** gives you an opportunity to explore your knowledge, thoughts, and feelings about the chapter content or applications to which it relates. You should complete the activity as you begin the chapter and then revisit it once you have finished the chapter to find out if and how your responses may have changed.

Skim each section using the subtitles and the visuals along with their captions. Then as you read carefully, focus on the boldfaced **Key Ideas** and use them to discover answers to the **Guide for Reading** questions at the beginning of each section. Use the **Section Review** to test your knowledge of the material presented in the section.

2–3 Matter

One of the simplest observations anyone can make about the world is that it is filled with "stuff"—tables, chairs, books, soil, plants, animals (including ourselves), and so on. The "stuff" that such objects are made of is called matter. Everything you see around you is made of matter. **Matter is anything that has mass and volume.** As you will recall from Chapter 1, mass is the amount of material in an object, and volume is the amount of space the object occupies. A tree has a certain mass and occupies space, so it is composed of matter. So are cars, buildings, people, and anything else you see around you. Even air is made of matter.

What is matter? Why does it exist? These questions have occupied philosophers and scientists for thousands of years, but the full answer has still not been found. We accept the existence of matter, although we do not completely understand it. This textbook is devoted to studying the characteristics of matter. As part of this examination, we will describe the composition of matter at more and more microscopic levels. But we cannot answer all the questions about matter. Some of these questions have been answered by the work of physicists, and we hope you pursue this knowledge in further science courses. Other answers, however, still lie beyond the probing of science.

What humans have learned about the nature of matter is a fascinating story of discovery and painstaking effort. Some of the crucial experiments that were performed in an effort to understand matter are among the most important contributions of science to our understanding of the universe. You will learn about these experiments in upcoming chapters.

Guide for Reading
- What is matter?
- What is the law of conservation of matter?

Figure 2–11 *What do a bridge, a wolf, and redwood trees have in common? They are all made of matter. Matter—its structure and interactions—is the subject of this textbook.*

Chapter 2 *Energy and Matter* 65

15–2 Section Review

1. Define the concentration of a solution. Describe three methods of measuring concentration.
2. What is a saturated solution? An unsaturated solution? A supersaturated solution?
3. **Connection—Economics** When too many restaurants open in the same neighborhood, you may hear someone say that the market for restaurants is saturated. Explain what is meant by the statement and relate it to saturated solutions.

MATH TOOL KIT
Focusing on the Basics

The lake near your home is slowly becoming polluted by an oil-tank leak. You want to determine how quickly the water is being polluted. Each time you return from the lake, you carefully analyze the water and soil samples to determine the amounts of various chemicals present. You then compare these measurements with the data from previous visits, and also with similar data from other sources. From these comparisons, you will be able to draw significant conclusions about the current condition of the lake. Your studies may raise other questions, leading to more and better experimentation.

Only by the use of accurate measurements can scientists like you *do science*. From making observations and gathering and analyzing data, to comparing and confirming results, scientists rely on accurately measured numbers. Almost always, a series of calculations must be performed on the data to obtain meaningful results.

To help you acquire the basic math skills that will enable you to succeed in chemistry, we have organized the rest of Chapter 1 into a Math Tool Kit. The Math Tool Kit will help you practice and apply simple math concepts to your study of chemistry. The Math Tool Kit contains the following topics:

1–4 Units of Measurement
1–5 Uncertainty in Measurement
1–6 Working With Numbers
1–7 Problem Solving

You may want to go through the next four sections of this chapter at your own pace, making sure that you have mastered the concepts and acquired the skills as you proceed.

MATH

As you read this textbook, look for the Math Tip feature in the margin. The Math Tip will provide information that will aid you in your study of chemistry. It will help you solve sample and practice problems or simplify mathematical operations or concepts presented in the textbook.

Visit the Prentice Hall Web site at **http://www.phschool.com** to find material that will support, enhance, and enrich your study of chemistry.

The **Math Tool Kit** introduces you to the sections in Chapter 1 that help you brush up on some basic math skills. Use the **Math Tip** features located in the margin throughout the text to get helpful hints on how to solve sample and practice problems, or how to clarify mathematical operations or concepts. The **Internet Resources** feature reminds you to visit our Web site to find more ways to be successful in your study of chemistry.

CONNECTION
SCIENCE TECHNOLOGY AND SOCIETY

Ups and Downs Down Under

Visit the beautiful continent of Australia and you will discover a cute and fuzzy problem—rabbits. Years ago, there were no rabbits at all in Australia. To fill the void, people eventually brought rabbits onto the continent. It may have seemed like a good idea at the time, but all too soon the flaw in the plan was evident. Within...

number of animals in a particular population is generally constant over time, the actual number changes in a continual cycle. The population increases and decreases away from the equilibrium value. At one part of the cycle, the prey population grows so large that prey are numerous and easy to find. As predators...

The relationship between predators and prey may be violent, but it serves to keep their populations in check.

Connection—Science, Technology, and Society will give you the opportunity to further apply the chemistry concepts you are learning and the thinking skills you are developing to understand and evaluate current topics in your world. Experience chemistry as a process as well as a body of knowledge as you conduct **Laboratory Investigations.** Some of these are "Design-an-Experiment" investigations that enable you to create and perform your own experimental setups.

Laboratory Investigation DESIGNING an EXPERIMENT

Experimenting With Voltaic Cells

Problem
How can you construct and compare voltaic cells?

Suggested Materials *(per group)*

voltmeter
4 plastic drinking cups
strips of the following metals:
  magnesium
  copper
  zinc
  lead
  aluminum
  iron
6 wire leads with alligator clips
electrolyte solutions:
  sports drink
  club soda
  cola
  salt water solution

Suggested Procedure

1. Devise an experiment to construct and compare several voltaic cells.
2. Write down the steps of your experimental procedure. The drawing may provide you with some help in writing your procedure. Try to make at least four different cells using different combinations of metals and electrolytes.
3. Prepare a data table similar to the one shown to record your data.
4. Conduct your experiment after having your teacher approve your procedure and data table.
5. From your data, determine the voltaic cell with the highest voltage.

Observations

Cell Number	Metal A	Metal B	Electrolyte	Voltmeter Reading
1				
2				
3				
4				
5				

Analysis and Conclusions

1. What metal combinations produced the highest voltage? The lowest voltage?
2. Use a table of reduction potentials as a reference. For each cell that you constructed, do you notice any relationship between relative locations of the two metals in the table and the voltmeter reading?
3. For each cell that you constructed, use the table of reduction potentials to write the two half reactions and calculate the cell potential. How do your voltmeter readings compare to this value? Give reasons for the differences.
4. Write the net ionic equation for each of your cells.
5. Identify the anode and cathode for each battery.
6. Compare your data with that of others in your class. Which metal combination that produces the highest voltage? Which electrolyte worked the best?
7. Describe what takes place at the electrodes and in the electrolyte in a voltaic cell.
8. Predict which would make a better cell—one with copper and zinc electrodes or one with copper and iron? Explain your answers.
9. **On Your Own** Test these two cells. Do your results support your predictions?

The **Integrating** feature located in the margin helps to identify areas where chemistry relates to other sciences such as biology, earth science, environmental science, and physics. Answer the questions provided in order to make sure that you fully understand the relationship. A list of Integrations for each chapter is provided below the Chapter Guide for Reading.

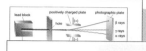

Figure 3–13 An electrical field splits the radiation emitted by a sample into three components. How do the three types of radiation differ from one another?

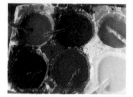

Figure 9-20 The artist using these paints must really get into her work! Paints are chemical compounds produced by double-replacement reactions.

INTEGRATING
ENVIRONMENTAL SCIENCE

How do you think burning gasohol instead of gasoline in your automobile helps the environment?

Activity

Atomic Models

1. Using simple materials—poster board, cardboard, construction paper, colored pencils, string, cotton balls—construct models of Thomson's plum pudding atom and Rutherford's nuclear atom.
2. Label the parts of your models and display them in your classroom. Include a brief description of Thomson's and Rutherford's experiments with each model.

100

Exploration

How Sweet It Is

1. Place one or two spoonfuls of sugar into an old pan.
2. Heat the sugar for about 3 to 5 minutes in the presence of an adult. Follow all applicable safety precautions when using heat.
3. Observe and record any changes that occur as the sugar is heated.
4. Let the pan cool for several minutes. What do you observe in the pan? What happened to the sugar? Did a chemical reaction take place? How do you know?
5. Meats such as beef and chicken brown when they are cooked. Use your observations from this activity to form a hypothesis as to why such browning occurs. Research this phenomenon to find out if your hypothesis is correct.

Some Exceptions to the Rule

As you know by now, just about every rule in science has an exception. The rules governing chemical reactions are no different. Although the majority of chemical reactions that you will encounter in your study of chemistry fit nicely into one of the four categories of chemical reactions, there are many reactions that do not. For example, many of the direct combination reactions we used as examples were combustion reactions—reactions in which something burned. But not all combustion reactions are necessarily direct combination reactions. The example of the combustion of methane, which we used to describe how to balance equations, is not a direct combination reaction. Two reactants combine, but more than one product is formed. In fact, this reaction does not fit into any of the four categories of reactions.

Consider another combustion reaction in which gasohol burns in a car's engine. Gasohol is a type of fuel that is made up of regular unleaded gasoline and alcohol. It is intended to burn a little more cleanly in order to release fewer pollutants and so protect the environment. The alcohol in gasohol burns according to the following equation:

$$C_2H_5OH + 3 O_2 \rightarrow 2 CO_2 + 3 H_2O \qquad (Eq. 29)$$

While the reactant side of this equation resembles many of the direct combination reactions we have described, the product side of the equation shows two products instead of one. This cannot be a direct combination, nor can it be a decomposition, single-replacement, or double-replacement reaction.

In later chapters, you will learn about other reactions that do not fit neatly into one of the four categories described in this section. For now all you need to recognize is that not every chemical reaction must fit into one of these four categories.

The **ChemActivity** and **ChemExploration** features located in the margin enable you to perform hands-on and minds-on activities to enhance your study of chemistry. These activities will also help you to understand that chemistry is a far-reaching science that impacts upon almost every aspect of life.

CHEMISTRY IN ACTION

YOU AND YOUR WORLD

Spare Tires

What happens to old automobile tires? The answer often is "not much." Today's tires are made from synthetic rubbers, which typically are complex hydrocarbon polymers. These polymers are designed to be strong, durable, airtight, and resistant to extremes in temperature. But while such qualities help the tires on the road, they make tires all the more difficult to dispose of. Used tires often end up piled on top of each other in dumps or landfills.

Call an auto junkyard or rubbish removal company and ask what they do with old tires. Find out if your community is trying any novel ways to use, destroy, or recycle tires.

Figure 25-27 An ethene monomer can undergo an addition polymerization reaction to form polyethylene, which is used to make trash bags and other products.

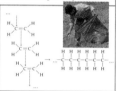

Other synthetic polymers have a wide variety of different properties and uses. Polyethylene is a lightweight, inexpensive polymer used to make such items as trash bags and plastic containers. Polyvinyl chloride is used as plastic wrap because it can be made into a thin film that adheres well to itself. Polymethyl methacrylate is a polymer valued for its transparency and resistance to shattering. It is used as a substitute for glass. Another well-known polymer is Teflon™, which is used as a nonstick finish on metal cookware.

The two principal methods of synthesizing polymers are addition polymerization and condensation polymerization. Addition polymerization begins with an unsaturated monomer that contains a double bond. In a catalyzed reaction, the double bond of one monomer breaks. Then one of its carbon atoms forms a single bond to a carbon atom on an adjacent monomer. This new single bond breaks the second monomer's double bond, which induces it to unite with a third monomer. The third monomer unites with a fourth, and on and on the reaction continues. The chain reaction is outlined in Figure 25–27. Addition polymerization can proceed almost indefinitely, uniting thousands and thousands of monomers into a single, enormous molecule.

Polyethylene is one polymer formed by the addition polymerization method. The monomer of polyethylene is ethene (CH_2=CH_2), which under the right circumstances will form a chain of thousands of –CH_2– groups, each united by a single bond to the next. Polyvinyl chloride, polystyrene, and Teflon are other polymers formed by addition polymerization.

828

CHEMISTRY IN ACTION

CONSUMER TIP

Microwave Ovens

A microwave oven is an appliance that heats food by penetrating it with short radio waves. These waves cause the water molecules in food to vibrate and rotate rapidly, thus creating heat. Because microwaves pass through glass, paper, and most types of china and plastics, containers made of these materials can be used to hold food in microwave ovens. Metal cookware not onl...

Chemistry in Action—Consumer Tip and **You and Your World** features enable you to discover some of the numerous ways in which chemistry is involved in your daily life, either directly or indirectly.

Problem Solving *Chemistry at Work*

A Fishy Situation

Your neighbor has gone on vacation for a week and has asked you to take care of her aquarium. The aquarium is filled with water and contains a few fishes and plants. Unfortunately, your neighbor forgot to tell you whether the water is fresh water or salt water and you need to know before adding any more water. You cannot analyze the water by smell and you certainly do not want to taste the water! Devise a method of determining which type of water is in the aquarium using only materials available in the kitchen.

An understanding of chemistry and an ability to think about and solve problems like a chemist will always be useful to you, no matter what goals you pursue in life. Use **Problem Solving—Chemistry at Work** to develop the thinking skills you will find necessary in all areas of learning.

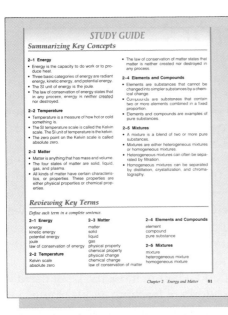

The key concepts in each section of a chapter are listed in the **Summarizing Key Concepts** to help you review the chapter content. Vocabulary terms are important to your understanding of chemistry. The key terms that were boldfaced throughout the chapter are listed in **Reviewing Key Terms**.

Throughout the chapter, you have several opportunities to solve a **Sample Problem** involving chemistry concepts. Follow along as the first problem is worked out for you and then solve two similar **Practice Problems** on your own.

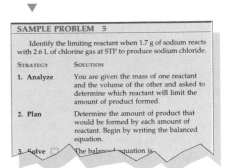

Test your knowledge of the facts presented in the chapter by answering the **Content Review** questions. Then evaluate your understanding of the concepts and apply your knowledge to the **Critical Thinking and Problem Solving** questions.

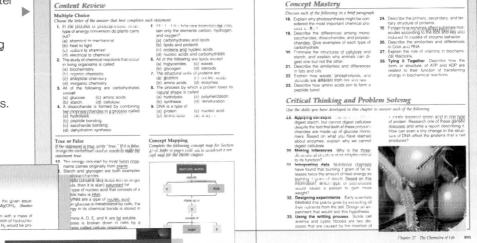

The **Problem Bank**, which appears in selected chapters, and the **Practice Problems**, which appear on pages 900–931, provide you with additional problems. The problems in the Problem Bank are divided into two groups, Group A and Group B. To check your solutions, the answers to selected problems in Group A and in Group B are provided in Appendix G at the back of the textbook. The Practice Problems are grouped according to chapter section.

About the Authors

H. Eugene LeMay, Jr., was born in 1940 in Tacoma, Washington. He attended public schools in the Tacoma area, graduating from Clover Park High School in 1958. Throughout his public schooling, he had an interest in science and mathematics as well as in writing. His earliest acquaintance with chemistry came through experiments with a chemistry set when he was in junior high school. It was the fun, logic, challenge, and excitement of his high-school chemistry course, however, that really focused his interests on chemistry. (Thank you, Mr. Reeves.)

LeMay attended Pacific Lutheran University in Tacoma, intending to take two years of study and then transfer to obtain a degree in chemical engineering. Instead, he stayed at P.L.U. and completed his Bachelor of Science degree in chemistry in 1962. He then entered graduate school at the University of Illinois, where he majored in inorganic chemistry. He obtained his Master of Science degree in 1964 and his Ph.D. degree in 1966. Since that time, he has taught at the University of Nevada in Reno, where he is presently Professor of Chemistry. He has also enjoyed Visiting Professorships in Chemistry at the University of North Carolina at Chapel Hill, the University College of Wales in Great Britain, and the University of California at Los Angeles.

LeMay is a popular and effective teacher, who has taught thousands of students and won several university teaching awards during more than 30 years of teaching. He is also a co-author of two college textbooks, *Chemistry: The Central Science*, which was first published in 1977 and is now in its sixth edition, and *Qualitative Inorganic Analysis*, which was published in 1985. *Chemistry: The Central Science* has been used by more than a million college and Advanced Placement students during its many editions, and it has been translated into Spanish, German, Russian, Italian, and Korean. LeMay is also the author of 30 research publications and review articles, mainly in the area of solid-phase reactions.

LeMay and his wife, Carla, live in Reno, where they have raised two sons and a daughter. When not teaching and writing, LeMay enjoys photography and hiking.

Herbert Beall was born in 1939 in Chatham, Ontario, Canada. His family moved to Appleton, Wisconsin, when he was six years old, and he now considers himself to be a Wisconsin native. He attended the University of Wisconsin in Madison where he received a Bachelor of Science degree in chemistry in 1961. Beall then attended Harvard University where he specialized in the chemistry of boron and received a Ph.D. in 1967. His first job was at Olin Corporation in New Haven, Connecticut, where he continued working on boron chemistry in the high-temperature polymers program.

After a year and a half in industry, Beall decided to return to the world of teaching and learning, and in 1968 joined the faculty of Worcester Polytechnic Institute in Worcester, Massachusetts, where he has been teaching ever since. In 1974 he spent an exciting year on leave from WPI as a visiting lecturer of chemistry at the University of Canterbury in Christchurch, New Zealand. At WPI he has taught inorganic chemistry courses and has been particularly active in teaching general chemistry to freshmen. Beall is very interested in finding ways to use writing in the teaching of chemistry and has published a number of articles on this subject in educational journals. In addition to this textbook, he is also the author of an introductory college chemistry textbook and a book on reading and writing about chemistry. His research is in the area of inorganic chemistry, particularly the chemistry of boron and the inorganic chemistry of coal. He has published more than 35 research papers and given talks throughout the United States, as well as in Europe and the South Pacific.

Beall enjoys running, cross-country skiing, and playing guitar. He and his wife, Barbara, spend part of the year in Worcester and part in Mineral Point, Wisconsin. They have three daughters, one of whom lives in Philadelphia, one in Chicago, and one who is on a Peace Corps assignment in Botswana in southern Africa.

Karen M. Robblee received a Bachelor of Science degree in biochemistry from the University of New Hampshire in 1985 and a Master of Arts in Teaching from the University of New Hampshire in 1987. She began teaching in Exeter, New Hampshire, in 1986 and currently teaches first year and Advanced Placement chemistry at Millbrook High School in Raleigh, North Carolina.

Robblee has conducted workshops on laboratory safety and writing in science, and has had articles published in *The Science Teacher*. She also served as science consultant for the development of the North Carolina Food Science curriculum and has worked with industry representatives from nearby Research Triangle Park to acquaint students with career opportunities in science.

Robblee has been active in Girl Scouts, Cub Scouts, and the PTA. She has also served as a class advisor and is currently the sponsor of her school's Chemistry Club. With her two children now in college, she has more time to devote to writing, reading, gardening, and getting her doctorate at Boston University.

Douglas C. Brower was born in Melbourne, Australia, in 1958. He attended high school in Jakarta, Indonesia, graduating from the Joint Embassy School in 1976. During his senior year, he was co-captain of the rugby team. His interest in chemistry was sparked by his chemistry teacher. Brower earned a Bachelor of Science degree in chemistry at Grinnell College in 1980, studying compounds containing amino acids and platinum ions. At the University of North Carolina at Chapel Hill, he earned a Ph.D. in chemistry in 1986, studying the interactions of small organic molecules with molybdenum and tungsten ions.

Brower has taught chemistry at the University of Wisconsin—Oshkosh, at Catawba College, and at Jordan-Matthews High School in Siler City, North Carolina. He is past Secretary of the Rowan-Cabarrus-Stanly Science Alliance, and he is a member of the North Carolina Science Teachers Association. He has published more than 12 scientific papers in journals such as *The Journal of the American Chemical Society, Inorganic Chemistry,* and *Organometallic Chemistry.*

With his wife, Debbie, Brower lives in a small house on 10 wooded acres in Chatham County, North Carolina. He enjoys playing guitar and penny whistle.

To the Student

Dear Reader,

We wrote this textbook to help you gain a greater knowledge of chemistry. We say "greater knowledge" because we know that your daily experiences have already taught you a lot about chemistry! The science of chemistry offers a point of view that organizes and explains many of the common observations of daily life. Your life will be richer when viewed from chemistry's powerful perspective.

But chemistry is more than a catalog of what has already been seen and explained by others. It encompasses a community of people working to expand what is known about the world. This is for us the most exciting aspect of chemistry. Searching for new scientific knowledge—by combining thoughtful questions, clever experiments, and careful analysis—is a gratifying and deeply human activity.

By taking up this textbook, you have joined the community of chemistry for a time. You will have many opportunities to hone your questioning and problem-solving skills as you study. These skills are crucial to making chemistry fun. Yes, we mean it: Chemistry is fun! And when you are finished, we hope you will consider chemistry in your future plans—the world needs good chemists!

H. Eugene LeMay, Jr.   Karen M. Robblee
Herbert Beall   Douglas C. Brower

Concept Mapping in Chemistry

Throughout your study of chemistry, you will learn a variety of terms, facts and figures, and concepts. Each new topic you encounter will provide its own collection of words and ideas—which, at times, you may think seem endless. But each of the ideas within a particular topic is related in some way to the others. No concept in chemistry is isolated. Thus, it will help you to understand the topic if you see the whole picture; that is, the interconnectedness of all the individual terms and ideas. This is a much more effective and satisfying way of learning than memorizing separate facts.

Actually, this should be a rather familiar process for you. Although you may not think about it in this way, you analyze many of the elements in your daily life by looking for relationships or connections. For example, when you look at a collection of birds, you may divide them into groups: pigeons, cardinals, and crows. You may then associate colors with these birds: gray, red, and black. The general topic is birds. The subtopic is types of birds. And the colors are specific terms that describe these birds. A topic makes more sense and is more easily understood if you understand how it is broken down into individual ideas and how these ideas are related to one another and to the entire topic.

It is often helpful to organize information visually so that you can see how it all fits together. One technique for describing related ideas is called a **concept map.** In a concept map, an idea is represented by a word or phrase enclosed in a box. There are several ideas in any concept map. A connection between two ideas is made with a line. A word or two that describes the connection may be written on or near the line. The general topic is located at the top of the map. That topic is then broken down into subtopics, or more specific ideas, by branching lines. The most specific topics are located at the bottom of the map.

To construct a concept map, first identify the important ideas or key terms in the chapter or section. Do not try to include too much information. Use your judgment as to what is really important. Write the general topic at the top of your map. Let's use an example to help illustrate this process. Suppose you decide that the key terms in a section you are reading are chemistry, chemical reactions, states of matter, acids and bases, chemical formulas, chemical equations, gases, liquids, solids, salts, sour, bitter. The general topic is chemistry. Write and enclose this word in a box at the top of your map.

CHEMISTRY

Now choose the subtopics—chemical reactions, states of matter, acids and bases. Figure out how they are related to the topic. Add these words to your map. Continue this procedure until you have included all the appropriate ideas and terms. Then use lines to make the appropriate connections between ideas and terms. Don't forget to write a word or two on or near the connecting lines to describe the nature of the connection.

Do not be concerned if you have to redraw your map (perhaps several times!) before you show all the important connections clearly. If, for example, you write chemical formulas for acids and bases as well as for chemical reactions, you may want to place these two subtopics next to each other so that the lines do not overlap.

One more thing you should know about concept mapping: Concepts can be correctly mapped in many different ways. In fact, it is unlikely that any two people will draw identical concept maps for a complex topic. Thus, there is no one correct concept map for any topic! Even though your concept map may not match those of your classmates, it will be correct as long as it shows the most important concepts and the clear relationships among them. Your concept map will also be correct if it has meaning to you and if it helps you understand the material you are reading. A concept map should be so clear that if some of the terms are erased, the missing terms could easily be filled in by following the logic of the concept map.

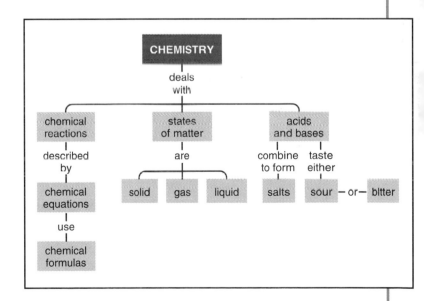

Unit 1 The Nature of Chemistry

What in the world, you may be thinking, does an ordinary candle have to do with the nature of chemistry? Well, you might be surprised! The great English chemist and physicist Michael Faraday has written, "There is no better, there is no more open door by which you can enter into the study of natural philosophy [science], than by considering the physical phenomena of a candle." In 1860, in fact, Faraday devoted his annual series of Christmas Lectures to "The Chemical History of a Candle." As Faraday knew, careful observations of even the simplest phenomena can tell you a lot about the world around you.

This unit is a sort of prelude—an introduction to the world of chemistry. In the chapters that follow, you will learn some of the basic techniques you will need as you proceed in your study of chemistry. You will learn how to work safely and efficiently in a chemistry laboratory, as well as how to make careful measurements and calculations. And you will learn about the interactions of the two basic concepts in chemistry—energy and matter—both of which are illustrated nicely by a burning candle!

DISCOVERY LEARNING

1. Fill a glass half full with water.

2. Light a small candle. Observe the flame until it appears to be burning steadily and evenly.

3. Hold the glass of water above the candle flame. Slowly lower the glass until the bottom of the glass is in the center of the flame. Hold the glass there for about 1 second, then lift it out of the flame.

4. Blow out the candle.

   ■ What do you observe on the bottom of the glass?

   ■ How can you explain your observations?

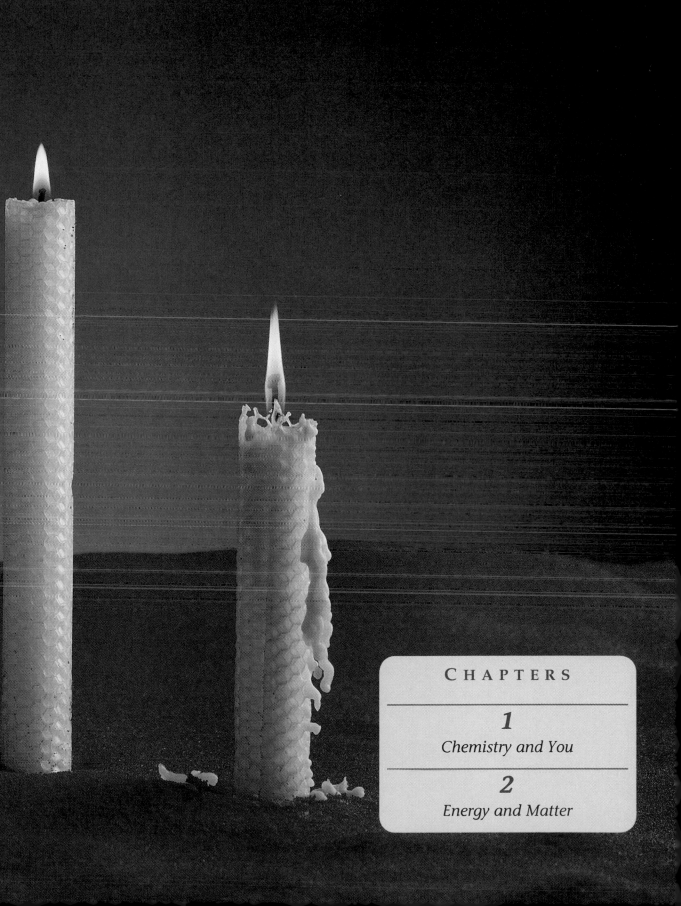

1 Chemistry and You

Think about how you have changed since you were born. Especially in the last few years, you may have noticed many wondrous changes taking place in your body. How did all these changes happen?

To fully understand these changes, you would have to look carefully at the substances that make up your body. You would have to follow a particle of food as it is digested and then changed into living tissue. You would have to learn how light and sound waves become chemical signals that your brain interprets and stores as memories.

In other words, you would have to study chemistry.

Chemistry is going on all around you—and inside you as well! The energy that allows these young people to work—and play—comes from chemical reactions.

Chem Journal

YOU AND YOUR WORLD
Do you think chemistry has anything to do with your day-to-day life? In your journal, describe a typical day. Then try to identify situations during the day in which chemistry somehow played a part. After you finish this chapter, go back to your journal and ask yourself if you would change or add to your entry based on what you learned in the chapter.

1–1 What Is Chemistry?

Guide for Reading
- Why is chemistry often called the central science?

Medicines that cure diseases, fibers that go into your clothing, even the complex substances that make up your body—all are chemicals. Chemistry is the study of substances such as these. In fact, **chemistry** is the study of all substances and the changes that they can undergo.

Like all sciences, chemistry begins with curiosity. Why does a match burst into flame when it is scraped against a rough surface? Why can a stain on your favorite shirt be removed by laundry bleach? As you know, even quite ordinary substances can undergo dramatic changes. In this textbook, you will learn the reasons for changes such as these and many others.

Chemistry in Action

Chemistry is a broad science that touches nearly every aspect of human life. Throughout this textbook you will find many examples of professions and hobbies that require or use a knowledge of chemistry. We will give just two examples here.

EXAMINING A WETLANDS HABITAT   As Joanie guides her canoe to an open patch of water, a light wind twitches the cattails

Figure 1–1   *Under hot, dry conditions, just one tiny spark—whether from lightning or from a neglected campfire—may result in a devastating forest fire. A fire is a drastic example of how everyday substances can undergo dramatic changes.*

Figure 1–2 This peaceful wetlands scene may look tranquil and inviting, but has the swamp been damaged by harmful chemicals from an oil spill? Careful analysis of samples in the chemistry laboratory may provide the answer.

on the banks of the swamp. Picking up a long-handled scoop, she leans over the side to collect some sediment. The black ooze she brings up goes into a collection jar, which joins other jars of water and soil samples in a box at her feet. The samples will help her decide how badly the swamp has been damaged by fuel oil that leaked from a storage tank some distance away.

Joanie does not call herself a chemist—she is a wetlands ecologist—but when she returns to the laboratory, she will focus on the chemicals in her samples. She will measure the amount of oil in the water and the soil. She is trying to determine how quickly the oil is breaking down into less toxic, or harmful, substances in the water and soil.

Joanie's chemical analysis suggests that oil-eating bacteria are active in the swamp. With help from these tiny organisms and other natural processes, Joanie hopes, the habitat will gradually rid itself of the contamination.

PRESERVING HISTORICAL ARTIFACTS Joanie is not the only person interested in the swamp. Linda and Spencer are also working there, studying a canoe that sank 300 years ago.

Like Joanie, Linda and Spencer are not chemists—they are archaeologists—but they are also concerned with chemistry. They must decide what chemicals they should use to preserve the canoe. The wood looks strong, but it is not. Tiny gaps have formed in the wood where some of the fibers have decayed. The canoe is like a house with every other brick knocked out. It will collapse if it is simply hauled out of the swamp and left to dry.

The method they choose for preserving the canoe is simple and inexpensive, and the process creates no chemical hazards. These are all important considerations. First the canoe is removed from the swamp and placed into a long tank. Over a period of months, Linda and Spencer soak the canoe in a sugar solution. The sugar gradually fills the gaps in the wood and hardens. Now the canoe can be safely dried and exhibited. But one potential problem still remains. Can you guess what this might be? At the museum, the canoe is put into a special "bug-proof" case. Why? Because to some insects, the canoe now looks like a huge candy bar!

The Central Science

As you have seen, archaeologists such as Linda and Spencer must understand the properties of the materials they are trying to preserve. Similarly, wetlands ecologists such as Joanie must know how to analyze substances that threaten the environment.

Chemistry plays a role in these professions and in many others as well. **Chemistry has been called the central science because it overlaps so many sciences.** Whether your career interests are in science, engineering, public service, or some other occupation, chances are good that you will need a knowledge of

chemistry. Hair stylists, for example, need to know some chemistry so that they can handle hair relaxers and permanent wave solutions safely and correctly. Construction engineers use chemistry when they select the right cement for a particular job. Biologists learn chemistry so that they will understand the chemical processes that go on in living things. Can you think of any other occupations in which a knowledge of chemistry might be helpful?

If you have a strong interest in chemistry itself, you may decide to become a professional chemist. But what kind of chemist? Chemists are employed in dozens of occupations. Chemists work for police departments to help solve crimes and for perfume makers to help formulate new fragrances. Some chemists, called research chemists, investigate new substances that may not have any practical use yet. Research chemists create new scientific knowledge. The applications of this knowledge, if any, lie in the future. It is research chemists who have given us many of the wonderful new materials that have made our lives easier.

Figure 1–3 *Here you see two different aspects of chemistry. A research chemist working in a pharmaceutical laboratory searches for new drugs to treat disease and improve the quality of human life. How do you think a knowledge of chemistry helps the firefighters in their job?*

Figure 1–4 *Autumn brings with it a spectacular transformation in the appearance of the northeastern forests, as leaves exchange their ordinary green color for a blaze of red, orange, and yellow.*

Why Study Chemistry?

You have seen that chemistry can play a role in many different areas of life. But there is another reason why you should learn chemistry. Chemistry is fun! Chemistry will help you to understand what makes leaves change color in the fall, why icebergs float, and how the food you eat turns into muscle (and sometimes fat) in your body. Chemistry can help you look at the world in ways you may never have imagined. We hope that by the time you finish this textbook, you will see why chemistry can and should play an important role in your life.

The work ahead may seem overwhelming now, but you should not be discouraged. Here are a few hints to keep in mind as you begin your study of chemistry. First, do not try to memorize a collection of isolated facts. You will find the task much easier if you concentrate on understanding concepts, not memorizing facts. Second, remember that chemistry is first and

Cleaning Priceless Art

The dramatic scenes that Michelangelo depicted on the ceiling and upper walls of the Sistine Chapel are among the finest artistic achievements in history. Since they were first unveiled in 1512, generations of art lovers have gone to Rome to see Michelangelo's masterpiece. Over time, however, dust and greasy soot from burning candles and oil lamps gradually covered Michelangelo's work, darkening the paintings.

A visitor to the Sistine Chapel when the paintings were new described a typical reaction: "It was such as to make everyone speechless with astonishment." Now, after nearly 500 years, visitors can once again view Michelangelo's paintings in the same bright, glowing colors that they originally had.

What took Michelangelo, working alone, four years to paint required a team of specialists more than 14 years to clean and restore. One of the most useful materials in the restoration effort was a mild cleanser made of baking soda and other ingredients mixed with water to form a dripless gel. Several applications of the cleanser were often needed to remove the grime completely from sections of the ceiling and walls. This cleaning agent, which has been

available to art restorers for only about 20 years, was particularly suited to the job of restoring the Sistine Chapel. Its dripless formula allowed exact quantities to be applied where they were needed without the chance of streaks spreading any dirt away from the area being cleaned.

But some people actually miss the old, dirty look. They feel that the paintings had more depth and mystery when they were covered with dust and soot. And some art historians fear that much of Michelangelo's original work has been damaged in the cleaning process. What do you think?

foremost a process of discovery. Think of it as a journey into the unknown. Many fascinating and exciting sights await you. So sit back, relax, and enjoy the trip!

1–1 Section Review

1. What is chemistry?
2. How can a knowledge of chemistry help a wetlands ecologist or an archaeologist do her job?
3. Suppose you know a hair stylist who tells you that in his profession he has no need to understand chemistry. What arguments would you use to convince him that he is mistaken?
4. **Theme Trace—Unity and Diversity**   In your own words, explain why chemistry is sometimes called the central science.

1–2 The Scientific Method

Guide for Reading
- What is the scientific method?
- What are the steps of the scientific method?

More than 150 years ago, the English chemist and physicist Michael Faraday (1791–1867) made crucial discoveries that led to the invention of the electric motor. Think how important electric motors are today: refrigerators, automobile starters, hair dryers, and video equipment all rely on electric motors. Yet when Faraday demonstrated his discoveries, none of these machines had been invented. Houses were not even wired for electricity! The new scientific knowledge Faraday gathered did not have any immediate practical value. The value of Faraday's work lay in its potential for further growth and future applications. As it turned out, although he could not have imagined it, Faraday's discoveries changed the world completely.

The tremendous potential of science comes from the way in which scientific knowledge is gathered. Scientists follow an orderly and systematic approach called the **scientific method** to gather knowledge. With this approach, new ideas about the world are constantly checked against reality. Just what is the scientific method? **The scientific method is a way of answering questions about the world we live in.** Refer to Figure 1–6 on page 8 as you read about the steps of the scientific method.

Figure 1–5 *When Michael Faraday made the basic discoveries that led to the invention of the electric motor, he could not possibly have imagined the many applications his work would have in the future.*

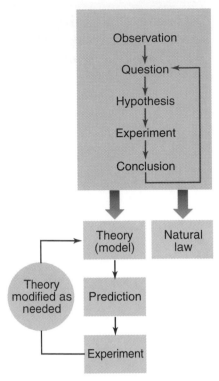

Figure 1–6 *This diagram outlines the steps of the scientific method. It is important to remember that although the scientific method appears clear-cut and orderly, in real life the process is not always so tidy! Scientists do not always follow the steps in exactly this order and they may occasionally skip a step. Remember that the real value of the scientific method is that it provides a framework for learning about nature.*

Steps of the Scientific Method

The scientific method consists of a series of steps that can be summarized as follows:

- First a scientist makes an **observation.**
- The observation leads to a question. (Because science begins with curiosity, the question may come first.)
- Thinking about the question produces a **hypothesis,** a tentative answer to the question.
- The scientist tests the hypothesis with an **experiment.** As part of an experiment, the scientist carefully records and analyzes data, or information, gathered in the experiment.
- The experiment produces a result, or a **conclusion,** which the scientist interprets carefully. The result may raise new questions and lead to new hypotheses and new experiments.
- After a number of experiments, the scientist may be able to summarize the results in a **natural law,** which describes how nature behaves but does not explain why nature behaves in that particular way.
- Finally, the scientist may be able to formulate a **theory.** The theory explains why nature behaves in the way described by the natural law. It answers not only the original question, but also any other questions that were raised during the process. The theory also predicts the results of further experiments, which is how it is checked.

Let's see how the scientific method might work in practice. Where could we go to make our first observation? The kitchen might be a good place to start!

Making an Observation

You are going to cook an onion. If you cannot actually do this activity now, read along anyway and perform it when you can.

Before you begin, a word of caution: Accidents can happen in the kitchen (and in the chemistry laboratory) when you are tired, trying to hurry, or unsure of the correct procedure. Read the recipe below carefully, stay alert, and work patiently. Ask an adult to help you get started if you are not accustomed to working alone in the kitchen. Working in a small group might also be helpful.

Obtain an onion, a knife and cutting board, a frying pan, a long-handled wooden spoon, and some vegetable oil or margarine. Chop the onion into pieces. Be very careful in using the knife. If the onion is fresh, watch out! Your eyes may sting from a sharp, smelly gas that is released when the onion is cut. Now taste a small piece of the onion. Some people actually like the strong taste of a raw onion. Do you?

Put a tablespoon of oil in the pan and cook the onion slowly over medium heat. Stir the pieces with the spoon so they heat evenly. In about 10 minutes, the onion should start turning brown. Continue cooking for another 10 minutes, then put the onion on a plate and let it cool.

Figure 1–7 *Have you ever wondered why cooked onions taste different from raw onions? It may surprise you to learn that you can follow the scientific method in your own kitchen in an attempt to answer this question. What observations can you make about sliced onions before (top) and after (bottom) they are cooked?*

Now taste the cooked onion. Notice that the flavor is completely different from the raw onion. In fact, it tastes sweet! But you never added sugar. All you did was heat the onion for a few minutes with a little oil. So here is your observation: The cooked onion tastes sweet. And the question is simply this: Why does a cooked onion taste sweet?

Forming a Hypothesis

Following the scientific method, you should now form a hypothesis to answer your question. Before you do, though, let's notice two things. First, the observation is not especially exotic or "scientific." All you have done is notice something curious about the flavor of a cooked onion. Scientific inquiries often start in this rather humble way—by simply wondering about day-to-day occurrences.

Second, notice that the question carries some emotional force. You want to know the answer. You have no idea whether it will be useful or important, but you want to know the answer anyway. Humans are naturally curious. The scientific method gives us a framework in which we can productively exercise our natural curiosity.

Recall that a hypothesis is a tentative answer to a question. A hypothesis is usually expressed in the form of a "cause-and-effect" statement. Remember, you must be able to test your hypothesis with an experiment. The experiment must be conducted openly, of course, with no hidden tricks or secret procedures, so that anyone who repeats the experiment can obtain the same results.

In this case, you want to know what causes the sweet taste of the cooked onion. One possibility is that the onion contains sugar. Because the raw onion does not taste sweet, the sugar might be in the form of starch. Starch is a substance made of sugar that many plants (such as potatoes) use to store food. You might guess that cooking the onion converts some of the starch into sugar. So your hypothesis would be as follows: The sweet taste is caused by the presence of starch in the onion, which is converted to sugar by cooking.

The next step is to test your hypothesis. Beware of hypotheses that cannot be tested! They are not true hypotheses at all because they break the chain of steps in the scientific method. Hypotheses that cannot be tested by an experiment do not belong in science. Let's stop for a moment to explore this important idea further in the following Sample Problem.

Activity
CHEM

Observations on Paper

A Frenchman visiting North America in 1719 observed some paper wasps building a nest. He made the following entry in his diary: "The American wasps form a very fine paper. . . . They teach us that paper can be made from the fibers of plants without the use of rags and linens, and seem to invite us to try whether we cannot make fine and good paper from the use of certain woods." How would you apply the scientific method to study this observation? Write a paragraph describing an investigation you could perform, including the question, hypothesis, and experiments you would propose.

SAMPLE PROBLEM 1

Which of the following hypotheses about the sweet taste of a cooked onion are testable? (More than one correct choice is possible.)

   (a) The sweet taste is caused by a chemical reaction between the onion and the oil.

   (b) A bitter spirit that inhabits the raw onion is driven away when the onion is cooked. The cooked onion tastes sweet because the bitter spirit is no longer present in the onion.

   (c) The sweet taste is caused by cooking the onion.

   (d) The sweet taste comes from the oil. It has nothing to do with the onion.

STRATEGY	SOLUTION
1. **Analyze**	You are given several possible hypotheses and asked to decide which are testable. Recall that a hypothesis is a "cause-and-effect" statement that poses a tentative answer to the question. The hypothesis is tested by an experiment. The experiment must be designed so that anyone can repeat it and obtain the same result.
2. **Plan**	Read each hypothesis carefully and try to imagine how it could be tested.
3. **Solve**	Answer (a) could be tested by cooking the onion without oil in a "no-stick" frying pan. Answer (b) cannot be tested because it is impossible to design an experiment to detect a "bitter spirit." Answer (c), although it is a true statement, merely restates the question, so it is not a hypothesis. Finally, answer (d) could be tested by heating the oil alone for the same length of time and at the same temperature used to cook the onion. Thus, the only testable hypotheses are (a) and (d).
4. **Evaluate**	The word cause is used in a particular way in science, whereas the word can have a broader meaning in general. Although answer (b) is not an acceptable hypothesis in a scientific sense, it is possible to imagine a society that did believe in such spirits. In that society, answer (b) could be thought correct. Should you dismiss the statement as

"wrong" because it cannot be tested? No. It is better to say instead that the statement is not scientific. Scientific knowledge, for all its power and potential, is just one branch of human understanding. Hypotheses that are not testable have no value in science, yet they may be very valuable in other aspects of human life.

PRACTICE PROBLEMS

1. In 1786, Benjamin Franklin wrote a letter to an English friend describing some observations he had made. Here is part of the letter:

   "In America I have often observ'd that on the Roofs of our shingled Houses, where Moss is apt to grow in northern Exposures, if there be anything on the Roof painted with white Lead, there is constantly a streak on the Shingles from such Paint down to the Eaves, on which no moss will grow, but the wood remains constantly clean and free from it."

   Think of a question and a hypothesis for this observation. *(Be sure your question is logical and your hypothesis is testable.)*

2. Think of a question and a hypothesis for each of the following observations:

   (a) You sneeze every time you visit your best friend's house.

   (b) On a cold morning, the air pressure in the tires of an automobile measures 34 pounds per square inch. After several hours of high-speed driving, the pressure measures 38 pounds per square inch. *(Be sure your question is logical and your hypothesis is testable.)*

Figure 1–8 Here you see the results of the starch-iodine test for onion, cornstarch, and potato. How would you describe the results of this test for each sample?

Performing an Experiment

How can you test your hypothesis about the sweet taste of a cooked onion? There are at least two ways. One way is to see whether onions do in fact contain starch. Can you think of another way?

Let's see what happens if you choose the first way to test your hypothesis. Starch will be the **variable,** or the factor being tested, in your experiment. A sensitive test for starch is called the starch-iodine test. A drop of iodine solution will turn blue-black in the presence of even tiny amounts of starch.

The result of the starch-iodine test on a slice of raw onion is shown in Figure 1–8. As you can see, a drop of iodine solution does not turn blue-black when it is added to a slice of onion.

Results of Iodine Test

Substance Tested	Color*
Onion slice	Red
Cornstarch	Blue-black
Potato slice	Blue-black

*Blue-black indicates presence of starch.

Figure 1–9 *The table lists the results of the starch-iodine test shown in Figure 1-8. Scientists often find it helpful to record their results in a data table such as this. Why do you think summarizing results in a table is a useful way to record data?*

Exploration

A Secret Message

1. Using a toothpick as a pen and milk as your ink, write a secret message on a blank sheet of white paper.

2. Observe what happens to your message as the milk dries.

3. Turn on a desk lamp and hold the paper close to the light bulb. Observe what happens.

4. State your observations in the form of a question and formulate a hypothesis to explain your observations.

5. Design an experiment to test your hypothesis.

Interpreting the Result

The result of the starch-iodine test on raw onion suggests that there is no starch in an onion after all. But you should be careful not to jump to this conclusion. How do you know that the starch-iodine test actually works? To answer this question, you could place a drop of iodine solution on a small amount of cornstarch, also shown in Figure 1–8. This test acts as an **experimental control.** A control responds in a predictable way to the experiment. In this case, the iodine turns blue-black in the presence of cornstarch, just as expected. So you can be confident that the iodine solution is capable of detecting starch in the onion. But just to be really certain, let's try one more test. You know that potatoes are "starchy" vegetables. In fact, potatoes are just one of many plants that store sugar in the form of starch. What do you think would happen if you placed a drop of iodine solution on a slice of raw potato? You are correct if you said that the iodine would turn blue-black. The table in Figure 1–9 summarizes the results of the starch-iodine test.

Even with an experimental control, however, you need to interpret the experiment carefully. All you can really say is that the amount of starch in the onion may be less than the smallest amount that the starch-iodine test can detect. Nevertheless, because the starch-iodine test is very sensitive, it seems doubtful that the hypothesis is correct.

To pursue the problem further, you would have to formulate a new hypothesis based on more thinking, questioning, and observing. As before, you would perform an experiment to test your new hypothesis. Finally, you might see the results of many experiments start to fit together like the scattered pieces of a jigsaw puzzle.

Laws and Theories

When the pieces of a jigsaw puzzle are in place, a picture emerges that could not be seen in the separate pieces. Likewise, a natural law draws together many observations and the results of many experiments into a "big picture." But the natural law does not explain what the picture means. A theory provides this explanation. You can think of a theory as a sort of "super-hypothesis."

Can a theory be wrong, even after all the work that goes into it? Yes. Knowledge gained through the scientific method is tentative. This means that it is open to revision. A theory about the flavor of cooked onions, for example, might make false predictions. If it did, you would have to modify the theory or discard it.

Some theories are so well established that their predictions are not expected to be disproven. The atomic theory, which underpins all of chemistry, is such a theory. Even the atomic theory continues to evolve, however, as scientists learn more about atomic structure. We will discuss the atomic theory in more detail in Chapter 3.

Are you still curious about what really makes a cooked onion taste sweet? The sweet flavor is due to several different kinds of sugar that are present in a raw onion, but not in the form of starch. It will probably surprise you to learn that a slice of onion can contain up to half as much sugar as a slice of ripe fruit! You cannot normally taste the sugar in a raw onion because the onion's sharp, tear-provoking gas overwhelms your sense of taste. Cooking destroys the ability of the onion to make the gas and allows you to taste the sugar.

Doing Science

Science is a process—something that people do. Do you think you can "do science" in your daily life? The answer is yes. You have many opportunities for observing and wondering about natural events around you. For example, suppose you are walking down a city street and you notice big blue garbage bags filled with plastic bottles piled high on the sidewalk. You might wonder: What happens to all the plastic products we throw away every day? How would you go about finding out?

It does not matter whether you live in a big city, in a small town, or on a farm in the country. It does not matter whether the events occur inside your kitchen or outside your home. When you notice something interesting, let your natural curiosity—and the scientific method—help you to investigate.

There is one more important thing to keep in mind when you think about doing science. You know that when you cook something in your kitchen, you must follow certain common-sense safety rules. In the same way, when you work in a laboratory, you must follow some safety rules and procedures. Because you will be performing many laboratory investigations as you study chemistry, we will examine safety in the chemistry laboratory next.

Figure 1–10 *Wherever you are—at home, at school, or just walking along a beach—try to find the time to observe and ask questions about the world around you.*

1–2 Section Review

1. What is the scientific method?
2. List the steps of the scientific method.
3. What is a variable? An experimental control?
4. What is the difference between a natural law and a scientific theory?
5. **Connection—You and Your World** Use the steps of the scientific method to explain this observation: A steel wool soap pad eventually becomes rusty after you use it several times.

Guide for Reading

- What are the basic safety rules you must follow in the chemistry laboratory?

YOU AND YOUR WORLD

Familiar Symbols

Before beginning your work in the chemistry laboratory, you must become familiar with the safety symbols used in this textbook. But the idea of using symbols to transmit information should come as no surprise to you. In fact, you are probably already familiar with the use of many different types of symbols in your everyday life—from traffic signs to road maps. What other types of symbols can you think of?

1–3 Safety in the Laboratory

As a part of daily living, you have a lot of experience working with tools. In the kitchen, for example, you may use a knife and a cutting board to chop vegetables for a salad. With a little common sense, these tools are safe to handle and the kitchen is a safe, even fun, place to be. The chemistry laboratory is very much the same.

Listed below are ten of the most important rules for safe conduct in the chemistry laboratory. An Appendix in the reference section provides further information and instructions regarding safety procedures.

- **Follow Your Teacher's Directions**
- **Notify Your Teacher of Problems**
- **Know How to Use the Safety Equipment in the Laboratory**
- **Wear Approved Safety Goggles**
- **If You Have Long Hair, Tie It Back**
- **Avoid Awkward Transfers of Chemicals**
- **If It's Hot, Let It Cool**
- **Carry Chemicals With Caution**
- **Dispose of Chemical Wastes Properly**
- **Clean up Afterward**

This short set of basic rules cannot anticipate every possible laboratory hazard, so your teacher will announce special safety precautions for particular experiments. Even so, having a safe laboratory environment always means more than just following rules. You should "think safety." That is, always keep safety in mind when you work in the laboratory.

The safety symbols that will be used in the laboratory investigations throughout this textbook are shown in Figure 1–12. An explanation of each symbol is also provided. As you may imagine, you should be familiar with these symbols before you first set foot in the laboratory.

Figure 1–11 *In the chemistry laboratory, as in a woodworking shop, safety should be a prime consideration! What safety precautions would you recommend in this situation?*

SAFETY CLOTHING
This symbol is to remind you to wear a laboratory apron over your street clothes to protect your skin and clothing from spills.

 SAFETY GOGGLES
This symbol is to remind you that safety goggles are to be worn *at all times* when working in the laboratory. For some activities, your teacher may also instruct you to wear protective gloves.

 GLOVES
This symbol is to remind you to wear gloves to protect your hands from contact with corrosive substances, broken glass, or hot objects.

 HEATING
This symbol indicates that you should be careful not to touch hot objects with your bare hands. Use either tongs or heat-proof gloves to pick up hot objects.

 FIRE
This symbol indicates the presence of an open flame. Loose hair should be tied back or covered, and bulky or loose clothing should be secured in some manner.

 CORROSIVE SUBSTANCE
This symbol indicates a caustic or corrosive substance—most frequently an acid. Avoid contact with skin, eyes, and clothing. Do not inhale vapors.

 BREAKAGE
This symbol indicates an activity in which the likelihood of breakage is greater than usual, such as working with glass tubing, funnels, and so forth.

 DANGEROUS VAPORS
This symbol indicates the presence of or production of poisonous or noxious vapors. *Use the fume hood* when directed to do so. Care should be taken not to inhale vapors directly. When testing an odor, use a wafting motion to direct the vapor toward your nose.

 EXPLOSION
This symbol indicates that the potential for an explosive situation is present. When you see this symbol, read the instructions carefully and *follow them exactly*.

 POISON
This symbol indicates the presence of a poisonous substance. Do not let such a substance come in contact with your skin and do not inhale its vapors.

 ELECTRICAL SHOCK
This symbol indicates that the potential for an electrical shock exists. Read all instructions carefully. Disconnect all apparatus when not in use.

 RADIATION
This symbol indicates a radioactive substance. Follow your teacher's instructions as to proper handling of such substances.

 DISPOSAL
This symbol indicates that a chemical should be disposed of in a special way. Dispose of these chemicals as directed by your teacher.

 HYGIENE
This symbol is to remind you to always wash your hands after completing a laboratory investigation. Never touch your face or eyes during a laboratory investigation.

Figure 1–12 *You will see many of these safety symbols again in the Laboratory Investigations at the end of each chapter in this textbook. Study the symbols carefully now so that you will know which safety precaution to follow as you proceed.*

1-3 Section Review

1. List ten basic safety rules that you must follow in the chemistry laboratory.

2. Why do you think it is important to tie back long hair and roll up loose sleeves when you are working in the laboratory?

3. **Connection—You and Your World**   How could you apply the basic safety rules for performing an experiment in a chemistry laboratory to baking a cake in your kitchen or changing a tire on a car?

MATH TOOL KIT
Focusing on the Basics

The lake near your home is slowly becoming polluted by an oil-tank leak. You want to determine how quickly the water is being polluted. Each time you return from the lake, you carefully analyze the water and soil samples to determine the amounts of various chemicals present. You then compare these measurements with the data from previous visits, and also with similar data from other sources. From these comparisons, you will be able to draw significant conclusions about the current condition of the lake. Your studies may raise other questions, leading to several hypotheses and further experimentation.

Only by the use of accurate measurements can scientists like you "do science." From making observations and gathering and analyzing data, to comparing and confirming results, scientists rely on accurately measured numbers. Almost always, a series of calculations must be performed on the data to obtain meaningful results.

To help you acquire the basic math skills that will enable you to succeed in chemistry, we have organized the rest of Chapter 1 into a Math Tool Kit. The Math Tool Kit will help you practice and apply simple math concepts to your study of chemistry. The Math Tool Kit contains the following topics:

1–4 Units of Measurement

1–5 Uncertainty in Measurement

1–6 Working With Numbers

1–7 Problem Solving

You may want to go through the next four sections of this chapter at your own pace, making sure that you have mastered the concepts and acquired the skills as you proceed.

Avogadro's number	6.02×10^{23}
Speed of light in a vacuum	3.00×10^{8} m/s
Atomic mass unit (amu)	1.66054×10^{-27} kg
Charge of an electron	1.60×10^{-19} C
Mass of an electron	9.11×10^{-31} kg 5.486×10^{-4} amu
Mass of a proton	1.6726×10^{-27} kg 1.0073 amu
Mass of a neutron	1.6749×10^{-27} kg 1.0087 amu
Planck's constant (h)	6.6262×10^{-34} J-s
Gas Constant (R)	0.08206 atm-L/mol-K 8.314 Pa-m³/mol-K 8.314 J/mol-K
Molar volume of a gas at STP	22.4 L

$T(K) = T(°C) + 273$
Density = Mass/Volume
Planck's Equation: $E = h\nu$
Ideal Gas Law: $PV = nRT$
$pH = -\log[H_3O^+]$
$\Delta G = \Delta H - T\Delta S$

1–4 Units of Measurement

Guide for Reading

- What units are used in science for measuring length, mass, and volume?
- What are metric prefixes? How are they used?

As you will find, measurements are an integral part of science. A measurement consists of a number and a unit. For example, a basketball player might easily be seven feet tall. In this measurement, "seven" is the number and "feet" is the unit. Both a number and a unit are always needed to make sense of a measurement. You would know there was something wrong if you read that someone was six inches tall. And what would you think if you read that someone was six tall?

How tall are you? You probably know this measurement best in units of feet and inches. These units are part of the English system of measurement. (Actually, this name is misleading because the English have now abandoned it.) The English system is not used in science. Instead, an international system of measurement called the **metric system** is preferred.

Recall what you read about Joanie's research in Section 1–1. When Joanie returned to the laboratory after collecting her soil and water samples, she made several measurements using the units of the metric system. This system is like an international language spoken by all scientists because it establishes a common system of measurement that all scientists understand. When Joanie uses the metric system for her measurements, other scientists who read her results will understand the significance of her work more easily.

Figure 1–13 *Workers at the New York Zoological Society must make careful temperature measurements in order to preserve the frozen embryos of endangered species (left). Without a system of measurement, you would have no way of knowing just how tall basketball star Alonzo Mourning (right) really is.*

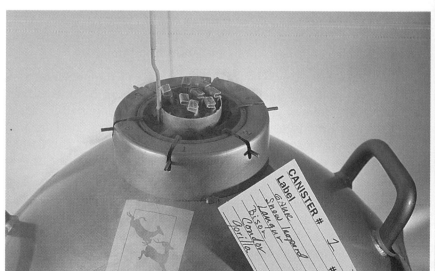

Figure 1–14 *The table lists the SI base units as well as some derived units. What is the basic SI unit of temperature?*

SI Base Units	
Physical Quantity	**Unit Name and Symbol**
mass	kilogram, kg
length	meter, m
time	second, s
count, quantity	mole, mol
temperature	kelvin, K
electric current	ampere, A
luminous intensity	candela, cd

Derived Units Commonly Used in Chemistry	
Physical Quantity	**Unit Name and Symbol**
area	square meter, m^2
volume	cubic meter, m^3
force	newton, N
pressure	pascal, Pa
energy	joule, J
power	watt, W
voltage	volt, V
frequency	hertz, Hz
electric charge	coulomb, C

Figure 1–15 *Although these floating astronauts have lost weight, their mass is the same in orbit as it was on Earth. What is the difference between mass and weight?*

The International System of Units

In 1960, the units of the metric system were streamlined by an international conference. The conference created a system of units called the **International System of Units,** abbreviated **SI** (after the French *Système International d'Unités*). The SI is built upon a set of seven metric units, which are called the **base units** of the SI. These base units are listed in Figure 1–14.

LENGTH The SI base units are carefully defined. **The meter (abbreviated m) is the basic SI unit of length.** One meter is currently defined as the distance that light travels in a vacuum during a time interval of 1/299,792,458 of a second. This is approximately the distance between a doorknob and the floor, or in English units, 3.3 feet—a little more than one yard.

MASS AND WEIGHT The amount of material in an object is called its **mass.** Like the unit of length, the SI unit of mass is carefully defined. **The unit of mass, the kilogram (abbreviated kg), is a base unit of the SI.** At the surface of the Earth, one kilogram weighs about 2.2 pounds. But note that mass and weight are not the same. As you have just read, the mass of an object is simply the amount of material in the object. The weight of an object is equal to the force of gravity pulling on the object.

If a 1-kilogram wrench is carried into space, it no longer weighs 2.2 pounds. The force of attraction due to Earth's gravity—the weight of the wrench—depends on the distance between the wrench and the Earth. In space, the wrench is "weightless" because it is so far from Earth that the force of gravity seems to disappear. The amount of material in the wrench, however, is the same on Earth and in space, so its mass does not change.

AREA AND VOLUME: DERIVED UNITS In addition to the seven base units, other SI units can be made from combinations of the base units. In the SI, a combination of base units is called a **derived unit.** To find the area of a rectangle, for example, you would multiply its length by its width. The area of a rectangle 5.0 meters long and 3.0 meters wide would be

$$\text{area} = \text{length} \times \text{width} \qquad \textbf{(Eq. 1)}$$
$$= 5.0 \text{ m} \times 3.0 \text{ m}$$
$$= 15 \, (\text{m} \times \text{m})$$
$$= 15 \text{ m}^2$$

Notice that both the numbers and the units are multiplied together in calculating the area. The derived SI unit for area is the square meter (m^2). It is a derived unit because it is a combination of base units.

Other common derived units are summarized in the table in Figure 1–14. **The SI unit of volume is the cubic meter (abbreviated m^3).** The **volume** of an object is the amount of space that it occupies. A washing machine has a volume of about one cubic meter (1 m^3).

The Units Used in This Textbook

Following international practice, most of the units used in this textbook will be SI units. However, there are some exceptions. These exceptions are listed in the table in Figure 1–16. This might be a good time to mention exceptions in science. We would like to be able to tell you that science is based on rules and that once you learn these rules, you will know everything there is to know about science. Unfortunately, this is not the case! Science is a process, not a collection of rules. You will find as you study chemistry that there are exceptions to most rules.

A non-SI unit frequently encountered in chemistry is the liter (L), which is a unit of volume. One liter is slightly larger than a quart. There are exactly 1000 liters (1000 L) in 1 cubic meter.

Another non-SI unit often used in chemistry is the Celsius degree (C°), which is a unit of temperature. We will discuss this unit and other non-SI units as they are needed in your study of chemistry.

INTEGRATING
PHYSICS

Have you ever wondered why astronauts in orbit appear weightless?

Figure 1–16 The table lists some common non-SI units that are often used in chemistry. You will encounter some of these units in this textbook.

Non-SI Units Frequently Encountered in Chemistry	
Physical Quantity	**Unit Name and Symbol***
volume pressure	liter, L atmosphere, atm millimeters of mercury, mm Hg
temperature energy	Celsius degree, C° calorie, cal

*For conversion factors between these units and SI units, see Figure 1–29 on page 38.

Figure 1–17 *Metric prefixes—word parts used to make a unit larger or smaller—are shown in this table. What is the prefix that means one thousandth?*

Common Metric Prefixes Used in Chemistry

Prefix	Abbreviation	Meaning*	
mega-	M	1 000 000	or 10^6
kilo-	k	1 000	or 10^3
		1	
deci-	d	0.1	or 10^{-1}
centi-	c	0.01	or 10^{-2}
milli-	m	0.001	or 10^{-3}
micro-	μ	0.000 001	or 10^{-6}
nano-	n	0.000 000 001	or 10^{-9}
pico-	p	0.000 000 000 001	or 10^{-12}

*Scientific, or exponential, notation used in the last column is reviewed in Section 1–6.

Figure 1–18 *Do you think milliliters would be an appropriate unit to use to measure the volume of oil that must be removed after a spill? What unit might you use to measure the mass of an iceberg?*

Metric Prefixes

The base SI units are not always convenient to use. For example, to travel from her laboratory to the swamp, Joanie must drive about 10,000 meters (a little more than 6 miles). This measurement can be written in a more compact way using a **metric prefix.** (Recall from your study of language arts that a prefix is a word attached to a base word to change its meaning.) A metric prefix is attached to the base unit, creating a more convenient, easier-to-use unit. Prefixes can make the new unit larger or smaller than the base unit.

PREFIXES THAT MAKE THE UNIT LARGER   The prefix *kilo-* (k) means 1000. Therefore, 1 kilometer (1 km) equals 1000 meters. In kilometer units, Joanie's 10,000-meter trip could be written as 10 kilometers.

$$10 \text{ km} = 10 \times 1000 \text{ m} = 10,000 \text{ m} \qquad \textbf{(Eq. 2)}$$

Other metric prefixes that make a unit larger are shown in the table in Figure 1–17.

PREFIXES THAT MAKE THE UNIT SMALLER   Metric prefixes can also decrease the size of a unit. As part of an experiment to measure the amount of oxygen dissolved in the swamp water, for instance, Joanie adds small volumes of several chemicals to a sample of the swamp water. The metric prefix *milli-* (m) means one thousandth, 1/1000, or 0.001. One milliliter (1 mL) is equal to 0.001 liter (0.001 L). When small volumes are involved, the milliliter unit is more convenient than the liter unit. For example, 3 milliliters is easier to write and remember than 0.003 liter.

Another common metric prefix is *centi-* (c) meaning one hundredth, 1/100, or 0.01. One cubic centimeter (1 cm^3) is the same volume as one milliliter (1 mL). Other metric prefixes that make a unit smaller are also shown in the table in Figure 1–17. What does the prefix *mega-* mean? What is the abbreviation for the prefix *nano-?*

SAMPLE PROBLEM 2

Express a time interval of 5 microseconds (5 μs) in seconds.

STRATEGY	SOLUTION
1. Analyze	You are asked to convert a measurement from units of microseconds (μs) to units of seconds (s).
2. Plan	Figure 1–17 gives the definition of the prefix *micro-*. You can use this definition to solve this problem.
3. Solve	According to Figure 1–17, the prefix *micro-* means 0.000 001. So 1 μs is 0.000 001 s:

$$1 \ \mu s = 0.000\ 001 \ s$$

Therefore,

$$5 \ \mu s = 0.000\ 001 \ s \times 5$$
$$= 0.000\ 005 \ s$$

4. Evaluate	According to the definition of the prefix *micro-*, 5 μs should be a much smaller unit of time than 5 s, as you have found.

PRACTICE PROBLEMS

3. Convert a volume of 8 deciliters into liters. Use the correct abbreviations for each unit. *(Answer: 0.8 L)*

4. Is 5 centimeters longer or shorter than 8 millimeters? Explain your answer. *(Answer: 5 cm is longer than 8 mm because 0.05 m (5 cm) is greater than 0.008 m (8 mm).)*

1–4 Section Review

1. What are the SI units for length, mass, and volume?

2. What is a metric prefix? What does the metric prefix *centi-* mean? The prefix *deci-?*

3. What is the difference between mass and weight?

4. **Critical Thinking—Making comparisons** What is the difference between a base unit and a derived unit in the metric system? Give one example of each type of unit.

Guide for Reading

- What causes uncertainty in measurements?
- What is the difference between accuracy and precision?

1–5 Uncertainty in Measurement

In this section, you will begin to explore a crucial aspect of science: making measurements. Many different kinds of measuring equipment are commonly found in the chemistry laboratory. Three simple kinds of measurements are frequently made in the laboratory: mass, volume, and temperature. Many other kinds of measurements are also made, including pressure, voltage, and time. Learning how to make different kinds of measurements correctly is an important part of learning chemistry.

Making Measurements

In making a measurement, you write down all of the certain (or exact) digits that the instrument can give you and also one uncertain digit that you estimate. Why, you might ask, are any digits in a measurement uncertain? **Measurements are uncertain for two reasons: Measuring instruments are never completely free of flaws and measuring always involves some estimation.** How the estimation is done depends on the instrument you are using. Instruments either have digital displays or they have scales (a kind of number line such as a ruler).

ESTIMATING WITH A DIGITAL DISPLAY Instruments such as electronic balances have digital displays. The final digit on a digital display is the estimated digit.

With a digital display, the estimation of the uncertain digit is done for you electronically. However, the estimated digit can sometimes flicker when the instrument cannot "make up its

Figure 1–19 *Chemists need to be able to make accurate and precise measurements.*

mind." If this happens, you should record the reading that the instrument seems to "prefer."

Remember that you must always include a number and a unit when you are recording a measurement. If an electronic balance reads 2.705, for example, check the instrument for the unit of the measurement. Is the measurement 2.705 grams, 2.705 kilograms, or what? Simply writing down 2.705 is not enough!

ESTIMATING WITH A SCALE   An example of an instrument that uses a scale is a graduated cylinder. A graduated cylinder measures liquid volume. With liquids such as water, the bottom of the curved surface of the liquid (called the meniscus) is the point where the reading is taken.

The graduated cylinder shown in Figure 1–20 has a scale that is marked in 1-milliliter increments. On this scale, every whole milliliter is an exact, or certain, digit in the measurement. You can see that the liquid in Figure 1–20 has a volume greater than 31 milliliters but less than 32 milliliters. To get a better reading of the volume, you must make an estimation. First, imagine ten more divisions on the scale between 31 milliliters and 32 milliliters. With these imaginary divisions, you can estimate the volume to be 31.7 milliliters. Which digit in this measurement is the estimated digit?

THE UNCERTAINTY OF A MEASUREMENT   It is doubtful that the volume of liquid in Figure 1–20 is exactly 31.7 milliliters. Because the last digit of the measurement was estimated, the true volume could be a little larger or a little smaller than 31.7 milliliters. In chemistry, the uncertainty of a measurement such as this one is usually taken to be 0.1 milliliter. In other words, we assume that the true volume could be somewhere between a high of 31.8 milliliters and a low of 31.6 milliliters.

A plus-or-minus symbol, ±, is sometimes used to show the uncertainty of a measurement as follows: 31.7 ± 0.1 milliliters. This measurement is read, "Thirty-one and seven tenths plus-or-minus one tenth milliliters." When this symbol is not used, you should assume that the uncertainty is plus-or-minus one in the estimated digit of the measurement.

Even though measurements are always uncertain, you should try to make your measurements as reliable as possible. Read the scales and digital displays of your instruments carefully and keep the instruments themselves clean and in top working order. Other steps should also be taken to ensure that your measurements are reliable, as we will now explain.

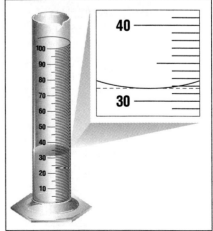

Figure 1–20   *In a digital display, the last digit shown is the estimated digit. Notice that the display also includes the unit for the measurement. The volume of liquid in this graduated cylinder is 31.7 mL. What is the curved surface of the liquid called?*

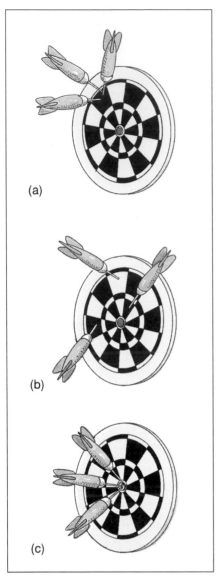

Reliability in Measurement

When a scientist like Joanie makes a measurement, she needs to know that it is reliable. There are two ways she can check her work.

PRECISION   One way is to repeat the measurement several times. A reliable measurement will give about the same result again and again under the same conditions. When it does, it is said to be precise, or to have high **precision.**

ACCURACY   The second way of checking a measurement's reliability is to test it against a standard. Joanie can make a standard by adding a known amount of oil to a sample of clean water. If she now measures how much oil is in the water, she knows what the result should be. The correct answer is called the **accepted value** for the measurement. If Joanie's measuring technique is good, she will obtain a result that is close to the accepted value. A measurement that is accurate, or that has high **accuracy,** is one that is close to the accepted value.

A DARTBOARD ANALOGY   A game of darts is a good analogy for the difference between precision and accuracy. (An analogy is a way of explaining something by comparing it to something else.) Throwing three darts at a dartboard could produce a number of different patterns, as shown in Figure 1–21.

As you can see from this analogy, reliable measurements should be both highly accurate and highly precise. Making reliable measurements is a source of pride as well as a practical necessity for scientists. In your own experiments, the quality of your laboratory work will be judged in part by the precision and accuracy of your measurements. What steps do you think you could take to ensure the precision and accuracy of the laboratory work you will do?

Figure 1–21   *In (a) the darts are clustered together (high precision), but they are far from the bull's-eye (low accuracy). In (b) the darts are closer to the bull's-eye (higher accuracy), but they are more widely scattered (lower precision). In (c) the darts are close to the bull's-eye (high accuracy) and clustered together (high precision).*

1–5 Section Review

1. Explain why measurements are always uncertain.
2. Describe two ways to check the reliability of a measurement.
3. How would you find the uncertain digit in a measurement using a digital display? Using a scale?
4. **Critical Thinking—Applying concepts**   The dartboard analogy is commonly used to explain the difference between accuracy and precision. Can you think of a different analogy to compare these two concepts?

1–6 Working With Numbers

A measurement is rarely meaningful by itself. More commonly, measurements are combined by adding, subtracting, multiplying, or dividing them to produce the values of mass, volume, or temperature needed in a scientific investigation. In your study of chemistry, you will often be asked to combine numbers and measurements mathematically. Several mathematical tools, which we will now describe, will help you in this process.

Significant Digits

When measurements are combined mathematically, the uncertainty of the separate measurements must be correctly reflected in the final result. A set of rules exists for this task, which depends on keeping track of the **significant digits,** or significant figures, in each separate measurement.

What are the significant digits in a measurement? **The certain digits and the estimated digit of a measurement are together called the significant digits of the measurement.** For example, there are three significant digits in 31.7 milliliters: two certain digits (the 3 and the 1) plus one estimated digit (the 7). When are digits significant or not significant? The rules for significant digits are given below. Here we have another example of "rules" in science. Remember that rules exist to help you understand a concept. They are not an end in themselves.

WHEN A ZERO IS NOT SIGNIFICANT A zero that is simply a place keeper in a measurement is not a significant digit. Suppose you wanted to find the mass of some fruit using a single-beam balance. To use the balance, a slider is moved along the scale until the arm balances horizontally. Since each division on the scale is 100 grams, the balance can determine the mass of the

Guide for Reading
- What are significant digits?
- How are the significant digits in a measurement found?
- What information is needed to calculate the density of an object?

Figure 1–22 Do you think you would be able to measure the mass of fruits and vegetables with a great deal of certainty using the balance shown in the photograph? Why or why not?

fruit to the nearest 10 grams by estimation. Now suppose the fruit has a mass of 1040 grams. How many of the digits in this measurement are significant?

From the way the measurement was made, you know that the 1 and the middle zero are exact digits and the 4 is the estimated digit. Thus, there are three significant digits in this mass measurement.

The final zero, though it is part of the measurement, is not a significant digit. Why not? It is a place keeper that only shows the location of the decimal point. The final zero is not significant because it is not one of the certain or estimated digits of the measurement.

THE ATLANTIC-PACIFIC RULE A rule that can help you identify the significant digits in a measurement is called the Atlantic-Pacific rule. The Atlantic-Pacific rule divides measurements into two kinds: those that are written with a decimal point, like 31.7 milliliters, and those that are written without a decimal point, like 1040 grams. To use the Atlantic-Pacific rule, first sketch (or imagine) a map of North America, similar to the one in Figure 1–23, with the Pacific Ocean on the left and the Atlantic Ocean on the right.

Now write the measurement on the map itself. If a decimal point is present in the measurement, count significant digits from the "Pacific" side; that is, from the left. (Think to yourself: "If the decimal point is **p**resent, count from the **P**acific side.") If a decimal point is absent, count from the "Atlantic" side; that is, from the right. ("If the decimal point is **a**bsent, count from the **A**tlantic side.") You should start counting with the first nonzero digit you find. All the digits from here to the end, including any zeros, are significant digits. An advantage of the Atlantic-Pacific rule is that you can tell which digits of a measurement are significant without knowing exactly how the measurement was carried out.

***Figure 1–23** Here you see an example of how to use the Atlantic-Pacific rule to help you determine the number of significant digits in a measurement.*

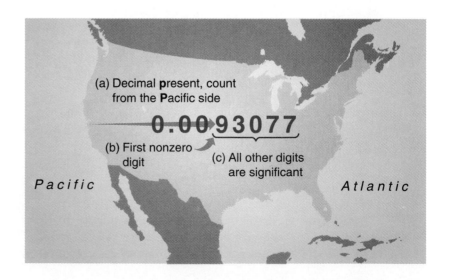

(a) Decimal **p**resent, count from the **P**acific side

0.0093077

(b) First nonzero digit

(c) All other digits are significant

Pacific

Atlantic

SAMPLE PROBLEM 3

Identify the number of significant digits in 0.057 010 gram.

STRATEGY	SOLUTION
1. Analyze	You are asked to find the number of significant digits in a measurement of mass.
2. Plan	You can use the Atlantic-Pacific rule to count significant digits. Figure 1–23 shows an example of how the Atlantic-Pacific rule is used.
3. Solve	The measurement 0.057 010 g has a decimal point, so you will count significant digits from the left. Start counting with the first nonzero digit. All the digits from there to the end of the number are significant:

$$0.057010$$
$$①②③④⑤$$

Thus, there are five significant digits in 0.057 010 g.

4. Evaluate	According to the Atlantic-Pacific rule, if a decimal point is present, you should start counting from the Pacific, or left, side beginning with the first nonzero digit, which you did. So the answer is reasonable.

PRACTICE PROBLEMS

5. Count the number of significant digits in the following measurements:

   (a) 0.002 6701 m   *(Answer: 5 significant digits)*

   (b) 19.0550 kg   *(Answer: 6 significant digits)*

   (c) 3500 V   *(Answer: 2 significant digits)*

   (d) 1,809,000 L   *(Answer: 4 significant digits)*

6. Explain why 2.07 mL is a different measurement from 2.070 mL. In your answer, be sure to compare the uncertainty and the number of significant digits in each measurement.   *(Answer: 2.07 mL has 3 significant digits and an uncertainty of ±0.01 mL; 2.070 mL has 4 significant digits and an uncertainty of ±0.001 mL.)*

In this textbook, you will often see measurements such as 100. milliliters and 250. grams. Why have we placed a decimal point after the numbers? By placing a decimal point after the number, the zeros become significant digits. According to the Atlantic-Pacific rule, 100. and 250. both have three significant digits. Without the decimal point, the number 100 has only one significant digit and 250 has only two.

Significant Digits in Calculations

Now that you know how to find the number of significant digits in a measurement, let's see what happens when several measurements with different numbers of significant digits are combined. When measurements are combined in a mathematical equation, the number of significant digits that are allowed in the final answer is found by applying the following rules:

- When an exact number appears in a calculation, it does not affect the number of significant digits in the final answer. Exact numbers are not measurements, but arise instead from a definition. For example, there are exactly 1000 meters in a kilometer. This is a definition, not a measurement. A definition has an infinite number of significant digits.
- In multiplication and division, the measurement with the smallest number of significant digits determines how many digits are allowed in the final answer. To find the volume of a box, for example, the length, width, and height of the box are multiplied.

$$\text{volume} = \text{length} \times \text{width} \times \text{height} \qquad \textbf{(Eq. 3)}$$
$$= 3.052 \text{ m} \times 2.10 \text{ m} \times 0.75 \text{ m}$$
$$= 4.8069 \text{ m}^3$$
$$= 4.8 \text{ m}^3$$

The final answer is rounded to two significant digits because your answer should have no more significant digits than the measurement with the fewest significant digits (0.75 meter). Electronic calculators typically give extra digits when they are used for multiplying and dividing. The numbers from a calculator must always be examined critically. Only a few of the digits will usually be significant.

- In addition and subtraction, the number of significant digits allowed depends on the number with the largest uncertainty. For example, suppose you added up the mass of everything you were wearing. Your list might look like this:

shoes	951.0 g
clothing	1407 g
ring	23.911 g
eyeglasses	158.18 g
total	2540. g

Figure 1–24 *Your answer to a calculation can never have more significant digits than the factor with the fewest significant digits. Which measurement in this example—length, width, or height—has the fewest significant digits? Explain.*

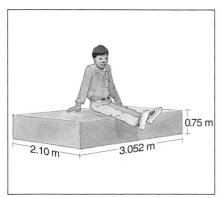

The measurements have different uncertainties (perhaps because they were made on different balances). The measurement with the largest uncertainty, ± 1 gram, is the mass of the clothing. Since the total mass cannot be known more accurately than the least accurate measurement in the sum, the total is rounded off to the nearest whole gram. (Notice that a decimal point was included with the total to show that the final zero in this measurement is a significant digit.)

When a calculation is performed in several steps, extra digits are carried in the intermediate results. Only the final answer is rounded to the proper number of significant digits.

To round off a number, look at the digit following the first digit to be rounded. If the digit is less than 5, round down. If the digit is 5 or more, round up.

SAMPLE PROBLEM 4

Perform the following calculation, then round off the answer to the proper number of significant digits: 6.15 m × 4.026 m = ?

STRATEGY	SOLUTION
1. Analyze	You are asked to multiply two numbers and to round off the answer to the correct number of significant digits.
2. Plan	Since the numbers are awkward, an electronic calculator would be a useful tool. You can then follow the rules for using significant digits in calculations to round off the answer. Be sure to include the units in your calculation as well as in your answer.

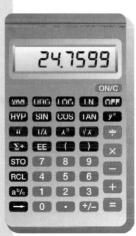

3. Solve Using a calculator, multiply the two numbers:

$$6.15 \text{ m} \times 4.026 \text{ m} = 24.7599 \text{ m}^2$$

This is the answer given by the calculator. You must now round off this answer to the correct number of significant digits:

$$24.7599 \text{ m}^2 = 24.8 \text{ m}^2$$

4. Evaluate According to the rules for significant digits, only three significant digits can be shown in the final answer. The digit to be rounded was the 7. The number was correctly rounded up to 8.

Practice Problems

7. Perform the following calculations and round the answers to the proper number of significant digits.

(a)
$$\begin{array}{r} 165.86\text{ g} \\ 4.0911\text{ g} \\ 27.32\text{ g} \\ +140.\text{ g} \\ \hline \end{array}$$
(Answer: 337 g)

(b)
$$\begin{array}{r} 150\text{ mL} \\ 76.9\text{ mL} \\ 209\text{ mL} \\ +0.036\text{ mL} \\ \hline \end{array}$$
(Answer: 440 mL)

(c) $\dfrac{12.7\text{ km}}{3.0} =$ *(Answer: 4.2 km)*

8. Perform the following calculations and round the answers to the proper number of significant digits.

(a) $\dfrac{35.6\text{ L} + 2.4\text{ L}}{4.803} =$ *(Answer: 7.91 L)*

(b) $2.542\text{ m} \times (16.408\text{ m} - 3.88\text{ m}) =$ *(Answer: 31.85 m^2)*

Scientific Notation

INTEGRATING **BIOLOGY**

Do you know that bacteria inhabit your digestive system? Do you know what one type of bacteria is called?

In science it is common to work with very large and very small numbers. For example, a drop of water contains approximately 1,700,000,000,000,000,000,000 molecules (or particles) of water. On the other hand, a single *E. coli* bacterium in your digestive tract is only about 0.000 002 meter long. To make numbers such as these easier to work with, they can be written in scientific notation.

When a number is written in scientific notation, it is separated into two parts. The first part is a number between 1 and 10. The second part is a power of ten.

For example, the number 0.00225 written in scientific notation is 2.25×10^{-3}. The first part, 2.25, is found from the original number by inspection. This part contains only the significant digits of the original number, which can be identified using the Atlantic-Pacific rule. The second part is a power of ten written in exponential form, that is, in the form of 10^n, where n is called the exponent. Let's find out more about exponents.

EXPONENTS Suppose you were going to write the number 1000 in exponential form. To do this, ask yourself: How many times must 10 be multiplied by itself to make 1000? After a bit of trial and error, you might come up with the following equation:

$$1000 = 10 \times 10 \times 10 \qquad \textbf{(Eq. 4)}$$

In other words, 10 multiplied by itself three times makes 1000. In exponential form this would be written as:

$$1000 = 10 \times 10 \times 10 = 10^3 \qquad \textbf{(Eq. 5)}$$

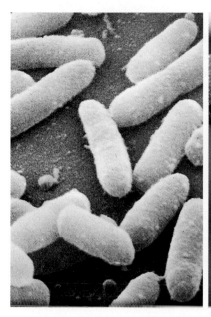

Figure 1–25 *Rod-shaped* E. coli *bacteria are normal inhabitants of the human intestine. Because they are so tiny, an instrument known as a scanning electron microscope must be used to observe these bacteria. Each water droplet contains billions of water molecules. How do scientists express very small or very large numbers?*

The exponent, $n = 3$, shows how many times ten is multiplied by itself.

Very large and very small numbers can be written in a compact way using exponents. The number 1,000,000 (one million), for example, is the same as 10 multiplied by itself six times:

$$1{,}000{,}000 = \underset{①}{10} \times \underset{②}{10} \times \underset{③}{10} \times \underset{④}{10} \times \underset{⑤}{10} \times \underset{⑥}{10} = 10^6 \quad \textbf{(Eq. 6)}$$

You can easily prove this to yourself with a pocket calculator.

Writing very small numbers (numbers less than one) involves the use of reciprocals. For example, 0.01 (one hundredth) is written in exponential form as

$$0.01 = \frac{1}{100} = \frac{1}{10 \times 10} = \frac{1}{10^2} = 10^{-2} \quad \textbf{(Eq. 7)}$$

Notice that in this case, the exponent, $n = -2$, is a negative number.

CONVERTING NUMBERS TO SCIENTIFIC NOTATION To write numbers in scientific notation, the proper exponent can be found by counting how many times the decimal point must be moved to bring it to its final position so that the number is between 1 and 10.

$$0 . \underset{①②③}{0\,0\,2{,}}25 \rightarrow 2.25 \times 10^{-3} \qquad \textbf{(Eq. 8)}$$

When the decimal point is moved to the right, the exponent is written as a negative number. Since it moves three times to the right in this case, the exponent is -3.

To express numbers greater than one in scientific notation, the exponent is positive. For instance, a horse might have a mass of 707 kilograms. This measurement written in scientific notation is 7.07×10^2 kilograms. The decimal point must be moved twice to the left, so the exponent is 2.

$$7\,0\,7 \rightarrow 7.07 \times 10^2 \qquad \textbf{(Eq. 9)}$$
②① (decimal point implied)

SAMPLE PROBLEM 5

A single tiny drop of water may contain approximately 1,700,000,000,000,000,000,000 molecules (or particles) of water. Express this number in scientific notation.

STRATEGY	SOLUTION
1. Analyze	You are given a very large number that must be rewritten in scientific notation. A number in scientific notation has two parts: The first part is between 1 and 10 and contains the significant digits of the measurement. The second part is a power of ten written in exponential form.
2. Plan	You can find the first part of the number by inspection and by applying the Atlantic-Pacific rule. To find the second part of the number, count the number of places you must move the decimal point to determine the exponent.
3. Solve	The first part will be 1.7. The decimal point must be moved to the left 21 times to put it in its final position, so the exponent will be 21. The final answer is $$1{,}700{,}000{,}000{,}000{,}000{,}000{,}000 = 1.7 \times 10^{21}$$
4. Evaluate	The number 1,700,000,000,000,000,000,000 has only two significant digits, so the first part of the answer should have two significant digits as well. The number is greater than 1, so the exponent should be positive. The number is very large, so you would expect the exponent to be large as well. Thus, 1.7×10^{21} is a reasonable answer.

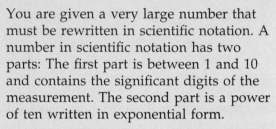

9. Write the following numbers in scientific notation:
   (a) 32,700   (Answer: 3.27×10^4)

   (b) 1,024,000   (Answer: 1.024×10^6)

   (c) 0.004 710 0   (Answer: 4.7100×10^{-3})

   (d) 0.000 000 003 901   (Answer: 3.901×10^{-9})

10. Are the following numbers written correctly in scientific notation? If any of the numbers are wrong, rewrite the number correctly:
    (a) $0.000\ 341\ 2 = 3.412 \times 10^{-3}$ (Answer: 3.412×10^{-4})

    (b) $475,500,000 = 4.75 \times 10^8$ (Answer: 4.755×10^8)

    (c) $0.000\ 056\ 0 = 5.6 \times 10^{-5}$ (Answer: 5.60×10^{-5})

    (d) $18,060,000 = 18.06 \times 10^6$ (Answer: 1.806×10^7)

Percents and Percent Error

In your study of chemistry, many of your results will be expressed as a percent. A fraction can be written as a percent by converting it to a decimal and then multiplying the decimal by 100 percent. For example, if 900 million kilograms of plastic soft drink bottles are produced each year and 180 million kilograms of them are recycled, the percentage of plastic soft drink bottles that are recycled is

$$\frac{180 \text{ million kilograms}}{900 \text{ million kilograms}} = 0.2 \times 100\% = 20\% \qquad \textbf{(Eq. 10)}$$

An example of the way percents are used in chemistry is the **percent error.** A measurement can be compared with its accepted value by calculating its percent error. The percent error is found from the following formula:

$$\text{percent error} = \frac{\text{measured value} - \text{accepted value}}{\text{accepted value}} \times 100 \text{ percent} \qquad \textbf{(Eq. 11)}$$

This formula first takes the difference between the measured value and the accepted value. This difference is then divided by the accepted value. The result is then multiplied by 100 percent to give a percent.

A percent error can be either positive or negative. If the measured value is greater than the accepted value, the difference (measured value − accepted value) will be positive and the percent error will be positive. If the measured value is less than the accepted value, the difference will be negative and the percent error will be negative.

CHEMISTRY IN ACTION

YOU AND YOUR WORLD

Recycling Plastics

The following data represent the amount of each type of plastic produced in the United States and the amount recycled.

Group 1 (PET)	872 million kilograms produced 207 million kilograms recycled
Group 2 (HDPE)	3978 million kilograms produced 200 million kilograms recycled
Group 3 (PVC)	3884 million kilograms produced 9 million kilograms recycled
Group 4 (LDPE)	5080 million kilograms produced 34 million kilograms recycled
Group 5 (PP)	3384 million kilograms produced 100 million kilograms recycled
Group 6 (PS)	2203 million kilograms produced 17 million kilograms recycled

You might want to calculate the percentages yourself. As you can see, we are still a long way from 100 percent recycling.

Visit our Web site at
http://www.phschool.com
to support your
study of chemistry.

Brand A vs. Brand B

Using ratios, you can find differences in cost between similar products, allowing you to buy the things you need and save money at the same time. For example, suppose a bottle of chocolate syrup (Brand A) costs $2.50 for 10 ounces, but Brand B costs $2.75 for 12 ounces. Which brand is cheaper by the ounce?

$$\text{Brand A} = \frac{\$2.50}{10.\ \text{oz}}$$
$$= \$0.25 \text{ per ounce}$$

$$\text{Brand B} = \frac{\$2.75}{12\ \text{oz.}}$$
$$= \$0.23 \text{ per ounce}$$

Brand B is 2 cents cheaper per ounce: A small difference, perhaps, but over a lifetime of eating chocolate sundaes the pennies would add up!

Ratios

Another common method of expressing results in chemistry is by the use of ratios. You are probably already familiar with ratios in your daily life. Riding in a car, for example, you have a sense of how fast you are going by observing how long it takes for the scenery to go by. In your mind you are forming a ratio, a kind of fraction. This ratio, called the speed, has a length or distance measurement in the numerator and a time measurement in the denominator:

$$\text{speed} = \frac{\text{distance}}{\text{time}} \qquad \textbf{(Eq. 12)}$$

The length measurement may be the distance between any two convenient objects, like streetlights, and the time measurement may be your heartbeat. With practice, your sense of speed can become very accurate and precise.

A ratio that is frequently used in chemistry is density. Density is a concept that is useful in many aspects of life. Like speed, density is a ratio because it is found by dividing one quantity by another quantity. A density is often a ratio of one measurement divided by a measurement of length, area, or volume. Have you ever heard the term population density? In a city with a high population density, many people live in each square kilometer

Figure 1–26 *Five people are standing on a square 2.0 m × 2.0 m in area. What is the population density?*

of the city. The population density is calculated by dividing the population of the city by its total area:

$$\text{population density} = \frac{\text{population}}{\text{area}} \qquad \textbf{(Eq. 13)}$$

Population density has units of people/km^2, which can be read as "people per square kilometer" or "the number of people in one square kilometer." Are you familiar with any cities that have a high population density?

In chemistry, **density** is one of the important properties of matter. Density is equal to the mass of a substance per unit volume. **The density of an object is calculated by dividing the mass of the object by its volume.**

$$\text{density} = \frac{\text{mass}}{\text{volume}} \qquad \textbf{(Eq. 14)}$$

Typically, density is expressed in units of g/cm^3, which can be read as "grams per cubic centimeter" or "the number of grams in one cubic centimeter." If a metal block has a mass of 75 grams and a volume of 22 cubic centimeters, the density of the block is

$$\text{density} = \frac{75\ \text{g}}{22\ \text{cm}^3} \qquad \textbf{(Eq. 15)}$$
$$= 3.4\ \text{g/cm}^3$$

This result means that each cubic centimeter of the block has a mass of 3.4 grams.

The densities of some common substances are shown in the table in Figure 1–27. The density of a substance determines whether that substance will float or sink in a liquid such as water.

The concept of density has many useful applications. For example, almost 50 different kinds of plastics are in use today. To help in recycling, the plastics industry has introduced a coding system based on density. All plastic products are imprinted with a number from 1 to 6 inside the three arrows of the recycling symbol. Each number represents a different type of plastic, based on density and ease of recycling.

USING DENSITIES IN CALCULATIONS Knowing the volume occupied by an object and its density, you can calculate the mass of the object. In the same way, knowing the mass of an object and its density, you can calculate the volume it occupies. To make these calculations, the definition of density must be rearranged using algebra, as the next Sample Problem will demonstrate.

Density of Some Common Substances

Substance	Density (g/cm³)
air	0.0013*
ice	0.917
water	1.00
aluminum	2.70
iron	7.86
gold	19.3

* at 0°C and 1 atm pressure

Figure 1–27 *The densities of some common substances are listed in the table. What is the density of iron?*

Figure 1–28 *The liquids and solids in the beaker have different densities. If you did not know their individual densities, how could you determine the relative density of each substance?*

Floating and Sinking

1. Study the drawing below. The liquid is water.
• Why does one can of soda float while the other can sinks?
2. Repeat this experiment yourself using a can of diet soda and a can of regular soda.
• Do the ingredients used in soft drinks affect their density? Write a brief essay describing your observations.

SAMPLE PROBLEM 6

Using the information in the table in Figure 1–27 and the definition of density, calculate the mass of 200. cm^3 of air.

STRATEGY	SOLUTION
1. Analyze	You are asked to calculate the mass of a given volume of air. You can solve this problem by substituting the known values in the equation for density.
2. Plan	According to the table, the density of air is 0.0013 g/cm^3. Organizing all the information into a list is helpful:

$$\text{density} = 0.0013 \text{ g/cm}^3$$

$$\text{volume} = 200. \text{ cm}^3$$

$$\text{mass} = \text{unknown}$$

The definition of density is given in Equation 14:

$$\text{density} = \frac{\text{mass}}{\text{volume}}$$

The only unknown quantity in this equation is the mass. Using algebra, you can rearrange the definition of density to solve for the mass:

$$\text{mass} = \text{volume} \times \text{density}$$

3. Solve   Since you know the volume and the density, you now have everything you need to calculate the mass.

$$\text{mass} = 200. \text{ cm}^3 \times 0.0013 \text{ g/cm}^3$$

$$= 0.26 \text{ g}$$

4. Evaluate   The answer is expressed in the correct unit (grams) for mass. Since each cubic centimeter of air has a very small mass (as shown by the density), it makes sense that 200. cm^3 would also have a small mass. Thus, your answer is reasonable.

PRACTICE PROBLEMS

11. Using the definition of density and the information in the table in Figure 1–27, find the mass of a 35-cm^3 sample of aluminum. *(Answer: 95 g)*

12. Using the definition of density and the information in the table in Figure 1–27, calculate the volume occupied by 160. g of iron. *(Answer: 20.4 cm^3)*

Hold Your Breath!

Raychelle loved visiting the community swimming pool with her older sister Tonya. This summer, Tonya had promised to teach Raychelle how to swim.

"Before you can swim," Tonya said, "you first have to learn how to float."

Tonya demonstrated how easy it was to float on the surface of the water: She just put her head back, spread her arms to the side, and let her feet rise from the bottom of the pool. Then it was Raychelle's turn. As Tonya stood behind her and held her shoulders, Raychelle tried to imitate what Tonya had done. It worked! Her feet bobbed to the surface and she was floating.

"Tonya, I'm floating!" she exclaimed.

Just then, Tonya let go of her shoulders and Raychelle started to sink. Quickly, Tonya grabbed her and gave her a hint: She told Raychelle to take a deep breath and hold her lungs fully inflated. This time, when Tonya let go, Raychelle continued to float. When she finally

exhaled, however, she again began to sink rapidly.

Forming a Hypothesis

1. Can you suggest a hypothesis to explain Raychelle's experience?
2. How could you test your hypothesis?

As you noticed in the last Sample Problem, the cubic centimeter (cm^3) units disappeared in the final answer. This "disappearance," or cancellation, of the units was no accident. The final answer is a mass, which has units of grams, not cubic centimeters. Learning how to cancel unwanted units in a calculation is very important for solving chemistry problems. In the next section, we will explain this problem-solving strategy in detail.

1–6 Section Review

1. What are significant digits?
2. Describe how the Atlantic-Pacific rule can be used to help find the significant digits in a measurement.
3. How can you calculate the density of an object?
4. **Critical Thinking—Applying concepts** The accepted value for the boiling point of water is 100.0°C at sea level. When students in San Diego, California, measured this value, their result was 98.5°C. What is the percent error? Is it positive or negative? Why?

Guide for Reading

- What is dimensional analysis?
- What are the four steps you should follow in solving a chemistry problem?

1–7 Problem Solving

Solving a chemistry problem is like taking a trip. Where are you? Where are you going? How are you going to get there? Like any journey, solving a chemistry problem is much easier and more enjoyable if you plan ahead and keep your destination in mind. In this section, we will discuss problem-solving techniques that can help you chart a smooth course through your chemistry homework.

Dimensional Analysis

Many chemistry problems involve converting measurements from one unit to another. Another name for the unit of a measurement is dimension. **The technique of converting between units is called dimensional analysis.**

It is easiest to explain **dimensional analysis** with an example. Suppose the people responsible for the oil leak we described at the beginning of the chapter told Joanie that 250 gallons of oil entered the swamp. To use this measurement in her scientific work, Joanie must convert 250 gallons to metric units. The liter is a metric unit of volume, so Joanie's problem is this: How many liters are in 250 gallons? You can use dimensional analysis to answer this question.

UNIT EQUALITIES A unit equality is the starting point for solving the problem. A **unit equality** is an equation that shows how different units are related. Some unit equalities are given in the table in Figure 1–29. Reading from the table, the unit

---

Unit Equalities

Metric to Metric*

1000 m = 1 km	1 cm = 0.01 m	1 L = 1000 cm^3
1 m = 100 cm	1 mm = 0.001 m	1 mL = 1 cm^3
1 m = 1000 mm	1 μm = 1×10^{-6} m	
1 m = 1×10^6 μm	1 nm = 1×10^{-9} m	
1 m = 1×10^9 nm	1 pm = 1×10^{-12} m	
1 m = 1×10^{12} pm		

English to Metric	Miscellaneous
1 in. = 2.54 cm	1 ft = 12 in.
1 gal = 3.785 L	1 mi = 5280 ft
1 cal = 4.184 J	1 min = 60 s
1 atm = 101,325 Pa	1 hr = 60 min
	1 atm = 760 mm Hg

*These unit equalities follow from the definitions of the metric prefixes in Figure 1–17 on page 20 and they apply to other metric units as well, for example, 1000. g = 1 kg.

Figure 1–29 *Some unit equalities used in dimensional analysis are listed in the table. What is the unit equality that relates liters and cubic centimeters?*

equality showing the relationship between gallons and liters is

$$1 \text{ gal} = 3.785 \text{ L} \qquad \textbf{(Eq. 16)}$$

In other words, 1 gallon is a little less than 4 liters.

CONVERSION FACTORS The next step in solving the problem is to write **conversion factors** from the unit equality. A conversion factor is an equation that is always equal to 1. Two conversion factors can be written from one unit equality. Starting with Equation 16, the first conversion factor is created by dividing both sides of the equation by 1 gallon:

$$\frac{1 \text{ gal}}{1 \text{ gal}} = \frac{3.785 \text{ L}}{1 \text{ gal}}$$

$$1 = \frac{3.785 \text{ L}}{1 \text{ gal}} \qquad \textbf{(Eq. 17)}$$

The second conversion factor is created by dividing both sides of Equation 16 by 3.785 liters:

$$\frac{1 \text{ gal}}{3.785 \text{ L}} = \frac{3.785 \text{ L}}{3.785 \text{ L}}$$

$$\frac{1 \text{ gal}}{3.785 \text{ L}} = 1 \qquad \textbf{(Eq. 18)}$$

One of these conversion factors will convert gallons to liters and the other will convert liters to gallons. The question now is this: Which one should you use?

USING CONVERSION FACTORS Conversion factors work in the following way. It is customary in algebra to use a symbol for the unknown quantity in a problem. In this case, the unknown is the number of liters. An appropriate symbol for the unknown is V, for volume, but you could pick any symbol that suited you. The unknown will go on one side of the equal sign. On the other side is the information you were given (250 gallons) and one of the conversion factors:

$$V = 250 \text{ gal} \times \frac{3.785 \text{ L}}{1 \text{ gal}}$$

$$V = 950 \text{ L} \qquad \textbf{(Eq. 19)}$$

So you have found that 250 gallons is equal to 950 liters.

CANCELLATION OF UNITS Notice that the gallon unit canceled from Equation 19, leaving just the liter unit on the right side of the equal sign. This cancellation must happen because your answer must be expressed in the correct units for the quantity you are trying to find, in this case, volume. If the units do not cancel correctly, the calculation was probably set up wrong.

To make the cancellation, the correct conversion factor must be used. In setting up Equation 19, you chose the conversion

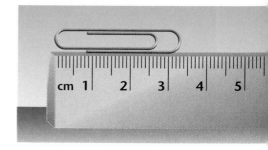

Figure 1–30 *The length of a paper clip is a little over 3 centimeters. How would you convert this measurement to meters? To millimeters?*

factor with the gallon unit on the bottom of the fraction bar. That way the gallon unit cancels from the equation.

Choosing the correct conversion factor requires looking carefully at the units involved in the problem. Studying the units and deciding which conversion factor to use are essential parts of performing a dimensional analysis.

Dimensional Analysis Applied to Unit Conversions

You can quickly and easily make conversions among English units and metric units by following these steps:

- Write down the unit equality for the units you need to convert.
- Write down the conversion factors corresponding to the unit equality.
- Use a symbol to represent the unknown quantity in the problem. Put this symbol on the left side of the equal sign.
- Write the given information on the right side of the equal sign and multiply by one of the conversion factors. Choose the correct conversion factor by performing a dimensional analysis. Units should cancel to give the desired unit. Units that are the same in the given measurement and below the fraction bar cancel from the equation.
- When the conversion is finished, the unit on the right side of the equal sign should be the unit you are converting to.

SAMPLE PROBLEM 7

How many inches are in 250. centimeters?

STRATEGY	SOLUTION
1. Analyze	This is a unit conversion problem, which you can solve by dimensional analysis. You can use the symbol d to represent the unknown number of inches. The unit equality you need is given in Figure 1–29: 1 in. = 2.54 cm. The two conversion factors you can write from this equality are

$$\frac{1 \text{ in.}}{2.54 \text{ cm}} \quad \text{and} \quad \frac{2.54 \text{ cm}}{1 \text{ in.}}$$

2. Plan	Choose the correct conversion factor by performing a dimensional analysis. Because you want centimeter units to cancel, use the conversion factor with centimeter units in the denominator. You are now ready to solve the problem.

3. Solve

$$d = 250.\ \text{cm} \times \frac{1\ \text{in.}}{2.54\ \text{cm}}$$

$$d = 98.4\ \text{in.}$$

4. Evaluate   To evaluate the answer, you should look at both the number and the unit. The centimeter unit canceled from the equation as required, leaving only units of inches. And since 1 in. has a length of about 2.5 cm, 250 cm should have a length of about 100 in. Thus, your answer is expressed in the correct units and has a reasonable value.

PRACTICE PROBLEMS _____

13. How many gallons are in 39 L?   *(Answer: 10. gal)*

14. How many centimeters are in 16 in.?   *(Answer: 41 cm)*

Lengthy Conversions

Sometimes several conversion factors are needed to complete a unit conversion. In such cases, the conversion could be performed in a series of separate steps. But it is usually more efficient to combine the steps, as the following example will illustrate.

How many seconds are in 5.0 hours? Checking the table in Figure 1–29, you will see that there is no unit equality that connects seconds and hours directly. However, there is a definition that relates hours and minutes, and another that relates minutes and seconds. Thus, you could perform the conversion from hours to seconds in two steps. But you can also solve the problem by combining the separate steps into one longer step.

First, list the definitions, as follows:

$$1\ \text{hr} = 60\ \text{min}$$

$$1\ \text{min} = 60\ \text{s}$$

Next, list the conversion factors you can use:

$$\frac{1\ \text{hr}}{60\ \text{min}} \quad \text{and} \quad \frac{60\ \text{min}}{1\ \text{hr}}$$

$$\frac{1\ \text{min}}{60\ \text{s}} \quad \text{and} \quad \frac{60\ \text{s}}{1\ \text{min}}$$

Use t as the variable to represent the number of seconds in 5.0 hours. Setting up the equation gives:

$$t = 5.0\ \text{hr} \times \frac{60\ \text{min}}{1\ \text{hr}} \times \frac{60\ \text{s}}{1\ \text{min}}$$

$$t = 18{,}000\ \text{s} \tag{Eq. 20}$$

Notice that the equation contains two conversion factors instead of just one. The first conversion factor changes hours to minutes. The second conversion factor changes minutes to seconds. The conversion factors were chosen by dimensional analysis so that the unwanted units, hours and minutes, would cancel.

SAMPLE PROBLEM   8

How many feet are in 86 centimeters?

STRATEGY	SOLUTION
1. Analyze	You are asked to convert centimeters to feet. There is no unit equality between centimeters and feet in Figure 1–29. However, there is an equality between centimeters and inches, and another between inches and feet.
2. Plan	Here are the unit equalities you will need:

$$1 \text{ in.} = 2.54 \text{ cm}$$

$$1 \text{ ft} = 12 \text{ in.}$$

The conversion factors you can use are

$$\frac{1 \text{ in.}}{2.54 \text{ cm}} \quad \text{and} \quad \frac{2.54 \text{ cm}}{1 \text{ in.}}$$

$$\frac{1 \text{ ft}}{12 \text{ in.}} \quad \text{and} \quad \frac{12 \text{ in.}}{1 \text{ ft}}$$

Choose the correct conversion factors by dimensional analysis. The symbol d can be used for the unknown quantity.

3. Solve

$$d = 86 \text{ cm} \times \frac{1 \text{ in.}}{2.54 \text{ cm}} \times \frac{1 \text{ ft}}{12 \text{ in.}}$$

$$d = 2.8 \text{ ft}$$

4. Evaluate   The unwanted units canceled from the equation as required, leaving only units of feet on both sides of the equal sign. Since 1 meter, or 100 cm, is about the same length as 1 yard (or 3 ft), it makes sense that 86 cm should be a little less than 3 ft.

PRACTICE PROBLEMS

15. How many cubic centimeters are in 2.3 gal?
    (Answer: 8700 cm³)

16. How many meters are in 3.5 mi?   *(Answer: 5600 m)*

Figure 1–31 *Suppose you were asked to convert seconds to kilograms. Could you do it? Why or why not?*

Impossible Conversions

Suppose you were asked, "How many seconds are in a kilogram?" Would you be able to answer this question? We hope your answer is a resounding "No!" This is a meaningless question and an impossible conversion to make because the units correspond to different quantities—the second is a unit of time, whereas the kilogram is a unit of mass. When you begin a unit conversion, first ask yourself: Do the units correspond to the same quantity? No one, not even the best chemist, can change apples to oranges! If the units in the problem do not correspond to the same quantity, it is impossible, no matter how hard you might try, to convert the units.

A Four-Step Problem-Solving Strategy

The Sample Problems we have worked out in this chapter have followed a four-step format. We recommend that you follow this same strategy, as outlined below, when working on your own problems.

1. **Analyze** Read the entire problem carefully. Identify the unknown quantity in the problem and choose a symbol to represent it. Organize the given information into a table or list. Sketch a picture or a diagram to help clarify the problem.
2. **Plan** Is the problem similar to any you have seen before? Review earlier problems for clues to connecting the unknown to the given information. Write down any equations that link the unknown and the given

information together. Make a plan for solving the problem. For example, you may have to rearrange an equation to isolate the unknown, as you saw in Sample Problem 6. Make an estimate of the answer. Ask yourself, What would be a reasonable answer in this case?

3. **Solve** Perform the mathematical steps outlined in your plan. Check units and significant digits.
4. **Evaluate** Ask yourself, Does the answer make sense? Compare the answer (numerical value and units) with your estimate.

Graphing

When an experiment generates many measurements, it can be difficult to see patterns in all the information. A graph can help clarify these patterns. Let's see how a graph can help by examining an example.

Suppose a balloon is filled with air and attached to the bottom of a large container of water. If the water temperature is changed, by heating or by adding ice, the volume of the air in the balloon also changes. The data in the table in Figure 1–32 were obtained by measuring the volume of the balloon at several temperatures. Is there a pattern in these measurements?

A graph of this information immediately reveals the answer. Yes! The volume of the air changes in a regular way when the temperature changes. This straight-line pattern is not obvious from the list of data in the table.

HOW TO DRAW A SCIENTIFIC GRAPH Scientific graphs show the relationship between two experimental variables. One variable is called the independent variable. The independent variable is the one that the scientist changes in the experiment. In the balloon experiment, the independent variable is the temperature. The independent variable is plotted on the horizontal,

Figure 1–32 The data table shows how the volume of air in a balloon changes as the temperature changes. Is it easy for you to see a pattern in these data?

Measurements of the Volume of a Sample Gas at Various Temperatures

Trial	Temperature (°C)	Volume (mL)
1	25	101.3
2	30.	102.2
3	35	103.4
4	40.	105.0
5	45	106.7
6	50.	108.4
7	55	110.0
8	60.	111.5
9	65	112.9
10	70.	114.2

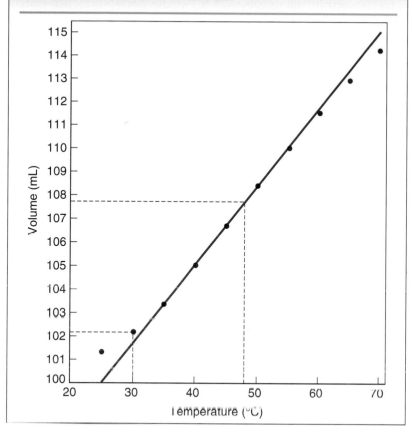

Effect of Changes in Temperature on the Volume of Air in a Balloon

Figure 1–33 *The pattern in the data becomes much clearer when the data are plotted on a graph. Which is the independent variable in this graph? The dependent variable?*

or x, axis of the graph. The second variable, called the dependent variable, is plotted on the vertical, or y, axis of the graph. The dependent variable responds to changes in the independent variable. The volume is the dependent variable in the balloon experiment. Here is a list of steps to follow in drawing a scientific graph. Refer to the graph in Figure 1–33 as you read these steps:

- Label each axis of the graph with the name of the variable and the units of the measurement. As shown in the graph, a simple numbering scheme is used for each axis, because it makes it easier for you to see relationships immediately.
- Convert each pair of measurements into a point on the graph. Mark the point by a clean dot. The second pair of measurements in the data table, for example, is plotted on the graph by locating 30°C on the horizontal axis and 102.2 mL on the vertical axis. The locations are projected onto the graph, as shown by the dotted lines, and the place where the lines intersect is marked with a dot as the data point.
- Connect the data points with a "best fit" line.
- Give the graph a suitable title when it is complete. The title of the graph in Figure 1–33 is "Effect of Changes in Temperature on the Volume of Air in a Balloon."

SPOTTING TRENDS IN A GRAPH A graph tells a "story" by showing a trend in the experimental data. After plotting all the measurements in the data table, a straight-line pattern is

MATH TIP

To draw a best-fit line, do not merely connect the data points. For data that display a linear pattern, use a ruler to draw a line that best accommodates all the data points. Because of uncertainty and errors in measurement, some of the data points will be above the best-fit line, while others will be below it. To obtain the slope of this line, calculate $\Delta y/\Delta x$.

clearly seen in the graph. Not all of the data points fall exactly on the line, but the trend is obvious. Drawing a line through the data points highlights the pattern.

A trend is different from the data that it is based on. A trend is an interpretation of the data. And like all interpretations, it may or may not be correct. It is possible for a graph to appear to follow a certain trend, but on further investigation you may find a different trend or even no trend at all.

In addition to straight lines (or linear trends), curves and other complicated trends are also found in science. A trend, whatever its shape, can be used to make predictions. Looking at the graph in Figure 1–33, you can easily predict the volume of the balloon at temperatures other than the ones actually measured. The Sample Problem that follows illustrates this idea.

SAMPLE PROBLEM 9

Using Figure 1–33 as a guide, what volume do you predict the balloon would have at 48°C?

STRATEGY	SOLUTION
1. **Analyze**	You are asked to find the volume of the balloon at a given temperature using the graph in Figure 1–33.
2. **Plan**	The straight line drawn through the data points in the graph includes a point corresponding to 48°C and the unknown volume. Reading this volume from the graph will give you the answer to the problem.
3. **Solve**	The procedure for reading the graph is illustrated in Figure 1–33. Following this procedure, you find that the volume of the balloon at 48°C is 107.7 mL.
4. **Evaluate**	According to the data table, the volume of the balloon at 45°C is 106.7 mL and at 50°C is 108.4 mL. Your answer is between these values, which is reasonable.

PRACTICE PROBLEMS

17. What volume would the balloon have at 57°C? *(Answer: 110.7 mL)*

18. Does the straight line in Figure 1–33 correctly predict the volume of the balloon at all temperatures? Within what range of temperatures does the line give accurate predictions for the volume of the balloon? *(Answer: No. The line is most accurate within a temperature range of 35°C to 60°C.)*

Figure 1–34 *Like Canada geese setting out on their annual migration, you, too, are beginning a journey—a journey into the fascinating world of chemistry. Good luck!*

The Road Ahead

As you read this, it is autumn in many parts of the United States. The leaves on certain trees are undergoing dramatic and colorful changes as the trees prepare for winter. Many birds are beginning their incredible annual migration southward. You, too, are embarking on an exciting journey—a journey into the world of chemistry. You are starting out on this journey equipped with the skills you learned in this chapter. You will have many chances to practice these skills in the chapters that follow. In the next chapter we turn our attention to the two basic entities of the universe: energy and matter.

1–7 Section Review

1. What is meant by dimensional analysis?
2. What is a unit equality? A conversion factor?
3. List and describe the four steps that can be used to solve problems in chemistry.
4. **Critical Thinking—Making judgments** Suppose you are asked as part of a chemistry problem to convert a measurement from units of milliliters to units of meters. Could you make such a unit conversion? Why or why not?

Laboratory Investigation

Accuracy of Measurements

Problem

What factors determine the accuracy of a measurement?

Materials (per group)

triple-beam balance
centimeter ruler
Celsius thermometer
100-mL graduated cylinder
coin
sheet of paper
water

Procedure

1. Using the triple-beam balance, measure the mass of the coin. Record your measurement in a data table similar to the one shown here.
2. Using the centimeter ruler, measure the length and width of the sheet of paper. Record your measurements in the data table.
3. Using the Celsius thermometer, record the temperature of the air in your classroom. Record your measurement in the data table.
4. Using the graduated cylinder, measure the volume of a sample of water. Record your measurement in the data table.
5. Repeat steps 1 to 4 two more times and record your results.

Observations

Instrument	Measurement	Results	Uncertainty
triple-beam balance	mass of coin		
centimeter ruler	length of paper		
	width of paper		
Celsius thermometer	temperature of air		
graduated cylinder	volume of water		

How precise were your measurements?

Analysis and Conclusions

1. Which instrument would be more accurate for measuring the volume of a liquid—a beaker or a graduated cylinder? Why?
2. Volume can be measured in units of cubic meters or milliliters. When would you use cubic meters? When would you use milliliters?
3. Is a precise measurement always accurate? Explain your answer.
4. What variables might have affected the accuracy of your measurements?
5. **On Your Own** Make additional measurements using calibrated pipets, burettes, a four-beam balance, a 10-mL graduated cylinder, a meterstick, and any other measuring instruments that are available. Record the uncertainty of each measurement.

STUDY GUIDE

Summarizing Key Concepts

1–1 What Is Chemistry?
- Chemistry is the study of all substances and the changes that they undergo.
- Chemistry is sometimes called the central science because it overlaps so many other sciences.

1–2 The Scientific Method
- The scientific method is a way of answering questions about the world around us.

1–3 Safety in the Laboratory
- There are several basic safety rules and procedures that must always be followed when working in a chemistry laboratory.

1–4 Units of Measurement
- Scientists use the metric system and a form of the metric system called the International System of Units, or SI.
- The SI units of length, mass, and volume are the meter, the kilogram, and the cubic meter, respectively.
- Metric prefixes are used to make units larger or smaller.

1–5 Uncertainty in Measurement
- Measurements are always uncertain because measuring instruments are never flawless and because measuring always involves some estimation.
- It is important that measurements in science have both high precision and high accuracy.

1–6 Working With Numbers
- The significant digits of a measurement include both the certain digits and the estimated digit.
- Scientific notation is used to write very large or very small numbers.
- The density of a substance is equal to its mass per unit volume.

1–7 Problem Solving
- Dimensional analysis is a technique for converting between units.
- The four steps that can be used to solve problems in chemistry are analyze, plan, solve, and evaluate.
- Graphs are often used to help clarify patterns in experimental data.

Reviewing Key Terms

Define each term in a complete sentence.

1–1 What Is Chemistry?
chemistry

1–2 The Scientific Method
scientific method
observation
hypothesis
experiment
conclusion
natural law
theory
variable
experimental control

1–4 Units of Measurement
metric system
International System of Units (SI)
base unit
mass
derived unit
volume
metric prefix

1–5 Uncertainty in Measurement
precision
accepted value
accuracy

1–6 Working With Numbers
significant digit
percent error
density

1–7 Problem Solving
dimensional analysis
unit equality
conversion factor

CHAPTER REVIEW

Content Review

Multiple Choice

Choose the letter of the answer that best completes each statement.

1. The study of matter and the changes that it undergoes describes the science of
   (a) biology.
   (c) chemistry.
   (b) ecology.
   (d) physics.

2. How many significant digits are in the measurement 5.0070 g?
   (a) two
   (c) four
   (b) three
   (d) five

3. When a chemist performs an experiment, the factor being tested is called the
   (a) control.
   (c) hypothesis.
   (b) variable.
   (d) theory.

4. After making observations and proposing a hypothesis, a scientist's next step is usually to
   (a) state a theory.
   (b) perform an experiment.
   (c) state a conclusion.
   (d) analyze data.

5. An appropriate metric unit to measure the distance between New York and Boston would be the
   (a) kilometer.
   (c) meter.
   (b) centimeter.
   (d) nanometer.

True or False

If the statement is true, write "true." If it is false, change the underlined word or words to make the statement true.

6. Chemistry has sometimes been called the <u>central</u> science.

7. After making observations that led to a question, a scientist may arrive at a <u>conclusion</u>.

8. It <u>is not</u> necessary to clean up your work area after completing an experiment if you have not spilled anything.

9. The cubic meter is an example of an SI <u>base</u> unit.

10. Measurements that you might make in the chemistry laboratory are <u>never</u> uncertain.

11. A measurement that is close to the accepted value has high <u>precision</u>.

12. A zero that is a place keeper in a measurement <u>is not</u> a significant digit.

13. The <u>density</u> of a substance is usually measured in units of grams per cubic centimeter.

14. When drawing a scientific graph, the independent variable is shown on the <u>y axis</u>.

Concept Mapping

Complete the following concept map for Section 1–1. Refer to pages xviii–xix to construct a concept map for the entire chapter.

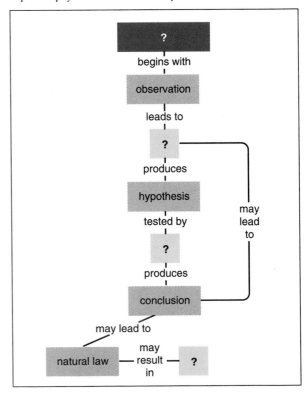

Concept Mastery

Discuss each of the following in a brief paragraph.

15. List the steps of the scientific method. Use specific examples to explain each step.
16. What is the importance of an experimental control in an experiment?
17. Describe ten important safety procedures that you should follow when working in the laboratory.
18. The metric system is like an international language that is spoken by all scientists. In your own words, explain what is meant by this statement.
19. What is the difference between an SI base unit and a derived unit? Give some examples of each type of unit.

20. What does a plus-or-minus symbol indicate when it is used in a measurement?
21. Explain how to use the Atlantic-Pacific rule to help identify the significant digits in a measurement.
22. What is percent error? Describe how to find the percent error in a calculation.
23. How is a scientific graph helpful in interpreting the results of an experiment?
24. **Tying it Together** In your own words, explain why chemistry is called the central science. Include some examples of the *diversity* of areas in which a knowledge of chemistry might be useful.

Critical Thinking and Problem Solving

Use the skills you have developed in this chapter to answer each of the following.

25. **Interpreting data** The following table lists the average water temperature of the ocean off the coast of Maine each month for a period of one year. Draw a graph to illustrate these data. Describe the pattern shown by your graph.

Average Ocean Water Temperature			
Month	**Temp. (°C)**	**Month**	**Temp. (°C)**
January	3.8	July	15.5
February	0.9	August	19.0
March	1.1	September	18.5
April	2.5	October	15.5
May	5.2	November	9.2
June	10.1	December	5.8

26. **Interpreting diagrams** What is the dependent variable in the graph you drew for the previous question? What is the independent variable?
27. **Designing experiments** Design an experiment to answer the following question:

What effect does the temperature at which milk is stored have on the rate at which the milk becomes sour?

28. **Interpreting data** Two students weighed the same sample on two different laboratory balances. The results were as follows:

Balance A	Balance B
12.11 g	12.1324 g
12.09 g	12.1322 g

Which balance is more precise? If the mass of the sample is actually 12.1036 g, which is more accurate?

29. **Using the writing process** One application of chemistry is in the restoration of artistic masterpieces, such as Michelangelo's Sistine Chapel ceiling. Very often, art restorers must touch up very old paintings using pigments that match those used in the original painting. Some of these pigments may be hundreds of years old. Using materials available in your school or local library, find out how art restorers analyze the chemicals that were used in old pigments.

PROBLEM BANK

Group A

30. Many SI units are named for influential scientists. Using the resources in your school library, prepare a short biography of one of the following scientists: Isaac Newton, James Watt, James Joule, Heinrich Hertz, Blaise Pascal, William Thomson (Lord Kelvin). *(Section 1–4)*

31. Applying what you have learned about metric prefixes, answer the following questions. *(Section 1–4)*
(a) How many watts are in 1 megawatt?
(b) How many grams are in 4 kilograms?
(c) What fraction of a joule is 1 millijoule?
(d) What fraction of a second is 1 picosecond?

32. Fill in the blank with the correct number or metric prefix. *(Section 1–4)*
(a) 1 centimeter = _____ meter
(b) 1 _____ liter = 0.001 liter
(c) 1 microgram = _____ gram
(d) 1 _____ volt = 1000 volts
(e) 1 nanosecond = _____ second

33. Complete the following table of SI base units. *(Section 1–4)*

Type of Measurement	SI Base Unit	Symbol
(a) _____	kilogram	_____
(b) length	_____	_____
(c) _____	_____	K
(d) count (or amount)	_____	_____

34. Complete the following table of metric units. *(Section 1–4)*

Type of Measurement	Metric Unit	Symbol
(a) _____	millimeter	_____
(b) _____	microliter	_____
(c) _____	_____	ng
(d) _____	_____	kPa
(e) _____	megahertz	_____
(f) _____	_____	cm³
(g) _____	_____	mA
(h) _____	picomole	_____

35. Of the following choices, which would be the most convenient unit to use for measuring the volume of a drop of water? (a) mL (b) m^3 (c) cm (d) mm *(Section 1–4)*

36. Classify the following units as SI or non-SI: (a) liter (b) calorie (c) volt (d) inch (e) joule *(Section 1–4)*

37. Write the following measurements in scientific notation: (a) 204,500 m (b) 0.003 57 J (c) 690,000,000 W (d) 101,325 Pa (e) 0.000 000 072 10 g *(Section 1–6)*

38. Explain why the measurement 600 g is not the same as 600. g. In your answer, compare the uncertainty and the number of significant digits in each measurement. *(Section 1–6)*

39. A brick used in the construction of pottery kilns is 11.0 cm wide, 6.0 cm tall, and 22.7 cm long. The brick has a mass of 2950 g. What is the density of the brick? *(Section 1–7)*

40. A classroom is 7.0 m wide, 10. m long, and holds 25 people (24 students plus 1 teacher). What is the population density of the classroom? *(Section 1–7)*

41. Mercury is a liquid at room temperature with a density of 13.6 g/cm^3. Would a bar of aluminum float or sink in a pool of mercury? Explain your answer. *(Section 1–7)*

42. The SI unit of density is kilograms per cubic meter. What is the density of iron expressed in units of kilograms per cubic meter? Refer to Figure 1–29. *(Section 1–7)*

43. Perform the following unit conversions. *(Section 1–7)*
(a) 0.001 348 g to milligrams
(b) 3560 N to kilonewtons
(c) 5.29 cs to seconds
(d) 81 mW to watts

44. Perform the following unit conversions. *(Section 1–7)*
(a) 12 in. to centimeters
(b) 3.76 hr to minutes
(c) 137 J to calories
(d) 0.085 490 atm to pascals

Group B

45. Using the information in Figure 1–27 and the definition of density, find the volume occupied by 15 g of aluminum.

46. A scale can be "bent" into a semicircle for use on a meter, as shown in the drawing of a voltmeter. What is the voltage on the meter?

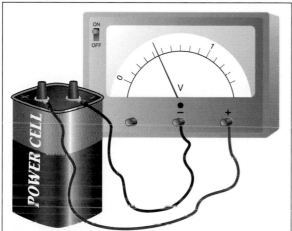

47. Of the following choices, which would be the most convenient unit to use for measuring the thickness of a penny? (a) cm^2 (b) mg (c) mm (d) km

48. A classmate records the following reading from an electronic balance: 15.1 g. Glancing at the digital display, you notice that it actually reads 15.10 g. In a sentence or two, describe what you would say to your friend to explain why it is wrong to ignore the final zero in the measurement.

49. Are the following numbers written correctly in scientific notation? Rewrite any that are incorrect.
(a) $84.029 = 84.029 \times 10^3$
(b) $0.000\ 004\ 70 = 4.7 \times 10^{-6}$
(c) $0.000\ 541 = 5.41 \times 10^4$
(d) $623.000 = 6.23 \times 10^5$
(e) $0.004\ 998 = 4.998 \times 10^{-2}$

50. A friend shows you a gift she has received—a gold ring! In the laboratory, you find its mass to be 58.21 g and its volume to be $3.64\ cm^3$. Calculate the density of the ring. Is it really pure gold? Why or why not?

51. Classify the following units as SI or non-SI: (a) atmosphere (b) newton (c) ampere (d) Celsius degree (e) mile

52. A student counts 320 cars along a 2.0-km stretch of road. In 5.0 min, another student counts 210 cars passing an observation point along the same road.
(a) What is the traffic density?
(b) What is the traffic rate?

53. The density of copper is $8.96\ g/cm^3$. If a rectangular sheet of copper is 10.3 cm wide, 46.1 cm long, and 0.14 cm thick, what is the mass of the copper?

54. Chloroform is a liquid with a sticky sweet odor that was once used as a surgical anesthetic. If the density of chloroform is $1.49\ g/cm^3$, what is the volume of 25 g of chloroform?

55. Perform the following unit conversions. Identify any that are impossible conversions.
(a) 75 mm to inches
(b) 18.69 m to feet
(c) 3 kg to liters
(d) 190 pm to centimeters
(e) 64.05 mL to seconds
(f) 392 mm Hg to atmospheres

56. Perform the following unit conversions. Identify any that are impossble conversions. Express your answers in scientific notation when necessary.
(a) 1.042×10^{-2} m to millimeters
(b) 5.83×10^5 L to cubic meters
(c) 2.56×10^4 Pa to atmospheres
(d) 45 km to inches
(e) 2.7 hr to milliseconds
(f) 7.9×10^3 K to milliamperes

57. The speed limit on many roads in the United States is 55 mi/hr.
(a) Convert 55 mi/hr to kilometers per hour.
(b) Convert 55 mi/hr to meters per second.

Energy and Matter

A hush of anticipation falls over the crowd. All eyes are on the weight lifter. Carefully, he grasps the barbell, prepares himself, and then, with a mighty effort, heaves the enormous weight over his head. The crowd roars its approval! The weight lifter savors his accomplishment!

Raising a massive object, as this Olympic weight lifter is doing in competition, requires more than careful training, natural ability, and a winning attitude. It requires chemical energy stored in the cells of the athlete's muscles. Energy gives us the ability to accomplish a task—lifting a barbell and winning a gold medal or playing a fast-paced game of soccer. Matter is the "stuff" that makes up all objects, including barbells and soccer balls. Energy and matter are intimately connected, as you will discover in this chapter.

From a weight-lifting competition to a high-school soccer game, the interactions of matter and energy are all around us.

Chem Journal

YOU AND YOUR WORLD

You know that everything around you is made of matter. But what about energy? In your journal, describe all the different forms of energy you are aware of in your surroundings. After you finish reading this chapter, return to your journal entry and evaluate your response.

2-1 Energy

Guide for Reading
- What is energy?
- What is the law of conservation of energy?

Everyone is familiar with the need for **energy**—to heat water for bathing, to provide nourishment for our bodies, and to give us the means to travel long distances in comfort. Without energy, we could not accomplish any of the countless tasks that make up our days. But just what is energy?

Energy is the capacity to do work or to produce heat. Work is the capacity to move an object over a distance against a resisting force. What do a speeding locomotive, sunlight, and a chocolate bar have in common? The answer is that they all represent forms of energy. The locomotive pulls a train against the resistance due to friction with the surrounding air and friction in the wheels and other moving parts of the train. Sunlight striking a solar collector can generate electricity to power an electric motor against the resistance of the load (or appliance) attached to the motor. And a chocolate bar gives you the energy to climb up a steep hill against the resisting force of gravity.

Figure 2-1   The solar panels on the Hubble Space Telescope transform radiant energy into electrical energy to power the telescope. What type of energy does a moving locomotive have?

Stored Energy Content of Plastics

The unit commonly used to measure the stored energy content of fuels such as coal and petroleum is called the British thermal unit (BTU). One BTU is the amount of heat necessary to raise the temperature of 1 pound of water 1 Fahrenheit degree. The stored energy content of fuel oil, for example, is 20,900 BTU/pound. For coal, the energy content is equal to 9600 BTU/pound. How do these numbers compare with the stored energy content of plastics (which are made from petroleum)? The plastic used to make soft drink bottles, called PET (polyethylene terephthalate), contains 10,900 BTU/pound of stored energy—more than the same amount of coal. High-density polyethylene (HDPE), which is used to make plastic milk jugs and "crinkly" plastic bags, has a stored energy content of 18,700 BTU/pound—almost as much as fuel oil. It might be possible to "capture" this stored energy by burning plastics in so-called waste-to-energy incinerators and using the energy to generate electricity.

Figure 2–2 *The potential energy of the water stored behind the Glen Canyon Dam is used to generate electricity.*

The Forms of Energy

Energy comes in many forms, but they can be conveniently classified into just three categories: radiant energy, kinetic energy, and potential energy.

Sunlight is an example of radiant energy. We will consider radiant energy in greater depth in Chapter 3.

The energy carried by objects in motion, like a locomotive, is called **kinetic energy,** or energy of motion. Another kind of kinetic energy, sometimes used for the energy carried by the moving parts of a machine, is mechanical energy. Thermal energy is a form of kinetic energy caused by the random internal motion of particles of matter.

The energy possessed by objects because of their position or the arrangement of their particles is called **potential energy,** or stored energy. When rainwater is collected in an elevated tank, the water can be channeled down a pipe so that it turns a wheel. The moving wheel can perform work such as grinding grain or generating electricity. Thus, the water in the tank has the capacity to perform work—it has energy—because of its position above the wheel. The kind of energy carried by the water is called gravitational potential energy. Gravity is responsible for converting the potential energy of the water into kinetic energy, which is then able to do work.

There are other kinds of potential energy. Electrical potential energy (often simply called electrical energy) is the energy that exists when objects with different electrical charges are separated. In this case, energy is required to overcome the force of attraction between the two different charges. Some electrical devices such as batteries operate on this principle. Chemical potential energy, or chemical energy, exists because of the arrangement of the particles that make up a substance. Fuels such as the gasoline in a car or the food you eat have chemical potential energy.

Measuring Energy

A common unit of energy is the calorie (cal). One calorie is the amount of heat needed to raise the temperature of 1 gram of water by 1 Celsius degree (1 cal = 1 g × 1 C°). How many calories of heat do you think would be needed to raise the temperature of 5 grams of water by 1 Celsius degree? You are correct if you said 5 calories (5 cal = 5 g × 1 C°).

The energy stored in food is often given in a unit that is related to the calorie. The Calorie (Cal), spelled with a capital C, is the same as exactly 1000 calories or 1 kilocalorie. A typical chocolate bar can supply 200 Calories, or 200 kilocalories, of energy. Depending on your weight and activity level, a typical student requires between 2000 and 3000 Calories per day.

The SI unit of energy is the **joule** (JOOL). To picture the size of 1 joule (J), imagine lifting a medium-sized apple a distance of 1 meter against the force of gravity. This task requires about 1 joule of energy. The joule is named for James Prescott Joule (1818–1889), an English physicist who made pioneering advances in our understanding of energy.

In the 1800s, it was not known whether heat was related to various forms of energy, such as the energy involved in lifting an apple. James Joule investigated this question. As a result of his observations and experiments, Joule realized that the changes produced by heating a substance could also be produced by mechanical energy. Expressed in modern units, Joule's work can be summarized by the following unit equality:

$$1 \text{ cal} = 4.184 \text{ J} \qquad \textbf{(Eq. 1)}$$

In other words, four medium-sized apples falling through a distance of 1 meter can supply the same energy as 1 calorie of heat. (Of course, Joule did not use apples in his experiments!) Joule had discovered that mechanical energy is indeed related to heat.

Law of Conservation of Energy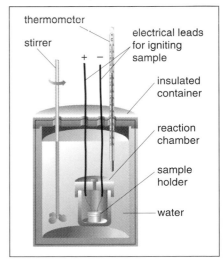

The implication of Joule's experiments is profound. Different forms of energy are equivalent, meaning that a particular amount of potential or radiant energy can be converted into an exactly equivalent amount of kinetic energy. In the process, no energy is lost and no energy is created.

Joule's results are summarized in a natural law called the **law of conservation of energy: In any process, energy is neither created nor destroyed.** By the term process, we mean any situation in which energy is transferred from one object to another or transformed from one kind of energy into another kind. For example, hitting a baseball transfers kinetic energy from the bat to the ball (and also to the air in the form of sound). Similarly, igniting a match transforms chemical energy into heat and light.

Figure 2–3 *The experiments of James Joule led to a greater understanding of the relationship between heat and energy.*

Figure 2–4 *This device, called a calorimeter, is used to measure the movement of heat into or out of a substance.*

thermometer

stirrer

electrical leads for igniting sample

insulated container

reaction chamber

sample holder

water

The law of conservation of energy is very general, but it does not apply to processes that occur in the sun and in nuclear reactors. These processes involve another form of energy called nuclear energy. You will learn more about nuclear energy in Chapter 24. As you probably know, the sun is the ultimate source of most of the energy we use.

SAMPLE PROBLEM 1

A student uses 30. J of energy putting books on a shelf in the classroom. Convert this amount of energy from joules to calories.

STRATEGY	SOLUTION
1. Analyze	The problem involves a conversion of units from joules to calories. Unit conversions were discussed in Chapter 1.
2. Plan	You can use the symbol E (for energy) to represent the unknown number of calories in 30. J. The unit equality for converting joules to calories is given in Equation 1. From the unit equality, two conversion factors can be written:

$$\frac{4.184\ J}{1\ cal} \quad \text{and} \quad \frac{1\ cal}{4.184\ J}$$

Choose the correct conversion factor by performing a dimensional analysis so that the joule units cancel, leaving only the calorie unit.

3. Solve

$$E = 30.\ J \times \frac{1\ cal}{4.184\ J}$$

$$= 7.2\ cal$$

4. Evaluate — The joule units canceled as required, leaving the calorie unit on the right side of the equal sign. Only two significant digits were kept in the final answer because there are only two significant digits in 30. J. Since there are slightly more than 4 J in 1 cal, it makes sense that 30. J should be slightly more than 7 cal.

PRACTICE PROBLEMS

1. Suppose you use 135 cal of energy to perform a task. How many joules have you used? *(Answer: 565 J)*

2. The energy content of a small tomato is about 17 Cal. Convert this measurement to joules. *(Answer: 7.1×10^4 J)*

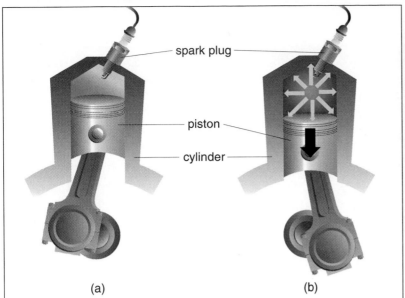

(a)   (b)

spark plug

piston

cylinder

The Energy Crisis

If energy is never created or destroyed as stated in the law of conservation of energy, why is it so common to hear that we are "running out of energy"? The answer is that our society depends on the chemical energy in two substances—coal and petroleum—for the majority of its energy needs. Coal and petroleum are two of the three so-called fossil fuels. (The third is natural gas.) About 90 percent of our energy comes from fossil fuels.

Although few people still burn coal directly for heat, coal is burned in power plants to generate electricity, which we consume in staggering amounts in our homes, offices, and schools. Petroleum is converted into the fuel that powers cars, trucks, and airplanes. When we say that we are "running out of energy," we are really expressing the fear that we will consume all of the potential energy of these fossil fuel resources.

Petroleum also has important nonfuel uses. One of the most important nonfuel uses of petroleum is to make petrochemicals, which are the source of plastics, synthetic fibers, and a variety of building materials. You will learn more about petroleum and plastics in Chapter 25.

What makes coal and petroleum so valuable? They are simple to get and easy to use—we dig or pump them out of the ground and then burn them. Burning releases their chemical energy. The energy from burning a kilogram of coal or a liter of gasoline can

Figure 2–5 *In an automobile engine, the firing of the spark plug ignites the fuel, which moves the piston, which transfers mechanical energy to the wheels of the car. When Jose Canseco hits a home run, the kinetic energy of the moving bat is transferred to the ball.*

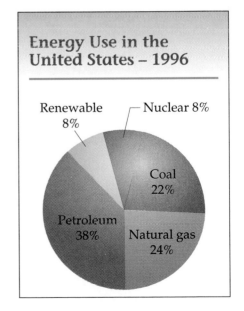

Energy Use in the United States – 1996

Renewable 8%
Nuclear 8%
Coal 22%
Petroleum 38%
Natural gas 24%

Figure 2–6 *This chart shows the sources of energy used in the United States. As you can see, about 84 percent of all energy is obtained from coal, oil, and natural gas. How much of our energy currently comes from nuclear power?*

Figure 2–7 *On this offshore oil rig, petroleum is obtained by drilling into the ocean floor. "Farms" of giant windmills, which convert the energy of the moving wind into electricity, are one alternative to burning fossil fuels for energy.*

be obtained from other sources, such as the sun and wind. Such alternatives, however, are less convenient and usually more expensive than coal and petroleum. With further research and development, alternative sources of energy will probably become more attractive to industries and consumers.

In the meantime, it is a good idea to reduce our consumption of coal and petroleum voluntarily. Conserving a little electricity and gasoline does not impose a hardship on most people, but it does help preserve an important resource for the benefit of future generations. What suggestions can you make to encourage people to conserve these resources?

2–1 Section Review

1. What is energy? Describe three basic forms of energy and give an example of each.
2. State the law of conservation of energy.
3. What is the SI unit of energy?
4. Why has it been said that our society is in the midst of an "energy crisis"?
5. **Theme Trace—Energy** Choose a common situation from your daily life—for example, waking up and getting ready to go to school—and describe all of the energy transformations involved.

2–2 Temperature

Guide for Reading

- What is the SI scale used to measure temperature?
- What is absolute zero?

Our bodies are well-adapted to detecting changes in temperature. Nerves on the surface of the skin are sensitive to the touch of an ice cube or a cup of hot chocolate. Even so, our sense of temperature is not precise. A room that feels too warm to one person may seem quite comfortable to someone else. So it is understandable that the sense of touch cannot be used to measure temperature. Instead we use a thermometer to measure temperature. A thermometer is an instrument that gives an accurate and precise reading of temperature.

Compared with other kinds of measurements, the idea of measuring temperature is relatively new. The Italian physicist Galileo Galilei (1564–1642) invented the first temperature-measuring instrument. A friend of Galileo's, a physician by profession, was one of the first to use the new instrument for measuring fevers in his patients.

The modern thermometer used in most homes and chemistry laboratories consists of a reservoir, or bulb, connected to a sealed tube, or stem. See Figure 2–8. The bulb is filled with a liquid such as mercury or colored alcohol. As the bulb is heated (or cooled), the liquid expands (or contracts) and rises (or falls) inside the stem. The stem is marked with a scale so that the level of the liquid can be read easily.

The Fahrenheit and Celsius Temperature Scales

The choice of a temperature scale is quite arbitrary. One scientist who made especially good thermometers was Gabriel Fahrenheit (1686–1736). Like many thermometer makers of his day, Fahrenheit devised his own temperature scale. His instruments became widely used and consequently so did his temperature scale.

Despite the popularity of Fahrenheit's thermometers, a different scale was gradually accepted by scientists for temperature measurements. The new scale, called the Celsius scale, was more compatible with the spirit of the metric system. The Celsius scale is named after its inventor, a Swedish astronomer named Anders Celsius (1701–1744). On the Celsius scale, the freezing point of pure water at sea level is 0°C and the boiling point of pure water at sea level is 100.°C. Figure 2–9 on page 62 compares the Fahrenheit and Celsius temperature scales.

Figure 2–8 You know that it is a cold winter day, but just how cold is it? Do you think you could make an accurate estimate of the air temperature without using a thermometer? A thermometer must be carefully calibrated, as shown in the diagram.

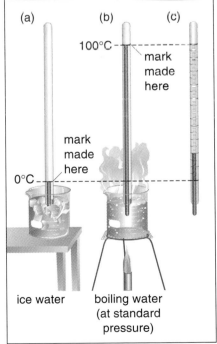

Figure 2–9 *The table shows a comparison between the Celsius and the Fahrenheit temperature scales. What is the boiling point of water on the Celsius scale? On the Fahrenheit scale?*

Comparison of Celsius and Fahrenheit Temperatures

Example	Temperature	
Lowest official temperature recorded in the United States* (Prospect Creek, AK, January 23, 1971)	−62°C	−80.°F
Melting ice	0°C	32°F
Typical room temperature	21°C	70°F
"Normal" body temperature	37.0°C	98.6°F
Highest official temperature recorded in the United States* (Death Valley, CA, July 10, 1913)	57°C	134°F
Boiling water	100.°C	212°F
Typical oven temperature for baking	163°C	325°F
Surface of the sun	6000°C	10,000°F

* Data from *World Almanac Book of Facts 1994.*

YOU AND YOUR WORLD

Making Candy

All candy starts out as a solution of sugar and water. The solution is heated to boiling and the water is gradually driven out of the resulting syrup. The less water, the higher the concentration of sugar and the harder and more brittle the candy will be. The boiling point of the solution increases as the water is driven out. So the boiling point of the solution is a good guide to the amount of water left in the syrup. Cooks use a candy thermometer to judge when the syrup has the correct amount of water for the type of candy they wish to make.

The Kelvin Temperature Scale

Although both the Fahrenheit and Celsius temperature scales are extremely useful for various applications, a third scale is part of the International System of Units. **The SI scale used to measure temperature is the Kelvin scale.** The **Kelvin scale** is named after the English physicist and mathematician William Thomson, Lord Kelvin (1824–1907). The unit of temperature on the Kelvin scale is the kelvin (K). Although the degree symbol (°) is not used with kelvins, the kelvin is the same size as the Celsius degree. In other words, a temperature change of 1 kelvin is the same as a change of 1 Celsius degree:

$$2\ K - 1\ K = 2°C - 1°C \qquad \textbf{(Eq. 2)}$$

The difference between the Kelvin and the Celsius scales is the location of the zero point. The zero point of the Kelvin scale, called **absolute zero,** corresponds to −273°C. See Figure 2–10. Absolute zero is the point at which the motion of particles of matter—their kinetic energy—ceases.

Because the zero points of the scales are different, to convert Kelvin temperatures to the Celsius scale you must subtract 273:

$$°C = K - 273 \qquad \textbf{(Eq. 3)}$$

To convert Celsius temperatures to the Kelvin scale, add 273:

$$K = °C + 273 \qquad \textbf{(Eq. 4)}$$

For example, the boiling point of water, 100.°C, is 373 K:

$$K = 100.°C + 273 \qquad \textbf{(Eq. 5)}$$
$$= 373\ K$$

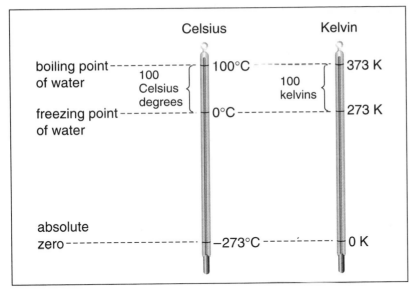

Notice that all temperatures on the Kelvin scale are positive. This is meaningful because temperature is an indicator of the kinetic energy (energy of motion) of particles within a sample, something that cannot be negative. Also notice that a Kelvin degree and a Celsius degree are identical in magnitude. A temperature on the Kelvin scale is always positive and is 273° higher than the parallel measure on the Celsius scale.

Figure 2–10 *The zero point on the Kelvin scale is called absolute zero. What is absolute zero?*

SAMPLE PROBLEM 2

Temperatures close to absolute zero are incredibly cold—at 50. K air will freeze into a solid! Convert 50. K to the Celsius scale.

STRATEGY	SOLUTION
1. **Analyze**	You are asked to convert a Kelvin temperature to a Celsius temperature.
2. **Plan**	Equation 3 is the correct equation to use to change a Kelvin temperature to a Celsius temperature.
3. **Solve**	$°C = K - 273$ $= 50. K - 273$ $= -223°C$
4. **Evaluate**	Check that you have subtracted correctly. You know that 50. K is an extremely cold temperature. Therefore, $-223°C$ is a reasonable answer.

PRACTICE PROBLEMS

3. Normal body temperature is 310. K. Convert 310. K to the Celsius scale.   *(Answer: 37°C)*

4. Antifreeze, or ethylene glycol, boils at 197°C. Convert 197°C to the Kelvin scale.   *(Answer: 470 K)*

CONNECTION

Pursuing Absolute Zero

Where do you think the coldest spot in the universe can be found? You might suggest that this spot exists not on Earth, but in deep space—in the black emptiness between the galaxies. But you would be wrong! In fact, the coldest spot in the universe is right here on Earth—in Boulder, Colorado, to be exact. At the University of Colorado, physicists have chilled 200 million cesium atoms to within a millionth of a degree of absolute zero (0 K or −273°C). Physicists at the Massachusetts Institute of Technology and at Stanford University are also pursuing the elusive goal of absolute zero. Why are scientists so interested in lowering the temperature of matter close to absolute zero? The answer is that some very strange things happen to matter when it is this cold. In fact, a new state of matter with as yet unknown properties may exist close to absolute zero. Some physicists call this unique state of matter "atom stuff" for want of a better term. The name reflects the prediction that at absolute zero, all the atoms in a sample of matter will condense into one big fuzzy atom!

Physicists can get closer and closer to absolute zero but they can never quite reach it. The reason absolute zero is unattainable is that as atoms are cooled, they lose energy. And as they lose energy, they slow down. (Remember that heat is a form of kinetic energy, or energy of motion.) So at absolute zero, the atoms would (if they could) stop moving entirely. The problem is that the closer the atoms get to absolute zero, the harder it becomes to remove any more heat. So absolute zero will always be the just-out-of-reach lower limit of temperature. So near and yet so far!

2–2 Section Review

1. Name three scales that are used to measure temperature. Which of these is the SI scale?

2. What point on the Kelvin scale corresponds to −273°C? What is this point called?

3. Write the equation you would use to convert a temperature measurement from the Celsius to the Kelvin temperature scale. From the Kelvin to the Celsius scale.

4. **Connection—You and Your World** Suppose your recipe for lasagna involves baking for 1 hour at 325°F. Convert this temperature to the Celsius scale and to the Kelvin scale.

2–3 Matter

Guide for Reading
- What is matter?
- What is the law of conservation of matter?

One of the simplest observations anyone can make about the world is that it is filled with "stuff"—tables, chairs, books, soil, plants, animals (including ourselves), and so on. The "stuff" that such objects are made of is called **matter.** Everything you see around you is made of matter. **Matter is anything that has mass and volume.** As you will recall from Chapter 1, mass is the amount of material in an object, and volume is the amount of space the object occupies. A tree has a certain mass and occupies space, so it is composed of matter. So are cars, buildings, people, and anything else you see around you. Even air is made of matter.

What is matter? Why does it exist? These questions have occupied philosophers and scientists for thousands of years, but the full answer has still not been found. We accept the existence of matter, although we do not completely understand it. This textbook is devoted to studying the characteristics of matter. As part of this examination, we will describe the composition of matter at more and more microscopic levels. But we cannot answer all the questions about matter. Some of these questions have been answered by the work of physicists, and we hope you pursue this knowledge in further science courses. Other answers, however, still lie beyond the probing of science.

What humans have learned about the nature of matter is a fascinating story of discovery and painstaking effort. Some of the crucial experiments that were performed in an effort to understand matter are among the most important contributions of science to our understanding of the universe. You will learn about these experiments in upcoming chapters.

Figure 2–11 *What do a bridge, a wolf, and redwood trees have in common? They are all made of matter. Matter—its structure and interactions—is the subject of this textbook.*

States of Matter

From everyday observation you know that matter exists in three states—solid, liquid, and gas. A fourth state of matter—plasma—is found inside stars. (We will not describe plasma in much detail in this textbook.) The table in Figure 2–12 shows examples of the four states of matter and indicates some ways in which they differ from one another.

ANALOGIES FOR THE STATES OF MATTER   Understanding the three common states of matter may be easier if you can picture an analogy for each state. An analogy is a way of describing something by comparing it to something else. As you read the following descriptions, remember that no analogy is perfect.

A **solid** holds a particular shape and has a definite volume. The appearance of certain solids, such as a crystal of salt, suggests an underlying orderliness to the arrangement of the particles of matter inside. A marching band arrayed in rigid formation serves as an analogy for the particles of a solid.

A **liquid** does not hold its own shape but it does occupy a definite volume. A liquid flows freely and takes the shape of its

The States of Matter

State	Example*	Characteristics
Solid	Gold	High density Density little affected by pressure Holds its own shape in a container
Liquid	Water	High density Density little affected by pressure Adopts the shape of its container
Gas	Nitrogen	Low density Density depends on pressure Expands to fill its container
Plasma	Interior of the sun	Low density Density depends on pressure Expands to fill its container** Exists only at high temperatures

*The example applies to conditions as they are found normally on Earth, i.e., at 25°C and 1 atmosphere, except in the case of plasmas, which require higher temperatures.
**The sun has no container, of course. The matter inside the sun is contained by its own gravity. In laboratories on Earth, plasma is contained by strong magnetic fields sometimes called "magnetic bottles."

Figure 2–12 *Matter exists in four forms, or states: solid, liquid, gas, and plasma.*

Figure 2–13 *It is often useful to use an analogy when you are trying to understand a concept. Here you see analogies for the three common states of matter.*

container. Spectators grouped in a disorderly bunch along the sidelines of a playing field are an analogy for the particles in a drop of liquid.

A **gas** has no definite shape or volume. It expands to fill the available volume of its container. A game of soccer, with the players spread far apart on the playing field, is an analogy for the particles of a gas. Compared with liquids and solids, the density of gases is extremely low. Thus there are relatively few particles of matter in a gas compared with a liquid or a solid.

CHANGES IN STATE By heating or cooling a sample of matter, any of the states we have just described—solid, liquid, and gas—can be observed. For example, mercury freezes to a solid at −39°C; it boils and becomes a gas at 357°C. Between these temperatures (including room temperature, around 21°C), mercury is a shiny, slippery liquid. Transitions from a solid to a liquid or from a liquid to a gas are called changes in state. Common changes in state are illustrated in Figure 2–14 on page 68.

Properties of Matter

Have you ever looked into a crowd of people and instantly recognized a friend? You learn to recognize people by the shape of their face, the color of their hair and eyes, the way they walk, and many other features. Their characteristics make them easy to identify even in a crowd. A sample of matter can be identified in a similar way—by observing its characteristics, or properties.

Figure 2–14 These dripping icicles illustrate the change of state from a solid to a liquid. When solid sulfur is heated, it turns into a liquid. When the liquid is poured into a beaker of cold water, it turns back into a solid.

Figure 2–15 How are these contortionists from Cirque du Soleil an analogy for a physical change in matter?

The characteristics of a substance that can be observed without altering the identity of the substance are called **physical properties.** Density, color, and melting point are examples of physical properties.

The characteristics of a substance that cannot be observed without altering the substance are called **chemical properties.** Flammability, which is the tendency of a substance to burn in air, is a chemical property.

Changes in Matter

Circus contortionists can train their bodies to adopt weird and fantastic shapes. The new shapes are surprising and entertaining, but you know (or hope!) the performers can get safely untangled when they want to. Throughout the act, each performer remains the same person despite many changes in shape.

PHYSICAL CHANGES Like the circus contortionist, some changes in matter involve startling alterations in form, but the matter itself is not altered. Changes of this kind, which do not alter the identity of a substance, are called **physical changes.** Crushing, tearing, and changes in state are examples of physical changes.

CHEMICAL CHANGES In contrast to physical changes, **chemical changes** (or chemical reactions) do alter the identity of a substance. A piece of wood undergoes a chemical change when it burns. Food undergoes chemical changes as it cooks. And a piece of iron exposed to moist air is chemically changed as it rusts. Figure 2–16 shows a variety of physical and chemical changes.

Figure 2–16 *Here you see some examples of physical and chemical changes in matter (clockwise from top left). Cars are crushed and turned into scrap metal. Metal drums rust away at an abandoned whaling station. Paper, plastics, and aluminum cans are recycled to be used again. An antacid tablet dissolves in a glass of water. A building burns to the ground. Which of these are physical changes? Which are chemical changes? Explain your reasoning.*

To distinguish between chemical and physical changes, you must ask yourself, Has the change altered the identity of the substance? A chemical change produces a different substance from what existed before. How do you know if the substance is different? You can tell by its characteristics, or properties. Rust is visibly different from iron: It is reddish and powdery, whereas iron is shiny and hard. Iron conducts electricity, but rust does not. These differences prove that rust is not the same substance as iron and so the process of rusting involves a chemical change.

Observing a Candle

1. Choose a location that is free of drafts. Light a candle and make a record, including drawings, of the physical and chemical changes you observe in the burning candle.

2. Extinguish the candle flame and immediately bring a lighted match close to the wick. What happens?

3. Let the candle cool completely. After at least 1 minute, light the tip of the wick and watch the progress of the flame. What do you observe?

4. Carefully trim a small piece of the wick with scissors. What effect does changing the length of the wick have on the appearance of the flame?

5. Summarize your observations in a brief essay. Include several questions and hypotheses for further investigation.

SAMPLE PROBLEM 3

Some phrases in the following letter have been underlined. Identify the phrases as describing chemical changes, physical changes, or neither.

Dear Aunt Linda,

Prom night was great fun! Tony, my date, looked very handsome in his rented tuxedo—it was a shame <u>the dog tore that little hole in his trousers</u>. First we went to dinner at Chez Chemie. I was a little surprised that we had to <u>light the candle</u> on our own table and <u>put ice water in the glasses</u>, but the restaurant was very busy and we didn't mind. (<u>The ice melted</u> right away, too, and we had to add more.)

STRATEGY	SOLUTION
1. Analyze	Each phrase may describe a chemical change, a physical change, or neither. You must identify the correct category for each phrase.
2. Plan	Take one phrase at a time and determine whether a substance has undergone a change. Ask, "Is it the same substance as it was before the change?"
3. Solve	<u>the dog tore that little hole in his trousers</u>: Tearing is a physical change because the identity of the fabric has not been altered. <u>light the candles</u>: A burning candle is an example of a chemical change because the candle is not the same substance after it is burned. <u>put ice water in the glasses</u>: No change in any substance occurs, so the phrase describes neither a chemical nor a physical change. <u>The ice melted</u>: This is a change in state, so it is a physical change.

4. Evaluate As with the properties of matter, the words that describe a change often disclose whether the change is chemical or physical. In this example, each description has been correctly identified based on the criteria stated in the problem.

PRACTICE PROBLEMS

5. Identify whether the underlined phrases in the following paragraph are chemical changes, physical changes, or neither.

> We both ordered shrimp Creole. While we waited, we <u>cut slices from a loaf</u> of warm French bread—yum! My shrimp Creole was delicious. But poor Tony! The waiter was hurrying so much that he <u>spilled the whole plate on him</u>. Tony was sweet about it, though. We got him cleaned up pretty well. He ordered a hamburger after that. He also ordered a baked potato, but he had to send it back <u>to be cooked some more</u> because it was still hard. It came back looking rather black, but Tony said it tasted fine. *(Answer: physical, neither, chemical)*

6. Identify at least one chemical change and one physical change mentioned in the following paragraphs:

> Thank goodness it was a warm evening. We had to drive with the windows rolled down because Tony was starting to smell a little like a fish market.
>
> At the prom, we actually danced in the moonlight! (We couldn't dance indoors on account of you know who.) We had a wonderful time. It really wasn't anyone's fault that Tony caught the edge of his sleeve on fire reaching over the snack table—I think too many little candles were burning on it. Mrs. Donaldson was mad that Tony dunked his arm in the punch bowl to put the fire out, but honestly what else could he do? He tipped over a vase of flowers to get to the punch bowl in time, and it shattered into a thousand pieces. Everyone stopped and stared, but no one got hurt.
>
> On the way home, we happened to pass the tuxedo rental store, and I saw a "Help Wanted" sign. That was lucky, said Tony—he was going to need a job to pay for what happened to his suit!
>
> Love, Janice
>
> P.S. Tony loves his new job, and he's just been promoted to assistant manager! *(Answer: Several answers are possible. Possibilities include setting his sleeve on fire: chemical; shattering a vase: physical.)*

CHEM Exploration

Why Does Popcorn Pop?

1. Add some unpopped kernels of popcorn to a large beaker.
2. Cover the beaker tightly with clear plastic wrap. Make a pinhole in the center of the plastic.
3. Place the beaker on a hot plate. Observe what happens as you heat the beaker.
- What do you observe forming in the beaker as the popcorn pops?
- What causes the popcorn to pop? Explain.
- How could you test your hypothesis?

The Mystery of the Spinning Pinwheel

Have you ever seen a device such as this in someone's home (maybe even yours) during the holiday season? These festive ornaments are usually made of metal. When the candles beneath the pinwheel are lit, the pinwheel begins to spin.

Making Inferences

1. What causes the pinwheel to spin?
2. What energy transformations or transfers are occurring?
3. What property of the air is being applied to make this device work?

Conservation of Matter

"One may take it for granted that in every reaction there is an equal quantity of matter before and after." With these words, Antoine Lavoisier (luhv-WAHZ-ee-ay) (1743–1794) started a revolution that overthrew a lot of old thinking and helped establish the science of modern chemistry. **Matter, like energy, is neither created nor destroyed in any process.** This statement is called the **law of conservation of matter,** a law that applies throughout the universe, in all branches of science.

A demonstration of this law can be seen in Figure 2–18. The spherical flask completely traps the smoke and other substances produced by the burning candle. As you can see, the balance pointer does not move as the candle burns. This proves that the total mass of the candle and the air in the flask is the same before, during, and after the chemical changes involved in burning. Thus, no matter has been created or destroyed in the process of burning.

Lavoisier performed careful experiments of this type to prove that the total mass does not change during any chemical reaction. For many reactions in which mass seemed to be lost or gained, Lavoisier showed that a gas was simply given off or taken from the air. For example, Lavoisier was the first to recognize the role of oxygen in burning and rusting. This discovery, which we take for granted today, was possible only because Lavoisier insisted on making exquisitely accurate and precise measurements. The balance was Lavoisier's chief scientific tool, as crucial to his work as a microscope is to a biologist.

Figure 2–17 *Here you see a portrait of Antoine Lavoisier with his wife, who collaborated with him on many of his experiments. Lavoisier is considered to be the father of modern chemistry because of his careful experiments and precise measurements.*

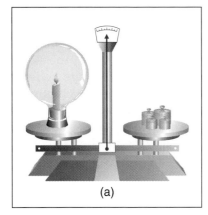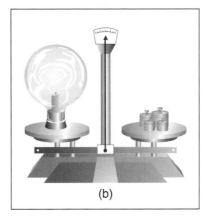

Figure 2–18 *As shown in this diagram, mass is neither gained nor lost when a candle burns in air.*

◄ *Historical Perspective*

Tragically, Lavoisier was guillotined during the Reign of Terror that followed the French Revolution. Like many of the French nobility, he was a member of the *Ferme Generale*, a private company that collected taxes for the government. The *Ferme Generale* was a hated institution, and Lavoisier's involvement in it marked him for death. His execution was a tragedy felt in all branches of science. The mathematician Lagrange, a contemporary of Lavoisier's, said: "It took them only an instant to cut off that head, and a hundred years may not produce another like it."

2–3 Section Review

1. Define matter. What is the law of conservation of matter?
2. What are the four states of matter? Give an example of each.
3. Briefly describe the characteristics of each of the four states of matter.
4. What is the difference between a physical property and a chemical property? Between a physical change and a chemical change?
5. **Critical Thinking—Classifying** Classify each of the following examples as a physical change or a chemical change: (a) plastic milk jugs are recycled to make plastic shopping bags; (b) plastic soft drink bottles are burned in an incinerator to generate electricity; (c) plastic soft drink bottles are recycled to make fiberfill for ski jackets.

Guide for Reading

- What is an element?
- What is the difference between an element and a compound?

Element Hunt

Many items in your home or classroom are made of common elements. For example, you might be able to identify items made of aluminum, copper, iron, or carbon.

1. Alone or with a partner, make a search of your home or classroom. See how many items you can find that are made of a single element.

2. Display all of the items that you collect. Label each item with the name and symbol of the element it is made of.

- What do you know about the properties of each element that might affect how that element is used?

Figure 2–19 *Several common elements and their symbols are listed in this table. What is an element?*

2–4 Elements and Compounds

Looking at the world, you find an overwhelming number of different substances—from clouds that float lazily in the sky to your own earthbound flesh and bones. Early thinkers believed that the variety of substances we see around us is actually the result of combinations of just a few simple forms of matter. These fundamental forms of matter were called elements. Although early philosophers had no scientific evidence for their belief, the concept of simple, fundamental elements was extremely appealing to them.

Elements

Our understanding of what defines a chemical **element** has changed radically since ancient times, but the basic concept of a fundamental kind of matter has endured. **An element is a substance that cannot be separated into simpler substances by a chemical change.** Today, slightly more than 100 chemical elements are known. Some familiar elements are listed in the table in Figure 2–19.

Names and Symbols of Selected Elements

Symbol	Element	Symbol	Element
Al	aluminum	Mn	manganese
Ar	argon	Hg	mercury (*hydrargyrum*)
As	arsenic	Ne	neon
Ba	barium	Ni	nickel
Be	beryllium	N	nitrogen
B	boron	O	oxygen
Br	bromine	P	phosphorus
Cd	cadmium	Pt	platinum
Ca	calcium	K	potassium (*kalium*)
C	carbon	Ra	radium
Cs	cesium	Rn	radon
Cl	chlorine	Rb	rubidium
Cr	chromium	Se	selenium
Co	cobalt	Si	silicon
Cu	copper (*cuprum*)	Ag	silver (*argentum*)
F	fluorine	Na	sodium (*natrium*)
Fr	francium	Sr	strontium
Au	gold (*aurum*)	S	sulfur
He	helium	Te	tellurium
H	hydrogen	Th	thorium
I	iodine	Sn	tin (*stannum*)
Fe	iron (*ferrum*)	W	tungsten (*wolfram*)
Kr	krypton	U	uranium
Pb	lead (*plumbum*)	Xe	xenon
Li	lithium	Zn	zinc
Mg	magnesium		

Some elements are named for famous scientists. The element einsteinium, for example, is named for Albert Einstein. One of the most recent elements to be discovered has been named seaborgium for the American chemist and Nobel Prize winner Glenn Seaborg. Countries, states, and even planets show up as the names of elements. Americium, californium, and plutonium are examples of elements that are named for a country (America), a state (California), and a planet (Pluto).

For convenience, chemical elements have abbreviations, called element symbols. Element symbols consist of one or two letters. The first letter of an element symbol is always capitalized and the second letter, if present, is never capitalized.

Some elements, like hydrogen, have symbols that are straightforward abbreviations of their English names. For hydrogen, the symbol is H. For aluminum, it is Al. Other elements are different. The element symbol for sodium, for example, is Na. This symbol is derived from the word *natrium,* an old word for sodium. The element symbol for gold is Au, the first two letters of the Latin name for gold—*aurum.* Refer to Figure 2–19. What is the symbol for chlorine? For potassium?

To help them organize information about the elements in a meaningful way, chemists developed the periodic table of the elements. The periodic table is essential for the study of chemistry. In fact, a large periodic table is probably hanging on the wall of your chemistry classroom right now! You will learn much more about the periodic table in Chapter 5. For now, it is enough for you to know that the periodic table organizes the elements according to their properties.

Compounds

When two or more elements combine in a chemical reaction, they form a **compound.** A compound is a substance that contains two or more elements combined in a fixed proportion.

An example of the formation of a compound is shown in Figure 2–20. When magnesium (a silvery metal) burns, it takes oxygen (a gas) out of the air. The white, powdery substance that forms in the reaction is different from either oxygen or magnesium. The powder, called magnesium oxide, is composed of magnesium and oxygen in a fixed proportion—60.32 percent is magnesium and 39.68 percent is oxygen. Magnesium oxide, therefore, is a compound of the elements magnesium and oxygen.

Chemists generally do not write out the names of compounds such as magnesium oxide. Instead, they use the symbols for the elements that comprise the compound to write the chemical formula for that compound. For example, you just read that the compound magnesium oxide contains the elements magnesium and oxygen. From Figure 2–19, you know that the symbol for magnesium is Mg and the symbol for oxygen is O. The chemical formula for magnesium oxide, therefore, is written MgO. In the

Visit our Web site at
http://www.phschool.com
to support your
study of chemistry.

Figure 2–20 *Here you see a burning magnesium ribbon. What is the name of the compound formed when magnesium burns in air?*

language of science, symbols are the letters of the chemical alphabet and chemical formulas are the words. Chemical formulas are the subject of Chapter 7.

Distinguishing Between Elements and Compounds

Elements and compounds are **pure substances.** Every pure substance has a unique set of chemical and physical properties. In Lavoisier's time, deciding whether a pure substance was a compound or an element was difficult. What is it about iron that makes it more "fundamental" than rust? This is not an easy question to answer, but the issue can be settled by making careful measurements of mass. The mass of a sample of iron increases when it changes to rust. On this basis, iron does appear to be the more fundamental substance.

A technique called electrolysis also helped chemists after Lavoisier to distinguish between elements and compounds. Electrolysis literally means "to tear apart with electricity." During electrolysis, an electric current is passed through a substance. If the substance is a compound, it may be broken down into the separate elements that form it. Electrolysis of water, for example, produces two gases. See Figure 2–21. Because water can be broken down by electrolysis, it is not an element. Instead, water is a compound of the two gases produced by electrolysis. One gas is called hydrogen ("water former") and the other is called oxygen ("acid former"). When mixed and ignited, these gases combine to form water once again.

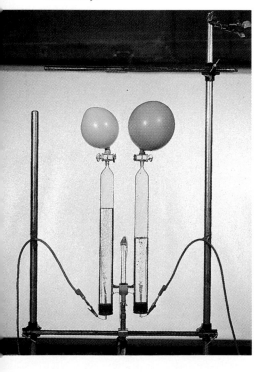

Figure 2–21 *The electrolysis of water produces hydrogen gas (captured in the blue balloon) and oxygen gas (in the yellow balloon).*

2–4 Section Review

1. What is an element? What is the difference between an element and a compound?

2. What is electrolysis? Describe how this process can be used to differentiate between an element and a compound.

3. Refer to Figure 2–19. Which element has the symbol C? Which has the symbol Cr? Why is the symbol for lead Pb?

4. Why are elements and compounds considered to be pure substances?

5. **Critical Thinking—Applying concepts** Sugar consists of carbon, hydrogen, and oxygen. Is sugar an element or a compound? Explain.

2-5 Mixtures

Look at a glass of fresh milk. It appears to be made of a pure substance. But if the milk has come straight from a cow, a layer of cream soon rises to the top of the glass. Apparently milk is not a pure substance after all! Milk is, in fact, a **mixture.** What is a mixture? **A mixture is a blend of two or more pure substances.**

Many objects that appear at first glance to be made of a single kind of matter turn out to be mixtures. A sample of seawater, for example, is largely a mixture of water and various salts. This can be shown by boiling the seawater until all the water is gone and then examining the white, powdery residue.

Types of Mixtures

Not all mixtures appear at first glance to be made of a single kind of matter. Sometimes, as in the case of certain salad dressings, you can see the different parts of a mixture. A mixture that has visibly different parts is called a **heterogeneous mixture.** Heterogeneous mixtures include chocolate chip cookies and granite.

Other mixtures do not contain visibly different parts. Such mixtures are called **homogeneous mixtures.** Seawater is a homogeneous mixture of water and salts. Air is a homogeneous mixture of several gases, including nitrogen and oxygen. Homogeneous mixtures are also called solutions. You will learn more about solutions in Chapter 15.

To tell whether a substance is a mixture, it is necessary to find out whether it can be separated into two (or more) pure substances. Let's see how this is done.

Separating the Components of a Mixture

In the chemistry laboratory, special equipment and techniques have been devised for separating mixtures. These methods, unlike electrolysis, do not cause any chemical changes in the mixture.

Heterogeneous mixtures composed of liquids and solids are often separated by filtration. The mixture is poured through a piece of paper (often shaped into a hollow cone), which lets the liquid part pass through but catches the solid. Figure 2-23 on page 78 shows a typical filtration setup.

Homogeneous mixtures, however, cannot be separated by filtration. Seawater is just as salty after filtering as it was before. Three techniques are commonly used in the laboratory to separate homogeneous mixtures. They are distillation, crystallization, and chromatography.

Guide for Reading
- What is a mixture?
- What are two basic types of mixtures?

Figure 2-22 *Granite is an example of a heterogeneous mixture made up of several different minerals, as can be seen in this photograph.*

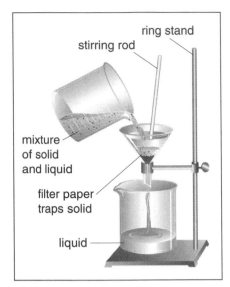

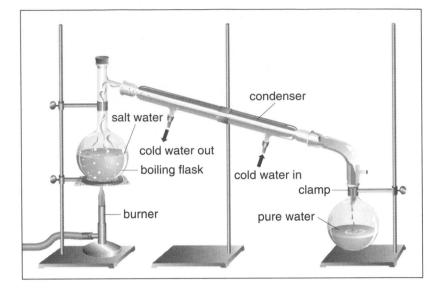

Figure 2–23 *Filtration can be used to separate the solid and liquid parts of a mixture (left). The process of distillation makes use of changes in state from a liquid to a gas and back to a liquid (right).*

INTEGRATING

EARTH **S**CIENCE

Have you ever wondered how diamonds, emeralds, and other beautiful gemstones were formed?

Figure 2–24 *As this photograph of paper chromatography illustrates, colored inks are made up of several different pigments. This beautiful amethyst geode formed deep within the Earth through the process of crystallization.*

The process of distillation takes advantage of differences in boiling points. In a mixture of two liquids, for example, the liquid with the lower boiling point boils and changes into a gas first. The gas is then changed back into a liquid and collected. Carefully performed, a distillation can separate liquids in a mixture that differ in boiling point by just a few degrees Celsius. A typical distillation arrangement is shown in Figure 2–23. Distillation is an important process in petroleum refining, in which petroleum is separated into its useful parts, such as fuel oils and gasoline. Distillation can also be used to separate solid impurities from water and other liquids. As the liquid is boiled in the distilling flask, the dissolved solids are left behind.

If a sample of seawater is allowed to evaporate partially, crystals of salt will form. This technique, called crystallization, can produce solids of very high purity. Crystallization is not limited to liquid solutions. Gemstones are crystals that formed as our young planet slowly cooled.

A solution can be separated by allowing it to flow along a stationary substance. This process is called chromatography. For instance, the pigments in an ink solution can be separated by passing the ink through a piece of paper. The pigments respond differently to the paper—some pigments are held back while others move ahead. Eventually, a pattern of colors results that shows the separated pigments. See Figure 2–24.

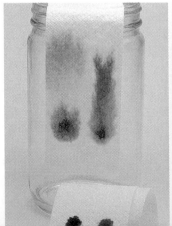

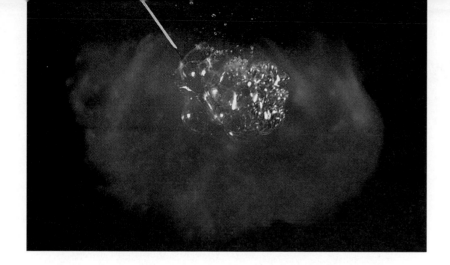

Figure 2–25 *When bubbles filled with hydrogen gas are ignited, the result is a spectacular display of the relationship between matter and energy!*

A Closer Look at Energy and Matter

In this chapter, we have explored the relationship between energy and matter. As you can see from Figure 2–25, there is an impressive amount of potential energy in a mixture of hydrogen and oxygen. The ignition of even a small quantity of these gases produces a burst of kinetic and radiant energy: a mighty thunderclap, a brilliant flame, and a wave of heat.

In fact, changes in matter, which are governed by the law of conservation of matter, are always accompanied by changes in energy. Heat must be added to a gold bar in order to melt it, and light must strike a green leaf to drive the chemical changes necessary for the plant to grow. Whenever matter undergoes a change, energy is involved.

These energy changes operate under the law of conservation of energy. All of the energy released by the explosion of hydrogen and oxygen is present as chemical energy in the original mixture. How is this energy stored? Where is it? These questions lead us deeper into the structure of matter itself, which is our next topic of study.

2–5 Section Review

1. What is a mixture?
2. What is the difference between a heterogeneous mixture and a homogeneous mixture? Give an example of each.
3. Describe how you would separate a mixture of sand and water. What is this process called?
4. Name three methods for separating homogeneous mixtures.
5. **Theme Trace—Energy** Explain how the process of distillation illustrates the relationship between matter and energy.

Laboratory Investigation

Conservation of Mass

Problem

Is mass conserved in a chemical reaction?

Materials (per group)

Erlenmeyer flask
small test tube
rubber stopper to fit flask
balance
graduated cylinder
copper sulfate solution ($CuSO_4$)
sodium hydroxide solution (NaOH)

Procedure

1. Find the mass of the empty Erlenmeyer flask, test tube, and rubber stopper. Record this mass in a data table similar to the one shown.
2. Using the graduated cylinder, measure 20 mL of copper sulfate solution. Pour the solution into the Erlenmeyer flask.
3. Measure 10 mL of sodium hydroxide solution and pour this solution into the test tube. CAUTION: Sodium hydroxide is extremely caustic. Follow all appropriate safety precautions.
4. Carefully place the test tube with the sodium hydroxide into the flask containing the copper sulfate, being careful not to mix the two solutions. Stopper the flask and record your observations of the two solutions in your data table.

5. Find the mass of the flask, test tube, rubber stopper, and the two solutions. Record this mass in your data table.
6. Carefully tip the flask so that the solution in the test tube mixes with the solution in the flask. Be careful not to spill the solutions.
7. Record any evidence of a reaction in your data table.
8. Find the mass of the flask, test tube, rubber stopper, and the products of the reaction. Record this mass in your data table.

Observations

1. Find the mass of the solutions (the reactants) by subtracting the mass with the empty flask (Step 1) from the mass before mixing (Step 5). What is the mass of the two reactants?
2. Find the mass of the products by subtracting the mass with the empty flask (Step 1) from the mass after mixing (Step 8). What is the mass of the products?

Analysis and Conclusions

1. What changes did you observe to indicate that a reaction took place?
2. How did the mass of the reactants (the two solutions) compare with the mass of the products in this reaction?
3. Was mass conserved in this reaction?
4. Was this reaction a chemical or a physical change? Explain.
5. **On Your Own** Repeat this experiment without stoppering the flask, and compare your results.

Mass of Flask, Test Tube, and Stopper (g)		Appearance of Solutions	
Empty flask		Copper sulfate	
Before mixing		Sodium hydroxide	
After mixing		After reaction	

STUDY GUIDE

Summarizing Key Concepts

2–1 Energy

- Energy is the capacity to do work or to produce heat.
- Three basic categories of energy are radiant energy, kinetic energy, and potential energy.
- The SI unit of energy is the joule.
- The law of conservation of energy states that in any process, energy is neither created nor destroyed.

2–2 Temperature

- Temperature is a measure of how hot or cold something is.
- The SI temperature scale is called the Kelvin scale. The SI unit of temperature is the kelvin.
- The zero point on the Kelvin scale is called absolute zero.

2–3 Matter

- Matter is anything that has mass and volume.
- The four states of matter are solid, liquid, gas, and plasma.
- All kinds of matter have certain characteristics, or properties. These properties are either physical properties or chemical properties.

- The law of conservation of matter states that matter is neither created nor destroyed in any process.

2–4 Elements and Compounds

- Elements are substances that cannot be changed into simpler substances by a chemical change.
- Compounds are substances that contain two or more elements combined in a fixed proportion.
- Elements and compounds are examples of pure substances.

2–5 Mixtures

- A mixture is a blend of two or more pure substances.
- Mixtures are either heterogeneous mixtures or homogeneous mixtures.
- Heterogeneous mixtures can often be separated by filtration.
- Homogeneous mixtures can be separated by distillation, crystallization, and chromatography.

Reviewing Key Terms

Define each term in a complete sentence.

2–1 Energy

energy
kinetic energy
potential energy
joule
law of conservation of energy

2–2 Temperature

Kelvin scale
absolute zero

2–3 Matter

matter
solid
liquid
gas
physical property
chemical property
physical change
chemical change
law of conservation of matter

2–4 Elements and Compounds

element
compound
pure substance

2–5 Mixtures

mixture
heterogeneous mixture
homogeneous mixture

CHAPTER REVIEW

Content Review

Multiple Choice
Choose the letter of the answer that best completes each statement.

1. The energy in sunlight is an example of
   (a) potential energy.
   (b) radiant energy.
   (c) kinetic energy.
   (d) chemical energy.
2. The SI unit used to measure energy is the
   (a) joule.   (c) Calorie.
   (b) kelvin.   (d) calorie.
3. The SI temperature scale is called the
   (a) Fahrenheit scale.
   (b) Joule scale.
   (c) Celsius scale.
   (d) Kelvin scale.
4. The state of matter that exists inside the sun and other stars is called
   (a) solid.   (c) gas.
   (b) liquid.   (d) plasma.

5. Which of the following is not an example of a chemical change in matter?
   (a) cooking food
   (b) crushing a can
   (c) burning a log
   (d) igniting a match
6. Which of the following is not a pure substance?
   (a) milk   (c) water
   (b) hydrogen   (d) oxygen
7. A homogeneous mixture can be separated by all of the following methods except
   (a) distillation.
   (b) chromatography.
   (c) crystallization.
   (d) filtration.

True or False
If the statement is true, write "true." If it is false, change the underlined word or words to make the statement true.

8. The type of energy stored in a battery is <u>chemical</u> potential energy.
9. The SI unit of energy is the <u>calorie</u>.
10. Absolute zero is equal to <u>0°C</u>.
11. The zero point on the <u>Kelvin</u> temperature scale is called absolute zero.
12. Matter and energy <u>can</u> be created or destroyed in any chemical process.
13. The color of a substance is an example of a <u>physical</u> property.
14. When solid ice melts to become a liquid, it has undergone a <u>chemical</u> change.
15. A substance that cannot be broken down into simpler substances is a(an) <u>compound</u>.
16. A bowl of breakfast cereal with slices of fresh fruit and milk is an example of a <u>homogeneous</u> mixture.
17. The process of distillation is based on differences in <u>melting</u> point.

Concept Mapping
Complete the following concept map for Section 2–1. Refer to pages xviii–xix to construct a concept map for the entire chapter.

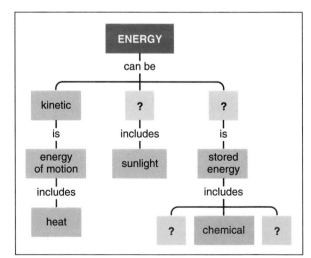

Concept Mastery

Discuss each of the following in a brief paragraph.

18. What is the difference between a homogeneous mixture and a heterogeneous mixture? Give one example of each.

19. What is meant by the physical properties of a substance? The chemical properties?

20. Describe some physical properties and some chemical properties of a copper wire.

21. Convert the following Celsius temperatures to the Kelvin scale:
(a) 37.0°C (b) 163°C (c) −62°C (d) 25°C

22. Convert the following Kelvin temperatures to the Celsius scale:
(a) 255 K (b) 25 K (c) 300. K (d) 273 K

23. Use a specific example to explain what is meant by the law of conservation of matter.

24. Tying it Together A typical automobile engine converts only about 10 percent of the chemical *energy* in gasoline into mechanical energy. Is this a violation of the law of conservation of energy? Explain.

Critical Thinking and Problem Solving

Use the skills you have developed in this chapter to answer each of the following.

25. Making Inferences How might recycling plastic containers help to conserve energy and avoid an energy crisis in our society? HINT: Where do plastics come from?

26. Classifying Classify each of the following examples as a physical change or a chemical change: (a) dissolving sugar in a glass of iced tea (b) a bicycle rusting on the lawn (c) scrambling an egg (d) cooking the scrambled egg.

27. Evaluating statements You complain to a friend one morning, "I have no energy today." She knows what you mean, but is your statement scientifically valid? Explain.

28. Interpreting data When a stick of butter is left on the kitchen table, it softens gradually rather than melting at a specific temperature, or melting point. Is butter a pure substance? Why or why not?

29. Interpreting data A 45.2-g sample of pyrite—a shiny yellow mineral also known as "fool's gold"—is completely broken down into iron and sulfur. The mass of iron produced is 21.0 g. What mass of sulfur is produced?

30. Making judgments René Descartes, a French intellectual who lived in the seventeenth century, once wrote, "Give me matter and motion, and I will construct the universe." Defend or attack Descartes' statement in light of the information presented in this chapter.

31. Using the writing process Geothermal energy is heat from inside the Earth. In some parts of the world, geothermal energy is used as an alternative to petroleum or natural gas as a means of generating electricity. Prepare a written report on where and how geothermal energy is currently being used.

FROM SCHOOL TO WORK

Connie Werner—Student

As a high-school chemistry student in St. Joseph, Missouri, Connie Werner remembers her resistance to learning the metric system of measurement. "I don't need to know this," she recalls thinking. "It's not at all relevant to my life."

Today, as a first-year nursing student, Connie realizes how wrong she was. "Nurses make metric conversions every day. For example, they might need to figure out how much of a drug to add to a patient's intravenous drip based on the dosage that a doctor orders—and it's important to get the right answer!"

Connie now knows how essential a good background in chemistry is to nurses. From making metric conversions to understanding the chemistry of the human body to knowing how X-ray machines and other medical equipment work, chemistry is now very relevant to Connie—and to her future patients.

Museum Conservation Technician

Museum conservation technicians repair and clean art objects, such as pottery, statues, and paintings, in an effort to restore them to their original or natural appearance. As part of this job, a conservation technician must perform standard chemical and physical tests to determine the age, composition, and original appearance of an object. The technician then plans and implements procedures for restoring the object. For example, a technician may clean a statue by applying a solvent or soap solution.

Museum conservation technicians must have completed high school with courses in chemistry and mathematics. For most jobs in this field, two to four years of training after high school are also required.

To receive additional information, write to the American Association of Museums, 1225 I Street, NW, Suite 200, Washington, DC 20005.

How to Find Out About Careers

School and community libraries are a good source of information about different types of jobs and careers. There you will find a number of sources that not only define specific titles but also describe the nature of the work, educational and training requirements, the employment outlook for that field, working conditions, and other necessary information. Two such publications are the *Occupational Outlook Handbook*, published by the United States government, and *The Encyclopedia of Careers and Vocational Guidance*.

In addition, many corporations provide career information to interested students. Your school counseling office may have information about some of these companies.

H. Eugene LeMay, Jr.

Doug Brower

Herbert Beall

Karen Robblee

From the Authors

Congratulations! You have just completed your first step on an exciting journey—a journey into the world of chemistry. By now, you have probably realized that the world of chemistry is not confined only to your chemistry classroom and laboratory. The world of chemistry is your world. It is the world you live in, work in, and play in every day.

Because chemistry is part of your life, we wrote this textbook with you—the student—in mind. Unit 1 is the foundation on which your study of chemistry will be built. As such, it was important to us that this unit provide the necessary background for the units that follow. We felt it was equally important, however, that this unit convey some of the excitement, the relevance, and even the fun of chemistry! We wanted to give you a glimpse of what it was that attracted us to careers in chemistry in the first place. Although these first two chapters turned out to be among the hardest for us to write, we hope we have succeeded in our goal.

Even if you decide not to pursue chemistry as a career, we hope that this textbook will help you make the vital connection between chemistry and our changing world—a world you will someday inherit. And now, on with the journey!

UNIT REVIEW

Concept Mastery

Discuss each of the following in a brief paragraph.

1. Explain why chemistry can be called the central science.
2. Describe the steps a chemist would follow in conducting a scientific investigation. Are some steps more important than others?
3. Why is it important to "think safety" while working in the laboratory?
4. Describe one or more advantages of the SI over the English system of measurement.

5. A basketball player must be able to shoot free throws reliably. Does a good free-throw shooter illustrate high precision, high accuracy, or both? Explain.
6. Why is a zero sometimes not a significant digit in a measurement? Include an example in your explanation.

7. Summarize the Atlantic-Pacific rule for finding the number of significant digits in a measurement. Include examples.
8. Design a simple experiment to determine whether the density of a block of plastic is greater than or less than $1.00 \ g/cm^3$.
9. You have just discovered a dusty chemistry notebook on the shelf of the school library. Flipping through its pages, you find the following problem: How many inches are in a flask with a volume of 400 milliliters? What is wrong with this problem?
10. Describe your activities from the time you wake up in the morning until the time you arrive at school in terms of energy transformations or transfers.
11. A thermometer is placed in a cup of water. When the reading stabilizes, is the temperature of the water or the temperature of the thermometer itself being measured? Does it make a difference?
12. An important property of matter is its heat capacity, which determines how much heat is required to raise the temperature of an object by 1 Celsius degree. Do you think heat capacity is a chemical property or a physical property of matter? Explain your answer.
13. A chemist carefully measures the mass of a beaker of water and the mass of an antacid tablet, then drops the tablet into the beaker of water. After the fizzing subsides, would you expect the total mass to have increased, decreased, or remained exactly the same? Explain your answer.
14. What methods can be used to help determine whether a substance is an element or a compound?
15. Suggest a method for separating the components of saliva, a homogeneous solution containing many different substances.
16. That dusty chemistry notebook from question 9 has other surprises. In it you read: A compound is any mixture of two or more elements. Why is this statement false?

Problem Bank

17. Convert 12 kg to grams (g).

18. Convert 0.050 m to millimeters (mm).

19. Convert 128 mL to liters (L).

20. Convert 81 μs to milliseconds (ms).

21. How many picograms are in 1 decigram?

22. Perform the following calculation. Then round off the result to the correct number of significant digits:

$$19.7 \times 20 =$$

23. Perform the following calculation. Then round off the result to the correct number of significant digits:

$$18.1 + 1012 + 0.772 + 0.01 =$$

24. A 10.00-cm^3 flask has a mass of 27.3114 g. When this flask is filled with cooking oil, the total mass is 37.1251 g. What is the density of the cooking oil in grams per cubic centimeter?

25. In the laboratory, liquids are often more easily measured by volume than by mass. If a certain experiment calls for 12 g of bromine, a red fuming liquid, what volume of bromine should you measure? The density of bromine is 3.1023 g/cm^3.

26. You take a certain dusty chemistry book to the beach and find that it weighs 6.3 pounds at sea level. What is the mass of the book in grams? (At sea level, 1 kg = 2.2 lb.)

27. The boiling point of lead is 1740.°C. Convert this temperature to the Kelvin scale.

28. The freezing point of nitrogen, a component of air, is 63 K. Convert this temperature to the Celsius scale.

Performance-Based Task

How Much Water Will Sink a Boat?

Imagine that you are in the middle of a lake and that your boat has sprung a leak. How much water can the boat hold before it sinks? Create a model of this situation so that you can show what information you need to answer the question.

1. Start by obtaining modeling clay, a metric measuring tape, a plastic tub, a pan balance, a plastic graduated cylinder, and tap water.

2. Draw a design for your boat and create it with the modeling clay. Create a tiny model of yourself as well.

3. State your hypothesis and then develop a procedure for testing it.

4. Carry out your experiment, measuring masses and volumes as accurately and precisely as possible.

5. Redesign your boat and test how a different design affects the results.

Going Further

6. Do you think your results would be different if your boat were in salt water rather than in fresh water? Explain.

7. How would your results differ if your boat were constructed of a different material, such as aluminum foil?

Unit 2 The Structure of Matter

Brilliant colors spring to life, dazzling your eyes for a few moments and then fading slowly away into the night sky. You watch in awe as shimmering flecks of gold, bright red streamers, and glittering green starbursts magically appear and then vanish without a trace. No doubt you have experienced the enchantment of a spectacular fireworks display. But have you ever wondered what gives rise to these glowing shapes and colors? Do you think that the behavior of certain chemicals might have something to do with it?

In the pages of this unit, you will discover the answers to these questions as you learn about the fundamental particles that constitute all matter. You will learn how chemists classify matter according to the makeup and structure of its tiniest part—the atom. Your study of the structure of matter will lead you inside the atom itself, to examine the particles found there. You will find out why the periodic table of the elements is a chemist's most valuable tool. Most importantly, you will learn how differences at the atomic level result in behaviors of matter that you are already very familiar with at the macroscopic level.

DISCOVERY LEARNING

1. Fill a plastic foam cup with hot, but not boiling, water. Be careful not to fill the cup to the brim.

2. Place a stainless steel spoon and a plastic spoon into the cup. Be sure that the tops of the spoons are above the water level.

3. After waiting at least 1 minute, carefully touch the exposed top of each spoon.

   ■ What difference do you observe between the stainless steel spoon and the plastic spoon?

   ■ How can you explain the difference?

Chapter

3 Atomic Structure

If you had lived 100 years ago, you might have regarded the everyday activities of this century as nothing short of miraculous. Household electricity was uncommon then, and many of the conveniences that we now take for granted were not even imagined—tape players, televisions, refrigerators, and computers, to name a few. Stop and think for a moment about all the technological advances of the twentieth century, and imagine how amazing they would seem to someone from the 1800s.

Why has so much technology been developed during the past 100 years? To a large measure, it is because of important advances in our understanding of the structure of matter. In this chapter, you will begin to examine some of the discoveries that help us understand atoms, the building blocks of matter.

When atomic particles collide, new and unusual particles may be produced. These particles leave tracks in a bubble chamber, as shown above. One of the first scientists to explain matter in terms of atoms was an English schoolteacher, John Dalton (inset).

Chem Journal

YOU AND YOUR WORLD

Write the word atom at the top of a page in your journal. Below it, list whatever ideas or thoughts about atoms you may have. Do you commonly hear or use the words atom or atomic? What do you think atoms are? What are they made of? When you finish this chapter, review your journal entry and see if you would answer these questions differently.

3-1 Early Models of the Atom

Guide for Reading
- What are atoms?
- What are the postulates of Dalton's atomic theory?

Imagine that you had the power—not to mention the time and interest—to cut a piece of aluminum foil into ever smaller pieces. First you would cut the piece in half, then cut the two halves into quarters, then cut the quarters into eighths, and so on. Do you think that you would ever finish this task—that you would eventually end up with the smallest possible pieces of aluminum foil? Or do you think that the task has no end—that you would forever be dividing aluminum foil into infinitely smaller and smaller pieces of aluminum?

If these questions intrigue you, then you are following a long line of thinkers and philosophers, a line that dates back to the ancient Greeks. About 450 BC, the Greek philosopher Democritus proposed that all matter, the "stuff" that makes up the world around us, is actually composed of tiny, indivisible particles. He called these particles *atomos*, from which we get the English word **atom.** In other words, Democritus would have said that you could not cut a piece of aluminum foil into infinitely smaller pieces. Eventually, you would divide the foil into individual

Figure 3-1 *A droplet of the element mercury can be divided into smaller and smaller drops, each possessing all the properties of mercury. What is the name of the smallest particle of an element that retains the chemical identity of that element?*

Figure 3–2 *Almost 2500 years ago, the Greek philosopher Democritus proposed that all matter is composed of tiny particles. He called these particles* atomos. *You know them as atoms.*

aluminum atoms, which Democritus thought could be divided no further. Today scientists define atoms in terms of elements. **An atom is the smallest particle of an element that retains the chemical identity of that element.**

Unfortunately, Aristotle and other well-known Greek philosophers did not agree with Democritus' ideas about atoms. If matter is composed of such particles, they asked, then what holds these particles together? Why does matter not fall apart, the way sand castles fall apart in the wind? Democritus could not answer such questions, and so his ideas about atoms were rejected. Not until the seventeenth and eighteenth centuries were these ideas reexamined. These years ushered in a new way of dealing with nature, one that relied not merely on logic but also on observations and experiments.

Particularly significant was the discovery of two important principles of chemical behavior, both made in the late 1700s. The first was Antoine Lavoisier's law of conservation of matter, which you studied in Chapter 2. Lavoisier carefully measured the mass of substances before and after a chemical reaction and found that the masses were always equal. No mass was gained or lost in the reaction. Lavoisier concluded that a chemical reaction neither creates nor destroys matter, but that matter is conserved. The second principle was the **law of constant composition,** established in 1799 by another French chemist, Joseph Louis Proust (1754–1826). Proust found that a given compound always contains the same elements in the same proportions by mass. For example, the mass of water is always 88.9 percent oxygen and 11.1 percent hydrogen.

In 1803, a modest English schoolteacher named John Dalton (1766–1844) studied these and other experimental observations. Dalton concluded that the properties of matter could be explained in terms of atoms. Dalton's **atomic theory of matter** was based on the following postulates:

- Each element is composed of extremely small particles called atoms.
- All atoms of a given element are identical, but they differ from those of any other element.
- Atoms are neither created nor destroyed in any chemical reaction.
- A given compound always has the same relative numbers and kinds of atoms.

As you read on, you will discover that there are small but important exceptions to some of Dalton's postulates. However, these postulates still form the basis for our understanding of chemistry.

Figure 3–3 *The Minnesota State Fair offers a bewildering collection of rides, exhibits, food, and people! Yet the diverse forms of matter at a fair—or anyplace else—come from a relatively few different kinds of atoms.*

There are about 100 elements, which means that there are about 100 different kinds of atoms. These atoms combine to form each of the vast number of substances that make up the world around us. In this sense, atoms are like the 26 letters of the alphabet, which in different combinations form the immense number of words in the English language. And just as the rules of spelling and phonics define how letters can combine to form a word, so do certain scientific laws govern how atoms combine to form matter.

Can we be sure that atoms exist? Even the largest atom is too small to be seen with an ordinary microscope, let alone the unaided eye. However, the evidence that atoms exist is overwhelming and conclusive. And in the years after Dalton, scientists devised experiments to reveal the composition of atoms. You will learn more about these experiments later in this chapter.

Today, we can come close to actually seeing an atom, thanks to a device called a scanning tunneling microscope. Invented in 1981, the scanning tunneling microscope provides pictures of atoms such as the one shown in Figure 3–4. As you can see, the scanning tunneling microscope provides a blurred picture of atoms, one that reveals little about what atoms are like inside. Even so, this microscope is a remarkable tool for visualizing atoms.

Figure 3–4 *Individual atoms of silicon appear as blue and black spheres in this color-enhanced image from a scanning tunneling microscope.*

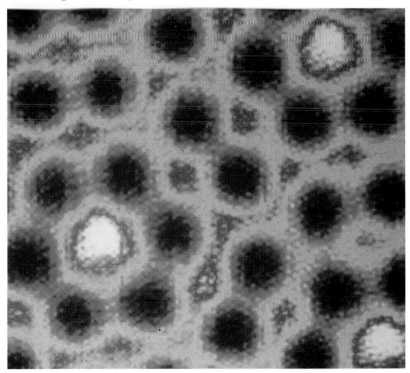

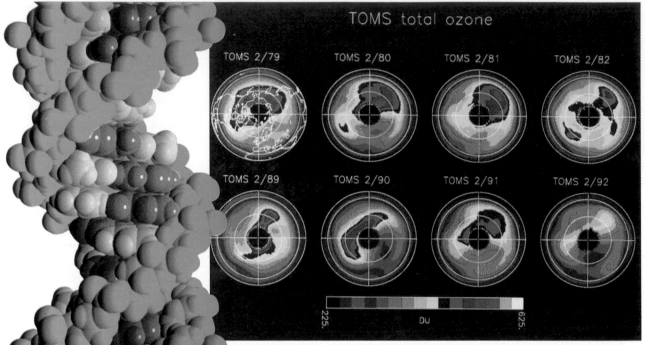

Figure 3–5 *Knowing about the submicroscopic world of atoms can help scientists to better understand holes in the Earth's ozone layer (top), integrated circuit chips (bottom left), and the genetic information encoded in DNA (top left).*

You can look at chemistry as the study of two worlds: the macroscopic world (the world of ordinary-sized objects) and the submicroscopic world of atoms. Chemists make their observations in the macroscopic world, the world in which we all live. However, in order to understand that world, the chemist's goal is to understand the atoms that compose it. So many of the scientific achievements of the twentieth century—deciphering the genetic code, designing plastics, understanding the ozone hole, and imprinting data on a silicon chip, to name only a few—stem from a fundamental knowledge of how atoms behave. You will explore this topic further in the next section.

3–1 Section Review

1. What is an atom?
2. List the postulates of Dalton's atomic theory of matter.
3. Why did the ancient Greeks reject Democritus' ideas about atoms?
4. **Critical Thinking—Applying concepts**   Why is there such diversity in nature if there are only about 100 different kinds of atoms?

3–2 Discovering Atomic Structure

Dalton and his contemporaries thought that atoms were hard and round, much like extremely tiny marbles or ball bearings. What puzzled them was why the atoms of one element behaved differently from those of another element. In 1839, the English chemist Michael Faraday (1791–1867) suggested that the structure of atoms was somehow related to electricity. A long series of experiments proved that Faraday was right. **Atoms contain particles that have electrical charge.** The story of electricity and the atom includes a certain American whose name you should find very familiar.

Static Electricity

The word electricity comes from *elektron,* the Greek word for amber. Amber is fossilized tree sap. The Greeks knew that if you rubbed amber with a piece of cloth, the amber would attract small pieces of dust or other particles. Today, this effect is commonly called static electricity. The word static means stationary; static electricity comes from electrical charges that are not in motion. No doubt you have encountered static electricity many times, such as when you take two socks out of the dryer and they stick together.

One of the scientists who studied static electricity was someone you know from American history, Benjamin Franklin (1706–1790). As a scientist, Franklin is perhaps most famous for the story of his flying a kite with a key on its string during a thunderstorm. As Franklin predicted, a bolt of lightning struck the key.

Guide for Reading

- How is atomic structure related to electricity?
- What did cathode rays indicate about atoms?
- What did Rutherford conclude from his alpha-scattering experiment?

Historical Perspective

Figure 3–6 *Dalton and his contemporaries thought that atoms were as hard, solid, and round as these marbles. However, the scientists of the century after Dalton discovered that atoms have a much more complicated structure.*

Figure 3–7 *Benjamin Franklin was a fine and careful scientist, so many historians question whether he actually performed his famous—and dangerous—kite-flying experiment.*

This experiment is very dangerous—please do not try it yourself! However, Franklin used the results of this experiment and other experiments to derive several important facts about electricity.

Franklin concluded that an object could have one of two kinds of electric charge. He could have given these charges any name, but he decided to call them positive (+) and negative (−). An essential feature of these charges is that two particles repel each other when they have like charges and attract each other when they have opposite charges, as illustrated in Figure 3–8. Some objects, such as your body when you walk across a carpet, readily pick up excess negative charges. These charges may suddenly jump to a metal doorknob or another object in a discharge of static electricity. Franklin also concluded that lightning is simply the result of static electricity on a larger scale. Lightning is the sudden discharge of electricity between clouds or between a cloud and the ground.

Where do these positive and negative charges come from? What are their physical properties? The answers to these questions came a century after Franklin's experiments, when scientists studied an intriguing device called a cathode ray tube.

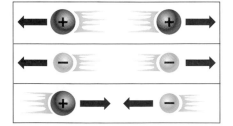

Figure 3–8 *Franklin identified two kinds of electrical charge, which he called positive (+) and negative (−). Objects that have similar charges repel each other and objects that have opposite charges attract each other.*

Cathode Rays and Electrons

A moving stream of electrical charges is called an electric current. You use electric currents whenever you use the electricity from a wall socket or a battery. Studying electric currents provided another key to understanding electrical charges.

In the mid-1800s, scientists began to investigate the way electric currents traveled through partially evacuated glass tubes, or tubes with very little air in them. One such tube is illustrated in Figure 3–9. The two electrodes in the figure are terminals connected to a battery. The negatively charged electrode is called the cathode and the positively charged electrode is called the anode. By lining the glass with a fluorescent material, or a material that glows in the presence of electricity, scientists discovered a kind of radiation streaming from the cathode to the anode. Because the radiation comes from the cathode, it was called a **cathode ray,** and the tube itself was called a **cathode ray tube,** or CRT. Today, you are familiar with a complex version of a cathode ray tube—a television picture tube.

By the end of the nineteenth century, scientists knew several facts about cathode rays. They discovered that a cathode ray could spin a small paddle wheel, which suggested that it was actually a stream of particles. They also discovered that a magnet deflects the cathode ray in the direction expected for negatively charged particles. This fact suggested that a cathode ray was not only made of particles, but that the particles carried a negative charge. But how can you prove that something is a particle? One way is to measure its mass. Remember from Chapter 2 that mass is a fundamental property of all matter.

Beginning in 1896, English physicist J. J. Thomson (1856–1940) conducted a series of systematic studies on cathode rays. The instrument he designed and used is illustrated in Figure 3–10. At one end of Thomson's instrument, a cathode ray is emitted from the cathode and moves toward the anode, positioned only

INTEGRATING
PHYSICS

What is a common version of a cathode ray tube?

Figure 3–9 *A stream of charged particles flows from the cathode to the anode in a cathode ray tube (left), causing the fluorescent material within the tube to glow (right). The picture tube in a television (top right) is actually a complex version of a cathode ray tube.*

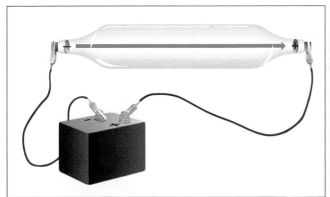

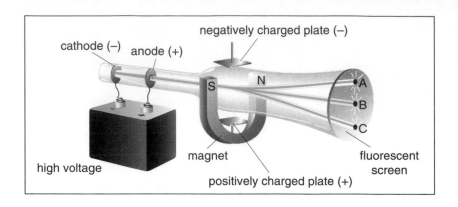

Figure 3–10 *The apparatus in J. J. Thomson's experiments consists of a cathode ray tube, a magnet, and electrically charged plates. When the magnetic field is on and the electric field is off, electrons strike point A on the screen. When the electric field is on and the magnetic field is off, electrons strike point C. When both fields are off, or balanced to cancel each other's effects, the electrons strike point B. What did Thomson conclude from his experiments?*

a short distance away. However, the anode has a hole in it, allowing a fraction of the cathode ray to pass through. This fraction travels the length of the tube, part of which is surrounded by both the poles of a magnet and electrically charged plates. Both the magnet and the plates can deflect the ray's path. The ray eventually hits the other end of the tube, which is coated with fluorescent material. When the ray hits this material, it produces a spot of green light.

Thomson carefully measured the degree to which both a magnetic field and an electric field deflected the ray, as shown in the diagram. He also repeated his experiments with different gases in the tube and with electrodes made of different materials. Thomson discovered that magnetic and electric fields deflected the ray's path in a mathematically predictable way. He also discovered that neither changing gases nor using different electrodes affected the results.

Thomson concluded that a cathode ray is composed of negative particles and that these particles come from the cathode. This meant that atoms were not indivisible balls but instead had a substructure. Thomson named these negative particles **electrons.** He was not able to compute the mass of an electron, but he did determine the ratio of an electron's electrical charge to its mass, which is 1.76×10^{8} coulombs per gram. (The coulomb, abbreviated C, is the SI unit of electrical charge.) Now if someone could determine the charge of a single electron, the electron's mass could be calculated easily.

In 1909, American physicist Robert Millikan (1868–1953) of the University of Chicago succeeded in measuring the charge of the electron. Millikan sprayed oil droplets into the apparatus shown in Figure 3–11. He used X-rays to give the droplets a negative charge. As the droplets fell between two electrically charged plates, Millikan measured how different charges on the plates changed the droplets' rate of fall. From these data, he calculated that the charge on every oil droplet is a multiple of 1.60×10^{-19} coulomb, which meant that 1.60×10^{-19} coulomb must be the charge of a single electron. Using this value and the electron's charge-to-mass ratio, Millikan calculated the mass of an electron to be 9.11×10^{-28} gram.

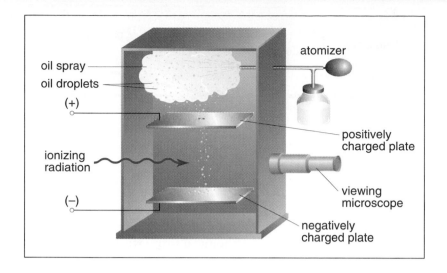

Figure 3–11 *Robert Millikan studied how negatively charged oil droplets fell between electrically charged plates. What did Millikan determine from his experiments?*

As Millikan's results show, an electron is an extremely light particle. It is about 2000 times lighter than an atom of hydrogen, the lightest atom.

Radioactivity

In 1896, French physicist Henri Becquerel (1852–1908) made a surprising discovery when he accidently placed a uranium sample on some unexposed photographic film. Becquerel found that an image had been produced on the film—an image caused by an unknown kind of radiation from the sample. Becquerel had discovered that uranium exhibits **radioactivity,** the spontaneous emission of radiation from an element. Uranium proved to be one of many naturally radioactive elements. Becquerel's colleagues Marie Sklodowska Curie (1867–1934) and her husband Pierre (1859–1906) isolated two other radioactive elements, radium and polonium. Other radioactive elements were discovered soon after.

Figure 3–12 *Radioactive material, such as a sample of uranium ore, can expose photographic film (left). Experiments performed by Marie and Pierre Curie (below) and other pioneers in the study of radioactivity provided insights about the nucleus.*

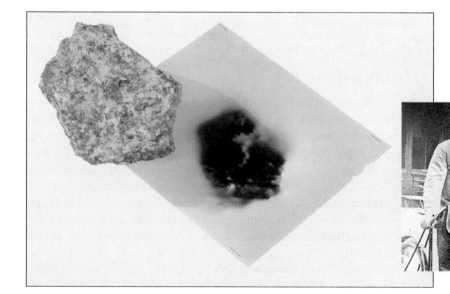

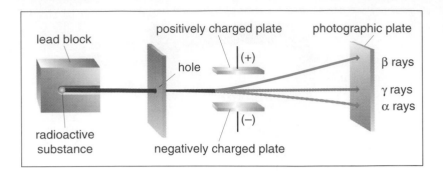

Figure 3–13 An electrical field splits the radiation emitted by a sample into three components. How do the three types of radiation differ from one another?

As scientists studied radioactivity, they made an important observation: Radioactivity accompanies fundamental changes in an atom. In other words, the chemical properties of a radioactive element change as it gives off radiation. Studying the nature of these changes gave scientists further clues about the substructure of the atom.

In the early 1900s, New Zealand scientist Ernest Rutherford (1871–1937) began an extensive study of radioactivity. Rutherford placed a radioactive sample in front of two electrically charged plates, as shown in Figure 3–13. Some of the radiation was deflected toward the negative plate. Rutherford called this alpha radiation. Other radiation was deflected towards the positive plate. Rutherford called this beta radiation. Scientists later discovered a third kind of radiation, called gamma radiation, which passes between electric plates without deflection.

Like cathode rays, alpha and beta radiation were shown to be made of particles. These particles are called alpha particles and beta particles, respectively. Alpha particles have a 2 + charge, or a charge twice that of an electron and with the opposite sign. Beta particles are high-speed electrons. Gamma radiation is similar to X-rays and is not composed of particles. You will learn more about these three kinds of radiation later in this chapter. Their existence provided further evidence that the atom was much more complex than Dalton had thought it to be. Additionally, alpha particles provided a way of probing the atom's structure.

The Nuclear Atom

J. J. Thomson had concluded that atoms contain electrons, or negatively charged particles. However, atoms themselves are electrically neutral. If they contain negatively charged particles, they must also contain particles with an equal amount of positive charge. How are positive and negative charges arranged in the atom? In 1909, Rutherford and his colleagues performed a famous experiment, called the alpha-scattering experiment, that answered this question. Running this experiment was tedious and time-consuming, but the researchers were rewarded with an exciting surprise.

Rutherford had designed an experiment to study how alpha particles interact with thin metal foils. He aimed a beam of high-

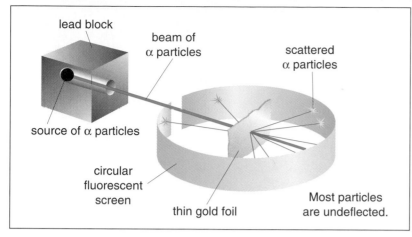

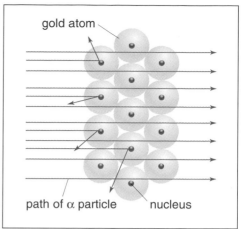

Figure 3–14 *When Rutherford shot a beam of alpha particles at a piece of very thin gold foil, most of the alpha particles passed straight through the foil. However, the foil scattered a fraction of the particles in almost every direction, as indicated by the bright spots on the fluorescent screen (above). These particles bounced off a tiny positively charged core, or nucleus, at the center of the atom (right).*

speed alpha particles at a piece of extremely thin gold foil, as shown in Figure 3–14. Rutherford found that almost all of the particles passed through the foil with no deflection, as if the foil were not there at all. But Rutherford was curious about the small fraction of alpha particles—approximately 1 in 8000—that the foil did deflect. What he expected was that most of these particles would be deflected only minimally, the way a bullet might be deflected by a tin can or some other loose object in its path. But to the great surprise of Rutherford and his students, they found that the foil scattered alpha particles in all directions. In fact, the foil completely reversed the direction of some of the particles, as if the particles bounced directly off it. Imagine how surprised you would be if you shot a bullet at a tin can only to have the bullet bounce right back at you!

Rutherford was convinced that his experiment was telling him something important about the atom. Within two years, he had solved the puzzle. Until then, scientists had accepted Thomson's so-called "plum pudding" model of an atom, named after a popular English dessert. According to this model, negative charges are distributed evenly throughout an atom's positively charged interior, similar to the way fruits and other objects are distributed in plum pudding. Rutherford's observations led him to conclude that this model was wrong. What he proposed instead was that all of an atom's positive charge, as well as most of its mass, is concentrated in a very small core at the atom's center. He gave this core the name that is still used, the **nucleus.**

How does this model of the atom explain Rutherford's experiment? As shown in Figure 3–14, most of the alpha particles pass through the gold foil because most of the atom is empty space.

Figure 3–15 *In both plum pudding and chocolate chip cookies, small objects are embedded in the dough. Is the plum pudding model of the atom accurate?*

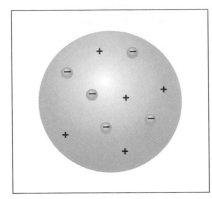

Figure 3–16 *The plum pudding model (left), in which negatively charged electrons are imbedded in a large, positively charged atom, was once the standard model of the atom. Rutherford proposed a new model (right), in which electrons orbited a positively charged nucleus.*

However, an alpha particle occasionally comes close enough to the tiny nucleus to be deflected. Both the alpha particle and the nucleus carry a positive charge, so they repel each other. And even though the nucleus is only a tiny fraction of the atom, a few alpha particles make a "direct hit" on the nucleus. A direct collision repels an alpha particle backward.

Rutherford's model of the atom is still accepted today, with negatively charged electrons moving around a very small, positively charged nucleus. How small are an atom's nucleus and electrons? Imagine that an atom were magnified to the size of a football stadium. The nucleus would be smaller than a dime in the center of the field. As for the electrons, each one would be smaller than the eye on the dime's portrait of Franklin Roosevelt! It is worth pondering that an atom—the building block of all matter in the universe—is mostly empty space.

Figure 3–17 *Imagine that you are standing on a nucleus that is the size of the Earth. The electron cloud surrounding the nucleus would be about as far away as the nearest stars are from Earth.*

3–2 Section Review

1. How is the structure of an atom related to electricity?

2. What is a cathode ray tube? What did scientists conclude about the composition of a cathode ray?

3. What is radioactivity? Describe the differences among alpha, beta, and gamma radiation.

4. **Theme Trace—Scale and Structure** How did Rutherford use the results of his alpha-scattering experiment to challenge the plum pudding model of the atom? How does Rutherford's model of the atom differ from the plum pudding model?

3–3 Modern Atomic Theory

Guide for Reading

- What are the names and properties of the three subatomic particles?
- How can you determine the number of protons, neutrons, and electrons in an atom or ion?
- What is an isotope? What is atomic mass?

As research progressed from the time of Rutherford, scientists discovered that an atom contains three fundamental particles. **Atoms are composed of protons, neutrons, and electrons.** In recent years, scientists have found some of these particles to be complicated entities with structures of their own. These "particles within particles" include quarks, gluons, mesons, muons, and an assortment of other exotic particles. Although these particles are fascinating, they have no immediate impact on chemistry. Chemical behavior is understood perfectly well in terms of protons, neutrons, and electrons.

The Structure of the Atom

As you have learned, an atom has a positively charged central core called a nucleus. The nucleus contains two kinds of particles: **protons** and **neutrons.** Protons carry the positive charge of the nucleus. An individual proton has a charge that is equal to the charge of an electron but with the opposite sign. Neutrons are similar to protons—their mass is only slightly greater—but neutrons carry no electrical charge. Neutrons get their name from the word neutral.

Electrons move in the space around the nucleus, their negative charge attracted to the nucleus' positive charge. In a neutral atom, the number of protons always equals the number of electrons. A proton, however, is much more massive than an electron. In fact, it would take almost 2000 electrons to equal the mass of a single proton.

Rutherford visualized the atom as a miniature solar system, with electrons circling the nucleus in much the same way that planets orbit the sun. While this model is pleasing, it is also inaccurate. As you will learn in Chapter 4, electrons do not orbit the nucleus in a well-defined path. In fact, it is impossible to know exactly where an electron is at any given time. For these reasons, scientists often picture the atom as shown in the bottom drawing in Figure 3–18, with the electrons' positions drawn as indistinct clouds around the nucleus.

The table in Figure 3–19 summarizes the locations, charges, and masses of the three subatomic particles. Notice that many of the numbers in this table are very cumbersome, to say the

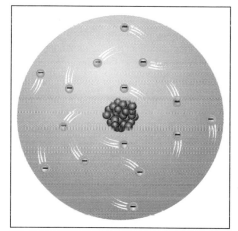

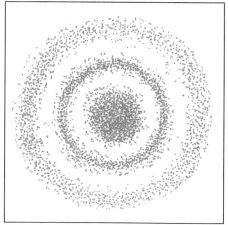

Figure 3–18 *The nucleus lies in the center of the atom and the electrons move in the space around it (top). However, the electrons do not orbit the nucleus in simple, well-defined paths. For this reason, chemists often show electron orbitals as indistinct clouds around a nucleus (bottom). The more dots in the cloud, the more likely an electron would be found there.*

Figure 3–19 *The table lists the fundamental subatomic particles and their characteristics. How does the mass of a proton compare with that of an electron? Of a neutron?*

Particle	Location	Charge (C)	Mass (g)	Mass (amu)
proton	inside nucleus	$+1.602 \times 10^{-19}$	1.673×10^{-24}	$1.0073 \approx 1$
neutron	inside nucleus	0	1.675×10^{-24}	$1.0087 \approx 1$
electron	outside nucleus	-1.602×10^{-19}	9.109×10^{-28}	$0.0006 \approx 0$

least. For the sake of convenience, the charge of a proton is simplified to $1+$ and the charge of an electron to $1-$. Likewise, their masses are expressed in **atomic mass units** (abbreviated amu). The mass of both a proton and a neutron is approximately 1 amu, and the mass of an electron is essentially 0 amu.

The diameters of atoms range from 0.100 to 0.500 nanometer. (A nanometer, abbreviated nm, is 10^{-9} meter.) How tiny is this diameter? Take a copper penny, which is about 1.9 centimeters in diameter, and draw a line across its center. Your line crosses approximately 810 million copper atoms! And if you strung together the nuclei of these 810 million atoms, their length would measure only 4×10^{-6} meter, or 4 millionths of a meter. Not only are atoms extraordinarily small, but their nuclei are smaller still.

Atomic Numbers

Soon after Rutherford's alpha-scattering experiment, a young English scientist named Henry Moseley (1887–1915) made an important discovery. Moseley, who was a student of Rutherford's, found that atoms of each element contain a unique positive charge in their nucleus. This discovery helped to solve the mystery of what makes the atoms of one element different from those of another: An atom's identity comes from the number of protons in its nucleus.

The number of protons in an atom is called its **atomic number.** Every element has a unique atomic number. For example, the atomic number of nitrogen is 7, indicating that every nitrogen atom has 7 protons. In the periodic table, each element's atomic number is written just above its chemical symbol. A complete periodic table is shown on pages 166–167. You will want to refer to that table in this chapter and throughout your study of chemistry. (The periodic table will be discussed in detail in Chapter 5.) Notice that the first element in the periodic table is hydrogen, which has an atomic number of 1. How many protons are in the nucleus of every hydrogen atom?

An individual atom is electrically neutral, which means the number of protons always equals the number of electrons. Thus, an element's atomic number also indicates the number of electrons in its atoms. For example, a hydrogen atom consists of 1 proton and 1 electron. However, under a variety of circumstances, an atom can gain or lose its electrons, giving it an overall positive or negative charge. As you will learn, an atom's ability to gain or lose electrons is responsible for a great many of its chemical properties.

7
N
Nitrogen

Figure 3–20 *Each square in the periodic table provides information about a particular element. What is nitrogen's atomic number? How many protons are in the nucleus of a nitrogen atom?*

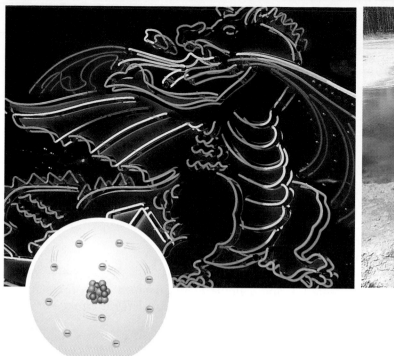

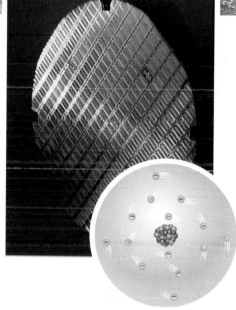

SAMPLE PROBLEM 1

How many protons and electrons are present in an oxygen atom?

STRATEGY	SOLUTION
1. Analyze	The answer to this question lies in oxygen's atomic number, which indicates the number of protons in an oxygen atom.
2. Plan	The periodic table gives an element's atomic number. Find oxygen in the table and identify its atomic number.
3. Solve	Oxygen is in the second row of the table. Its atomic number is 8, so oxygen has 8 protons. Because an oxygen atom is neutral, it also has 8 electrons.
4. Evaluate	The answer is reasonable, based on the definition of atomic number and the fact that a neutral atom has an equal number of protons and electrons.

Figure 3–21 *Neon, often used in lighted signs, has 10 protons in its nucleus (top left). Silicon, used in computer chips, has 14 protons (bottom). Sulfur combines with oxygen to form compounds that give the waters of Yellowstone National Park their characteristic smell (top right). How many protons are in a sulfur atom?*

PRACTICE PROBLEMS

1. How many protons and electrons are in a magnesium atom? *(Answer: 12 protons and 12 electrons)*

2. What is the name of the element that has atoms that contain 11 protons? *(Answer: sodium)*

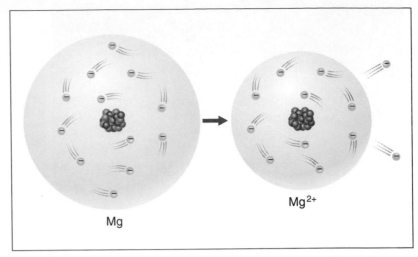

Figure 3–22 *When a neutral magnesium atom loses 2 electrons, it becomes a magnesium ion with a charge of 2+. What is the definition of an ion?*

Ions

When an atom loses or gains one or more electrons, it acquires a net electrical charge and is called an **ion** (IGH-ahn). An ion that has more electrons than protons has a negative charge. An ion that has fewer electrons than protons has a positive charge. The net charge on an ion is found by subtracting the number of electrons from the number of protons:

$$\text{charge of ion} = \text{number of protons} - \text{number of electrons}$$

(Eq. 1)

For example, a neutral magnesium atom (atomic number 12) has 12 protons and 12 electrons. If the atom loses 2 electrons, it becomes an ion with a charge of 2+:

$$
\begin{array}{lr}
\text{number of protons} & 12 \\
-\,\text{number of electrons} & -10 \\
\hline
\text{charge of ion} & +\ 2
\end{array}
$$

Sometimes the charge of an ion is written with the plus or minus sign before the number (as in +2) and sometimes after it (as in 2+). In this textbook you will see the charge sign written after the number. When the charge of an ion is 1+ or 1−, the number 1 is generally omitted, and the charge is written simply as + or −.

To write an ion with chemical symbols, place its charge to the upper right of the chemical symbol for the element. For example, the magnesium ion discussed above is written as Mg^{2+}. Notice that the ion is a magnesium ion because it still has 12 protons. The element name is always determined by the number of protons in the nucleus, a number that does not change when an atom becomes an ion.

SAMPLE PROBLEM 2

Write the chemical symbol for the ion with 9 protons and 10 electrons.

STRATEGY	SOLUTION
1. **Analyze**	The number of protons does not equal the number of electrons, so the problem specifies an ion. The ion has a negative charge because it has more electrons than protons.
2. **Plan**	The number of protons determines the atomic number and the element's identity, which can be found in the periodic table. The charge of the ion is the difference between the number of protons and the number of electrons.
3. **Solve**	The ion has 9 protons, so it is an ion of the element with atomic number 9. That element is fluorine (F). The net charge of the ion equals the number of protons minus the number of electrons: $9 - 10 = -1$. The symbol for this ion is F^{1-}, or simply F^-.
4. **Evaluate**	The element and its chemical symbol were correctly identified and the charge was correctly placed in the upper right corner.

PRACTICE PROBLEMS

3. What is the chemical symbol for the ion with (a) 13 protons and 10 electrons? (b) 7 protons and 10 electrons? *(Answer: (a) Al^{3+} (b) N^{3-})*

4. How many protons and electrons are present in (a) the S^{2-} ion? (b) the Li^+ ion? *(Answer: (a) 16 protons and 18 electrons (b) 3 protons and 2 electrons)*

Isotopes

Do you recall the second of Dalton's postulates? It states that all atoms of a given element are identical. In fact, this postulate is not entirely true. All atoms of a given element do have the same number of protons in their nuclei. However, these nuclei do not necessarily have the same number of neutrons. For example, all atoms of chlorine have a nucleus with 17 protons. But some chlorine nuclei have 18 neutrons whereas others have 20 neutrons. Atoms that have the same number of protons but different numbers of neutrons are called **isotopes.** Most elements in the first two rows of the periodic table have at least two isotopes,

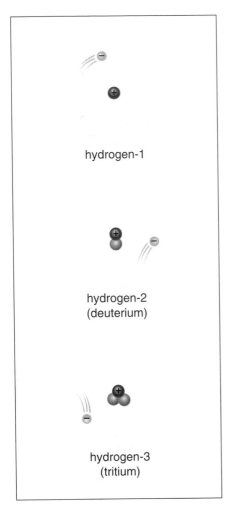

Figure 3–23 *Atoms with the same number of protons but different numbers of neutrons are called isotopes. How do the three hydrogen isotopes differ from one another in structure? In mass?*

one of which is much more common than the other. For example, the most common isotope of hydrogen has a nucleus of 1 proton and no neutrons. A rarer hydrogen isotope, which is called deuterium, has a nucleus of 1 proton and 1 neutron. A third, even rarer, hydrogen isotope called tritium has a nucleus of 1 proton and 2 neutrons.

In nature, elements are almost always found as a mixture of isotopes, and an element's isotopes typically are found in the same percentages. For example, suppose you were to examine any natural collection of hydrogen atoms, such as those in a drop of water. (Water contains hydrogen atoms and oxygen atoms. You will learn more about the composition and properties of water in the chapters that follow.) In a drop of water, 99.9844 percent of the hydrogen atoms are the isotope with no neutrons. Most of the remaining 0.0156 percent are the isotope with 1 neutron. These ratios are the same in any drop of water, or in any other natural compound that contains atoms of hydrogen.

How different are the two isotopes of hydrogen? They are almost indistinguishable. The chemical properties of an element depend primarily on its electrons and protons. Isotopes of the same element, which differ only in their number of neutrons, have essentially identical chemical properties. The major difference between two isotopes is their mass. Isotopes with more neutrons have a higher mass than those with fewer neutrons. For this reason, the adjectives heavy and light are often used to describe an isotope. Deuterium is sometimes called the "heavy" isotope of hydrogen and water made with deuterium is sometimes called heavy water.

To identify an isotope more specifically, chemists add a number after the element's name. This number is called the isotope's **mass number** and is the sum of the isotope's number of protons and neutrons. For example, an atom with 17 protons and 20 neutrons has a mass number of 37. From the number of protons you know that this is a chlorine atom, so the isotope is named chlorine-37. The isotope of chlorine with 17 protons and 18 neutrons is named chlorine-35. What is the name of the nitrogen isotope with 7 protons and 8 neutrons? Of the sodium isotope with 11 protons and 12 neutrons?

To name an isotope using chemical symbols, you simply place the atom's mass number to the upper left of the element symbol. For example, the chemical symbol for chlorine-37 is ^{37}Cl. In addition, chemists often include an atom's atomic number in the symbol. The atomic number is written to the lower left of the element symbol. The complete symbol for chlorine-37 is written like this:

$$\text{mass number} \rightarrow \quad ^{37}_{17}Cl \quad \leftarrow \text{element symbol}$$
$$\text{atomic number} \rightarrow$$

Using this notation, you can determine the number of neutrons in an isotope by subtracting the atomic number from the mass number. For $_{17}^{37}\text{Cl}$, subtract 17 from 37 to find that this chlorine isotope has 20 neutrons. For $_{8}^{18}\text{O}$, subtract 8 from 18. This isotope has 10 neutrons.

Confused? Understanding mass numbers, atomic numbers, and isotopes takes practice. Try solving the following Sample Problem and Practice Problems.

SAMPLE PROBLEM 3

How many protons, neutrons, and electrons are present in the $_{26}^{56}\text{Fe}^{2+}$ ion?

STRATEGY	SOLUTION
1. Analyze	The problem gives the complete chemical symbol for the ion. The solution lies in the definitions of mass number and atomic number.
2. Plan	The atomic number equals the number of protons. The number of neutrons is the difference between the mass number and the atomic number. The positive charge of the ion indicates that it has more protons than electrons.
3. Solve	The atomic number is the number on the lower left, 26. This means that there are 26 protons. The difference between the mass number and the atomic number is $56 - 26 = 30$. There are 30 neutrons. The charge on the ion, 2+, indicates that there are two more protons than electrons. Thus, there are 24 electrons.
4. Evaluate	The sum of the number of protons and neutrons gives the correct mass number ($26 + 30 = 56$). The difference between the number of protons and the number of electrons gives the correct charge ($26 - 24 = 2+$).

PRACTICE PROBLEMS

5. How many protons, neutrons, and electrons are present in (a) $_{13}^{27}\text{Al}^{3+}$ (b) $_{34}^{79}\text{Se}^{2-}$?

   (Answer: (a) 13 protons, 14 neutrons, and 10 electrons (b) 34 protons, 45 neutrons, and 36 electrons)

6. Write the complete chemical symbol for the ion with (a) 21 protons, 24 neutrons, and 18 electrons (b) 53 protons, 74 neutrons, and 54 electrons.

   (Answer: (a) $_{21}^{45}\text{Sc}^{3+}$ (b) $_{53}^{127}\text{I}^{-}$)

MATH TIP

A chemical symbol conveys a great deal of useful information. In addition to representing an element, a complete symbol can tell you the number of protons, neutrons, and electrons in an atom or ion by the numbers around the symbol. Look at the complete symbol for the 2+ ion of the barium-141 isotope.

mass number (M) $\qquad$ charge

$$_{56}^{141}\text{Ba}^{2+}$$

atomic number (Z)

number of protons $= Z$
number of neutrons $= M - Z$
number of electrons $= Z -$ charge

(Remember to pay attention to the sign of the charge!)

The Mass of an Atom

Chemists measure the mass of an individual atom not in grams but in atomic mass units, which were introduced earlier in this section. What is an atomic mass unit? It is roughly equal to the mass of a proton or a neutron. Recall that a proton and neutron have almost identical mass and that the mass of an electron is extremely small in comparison. Therefore, the mass of an atom in atomic mass units is approximately the same as the sum of its number of protons and neutrons, which is its mass number. For example, the mass of a copper-65 atom is approximately 65 amu, and the mass of a nitrogen-14 atom is approximately 14 amu. For most purposes, this simple way of expressing an atom's mass works very well.

But as you may have begun to realize, scientists prefer to define units precisely. It is not precise to define an atomic mass unit as the mass of a proton or neutron because protons and neutrons do not have exactly the same mass. Instead, scientists chose to define an atomic mass unit in terms of an arbitrary standard—a carbon-12 atom. Scientists set the mass of a carbon-12 atom to be exactly equal to 12 amu. This means that 1 atomic mass unit is $\frac{1}{12}$ of the mass of a carbon-12 atom.

$$1 \text{ amu} = \frac{1}{12} \text{ (mass of } {}^{12}_{6}\text{C atom)} = 1.66 \times 10^{-24} \text{ g}$$

With the exception of carbon-12, an atom's mass in atomic mass units is never precisely the same as its mass number, in part because 1 amu is not precisely the same as the mass of 1 proton or neutron. For example, the mass of a chlorine-35 atom is not 35 amu, but 34.969 amu. The mass of a chlorine-37 atom is 36.966 amu. Figure 3–25 lists further examples of the masses and mass numbers of different atoms.

Now suppose that you wanted to calculate the mass of a large number of atoms. For example, suppose you had 1000 chlorine atoms. What is their total mass? To answer this question,

Figure 3–24 *This Russian woman is using a scale to measure the mass of fruits and vegetables. But determining the mass of something as small as an atom is not as easy. Why not?*

Figure 3–25 *You can calculate an element's average atomic mass, often simply called the atomic mass, by multiplying each isotope's fractional abundance by its mass, then adding the results.*

Isotopes of Three Common Elements

Element	Symbol	Mass Number	Mass (amu)	Fractional Abundance	Average Atomic Mass
Carbon	${}^{12}_{6}\text{C}$	12	12 (exactly)	98.89%	12.01
	${}^{13}_{6}\text{C}$	13	13.003	1.11	
Chlorine	${}^{35}_{17}\text{Cl}$	35	34.969	75.53	35.45
	${}^{37}_{17}\text{Cl}$	37	36.966	24.47	
Silicon	${}^{28}_{14}\text{Si}$	28	27.977	92.21	28.09
	${}^{29}_{14}\text{Si}$	29	28.976	4.70	
	${}^{30}_{14}\text{Si}$	30	29.974	3.09	

you might be tempted to take the mass of one chlorine atom and multiply it by 1000. However, recall that elements have different isotopes. Chlorine exists as two common isotopes, chlorine-35 and chlorine-37, which have masses of approximately 35 amu and 37 amu, respectively. A collection of 1000 chlorine atoms would contain a mixture of these two isotopes, which means that its mass is somewhere between 35,000 amu and 37,000 amu.

To compute the mass of a large number of chlorine atoms, you would need to find the mass of an "average" chlorine atom. Fortunately, the isotopes of chlorine—and of other elements—are typically found in constant ratios. These ratios, which are called fractional abundances, are listed for the isotopes of several elements in Figure 3–25. The fractional abundances of the two common isotopes of chlorine are approximately 75 percent and 25 percent. In other words, in any collection of chlorine atoms, 75 percent of the atoms are the lighter isotope, chlorine-35, and the remaining 25 percent are the heavier isotope, chlorine-37. Logically, the average mass of chlorine atoms is somewhere between 35 amu and 37 amu. However, the average is closer to 35 amu, because chlorine-35 is more abundant.

The average mass of an element's atoms is called the **atomic mass,** which is also called the average atomic mass or the atomic weight. The atomic mass for each element is listed in the periodic table. It is the number written just below the element symbol.

Take a look at the atomic masses of helium, neon, argon, and krypton, which are the first four elements in the column at the right of the periodic table. Argon's atomic mass is 39.948 amu, from which you can conclude that its most common isotope is argon-40. What do you think are the most common isotopes of helium, neon, and krypton?

3–3 Section Review

1. Name the three fundamental particles of the atom. Discuss their important properties.

2. If you are given the complete chemical symbol for an atom or ion, how can you determine the number of each kind of particle in the atom or ion?

3. Define the term isotope. Explain how an element's atomic mass is related to the abundances of its different isotopes.

4. **Critical Thinking—Interpreting data** In the periodic table, some atomic masses are written with only a few significant figures. Others are written with as many as 7 or 8 significant figures. Use your knowledge of how atomic mass is calculated to explain these differences.

Figure 3–26 *The periodic table gives the atomic mass of each element. How does atomic mass reflect the abundance of an element's isotopes?*

3–4 Changes in the Nucleus

As you continue to read this textbook, you will learn about a wide variety of chemical reactions. In chemical reactions, atoms interact only through their outer electrons while their nuclei remain unchanged. But there are other types of reactions, called **nuclear reactions,** in which changes do occur in an atom's nucleus. **Nuclear reactions change the composition of an atom's nucleus.** All three kinds of radiation—alpha, beta, and gamma—are produced by nuclear reactions. In fact, alpha and beta radiation consist of particles that are emitted from the nucleus. Radioactivity is the spontaneous emission of radiation from an atom.

Nuclear Stability

Almost all the atoms that you encounter have stable nuclei, which is another way of saying that they are not radioactive. Only a few atoms in nature are radioactive. This rarity is fortunate because radiation can cause a variety of harmful effects.

Why are some nuclei stable and others unstable? Part of the reason has to do with the number of protons and neutrons that they contain. Not all combinations of protons and neutrons make a stable nucleus.

A nucleus consists of protons and neutrons packed together in a very small space. But as you learned earlier in this chapter, all protons have a positive charge and similarly charged particles repel each other. Why do protons in a nucleus not fly apart? Logically, some force must hold the nucleus together—an attractive force that overcomes the electric repulsion between protons. Scientists have named this force the **strong nuclear force.** The strong nuclear force is not a force that you encounter in your daily life. It is significantly strong only between subatomic particles that are extremely close.

As you can see in Figure 3–27, adjacent protons experience two forces: the electrical force repelling them and the strong nuclear force attracting them. But neutrons, which have no charge, experience no electrical repulsion. In a nucleus, both an adjacent neutron and proton and two adjacent neutrons have only the strong nuclear force acting on them. This force holds the particles together. In other words, the presence of neutrons adds a net attractive force to the inside of a nucleus. For this reason, you can think of neutrons as the glue that holds the nucleus together.

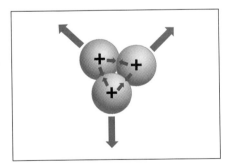

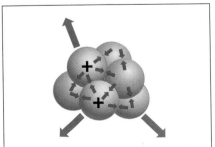

Figure 3–27 *In these diagrams, the black arrows represent the force of electrical repulsion and the blue arrows represent the strong nuclear force. If these diagrams represent nuclei, which nucleus is stable and which is unstable? Why?*

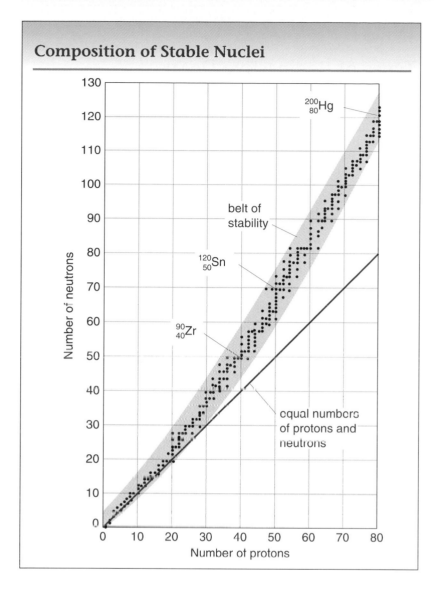

Composition of Stable Nuclei

Number of neutrons (y-axis, values: 0, 10, 20, 30, 40, 50, 60, 70, 80, 90, 100, 110, 120, 130)

Number of protons (x-axis, values: 0, 10, 20, 30, 40, 50, 60, 70, 80)

$^{200}_{80}Hg$

belt of stability

$^{120}_{50}Sn$

$^{90}_{40}Zr$

equal numbers of protons and neutrons

Figure 3–28 *This graph shows the number of protons and neutrons for stable nuclei. Beyond 20 protons, nuclei need increasingly more neutrons than protons to be stable. At what point is no number of neutrons sufficient to "glue" the nucleus together indefinitely?*

All stable nuclei follow a distinct pattern. For elements with atomic numbers between 1 and 20 (from hydrogen to calcium), stable nuclei have almost equal numbers of protons and neutrons. Beyond 20 protons, nuclei need increasingly more neutrons than protons to be stable. You can see this pattern in Figure 3–28, which shows the relationship between the number of neutrons and the number of protons for stable nuclei. When the atomic number exceeds 83 (the element bismuth), no number of neutrons is sufficient to glue the nucleus together indefinitely. All nuclei with atomic numbers greater than 83 are radioactive. What are some elements that fall into this category?

Interestingly, nuclei are unstable not only if they contain too few neutrons, but also if they contain too many. Nuclei that have excess neutrons are likely to emit beta radiation. As a general rule, isotopes that are much heavier (that contain more neutrons) or much lighter (that contain fewer neutrons) than the most common isotope are likely to be radioactive.

Types of Radioactive Decay

As you should recall, radioactive elements emit different kinds of radiation, three of which are alpha (α), beta (β), and gamma (γ) radiation. These three kinds of radiation are distinguished by their charge, mass, and penetrating power. Their properties are summarized for you in Figure 3–29.

Alpha radiation consists of a stream of high-energy alpha particles. An alpha particle consists of 2 protons and 2 neutrons and is identical to a helium-4 nucleus. An alpha particle is represented as $_2^4\text{He}^{2+}$ or merely $_2^4\text{He}$ or $_2^4\alpha$. These particles do not have much penetrating power. Most alpha particles are able to travel only a few centimeters through air and are easily stopped by paper or clothing. As a result, they usually do not pose a health hazard unless the source of the radiation actually enters the body.

Beta radiation consists of a stream of high-speed electrons. These electrons, however, are not the ones in motion around an atom's nucleus. Like all radioactivity, beta radiation comes from changes inside the nucleus. In the process that produces beta radiation, a neutron changes into a proton and an electron. The proton remains in the nucleus, and the electron—or beta particle—is propelled out of the nucleus at high speed.

Beta radiation is represented by the symbol $_{-1}^{0}\text{e}^-$ or merely $_{-1}^{0}\text{e}$ or $_{-1}^{0}\beta$. The mass number is zero because an electron has an exceedingly small mass compared to a proton or a neutron. Beta radiation is about 100 times more penetrating than alpha radiation and is able to penetrate 1 to 2 millimeters into solid material. It is able to pass through clothing and damage the skin.

Gamma rays are a very energetic form of light that our eyes cannot see, which makes them similar to X-rays. A gamma ray does not consist of particles, so it is symbolized by $_0^0\gamma$. Gamma radiation accompanies alpha and beta radiation and is much more penetrating than either of them. It is able to penetrate deeply into solid material, including body tissue, and is stopped only by heavy shielding, such as concrete or lead. Gamma rays are very dangerous, and scientists who work with them follow a strict set of precautions.

Figure 3–29 *The three types of radiation differ in composition, charge, and penetrating ability. What is the charge on a beta particle?*

Types of Radiation

Name	Identity	Charge	Penetrating Ability
alpha (α)	helium-4 nuclei	2+	low, stopped by paper
beta (β)	electrons	1–	medium, stopped by heavy clothing
gamma (γ)	high energy non-particle radiation	none	high, stopped by lead

Figure 3–30 *Protective clothing is essential for individuals who work with radioactive materials.*

When an atom emits one of these kinds of radiation, it is said to be undergoing a **radioactive decay.** Specifically, an atom may undergo an alpha, beta, or gamma decay. The radiation is called decay because the original nucleus decomposes, or decays, to form a new nucleus, releasing radiation in the process.

The best way to understand a radioactive decay is with a **nuclear equation,** or an equation that keeps track of the reaction's components. For example, here is the nuclear equation that describes the alpha decay of an isotope of radium, element number 88:

$$^{226}_{88}\text{Ra} \rightarrow {}^{222}_{86}\text{Rn} + {}^{4}_{2}\alpha \qquad \textbf{(Eq. 2)}$$

In a nuclear equation, the arrow is read as "yields" or "produces," and it points in the direction of the reaction. Equation 2 indicates that the nucleus of a radium-226 atom produces a radon-222 nucleus and an alpha particle.

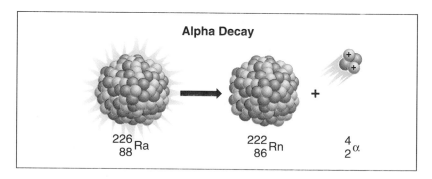

Alpha Decay

$^{226}_{88}\text{Ra}$ → $^{222}_{86}\text{Rn}$ + $^{4}_{2}\alpha$

Figure 3–31 *In alpha decay, a nucleus ejects a helium nucleus, or alpha particle, and becomes a smaller nucleus with less positive charge.*

You Are a Model Maker!

Today you start a new job: You are in charge of designing new exhibits for a science museum. Because of your expertise on the structure of atoms, you decide that your first exhibit will be a large, three-dimensional model of a helium atom. You tell your staff that you want this model to be as accurate, informative, and attractive as possible.

Right away, your staff barrages you with questions. Which isotope of helium do you want? Should the protons and neutrons be larger than the electrons? If so, how much larger? How should the particles be colored or labeled? Should the electrons be stationary or in motion around the nucleus? If you want the electrons to move, what kind of path should they follow?

You need to answer each of these questions before the exhibit is built. You can pretend that you have unlimited funding for this project, but your boss, the museum director, will want you to justify each expense.

Developing Models

1. Answer each question raised in the above paragraphs. In what ways is your model an accurate model of a helium atom? In what ways is it inaccurate?

2. Is it possible to accurately represent the motion of an electron? Explain your answer.

3. The museum director is so pleased with your work that she asks you to make a model of a uranium atom. What questions do you have in undertaking this task?

Figure 3–32 *Beta decay has the effect of turning a neutron in the nucleus into a proton, ejecting a beta particle—or electron—in the process.*

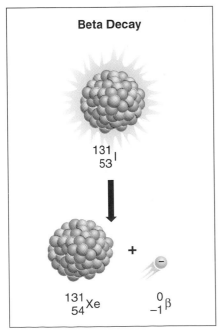

Beta Decay

$$^{131}_{53}I$$

$$^{131}_{54}Xe \qquad + \qquad ^{0}_{-1}\beta$$

Here is a nuclear equation that describes the beta decay of iodine-131:

$$^{131}_{53}I \rightarrow \,^{131}_{54}Xe + \,^{0}_{-1}\beta \qquad \textbf{(Eq. 3)}$$

In this reaction, the nucleus of an iodine-131 atom produces a xenon-131 nucleus and a beta particle.

As you look at Equations 2 and 3, do you notice anything interesting about their mass numbers and atomic numbers? In each equation, the sums of the mass numbers are the same on both sides of the arrow, as are the sums of the atomic numbers. In Equation 2, the mass number on the left side of the arrow is 226, which equals the sum of the mass numbers on the right side of the arrow, 222 and 4. The atomic numbers also balance: 88 = 86 + 2. How do the mass numbers and atomic numbers balance in Equation 3?

In any radioactive decay, the sums of the mass numbers and atomic numbers are the same before and after the reaction. This important fact will help you to write a nuclear equation when you do not know the products of the reaction. If you use the proper symbol for the radiation ($^{4}_{2}\alpha$ for alpha, $^{0}_{-1}\beta$ for beta, $^{0}_{0}\gamma$ for gamma), an equation's mass numbers and atomic numbers will always balance.

SAMPLE PROBLEM 4

Write the nuclear equation for the alpha decay of gold-185 ($^{185}_{79}$Au).

STRATEGY	SOLUTION
1. **Analyze**	The mass numbers and atomic numbers in a nuclear equation must balance.
2. **Plan**	The nuclear equation has the following form:

$$^{185}_{79}\text{Au} \rightarrow ^{M}_{Z}\text{X} + ^{4}_{2}\alpha$$

where M represents the mass number of the new atom, Z represents the atomic number, and X represents the element symbol.

3. Solve   The sum of the mass numbers must be equal, so write the algebraic equation:

$$185 = M + 4.$$

Solve to find that $M = 185 - 4$, or $M = 181$. For the atomic numbers, write the equation:

$$79 = Z + 2.$$

Solving gives $Z = 77$. From the periodic table, the element with atomic number 77 is Ir (iridium). Therefore, the symbol of the product is $^{181}_{77}$Ir, and the nuclear equation is

$$^{185}_{79}\text{Au} \rightarrow ^{181}_{77}\text{Ir} + ^{4}_{2}\alpha$$

4. Evaluate   Check the nuclear equation by adding both the mass numbers and the atomic numbers on each side of the arrow: $185 = 181 + 4$ and $79 = 77 + 2$. The equation has the correct mass numbers and atomic numbers. The element symbol is correct for the element with atomic number 77.

In a balanced nuclear equation, the sums of the atomic numbers (Z) and the mass numbers (M) on each side of the equation must be equal.

PRACTICE PROBLEMS

7. Write a nuclear equation for the alpha decay of uranium-238.   (Answer: $^{238}_{92}U \rightarrow ^{234}_{90}Th + ^{4}_{2}\alpha$)

8. Write a nuclear equation for the beta decay of sodium-24.   (Answer: $^{24}_{11}Na \rightarrow ^{24}_{12}Mg + ^{0}_{-1}\beta$)

Artifact or Art Fake?

A museum curator carefully examines a clay urn. It looks authentic, but the curator has some doubts. Is the urn an ancient art treasure or a modern forgery?

Can chemistry help a museum curator determine the age of a work of art? If there were no exceptions to Dalton's atomic theory, the answer might be no. Dalton's third postulate states that atoms are neither created nor destroyed in chemical reactions. This means that a perfectly preserved object would be composed of the same atoms today as when it was made.

However, an atom's identity can change through radioactive decay. Almost all objects on Earth contain at least some radioactive atoms and these atoms always decay at a predictable rate. For these reasons, scientists can estimate the age of an object simply by analyzing it for certain radioactive isotopes. For objects less than approximately 60,000 years old, scientists typically measure for carbon-14, a radioactive isotope of carbon. The procedure is called carbon-14 dating, or carbon dating for short.

How does an object acquire carbon-14 in the first place? As you may know from a biology course, plants take up carbon dioxide from the atmosphere. The carbon from carbon dioxide is incorporated not only into plant matter, but into animals that eat plants, and animals that eat other animals. Because all living organisms ultimately rely on plants for food, they all incorporate carbon atoms that were once in the atmosphere—atoms that include some carbon-14.

When an organism dies, it stops taking in carbon. Over time, the dead organism actually loses carbon because carbon-14 undergoes a slow beta decay:

$$^{14}_{6}C \rightarrow {}^{14}_{7}N + {}^{0}_{-1}\beta$$

This reaction proceeds at a known rate: After approximately 5730 years, one half of an object's carbon-14 atoms decay into nitrogen-14

atoms. In other words, a piece of wood that originally contained 20 grams of carbon-14 would contain 10 grams after 5730 years, 5.0 grams after 5730 more years, 2.5 grams after another 5730 years, and so on. By determining what percentage of a substance's carbon atoms are the carbon-14 isotope, scientists can calculate its age.

Carbon dating is useful for studying artifacts made of wood, bone, animal skins, or fabrics such as wool or linen. Carbon dating can also be used on clay objects because clay often contains bits of straw that were used to hold it together. The carbon atoms in the straw make dating clay objects possible.

- Suppose you found an artifact that contained one fourth as much carbon-14 as it contained when it was made. Estimate the age of this artifact.
- How might you determine whether a collector has perfectly legal replicas of valuable artifacts or may be guilty of robbing archaeological sites?
- Would carbon-14 dating help you to identify the age of any artifact? Give reasons to explain your answer.

Figure 3–33 *Radiation from the sun, which we perceive as heat and light, is produced as the sun's atoms undergo nuclear reactions.*

Other Nuclear Reactions

Radioactive decay is only one kind of nuclear reaction. As you will learn in Chapter 24, nuclei and nuclear particles can react in a variety of different ways. For example, hydrogen atoms inside the sun take part in nuclear fusion reactions. In this reaction, two hydrogen nuclei collide to form a helium nucleus, releasing a great amount of energy in the process. Other nuclear reactions involve splitting a nucleus, a process called nuclear fission. A nuclear reactor produces energy by splitting the nuclei of large atoms, such as uranium-235.

Although atoms are invisible to the unaided eye, studying their structure led scientists to a wealth of information about the world around us. When Democritus argued for the existence of atoms in ancient Greece, he could not have imagined that the study of atoms would help give rise to television picture tubes, smoke detectors, or nuclear power. Today, scientists still have questions about atomic structure, especially about the composition of the particles in the nucleus. Who knows what knowledge will come from the studies and experiments of the future?

3–4 Section Review

1. What changes accompany a nuclear reaction?
2. Define radioactivity. Is all radiation composed of particles? Explain.
3. Describe the force that holds the nucleus together. Explain why neutrons are the "glue" of the nucleus.
4. **Connection—You and Your World**   Why are gamma rays and not alpha or beta radiation used in treating cancer?

Laboratory Investigation

What's Inside?

Problem

How can you determine the structure of something that you cannot directly observe?

Materials (per group)

two mystery boxes

Procedure

1. On a separate sheet of paper, prepare a data table similar to the one shown. Make sure that the boxes are large enough for you to make drawings in them.
2. Obtain a mystery box.
3. Record the number of the mystery box in your data table.
4. The interior of each mystery box contains a unique arrangement of partitions and one or more marbles. Tilt, turn, and rotate the mystery box to move the marbles inside. The way the marbles move will provide clues about the arrangement of partitions inside the box.
5. In the appropriate place in your data table, record your hypothesis about the shape and location of the partitions inside the mystery box.
6. Repeat Steps 1 to 5 for a second mystery box.
7. Peek inside each of the two mystery boxes and record their actual internal structure in the appropriate places in your data table.

Observations

Mystery Box number: _____

Hypothesized Structure	Actual Structure

1. How did the marbles help you to infer the internal structure of the mystery boxes?
2. How did your hypothesized structures differ from the actual internal structures?

Analysis and Conclusions

1. Could you have inferred the internal structure of a mystery box that did not contain marbles (and without peeking)? Explain why or why not.
2. How is the process you used in this investigation similar to the method Ernest Rutherford used to determine the structure of an atom?
3. Which of your senses did you use to make observations in this experiment?
4. Why are your observations considered to be indirect?
5. **On Your Own** Have a friend put an unknown material into a nontransparent container. Try to determine the identity of the unknown material. What methods are available to you?

STUDY GUIDE

Summarizing Key Concepts

3–1 Early Models of the Atom

- Atoms are the smallest particles of an element that retain the chemical identity of that element.
- Dalton's atomic theory of matter forms the basis of our understanding of chemistry.
- There are about 100 different kinds of atoms that combine to form all matter.

3–2 Discovering Atomic Structure

- Atoms contain particles that have electrical charge.
- Franklin concluded that electricity was based on two kinds of charge, which he called positive and negative. Particles that have different charges attract each other. Those with similar charges repel each other.
- Thomson concluded that a cathode ray consists of negatively charged particles, which he named electrons. Millikan, from his oil-drop experiment, calculated the mass of an electron.
- Becquerel discovered radioactivity, the spontaneous emission of energy from an element. Radioactivity is the product of fundamental changes in an atom's nucleus.

- In his alpha-scattering experiment, Rutherford discovered that an atom contains a tiny, positively charged nucleus at its center.

3–3 Modern Atomic Theory

- Atoms are composed of protons, neutrons, and electrons. Protons and neutrons are found in an atom's nucleus. Electrons move in the space around the nucleus.
- The number of protons in an atom is called its atomic number.
- An atom or group of atoms with a net electrical charge is called an ion. Atoms that have the same number of protons but different numbers of neutrons are called isotopes.

3–4 Changes in the Nucleus

- Nuclear reactions change the composition of an atom's nucleus.
- In a stable nucleus, the strong nuclear force overcomes the electrical repulsion force.
- Unstable nuclei may emit alpha, beta, or gamma radiation. Alpha and beta radiation consist of particles. Gamma radiation is a very energetic form of light.

Reviewing Key Terms

Define each term in a complete sentence.

3–1 Early Models of the Atom

atom
law of constant composition
atomic theory of matter

3–2 Discovering Atomic Structure

cathode ray
cathode ray tube
electron
radioactivity
nucleus

3–3 Modern Atomic Theory

proton
neutron
atomic mass unit
atomic number
ion
isotope
mass number
atomic mass

3–4 Changes in the Nucleus

nuclear reaction
strong nuclear force
radioactive decay
nuclear equation

CHAPTER REVIEW

Content Review

Multiple Choice
Choose the letter of the answer that best completes each statement.

1. Who first proposed that matter is composed of tiny, indivisible particles?
   (a) Aristotle   (c) Franklin
   (b) Democritus   (d) Rutherford

2. Which scientist developed the atomic theory of matter?
   (a) Antoine Lavoisier   (c) Aristotle
   (b) John Dalton   (d) Joseph Proust

3. A nucleus of 4 neutrons and 4 protons that is surrounded by 2 orbiting electrons is
   (a) a positive ion.   (c) an alpha particle.
   (b) a negative ion.   (d) a beta particle.

4. Which of the following represents an ion?
   (a) Mg   (c) Na^+
   (b) ^4He (d) $^{40}_{20}Ca$

5. A positive charge will
   (a) attract another positive charge.
   (b) repel another positive charge.
   (c) repel a negative charge.
   (d) neither attract nor repel a negative charge.

6. A cathode ray
   (a) streams from anode to cathode.
   (b) cannot be deflected.
   (c) carries a positive charge.
   (d) could spin a small paddle wheel.

7. An alpha particle is
   (a) $^4_4\alpha$.   (c) $^2_4\alpha$.
   (b) ^4_2He.   (d) $^{\ 0}_{-1}\beta$.

8. Electrons were discovered by
   (a) Thomson, in his studies of magnetic and electric fields on cathode rays.
   (b) Franklin, in his kite-flying experiment.
   (c) Rutherford, in his experiments with alpha-particle beams and gold foil.
   (d) Becquerel, in his oil-drop experiment.

9. A hydrogen atom has a charge of
   (a) $+1$.   (c) $+2$.
   (b) -1.   (d) 0.

10. Isotopes contain different numbers of
    (a) electrons.   (c) neutrons.
    (b) protons.   (d) nuclei.

True or False
If the statement is true, write "true." If it is false, change the underlined word or words to make the statement true.

11. Radioactivity results from changes in an atom's <u>nucleus</u>.

12. The force that holds nuclear particles together is called the <u>electrical</u> force.

13. <u>Gamma</u> radiation consists of particles with a 2+ charge.

14. In a cathode ray tube, the cathode ray comes from the <u>anode</u>.

15. An electron's mass is essentially <u>1</u> amu.

16. The number of protons in an atom is called its <u>atomic mass</u>.

17. A(An) <u>isotope</u> is an atom or a group of atoms having a net electrical charge.

18. An atom's <u>mass number</u> is the sum of its protons and neutrons.

Concept Mapping
Complete the following concept map for Section 3–1. Refer to pages xviii–xix to construct a concept map for the entire chapter.

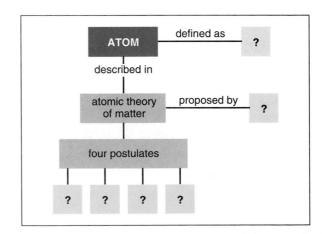

Concept Mastery

Discuss each of the following in a brief paragraph.

19. Why is a nucleus with too few neutrons unstable?

20. Write the nuclear equation for the alpha decay of astatine-213 ($^{213}_{85}At$).

21. Write the nuclear equation for the beta decay of titanium-50 ($^{50}_{22}Ti$).

22. List the three kinds of subatomic particles in an atom. What are the major characteristics of these particles?

23. Describe Rutherford's alpha-scattering experiment. What did the results of this experiment reveal about atoms?

24. What is a cathode-ray tube? What role did this device play in the discovery of atomic structure?

25. Define radioactivity. List the three important types of radiation and describe their characteristics. Does all radiation consist of particles?

26. Tying it Together Describe the changes in *structure* that an atom undergoes during an alpha decay. Do these changes challenge any part of Dalton's atomic theory of matter?

Critical Thinking and Problem Solving

Use the skills you have developed in this chapter to answer each of the following.

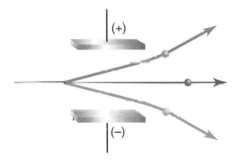

27. Interpreting diagrams Consider the movement of three kinds of particles between electrically charged plates as shown in the diagram. What can you conclude about the charge of each particle?

28. Making inferences Before Rutherford's alpha-scattering experiment, Rutherford and other scientists accepted the plum pudding model of the atom. Describe this model and use it to explain the results Rutherford expected for his experiment.

29. Drawing conclusions Why does splitting a nucleus produce tremendous amounts of energy?

30. Making predictions Molybdenum is element number 42 and its atomic mass is 95.94. Use these numbers to predict the relative abundances of molybdenum's different isotopes. How certain can you be about your answers?

31. Developing models Draw an illustration of a beryllium-8 atom, which contains 4 protons, 4 neutrons, and 4 electrons. In what ways does your drawing accurately represent a beryllium atom? In what ways is it inaccurate?

32. Interpreting data Some radioactive nuclei emit positrons, particles that have the same mass as electrons but the opposite charge. A positron is symbolized by $^{0}_{1}e$ or sometimes $^{0}_{1}\beta^{+}$. Write the nuclear equation for the reaction in which a carbon-11 atom decays by emitting a positron.

33. Using the writing process Imagine that you are a subatomic particle in a nuclear reaction. Write a short story or play about your experiences. How do you react to the different forces you encounter? What is your opinion of other particles?

Chapter 4

Electron Configurations

Perhaps you are wondering what a drawing of a woman has to do with the topic of this chapter. Actually, the drawing itself has nothing to do with atoms and electrons. But later in this chapter, you will take a second look at this picture and possibly astonish yourself.

Something similar happened to scientists in the early twentieth century. They thought they understood the basic laws of nature only to uncover some surprising facts about the behavior of electrons and other small particles. In this chapter, we will examine some of the clues explored by scientists and the conclusions they reached. The result of their work was a new, interesting, and highly useful model of the atom—a model that helps explain the arrangement of electrons in atoms, or electronic structure.

Look closely at the sketch of the woman shown in the inset. Now look at the larger drawing. Do you see a woman? How old do you think she is? What does she look like? What is she wearing? How do your impressions compare with those of your friends?

4–1 Radiant Energy

Guide for Reading
- What are the four characteristics of an electromagnetic wave?
- What are the major regions of the electromagnetic spectrum?

Much of the understanding of how electrons behave in atoms comes from studies of how light interacts with matter. To make sense of these studies, you must first consider some aspects of light. Light travels through space and is a form of radiant energy, as you learned in Chapter 2. It is this energy that causes you to feel hot when you stand in bright sunlight. But how does light carry energy through space?

Throughout the past 200 years there has been considerable scientific debate over the nature of light. Until the 1900s, scientists believed that light was a beam of energy moving through space in the form of waves, much like the waves you see on the surface of a lake. But in the 1900s, scientists observed another side to the nature of light. They found that in some experiments light behaved like a stream of extremely tiny, fast-moving particles. Today, scientists recognize that light has both the properties of waves and the properties of particles, and they use both models to describe it.

Figure 4–1 *Earth's ultimate source of energy is the sun. The sun's radiant energy is the result of nuclear fusion reactions. How does nuclear fusion differ from nuclear fission?*

Figure 4–2 *Electromagnetic radiation consists of oscillating electric and magnetic fields that are perpendicular to the direction of propagation of the wave. What is the angle between the electric and the magnetic fields?*

electric field

magnetic field

direction of electromagnetic wave

Waves

Light travels in waves similar to the waves caused by a moving boat. Light waves, however, are electromagnetic waves and light is a form of **electromagnetic radiation.** X-rays, gamma rays, and radio waves are other forms of electromagnetic radiation. An electromagnetic wave consists of electric and magnetic fields oscillating at right angles to each other and to the direction of motion of the wave. **All waves, whether they are water waves or electromagnetic waves, can be described in terms of four characteristics—amplitude, wavelength, frequency, and speed.**

The **amplitude** of a wave is the height of the wave measured from the origin to its crest, or peak. See Figure 4–3. The brightness, or intensity, of light depends on the amplitude of the light wave.

The **wavelength,** also shown in Figure 4–3, is the distance between successive crests of the wave. It is the distance that the wave travels as it completes one full cycle of upward and downward motion. The light, or electromagnetic radiation, that your eyes can see—visible light—has wavelengths in the range of 400 to 750 nanometers. (Recall that a nanometer is 10^{-9} meter.)

Figure 4–3 *The amplitude, wavelength, and frequency of a wave are illustrated here. The frequency of a wave is the number of complete waves passing a fixed point in a given time. How are the wavelength and frequency of an electromagnetic wave related?*

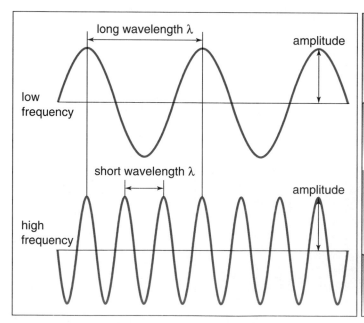

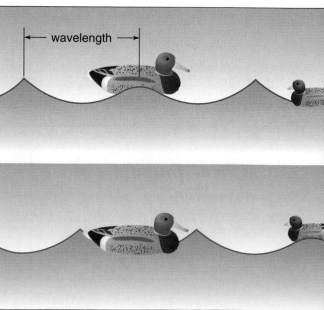

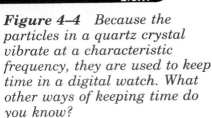

Figure 4–4 *Because the particles in a quartz crystal vibrate at a characteristic frequency, they are used to keep time in a digital watch. What other ways of keeping time do you know?*

You perceive visible light because of the chemical reactions it causes in your eyes.

The **frequency** of a wave tells how fast the wave oscillates up and down. The frequency of light is measured by the number of times a light wave completes a cycle of upward and downward motion in one second. Thus, the unit for frequency is cycles per second. Because it is understood that cycles are involved, frequency is commonly expressed simply as "per second," which is written as s^{-1}, or $1/s$. (The quantities $1/s$ and s^{-1} are equal. They are two ways of representing the same unit.) A cycle per second is also called a hertz (Hz): $1 \text{ Hz} = 1 \text{ s}^{-1}$. When an FM radio station identifies itself as broadcasting at 93.1 megahertz (MHz), it means that the radio waves have a frequency of 93.1 $\times$ 10^6 cycles per second. (The frequency is 93.1 $\times$ 10^6 s^{-1}; *mega-* is the metric prefix meaning 10^6.) The frequency of visible light varies from about 4 $\times$ 10^{14} s^{-1} to about 7 $\times$ 10^{14} s^{-1}.

Light, regardless of its wavelength, moves through space at a constant speed of 3.00 $\times$ 10^8 meters per second (m/s), which is the **speed of light**. Because light moves at a constant speed, there is a relationship between its wavelength and its frequency. As Figure 4–3 shows, the shorter the distance between the crests of the wave, the faster the wave oscillates up and down. That is, the shorter the wavelength, the greater the frequency. This relationship can be expressed in a simple equation. Using the symbol λ (the Greek letter lambda) for wavelength, ν (the Greek letter nu) for frequency, and c for the speed of light, the relationship between wavelength and frequency is

$$\lambda = c/\nu \qquad \textbf{(Eq. 1)}$$

For example, the truck-mounted helium-neon laser shown in Figure 4–5 produces red light whose wavelength is 633 nanometers. The frequency of this radiation, 4.74 $\times$ 10^{14} s^{-1}, can be easily calculated using a slightly rearranged Equation 1. What is the form of the rearranged equation?

MATH TIP

The frequency (ν) and the wavelength (λ) of electromagnetic radiation are inversely related.

$$\nu \cdot \lambda = c$$

Thus, high frequency radiation has short wavelengths, whereas long wavelength radiation has low frequencies.

Figure 4–5 *The helium-neon lasers mounted on a truck are used to measure precisely the clearance in tunnels. Why are such measurements important?*

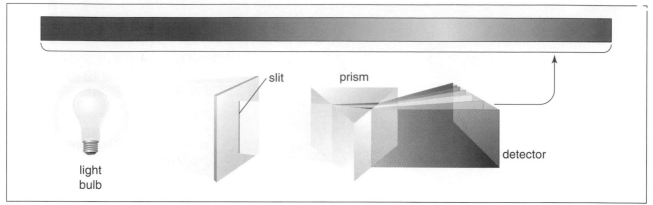

Figure 4–6 A continuous visible spectrum results when light passes through a prism or through raindrops. Which color is refracted the most?

Electromagnetic Spectrum

You have probably seen a glass prism spread ordinary sunlight into a rainbow of colors, as shown in Figure 4–6. The same phenomenon happens when sunlight passes through raindrops, creating a familiar sight: a rainbow. At the inner curve of the rainbow is the color violet and at the outer curve is the color red. In between are the colors indigo, blue, green, yellow, and orange, each color gradually fading into the next. This array of colors is called the **visible spectrum.** The visible spectrum is an example of a continuous spectrum because one color fades gradually into the next color. The different colors have different wavelengths (and therefore also different frequencies). Violet has the shortest wavelength (and the highest frequency). Red has the longest wavelength (and the lowest frequency).

Visible light constitutes a very small portion of the total electromagnetic spectrum. The rest of the electromagnetic spectrum is invisible to the human eye. You are probably familiar with the words microwaves, radio waves, and X-rays. These are some other examples of electromagnetic radiation. Radio waves and microwaves have longer wavelengths than visible light. X-rays, on the other hand, have wavelengths that are much shorter than the wavelengths of visible light. Figure 4–7 shows the relative positions of the various types of electromagnetic radiation in the electromagnetic spectrum.

Using visible light as the point of reference, notice how the wavelengths of the various kinds of electromagnetic radiation differ. Beyond the red portion of the visible spectrum, at longer wavelengths, is infrared radiation. Infrared radiation is also known as radiant heat. A heat lamp produces infrared radiation. As wavelengths continue to increase, the radiation becomes microwaves and then radio waves. Microwaves are used for quickly heating food in a microwave oven. The microwaves heat only

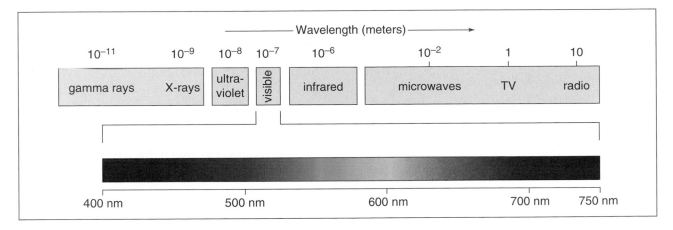

Figure 4–7 *The visible spectrum is only a small portion of the electromagnetic spectrum, which ranges from the long-wavelength radio waves to the short-wavelength cosmic rays. Which waves are responsible for sunburn?*

the food (not the entire oven space) by transferring their energy to the moisture present in the food. On the other side of the visible spectrum, beyond the violet portion, is ultraviolet or UV radiation. This form of radiation is responsible for sunburns and skin cancer. X-rays and gamma rays are forms of electromagnetic radiation with even shorter wavelengths than UV.

Figure 4–8 *This photograph of a house was taken with an infrared camera. The hotter areas appear as yellow and orange and the cooler areas as blue. X-rays, which pass through soft human tissues, are blocked by dense bone tissue. The picture that results allows a physician to see the consequence of an accident—two broken arm bones.*

*I*NTEGRATING *B*IOLOGY

What type of damage is caused by high-energy radiation?

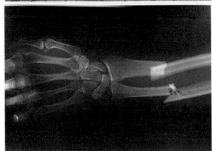

4-1 Section Review

1. Define the terms amplitude, wavelength, frequency, and wave speed.
2. How are wavelength and frequency related to each other?
3. List the major regions of the electromagnetic spectrum in order of increasing wavelength.
4. **Connection—Physics** Using Equation 1, calculate the wavelength of a radio wave with a frequency of $93.1 \times 10^6 \text{ s}^{-1}$.

Guide for Reading

- What is meant by energy quantization?
- How is the energy of radiation related to its wavelength?
- How does the idea of photons of light explain the photoelectric effect?

4–2 Quantum Theory

By the beginning of the twentieth century, the wave model of light was just about universally accepted by scientists. But several observations were beginning to puzzle them. One of these was the way in which electromagnetic radiation is emitted by hot objects. For example, as a metal is heated, it first emits invisible infrared radiation (heat), but no visible light. Upon further heating, it begins to glow red, then yellow, and finally becomes "white hot," as illustrated in Figure 4–9. Scientists wondered why a different range of wavelengths is emitted at different temperatures. The well-known, or "classical," ideas of physics simply could not explain this phenomenon. A new model had to be developed in order to account for these observations.

Some other questions that scientists in those days could not answer included how elements such as barium and strontium gave rise to green and red colors when heated, and what caused devices such as "neon" lights to give off characteristic colors of light. The search for answers to these and other questions led scientists on a fascinating voyage of scientific discovery. The rest of this chapter gives a glimpse of the work of these brilliant science detectives.

Figure 4–9 *Why does the heating element of a stove glow red-hot and the horseshoe on the blacksmith's anvil glow white-hot? The graph, which shows how the wavelengths of the radiation emitted by a hot object shift as its temperature is increased, may provide the answer.*

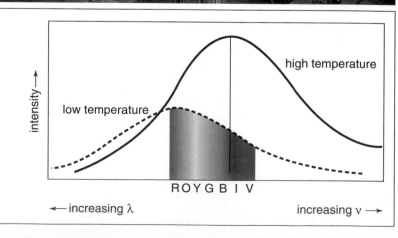

Planck's Theory

In 1900, the German physicist Max Planck (1858–1947) was able to predict accurately how the spectrum of radiation emitted by an object changes with its temperature. To do so, however, he had to make a radical suggestion, one that carried the seeds of a scientific revolution. Planck suggested that the energy emitted or absorbed by an object—any object—is restricted to "pieces" of particular sizes. **Planck proposed that there is a fundamental restriction on the amounts of energy that an object emits or absorbs, and he called each of these pieces of energy a quantum.** The word **quantum** means a fixed amount, and the plural of quantum is quanta. The quantization of energy is the basis of the currently accepted model of electronic structure. This idea completely contradicts one of the assumptions of the old classical physics—that an object can absorb and emit any amount of energy so that the energy it can possess forms a continuum of values.

The essence of Planck's theory is the relationship between the frequency (and also the wavelength) of a particular radiation and the energy with which it is associated. Planck's fundamental equation is quite simple, relating the amount of energy, E, to the frequency, v, of the radiation:

$$E = hv \qquad \text{(Eq. 2)}$$

The constant h, now called **Planck's constant,** has a value of 6.6262×10^{-34} J-s. (J-s is read joule-second.) The joule (J) is the SI unit for energy as you learned in Chapter 2. Using Planck's theory, scientists today can determine the temperatures of distant planets and stars by measuring the wavelengths of the electromagnetic radiation that they emit.

Planck's theory proposes that the energies absorbed or emitted by atoms are quantized, which means that their values are restricted to certain quantities. What do you think would happen if the energy of a car were quantized? You are correct if you said that the car would only be able to move at certain speeds. For example, suppose that a car's fundamental quantum of energy corresponds to a speed of 10 km/hr. If the car has 7 quanta of energy, it will move at a speed of 70 km/hr. If it has 9 quanta of energy, it will move at a speed of 90 km/hr. The car can gain or lose its energy only in multiples of its fundamental energy quantum. Thus, the car will not be able to move at any speed that is not a multiple of 10 km/hr. The car's speed will not vary continuously, and speeds such as 13 km/hr and 47 km/hr will be impossible. Would a speed of 88 km/hr be possible?

You know from your experience that cars do not move in this jumpy, jerky fashion. Why, then, should scientists accept Planck's quantum theory? Is Planck's explanation of the emission of energy by hot objects sufficient to support this bold concept? Very shortly you will learn about the photoelectric effect observed in metals. As you will see, the photoelectric effect offers

Figure 4-10 *Max Karl Ernst Ludwig Planck was awarded the Nobel Prize in 1918 for his quantum hypothesis. Planck decided to pursue physics in spite of the advice that he received from the head of the physics department at Munich who said that "The important discoveries [in physics] have been made."*

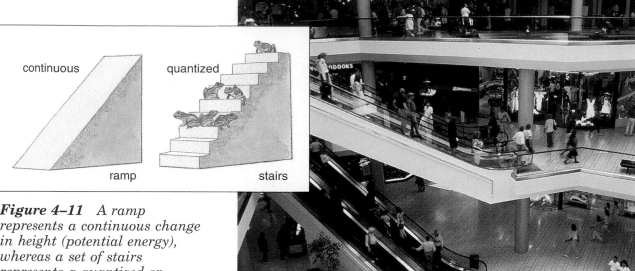

Figure 4–11 *A ramp represents a continuous change in height (potential energy), whereas a set of stairs represents a quantized or discrete change in height. What conclusions can you draw regarding the change in height of a person on a moving escalator? A person climbing a set of stairs?*

further evidence to support the idea of quantized energy. In time, scientists performed other experiments which gave a greater validity to Planck's quantum idea.

So why are you not aware of quantum effects in the world around you? Why does it appear that the speed of a car can change continuously without jumps? The answer is hidden in the size of Planck's constant. Notice that Planck's constant, h, is a very small number. Therefore, each quantum of energy ($E = h\nu$) is extremely small. This makes energy seem continuous because the quanta are too small to notice in the everyday world. For you, the quanta seem insignificant. For atoms, which are themselves very small, the quanta are of tremendous significance.

The Photoelectric Effect

Although Planck's discovery of energy quanta was a major turning point in science, it did not attract much attention at first. Even Planck was uncomfortable with the concept he had proposed and did not fully appreciate its importance. Albert Einstein (1879–1955), however, saw in this idea a new way of thinking about light. In 1905, just two years after obtaining his Ph.D. degree, Einstein used Planck's equation to explain another puzzling phenomenon, the **photoelectric effect.**

In the photoelectric effect, electrons are ejected from the surface of a metal when light shines on the metal. See Figure 4–12. The operation of numerous electronic devices, such as photocells used in camera light meters, is based on the photoelectric effect. For each metal, a minimum frequency of light is needed to release electrons. For example, red light is incapable of releasing electrons from sodium metal, even if the light is extremely intense. On the other hand, violet light, even if relatively faint, releases electrons easily.

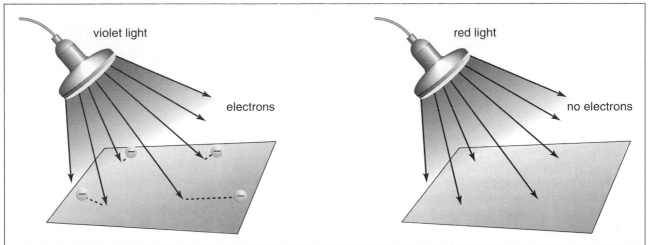

Einstein realized that Planck's idea of energy quanta was the key to understanding this phenomenon. He proposed that light consists of quanta of energy that behave like tiny particles of light. He called these energy quanta **photons.** Einstein proposed that each photon carries an amount of energy that is given by Planck's equation, $E = h\nu$.

How did Einstein's idea explain the photoelectric effect? When a photon strikes the surface of a metal, it transfers its energy to an electron in a metal atom. Einstein reasoned that an electron either "swallows" the entire photon or does not swallow any of it. The electron cannot use just part of the energy from a photon, and it cannot collect energy from several photons. If the energy of the photon is too small, an electron will not have enough energy to escape from the metal—no matter how many photons strike the surface. What is important is the energy (and thus the frequency) of the photon, not the number of photons (the intensity of the light). So why does violet light free electrons from sodium metal but red light does not? Violet light has a greater frequency and, as a result, a greater amount of energy per photon.

The relationship between the frequency of light and the energy of a photon helps explain some of the effects of different kinds of electromagnetic radiation. For example, wherever X-rays are used, such as in hospitals or other locations, signs are posted warning of high-energy radiation. X-rays have high frequencies. Thus their photons have high energies—high enough to be capable of damaging organisms. Radio waves, on the other hand, have low frequencies. Their photons have low energies and therefore appear to pose no health hazard. This is quite fortunate for humans because we are surrounded by radio waves!

Figure 4-12 Although violet light is able to eject electrons from sodium metal, red light is not. This is because the energy of violet photons is greater than the energy of red photons. Will infrared photons release electrons from sodium? The photograph shows a panel of solar cells that produce a photoelectric current.

Dual Nature of Radiant Energy

The idea that light consists of tiny particles, or photons, was convincingly proven in 1923 when the American physicist Arthur Compton (1892–1962) demonstrated that a photon could collide

The Darkroom Mystery

You have a friend who is taking a photography class at school. She is learning to be a good photographer as well as how to process her film. So she regularly uses a darkroom for developing her pictures. The darkroom is equipped with a dim red light so that your friend can see enough to handle the film and the developing solutions. One day when the red bulb burned out, your friend replaced it with a dim yellow bulb that she found. She and several other students were later dismayed when they ruined their film while using the darkroom. When your friend told you of this disaster, you immediately understood what had happened. Explain to your friend why the red light was safe but the yellow one was not.

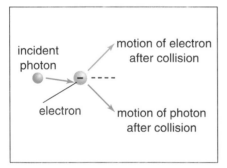

Figure 4–13   *The Compton effect helped prove the dual nature theory of light.*

with an electron much as two tiny balls might collide. As you can see from Figure 4–13, the collision acts in every way like the collisions between marbles or between billiard balls. Thus a photon behaves like a particle—but a very special particle that always travels at the speed of light and has an associated frequency and wavelength. So the question of whether light is a particle or a wave is really inappropriate. You might as well ask if books are made of words or pages. It is not a matter of one or the other—books have both words and pages. Likewise, light somehow has a dual nature, possessing the properties of both particles and waves.

4–2 Section Review

1. What does it mean to say that energy is quantized?
2. How is the energy of a quantum of radiant energy related to its frequency?
3. Why do you not ordinarily observe the quantization of energy in the world around you?
4. **Connection—Biology**   People who work around X-rays often wear film badges to monitor the amount of radiation to which they are exposed. Why do X-rays expose the film in the badge when other kinds of electromagnetic radiation do not?

4-3 Another Look at the Atom

Guide for Reading

• What is a line spectrum?
• How does the Bohr model explain the line spectrum of hydrogen?

The fact that atoms can gain or lose energy only in chunks, or quanta, brings us closer to answering the question of how electrons are arranged in atoms. But before we arrive at that answer, we must first consider another observation that puzzled scientists at the beginning of this century.

Line Spectra

If you dip the end of a heat-resistant wire into a saltwater solution and then place it in the flame of a burner, a yellow light is emitted, as shown in Figure 4–14. When this light is passed through a prism, a spectrum is formed that contains only a few colors, including the yellow seen in the burner flame. **A spectrum that contains only certain colors, or wavelengths, is called a line spectrum.** A **line spectrum** is quite different from the continuous spectrum of sunlight or the light from a filament bulb.

Samples of all elements emit light when they are vaporized in an intense flame or when electricity is passed through their gaseous state. How is this light produced? The atoms must somehow absorb energy and then give the energy off in the form of light. For every element, the emitted light contains only certain wavelengths, giving each element a unique line spectrum. See Figure 4–15. The line spectrum is also referred to as the atomic emission spectrum of the element. An atomic emission spectrum of an element is a kind of atomic fingerprint that is extremely useful in identifying elements. The yellow light emitted by salt (sodium chloride) is characteristic of sodium. This yellow light

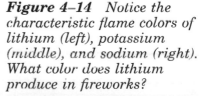

Figure 4–14 *Notice the characteristic flame colors of lithium (left), potassium (middle), and sodium (right). What color does lithium produce in fireworks?*

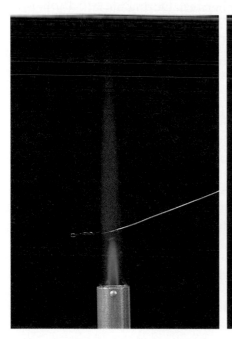
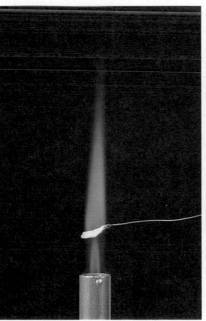
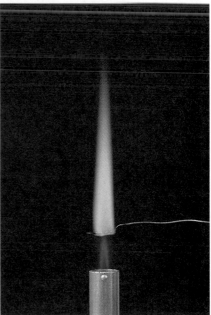

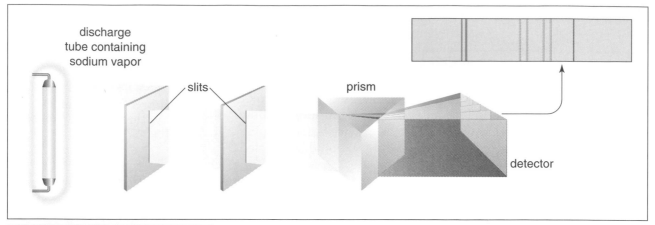

discharge
tube containing
sodium vapor

slits

prism

detector

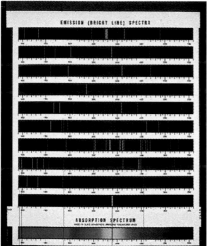

Figure 4–15 *The line spectra of several elements such as mercury, helium, and strontium are shown. A continuous visible spectrum is provided at the bottom of the line spectra for easy comparison of the lines. Notice the characteristic yellow color of sodium given off by a sodium-vapor street lamp.*

is also produced by sodium-vapor lamps, which are widely used for street lighting. The different colors seen in "neon" lights are produced by using different gases or vapors in the lights. For example, neon itself gives off a red light, as does hydrogen. Nitrogen emission is orange. Mercury emission is blue.

The Bohr Model of the Hydrogen Atom

How do scientists explain the fact that each element is capable of emitting its own characteristic wavelengths of radiation? Is there some connection between the wavelengths an element emits and its atomic structure? It was the Danish physicist Niels Bohr (1885–1962) who first saw the connection. In 1911, Bohr attended a lecture given by Ernest Rutherford. During his talk, Rutherford described his new planetary model of the atom with its nucleus and circling electrons. Recall that you learned about Rutherford's model in Chapter 3. Bohr realized how Planck's idea of quantization could be applied to this model to explain the line spectra of elements.

Bohr started with the simplest atom, a hydrogen atom, which has only one electron. Bohr postulated that to get spectral lines, the energy of the electron in the atom must be quantized. In terms of Rutherford's planetary model, this means that the electron is allowed to have only certain orbits corresponding to different amounts of energy. Bohr labeled each energy level, and consequently each orbit, by a **quantum number,** n. For the lowest energy level, or **ground state,** $n = 1$. This energy level corresponds to the orbit closest to the nucleus. When the electron absorbs the appropriate amount of energy, it jumps to a level of higher energy, called an **excited state.** The excited states have quantum numbers $n = 2$, $n = 3$, $n = 4$, and so forth. The excited states represent larger orbits with the electron farther from the nucleus, as shown in Figure 4–16.

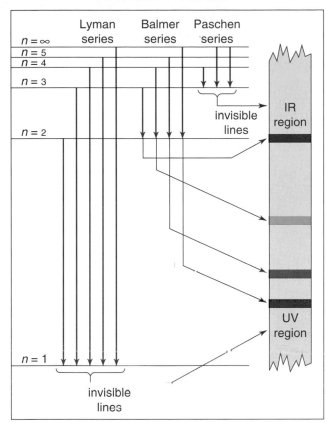

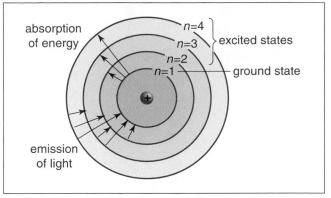

Figure 4–16 *In the Bohr model of a hydrogen atom, the electron in the* n = *1 level represents the ground state. As the electron absorbs a quantum of energy, it jumps to a higher level (excited state). When the electron jumps down to the* n = *1 level, it is accompanied by an emission of radiation. What transitions lead to visible emissions?*

To explain hydrogen's spectral lines, Bohr proposed that when radiation is absorbed, an electron jumps from the ground state to an excited state. Radiation is emitted when the electron falls back from the higher energy level to a lower one. The energy of the absorbed or emitted radiation equals the difference between the two energy levels involved. Bohr was able to use this model and Planck's equation, $E = h\nu$, to calculate the frequencies observed in the line spectrum of hydrogen. The fact that the results of the calculation matched the observed emission spectrum for hydrogen was powerful evidence in support of his model.

Although the Bohr model worked well for hydrogen, it could not explain the spectra of atoms with more than one electron, except in a rather approximate way. Further observations and suggestions pointed to a more generally useful way to describe electrons. Because the Bohr model introduced the idea of quantized energy levels for electrons in atoms, it represents an important initial step in the development of the current model for electronic structure.

Matter Waves

Until 1900, scientists believed that there was a clear distinction between matter and energy. Dalton's atomic theory was the framework for thinking about matter. Matter was considered to be a collection of particles—particles that are discrete, or quantized. Think for a moment about atoms of copper. You can have

Figure 4–17 This photograph shows the two famous scientists Albert Einstein (left) and Niels Bohr (right) walking together in Brussels, Belgium, in 1933.

1 atom, 2 atoms, 1000 atoms, or even 810 million atoms of copper. But you cannot have 1.374 or 38.79 or even 2.5 atoms! At the same time, energy in the form of radiation was considered to be a collection of waves. Wavelength—and therefore frequency—could change continuously and thus energy itself was believed to be continuous.

As you have just learned, first Planck in 1900, then Einstein in 1905, and again Bohr in 1913 were forced to describe light as consisting of photons—quanta of energy that have some of the characteristics of particles. When light travels through space, it behaves like a wave. When light interacts with matter, its behavior can be like that of a stream of particles. If energy has a dual nature, do you think matter does too? Does nature show such symmetry?

In 1924, a French graduate student named Louis de Broglie (1892–1987) thought so. He reasoned that particles of matter should behave like waves and exhibit a wavelength, just as waves of light behave like particles of matter. De Broglie referred to the wavelike behavior of particles as **matter waves.** He went on to derive a mathematical relationship between the mass and velocity of a moving particle and the wavelength that it would exhibit. While exciting, this mathematical relationship would not have been accepted without experiments that demonstrated its validity. Only three years later, experiments performed by Clinton Davisson and Lester Germer at Bell Labs in New Jersey did just that. The two scientists had been studying the bombardment of metals with beams of electrons. They had noticed that curious patterns were produced by the electrons reflected from the metal

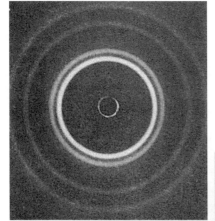

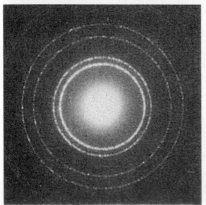

Figure 4–18 The diffraction pattern in the top photograph is produced by a beam of electrons. The diffraction pattern in the bottom photograph is produced by a beam of X-rays. The electron micrograph of a Mediterranean fruit fly is produced by an electron microscope that makes use of the wave nature of electrons.

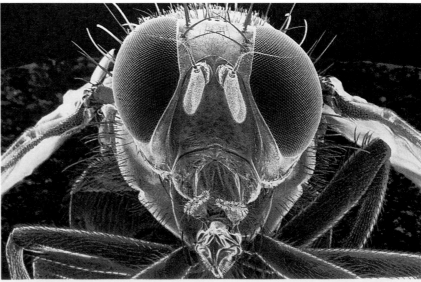

surfaces. See Figure 4–18. The patterns were like those obtained when X-rays (waves of electromagnetic radiation) are reflected from metal surfaces. And indeed, de Broglie's mathematical equation predicted precisely the patterns produced. The electrons— believed to be particles—were reflected as if they were waves! De Broglie was awarded the Nobel Prize for his work on the wave nature of matter. Davisson also recieved the Nobel Prize for his experiments demonstrating the wave nature of electrons.

Today, scientists routinely take advantage of the wavelike properties of beams of electrons to magnify objects using electron microscopes. Electrons behaving as waves are also used to determine distances between atoms or ions.

De Broglie's equation predicts that all moving objects have wavelike behavior. Why are you unable to observe the effects of this wave motion for ordinary objects like golf balls or trains? The answer is that the mass of the object, m, must be very small in order for its wavelength, λ, to be large enough to observe. For example, a 50-gram golf ball traveling at 40 meters/second (about 90 mi/hr) has a wavelength of only 3×10^{-34} meter, far too small to detect experimentally. On the other hand, an electron has a mass of only 9.11×10^{-28} gram. If it were moving at a velocity of 40 meters/second, it would have a wavelength of 2×10^{-5} meter, which is comparable to infrared radiation and readily measured.

Let's pause here for a few moments and revisit the chapter opener drawing. Look carefully at the sketch in Figure 4–19. Now turn to the chapter opener on page 124. What do you see? Do you see the same woman you saw when you began reading this chapter? Can you see a tired, sad, old woman as well as a sophisticated, fashionable, young one? If not, look at the sketch in Figure 4–19 again and try to capture that image in the chapter opener drawing. Just as the chapter opener drawing contains the "attributes" of the two different personalities, so do matter and energy simultaneously contain the attributes of particles and waves. The dual nature of the chapter opener drawing serves as a fascinating analogy for the dual nature of matter and energy.

Figure 4–19 *After carefully looking at the sketch of this old woman, refer back to the sketch at the beginning of the chapter. How does this impression compare with your first impression?*

Heisenberg's Uncertainty Principle

There is yet another concept to be considered before we can discuss the current model for electronic structure. In 1927, Werner Heisenberg (1901–1976) proposed his **uncertainty principle,** which states that the position and the momentum of a moving object cannot simultaneously be measured and known exactly. This means that there is an inherent limitation to knowing both where a particle is at a particular moment and how it is moving in order to predict where it will be in the future. This limitation is inherent in the dual nature of matter and energy and becomes critical in dealing with small particles like electrons. However,

Figure 4–20 *Although it may be possible to obtain a sharp image of this cheetah using a very fast film and a very fast shutter speed, Heisenberg's uncertainty principle states that it is impossible to know the exact position and momentum of any object simultaneously.*

with ordinary sized objects like cars or airplanes or even cheetahs, it is inconsequential.

To understand this principle, consider how you determine the location of an object. To locate a set of keys in a dark room, for example, you can use a flashlight. You see the keys when the light bounces off them and strikes your eyes. Likewise, to locate an electron, you must strike it with a photon or another particle, which then bounces back to some detection device. Because the electron has such a small mass, the collision moves it in some unpredictable way. So in this case, the very act of measurement changes in some way that which you are trying to measure.

One of the problems with the Bohr model is that there is no way to observe or to measure the orbit of an electron in an atom. Indeed, the uncertainty principle states that it is not even appropriate to think in terms of electrons moving in well-defined orbits because there is no way to test this idea. To scientists, however, experiments are the ultimate test of ideas. As you will learn in the next section, the way around this problem is to discuss the arrangement of electrons in atoms in terms of the probability of finding an electron in certain locations within the atom. Thus the concept of probability provides an escape from the limitations of uncertainty.

4–3 Section Review

1. What is the difference between a line spectrum and a continuous spectrum?

2. How does the Bohr model account for the line spectrum of the hydrogen atom?

3. What is the Heisenberg uncertainty principle?

4. **Critical Thinking—Applying concepts** You have learned that in attempting to locate an electron, the act of measurement changes the system. Suppose that you measure the temperature of a cup of hot tea with a cold thermometer. How does the use of the cold thermometer affect the temperature reading? Is this an example of the uncertainty principle? Explain.

4–4 A New Approach to the Atom

Guide for Reading

• What is an atomic orbital?
• How do the *s, p, d,* and *f* orbitals compare in size, shape, and energy?

Let's take a moment to review what you have learned so far about electrons in atoms. First, you know that the energy of electrons is quantized. This means that electrons can have only certain specific amounts of energy. Second, you know that electrons exhibit wavelike behavior. Third, you know what you cannot know about electrons: It is impossible to know the exact position as well as momentum of an electron at any given instant. Scientists have developed the **quantum-mechanical model** of an atom, which includes all of these ideas. The quantum-mechanical model explains the properties of atoms by treating the electron as a wave that has quantized its energy. Although it is impossible to describe the exact positions of electrons or to describe how they are moving, the model does describe the probability that electrons will be found in certain locations around the nucleus. Just how, then, can you visualize these electrons? Read on for the answer to this question.

Probability and Orbitals

The probability of finding an electron in various locations around the nucleus can be pictured in terms of a blurry cloud of negative charge. The cloud is most dense where the probability of finding the electron is highest. The cloud is least dense where the probability of finding the electron is lowest. The density of an electron cloud is referred to as **electron density.** Those regions of high probability are said to have high electron density. Conversely, regions of low probability are said to have low electron density.

The probability of finding electrons in certain regions of an atom is described by **orbitals. An atomic orbital is a region around the nucleus of an atom where an electron with a given energy is likely to be found.** Be careful to distinguish between the terms orbital (quantum-mechanical model) and orbit (Bohr model). Orbitals have characteristic shapes, sizes, and energies. But orbitals do not describe how the electron actually moves.

Rather than drawing electron clouds to represent orbitals, it is more convenient to merely draw the surface within which an electron is found 90 percent of the time. For the electron cloud shown to the left in Figure 4–22 on the following page, a sphere can be drawn that encloses 90 percent of the electron density. The probability of finding the electron is the same for all points on the surface, and there is a 90-percent chance of finding the electron within the sphere.

Figure 4–21 The quantum mechanical model of an atom (bottom) is compared to the Bohr model of an atom (top). According to the quantum mechanical model, electrons have no precise orbits. Instead, their motion can only be described by the probability of finding them in certain regions surrounding the nucleus. What are these regions called?

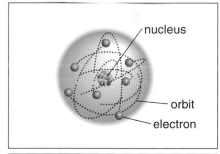

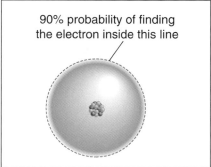

90% probability of finding the electron inside this line

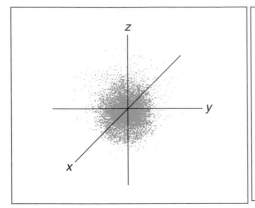 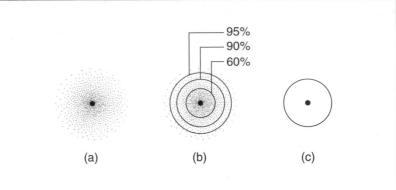

Figure 4–22 *The electron density distribution in the ground state of the hydrogen atom is shown in diagram (a). In diagram (b), the contours for 60, 90, and 95 percent are superimposed to show how electron density decreases as the distance from the nucleus increases. Diagram (c) shows only the 90-percent contour, which represents the s orbital.*

Figure 4–23 *The diagram illustrates the electron density of the p orbital. How would you describe this orbital shape?*

There are several different kinds of orbitals, each having a different fundamental shape. These different kinds of orbitals are designated by the letters *s, p, d,* and *f.* All *s* orbitals are spherical in shape, whereas *p* orbitals are dumbbell shaped. The shapes of *d* and *f* orbitals are more complex. Figure 4–23 shows the electron density and the 90-percent contour for a *p* orbital. The amount of energy that an electron has determines the kind of orbital it occupies.

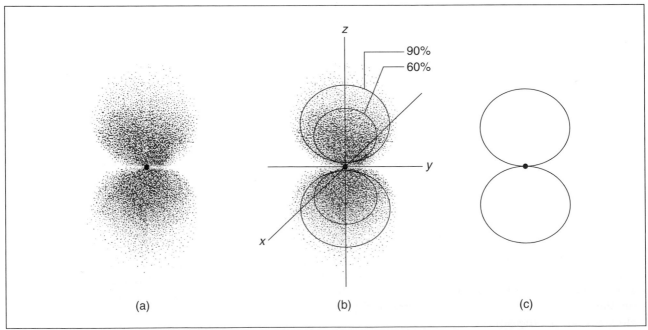

Orbitals and Energy

As you learned previously, Bohr proposed that the energies of the electrons in atoms are quantized. This means that their energies are limited to certain values. You can begin to visualize electrons with the idea of energy levels introduced by Bohr. The main or **principal energy levels** in an atom are designated by the quantum number n, which is called the principal quantum number. (The quantum-mechanical model also introduces other quantum numbers that will not be discussed here.)

Just as proposed in the Bohr model, the energy of the electron increases as n increases from 1 to 2 to 3, and so forth. Unlike the Bohr model, however, each principal energy level is divided into one or more **sublevels.** There is a distinct and important pattern of these sublevels. The number of sublevels in each principal energy level equals the quantum number n for that energy level. Thus, there is one sublevel when $n = 1$, two sublevels when $n = 2$, three sublevels when $n = 3$, and so forth. As you can see in Figure 4–24, these sublevels are labeled with a number that is the value of the quantum number n and a letter (s, p, d, or f) that corresponds to the type of sublevel. For example, $2p$ is the designation of the p sublevel in the principal energy level 2. Likewise, $3s$ is the designation of the s sublevel in the principal energy level 3. If all of this sounds rather confusing to you, do not despair. In the next few paragraphs, you will take a step-by-step "trip" through the sublevels and orbitals of the first few principal energy levels. As you proceed, keep in mind the definition of an orbital—a region in which an electron with a particular energy is likely to be found.

Each principal energy level consists of one or more sublevels and each sublevel consists of one or more orbitals. Just as your

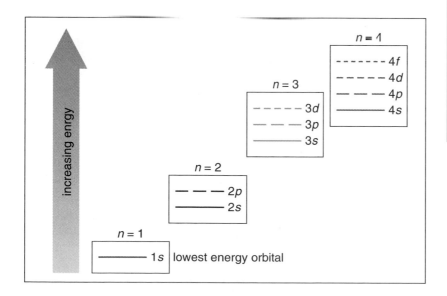

Figure 4–24 *The principal energy levels (n = 1, n = 2, and so forth), sublevels (s, p, d, and f), and orbitals are shown in terms of their relative energies. Is the 4s sublevel lower or higher in energy than the 3d?*

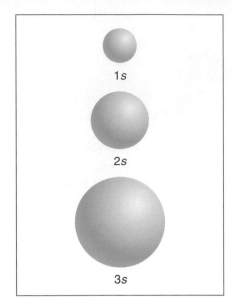

1s

2s

3s

Figure 4–25 *The 1s, 2s, and 3s orbitals shown represent 90-percent contours of electron density. How does an electron in a 3s orbital differ from an electron in a 1s orbital?*

mailing address consists of a state, a city, and a street name within the city, the "address" of an electron consists of its principal energy level, its sublevel, and its orbital within that sublevel. The first energy level ($n = 1$) consists of only one sublevel. (Remember that there are as many sublevels in a principal energy level as the value of n for that principal energy level.) That sublevel contains a single s orbital with its characteristic spherical shape. That sublevel is therefore called the 1s sublevel and its orbital is called the 1s orbital.

The second principal energy level ($n = 2$) consists of two sublevels—the 2s and 2p sublevels. They are called the 2s and 2p sublevels because of the kinds of orbitals they contain. The 2s sublevel consists of a single s orbital, which is called the 2s orbital. Like the 1s orbital, the 2s orbital is spherical in shape. The 2s orbital, however, is larger than the 1s orbital. An electron in a 2s orbital is free to roam over a larger space because it has more energy. See Figure 4–25. The 2p sublevel is slightly higher in energy than the 2s sublevel. The 2p sublevel consists of three p orbitals of equal energy. Each 2p orbital is dumbbell shaped, as shown in Figure 4–26, and extends from the nucleus at a 90° angle from each of the other two orbitals. It is convenient to label these orbitals $2p_x$, $2p_y$, and $2p_z$, based on the axes along which they lie.

The third principal energy level ($n = 3$) has three sublevels—the 3s, 3p, and 3d. The 3s sublevel is composed of a single 3s orbital. How, then, does it differ from the 2s orbital? The 3p sublevel, which is higher in energy than the 3s sublevel, is composed of three equal-energy p orbitals. The $3p_x$, $3p_y$, and $3p_z$ orbitals are identical in shape and orientation to the 2p orbitals

Figure 4–26 *The 90-percent contour representations of $2p_x$, $2p_y$, and $2p_z$ orbitals are shown first separately and then superimposed, centered on the nucleus. How is a 3p orbital different from a 2p orbital?*

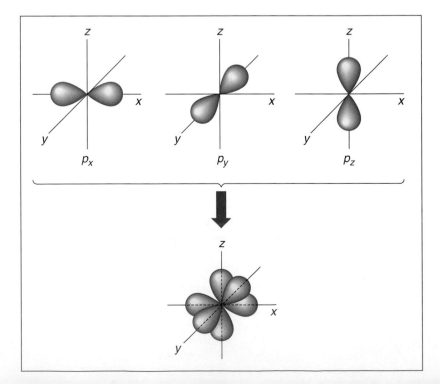

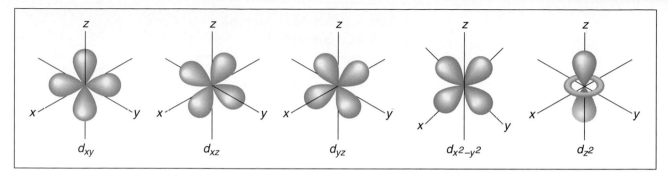

d_{xy} d_{xz} d_{yz} $d_{x^2-y^2}$ d_{z^2}

of the second level. The 3p orbitals are, however, larger than the 2p orbitals, and their electrons can be found farther from the nucleus due to their greater energy. The 3d sublevel, which is higher in energy than the 3p sublevel, is composed of five equal-energy orbitals, as shown in Figure 4–27.

The fourth principal energy level ($n = 4$) consists of four sublevels: 4s, 4p, 4d, and 4f. The 4s sublevel consists of one 4s orbital, the 4p sublevel consists of three 4p orbitals, the 4d sublevel consists of five 4d orbitals, and the 4f sublevel consists of seven 4f orbitals. The shapes of the 4f orbitals are not shown here.

The division of the principal energy levels into sublevels and orbitals is summarized in Figure 4–28. Notice that the number of sublevels always equals the quantum number n. Notice also that the number of orbitals in each sublevel is always an odd number. There is 1 orbital in an s sublevel, 3 orbitals in a p sublevel, 5 orbitals in a d sublevel, and 7 orbitals in an f sublevel. As the value of n increases, the electron energy increases. The electrons also spend more time farther from the nucleus, making the orbital larger.

Electron Spin

Electrons not only have characteristic energies, but they also possess another important property. They behave as though they were spinning on their own axis. The spin can be either clockwise or counterclockwise.

A spinning charge creates a magnetic field. Thus, when a negatively charged electron spins clockwise, it behaves like a tiny magnet whose north pole is pointing up. When it spins counterclockwise, it behaves like a tiny magnet whose north pole is pointing down. As you read these descriptions of electron spin, keep in mind that the terms clockwise and counterclockwise are

Figure 4–27 *The diagram shows the shapes of the five equal-energy d orbitals. Can you visualize these orbitals superimposed upon one another centered at the atom's nucleus?*

Figure 4–28 *The principal energy levels, sublevels, and orbitals are summarized in this table. How many orbitals are found in the second principal energy level?*

Summary of Energy Levels, Sublevels, and Orbitals

Principal Energy Level	Sublevels	Orbitals
$n = 1$	1s	1s (one)
$n = 2$	2s, 2p	2s (one) + 2p (three)
$n = 3$	3s, 3p, 3d	3s (one) + 3p (three) + 3d (five)
$n = 4$	4s, 4p, 4d, 4f	4s (one) + 4p (three) + 4d (five) + 4f (seven)

Maximum Number of Electrons in Each Sublevel

Sublevel	Number of Orbitals	Maximum Number of Electrons
s	1	2
p	3	6
d	5	10
f	7	14

Figure 4–29 *The table lists the maximum number of electrons in each sublevel. Can you predict the number of orbitals in a g sublevel?*

used only for your benefit—so that you can visualize the spinning electron and its effect. The important point here is that there are only two possible ways in which electrons can spin. These two ways are mutually opposite and have been designated as clockwise and counterclockwise. A pair of electrons can have parallel spins (meaning that both are clockwise or both are counterclockwise) or opposite spins (one clockwise and one counterclockwise). If 2 electrons have opposite spins, the effects of their spins cancel each other. If 2 electrons have parallel spins, the spins result in a net magnetic effect that can be experimentally observed. Can you predict the result of a single spinning electron?

In 1925, the Austrian-born physicist Wolfgang Pauli (1900–1958) expressed the importance of electron spin in determining how electrons are arranged in atoms. The Pauli exclusion principle states that each orbital in an atom can hold at most 2 electrons and that these electrons must have opposite spins. Two electrons with opposite spins are said to be paired. The capacity of an atomic orbital to hold a maximum of 2 electrons determines the maximum number of electrons allowed in each energy level and sublevel. The electron capacities of each sublevel in an atom are listed in Figure 4–29.

4–4 Section Review

1. What is an atomic orbital? An electron orbit?
2. Sketch the general shape of an *s* orbital and of a *p* orbital.
3. List the kinds of sublevels in the fourth principal energy level of an atom.
4. How many electrons can be found in any orbital of an atom? Are their spins parallel or opposite?
5. **Theme Trace—Scale and Structure**   How many sublevels are in the fifth principal energy level of an atom? How many orbitals are in each sublevel? How many electrons can each sublevel hold?

4–5 Electron Configurations

The distribution of electrons among the orbitals of an atom is called the **electron configuration** of the atom. The electron configuration of an atom describes where the electrons are found and what energies they possess. As you read earlier, this information is vital to chemists' understanding of how atoms of elements differ and why they interact with one another as they do. These interactions are the subject of the next unit.

When atoms encounter each other, it is their outer parts—their electrons—that come in contact. These contacts often cause the atoms to "stick together." For example, when hydrogen (H) atoms collide, they join to form tightly bound pairs of atoms as shown in Figure 4–30. Chemists represent this combination by the chemical formula H_2. Such a combination of atoms is called a molecule. You may remember that atoms sometimes lose or gain one or more of their electrons and the resulting charged particles are called ions. The formation of ions is another type of interaction between atoms that involves only their electrons. You will study these and other types of atomic interactions in greater depth in Chapter 7. To prepare for that study, you must first understand how an atom's electrons are arranged around its nucleus and how this arrangement relates to the energy of the electrons. **Electron configurations of atoms are determined by distributing the atom's electrons among levels, sublevels, and orbitals based on a set of stated principles.**

Determining Electron Configurations

Determining the electron configuration of an atom is easy once you know the relative energies of the orbitals. Figure 4–31 on the following page shows the relative energies of the various energy levels, sublevels, and orbitals. Each box represents an orbital. Notice that within each principal energy level, the *s* sublevel is always lowest in energy, followed by the *p*, then the *d*, and finally the *f*. Notice also that above the 3*p* sublevel, the energies of the different principal energy levels begin to overlap. Thus the 4*s* sublevel is actually lower in energy than the 3*d*. In the next chapter you will see how the periodic table contains within its very arrangement the energy ranking of sublevels so that electron configurations can be determined easily. This means that you will not need to memorize the energy ranking shown in Figure 4–31!

When electrons populate the lowest energy orbitals available, the atom is said to be in its ground state. The ground state is the most stable, lowest energy state of the atom. It is the way atoms normally exist. The location of the electrons in the ground state of an atom can be predicted by using Figure 4–31 and applying three important principles: the Aufbau principle, the Pauli exclusion principle, and Hund's rule.

Guide for Reading
- How is an atom's electron configuration determined?

Figure 4–30 *Hydrogen, the simplest element, consists of 2-atom molecules (H_2) in a gaseous state. Because hydrogen reacts explosively with oxygen (O_2) releasing huge amounts of energy, these elements are used to fuel the main engines of the space shuttle.*

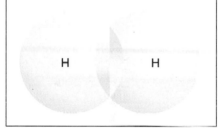

Figure 4-31 *The diagram on the top arranges the atomic orbitals in order of increasing energy. The diagram on the bottom shows the placement of the 6 carbon electrons in the proper atomic orbitals, representing the ground state of the carbon atom. What is a possible excited state configuration for carbon?*

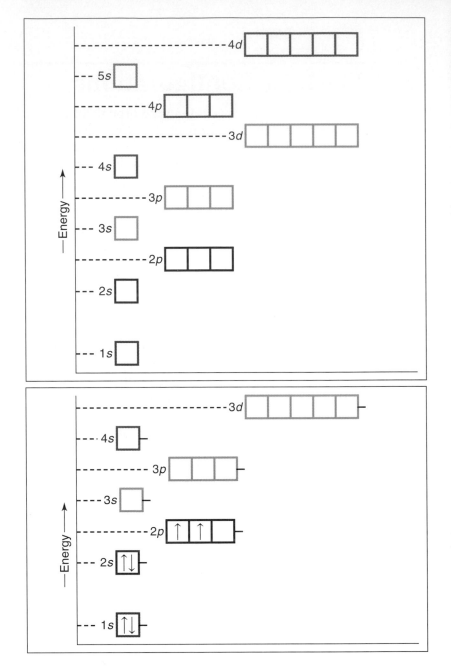

THE AUFBAU PRINCIPLE Electrons are added one at a time to the lowest energy orbitals available until all the electrons of the atom have been accounted for. (The word *Aufbau* is German for building up.) Recall that the number of electrons in a neutral atom equals the atomic number of the element. Thus the electron configuration for the ground state of carbon (atomic number = 6), for example, must account for 6 electrons.

THE PAULI EXCLUSION PRINCIPLE An orbital can hold a maximum of 2 electrons. To occupy the same orbital, 2 electrons must spin in opposite directions. When electrons with opposite spins occupy an orbital, the electrons are said to be paired. A single electron present in an orbital is said to be unpaired.

HUND'S RULE   Electrons occupy equal-energy orbitals so that a maximum number of unpaired electrons results. This rule will help you decide how to fill a sublevel consisting of more than one orbital, for example, a $2p$ sublevel with its three equal-energy orbitals. According to Hund's rule, you would first place electrons into $2p$ orbitals one by one until all three orbitals had 1 electron. Then you would place the next electrons to pair up with the existing electrons. This process will become clearer as you practice writing the electron configurations of some familiar elements.

Let's start with the element carbon. The atomic number of carbon is 6. This tells you that carbon atoms have 6 protons in the nucleus and 6 electrons distributed in orbitals outside the nucleus. You can use Figure 4–31 in placing the 6 electrons into the lowest energy orbitals. The first 2 electrons go into the $1s$ orbital with their spins paired. The next 2 electrons go into the $2s$ orbital, also with their spins paired. You know this is the correct arrangement because the capacity of an orbital is only 2 electrons and subsequent electrons must occupy a higher energy orbital. The fifth and the sixth electrons occupy two separate $2p$ orbitals. Hund's rule further tells you that the 2 electrons in the two separate $2p$ orbitals have parallel spins.

The resulting occupied sublevels are shown at the bottom in Figure 4–31. Each electron is represented by an arrow. By convention, the arrow points upward when the electron spin is counterclockwise and downward when the electron spin is clockwise. The direction of the arrows is based on the magnetic properties of the spinning electron. The first electron entering an orbital is usually represented by an arrow that points upward.

To save space, the way electrons populate orbitals is often shown by a horizontal diagram:

C   1s   2s   2p
    [↑↓] [↑↓] [↑|↑|]

This type of representation is called an **orbital diagram**, whereas Figure 4–31 is called an orbital energy diagram. Electron configurations are generally given in an even more compact form by

Figure 4–32   *The ground state electron configurations of several elements are listed in the table. How many unpaired electrons does a nitrogen atom have?*

Electron Configurations of Selected Elements

Element	Total Electrons	Orbital Diagram 1s	2s	2p	3s	Electron Configuration
H	1	↑				$1s^1$
He	2	↑↓				$1s^2$
Li	3	↑↓	↑			$1s^2 2s^1$
N	7	↑↓	↑↓	↑ ↑ ↑		$1s^2 2s^2 2p^3$
O	8	↑↓	↑↓	↑↓ ↑ ↑		$1s^2 2s^2 2p^4$
Ne	10	↑↓	↑↓	↑↓ ↑↓ ↑↓		$1s^2 2s^2 2p^6$
Na	11	↑↓	↑↓	↑↓ ↑↓ ↑↓	↑	$1s^2 2s^2 2p^6 3s^1$

Sunlight—Friend or Foe?

It's been a long, cold, and snowy winter. You dream of lying in the sun, "soaking up some rays," and getting a tan. The thought of feeling the sun's warmth on your skin brings a smile to your face. But don't spread out your beach blanket just yet. There are some things that you should know about sunlight.

The sun is the major natural source of ultraviolet rays. As you have learned, ultraviolet rays are an invisible form of light. They are found just beyond the violet end of the spectrum. Ultraviolet rays are high-energy rays that can cause sunburn. And overexposure to these rays can cause skin cancer. This year alone, doctors will diagnose more than 700,000 cases of highly curable but sometimes fatal skin cancer caused by sunlight! Ozone, which is a form of oxygen in the Earth's upper atmosphere, absorbs most of the sun's ultraviolet radiation. Without the layer of ozone, ultraviolet radiation would probably destroy most plant and animal life on the Earth. Although this information may seem a little unnerving, there are precautions that you can take before going out in the sun.

One precaution is to apply sunscreen with a sun protection factor (S.P.F.) of 15 or higher to your skin about 30 minutes before going out. This action allows sufficient time for the protective ingredients in the sunscreen to inter-act with the skin. In addition, the sunscreen should be reapplied every two hours, and more often if you go into the water or perspire a lot.

After reading about the harm that ultraviolet radiation can do, you may be wondering if it can do any good. Yes, it can. When the skin is exposed to the ultraviolet rays of sunlight, for example, substances in the skin react with the rays to produce vitamin D. For this reason, vitamin D is also known as the sunshine vitamin. Vitamin D prevents and treats rickets, which is a serious bone disease. Medical researchers also use ultraviolet rays to analyze substances in the human body, including amino acids, enzymes, and other proteins.

Now that you are more aware of the effects of ultraviolet radiation on the skin, you may think twice before lying out in the sun. But if you decide that you still want to "soak up some rays," remember two things—put on an effective sunscreen and have fun!

writing the label for each occupied sublevel and adding superscripts to indicate the number of electrons in each sublevel. Using this sublevel notation, the electron configuration for carbon is

$$\text{C} \qquad 1s^2 2s^2 2p^2$$

Because the superscripts represent electrons, the sum of the superscripts equals the number of electrons in the atom, which is the atomic number of the element. Figure 4–32 on the previous page shows the orbital diagrams and the sublevel notation for the electron configurations of several other elements. Sample Problem 1 shows you how to arrive at the electron configuration for iron. Use the Practice Problems to check your understanding of electron configurations.

SAMPLE PROBLEM 1

Use Figure 4–31 to write the orbital diagram and determine the number of unpaired electrons for iron.

STRATEGY	SOLUTION
1. Analyze	You are asked to determine how the electrons in an atom of iron are distributed among atomic orbitals.
2. Plan	You must first determine how many electrons are in an atom of iron. The atomic number gives the number of electrons in a neutral atom. Next the electrons must be placed into the orbital energy diagram given in Figure 4–31 using the Aufbau principle, the Pauli exclusion principle, and Hund's rule.
3. Solve	Iron (Fe, atomic number = 26) has 26 electrons. Accounting for 26 electrons gives

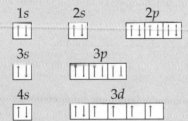

An iron atom has 4 unpaired electrons (in the $3d$ sublevel). The electron configuration is $1s^2 2s^2 2p^6 3s^2 3p^6 4s^2 3d^6$. You may also write the electron configuration of iron as $1s^2 2s^2 2p^6 3s^2 3p^6 3d^6 4s^2$.

4. Evaluate The electron configurations can be checked by adding the number of electrons to ensure that they equal the atomic number of the element.

PRACTICE PROBLEMS

1. Write the electron configurations for (a) magnesium and (b) nickel. How many unpaired electrons does each possess? *(Answer: (a) Mg: $1s^2 2s^2 2p^6 3s^2$, no unpaired electrons (b) Ni: $1s^2 2s^2 2p^6 3s^2 3p^6 4s^2 3d^8$, 2 unpaired electrons)*

2. Which element has the following electron configuration: $1s^2 2s^2 2p^6 3s^2 3p^6 3d^{10} 4s^2 4p^5$? *(Answer: bromine)*

CONSUMER TIP

Sunglasses

Sunglasses protect against sun glare, which is caused by sunlight reflecting off surfaces, such as snow, water, and sand. Sun glare can cause your eyes to receive ten times as much light as they receive under ordinary conditions. Sun glare can be almost eliminated by sunglasses fitted with polarizing lenses. Polarizing lenses contain a tinted plastic filter with tiny crystals that have been stretched into a series of lines. This arrangement effectively blocks out the horizontal rays of light, while permitting enough vertical rays to get through for you to be able to see. Thus, glare is significantly reduced and you can see well enough to read or to drive.

Now that you have an understanding of what electron configurations are and how to determine them, let's see how the exciting colors of fireworks and neon lights are produced.

The electron configurations that you have learned to write represent ground states of atoms. What happens when an atom in its ground state is heated or supplied with energy from some other source? One of its electrons can absorb an amount of energy that corresponds to the energy difference between its present orbital and a higher energy orbital. The atom is now in an excited state. This is an unstable state and the electron "jumps" back to

Figure 4–33 *As excited electronic state atoms return to their ground electronic states, they emit energy in the form of visible light. The visible light is evident in the bright colors of fireworks high above Mount Rushmore in South Dakota. Why does neon exhibit a characteristic red color, whereas sodium is well known for its yellow emission?*

its initial state by emitting the extra energy in the form of light. Remember that the different wavelengths of radiation represent photons with different energy. So the color of light emitted by an element depends on the energy gap between its sublevels.

"Neon" lights consist of sealed gas-filled tubes with electrodes at each end. Different gases absorb the electrical energy, exciting several of the gas atoms. These excited atoms promptly emit the energy in the form of visible light and return to their original ground states. As long as the neon light is switched on, this process of electrons jumping up to excited states and returning to the ground state goes on and on.

Exceptions to the Aufbau Principle

If you apply the Aufbau principle to all known elements, you will find that their electron configurations do not always agree with those determined experimentally. These exceptions do not have any major chemical consequences, though they are interesting to chemists. The first exceptions occur with chromium (atomic number 24) and copper (atomic number 29). Using the Aufbau principle, you would expect the following electron configurations for Cr and Cu:

$$Cr \quad 1s^2 2s^2 2p^6 3s^2 3p^6 4s^2 3d^4$$
$$Cu \quad 1s^2 2s^2 2p^6 3s^2 3p^6 4s^2 3d^9$$

Chemists find instead that the actual configurations are

$$Cr \quad 1s^2 2s^2 2p^6 3s^2 3p^6 4s^1 3d^5$$
$$Cu \quad 1s^2 2s^2 2p^6 3s^2 3p^6 4s^1 3d^{10}$$

Exceptions to the Aufbau principle are due to subtle electron-electron interactions in orbitals with very similar energies. Although it is worth knowing that such exceptions occur, it is more important to understand the general rules for determining electron configurations.

4–5 Section Review

1. What is meant by the electron configuration of an atom?

2. State the three rules that allow you to write the electron configuration of an atom.

3. **Critical Thinking—Developing hypotheses**   Why do electrons occupy equal energy orbitals singly before beginning to pair up in twos?

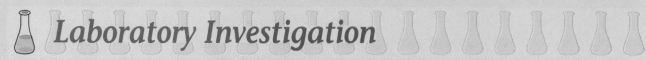

Laboratory Investigation

Predicting the Location of a 1s Electron

Problem

Where is a 1s electron most likely to be found?

Materials (per group)

sheet of paper
felt-tipped marking pen
compass

Procedure

1. Working with a partner, draw a target on the sheet of paper. The center of the target represents the atom's nucleus, which is very small in comparison to the rest of the atom. The nucleus should be represented by a single dot in the center of the paper. Draw concentric circles around the dot so that the radius of each circle is 2.0 cm greater than that of the preceding circle.
2. Tape the paper to the floor so that it will not move.
3. Stand on the opposite side of the target from your partner. Holding a felt-tipped marker at shoulder height above the target center, take turns dropping the marker so that it leaves a dot when it hits the paper. Each dot represents the location of an electron at that moment.
4. Continue dropping the marker until you each have 50 "electron" dots on your paper.
5. Count the number of dots in each ring and record that number in your data table.

Observations

1. Record the number of dots in each ring of the target and calculate the number of dots per cm².
2. What happens to the number of dots per unit area as the distance from the center increases?

Ring Number	Average Distance From Center	Area of Ring	Number of Dots in Ring	Dots per cm²
1	1.0 cm	13 cm²		
2	3.0 cm	37 cm²		
3	5.0 cm	63 cm²		
4	7.0 cm	88 cm²		
5	9.0 cm	113 cm²		

3. Make a graph of your observations by plotting the average distance from the center on the x-axis and number of dots per cm² on the y-axis.

Analysis and Conclusions

1. Determine the probability of finding a dot in each of the rings in the target by dividing the number of dots in the ring by the total number of dots (100). Multiplying this fraction by 100 will give you the percent probability.
2. Based on your graph, what is the distance with the highest probability of finding a dot?
3. How many dots are actually located at the distance of highest probability?
4. Will there necessarily be an electron at the distance with the highest probability of finding an electron? Explain your answer.
5. In what ways is this model similar to the structure of an atom? In what ways is it different?
6. **On Your Own** An atomic orbital is defined as the region within which an electron is found 90 percent of the time. On your target, draw a circle within which 90 percent of the dots are found. What is the distance of this circle from the center? What is the area of this circle?

STUDY GUIDE

Summarizing Key Concepts

4–1 Radiant Energy

- Light is a form of electromagnetic radiation. Its energy is transmitted in the form of waves.
- The electromagnetic spectrum spans a wide range of wavelengths, from radio waves to X-rays.

4–2 Quantum Theory

- The photoelectric effect can be explained in terms of quanta, or photons, of light.
- Light exhibits properties of both particles and waves.

4–3 Another Look at the Atom

- When sunlight is passed through a prism, the resulting visible spectrum is continuous.
- When a sample of an element is heated and the emitted light is passed through a prism, a line spectrum is observed.
- The Bohr model proposes that the energy of electrons is quantized.
- Matter exhibits properties of particles and waves.
- Heisenberg's uncertainty principle states that it is impossible to know the position and momentum of particles exactly.

4–4 A New Approach to the Atom

- The quantum mechanical model of the atom explains the properties of atoms by treating the electron as a wave and by including the idea of quantized energies.
- An orbital is a region in the space around an atom's nucleus where an electron with a particular energy is likely to be found.
- Principal energy levels consist of sublevels such as *s, p, d,* and *f.* The shape of the orbitals depends on the kind of sublevel.
- Two electrons with opposite spins may occupy a single atomic orbital.

4–5 Electron Configurations

- The distribution of electrons among the orbitals of an atom is its electron configuration.
- The Aufbau principle states that in the ground state of an atom, the electrons occupy the lowest energy orbitals available. The Pauli exclusion principle states that only 2 electrons occupy an orbital. Hund's rule describes how electrons fill orbitals of equal energy so that a maximum number of unpaired electrons results.

Reviewing Key Terms

Define each term in a complete sentence.

4–1 Radiant Energy

electromagnetic radiation
amplitude
wavelength
frequency
speed of light
visible spectrum

4–2 Quantum Theory

quantum
Planck's constant

photoelectric effect
photon

4–3 Another Look at the Atom

line spectrum
quantum number
ground state
excited state
matter wave
uncertainty principle

4–4 A New Approach to the Atom

quantum-mechanical model
electron density
orbital
principal energy level
sublevel

4–5 Electron Configurations

electron configuration
orbital diagram

CHAPTER REVIEW

Content Review

Multiple Choice
Choose the letter of the answer that best completes each statement.

1. Which of the following radiations is not a part of the electromagnetic spectrum?
   (a) microwave (c) beta ray
   (b) X-ray (d) infrared

2. The characteristic of an electromagnetic wave that is associated with the energy of that radiation is its
   (a) amplitude. (c) speed.
   (b) frequency. (d) momentum.

3. Which has the greatest energy?
   (a) ultraviolet (c) green light
   (b) infrared (d) blue light

4. Which of the following will give rise to a spectrum most different from the other three?
   (a) sunlight (c) red fireworks
   (b) moonlight (d) white fireworks

5. "Pieces" of energy are known as
   (a) isotopes. (c) quanta.
   (b) particles. (d) line spectra.

6. The lowest sublevel in each principal energy level is represented by the symbol
   (a) f (c) s
   (b) p (d) d

7. Which electron transition results in the emission of energy?
   (a) $3p$ to $3s$ (c) $2s$ to $2p$
   (b) $3p$ to $4p$ (d) $1s$ to $2s$

8. Which is the ground state electron configuration of a magnesium atom?
   (a) $1s^2 2s^2 2p^6 3s^2$ (c) $1s^2 2s^2 3s^2 2p^6$
   (b) $1s^2 2s^2 2p^6 3s^1$ (d) $1s^2 2s^2 2p^4 3s^2$

True or False
If the statement is true, write "true." If it is false, change the underlined word or words to make the statement true.

9. The longer the wavelength of light, the <u>higher</u> its frequency.

10. The <u>greater</u> the frequency of light, the higher the energy of its photons.

11. The shape of a typical p orbital is similar to a <u>four-leaf clover</u>.

12. The electron configuration of an atom gives the distribution of electrons in the <u>ground state</u>.

13. The energy of an atom in an excited state is <u>less</u> than its energy in the ground state.

14. Compared to a $2p$ orbital, a $3p$ orbital can contain <u>2 more</u> electrons.

15. The second principal energy level of an atom can hold a total of <u>10</u> electrons.

Concept Mapping

Complete the following concept map for Section 4–1. Refer to pages xviii–xix to construct a concept map for the entire chapter.

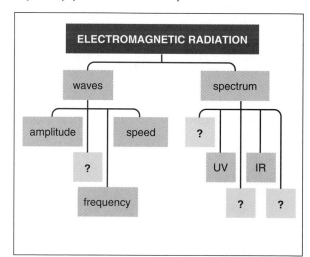

156

Concept Mastery

Discuss each of the following in a brief paragraph.

16. What is a continuous spectrum? Give some examples of sources of continuous spectra.

17. Describe the photoelectric effect and explain how it supports the particle nature of light.

18. Explain the difference between an orbit and an orbital.

19. What is a line spectrum? Describe some ways in which a line spectrum is produced.

20. What is the maximum number of electrons that can go into the following sublevels?
(a) $2s$ (c) $3p$ (e) $4f$ (g) $5d$
(b) $5s$ (d) $4d$ (f) $4p$ (h) $5f$

21. Distinguish between an excited state and a ground state of an atom.

22. Describe the three rules that govern the filling of atomic orbitals by electrons.

23. Using Figure 4–31, write the orbital diagram for the atoms of each element.
(a) boron   (d) phosphorus
(b) chlorine   (e) manganese
(c) zinc   (f) calcium

24. Tying it Together How does the organization of the periodic table correspond to the *scale and structure* represented by electron energy levels?

Critical Thinking and Problem Solving

Use the skills you have developed in this chapter to answer each of the following.

25. Applying concepts Picture two hydrogen atoms. The electron in the first hydrogen atom is in the $n = 1$ level. The electron in the second hydrogen atom is in the $n = 4$ level.
(a) Which atom has the ground state electron configuration?
(b) Which atom can emit electromagnetic radiation?
(c) In which atom is the electron in a larger orbital?
(d) Which atom has a lower energy?

26. Interpreting diagrams Orbital diagrams for the ground states of two elements are shown below. Each diagram shows something that is incorrect. Identify the error in each orbital diagram and then draw the correct diagram.
(a) nitrogen

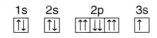

(b) magnesium

27. Applying concepts Identify the elements that have the following electron configurations:
(a) $1s^2 2s^2 2p^5$
(b) $1s^2 2s^2 2p^6 3s^2 3p^6 4s^2 3d^{10} 4p^2$
(c) $1s^2 2s^2 2p^6 3s^2 3p^6 3d^3 4s^2$

28. Making inferences Which of the following is the ground state of an atom? Which is its excited state? Which is an impossible electron configuration? Identify the element and briefly explain your choices.
(a) $1s^2 2s^2 2p^6 3s^2 3p^6 5p^1$
(b) $1s^2 2s^2 2p^6 3s^2 3p^6 4s^1$
(c) $1s^2 2s^2 2p^6 3s^2 3p^7$

29. Using the writing process Describe an event that you experienced in which you were taken by surprise—just as you were surprised by the presence of the two women in the chapter opener drawing.

Chapter 5

The Periodic Table

There is a joy to be felt in looking at the world—the joy of observing the grandeur of a mountain or the delicate beauty of a snowflake. That delight can be heightened when you begin to see the fundamental orders, relationships, and patterns that are found in nature. The more you study the natural world, the more connections you find between events that you once thought were unrelated.

Scientists work hard to discover patterns and relationships in order to organize facts and to gain insight into the workings of nature. In this chapter, you will examine an extremely important pattern among the elements, the pattern that gave rise to the periodic table. As you will discover, the periodic table is very useful for discovering, learning, and remembering the different properties of the elements.

Gaze up at Mount Rainier and you can see distinct changes in the terrain. Beautiful flowers thrive at the bottom, tall trees scale the mountainside, and only snow and rocks can be seen on the mountaintop. What do you think causes such a pattern?

Chem Journal

YOU AND YOUR WORLD

Take a look at the periodic table on pages 166–167. Does it resemble any other tables that you know of? Do you wonder why it has such an unusual shape?

In your journal, propose answers to these and any other questions you may have about the periodic table. When you finish the chapter, review this entry and see if you would answer the questions differently.

5–1 Development of the Periodic Table

Guide for Reading
- What is the periodic law?
- How did Dobereiner, Newlands, Mendeleev, and Moseley each help to develop the modern periodic table?

Do you collect anything? Baseball cards? Coins? Cassette tapes of your favorite music? If so, you probably have a way of organizing your collection. Perhaps you group baseball cards by the players' teams or by the years in which the cards were issued. Perhaps you alphabetize cassette tapes according to the musicians' names. Whatever you collect, organizing your collection becomes more important as the collection grows larger.

Chemists also have a collection—a collection of elements. And as the number of known elements grew, chemists developed the periodic table to organize and classify them. The development of the periodic table is one of the milestones in the history of chemistry because it brought order to what had seemed to be a collection of thousands of unrelated facts. And it did something equally impressive: It helped chemists to predict the existence of elements that had yet to be discovered!

Figure 5–1   As a collection grows larger, it becomes increasingly important to organize it. This is true whether you collect baseball cards or chemical elements.

Figure 5–2 *The gleaming handle of this ceremonial knife (left) is made of gold, one of the handful of elements known since ancient times. Most elements were discovered within the last two hundred years. Titanium, which is used in aircraft parts (right), was discovered in 1791.*

Figure 5–3 *J. W. Dobereiner observed that some elements could be arranged in triads. How do the mass and density of strontium (Sr) compare with those of calcium (Ca) and barium (Ba)?*

Two of Dobereiner's Triads

Element	Atomic Mass (amu)	Density
Cl	35.5	1.56 g/L
Br	79.9	3.12 g/L
I	126.9	4.95 g/L
Ca	40.1	1.55 g/cm³
Sr	87.6	2.6 g/cm³
Ba	137	3.5 g/cm³

Forerunners of the Periodic Table

By the end of the 1700s, scientists had identified only about 30 elements. These elements included metals that had been known since prehistoric times—metals such as copper, silver, and gold—as well as some common nonmetallic elements, such as hydrogen, oxygen, nitrogen, and carbon. By the early 1800s, scientists were using new laboratory techniques to discover additional elements. One of these techniques was atomic spectroscopy, in which elements are identified from their line spectra. As you learned in Chapter 4, each element produces a unique line spectrum. In less than 100 years, scientists doubled the number of known elements. As their list of elements increased, scientists needed better ways of classifying the elements.

In the early 1800s, German chemist J. W. Dobereiner (1780–1849) observed that several elements could be classified into sets of three, which he called triads (the prefix *tri-* means three.) His triads included lithium, sodium, and potassium; calcium, strontium, and barium; and chlorine, bromine, and iodine. The elements within each triad have similar chemical properties. Furthermore, many of the properties of the middle element in each triad are approximate averages of the properties of the first and third elements. For example, in the chlorine, bromine, and iodine triad, the atomic mass of bromine is the approximate average of the atomic mass of chlorine and the atomic mass of iodine:

atomic mass of bromine	79.9
average of atomic masses of chlorine and iodine	$\dfrac{35.5 + 126.9}{2} = 81.2$

Figure 5–3 shows the atomic masses and densities of the elements in two of Dobereiner's triads. Notice that in each triad, the properties of the middle element are close to the averages of the properties of the first and third elements.

In 1865, English chemist J.A.R. Newlands (1837–1898) presented another way of classifying and organizing elements. By that time, 62 elements were known. Newlands observed that when these elements were arranged in order of increasing atomic mass, the properties of the eighth element were like those of the first, the ninth like those of the second, the tenth like those of the third, and so on. Because the pattern repeats every 8 elements, Newlands called the pattern the law of octaves, after the 8 notes of the musical scale.

Newlands' choice of the word octave was unfortunate! The idea of a relationship between chemistry and music seemed ridiculous to Newlands' colleagues, and they did not take his ideas seriously. It took nearly 20 years for Newlands to receive proper credit for his idea that there was a periodic pattern, or repetition, to the properties of the elements.

In 1869, Russian chemist Dmitri Mendeleev (1834–1907) and German chemist Lothar Meyer (1830–1895) published nearly identical schemes for classifying the elements. However, Mendeleev is usually given more credit than Meyer because Mendeleev published his scheme first and was more successful at demonstrating its value. Mendeleev wanted to organize the elements in a way that would help his students learn them more easily. He approached this task by writing the names of the elements and some of their properties on cards, then arranging the cards in various ways. Like Newlands, Mendeleev noticed that when he arranged the elements by increasing atomic mass he could see a periodic repetition of their properties. Mendeleev eventually produced the first **periodic table** of the elements, one similar to the one shown in Figure 5–4. Mendeleev arranged his table so that elements in the same column have similar properties.

Figure 5–4 *Dmitri Mendeleev (right) was not the first to recognize periodic properties in the elements. But his periodic table was more accurate than the tables of other scientists, and he successfully convinced his colleagues of his table's value. In this table from the nineteenth century (left), which elements had yet to be discovered?*

ПЕРИОДИЧЕСКАЯ СИСТЕМА ЭЛЕМЕНТОВ

ПЕРИОДЫ	РЯДЫ	I	II	III	IV	V	VI	VII	VIII			0
1	I	H 1 — 1,008										He 2 — 4,003
2	II	Li 3 — 6.940	Be 4 — 9,02	B 5 — 10.82	C 6 — 12,010	N 7 — 14,008	O 8 — 16,000	F 9 — 19,00				Ne 10 — 20,183
3	III	Na 11 — 22,997	Mg 12 — 24,32	Al 13 — 26,97	Si 14 — 28,06	P 15 — 30,98	S 16 — 32,06	Cl 17 — 35,457				Ar 18 — 39,944
4	IV	K 19 — 39,096	Ca 20 — 40,08	Sc 21 — 45,10	Ti 22 — 47,90	V 23 — 50,95	Cr 24 — 52,01	Mn 25 — 54,93	Fe 26 — 55,85	Co 27 — 58,94	Ni 28 — 58,69	
	V	Cu 29 — 63,57	Zn 30 — 65,38	Ga 31 — 69,72	Ge 32 — 72,60	As 33 — 74,91	Se 34 — 78,96	Br 35 — 79,916				Kr 36 — 83,7
5	VI	Rb 37 — 85,48	Sr 38 — 87,63	Y 39 — 88,92	Zr 40 — 91,22	Nb 41 — 92,91	Mo 42 — 95,95	Ma 43 — —	Ru 44 — 101,7	Rh 45 — 102,91	Pd 46 — 106,7	
	VII	Ag 47 — 107,88	Cd 48 — 112,41	In 49 — 114,76	Sn 50 — 118,70	Sb 51 — 121,76	Te 52 — 127,61	J 53 — 126,92				Xe 54 — 131,3
6	VIII	Cs 55 — 132,91	Ba 56 — 137,36	La 57 — 138,92	Hf 72 — 178,6	Ta 73 — 180,88	W 74 — 183,92	Re 75 — 186,31	Os 76 — 190,2	Ir 77 — 193,1	Pt 78 — 195,23	
	IX	Au 79 — 197,2	Hg 80 — 200,61	Tl 81 — 204,39	Pb 82 — 207,21	Bi 83 — 209,00	Po 84 — 210	85 — —				Rn 86 — 222
7	X		Ra 88 — 226,05	Ac 89 — 227	Th 90 — 232,12	Pa 91 — 231	U 92 — 238,07					

* ЛАНТАНИДЫ 58—71

Ce 58 — 140,13	Pr 59 — 140,92	Nd 60 — 144,27	61	Sm 62 — 150,43	Eu 63 — 152,0	Gd 64 — 156,9
Tb 65 — 159,2	Dy 66 — 162,46	Ho 67 — 164,94	Er 68 — 167,2	Tu 69 — 169,4	Yb 70 — 173,04	Cp 71 — 174,99

161

Ekasilicon and Germanium

Property	Ekasilicon	Germanium
atomic mass (amu)	72	72.59
density (g/cm^3)	5.5	5.35
melting point (°C)	high	947
color	gray	gray

Figure 5–5 *The properties that Mendeleev predicted for ekasilicon closely match the actual properties of germanium. Why was Mendeleev able to make such accurate predictions?*

Why is Mendeleev and not Newlands given credit for the first periodic table? One reason is that Mendeleev sometimes broke the pattern of arranging elements by increasing atomic mass in order to keep elements with similar properties in the same columns. When Mendeleev constructed the periodic table shown in Figure 5–4, he switched the order of three pairs of elements. Why did he do so? Mendeleev boldly suggested that the atomic masses of these elements were incorrect and needed to be remeasured.

Mendeleev also had the insight to predict the existence and some of the properties of three new elements. These elements fit into the gaps in his early tables—the places he left empty in order to keep similar elements in the same columns. He named one of the missing elements ekasilicon. The prefix *eka-* comes from the Sanskrit language and means one. Mendeleev's ekasilicon fit just below silicon in his table.

In 1886, fifteen years after Mendeleev's prediction, a new element was discovered in Germany and given the name germanium. As you can see from Figure 5–5, germanium is very similar to Mendeleev's ekasilicon! Mendeleev's accurate prediction did much to ensure the success of his periodic table.

CHEM Activity

Mimicking Mendeleev?

Choose any 10 elements and assign them numbers from 1 to 10. On an index card for each element, write the number that you assigned the element and some of its properties. Do not include the name of the element or its atomic number. You may select from the properties presented in this chapter, or you may consult a reference book to find other properties.

Exchange your index cards with a partner. Can you identify each element? Which properties are the most helpful in identifying the elements?

The Periodic Law

Did all of Mendeleev's ideas prove to be correct? No, not exactly. Remember that Mendeleev believed that the atomic masses of some elements had been miscalculated. Yet even when scientists obtained more accurate values for those atomic masses and filled all of the gaps in Mendeleev's table, some elements in the table were still out of order. Why is this the case? The answer has to do with a property of atoms that was not identified until 1913. It is a property that you know already—atomic number.

The man who developed the concept of atomic number was English chemist H.G.J. Moseley (1887–1915). Moseley was a postdoctoral student working in Ernest Rutherford's laboratory. He observed that metals produce X-rays when bombarded with energetic electrons and that the frequencies of the X-rays differed for each metal. These different frequencies, Moseley correctly hypothesized, resulted from differences in a fundamental property of each element—the amount of positive charge in the nucleus. Moseley correlated these frequencies to a series of whole numbers that he assigned to each element. He called each element's whole number its atomic number.

The correct way to arrange elements is not by atomic mass, but by atomic number. So why was Mendeleev's periodic table valid at all? The answer is that atomic masses generally increase with atomic number. Mendeleev may have arranged the elements according to the wrong property—but he found the correct pattern. Sometimes this is the way science works!

As chemists now know, and as you learned in Chapter 3, the atomic number equals both the number of protons in an atom's nucleus and the number of electrons in the atom. The **periodic law,** which is the basis for the periodic table, states the following relationship between the properties of the elements and their atomic number: **When elements are arranged in order of increasing atomic number, their physical and chemical properties show a periodic pattern.** You will learn more about these periodic patterns, or trends, in the sections that follow.

Figure 5–6 *English chemist Henry Moseley had a promising career ahead of him, but his life ended tragically in the infamous World War I battle of Gallipoli. How did this young chemist contribute to the development of the periodic table?*

5–1 Section Review

1. What is the periodic law?

2. Discuss how Dobereiner and Newlands helped to develop the periodic table.

3. How did Mendeleev demonstrate that his periodic table was valid? What did Moseley's work contribute to the development of the periodic table?

4. By which property of the elements did Mendeleev arrange his periodic table? Is this the correct property for the periodic table? Explain.

5. **Critical Thinking—Interpreting data** The atomic mass of aluminum is 27.0, which is close to the average of the atomic masses of fluorine (19.0) and chlorine (35.5). From these data, do you think that aluminum should be placed between fluorine and chlorine in a column of the periodic table? Explain.

Guide for Reading

- Why do the elements in a group have similar properties?
- What are the four blocks of the periodic table?

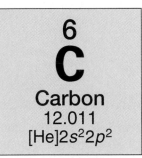

Figure 5–7 *Each square in the periodic table provides information about a particular element. What information does this square provide about carbon?*

5–2 Reading the Periodic Table

Take a look at the modern periodic table shown on pages 166–167. You are about to go on a "tour" of this table. This trip will teach you how the periodic table is organized and acquaint you with the basic properties of the elements. Remember, you do not need to memorize lots of facts about each element. Instead, you can predict an element's properties by knowing its position in the periodic table and understanding what that position signifies.

Organizing the Squares

The modern periodic table has 112 squares, each of which represents a unique element. Inside the squares is the same kind of information for each element. In the large periodic table on pages 166–167, each element symbol is in the center of a square. Above the element symbol is the atomic number, and below it is the element's name and atomic mass. At the bottom of the square is the element's abbreviated electron configuration. (You will learn more about abbreviated electron configurations and their importance as you read on in this chapter.) You should also know that different periodic tables may present different kinds of information or present information in different ways.

The shape of the periodic table comes in part from the periodic law. Elements that have similar properties are aligned in vertical columns, called **groups** or **families.** The horizontal rows in the table are called **periods.** The periodic table has 7 periods and 18 labeled groups.

Take a close look at the periodic table's seven periods, or horizontal rows. Notice that each period contains more and more elements. The first period has only 2 elements: hydrogen (H) and helium (He). The second and third periods each have 8 elements: lithium (Li) through neon (Ne) in the second period and sodium (Na) through argon (Ar) in the third period. The fourth and fifth periods each have 18 elements. How many elements are in the sixth period? If you count 18, look closely at the elements on the left side of the period. The correct answer is 32. To keep the periodic table from being too wide, 14 of the elements in the sixth period are placed under the main part of the table, together with the 14 corresponding elements from the seventh period. Figure 5–8 shows how the periodic table would look if these elements were reinserted into the sixth and seventh rows.

Why does the periodic table get wider and wider with each period? You will learn the answer very soon!

Figure 5–8 *When the inner transition metals are inserted into their proper places, the periodic table becomes extremely wide and unwieldy.*

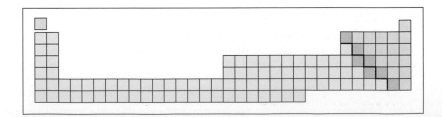

Labeling and Naming Groups

Chemists label the groups of the periodic table in a variety of ways. Three common schemes are shown in Figure 5–9. Traditionally, chemists label groups with Roman numerals together with the letters A and B. In Europe, the groups on the left are labeled IA through VIIIA, and those on the right are labeled IB through VIIIB. In Figure 5–9, the European designations are shown in blue. In the United States, the longer columns on the left and right are labeled IA through VIIIA, and the shorter columns in the middle are labeled IB through VIIIB. Some chemists, however, have switched from Roman to Arabic numerals. For example, Group IIA is now often labeled 2A. We will be using the American system with Arabic numerals in this textbook. In Figure 5–9, the American designations are shown in red.

In 1985, The International Union of Pure and Applied Chemistry (IUPAC) sought to resolve the controversy between the American and European systems by proposing a new labeling scheme. They proposed that the groups be designated by the numerals 1 through 18, as shown by the black labels in Figure 5–9. Unfortunately, this scheme has not yet been widely adopted, so now there are three schemes. The periodic table on pages 166–167 includes both the IUPAC and the American designations for the groups.

Figure 5–9 *Different chemists prefer different labeling systems for the groups of the periodic table. How does the European system (in blue) differ from the American system (in red) and the IUPAC system (in black)?*

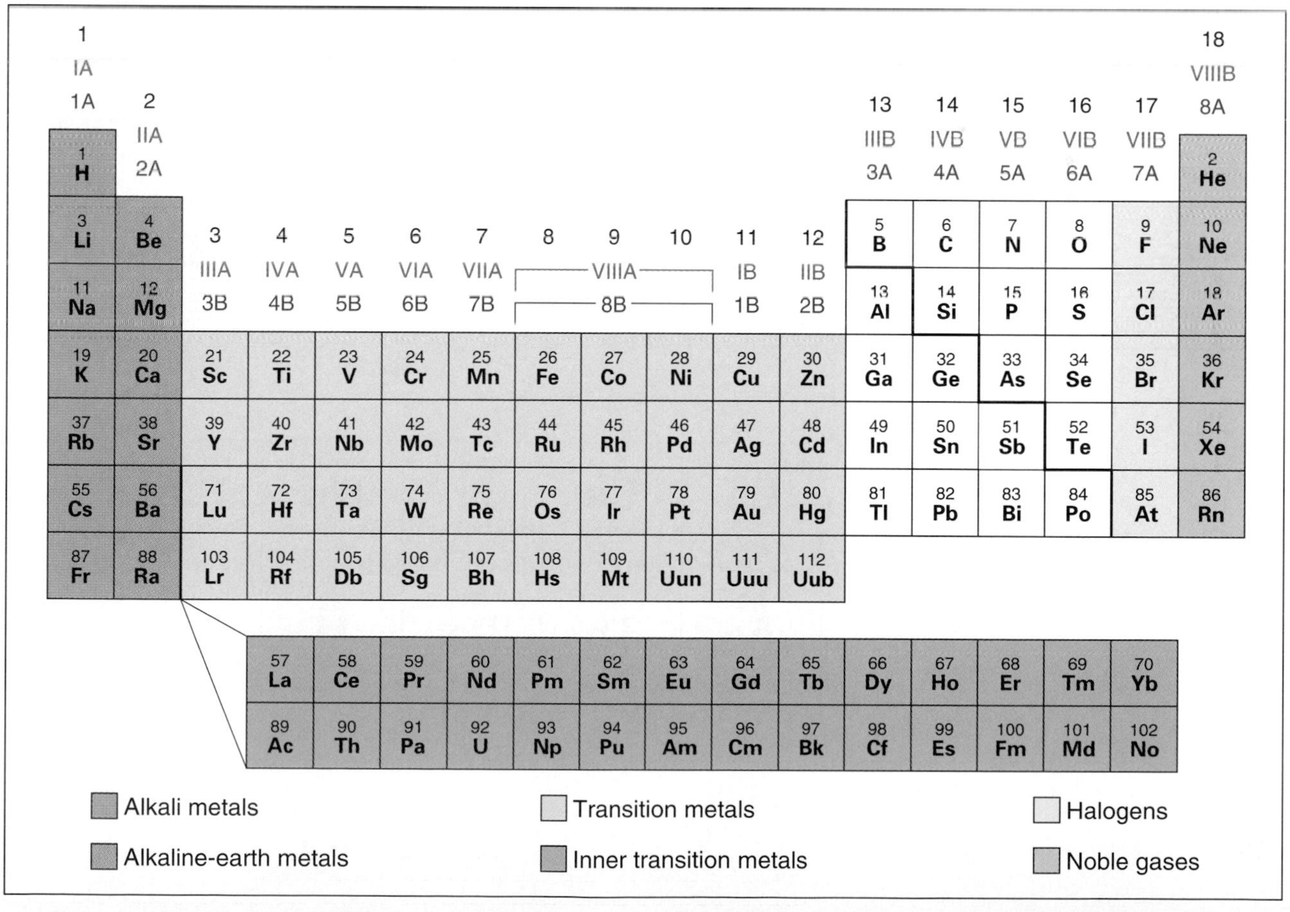

Figure 5–10 *The periodic table of the elements*

1 1A							

1
H
Hydrogen
1.00794
$1s^1$

Key

6
C
Carbon
12.011
$[He]2s^22p^2$

— Atomic number
— Element symbol
— Element name
— Atomic mass
— Electron configuration

2 2A

3
Li
Lithium
6.941
$[He]2s^1$

4
Be
Beryllium
9.01218
$[He]2s^2$

11
Na
Sodium
22.98977
$[Ne]3s^1$

12
Mg
Magnesium
24.305
$[Ne]3s^2$

3 3B	4 4B	5 5B	6 6B	7 7B	8	9 8B

19
K
Potassium
39.0983
$[Ar]4s^1$

20
Ca
Calcium
40.078
$[Ar]4s^2$

21
Sc
Scandium
44.9559
$[Ar]4s^23d^1$

22
Ti
Titanium
47.88
$[Ar]4s^23d^2$

23
V
Vanadium
50.9415
$[Ar]4s^23d^3$

24
Cr
Chromium
51.996
$[Ar]4s^13d^5$

25
Mn
Manganese
54.9380
$[Ar]4s^23d^5$

26
Fe
Iron
55.847
$[Ar]4s^23d^6$

27
Co
Cobalt
58.9332
$[Ar]4s^23d^7$

37
Rb
Rubidium
85.4678
$[Kr]5s^1$

38
Sr
Strontium
87.62
$[Kr]5s^2$

39
Y
Yttrium
88.9059
$[Kr]5s^24d^1$

40
Zr
Zirconium
91.224
$[Kr]5s^24d^2$

41
Nb
Niobium
92.9064
$[Kr]5s^14d^4$

42
Mo
Molybdenum
95.94
$[Kr]5s^14d^5$

43
Tc
Technetium
(98)
$[Kr]5s^24d^5$

44
Ru
Ruthenium
101.07
$[Kr]5s^14d^7$

45
Rh
Rhodium
102.9055
$[Kr]5s^14d^8$

55
Cs
Cesium
132.9054
$[Xe]6s^1$

56
Ba
Barium
137.33
$[Xe]6s^2$

71
Lu
Lutetium
174.967
$[Xe]6s^24f^{14}5d^1$

72
Hf
Hafnium
178.49
$[Xe]6s^24f^{14}5d^2$

73
Ta
Tantalum
180.9479
$[Xe]6s^24f^{14}5d^3$

74
W
Tungsten
183.85
$[Xe]6s^24f^{14}5d^4$

75
Re
Rhenium
186.207
$[Xe]6s^24f^{14}5d^5$

76
Os
Osmium
190.2
$[Xe]6s^24f^{14}5d^6$

77
Ir
Iridium
192.22
$[Xe]6s^24f^{14}5d^7$

87
Fr
Francium
(223)
$[Rn]7s^1$

88
Ra
Radium
226.0254
$[Rn]7s^2$

103
Lr
Lawrencium
(260)
$[Rn]7s^25f^{14}6d^1$

104
Rf
Rutherfordium
(261)
$[Rn]7s^25f^{14}6d^2$

105
Db
Dubnium
(262)
$[Rn]7s^25f^{14}6d^3$

106
Sg
Seaborgium
(263)
$[Rn]7s^25f^{14}6d^4$

107
Bh
Bohrium
(262)
$[Rn]7s^25f^{14}6d^5$

108
Hs
Hassium
(265)
$[Rn]7s^25f^{14}6d^6$

109
Mt
Meitnerium
(266)
$[Rn]7s^25f^{14}6d^7$

57
La
Lanthanum
138.9055
$[Xe]6s^25d^1$

58
Ce
Cerium
140.12
$[Xe]6s^24f^15d^1$

59
Pr
Praseodymium
140.9077
$[Xe]6s^24f^3$

60
Nd
Neodymium
144.24
$[Xe]6s^24f^4$

61
Pm
Promethium
(145)
$[Xe]6s^24f^5$

62
Sm
Samarium
150.36
$[Xe]6s^24f^6$

89
Ac
Actinium
227.0278
$[Rn]7s^26d^1$

90
Th
Thorium
232.0381
$[Rn]7s^26d^2$

91
Pa
Protactinium
231.0359
$[Rn]7s^25f^26d^1$

92
U
Uranium
238.0289
$[Rn]7s^25f^36d^1$

93
Np
Neptunium
237.048
$[Rn]7s^25f^46d^1$

94
Pu
Plutonium
(244)
$[Rn]7s^25f^6$

Phase at 20°C

C	Solid
Br	Liquid
H	Gas

Metallic Properties

Li	Metal
B	Semimetal
C	Nonmetal

	18 8A
	2 **He** Helium 4.00260 $1s^2$

13 3A	14 4A	15 5A	16 6A	17 7A	
5 **B** Boron 10.81 [He]$2s^22p^1$	**6** **C** Carbon 12.011 [He]$2s^22p^2$	**7** **N** Nitrogen 14.0067 [He]$2s^22p^3$	**8** **O** Oxygen 15.9994 [He]$2s^22p^4$	**9** **F** Fluorine 18.998403 [He]$2s^22p^5$	**10** **Ne** Neon 20.1797 [He]$2s^22p^6$
13 **Al** Aluminum 26.98154 [Ne]$3s^23p^1$	**14** **Si** Silicon 28.0855 [Ne]$3s^23p^2$	**15** **P** Phosphorus 30.97376 [Ne]$3s^23p^3$	**16** **S** Sulfur 32.066 [Ne]$3s^23p^4$	**17** **Cl** Chlorine 35.453 [Ne]$3s^23p^5$	**18** **Ar** Argon 39.948 [Ne]$3s^23p^6$

10	11 1B	12 2B					
28 **Ni** Nickel 58.69 [Ar]$4s^23d^8$	**29** **Cu** Copper 63.546 [Ar]$4s^13d^{10}$	**30** **Zn** Zinc 65.39 [Ar]$4s^23d^{10}$	**31** **Ga** Gallium 69.72 [Ar]$4s^23d^{10}4p^1$	**32** **Ge** Germanium 72.61 [Ar]$4s^23d^{10}4p^2$	**33** **As** Arsenic 74.9216 [Ar]$4s^23d^{10}4p^3$	**34** **Se** Selenium 78.96 [Ar]$4s^23d^{10}4p^4$	**35** **Br** Bromine 79.904 [Ar]$4s^23d^{10}4p^5$
46 **Pd** Palladium 106.42 [Kr]$4d^{10}$	**47** **Ag** Silver 107.8682 [Kr]$5s^14d^{10}$	**48** **Cd** Cadmium 112.41 [Kr]$5s^24d^{10}$	**49** **In** Indium 114.82 [Kr]$5s^24d^{10}5p^1$	**50** **Sn** Tin 118.710 [Kr]$5s^24d^{10}5p^2$	**51** **Sb** Antimony 121.757 [Kr]$5s^24d^{10}5p^3$	**52** **Te** Tellurium 127.60 [Kr]$5s^24d^{10}5p^4$	**53** **I** Iodine 126.9045 [Kr]$5s^24d^{10}5p^5$
78 **Pt** Platinum 195.08 [Xe]$6s^14f^{14}5d^9$	**79** **Au** Gold 196.9665 [Xe]$6s^14f^{14}5d^{10}$	**80** **Hg** Mercury 200.59 [Xe]$6s^24f^{14}5d^{10}$	**81** **Tl** Thallium 204.383 [Xe]$6s^24f^{14}5d^{10}6p^1$	**82** **Pb** Lead 207.2 [Xe]$6s^24f^{14}5d^{10}6p^2$	**83** **Bi** Bismuth 208.9804 [Xe]$6s^24f^{14}5d^{10}6p^3$	**84** **Po** Polonium (209) [Xe]$6s^24f^{14}5d^{10}6p^4$	**85** **At** Astatine (210) [Xe]$6s^24f^{14}5d^{10}6p^5$
110 **Uun** Ununnilium (269) [Rn]$7s^25f^{14}6d^8$	**111** **Uuu** Unununium (272) [Rn]$7s^25f^{14}6d^9$	**112** **Uub** Ununbium (277) [Rn]$7s^25f^{14}6d^{10}$					

Additional right-column elements:

36	54	86
36 **Kr** Krypton 83.80 [Ar]$4s^23d^{10}4p^6$	**54** **Xe** Xenon 131.29 [Kr]$5s^24d^{10}5p^6$	**86** **Rn** Radon (222) [Xe]$6s^24f^{14}5d^{10}6p^6$

63 **Eu** Europium 151.96 [Xe]$6s^24f^7$	**64** **Gd** Gadolinium 157.25 [Xe]$6s^24f^75d^1$	**65** **Tb** Terbium 158.9254 [Xe]$6s^24f^9$	**66** **Dy** Dysprosium 162.50 [Xe]$6s^24f^{10}$	**67** **Ho** Holmium 164.9304 [Xe]$6s^24f^{11}$	**68** **Er** Erbium 167.26 [Xe]$6s^24f^{12}$	**69** **Tm** Thulium 168.9342 [Xe]$6s^24f^{13}$	**70** **Yb** Ytterbium 173.04 [Xe]$6s^24f^{14}$
95 **Am** Americium (243) [Rn]$7s^25f^7$	**96** **Cm** Curium (247) [Rn]$7s^25f^76d^1$	**97** **Bk** Berkelium (247) [Rn]$7s^25f^9$	**98** **Cf** Californium (251) [Rn]$7s^25f^{10}$	**99** **Es** Einsteinium (252) [Rn]$7s^25f^{11}$	**100** **Fm** Fermium (257) [Rn]$7s^25f^{12}$	**101** **Md** Mendelevium (258) [Rn]$7s^25f^{13}$	**102** **No** Nobelium (259) [Rn]$7s^25f^{14}$

In addition to group labels, some groups are also given family names. The groups at the left and right sides of the periodic table show particularly strong resemblances among their members, so they are the ones most frequently referred to by family names. The elements in Group 1A are called the **alkali metals** and those in Group 2A are called the **alkaline earth metals.** The elements in Group 7A are called the **halogens,** and those in Group 8A are called the **noble gases.** You will become more familiar with these names as you see and use them. Other families are sometimes identified by the name of the first element in the group. For example, Group 4A is sometimes called the carbon group or the carbon family.

As you look at the periodic table, do you notice anything unusual about the square for hydrogen? It is separated slightly from the other squares. The reason for this separation is that hydrogen is a unique element. Hydrogen is really not a member of any family, although it is often considered together with the members of Group 1A, the alkali metals. However, hydrogen is definitely a nonmetal. In fact, in some ways it more closely resembles the elements of Group 7A, the halogens. For these reasons, some textbooks place hydrogen in Group 7A or even in both Groups 1A and 7A.

Figure 5–11 Aluminum is ductile, which means it can be drawn into wire (bottom left). Gold is unusually malleable. Some of the gold leaf on this sculpture (bottom right) is thinner than paper. In this periodic table (right), metals are shaded blue, nonmetals are shaded red, and semimetals are shaded purple.

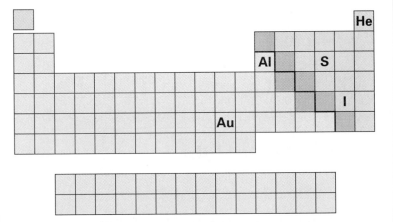

Metals, Nonmetals, and Semimetals

As you may have noticed, the squares in the large periodic table in this chapter are shaded with three different colors. Most squares are shaded light blue, which signifies that the element is a **metal.** Metals share many properties and are easily recognized by their characteristic luster or shine. Metals are also good conductors of heat and electricity. They typically are solids at room temperature, although mercury is an important exception. Additionally, most metals are malleable, which means that they can be hammered into thin sheets, and many are ductile, which means that they can be drawn into fine wires. Figure 5–11 illustrates these qualities. Have you ever taken advantage of the malleable or ductile qualities of a metal?

Elements that are clearly not metals are called **nonmetals** and are shaded light red in the periodic table. As illustrated in Figure 5–12, nonmetals do not possess a metallic luster. Most nonmetals are poor conductors of heat and electricity and are neither malleable nor ductile. Many nonmetals are gases at room temperature. Others are solids. And one nonmetal—bromine—is a liquid. Nonmetals show quite a variation in physical properties: Some are colored, others are colorless; some exist as soft solids, others form hard solids. Carbon, a nonmetal, can be found in the form of diamond—the hardest natural substance on Earth.

The periodic table provides an easy way to group metals and nonmetals: The metals are on the left side of the table and, with the exception of hydrogen, the nonmetals are on the far right. Notice that between the metals and nonmetals is a third category of elements called the **semimetals,** or metalloids. The semimetals may have some properties of metals and some properties of nonmetals, or they may have properties that are intermediate between metallic and nonmetallic properties. In the periodic table in this textbook, the semimetals are shaded light purple. Where have you encountered one of the semimetals?

*I*NTEGRATING
*E*ARTH *S*CIENCE

What is the hardest natural substance on Earth?

Figure 5–12 *Nonmetallic elements come in many different forms. Yellow spikes of sulfur crystals decorate the opening of a volcanic steam vent (far left). Under the right conditions, solid crystals of iodine transform into purple iodine gas (near left). Colorless helium gas fills these balloons (top), allowing them to float in the air.*

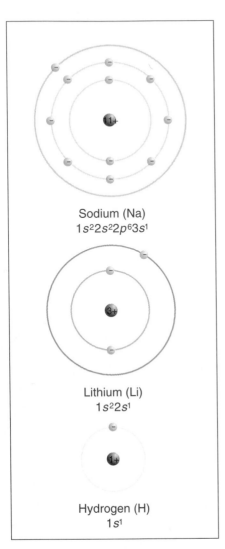

Figure 5–13 *Valence electrons are an atom's outermost electrons. How many valence electrons are in a hydrogen atom? In a lithium atom? In a sodium atom? What do the answers to these questions tell you about these elements?*

Sodium (Na)
$1s^2 2s^2 2p^6 3s^1$

Lithium (Li)
$1s^2 2s^1$

Hydrogen (H)
$1s^1$

Electron Configurations and the Periodic Table

The periodic table is one of the most useful tools in chemistry for organizing and remembering facts about the elements. But why does it work? Why are there families of elements with similar properties? And why does the table have its characteristic shape, with 7 periods of increasing width?

You might be tempted to answer these questions by counting the number of protons in different atoms, because you now know that the elements in the periodic table are arranged by increasing atomic number. But as you learned in Chapter 3, the atomic number equals not only an atom's number of protons but also its number of electrons. Furthermore, electrons reside at the outer boundary of an atom, which is where atoms come in contact with each other. To understand the periodic table, you need to examine how an atom's electrons are arranged.

For example, consider the electron configurations of the first three elements in Group 1A, shown in Figure 5–13. Notice that the highest-energy electron in each element is in an *s* orbital. As you learned in Chapter 4, electrons that occupy the highest principal energy level are the atom's outermost electrons. These electrons, which are largely responsible for an atom's chemical behavior, are called **valence electrons.** Each element in Group 1A has one outermost electron, or valence electron, and it resides in an *s* orbital. **The elements in a group have similar properties because they have valence electrons in similar configurations.** The periodic table is structured so that elements with similar valence electrons are placed in the same column, or group.

To save space in writing electron configurations and to focus attention on valence electrons, chemists often use **abbreviated electron configurations.** We have included each element's abbreviated electron configuration in the periodic table on pages 166–167. In abbreviated electron configurations, an atom's inner electrons are represented by the symbol for the nearest noble gas with a lower atomic number. These electrons are called the **noble gas inner core** of the atom. For example, the abbreviated electron configuration of lithium is $[He]2s^1$. The symbol [He] represents helium's electron configuration: $1s^2$. Outside this helium inner core, lithium has a single valence electron in a 2*s* orbital.

The abbreviated electron configurations for the first six elements in Group 1A are:

H	Li	Na	K	Rb	Cs
$1s^1$	$[He]2s^1$	$[Ne]3s^1$	$[Ar]4s^1$	$[Kr]5s^1$	$[Xe]6s^1$

Do you see what these elements have in common? Each has a single valence electron that resides in an *s* orbital. Also, notice that the principal quantum number of this *s* orbital is the same as the element's period number, or row, in the periodic table.

The *s-*, *p-*, *d-*, and *f*-block Elements

The key to understanding the shape of the periodic table is to examine the elements' electron configurations. The simplest way to look at these electron configurations is to divide the periodic table into four sections, or blocks. These sections are illustrated in Figure 5–14 and are described below.

The *s*-block elements   This block is composed of hydrogen, helium, and the elements of Groups 1A and 2A (the alkali metals and alkaline earth metals). In this block, valence electrons are in *s* orbitals only. Look at the elements in Group 1A, and you will see that each electron configuration ends in s^1. In this group, each element has 1 valence electron in an *s* orbital. In Group 2A, each electron configuration ends in s^2. Each element in Group 2A has 2 valence electrons in an *s* orbital. The *s*-block contains only two groups because an *s* orbital can hold a maximum of 2 electrons.

The *p*-block elements   As you move from left to right across this block, the elements' valence electrons fill *p* orbitals. Look at the elements from Group 3A to Group 8A of any period, and you will see that the last sublevels in their electron configurations progress from p^1 to p^6. Remember that the first principal energy level has no *p* sublevels, which is why the first period of the table has no *p*-block elements. The first *p* orbital is the 2*p* orbital, which begins filling with the element boron (B) in the second period of the table. The *p*-block is 6 elements wide because *p* orbitals can hold up to 6 electrons.

Figure 5–14 *The periodic table can be divided into s-, p-, d-, and f-blocks. As you move across any of these blocks, the elements' electrons fill the block's characteristic type of orbital.*

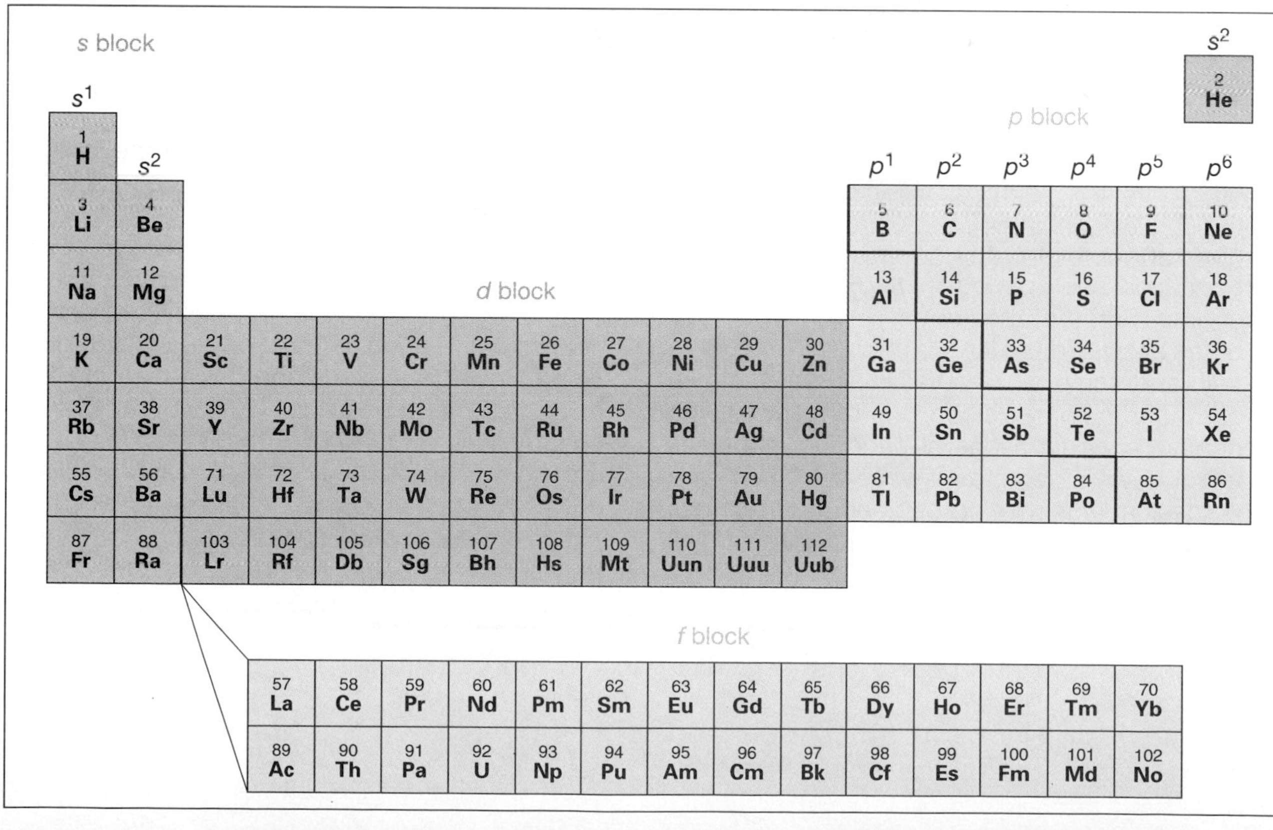

Metal Ions in the Body

Of the atoms that make up the human body, do you think that most are metals, semimetals, or nonmetals? By far, the answer is nonmetals. In any living organism, almost all of the matter is made from carbon, oxygen, hydrogen, nitrogen, and phosphorus. Organisms also contain a few other nonmetals—including chlorine and sulfur.

However, a number of metals—in the form of ions—play essential roles in most organisms. Perhaps the most important of these metallic ions are sodium and potassium. In humans and other animals, sodium ions are found mainly in extracellular fluids, or the fluids outside cells. Potassium ions are more common in intracellular fluids, or the fluids inside cells. This difference exists throughout the body, but it is particularly significant in nerve cells. When a nerve is stimulated, gates in its membrane open for a short period of time. Some of these gates allow sodium ions to move into the nerve cell, and some allow potassium ions to move out. After the gates close, a pump restores the original concentrations of each ion. Impulses travel down a nerve as a wave of sodium and potassium ions moving back and forth across the nerve's membrane. Some impulses travel at 300 kilometers per hour!

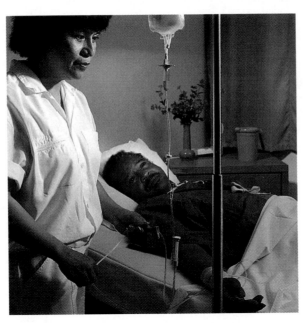

This patient receives a salt solution from a plastic tube attached to a vein in his arm.

For nerves and other cells to function properly, the concentrations of sodium and potassium ions must lie within certain limits. For this reason, physicians track and regulate the concentrations of these ions in patients receiving intravenous fluids. Abnormal potassium levels can be particularly serious. Too low a potassium concentration can cause a weak or irregular heartbeat as well as paralysis. A high potassium concentration can lead to cardiac arrest.

Two other vital metallic ions are iron and calcium. Iron is a part of hemoglobin, the oxygen-carrying molecule in red blood cells. Calcium is important for strong bones and teeth. Both iron and calcium are a part of a healthy diet. Iron is found in meat and fish, and calcium is found in milk and milk products. Of less importance, but still used by the body, are zinc, magnesium, and copper.

As you have learned in this chapter, elements in the same column of the periodic table have similar properties. However, those properties are not identical. Sodium and potassium reside in adjacent squares in Group 1A, but living organisms are able to distinguish their ions. As you will discover in later chapters of this textbook, the chemistry inside any living organism is remarkably complex, efficient, and sophisticated.

The _d_-block elements This block takes up most of the middle of the table. As you move from left to right across this block, the elements' electrons fill the _d_ orbitals. A _d_ orbital can hold up to 10 electrons, which is why the _d_-block is 10 elements wide. The first _d_ orbital is the 3_d_ orbital, which begins filling with scandium (Sc), element number 21.

The _f_-block elements Move across this block and electrons fill the _f_ orbitals. The first _f_ orbital is the 4_f_ orbital, which begins filling with elements in the sixth period. Essentially, the _f_-block elements are the 28 elements that are placed below the main body of the periodic table. The _f_-block is 14 elements wide because an _f_ sublevel can hold up to 14 electrons. However, electrons do not fill _f_ orbitals in a regular sequence. Look at the electron configurations of the elements in the _f_-block, and you will see that they do not progress sequentially from f^1 to f^{14}.

Notice that as you progress down the periodic table, the periods contain an increasing number of blocks: The first period contains only the _s_-block, the second and third periods contain the _s_- and _p_-blocks, the fourth and fifth periods contain the _s_-, _p_, and _d_ blocks, and the sixth and seventh periods include all four blocks. This pattern arises from the principles of the quantum theory. The shape of the periodic table is a result of the way electrons fill the _s_, _p_, _d_, and _f_ orbitals of different energy levels.

The four blocks have other names as well. The elements in the _s_- and _p_-blocks are collectively called the representative elements (or main-group elements). The elements in the _d_-block are called the transition metals. Those in the _f_-block are known as the inner transition metals.

5–2 Section Review

1. Why do elements in a group have similar properties?

2. Sketch the general shape of the periodic table and label the _s_-, _p_-, _d_-, and _f_-blocks.

3. Describe the general differences between the elements on the right side of the periodic table and those on the left.

4. What information is presented inside each square of the periodic table?

5. **Theme Trace—Unity and Diversity** A chemistry experiment calls for a compound that supplies ions of bromine, but unfortunately this compound is not available. Ruth substitutes a compound that supplies ions of chlorine. Betsy uses a compound that contains selenium. From what you know about the periodic table, predict whether Ruth or Betsy will run a more successful experiment.

Visit our Web site at
http://www.phschool.com
to support your
study of chemistry.

Guide for Reading

- What is a periodic trend?
- Name four important periodic trends. How does each trend reflect the electron configurations of the elements?

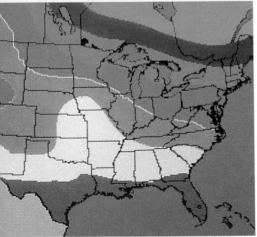

5–3 Periodic Trends

As you have learned, many of an element's properties are determined by its electron configuration. In addition, the periodic table is organized so that elements with similar electron configurations are in the same column. For these reasons, you can use an element's location in the periodic table to predict many facts about it. **Many properties of the elements change in a predictable way as you move through the periodic table.** These systematic variations are called **periodic trends.** There are many periodic trends, several of which you will study in this section.

Atomic Radius

You may already be familiar with the word radius (plural: radii). For a sphere, or ball, the radius is the distance from the center to the outer edge. Because atoms can be thought of as spheres, they also have a radius. The **atomic radius** is the distance from the center of an atom's nucleus to its outermost electron.

Unfortunately, the definition of atomic radius is not precise. The electron cloud that surrounds the nucleus is spherical, but it does not have an exact boundary. Nevertheless, there are several ways to estimate the radius of an atom. These methods are based on a variety of techniques used to measure the distance between the centers of atoms in various materials. For example, the distance between two chlorine nuclei in a Cl_2 molecule is found to be 0.198 nanometer. Therefore, a value of $0.198 \div 2 = 0.099$ nanometer is a good estimate of the radius of a chlorine atom. Similarly, the distance between carbon atoms in diamond (a form of pure carbon) is 0.154 nanometer. The radius of a carbon atom is $0.154 \div 2 = 0.077$ nanometer.

You might think that atoms with more electrons would have larger atomic radii. However, this idea is only half true at best. Study Figure 5–16, and you will notice two distinct trends:

1. Atoms get larger going down a group. In Group 1A, the atomic radii progress from 0.152 nanometer for a lithium atom to 0.262 nanometer for a cesium atom.
2. Atoms get smaller moving from left to right across each period. For example, across the second period, the atomic radii decrease from 0.152 nanometer for a lithium atom to 0.064 nanometer for a fluorine atom.

Figure 5–15 *Periodic trends occur throughout nature. Each autumn, many trees change from green to fiery red (top). The farther south you travel in the United States, the warmer the temperatures generally become (middle). And ocean tides gradually rise to their highest levels and then decrease (bottom).*

Why do these trends exist? The first trend is the easier to explain. As you move down a group, the principal quantum number of the outermost electrons increases. For example, as you move down Group 1A, the outermost electron resides in orbitals from $1s^1$ to $2s^1$ to $3s^1$ and up to $7s^1$. Electrons with a larger principal quantum number are found in orbitals that extend farther away from the nucleus, which makes the atomic radius larger.

The second trend requires a bit more thought to understand. Recall that in any period, the outer electrons of each element are in orbitals with the same principal quantum number. If principal quantum number were the only factor that influenced the size of an orbital, then all the elements in a period would have atoms of the same size. So, another factor must be at work.

Recall that as you move from left to right across a period, the atoms' nuclei gain more protons. As a rule, atoms that have more positive charge in their nuclei exert a stronger pull on the electrons in a given principal quantum level. In other words, as you look at the elements from left to right across a period, the atoms' outer electrons are increasingly attracted to the nucleus. A stronger attractive force shrinks the electrons' orbitals and makes the atom smaller.

Figure 5–16 *How does atomic radius change as you move down a group? As you move across a period?*

Atomic Radii of Representative Elements (nm)

1A	2A	3A	4A	5A	6A	7A
Li	Be	B	C	N	O	F
0.152	0.111	0.088	0.077	0.070	0.066	0.064
Na	Mg	Al	Si	P	S	Cl
0.186	0.160	0.143	0.117	0.110	0.104	0.099
K	Ca	Ga	Ge	As	Se	Br
0.231	0.197	0.122	0.122	0.121	0.116	0.115
Rb	Sr	In	Sn	Sb	Te	I
0.244	0.215	0.162	0.14	0.141	0.137	0.133
Cs	Ba	Tl	Pb	Bi	Po	At
0.262	0.217	0.171	0.175	0.146	0.14	0.140

Ionic Size

As you learned in Chapter 3, an atom can gain or lose electrons to form an ion. How does the size of an atom change when electrons are added or removed? When an atom loses electrons—or becomes a positive ion—it becomes smaller. For example, the radius of a lithium atom (Li) is 0.152 nanometer, whereas the radius of a Li^+ ion is 0.060 nanometer. A lithium ion is smaller than a lithium atom because it has 1 fewer electron, which was the atom's outermost electron. Loss of electrons not only vacates the atom's largest orbitals, it also reduces the repulsive force between the remaining electrons, allowing them to be pulled closer to the nucleus.

When an atom gains electrons—or becomes a negative ion—it becomes larger. For example, the radius of a fluorine (F) atom is 0.064 nanometer, whereas the radius of a F^- ion is 0.136 nanometer. A fluoride ion is larger than a fluorine atom mainly because of the greater number of electrons, which increases the electric

Figure 5–17 *Notice that the elements on the left side of the table form positive ions and those on the right form negative ions. What other periodic trends do you see?*

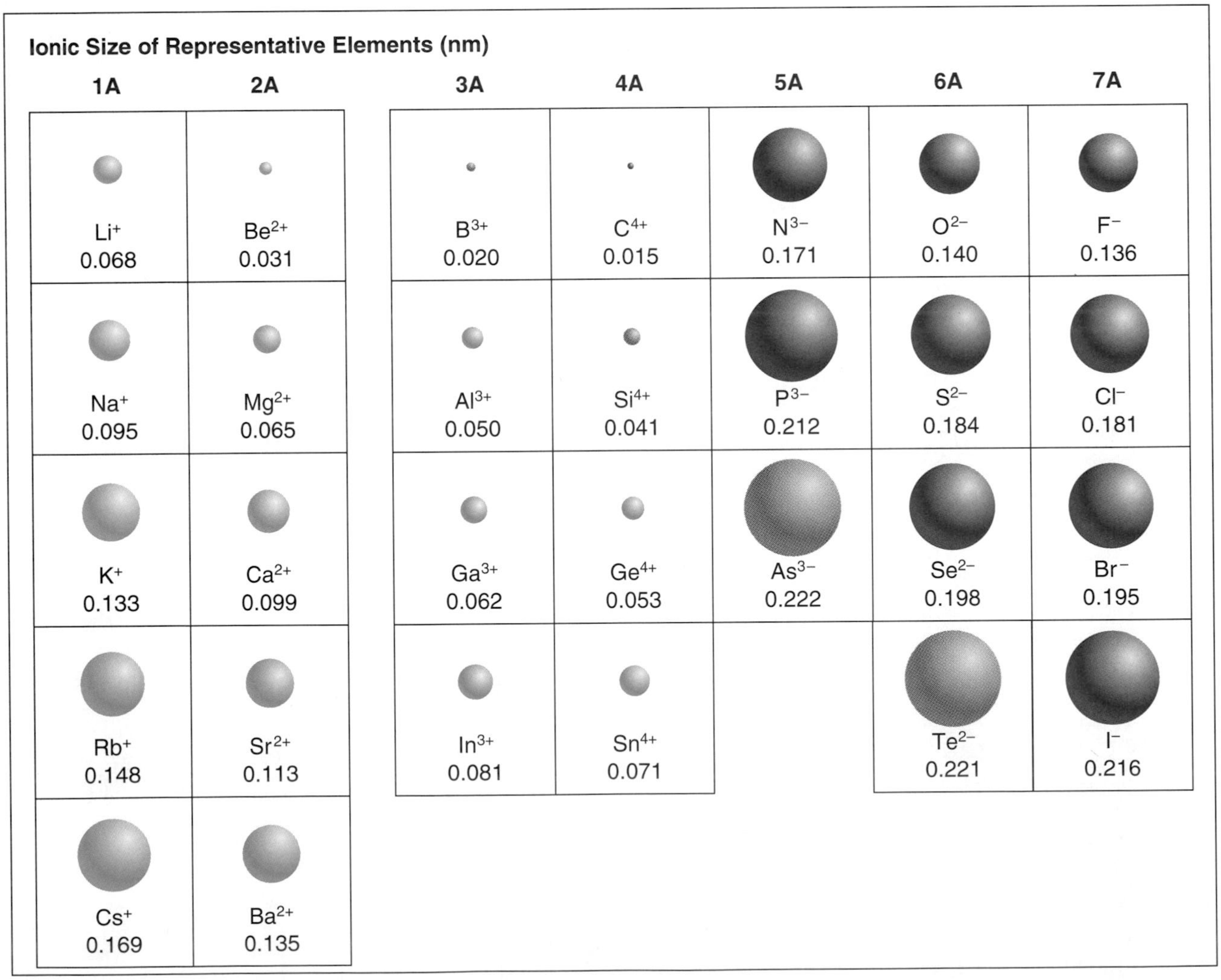

Ionic Size of Representative Elements (nm)

1A	2A	3A	4A	5A	6A	7A
Li^+ 0.068	Be^{2+} 0.031	B^{3+} 0.020	C^{4+} 0.015	N^{3-} 0.171	O^{2-} 0.140	F^- 0.136
Na^+ 0.095	Mg^{2+} 0.065	Al^{3+} 0.050	Si^{4+} 0.041	P^{3-} 0.212	S^{2-} 0.184	Cl^- 0.181
K^+ 0.133	Ca^{2+} 0.099	Ga^{3+} 0.062	Ge^{4+} 0.053	As^{3-} 0.222	Se^{2-} 0.198	Br^- 0.195
Rb^+ 0.148	Sr^{2+} 0.113	In^{3+} 0.081	Sn^{4+} 0.071		Te^{2-} 0.221	I^- 0.216
Cs^+ 0.169	Ba^{2+} 0.135					

repulsion forces among them. The increased repulsions spread out the electrons, thus making the ion larger than the atom.

Are some ions more common than others? The answer is definitely yes. In nature, the atoms of a particular element typically form only certain ions. The table in Figure 5–17 shows the common ions of the representative elements. What is the common ion of magnesium (Mg)? Of bromine (Br)?

In addition to their different sizes, Figure 5–17 illustrates another periodic trend for the common ions: Elements in a group form ions of the same charge. In addition, these charges follow a specific pattern. The elements on the left side of the table form positive ions. Moving from left to right across the table, the ions' charges increase sequentially from 1+ to 2+ and so forth. In contrast, the elements on the right side of the table form negative ions. Starting with Group 7A and moving to the left, the ions' charges progress from 1− to 2− to 3−. As for the elements at the far right of the table—the noble gases—they do not form ions at all.

As you might imagine, the principles of chemistry can explain these trends. First, you need to understand why atoms hold some electrons more strongly than they hold others.

Ionization Energy

An atom's **ionization energy** is the energy needed to remove one of its electrons. For example, 8.64×10^{-19} joules are required to remove 1 electron from a lithium (Li) atom, so the ionization energy for lithium is 8.64×10^{-19} joules per atom. (Recall that the joule, abbreviated J, is the SI unit for energy.) In the form of a chemical equation, removing an electron from lithium is written as

$$\text{Li}\,(g) \rightarrow \text{Li}^+\,(g) + \text{e}^- \quad \text{ionization energy} = 8.64 \times 10^{-19}\,\text{J/atom}$$
$$\textbf{(Eq. 1)}$$

This chemical equation tells you that when a lithium atom loses an electron, it becomes a lithium ion with a 1+ charge. The ionization energy is measured on atoms in the gas state—signified by the letter g in parentheses—because the electrons of different atoms must be far away from one other for an accurate measurement to be made.

You can think of ionization energy as a reflection of how strongly an atom holds onto its outermost electron. Atoms with high ionization energies hold onto their electrons very tightly, whereas atoms with low ionization energies are more likely to lose one or more of their outermost electrons and gain a positive charge.

As you have just seen, ionization energy can be stated in units of joules per atom. However, ionization energies are usually reported for a very large collection of atoms, not just a single atom. In chemistry, the commonly used unit for a large collection

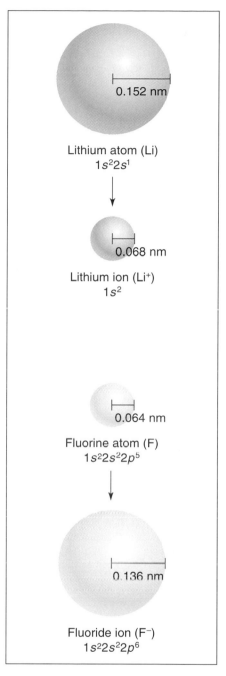

Lithium atom (Li)
$1s^2 2s^1$

0.152 nm

Lithium ion (Li⁺)
$1s^2$

0.068 nm

Fluorine atom (F)
$1s^2 2s^2 2p^5$

0.064 nm

Fluoride ion (F⁻)
$1s^2 2s^2 2p^6$

0.136 nm

Figure 5–18 *Atoms can gain or lose electrons to become ions. How does the size of an atom change when electrons are added or removed?*

of atoms is the mole, abbreviated mol. You will learn much more about this unit in Chapter 10. A mole of atoms is a collection of 6.02×10^{23} atoms—a very large collection indeed. To ionize a mole of lithium atoms, 521 kilojoules of energy are required:

$$\text{Li } (g) \rightarrow \text{Li}^+ (g) + e^- \quad \text{ionization energy} = 521 \text{ kJ/mol}$$
(Eq. 2)

The graph in Figure 5–19 shows how ionization energies vary with atomic number. What trends do you see in this graph?

With respect to the periodic table, ionization energies show two important trends:

1. Ionization energies decrease as you move down a group.
2. Ionization energies increase as you move from left to right across a period.

Do these trends remind you of any other trends? They are the exact opposite of the trends for atomic radius! This fact is not a coincidence. Both an atom's size and its ionization energy depend on how strongly its electrons are attracted to the nucleus. The electrons in smaller atoms are held more strongly by the nucleus, so more energy is required to remove 1 electron. The electrons in larger atoms are held less strongly, so less energy is required to remove 1 electron.

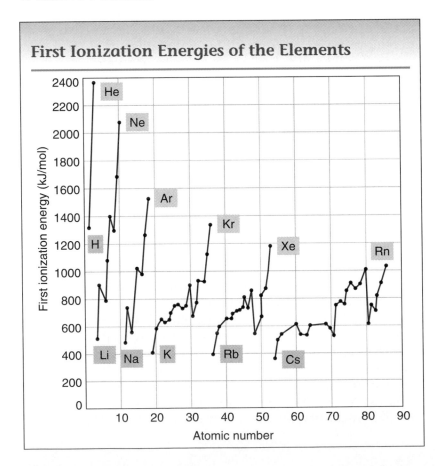

Figure 5–19 *Ionization energy is the energy required to remove one electron from an isolated atom. Which elements have the highest ionization energies? Which have the lowest?*

SAMPLE PROBLEM 1

Boron, carbon, and aluminum occur near each other in the periodic table. Use the periodic table to identify which of these elements is (a) the largest atom, and (b) the atom with the highest ionization energy.

STRATEGY	SOLUTION
1. Analyze	Both atomic radius and ionization energy are periodic trends. They are properties that can be predicted from an element's position in the periodic table.
2. Plan	Moving down a group, atoms get larger and the ionization energy decreases. Moving from left to right across a period, atoms get smaller and the ionization energy increases.
3. Solve	From the periodic trends for atomic radius, a boron atom is larger than the atom to its right in the periodic table, a carbon atom. Likewise, a boron atom is smaller than an aluminum atom, which is just below it. Therefore, the aluminum atom is the largest of the three atoms and the carbon atom is the smallest. Because the trends for ionization energy are the opposite of the trends for atomic radius, the carbon atom has the highest ionization energy.
4. Evaluate	Consult the table of atomic radius in Figure 5–16 and first ionization energies in Figure 5–19 to confirm your answer.

PRACTICE PROBLEMS

1. (a) Which of the following atoms is smallest: lithium, beryllium, or magnesium? (b) Which of these atoms has the highest ionization energy?   *(Answer: (a) beryllium (b) beryllium)*

2. Which of the following is the largest: a sodium atom, a sodium ion with a charge of $1+$, or a potassium atom? *(Answer: a potassium atom)*

Successive Ionization Energies of Period 3 Elements (kJ/mol)

Element	First	Second	Third	Fourth	Fifth	Sixth	Seventh
Na	496	4560					
Mg	738	1450	7730				
Al	577	1816	2744	11,600			
Si	786	1577	3228	4354	16,100		
P	1060	1890	2905	4950	6270	21,200	
S	999	2260	3375	4565	6950	8490	27,000
Cl	1256	2295	3850	5160	6560	9360	11,000
Ar	1520	2665	3945	5770	7230	8780	12,000

Figure 5–20 *Successive ionization energies are the energies required to remove electrons beyond the first electron. What does the stair-step line signify in the table?*

Successive Ionization Energies

The energy required to remove the first electron from an isolated atom is called the first ionization energy (or simply the ionization energy). The successive ionization energies are the energies required to remove electrons beyond the first electron. In other words, the energy required to remove a second electron from an atom is called the second ionization energy, the energy required to remove a third electron is the third ionization energy, and so on. Here are the reactions that show the first three ionization energies of a lithium atom:

$$Li\ (g) \rightarrow Li^+\ (g) + e^- \quad \text{1st ionization energy} = 521 \text{ kJ/mol}$$
(Eq. 3)

$$Li^+\ (g) \rightarrow Li^{2+}\ (g) + e^- \quad \text{2nd ionization energy} = 7304 \text{ kJ/mol}$$
(Eq. 4)

$$Li^{2+}\ (g) \rightarrow Li^{3+}\ (g) + e^- \quad \text{3rd ionization energy} = 11{,}752 \text{ kJ/mol}$$
(Eq. 5)

The table in Figure 5–20 lists the ionization energies for the elements in the third period of the periodic table. Notice that for each of these elements, the ionization energies increase for every electron removed. Each increase in energy is due in part to reduced electron-electron repulsions. However, an element's successive ionization energies do not increase smoothly. For each element you can find one very large increase between a different pair of ionization energies. For sodium, this large increase is between the first and second ionization energies. For magnesium, the large increase is between the second and third ionization energies. Where is the large increase for aluminum?

Ionization energies show that an atom holds the electrons in its noble gas inner core much more strongly than it holds its valence electrons. For example, consider a sodium atom, which has an electron configuration of $[Ne]3s^1$. As you can tell from Figure 5–20, sodium has a relatively small first ionization energy but a much larger second ionization energy. Sodium is likely to lose its 1 valence electron and become Na^+, but its other electrons are in its noble gas inner core, so sodium is not found as Na^{2+}. Similarly, the other elements in sodium's group have 1 valence electron beyond their noble gas inner core, so they also typically exist as ions with a $1+$ charge.

For a second example, consider a magnesium atom, which has an electron configuration of $[Ne]3s^2$. A magnesium atom has two valence electrons, which explains why magnesium has relatively small first and second ionization energies and a very large third ionization energy. As a result, magnesium is commonly found as Mg^{2+}, but not Mg^{3+}. All of the elements in magnesium's group are also found as ions with a $2+$ charge. What ions would you expect from the elements in aluminum's group?

At this point, you may expect to see silicon atoms form Si^{4+} ions, phosphorus atoms form P^{5+} ions, and so on for the atoms across the third period. However, the elements on the right side of the periodic table are less likely to lose their valence electrons and form positive ions. You will learn the reasons why very soon as you read on.

Electron Affinity

An atom's **electron affinity** is the energy change that occurs when it gains an extra electron. For example, the electron affinity of a neon atom is 4.8×10^{-20} joule, which means that 4.8×10^{-20} joules of energy is needed to add another electron to a neon atom. However, as with ionization energies, electron affinities are usually reported for a mole of atoms. The electron affinity of a mole of neon atoms is 29 kilojoules. In the form of a chemical equation, adding an electron to neon is written as

$$Ne\ (g) + e^- \rightarrow Ne^-\ (g) \quad \text{electron affinity} = 29\ kJ/mol$$
(Eq. 6)

The periodic table in Figure 5–21 on page 182 shows the electron affinities of many of the elements. As you study this diagram, do you notice that most of the electron affinities are negative numbers? For example, the electron affinity of fluorine is -328 kilojoules per mole:

$$F\ (g) + e^- \rightarrow F^-\ (g) \quad \text{electron affinity} = -328\ kJ/mol$$
(Eq. 7)

Why do fluorine and other elements have a negative electron affinity? The answer is that these elements do not require energy to gain an electron. Instead, they release energy. A mole of fluorine atoms releases 328 kilojoules of energy when each atom gains an electron.

You can think of electron affinity as a measure of an atom's attraction, or affinity, for an extra electron. However, be sure that you understand the sign convention. Atoms that have a greater attraction for an added electron have a more negative electron

Just as ionization energy is the energy required to **remove** an electron from an atom, electron affinity is the energy required to **add** an electron to an atom. While ionization energies of the elements are typically positive, electron affinities can be positive as well as negative. A negative value for electron affinity indicates that energy is **released** as the electron is added.

Electron Affinity (kJ/mol)

1	2	3	4	5	6	7	8	9	10	11	12	13	14	15	16	17	18
1 H −73																	2 He 21
3 Li −60	4 Be 19											5 B −27	6 C −122	7 N 7	8 O −141	9 F −328	10 Ne 29
11 Na −53	12 Mg 19											13 Al −43	14 Si −134	15 P −72	16 S −200	17 Cl −349	18 Ar 35
19 K −48	20 Ca 10	21 Sc −18	22 Ti −8	23 V −51	24 Cr −64	25 Mn	26 Fe −16	27 Co −64	28 Ni −112	29 Cu −118	30 Zn 47	31 Ga −29	32 Ge −116	33 As −78	34 Se −195	35 Br −325	36 Kr 39
37 Rb −47	38 Sr	39 Y −30	40 Zr −41	41 Nb −86	42 Mo −72	43 Tc −53	44 Ru −101	45 Rh −110	46 Pd −54	47 Ag −126	48 Cd 32	49 In −29	50 Sn −116	51 Sb −103	52 Te −190	53 I −295	54 Xe 41
55 Cs −45	56 Ba	71 Lu	72 Hf	73 Ta −31	74 W −79	75 Re −14	76 Os −106	77 Ir −151	78 Pt −205	79 Au −223	80 Hg 61	81 Tl −20	82 Pb −35	83 Bi −91	84 Po −183	85 At −270	86 Rn 41
87 Fr −44	88 Ra	103 Lr	104 Rf	105 Db	106 Sg	107 Bh	108 Hs	109 Mt	110 Uun	111 Uuu	112 Uub						

Figure 5–21 *The electron affinity of an atom is the energy change when it gains an extra electron. How does the electron affinity of beryllium compare with that of chlorine?*

affinity. Of the elements represented in Figure 5–21, which element most strongly attracts an added electron? Which element most weakly attracts an added electron?

Perhaps you have noticed that electron affinities change in a very irregular way across a period or down a group of the periodic table. However, as a general rule, the nonmetals (the elements on the right side of the table) have more negative electron affinities than do the metals (the elements on the left side of the table). The most important exception to this rule is the noble gases, which have positive electron affinities.

What can you conclude from the general trends in electron affinity? Again, you need to look at electron configurations. First, consider the electron configuration of a fluorine atom, which is $[He]2s^2 2p^5$. Fluorine has a very negative electron affinity, which means that a fluorine atom strongly attracts an additional electron. Adding an electron to a fluorine atom gives a fluorine ion with the electron configuration $[He]2s^2 2p^6$. This is the same as the electron configuration of a neon atom. Adding an electron to a neon atom, however, requires a great deal of energy. (Remember that neon has a positive electron affinity.) An additional electron in a neon atom would be placed in a $3s$ orbital, which is an orbital of much higher energy than the orbitals in the $n = 2$ level.

As the data in Figure 5–21 show, an atom's electron affinity is related to the number of electrons it needs to fill its outer energy level. Fluorine and the other members of Group 7A are each 1 electron short of a full outer energy level—they are each 1 electron away from the electron configuration of a noble gas.

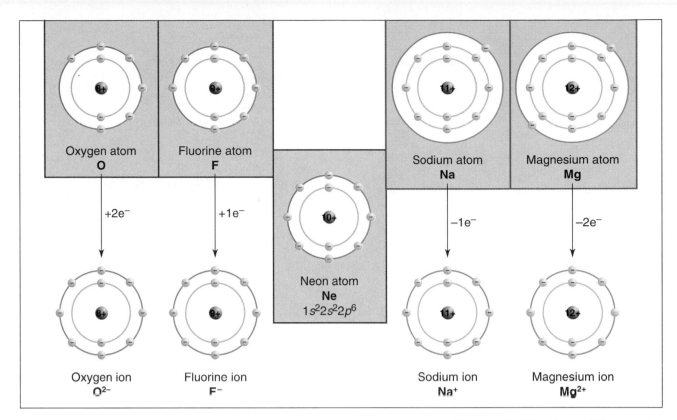

| Oxygen atom O | Fluorine atom F | Neon atom Ne $1s^2 2s^2 2p^6$ | Sodium atom Na | Magnesium atom Mg |

$+2e^-$ $+1e^-$ $-1e^-$ $-2e^-$

Oxygen ion O^{2-} Fluorine ion F^- Sodium ion Na^+ Magnesium ion Mg^{2+}

As a result, they each have a strong electron affinity. These facts explain why the members of Group 7A all commonly exist as ions with a 1− charge. Similarly, the elements in Group 6A are 2 electrons short of full outer energy levels, so they commonly form ions with a 2− charge. What ions would you expect to see among the elements in Group 5A?

Using the elements' ionization energies and electron affinities, we can derive an important principle about atoms, a principle that you will use throughout your study of chemistry. This principle is the octet rule, which states that atoms tend to gain, lose, or share electrons in order to acquire a full set of valence electrons. An octet is a group of eight. You may recognize the prefix *oct-* from words such as octopus (an eight-legged animal) and octave (a distance of eight notes on a musical scale). For most energy levels there are 8 valence electrons in a full set of valence electrons—2 in the *s* orbitals and 6 in the *p* orbitals. An exception is for the first energy level, which is full with only 2 electrons.

You will learn more about the octet rule and its importance when you study Chapter 7. For now, you can use the octet rule to help you to learn some of the important properties of the elements. The elements on the right side of the periodic table tend to gain electrons—or become negative ions—in order to acquire a complete set of valence electrons. The elements on the left side of the periodic table tend to lose electrons—or become positive ions—in order to expose a complete set of valence electrons from their noble gas inner core. As for the noble gases themselves, they neither gain nor lose electrons. Can you explain why noble gases do not form ions?

Figure 5–22 *One of the most important rules in chemistry is the octet rule, which states that atoms tend to gain, lose, or share electrons in order to acquire a full set of valence electrons. How does the octet rule explain the common ions of oxygen, fluorine, sodium, and magnesium?*

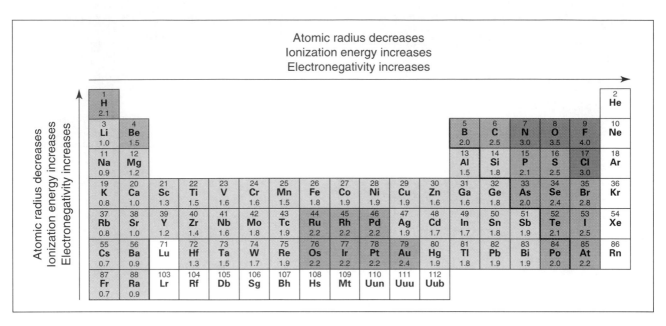

Figure 5–23 *This periodic table shows the electronegativities of the atoms and summarizes three important periodic trends. Which are the most electronegative elements? What periodic trends are seen in electronegativity?*

Electronegativity

An atom's **electronegativity** reflects its ability to attract electrons in a chemical bond. The periodic table in Figure 5–23 lists the electronegativities of the elements. Notice that electronegativity values have no units. Unlike ionization energy and electron affinity, electronegativity is not an amount of energy. Nor is it a property of an atom that can be directly measured.

Fluorine is the most electronegative element, with an electronegativity of 4.0. The least electronegative elements are in the lower left corner of the periodic table. Both cesium and francium have electronegativities of 0.7. If a cesium atom and a fluorine atom were to form a chemical bond, the atom with the higher electronegativity—the fluorine atom—would more strongly attract the bond's electrons. You will learn more about electronegativity and chemical bonds in Chapter 7.

An atom's electronegativity is related to its ionization energy and electron affinity. And although electron affinity changes somewhat randomly across the periodic table, the trends of ionization energy and electronegativity are similar: Both increase as you move from left to right across a period and decrease as you move down a group. The long arrows in Figure 5–23 summarize these important periodic trends for you and relate them to another periodic trend, the trend in atomic radii.

Problem Solving   *Chemistry at Work*

Turning the Table on Another Planet!

Welcome to the planet Merullo! As an ambassador from Earth and a student of chemistry, you have been given the task of deciphering the Merullan periodic table, which is shown below.

As you can see, the Merullans have discovered only 42 elements—or perhaps these are the only elements on Merullo. Unfortunately, you have not been able to decipher the Merullan numbering system, which is why you do not know the elements' atomic numbers or atomic masses. However, you have learned the following information about three elements:

- **Ondichium (Od)** is a silvery-white, metallic element that reacts readily with atoms in the air. Ondichium exists in many different isotopes. It has a low ionization energy.

- **Eigerium (E)** exists as a colorless, odorless gas, and is common in the Merullan atmosphere. Eigerium is very electronegative.

- **Petersia (P)** is also found as a gas, but never as a positive or negative ion. It is one of the lightest elements known on Merullo.

Reaching Conclusions

1. Explain how the Merullans organize their periodic table. Give the English names for the three elements discussed.

2. What elements are missing on the planet Merullo? Suggest ways that life on Merullo might be different from life on Earth because of the missing elements.

3. Do you think it is possible that a planet would have only the 42 elements in the Merullan periodic table? Give reasons for your answer.

Np Poppah	Kv Venturia	Bb Bostwicklum	Hb Bakalian	Ph Pamium	Vw Vickium	Od Ondichium	M Momm
Rb Bassoonium	Jw Janium	Lb Birdia	Ls Lorranium	Pl Letendrium	An Andium	Ta Tanickium	Hg Hagassium
Ro Rostonium	Rs Rosellium	Sb Bellisima	Cc Christinogen	Mg Maureenium	Di Dianium	Fx Dafinks	Tl Talchinsky
Me Meghanium	Mh Maggium	Ml Melanium	Rk Rokha	Tm Tanium	Ju Julium	Wi Wilsine	Cg Claranglen
I Tedogen	Ng Natalium	E Figerium	Ag Arturo	R Rebeckium	Mk Markanium	Ge Gendlerium	W Wendella
P Petersia							Mi Mindriklum

5–3 Section Review

1. What is a periodic trend?

2. Name four periodic trends. Discuss how each trend reflects the elements' electron configurations.

3. Do an atom's successive ionization energies increase regularly? Explain your answer.

4. **Connection—You and Your World**   A strip of sodium metal reacts with chlorine gas to form sodium chloride, better known as table salt. From your knowledge of periodic trends, explain why elemental sodium and chlorine react so readily. Would you expect any energy to be released in this reaction?

Laboratory Investigation DESIGNING an EXPERIMENT

Determining Trends in a Group

Problem

How does density change going down a group in the periodic table?

Suggested Materials (per group)

10-mL graduated cylinder
plastic weighing dishes
lead shot (Pb)
silicon pieces (Si)
tin pieces (Sn)
graph paper
metric ruler
balance

Suggested Procedure 👓

1. Devise an experiment to determine the density of three or more elements within the same group of the periodic table. Silicon (Si), tin (Sn), and lead (Pb) are suggested.
2. Write down the steps of your experimental procedure.
3. Prepare a table, such as the one shown, to record your data.
4. Conduct your experiment after having your teacher approve your procedure and data table.
5. From your data, calculate the densities of the elements you used in your experiment.

Observations

Measurement	Silicon (Si)	Tin (Sn)	Lead (Pb)
Density of element (g/cm³)			

 Prepare a graph of density vs. period number for silicon, tin, and lead.

Analysis and Conclusions

1. How does density change going down a group in the periodic table?
2. Use your graph to estimate the density of germanium (Ge, atomic number 32) and carbon (C, atomic number 6).
3. Calculate the percent error of the densities you determined as compared with accepted values.
4. What are some possible sources of error in your procedure?
5. **On Your Own** Choose another group in the periodic table and look up the densities of the elements in that group. Do you observe the same periodic trend as you found in this experiment?

STUDY GUIDE

Summarizing Key Concepts

5–1 Development of the Periodic Table

- Dobereiner classified elements in sets of three, or triads. Newlands arranged the elements according to atomic mass, and suggested that every eighth element has similar properties. Mendeleev constructed the first periodic table, which he used to predict three new elements.
- The periodic law states that when the elements are arranged in order of increasing atomic number, their properties show a periodic pattern.

5–2 Reading the Periodic Table

- The periodic table is organized into 7 periods, or rows, and 18 major groups, or columns. Elements in a group have similar properties, especially those elements in four of the groups: the alkali metals, alkaline earth metals, halogens, and noble gases.
- Metals are lustrous, ductile, malleable, and are good conductors of heat and electricity. Metals are found on the left side of the periodic table. Nonmetals have a diverse set of properties but do not resemble metals. Nonmetals are found on the upper right side of the periodic table. Semimetals have some of the properties of metals and nonmetals.
- Elements in a group have similar properties because they have the same number of valence electrons. The groups can be organized into s-, p-, d-, and f-blocks based on how valence electrons fill each sublevel.

5–3 Periodic Trends

- A periodic trend is a property that changes predictably as you move across a period or down a group of the periodic table.
- Atomic radius increases moving down a group because the atoms' electrons fill more principal energy levels. Atomic radius decreases moving from left to right across a period because the atoms' nuclei have increasing positive charge, which attracts electrons more strongly.
- Ionization energy is the energy needed to remove an electron, forming a positive ion. Electron affinity is the energy change that occurs when an atom gains an electron, forming a negative ion. An element's electronegativity reflects its attraction for electrons in a chemical bond.

Reviewing Key Terms

Define each term in a complete sentence.

5–1 Development of the Periodic Table
periodic table
periodic law

5–2 Reading the Periodic Table
group
family
period
alkali metal
alkaline earth metal
halogen
noble gas
metal

nonmetal
semimetal
valence electron
abbreviated electron configuration
noble gas inner core

5–3 Periodic Trends
periodic trend
atomic radius
ionization energy
electron affinity
electronegativity

CHAPTER REVIEW

Content Review

Multiple Choice

Choose the letter of the answer that best completes each statement.

1. The scientist who classified elements in triads, or groups of three, was
   - (a) Dobereiner.
   - (b) Moseley.
   - (c) Mendeleev.
   - (d) Rutherford.

2. The element germanium is very similar to an element that Mendeleev called
   - (a) hydrogen.
   - (b) silicon.
   - (c) phosphorus.
   - (d) ekasilicon.

3. How many elements are in the first period of the periodic table?
   - (a) 2
   - (b) 7
   - (c) 8
   - (d) 16

4. The elements in Group 8A, the column at the far right of the periodic table, are called
   - (a) alkali metals.
   - (b) halogens.
   - (c) reactive gases.
   - (d) noble gases.

5. The nonmetals
   - (a) are good conductors of electricity.
   - (b) are ductile and malleable.
   - (c) form soft solids.
   - (d) have diverse physical properties.

6. $[Ar]4s^1$ represents an element of
   - (a) Group 2A.
   - (b) Group 1A.
   - (c) Group 7A.
   - (d) a noble gas.

7. The inner transition elements
   - (a) are listed below the main body of the periodic table.
   - (b) are the p-block elements.
   - (c) include the noble gases.
   - (d) each have full f sublevels.

8. As you move from left to right across a row of the periodic table, the elements
   - (a) increase in atomic radius.
   - (b) have an increasing ionization energy.
   - (c) have a decreasing electron affinity.
   - (d) show no periodic trends.

9. The energy change from an added electron is called
   - (a) ionization energy.
   - (b) electronegativity.
   - (c) electron affinity.
   - (d) second ionization energy.

True or False

If the statement is true, write "true." If it is false, change the underlined word or words to make the statement true.

10. Elements arranged in order of <u>increasing atomic number</u> show a periodic pattern in their properties.

11. The modern periodic table includes seven rows, or <u>families</u>.

12. The elements in Group 1A of the periodic table are the <u>halogens</u>.

13. Elements on the <u>left</u> side of the periodic table are nonmetals.

14. In $[Ne]3s^23p^4$, the symbol [Ne] represents the <u>valence electron</u> core.

15. Elements in a group have similar properties because they have similar <u>valence</u> electrons.

16. Move from left to right across a period, and atomic radius <u>increases</u>.

17. <u>Ionization energy</u> is the energy needed to remove an electron from an atom.

Concept Mapping

Complete the following concept map for Section 5–1. Refer to pages xviii–xix to construct a concept map for the entire chapter.

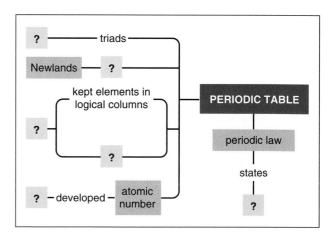

188

Concept Mastery

Discuss each of the following in a brief paragraph.

18. Why did Mendeleev leave gaps in his early periodic table?

19. In his periodic table, Mendeleev placed the elements in order of increasing atomic mass. Explain why this approach is not entirely valid.

20. Why do lower rows of the periodic table contain more elements?

21. Why is the square for hydrogen separated slightly from the squares for the other elements in the periodic table?

22. Why are the atoms of elements in Group 1A likely to form ions with a 1+ charge?

23. Why are the atoms of elements in Group 7A likely to form ions with a 1− charge?

24. Identify three ways to number the groups of the periodic table.

25. Why does atomic radius decrease as you move from left to right across a period?

26. Explain why atoms become smaller as positive ions. Explain why they become larger as negative ions.

27. Why do an atom's successive ionization energies not increase smoothly?

28. **Tying it Together** The elements have *diverse* properties, but can be *united* into periods and groups. Discuss how you can predict an element's properties from its position in the periodic table.

Critical Thinking and Problem Solving

Use the skills you have developed in this chapter to help you answer each of the following.

29. **Classifying** An element has the electron configuration $[Ne]3s^23p^5$. Without consulting the periodic table, determine this element's group and period number.

30. **Making inferences** In Figure 5–23, no electronegativity values are given for the noble gases. Explain why this is the case.

31. **Making predictions** The electronegativity of carbon is 2.5 and that of hydrogen is 2.1. Predict the distribution of electrons in methane, a molecule that contains only carbon and hydrogen atoms.

32. **Drawing conclusions** A chemistry student believes that he has isolated a new element. This proposed element has an atomic mass that is close to the average of the atomic masses of nitrogen and phosphorus, and it shares many properties with these two elements. Nitrogen and phosphorus are adjacent elements in Group 5A. Do you think that the student has discovered a new element in Group 5A? Explain your answer.

33. **Interpreting data** An unknown element has the following successive ionization energies:

1st ionization energy:	589 kJ/mol
2nd ionization energy:	1144 kJ/mol
3rd ionization energy:	4905 kJ/mol
4th ionization energy:	6465 kJ/mol

Predict this element's family.

34. **Interpreting data** An unknown element has a positive electron affinity, a very high first ionization energy, and one of the smallest atomic radii in its period. Predict this element's family in the periodic table.

35. **Using the writing process** The periodic table can be presented in different ways and with a variety of different information. Research the periodic tables in encyclopedias, dictionaries, magazines, and books. Notice their similarities and differences, and report your findings in a short paper.

Chapter 6
Groups of Elements

Imagine that you have just discovered a new element. How would you describe it to your friends? After you modestly name the element after yourself, you might want to tell them where and how you found it. If you reported your discovery in a scientific journal, you would probably describe how the element behaves in air and water because these are important components of our environment. As the element is studied more widely, important uses for it may emerge.

Over the centuries, chemists have gathered a great deal of information about each known element. In this chapter the periodic table will guide your study of some of the more common elements.

The elements that make up the Grand Canyon, shown in this magnificent view of Arizona's Yaki Point National Park, are also present in other parts of the universe such as Jupiter, shown here in an artist's rendering of the planet's collision with Comet Shoemaker-Levy 9.

Chem Journal

YOU AND YOUR WORLD

Perhaps some of the elements in the periodic table were already familiar to you because of their use in your world. Write a short poem of about 8 to 10 lines that links some of these elements with the way in which they are commonly used.

6–1 Reactive Metals: The *s*-block Elements

Guide for Reading

- What are the most reactive metals?
- What are some important characteristics of the alkali metals? Alkaline earth metals?

When you hear the word metal, what comes to mind—iron, aluminum, copper? These elements are just a few of the more commonly used metals. Because of their strength, metals are widely used as building materials in our society. For example, iron is used to make engine blocks, aluminum to make ladders, copper to make tubing, and titanium to make airplanes. Because metals are so common, it may surprise you to learn that some cannot be used as structural materials because of their extreme reactivity. Imagine a metal that would start a fire if it came in contact with water! There are actually several metals that do just that. **The metals that are most reactive are found in the two-column *s*-block of the periodic table. These are called the alkali metals and the alkaline earth metals.**

Alkali Metals

The members of Group 1A, or the alkali metal family, are lithium (Li), sodium (Na), potassium (K), rubidium (Rb), cesium

Figure 6–1 *The vigorous reaction of potassium with water (left) illustrates the intense chemical reactivity possessed by all members of the alkali metal family. Alkaline earth metals such as calcium (right) are not quite as reactive as the alkali metals. Why might this be the case?*

Figure 6–2 *Like all alkali metals, sodium is soft enough to be cut with a knife (top). Because of strontium's reactivity with cold water, it is usually stored in mineral oil (bottom). To which group of elements does strontium belong?*

(Cs), and francium (Fr). The name alkali comes from an Arabic word that means ashes. Sodium and potassium compounds are present in the ashes of burned plants.

PROPERTIES Just as human family members resemble one another, so the elements in the alkali metal family show a striking resemblance to one another. Like most metals, the alkali metals are shiny solids that are malleable, ductile, and good conductors of electricity. (Do you remember from Chapter 5 what the terms malleable and ductile mean?) In addition, the alkali metals have low densities and low melting points.

All of the alkali metals are soft enough to be cut by a knife. When cut, their shiny metallic surfaces become exposed to the oxygen in the air. This causes the reactive metals to tarnish rapidly. Indeed, one of the most remarkable characteristics of the members of this family is their intense chemical reactivity. All of the alkali metals react with water as well as with air. As you might imagine, this behavior causes storage problems. The alkali metals are commonly stored in evacuated metal containers. Once a container is opened, the metals must be placed in oil to protect them from oxygen and moisture.

Why do you suppose the alkali metals are the most reactive family of metals? You know that all of these elements possess a single valence electron. Because of their low ionization energies, the alkali metals readily lose this electron, forming ions with a 1+ charge. The ease with which an atom loses a valence electron increases as the size of the atom increases. As a result, the reactivity of alkali metals increases going down the family. Thus lithium reacts moderately with water, whereas cesium and francium react more explosively with water.

Figure 6–3 *A comparison of the physical properties of the alkali metals shows the trend going down a column of the periodic table. Why does cesium have a low ionization energy?*

Properties of the Alkali Metals

Element	Electron Configuration	Ionization Energy (kJ/mol)	Density (g/cm³)	Melting Point (°C)
Lithium	[He]$2s^1$	521	0.534	180.5
Sodium	[Ne]$3s^1$	496	0.971	97.8
Potassium	[Ar]$4s^1$	419	0.862	63.7
Rubidium	[Kr]$5s^1$	403	1.53	39.0
Cesium	[Xe]$6s^1$	376	1.83	28.6
Francium*	[Rn]$7s^1$			

* The data for francium are not accurately known.

Because of their similar electron configurations, the elements in a given group of the periodic table generally react with other elements to form similar compounds. For example, all of the alkali metals react with the halogens (Group 7A) to form compounds whose chemical formulas are of the type MX. (That is, they all contain 1 alkali metal ion, M^+, for each halogen ion, X^-.) Probably the most familiar compound of this type is sodium chloride (NaCl), which you know as table salt. Another common example is potassium iodide (KI), which is added in small amounts to table salt to form iodized table salt. Other examples of compounds formed by the alkali metals and halogens include lithium chloride (LiCl), rubidium iodide (RbI), and cesium bromide (CsBr). What would you predict as a chemical formula for the compound containing francium and bromine? If you said FrBr, you are correct. As you can see, the periodic table is a very powerful tool to help chemists predict and remember the chemical formulas of compounds formed by the elements. You will learn to rely increasingly on this tool as you study the chapters that follow.

SOURCES AND USES   Of all the alkali metals, sodium and potassium are by far the most abundant. By mass, they rank seventh and eighth among the elements in the Earth's crust.

Because the alkali metals are very reactive, they are never found as free, or uncombined, elements in nature. Instead, they are found as compounds that are widely distributed throughout many parts of the world. These compounds are very soluble in water. As a result, they are easily dissolved by groundwater and then carried by rivers and streams to the ocean. In the ocean, these alkali metal compounds make up about 3 percent of seawater. In fact, in many parts of the world, sea water is the primary source of table salt.

Sodium is the only metal of the group that is prepared commercially in large amounts. The metal is obtained by passing electricity through molten sodium chloride, using a specially designed electrolysis cell. You will learn more about the electrolysis of molten sodium chloride in Chapter 21.

Several compounds of sodium are important commercially. Examples include compounds that you may recognize by their common name: table salt (NaCl), lye, or caustic soda (NaOH), bleach (NaClO), and soda ash (Na_2CO_3). Baking soda, or sodium bicarbonate ($NaHCO_3$), is used in baking because it reacts with an acid to form carbon dioxide gas (CO_2). The gas forms bubbles in the dough, causing it to leaven, or rise. The source of the acid can be sour milk, cream of tartar, or any of a number of other acidic substances.

A far less common, but nevertheless interesting, alkali metal compound is lithium carbonate (Li_2CO_3). Lithium carbonate is used to treat manic depression, which is a type of mental disorder. Although how lithium carbonate works is not totally understood,

Figure 6–4 The Dead Sea, shown here in a satellite image, has some of the highest levels of dissolved salts found in any body of water on Earth. As water evaporates, salts crystallize out on the shores of the sea. Sodium chloride makes up a large percentage of these salts. How does salt get into the waters of the Dead Sea?

Figure 6–5 Sodium compounds have many commercial uses. When baking soda, or sodium bicarbonate, is added to bread dough, it reacts with an acid (also included in baking powder) producing carbon dioxide gas. The gas forms bubbles that lighten, or leaven, breads and other baking products so that they rise.

it is thought that the lithium ions interfere with complex chemical reactions that relay and amplify messages carried to the cells of the brain. It is interesting that such a simple compound has such a profound effect on the chemistry of the brain.

Alkaline Earth Metals

Elements of Group 2A are known as the alkaline earth metals. The term earth came from the alchemists of the Middle Ages who referred to substances that are unchanged by fire, such as lime (CaO) and magnesia (MgO), as earths. The term alkaline was used because the behavior of these Group 2A oxides is similar to that of the alkali metal oxides. When the pure metals were obtained from the alkaline earths, they were called alkaline earth metals, a name that has remained. The elements of Group 2A are beryllium (Be), magnesium (Mg), calcium (Ca), strontium (Sr), barium (Ba), and radium (Ra).

PROPERTIES   There are strong similarities among the members of this family, although the similarities are not quite as striking as those among the Group 1A elements. Beryllium in particular shows many characteristics that distinguish it from the other members of the family.

Figure 6–6   *Emeralds are crystals of the mineral beryl, a silicate of the element beryllium. Marie and Pierre Curie, the discoverers of radium, placed a pinch of the radioactive element a distance of 1 foot from this purse for 1 hour to obtain the first radiograph. What are some characteristics of alkaline earth metals?*

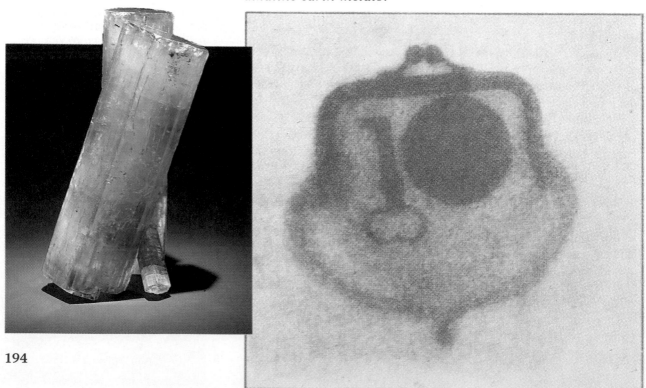

Properties of the Alkaline Earth Metals

Element	Electron Configuration	Ionization Energy (kJ/mol)	Density (g/cm³)	Melting Point (°C)
Beryllium	$[He]2s^2$	899	1.85	1287
Magnesium	$[Ne]3s^2$	738	1.74	649
Calcium	$[Ar]4s^2$	590	1.55	839
Strontium	$[Kr]5s^2$	549	2.63	768
Barium	$[Xe]6s^2$	503	3.62	727
Radium*	$[Rn]7s^2$			

* The data for radium are not accurately known.

Figure 6–7 *The physical properties of the alkaline earth metals are listed in the table. Which metal is radioactive?*

The alkaline earth metals have higher densities and melting points than the alkali metals. As reflected in their higher ionization energies, the alkaline earth metals are not quite as reactive as the alkali metals. The heavier alkaline earth metals, however, do react with water. Although it is inherently reactive, magnesium metal is protected from its environment by a tough coating of magnesium oxide (MgO). The oxide is formed when the metal surface reacts with the oxygen in the air. All of the alkaline earth metals have 2 valence electrons that they readily lose to form ions with a 2+ charge, such as Mg^{2+}. When the alkaline earth metals react with the halogens, they form compounds, such as $MgCl_2$, that contain 1 alkaline earth metal ion for every 2 halide ions.

SOURCES AND USES Because the alkaline earth metals are almost as reactive as the alkali metals, they too are not found in nature in the elemental state. The most abundant of these elements, calcium and magnesium, occur widely in various mineral deposits such as limestone ($CaCO_3$) and magnesite ($MgCO_3$). The metal ions are also found in seawater. Calcium ranks fifth and magnesium ranks sixth in their abundance on Earth.

The only alkaline earth metal produced in significant quantities is magnesium. It is recovered from seawater as well as from mineral deposits. Because it has a low density and moderate strength, particularly when combined with aluminum, magnesium is an important structural metal. When one metal is added to another metal, the resulting combination is called an **alloy.** An alloy can be a combination of several metals. Adding up to 10 percent of aluminum or zinc to magnesium increases its hardness, strength, and resistance to corrosion. Magnesium metal is used to make aircraft, automobile wheels, tools, and even garden furniture. Although it does not react with cold water, magnesium does react with hot water or steam, making magnesium fires very difficult to fight. In contrast, the heavier alkaline earth metals—calcium, barium, strontium, and radium—react

CONSUMER TIP

Iodized Salt

In the human body, the thyroid gland, which is located in the neck, uses iodine to produce the hormone thyroxine. Thyroxine controls the body's rate of metabolism. A deficiency in iodine can hinder physical growth and also produce an enlargement of the thyroid gland called a goiter. For these reasons, manufacturers add small amounts of potassium iodide or sodium iodide to table salt in areas where the levels of iodine in food and water are low.

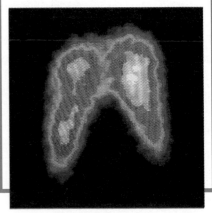

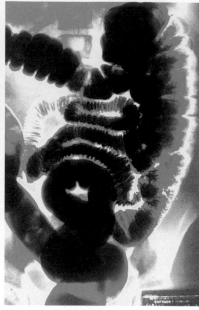

Figure 6–8 *This vase from the Tutankhamen exhibit is made of alabaster, which is a form of the calcium-containing mineral gypsum. The color-enhanced X-ray photograph shows parts of a human large intestine and small intestine. These organs are visible only because the person has ingested some barium sulfate, a substance that is opaque to X-rays.*

even with cold water. Can you explain why reactivity increases going down the alkaline earth family?

Beryllium is a fascinating element, although it is not very abundant. It has a very high melting point and is as strong as steel. At the same time, it is very lightweight with a density of only 1.85 g/cm^3. Iron, by contrast, is four times as dense! Beryllium is used in combination with other metals to make alloys that are durable and lightweight.

There are many important compounds of the alkaline earth metals. Magnesium hydroxide ($Mg(OH)_2$) is only slightly soluble in water, and suspensions of the solid are sold as a popular antacid. Calcium carbonate ($CaCO_3$) forms the shells of marine organisms and is also found as limestone, marble, and chalk.

6–1 Section Review

1. What important characteristic do the alkali metals and alkaline earth metals have in common?
2. Why are the alkali metals very reactive?
3. What are some common uses of alkali metal compounds? Of alkaline earth metal compounds?
4. **Theme Trace—Unity and Diversity** Identify the similarities and differences in the electronic configurations of Group 1A and 2A atoms and Group 1A and 2A ions.

6–2 Transition Metals: The *d*-block Elements

The elements in the middle, or the *d*-block, of the periodic table are called the transition metals. Many of these metals should be quite familiar. **Transition metals play an important role in living organisms, and are also extremely valuable as strong, structurally useful materials.** For example, iron is the primary building metal in our society. Chromium is used as a protective coating on metals. Silver and gold are used in jewelry and coins. Cobalt is found in vitamin B_{12}, and iron is an essential part of the hemoglobin required for oxygen transport.

The transition metals vary greatly in their abundance. Iron and titanium are quite abundant, ranking fourth and tenth among the elements in the Earth's crust. Platinum and iridium are very rare.

The properties of the transition metals vary from family to family. Most of these metals, however, have high densities and high melting points. For example, the most dense of all the elements are iridium (22.65 g/cm^3) and osmium (22.61 g/cm^3). The metal with the highest melting point is tungsten ($3410°C$). We will now consider a few of the common transition metals—chromium, iron, copper, silver, and gold.

Chromium

Chromium occurs in nature in a variety of compounds. It is obtained principally from deposits of these compounds in Russia, the Philippines, and southern Africa.

Chromium may be familiar to you as chrome because metal parts such as the grilles of automobiles are plated with chromium. A hard, silvery metal, chromium is very resistant to **corrosion.** Corrosion is the term used to describe the reaction between a metal and water, oxygen, or an acid. In addition to its use as a protective coating over other metals, chromium is also used to produce a variety of alloys. The best known of the chromium alloys is stainless steel, which contains mainly iron, chromium, and nickel.

One of the characteristics of chromium compounds is the variety of colors they exhibit. Indeed, the name chromium comes from the Greek word meaning color. Color is a common feature of transition metal ions with d^1 to d^9 valence electron configurations. The gemstones emerald and ruby owe their colors to the presence of trace amounts of Cr^{3+} ions. One of the common uses of chromium compounds is in paint pigments. For example, Cr_2O_3, which is green, is used for coloring not only paints but also roofing granules and other materials. Lead chromate ($PbCrO_4$) is a yellow compound that is used in artists' oil paints. About 35 percent of the chromium chemicals produced annually is used in pigments.

Guide for Reading

- What are some important uses of transition metals?

Visit our Web site at
http://www.phschool.com
to support your
study of chemistry.

Activity

It's Elementary!

1. Collect some samples of elements that are easily obtained, such as copper, aluminum, nickel, and carbon.

2. Attach each element to a large square of stiff paper or cardboard. Each square will represent a square of the periodic table.

3. On the paper or cardboard square, include the atomic number, atomic mass, name, and chemical symbol for the element displayed.

Working with your classmates, see how complete a periodic table you are able to create. (You may use samples of compounds of elements to represent the element.)

Lightweight titanium alloys are used in supersonic aircraft.

The Iron Pillar of Mehauli in India, has not rusted in 1600 years.

The Statue of Liberty in New York harbor is made of copper.

William Henr Fox Talbot, th inventor of a photographic process that uses light-sensitive compounds of silver, took this photograph of his home in 1840.

Chromium and its compounds are used in paints and as protective coatings over metal parts such as automobile grilles.

Figure 6–9 *Uses of transition metals.*

Iron

The Iron Age in history refers to that important time when humanity found ways to obtain the metal from its naturally occurring compounds and to use it for making weapons and tools. Iron is now the least expensive of all metals. Iron is combined with different amounts of other elements to produce alloys with various desirable qualities—qualities such as strength, durability, and resistance to corrosion. These alloys typically contain small amounts of carbon and are called steel.

Iron is the fourth most abundant element in the Earth's crust. Because it is so common, iron has been used by human society for thousands of years. Iron occurs in nature as hematite (Fe_2O_3), magnetite (Fe_3O_4), siderite ($FeCO_3$), and iron pyrite (FeS_2). The free element is obtained from Fe_2O_3 or Fe_3O_4 in a huge reactor called a blast furnace. A typical blast furnace, shown in Figure 6–10, is more than 30 meters high, about 8 meters wide, and produces in excess of 2000 kilograms of iron daily.

One of the disadvantages of iron is that it readily corrodes to form iron oxide (Fe_2O_3), or rust. Numerous procedures, including chromium plating, are used to prevent iron from rusting. (You will have an opportunity to study these methods in Unit 8.) The familiar red-brown color of rust again brings to mind the colors of transition metal ions with d^1 to d^9 valence electron configurations. Like many other transition metal ions, iron compounds have a variety of colors.

You probably know that in the proper amount iron is an essential part of a healthful diet. One of its roles in your body is as a component of the complex compound in red blood cells called hemoglobin. This iron-containing substance is responsible for carrying oxygen from your lungs to the cells of your body, where the oxygen reacts with sugars to produce energy.

The Coinage Metals

Copper, silver, and gold are often called the coinage metals because at one time they were used primarily to make coins. These metals are often found in the free, elemental state in nature and are also easily obtained from their compounds. As a consequence, they were the first metals known to early humans. Copper has been used since about 5000 BC. By 3000 BC, it was discovered that adding tin to copper forms a harder alloy, which is known as bronze. The introduction of this alloy marks the beginning of the Bronze Age. Silver and gold have been known at least as long as copper has—and perhaps even longer.

The coinage metals, prized for their resistance to corrosion and for their beauty, are all commercially important. However, they are not particularly abundant elements. In terms of their crustal abundance, copper ranks 25th, silver 64th, and gold 71st among the elements. Do you think their value has anything to do with their abundance? Why or why not?

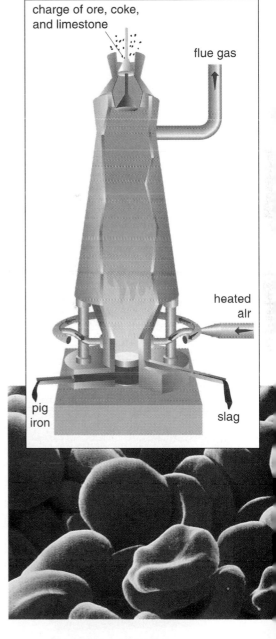

Figure 6–10 *For hundreds of years, a blast furnace has been used to extract iron by reacting iron ore with coke, which is essentially carbon. The red disc-shaped objects in this electronmicrograph are human red blood cells, which consist mainly of the iron-containing protein known as hemoglobin.*

charge of ore, coke, and limestone

flue gas

heated air

pig iron

slag

Figure 6–11 *This etching by the sixteenth-century Flemish artist Pieter Brueghel depicts an alchemist's laboratory. Alchemists were convinced that they could turn base metals, such as iron, into gold. Why were their efforts unsuccessful?*

Figure 6–12 *In 1860, George W. Northrup, a gold miner from Minnesota, posed with his tools and his bag of gold.*

COPPER   Copper is a soft metal with a distinctive reddish color. It is alloyed with tin to make bronze and with zinc to make brass. Both alloys have a wide range of use. Copper is used in the United States to make pennies, although pennies minted since 1982 are actually made of zinc with just a thin copper coating. The major use of copper is in making electrical wiring. Silver is the only metal that is a better electrical conductor than copper. Copper is also used to make water pipes for homes.

Although relatively resistant to corrosion, copper does react slowly with oxygen and carbon dioxide in the air to take on a green coating called patina. This thin, green coating is seen on numerous statues, the Statue of Liberty being the best-known example. Many compounds of copper have green or blue colors. Indeed, copper compounds are used in fireworks to serve as the source of blue color.

SILVER   Silver is a lustrous, white metal that is very ductile and malleable. Pure silver is relatively soft and is therefore usually alloyed with other metals. For example, sterling silver contains about 7.5 percent copper.

Silver is used in photography, coinage, jewelry, silverware, and to make electrical contacts in electrical equipment. Although the metal is highly resistant to ordinary corrosion, it is tarnished by sulfide ions in the presence of air. The tarnishing of silver to form a black coating of Ag_2S is evident when silverware is left in contact with sulfur-containing foods such as eggs.

GOLD   Gold is a highly dense (19.3 g/cm^3), yet very soft metal with a lovely yellow luster. It is widely prized and used in jewelry because of its appearance and resistance to corrosion. Because pure gold is very soft, it is alloyed to form a harder metal. The amount of gold in an alloy is expressed in karats. Pure gold is 24 karat. A piece of jewelry made of 18 karat gold contains $\frac{18}{24} \times 100$, or 75 percent, gold. Gold alloyed with silver is yellow, whereas gold alloyed with nickel is white.

CONNECTION

Get the Lead Out

Lead, a naturally occurring element, was first mined more than 5000 years ago when it was discovered that small amounts of silver could be extracted from lead ore. The ancient civilizations of Phoenicia, Egypt, Greece, India, and China used lead for vessels, roofs, water ducts, utensils, ornaments, and weights. The Romans used lead extensively in the transport of water and in the storage of food and wine. This extensive use of lead resulted in what many people today believe played a part in the decline of the early Greek and Roman civilizations—lead poisoning.

Lead poisoning is a condition that affects many systems of the human body, including the nervous and reproductive systems, the kidneys, the production of blood cells, and even behavior. Even in small amounts in the body, lead can cause severe health problems, including irreversible brain damage and injury to the blood-forming organs. Unless lead poisoning is acute, its symptoms are often vague and may mimic other conditions.

One of the main sources of lead in our environment has been the use of leaded gasoline in automobile engines. The use of leaded gasoline substantially improves engine performance. However, the lead that is released into the air forms deposits on soils, plants, and water and may eventually get into our food.

For preschool-age children, soil, dust, and lead based paints are significant sources of exposure to lead. Children of this age spend a great deal of time on the ground, putting their fingers in their mouths, and tasting and swallowing any object within reach. If a child unknowingly eats chips, flakes, or dust from

lead-based paints, he or she can risk developing lead poisoning.

What is being done to reduce the amount of lead in our environment? Fortunately, emissions of lead into the air have dropped dramatically in recent years because of the restrictions put on the lead content of gasoline by the Environmental Protection Agency (EPA). Since 1976, the year of peak emissions, the release of lead into the air has declined more than 94 percent from all sources and more than 97 percent from vehicles! The EPA also regulates the concentration of lead in drinking water. Another group, the Consumer Product Safety Commission, has banned the use of lead in toys and other articles used by children.

What can you do to protect against lead poisoning? A few ways to protect against lead poisoning are to wash food before cooking; wash hands before eating, particularly those of young children; flush water that has been standing overnight in pipes for three minutes before using it for cooking or drinking; and have old, flaking paint removed by a professional.

6–2 Section Review

1. Name two transition metals and describe their uses.
2. What is an alloy? Name several important alloys of the transition metals.
3. **Critical Thinking—Making inferences** Explain why many compounds containing transition metal ions are colored.

Guide for Reading

- What series of elements make up the *f*-block of the periodic table?

- What are some general properties of the inner transition metals?

6–3 Inner Transition Metals: The *f*-block Elements

Set somewhat apart from the transition metals is a group of elements called the inner transition metals, or *f*-block elements. **The elements of the 4*f* series are generally called lanthanides, after the element lanthanum (La), which is the first member of the series. Similarly, the elements of the 5*f* series are called actinides, after the first member of that series, actinium (Ac).**

Chemists do not agree upon how these elements should be placed in the periodic table. Some chemists favor placing them immediately after the *s*-block, as we have done in Chapter 5. Others prefer to place them immediately after La and Ac, with cerium (Ce) as the first member of the lanthanides and thorium (Th) as the first member of the actinides. The conflict stems from the fact that all the elements from lanthanum to lutetium have extremely similar properties. Their electron configurations, however, are not perfectly regular across the series. For example, the electron configuration of lanthanum (La) is $[Xe]6s^25d^1$, whereas that of the next element cerium (Ce) is $[Xe]6s^24f^15d^1$.

The Lanthanides

These elements are all very similar to one another because they differ principally in the number of electrons in the 4*f* and 5*d* sublevels rather than in their outer 6*s* sublevel. They all readily lose 3 electrons to form 3+ ions. They are all rather soft, silvery metals. Somewhat less reactive than the heavier alkaline earth metals, they are still too reactive to be used as structural materials. They tarnish readily in air and even react slowly with water.

The lanthanides are widely distributed in nature. They occur together in nature and because their properties are very similar, they are difficult to separate. One of the main reasons they are rather unfamiliar is that they have little commercial importance. Their primary use is in making special steel alloys. Some lanthanide compounds are used to produce the color in color television screens.

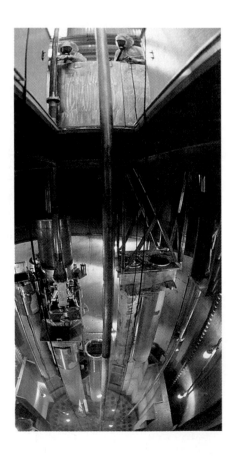

Figure 6–13 *Like all actinides, uranium is radioactive. Uranium is extracted in large quantities for use as fuel in nuclear reactors. What kind of a nuclear reaction provides the energy at a nuclear power plant?*

Fool's Gold?

While hiking, you discover a large piece of a gold-colored material that you suspect might actually be gold. You bring it to school and ask your chemistry teacher how you might test the material. He suggests that you determine its density and also see if it reacts with acids. You find that the solid has a mass of 15.5 g and occupies a volume of about 3 mL. When you add some sulfuric acid to a piece of the material, it dissolves, giving off a slight odor and producing a brownish solution. Your teacher then directs your attention to a chemistry handbook and another textbook to read about the properties of gold. What information should you look for? When you find it, what conclusions can you reach concerning the identity of the material? Should you begin making plans to buy that new stereo system you've been wanting to set up in your room?

The Actinides

Actinides are of greatest interest because of their radioactivity. All isotopes of these elements are radioactive. Only thorium (Th) and uranium (U) occur to any extent in nature. All the elements after uranium are artificial elements, produced by nuclear bombardment reactions. Uranium might be familiar to you as the radioactive element used as fuel in nuclear power plants. You will learn more about uranium in Chapter 24.

6–3 Section Review

1. Where is the lanthanide series of elements found in the periodic table? The actinide series?

2. Which elements in the actinide series are artificial?

3. **Critical Thinking—Making inferences** Explain why Ce is able to form a 4+ ion, whereas most other lanthanides form only 3+ ions.

Guide for Reading
- What are the most important *p*-block elements?
- What are the uses of the more common *p*-block elements?

6–4 From Metals to Nonmetals: The *p*-block Elements

The *p*-block contains both metals and nonmetals. **Some of the most important elements in the *p*-block of the periodic table are aluminum, carbon, silicon, nitrogen, oxygen, and chlorine.** You will encounter many of these elements and their compounds in the following chapters.

The Boron Group (Group 3A)

The elements of Group 3A are boron (B), aluminum (Al), gallium (Ga), indium (In), and thallium (Tl). Boron is a semimetal; aluminum, gallium, indium, and thallium are metals. All have an outer ns^2np^1 electron configuration and form $3+$ ions by loss of these valence electrons.

The most important element is aluminum, which is the third most abundant element in the Earth's crust. Unfortunately, most aluminum occurs combined with silicon and oxygen in compounds from which pure aluminum is difficult to extract. Aluminum metal is obtained commercially from aluminum oxide (Al_2O_3), which occurs in an ore known as bauxite.

Until the late 1800s, aluminum was very costly. Charles Hall (1863–1914), a student at Oberlin College in Ohio, became interested in the metal when his chemistry professor spoke of the fortune awaiting anyone who found a simple way of extracting Al from Al_2O_3. Using borrowed equipment, Hall began to investigate inexpensive ways of obtaining the metal from its compounds. He found that Al could be obtained from Al_2O_3 by

Figure 6–14 *This aluminum pendant, called the "Crown Jewel," was one of the few pieces of aluminum that was extracted by Charles Hall. Today, using the same process that Hall used more than 100 years ago, workers in an aluminum extraction plant monitor one phase of the process, which produces the shiny ingots awaiting delivery to various manufacturing plants. What are some uses of aluminum?*

dissolving this compound in molten Na_3AlF_6 and passing electricity through the solution. As a result of his research, large-scale production of aluminum metal became commercially feasible, and aluminum became a common and inexpensive metal. Hall filed his patent in 1886, and the price of aluminum soon fell from several hundred dollars a pound to about two dollars a pound.

Aluminum has a low density, but when it is alloyed with other metals, it is quite strong. It does not corrode extensively in air because a thin, tough, protective layer of Al_2O_3 forms on its surface. Aluminum is widely used as a structural metal. No doubt its use in beverage cans, pots and pans, and aluminum foil is quite familiar to you. Among metals, aluminum ranks second in production and consumption. What metal ranks first?

The Carbon Group (Group 4A)

The Group 4A elements are carbon (C), silicon (Si), germanium (Ge), tin (Sn), and lead (Pb). Carbon is nonmetallic (although, in the form of graphite, it does conduct electricity), silicon and germanium are semimetals, and tin and lead are metals.

CARBON Carbon is widely distributed throughout the Earth's crust. More than 50 percent of the Earth's carbon is found in limestone ($CaCO_3$). Carbon and carbon compounds are a major component of fossil fuels—coal, petroleum, and natural gas. Carbon forms an incredible number of compounds and occurs in all living organisms. The pure element exists in several forms, the most familiar being diamond and graphite. The difference between these two forms of the element results from the way the carbon atoms attach to each other.

Compounds of carbon and hydrogen are called hydrocarbons. Hydrocarbons are the major components of coal, petroleum, and natural gas. They are often burned as fuels. They are also used as raw materials for the manufacture of plastics, medicines, and a vast variety of other commercially important substances. The study of these and related compounds is called organic chemistry. Organic chemistry will be the topic of your study in Chapters 25 and 26.

When hydrocarbons and other organic compounds are burned in a limited supply of oxygen, carbon monoxide (CO) is produced. Carbon monoxide is a colorless, odorless gas that is highly poisonous. It is a common air pollutant associated with combustion reactions in automobiles and other vehicles. Carbon monoxide levels can become dangerously high in rush-hour traffic. Ways to reduce these levels include car pooling and using mass transportation. Carbon dioxide (CO_2) is produced in combustion reactions in which oxygen is plentiful. Carbon dioxide

Figure 6–15 *Carbon is unique among the elements in the number and variety of compounds it can form. Many of these compounds are the basis of all living things, including giraffes and trees. How does carbon differ from the other members of Group 4A?*

INTEGRATING
ENVIRONMENTAL SCIENCE

How can CO emissions from cars be reduced?

Figure 6-16 *When the supply of oxygen is limited, carbon burns to form a highly poisonous gas called carbon monoxide. Carbon monoxide is a common air pollutant associated with the burning of fossil fuels. What gas is produced if the oxygen supply is not limited?*

Figure 6-17 *The inviting sands on a beach in Florida and the intricate stained-glass windows in a mansion in Barcelona, Spain, consist largely of silica, a silicon compound. What is the chemical formula for silica?*

is also a colorless, odorless gas, but it is not toxic. It has a faintly sour taste when dissolved in water. One of the leading uses of CO_2 is to form the "fizz" in carbonated beverages, such as soft drinks. When carbon dioxide is cooled below $-78.5°C$ it becomes solid. Solid CO_2, known as dry ice, is a popular refrigerant.

SILICON Silicon is the second most abundant element in the Earth's crust. It occurs as silica (SiO_2), the principal component of sand, and in an enormous variety of other compounds called silicates that contain oxygen and other elements. These compounds are the structural materials of most rocks. The pure element is a semiconductor and is used to make transistors and solar cells.

Silica is the major component of glass. Other inexpensive chemicals, such as CaO and Na_2O, are added to the SiO_2 to make it melt at a lower temperature and to make the molten material easier to shape. A wide variety of glass properties can be obtained by adding other substances. Replacing some CaO and Na_2O with B_2O_3 results in borosilicate glass, which is used to make cooking utensils and laboratory glassware. To give the glass some color, transition metal oxides are added. For example, adding cobalt oxide results in a blue glass called cobalt glass.

GERMANIUM, TIN, AND LEAD Germanium, which is found in nature with silicon, is also used to make electronic devices. It is not as important or common, however, as tin and lead, which have been used for hundreds of years. Today, tin is used to coat the steel cans that you know as "tin cans" found on your supermarket shelves. The Romans used lead extensively for water pipes and plumbing. Indeed, the word plumber comes from the Latin word for lead, *plumbum*. This is also the reason that the symbol for lead is Pb. The major use of lead today is in the manufacture of lead storage batteries, which are used in automobiles.

Figure 6–18 *Nitrogen-fixing bacteria found in small round structures called nodules in the roots of plants use nitrogen from the environment for the manufacture of proteins. Fertilizers represent artificially fixed nitrogen.*

The Nitrogen Group (Group 5A)

Nitrogen (N), phosphorus (P), arsenic (As), antimony (Sb), and bismuth (Bi) are the members of Group 5A. Nitrogen and phosphorus are nonmetals, arsenic and antimony are semimetals, and bismuth is a metal. Arsenic, antimony, and bismuth are less abundant and commercially less important than nitrogen and phosphorus.

NITROGEN Nitrogen makes up approximately 80 percent of the Earth's atmosphere. Atmospheric nitrogen accounts for nearly all of the Earth's nitrogen. Nitrogen is a colorless, odorless gas composed of N_2 molecules. Although nitrogen is essential to life, few organisms can use nitrogen directly because the molecules are not very reactive. Instead, most organisms rely on nitrogen compounds as the source of their nitrogen. In nature, bacteria that live on the roots of certain plants convert atmospheric nitrogen into nitrogen compounds. The formation of nitrogen compounds from nitrogen is called nitrogen fixation.

Nitrogen is used primarily in the manufacture of compounds that are the main components of plant fertilizers. Ammonia (NH_3), which is manufactured from nitrogen and hydrogen, is used either directly as a fertilizer, or to manufacture other nitrogen-containing compounds. More than 15 billion kilograms of ammonia are manufactured each year in the United States. The characteristic odor of ammonia may be familiar to you because household ammonia, a water solution of NH_3 and a detergent, is widely used as a cleaning agent.

PHOSPHORUS Phosphorus, another abundant crustal element, is found combined with oxygen and other elements in minerals known as phosphates. Phosphorus also occurs in all living organisms. The bones in your body, for example, are made up of a calcium-phosphorus compound called calcium hydroxyapatite ($Ca_5(PO_4)_3OH$).

The most significant compounds of phosphorus are those in which the phosphorus is combined with oxygen. More than 10 billion kilograms of phosphoric acid (H_3PO_4) are manufactured in the United States each year. Phosphoric acid is used to manufacture fertilizers, detergents, and a host of other products. When diluted, phosphoric acid becomes nontoxic and is used to give various soft drinks their tart or sour taste. The next time you drink a can of cola, look for phosphoric acid in the list of ingredients.

Figure 6–19 *Like the once-living bones of this dinosaur, human bones contain a calcium-phosphorus compound.*

*I*NTEGRATING
*B*IOLOGY

What is nitrogen fixation?

Fertilizers

Farmers and home gardeners use fertilizers to replace nutrients lost from the soil and to increase crop production. The three primary plant nutrients in fertilizers are nitrogen, phosphorus, and potassium. For example, a fertilizer might be labeled 15-10-4. The first number represents the percentage of nitrogen, the second the percentage of phosphorus (in the form of P_2O_5), and the third, the percentage of potassium (in the form of K_2O). The choice of fertilizer depends on the crop being grown as well as on the condition of the soil. Lawns need a lot of nitrogen, so the choice might be a 20-5-5 fertilizer. Fruits and vegetables require more phosphorus, so the choice for them might be a 10-30-10 fertilizer.

The Oxygen Group (Group 6A)

Oxygen and sulfur are by far the most important of the Group 6A elements. Other members of this group include selenium (Se), tellurium (Te), and polonium (Po). Oxygen, sulfur, and selenium are nonmetals, tellurium is a semimetal, and polonium is a metal.

OXYGEN Oxygen is the most abundant element on Earth. It makes up 23 percent of the mass of air, 89 percent of the mass of water, and about 46 percent of the mass of the crustal rocks of our planet. The most readily available source of the element is the atmosphere, where oxygen occurs as O_2 molecules.

Elemental oxygen (O_2) is a colorless, odorless, and tasteless gas. It is relatively reactive and combines with most elements to form compounds called oxides. Oxygen is required for respiration and is consumed by combustion, or burning, reactions. In fact, one way to fight fires is to exclude oxygen by smothering the fire. One of the largest uses of oxygen is in the steelmaking industry.

Elemental oxygen also exists as O_3, which is known as ozone. Ozone is a colorless gas with a strongly irritating odor. It is formed when oxygen in the air is subjected to an electrical discharge, such as a bolt of lightning. This is why the odor of ozone is often evident around electrical equipment and during electrical storms. Because it attacks structural materials, as well as the tissues of plants and animals, ozone is considered an air pollutant. However, it does play an important role in the upper atmosphere, where it absorbs a great deal of the high-energy ultraviolet radiation from the sun. Without this natural sunscreen, ultraviolet radiation would be harmful to living things.

Figure 6–20 *A fire is most commonly a reaction of a fuel with oxygen. What are some causes of forest fires?*

Figure 6–21 *Sulfur has been known for a long time because it occurs as a free solid in nature. In the United States sulfur deposits are found in Texas and Louisiana. In addition to producing sulfuric acid, sulfur is heavily used in the rubber industry.*

SULFUR   Sulfur occurs in the elemental form in nature and has been known since ancient times as brimstone. Most sulfur, however, occurs in compounds such as iron pyrite (FeS_2), which is commonly called "fool's gold."

Many compounds of sulfur have a characteristic unpleasant odor. Hydrogen sulfide (H_2S), for example, smells like rotten eggs. Small amounts of sulfur-containing compounds are added to natural gas to give the gas an odor that can be easily detected in case of leaks. Even the odor associated with skunks is due to sulfur-containing compounds.

The largest use of sulfur is in the production of sulfuric acid (H_2SO_4). More than 40 billion kilograms of sulfuric acid are produced annually in the United States. Sulfuric acid is used in almost all manufacturing processes. The manufacture of detergents, lubricants, paints, plastics, insecticides, pharmaceuticals, food additives, and explosives involves the use of sulfuric acid. A direct use of sulfuric acid is in lead storage batteries.

The Halogens (Group 7A)

The name halogen comes from the Greek language and literally means salt former. In Chapter 7, you will learn how the reaction of most metals with the halogens results in the formation of compounds called salts. The halogens consist of the nonmetals fluorine (F), chlorine (Cl), bromine (Br), iodine (I), and astatine (At).

Halogen Lamps

Halogen lamps contain metal halides—chemical compounds of a metal and a halogen. These compounds produce a more natural color balance than mercury vapor lamps. Halogen lamps also last a long time and produce more light for the same amount of electrical input. For these reasons, halogen lamps are excellent light sources for outdoor use. They are also commonly used in automobile headlights.

All of the halogens exist in elemental form as diatomic (2-atom) molecules—F_2, Cl_2, Br_2, I_2, and At_2. Fluorine is a pale yellow gas, chlorine is a green-yellow gas, bromine is a dark red-brown liquid that readily forms a red-brown vapor, and iodine is a dark gray solid that readily forms a violet vapor. Astatine is an extremely rare element whose isotopes are all radioactive.

The halogens react with most metals and with many nonmetals. Because they are all highly reactive, they do not occur as free elements in nature. The feature that accounts for their reactivity is their strong attraction for electrons. The reactivity of halogens decreases from fluorine to iodine. This is because fluorine has the strongest attraction for electrons, as you learned in the discussion of electron affinities in Chapter 5. In nature, the halogens occur mainly as halides, compounds that contain F^-, Cl^-, Br^-, or I^- ions.

FLUORINE Fluorine, a very corrosive gas, is the most reactive of all the elements. It is a fairly abundant element in the Earth's crust, occurring in several minerals. The most important source of fluorine is the mineral fluorite (CaF_2). Fluorine is used to manufacture many carbon-fluorine compounds, including chlorofluorocarbons (CFCs), which are used as refrigerants in air-conditioners and refrigerators. The release of CFCs in the environment has been linked to the formation of the ozone hole in Earth's upper atmosphere. Fluorine is also used to make lubricants and plastics such as Teflon.

CHLORINE Chlorine, the most industrially useful of the halogens, occurs as NaCl in natural salt deposits. The element is added to drinking water and to swimming pools to serve as

Figure 6–22 *Chlorine is a fairly reactive, widely used halogen. Because of its germicidal properties, chlorine is added to swimming pools to kill bacteria.*

a disinfectant. It is also used as a bleach, and in the manufacture of polyvinyl chloride (PVC) plastic, and many other chlorine-containing organic compounds. Many chlorinated organic compounds are hazardous to humans and other animals, and thus their manufacture and use have been severely limited.

BROMINE AND IODINE Bromine and iodine are less abundant than fluorine and chlorine and are not widely used. Bromine is used to manufacture compounds that are used as fire-retardants, pesticides, and components of photographic film. Iodine is used to make iodized salt, which contains small amounts of KI mixed with NaCl. Iodine is also used to make tincture of iodine, an alcohol solution of I_2 that is an effective household antiseptic for treating minor cuts and scratches.

The Noble Gases (Group 8A)

The noble gases are helium (He), neon (Ne), argon (Ar), krypton (Kr), xenon (Xe), and radon (Rn). They are the least reactive elements. The name noble gases comes from the idea that the lack of reactivity—a tendency to remain apart—was characteristic of nobility.

The most abundant noble gas is argon, which makes up about 1 percent of the Earth's atmosphere. Argon was the first noble gas to be discovered. Because it forms no compounds, it was named argon, which means the lazy one in Greek. With the

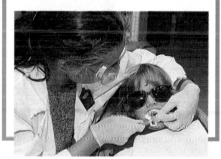
Figure 6–23 *Crystals of xenon tetrafluoride were first prepared in 1962. Before that time, it was believed that noble gases could not form compounds. How did the noble gases get their name?*

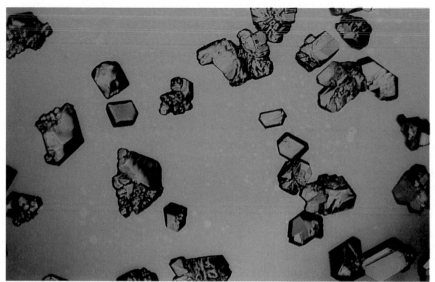

Figure 6–24 *Because helium is less dense than air, it is used to inflate weather balloons.*

discovery of argon in 1894, it became apparent that a previously unknown and unsuspected family of elements must exist. By 1898, helium, neon, krypton, and xenon had been discovered. Neon, krypton, and xenon were isolated from air. Although first identified in the sun's spectrum, helium was isolated from uranium ores. (Indeed, the name helium comes from the Greek word *helios* meaning the sun.) As you may recall from Chapter 3, the radioactive uranium in such ores emits alpha particles, which consist of helium-4 nuclei. When they pick up electrons, the helium-4 nuclei form helium gas. Helium also occurs in many natural gas wells, which today represent the major source of this noble gas.

Prior to 1962, all chemistry textbooks proclaimed that the noble gases formed no compounds. In that year, however, Neil Bartlett, then working at the University of British Columbia, succeeded in reacting xenon with a fluorine-containing chemical, PtF_6. Shortly after he announced his results, other researchers succeeded in reacting xenon directly with fluorine to form XeF_2, XeF_4, and XeF_6. The only known compound of krypton is KrF_2. And to date, there are no known compounds of helium, neon, or argon. Although radon can form compounds, its high radioactivity inhibits any study of its chemical reactions. Nevertheless, it is evident that the chemical reactivity of the noble gases, although minor, increases as the size of the atoms increases, from helium to radon.

Helium is commercially the most important of the noble gases. It is used as a coolant to perform experiments at very low temperatures. Helium has the lowest boiling point of any known substance ($-269°C$), so liquid helium is the coldest liquid refrigerant available. Argon is used in light bulbs, where it conducts heat away from the filament but does not react with it. Argon is also used as an inert blanketing atmosphere in working with very reactive substances. Neon is the well-known gas that produces the red light in "neon" signs. Krypton, xenon, and radon are not very important commercially.

6–4 Section Review

1. List the most important p-block elements.
2. What properties of aluminum make it an important commercial metal?
3. What is the major component of glass?
4. Why are Group 8A elements known as the noble gases?
5. **Connection—Biology** Nitrogen fixation can occur naturally as well as artificially. Explain.

6–5 Hydrogen: One of a Kind

Guide for Reading
- What are the sources of hydrogen on Earth?
- What are some uses of hydrogen?

We end our dicussion of the elements by examining the very first element in the periodic table, hydrogen (H). In Chapter 5 you saw it placed at the top of the Group 1A column of elements. But is hydrogen a metal? You probably know that it is not. Although it has 1 valence electron, the ionization energy of hydrogen is even greater than that of lithium. What does this indicate to you?

Hydrogen is a nonmetal that exists as a gas under normal conditions. It is colorless, odorless, and composed of H_2 molecules. Hydrogen is rare in the atmosphere because it is light enough to escape Earth's gravitational attraction. **Most of the Earth's hydrogen is combined with oxygen as water (H_2O).** Hydrogen also occurs frequently in combination with carbon in a large variety of organic compounds. Such compounds are found in coal, petroleum, natural gas, and all plants and animals. In terms of mass, hydrogen is the ninth most abundant element on the Earth's surface, which includes the crust, the oceans, and the atmosphere. However, it is by far the most abundant element in the universe.

Most elemental hydrogen is obtained commercially from hydrocarbons. Recall that hydrocarbons are compounds of carbon and hydrogen such as those found in natural gas and petroleum. The major use of hydrogen is in the manufacture of ammonia (NH_3), which is used as a fertilizer or converted into other nitrogen-containing fertilizers. Large quantities of hydrogen are also used to prepare various organic compounds, notably methanol (CH_3OH). Methanol is used in place of gasoline to power the engines of race cars.

Figure 6–25 *Hydrogen, the first element in the periodic table, has the simplest atomic structure. Hydrogen can be produced in large quantities from water and currently is being tested as an alternative fuel in automobiles. What are some other uses of hydrogen?*

6–5 Section Review

1. What are the sources of hydrogen on Earth?
2. What is the major use of hydrogen?
3. **Critical Thinking—Making comparisons** In what way is hydrogen like the alkali metals? In what way is it like the halogens?

Laboratory Investigation

Periodicity and Chemical Reactivity

Problem

Is there a pattern of reactivity and solubility within a family of elements?

Materials (per group)

balance	distilled water
3 test tubes,	phenolphthalein
13 × 100 mm	solution
test-tube holder	saturated solutions of:
test-tube rack	$Ca(OH)_2$
wood splints	$Mg(OH)_2$
glass stirring rod	$Ba(OH)_2$
calcium turnings	0.1 M solutions of:
magnesium ribbon	Na_2CO_3
$MgSO_4$ crystals	$MgCl_2$
$CaSO_4$ crystals	$CaCl_2$
$BaSO_4$ crystals	$BaCl_2$
pH paper	

Procedure

1. Pour about 5 mL of distilled water into a clean, dry test tube. Add a calcium turning to the water in the tube. Using a test-tube holder, invert a clean, dry test tube over the reactant test tube to collect the gas being given off during the reaction.
2. Test for hydrogen gas by inserting a burning wooden splint into the upper part of the test tube. *CAUTION: Be careful when using an open flame.* Record your observations in a data table similar to the one shown.
3. Add a few drops of phenolphthalein solution to the reactant test tube. After recording your observations, discard the contents of the test tube as directed by your teacher and clean and dry the tube.
4. Repeat steps 1 to 3 using a 10-cm piece of magnesium ribbon in place of the calcium. If no visible reaction takes place, heat the water to boiling, using a test tube holder to hold the tube over the burner flame. *CAUTION: Be careful when using an open flame.* Record the results in your data table.
5. Obtain 5-mL samples of saturated solutions of $Ca(OH)_2$, $Mg(OH)_2$, and $Ba(OH)_2$. Test each solution with pH paper and record the results.

6. Using a laboratory balance, measure out 1-g samples of $MgSO_4$, $CaSO_4$, and $BaSO_4$. Place each sample in a clean, dry, labeled test tube.
7. Add 5 mL of distilled water to each test tube. Use a glass stirring rod to dissolve as much of the sample as you possibly can in each test tube. Record your observations of the relative solubilities of each of these compounds in your data table.
8. Add about 5 mL of the 0.1 M solution of $MgCl_2$, $CaCl_2$, and $BaCl_2$ to three labeled test tubes.
9. To each of the solutions in the test tubes, add about 1 mL of the Na_2CO_3 solution. Record your observations in your data table.

Observations

Test for H₂ Gas			
$Ca + H_2O$		$Mg + H_2O$	
Phenolphthalein Test			
$Ca(OH)_2$		$Mg(OH)_2$	
pH Test			
$MG(OH)_2$	$Ca(OH)_2$		$Ba(OH)_2$
Solubility			
$MgSO_4$	$CaSO_4$		$BaSO_4$
$MgCO_3$	$CaCO_3$		$BaCO_3$

1. Write balanced equations for each chemical reaction that took place.
2. What pattern can you observe for the solubility of each of the hydroxides? The sulfates?

Analysis and Conclusions

1. Describe the reactivity of the metals in Group 2 in terms of their location in the Group.
2. Why do Group 2 metals form ions with a 2+ charge?
3. Why does the metallic character of the alkaline earth metals increase as you go down the Group?
4. Suggest why the Group 2 elements are called the alkaline earth metals.
5. **On Your Own** How would you extend this experiment to the study of Group 1 metals? What types of reactions would be most useful in characterizing the alkali metals?

STUDY GUIDE

Summarizing Key Concepts

6–1 Reactive Metals: The *s*-block Elements

- The alkali metals are all very reactive metals and, therefore, they do not exist free in nature. Group 1A elements form ions with a 1+ charge. Many compounds of sodium are important commercially.
- The alkaline earth metals are reactive metals. They form ions with a 2+ charge. Magnesium and calcium are the most abundant of this group of elements. Magnesium is an important structural metal. Several calcium compounds are important commercially.

6–2 Transition Metals: The *d*-block Elements

- Transition metals have *d* orbital valence electrons. As a result, many of these metals have highly colored compounds.
- Several transition metals are widely used. Iron is the main structural metal, and copper, silver, and gold are coinage metals.

6–3 Inner Transition Metals: The *f*-block Elements

- The inner transition elements consist of the two series of elements called the lanthanides and the actinides.

- The lanthanides are very similar to one another in their properties and are a little less reactive than the alkaline earth metals. All of the actinides are radioactive.

6–4 From Metals to Nonmetals: The *p*-block Elements

- The *p*-block consists of six groups of elements, Group 3A to Group 8A. The metallic character of the elements increases going down a group.
- Carbon, nitrogen, and oxygen are the most important nonmetals. Silicon is an important semimetal. Aluminum, tin, and lead are the most commonly used metals.

6–5 Hydrogen: One of a Kind

- Hydrogen is the most abundant element in the universe. On the Earth it is found primarily in combination with oxygen in water.
- Hydrogen is used mainly in the manufacture of ammonia and hydrocarbons.

Reviewing Key Terms

Define each term in a complete sentence.

6–1 Reactive Metals: The *s*-block Elements

alloy

6–2 Transition Metals: The *d*-block Elements

corrosion

CHAPTER REVIEW

Content Review

Multiple Choice

Choose the letter of the answer that best completes each statement.

1. Which element is an alkali metal?
   (a) boron
   (b) magnesium
   (c) sodium
   (d) oxygen

2. Which metals are soft enough to be cut by a knife?
   (a) inner transition metals
   (b) transition metals
   (c) semimetals
   (d) alkali metals

3. The least reactive family of elements in the periodic table is the
   (a) alkali metals.
   (b) transition metals.
   (c) noble gases.
   (d) halogens.

4. The transition metal with the highest melting point is
   (a) magnesium.
   (b) gold.
   (c) tungsten.
   (d) chromium.

5. Which of the following is not an alloy?
   (a) bronze
   (b) brass
   (c) steel
   (d) lanthanum

6. The transition metal that is the best conductor of electricity is
   (a) chromium.
   (b) silver.
   (c) copper.
   (d) iron.

7. Members of the 4*f* series are called
   (a) lanthanides.
   (b) actinides.
   (c) metalloids.
   (d) halides.

8. Aluminum is obtained commercially from
   (a) siderite.
   (b) magnetite.
   (c) bauxite.
   (d) hematite.

9. The most abundant element in the universe is
   (a) oxygen.
   (b) carbon.
   (c) hydrogen.
   (d) silicon.

True or False

If the statement is true, write "true." If it is false, change the underlined word or words to make the statement true.

10. <u>Alkaline earth metals</u> are the most reactive metals.

11. The element sodium is found mainly as <u>sodium chloride</u>.

12. Most <u>transition metals</u> have high densities and high boiling points.

13. Iron and small amounts of carbon form the alloy <u>bronze</u>.

14. The Group 8A element that is used to fill light bulbs is <u>argon</u>.

15. The most abundant element on Earth is <u>nitrogen</u>.

16. The <u>least</u> reactive element in Group 7A is fluorine.

17. The most abundant of the noble gases is <u>xenon</u>.

18. Hydrogen is mainly used to manufacture <u>ammonia</u>.

19. Most <u>nonmetals</u> are good structural materials.

Concept Mapping

Complete the following concept map for Section 6–1. Refer to pages xviii–xix to construct a concept map for the entire chapter.

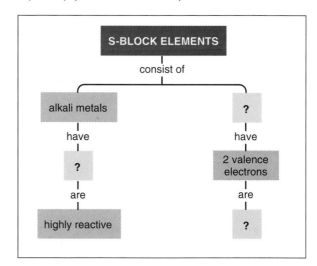

216

Concept Mastery

Discuss each of the following in a brief paragraph.

20. Why do the alkali metals have the largest atoms in each period?
21. How do the alkaline earth metals differ from the alkali metals?
22. What are the sources of the alkali metals? Why are these metals not found free in nature?
23. List five transition metals and describe a use for each.
24. Explain why chemists do not agree upon where to place the inner transition metals in the periodic table.
25. Describe how Charles Hall produced aluminum inexpensively.
26. What happens when hydrocarbons burn in the air?
27. What are the major uses of the elements of the halogen family?
28. Why are the noble gases the least reactive of any of the elements?
29. Describe the role of oxygen, sulfur, and nitrogen in your world.
30. What are some characteristics of the element hydrogen?

31. **Tying it Together** Explain how the organization of the periodic table represents *unity and diversity* of the elements.

Critical Thinking and Problem Solving

Use the skills you have developed in this chapter to answer each of the following.

32. **Developing hypotheses** Explain why a person suffering from an iron deficiency would feel tired all the time.
33. **Giving an example** Metals are ductile and malleable. How have these properties affected your daily life?
34. **Applying concepts** How can the arrangement of elements in the periodic table be used to predict how they will react with other elements to form compounds?
35. **Evaluating results** Why is it most unlikely for a scientist to have discovered a new element between nitrogen and oxygen?

36. **Applying concepts** Why is it advisable to paint metal outdoor furniture?
37. **Making predictions** How would a diet with an insufficient amount of phosphorus affect the body?
38. **Using the writing process** Some science fiction stories have proposed the existence of silicon-based life on other planets. Do you think this is possible? Write your own science fiction story about alien organisms that are based on silicon instead of carbon. How would such organisms be different from Earth organisms? How would they be similar?

FROM SCHOOL TO WORK

Vikram Goghari—Student

Vikram Goghari, of Vancouver, British Columbia, Canada, has taken several chemistry courses at Sir Charles Tupper Secondary School and has enjoyed them all. He began the subject expecting it to be interesting but extremely challenging, but in fact found it easier than expected. Vikram explains, "It is fascinating how everything can be calculated and how useful these numbers are. There are stories we see on television and read in the newspaper that demand the knowledge gained through an introductory chemistry course. It is an exciting world of knowledge that should be the first branch of science."

When asked about the chemistry knowledge he now uses in his everyday life, Vikram cites information as diverse as "why iron rusts, and how to prevent it" and "the structures of atoms, and how they affect the properties of common materials."

Pharmacologist

Pharmacologists study the effects of drugs, chemicals, and other substances on the human body. They perform tests to determine how drugs should be used most effectively and to standardize dosages. They also analyze chemicals, food additives, poisons, and pesticides to determine their effects.

Much of the research work of a pharmacologist is done in the laboratory. Most pharmacologists earn a doctorate in pharmacology and many are also medical doctors or doctors of veterinary medicine. A good high-school background in mathematics and science, including courses in physical and organic chemistry, is essential if you are interested in a career in pharmacology.

To receive additional information, write to the American College of Clinical Pharmacology, 175 Strafford Avenue, Suite 1, Wayne, PA 19087.

How to Choose a Technical School

Technicians are workers who are trained beyond high school in a specialized field of technology. A technical education mixes theory with practice and usually takes from one to three years to complete, depending on the field. Technicians receive either a certificate or an Associate degree.

When choosing a technical school, seek reliable evaluations from past graduates and job placement statistics. Although many schools advertise, only the better schools are accredited by the government.

For information write to the National Association of Trade and Technical Schools, 2251 Wisconsin Avenue, NW, Washington, DC 20007 and ask for a copy of the *Handbook of Trade and Technical Careers and Training*.

H. Eugene LeMay, Jr

From the Author

I became interested in chemistry when I took high-school chemistry. That was my senior year in high school. I had taken physics my junior year and I thought it was all right. But I really enjoyed chemistry. I liked the smells and color changes. Most of all, though, I liked the logic of it and the way it helped me see and understand my world in a new way.

I remember being fascinated by the fact that so few different kinds of atoms could create such marvelous diversity around us. Then there was the matter of learning how things worked—neon lights, fireworks, pressure cookers, batteries, antacids. The list goes on and on. In fact, learning how things work still fascinates me.

I continue to enjoy chemistry. I feel incredibly fortunate to be able to spend my life learning about the world, using my imagination, and interacting with young, vibrant students. My wish for you as you study chemistry is that you not let the work of mastering the material interfere with your joy and excitement in learning. Let your imagination soar! You may be surprised by what you discover and where it leads you.

UNIT REVIEW

Concept Mastery

Discuss each of the following in a brief paragraph.

1. How does the atomic theory of matter explain the law of conservation of mass and the law of constant composition?
2. How did Dalton's concept of the atom differ from that of modern chemists?
3. If a piece of fur somehow has a negative electrical charge, what does this indicate about its fundamental composition?
4. What are cathode rays, and what role did they play in the discovery of the electron?
5. What experiment led to the discovery of the atomic nucleus?
6. Describe the basic substructure of the atom.
7. What is the nature of alpha, beta, and gamma radiation?
8. What are the properties and locations of the three kinds of subatomic particles in an atom?
9. What information do the atomic number, mass number, and electrical charge provide about an atom?
10. What does it mean when chemists say that two atoms are isotopes of each other?
11. What experimental information is necessary to determine the atomic mass of an element?
12. How can the relative number of protons and neutrons in a nucleus provide a clue to nuclear stability?
13. What type of radioactivity would you expect from an unstable nucleus that contains more protons than neutrons? That contains fewer protons than neutrons?
14. List four characteristic properties of light.
15. What is the difference between a continuous spectrum and a line spectrum? Which is produced by the heating of a tungsten wire inside a light bulb? Which is produced by a neon light?
16. What is a photon? What properties of a photon can be related to its energy?
17. Explain why X-rays can have a much more damaging effect on biological cells than infrared radiation.
18. Explain why violet light but not red light will free an electron from the surface of sodium metal.
19. How did Bohr explain the existence of line spectra?
20. What is the difference between (a) a $2s$ orbital and a $3s$ orbital? (b) a $2p_z$ orbital and a $2p_y$ orbital?
21. What principles determine how electrons are arranged in atoms?
22. In general, do larger or smaller atoms have greater ionization energies? Explain.
23. Which are the easiest electrons to remove from a magnesium atom? How is this fact related to a magnesium atom's electron configuration?
24. When a P atom is bonded to a Cl atom, they share a pair of electrons, which act as the glue to hold the atoms together. Using electronegativity, predict whether these electrons are more likely to be closer to P or to Cl most of the time.
25. Why are the alkali metals never used as structural materials?
26. Using abbreviated electron configurations, explain why the alkali metals form ions with 1+ charges and not 2+.

Problem Bank

27. Determine the number of protons, neutrons, and electrons in (a) the $^{201}_{80}Hg^{2+}$ ion (b) an ion of iodine-127 that has a charge of 1−.
28. The element copper contains two naturally occurring isotopes, $^{63}_{29}Cu$ and $^{65}_{29}Cu$. Their masses are 62.93 amu and 64.93 amu and their relative abundances are 69.09 percent and 30.91 percent, respectively. Calculate the atomic mass of copper.
29. Calculate the mass, in grams, of one atom of oxygen-16 if its mass is reported as 16.0 amu.

30. Write balanced nuclear equations for each of the following processes: (a) nickel-66 undergoes beta decay (b) polonium-211 undergoes alpha decay.

31. Determine the missing isotope in the following nuclear reaction:
$$^{66}_{29}Cu \rightarrow {}^{0}_{-1}e + ?$$

32. If the electromagnetic radiation used to send television signals has a frequency of 3.0×10^9 Hz, what is its wavelength?

33. An amateur radio operator transmits radio waves with a wavelength of 10 meters. What is the energy of a single photon of this radio wave?

34. Draw the orbital diagram and determine the number of unpaired electrons in (a) vanadium (b) indium.

35. Write the electron configuration for (a) strontium (b) lutetium.

36. Identify (a) the alkaline earth metal in the fourth period (b) the halogen in the fifth period of the periodic table.

37. Write the abbreviated electron configuration of (a) S (b) Hg.

38. Arrange the following atoms in order of increasing size: P, Ge, As.

39. Arrange the following particles in order of increasing size: I, I$^-$, I$^+$.

40. Arrange the following atoms in order of increasing ionization energy: S, Cl, Se.

41. Write the chemical formulas of compounds formed from (a) 1 Cr atom and 3 Cl atoms (b) 3 Mg atoms and 2 PO$_4$ groups.

42. Given that magnesium forms the compounds MgO and Mg(NO$_3$)$_2$, use your knowledge of the periodic table to predict the chemical formula of a compound containing (a) Ca and O (b) Mg and S (c) Sr and NO$_3$ groups.

43. Determine the abbreviated electron configuration of the In^{3+} ion.

Performance-Based Task

Which Metals Corrode Less in an Aquarium?

In cleaning your fish tank, you notice excessive corrosion of the metal fittings in the aquarium. How can you determine which metals would be more suitable? Design an experiment to answer the question.

1. Start by obtaining safety goggles, a lab apron, samples of various metals and their ions in solution, a copy of the periodic table, a spot plate, forceps, a dropper or pipette, and tap water.

2. State your hypothesis and then develop a procedure for testing it.

3. Carry out your experiment. Record your observations in order to determine patterns of reactivity of the metals.

4. Test how other metals and solutions fit into the pattern you observed.

Going Further

5. Do you think your results would be different if you changed the concentrations of the solutions? Explain.

6. How would your results be different if you used the metals in a saltwater, instead of a freshwater, aquarium?

3 Interactions of Matter

Framed by the glowing hands of a forensics laboratory techni-cian, DNA sequences appear mysterious and intriguing. Actually, although DNA itself was a mystery for many years, today the inter-pretation of DNA sequences can be used to solve mysteries. Through DNA fingerprinting, as the technique is called, police can often identify a murderer based on evidence as small as a strand of hair or a drop of blood!

In this unit, you will learn how chemists were able to unravel the secrets of many important molecules—including DNA—by studying the interactions of matter as they occur at the atomic level. You will learn how atoms join together to form molecules and how molecules interact with one another. By visualizing the characteris-tic shapes of typical molecules, you will begin to understand the properties of many different chemical compounds. And you will learn how to describe the interactions of matter through the use of chemical equations. By the time you finish reading the chapters that follow, you may even think that solving problems in chemistry is as fascinating as solving crimes!

DISCOVERY LEARNING

1. Place a piece of steel wool in the bottom of a clear plastic cup.

2. Pour equal amounts of water into each of two shallow bowls.

3. Invert the plastic cup with the steel wool into one of the bowls. Invert an empty plastic cup into the other bowl.

4. Observe the cups every day for 1 week.

   ■ What changes did you observe in the steel wool?

   ■ What changes did you observe in the water level?

   ■ How can you explain your observations?

Chapter 7 Chemical Formulas and Bonding

The material that makes up a spider's web has some very impressive properties: It is thin and lightweight, yet strong enough to withstand wind, rain, and other stresses. And, of course, the web is sticky enough to trap a passing fly or other small insect—a nutritious meal for the spider!

Why are spider webs so strong, sticky, and flexible? The answer lies with the nature of the chemical bonds that bind the web's atoms. In this chapter, you will learn all about chemical bonds—what they are, why atoms form them, and why some bonds are stronger than others. When you finish the chapter, you may not be able to re-create a spider's web, but you should appreciate its qualities all the more.

Suppose you knit this yarn into an intricate web, such as this spider web. Would the two webs have similar properties? To understand the properties of any material, you need to understand the bonds that join its atoms.

7-1 Ionic Bonding

Guide for Reading
- What is an ionic bond?
- What is the octet rule?

The great diversity of matter—the different kinds of "stuff" that make up our world—comes from only about 100 different kinds of atoms. If atoms did not interact with each other, then perhaps such diversity would not be possible. But as you have learned, atoms are not the tiny, indivisible spheres they once were imagined to be. Rather, they are composed of subatomic particles called protons, neutrons, and electrons. And the tiniest of these particles—the electrons—play a crucial role in the forces that link atoms together to form the different kinds of matter that you see around you. These links are called chemical bonds.

In this chapter you will learn about two kinds of chemical bonds: **ionic bonds** and **covalent bonds.** You will learn about other types of bonds, such as the bonds that hold metals together, in later chapters.

Ionic Bonds and Ionic Compounds

As you learned in Chapter 3, static electricity is the effect you might encounter when you pull clothes from a dryer. Your clothes stick together because they acquire small electrical

Figure 7-1 *Van de Graaf generators the metal balls at the bottom of this photograph—are a source of static electricity. Electrical charges have accumulated on this young woman's hair, causing the strands to separate from each other.*

Lose that Cling!

Many consumers buy products that rid their laundry of static electricity. One such product is a small, foamlike sheet that tumbles with clothing in the dryer. This sheet acts as an electrical conductor, redistributing the electrical charges that build up among the clothing. It thus neutralizes the static electricity.

charges from tumbling and rubbing against each other. Perhaps a sock with a slight negative charge clings to a shirt with a slight positive charge.

Static electrical attraction is the basis for ionic bonds. **In an ionic bond, a positively charged ion is attracted to a negatively charged ion.** As you may remember from Chapter 5, metals tend to form positive ions and nonmetals tend to form negative ions. As a result, ionic bonds commonly form between the ions of a metallic element, such as sodium, and a nonmetallic element, such as chlorine. What other pairs of elements do you think would form ionic bonds?

A compound that is composed entirely of ions is called an **ionic compound.** All ionic compounds consist of positively charged ions, called **cations** (KAT-igh-ahnz), and negatively charged ions, called **anions** (AN-igh-ahnz). Ionic compounds are electrically neutral, so the electrical charges of the cations and anions must balance. As you will discover as you read on, this fact helps you to predict the ratio of cations to anions in any ionic compound.

The ionic compound formed from sodium ions and chloride ions is named sodium chloride. Although you may not have realized it, you have already seen and used sodium chloride many times: Sodium chloride is ordinary table salt! However, as you will discover, there is more to learn about this compound than what you know from the dinner table.

If you could see the individual sodium and chloride ions in a crystal of sodium chloride, you would find that they are arranged in a specific pattern. This pattern is illustrated in Figure 7–2. Notice that each sodium ion is surrounded by chloride ions and that each chloride ion is surrounded by sodium ions. (If we colored the atoms differently, the picture might look like an alternating arrangement of oranges and grapefruit at the supermarket!) The ions form this pattern to maximize the electrical attraction among them. Take a close look at Figure 7–2. How many chloride ions surround each sodium ion?

Figure 7–2 *These diagrams show how sodium ions (gray) and chloride ions (green) stack in a crystal of sodium chloride—also known as table salt. The diagram on the right emphasizes the ions' cubic arrangement. How many sodium ions surround each chloride ion?*

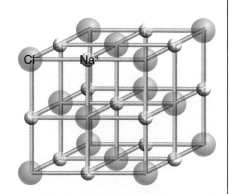

Ionic compounds have a variety of properties. They usually have high melting points, which indicates that ionic bonding is very strong. However, ionic compounds tend to be brittle. Strike an ionic compound sharply and it will shatter, or cleave, in distinct directions, as illustrated in Figure 7–3.

Many ionic compounds dissolve in water, a process that breaks the ionic bonds and separates the ions. The separated ions move freely in water, which makes such solutions good conductors of electricity. Molten ionic compounds, or ionic compounds in a liquid state, are also good conductors of electricity. As solids, however, ionic compounds do not conduct electricity because the ions are held in position more firmly and cannot move freely.

The Octet Rule

When elemental chlorine, a nonmetal, is mixed with elemental sodium, a metal, they react to form sodium chloride, the ionic compound that you just studied. This reaction is illustrated in Figure 7–4. Notice that the reaction also produces energy in the form of light. Indeed, this reaction yields a great deal of energy, which indicates that its product—sodium chloride—is much more stable than elemental chlorine and sodium, the materials that started the reaction.

Are you surprised that a soft, silvery metal and a poisonous gas react to produce table salt, a compound quite different from either starting material? You will learn much more about chemical reactions—and some of the other surprises they hold—when you study Chapter 9.

Why is sodium chloride more stable than elemental sodium and chlorine? To answer this question, you need to study the

Figure 7–3 *Like other ionic compounds, sodium chloride cleaves in different directions when hit by a hammer.*

Figure 7–4 *Chlorine is a green gas and sodium is a silvery metal (left). Bring them together and they react violently, releasing a great deal of energy (middle and right). The result is an ionic compound—sodium chloride—which has very different properties from either starting material.*

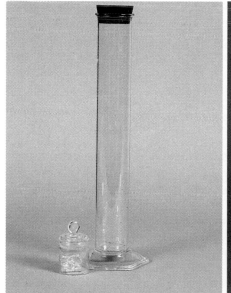
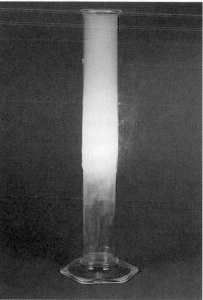
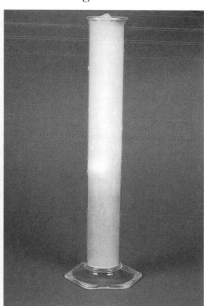

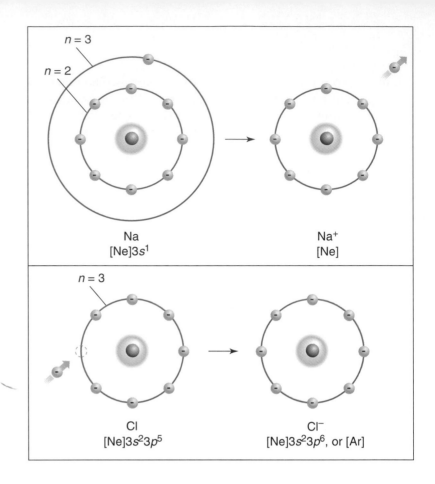

Figure 7–5 *A sodium atom readily loses one of its electrons (top) whereas a chlorine atom readily gains an electron (bottom). In both cases, the ion that forms has the electron configuration of a noble gas.*

electron configurations of these elements. First, consider the electron configuration of chlorine, which is $[Ne]3s^23p^5$. When a chlorine atom gains an extra electron, it becomes a chloride ion with an electron configuration of $[Ne]3s^23p^6$. Notice that the electron configuration for the chloride ion is the same as the electron configuration for argon, the nearest noble gas to chlorine in the periodic table. Remember from Chapter 6 that noble gases are particularly stable. So, because the chloride ion (Cl^-) has the same electron configuration as a noble gas, it is stable as well.

Next, consider the sodium atom, which has an electron configuration of $[Ne]3s^1$. When a sodium atom loses 1 electron, it becomes a sodium ion with the electron configuration $[Ne]$, the electron configuration of a neon atom. Neon is the nearest noble gas to sodium in the periodic table. Both neon and the sodium ion (Na^+) are stable.

Like sodium and chlorine, other elements tend to gain or lose electrons in order to acquire the electron configuration of a noble gas. These elements include those listed in the reconfigured periodic table in Figure 7–6. In this diagram, the green numbers over each column indicate the charge of the common ions of that group. Study the electron configurations of the elements in this diagram and the charges of their common ions. What relationship do you see?

3–	2–	1–	0	1+	2+	3+
			2 **He** $1s^2$ or [He]	3 **Li** [He]$2s^1$	4 **Be** [He]$2s^2$	5 **B** [He]$2s^2 2p^1$
7 **N** [He]$2s^2 2p^3$	8 **O** [He]$2s^2 2p^4$	9 **F** [He]$2s^2 2p^5$	10 **Ne** [He]$2s^2 2p^6$ or [Ne]	11 **Na** [Ne]$3s^1$	12 **Mg** [Ne]$3s^2$	13 **Al** [Ne]$3s^2 3p^1$
15 **P** [Ne]$3s^2 3p^3$	16 **S** [Ne]$3s^2 3p^4$	17 **Cl** [Ne]$3s^2 3p^5$	18 **Ar** [Ne]$3s^2 3p^6$ or [Ar]	19 **K** [Ar]$4s^1$	20 **Ca** [Ar]$4s^2$	
	34 **Se** [Ar]$4s^2 3d^{10} 4p^4$	35 **Br** [Ar]$4s^2 3d^{10} 4p^5$	36 **Kr** [Ar]$4s^2 3d^{10} 4p^6$ or [Kr]	37 **Rb** [Kr]$5s^1$	38 **Sr** [Kr]$5s^2$	
		53 **I** [Kr]$5s^2 4d^{10} 5p^5$	54 **Xe** [Kr]$5s^2 4d^{10} 5p^6$ or [Xe]	55 **Cs** [Xe]$6s^1$	56 **Ba** [Xe]$6s^2$	

Figure 7–6 *This is a reconfigured version of part of the periodic table. What do the green labels above each column signify? What principle explains why many atoms form ions?*

The transition metals and inner transition metals do not form ions that follow this pattern. However, most of the representative elements follow this trend. And this gives rise to the **octet rule**—one of the most important rules in chemistry. **The octet rule states that atoms tend to gain, lose, or share electrons in order to acquire a full set of valence electrons.** The octet rule gets its name because most atoms have 8 valence electrons, or an octet, in a full set. The exceptions include hydrogen and helium, the two elements that have valence electrons in the $n = 1$ energy level. The first principal energy level is full with only 2 electrons.

The atoms with a full set of valence electrons are the noble gases, so students sometimes think of the octet rule as the "noble gas rule." But no matter what it is called, the octet rule helps to explain why a chlorine atom—or an atom of any element in Group 7A—gains 1 electron to become an anion with a 1– charge. And it helps to explain why a sodium atom—or an atom of any element in Group 1A—loses 1 electron to become a cation with a 1+ charge. What kind of ions do you expect from the elements in Group 6A? From the elements in Group 2A?

Figure 7–7 *In music, an octet is a group of eight musicians. Why are octets important in chemistry? What is the octet rule?*

Figure 7–8 *American chemist Gilbert Lewis (left) created what we now call Lewis dot diagrams and Lewis structures.*

Lewis Dot Diagrams

As you may already have concluded, an atom's valence electrons are the stars in the drama of chemical bonding. The atom's inner electrons—the noble gas inner core—do not form bonds. For this reason, when chemists describe chemical bonds and reactions, they focus their attention on the atoms' valence, or outer, electrons only.

One popular way to emphasize an atom's valence electrons was developed by American chemist Gilbert Lewis (1875–1946). Lewis developed what we now call Lewis dot diagrams or electron dot diagrams. In these diagrams, valence electrons are represented as dots placed around the element symbol. Small x's or o's can also be used instead of dots.

In atoms with more than 1 valence electron, the dots are placed alone or in pairs around the element symbol. Traditionally, the dots are written along the sides of an imaginary box, and no more than two dots are placed on any side of the box. Figure 7–9 illustrates the Lewis dot diagram for several common elements. Lewis dot diagrams are a fast and simple way to represent valence electrons, which is why they are so popular with chemists. You will see and use Lewis dot diagrams in this chapter and throughout your study of chemistry.

Chemists also use Lewis dot diagrams to illustrate how electrons rearrange during chemical reactions. For example, the reaction between sodium and chlorine to produce sodium chloride can be represented this way:

Figure 7–9 *This table shows the electron configurations and Lewis dot diagrams for elements in the second and third periods. How is an atom's Lewis dot diagram related to its group in the periodic table?*

Lewis Dot Diagrams for Elements in Periods 2 and 3

Element	Electron Configuration	Lewis Dot Diagram	Element	Electron Configuration	Lewis Dot Diagram
Li	$[He]2s^1$	Li·	Na	$[Ne]3s^1$	Na·
Be	$[He]2s^2$	·Be·	Mg	$[Ne]3s^2$	·Mg·
B	$[He]2s^22p^1$	·Ḃ·	Al	$[Ne]3s^23p^1$	·Ȧl·
C	$[He]2s^22p^2$	·Ċ·	Si	$[Ne]3s^23p^2$	·Ṡi·
N	$[He]2s^22p^3$	·Ṅ:	P	$[Ne]3s^23p^3$	·Ṗ:
O	$[He]2s^22p^4$	:Ȯ:	S	$[Ne]3s^23p^4$	:Ṡ:
F	$[He]2s^22p^5$	·F̈:	Cl	$[Ne]3s^23p^5$	·C̈l:
Ne	$[He]2s^22p^6$	:N̈e:	Ar	$[Ne]3s^23p^6$	:Är:

$$\text{Na} \cdot \quad \cdot \ddot{\underset{\cdot\cdot}{\text{Cl}}} : \quad \longrightarrow \quad \text{Na} \cdot \overset{\frown}{} \cdot \ddot{\underset{\cdot\cdot}{\text{Cl}}} : \quad \longrightarrow \quad \text{Na}^+ \quad : \ddot{\underset{\cdot\cdot}{\text{Cl}}} :^- \quad \textbf{(Eq. 1)}$$

The diagram above shows that 1 electron is transferred from a sodium atom to a chlorine atom, changing both atoms into ions. Notice that the chloride ion is drawn with 8 dots around it and the sodium ion is drawn with no dots around it. Is the octet rule satisfied for each ion?

Types of Ions

The ions you have seen so far in this chapter are each formed from 1 atom. Such ions are called **monatomic ions,** or "one-atom" ions (the prefix *mono-* means one). Other common ions are formed from a group of atoms. These ions are called **polyatomic ions** (the prefix *poly-* means many). A polyatomic ion is an ion made from more than 1 atom.

MONATOMIC CATIONS. The table in Figure 7–10 lists several monatomic cations. These cations have the same name as the element. For example, Na^+ is a sodium ion and Mg^{2+} is a magnesium ion. Notice that the elements of Group 1A—which includes lithium, sodium, and potassium—each form monatomic cations with a charge of 1+. These elements need to lose only 1 electron to reach the electron configuration of the nearest noble gas. The elements of Group 2A—which includes beryllium, magnesium, and calcium—form monatomic cations with a 2+ charge. These elements need to lose 2 electrons to reach the electron configuration of the nearest noble gas.

Some elements commonly form more than one kind of cation. These elements include the transition metals, which do not follow the octet rule in forming cations. Iron, for example, can form cations with charges of 2+ or 3+. To distinguish the different cations of a transition metal, chemists add Roman numerals to the element name. Thus, Fe^{2+} is named iron(II) and Fe^{3+} is named iron(III). These names are read as "iron two" and "iron three." What do you call a Cu^+ cation? A Cu^{2+} cation?

Figure 7–10 *This table lists several common cations. Where in the periodic table do you find atoms that form more than one kind of cation?*

Some Common Cations

1+		2+		3+	
H^+	hydrogen	Mg^{2+}	magnesium	Al^{3+}	aluminum
Na^+	sodium	Fe^{2+}	iron(II)	Fe^{3+}	iron(III)
K^+	potassium	Co^{2+}	cobalt(II)	Co^{3+}	cobalt(III)
NH_4^+	ammonium	Ni^{2+}	nickel(II)	Ni^{3+}	nickel(III)
Li^+	lithium	Ca^{2+}	calcium		
Ag^+	silver	Zn^{2+}	zinc		
Cu^+	copper(I)	Cu^{2+}	copper(II)		

Some Common Anions

	1–			2–	3–	
F^-	fluoride	ClO^-	hypochlorite	O^{2-} oxide	N^{3-}	nitride
Cl^-	chloride	NO_3^-	nitrate	S^{2-} sulfide	P^{3-}	phosphide
Br^-	bromide	HCO_3^-	bicarbonate (or	SO_4^{2-} sulfate	PO_4^{3-}	phosphate
I^-	iodide		hydrogen carbonate)	CO_3^{2-} carbonate		
OH^-	hydroxide	$C_2H_3O_2^-$	acetate			

Figure 7–11   This table lists several monatomic and polyatomic anions. Why do nonmetals form anions more readily than do metals?

Visit our Web site at
http://www.phschool.com
to support your
study of chemistry.

MONATOMIC ANIONS   The table in Figure 7–11 lists several common monatomic anions. Nonmetals, the elements on the right side of the periodic table, form anions most easily. Notice that the elements in Group 7A—which includes fluorine, chlorine, bromine, and iodine—form monatomic anions with a 1– charge. These elements need to gain 1 electron to reach the electron configuration of the nearest noble gas. What kinds of anions are formed by the elements of Group 6A?

To name a monatomic anion, you need to replace the suffix of the element name with the suffix *-ide*. For example, a chlorine atom becomes a chloride ion, and an oxygen atom becomes an oxide ion. Unfortunately, there is no rule to tell you exactly how to add the *-ide* ending! But with practice, you will begin to recognize the correct names of the common monatomic anions.

POLYATOMIC IONS   The tables in Figures 7–10 and 7–11 also include several polyatomic ions, or ions that consist of more than 1 atom. For example, a sulfate ion consists of 4 oxygen atoms and 1 sulfur atom, and it has an overall charge of 2–. The atoms that make up polyatomic ions are bonded together by covalent bonds. (You will learn more about covalent bonds in the next section.) But as a unit, a polyatomic ion forms an ionic bond with an ion of the opposite charge.

Binary Ionic Compounds

Almost any combination of cations and anions can form an ionic compound. The simplest of these compounds are the **binary ionic compounds,** which contain the ions of only two elements. To name a binary ionic compound, simply write the name of the cation followed by the name of the anion. For example, the binary ionic compound made from calcium cations and fluoride anions is called calcium fluoride. The compound made from magnesium cations and oxygen anions is called magnesium oxide.

A compound's name, however, does not provide you all the information you might want to know about the compound. For example, earlier in this section you learned that sodium and chloride ions are found in a 1:1 ratio in a crystal of sodium chloride. But in what ratio are the ions found in calcium fluoride? In magnesium oxide? In lithium oxide? The names of these compounds do not directly indicate the ratio of the ions.

To denote the ratio of ions in a compound, chemists use an **empirical formula.** For ionic compounds, the empirical formula is called the chemical formula, or just formula for short. An empirical formula uses element symbols to indicate the atoms or ions in a compound, with subscripts added to indicate their ratios. For example, aluminum oxide has the formula Al_2O_3, which indicates that the compound contains 2 aluminum ions for every 3 oxide ions. The formula for lithium oxide is Li_2O, which indicates that 2 lithium ions are present for every 1 oxide ion. Notice that when element symbols are written without a subscript, a subscript of 1 is assumed.

As you can see from these examples, not all ionic compounds have ions that are present in a 1:1 ratio. Why not? The reason is that all ionic compounds are electrically neutral. For example, calcium forms an ion with a 2+ charge and fluorine forms an ion with a 1− charge, so 2 fluoride ions are needed to balance the electrical charge of 1 calcium ion. Therefore, the formula for calcium fluoride is CaF_2.

You are now ready to learn a simple method of writing the formulas for binary ionic compounds, a method that is popularly called the crisscross method. To use the crisscross method, first write the element symbols for the cation and for the anion, with the cation to the left of the anion. Then, write each ion's charge as a superscript. Now criss-cross the two charges, moving them diagonally downward from one ion's superscript to the other ion's subscript.

Let's use the crisscross method to write a formula that you already know, the formula for calcium fluoride. The calcium ion has a charge of 2+ and the fluoride ion has a charge of 1−, so begin by writing $Ca^{2+}F^{1-}$. Then diagonally criss-cross the charges—without the plus and minus signs—to produce the formula:

$$Ca^{2+}F^{1-} \longrightarrow Ca^{2+}F^{1-} \longrightarrow Ca_1F_2$$

This is close to the correct formula: Remember that formulas do not include the number 1 as a subscript. The actual formula for calcium fluoride is CaF_2.

Sometimes the crisscross method gives a ratio that is not in the smallest whole numbers. In such a case, the formula needs to be simplified. For example, here is what the crisscross method gives for the formula for magnesium oxide:

$$Mg^{2+}O^{2-} \longrightarrow Mg^{2+}O^{2-} \longrightarrow Mg_2O_2$$

However, the formula Mg_2O_2 should be simplified to just MgO. Remember that formulas for ionic compounds usually give the smallest whole-number ratio of the ions.

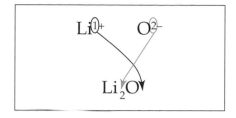

Figure 7–12 *You can write the formula for a binary ionic compound, such as lithium oxide, by criss-crossing the ions' charges. What is the formula for aluminum oxide?*

Figure 7–13 *Old-fashioned flash bulbs, such as the ones shown here, used magnesium oxide. What is the formula for magnesium oxide?*

You can also use the crisscross method for compounds that include polyatomic ions, such as calcium nitrate and aluminum sulfate. However, when you add a subscript to a polyatomic ion, you must remember to put parentheses around the ion. For example, calcium nitrate has the formula $Ca(NO_3)_2$, and aluminum nitrate has the formula $Al(NO_3)_3$.

Correctly writing the formulas for ionic compounds takes practice. The following problems will give you a good start.

SAMPLE PROBLEM 1

What is the formula for (a) potassium phosphide (b) aluminum sulfate?

STRATEGY	SOLUTION
1. **Analyze**	The problem specifies two ionic compounds. The names and charges of the ions are listed in Figures 7–10 and 7–11.
2. **Plan**	Use the crisscross method. Remember that an ionic compound must be electrically neutral.
3. **Solve**	(a) The potassium ion is K^+ and the phosphide ion is P^{3-}. Use the crisscross method to write the formula $$K^{1+}P^{3-} \rightarrow K_3P$$
	(b) The aluminum ion is Al^{3+} and the polyatomic sulfate ion is SO_4^{2-}. Use the crisscross method to write the formula. Remember to add parentheses around the sulfate ion when you add its subscript. $$Al^{3+}SO_4^{2-} \rightarrow Al_2(SO_4)_3$$
4. **Evaluate**	Both formulas must specify electrically neutral compounds. For $Al_2(SO_4)_3$, each aluminum ion has a charge of $3+$ and $2 \times 3+ = 6+$. Each sulfate ion has a charge of $2-$ and $3 \times 2- = 6-$. The formula's net charge is 0. The net charge of K_3P is also 0. So, both formulas are reasonable.

PRACTICE PROBLEMS

1. What is the formula for (a) potassium nitride (b) aluminum sulfide? *(Answer: (a) K_3N (b) Al_2S_3)*

2. What is the formula for (a) calcium nitrate (b) calcium sulfate? *(Answers: (a) $Ca(NO_3)_2$ (b) $CaSO_4$)*

All About Salt

Salt—sodium chloride—has always been a valued mineral, mainly because it adds flavor to food and helps to preserve perishable food. In ancient Rome, salt was so valuable that soldiers were often paid in salt. The Latin word for such a payment is *salarium*, from which the English word salary was derived.

Today, salt is inexpensive and plentiful. Underground salt deposits have been found all over the world, and salt is mined from many of them. In the United States, the largest salt deposits are found near the Great Lakes, in western Kansas and Oklahoma, and along the coast of the Gulf of Mexico. Salt can also be evaporated from seawater or from other salt-containing water. One company harvests salt from the Great Salt Lake in Utah.

Salt is vital to the diet of almost every animal, including humans. The body depends on sodium and chloride ions for many purposes, including the transmission of impulses in the nervous system. However, the danger for most people lies in taking in too much salt, not too little. A high-salt diet has been linked with high blood pressure and other medical problems.

Is the salt you buy at the grocery store pure, 100 percent sodium chloride? Usually it is not. Manufacturers typically add other ionic compounds to salt to keep it from clumping together. These compounds, called free-flowing agents, include magnesium carbonate, cal-

cium carbonate, and calcium silicate. Each is colorless, tasteless, odorless—and quite harmless in small quantities. Also, most salt on the market today is iodized salt, or salt to which small amounts of potassium iodide or sodium iodide have been added. The thyroid gland uses iodide ions to make thyroxine, an important hormone.

Open a dictionary and read the definition for salt. Then look for words or phrases that include the term salt or that are derived from the same origins as salt. (Many such words begin with the prefix *sal-*) From the dictionary alone, what can you conclude about how humans have valued salt over the years?

7–1 Section Review

1. What is an ionic bond?

2. State the octet rule. Use the octet rule to describe the reaction between elemental chlorine and sodium.

3. Describe the crisscross method of writing formulas for binary ionic compounds. What extra step must be added for a polyatomic ion?

4. **Critical Thinking—Interpreting diagrams** Nancy wants to model a crystal of magnesium bromide. She decides to copy Figure 7–2, labeling the gray globes Mg^{2+} and the green globes Br^-. Will Nancy produce an accurate model? Explain.

Guide for Reading

- What is a covalent bond?
- What is the difference between a polar and a nonpolar covalent bond?

7–2 Covalent Bonding

As you learned earlier in this chapter, ionic compounds are characterized by high melting points, brittleness, and in many cases, solubility in water. However, our world is full of substances that have none of these properties. Cork, hair, perfume, rubber, fabrics, chewing gum—none of these is a brittle substance with a high melting point. Can you name other substances that do not have the properties of ionic compounds?

The bonds between the atoms in the materials just mentioned are not ionic. Rather, these bonds are covalent bonds; they arise from electrons that are shared, not transferred, between atoms. **A covalent bond is formed by a shared pair of electrons between two atoms.** Covalent bonds are found in a long list of common substances—including paper, plastic, plant matter, and every tissue in the human body!

Molecules and Their Formulas

A group of atoms that are united by covalent bonds is called a **molecule,** and a substance that is made of molecules is called a **molecular substance.** Molecules may contain as few as 2 atoms or as many as a thousand or even a million atoms! Examples of molecules that contain only 2 atoms include molecular oxygen, a gas that travels through your bloodstream, and carbon monoxide, a poisonous gas found in automobile exhaust. Much larger molecules include DNA, the molecule that encodes genetic information in all forms of life, and artificially made compounds such as polyethylene, a plastic used to make garbage bags and other products. As you will learn as you read on, molecules can have

Figure 7–14 *Paper can be easily colored, cut, and folded. These properties are put to attractive use in the Japanese art of origami. What kind of bonds unite the atoms in the molecules of a sheet of paper?*

$C_{12}H_{22}O_{11}$

Figure 7–15 *Sucrose, or table sugar, is an important molecule for humans. Sugar cane is a profitable crop in tropical climates.*

an enormous variety of sizes, shapes, and physical and chemical properties.

To describe the composition of a molecular compound, chemists often use a **molecular formula.** A molecular formula tells you how many atoms are in a single molecule of the compound. For example, the molecular formula for molecular oxygen is O_2, which tells you that this molecule contains 2 oxygen atoms. The molecular formula for sucrose, or ordinary table sugar, is $C_{12}H_{22}O_{11}$. This formula indicates that a sucrose molecule contains 12 carbon atoms, 22 hydrogen atoms, and 11 oxygen atoms.

You can also write an empirical formula for a molecule. Recall that an empirical formula lists the atoms' ratios, or relative numbers in a compound. For example, the molecular formula for glucose, a simple type of sugar, is $C_6H_{12}O_6$. In a molecule of glucose, the carbon, hydrogen, and oxygen atoms are present in a 1:2:1 ratio, so the empirical formula for glucose is CH_2O. A molecule of lactic acid, a product of the digestion of milk, has the molecular formula $C_3H_6O_3$. What is the empirical formula for this molecule?

As the previous examples illustrate, different compounds can have the same empirical formula. In fact, different compounds may have the same molecular formula. (Glucose is part of a whole family of sugars, for example, in which each member has the molecular formula $C_6H_{12}O_6$.) In part for this reason, chemists often depict molecules with a **structural formula.** A structural formula specifies which atoms are bonded to each other in a molecule.

There are several different kinds of structural formulas, but the ones used in this chapter are called **Lewis structures.** The

$$:\overset{\displaystyle ..}{\underset{\displaystyle ..}{F}}\!\!:\!\!\overset{\displaystyle ..}{\underset{\displaystyle ..}{F}}:$$

Figure 7–16 *This diagram is the Lewis dot formula for molecular fluorine (F_2). The circled dots signify the electrons in a single bond.*

Figure 7–17 *Ammonia is often used in cleaning solutions. Is the octet rule satisfied for each atom in the ammonia molecule?*

Lewis structure for molecules is based on the Lewis dot diagrams for atoms. Figure 7–16 shows you the Lewis structure for a very simple molecule—molecular fluorine (F_2). As before, the dots placed around the element symbol represent the atom's valence electrons. But in addition, the dots placed between the two element symbols represent the electrons in a covalent bond. Sometimes you will see these dots circled, as they are in Figure 7–16. The Lewis structure for molecular fluorine tells you that the molecule contains 2 fluorine atoms joined by a single covalent bond.

Describing Covalent Bonds

The principle that describes covalent bonding is the octet rule—the same principle that describes ionic bonding. Consider again the covalent bond in molecular fluorine (F_2). The electron configuration for fluorine is $[He]2s^2 2p^5$, so a fluorine atom has 7 valence electrons. From the octet rule, you know that a fluorine atom is most stable with an additional valence electron. So in order to satisfy the octet rule, each fluorine atom in molecular fluorine shares 1 electron with the other fluorine atom. The result is a shared pair of electrons, or a covalent bond. Look closely at the illustration in Figure 7–16. Is the octet rule satisfied for both fluorine atoms?

Let's draw the Lewis structure for a more complicated compound, ammonia, which has the molecular formula NH_3. The first step is to draw the Lewis dot diagrams for each atom. From their electron configurations and their groups in the periodic table, you know that a nitrogen atom has 5 valence electrons and a hydrogen atom has 1 valence electron. To keep track of the individual electrons, we will represent the hydrogen atom's electrons with red dots and the nitrogen atom's electrons with blue dots:

$$H\cdot \quad H\cdot \quad H\cdot \qquad \cdot\overset{\displaystyle ..}{N}\cdot$$

As unbonded atoms, neither the hydrogen atoms nor the nitrogen atom satisfy the octet rule. However, the octet rule is satisfied for each atom when each hydrogen atom forms a covalent bond with the nitrogen atom, as shown below:

$$H:\overset{\displaystyle ..}{N}:H$$
$$H$$

This is the Lewis structure for ammonia. Notice that 2 of nitrogen's valence electrons are not shared in bonds. These two electrons are called an **unshared pair.** The unshared pair and the 3 shared pairs, or covalent bonds, provide the nitrogen atom with a total of 8 valence electrons, which satisfies the octet rule.

The octet rule is also satisfied for each hydrogen atom. Why does a hydrogen atom need only 2 electrons to satisfy the octet rule?

Multiple Bonds

Until now, you have only seen examples of **single covalent bonds**—or single bonds, for short. In a single bond, 2 atoms share exactly one pair of electrons. However, 2 atoms may also form a multiple bond, or a bond that is made of more than one pair of shared electrons. A **double covalent bond**—or double bond—consists of two pairs of shared electrons. A **triple covalent bond**—or triple bond—consists of three pairs of shared electrons. Let's take a closer look at each kind of multiple bond.

DOUBLE BONDS Formaldehyde, which has a molecular formula of H_2CO, is an example of a molecule that contains a double bond. Formaldehyde was once a familiar substance to biology students because it was used to preserve specimens. Today, biologists typically use less toxic preservatives. Here are the Lewis dot diagrams for the component atoms of formaldehyde and the Lewis structure for the molecule:

$$H \cdot \quad H \cdot \quad \cdot \overset{\cdot}{\underset{\cdot}{C}} \cdot \quad \cdot \overset{\cdot \cdot}{\underset{\cdot \cdot}{O}} : \quad \longrightarrow \quad H : \overset{}{\underset{H}{C}} : : \overset{\cdot \cdot}{O} : \qquad \textbf{(Eq. 4)}$$

In the Lewis structure, notice that a total of 4 dots are written between the carbon atom and the oxygen atom. This signifies a double bond, or 2 pairs of shared electrons.

Is the octet rule satisfied around every atom in formaldehyde? The answer is yes. Two electrons surround each hydrogen atom, and 8 electrons surround both the carbon atom and the oxygen atom. Remember that the carbon atom and the oxygen atom share the 4 electrons in a double bond, so these electrons count as part of the octet for both atoms.

TRIPLE BONDS Ethyne, which has a molecular formula of C_2H_2, is an example of a molecule that contains a triple bond. Ethyne is also known as acetylene. Ethyne is a common fuel for the flame of welding torches, as shown in Figure 7–18. Here are the Lewis dot diagrams for the component atoms of ethyne and the Lewis structure for the ethyne molecule:

$$H \cdot \quad \cdot \overset{\cdot}{\underset{\cdot}{C}} \cdot \quad \cdot \overset{\cdot}{\underset{\cdot}{C}} \cdot \quad \cdot H \quad \longrightarrow \quad H : C : : : C : H \quad \textbf{(Eq. 5)}$$

In this Lewis structure, the total of 6 dots between the carbon atoms denotes a triple bond, or three shared electron pairs. Each carbon atom in ethyne satisfies the octet rule because each is surrounded by 8 valence electrons. Again, the 6 electrons in the triple bond count as part of the octet for both carbon atoms.

At this point in the discussion, you may expect to see examples of quadruple bonds (4 shared pairs of electrons), quintuple bonds (5 shared pairs of electrons), and so forth. However, under all but the most unusual circumstances, 2 atoms can share at most three pairs of electrons between them. In other words, you commonly see single, double, and triple bonds in natural compounds, but not bonds of any higher multiple.

INTEGRATING
BIOLOGY

Do today's biologists use formaldehyde to preserve specimens?

Figure 7–18 *Ethyne, also known as acetylene, is used as a fuel in welding torches. What kind of bond unites the carbon atoms in ethyne?*

Dots or Dashes?

The Lewis structures that you have seen so far use a pair of dots to represent a covalent bond. Another kind of Lewis structure uses dashes to represent covalent bonds. Using dashes, here are the Lewis structures for the three molecules we just discussed:

$$H-\overset{\cdot\cdot}{N}-H \qquad\qquad H-C=\overset{\cdot\cdot}{\underset{\cdot\cdot}{O}}: \qquad\qquad H-C\equiv C-H$$
$$\hspace{0.8em}|\hspace{6em}|$$
$$\hspace{0.8em}H\hspace{6em}H$$

ammonia   formaldehyde   ethyne

In these formulas, a single dash represents a single bond, a double dash represents a double bond, and a triple dash represents a triple bond. Dots are used only to represent valence electrons that are not involved in bonds, such as the unshared pairs on the nitrogen atom in ammonia and on the oxygen atom in formaldehyde.

For the ammonia molecule, the Lewis structure tells you that 1 nitrogen atom forms single bonds with each of 3 hydrogen atoms. The nitrogen atom also has an unshared pair of electrons. What does the Lewis structure for formaldehyde tell you about the formaldehyde molecule? What does the Lewis structure for ethyne tell you about the ethyne molecule?

Lewis structures that use dashes are a simple, easy way to write structural formulas. You will see them in this section and in many of the upcoming chapters in this textbook.

Exceptions to the Octet Rule

Although the octet rule can be used to predict the structural formulas for millions of molecules, there are exceptions. This probably comes as no surprise to you, as you are learning that even in chemistry there often are exceptions to the rules!

ATOMS WITH LESS THAN AN OCTET Many compounds of boron do not follow the octet rule. An example is boron trifluoride (BF_3).

$$:\overset{\cdot\cdot}{\underset{\cdot\cdot}{F}}:$$
$$|$$
$$B$$
$$:\overset{\cdot\cdot}{\underset{\cdot\cdot}{F}}\qquad\overset{\cdot\cdot}{\underset{\cdot\cdot}{F}}:$$

In the structure above, only 6 valence electrons surround the boron atom.

ATOMS WITH MORE THAN AN OCTET Some atoms that are found beyond the second row of the periodic table—most notably phosphorus and sulfur—sometimes form bonds that give them more than an octet of electrons. The additional electrons fill the $3d$ orbitals of these atoms. An example is the sulfur atom in the molecule SF_4. This molecule has the following Lewis structure:

$$:\ddot{F}-\overset{\cdot\cdot}{S}-\ddot{F}:$$
$$:\underset{\cdot\cdot}{\ddot{F}}: \quad :\underset{\cdot\cdot}{\ddot{F}}:$$

Count the valence electrons around the sulfur atom. You will see that there are 10 of them, 2 more than an octet.

MOLECULES WITH AN ODD NUMBER OF ELECTRONS A molecule that has an odd number of electrons cannot follow the octet rule. For example, nitrogen monoxide (NO) has a total of 11 valence electrons. From some carefully run experiments, chemists know that the "odd" electron is usually on the nitrogen atom:

$$\cdot\ddot{N}\cdot \quad + \quad \cdot\ddot{O}: \quad \longrightarrow \quad \cdot\dot{N}=\ddot{O}: \qquad \textbf{(Eq. 6)}$$

The nitrogen atom in this molecule does not have an octet. As a result, nitrogen monoxide is an unstable molecule; it is short-lived and very reactive. Nevertheless, nitrogen monoxide can be found in nature. In fact, it is a vital messenger molecule in the human body.

Properties of Covalent Bonds

As you have learned, a covalent bond is a shared pair of electrons between 2 atoms. But do atoms share these electrons equally? No, not necessarily. Different atoms can have different electronegativities. As you learned in Chapter 5, electronegativity is a measure of an atom's attraction for electrons in a chemical bond. When atoms with different electronegativities form a covalent bond, the shared electrons are more strongly attracted to the atom that is more electronegative. The table in Figure 7–19 lists the electronegativies of several atoms.

When one atom is significantly more electronegative than another, a covalent bond between them is said to be **polar.** In a polar covalent bond, the atom with greater electronegativity gains a slight negative charge because it has a slight excess of electron density. At the same time, electron density is lost from the atom with lower electronegativity, and that atom gains a slight positive charge.

The diagram in Figure 7–20 on page 242 illustrates a polar bond between a hydrogen atom and an oxygen atom in a molecule of water. Because an oxygen atom is more electronegative than a hydrogen atom, the electron pair that forms the bond between them is pulled closer to the oxygen atom. As a result, the oxygen atom in a water molecule has a slight negative charge, and the hydrogen atom has a slight positive charge.

Electronegativities of Representative Elements	
Element	**Eletronegativity**
Fluorine	4.0
Oxygen	3.5
Chlorine	3.0
Nitrogen	3.0
Bromine	2.8
Carbon	2.5
Sulfur	2.5
Hydrogen	2.1
Phosphorus	2.1
Boron	2.0
Cobalt	1.9
Copper	1.9
Nickel	1.9
Iron	1.8
Silicon	1.8
Aluminum	1.5
Magnesium	1.2
Calcium	1.0
Lithium	1.0
Sodium	0.9
Potassium	0.8

Figure 7–19 *This table lists the electronegativities of many elements. When two atoms form a bond, what do their electronegativities indicate about the bond?*

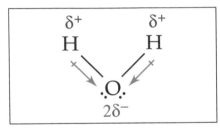

Figure 7–20 *In a molecule of water, each oxygen-hydrogen bond is a polar bond, or a bond in which the electrons are shared unevenly between the atoms. What do both the arrows and the delta symbols (δ+, δ−) indicate?*

In mathematics, a quantity having a magnitude as well as a direction is called a vector quantity. Velocity is an example of a vector quantity. A car that is travelling at 80 km/hr southward is said to have a speed of 80 km/hr and a velocity of 80 km/hr south. Bond polarity is also a vector quantity. Its magnitude depends on the electronegativity difference between the bonding atoms. Its direction is along the line joining the two atoms.

To signify these slight charges, which are also called partial charges, chemists use the Greek delta (δ). The symbol δ+ signifies a partial positive charge, and the symbol δ− signifies a partial negative charge. In addition, chemists sometimes use arrows to signify a charge shift between bonding atoms. Both ways of showing partial charges are illustrated for you in Figure 7–20.

Can you think of a covalent bond that is not polar? You are right if you chose a bond between 2 atoms that have similar or equal electronegativities. In such a bond, both atoms exert an approximately equal pull on the electrons in the bond. This kind of bond is called a **nonpolar** covalent bond. The best examples of nonpolar bonds are found between atoms of the same element, such as the single bond between two fluorine atoms in molecular fluorine (F–F) or the triple bond between two nitrogen atoms in molecular nitrogen ($N \equiv N$). In each of these molecules, electrons are shared equally between the atoms.

The three different types of bonds that you have learned about so far—ionic bonds, polar covalent bonds, and nonpolar covalent bonds—actually form a spectrum of bond types. At one end of the spectrum are ionic bonds, in which electrons are transferred from one atom to another. At the other end of the spectrum are the nonpolar covalent bonds, in which electrons are shared equally between 2 atoms. Polar covalent bonds are found between these two extremes.

You can use electronegativity to predict whether a bond will be nonpolar, polar, or ionic. If the electronegativity difference between two atoms is 0.4 or less, chemists generally consider the bond between the atoms to be nonpolar. If the electronegativity difference is 2.0 or greater, the bond is generally considered to be very polar, or ionic. Between these extremes, the greater the difference in electronegativity, the more polar the bond. These categories are summarized for you in the table in Figure 7–21.

Figure 7–21 *If you know the electronegativities of the atoms in a bond, you can use this table to predict the bond's polarity. What kind of bond forms between a hydrogen atom and a bromine atom?*

Bond Type by Electronegativity

Electronegativity Difference	Bond Type
≤ 0.4	nonpolar covalent
between 0.4 and 2.0	polar covalent
≥ 2.0	ionic

I Dream of Benzene

$$
\text{H}-\text{C}=\text{C}=\text{C}-\overset{\displaystyle \overset{\text{H}}{|}}{\text{C}}=\text{C}=\overset{\displaystyle \overset{\text{H}}{|}}{\text{C}}-\text{H}
$$

$$
\text{H}-\overset{\displaystyle \overset{\text{H}}{|}}{\text{C}}=\overset{\displaystyle \overset{\text{H}}{|}}{\text{C}}-\text{C}=\text{C}=\text{C}=\text{C}-\text{H}
$$

$$
\text{H}-\text{C}\equiv\text{C}-\text{C}=\text{C}-\text{C}=\text{C}-\text{H}
$$

Imagine that the year is 1865 and you are the German chemist August Kekulé (1829–1896). You have been working hard to determine the structural formula for benzene, a compound that was first isolated 40 years ago. You know that the molecular formula for benzene is C_6H_6. However, none of the structural formulas that you consider, such as those shown above, adequately account for benzene's properties. Some of these structures have adjacent double bonds, which make molecules especially unstable and reactive. Benzene is stable and nonreactive. You doubt that any of the structures shown above represents a benzene molecule.

One night you have an interesting dream. You dream about a snake that is whirling and twisting in front of you. Suddenly the snake swallows its own tail, forming a circle. When you wake up, you believe that your dream told you something important about benzene's structure.

Developing Models

1. How do you think Kekulé's dream applies to the structure of benzene? What does the "snake circle" represent?

2. From the information presented in the problem, hypothesize the structural formula for benzene. Remember that the octet rule must be satisfied for each atom.

3. Describe the bonds between carbon atoms in the benzene molecule. Are they single, double, or triple covalent bonds?

7–2 Section Review

1. Describe a covalent bond.

2. What is a molecule? What does a molecule's structural formula indicate?

3. How does a polar covalent bond differ from a nonpolar covalent bond? Which type of bond is found in molecular oxygen (O_2)? In carbon monoxide (CO)?

4. **Theme Trace—Scale and Structure** Dinitrogen monoxide is also called nitrous oxide or laughing gas. This compound was once a popular dental anesthetic, but is now mainly used to relax patients. Write the molecular formula and the structural formula for dinitrogen monoxide. Does the structure that you drew satisfy the octet rule for each atom?

Guide for Reading

- How do chemists name compounds?
- How are ionic compounds, molecular compounds, and acids named?

7–3 Naming Chemical Compounds

Can you remember the name of every student in your class? How about every student in your school? Trying to remember even 30 or 40 names is not always easy. So, imagine memorizing the names of all the chemical compounds! Chemists have identified millions of compounds, and the number of imaginable compounds is almost limitless.

Fortunately, you do not need to memorize the names of these compounds—and neither does any other chemistry student or chemist. Why not? The answer is that chemists have developed a system of naming compounds, a system based on a series of logical rules and principles. **Chemists name a compound according to the atoms and bonds that compose it.**

In this section, you will begin to learn the rules for naming compounds. Let's start with the simplest rules—the rules for naming ionic compounds.

Naming Ionic Compounds

As you learned earlier in this chapter, the name of an ionic compound is determined by the names of its component ions. For example, KI is called potassium iodide, and $MgCl_2$ is called magnesium chloride. Notice that the name of the cation comes first, just as the cation is listed first in the formula.

Sometimes you must study a formula carefully to figure out its name. For example, what would you call $Cu(NO_3)_2$? From

Figure 7–22 *Imagine how long it would take you to memorize the names of everyone in this photograph! Fortunately, naming chemical compounds is much easier. Compounds are named with a system of logical rules.*

the formula and from the tables of common ions in Figures 7–10 and 7–11, you know that the cation is copper and the polyatomic anion is nitrate. But a copper cation can exist with a charge of either 1+ or 2+. What is the correct charge on the copper ion in this case? The answer lies with the nitrate ion. Nitrate has a charge of 1− and the formula specifies 2 nitrate ions for every 1 copper ion. So the charge on the copper ion must be 2+. (Remember that the formula must have a net charge of 0.) Thus the name of $Cu(NO_3)_2$ is copper(II) nitrate. What is the name of the compound with the formula $CuNO_3$? With the formula $FeCl_2$?

To practice naming ionic compounds, try the following problems:

YOU AND YOUR WORLD

Rust

When iron atoms in steel react with oxygen in the air, the result is the compound iron(III) oxide, the principal component of rust. Iron(III) oxide is very stable, which explains why rust does not readily change back to steel and oxygen.

Can you write the formula for iron(III) oxide?

SAMPLE PROBLEM 2

Name the compound with the formula $Fe(OH)_3$

STRATEGY	SOLUTION
1. Analyze	The name of an ionic compound comes from the ions in its formula. However, the transition metal iron (Fe) can form ions with different charges.
2. Plan	Figures 7–10 and 7–11 list the names and charges of many common ions. For iron, choose the ion that gives the compound a net 0 charge.
3. Solve	Iron can exist as iron(II) or iron(III). Because the formula indicates 3 hydroxide (OH^-) ions, which together give a charge of 3−, the iron ion must have a charge of 3+. The compound is named iron(III) hydroxide.
4. Evaluate	Look again at the formula $Fe(OH)_3$. If the iron ion has a charge of 3+, the formula specifies a neutral compound. You also can use the crisscross method to write the formula for the compound formed from Fe^{3+} and OH^- ions: $$Fe^{3+}OH^- \rightarrow Fe(OH)_3$$

PRACTICE PROBLEMS

3. Write the names of the following ionic compounds: (a) KNO_3 (b) NH_4Br (c) $Ca(OH)_2$ *(Answers: (a) potassium nitrate (b) ammonium bromide (c) calcium hydroxide)*

4. Write the names of the following ionic compounds: (a) $CuSO_4$ (b) Cu_2O (c) Al_2S_3 *(Answers: (a) copper(II) sulfate (b) copper(I) oxide (c) aluminum sulfide)*

Figure 7–23 *Anhydrous copper(II) sulfate is nearly colorless. But as a hydrate, it acquires a bright blue color.*

I**NTEGRATING**

B**IOLOGY**

Where does carbon dioxide come from?

Figure 7–24 *Now is a good time to learn these numerical prefixes. What is the name of the molecule with the formula N_2O_3?*

Numerical Prefixes

mono-	1
di-	2
tri-	3
tetra-	4
penta-	5
hexa-	6
hepta-	7
octa-	8
nona-	9
deca-	10

Hydrates

Ionic compounds that absorb water into their solid structures form substances called **hydrates.** Hydrates typically have properties different from **anhydrous substances,** which are water-free substances. For example, anhydrous copper(II) sulfate is nearly colorless. When it absorbs water, however, it becomes bright blue, as you can see in Figure 7–23. When copper(II) sulfate is fully hydrated, 5 water molecules (H_2O) are present for every copper ion, and the formula is written $CuSO_4 \cdot 5\ H_2O$. Notice that the formula includes a dot to separate the water molecules from the rest of the compound.

Because the properties of an ionic compound depend on whether or not it is hydrated, the name of the compound must reflect the degree of hydration. The name for $CuSO_4 \cdot 5\ H_2O$ is copper(II) sulfate pentahydrate. The prefix *penta-* means five. Other prefixes used to show the degree of hydration are listed in the table in Figure 7–24. For example, $MgSO_4 \cdot 7\ H_2O$ is magnesium sulphate heptahydrate.

Naming Molecular Compounds

The rules for naming binary molecular compounds are similar to those for naming ionic compounds. However, the names of molecular compounds include prefixes that indicate the number of atoms in the molecule. The prefixes are the same ones as those listed in the table in Figure 7–24.

According to these rules, the molecule with the formula CO_2 is named carbon dioxide. The prefix *di-* means two; this molecule contains 2 oxygen atoms. Carbon dioxide is one of the end products of animal metabolism. You exhale molecules of carbon dioxide with every breath. A very different molecular compound consists of carbon bonded to 4 chlorine atoms, or CCl_4. This compound is named carbon tetrachloride. The prefix *tetra-* means four; this molecule contains 4 chlorine atoms. Chemists often use carbon tetrachloride to dissolve other compounds, and it was once used in cleaning solutions.

Notice that in both these examples the suffix *-ide* is added to the name of the more electronegative element. Also, the more electronegative element is usually written last in both the name and the formula for these compounds. These rules are similar to those followed in naming ionic compounds.

Before you begin the following Sample Problem and Practice Problems, you need to be aware of a few exceptions to the rules you have just learned. First, the prefix *mono-* is usually not written with the first word of a compound's name. The compound CO_2 is called carbon dioxide, not monocarbon dioxide. Second, prefixes are sometimes shortened to make a name easier to say.

Thus, the compound CO is called carbon monoxide, not "carbon monooxide." And third, chemists use common names other than the formal names for some compounds. The oxygen in our atmosphere exists as molecules of O_2, so perhaps we should call this substance "dioxygen." However, this name is rarely used. Instead, this molecule is called diatomic oxygen, molecular oxygen, or often just oxygen, for short. In addition, the compound NH_3 is so important in chemistry that it is called by its common name—ammonia. And although H_2O might be called "dihydrogen monoxide," even the most formal chemists do not use this name. English-speakers everywhere recognize H_2O as water!

SAMPLE PROBLEM 3

Name the following molecular substances: (a) N_2O_4 (b) PCl_5.

STRATEGY	SOLUTION
1. Analyze	Naming molecular compounds is similar to naming ionic compounds, but prefixes are added to denote the relative numbers of each atom.
2. Plan	Consult the table of prefixes in Figure 7–24 and the rules given in the chapter for naming molecular compounds.
3. Solve	(a) The prefix for 2 is *di-* and the prefix for 4 is *tetra* . The name tetraoxide should be shortened to tetroxide to make it easier to pronounce. N_2O_4 is named dinitrogen tetroxide. (b) The prefix for 1 is *mono-*, but the name of a compound usually does not begin with the *mono-* prefix. PCl_5 is named phosphorus pentachloride.
4. Evaluate	For both (a) and (b), the molecular formula and name of the compound specify the same kinds of atoms and numbers of atoms.

Figure 7–25 *Carbon dioxide is an invisible, odorless gas that is exhaled by animals, including chimpanzees (top). Water, another small molecule, is Earth's most common liquid (bottom).*

PRACTICE PROBLEMS

5. Name the following molecular substances: (a) NO_2 (b) BF_3.
   (Answers: (a) nitrogen dioxide (b) boron trifluoride)

6. Name the following molecular substances: (a) NF_3 (b) P_2O_5.
   (Answers: (a) nitrogen trifluoride (b) diphosphorus pentoxide)

Acids

Acids are a very important group of compounds. If you look around your home, you can find products that contain a variety of different acids. Acids are found in aspirin, antiseptics, and solutions to clean contact lenses. Fruits such as oranges, apples, grapes, and lemons contain acids, as do carbonated beverages, vinegar, and tea. Many vitamins, including Vitamin C and some of the B vitamins, are acids. Other acids are found in batteries, dyes, and paints. You will learn more about these and other acids in Unit 7.

An acid can be defined in various ways. For now, we will use one simple definition: An acid is a molecular substance that dissolves in water to produce hydrogen ions (H^+). Although acids are molecular compounds, in water they behave somewhat like ionic compounds because they separate into a cation and an anion. The cation is always H^+, and the anion depends on the particular acid. For example, when the acid with the formula HCl dissolves in water, it yields H^+ cations and Cl^- anions. When the acid with the formula HNO_3 dissolves in water, it yields H^+ cations and NO_3^- anions.

Most acids, such as the ones just discussed, produce a characteristic anion when they dissolve in water. As a result, the name

Figure 7–26 *Both plants and animals produce acids. Citric acid is a mild acid found in many fruits, including oranges (left and center). A much stronger acid— hydrochloric acid—is produced in the walls of the stomach (right). Hydrochloric acid in the stomach helps to break down proteins.*

Concept Mastery

Discuss each of the following in a brief paragraph.

19. What is the octet rule? Why is it important?

20. Why are many elements more stable as ions than they are as atoms?

21. Define and compare cations, anions, monatomic ions, and polyatomic ions.

22. Describe single, double, and triple covalent bonds.

23. Explain the difference between copper(I) nitrate and copper(II) nitrate. What do the Roman numerals signify in these names?

24. What is an acid? How are acids similar to ionic compounds?

25. Why are some covalent bonds polar and others nonpolar?

26. Tying it Together Draw Lewis structures for sodium chloride, water, and hydrochloric acid. Identify the bond type in each *structure*. Is the octet rule satisfied for each atom or ion?

Critical Thinking and Problem Solving

Use the skills you have developed in this chapter to answer each of the following.

27. Making comparisons How do ionic bonds and ionic substances differ from covalent bonds and molecules?

28. Applying concepts Determine the formulas for the following compounds.
(a) silver nitrate
(b) magnesium hydroxide
(c) carbon tetrachloride
(d) sulfuric acid
(e) lead(II) acetate
(f) iron(III) nitrate

29. Drawing conclusions A compound called acetone has the molecular formula C_3H_6O. A chemistry student has isolated a compound that has this same formula. Is this compound acetone? Explain.

30. Applying concepts Draw Lewis dot diagrams for the following elements:
(a) carbon   (d) sulfur
(b) hydrogen   (e) magnesium
(c) potassium   (f) iodine

31. Making comparisons Compare empirical, molecular, and structural formulas. Under what circumstances is each type of formula most useful?

32. Developing models Draw Lewis structures for each of the following compounds. Identify each bond as polar or nonpolar.
(a) H_2O (d) HCN
(b) CO_2 (e) NCl_3
(c) Cl_2 (f) N_2

33. Drawing conclusions Ozone has the molecular formula O_3. Does ozone contain nonpolar, polar, or ionic bonds?

34. Applying concepts Determine the name of each of the following compounds:
(a) Sb_2S_3 (d) H_2CO_3
(b) FeS   (e) $SiO_2 \cdot 8\ H_2O$
(c) Na_2O (f) $CaSO_4 \cdot 2\ H_2O$

35. Using the writing process Prepare a poster that presents the rules for naming ionic compounds and for naming molecular compounds. Include examples of both kinds of compounds and include some compounds that are exceptions to the rules, such as water and ammonia.

8 Molecular Shape

Can you describe water? The task is not so simple! You might describe water as a wet, shapeless liquid. But water can also exist as an invisible gas, which is called water vapor. And in its solid form, water can be opaque and hard, like a block of ice— or it can be powdery and delicate, like a snowflake.

Water takes on many different shapes and forms in the macroscopic world. But in the microscopic world of atoms and molecules, water is much easier to describe. In this chapter, you will learn the shape of a water molecule and other small molecules, and you will see how a molecule's shape helps to determine its properties. By the time you are finished, you may never look at a block of ice in the same way again!

This beautiful ice palace of a Minnesota winter could become the cooling water of a New York City summer. To understand the properties of water, you need to understand its molecular shape.

Chem Journal

YOU AND YOUR WORLD
Think of three animals that have distinctive or unusual body shapes. For each of these animals, describe how its body shape helps it to live in its environment.

8–1 The Shape of Small Molecules

Guide for Reading
- What is the VSEPR theory?
- What are some common shapes of small molecules?

When you were younger, did you ever play with building blocks? Or with plastic beads? Or with track for a model railroad? If so, then you know that part of the fun of such toys is putting the pieces together in different ways. From the same set of blocks, you could build a model of a house, an animal, or a skyscraper. From the same set of beads, you could make a necklace, a bracelet, or decoration for a jacket. And even fifty pieces of track can form a huge number of layouts for a model railroad.

Part of the fun of chemistry also comes from putting different pieces together. And as you know by now, the "pieces" that chemists study are the atoms of the different elements, atoms that bond together to form different molecules. In Chapter 7, you learned about the various kinds of bonds that atoms can form. Now you are ready to learn more about how bonds are arranged in a molecule, arrangements that determine a molecule's shape. You may discover that you enjoy building models of molecules just as much as you enjoyed building with blocks many years ago.

Figure 8–1 *You can combine a large number of snap-together blocks to model almost anything, including a smiling dinosaur. Similarly, atoms combine to form an almost infinite number of molecules.*

H—N̈—H
|
H

Figure 8–2 *From the structural formula for ammonia, you might conclude that an ammonia molecule has a T-shape. Is this correct?*

Figure 8–3 *Chemists use ball-and-stick models (right) to indicate molecular shape. A molecule of ammonia has the shape of an easel with a triangular base, similar to the easel this artist is using (left).*

Molecular Geometry

Figure 8–2 shows you the structural formula for ammonia (NH_3). The structural formula tells you that an ammonia molecule contains 1 nitrogen atom that forms single bonds with each of 3 hydrogen atoms. It also tells you that the nitrogen atom has one unshared pair of electrons, or a pair of valence electrons that is not involved in a chemical bond.

Although the structural formula for ammonia provides considerable information, it does not indicate the shape of an ammonia molecule. This is because a structural formula only identifies the bonds in a molecule. It does not provide direct information about how those bonds are arranged in space. So, when you look at the structural formula for ammonia, you should not conclude that the atoms are arranged in a T-shape, with the hydrogen atoms placed on the left, right, and bottom sides of a nitrogen atom. The actual shape of an ammonia molecule is quite different!

Instead of using structural formulas, chemists often indicate molecular shape with what are popularly called **ball-and-stick models.** In these models, a ball represents an atom's nucleus and inner-level electrons. The balls are connected either with straight sticks, which represent single bonds, or with curved springs, which represent multiple bonds.

Figure 8–3 shows you the ball-and-stick model for ammonia. Notice that this model is three-dimensional. The 4 atoms in an ammonia molecule are arranged in a three-dimensional shape that resembles an easel with a triangular base, just like the one the artist is using in the photograph. You will learn more about the shape of ammonia as you read on in this section.

Figures 8–4, 8–5, and 8–7 show ball-and-stick models for other small molecules. Some of these molecules have a linear shape, which means that the centers of their atoms fall in a straight line. Others have a triangular shape. Still others have the shape of pyramids or other three-dimensional shapes. Very soon, we will discuss each of these shapes individually. But first, you should notice one thing that these shapes have in common: Each of these shapes is symmetrical. That is, the bonds and atoms are arranged in a regular pattern, with equal distances separating the atoms that are not bonded to each other.

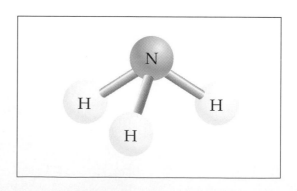

Why are the atoms in many small molecules arranged symmetrically? The answer has to do with the forces that arrange valence electrons around atoms. When atoms combine to form molecules, their valence electrons are usually found in pairs. A pair of valence electrons may be shared between 2 atoms, forming a chemical bond. Or the pair may be found on 1 atom only, which is called an unshared pair. But whether a valence electron pair is in a bond or is unshared, it will repel other valence electron pairs because of similar electrical charges.

This repulsion force between electron pairs gives rise to the **valence-shell electron pair repulsion theory,** or VSEPR theory, for short. (The letters in VSEPR are the first letters of the words in the theory's name.) **The VSEPR theory states that in a small molecule, the pairs of valence electrons are arranged as far apart from each other as possible.** The VSEPR theory—like other theories in science—does not apply in all circumstances. Molecules that contain transition metals, for example, are found in a variety of asymmetrical shapes that often do not follow from the VSEPR theory. However, the VSEPR theory does explain a wide variety of molecular shapes. Let's take a close look at the five most common of them.

LINEAR In a linear molecule, the atoms can be connected in a straight line. Clearly, all molecules that contain only 2 atoms, such as molecular oxygen (O_2) and hydrochloric acid (HCl), are linear. But many molecules that contain 3 atoms are also linear. Figure 8–4 shows a ball-and-stick model for a very common linear molecule: carbon dioxide (CO_2). In this model, each pair of springs represents a double bond, or two pairs of valence electrons, between the carbon atom and an oxygen atom. As VSEPR theory predicts, these pairs of valence electrons are arranged to be as far apart from each other as possible. Thus, the molecule has a linear shape.

Another way to discuss the way bonds are arranged is to look at the **bond angles** that they form. A bond angle is simply the geometric angle between two adjacent bonds. When the angle between two bonds is a straight line, as it is in carbon dioxide, the bond angle is 180°.

CHEMISTRY IN ACTION

YOU AND YOUR WORLD

Smelling Shapes

How does your nose distinguish one smell from another? Part of the answer lies with molecular shape. Researchers have identified molecules with similar shapes that have the same smell, and molecules with different shapes that have different smells.

From this evidence, can you suggest a hypothesis about the smell receptors in your nose? How could this hypothesis be tested?

Figure 8–4 *Carbon dioxide (CO_2) has a linear shape, similar to a section of a lane divider in a swimming pool.*

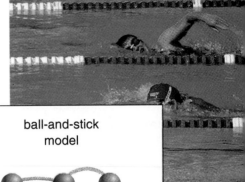

molecular formula	structural formula	molecular shape	ball-and-stick model
CO_2	$:\ddot{O}=C=\ddot{O}:$	O=C=O 180°	

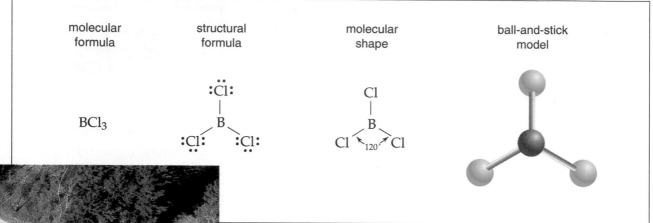

molecular formula	structural formula	molecular shape	ball-and-stick model

BCl_3

Figure 8–5 *Boron trichloride (BCl_3) has a trigonal planar shape. Its three bonds form a "Y" shape, or the shape of a fork in the road.*

TRIGONAL PLANAR   The word trigonal means triangular, and the word planar means flat. (A plane can be any flat surface.) Therefore, a molecule that is trigonal planar has a triangular, flat shape. Figure 8–5 shows a ball-and-stick model for one trigonal planar molecule, boron trichloride (BCl_3). As with the ball-and-stick model for ammonia, each stick represents a single bond, or pair of valence electrons. Again, these pairs of valence electrons are arranged to be as far apart from each other as possible. This arrangement places the 3 chlorine atoms in the shape of an equilateral triangle, or a triangle that has three sides of the same length. The bond angle between any two boron-chlorine bonds is 120°.

In general, a trigonal planar molecule has a central atom that is bonded to three other atoms, and the central atom has no unshaired pairs of electrons. Notice that the trigonal planar shape is different from the three-dimensional, pyramidal shape of ammonia. You will learn more about this difference as you read on.

TETRAHEDRAL   The prefix *tetra-* signifies the number 4 and the suffix *-hedral* refers to a surface. Thus, a tetrahedron is a shape that has four surfaces. One molecule that has a tetrahedral shape is methane (CH_4). Methane is the principal component of natural gas and is an important fuel. You will learn more about methane and other compounds of carbon and hydrogen atoms in Chapter 25.

The ball-and-stick model for a methane molecule is shown in Figure 8–7. In this model, the four sticks represent the four single bonds, or pairs of valence electrons, between the carbon atom and the hydrogen atoms. As before, these pairs of valence electrons are arranged to be as far apart from each other as possible, an arrangement that places the 4 hydrogen atoms of methane in the shape of a tetrahedron.

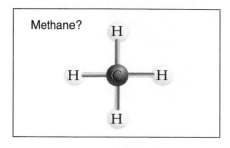

*I*NTEGRATING

*E*ARTH *S*CIENCE

What is the principal component of natural gas?

Figure 8–6 *Does this ball-and-stick model illustrate the correct shape of methane? Why or why not?*

Methane?

258

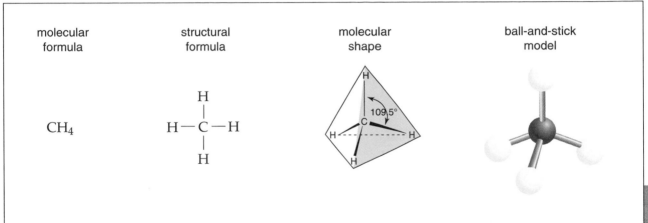

| molecular formula | structural formula | molecular shape | ball-and-stick model |

CH_4

H—C—H with H above and H below (structural formula)

109.5°

Figure 8–7 *The four carbon-hydrogen bonds of methane are arranged in a tetrahedral pattern. A surveyor's tripod has a similar shape.*

You may be wondering why the hydrogen atoms of methane do not fit into the shape of a square, as shown in Figure 8–6. The answer is that pairs of valence electrons can be arranged in three dimensions, not just two dimensions! In the other small molecules you have seen, the pairs of valence electrons only needed two dimensions to best separate from each other. However, if methane had a two-dimensional, square shape, the angle between any two bonds would be 90°. By arranging pairs of valence electrons in three dimensions, the bonds in methane can separate farther away from each other. As illustrated in Figure 8–7, the angle between any two bonds in an actual molecule of methane is 109.5°. This is the characteristic bond angle of the tetrahedral shape.

PYRAMIDAL   What is a pyramid? Outside of chemistry, the term pyramid describes a variety of three-dimensional shapes with triangular sides. Some pyramids have three sides and a triangular base, like a tetrahedron, and others have four sides and a rectangular base, like the pyramid that you see on the back of a one-dollar bill. However, we will use the terms pyramid and pyramidal to describe a specific shape, not just any pyramid.

As you learned earlier, one example of a molecule with a pyramidal shape is ammonia (NH_3). The ball-and-stick model for an ammonia molecule is shown in Figure 8–8 on page 260. In this model, the three sticks represent single bonds, or pairs of valence electrons, between the nitrogen atom and hydrogen atoms. However, remember that the nitrogen atom has a fourth pair of valence electrons around it. This is an unshared pair, or a pair of valence electrons that is not involved in a bond.

If all pairs of valence electrons repelled each other equally, then a molecule of ammonia would have the same tetrahedral

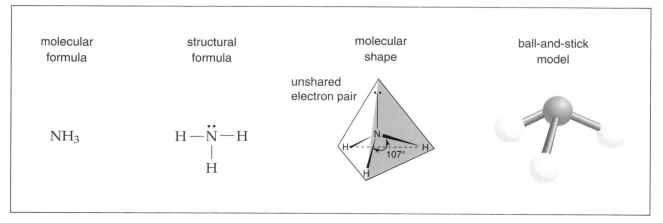

| molecular formula | structural formula | molecular shape | ball-and-stick model |

NH_3

H—N̈—H
|
H

unshared electron pair

N

107°

Figure 8–8 *Like BCl_3, an ammonia molecule contains three bonds. But the nitrogen atom in ammonia has an unshared pair of electrons, which gives it a pyramidal shape. How does this differ from methane's shape?*

shape as a molecule of methane. However, unshared pairs exert a greater repulsion force—they take up "more room" around an atom—because they are held by 1 atom's nucleus only. As a result, the angle between the nitrogen-hydrogen bonds in ammonia is 107°, which is slightly less than the bond angle in a tetrahedral molecule.

In general, a pyramidal molecule has a central atom that is bonded to 3 other atoms and has an unshared pair of valence electrons. (To be specific, chemists sometimes describe this shape as trigonal pyramidal. The word trigonal means three-sided.) In what ways is a pyramidal shape similar to a tetrahedral shape? In what ways is it different?

BENT Of all the molecular shapes you are studying in this chapter, perhaps none is more important than the shape of a molecule of water (H_2O). At first glance, you may be tempted to think that water has a linear shape, like carbon dioxide. Indeed, chemists of 100 years ago suspected this to be the case. The evidence, however, shows that a water molecule is not linear. Rather, a water molecule has a bent shape, as shown in Figure 8–9. The bond angle in water—the angle between the two oxygen-hydrogen bonds—is 105°.

To understand this shape, take a look at the pairs of valence electrons around the central atom of the molecule—the oxygen atom. How many pairs of valence electrons surround this atom? You are correct if you counted four pairs: two pairs that form the single bonds to hydrogen atoms and two unshared pairs. If these electron pairs were arranged as far apart from each other as possible, then the bond angle in water would be 109.5°, as are the bond angles in methane. However, just like the unshared pair around the nitrogen atom in ammonia, the two unshared pairs around the oxygen atom exert a greater repulsion force

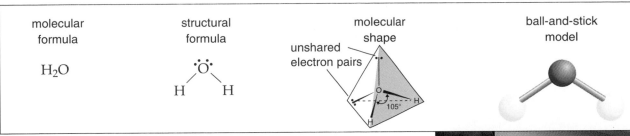

molecular formula	structural formula	molecular shape	ball-and-stick model
H_2O		unshared electron pairs	

Figure 8–9 *The bent shape of a water molecule is similar to the shape of the chevron insignia on this cadet's uniform. Why does a water molecule have this shape?*

than do the two electron pairs in the bonds. As a result, the 2 hydrogen atoms in a water molecule are separated by a slightly smaller angle than they would be in a tetrahedral or pyramidal molecule.

The bent shape of a water molecule is very significant! This shape is the key to understanding many of water's important properties. You will learn why this is so in the next section.

A few small molecules have other shapes, and some of these shapes are shown in Figure 8–10. However, the five shapes you have just studied—linear, trigonal planar, tetrahedral, pyramidal, and bent—are by far the most common. You can use these shapes and the VSEPR theory to identify the shapes of many different compounds. Try solving the problems on the next page.

Figure 8–10 *Small molecules can take on a variety of interesting shapes. How many sides does an octahedron have?*

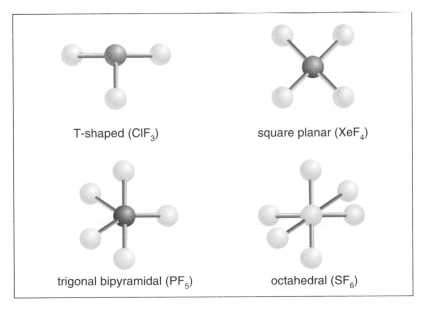

T-shaped (ClF_3)

square planar (XeF_4)

trigonal bipyramidal (PF_5)

octahedral (SF_6)

SAMPLE PROBLEM 1

Describe the shapes and approximate bond angles of the following molecules:

$$H-C\equiv C-H$$
(a) ethyne

$$H-\overset{\overset{\displaystyle O}{\|}}{C}-H$$
(b) formaldehyde

$$Cl-\overset{\overset{\displaystyle Cl}{|}}{\underset{\displaystyle\cdot\cdot}{N}}-Cl$$
(c) nitrogen trichloride

STRATEGY	SOLUTION
1. **Analyze**	The problem provides structural formulas for each molecule. However, a molecule's shape differs from the shape of its structural formula.
2. **Plan**	Use the VSEPR theory, which explains how pairs of valence electrons are arranged in small molecules. For each molecule focus on the central atom or atoms.
3. **Solve**	(a) In ethyne, the valence electrons around each carbon atom form two bonds. By the VSEPR theory, these bonds are arranged as far apart from each other as possible, forming a linear molecule. Both bond angles in ethyne are 180°. (b) In formaldehyde, the valence electrons around the carbon atom form three bonds. By the VSEPR theory, these bonds form a trigonal planar molecule. Each bond angle in formaldehyde is close to 120°. (c) In nitrogen trichloride, the valence electrons around the nitrogen atom form three bonds and one unshared pair. By the VSEPR theory, this molecule is pyramidal. The bond angles are approximately 107°.
4. **Evaluate**	Review the examples given in the chapter for linear, trigonal planar, and pyramidal molecules. For each molecule in this problem and the appropriate example in the chapter, the valence electrons form similar bonds and unshared pairs.

Hybrid Orbitals

Remember from Chapter 4 that an atom's electrons occupy specific orbitals, which are called atomic orbitals. Atomic orbitals have names such as the 1s orbital, the 2s orbital, the 2p orbital, and so on. But atomic orbitals usually apply only to the electrons in an unbonded atom. As a rule, they do not explain the electrons in the bonds of a molecule.

When an atom approaches another atom to form a bond, the orbitals of its electrons may be perturbed, or changed. To describe this process, chemists suggest that the atom's atomic orbitals mix together, forming **hybrid orbitals.** An atom's hybrid orbitals have a combination of the properties of the atomic orbitals that formed them. (The word hybrid comes from biology. A hybrid variety of corn, for example, is a cross between two different types of corn plant.)

INTEGRATING

BIOLOGY

What does the term hybrid mean?

Hybrid Orbital	Geometry	Examples
sp	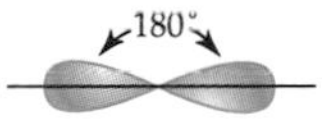 180° linear	BeF_2
sp²	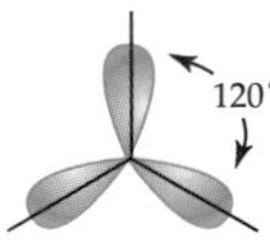 120° trigonal planar	BCl_3
sp³	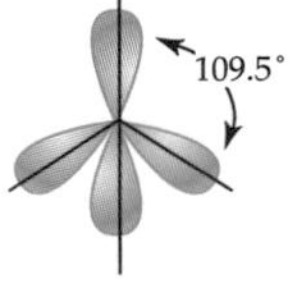 109.5° tetrahedral	CH_4

Figure 8–11 *Hybrid orbitals are another way to define molecular shape. Can you think of examples other than those listed here for sp, sp², and sp³ hybridization?*

CHEM Activity

Balloon Orbitals

1. Inflate two pear-shaped latex balloons. Use string to tie the balloons together at their ends. Sketch the two balloons.
2. Inflate a third balloon. Tie its end to the ends of the other balloons. Sketch the result.
3. Add a fourth balloon to the collection. Sketch the result.

Are the shapes of small molecules similar to the shapes of joined balloons? Why or why not?

Many hybrid orbitals are possible, but three important kinds are illustrated for you in Figure 8–11. In a linear molecule, such as beryllium fluoride, the two orbitals around the central atom form from mixing an s orbital and a p orbital. These orbitals are called sp orbitals. In a trigonal planar molecule, the three orbitals around the central atom form from mixing an s orbital and two p orbitals. These orbitals are called sp^2 orbitals. And when an atom has 4 pairs of valence electrons surrounding it, and none of these electrons is in a multiple bond, four hybrid orbitals form from mixing an s orbital and three p orbitals. These orbitals are called sp^3 orbitals. Figure 8–11 shows you the sp^3 orbitals in a tetrahedral molecule, in which all four orbitals are separated from each other by the same angle. However, the central atoms in pyramidal and bent molecules also have sp^3 orbitals. Can you explain why?

Hybrid orbitals are often used to categorize molecular shape. What kind of hybrid orbitals are in a molecule of boron trichloride (BCl_3)? In a molecule of methane (CH_4)? In a molecule of water (H_2O)?

Bond Length

In the ball-and-stick models that you see in this chapter, the sticks have been drawn to the same length. In real molecules, however, different pairs of atoms form bonds of different length. The bond lengths for a number of covalent bonds are shown in Figure 8–12. Notice that these bond lengths are extremely small. The bond length in a molecule of diatomic hydrogen (H_2) is 0.075 nanometer, which is smaller than the wavelength of visible light.

You should be aware of two important trends in bond length, both of which you can discover from the table in Figure 8–12. First, as you move down a group of the periodic table, the atoms form longer bonds. For example, in the halogen family (Group 7A), a bond between 2 fluorine atoms is shorter than a bond

Figure 8–12 *What trends can you find in the bond lengths between atoms?*

Average Bond Lengths

Bond	Distance (nm)	Bond	Distance (nm)
H—H	0.075	C—O	0.143
C—H	0.109	C=O	0.121
F—F	0.128	C—N	0.147
Cl—Cl	0.198	C=N	0.138
Br—Br	0.228	C≡N	0.116
I—I	0.266	C—C	0.154
O=O	0.121	C=C	0.134
S=S	0.189	C≡C	0.120

$$\begin{array}{ccc} & H & \ddot{\overset{\displaystyle\cdot\,\cdot}{O}} \\ & | & \| \\ H - & C - C - & \ddot{\underset{\displaystyle\cdot\,\cdot}{O}} - H \\ & | & \\ & H & \end{array}$$

Figure 8–13 *Acetic acid is the principal component of vinegar. How does the structural formula shown here compare to an actual molecule of this compound?*

between 2 chlorine atoms, which is shorter than a bond between 2 iodine atoms. This trend makes sense because, as you learned in Chapter 5, the atoms become larger as you move down a group.

Second, multiple bonds are shorter than single bonds. Compare a single, double, and triple bond between 2 carbon atoms, and you will see that the bond length decreases from 0.154 to 0.134 to 0.120 nanometer. We can explain this decrease by looking at the electrical forces between nuclei and electrons. As you learned in earlier chapters, two nuclei repel each other because they both have positive charge. But a bond is made of electrons, which have negative charge. The more electrons in a bond, the stronger that bond attracts the positively charged nuclei of the bonding atoms. In other words, you can think of the electrons in a bond as an "electrical glue" between two nuclei, allowing the nuclei to draw closer together.

Take a look at Figure 8–13, which shows the structural formula for a molecule of acetic acid. (As you may remember from Chapter 7, acetic acid is the principal component of vinegar.) Suppose you were to assemble a ball and-stick model of this molecule, a model that accurately reflects both the structure and length of the bonds. What kinds of balls and sticks would you need?

8–1 Section Review

1. What is the VSEPR theory? How does this theory explain the shape of small molecules?

2. Describe five common shapes of small molecules. Give an example for each shape.

3. Describe two factors that influence the length of a bond. What periodic trend exists for bond length?

4. **Theme Trace—Models and Organization** Many fruits produce ethene, which helps them to ripen. The molecular formula for ethene is C_2H_4, and the 2 carbon atoms are joined by a double bond. Draw a structural formula and a ball-and-stick model for ethene. Identify the hybrid orbitals on each carbon atom and estimate the bond angles.

Guide for Reading

- What factors determine the polarity of a molecule?
- Why is water a polar molecule?

8–2 Polarity

In Chapter 7, you learned how to determine whether a bond is polar or nonpolar. In a polar bond, the electrons are shared unequally between 2 atoms. The electrons are pulled closer to the more electronegative atom, giving that atom a slight negative charge and the other atom a slight positive charge. In a nonpolar bond, the electrons are shared equally between 2 atoms, which means the bond has no positive or negative end.

Just as a bond can be polar or nonpolar, a molecule also can be polar or nonpolar. A polar molecule has one end with a positive charge and another end with a negative charge. Polar molecules are also called **dipoles** (the prefix *di-* means two) because they have two charged ends. A molecule that does not have positive or negative ends—or that is not a dipole—is a nonpolar molecule. You will learn how to identify polar and nonpolar molecules very soon.

Being polar or nonpolar gives a molecule a variety of different properties. As shown in Figure 8–14, a collection of polar molecules will align in an electric field, whereas a collection of nonpolar molecules will not align. Polar molecules will also be attracted to a charged rod or be deflected by a magnetic field. In Figure 8–15, the blue liquid is composed of polar molecules and the red liquid is composed of nonpolar molecules.

Determining Polarity

If a molecule contains only nonpolar bonds, it will be a nonpolar molecule. For example, any molecule that is composed of only one kind of atom is a nonpolar molecule. These molecules include molecular hydrogen (H_2), molecular oxygen (O_2), ozone (O_3), and diamond (an arrangement of carbon atoms). However, a molecule that contains polar bonds is not necessarily a polar molecule! As you learned in Chapter 7, a molecule of carbon

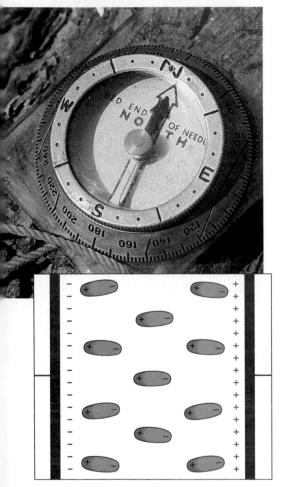

Figure 8–14 *The needle of a compass (top) aligns with the magnetic polarity of the Earth. Certain molecules also have polarity. They align in the presence of an electric field (bottom).*

Figure 8–15 *In both photographs, the rod has an electrical charge. Can you tell which liquid is polar and which is nonpolar? Explain.*

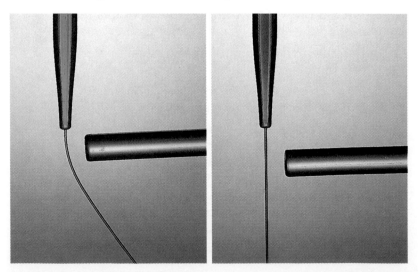

dioxide (CO_2) contains two carbon-oxygen bonds, each of which is polar. But experimental evidence shows that carbon dioxide is a nonpolar molecule.

To determine whether a molecule is polar, you need to look at more than just the polarity of its bonds. You also need to look at the shape of the molecule. **The shape of a molecule and the polarity of its bonds together determine whether the molecule is polar or nonpolar.** Let's look at the shapes and polarities of three small molecules that you have already studied: formaldehyde, carbon dioxide, and water.

FORMALDEHYDE   Figure 8–16 shows the structural formula for formaldehyde. Notice that the carbon atom in this molecule forms bonds with 3 other atoms: 1 oxygen atom and 2 hydrogen atoms. Of these atoms, which do you think most strongly attracts the electrons in its bond with the carbon atom? (Hint: See the table of electronegativities in Figure 7-19 on page 241.)

You are correct if you chose the oxygen atom. Oxygen's electronegativity is 3.5, which makes oxygen more electronegative than either carbon or hydrogen. As a result, the electrons in the carbon-oxygen bond are attracted more toward the oxygen atom. This attraction causes a shift in charge: The oxygen atom gains a partial negative charge and the carbon atom gains a partial positive charge. In Figure 8–16, this charge shift is signified by the green arrow written beside the carbon-oxygen bond.

The other bonds in the molecule are carbon-hydrogen bonds, which are not nearly as polar as the carbon-oxygen bond. Hydrogen is less electronegative than carbon, but the difference is not a large one. So, only a very small charge shift takes place in a bond between these 2 atoms. This shift is signified by the small green arrows in Figure 8–16.

Taken together, the three arrows shown in Figure 8–16 show a distinct charge shift in a molecule of formaldehyde. One end of the molecule has the center of positive charge—a point next

Figure 8–16 *Chemists use arrows to represent the polarity of a bond. By combining the arrows for each bond in a molecule, you can predict the polarity of the molecule. Formaldehyde, which once was a common preservative for biology specimens, is polar.*

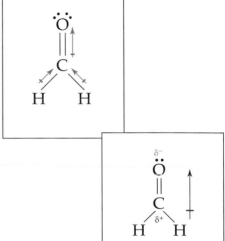

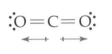

Figure 8–17 *As the green arrows indicate, both bonds in carbon dioxide are polar. But is carbon dioxide a polar molecule? Why or why not?*

to the carbon atom and between the 2 hydrogen atoms. The other end of the molecule has the center of negative charge—the oxygen atom. These separate ends of positive and negative charge mean that formaldehyde is a dipole, or a polar molecule.

Formaldehyde is an ingredient in certain embalming fluids, in antiseptics and disinfectants, and in a solution used to preserve biological specimens. Formaldehyde is toxic, however, so it is not as widely used today as it was in the past.

CARBON DIOXIDE Figure 8–17 shows the structural formula for a linear molecule, carbon dioxide (CO_2). This molecule consists of two carbon-oxygen double bonds. As you have just seen, a carbon-oxygen bond is polar. The electrons in the bond are drawn closer to the more electronegative atom—the oxygen atom—and away from the less electronegative atom—the carbon atom. In Figure 8–17, this electron shift is signified the same way it was in earlier figures, by arrows written next to the bonds.

Because carbon dioxide contains only polar bonds, you might conclude that it is a polar molecule. But this is not correct! Remember that a polar molecule has separate positive and negative ends. In a molecule of carbon dioxide, the positive charge is concentrated in the center and the negative charge is divided equally on both sides. While the electrons are not distributed evenly among the atoms of carbon dioxide, it is impossible to label one end of the molecule positive and another end negative. Therefore, carbon dioxide is a nonpolar molecule.

Another way to determine a molecule's polarity is to add together the arrows that show the polarity of its bonds. For carbon dioxide, the arrows for the two carbon-oxygen bonds cancel each other out. (In other words, they are equal in magnitude but opposite in direction.) These arrows add together to form a "zero arrow," which signifies a nonpolar molecule.

Being nonpolar gives carbon dioxide many of its important properties. Because a carbon dioxide molecule has no positive or negative end, there is little attraction between one carbon dioxide molecule and another. As a result, carbon dioxide is a gas at room temperature. You exhale carbon dioxide gas with every breath, and plants take in carbon dioxide from the atmosphere to make sugars and other compounds.

INTEGRATING
BIOLOGY

Do humans inhale or exhale carbon dioxide gas? How do plants use this gas?

Figure 8–18 *Molecules of carbon dioxide have little attraction for each other because they are nonpolar. As a result, carbon dioxide is a gas at room temperature.*

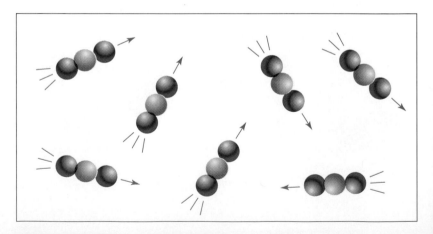

The Shape of Things to Come

One of the most recent molecular shapes to be discovered is also one of the most interesting: the shape of a soccer ball. Under specific conditions, a collection of carbon atoms can bond to form a ball-like arrangement of pentagons and hexagons. These carbon molecules are called fullerenes. Scientists have suggested that fullerenes could be used for superconductors, lubricants, parts of batteries, drug therapies, and other applications. But perhaps even more interesting than fullerenes themselves is the eccentric architect, inventor, poet, and futurist for whom these molecules are named.

R. Buckminster Fuller (1895–1983) is best known for designing the geodesic dome. The dome's interlocking pentagons or hexagons distribute stress more efficiently than any other architectural design, which makes a geodesic dome the only kind of building that has no limiting dimensions. Geodesic domes are ideal for enclosing arenas, exhibit halls,

botanical collections, and other large open spaces. Fuller himself envisioned the domes enclosing entire cities, sheltering people from disease and extremes of climate, and permitting people to live comfortably in environments as hostile as Antarctica.

In 1927, in the wake of personal tragedy and professional setbacks, Fuller decided to devote himself to improving human life through engineering and design. He was perhaps the first person to form global, long-range plans for technological and economic development. With the ultimate goal of "mak[ing] man a success in the universe," Fuller invented a self-contained, prefabricated house, a domed underwater farm, and the first streamlined car, which produced little pollution and had better gas mileage than many cars available today.

The first fullerene was identified in 1985, decades after Buckminster Fuller designed his first geodesic dome. Nature, it seemed, was imitating art!

Figure 8–19 *Both bonds in water are polar. But unlike the bonds in carbon dioxide, the bonds in water are not directly opposite each other. Therefore, water is a polar molecule.*

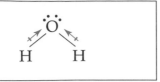

Molecules with polar bonds are nonpolar if the bond polarities add up to zero, which means that they cancel out. This happens when a molecule has polar bonds of equal magnitude that are symmetrically arranged about the central atom. When bond polarities do not cancel out, the molecule and the compound will be polar.

WATER In some ways, a molecule of water is similar to a molecule of carbon dioxide. Both molecules consist of 3 atoms that form two polar bonds. As you learned in Section 8–1, however, these molecules differ in one very important way: They have different molecular shapes. A molecule of carbon dioxide is linear; a molecule of water has a bent shape.

Figure 8–19 shows the structural formula for water in the correct shape, and it includes arrows to show the polarity of the bonds. If a water molecule had a linear shape, like carbon dioxide, the two arrows in the figure would point in opposite directions and cancel each other out. In other words, if water were a linear molecule it would be nonpolar, just like carbon dioxide. However, the bent shape of the water molecule means that the polarities of its bonds do not cancel out. Because of its bent shape, a water molecule has separate positive and negative ends: A negative end at the oxygen atom and a positive end alongside the 2 hydrogen atoms. Thus a molecule of water is polar.

Water is an extremely important molecule—as you no doubt already know. While most small molecules are gases at room temperature, water is a liquid. In fact, water is a part of almost every liquid seen on Earth, including the salt water of the ocean, the blood that circulates through your body, and the juices that fill many fruits and vegetables. It is indeed difficult to imagine life on Earth without water in its liquid state.

So why does water form a liquid? Part of the reason is that it is a polar molecule. The positive hydrogen end of one water molecule attracts the negative oxygen end of another water molecule. At room temperature, this attraction helps to loosely bind water molecules together, a loose binding that we recognize as a liquid state. If a molecule as small as water had a linear shape, it probably would be a nonpolar gas at room temperature.

Water is one of the few compounds that can be found in nature as either a solid, liquid, or gas. You will learn much more about these three states of matter in Unit 5.

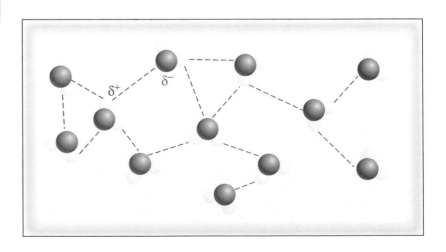

Figure 8–20 *The positive end of one water molecule attracts the negative end of another water molecule. As a result, water is a liquid at room temperature. Why is water a polar molecule?*

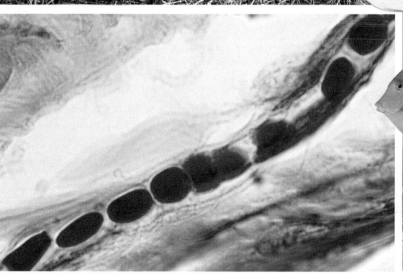

Figure 8–21 *In what ways is the water shown in these photographs different? In what ways is it the same?*

Large Molecules

As you have seen, the shape of a small molecule helps to determine the molecule's polarity. For a large molecule, however, the exact opposite is sometimes true: The polarity of a large molecule often helps to determine its shape!

One example of such a molecule is a protein. Proteins are essential to all living organisms. They help to build and repair cells, and they are important components of skin, hair, and other tissues. Proteins are extremely large and complex molecules, often containing thousands of atoms.

As you can see in Figure 8–22, a protein is composed of individual subunits linked together in a chain. Notice that some of these subunits have polar sidechains (shaded green) and others have nonpolar sidechains (shaded blue). These different polarities cause the molecule to kink and bend in a complicated pattern. As you will learn in Chapter 15, molecules with similar polarity attract each other. For a protein, these attractions tend to group the nonpolar subunits on the inside of the molecule and the polar subunits on the outside of the molecule. These attractions, along with other factors, give a protein molecule a complex, three-dimensional shape. Such shapes allow proteins and similar molecules to serve a variety of important, specialized functions.

Large molecules can have a variety of shapes—chains, rings, and even soccer balls. In 1994, one group of chemists succeeded in making a molecule of five interlocking rings, similar to the symbol for the Olympic games! But even in the largest molecule, the geometry around individual atoms is similar, if not identical, to the geometry you learned in this chapter. In chemistry, as in other sciences, you need to first study the small, simple examples in order to understand those that are more complex.

INTEGRATING
BIOLOGY

What are proteins?

Figure 8–22 *Proteins are large molecules that contain polar sidechains (shaded green) and nonpolar sidechains (shaded blue). For several reasons, including polarity, a protein bends and twists itself into a complex, three-dimensional shape, such as the shape shown in this figure.*

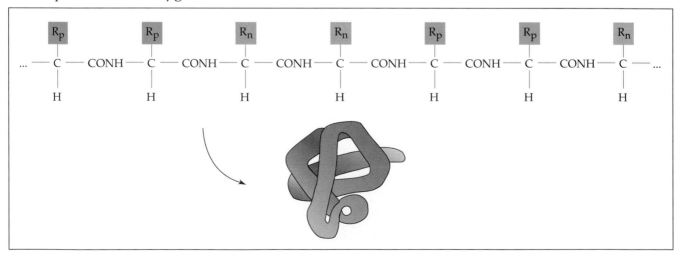

Which Is Ether?

The compound diethyl ether—or just ether, for short—was once a popular general anesthetic (or "knock-out" drug) for patients undergoing surgery. Ether is easy for doctors to administer, provides excellent muscle relaxation, and has only minimal effects on blood pressure and other vital signs. But ether can irritate respiratory passages and leaves many patients feeling nauseated after they regain consciousness. Ether is also highly flammable.

Ether has a boiling point of 35°C, which is only 10°C above normal room temperature. It does not mix well with water, but does dissolve many nonpolar compounds. The structural formula for ether is shown below:

$$\begin{array}{ccccc} H & H & & H & H \\ | & | & & | & | \\ H-C & -C & -\overset{..}{\underset{..}{O}} & -C & -C-H \\ | & | & & | & | \\ H & H & & H & H \end{array}$$

As your class discusses ether, a debate unfolds about its molecular shape. Some of your classmates say that the oxygen atom in ether is similar to the oxygen atom in water, so the bond angle between the two carbon-oxygen bonds should be 105°. Others say that ether's properties are more like the properties of a linear molecule. They say that the bond angle around the oxygen atom should be 180°.

To resolve the issue, you ask your chemistry teacher. She says that she knows the correct answer, but suggests that you discover it for yourself!

Making Predictions

1. From the information presented above and elsewhere in this chapter, predict the bond angle around the oxygen atom in a molecule of ether. Explain your prediction.

2. Why are bond angles important? How does the bond angle around the oxygen atom affect ether's properties?

3. Consult a reference book to learn the actual bond angle around the oxygen atom in a molecule of ether. Was your prediction accurate? Why or why not?

8–2 Section Review

1. What two factors determine the polarity of a molecule?

2. Why is water a polar molecule? Why does water have different properties than carbon dioxide?

3. How does polarity help to give proteins their three–dimensional shape?

4. **Connection—You and Your World** Ammonia is a common ingredient in cleaning solutions. Is ammonia a polar or nonpolar molecule? Explain your answer.

Visit our Web site at
http://www.phschool.com
to support your
study of chemistry.

Laboratory Investigation

Molecular Models

Problem

What shapes do small molecules have?

Materials (per group)

ruler	tape
scissors	sheet of notebook paper
protractor	sheet of construction paper
small balls made of modeling clay.	
one box of multicolored toothpicks	

Procedure

Part A: Methane (CH₄)

1. Select four toothpicks of different colors. Select one ball to represent a carbon atom.
2. Prepare a data table similar to the one shown. Substitute colors as necessary.
3. Stick one end of each toothpick into the ball. The toothpicks should touch each other at the center of the ball. Outside the ball, the toothpicks should be as far apart from each other as possible.
4. Measure the distance between the ends of two toothpicks. Record this distance in the appropriate column of your data table.
5. On a sheet of notebook paper, draw a straight line of the same length that you recorded in Step 4. Arrange two extra toothpicks in a triangle, with the straight line as the third side. Use the protractor to measure the angle between the two toothpicks. This angle is the same as the bond angle in your model. Record the bond angle in your data table.
6. Repeat Steps 4 and 5 for each pair of toothpicks.
7. To complete the model, attach balls to represent hydrogen atoms.

Part B: Other Molecules

1. Use balls and toothpicks to assemble models of the following molecules:
   ammonia (NH_3)
   water (H_2O)
   carbon dioxide (CO_2)
   boron trichloride (BCl_3)
   molecular oxygen (O_2)
2. Cut the construction paper into at least 10 narrow strips. The strips should fit along the lengths of the toothpicks of your models. On one side of each strip, draw an arrow pointing down the length of the strip.
3. For each model, tape a strip onto each toothpick that represents a polar bond. The arrows should point toward the negative end of the bond.

Observations

Toothpicks	red and blue	red and green	red and gray	blue and green	blue and gray	green and gray
Distance						
Bond angle						

Analysis and Conclusions

1. For methane, compare the bond angles in your model with those in the actual molecule.
2. Compare your models of methane, ammonia, and water. Should the bond angles in these models be equal? Why or why not?
3. In Part B, which are polar molecules and which are nonpolar molecules? Can a molecule with polar bonds be nonpolar?
4. **On Your Own** Use balls and toothpicks to make other molecular models.

STUDY GUIDE

Summarizing Key Concepts

8–1 The Shape of Small Molecules

- The VSEPR (valence-shell electron pair repulsion) theory states that pairs of valence electrons are arranged as far apart from each other as possible. VSEPR theory can be used to predict the shapes of a wide variety of molecules.
- The common shapes of small molecules are linear, trigonal planar, tetrahedral, pyramidal, and bent. These shapes each have characteristic bond angles.
- When an atom forms a bond, its atomic orbitals combine to form hybrid orbitals, which have a combination of the shapes and properties of atomic orbitals. Small molecules with sp orbitals are linear, those with sp^2 orbitals are trigonal planar, and those with sp^3 orbitals are tetrahedral, pyramidal, or bent.
- Atoms farther down a group of the periodic table form longer bonds. Multiple bonds are shorter than single bonds because bonds with more electrons attract the nuclei of the bonding atoms more strongly.

8–2 Polarity

- A polar molecule, or dipole, has one end with a positive charge and one end with a negative charge.
- A molecule's polarity is determined by its shape and the polarity of its bonds. A molecule that contains only nonpolar bonds is always nonpolar, whereas a molecule with polar bonds may be either polar or nonpolar.
- You can signify the polarity of a bond with an arrow. By combining the arrows for each bond, you can determine the polarity of the molecule.
- Water is a polar molecule because of its bent shape. The polarities of the two hydrogen-oxygen bonds are signified by arrows of the same magnitude, but these arrows do not point in opposite directions.
- The polarity of individual units of a large molecule, such as a protein, helps to determine the molecule's shape.

Reviewing Key Terms

Define each term in a complete sentence.

8–1 The Shape of Small Molecules

ball-and-stick model
valence-shell electron pair repulsion theory
bond angle
hybrid orbital

8–2 Polarity

dipole

CHAPTER REVIEW

Content Review

Multiple Choice
Choose the letter of the answer that best completes each statement.

1. One example of a molecule with a bent shape is
   (a) oxygen.
   (c) carbon dioxide.
   (b) nitrogen.
   (d) water.

2. An example of a nonpolar molecule is
   (a) formaldehyde.
   (c) water.
   (b) N_2.
   (d) NH_3.

3. The bond angle associated with sp^2 hybrid orbitals is
   (a) 180°.
   (c) 109°.
   (b) 120°.
   (d) 90°.

4. Which of the following types of molecules does not have sp^3 orbitals?
   (a) pyramidal
   (c) tetrahedral
   (b) bent
   (d) linear

5. Compared with shared pairs of valence electrons, unshared pairs exert
   (a) a greater repulsion force.
   (b) a lesser repulsion force.
   (c) the same repulsion force.
   (d) no repulsion force.

6. Carbon dioxide is nonpolar because it
   (a) has a pyramidal shape.
   (b) contains only nonpolar bonds.
   (c) has a linear shape.
   (d) has positive ends only.

7. A ball-and-stick model for ammonia
   (a) has a linear shape.
   (b) is the same as a structural formula.
   (c) uses four sticks.
   (d) uses three sticks.

8. The hybrid orbitals in CO_2 are
   (a) sp.
   (c) sp^3.
   (b) sp^2.
   (d) sp^4.

9. The shape of methane (CH_4) is
   (a) tetrahedral.
   (c) square.
   (b) pyramidal.
   (d) T-shaped.

10. Polar molecules tend to
    (a) attract one another.
    (b) repel one another.
    (c) have identical shapes.
    (d) be similar in size.

True or False
If the statement is true, write "true." If it is false, change the underlined word or words to make the statement true.

11. A dipole is a <u>polar</u> molecule.
12. Boron trichloride (BCl_3) is an example of a <u>trigonal planar</u> molecule.
13. Water is an example of a <u>nonpolar</u>, <u>linear</u> molecule.
14. The geometric angle between two adjacent bonds is called a(an) <u>atomic orbital</u>.
15. In a trigonal planar molecule, the orbitals around the central atom are <u>sp</u> orbitals.
16. The bond angles in a linear molecule are <u>109.5°</u>.
17. In a small molecule, the electrons' atomic orbitals combine to form <u>nuclear</u> orbitals.
18. A single bond between 2 atoms is probably <u>shorter</u> than a double bond between the same 2 atoms.

Concept Mapping
Complete the following concept map for Section 8–1. Refer to pages xviii–xix to construct a concept map for the entire chapter.

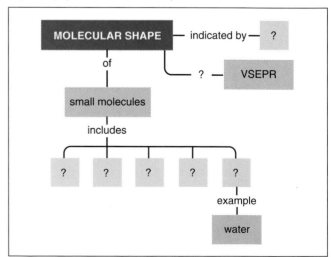

Concept Mastery

Discuss each of the following in a brief paragraph.

19. What are ball-and-stick models? Why are they useful?
20. The bond angles in NH_3 are 107° and in NH_4^+ are 109.5°. Explain this difference between bond angles.
21. What factors determine the polarity of a molecule? Explain.
22. What does each letter in VSEPR stand for? What is the VSEPR theory?
23. How does water's shape determine its properties?
24. How can drawing arrows help you decide whether a molecule is polar or nonpolar?

25. Are the following molecules polar or non-polar? Explain your answer.
    (a) Br_2 (d) SF_6
    (b) CO   (e) $BeCl_2$
    (c) OF_2 (f) IF
26. Describe two important trends in bond length.
27. **Tying it Together**   Choose 3 small molecules that have different molecular shapes. Draw ball-and-stick *models* for them. Do not choose molecules that already are modeled in this chapter.

Critical Thinking and Problem Solving

Use the skills you have developed in this chapter to answer each of the following.

28. **Interpreting diagrams** Examine the molecule below. What kind of shape does it have? Is the molecule polar or nonpolar? How can you tell?

29. **Applying concepts**   The molecules NF_3 and BF_3 have different shapes. What are the shapes of these two molecules? Why are they different?
30. **Classifying** Identify the molecular shapes of the following molecules. In which molecules do you find sp^3 hybrid orbitals?

    (a)   (b)

    (c)   (d) $O{=}C{=}O$

31. **Making comparisons** Prepare a table that names, describes, and gives at least one example of each of the five common shapes of small molecules. Use this table to briefly compare and contrast the five shapes.
32. **Making predictions** Molecules called phospholipids are found in the membranes of cells. A phospholipid contains a polar phosphate group and two long, nonpolar chains of carbon atoms and hydrogen atoms. Predict how phospholipid molecules might behave in water.
33. **Using the writing process** Describe some of the common, simple shapes that you see in the macroscopic world—either in nature or in objects that humans make. Do these shapes suit any purpose? Do you find some shapes more attractive than others? Do you see any molecular shapes reflected in the macroscopic world? You may choose to respond to these questions with a poem, short story, or essay.

Chapter

9

Chemical Reactions and Equations

Beneath the surface of the ocean in the South Pacific lies a unique structure known as the Great Barrier Reef. Within the reef can be found tunnels, caves, and deep channels in which live some of the most beautiful and fascinating animals in the world.

The reef was not built by any human architect or engineer, but by organisms known as corals. Corals grow in shallow tropical waters around the world. Through various chemical reactions, corals produce skeletons of calcium carbonate, or limestone, which makes up the huge reef.

Chemical reactions play an enormous role in your life too. Chemical reactions make it possible for your body to use the air you breathe and the food you eat. In this chapter, you will find out about chemical reactions— what they are, why they are important, how they are described and classified.

The beautiful world of a coral reef is as dependent on chemical reactions as is the human body.

9–1 The Nature of Chemical Reactions

Guide for Reading

- What are chemical reactions and why do they occur?

You probably do not give much thought to the eggs you may occasionally eat for breakfast. Nonetheless, it is likely that you would rather eat a cooked egg than a raw egg. Crack open a raw egg and you will see a runny combination of a semiliquid yolk and a gelatinous clear "goop," usually known as the white part of the egg. Drop the egg into a hot frying pan, however, and it becomes more solid, and the clear goop turns white.

Unlike a melted ice cube, which can be refrozen, a cooked egg cannot be "uncooked"—it can no longer be returned to its original form. The egg has undergone a chemical change. A **chemical reaction** caused by the act of cooking the egg produced the chemical change. **A chemical reaction is a process in which one or more substances are converted into new substances with different physical and chemical properties.** After it is cooked, the egg has different physical and chemical properties.

Figure 9–1 *The corrosion of metal, such as the copper used to make the Statue of Liberty in New York Harbor, is a chemical reaction. The formation of stalactites that hang dramatically in limestone caverns is also the result of chemical reactions.*

1. Obtain a tarnished piece of silver. Describe its characteristics.

2. Crumple a small sheet (about 20 cm × 20 cm) of aluminum foil into a ball.

3. Place the aluminum foil ball into a dishpan filled with soapy water.

4. Position the tarnished piece of silver in the dishpan so that it is underwater and touching the aluminum foil.

5. Wait about 30 minutes and observe the piece of silver.

- What happens to the piece of silver during this activity?
- Did a chemical reaction occur? How do you know?
- What must occur when silver tarnishes? When it is polished?

6. Silver will tarnish when it is exposed to air, egg white, or rubber bands. Each of these substances contains some form of sulfur. Use this information to describe what happens when silver tarnishes and what happened during this activity.

INTERNET RESOURCES

Visit our Web site at
http://www.phschool.com
to support your
study of chemistry.

Chemical Reactions

An incredible number of different chemical reactions are occurring all around you, and even inside you, all the time. The burning of gasoline, the rusting of iron, the ripening of bananas, the tarnishing of silver, and the baking of bread are all examples of chemical reactions. The process by which your body utilizes the oxygen you breathe is a chemical reaction. So, too, is photosynthesis, the food-making process in green plants. And, as we write these words, chemists throughout the world are working in laboratories to simulate or create chemical reactions with products that can be of use in medicine, agriculture, and industry.

Do these and other chemical reactions share certain characteristics? Fortunately, the answer is yes. All chemical reactions involve two types of substances: those present before the chemical reaction and those created by the chemical reaction. A substance that enters into a chemical reaction is called a **reactant.** A substance that is produced by a chemical reaction is called a **product.** A general description of a chemical reaction can thus be stated as reactants changing into products. In one such reaction, hydrogen gas reacts with chlorine gas to produce hydrogen chloride, a gas with a sharp odor. What are the reactants in this reaction? What is the product?

The Reason for Reactions

If chemical reactions are so common, why is it that so many substances do not take part in chemical reactions? Your textbook, for example, will not (we hope) enter into a chemical reaction

Figure 9–2 *You may find it hard to believe that tiny grains of wheat stored in a grain elevator can cause the amount of destruction you see here. But this devastating blast was caused by a spontaneous chemical reaction.*

Figure 9–3 *When a match is burned, it undergoes a chemical reaction. Yet an unburned match will remain unchanged indefinitely until someone strikes it. The act of striking a match creates friction, which produces heat, causing the match to ignite. It is the addition of energy, in the form of heat, that initiates this chemical reaction.*

while you are reading it, nor will your desk, chair, or most other objects that surround you. The water in a lake and the air around you may remain unchanged indefinitely without undergoing chemical reactions. In fact, had the egg described earlier not been cooked, it would not have been involved in a chemical reaction either. What then accounts for the ability of different substances to undergo certain chemical reactions?

In order to answer this question, you must think back to what you learned about atoms and bonding. The arrangement of electrons in an atom determines whether it will bond with other atoms and with which atoms it will bond. An atom with a full set of valence electrons will not bond with other atoms. But an atom with an incomplete set of valence electrons will bond. Through a chemical reaction, atoms have the opportunity to obtain a complete set of valence electrons and become more stable. During a chemical reaction, atoms can form molecules, molecules can break apart to form atoms, or molecules can react with other molecules. In any case, new substances are produced as existing bonds are broken, atoms are rearranged, and new bonds are formed.

There are other factors that determine whether or not a reaction will occur. You will learn more about these factors in later chapters, but you will begin to recognize them as you learn about chemical reactions. For example, consider what caused the chemical reaction in the egg. It was the process of cooking—a process in which heat was applied to the egg. You will learn more about the role of heat in chemical reactions in Chapter 12. As you learned in Chapter 2, heat is transferred when energy is added to a substance. The addition of energy in some form is often necessary to initiate a chemical reaction.

9–1 Section Review

1. What is a chemical reaction?
2. What is a reactant? A product?
3. Why do substances react with each other?
4. **Connection—You and Your World** Explain why burning a log in the fireplace involves a chemical reaction while sawing a log in half does not.

Guide for Reading

- How can a chemical reaction be represented?
- How does a balanced chemical equation demonstrate the law of conservation of matter?

9–2 Chemical Equations

It is important to be able to describe the details of a chemical reaction. One way of doing this is to use words. The chemical reactions we have talked about thus far were described in words. But describing a chemical reaction with words can be awkward. Many atoms may be involved and the changes may be complicated. Furthermore, different people might describe the same reaction differently. So chemists have developed a more convenient way to represent a chemical reaction. **Chemical reactions are represented by sentences known as chemical equations.** A **chemical equation** is similar to the equations you have learned in mathematics. Just as a mathematical equation describes what happens in a mathematical operation, a chemical equation describes exactly what happens in a chemical reaction. More specifically, a chemical equation identifies the reactants and products in a chemical reaction.

Word Equations

The simplest type of chemical equation is a word equation. Such equations give the names of the reactants and the names of the products. Let's consider an example. Suppose a piece of calcium reacts with, or is burned in, oxygen. To describe the reaction you could say that calcium burns in oxygen to produce calcium oxide. This reaction, which is shown in Figure 9–4, would be written as

$$\text{calcium} + \text{oxygen} \rightarrow \text{calcium oxide} \qquad \textbf{(Eq. 1)}$$

The + sign means reacts with and the → means yields, or produces. The equation would be read as calcium reacts with, or in this case burns in, oxygen to yield calcium oxide. The arrow indicates the direction of the reaction. The arrow points away from the reactants and toward the products. Calcium and oxygen are the reactants and calcium oxide is the product. So without using any chemical symbols or formulas to describe the reactants and products, we have described a chemical reaction.

Formula Equations

Chemical equations are more commonly written with chemical symbols and formulas replacing the names of the reactants and products. This type of chemical equation is called a formula equation, or simply a chemical equation. The formula equation for the burning of calcium described earlier can be written by first determining the symbols and formulas that describe the reactants and products and then substituting them into the word equation. The symbol for calcium is Ca, the formula for oxygen

Figure 9–4 *Calcium reacts with oxygen to produce calcium oxide. Notice the bright glow created by the reaction.*

gas is O_2, and the formula for calcium oxide is CaO. By replacing the words with the symbols and formulas we get

$$\text{calcium} + \text{oxygen} \rightarrow \text{calcium oxide} \quad \textbf{(Eq. 2)}$$
$$\text{Ca} + \text{O}_2 \rightarrow \text{CaO}$$

The formula equation is read in exactly the same way as the word equation—calcium reacts with, or burns in, oxygen to yield calcium oxide.

The key to writing formula equations is to be very careful to use the correct chemical symbols and formulas for the reactants and products. You may want to practice converting a few word equations to formula equations before going on.

CONSUMER TIP

Dangerously Clean

Suppose one household cleaning product makes a surface sparkle and another one disinfects the surface. Mixing the two products together will make the surface brighter and cleaner than ever, right? Wrong! Many household chemicals can react to form potentially dangerous products. One such combination is the reaction between household ammonia and liquid bleach. When these two common cleansers are combined, they react to produce a toxic gas. Manufacturers provide warnings to consumers of possible harmful reactions. Be sure you read all product labels both in the laboratory and at home.

remove contaminated clothing and wash skin thoroughly with water.
Physical and chemical hazards. Bleach contains a strong oxidizer. Always flush drains before and after use. **Do not use or mix with other household chemicals,** such as toilet bowl cleaners, rust removers, acid or products containing ammonia. To do so will release hazardous gases. Prolonged contact with metal may cause pitting or discoloration.
Storage and disposal. Store bleach in a cool, dry place. Do not reuse empty container; instead, rinse and put in trash collection.

SAMPLE PROBLEM 1

Write the formula equation for the reaction in which magnesium reacts with nitrogen to produce magnesium nitride.

STRATEGY	SOLUTION
1. Analyze	The problem provides the names of the reactants and products and asks for the formula equation.
2. Plan	You must first determine the word equation to describe the chemical reaction and then replace the names of the substances with symbols or formulas.
3. Solve	Magnesium and nitrogen are the reactants. Magnesium nitride is the product. The word equation is

magnesium + nitrogen →

magnesium nitride

The symbol for magnesium is Mg. Because atmospheric nitrogen is diatomic, its formula includes a subscript of 2. The formula for magnesium nitride is Mg_3N_2.

The formula equation is

$$Mg + N_2 \rightarrow Mg_3N_2$$

4. Evaluate	The equation correctly describes the chemical reaction in the problem.

PRACTICE PROBLEMS

1. Write the formula equation for the following reaction: Silver(I) nitrate reacts with copper to form copper(II) nitrate and silver. *(Answer: $AgNO_3 + Cu \rightarrow Cu(NO_3)_2 + Ag$)*

2. Hydrogen peroxide (H_2O_2) must be kept in an opaque container because when it is exposed to light, it decomposes to form water and oxygen. Write an equation that describes this reaction. *(Answer: $H_2O_2 \rightarrow H_2O + O_2$)*

Balancing Chemical Equations

When writing chemical equations, it is essential that you remember the law of conservation of matter, or mass. According to this law, which you learned in Chapter 2, matter is neither created nor destroyed. Because all matter has mass, this means that mass can neither be gained nor lost through a chemical reaction. Thus, the total mass of the reactants must be equal to the total mass of the products. **For mass to remain constant** before and after a chemical reaction, **the number of atoms of each element must be the same before and after a chemical reaction.** As a result, the same number of atoms of each element must appear on both sides of the arrow in a chemical equation. For example, if the reactants in a chemical equation contain 1 carbon atom, 4 hydrogen atoms, and 4 oxygen atoms, then the products will also contain 1 carbon atom, 4 hydrogen atoms, and 4 oxygen atoms. When the law of conservation of matter is observed in a chemical equation, the equation is called a **balanced chemical equation**.

Consider again the example of calcium burning to produce calcium oxide. We determined the formula equation to be $Ca + O_2 \rightarrow CaO$, as shown in Equation 2. Is this equation balanced? You are correct if you said no. The number of atoms of each element is not the same on both sides of the equation. To count the number of atoms of each element, multiply the subscript by the number to the left of the symbol or formula. If there is no number to the left of the symbol or formula, assume that it is 1. The equation is not balanced because, although there is 1 calcium atom on each side of the equation, there are 2 oxygen atoms on the reactant side and only 1 oxygen atom on the product side.

The problem now is to show that the number of atoms of each element is the same on both sides of the equation. Although it might seem tempting, one solution you should not consider is changing the subscripts in the formulas you have written for the reactants or products. If you change the subscript in a formula, you are changing the identity of the substance.

What is the correct way to balance an equation? The correct way is to use **coefficients,** or whole numbers written before the formulas for reactants and products. Let's apply this idea to the original equation. There are 2 oxygen atoms on the left but only 1 on the right. Because the oxygen molecule on the reactant side of the equation must have a subscript of 2 to maintain its identity, you must make the product side match the reactant side. To do this, place a coefficient of 2 to the left of the product.

Figure 9–5 *Here's a home cleaning tip: Vinegar added to baking soda can be used to clean a clogged drain. The cleaning action comes from the bubbles formed when the two ingredients react. In this—as in all chemical reactions—mass is conserved.*

Figure 9–6 *Chemical reactions in the body use oxygen to produce energy and give off carbon dioxide. How do you take in oxygen from the air? How do you release carbon dioxide?*

Figure 9–7 *These grapes will soon be turned into wine when microscopic fungi called yeast, which grow naturally on grape skins, convert the sugar content of grape juice into alcohol and carbon dioxide. In this chemical reaction, called fermentation, the number of atoms that enter into the reaction equals the number of atoms produced by the reaction.*

Figure 9–8 *When 2 calcium atoms combine with an oxygen molecule, the result is 2 formula units of calcium oxide. Notice that all of the atoms in the reactants also appear in the product; they are just rearranged.*

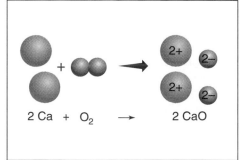

$$Ca + O_2 \rightarrow 2\,CaO \qquad \text{(Eq. 3)}$$

Now the equation has 2 oxygen atoms on the left and 2 oxygen atoms on the right. But do you notice a problem? There is now 1 calcium atom on the left and there are 2 calcium atoms on the right. To correct this inequality, do not be tempted to place the coefficient in the middle of the calcium oxide formula. Why not? Because doing so would change the formula. To balance calcium you must place a coefficient of 2 to the left of the calcium symbol on the reactant side of the equation.

$$2\,Ca + O_2 \rightarrow 2\,CaO \qquad \text{(Eq. 4)}$$

Now the chemical equation is balanced. There are 2 calcium atoms on the reactant side and 2 on the product side. And there are 2 oxygen atoms on the reactant side and 2 on the product side.

This equation was relatively simple to balance because it involved only two elements. Other equations may be a bit more complicated, but the procedure for balancing them is the same. It might be helpful for you to balance a more difficult equation in a step-by-step fashion so that you can become comfortable with the procedure. The example we will use is the combustion, or burning, of methane gas (CH_4). Methane is a component of natural gas. The combustion of methane in oxygen produces carbon dioxide and water. Follow these steps to write a balanced equation:

1. Write the word equation that describes the reaction.

$$\text{methane} + \text{oxygen} \rightarrow \text{carbon dioxide} + \text{water} \quad \text{(Eq. 5)}$$

2. Replace the words in the equation with symbols and formulas.

$$CH_4 + O_2 \rightarrow CO_2 + H_2O \qquad \text{(Eq. 6)}$$

3. Count the number of atoms of each element on both sides of the equation. The reactant side of the equation shows 1 carbon atom, 4 hydrogen atoms, and 2 oxygen atoms. The product side shows 1 carbon atom, 2 hydrogen atoms, and 3 oxygen atoms. The equation is unbalanced.

4. To balance the equation, it is usually best to begin with those elements that occur in only one substance on each side of the equation. In this example you could start with either carbon or hydrogen because each is found in one reactant and one product. Oxygen is more difficult to balance because it is found in three different substances in the equation. Let's start balancing this equation with carbon, then proceed to hydrogen, and finally to oxygen.

There is 1 carbon atom on each side of the equation, so carbon is already balanced.

$$CH_4 + O_2 \rightarrow CO_2 + H_2O \qquad \text{(Eq. 7)}$$
$$\quad\downarrow \qquad\qquad\quad \downarrow$$
$$1\,C \qquad\qquad\quad 1\,C$$

There are 4 hydrogen atoms on the reactant side and only 2 hydrogen atoms on the product side.

$$CH_4 + O_2 \rightarrow CO_2 + H_2O \qquad \textbf{(Eq. 8)}$$
$$\underset{4\,H}{} \qquad\qquad\qquad \underset{2\,H}{}$$

To balance hydrogen, place a coefficient of 2 in front of the H_2O on the product side of the equation.

$$CH_4 + O_2 \rightarrow CO_2 + 2\,H_2O \qquad \textbf{(Eq. 9)}$$
$$\underset{4\,H}{} \qquad\qquad\qquad \underset{4\,H}{}$$

There are now 4 hydrogen atoms on each side of the equation. Remember that the number of atoms is found by multiplying the subscript by the coefficient. The subscript of 2 next to the hydrogen on the product side of the equation times the coefficient of 2 gives 4 hydrogen atoms.

Now balance oxygen. You should be aware that each adjustment you make may affect elements that are already balanced. By placing a coefficient of 2 in front of the H_2O, the number of oxygen atoms was also changed. There are now 2 oxygen atoms on the reactant side of the equation and 4 oxygen atoms on the product side of the equation.

$$CH_4 + O_2 \rightarrow CO_2 + 2\,H_2O \qquad \textbf{(Eq. 10)}$$
$$\qquad \underset{2\,O}{} \quad \underset{2\,O}{} \quad \underset{2\,O}{}$$

To balance oxygen, place a coefficient of 2 in front of O_2 on the reactant side of the equation.

$$CH_4 + 2\,O_2 \rightarrow CO_2 + 2\,H_2O \qquad \textbf{(Eq. 11)}$$
$$\qquad \underset{4\,O}{} \qquad \underset{4\,O}{}$$

There are now 4 oxygen atoms on each side of the equation. Because the coefficient was placed in front of the oxygen molecule only, no other elements are affected.

5. The final step is to verify that the equation is balanced. The fully balanced equation is

$$CH_4 + 2\,O_2 \rightarrow CO_2 + 2\,H_2O \qquad \textbf{(Eq. 12)}$$

You will find that the best approach to balancing equations is primarily trial and error. You balance each kind of atom in succession and then adjust coefficients as necessary. If you are having extreme difficulty balancing a particular equation, you might need to recheck your formulas. An incorrect subscript can make an equation impossible to balance. One final note: The balanced equation should have coefficients in the lowest whole-number ratio possible. In other words, had you balanced this equation differently, you might have written

$$2\,CH_4 + 4\,O_2 \rightarrow 2\,CO_2 + 4\,H_2O \qquad \textbf{(Eq. 13)}$$

The equation is balanced, but the coefficients are not in the lowest whole-number ratio. You need to divide each coefficient by the largest common factor, which in this case is 2.

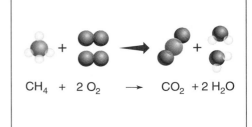

$$CH_4 + 2\,O_2 \longrightarrow CO_2 + 2\,H_2O$$

Figure 9–9 *An unbalanced equation describing the reaction between methane and oxygen would show 1 molecule of each substance.*

Figure 9–10 *Here you see a list of steps to follow in balancing a chemical equation. Why must a chemical equation be balanced?*

BALANCING EQUATIONS

1. Write a formula equation with correct symbols and formulas.

$$Na + Cl_2 \longrightarrow NaCl$$

2. Count the number of atoms of each element on each side of the arrow.

3. Balance atoms by using coefficients.

$$2\,Na + Cl_2 \longrightarrow 2\,NaCl$$

4. Check your work by counting atoms of each element.

Activity

Edible Equations

1. Gather several thin pretzel sticks and a package of candy that comes in at least three different colors.

2. Use the pretzels and candy to make models of the following chemical reactions:

$$2 \ KClO_3 \rightarrow 2 \ KCl + 3 \ O_2$$

$$U + 3 \ F_2 \rightarrow UF_6$$

3. Use your models to balance the following additional chemical reactions:

$$Cd + HCl \rightarrow CdCl_2 + H_2$$

$$CS_2 + O_2 \rightarrow CO_2 + SO_2$$

4. How do your models illustrate the law of conservation of matter?

Visit our Web site at
http://www.phschool.com
to support your
study of chemistry.

SAMPLE PROBLEM 2

Sodium phosphate (Na_3PO_4) is used to cut grease. Write a balanced equation for the reaction in which iron(II) chloride reacts with sodium phosphate to produce sodium chloride and iron(II) phosphate.

STRATEGY	SOLUTION
1. Analyze	The names of reactants and products are given. The balanced equation will have the same number of atoms on each side.
2. Plan	Write the word equation and then replace the names with formulas. Use coefficients to balance the number of each kind of atom or ion on both sides of the equation.
3. Solve	The reactants are iron(II) chloride and sodium phosphate. The products are sodium chloride and iron(II) phosphate. The formula for iron(II) chloride is $FeCl_2$, sodium chloride is $NaCl$, and iron(II) phosphate is $Fe_3(PO_4)_2$. The word equation is

iron(II) chloride + sodium phosphate →
   sodium chloride + iron(II) phosphate

The unbalanced equation is

$$FeCl_2 + Na_3PO_4 \rightarrow NaCl + Fe_3(PO_4)_2$$

You could start balancing with any element because each is found in only one reactant and one product, but in this example we will start with Fe:

$$3 \ FeCl_2 + Na_3PO_4 \rightarrow NaCl + Fe_3(PO_4)_2$$

Balancing Cl:

$$3 \ FeCl_2 + Na_3PO_4 \rightarrow 6 \ NaCl + Fe_3(PO_4)_2$$

Balancing Na:

$$3 \ FeCl_2 + 2 \ Na_3PO_4 \rightarrow$$
$$6 \ NaCl + Fe_3(PO_4)_2$$

(PO_4), which can be treated as a single unit, is now balanced as well.

4. Evaluate	The total number of each kind of atom on each side of the equation is the same and the coefficients are in lowest whole number ratio. Thus the equation is balanced.

3. Write a balanced chemical equation for the reaction in which aluminum reacts with oxygen to produce aluminum oxide. *(Answer: 4 Al + 3 O$_2$ → 2 Al$_2$O$_3$)*

4. Chlorine reacts with lithium bromide (LiBr) to produce lithium chloride (LiCl) and bromine. Write the balanced equation for this reaction. *(Answer: Cl$_2$ + 2 LiBr → 2 LiCl + Br$_2$)*

Writing Complete Chemical Equations

In addition to verifying the law of conservation of matter, there is another important reason for writing a balanced equation. When you write a balanced equation, you are not deciding how the reactants should combine. After all, the reaction will occur in a certain way whether or not you write a balanced equation. You are simply describing how that reaction actually does occur. Thus a balanced chemical equation relates the macroscopic, observable, reaction to the interactions on a microscopic level.

Because a chemical equation describes how a chemical reaction actually occurs, there is one other important piece of information that is often included in a complete chemical equation. This information is the physical state of each reactant and product. Recall from Chapter 2 that the three states of matter are solid, liquid, and gas. In later chapters, you may see the symbol (s) to indicate a solid, (l) to indicate a liquid, and (g) to indicate a gas in various chemical equations. These symbols are written after the chemical formulas in a chemical equation. Thus, the complete chemical equation for the combustion of methane in oxygen would be written as follows:

$$CH_4\ (g)\ +\ 2\ O_2\ (g)\ \rightarrow\ CO_2\ (g)\ +\ 2\ H_2O\ (g)\quad \textbf{(Eq. 14)}$$

This equation tells you that methane gas reacts with oxygen gas to produce carbon dioxide gas and liquid water.

In addition to the symbols for solid, liquid, and gas, you may see another symbol used in some chemical equations. Many solids will not react unless they are dissolved in water. For this reason, the symbol (*aq*) is used to indicate that a solid exists in an aqueous, or water, solution. You will learn more about aqueous solutions in Chapter 15.

Figure 9–11 *As in other chemical reactions, the atoms taking part in this reaction are rearranged in certain ways. If additional atoms were present, they would not simply add on to the product. Only these 5 atoms can join together to form this product—no more and no less.*

When balancing a chemical equation, always remember how a coefficient differs from a subscript. A coefficient is a number in front of a chemical formula that refers to the number of units of the formula after it. A subscript is a number to the lower right of a symbol or group of symbols that indicates the number of times the particular atom, ion, or group of atoms occurs in the chemical formula.

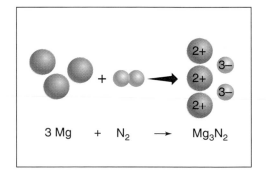

3 Mg   +   N$_2$ →   Mg$_3$N$_2$

True Colors

The colors of leaves at any time of year are caused by pigments, which are chemicals that reflect and absorb light. White light, such as sunlight, is made up of all the different colors of light (red, orange, yellow, green, blue, indigo, and violet). When light strikes a pigment, some colors are reflected (bounced back) to your eyes and others are absorbed (taken into the material). An apple appears red because the pigments in the apple absorb all of the colors of light except red, which is reflected to your eyes. The green leaf of a tree appears green because the pigments in the leaf absorb all of the colors of light except green, which is reflected to your eyes.

Anything that has color contains some type of pigment. There are pigments in paint, in the dyes in your clothing, even in your hair and skin. The pigment that is responsible for giving plants and leaves their green color is called chlorophyll.

In addition to chlorophyll, two other major pigments are present in tree leaves. Carotenoid pigments give leaves the orange, yellow, and some of the red colors seen in autumn. Anthocyanin pigments, which are less prevalent but are the most colorful, create bright red leaves and blue colors in other plants. Both of these pigments are present and active throughout the summer. So why don't you see them?

The answer is that they are covered up by the chlorophyll. In the autumn, however,

conditions change as trees prepare for the harsh elements of winter. As part of this preparation, trees signal their leaves to cease photosynthetic activity in a way that is not totally understood. As activity comes to a stop, the chlorophyll pigments decompose and the green color fades. Now the other pigments show through. It is as if the leaves take off their green coats to uncover the beautiful colors beneath. The more photosynthesis that took place during the growing season, the more brilliant the underlying colors. A wet summer followed by sunny autumn days and chilly autumn nights makes for the most spectacular fall foliage.

9–2 Section Review

1. How are chemical reactions described?
2. What constraints does the law of conservation of matter place on chemical equations?
3. Write a balanced chemical equation for the chemical reaction in which sodium and oxygen combine to form sodium oxide (Na_2O).
4. **Critical Thinking—Making comparisons** What is the difference between O_2 and $2\ O$ in a chemical equation?

9–3 Classifying Chemical Reactions

Guide for Reading
- What are the four general types of chemical reactions?
- What characteristics identify each type of chemical reaction?

As you read this sentence, an incredible number of chemical reactions are occurring. In some reactions, elements combine to form compounds. In other reactions, compounds break down into elements. And in still other reactions, one element replaces another in a compound.

Fortunately, chemists have organized this multitude of reactions into just a few categories. Most of the reactions you will encounter can be classified as one of four general types. **The four general types of chemical reactions are direct combination, decomposition, single-replacement, and double-replacement.** By knowing the type of chemical reaction that is occurring, you can predict the products that will be formed.

Direct Combination Reactions

In a **direct combination reaction** two or more reactants come together to form a single product. Direct combination reactions are also known as synthesis reactions. It is helpful to remember this type of reaction (as well as the other types of reactions) by a general form. The general form for a direct combination, or synthesis, reaction is

$$A + B \rightarrow AB \qquad \text{(Eq. 15)}$$

The letters A and B stand for either elements or compounds, and AB stands for a compound consisting of A and B. This is the only one of the four types of reactions in which there is a single product. And this single product is always more complex than either of the reactants.

There are many examples of direct combination reactions. You are already familiar with one of them. Remember the example that we introduced earlier of calcium burning in oxygen to form calcium oxide? That was a direct combination reaction. Two elements, calcium and oxygen, joined together to form a compound, calcium oxide.

Another direct combination reaction results in the formation of common table salt. In this case, sodium and chlorine react to form sodium chloride. The equation for this reaction is written as follows:

$$2 \, Na + Cl_2 \rightarrow 2 \, NaCl \qquad \textbf{(Eq. 16)}$$

Notice again that two elements joined together to form a single product.

One particular direct combination reaction results in the production of a dangerous air pollutant, sulfur dioxide. In this reaction, sulfur and oxygen gas react to form sulfur dioxide. Why do you think this direct combination is of great importance?

Figure 9–12 *When sodium metal burns in chlorine gas, a direct combination reaction takes place, producing white sodium chloride smoke and a bright yellow flame. How many atoms are on each side of the chemical equation describing this reaction?*

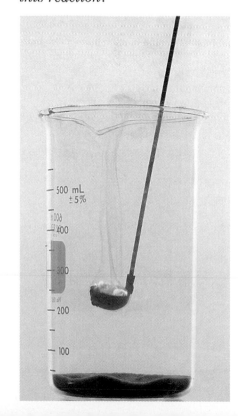

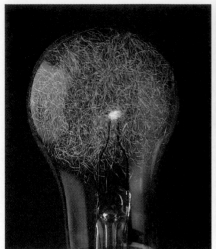
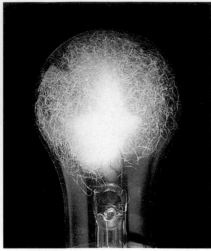
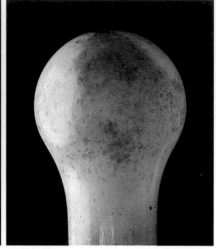

Figure 9–13 *The direct combination reaction between magnesium and oxygen produces a brilliant white light. The light is so bright that this reaction was once used in camera flashbulbs. Inside a flashbulb, oxygen surrounds a thin coil of magnesium. When the bulb is flashed, an electrical charge ignites the magnesium, which then reacts with oxygen. How can you tell that a chemical reaction has taken place?*

$$S + O_2 \rightarrow SO_2 \qquad \textbf{(Eq. 17)}$$

During another direct combination reaction, iron combines with oxygen to form iron(III) oxide. The equation for this reaction is written as

$$4\ Fe + 3\ O_2 \rightarrow 2\ Fe_2O_3 \qquad \textbf{(Eq. 18)}$$

Is this reaction familiar to you? If not, look at Figure 9–14.

The examples we have considered so far all involve two elements joining together to form a compound. These are not the only possible direct combination reactions, however. A direct combination reaction may also involve two simple compounds forming a more complex compound. For example, carbon dioxide reacts with water to form carbonic acid, which is a weak acid. The equation for this reaction is

$$CO_2 + H_2O \rightarrow H_2CO_3 \qquad \textbf{(Eq. 19)}$$

Notice that no matter how different these assorted direct combination reactions may be, they all follow the same general form of two or more simple reactants reacting to form a single, more complex product.

Decomposition Reactions

If something decomposes, it breaks down into smaller parts. For example, when plants die, they decompose by the action of microorganisms and their compounds are converted into smaller, simpler substances. A **decomposition reaction** is a reaction in which a single compound is broken down into two or more smaller compounds or elements. A decomposition reaction is the reverse of a direct combination reaction. The identifying characteristic of a decomposition reaction is the presence of only one reactant. The general form for a decomposition reaction is

$$AB \rightarrow A + B \qquad \textbf{(Eq. 20)}$$

As in a direct combination reaction, AB represents a compound. A and B represent elements or compounds.

Figure 9–14 *Believe it or not, these rusty items were once bright and shiny! Their original shine cannot be restored simply by washing them, however, because rusting is a chemical reaction.*

A simple decomposition reaction is the decomposition of water. The balanced equation for this reaction is

$$2 \ H_2O \rightarrow 2 \ H_2 + O_2 \qquad \textbf{(Eq. 21)}$$

Notice that the decomposition of water is the reverse reaction of the synthesis of water shown earlier.

As you know, the marble (calcium carbonate) in a statue or building does not readily decompose. When heated, however, it can be made to decompose to form calcium oxide and carbon dioxide. The balanced equation for this reaction is

$$CaCO_3 \rightarrow CaO + CO_2 \qquad \textbf{(Eq. 22)}$$

In each example, notice that a single complex reactant breaks down to form two or more simpler products.

Single-Replacement Reactions

In a **single-replacement reaction,** an uncombined element displaces an element that is part of a compound. The reactants in a single-replacement reaction are always one element and one compound. The general form for a single-replacement reaction is

$$A + BX \rightarrow AX + B \qquad \textbf{(Eq. 23)}$$

where BX and AX are generally ionic compounds and A and B are elements. Notice that the atom represented by the letter X switches its "partner" from B to A.

An example of a single-replacement reaction is the reaction that occurs when a piece of magnesium is placed in a solution of copper(II) sulfate. The magnesium replaces the copper in the compound, forming magnesium sulfate. The other product of the reaction is copper metal. The balanced equation for this reaction is

$$Mg + CuSO_4 \rightarrow MgSO_4 + Cu \qquad \textbf{(Eq. 24)}$$

If an iron nail is placed in a solution containing copper(II) sulfate, the iron will begin to replace the copper. Slowly, the displaced copper will accumulate on the remaining part of the nail. The reaction is

$$Fe + CuSO_4 \rightarrow FeSO_4 + Cu \qquad \textbf{(Eq. 25)}$$

What would happen if you switched this reaction around? For example, instead of placing iron into copper(II) sulfate, you place copper into iron(II) sulfate. Will a single-replacement reaction occur in which copper replaces iron? The answer is no. Not

Figure 9–15 *The explosion of dynamite is a decomposition reaction. What is the general form for a decomposition reaction?*

Figure 9–16 *This football player is thankful for the oxygen he is inhaling while he recovers on the sidelines during a game. We have come to rely on the availability of oxygen everywhere from airplanes to hospitals. But supplies of oxygen were not always so common. Oxygen was discovered by Joseph Priestley in 1774 when he decomposed mercury(II) oxide into its elements by heating it. What is the equation describing this reaction?*

Joseph Priestley
USA 20c

Figure 9–17 *When an iron nail is dipped into copper(II) sulfate, a reddish-brown substance begins to coat the nail. What is happening in this reaction?*

all elements can replace all other elements. Whether one element will replace another depends on the tendency of each element to react, or their chemical activity. A more active element will replace a less active element. In this case, iron is more active than copper. When copper is in a compound, it can be replaced by the more active iron. But when iron is in a compound, copper is not active enough to replace it. Thus no reaction will occur.

Figure 9-19 provides a list of metals in order of chemical activity. This list is known as the activity series, and it can be used to predict whether or not a single-replacement reaction will occur. You will learn more about the activity series in Chapter 20. For now what is important is that you realize that not all elements can be replaced through single-replacement reactions.

Let's work through one more example—the reaction between chlorine and potassium iodide. The reactants do take part in a single-replacement reaction, but which element is replaced? Figure 9-19 lists only metals. And there's your clue. Potassium is a metal and chlorine is a nonmetal. In a single-replacement reaction, metals usually replace metals or hydrogen and nonmetals usually replace nonmetals. The correct equation for this reaction is

$$Cl_2 + 2 KI \rightarrow 2 KCl + I_2 \qquad \textbf{(Eq. 26)}$$

Figure 9–18 *When a piece of copper is placed into silver nitrate, the copper replaces the silver. In these photographs, you can see the gradual build-up of silver on the copper coil. What type of reaction is this?*

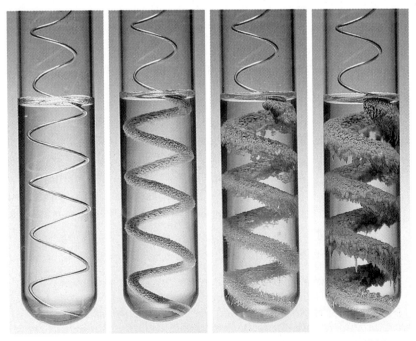

Figure 9–19 *The activity series shown here, which is used to determine which element replaces another in a single-replacement reaction, lists metal elements according to their ability to react. The series goes from the most active element at the top of the list to the least active element on the bottom. An element can replace any element that is below it in the list. Lithium, for example, can replace potassium, which can replace barium. Although hydrogen is not a metal, it is included in the series because it acts like a metal in replacement reactions.*

Activity Series
Metals
Li
K
Ba
Sr
Ca
Na
Mg
Al
Mn
Zn
Fe
Cd
Co
Ni
Sn
Pb
H
Cu
Ag
Hg
Au

Double-Replacement Reactions

In a **double-replacement reaction,** atoms or ions from two different compounds replace each other. An identifying characteristic of a double-replacement reaction is the presence of two compounds as reactants and two compounds as products. The reactants in a double-replacement reaction are generally ionic compounds. The general form for a double-replacement reaction is

$$AX + BY \rightarrow AY + BX \qquad \text{(Eq. 27)}$$

Notice that in this type of equation, the two atoms or ions represented by the letters X and Y "switch partners."

If you have ever had an upset stomach, you may have taken a tablet that contains the compound calcium carbonate ($CaCO_3$). Calcium carbonate reacts with the hydrochloric acid in your stomach in the following double-replacement reaction:

$$CaCO_3 + 2\ HCl \rightarrow CaCl_2 + H_2CO_3 \qquad \textbf{(Eq. 28)}$$

In this reaction, the calcium and hydrogen replace each other, or switch partners. One product is calcium chloride, which is a harmless compound. The other product is carbonic acid. Carbonic acid decomposes into water and carbon dioxide.

Just as in single-replacement reactions, not all pairs of compounds will react in a double-replacement reaction. There are several factors that determine whether or not such a reaction will proceed. For example, most double-replacement reactions will not occur unless the reactants are dissolved in water so that the compounds can separate into ions. A double-replacement reaction is likely to proceed if at least one of the products is a molecular compound, a precipitate (a solid that separates from a solution), or a gas that cannot be dissolved in water. You will learn more about these factors in later chapters. For now, you need only recognize that not all combinations of reactants will take part in a double-replacement reaction.

*I*NTEGRATING
*B*IOLOGY

Did you ever wonder how an antacid tablet helps relieve an upset stomach?

Figure 9–20 *The artist using these paints must really get into her work! Paints are chemical compounds produced by double-replacement reactions.*

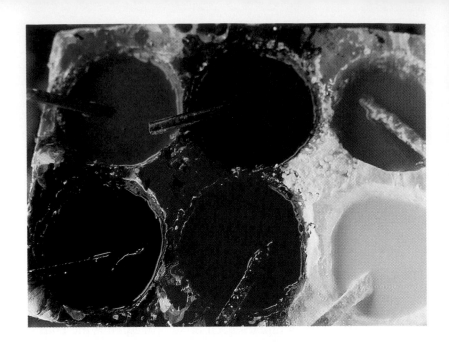

INTEGRATING
ENVIRONMENTAL **S**CIENCE

How do you think burning gasohol instead of gasoline in your automobile helps the environment?

CHEM Exploration

How Sweet It Is

1. Place one or two spoonfuls of sugar into an old pan.
2. Heat the sugar for about 3 to 5 minutes in the presence of an adult. *Follow all applicable safety precautions when using heat.*
3. Observe and record any changes that occur as the sugar is heated.
4. Let the pan cool for several minutes. What do you observe in the pan? What happened to the sugar? Did a chemical reaction take place? How do you know?
5. Meats such as beef and chicken brown when they are cooked. Use your observations from this activity to form a hypothesis as to why such browning occurs. Research this phenomenon to find out if your hypothesis is correct.

Some Exceptions to the Rule

As you know by now, just about every rule in science has an exception. The rules governing chemical reactions are no different. Although the majority of chemical reactions that you will encounter in your study of chemistry fit nicely into one of the four categories of chemical reactions, there are many reactions that do not. For example, many of the direct combination reactions we used as examples were combustion reactions—reactions in which something burned. But not all combustion reactions are necessarily direct combination reactions. The example of the combustion of methane, which we used to describe how to balance equations, is not a direct combination reaction. Two reactants combine, but more than one product is formed. In fact, this reaction does not fit into any of the four categories of reactions.

Consider another combustion reaction in which gasohol burns in a car's engine. Gasohol is a type of fuel that is made up of regular unleaded gasoline and alcohol. It is intended to burn a little more cleanly in order to release fewer pollutants and so protect the environment. The alcohol in gasohol burns according to the following equation:

$$C_2H_5OH + 3\,O_2 \rightarrow 2\,CO_2 + 3\,H_2O \qquad \textbf{(Eq. 29)}$$

While the reactant side of this equation resembles many of the direct combination reactions we have described, the product side of the equation shows two products instead of one. This cannot be a direct combination reaction, nor can it be a decomposition, single-replacement, or double-replacement reaction.

In later chapters, you will learn about other reactions that do not fit neatly into one of the four categories described in this section. For now all you need to recognize is that not every chemical reaction must fit into one of these four categories.

A Volatile Situation

Taneeka's younger brother Omar is making a model of a volcano for his sixth-grade science fair. Taneeka is worried that the gas produced by the volcano's eruption may be harmful to him. She asks Omar what chemicals he is mixing to produce the gas in the volcano. He tells her that he is using baking soda and vinegar. Although these seem like harmless reactants, Taneeka knows from her chemistry class that the products of a reaction are very different from the reactants. She checks the labels on the containers to determine the compounds contained in baking soda and vinegar. The labels say that baking soda contains sodium bicarbonate ($NaHCO_3$) and vinegar is a solution of acetic acid ($HC_2H_3O_2$).

1. What type of reaction is most likely to occur between these two compounds?

2. What gases could possibly be produced from these two reactants?

3. Do you think the gases are harmful?

4. How might you obtain further information about the products to determine if they are safe?

5. What should Taneeka tell her brother about his science fair project?

9–3 Section Review

1. Describe each of the four types of chemical reactions.

2. Contrast direct combination reactions with decomposition reactions.

3. Given two chemical equations, how can you determine which equation describes a single-replacement reaction and which describes a double-replacement reaction?

4. Based on what you have learned about types of reactions, classify the type of reaction that will occur given the following reactants:
   (a) element + element →
   (b) element + ionic compound →
   (c) ionic compound + ionic compound →
   (d) compound →

5. **Theme Trace—Patterns of Change** Although the reaction in which two elements join together to form a compound is very different from the reaction in which a compound breaks down into two elements, all reactions share certain characteristics. Explain how chemical reactions can be similar and different at the same time. Include specific examples in your explanation.

Visit our Web site at
http://www.phschool.com
to support your
study of chemistry.

Laboratory Investigation

Reactivity of Metals in Single-Replacement Reactions

Problem

Which metals will replace each other in single-replacement reactions?

Materials (per group)

four small pieces of the following metals:
   copper, magnesium, iron
dilute solutions of the following
   compounds: HCl, $CuCl_2$, $MgCl_2$, $FeCl_3$
12-well spot plate (or 12 small test tubes)
paper and pencil

Procedure

1. Make small labels for each of the wells on the spot plate. Each label should list one of the metals being used and one of the compounds. There should be 12 labels in all.
2. Place a piece of copper in each of four wells on the spot plate.
3. Add enough HCl to cover the copper in the first well. Label this well with the label that lists copper and HCl. Cover the copper in the second well with $CuCl_2$, the copper in the third well with $MgCl_2$, and the copper in the fourth well with $FeCl_3$. Label each well accordingly
4. Repeat Steps 2 and 3 using magnesium in clean wells on the spot plate.
5. Repeat Steps 2 and 3 using iron in clean wells on the spot plate.
6. In a data table similar to the one shown, record any signs of chemical change that you observe in each of the wells. Possible changes could include changes in color or state, or the production of bubbles.

Observations

Metals	Compounds			
	HCl	**$CuCl_2$**	**$MgCl_2$**	**$FeCl_3$**
Cu				
Mg				
Fe				

1. Which of the metals reacted with the most compounds?
2. Which reacted with the fewest compounds?

Analysis and Conclusions

1. Describe what happened in the chemical reactions you observed.
2. List the metals you tested from most reactive to least reactive.
3. Which of the metals you tested were able to replace the hydrogen in HCl?
4. Where would hydrogen, as in an acid, be placed in the activity series you listed?
5. Compare your results with Figure 9–19 on p. 295. Do your experimental results agree with the table? Explain possible reasons for disagreement.
6. **On Your Own** Test the same three metals for reactivity with water. Can any of these metals replace hydrogen in water? Is any metal capable of replacing hydrogen in water?

STUDY GUIDE

Summarizing Key Concepts

9–1 The Nature of Chemical Reactions

- Substances that undergo a chemical reaction experience a change in their physical and chemical properties.
- Reactants are the substances present before a chemical reaction occurs, and products are the substances that result from the chemical reaction.
- Chemical reactions occur so that atoms can become more stable.

9–2 Chemical Equations

- Chemical reactions are described by chemical equations.
- Because the number and kind of atoms on the reactant side are the same as the number and kind of atoms on the product side, a balanced chemical equation demonstrates conservation of matter.

- A coefficient is a number written before the formula for a substance in a balanced chemical equation to represent the quantities of reactants and products involved in the chemical reaction.

9–3 Classifying Chemical Reactions

- Direct combination reactions occur when two or more substances combine to form one compound.
- In a decomposition reaction, a complex substance breaks down into two or more simpler products.
- Single-replacement reactions occur when an uncombined element replaces an element that is part of a compound.
- In a double-replacement reaction, atoms or ions from two different compounds replace each other.

Reviewing Key Terms

Define each term in a complete sentence.

9–1 The Nature of Chemical Reactions

chemical reaction
reactant
product

9–2 Chemical Equations

chemical equation
balanced chemical equation
coefficient

9–3 Classifying Chemical Reactions

direct combination reaction
decomposition reaction
single-replacement reaction
double-replacement reaction

CHAPTER REVIEW

Content Review

Multiple Choice
Choose the letter of the answer that best completes each statement.

1. During a chemical reaction,
   - (a) new elements are produced.
   - (b) atoms are destroyed.
   - (c) atoms are rearranged.
   - (d) elements are destroyed.

2. The unbalanced chemical equation for the reaction in which carbon monoxide burns in oxygen to form carbon dioxide is
   - (a) $CO \rightarrow O_2 + CO_2$
   - (b) $CO + O \rightarrow CO_2$
   - (c) $CO_2 \rightarrow CO + O_2$
   - (d) $CO + O_2 \rightarrow CO_2$

3. An equation is balanced by
   - (a) changing subscripts.
   - (b) erasing elements as necessary.
   - (c) adding coefficients.
   - (d) adding elements as necessary.

4. A reaction that has two compounds as reactants and two compounds as products might be described as a
   - (a) direct combination reaction.
   - (b) single-replacement reaction.
   - (c) decomposition reaction.
   - (d) double-replacement reaction.

5. An atom's ability to undergo chemical reactions is determined by its
   - (a) protons.
   - (b) innermost electrons.
   - (c) neutrons.
   - (d) outermost electrons.

6. When the equation $Al + Br_2 \rightarrow AlBr_3$ is balanced, the coefficient for Al is
   - (a) 1.
   - (b) 2.
   - (c) 3.
   - (d) 4.

7. Two or more substances combine to form one substance in a
   - (a) direct combination reaction.
   - (b) single-replacement reaction.
   - (c) decomposition reaction.
   - (d) double-replacement reaction.

8. $Mg + 2 HCl \rightarrow MgCl_2 + H_2$ is a
   - (a) direct combination reaction.
   - (b) single-replacement reaction.
   - (c) decomposition reaction.
   - (d) double-replacement reaction.

True or False
If the statement is true, write "true." If it is false, change the underlined word or words to make the statement true.

9. Chemical <u>equations</u> are written to describe chemical reactions.

10. The substances formed as a result of a chemical reaction are called <u>reactants</u>.

11. Chemical equations are balanced to reflect the law of <u>multiple proportions</u>.

12. <u>Coefficients</u> are written in front of chemical formulas to balance equations.

13. In <u>direct combination</u> reactions, complex substances form simpler substances.

14. In a <u>single-replacement</u> reaction, there is only one product.

15. When Mg reacts with $FeCl_3$, magnesium will replace <u>chlorine</u> in the compound.

Concept Mapping
Complete the following concept map for Section 9–2. Refer to pages xviii–xix to construct a concept map for the entire chapter.

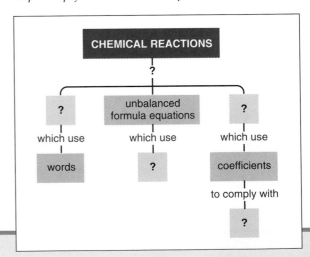

Concept Mastery

Discuss each of the following in a brief paragraph.

16. What occurs during a chemical reaction? What are the names given to the various substances that are involved in a chemical reaction?

17. When oil and water are mixed, they never react with each other. But when hydrogen gas and oxygen gas are mixed together, they can react to produce water. Why do some substances react with each other, while others do not?

18. How are chemical reactions described? Give an example.

19. What are coefficients and why are they used?

20. Describe the steps you would follow to balance a chemical equation.

21. If a chemical equation is impossible to balance, what is most likely the problem?

22. Explain how a balanced equation verifies the law of conservation of matter.

23. Tying it Together Chemical changes occur as a result of chemical reactions. The changes that occur in each of the four types of chemical reactions follow certain patterns. Explain how you can use those *patterns of change* to predict the results of a chemical reaction when the products are not given.

Critical Thinking and Problem Solving

Use the skills you have developed in this chapter to answer each of the following.

24. Applying concepts Balance each of the following equations:
(a) $P + O_2 \rightarrow P_2O_5$
(b) $NaNO_3 \rightarrow NaNO_2 + O_2$
(c) $C_8H_{18} + O_2 \rightarrow CO_2 + H_2O$
(d) $H_2SO_4 + NaOH \rightarrow Na_2SO_4 + 2 H_2O$

25. Classifying Identify the type of reaction represented by each equation. Explain your answers.
(a) $MnSO_4 \rightarrow MnO + SO_3$
(b) $3 NiSO_4 + 2 Li_3PO_4 \rightarrow$
$$Ni_3(PO_4)_2 + 3 Li_2SO_4$$
(c) $Cd + 2 HCl \rightarrow CdCl_2 + H_2$
(d) $4 Co + 3 O_2 \rightarrow 2 Co_2O_3$

26. Making inferences Fish need oxygen to breathe. Where does this oxygen come from? Is this a decomposition reaction? Why?

27. Applying concepts Given the unbalanced equation $PCl_5 + H_2O \rightarrow H_3PO_4 + HCl$, a student balances it by writing the following: $PCl_5 + 2 H_2O_2 \rightarrow H_3PO_4 + H_5Cl$. Has it been balanced correctly? Why or why not?

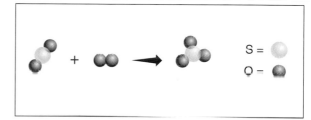

S = ○
O = ●

28. Interpreting diagrams Given the balanced equation $2 SO_2 + O_2 \rightarrow 2 SO_3$, a student depicts it using spheres to represent atoms. Has it been depicted correctly? Why or why not?

29. Evaluating A student is asked to give the sum of the coefficients in the following balanced equation: $3 FeO + 2 Al \rightarrow Al_2O_3 + 3 Fe$. The student's answer is 8. Why is the answer incorrect?

30. Using the writing process Acid rain is a serious environmental problem that results from two successive direct combination reactions. Research the acid rain problem. Summarize your findings in a report, brochure, or pamphlet that you can show to others to make them aware of the situation.

CHAPTER REVIEW — PROBLEM BANK

Group A

31. Identify the reactants and products in the following chemical reactions: *(Section 9–2)*
 (a) Manganese metal reacts with sulfuric acid to produce manganese(II) sulfate and hydrogen gas.
 (b) Silver chlorate is decomposed with heat to give silver chloride and oxygen gas.
 (c) Chromium metal is heated in oxygen to produce chromium(III) oxide.

32. Write unbalanced formula equations for the following reactions: *(Section 9–2)*
 (a) Sodium hydroxide and hydrogen chloride react to yield water and sodium chloride.
 (b) Lithium metal reacts with water to produce lithium hydroxide and hydrogen gas.

33. Write the balanced equation for each of the reactions described in question 32. *(Section 9–2)*

34. Write balanced chemical equations describing the reactions depicted in the diagram below. *(Section 9–2)*

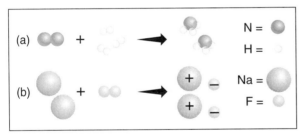

35. Write a balanced equation for each of the following direct combination reactions: *(Sections 9–2 and 9–3)*
 (a) Lithium reacts with oxygen to produce lithium oxide.
 (b) Silver(I) nitride is produced when silver reacts with atmospheric nitrogen.

36. Write a balanced equation for each of the following decomposition reactions: *(Sections 9–2 and 9–3)*
 (a) Magnesium hydroxide decomposes to form magnesium oxide and water.

 (b) Hydrogen and oxygen are produced by the decomposition of water.

37. Write balanced equations for the following single-replacement reactions: *(Sections 9–2 and 9–3)*
 (a) Aluminum reacts with iron(II) nitrate to form aluminum nitrate and iron.
 (b) Potassium reacts with water to produce hydrogen and potassium hydroxide.

38. Write balanced equations for the following double-replacement reactions: *(Sections 9–2 and 9–3)*
 (a) Copper(II) hydroxide and potassium sulfate are produced when potassium hydroxide reacts with copper(II) sulfate.
 (b) Sodium hydroxide reacts with phosphoric acid to produce trisodium phosphate and water.

39. Balance these equations and indicate the type of reaction each equation represents: *(Sections 9–2 and 9–3)*
 (a) $NH_3 \rightarrow N_2 + H_2$
 (b) $Ba(C_2H_3O_2)_2 + Na_3PO_4 \rightarrow$
$$Ba_3(PO_4)_2 + NaC_2H_3O_2$$
 (c) $Zn + HCl \rightarrow ZnCl_2 + H_2$
 (d) $Hg + O_2 \rightarrow HgO$

40. Complete and balance the following chemical equations: *(Sections 9–2 and 9–3)*
 (a) $Sr + S \rightarrow$
 (b) $Bi + S \rightarrow$
 (c) $Al + Cl_2 \rightarrow$

41. Identify the type of reaction for each of the following: *(Section 9–3)*
 (a) An element reacts with an ionic compound, producing a different compound and element.
 (b) When an electric current is passed through a compound, two elements are produced.
 (c) Two ionic compounds are combined to form a solid compound and a different ionic compound.

(d) Two compounds combine to form one compound.

42. Identify the type of reaction for each of the following: *(Section 9–3)*

(a) $Sb_2S_3 + 6\ HCl \rightarrow 2\ SbCl_3 + 3\ H_2S$

(b) $3\ Sn + 2\ P \rightarrow Sn_3P_2$

(c) $2\ PbO_2 \rightarrow 2\ PbO + O_2$

(d) $Zn + 2\ HCl \rightarrow ZnCl_2 + H_2$

43. For each of the following sets of reactants, predict the products and identify the type of reaction: *(Section 9–3)*

(a) potassium phosphate + barium chloride →

(b) calcium + water →

(c) aluminum + chlorine →

Group B

44. Identify the reactants and products in the following reactions:

(a) Copper metal heated with fluorine gas yields copper(II) fluoride.

(b) Heating orange HgO powder produces colorless oxygen gas and beads of silver mercury.

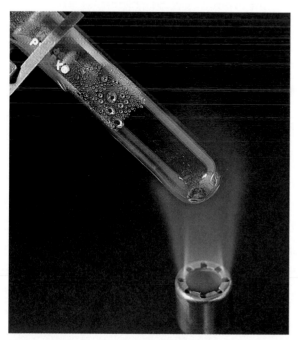

45. Write unbalanced formula equations for each of the following reactions:

(a) Mercury is heated with chlorine to give mercury(II) chloride.

(b) Cobalt is heated with sulfur to produce cobalt(II) sulfide.

46. Write a balanced equation for each of the following direct combination reactions:

(a) Magnesium chloride is the product of a reaction between magnesium and chlorine.

(b) When sulfur dioxide reacts with water, sulfurous acid is formed.

47. Write a balanced equation for each of the following decomposition reactions:

(a) When hydrogen peroxide decomposes, the products are water and oxygen.

(b) Potassium chloride decomposes to form potassium and chlorine.

48. Write a balanced equation for the following single-replacement reactions:

(a) Chlorine reacts with sodium oxide to produce oxygen and sodium chloride.

(b) Nickel(II) chloride and lead are formed when lead(II) chloride reacts with nickel.

49. Reusable booster rockets are employed to launch United States space shuttles. The rockets use a mixture of aluminum and ammonium perchlorate for fuel. Balance the equation that shows the chemical reaction between these two substances.

$$Al + NH_4ClO_4 \rightarrow$$
$$Al_2O_3 + AlCl_3 + NO + H_2O$$

50. Propane (C_3H_8) is a common fuel used for cooking and home heating. The combustion of propane releases carbon dioxide and water vapor into the atmosphere. Balance the equation for the combustion of propane.

$$C_3H_8 + O_2 \rightarrow CO_2 + H_2O$$

FROM SCHOOL TO WORK

Natalie Clemons—Student

Natalie Clemons of Raleigh, North Carolina, uses her knowledge of chemistry every day in her job as a technician in a neighborhood pharmacy. "If you don't know the names of the elements and their symbols, and if you can't read chemical formulas, you're in trouble," explains Natalie about her most important responsibility—reading prescriptions and preparing medications accurately. To do this, Natalie uses many of the laboratory skills that she learned in chemistry class: using balances, making dilutions, measuring volumes, and many others.

What Natalie finds most rewarding about her job is the one-on-one interaction with the customers. "People have a lot of questions about their prescriptions. They want to know how to take the medicine, what side effects to expect, and how the medicine might interact with their other medications."

Forensic Chemist

Forensic chemists apply the scientific method to the analysis, identification, and classification of physical evidence from crime scenes. Much of the work of forensic chemists is done in laboratories using various instruments to analyze fabric, paint, paper, and ink. Although forensic chemists spend most of their time in the laboratory, they often visit crime scenes and may be called on to present scientific evidence in court.

Most jobs in the field of forensic chemistry require at least a Bachelor of Science or Arts. High-school students interested in becoming forensic chemists should concentrate on taking courses in chemistry, physics, biology, and physiology. Communication and computer skills are also important.

To receive additional information, write to the American Academy of Forensic Sciences, 218 East Cache La Poudre, Colorado Springs, CO 80901.

How to Find the Right College

When choosing a college, first consider what type of career or academic program interests you. Also decide what geographic location and student-body size would make you most comfortable. Other things to consider are financial constraints, availability of housing, and ease with which you can travel back and forth to school. Once you have a list of potential colleges, compare the courses they offer, their job placement records, and their extracurricular activities.

In addition to talking with counselors, you might want to read some college guides to learn about specific institutions. Two popular examples are *Peterson's Guide to Four-Year Colleges* and *Barron's Profiles of American Colleges*.

Doug Brown

From the Author

At one point during Shakespeare's masterpiece *Hamlet*, the gloomy Prince of Denmark says, "I could be bounded in a nutshell, and call myself king of infinite space." I doubt that Hamlet is telling the truth about himself, but his words ring true for me all the same. When I think about the tiny world inside a molecule, I wonder at the vast realm there. I'm not the king of it exactly, but a kind of visitor. There's so much to see. The balance of attractions and repulsions that determine the shape of a molecule seem more like dancing than science. And the variety of shapes! Some beautifully geometric, some not quite so pure (and all the more interesting for their imperfection)—they seem to exist as much to amaze me as for any other purpose.

Is there a reason for so much beauty, so much variety on a scale that is so much smaller than the eye can see? The richness of the visible world reflects the richness of the invisible one. A hand, a flower, a gemstone flashing in the sunlight—all owe their shapes to a dance of electrons. But this fact makes the question even harder to answer: Does the tiny world exist to make the bigger one possible? I don't know, but I am grateful all the same.

UNIT REVIEW

Concept Mastery

Discuss each of the following in a brief paragraph.

1. Explain the difference between ionic and covalent bonds. Give examples of compounds that contain these bonds.

2. Explain the difference between polar covalent and nonpolar covalent bonds. Give examples of compounds that contain these bonds.

3. What is the octet rule? How does this rule explain the common ion of fluorine (F^-)? Of calcium (Ca^{2+})?

4. When naming ions of the transition metals, what extra information must you provide? Why is providing this information necessary?

5. Choose a molecule and write its molecular formula and Lewis structure. What information does a Lewis structure provide that a molecular formula does not?

6. What is the shape of a water molecule? Why is this shape significant?

7. Give examples for 5 different molecular shapes. How does the VSEPR theory explain each of these shapes?

8. Can a nonpolar molecule have polar bonds? Use an example to explain your answer.

9. Give examples of molecules with sp, sp^2, and sp^3 hybrid orbitals.

10. Which is longer: a carbon–carbon single bond or a carbon–carbon double bond? Explain.

11. Harriet folds a piece of paper into the shape of an elephant. Sam burns a piece of paper with a match. Which of them has performed a chemical reaction on paper? Explain.

12. What are the reactants and products of a chemical reaction?

13. Are the expressions 2 NO and N_2O_2 identical? Explain.

14. What is the difference between the following: a single-replacement reaction and a double-replacement reaction?

Problem Bank

For Questions 15 to 22 write the name of the compound and identify it as an ionic compound, a molecule, or an acid.

15. HNO_3
16. CaI_2
17. Fe_2O_3
18. N_2O_4
19. HF
20. $Cu_3(PO_4)_2$
21. NH_4Cl
22. CO

For Questions 23 to 29 identify the molecule's shape and whether it is polar or nonpolar.

23. CCl_4
24. H_2O
25. CO_2
26. HCN
27. NBr_3
28. BF_3
29. CH_2O

30. A molecule of formic acid consists of a carbon atom bonded to a hydrogen atom, an oxygen atom, and a hydroxyl ($-OH$) group. Write the molecular formula and Lewis structure for formic acid.

31. Explain why the octet rule cannot be satisfied in a molecule of nitrogen monoxide.

THE JUNGLE

For Questions 32 to 40 classify the reaction as a direct combination, decomposition, single-replacement, or double-replacement. Then add coefficients to balance the reaction, when necessary.

32. Aluminum hydroxide becomes aluminum oxide and water.

33. Iron metal reacts with oxygen in the atmosphere to become iron(III) oxide.

34. $Zn + H_2SO_4 \rightarrow ZnSO_4 + H_2$

35. $H_2 + O_2 \rightarrow H_2O$

36. $Na + Cl_2 \rightarrow NaCl$

37. $H_2CO_3 \rightarrow CO_2 + H_2O$

38. $KCl + AgNO_3 \rightarrow KNO_3 + AgCl$

39. $AgNO_3 + Zn \rightarrow Zn(NO_3)_2 + Ag$

40. $Al_2(SO_4)_3 + BaCl_2 \rightarrow AlCl_3 + BaSO_4$

41. Write a balanced chemical equation for the complete combustion of ethane (C_2H_6).

42. Write a balanced chemical equation for the complete combustion of butane (C_4H_{10}).

43. Holly wants to extract pure iron from a sample of iron(II) sulfate. Explain why she should use aluminum metal rather than copper metal. Write a balanced equation for the reaction between iron(II) sulfate and aluminum.

Performance-Based Task

Can You Make Matter Vanish?

Imagine that you are a medieval alchemist. You are trying to devise a procedure to change one substance into another substance. Are new substances with different properties produced in a chemical reaction? Design an experiment to answer this question.

1. Start by obtaining safety goggles, a lab apron, 0.5 g of ammonium carbonate, limewater (aqueous calcium hydroxide), and the equipment shown in the diagram.

2. State your hypothesis and then design a procedure for testing it.

3. Carry out your experiment, making careful observations to determine if new substances were produced with properties unlike those of the substances present before the reaction.

4. Based on your observations, identify any new substances produced in the reaction.

Going Further

5. Design an experiment to prove or disprove the law of conservation of matter.

6. When the gaseous products of this reaction are bubbled through water, no change is observed in the water. Design an experiment to determine if any of the products interact with water.

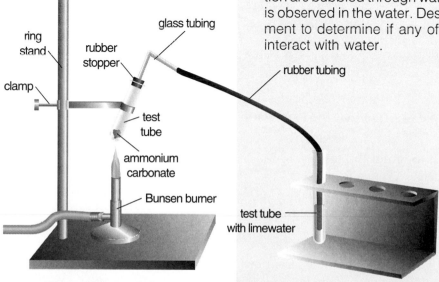

ring stand

rubber stopper

glass tubing

clamp

test tube

ammonium carbonate

Bunsen burner

rubber tubing

test tube with limewater

Unit 4 *Stoichiometry*

As if suspended from the ceiling on fine wires, two dancers soar above the floor of a rehearsal studio. After hours of practice, they will be ready to repeat this dazzling feat on stage before an admiring audience. In performance, professional dancers are able to make their astonishing leaps, lifts, and turns look effortless and graceful. In reality, dancing is hard work! And dancers must train just as hard as any football player, gymnast, or other athlete. As with other athletes, proper diet and nutrition are an important part of a dancer's training regimen. Eating a balanced diet ensures that the food you eat will provide your body with the energy you need every day—whether you use that energy for dancing, playing football, or studying.

How is the food you eat converted into energy by your body? The answer is that chemical reactions in the body break down the substances in food and produce simpler substances and energy as byproducts. The topic of this unit—stoichiometry—refers to the study of the amounts of substances consumed and produced in chemical reactions, such as the ones that take place in your body.

DISCOVERY LEARNING

1. Carefully straighten a paper clip and stick a sample of food on it.

2. Rest the ends of the paper clip on the edges of an aluminum pie plate so that the food sample is suspended above the center of the plate.

3. Use a match to ignite the food sample. Dispose of the used match properly.

4. Half fill a glass with water and hold the glass above the burning food sample for several minutes.

   - What do you observe?

   - How can you explain your observations?

Chapter

10

The Mole

David McCord wrote in 1929, "A handful of sand is an anthology of the universe." An anthology is a collection of pieces that provides meaning to the compiler.

The grains of sand in McCord's anthology tell an important story about our universe. Similarly, the particles with which chemists work tell their own story.

The number of items in an anthology can vary, just as the number of grains in a handful of sand and the number of chemical particles in a sample do. Just how does one go about counting them?

In this chapter, you will find out how chemists count particles more numerous than the grains in a handful of sand—more numerous in fact than the grains of sand in an entire desert!

The setting sun glistens off ripples of sand shaped by the powerful wind. In a different part of the world, a small mole pokes its head out of its burrow for some fresh air.

Chem Journal

YOU AND YOUR WORLD

You make many measurements throughout each day, many without even realizing it. You might take a glassful of juice, a handful of raisins, or a foot of licorice. Although the amounts may not be exact, they still involve volume, mass, or length. In your journal describe several measurements you make during the day. In each case, list another way that you could have described the same amount.

10-1 Chemical Measurements

Guide for Reading
- What is a mole and how does it relate to Avogadro's number?
- What is molar mass?

Imagine trying to purchase fruit without being able to count the number or measure the mass of the pieces you choose. Sounds pretty difficult, doesn't it? Every day people perform a variety of tasks that require the ability to count or measure. In some cases the job is easier than in others—but it is always important. A chef, for example, knows that using the proper amounts of ingredients is essential to the success of any recipe. A construction worker knows that mixing the correct proportions of cement, sand, gravel, and water will determine the consistency of concrete. And a painter knows that combining just the right mixture of colors will create the perfect shade of amber. Just as these measurements are important, so too are the amounts of substances essential in chemistry.

One of the many measurements used to describe substances in chemistry is atomic mass. You were introduced to it in Chapter 3. Because it has been some time since you read about atomic mass, it might be helpful to review it before going on to discuss additional measurements.

Figure 10-1 *The sale of fruit, production of cement, and mixing of paint all depend upon being able to measure amounts. What would happen if too much water was added to this cement? What about adding too much white to the blue of the sky in a painting?*

Atomic Mass and Formula Mass

As you should recall, the atoms of different elements have different masses. Because the actual mass of a single atom is so small (on the order of 10^{-23} gram), a special unit—the atomic mass unit (amu)—is used to describe the mass of an atom. In addition, a system has been devised for expressing the masses of atoms on a relative scale—that is, a scale based on experimental comparison with a standard. The scale for expressing atomic masses is based on the mass of carbon-12. The mass of an atom expressed relative to the mass assigned to carbon-12 is the **atomic mass** of the atom.

Now that you know how to describe the atomic mass, in amu, of an element, how do you think you would go about finding the mass of an entire molecule of a compound? To answer this question, let's look at a molecule of water (H_2O). It contains 2 hydrogen atoms and 1 oxygen atom. You know from the periodic table that the atomic mass of a hydrogen atom is 1.0 amu. To find the atomic mass of 2 hydrogen atoms then, you would multiply the atomic mass of a single hydrogen atom by 2. Thus the atomic mass of 2 hydrogen atoms is 2.0 amu (2 $\times$ 1.0 amu). The atomic mass of 1 oxygen atom is 16.0 amu. To find the total mass of the molecule, you would add the mass of each atom in the molecule. The atomic mass of 2 hydrogen atoms added to the atomic mass of 1 oxygen atom gives a total of 18.0 amu (2.0 amu + 16.0 amu). The sum of the atomic masses of all the atoms in a compound is called the **formula mass** of the compound. The formula mass of water is 18.0 amu. What is the formula mass of SO_2?

Figure 10–2 *The atomic mass of every element is listed in the periodic table. The atomic mass is usually found below the element's chemical symbol. Notice that in this table, the atomic masses of helium and bismuth have been highlighted. What is the atomic mass of Be? Of Kr?*

1A	2A	3B	4B	5B	6B	7B	8B	8B	8B	1B	2B	3A	4A	5A	6A	7A	8A
1 H 1.00794																	2 **He** **4.0026**
3 Li 6.941	4 Be 9.0122											5 B 10.81	6 C 12.011	7 N 14.007	8 O 15.999	9 F 18.9984	10 Ne 20.180
11 Na 22.990	12 Mg 24.305											13 Al 26.98	14 Si 28.086	15 P 30.974	16 S 32.07	17 Cl 35.453	18 Ar 39.948
19 K 39.098	20 Ca 40.08	21 Sc 44.956	22 Ti 47.88	23 V 50.94	24 Cr 51.996	25 Mn 54.938	26 Fe 55.847	27 Co 58.9332	28 Ni 58.69	29 Cu 63.546	30 Zn 65.39	31 Ga 69.72	32 Ge 72.61	33 As 74.922	34 Se 78.96	35 Br 79.904	36 Kr 83.80
37 Rb 85.468	38 Sr 87.62	39 Y 88.9059	40 Zr 91.224	41 Nb 92.91	42 Mo 95.94	43 Tc (98)	44 Ru 101.07	45 Rh 102.906	46 Pd 106.42	47 Ag 107.868	48 Cd 112.41	49 In 114.82	50 Sn 118.71	51 Sb 121.76	52 Te 127.60	53 I 126.905	54 Xe 131.29
55 Cs 132.91	56 Ba 137.33	71 Lu 174.967	72 Hf 178.49	73 Ta 180.95	74 W 183.85	75 Re 186.207	76 Os 190.2	77 Ir 192.22	78 Pt 195.08	79 Au 196.967	80 Hg 200.59	81 Tl 204.383	82 Pb 207.2	83 **Bi** **208.98**	84 Po (209)	85 At (210)	86 Rn (222)
87 Fr (223)	88 Ra 226.025	103 Lr (260)	104 Rf (261)	105 Db (262)	106 Sg (263)	107 Bh (262)	108 Hs (265)	109 Mt (266)	110 Uun (269)	111 Uuu (272)	112 Uub (277)						

57 La 138.906	58 Ce 140.12	59 Pr 140.908	60 Nd 144.24	61 Pm (145)	62 Sm 150.36	63 Eu 151.96	64 Gd 157.25	65 Tb 158.925	66 Dy 162.50	67 Ho 164.93	68 Er 167.26	69 Tm 168.934	70 Yb 173.04
89 Ac 227.028	90 Th 232.038	91 Pa 231.036	92 U 238.029	93 Np 237.048	94 Pu (244)	95 Am (243)	96 Cm (247)	97 Bk (247)	98 Cf (251)	99 Es (252)	100 Fm (257)	101 Md (258)	102 No (259)

SAMPLE PROBLEM   1

The vinegar you might find in your salad dressing is a solution of acetic acid ($HC_2H_3O_2$). What is the formula mass of acetic acid?

STRATEGY	SOLUTION
1. Analyze	You are given the chemical formula and are asked to determine the formula mass.
2. Plan	The formula mass is found by first multiplying the atomic mass of each element by the number of atoms of that element in the formula. The products of these numbers are then added together to find the mass of the entire formula.
3. Solve	H: 4 atoms × 1.0 amu = 4.0 amu C: 2 atoms × 12 amu = 24 amu O: 2 atoms × 16 amu = 32 amu Formula mass = 60 amu
4. Evaluate	The formula mass of acetic acid should be greater than the atomic masses of any of the individual elements, which it is. If the atomic mass of each atom were subtracted one by one from the formula mass, the result should be zero, which it is. Thus the answer makes sense.

PRACTICE PROBLEMS

1. What is the atomic mass of bromine (Br)? *(Answer: 79.9 amu)*

2. Carbonic acid (H_2CO_3) is found in carbonated drinks. What is the formula mass of carbonic acid? *(Answer: 62.0 amu)*

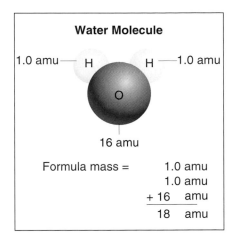

Water Molecule

1.0 amu — H   H — 1.0 amu

O

16 amu

Formula mass =   1.0 amu
                    1.0 amu
                 + 16   amu
                   18   amu

Figure 10–3 *The formula mass of a substance is found by adding the masses of each of the individual atoms in the molecule. The formula mass of a water molecule is found by adding the mass of 2 hydrogen atoms to the mass of an oxygen atom. What would be the formula mass of hydrogen peroxide (H_2O_2)?*

What Is a Mole?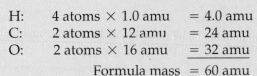

Although knowing the mass of 1 atom or 1 molecule in atomic mass units is important, it is not practical to use such units in the laboratory. Instead, the gram is the desired unit of mass. In the early 1900s, chemists recognized this fact and realized that they needed to find a way to relate the atomic mass of 1 atom of an element in atomic mass units to an amount of that element in grams.

To establish this relationship, scientists first had to identify what they already knew about atoms and mass. They knew the mass of 1 atom of every element in atomic mass units. They also knew that they could determine the mass of more than 1 atom

Figure 10–4 *The ratio of the mass of hydrogen to the mass of oxygen is 1:16. No matter how many atoms of hydrogen and oxygen you have, as long as the number of hydrogen atoms equals the number of oxygen atoms, you know that the mass ratio of hydrogen atoms to oxygen atoms is the same—1:16. What would be the ratio of the mass of 1000 hydrogen atoms to the mass of 1000 oxygen atoms?*

Mass Ratio of Hydrogen to Oxygen

Number of Atoms	Mass of Hydrogen (amu)	Mass of Oxygen (amu)	Ratio of Masses
1	1.0	16	1:16
2	2.0	32	1:16
5	5.0	80	1:16
10	10.	160	1:16
20	20.	320	1:16

of an element by multiplying the atomic mass of that element by the number of atoms, as you did when you were finding formula mass. Knowing this, they recognized an important relationship. They could determine the ratio of the mass of one element to the mass of another element. The ratio of the mass of hydrogen to the mass of oxygen is 1:16. Notice that even when the number of hydrogen and oxygen atoms is doubled, the ratio of their masses remains the same, 1:16. This mass ratio will be true for any number of hydrogen and oxygen atoms as long as there is an equal number of them. Ten atoms of hydrogen have a mass of 10.0 amu (10 atoms × 1.0 amu) and 10 atoms of oxygen have a mass of 160 amu (10 atoms × 16.0 amu). The ratio of the mass of the atoms is 1:16.

So far, chemists had established the following: As long as the masses of the element samples are in the same ratio as their atomic masses, there are equal numbers of atoms of each element. Knowing this, they were then able to approach the problem from the other direction. Rather than trying to measure the masses of individual atoms in grams, they measured quantities of each substance in grams according to the ratio of the atomic masses. For example, chemists might have chosen 1.0 gram of hydrogen atoms and 16.0 grams of oxygen atoms. As long as the masses of the elements in grams were in the same ratio as their atomic masses, the samples contained exactly the same number of atoms of each element.

The problem then was to determine the number of atoms in each sample. In other words, how many atoms are necessary to make up a mass in grams that is equal to an element's atomic mass in atomic mass units? For example, how many atoms would be necessary to make up a mass of 1.0 gram of hydrogen (atomic mass = 1.0 amu), 16.0 grams of oxygen (atomic mass = 16.0 amu), or 207.2 grams of lead (atomic mass = 207.2 amu)?

Counting atoms, like counting sand particles, is no easy task! Perhaps you are wondering if it is even possible, considering how very small atoms are. The answer is yes, but you do not count the number of atoms as you might count the number of baseballs in a bin or marbles in a box. Over the past 50 years, scientists have devised many direct and indirect methods for determining this number using sophisticated equipment. To find the number of atoms in a given mass of an element, chemists decided to use the element carbon as a standard. Recall from your earlier reading that the element carbon was also used as the standard for determining atomic mass. The atomic mass of the isotope carbon-12 is 12.0 amu. The number of atoms in 12.0 grams of carbon-12 was determined experimentally. From such experiments it was found that the number of atoms of an element whose mass in grams is numerically equal (has the same number value but different units) to its atomic mass is 6.02×10^{23}. This number is called a **mole** (abbreviated mol). **A mole of any element is defined as the number of atoms of that element equal to the number of atoms in exactly 12.0 grams of carbon-12.** The number of atoms in one mole of atoms is always the same— 6.02×10^{23}. See Figure 10–6. Thus, there are 6.02×10^{23} hydrogen atoms in 1.0 gram of hydrogen, 6.02×10^{23} oxygen atoms in 16.0 grams of oxygen, and 6.02×10^{23} lead atoms in 207 grams of lead. How many atoms are in 39.1 grams of potassium?

Figure 10–5 *You wouldn't want to lose a friend in this crowd! Majestic King penguins gather in groups too numerous to count. Similarly large numbers of spores are expelled from this puffball fungus after it is hit by a raindrop. Attempting to count such huge numbers as these would be a daunting task.*

Mass of One Mole of Selected Elements

	Number of Atoms in 1 Mole	Mass of 1 Mole
Copper (Cu)	6.02×10^{23} atoms Cu	63.5 g
Mercury (Hg)	6.02×10^{23} atoms Hg	201 g
Sulfur (S)	6.02×10^{23} atoms S	32.1 g
Iron (Fe)	6.02×10^{23} atoms Fe	55.8 g

Figure 10–6 *This photo shows 1-mole samples of copper (left), mercury (top), sulfur (right), and iron (bottom). Although each sample contains exactly the same number of atoms—6.02×10^{23}—each sample has a different mass. As the table indicates, the mass of 1 mole of each of the elements shown in the photograph varies greatly—from 32.1 g for sulfur to 201 g for mercury.*

The mole establishes a relationship between the atomic mass unit and the gram. The mass in grams of 1 mole of a substance is numerically equal to its atomic mass or formula mass in atomic mass units. Notice that any unit of mass could have been used. Had a unit other than the gram been chosen, however, the number of atoms in a mole would also have been different. For example, if scientists had chosen the kilogram as the unit, the number would have been a thousand times larger. In any case, chemists at the time chose the gram purposely, and thus the gram is the unit on which the mole is based.

The mole might seem to be a strange term. By now you know that this mole is not the furry little animal you saw at the beginning of the chapter (although it is filled with moles of atoms). Actually, although the term may be unusual, the concept is not. Every day you encounter many items that are usually packaged together and described as a group. For example, when you buy 12 of the same item, such as eggs, you say that you have bought a dozen. Similarly, a store owner who has purchased 144 pens will say that she has a gross of pens. And an office manager would order a ream of paper rather than asking for 500 sheets. Dozen, gross, and ream are three terms that describe groups. Like dozen, gross, or ream, it is convenient to have a special name to describe a group of atoms. The group in chemistry is the mole, and it contains 6.02×10^{23} items. The mole is so similar, in fact, to the other terms that it is sometimes referred to as the chemist's dozen!

6.02 × 10²³ particles

Mole

Figure 10–7 *Just as a dozen eggs are placed in a carton, many items are grouped together to make them easier to handle or measure. For example, clothes are packed in a suitcase before a trip and aluminum cans are bundled in a bag for recycling. Similarly, chemical particles are described and measured in groups called moles.*

What's in a Mole?

Because the mole is such a huge counting group, it is used to count only the extremely small particles that make up matter. The particles could be atoms, molecules, or formula units. The type of particles in a mole of a substance depends on the identity of the substance.

ATOMS AND MOLES So far you have learned that the number of atoms in 1 mole of an element is always 6.02×10^{23}. You will recall from Chapter 3 that an atom is the smallest particle of an element that retains the identity of that element. Thus when you are talking about a mole of particles in an element, the particles are usually atoms.

MOLECULES AND MOLES If a substance exists in a molecular form because its atoms are joined by covalent bonds, then its smallest particle is a molecule. A mole describes the number of molecules in such a substance. The number of molecules in a mole of any molecular compound is 6.02×10^{23}.

What type of particles are you describing when you say 1 mole of hydrogen? There are two answers to this question. You might mean hydrogen atoms if the sample contains hydrogen atoms. But more than likely, you are describing hydrogen molecules (H_2) because hydrogen is one of the seven elements that exist as diatomic molecules. Recall that the other six elements are oxygen, fluorine, chlorine, bromine, iodine, and nitrogen. You

Figure 10–8 *The cascading water that makes up this beautiful waterfall is a molecular compound. The representative particle of a molecular compound is a molecule. How many water molecules are in 1 mole of water?*

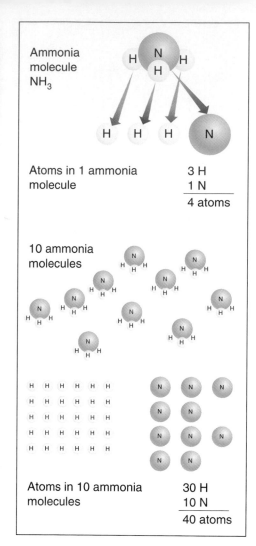

Ammonia molecule NH_3

Atoms in 1 ammonia molecule	3 H
	1 N
	4 atoms

10 ammonia molecules

Atoms in 10 ammonia molecules	30 H
	10 N
	40 atoms

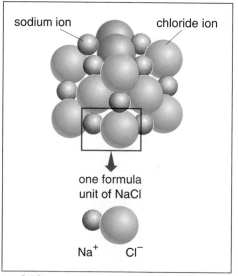

sodium ion   chloride ion

one formula unit of NaCl

Na^+ Cl^-

Figure 10–9 *Because molecules are made up of atoms, you can determine the number of atoms in a given number of molecules. For example, there are 4 atoms in 1 molecule of ammonia and there are 10 times as many, or 40 atoms, in 10 molecules of ammonia. One mole of ammonia molecules would contain 6.02×10^{23} times as many atoms as are in 1 molecule, or 4 moles of atoms ($4 \times 6.02 \times 10^{23}$). How many moles of atoms are in 5 moles of ammonia molecules?*

will have to be specific when describing these elements so that the type of sample you are referring to is obvious. In any case, 1 mole of H_2 contains 6.02×10^{23} H_2 molecules.

This relationship tells you more than the number of molecules in a mole, however. Can you see what other information it provides? Consider how many atoms are in each molecule of ammonia (NH_3). If your answer is 4 atoms you are correct—1 nitrogen atom and 3 hydrogen atoms. In each molecule of ammonia, there are 4 atoms. So 1 mole of ammonia contains 1 mole of NH_3 molecules, but four times as many atoms, or 4 moles of atoms (1 mole of nitrogen atoms and 3 moles of hydrogen atoms). One mole of water (H_2O) contains 1 mole of water molecules, but 3 moles of atoms. You can determine the number of moles of atoms in a mole of molecules by looking at the subscripts of the elements in the chemical formula for the substance.

FORMULA UNITS AND MOLES   A mole can also describe the number of ions in an ionic compound. As you may recall from Chapter 7, unlike molecular compounds, ionic compounds do not exist as distinct units. Ionic compounds are three-dimensional crystals composed of alternating cations and anions. For example, sodium chloride (NaCl) does not exist as a single sodium ion bonded to a single chloride ion. Instead, trillions of sodium ions alternate with trillions of chloride ions to form a single grain of salt.

If a substance is an ionic compound, it is represented by a formula unit. The formula unit is the lowest whole-number ratio of elements in an ionic compound. One mole of an ionic compound contains 6.02×10^{23} formula units of the compound. This means that 1 mole of sodium chloride contains 6.02×10^{23} formula units of NaCl and 1 mole of calcium chloride contains 6.02×10^{23} formula units of $CaCl_2$.

Because formula units can be described in terms of ions, it is possible to determine the number of moles of ions in 1 mole of formula units or in 1 mole of an ionic compound. For example,

Figure 10–10   *The representative particle of an ionic compound is a formula unit. Common table salt, sodium chloride, is an ionic compound made up of sodium and chloride ions. Notice how formula units join to form a crystal of sodium chloride.*

each formula unit of NaCl contains 2 ions, 1 Na$^+$ and 1 Cl$^-$. Therefore, 1 mole of formula units of NaCl (1 mole of the ionic compound) contains 1 mole of Na$^+$ ions and 1 mole of Cl$^-$ ions, or 2 moles of ions. Each formula unit of CaCl$_2$ contains 3 ions, 1 Ca^{2+} and 2 Cl$^-$. One mole of formula units of CaCl$_2$ (1 mole of the ionic compound) contains 1 mole of Ca^{2+} ions and 2 moles of Cl$^-$ ions, or 3 moles of ions. How many moles of Ca^{2+} and F$^-$ are in 1 mole of calcium fluoride (CaF$_2$)?

Avogadro's Number

By now you have seen the number of items in a mole, 6.02 × 10^{23}, many times. This number is extremely important and is known by heart by even the novice chemist. In fact, the quantity of items in a mole is so important in science that it has been given a special name. This number is known as **Avogadro's number** (abbreviated N) in honor of Amadeo Avogadro (1776–1856), an Italian chemist and physicist.

The enormity of this number may be difficult to imagine at first, but you can begin to appreciate it if you consider the following: Written in standard form, Avogadro's number is 602,000,000,000,000,000,000,000. Avogadro's number of sheets of paper stacked one sheet on top of another would reach beyond our solar system. Avogadro's number of basketballs could create a new planet the size of the Earth. Avogadro's number of grains of rice would cover the land masses of the Earth to a depth of 75 meters.

Now think about this. If you had Avogadro's number, 6.02 × 10^{23}, of pennies and decided to give away $1 million (that's 100,000,000 pennies) a day to every person on Earth, it would take you more than 3000 years to distribute all your money. Do you see now why a mole, which contains Avogadro's number of particles, is used only to count tiny particles such as atoms, molecules, and formula units?

Figure 10–11 *The marble that gives the Lincoln Memorial in Washington, D.C., its strength and beauty is an ionic compound called calcium carbonate (CaCO$_3$). How many formula units are in 1 mole of marble?*

Mass of One Mole of Selected Substances

Substance	Representative Particle	Number of Particles in 1 Mole	Mass of 1 Mole
Neon (Ne)	atom	6.02 × 10^{23}	20.2 g
Zinc (Zn)	atom	6.02 × 10^{23}	65.4 g
Oxygen (O$_2$)	molecule	6.02 × 10^{23}	32.0 g
Water (H$_2$O)	molecule	6.02 × 10^{23}	18.0 g
Magnesium oxide (MgO)	formula unit	6.02 × 10^{23}	40.3 g
Calcium fluoride (CaF$_2$)	formula unit	6.02 × 10^{23}	78.1 g

Figure 10–12 *The table lists several chemical substances, the representative particle for each, and the number of particles in and the mass of 1 mole of each substance. Notice that no matter which type of substance, the number of particles in a mole remains the same. The mass of 1 mole of each substance, however, is different. Why?*

Figure 10–13 This pile of shiny pennies seems endless, yet it is only a small fraction of the number that would be in a mole of pennies. Let's exaggerate and suppose there were 5 million pennies ($50,000) in this pile. What fraction of a mole would this be?

Molar Mass

You now know that while the number of items in a mole of a substance is always the same, the mass of that mole varies. **The mass in grams of 1 mole of a substance is called the molar mass of the substance.** The **molar mass** (abbreviated M) depends upon the masses of the particles—atoms, molecules, or formula units—that make up the substance.

Figure 10–14 Although the number of particles in a mole of any substance is constant, the mass of 1 mole varies. Notice that the mass in grams of 1 mole of a substance is numerically equal to the atomic mass or formula mass in atomic mass units.

Molar Mass of Selected Substances

Substance	Type of Substance	Atomic or Formula Mass	Molar Mass
Calcium (Ca)	atomic element	40 amu	40 g
Carbon (C)	atomic element	12 amu	12 g
Hydrogen (H_2)	diatomic element	2 amu	2 g
Hydrogen peroxide (H_2O_2)	molecular compound	34 amu	34 g
Sodium chloride (NaCl)	ionic compound	58.5 amu	58.5 g
Calcium chloride ($CaCl_2$)	ionic compound	111 amu	111 g

The molar mass of a substance can be determined from its atomic mass or formula mass. Because you know that 1 mole of any element is the amount of that substance that has a mass in grams numerically equal to the atomic mass or formula mass, the molar mass (the mass of 1 mole) must also be numerically equal to the atomic mass or formula mass.

SAMPLE PROBLEM 2

During photosynthesis, plants produce glucose ($C_6H_{12}O_6$), which is a sugar that can be broken down for energy. What is the molar mass of glucose?

STRATEGY	SOLUTION
1. Analyze	You are given the chemical formula and need to find the molar mass, or mass in grams of 1 mole of the substance.
2. Plan	The molar mass is numerically equal to the formula mass of the compound. The formula mass is found by first multiplying the atomic mass of each element by the number of atoms of that element in the compound. The sum of these products is the formula mass.

3. Solve

C: 12.0 amu/atom × 6 atoms = 72 amu
H: 1.0 amu/atom × 12 atoms = 12 amu
O: 16.0 amu/atom × 6 atoms = <u>96 amu</u>

Formula mass $C_6H_{12}O_6$ = 180 amu
Molar mass $C_6H_{12}O_6$ = 180 g/mol

4. Evaluate   The answer should be the mass of 1 mole of glucose. The answer is reasonable because it is the same as the mass of 6 moles of carbon atoms, 12 moles of hydrogen atoms, and 6 moles of oxygen atoms.

PRACTICE PROBLEMS

3. Find the molar mass of carbon monoxide (CO).   *(Answer: 28.0 g/mol)*

4. Stomach acid is made up of hydrochloric acid (HCl). What is the molar mass of HCl?   *(Answer: 36.5 g/mol)*

How Many Pages Is That?

Steve is in the process of writing a 3000-word term paper. He has done his research and thinks he has an interesting approach to his topic. His biggest worry is whether he can write a paper with 3000 words. That seems like so many words!

Steve thinks that if he can find out how many

pages his paper should be, it won't seem like such a big task. The number of pages will be smaller than the number of words he needs to write. Steve begins counting the words he has written, but loses track of the number by the time he gets to the fourth page.

Steve's sister Katie asks what he is doing. When Steve explains that he is trying to count all the words he has written so far, Katie has an idea. She asks how many lines of type are on one page and how many words are in an average line. She is thinking of a way to simplify counting every word in the paper. How is Katie planning to find the number of pages in a 3000-word paper?

Reaching Conclusions

1. How could Steve find the number of pages he needs to write based on the number of words per page?

2. What are some advantages in working with units that represent a large number of individual items?

10–1 Section Review

1. What is a mole?

2. How does the mole relate to atoms, molecules, and ions?

3. What is Avogadro's number and why is it significant?

4. If you wanted to produce carbon dioxide from 12 grams of carbon, how many grams of oxygen would you need?

5. **Connection—Language Arts**   There are many words, such as pair, dozen, and gross, that represent an accepted number of items. What might be the purpose of using a standard term to describe a certain number?

10–2 Mole Conversions

Can you imagine following a cookbook recipe that reads, "Place 500,000 particles of flour into a mixing bowl"? Of course not. For while it is possible to measure flour by counting individual particles, it is just not practical. Just think about how much time it would take to measure out 500,000 particles. You probably measure flour by volume or mass. Similarly, scientists working with chemicals do not try to count the particles. Rather, they measure amounts of substances by volume or mass. Yet chemical samples are described by moles, and the mole was defined as a number of particles. How, then, do scientists relate a number of particles to a mass or volume? The answer is that they can convert among the various measurements.

Although a baker does not have a unit by which to convert among the number of particles, mass, and volume, the chemist does. **Because the mole measures both a mass and a number of particles (and as you will soon learn, a volume of a gas), it is the central unit in converting the amount of a substance from one type of measurement to another.** Understanding how to use the mole, then, is essential to the study of chemistry.

Mass and Moles

If you know the mass of a given amount of a substance, you can calculate the number of moles of the substance. For example, suppose you have a sample of sodium chloride (NaCl) that has

Guide for Reading

- How can you convert among the number of moles, the number of particles, and the mass of a sample?
- What is the relationship between 1 mole of a gas and its volume at standard temperature and pressure?

Figure 10–15 *Fortunately, cooks can measure flour by mass or volume rather than by counting individual particles. The cost of grapes at a fruit market and the cost of bolts in a hardware store are usually dependent on the mass (and in turn the weight) of the package rather than on the exact number of each purchased. What is another substance that you would rather measure by mass or volume than by the number of particles? Can you think of anything that you would rather count by pieces than measure by mass or volume?*

Figure 10–16 *Many animals, including this huge elephant, gather at salt licks to obtain the salt needed by their bodies. How many moles of NaCl does an elephant take in if it consumes 60 grams of NaCl?*

a mass of 11.2 grams. You need to know how many moles of sodium chloride this is. What do you do? You must first determine the molar mass of sodium chloride. (Remember that the molar mass is numerically equal to the formula mass.) The formula mass of sodium chloride is 58.5 amu (23.0 amu + 35.5 amu). The molar mass of sodium chloride is then 58.5 grams/mole. In other words, 1 mole of NaCl has a mass of 58.5 grams.

You can now determine the number of moles by setting up an equation. Recall from dimensional analysis that when you are converting units, you need a conversion factor, which is a fraction whose value is equal to 1. The conversion factor should have the units you are seeking in the numerator and the units you already know in the denominator. Because you are looking for the number of moles, the conversion factor should be 1 mol NaCl/58.5 g NaCl. The equation can be written as

$$11.2 \text{ g NaCl} \times \frac{1 \text{ mol NaCl}}{58.5 \text{ g NaCl}} = 0.191 \text{ mol NaCl} \quad \textbf{(Eq. 1)}$$

Thus there is 0.191 mole of NaCl in an 11.2-gram sample.

In a similar way, you can determine the mass of a sample if you know the number of moles in that sample. This time suppose you have 2.50 moles of NaCl for an experiment. How many grams do you have? Again you first find the molar mass, which you know is 58.5 grams/mole. This time your conversion factor is 58.5 g NaCl/1 mol NaCl. Now you can set up an equation.

$$2.50 \text{ mol NaCl} \times \frac{58.5 \text{ g NaCl}}{1 \text{ mol NaCl}} = 146 \text{ g NaCl} \quad \textbf{(Eq. 2)}$$

The mass of 2.50 moles of NaCl is 146 grams.

Figure 10–17 shows the relationship between mass and moles. You should become familiar with these conversions, as it will make calculations easier to do as you complete the problems in this section.

Figure 10–17 *The mass of a sample can be determined if the number of moles of substance in that sample is known. The reverse is also true. The number of moles in a sample can be determined if the mass of the sample is known. The molar mass of the substance in the sample makes these conversions possible. How does the conversion factor differ depending on which information is given?*

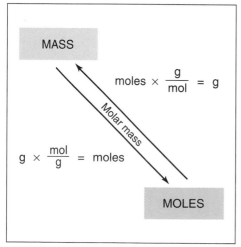

The Search for an Accurate Value

Determining a number as huge as Avogadro's number is no simple task. Nonetheless, Avogadro's number has been derived by scientists using a variety of experimental methods.

One of the earliest experiments to determine the number of particles in a mole was performed by Austrian chemist Johann Loschmidt in 1865. Loschmidt found that there were approximately 1×10^{24} molecules in a mole of gas. Shortly after, French scientist Jean Baptiste Perrin concluded that the number of molecules in a mole was 6.8×10^{23} during an investigation in which he studied how gravity altered the rate at which particles settle in a colloid.

In 1911, British chemist and physicist Ernest Rutherford tried his hand at searching for Avogadro's number while measuring the alpha particles emitted by radioactive radium. Rutherford was able to count alpha particles with the use of a gadget invented by his assistant, Hans Geiger. That gadget was the Geiger counter. By counting alpha particles and then measuring the volume of helium gas formed when the alpha particles decayed, Rutherford calculated the number of particles in a mole to be 6.11×10^{23}. The next scientist to try was American physicist Robert Millikan. He determined the number of electrons in a mole to be 6.02×10^{23} through his famous oil drop experiment, in which he suspended small charged oil drops using an electric field to counter the force of gravity.

A more modern method that is used to determine Avogadro's number uses the fact that light is scattered as it travels through the Earth's atmosphere.

The most accurate method for arriving at Avogadro's number, however, is using X-ray diffraction. In this method, X-ray beams are directed at a crystalline substance. When the X-ray beams strike the nuclei of atoms in the crystal, the paths of the beams are changed, or diffracted. Computer analysis of the angles at which the beams are diffracted, as well as the structure of the crystal, provides enough information to determine the number of atoms in a given sample. This method has generated a value of 6.0221367×10^{23} particles per mole—the most accurate value to date.

While it is not necessary to understand the details of these methods, it is important for you to recognize how the development of technology went hand-in-hand with the search for an accurate value of Avogadro's number. As scientific instruments became more sophisticated, the value of Avogadro's number was determined with greater accuracy. Maybe you will be the next scientist to calculate the number with even more accuracy!

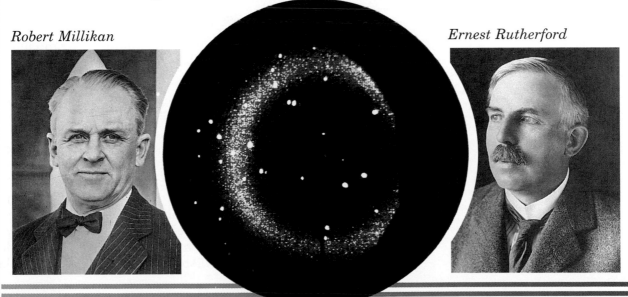

Robert Millikan

Ernest Rutherford

SAMPLE PROBLEM 3

To carry out a chemical reaction you need 3.20 moles of zinc nitrate ($Zn(NO_3)_2$). What is the mass of 3.20 moles of $Zn(NO_3)_2$?

STRATEGY	SOLUTION
1. **Analyze**	You are given the number of moles of $Zn(NO_3)_2$ and are asked to find the mass.
2. **Plan**	You can solve this problem by determining the conversion factor that will enable you to convert moles to mass. The conversion factor will need to have moles in the denominator and mass in the numerator. The conversion factor will include the molar mass of $Zn(NO_3)_2$.
3. **Solve**	The molar mass of $Zn(NO_3)_2$ is 189.4 g/mol.

Zn: 65.4 amu/atom $\times$ 1 atom = 65.4 amu
N: 14.0 amu/atom $\times$ 2 atoms = 28.0 amu
O: 16.0 amu/atom $\times$ 6 atoms = 96.0 amu
$\underline{\qquad\qquad\qquad\qquad\qquad\qquad}$
Formula mass $Zn(NO_3)_2$ = 189.4 amu
Molar mass $Zn(NO_3)_2$ = 189.4 g/mol

Thus the equation is

$$3.20 \; \cancel{mol \; Zn(NO_3)_2} \times \frac{189.4 \text{ g } Zn(NO_3)_2}{1 \; \cancel{mol \; Zn(NO_3)_2}}$$

$$= 606 \text{ g } Zn(NO_3)_2$$

4. **Evaluate**   The answer is reasonable. Because the mass of 1 mole of $Zn(NO_3)_2$ is 189.4 g, the mass of 3.20 moles should be more than three times greater, which it is.

PRACTICE PROBLEMS

5. Find the mass of 0.650 mol P_2O_5.   *(Answer: 92.3 g)*

6. A bottle of $NaNO_3$ contains 100.0 grams of the compound. How many moles of $NaNO_3$ does it contain?   *(Answer: 1.176 moles)*

Particles and Moles

Just as you can convert between moles and mass, you can also convert between moles and particles. This conversion is somewhat simpler, however, because you do not need to calculate molar mass. In fact, it is not even necessary to know the identity of the substance because the number of particles in 1 mole of any substance is always the same—Avogadro's number. If you know how many moles are in a given amount of a substance, then the number of particles will be 6.02×10^{23} times that number of moles. Let's try an example. How many molecules are in 2 moles of water (H_2O)? To find the answer, you simply multiply the number of molecules in 1 mole of water (6.02×10^{23}) by 2. The answer is 12.0×10^{23}. This number should be rewritten as 1.20×10^{24}. How many formula units are in 3 moles of $Zn(NO_3)_2$?

The reverse is also true: If you know how many particles are in a given sample of a substance, you can calculate the number of moles in the substance. This is essentially done by dividing the number of particles by Avogadro's number.

Figure 10–18 shows the relationship between moles and particles. As before, you should become familiar with the relationship as you solve the problems provided here.

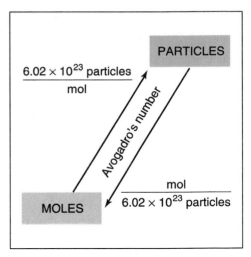

Figure 10–18 *The number of particles in a sample can be determined from the number of moles just as the number of moles can be determined from the number of particles. Knowing the number of representative particles in a mole of any substance—6.02×10^{23}—makes these conversions possible. How many atoms are in 3.2 moles of silver?*

SAMPLE PROBLEM 4

A piece of marble contains 8.74×10^{23} formula units of calcium carbonate ($CaCO_3$). How many moles of $CaCO_3$ is that?

STRATEGY	SOLUTION
1. Analyze	You know the number of formula units and need to determine the number of moles.
2. Plan	The conversion factor you need will have formula units in the denominator and moles in the numerator. The conversion factor will include the number of formula units (u) in 1 mole of $CaCO_3$.
3. Solve	Set up your equation, cancel units, and perform the necessary arithmetic.

$$8.74 \times 10^{23} \text{ u } CaCO_3 \times \frac{1 \text{ mol } CaCO_3}{6.02 \times 10^{23} \text{ u } CaCO_3}$$

$$= 1.45 \text{ mol } CaCO_3$$

4. Evaluate	In this problem you divided the number of formula units you had by the number of formula units in each mole. Because 8.74 is almost 9, when you divide this number by 6.02 you expect the answer to be about 1.5, which it is. The exponential (10^{23}) cancels out.

PRACTICE PROBLEMS

7. Determine the number of atoms in 0.36 mol Al. *(Answer: 2.2×10^{23} atoms)*

8. How many moles of sodium carbonate (Na_2CO_3) contain 7.9×10^{24} formula units? *(Answer: 13 moles)*

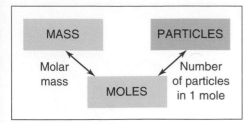

Figure 10–19 *The mole serves as a bridge between the mass of a sample and the number of particles in that sample. Whether you know the mass of the sample and are looking for the number of particles or vice versa, the first step is always to convert the given information to moles and then from moles to the information you are seeking. What must you know to complete these conversions?*

Multistep Conversions

So far you have learned how to convert between moles and mass and between moles and particles. But what if you want to convert between mass and particles? You can complete such a calculation in much the same way with the only difference being that two conversion factors instead of one are needed. Figure 10–19 combines the two relationships described previously.

Suppose you know that a given sample contains 7.2×10^{22} atoms of Ca. How can you determine the mass of the sample? The first step is to realize that you know everything you need to know to solve the problem! The next step is to convert the number of atoms of calcium to moles. And the final step is to convert the number of moles to mass. The mole is the "bridge" to get from one "side" of a problem to the other—whether from particles to mass or mass to particles. Recall from Chapter 1 that for lengthy conversions, it is more efficient to combine the steps.

$$7.2 \times 10^{22} \text{ atoms Ca} \times \frac{1 \text{ mol Ca}}{6.02 \times 10^{23} \text{ atoms Ca}}$$
$$\times \frac{40.1 \text{ g Ca}}{1 \text{ mol Ca}} = 4.8 \text{ g Ca} \quad \textbf{(Eq. 3)}$$

Thus the sample of Ca has a mass of 4.8 grams. You can use the same steps in the reverse direction to convert the mass of a sample to the number of particles it contains.

At this point you should be getting used to the procedure: Convert the information to moles and then convert the number of moles to the unit you are seeking. If you get confused, refer back to Figure 10–19.

Figure 10–20 *This color-enhanced computer X-ray shows the wrist bones in a human hand. The health of bones depends upon a good supply of calcium. If a person consumes 0.05 gram of calcium, how many atoms of calcium is that?*

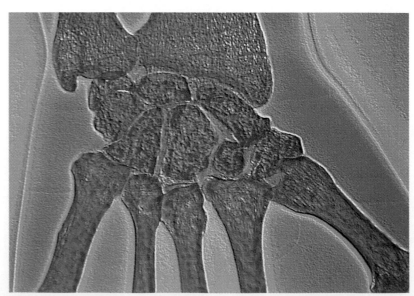

SAMPLE PROBLEM 5

You need 250 grams of table sugar, or sucrose ($C_{12}H_{22}O_{11}$), to bake a cake. How many sucrose molecules will be in the cake?

STRATEGY	SOLUTION
1. Analyze	You know the mass of the sample and want to find the number of molecules in that mass.
2. Plan	You must convert the mass to moles using the molar mass of $C_{12}H_{22}O_{11}$ and then convert the moles to the number of molecules using Avogadro's number.

3. Solve

$$250 \text{ g } C_{12}H_{22}O_{11} \times \frac{1 \text{ mol } C_{12}H_{22}O_{11}}{342.3 \text{ g } C_{12}H_{22}O_{11}}$$

$$\times \frac{6.02 \times 10^{23} \text{ molecules}}{1 \text{ mol } C_{12}H_{22}O_{11}}$$

$$= 4.4 \times 10^{23} \text{ molecules } C_{12}H_{22}O_{11}$$

4. Evaluate Because the mass of sucrose in the cake is less than the formula mass of sucrose, the number of molecules used should also be less than the number of molecules in 1 mole; 4.4×10^{23} is less than 6.02×10^{23}. Therefore, this answer is reasonable.

PRACTICE PROBLEMS

9. How many formula units of $NaHCO_3$ are in 1.8 g of sodium bicarbonate (baking soda)? *(Answer: 1.3 × 10²² formula units)*

10. If you burned 4.0×10^{24} molecules of natural gas, or methane (CH_4), during a laboratory experiment, what mass of methane did you burn? *(Answer: 110 g)*

The molar mass of a substance allows you to relate mass, moles, and the number of particles of that substance. By knowing the molar mass of a substance, such as methane, CH_4, you have the following conversion factors: molar mass = 16.0 g CH_4 = 1 mol CH_4 = 6.02×10^{23} molecules of CH_4.
To convert 9.03×10^{23} molecules of CH_4 to the mass of CH_4, you would use the following dimensional analysis:

$$9.03 \times 10^{23} \text{ molecules } CH_4$$

$$\times \frac{1 \text{ mol}}{6.02 \times 10^{23} \text{ molecules of } CH_4}$$

$$\times \frac{16.0 \text{ g } CH_4}{1 \text{ mol } CH_4}$$

Moles and Gases

There is one more important measurement related to the mole. It is the volume of a gas. Recall from Chapter 2 that in a gas, the particles are spread out from one another. Avogadro proposed that at the same temperature and pressure, equal volumes of gases contain the same number of gas particles. Therefore, 1 mole of a gas would occupy the same volume as 1 mole of any other gas at the same temperature and pressure. It was later found experimentally that 1 mole of any gas at standard temperature and pressure (STP, 0°C and 1 atmosphere) has a volume of 22.4 cubic decimeters (dm^3), which is the same as 22.4 liters (L). This volume of gas is called a **molar volume** because it is the volume of 1 mole of a gas at STP.

Figure 10–21 *In the photograph are shown 1-mole samples of a solid, a liquid, and a gas. How many liters of air must be in the balloon at STP?*

Figure 10–22 *The mole enables you to convert among the mass, number of particles, and volume of a gas at STP. Remember that it can be thought of as a bridge used to get from one unit of measurement to another.*

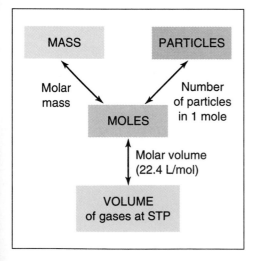

The molar volume relationship can be used to convert between the volume of that gas at standard temperature and pressure (STP), the number of moles of the gas, the number of particles in the gas, and the mass of the gas. But you must remember that the value of 22.4 L/mol of gas applies only to gases and only at standard temperature and pressure. Figure 10–22 now shows the total relationship among moles, mass, particles, and the volume of a gas. You can use this additional information to solve more problems—which you are probably eager to do now that you are getting so good at it!

SAMPLE PROBLEM 6

A student fills a 1.0-L flask with carbon dioxide (CO_2) at standard temperature and pressure. How many molecules of gas are in the flask?

STRATEGY	SOLUTION
1. Analyze	You know the volume of the gas at standard conditions and need to determine the number of molecules in that volume.

2. Plan You need to convert from volume to moles using the molar volume of a gas at STP as a conversion factor. Then you need to convert from moles to molecules using Avogadro's number.

3. Solve Set up your equation. Cancel units and perform the necessary arithmetic.

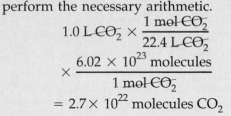

$$1.0 \text{ L } CO_2 \times \frac{1 \text{ mol } CO_2}{22.4 \text{ L } CO_2}$$
$$\times \frac{6.02 \times 10^{23} \text{ molecules}}{1 \text{ mol } CO_2}$$
$$= 2.7 \times 10^{22} \text{ molecules } CO_2$$

4. Evaluate The answer makes sense because the volume of gas collected is about 20 times less than the volume occupied by 1 mole of a gas. This means that the number of molecules should be about one twentieth of Avogadro's number.

PRACTICE PROBLEMS

11. A room with a volume of 4000. L contains how many moles of air at STP? *(Answer: 178.6 moles of air)*

12. A chemical reaction produces 0.82 mole of oxygen gas. What volume will that gas occupy at STP? *(Answer: 18 L)*

10–2 Section Review

1. Describe how to convert from moles to mass. From moles to particles.

2. Explain the importance of the mole in converting from one unit of measurement to another.

3. What is molar volume?

4. **Theme Trace—Unity and Diversity** You know that for a gas at standard temperature and pressure there is a direct relationship between the volume of the gas and the number of moles present. For liquids and solids, what other property must be considered if you want to find the number of moles and you are given the volume of the substance?

- What is percentage composition of a substance?
- How are empirical formulas calculated?
- What is a molecular formula and how is it found?

Figure 10–23 *Teachers often base a class grade on several components. Each component is responsible for a percentage of the final grade. What percentage of the final grade in this teacher's class is determined by the science project and class participation?*

SCIENCE

Your science grade will be made up of the following:

class participation	20%
science project	20%
quizzes	15 %
exams	20%
midterm/final	25%
	100%

10–3 Empirical and Molecular Formulas

The formula for a compound indicates the number and kind of each atom in a representative particle of the compound. You have learned how to perform a number of useful calculations based on the formula for a substance and various mole relationships. But what you may not realize is that there are different types of formulas and different information you can learn from them. So how is a chemical formula determined in the first place? Before you can understand how formulas are determined, you must first learn about the relationships among the various elements in a compound.

Percentage Composition

Suppose you sleep seven hours each night. What percentage of each day do you spend sleeping? To find the answer you first divide the number of hours you spend asleep by the total number of hours in a day ($7 \div 24 = 0.29$). Then you multiply the answer by 100 percent to get the percentage ($0.29 \times 100\% = 29\%$). If you sleep seven hours, you are asleep for 29 percent of each day.

Just as the length of a day is made up of smaller units such as hours, the mass of a compound is made up of smaller amounts of different elements. So in much the same way as you calculated the percentage of the day you slept, you can determine what part of the total mass of a compound is made up by each element in a compound. **The mass of each element in a compound compared to the entire mass of the compound and multiplied by 100 percent is called the percentage composition of the compound.** Thus the **percentage composition** of a compound tells you the percent of the mass made up by each element in the compound.

The percentage composition of a compound can be determined in one of two ways. The first is by calculating percentage composition from a given chemical formula. For example, suppose you have 1 mole of water. One mole of water has a mass of 18 grams. Recall that 1 mole of water molecules contains 2 moles of hydrogen atoms and 1 mole of oxygen atoms. To find the percentage composition, then, you need to determine what part of the total mass, 18 grams, is made up of hydrogen atoms and what part is made up of oxygen atoms. To do this, first find the mass of the hydrogen atoms. Two moles of hydrogen atoms have a mass of 2.0 grams. Then divide the mass of the hydrogen atoms by the mass of the water and multiply the answer by 100 percent.

$$\text{percentage of hydrogen} = \frac{2.0 \text{ g H}}{18 \text{ g H}_2\text{O}} \times 100\%$$

$$= 11\% \qquad \textbf{(Eq. 4)}$$

Figure 10–24 *Whether a given amount of water is as tiny as a drop on a leaf or as great as the amount in a lake, the percentage composition of water is always the same. You know that hydrogen will always make up 11 percent of the water's mass and oxygen will make up the remaining 89 percent. Although the masses of the samples will vary, the percentage composition will not.*

Now repeat the procedure for oxygen. One mole of oxygen atoms has a mass of 16.0 grams.

$$\text{percentage of oxygen} = \frac{16 \text{ g O}}{18 \text{ g H}_2\text{O}} \times 100\%$$

$$= 89\% \qquad \textbf{(Eq. 5)}$$

The second way to find the percentage composition of a compound is by experimental analysis. In this method, the mass of the sample is measured. The sample is then decomposed, or chemically separated, into its component elements. The masses of the component elements are then determined and the percentage composition is calculated as before—by dividing the mass of each element by the mass of the sample and multiplying by 100 percent.

SAMPLE PROBLEM 7

A sample of an unknown compound with a mass of 0.2370 g is extracted from the roots of a plant. Decomposition of the sample produces 0.09480 g of carbon, 0.1264 g of oxygen, and 0.0158 g of hydrogen. What is the percentage composition of the compound?

STRATEGY	SOLUTION
1. Analyze	You know the mass of the sample as well as the masses of the component elements. You need to determine what percentage of the total mass is made up by each element.
2. Plan	Determine the percentage of each element in the compound by dividing the mass of each element by the total mass of the sample, then multiplying by 100 percent.

3. Solve

$$\text{percentage C} = \frac{0.0948 \text{ g}}{0.2370 \text{ g}} \times 100\%$$

$$= 40.00\%$$

$$\text{percentage O} = \frac{0.1264 \text{ g}}{0.2370 \text{ g}} \times 100\%$$

$$= 53.33\%$$

$$\text{percentage H} = \frac{0.0158 \text{ g}}{0.2370 \text{ g}} \times 100\%$$

$$= 6.67\%$$

4. Evaluate   If the percentages were calculated accurately, the sum of all the percentages should equal 100 percent. The sum of the percentages in this problem does equal 100 percent after rounding up.

PRACTICE PROBLEMS

13. Find the percentage composition of a compound that contains 2.30 g of sodium, 1.60 g of oxygen, and 0.100 g of hydrogen in a 4.00-g sample of the compound.   *(Answer: 57.5% Na, 40.0% O, 2.50% H)*

14. A sample of an unknown compound with a mass of 0.562 g has the following percentage composition: 13.0% carbon, 2.20% hydrogen, and 84.8% fluorine. When this compound is decomposed into its elements, what mass of each element would be recovered?   *(Answer: 0.0731 g C, 0.0124 g H, 0.477 g F)*

Determining Empirical Formula

You have learned how to determine the percentage composition by mass of a compound from a chemical formula and from experimental data. Do you think you can go in the other direction—use the percentage composition to determine the chemical formula? The answer is yes. You can go from a ratio of masses (percentage composition) to a ratio of atoms (chemical formula). The ratio of atoms will be the simplest whole-number ratio of atoms of the elements. **A formula that gives the simplest whole-number ratio of the atoms of the elements is called an empirical formula.**

You may recall having seen some **empirical formulas** in the previous chapters. The empirical formula for hydrogen peroxide is HO. This means that a molecule of hydrogen peroxide always has equal numbers of hydrogen and oxygen atoms. However, it does not necessarily mean that a molecule of hydrogen peroxide has only 1 of each atom. The empirical formula simply tells you the ratio of the atoms, in this case 1:1.

Suppose you are given a compound with a percentage composition by mass that is 80 percent carbon and 20 percent hydrogen. To begin, assume you are dealing with 100.0 grams of the compound. If you have 100.0 grams of the compound, then the mass of each element will have the same numerical value as the percentage of that element. Thus a 100-gram sample of the unknown compound contains 80 grams of carbon and 20 grams of hydrogen.

The next step is based on the fact that the ratio of atoms in a chemical formula is the ratio of moles of atoms in a mole of the compound. Remember that the subscripts indicate the number of moles of atoms in a compound. The empirical formula is found by converting the mass of each element in the sample to the number of moles of atoms of that element. Recall that to convert from mass to moles you need to use a conversion factor that includes the molar mass of the element. In this case

$$80 \text{ g C} \times \frac{1 \text{ mol C}}{12.0 \text{ g C}} = 6.7 \text{ mol C atoms} \qquad \textbf{(Eq. 6)}$$

$$20 \text{ g H} \times \frac{1 \text{ mol H}}{1.0 \text{ g H}} = 20 \text{ mol H atoms} \qquad \textbf{(Eq. 7)}$$

Thus 100 grams of this compound contains 6.7 moles of carbon atoms and 20 moles of hydrogen atoms. The smallest whole-number ratio of these amounts can be found by dividing each mole value by the smaller of the two values.

$$\text{C: } \frac{6.7}{6.7} = 1 \qquad\qquad \text{H: } \frac{20}{6.7} = 2.98 \qquad \textbf{(Eq. 8)}$$

Because you are looking for whole numbers, 2.98 must be rounded to 3. Thus the ratio of carbon atoms to hydrogen atoms is 1:3. The empirical formula for this compound is CH_3. If there were more than two elements in the compound, you would divide all the mole amounts by the smallest amount.

Exploration

Eggshell Analysis

1. Find the mass of a clean, dry eggshell.
2. Break the eggshell into pieces and place the pieces in a beaker or dish.
3. Pour vinegar over the shell pieces and set the dish aside for several days. Make sure all of the shell pieces are covered with vinegar.
4. After several days, rinse and dry the remaining eggshell pieces. Find the mass of the dried shell pieces.
5. Compare the mass of the shell before and after adding vinegar. The difference in mass is the loss of the calcium carbonate that was in the eggshell.
6. Using the formula mass of $CaCO_3$, determine how many moles of $CaCO_3$ were in the eggshell. How many formula units would that be?
On Your Own In some regions of the country acid rain reacts with eggshells to remove some of the calcium carbonate and soften the shells. Collect some rainwater and try this activity using rainwater instead of vinegar. Is there a change in mass?

SAMPLE PROBLEM 8

A compound was analyzed and found to contain 13.5 g Ca, 10.8 g O, and 0.675 g H. What is the empirical formula for the compound?

STRATEGY

SOLUTION

1. Analyze

You are given the mass of each element in the compound and are asked to find the empirical formula.

2. Plan

First convert the mass of each element to a number of moles using molar mass. Then find the lowest whole-number ratio of moles.

3. Solve

Find mole amounts:

$$13.5 \text{ g Ca} \times \frac{1 \text{ mol Ca}}{40.08 \text{ g Ca}} = 0.337 \text{ mol Ca}$$

$$10.8 \text{ g O} \times \frac{1 \text{ mol O}}{16.0 \text{ g O}} = 0.675 \text{ mol O}$$

$$0.675 \text{ g H} \times \frac{1 \text{ mol H}}{1.01 \text{ g H}} = 0.668 \text{ mol H}$$

Divide each mole value by the smallest number of moles (0.337 mole):

$$\frac{0.337 \text{ mol Ca}}{0.337} = 1.00 \text{ mol Ca}$$

$$\frac{0.675 \text{ mol O}}{0.337} = 2.00 \text{ mol O}$$

$$\frac{0.668 \text{ mol H}}{0.337} = 1.98 \text{ mol H}$$

This mole ratio of the elements can be rounded to 1 Ca : 2 O : 2 H and is represented by the subscripts in the empirical formula. The empirical formula is CaO_2H_2. Because 2 moles of O and 2 moles of H in an ionic compound probably means 2 moles of OH^- ions, the empirical formula can be rewritten as $Ca(OH)_2$

4. Evaluate

The empirical formula can be confirmed by comparing the percentage composition of the elements given in the problem to the percentage composition of $Ca(OH)_2$. In both cases Ca = 54.1%, O = 43.2%, and H = 2.70%.

15. Determine the empirical formula for a compound containing 2.128 g Cl and 1.203 g Ca. *(Answer: $CaCl_2$)*

16. Determine the empirical formula for a compound containing 7.30 g Na, 5.08 g S, and 7.62 g O. *(Answer: Na_2SO_3)*

Determining Molecular Formula

The empirical formula for a compound indicates the simplest ratio of the atoms in the compound. However, it does not tell you the actual numbers of atoms in each molecule of the compound. Recall that the empirical formula for hydrogen peroxide is HO. In actuality, hydrogen peroxide has 2 atoms of each element per molecule (H_2O_2). While the ratio is 1:1, the number of atoms of each element is not necessarily 1 and 1. This information is extremely important. The exact number of atoms in each molecule of a compound determines the properties, or characteristics, of that compound.

The formula that gives the actual number of atoms of each element in a molecular compound is called the molecular formula. The **molecular formula** is always a whole-number multiple of the empirical formula. You can determine the molecular formula for an unknown compound by comparing the molar mass of the unknown compound with the molar mass of the empirical formula, or the empirical formula mass. This will tell you what

Figure 10–25 Acetylene used in a torch, styrene used in packing materials, and benzene, a dangerous chemical once used in insecticides, all share the same empirical formula. How does an empirical formula differ from a molecular formula?

Figure 10–26 *Most plant leaves contain glucose, the sugar produced during photosynthesis. When you eat plants, in the form of fruits and vegetables, your body uses that glucose for energy. Lettuce leaves contain mostly cellulose, which your body cannot use for energy.*

multiple of the empirical formula is the formula for the unknown compound. The molar mass of the compound is determined experimentally. The empirical formula mass is found just as you found the molar mass of other formulas.

Now let's consider an example. The empirical formula for glucose is CH_2O. Its empirical formula mass is 30 g/mol (12 g/mol C + 2(1.0 g/mol H) + 16 g/mol O). Experiments show that the molar mass of glucose is 180 g/mol. So

$$\frac{180 \text{ g/mol glucose}}{30.0 \text{ g/mol } CH_2O} = 6 \text{ mol } CH_2O/\text{mol glucose} \qquad \textbf{(Eq. 9)}$$

The molar mass of glucose is six times greater than its empirical formula mass. The molecular formula for glucose must therefore contain six times as many atoms as are in the empirical formula. By multiplying each subscript in the empirical formula by 6, you obtain the molecular formula for glucose, $C_6H_{12}O_6$.

You may be wondering why you have not read about the molecular formulas for ionic substances. The answer is that molecular formulas cannot be used to describe ionic substances. Just as the name implies, molecular formulas are only for molecular substances. Because ionic substances are not made up of molecules, they cannot be described by molecular formulas.

SAMPLE PROBLEM 9

Ribose is an important sugar that is found in DNA and RNA. Ribose has a molar mass of 150 g/mol and a chemical composition of 40.0% carbon, 6.67% hydrogen, and 53.3% oxygen. What is the molecular formula for ribose?

STRATEGY	SOLUTION
1. Analyze	You know the percentage composition and molar mass of the compound. You need to use this information to determine the molecular formula for the compound.
2. Plan	First, you need to find the empirical formula for ribose using the percentage composition. You then need to determine the empirical formula mass. Finally, you will compare the empirical formula mass with the molar mass given in the problem.

3. Solve Find the empirical formula.

40.0% C: $40.0 \text{ g C} \times \dfrac{1 \text{ mol C}}{12.0 \text{ g C}} = 3.33 \text{ mol C}$

6.67% H: $6.67 \text{ g H} \times \dfrac{1 \text{ mol H}}{1.01 \text{ g H}} =$

6.60 mol H

53.3% O: $53.3 \text{ g O} \times \dfrac{1 \text{ mol O}}{16.0 \text{ g O}} =$

3.33 mol O

mole ratio = 1 mol C : 2 mol H : 1 mol O
empirical formula = CH_2O
empirical formula mass = 30.0 g/mol

$$\dfrac{\text{molar mass}}{\text{empirical formula mass}} = \dfrac{150 \text{ g/mol}}{30.0 \text{ g/mol}} = 5$$

molecular formula = 5 × empirical
formula = $C_5H_{10}O_5$

4. Evaluate Confirm the percentages in the molecular formula by finding the percentage composition of $C_5H_{10}O_5$. Also check the formula mass to be sure it agrees with the given formula mass of ribose.

PRACTICE PROBLEMS

17. Find the molecular formula for a compound that contains 4.90 g N and 11.2 g O. The molar mass of the compound is 92.0 g/mol. *(Answer: N_2O_4)*

18. β-carotene, a compound found in carrots, can be broken down to form vitamin A. The empirical formula for β-carotene is C_5H_7. The molar mass of β-carotene is 536 g/mol. What is the molecular formula for β-carotene? *(Answer: $C_{40}H_{56}$)*

10–3 Section Review

1. What is the percentage composition of a compound?

2. Which formula provides more information about a molecular compound, the molecular formula or the empirical formula? Explain your answer.

3. **Critical Thinking—Interpreting data** A plant extract is analyzed and found to contain 59% carbon, 5.0% hydrogen, 23% nitrogen, and 13% oxygen. On the basis of these data, the researcher reported that the plant extract has the molecular formula $C_6H_6N_2O$. Discuss this conclusion.

Laboratory Investigation

DESIGNING an EXPERIMENT

Molar Quantities

Problem

How are the mass, the number of moles, and the number of particles in a substance related?

Suggested Materials *(per group)*

similar-sized pieces of lead, copper, zinc, sulfur
salt (sodium chloride)
sugar (sucrose)
water
balance
10-mL graduated cylinder
tare paper or dishes

Suggested Procedure

1. Design an experiment that determines the mass, the number of moles, and the number of particles of substances, such as the elements lead, copper, zinc, and sulfur, and the compounds salt, sugar, and water.
2. On a sheet of paper, write down the steps of your experimental procedure.
3. Prepare a table, such as the one shown, to record your data.
4. After having your teacher approve your procedure and data table, conduct your experiment.
5. From your data, calculate the number of moles and the number of particles in each sample.

Analysis and Conclusions

1. List the elements you investigated in order from smallest to greatest mass.
2. List the elements you investigated in order from smallest to greatest number of moles.
3. List the elements you investigated in order from smallest to greatest number of particles.
4. Is the number of particles in a sample directly proportional to the mass or to the number of moles?
5. Compare the number of particles in each of the 5.0-gram samples of the compounds you investigated. Explain why a 5.0-gram sample of water does not have the same number of particles as 5.0 grams of sugar.
6. **On Your Own** How many grams of sugar would you need to have the same number of particles as 5.0 grams of salt?

Observations

Substance	Lead	Copper	Zinc	Sulfur	Salt	Sugar	Water
Mass (g)							
Moles							
Particles							

STUDY GUIDE

Summarizing Key Concepts

10–1 Chemical Measurements

- A mole is the amount of a substance that contains 6.02×10^{23} particles. The particle that represents a substance depends on the type of substance. Atoms are representative particles for monatomic elements. Molecules are representative particles for molecular compounds and diatomic elements. Formula units are representative particles for ionic compounds.
- The number of particles in a mole of a substance is known as Avogadro's number.
- The mass of 1 mole of a substance is called its molar mass.

10–2 Mole Conversions

- A mole can be defined in terms of the number of particles in a substance or by the mass in grams of the substance. Thus the mole can be used as a means of converting among different units.
- The volume of 1 mole of any gaseous substance at standard conditions is called the molar volume. The molar volume of a gas at 0°C and 1 atmosphere of pressure is 22.4 liters.

10–3 Empirical and Molecular Formulas

- The percentage composition of a compound is the percentage by mass of each element in the compound. It is determined by dividing the mass of each element by the mass of the entire compound and multiplying by 100 percent.
- The empirical formula is the simplest whole-number ratio of atoms of elements in a compound. It can be determined by using the mass of each element in the compound to calculate the moles of each element, then comparing the mole ratios. The empirical formula can also be calculated from the percentage composition of the compound.
- The molecular formula gives the actual number of atoms of each element in a molecular compound. The molecular formula for a compound can be determined by dividing the molar mass of the compound by the empirical formula mass.

Reviewing Key Terms

Define each term in a complete sentence.

10–1 Chemical Measurements

atomic mass
formula mass
mole
Avogadro's number
molar mass

10–2 Mole Conversions

molar volume

10–3 Empirical and Molecular Formulas

percentage composition
empirical formula
molecular formula

CHAPTER REVIEW

Content Review

Multiple Choice
Choose the letter of the answer that best completes each statement.

1. While a molecule is the smallest representative particle of a molecular compound, a formula unit is the smallest particle in a(an)
   (a) ionic compound.
   (b) monatomic element.
   (c) diatomic element.
   (d) ion.

2. The mass of 1 mole of lithium hydroxide (LiOH) is
   (a) 24 g.   (c) 25 g.
   (b) 31 g.   (d) 47 g.

3. The number of atoms in 24 g calcium is
   (a) 24.   (c) 6.02×10^{23}.
   (b) 3.6×10^{23}. (d) 48.

4. A salt shaker filled with 17.0 g sodium chloride contains
   (a) 17.0 mol NaCl.
   (b) 5.85 mol NaCl.
   (c) 3.52×10^{20} mol NaCl.
   (d) 0.291 mol NaCl.

5. The empirical formula for a compound that contains 36 g carbon, 8 g oxygen, and 6 g hydrogen is

   (a) C_4H_6O.   (c) $C_9H_2O_4$.
   (b) $C_6H_{12}O$.   (d) $C_6H_{12}O_6$.

6. Which of the following has the greatest mass?
   (a) 4.2 mol of carbon
   (b) 8.34×10^{24} atoms of lead
   (c) 9500 formula units of calcium carbonate ($CaCO_3$)
   (d) 12.6 g aluminum nitrate ($Al_2(NO_3)_3$)

7. How many grams of magnesium are in 97.4 g magnesium hydroxide ($Mg(OH)_2$)?
   (a) 40.6   (c) 57.3
   (b) 24.3   (d) 72.8

8. In 60.0 g of N_2O there are
   (a) 3.61×10^{25} atoms.
   (b) 1.00×10^{23} molecules.
   (c) 8.21×10^{23} molecules.
   (d) 2.77×10^{25} formula units.

9. The molecular formula for a compound with a molar mass of 472.2 g/mol and an empirical formula of HgCl is
   (a) HgCl.   (c) Hg_2Cl.
   (b) Hg_2Cl_2.   (d) $HgCl_2$.

True or False
If the statement is true, write "true." If it is false, change the underlined word or words to make the statement true.

10. One mole of calcium carbonate contains 6.02×10^{23} <u>atoms</u>.

11. Diatomic elements are represented by <u>ions</u>.

12. One mole of any gas occupies a volume of <u>22.4 L</u> at STP.

13. The empirical formula for a <u>molecular</u> compound is generally the same as its chemical formula.

14. The percentage composition of a compound is the percent by <u>mass</u> of each element in the compound.

15. A <u>molecular</u> formula is the simplest whole-number ratio of atoms in a compound.

Concept Mapping
Complete the following concept map for Section 10–1. Refer to pages xviii–xix to construct a concept map for the entire chapter.

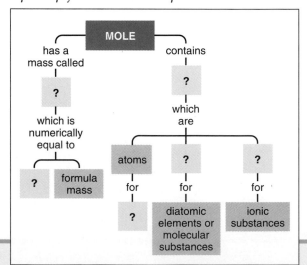

Concept Mastery

Discuss each of the following in a brief paragraph.

16. What is a mole and how is the mole used in chemistry?

17. Explain how 1 mole of a substance can be described by mass, volume, or a number of particles.

18. Explain what is wrong with this statement, "One mole of any substance contains 6.02×10^{23} atoms." Rewrite the statement to make it correct.

19. How is the atomic mass of a monatomic element related to its molar mass?

20. Why is Avogadro's number important?

21. Describe the conditions necessary for 6.02×10^{23} gas particles to occupy a volume of 22.4 dm^3.

22. What is the difference between an empirical formula and a molecular formula?

23. **Tying it Together** One mole of substance A has a mass of 9 grams and 1 mole of substance B has a mass of 32 grams. Compare the amounts of each substance in terms of *unity and diversity:* How are they similar? How are they different?

Critical Thinking and Problem Solving

Use the skills you have developed in this chapter to answer each of the following.

24. **Drawing conclusions** The metric system is based on multiples of 10, yet scientists prefer to use 6.02×10^{23} particles per mole. Can you think of reasons why this is true? What would be the effect of creating a new definition to describe the "amount of a substance" whose value would be a multiple of 10?

25. **Designing experiments** Aluminum cans are easily recycled. Describe how you would determine how many atoms of aluminum can be recycled from one aluminum soda can.

26. **Applying concepts** Supercomputers can perform calculations at amazingly fast speeds, but it would take even the fastest computer over a million years to count up to Avogadro's number. How many numbers per second would a computer need to count in order to reach Avogadro's number in only 100 years?

27. **Evaluating data** The value for Avogadro's number has been determined through a number of different experiments.

Each experiment focused on a different property of matter in order to determine the number of particles in 1 mole of a substance. Does the fact that the value 6.02×10^{23} particles/mole was derived through different means affect its reliability as a standard value? Explain your answer.

28. **Designing experiments** A mixture of silicon dioxide (sand) and sodium chloride (salt) contains exactly 1 mole of particles. Describe how you can determine the percentage of the mixture that is sand and the percentage that is salt if your only equipment is a balance.

29. **Using the writing process** The amount of a substance can be measured in a number of different ways: mass, volume, number of items. There are other things in your life that can be measured by different methods. Write a short story about how you can measure the same thing by different methods. For example, describe how you would measure your progress in school.

PROBLEM BANK

Group A

30. Find the atomic mass or formula mass for each of the following: (a) Mn (b) Se (c) $BaBr_2$ (d) NaOH *(Section 10–1)*

31. Name the type of representative particle for each of the following substances: (a) Al (b) $Pb(NO_3)_2$ (c) H_2O_2 (d) Fe (e) Cl_2 (f) Kr (g) $CaBr_2$ (h) $MgSO_4$ *(Section 10–1)*

32. Find the number of moles in each of the following: (a) 25.0 g Ar (b) 38.6 g Mg (c) 182.7 g Fe (d) 524.0 g Pb *(Section 10–2)*

33. Find the number of moles in each of the following: (a) 67.6 g H_2O (b) 264.5 g $Ca(OH)_2$ (c) 76.5 g SO_3 (d) 229.0 g $NaNO_3$ *(Section 10–2)*

34. Find the mass of each of the following: (a) 3.2 moles Li (b) 0.76 mole Ne (c) 5.26 moles Au (d) 3.78 moles Zn *(Section 10–2)*

35. Find the mass of each of the following: (a) 0.882 moles O_2 (b) 1.62 moles $CaCO_3$ (c) 3.24 moles CF_4 (d) 0.090 mole $BaCl_2$ *(Section 10–2)*

36. Find the number of atoms in each of the following: (a) 0.28 mole Ni (b) 1.84 moles S (c) 3.24 moles K (d) 2.26 moles He *(Section 10–2)*

37. Find the number of molecules in each of the following: (a) 1.5 moles CH_4 (b) 0.116 mole NO_2 (c) 1.32 moles F_2 (d) 0.92 mole H_2 *(Section 10–2)*

38. Find the number of formula units in each of the following: (a) 2.37 moles $CuSO_4$ (b) 3.15 moles K_3PO_4 (c) 0.025 mole Fe_2O_3 (d) 0.16 mole KCl *(Section 10–2)*

39. Find the number of moles in each of the following: (a) 2.67×10^{22} atoms of Mg (b) 3.25×10^{23} formula units of $FeSO_4$ (c) 9.25×10^{23} molecules of O_2 (d) 8.17×10^{24} molecules of NH_3 *(Section 10–2)*

40. Find the volume of each of the following amounts of gas at STP: (a) 0.72 mole O_2 (b) 3.4 moles N_2 (c) 57 grams CO_2 (d) 320 grams Rn *(Section 10–2)*

41. How many moles are in each of the following volumes of gas at STP? (a) 83.5 L CO_2 (b) 15.8 L NH_3 (c) 55.2 L He (d) 34.5 L H_2 *(Section 10–2)*

42. Find the mass of each of the gas samples in question 41. *(Section 10–2)*

43. (a) Determine the percentage composition of $CaCO_3$.
(b) How many grams of calcium would be produced from the decomposition of 200 g $CaCO_3$? *(Section 10–3)*

44. Find the empirical formula for a compound which contains 6.5 g potassium, 5.9 g chlorine, and 8.0 g oxygen. *(Section 10–3)*

45. The explosive, TNT, is composed of 37.0% carbon, 2.20% hydrogen, 18.5% nitrogen, and 42.3% oxygen.
(a) Determine the empirical formula for TNT.
(b) The molar mass for TNT is 227 g/mol. What is the molecular formula for TNT? *(Section 10–3)*

Group B

46. Determine the number and type of particles in each of the following:
    (a) 76 g $Mg(OH)_2$
    (b) 2.95 g H_2
    (c) 125 g Ag
    (d) 8.26 g PCl_3

47. Which of the following has the greatest mass?
    (a) 9.5×10^{24} atoms of C
    (b) 2.1 mol Br_2
    (c) 1.86×10^{22} molecules of CCl_4
    (d) 59.5 g Hg

48. An extra-strength aspirin tablet contains 500. mg of aspirin ($C_9H_8O_4$). How many molecules of aspirin are in one extra-strength tablet?

49. If gold is selling for $320 per ounce, how many atoms of gold can you buy for one penny? (1 ounce = 31.1 grams)

50. If your chemistry classroom has a volume of 1.8×10^5 dm^3, how many gas particles are in the room at standard temperature and pressure? (Remember that 1 mole of any gas occupies 22.4 dm^3 at STP.)

51. One cup of water is equivalent to 236 mL, and the density of water is 1.0 g/mL.
    (a) How many moles of water are in 1 cup of water?
    (b) How many molecules are in 1 cup of water?

52. The human body is approximately 9.5% carbon. How many moles of carbon are in the body of a student with a mass of 59 kg (130 lb)? How many carbon atoms are in that student?

53. Of the four taste sensations, humans can identify sweetness and saltiness in the lowest concentrations. The minimum concentration necessary to detect these tastes is 1.0×10^{-5} mole in 1 mL.
    (a) How many grams of sucrose (table sugar: $C_{12}H_{22}O_{11}$) would need to be dissolved in 1 mL in order for you to taste the sweetness?
    (b) How many grams of sodium chloride (table salt) would need to be dissolved in 1 mL for you to taste the saltiness?

54. A compound was analyzed in a lab to determine its empirical formula. Decomposition of the compound at standard temperature and pressure produced 9.00 g carbon, 16.8 L hydrogen, and 2.80 L oxygen.
    (a) What is the empirical formula for this compound?
    (b) The molar mass of the compound is 116 g/mol. What is its molecular formula?

55. Phenylalanine is an essential amino acid whose chemical composition is 65.5% carbon, 6.67% hydrogen, 8.48% nitrogen, and 19.4% oxygen. What is the empirical formula for phenylalanine?

The Mathematics of Chemical Equations

Three. Two. One. Liftoff! The ground rumbles. Fire explodes in every direction. Crowds cheer. And a thunderous roar is heard as the space shuttle lifts off the ground, leaving a huge cloud of billowing smoke in its wake.

The flight of a space shuttle is made possible in part by the fuel that powers its ascent. The fuel, which takes part in an explosive chemical reaction, is extremely unstable. The substances that comprise the fuel must be combined in exactly the right proportions, otherwise the results could be disastrous.

In this chapter you will discover how a balanced chemical equation is used to determine the amounts of reactants needed and the amounts of products produced by any chemical reaction.

A wide variety of events—from the launch of a space shuttle to the baking of bread—depend on chemical reactions.

11–1 Stoichiometry

Guide for Reading

- What is stoichiometry?
- How are molar relationships represented in a balanced chemical equation?

If you have ever followed a recipe, you know that it is essential to use the exact amounts of the ingredients indicated. Recipes are written so that the ingredients combine in just the right way to produce a delicious treat. Every day a huge variety of products are used in which the ingredients were carefully measured or counted to achieve the desired result. You can build a table from a top and legs, but not if you have two tops and one leg. You can make a glass of chocolate milk from powdered chocolate and milk, but not if you have a kilogram of powdered chocolate and only 1 milliliter of milk. The same is true for products that are a result of chemical reactions. The plastic in a bicycle helmet, the metal that makes up the utensils with which you eat, and the wintergreen flavoring in your favorite candy are all produced by chemical reactions in which the ingredients combine in particular amounts.

Knowing the amounts of substances that enter into a chemical reaction as well as the amounts of products that result is crucial. In the previous chapter, you learned how to use the mole to analyze chemical formulas in terms of particles, mass, and volume. In this chapter, you will find that you can also apply the mole concept to relate quantities of reactants and products in chemical reactions.

Figure 11–1 *The potatoes and yams sold in this market in Papua New Guinea provide a good source of carbohydrates for the local residents. Chemical reactions that occur in the human body require certain amounts of carbohydrates to produce the energy needed by the body. The measurable quantities involved in chemical reactions, such as those that take place in the body, are the subject of stoichiometry.*

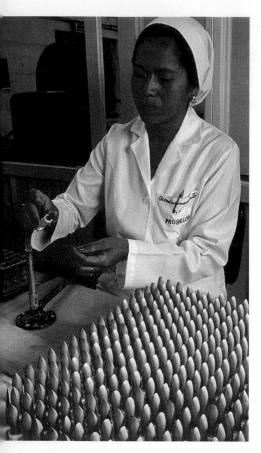

Figure 11–2 *In industry, profits depend on the amount of product made from a given amount of materials. If selling all the lipstick produced earns only as much as the cost of the ingredients used to make them, the manufacturers will not make any money. For this reason, they need to be able to calculate the amount of lipstick that will result from the manufacturing process.*

What Is Stoichiometry?

In chemistry, calculations that relate quantities of substances are known as **stoichiometry** (stoi-kee-AHM-uh-tree) problems. **Stoichiometry is the study of the quantitative, or measurable, relationships that exist in chemical formulas and chemical reactions.** The term is derived from the Greek words *stoicheion,* meaning element, and *metron,* meaning measure. The calculations you completed in Chapter 10 when converting among moles, particles, mass, and volume of chemical formulas comprise one aspect of stoichiometry. Another aspect of stoichiometry is concerned with chemical reactions and involves the relationships between reactants and products in a chemical reaction.

Although the term stoichiometry may be unfamiliar to you, the topic is one of the most important quantitative topics you will encounter in chemistry, and one we hope you will enjoy learning and practicing. A great deal of valuable information relies on stoichiometric calculations. For example, determining the nutritional value of food as required by the body, measuring the concentration of pollutants in the atmosphere, and determining the amount of copper that can be retrieved from ore all depend upon stoichiometric calculations. Furthermore, manufacturing processes are financed according to the cost of reactants and the value of products as determined stoichiometrically.

Interpreting Balanced Chemical Equations

Before going any further, you need to take another look at balanced chemical equations. Although you learned about them in Chapter 9, now that you know about the mole, you need to discover how much more you really know about them. Recall that chemical equations indicate the reactants and products involved in a chemical reaction. The coefficients in a balanced equation indicate the number of particles of each substance taking part in the reaction. They do not indicate the actual number of grams or liters of that substance, yet these are precisely the measurements that are needed in the laboratory and in industry. So how do you relate coefficients to actual amounts in grams or liters? The answer is through the use of the mole. Let's use an example to help you find out what moles have to do with chemical equations.

Have you ever used hydrogen peroxide to sterilize a minor cut? How hydrogen peroxide is used depends upon the amount of it in a solution, or the strength of the solution. A weak solution of hydrogen peroxide is perfect for cleaning small cuts. A stronger solution can be used to bleach hair. And at full strength, hydrogen peroxide can be used to power a rocket similar to the shuttle you read about at the beginning of the chapter. The fuel of some rockets is a mixture of hydrazine (N_2H_4) and hydrogen peroxide

(H_2O_2). The balanced equation for the reaction between these two substances is

$$N_2H_4 + 2\ H_2O_2 \rightarrow N_2 + 4\ H_2O \qquad \textbf{(Eq. 1)}$$

The coefficients in the balanced equation indicate that 1 molecule of N_2H_4 reacts with 2 molecules of H_2O_2 to produce 1 molecule of N_2 and 4 molecules of H_2O.

Recall from Chapter 9 that a standard chemical reaction gives coefficients in the least common multiple. Thus you could multiply every coefficient in the equation by the same number and still have a balanced equation. If, for example, you multiplied all the coefficients by 2, 20, 200, or even 2000, the equation would still be balanced. Because molecules are so small, let's consider a number even greater than 2000, such as Avogadro's number (6.02×10^{23}), or a mole. Using a mole as the multiple gives the equation

1 mole N_2H_4 + 2 moles $H_2O_2 \rightarrow$

$$1 \text{ mole } N_2 + 4 \text{ moles } H_2O \qquad \textbf{(Eq. 2)}$$

This equation reads 1 mole of hydrazine reacts with 2 moles of hydrogen peroxide to produce 1 mole of nitrogen and 4 moles of water.

Thus it is possible to interpret a balanced chemical equation in terms of moles using the coefficients. The coefficients in a balanced chemical equation, then, can be interpreted both as the relative number of particles involved in the reaction—be they atoms, molecules, or formula units—and as the relative number of moles. Later on, after you become more familiar with the role of moles in chemical equations, you will learn to use the mole to find the actual amounts of substances involved in chemical reactions.

Mole-Mole Problems

Imagine working in a paint store. A customer asks for a particular shade of pink paint that you produce by mixing 3 liters of white paint with 1 liter of red paint. This exact mixture

Figure 11–3 The photograph shows ground beef liver being added to hydrogen peroxide in a beaker. Notice the bubbles that are formed as chemicals in the liver cause the hydrogen peroxide to decompose into water and oxygen. In a similar way, hydrogen peroxide bubbles when it is poured on a minor cut as it reacts with blood. Do you know why hydrogen peroxide is always stored in light-proof containers?

Figure 11–4 Green, yellow, white, blue, pink—these beautiful homes on Martha's Vineyard in Massachusetts have been artistically decorated with vivid colors of paint. Each shade is the result of mixing particular amounts of different colors.

produces 4 liters of pink paint. What do you do to produce more or less pink paint? You probably know already that instead of always mixing 3 liters with 1 liter, you can determine the ratio between the amounts. Ratios are relationships between numbers. The ratio of white paint to red paint is 3 liters to 1 liter, or 3:1. Using this ratio, you can mix different amounts of paint to produce the same shade of pink. For example, you can mix 1.5 liters of white paint with 0.5 liter of red paint, 6 liters of white paint with 2 liters of red paint, or 9 liters of white paint with 3 liters of red paint. No matter what the amounts of paint you use, as long as the ratio between the two colors remains the same, you will wind up with the correct color.

The same information about ratios is true for chemical reactions. You just learned that the coefficients in a balanced chemical equation can be interpreted both as the relative number of particles involved in the reaction and as the relative number of moles. Notice the use of the word relative. Each coefficient is related to the others. The coefficients in a chemical reaction do not necessarily show the exact number of moles involved; instead the coefficients indicate the relationship among the various amounts. Just as you do not always have to use exactly 3 liters of white paint and 1 liter of red paint, any amount of each substance may be involved in a chemical reaction as long as the ratios shown by the coefficients do not change.

The ratio of moles, or molar ratios, in a balanced equation is essential for solving any stoichiometry problem. Using the molar ratios, you can determine the number of moles of any substance in the reaction if you know the number of moles of at least one other substance in the reaction. As an example, let's consider the reaction in which nitrous oxide (N_2O) is produced by the decomposition of ammonium nitrate (NH_4NO_3). The equation for the reaction is

$$NH_4NO_3 \rightarrow N_2O + 2\ H_2O \qquad \textbf{(Eq. 3)}$$

According to the equation, 1 mole of ammonium nitrate produces 1 mole of nitrous oxide and 2 moles of water. Suppose you want to find out how many moles of N_2O and H_2O are produced from 2.25 moles of NH_4NO_3. You first need to determine the molar ratios indicated by the equation. The molar ratio of NH_4NO_3 to N_2O is 1:1 and the molar ratio of NH_4NO_3 to H_2O is 1:2. What is the molar ratio of N_2O to H_2O?

Figure 11–5 *The mound of whipped cream on this mouthwatering ice cream sundae was made possible by the use of nitrous oxide, which forces the cream out of the can in a light, airy foam. In greater amounts, nitrous oxide is used as the "laughing gas" that can make a trip to the dentist a little less painful. And in even greater amounts, nitrous oxide provides an extra burst of power in race car engines.*

Next you must set up equations to convert the number of moles of the reactant to the number of moles of each of the products using dimensional analysis. Remember that in dimensional analysis you want to use a conversion factor that has the unit or substance you want in the numerator and the unit or substance you are trying to cancel in the denominator. In this case, the conversion factor is the molar ratio between the reactant and each product.

$$2.25 \text{ mol } \cancel{NH_4NO_3} \times \frac{1 \text{ mol } N_2O}{1 \text{ mol } \cancel{NH_4NO_3}} = 2.25 \text{ mol } N_2O$$

(Eq. 4)

$$2.25 \text{ mol } \cancel{NH_4NO_3} \times \frac{2 \text{ mol } H_2O}{1 \text{ mol } \cancel{NH_4NO_3}} = 4.50 \text{ mol } H_2O$$

(Eq. 5)

So the decomposition of 2.25 moles of ammonium nitrate produces 2.25 moles of nitrous oxide and 4.50 moles of water.

If you get confused by the conversion factor, stop for a moment and think it out logically. For example, in the case of water you know from the equation that the ratio of ammonium nitrate to water is 1:2. That means that for every mole of ammonium nitrate there are twice as many moles of water. If 8.2 moles of water are produced, how many moles of ammonium nitrate must there have been?

In this problem, you converted from moles of one substance to moles of another. For this reason, these types of problems are referred to as **mole-mole problems.** The ability to convert moles of one substance in a reaction to moles of another substance is essential to solving more complex types of stoichiometry problems.

Figure 11–6 Whales and other marine animals have the ability to hold their breath for long periods of time. Unlike a whale, you are prevented from holding your breath too long by chemical reactions in your body. When you hold your breath, carbon dioxide reacts with water in your blood to form carbonic acid (H_2CO_3). This carbonic acid quickly breaks down, sending a message to your brain that forces you to breathe in fresh air. How many moles of carbonic acid are produced by each mole of carbon dioxide?

SAMPLE PROBLEM 1

How many moles of HCl are needed to react with 2.3 moles of Zn? The equation for this reaction is $2\ HCl + Zn \rightarrow ZnCl_2 + H_2$.

STRATEGY	SOLUTION
1. **Analyze**	The number of moles of one reactant is given and you are asked to calculate the number of moles of the other reactant.
2. **Plan**	You must first determine the molar ratio between the two reactants and then use this ratio to solve the problem.
3. **Solve**	The molar ratio of Zn to HCl is 1:2. There are 2.3 moles of Zn. Therefore,

$$2.3\ \text{mol Zn} \times \frac{2\ \text{mol HCl}}{1\ \text{mol Zn}} = 4.6\ \text{mol HCl}$$

So 4.6 moles of HCl are needed to react completely with 2.3 moles of Zn.

4. **Evaluate**	Because the molar ratio of HCl to Zn is 2:1, twice as many moles of HCl react with Zn. The answer should be twice as much as the amount of Zn, which it is.

PRACTICE PROBLEMS

1. Magnesium burns in oxygen to produce magnesium oxide. How many moles of oxygen are needed to burn 0.52 mole of magnesium?   *(Answer: 0.26 mol O_2)*

2. How many moles of $Al(NO_3)_3$ will be produced when 0.75 mol $AgNO_3$ reacts according to the following equation: $3\ AgNO_3 + Al \rightarrow Al(NO_3)_3 + 3\ Ag$?   *(Answer: 0.25 mol $Al(NO_3)_3$)*

Verifying the Law of Conservation of Matter

As you know, a balanced equation "obeys" the law of conservation of matter. Now you can verify that mass is conserved by using what you know about moles to examine a chemical equation. Consider another example and you will see how. In this example, water is produced from hydrogen and oxygen as shown by the following equation:

$$2\ H_2 + O_2 \rightarrow 2\ H_2O \qquad \textbf{(Eq. 6)}$$

The coefficients indicate that 2 moles of H_2 react with each mole of O_2 to form 2 moles of H_2O.

Figure 11–7 *Nitrogen in the atmosphere combines with oxygen during lightning flashes to form nitrogen monoxide (NO), which then reacts with oxygen to produce nitrogen dioxide (NO_2). Is mass conserved in each of these reactions? Write chemical equations to illustrate your answer.*

The mass of each reactant and product is found by multiplying the molar mass of the substance by the number of moles of that substance in the balanced equation. The molar mass of H_2 is 2 g/mol, of O_2 is 32 g/mol, and of H_2O is 18 g/mol. So

$$2 \text{ mol } H_2 \left(\frac{2 \text{ g } H_2}{\text{mol } H_2}\right) + 1 \text{ mol } O_2 \left(\frac{32 \text{ g } O_2}{\text{mol } O_2}\right)$$

$$4 \text{ g} \quad\quad + \quad\quad 32 \text{ g}$$

$$\rightarrow 2 \text{ mol } H_2O \left(\frac{18 \text{ g } H_2O}{\text{mol } H_2O}\right)$$

$$\rightarrow \quad\quad 36 \text{ g} \quad\quad\quad\quad\quad \textbf{(Eq. 7)}$$

The total mass of the reactants is 36 grams (4 g + 32 g) and the total mass of the product is also 36 grams. Thus mass is conserved.

11–1 Section Review

1. Define stoichiometry and describe its significance.

2. What information is given by the coefficients in a chemical equation?

3. What is a ratio? Give an everyday example of a ratio. How are ratios related to chemical equations?

4. How can you show that mass is conserved in a chemical equation?

5. **Critical Thinking—Applying concepts** Acetylene gas (C_2H_2) burns with a hot flame. The equation for this reaction is $2 \text{ C}_2\text{H}_2 + 5 \text{ O}_2 \rightarrow 4 \text{ CO}_2 + 2 \text{ H}_2\text{O}$. Describe all the information that you can obtain from this equation.

Guide for Reading

- What are the main types of stoichiometry problems?

11–2 Solving Stoichiometry Problems

In Chapter 10 you learned that the mole could be used to convert between the number of particles, the mass, or the volume of a substance using its chemical formula. And in the last section you learned that even chemical reactions can be interpreted in terms of the mole. It stands to reason, then, that any mole conversions possible using chemical formulas can also be applied to chemical reactions. Thus, a chemical equation can be further interpreted in terms of mass, volume, or number of particles through stoichiometry problems.

In general, stoichiometry problems can be classified according to the given and unknown quantities. **The major categories of stoichiometry problems are mass-mass, mass-volume, and volume-volume problems.** Despite the different information given or sought in these problems, you will discover that they all follow the same basic logic. You must convert the information you are given to moles, then convert this number of moles to the number of moles of the quantity you are seeking, and then finally convert the number of moles of the unknown quantity to the units you are seeking. The steps are outlined in Figure 11–9. How is this logic similar to the logic you used for mole conversions in Chapter 10?

Figure 11–8 *Goods and services around the world are assigned prices in terms of money. Thus, money is a method of conversion between different goods and services. On the floor of the Chicago Board of Trade, people make and lose fortunes by converting money into goods and goods into money. What is a method of conversion used in chemistry?*

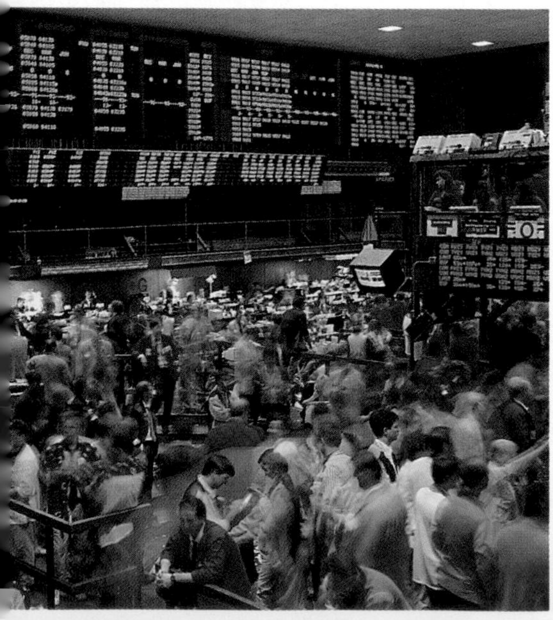

Figure 11–9 *No matter what the type of stoichiometry problem, you always begin by converting the given information to moles. The next step is to determine the molar ratio between the given and unknown quantity and then use this ratio to determine the number of moles of the unknown quantity. The final step is to convert the number of moles of the unknown quantity to the units you are seeking.*

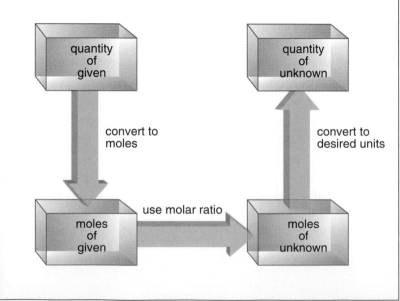

Mass-Mass Problems

In a **mass-mass problem,** you are given the mass of one substance and are asked to find the mass of another substance involved in the same reaction. Although you may be tempted to use the coefficients as masses, you must remember that the coefficients in the balanced equation represent the relative number of moles of reactants and products. They do not tell you about the relative masses of reactants and products.

Let's look at the method for finding the mass of a product by considering an example. The average person drinks 2 liters of water each day, yet eliminates about 2.5 liters. Where do you think the extra water comes from? It is produced when food is metabolized in the body. Metabolism is the sum of all the chemical reactions that occur in the body. In one series of reactions, glucose ($C_6H_{12}O_6$) is burned in oxygen to produce carbon dioxide and water. What mass of water is produced from 1.5 grams of glucose? The balanced equation for this reaction is

$$C_6H_{12}O_6 + 6\ O_2 \rightarrow 6\ CO_2 + 6\ H_2O \qquad \textbf{(Eq. 8)}$$

The first step is to convert the given mass to moles using the molar mass of glucose, which is 180 g/mol. Remember that the molar mass of a compound is numerically equal to the sum of the atomic masses of the atoms in the compound.

$$1.5\ \text{g}\ C_6H_{12}O_6 \times \frac{1\ \text{mol}\ C_6H_{12}O_6}{180\ \text{g}\ C_6H_{12}O_6} = 0.0083\ \text{mol}\ C_6H_{12}O_6$$

$$\textbf{(Eq. 9)}$$

Figure 11–11 *To solve a mass-mass stoichiometry problem, begin by converting the amount of the given substance to moles using the molar mass. Then use the molar ratio given in the balanced equation to determine the number of moles of the unknown quantity. Finally, convert the number of moles of the unknown quantity to mass using its molar mass.*

Figure 11–10 *Most of the foods you eat are broken down into a type of sugar known as glucose. In the body, glucose is burned and energy is released in a chemical reaction known as glycolysis. If you are engaged in activities that require a lot of energy, the energy will be used. Do you know what happens if the energy is not used?*

*I*NTEGRATING
*B*IOLOGY

Did you ever wonder how the food you eat is used, or metabolized, by your body?

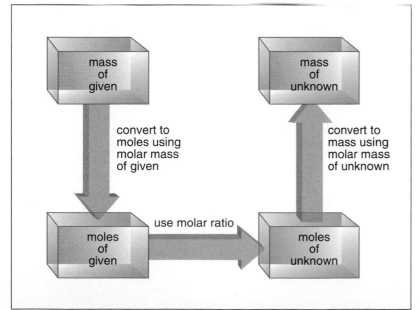

Now you know that there is 0.0083 mole of $C_6H_{12}O_6$. The next step is to determine the number of moles of water that are produced. This is accomplished by using the molar ratio of the coefficients in the balanced equation. The ratio between $C_6H_{12}O_6$ and H_2O is 1:6. You can now set up a mole-mole problem.

$$0.0083 \text{ mol } C_6H_{12}O_6 \times \frac{6 \text{ mol } H_2O}{1 \text{ mol } C_6H_{12}O_6} = 0.050 \text{ mol } H_2O$$

(Eq. 10)

The last step is to convert the number of moles of H_2O into grams using molar mass. This time you need to use the molar mass of water, which is 18 g/mol.

$$0.050 \text{ mol } H_2O \times \frac{18 \text{ g } H_2O}{1 \text{ mol } H_2O} = 0.90 \text{ g } H_2O \qquad \textbf{(Eq. 11)}$$

Thus 1.5 grams of glucose produce 0.90 gram of water. You have solved the problem. The process for solving mass-mass stoichiometry problems such as this one is outlined in Figure 11–11 on the previous page.

As in Chapter 10, problems such as these are more efficiently solved in one step. This problem could be solved as follows:

$$1.5 \text{ g } C_6H_{12}O_6 \times \frac{1 \text{ mol } C_6H_{12}O_6}{180 \text{ g } C_6H_{12}O_6} \times \frac{6 \text{ mol } H_2O}{1 \text{ mol } C_6H_{12}O_6} \times \frac{18 \text{ g } H_2O}{1 \text{ mol } H_2O}$$

$$= 0.90 \text{ g } H_2O \quad \textbf{(Eq. 12)}$$

Make sure you follow how the individual steps have been combined and how the units cancel.

Figure 11–12 *Small quantities of molten iron are produced when iron(III) oxide reacts with aluminum in a thermite reaction. The molten iron is used for special purposes such as repairing railway lines. Why would it be important to be able to calculate the amount of iron produced in this reaction?*

SAMPLE PROBLEM 2

In a thermite reaction, powdered aluminum reacts with iron(III) oxide to produce aluminum oxide and molten iron. What mass of aluminum oxide is produced when 2.3 g of aluminum reacts with iron(III) oxide?

STRATEGY	SOLUTION
1. Analyze	The mass of one reactant is given and you are asked to find the mass of one of the products.
2. Plan	You must first write a balanced equation for the reaction. Then you can use the coefficients in the equation to convert the given mass to moles, find the molar relationship between the given and unknown quantity, and convert the molar value of the unknown quantity to mass.
3. Solve	The balanced equation is

$$2\,Al + Fe_2O_3 \rightarrow 2\,Fe + Al_2O_3$$

You know that there are 2.3 g Al and that the molar mass of Al is 27 g/mol and the molar mass of Al_2O_3 is 102 g/mol. The molar ratio of Al to Al_2O_3 is 2:1. So the mass of the Al_2O_3 produced is

$$2.3\ \text{g Al} \times \frac{1\ \text{mol Al}}{27\ \text{g Al}} \times \frac{1\ \text{mol Al}_2O_3}{2\ \text{mol Al}} \times$$

$$\frac{102\ \text{g Al}_2O_3}{1\ \text{mol Al}_2O_3} = 4.3\ \text{g Al}_2O_3$$

4. Evaluate The mass of 1 mole of Al_2O_3 is about four times the mass of 1 mole of Al. In this reaction, there are 2 moles of Al for every mole of Al_2O_3. So the mass of 1 mole of Al_2O_3 should be about twice the mass of 2 moles of Al, which it is.

PRACTICE PROBLEMS

3. Determine the mass of sodium hydroxide produced when 0.25 g of sodium reacts with water according to the following equation: $2\,Na + 2\,H_2O \rightarrow 2\,NaOH + H_2$. *(Answer: 0.43 g NaOH)*

4. What mass of bromine (Br_2) is produced when fluorine reacts with 1.72 g of potassium bromide? *(Answer: 1.15 g Br$_2$)*

Mass-Volume Problems

In many chemical reactions, solid reactants can yield products that are gases. In **mass-volume problems,** you are given the mass of one substance in a chemical reaction and are asked to find the volume of another substance—in this case a gas. The procedure is similar to the steps you followed for mass-mass problems, except that instead of converting the moles of the unknown to mass, you convert them to volume. The process is outlined in Figure 11–13.

Consider the example of inflatable air bags, which have been a revolutionary safety feature in the automobile industry. Did you ever wonder what makes it possible for an air bag to inflate so quickly in the event of an accident? When folded up inside the dashboard or steering wheel of a car, air bags contain a compound called sodium azide (NaN_3). When the car is involved in a collision, a motion sensor sets off a spark that causes sodium azide to decompose explosively. The result is the production of nitrogen gas, which quickly inflates the bag. The chemical equation for this reaction is

$$2\ NaN_3 \rightarrow 2\ Na + 3\ N_2 \qquad \textbf{(Eq. 13)}$$

Assume that a particular air bag contains 125 grams of sodium azide. What volume of nitrogen gas is produced at STP? Recall that STP is standard temperature and pressure (0°C and 1 atm).

To solve this problem you must begin as you always do—by converting the given information to moles. You are given the mass of NaN_3. The molar mass of NaN_3 is 65.0 g/mol. The next step is to calculate the relative number of moles of N_2 produced using the balanced equation. The ratio between moles of NaN_3 and moles of N_2 is 2:3. The last step is to convert the number of moles of N_2 to volume. Remember that the molar volume of a gas at STP is 22.4 L/mol.

Figure 11–13 *To solve a mass-volume stoichiometry problem, begin by converting the given information to moles using the molar mass. Then use the molar ratio in the balanced equation to determine the number of moles of the unknown quantity. Finally, convert the number of moles of the unknown quantity to volume using the molar volume of a gas.*

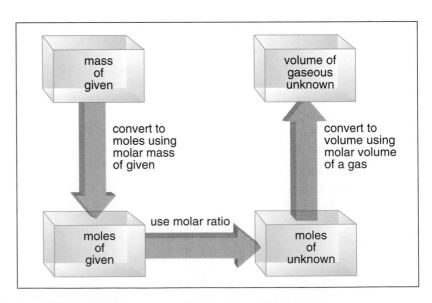

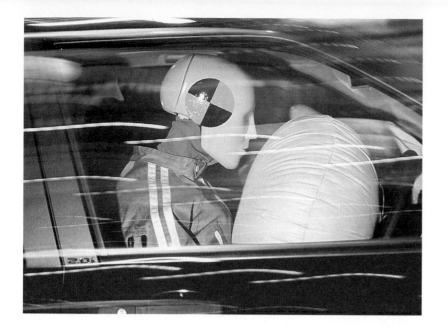

Figure 11–14 *Air bags are designed to save the lives of the people in a car in the event of an accident. The effectiveness of air bags depends on a reaction that produces a large volume of gas from a small mass of a substance called sodium azide in a short span of time. How can manufacturers design air bags so that a specific volume of gas will be produced?*

$$125 \text{ g NaN}_3 \times \frac{1 \text{ mol NaN}_3}{65.0 \text{ g NaN}_3} \times \frac{3 \text{ mol N}_2}{2 \text{ mol NaN}_3} \times \frac{22.4 \text{ L N}_2}{1 \text{ mol N}_2}$$
$$= 64.6 \text{ L N}_2 \text{ (STP)} \quad \textbf{(Eq. 14)}$$

So, in a fraction of second, the air bag fills with 64.6 liters of nitrogen gas!

The opposite type of problem in which a volume is given and you are asked to find a mass is also possible. This type of problem is still considered to be a mass-volume problem even though the steps are reversed. How would you solve this type of problem?

Figure 11–15 *A fire needs oxygen to continue burning. When carbon dioxide is used to smother a fire, the combustion reaction comes to an end and the fire dies out. African American chemist Percy Julian, commemorated in this postage stamp, made use of this principle to develop a fire-fighting chemical foam from soybeans.*

Percy Lavon Julian
29
Black Heritage USA

359

SAMPLE PROBLEM 3

Sodium bicarbonate ($NaHCO_3$) can be used to extinguish a fire. When heated, it decomposes to give carbon dioxide gas, which smothers the fire. If a sample contains 4.0 g of $NaHCO_3$, what volume of carbon dioxide gas is produced at STP? The balanced equation for the reaction is $2\ NaHCO_3 \rightarrow Na_2CO_3 + H_2O + CO_2$.

STRATEGY	SOLUTION
1. **Analyze**	You are given the mass of the reactant and asked to find the volume of one of the products.
2. **Plan**	Convert the given mass to a number of moles of $NaHCO_3$ using molar mass. Then determine the number of moles of CO_2 from the molar ratio indicated in the balanced equation. Finally convert the number of moles of CO_2 to a volume using the molar volume of a gas.
3. **Solve**	The molar mass of sodium bicarbonate is 84 g/mol. The ratio between the number of moles of $NaHCO_3$ and CO_2 is 2:1.

$$4.0\ \text{g } NaHCO_3 \times \frac{1\ \text{mol } NaHCO_3}{84\ \text{g } NaHCO_3} \times$$

$$\frac{1\ \text{mol } CO_2}{2\ \text{mol } NaHCO_3} \times \frac{22.4\ \text{L } CO_2}{1\ \text{mol } CO_2} =$$

$$0.53\ \text{L } CO_2$$

4. **Evaluate**	The steps of the process are logical. The units canceled so that the answer is in the desired unit of volume.

PRACTICE PROBLEMS

5. Find the mass of aluminum required to produce 1.32 L of hydrogen gas at STP from the reaction described by the following equation: $2\ Al + 3\ H_2SO_4 \rightarrow Al_2(SO_4)_3 + 3\ H_2$. *(Answer: 1.06 g Al)*

6. How many liters of oxygen are necessary for the combustion of 340. g of ethanol (C_2H_5OH) assuming that the reaction occurs at STP? The balanced equation is $C_2H_5OH + 3\ O_2 \rightarrow 2\ CO_2 + 3\ H_2O$. *(Answer: 497 L O_2)*

Volume-Volume Problems

In the previous chapter, you learned that 1 mole of any gas occupies the same volume as 1 mole of any other gas. Thus if the coefficients in a chemical equation represent the ratio of moles, they also represent the ratio of the volumes of gases involved in the reaction. Problems in which you are given a volume and are asked to find a volume, then, are much like the mole-mole problems you completed earlier. These problems are referred to as **volume-volume problems.**

Consider the industrial production of ammonia. The manufacture of ammonia from nitrogen and hydrogen is an important industrial process because ammonia can be used to produce a wide range of chemicals, from fertilizers to explosives. The balanced equation for ammonia synthesis is

$$N_2 + 3 H_2 \rightarrow 2 NH_3 \qquad \textbf{(Eq. 15)}$$

The balanced equation can be interpreted as follows: 1 mole of nitrogen (N_2) reacts with 3 moles of hydrogen (H_2) to produce 2 moles of ammonia (NH_3). But because the reactants and products are all gases, this equation can also be interpreted as 1 volume of N_2 reacts with 3 volumes of H_2 to produce 2 volumes of NH_3. The unit of volume does not matter. As long as the same unit is selected, the ratio will always be true. So, for these calculations we will make that unit 1 liter.

Let's calculate the volume of hydrogen gas that reacts with 15.5 liters of nitrogen. Just as you did when calculating mole-mole problems, you must use the ratio of the coefficients to determine the answer. The ratio of the volume of N_2 to H_2 is 1:3.

Figure 11–16 *This attractive flower garden might not have been possible without the use of fertilizers to ensure that each plant obtains the nutrients it requires. Most fertilizers contain ammonia. The ability to produce large quantities of ammonia for such products as fertilizer is thus very important to industry. How can manufacturers determine the volume of ammonia that will be produced from any given volume of reactants?*

$$15.5 \text{ L N}_2 \times \frac{3 \text{ L H}_2}{1 \text{ L N}_2} = 46.5 \text{ L H}_2 \qquad \textbf{(Eq. 16)}$$

Thus 46.5 liters of hydrogen reacts with 15.5 liters of nitrogen. The answer makes sense because the equation indicates that three times as much hydrogen as nitrogen is used in the reaction.

SAMPLE PROBLEM 4

If 0.38 L of hydrogen reacts with chlorine gas, what volume of hydrogen chloride gas will be produced?

STRATEGY	SOLUTION
1. Analyze	The reactants and products are all gases. The volume of one reactant is given and the volume of the product must be determined.
2. Plan	The balanced equation must be written first. Then the volume of the product can be calculated using the ratio of volumes as indicated by the coefficients of the equation.
3. Solve	The balanced equation is

$$H_2 + Cl_2 \rightarrow 2 \text{ HCl}$$

The ratio between the volume of H_2 and the volume of HCl is 1:2.

$$0.38 \text{ L H}_2 \times \frac{2 \text{ L HCl}}{1 \text{ L H}_2} = 0.76 \text{ L HCl}$$

| **4. Evaluate** | Because 2 moles of HCl are produced for every 1 mole of H_2, the volume of HCl is also twice that of H_2. So the answer makes sense. |

PRACTICE PROBLEMS

7. Methane (CH_4) burns in oxygen to produce carbon dioxide and water vapor. The balanced equation is $CH_4 + 2 O_2 \rightarrow CO_2 + 2 H_2O$. What volume of carbon dioxide is produced when 3.2 L of oxygen are consumed? *(Answer: 1.6 L CO_2)*

8. What volumes of hydrogen and nitrogen gases are necessary to produce 16.0 L of ammonia gas? *(Answer: 24.0 L H_2 and 8.00 L N_2)*

Smooth as Silk

Some of the most beautiful clothes in the world are made of silk. For thousands of years, silk has been considered the most precious of fabrics. Chinese legend dates the discovery of silk to the year 2640 BC. Clothing made of silk continues to command high prices. But what makes silk so special? Silk is unusual in that its shimmering texture is created by fibers that are triangular, instead of round, and so reflect light.

In addition to its beauty, the value placed on silk has to do with the way in which it is produced. Unlike cotton or wool, silk is not made from plants or animal hair—it is spun by tiny animals known as silkworms.

Silkworms have the unique ability to convert the cellulose in tree leaves into thin strands of silk. This feat is made possible by chemical reactions that occur within the bodies of the silkworms. Silkworms eat the leaves of a variety of trees, but it is mulberry leaves that yield the finest silk. In China, where the greatest amount of silk is produced, mulberry trees are cultivated as low bushes so that the leaves can be easily harvested and fed to silkworms.

Each year silkworm eggs are carefully preserved through the winter so that in the spring, when leaves appear on the mulberry bushes, the eggs can be incubated, or prepared for hatching. When they hatch, the tiny worms feed continuously on the mulberry leaves for about a month. During this period, their body weight can increase as much as 10,000 times. Because the silkworms breathe through holes in their bodies rather than through their mouths, they need not stop eating even to breathe!

Like caterpillars, silkworms must eventually make cocoons so that they can turn into moths. They begin by secreting a semiliquid mixture from two glands that run the length of their body. The secretion forms an extremely thin thread. The threads from each gland join together to form a single thread, which the silkworm uses to build a waterproof cocoon around itself. The cocoon is completed in about three days. To obtain the silk, each cocoon is soaked in warm water. Then the end of the silk thread is found and wound onto a reel. Each thread is so thin that the threads from several cocoons are wound onto the same reel to make a single thicker thread. At one time, this entire process was done by hand. Today machines do much of the work.

Amazingly, each cocoon produces about 1.6 kilometers of thread! (That's about the length of $17\frac{1}{2}$ football fields placed end-to-end.) Even so, it takes about 100 cocoons to make a silk tie, 600 to make a silk blouse, and 3000 to make a Japanese kimono. No matter how much silk is produced, no mass is lost during the chemical reactions during which the silk is formed. And the amount of silk produced is proportional to the substances that reacted to form it. Silk—a beautiful fabric—is made possible by chemical reactions that occur in the bodies of what might otherwise be considered less-than-beautiful creatures!

More Relationships

Not all the problems you encounter will be exactly like those we have covered in this section. Some may be a variation of the types shown here. You will still be able to solve them, however, if you have a good understanding of the general steps. For example, consider a problem in which you are given an amount of a product in moles and are asked to determine the mass of one of the reactants. Although this is not exactly a mass-mass problem, you can still solve it. In fact, it is a little easier to solve because the first step has already been done for you! The first step of a mass-mass problem is to convert the given quantity to moles, but here you have already been given the information in moles. For any of the problems we have covered in this section, if the information is given in moles or requested in moles, you can solve the problem just as you did before.

Similarly, because you know the number of representative particles in each mole of a substance, you can use information in terms of the number of particles. Recall from Chapter 10 that to convert moles of a substance into particles of that substance you must multiply the number of moles by 6.02×10^{23} particles per mole. You would solve the problem as you did the others, but instead of converting from or to mass and volume, you would convert from or to the number of particles.

11–2 Section Review

1. What are the major types of stoichiometry problems? Describe each type in terms of the given and unknown information.

2. Explain how a balanced equation can be used to determine the mass or volume of an unknown quantity in a stoichiometry problem.

3. A piece of carbon with a mass of 24 g is burned. What is the mass of the carbon dioxide that is produced? Assume CO_2 is the only product.

4. Outline the steps involved in solving this problem: How many milliliters of oxygen gas at STP are released from the decomposition of 3.2 grams of calcium chlorate as described by the equation $Ca(ClO_3)_2 \rightarrow CaCl_2 + 3O_2$?

5. **Theme Trace—Scale and Structure** Explain how you can determine the amount of a product that will result from a given amount of reactant no matter how small or large the amount.

11–3 Limiting Reactants and Percent Yield

Guide for Reading
- What determines the amount of products formed in a chemical reaction?
- How is the percent yield of a chemical reaction determined?

Think back to the paint example used earlier. Recall that to make pink paint you had to mix white paint and red paint in a ratio of 3:1. Suppose now that you have 6 liters of white paint and 1.5 liters of red paint. How many liters of pink paint can you produce? Your first reaction might be to say 7.5 liters because that is the sum of the two amounts of paint. But remember that the two paints must be mixed in a ratio of 3:1 to produce the desired shade. If you use all 6 liters of white paint, you would need 2 liters of red paint. But you have only 1.5 liters of red paint. So the amount of pink paint you can produce is limited by the amount of red paint you have. You can use the entire 1.5 liters of red paint and three times as much, or 4.5 liters, of white paint. The result is 6 liters of pink paint, with 1.5 liters of white paint left over.

The amount of many different kinds of products is dependent on the amounts of ingredients available. The number of cookies baked for a sale is limited by the number of eggs you use. The number of cars washed at a fund raiser is limited by the amount of soap you have. The number of people who can sit down in a game of musical chairs is limited by the number of chairs available. The same is true for chemical reactions. The amount of the products formed by a reaction is dependent on the amounts of reactants available. For example, the gasoline in a car's gas tank reacts with oxygen in the air to run the car's engine. Once the gasoline is used up, however, the car will not run even though there is plenty of oxygen available. The amount of gasoline available limits the extent of the reaction. The amount of oxygen is in excess.

When quantities of reactants are available in the exact ratio described by the balanced equation, chemists say that the reactants are in stoichiometric proportions. When this is the case, all of the reactants will take part in the reaction and there will be no reactants left over once the reaction is completed. Most often, however, reactants are available in other than stoichiometric proportions. There is more of one reactant than can be used, and the reactants are said to be in nonstoichiometric proportions.

Figure 11–17 The number of bicycles that this bicycle shop can produce is limited by the number of tires available. How many bicycles can be put together if the shop has 7 bicycle frames and 11 tires?

Identifying Limiting Reactants

When chemicals are combined in nonstoichiometric proportions, the ratio in which the reactants combine must still hold true. This means that one reactant will limit the amount of product formed. The reactant that limits the amount of product formed in a chemical reaction is called the **limiting reactant.** The limiting reactant will be completely used up by the reaction. The other reactant (or reactants) will have some amount unchanged, or left over, after the reaction. Such a reactant (or reactants) is said to be in excess. **The quantities of products formed in a reaction are always determined by the quantity of the limiting reactant.** The given amounts of other reactants cannot be used to predict the amount of product that will be formed.

When you are given a stoichiometry problem, the identity of the limiting reactant may not be immediately obvious to you. Most likely you will know the amounts of reactants in grams or liters, but whether or not the reaction is limited depends upon the molar ratios. Let's examine a method of determining the limiting reactant using a reaction in which 3.5 grams of copper is added to a solution containing 6.0 grams of silver(I) nitrate.

Notice that the information given is similar to the information given in the mass-mass problems you solved earlier. This time, however, instead of having only one mass to work with, you have two. To determine the limiting reactant, you must complete two separate mass-mass problems. In the first one, you will calculate the mass of product formed using the given mass of one reactant. Then you will repeat the calculation using the given mass of the other reactant. The reactant that produces the smaller amount of product is the limiting reactant.

As before, the first step is always to write the balanced chemical equation. The balanced equation for this reaction is

Figure 11–18 Hydrogen can react with bromine to produce hydrogen bromide. Under the proper conditions, each hydrogen atom will combine with only 1 bromine atom. If there are more hydrogen atoms than bromine atoms, the extra hydrogen atoms will be left over when the reaction is complete. In this case, which reactant limits the amount of hydrogen bromide that can be produced?

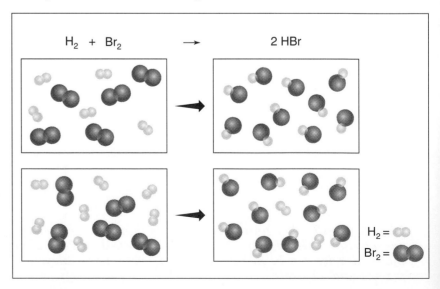

$$Cu + 2\,AgNO_3 \rightarrow Cu(NO_3)_2 + 2\,Ag \quad \textbf{(Eq. 17)}$$

The next step is to calculate the mass of product formed by each amount of reactant. Although you can calculate the amount of either product, in this example you will find the amount of silver because its molar mass is more easily determined.

$$3.5\ \text{g Cu} \times \frac{1\ \text{mol Cu}}{63.5\ \text{g Cu}} \times \frac{2\ \text{mol Ag}}{1\ \text{mol Cu}} \times \frac{108\ \text{g Ag}}{1\ \text{mol Ag}}$$

$$= 12\ \text{g Ag} \quad \textbf{(Eq. 18)}$$

$$6.0\ \text{g AgNO}_3 \times \frac{1\ \text{mol AgNO}_3}{169.9\ \text{g AgNO}_3} \times \frac{2\ \text{mol Ag}}{2\ \text{mol AgNO}_3} \times \frac{108\ \text{g Ag}}{1\ \text{mol Ag}}$$

$$= 3.8\ \text{g Ag} \quad \textbf{(Eq. 19)}$$

The reactant that would produce the smaller amount of product is the limiting reactant. In this case, the limiting reactant is silver(I) nitrate, which produces 3.8 grams of silver.

When the reactants are combined in this proportion, some copper remains after the reaction is completed, whereas all of the silver(I) nitrate is used up in the reaction. Do not be fooled into thinking that the reactant present in a smaller amount by mass or volume is necessarily the limiting reactant. Notice, for example, that silver(I) nitrate is available in a greater amount by mass, but it is in a smaller amount by moles relative to the ratio.

MATH TIP

Whenever you are given the quantity of both reactants, you need to determine which of the reactants will be used up first. The moles of this reactant form the basis for calculating the quantity of the product produced.

Figure 11–19 *This photograph shows what happens when a copper wire is immersed in a solution of silver(I) nitrate. The solid silver formed as a result of the reaction has begun to build up on the copper wire. By analyzing the balanced equation for this reaction in terms of the masses of the two reactants, it is possible to determine which reactant is the limiting reactant.*

SAMPLE PROBLEM 5

Identify the limiting reactant when 1.7 g of sodium reacts with 2.6 L of chlorine gas at STP to produce sodium chloride.

STRATEGY	SOLUTION
1. Analyze	You are given the mass of one reactant and the volume of the other and asked to determine which reactant will limit the amount of product formed.
2. Plan	Determine the amount of product that would be formed by each amount of reactant. Begin by writing the balanced equation.
3. Solve	The balanced equation is

$$2 \, Na + Cl_2 \rightarrow 2 \, NaCl$$

$$1.7 \, g \, Na \times \frac{1 \, mol \, Na}{23 \, g \, Na} \times \frac{2 \, mol \, NaCl}{2 \, mol \, Na}$$

$$\times \frac{58 \, g \, NaCl}{1 \, mol \, NaCl} = 4.3 \, g \, NaCl$$

$$2.6 \, L \, Cl_2 \times \frac{1 \, mol \, Cl_2}{22.4 \, L \, Cl_2} \times \frac{2 \, mol \, NaCl}{1 \, mol \, Cl_2}$$

$$\times \frac{58 \, g \, NaCl}{1 \, mol \, NaCl} = 13 \, g \, NaCl$$

Sodium is the limiting reactant.

| **4. Evaluate** | The limiting reactant is the reactant that is present in the smallest number of moles compared with the number of moles in the balanced equation. The answer supports this. |

PRACTICE PROBLEMS

9. Identify the limiting reactant when 10.0 g H_2O reacts with 4.5 g Na to produce NaOH and H_2. *(Answer: Na)*

10. Identify the limiting reactant when 12.5 L H_2S at STP is bubbled through a solution containing 24.0 g KOH to form K_2S and H_2O. *(Answer: KOH)*

Limiting Reactant Problems

The fizz produced when some antacid tablets are dropped into water is created by the production of carbon dioxide during the reaction between sodium bicarbonate ($NaHCO_3$) and citric acid ($H_3C_6H_5O_7$). Suppose 2.0 grams of sodium bicarbonate and 0.5 gram of citric acid are present. Which is the limiting reactant, and what volume of carbon dioxide will be produced? Although the reaction is a little more complicated than most you have seen so far, the problem is solved in the same way. The balanced equation for this reaction is

$$3 \text{ NaHCO}_3 + \text{H}_3\text{C}_6\text{H}_5\text{O}_7 \rightarrow 3 \text{ CO}_2 + 3 \text{ H}_2\text{O} + \text{Na}_3\text{C}_6\text{H}_5\text{O}_7$$

(Eq. 20)

First determine the limiting reactant.

$$2.0 \text{ g NaHCO}_3 \times \frac{1 \text{ mol NaHCO}_3}{84 \text{ g NaHCO}_3} \times \frac{3 \text{ mol CO}_2}{3 \text{ mol NaHCO}_3} \times$$

$$\frac{22.4 \text{ L CO}_2}{1 \text{ mol CO}_2} = 0.53 \text{ L CO}_2 \quad \textbf{(Eq. 21)}$$

$$0.5 \text{ g H}_3\text{C}_6\text{H}_5\text{O}_7 \times \frac{1 \text{ mol H}_3\text{C}_6\text{H}_5\text{O}_7}{192 \text{ g H}_3\text{C}_6\text{H}_5\text{O}_7} \times \frac{3 \text{ mol CO}_2}{1 \text{ mol H}_3\text{C}_6\text{H}_5\text{O}_7} \times$$

$$\frac{22.4 \text{ L CO}_2}{1 \text{ mol CO}_2} = 0.2 \text{ L CO}_2 \quad \textbf{(Eq. 22)}$$

Because citric acid produces the smaller volume of CO_2, you know that citric acid is the limiting reactant. The amount of carbon dioxide that will be produced is then the amount limited by citric acid, or 0.2 liter.

There is one more piece of information you can determine and that is the amount of sodium bicarbonate left over. Since citric acid is the limiting reactant, you know that it is totally consumed in the reaction but that some sodium bicarbonate is left over. This amount is determined by calculating the amount of sodium bicarbonate that would react with 0.5 gram $H_3C_6H_5O_7$ and subtracting this amount from the starting amount.

$$0.5 \text{ g H}_3\text{C}_6\text{H}_5\text{O}_7 \times \frac{1 \text{ mol H}_3\text{C}_6\text{H}_5\text{O}_7}{192 \text{ g H}_3\text{C}_6\text{H}_5\text{O}_7} \times \frac{3 \text{ mol NaHCO}_3}{1 \text{ mol H}_3\text{C}_6\text{H}_5\text{O}_7} \times$$

$$\frac{84 \text{ g NaHCO}_3}{1 \text{ mol NaHCO}_3} = 0.7 \text{ g NaHCO}_3 \quad \textbf{(Eq. 23)}$$

The difference between the amount of sodium bicarbonate that you have and the amount used is 1.3 grams (2.0 g − 0.7 g). This means that 1.3 grams of sodium bicarbonate is left over.

Figure 11–20 *An antacid tablet dropped into a glass of water produces a characteristic trail of bubbles. The tablet's effectiveness results from a reaction between sodium bicarbonate and citric acid. How can you determine which ingredient is the limiting reactant?*

Figure 11–21 *Cement is widely used to support many structures, such as this beautiful lighthouse. But if too much water is added to the cement, it will not harden properly. Luckily for builders, English engineer Joseph Aspdin patented a type of cement that actually limits the amount of water that takes part in the chemical reaction during which the cement hardens.*

SAMPLE PROBLEM 6

What mass of lead(II) iodide will be produced when 16.4 g of lead(II) nitrate is added to 28.5 g of potassium iodide? What is the limiting reactant?

STRATEGY	SOLUTION
1. Analyze	The mass of each reactant is given and you are asked to find the mass of one of the products as well as to identify the limiting reactant.
2. Plan	The first step is to write a balanced equation for the reaction. The next step is to determine the limiting reactant and the amount of the product formed by that limiting reactant.
3. Solve	The balanced equation is

$$Pb(NO_3)_2 + 2\ KI \rightarrow PbI_2 + 2\ KNO_3$$

$$16.4\ g\ Pb(NO_3)_2 \times \frac{1\ mol\ Pb(NO_3)_2}{331\ g\ Pb(NO_3)_2} \times$$

$$\frac{1\ mol\ PbI_2}{1\ mol\ Pb(NO_3)_2} \times \frac{461\ g\ PbI_2}{1\ mol\ PbI_2}$$

$$= 22.8\ g\ PbI_2$$

$$28.5\ g\ KI \times \frac{1\ mol\ KI}{166\ g\ KI} \times \frac{1\ mol\ PbI_2}{2\ mol\ KI} \times$$

$$\frac{461\ g\ PbI_2}{1\ mol\ PbI_2} = 39.6\ g\ PbI_2$$

Pb(NO$_3$)$_2$ is the limiting reactant and 22.8 grams of PbI$_2$ are produced.

4. Evaluate   The Pb(NO$_3$)$_2$ is present in a smaller quantity than can react with all the KI available. Thus it limits the amount of product formed.

PRACTICE PROBLEMS

11. If 3.5 g Zn and 3.5 g S are mixed together and heated, what mass of ZnS will be produced? *(Answer: 5.2 g ZnS)*

12. What mass of barium nitride (Ba$_3$N$_2$) is produced from the reaction between 22.6 g barium and 4.2 g nitrogen gas? *(Answer: 24.1 g Ba$_3$N$_2$)*

Percent Yield

Although you have learned how to determine the amount of product that will be produced in a chemical reaction, in reality, that calculated amount is not always the actual amount obtained from the reaction. The amount of a product that should be produced based on calculations is called the **expected yield.** The amount of a product that is really obtained from a chemical reaction is called the **actual yield.** There are many reasons why the actual yield may differ from the expected yield. Some portion of the reactants may simply not react. Some of the reactants may take part in side reactions that differ from the reaction on which the calculations are based. Some of the product may be lost during the process of recovering it or transferring it from one container to another.

Chemists often find it useful to determine what percent of the expected yield was actually obtained. This percentage is called **percent yield.** To calculate the percent yield, you divide the actual yield obtained in the laboratory by the expected yield predicted by stoichiometry calculations. The decimal number obtained is then multiplied by 100 percent to give a percentage. The general formula can be written as

$$\text{percent yield} = \frac{\text{actual yield}}{\text{expected yield}} \times 100\% \qquad \textbf{(Eq. 24)}$$

For example, you might burn 4.9 grams of magnesium in oxygen and find that the actual yield of magnesium oxide is 6.5 grams. The stoichiometry calculations give an expected yield of 8.2 grams of magnesium oxide. The percent yield is then 6.5 g/8.2 g $\times$ 100%, or 80 percent. Eighty percent of the expected amount of product was recovered and 20 percent was lost or not produced.

SAMPLE PROBLEM 7

A piece of copper with a mass of 5.00 g is placed in a solution of silver(I) nitrate containing excess $AgNO_3$. The silver metal produced has a mass of 15.2 g. What is the percent yield for this reaction?

STRATEGY	SOLUTION
1. Analyze	You are given the mass of the product and are asked to compare the actual mass with the expected mass.
2. Plan	The expected mass is determined from a stoichiometry, or mass-mass, problem. First find the expected mass and then compare it with the actual mass as given in the problem.
3. Solve	The balanced equation is

$$Cu + 2\,AgNO_3 \rightarrow 2\,Ag + Cu(NO_3)_2$$

$$5.00 \text{ g Cu} \times \frac{1 \text{ mol Cu}}{63.5 \text{ g Cu}} \times \frac{2 \text{ mol Ag}}{1 \text{ mol Cu}} \times$$

$$\frac{107.9 \text{ g Ag}}{1 \text{ mol Ag}} = 17.0 \text{ g Ag}$$

The expected yield is 17.0 g Ag.

$$\text{percent yield} = \frac{\text{actual yield}}{\text{expected yield}} \times 100\%$$

$$= \frac{15.2 \text{ g Ag}}{17.0 \text{ g Ag}} \times 100\%$$

$$= 89.4\%$$

4. Evaluate	The mass of silver actually produced is less than the calculated mass. Therefore, the percent yield is less than 100 percent. So the answer is reasonable.

PRACTICE PROBLEMS

13. Determine the percent yield for the reaction between 2.80 g $Al(NO_3)_3$ and excess NaOH if 0.966 g $Al(OH)_3$ is recovered. *(Answer: 93.8%)*

14. Determine the percent yield for the reaction between 15.0 g N_2 and 15.0 g H_2 if 10.5 g NH_3 is produced. *(Answer: 57.7%)*

An Explosive Mistake

While the rest of the family was finishing up a game of volleyball in the bright afternoon sunshine, Brendon attempted to start a fire in the charcoal grill. He arranged the charcoal briquettes and squirted them with lighter fluid. He waited a few minutes for the fuel to soak into the charcoal and then he lit the pile of charcoal briquettes with a match. Flames from the match quickly began to ignite the briquettes.

Just as the fire got going, Brendon's brother knocked the volleyball out of bounds and Brendon ran to get it. By the time he returned the ball and chatted with the family, the fire appeared to have gone out. Brendon grabbed the can of lighter fluid and squeezed its sides to douse the charcoal again. Suddenly, the can of lighter fluid exploded, spewing burning fluid everywhere. Luckily, Brendon dropped the can—not a fraction of a second too soon—and was spared serious injury.

The moral of this story is never to add lighter fluid to charcoal twice. Use the following information to determine exactly why this is true: A typical molecule of lighter fluid might be C_7H_{16}. A molecule like this one, consisting of carbon and hydrogen, is called a hydrocarbon. When hydrocarbons are ignited by heat, as from the flame of a match, they combine with oxygen in the air in a combustion reaction.

- Write a balanced chemical equation that describes the reactions that took place. What volume of oxygen is necessary to burn 0.1 g of lighter fluid? What volume of carbon dioxide is produced?

- Form a hypothesis to explain what happened to Brendon. Why was this reaction so violent compared with the reaction that occurs normally when charcoal briquettes are burned in a barbecue grill?

- If circumstances had been more fortunate, what conditions could have limited the extent of the reaction?

11–3 Section Review

1. What is a limiting reactant? Why is the amount of product formed determined only by the amount of limiting reactant?

2. How are quantities of products determined when there is an excess of one or more reactants?

3. What is percent yield and how is it determined?

4. **Connection—Economics**   You invest $100 and expect to earn $350 in 5 years. At the end of 5 years, your account shows $1220. What percent of the expected yield is the actual yield? Are you happy with your investment? Relate this example to chemical reactions.

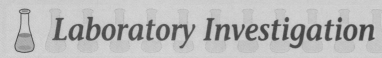

Laboratory Investigation

Determining Percent Yield in a Chemical Reaction

Problem

What is the percent yield of copper in the reaction between copper sulfate and iron: $Fe + CuSO_4 \rightarrow FeSO_4 + Cu$?

Materials (per group)

> balance
> beakers, 100-mL and 250-mL
> Bunsen burner
> anhydrous copper sulfate crystals ($CuSO_4$)
> glass stirring rod
> 10-mL graduated cylinder
> water
> iron filings (Fe)
> ring stand and ring
> wire gauze

Procedure

1. Determine the mass of a clean, dry 100-mL beaker. Record the mass in a data table similar to the one shown.
2. Measure 8.0 g of copper sulfate crystals and add these to the beaker.
3. Measure 50.0 mL of water in a graduated cylinder and add the water to the crystals in the beaker.
4. Set up the ring stand and ring with the wire gauze on the ring. Place the Bunsen burner below the ring. Place the beaker on the wire gauze. Carefully heat the mixture in the beaker, but do not allow the mixture to boil.
5. Continue heating and stirring the mixture with the stirring rod until the crystals are completely dissolved.
6. Measure 2.24 g of iron filings. Add the iron filings, a little at a time, to the hot copper sulfate solution, stirring continuously. Allow the beaker to cool for 10 min.
7. Decant the liquid into a 250-mL beaker by gently pouring the liquid down the stirring rod into the beaker. Do not disturb the solid at the bottom of the beaker.

8. Add about 10 mL of water to the solid in the 100-mL beaker, stirring vigorously. Allow the solid to settle and decant again.
9. Spread the solid over the bottom of the beaker and allow the solid to dry.
10. After the solid is completely dry, find the mass of the beaker and the solid copper. Record this mass in your data table.

Observations

Mass of empty beaker	
Mass of beaker plus copper	
Actual yield of copper	
Expected yield of copper	
Percent yield of copper	

1. What signs indicate that a chemical reaction occurred?
2. What is the expected yield of copper from stoichiometry calculations? Is the reaction limited by either reactant?
3. Determine the actual yield of copper.
4. What is the percent yield of copper?

Analysis and Conclusions

1. What changes indicate that all of the iron reacted?
2. Was your actual yield close to the expected yield? If not, explain why you think it was not.
3. **On Your Own** Repeat this reaction using different proportions of iron and copper sulfate.

STUDY GUIDE

Summarizing Key Concepts

11–1 Stoichiometry

- Stoichiometry involves the quantitative relationships that exist between the reactants and products in a chemical reaction.
- The coefficients in a balanced chemical equation represent the relative number of moles of each substance. This molar ratio can be used to analyze a chemical reaction more closely and to determine the number of moles of any reactant or product given the number of moles of any other reactant or product. Such calculations are known as mole-mole problems.
- Mole calculations can be used to verify that mass is conserved in a chemical reaction.

11–2 Solving Stoichiometry Problems

- There are three major types of stoichiometry problems: mass-mass, mass-volume, and volume-volume. All three involve using the molar ratio described by the coefficients in a balanced chemical equation.
- Most stoichiometry problems follow the basic steps of converting the given information to moles, using the molar ratio to determine the number of moles of the reactant or product, and finally converting the calculated number of moles to the desired unit of the reactant or product.
- Volume-volume problems are very similar to mole-mole problems in that the coefficients describe the ratio of volumes of gases as well as the ratio of moles.

11–3 Limiting Reactants and Percent Yield

- The limiting reactant in a chemical reaction is the reactant that limits the amount of product formed. The limiting reactant is the reactant present in the smallest quantity relative to the molar ratio indicated by the balanced chemical equation.
- The percent yield of a reaction is the ratio of the actual yield to the expected yield times 100 percent.

Reviewing Key Terms

Define each term in a complete sentence.

11–1 Stoichiometry

stoichiometry
mole-mole problem

11–2 Solving Stoichiometry Problems

mass-mass problem
mass-volume problem
volume-volume problem

11–3 Limiting Reactants and Percent Yield

limiting reactant
expected yield
actual yield
percent yield

CHAPTER REVIEW

Content Review

Multiple Choice
Choose the letter of the answer that best completes each statement.

1. The coefficients in a balanced chemical equation represent ratios of all of the following except
   (a) mass.
   (b) moles.
   (c) volumes.
   (d) particles.

2. The equation for the synthesis of ammonia is $N_2 + 3 H_2 \rightarrow 2 NH_3$. How many moles of H_2 are needed to produce 6 mol NH_3?
   (a) 4
   (b) 6
   (c) 8
   (d) 9

3. What mass of copper is produced when 3.8 g of iron reacts with excess copper(II) sulfate according to the equation $Fe + CuSO_4 \rightarrow FeSO_4 + Cu$?
   (a) 6.4 g
   (b) 4.3 g
   (c) 3.3 g
   (d) 3.8 g

4. If 16.4 g Na_2CrO_4 are combined with 26.2 g $AgNO_3$ in a double-replacement reaction, what will be the limiting reactant?
   (a) Na_2CrO_4
   (b) $AgNO_3$
   (c) $NaNO_3$
   (d) Ag_2CrO_4

5. Magnesium reacts with hydrochloric acid according to the following equation: $Mg + 2 HCl \rightarrow MgCl_2 + H_2$. If 0.30 mole of Mg reacts, how many molecules of HCl will also react?
   (a) 2.0×10^{24}
   (b) 1.8×10^{23}
   (c) 3.0×10^{23}
   (d) 3.6×10^{23}

6. If 3.0 L CH_4 are burned according to the equation $CH_4 + 2 O_2 \rightarrow CO_2 + 2 H_2O$, what volume of carbon dioxide will be produced at STP?
   (a) 3.0 L
   (b) 44 L
   (c) 132 L
   (d) 6.0 L

7. Percent yield is the quantity of product actually produced compared with the quantity
   (a) of product expected.
   (b) of the limiting reactant.
   (c) usually produced on average.
   (d) of the reactant in excess.

True or False
If the statement is true, write "true." If it is false, change the underlined word or words to make the statement true.

8. The total <u>number of moles</u> of reactants is always equal to that of the products.

9. All stoichiometry problems are based upon the <u>molar</u> ratios that exist between the substances in a reaction.

10. When 3 moles of calcium chlorate are decomposed in the reaction $Ca(ClO_3)_2 \rightarrow CaCl_2 + 3 O_2$, <u>6</u> moles of oxygen gas are produced.

11. The <u>limiting reactant</u> determines the quantity of products in a chemical reaction.

12. When 5.0 g of aluminum combine with 3.0 g of sulfur to produce aluminum sulfide (Al_2S_3), the limiting reactant is <u>sulfur</u>.

13. The amount of product recovered from a chemical reaction is the <u>estimated</u> yield.

Concept Mapping
Complete the following concept map for Section 11–2. Refer to pages xviii–xix to construct a concept map for the entire chapter.

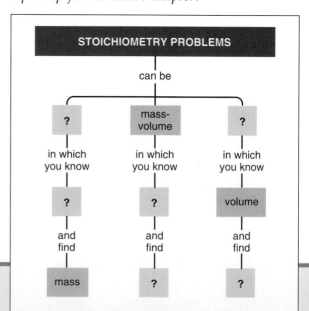

Concept Mastery

Discuss each of the following in a brief paragraph.

14. Describe stoichiometry and its role in chemistry.
15. Explain why a balanced chemical equation is necessary to solve a stoichiometry problem.
16. Explain why it is necessary to convert the given units of substances to moles when solving a stoichiometry problem.
17. The coefficients in a balanced chemical equation represent the ratio of moles, particles, or volumes of gases. However, coefficients do not represent the ratio of the masses of reactants or products. Explain.
18. Describe the procedure you would follow and the information you would need to find the mass of a reactant in a chemical reaction when you are given the mass of one product.

19. Explain why all of the available reactants might not be converted to products in a chemical reaction.
20. Explain what is meant by stoichiometric proportions.
21. What are the steps involved in determining a limiting reactant?
22. Describe the differences among the terms expected yield, actual yield, and percent yield.
23. **Tying it Together** While the formulas and coefficients of reactants and products in a chemical reaction remain the same, the *scale* on which that reaction takes place can vary depending upon the amounts of the various reactants and products involved. Explain the meaning and importance of this statement.

Critical Thinking and Problem Solving

Use the skills you have developed in this chapter to answer each of the following.

24. **Designing experiments** Given a solution of HCl, describe an experiment that would allow you to determine the number of moles of HCl in 100 mL of the solution.
25. **Making comparisons** A farmer has 450 oranges and needs to place them into mesh bags for sale. Each bag can hold 8 oranges. How many full bags of oranges can be prepared? Relate the farmer's situation to an experimental situation a chemist might face.

26. **Making comparisons** How is the mole ratio in a balanced equation like a bridge spanning a river that separates one city from another?
27. **Developing hypotheses** Even after the most precise measurements possible and under tightly controlled experimental conditions, the percent yield for a reaction is not likely to be 100 percent. What factors might cause the yield to be less than 100 percent?
28. **Using the writing process** Astronauts in space carry on the same biological processes as they do on Earth. What processes must be taken into account for space travel? Write a short story in which you describe the chemical reactions that help maintain a stable environment on a space mission from the point of view of an astronaut.

PROBLEM BANK

Group A

29. In the reaction that follows, how many moles of copper will be produced from 2 moles of Al? $3 CuSO_4 + 2 Al \rightarrow Al_2(SO_4)_3 + 3 Cu$ *(Section 11–1)*

30. According to the equation that follows, how many moles of $FeCl_3$ will be produced from 6 moles of Cl_2? $2 FeBr_3 + 3 Cl_2 \rightarrow 2 FeCl_3 + 3 Br_2$ *(Section 11–1)*

31. How many moles of water are needed to react completely with 12 moles of sodium according to the balanced equation that follows? $2 Na + 2 H_2O \rightarrow 2 NaOH + H_2$ *(Section 11–1)*

32. Determine the mass of each reactant and product based on their molar mass. *(Section 11–1)*
    (a) $2 Na + Cl_2 \rightarrow 2 NaCl$
    (b) $Na_2SO_4 + MgBr_2 \rightarrow 2 NaBr + MgSO_4$

33. Show that mass is conserved in the following reactions: *(Section 11–1)*
    (a) $3 PbCl_2 + Al_2(SO_4)_3 \rightarrow 3 PbSO_4 + 2 AlCl_3$
    (b) $C_3H_8 + 5 O_2 \rightarrow 4 H_2O + 3 CO_2$

34. How many grams of lead(II) iodide are produced from 6.0 mol NaI according to the balanced equation given? $Pb(NO_3)_2 + 2 NaI \rightarrow 2 NaNO_3 + PbI_2$ *(Section 11–2)*

35. How many moles of oxygen are needed to combine with 87 g of lithium according to the given equation? $4 Li + O_2 \rightarrow 2 Li_2O$? *(Section 11–2)*

36. Use the equation given to determine how many grams of aluminum chloride will be produced from 92 g of Cl_2. $2 AlBr_3 + 3 Cl_2 \rightarrow 3 Br_2 + 2 AlCl_3$ *(Section 11–2)*

37. Use the equation to determine what mass of FeS must react to form 326 g of $FeCl_2$. $FeS + 2 HCl \rightarrow H_2S + FeCl_2$ *(Section 11–2)*

38. What mass of barium chloride is needed to react completely with 46.8 g of sodium phosphate according to the given equation? $3 BaCl_2 + 2 Na_3PO_4 \rightarrow Ba_3(PO_4)_2 + 6 NaCl$ *(Section 11–2)*

39. How many grams of magnesium oxide are needed to produce 264 g of magnesium hydroxide according to the given equation? $MgO + H_2O \rightarrow Mg(OH)_2$ *(Section 11–2)*

40. If a piece of magnesium with a mass of 2.76 g is added to a solution of hydrochloric acid, what volume of H_2 would be produced at STP? *(Section 11–2)*

41. Candles are made of paraffin wax ($C_{25}H_{52}$). When paraffin burns in oxygen, carbon dioxide and water are produced. If 5.5 g of paraffin burn, what volume of carbon dioxide is produced at STP? The balanced equation is $C_{25}H_{52} + 38 O_2 \rightarrow 25 CO_2 + 26 H_2O$. *(Section 11–2)*

42. The body metabolizes sucrose, or table sugar, by burning it with oxygen to produce carbon dioxide, water, and energy. If 3 moles of sucrose are burned according to the following equation, what volume of carbon dioxide is produced at STP: $C_{12}H_{22}O_{11} + 12 O_2 \rightarrow 12 CO_2 + 11 H_2O$? *(Section 11–2)*

43. Hydrogen gas reacts with oxygen gas to produce water. If a student fills a 250-mL flask with hydrogen at STP, what volume of oxygen is necessary for the reaction? *(Section 11–2)*

44. Toluene (C_7H_8) burns in oxygen to produce carbon dioxide and water. *(Section 11–2)*
    (a) How many grams of oxygen are necessary for the combustion of 94.5 g of toluene?
    (b) What volume of oxygen would be necessary for this reaction at STP?

45. How many molecules of sulfuric acid are needed to react with 15 moles of ammonium hydroxide? The equation that describes this reaction is $2 NH_4OH + H_2SO_4 \rightarrow (NH_4)_2SO_4 + 2 H_2O$. *(Section 11–2)*

46. How many formula units of magnesium phosphate will be produced from 35.8 g of sodium triphosphate? The equation is $2 Na_3PO_4 + 3 Mg(NO_3)_2 \rightarrow Mg_3(PO_4)_2 + 6 NaNO_3$. *(Section 11–2)*

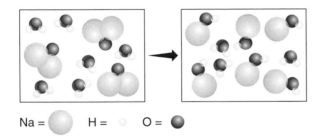

Na = ◯ H = ○ O = ●

47. The diagram above shows the substances that take part in a chemical reaction before and after the reaction. Explain what is happening in the diagram. Then write an equation to describe the reaction. Use your equation to make up and solve your own stoichiometry problem. *(Section 11–3)*

48. Using the reaction shown, identify the limiting reactant in each of the following examples. *(Section 11–3)*

$$4\ Al + 3\ O_2 \rightarrow 2\ Al_2O_3$$

(a) 0.25 mol Al and 0.40 mol O_2
(b) 58.5 g Al and 98.0 g O_2
(c) 78.2 g Al and 113.1 g O_2

49. When octane (C_8H_{18}) is burned in oxygen, carbon dioxide and water are produced. If 320 g of octane are burned and 392 g of water are recovered, what is the percent yield of the experiment? The equation is $2\ C_8H_{18} + 25\ O_2 \rightarrow 16\ CO_2 + 18\ H_2O$. *(Section 11–3)*

Group B

50. Antacid tablets react with the hydrochloric acid in the stomach to ease indigestion. Baking soda ($NaHCO_3$) is often used as an antacid because it takes part in the following reaction:

$$NaHCO_3 + HCl \rightarrow NaCl + H_2O + CO_2$$

Milk of magnesia ($Mg(OH)_2$) is also used as an antacid because it takes part in the following reaction:

$$Mg(OH)_2 + 2\ HCl \rightarrow 2\ H_2O + MgCl_2$$

Determine which antacid is more effective (reacts with more HCl) per gram.

51. Ethylene glycol is used in automobile antifreeze and in the preparation of polyester fiber. Ethylene glycol is produced in the following reaction: $C_2H_4O + H_2O \rightarrow C_2H_6O_2$. If 5 moles of water are used completely in the reaction how many moles of ethylene glycol are produced?

52. How many grams of calcium are needed to produce 16 moles of iron? The equation for the reaction is $2\ FeBr_3 + 3\ Ca \rightarrow 3\ CaBr_2 + 2\ Fe$.

53. How many grams of magnesium nitrate are needed to react with 549.6 g of potassium carbonate? The equation for the reaction is $K_2CO_3 + Mg(NO_3)_2 \rightarrow 2\ KNO_3 + MgCO_3$.

54. To produce 196.5 g of aluminum sulfate, what mass of aluminum must react with sulfuric acid? The equation for the reaction is $2\ Al + 3\ H_2SO_4 \rightarrow Al_2(SO_4)_3 + 3\ H_2$.

55. Solid lithium hydroxide (LiOH) is used in spacecraft to remove exhaled carbon dioxide from the air. The lithium hydroxide reacts with carbon dioxide to form lithium carbonate (Li_2CO_3) and water. How many grams of carbon dioxide can be absorbed by each gram of lithium hydroxide?

56. What volume of oxygen at STP is necessary to burn 500. g of glucose? The equation for this reaction is $C_6H_{12}O_6 + 6\ O_2 \rightarrow 6\ CO_2 + 6\ H_2O$.

57. Hexane (C_6H_{14}) burns in oxygen to produce carbon dioxide and water. How many moles of oxygen are needed for the complete combustion of 9.88×10^{21} molecules of hexane?

58. A student places an iron nail with a mass of 2.32 g into a flask of $CuSO_4$. The nail reacts completely, leaving a quantity of copper metal in the bottom of the flask. The student finds the mass of the recovered copper to be 2.51 g. The equation for this reaction is $Fe + CuSO_4 \rightarrow FeSO_4 + Cu$.
(a) What is the expected yield?
(b) What is the percent yield?

Chapter
12
Heat in Chemical Reactions

What do you visualize when you hear the words chemical reaction? It is probably one of two images: chemicals combining to produce a dramatic color change or chemicals uniting explosively to create lots of light, sound, and heat! The thermite reaction shown here is a classic example of the latter image. Talk to any chemistry teacher and you will most likely hear an exciting "thermite" story—complete with anticipation, unexpected drama, and perhaps even panic. The thermite reaction generates so much heat that the iron produced is in a molten state.

Most chemical reactions involve a transfer of heat, although not always as dramatically as in the thermite reaction. Heat produced and consumed by chemical reactions is the subject of this chapter.

Not all chemical reactions liberate energy as noticeably as in this thermite reaction. Many reactions, such as those that occur within the human body, give off large quantities of energy that can be used in activities such as swimming.

Chem Journal

YOU AND YOUR WORLD

Make a list of the chemical and physical changes taking place around you for one day. Try to identify them as releasing heat or absorbing heat. After you complete this chapter, go back to your list and see if you identified the processes correctly. Ask your teacher if you are not sure of some of the processes on your list.

12–1 Chemical Reactions That Involve Heat

Guide for Reading
- What are exothermic and endothermic reactions?

How much fun is a cookout if the chef cannot start a fire in the grill? How refreshing is iced tea if there are no ice cubes to cool the tea? In each of these situations, heat is involved. In the first case, heat is needed to cook food. In the second case, ice cubes are needed to cool the tea. As you probably know, energy and heat play an important role in your daily life. In fact, it is energy that maintains your body temperature close to 37°C, enables your heart and lungs to carry on circulation and respiration, and generates the electrical impulses necessary for your nervous system to function.

Most chemical reactions involve energy—more specifically, changes in energy. Remember from Chapter 9 that in a chemical reaction existing bonds are broken, atoms are rearranged, and new bonds are formed. Because bond breaking requires energy and bond formation releases energy, almost all chemical reactions either absorb or release energy. This results in energy flow that is familiar to you as heat. Heat is defined as the energy that is transferred from one object to another due to a difference in temperature.

Figure 12–1 *Most chemical reactions, such as the violent eruption of an explosive, involve changes in energy. Sometimes this energy may take on other forms—such as light, as in the eerie glow given off by this chemiluminescent reaction.*

The study of the changes in heat in chemical reactions is called **thermochemistry.** The word is derived from the Greek word *thermes* meaning heat. Thermochemistry is part of a larger subject area called thermodynamics, which examines energy and work transformations in systems. You will learn more about thermodynamics in Chapter 23.

Reactions that release heat are called exothermic reactions. The prefix *exo-* means outside, so an **exothermic reaction** releases heat to its surroundings. The opposite of an exothermic reaction is a reaction that absorbs heat. **Reactions that absorb heat are called endothermic reactions.** The prefix *endo-* means inside. What is the source of heat in an **endothermic reaction**?

Exothermic Reactions

A camping stove uses oxygen from the air and a fuel such as propane to heat food and water. When mixed and ignited, propane and oxygen undergo a chemical reaction that generates quite a bit of heat. This reaction, like all combustion reactions, is exothermic.

$$C_3H_8\,(g) + 5\,O_2\,(g) \rightarrow 3\,CO_2\,(g) + 4\,H_2O\,(g) + 2043\ \text{kJ}$$

(Eq. 1)

The balanced equation shows that carbon dioxide and water are produced in the reaction. But to a cold, hungry camper these reaction products are not nearly as important as the heat that is generated. Equation 1 also shows that 2043 kilojoules of heat is produced (released) when 1 mole of propane reacts completely with 5 moles of oxygen. In a sense, heat is one of the products of this reaction. Heat is produced in this combustion reaction because the energy released as new bonds are formed in the products is greater than the energy required to break the old bonds in the reactants. Because heat and energy are related, the base SI unit of energy, the joule (J), also serves as the unit of heat.

Figure 12–2 Thanks to the greater stability of bonds in carbon dioxide and water compared to those in propane and oxygen, the camping stove generates enough heat to provide these cold, hungry campers with warmth and hot food. Is this combustion reaction endothermic or exothermic?

Figure 12–3 *In a chemical plant, the production of water gas from the reaction between coal and steam is an endothermic reaction. So too is the reaction between the chemicals in this cold pack, which will help reduce swelling when applied to the skin. What happens to the heat that is absorbed in an endothermic reaction?*

Endothermic Reactions

An important industrial fuel called water gas, which is a mixture of carbon monoxide and hydrogen, is prepared by passing steam over hot coal (coal is mostly carbon). This reaction absorbs heat, so it is endothermic.

$$C\,(s) + H_2O\,(g) + 113\text{ kJ} \rightarrow CO\,(g) + H_2\,(g)$$

(Eq. 2)

In Equation 2, the amount of heat—113 kJ—appears on the left side of the arrow, indicating that heat is a reactant and not a product. In this reaction, 1 mole of carbon and 1 mole of water vapor require an input of 113 kilojoules of heat to form 1 mole of carbon monoxide and 1 mole of hydrogen. Another example of an endothermic reaction is the decomposition of water into oxygen gas and hydrogen gas. In this reaction, 1 mole of water requires 286 kilojoules of heat to decompose into its elements. What is the balanced equation for this reaction?

Exactly what happens to the heat that is absorbed in reactions such as the production of water gas or the decomposition of water? In an endothermic reaction, the energy released as new bonds are formed in the products is less than the energy required to break the bonds in the reactants. This energy must be supplied in order for the reaction to proceed. The added heat does not disappear, of course, because energy is conserved. Instead, it becomes stored in the chemical bonds of the products.

12–1 Section Review

1. What is an exothermic reaction? An endothermic reaction?

2. Why do almost all chemical reactions involve changes in energy?

3. On which side of a chemical equation does the energy term appear in an exothermic reaction? An endothermic reaction?

4. **Connection—Earth Science** Is cloud formation an exothermic or endothermic process? Explain your reasoning. What happens when raindrops form from clouds?

Guide for Reading

• What is the significance of the enthalpy change of a reaction?

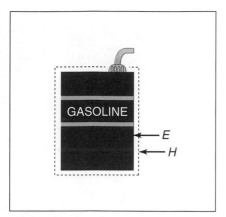

Figure 12–4 To help you better understand the concept of enthalpy, think of the volume inside this gasoline can as representing the total energy of a gallon of gasoline. Then think of the volume within the dotted line as representing the total enthalpy of the gasoline. What is the symbol for enthalpy?

12–2 Heat and Enthalpy Changes

You now know that the heat absorbed by the reactants in an endothermic reaction becomes the added energy of the products. In a similar way, the heat released in an exothermic reaction is the extra energy that reactants have compared to the energy of the products. This might lead you to expect that the heat transferred in a reaction is the difference in the energies of reactants and products. Although this explanation is close, it is not exactly true under all conditions. The heat absorbed or released in a reaction depends on the difference in a quantity called **enthalpy.** Enthalpy is represented by the capital letter H. Just what is a substance's enthalpy and how is it related to its energy? Recall that the total energy of a substance is the sum of all the kinetic energy and the potential energy of its particles. The enthalpy of a substance is its energy plus a small added term that takes into account the pressure and volume of the substance. Like energy, the enthalpy of a substance depends on its temperature, physical state, and composition. The most important fact for you to understand about the energy and enthalpy of a substance is that they are numerically very close to each other. In other words, the difference between energy and enthalpy is always very small. Why, then, do chemists bother with two very similar concepts?

To chemists, a substance's enthalpy is a much more useful concept than its energy when dealing with the heat transferred in chemical reactions. This is because the heat absorbed or released in a reaction at constant pressure is the enthalpy difference between the reactants and products—not the energy difference between the reactants and products. Because most everyday reactions—reactions that occur in living organisms or in a beaker in a laboratory—take place under atmospheric pressure, which does not change significantly over the course of the reactions, enthalpy and enthalpy changes are very useful. **When the pressure remains constant, the heat absorbed or released during a chemical reaction is equal to the enthalpy change for the reaction.**

Enthalpy Change, ΔH

As you just learned, the enthalpy change for a chemical reaction is equal to the heat absorbed or gained during the reaction. The enthalpy change for a reaction is written as the enthalpy of the products minus the enthalpy of the reactants. Enthalpy changes are represented by the symbol ΔH, which is read delta H. The Greek letter Δ is used in science to mean a change or a difference. Thus, the symbol ΔH literally means a change (or a difference) in enthalpy.

$$\Delta H = H_{\text{products}} - H_{\text{reactants}} \qquad \textbf{(Eq. 3)}$$

When 1 mole of carbon and 1 mole of water react according to Equation 2, 113 kilojoules of heat is absorbed. Enthalpy changes are graphically illustrated in Figure 12–5. The heat absorbed in an endothermic reaction ends up as the "extra" enthalpy of the products compared with the enthalpy of the reactants. In other words, H_{products} is greater than $H_{\text{reactants}}$. Thus ΔH for an endothermic reaction always has a positive sign. In an exothermic reaction, the enthalpy of the products, H_{products}, is less than the enthalpy of the reactants, $H_{\text{reactants}}$. Thus ΔH has a negative sign and its numerical value is the amount of heat released in the exothermic reaction. The table in Figure 12–5 summarizes the relationship between the sign of ΔH and the direction of heat flow in a chemical process.

The amount of heat that a reaction absorbs or releases depends on the conditions under which the reaction is carried out—conditions such as the temperature, pressure, and physical states of the reactants and products. To make comparing enthalpy changes easier, chemists have chosen 1 atmosphere as the standard pressure and conventionally use 25°C as the temperature for reporting enthalpy changes. In addition, an important condition for the reaction is that the reactants and products are in their standard states. The standard state of a substance is defined as its pure form at the standard pressure of 1 atmosphere. When a pure element is involved, it must be present in its most stable form at standard pressure. For example, the two most common forms of carbon at 25°C and 1 atmosphere are graphite (used in pencil "lead") and diamond. Of the two forms, graphite is slightly more stable. Thus, in reactions where pure carbon is present under standard conditions, it is present in the form of graphite. The most stable form of an element under standard conditions is called the standard state of the element.

An enthalpy change that is measured when reactants in their standard states change to products in their standard states is called a **standard enthalpy change.** A standard enthalpy change is denoted with a superscript o, $\Delta H°$. As you just read, chemists have chosen to report enthalpy data at the temperature of 25°C. You may be wondering how a reaction such as the combustion

Figure 12–5   The enthalpy diagrams for Equations 1 and 2 on pages 382 and 383 show the relative enthalpies of reactants and products for an exothermic and an endothermic reaction. A summary of the characteristics of an enthalpy change is presented in the table. What can you conclude about the reverse of an endothermic reaction?

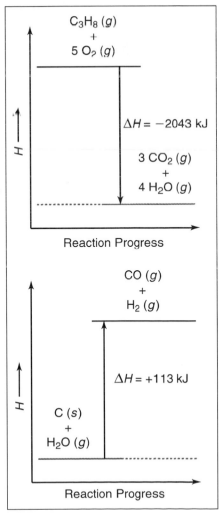

Heat Transfer and the Sign of ΔH

Sign of ΔH	Process	Heat
positive	endothermic	absorbed
negative	exothermic	released

Figure 12–6 *The standard states of iron and iodine are illustrated in the photographs. What is the definition of standard state?*

of propane can be carried out under standard conditions at 25°C. After all, as soon as a combustion reaction starts, the heat it produces raises the temperature of the reactants and products above 25°C! The answer is that if the reaction occurs at a temperature other than 25°C, the standard enthalpy change takes into account the heat involved in restoring the products to standard conditions after the reaction is complete.

An appropriate way to rewrite Equations 1 and 2, including the standard enthalpy change, is shown by Equations 4 and 5.

$$C_3H_8\,(g) + 5\,O_2\,(g) \rightarrow 3\,CO_2\,(g) + 4\,H_2O\,(g)$$
$$\Delta H° = -2043\text{ kJ} \qquad \textbf{(Eq. 4)}$$

$$C\,(s) + H_2O\,(g) \rightarrow CO\,(g) + H_2\,(g) \qquad \Delta H° = +113\text{kJ}$$
$$\textbf{(Eq. 5)}$$

Using Enthalpy Changes

Chemistry problems involving enthalpy changes are similar to the stoichiometry problems that you learned to solve in Chapter 11. The amount of heat that is absorbed or released in a reaction depends on the number of moles of reactants involved. For example, according to Equation 2, 113 kilojoules of heat is absorbed when 1 mole of carbon reacts with 1 mole of water. How much heat will be absorbed if 2 moles of carbon combine with 2 moles of water? If you said 226 kilojoules of heat are absorbed—twice the amount absorbed by 1 mole of each of the reactants—you are correct.

The enthalpy change for a reaction is proportionately smaller or larger depending on the quantities of the reactants and products involved. This is illustrated in the following Sample Problem that builds on the skills you learned in Chapter 11. After you understand the steps in the Sample Problem, solve the Practice Problems on your own.

SAMPLE PROBLEM 1

How much heat will be released if 1.0 g of hydrogen peroxide (H_2O_2) decomposes in a bombardier beetle to produce a steam spray such as the one shown in the photograph on the opposite page?

$$2\,H_2O_2\,(l) \rightarrow 2\,H_2O\,(l) + O_2\,(g) \qquad \Delta H° = -190\text{ kJ}$$

STRATEGY   **SOLUTION**

1. Analyze   You are asked to calculate the heat released when 1.0 g of H_2O_2 decomposes. You are given the balanced equation, which includes $\Delta H°$.

2. Plan
The given ΔH° corresponds to the reaction in which 2 mol H_2O_2 decompose. This gives the conversion factor relating moles of H_2O_2 to heat produced. You must first convert grams of H_2O_2 to moles of H_2O_2 and then use the conversion factor to find the heat released.

3. Solve
$$1.0 \text{ g } H_2O_2 \times \frac{1 \text{ mol } H_2O_2}{34.0 \text{ g } H_2O_2} = 0.029 \text{ mol } H_2O_2$$

heat transferred $= 0.029 \text{ mol } H_2O_2 \times$
$$\frac{-190 \text{ kJ}}{2 \text{ mol } H_2O_2} = -2.8 \text{ kJ}$$

4. Evaluate
The minus sign tells you that heat is released in this reaction. The quantity of heat that is released, 2.8 kJ, is much less than the amount in the balanced equation. This makes sense, because the balanced equation requires 2 mol H_2O_2 and only 0.029 mol is present.

PRACTICE PROBLEMS

1. How much heat is transferred when 9.22 g of glucose $(C_6H_{12}O_6)$ in your body reacts with O_2 according to the following equation?

$$C_6H_{12}O_6 (s) + 6 O_2 (g) \rightarrow 6 CO_2 (g) + 6 H_2O (l)$$
$$\Delta H^\circ = -2803 \text{ kJ}$$

(Answer: 144 kJ released)

2. How much heat is transferred when 147 g of NO_2 (g) is dissolved in 100 g of water?

$$3 NO_2 (g) + H_2O (l) \rightarrow 2 HNO_3 (aq) + NO (g)$$
$$\Delta H^\circ = -138 \text{ kJ}$$

(Answer: 147 kJ released)

12–2 Section Review

1. What information is provided by the enthalpy change, ΔH, of a reaction?

2. Compare standard enthalpy change ΔH° and enthalpy change ΔH.

3. Explain the significance of the sign of the enthalpy change for a reaction.

4. **Critical Thinking—Applying concepts** Why is the ΔH for a reaction proportional to the quantity of reactants?

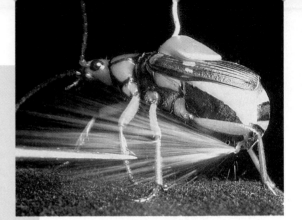

12–3 Hess's Law

In the nineteenth century, Swiss chemist G. H. Hess (1802–1850) proposed a way of finding the enthalpy change for a reaction even if the reaction could not be performed directly. In 1840, Hess demonstrated experimentally that the heat transferred during a given reaction is the same whether the reaction occurs in one step or several steps. His method is now called Hess's law of heat summation. **Hess's law states that if a series of reactions are added together, the enthalpy change for the net reaction will be the sum of the enthalpy changes for the individual steps.** A simple analogy might help you with this concept. Assume that your bank balance was $200 at the beginning of the month. If you made no deposits but did make a $100 withdrawal, your balance at the end of the month would be $100. Now suppose, instead, that you deposited $200 into your account and then withdrew $300. Your balance at the end of the month would still be $100. This is because in both instances the net effect was a withdrawal of $100.

Now let's consider a chemical situation. The brown haze often seen in the air above large cities is caused by NO_2 (nitrogen dioxide), a noxious gas that forms when the elements N_2 and O_2 combine. The overall, or net, reaction for the formation of NO_2 is the sum of the two steps as shown.

$$N_2\,(g) + O_2\,(g) \rightarrow 2\,NO\,(g) \qquad \Delta H_1 = +181\ kJ \quad \textbf{(Eq. 6)}$$
$$+\ 2\,NO\,(g) + O_2\,(g) \rightarrow 2\,NO_2\,(g) \qquad \Delta H_2 = -113\ kJ \quad \textbf{(Eq. 7)}$$

$$N_2\,(g) + 2\,O_2\,(g) + 2\,NO\,(g) \rightarrow 2\,NO\,(g) + 2\,NO_2\,(g)$$
$$\Delta H_{net} = \Delta H_1 + \Delta H_2$$

Figure 12–7 *The brownish haze found in the air above many cities is due to the gas nitrogen dioxide (NO_2). This gas is produced whenever any combustion takes place in air, allowing the nitrogen and the oxygen in air to react at high temperature. Hess's law can be applied to the two-step production of NO_2. What fundamental principle does Hess's law represent?*

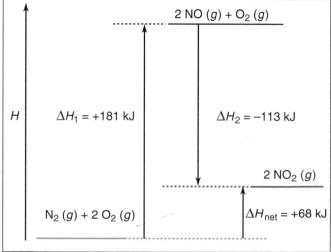

The net equation is

$$N_2\,(g) + 2\,O_2\,(g) \rightarrow 2\,NO_2\,(g) \qquad \Delta H_{net} = \Delta H_1 + \Delta H_2$$

(Eq. 8)

To write the net equation, the sum of the reactants is placed on the left side of the reaction arrow, and the sum of the products is placed on the right side. Substances that appear on both sides of the arrow cancel from the net equation just as they do in algebra. Notice in the example that NO cancels completely from the net equation because it is present in equal quantities on both sides of the reaction arrow.

According to Hess's law, the enthalpy change for the net reaction, ΔH_{net}, will be the sum of the enthalpy changes of the individual steps.

$$\begin{aligned}
\Delta H_{net} &= \Delta H_1 + \Delta H_2 \\
&= (+181\ kJ) + (-113\ kJ) \\
&= +68\ kJ
\end{aligned}$$

(Eq. 9)

Overall, the formation of NO_2 from N_2 and O_2 is an endothermic process, although one of the steps is exothermic.

Applying Hess's Law

Hess's law is very useful when a given reaction can be written as the sum of two or more reactions for which the ΔH's are known. To successfully apply Hess's law, the following two rules for manipulating reactions are important. (These rules should seem familiar to you because they are applied in algebra.)

1. If the coefficients of an equation are multiplied by a factor, the enthalpy change for the reaction is multiplied by the same factor. Doubling the coefficients of an equation, for example, means that the enthalpy change for the reaction also doubles. This rule makes sense because the amount of heat absorbed or released by a reaction depends on the quantity of reactants and products.

2. If an equation is reversed, the sign of ΔH changes also. When a reaction releases heat in one direction, it must absorb the same amount of heat in the reverse direction. In other words, changing the direction of a reaction changes the sign of ΔH. Suppose you wanted to know the value of ΔH for the following reaction:

$$H_2\,(g) + CO\,(g) \rightarrow C\,(s) + H_2O\,(g) \qquad \Delta H^\circ = ?$$

(Eq. 10)

This equation is the reverse of Equation 5 on page 386. Thus $\Delta H^\circ = -113\ kJ$ for this reaction.

CHEM Exploration

Hot and Cold Packs

You may work in a team for this activity. Obtain one hot pack and one cold pack. Activate a pack by following its label instructions. Quickly wrap the pack around a thermometer. Monitor the temperature of the pack until it reaches its maximum (or minimum) value. Now do the same with the other pack.

Which pack produced a greater change in the surrounding temperature? Compare your results with those of other teams. What is the principle on which this reaction is based? What are the advantages of these hot and cold packs over ice packs and hot water bottles?

SAMPLE PROBLEM 2

The combustion of sulfur, pictured in the photograph on the opposite page, can produce SO_2 as well as SO_3 depending upon the supply of oxygen.

From the following reactions and their enthalpy changes,

$$2 SO_2 (g) + O_2 (g) \rightarrow 2 SO_3 (g) \qquad \Delta H^\circ = -196 \text{ kJ}$$
$$2 S (s) + 3 O_2 (g) \rightarrow 2 SO_3 (g) \qquad \Delta H^\circ = -790 \text{ kJ}$$

calculate the standard enthalpy change for the combustion of sulfur to produce SO_2.

$$S (s) + O_2 (g) \rightarrow SO_2 (g)$$

STRATEGY	SOLUTION
1. Analyze	This is a Hess's law problem. You must calculate ΔH° for a reaction by adding a series of reactions together.
2. Plan	The equations with the known values of ΔH° must be manipulated so that they add to yield the equation whose ΔH° is to be determined.
3. Solve	In the net equation, $SO_2 (g)$ is a reaction product. Therefore, it is necessary to reverse the first equation to get $SO_2 (g)$ on the right side of the reaction arrow. Remember that when an equation is reversed, the sign of ΔH changes.

$$2 SO_3 (g) \rightarrow 2 SO_2 (g) + O_2 (g)$$
$$\Delta H^\circ = +196 \text{ kJ}$$

$$+ 2 S(s) + 3 O_2 (g) \rightarrow 2 SO_3 (g)$$
$$\Delta H^\circ = -790 \text{ kJ}$$

$$2 SO_3 (g) + 2 S (s) + 3 O_2 (g) \rightarrow$$
$$2 SO_2 (g) + O_2 (g) + 2 SO_3 (g)$$

The net reaction after cancellations is

$$2 S(s) + 2 O_2 (g) \rightarrow 2 SO_2 (g)$$
$$\Delta H^\circ = (+196 \text{ kJ}) + (-790 \text{ kJ})$$
$$\Delta H^\circ = -594 \text{ kJ}$$

The net equation is close to the reaction you were asked to find but the coefficients of the reactants and products differ. The net equation must be

multiplied by $\frac{1}{2}$ so that it will match the equation given in the problem.

$$\frac{1}{2}[2\,S(s) + 2\,O_2\,(g) \rightarrow 2\,SO_2\,(g)]$$
$$\Delta H^\circ - \frac{1}{2}(-594\text{ kJ})$$

$$S\,(s) + O_2\,(g) \rightarrow SO_2\,(g)$$
$$\Delta H^\circ = -297\text{ kJ}$$

4. Evaluate   Draw an enthalpy diagram to help you evaluate your answer.

PRACTICE PROBLEMS

3. From the following enthalpy changes,

$$H_2S\,(g) + \tfrac{3}{2}O_2\,(g) \rightarrow H_2O\,(l) + SO_2\,(g) \quad \Delta H^\circ = -563 \text{ kJ}$$
$$CS_2\,(l) + 3\,O_2\,(g) \rightarrow CO_2\,(g) + 2\,SO_2\,(g)$$
$$\Delta H^\circ = -1075 \text{ kJ}$$

calculate the value of ΔH° for

$$CS_2\,(l) + 2\,H_2O\,(l) \rightarrow CO_2\,(g) + 2\,H_2S\,(g) \quad \textit{(Answer: 51 kJ)}$$

4. From the following enthalpy changes,

$$OF_2\,(g) + H_2O\,(l) \rightarrow O_2\,(g) + 2\,HF\,(g) \quad \Delta H^\circ = -277 \text{ kJ}$$
$$SF_4\,(g) + 2\,H_2O\,(l) \rightarrow SO_2\,(g) + 4\,HF\,(g) \quad \Delta H^\circ = -828 \text{ kJ}$$
$$S\,(s) + O_2\,(g) \rightarrow SO_2\,(g) \quad \Delta H^\circ = -297 \text{ kJ}$$

calculate the value of ΔH° for

$$2\,S\,(s) + 2\,OF_2\,(g) \rightarrow SO_2\,(g) + SF_4\,(g)$$

(Answer: $\Delta H^\circ = -320$ kJ)

Figure 12-8 *The freezing of water to form ice and the condensation of water vapor to form dew are examples of an exothermic physical change. Can you think of some examples of an endothermic physical change?*

So far you have practiced manipulating equations and their ΔH's to determine new ΔH's. You learned that you can write a reaction in both directions as long as you reverse the sign of ΔH. Although this is possible on paper, perhaps you are wondering if a reaction really can take place in either direction. And you are quite right to wonder. Most reactions can proceed in only one direction on their own. Chemists are interested in knowing what this direction is, as well as what is required to have the reverse reaction take place. It is in answering these questions that the enthalpy change for a reaction is most useful, as you will learn in Chapter 23.

Remember that enthalpy changes represent the heat absorbed or released in reactions—reactions such as the production of metals from their ores, the combustion of fossil fuels, and the metabolism of living organisms. So they span a wide range of applications. In this chapter we have dealt mainly with chemical reactions. However, heat is transferred in physical changes too. Think about what happens when ice melts or water boils. These are probably the two most familiar examples of endothermic processes.

$$H_2O\ (s) \rightarrow H_2O\ (l) \qquad \Delta H^\circ = +\ 6.01\ \text{kJ} \qquad \textbf{(Eq. 11)}$$
$$H_2O\ (l) \rightarrow H_2O\ (g) \qquad \Delta H^\circ = +44.0\ \text{kJ} \qquad \textbf{(Eq. 12)}$$

The enthalpy change for the melting of ice is called the heat of fusion. The enthalpy change for the vaporization of water is called the heat of vaporization. You will learn more about the heat transferred in a change of state in Chapter 14.

12-3 Section Review

1. Explain how Hess's law can be used to find the ΔH° of a reaction.

2. Identify the following reactions as endothermic or exothermic.

$$\text{(a)} \qquad Br_2\ (s) \rightarrow Br_2\ (l)$$
$$\text{(b)} \qquad Br_2\ (g) \rightarrow Br_2\ (l)$$

3. **Theme Trace—Energy** Explain how Hess's law is really a statement of the law of conservation of energy.

12-4 Calorimetry

Just how do chemists measure the enthalpy change for a reaction? To answer this question, think of what happens to the surroundings after an exothermic reaction takes place. An exothermic reaction releases heat, so the temperature of the surroundings increases. What about when an endothermic reaction takes place? An endothermic reaction absorbs heat, so the temperature of the surroundings decreases. Thus a change in temperature is a clear sign that some heat has been absorbed or released. But how much heat? This is the subject of **calorimetry,** the study of heat flow and heat measurement. **Calorimetry experiments determine the heats (enthalpy changes) of reactions by making accurate measurements of temperature changes produced in a calorimeter.** The words calorimeter, calorimetry, and the energy unit calorie are derived from the Latin word *calor,* which means heat.

Heat and Temperature

When an exothermic reaction releases heat to its surroundings, the temperature of the surroundings increases. The size of the temperature increase depends on how much heat is released and on the **heat capacity** of the surroundings. The heat capacity of an object is the amount of heat needed to raise the temperature of the object by 1 Celsius degree. The heat capacity of a cup of water at 18°C, for example, is the number of joules needed to raise the temperature of the water in the cup to 19°C. The heat capacity of an object depends on its mass and its composition. A large mass of water can absorb a large quantity of heat with only a small temperature increase. The flame from a match can heat a drop of water to boiling, but it will only warm a full cup of water slightly.

The heat capacity of 1 gram of a substance is called its **specific heat.** The specific heat is a physical property of the substance, like its color and melting point. The specific heats of some familiar substances are listed in the table in Figure 12-11 on the next page. Some substances, particularly metals, have low specific heats. Water, on the other hand, has one of the highest specific heats of any common substance. In Chapter 14 you will read about the significance of this property of water for life on Earth. The specific heat of liquid water is 4.184 J/g • C°. To raise the temperature of 1 gram of H_2O (*l*) by 1 Celsius degree, 4.184 joules of heat must be added. (You may remember the definition of a calorie as the amount of heat that increases the temperature of 1 gram of water by 1 Celsius degree; 4.184 joules = 1 calorie. As you learned in Chapter 2, 1000 calories, or 1 kilocalorie, is recognized as a nutritional calorie and given the symbol Cal.)

Figure 12-9 *In an exothermic reaction, the release of heat increases the temperature of the surroundings. In an endothermic reaction, the absorption of heat decreases the temperature of the surroundings. Which reaction has a positive ΔH? A negative ΔH?*

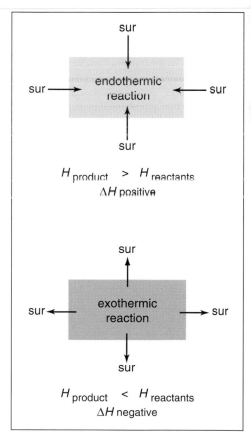

Figure 12–10 *If you have ever gone swimming in a lake and in an ocean during the summer, you know that a lake is generally warmer than the ocean. In winter, the lake freezes more quickly than the ocean. How can you explain these observations?*

INTEGRATING

PHYSICS

Why do metals heat up more quickly than water?

Perhaps you are beginning to see that heat and temperature are two related but distinct concepts. A transfer of heat is detected by measuring a temperature change. But a small temperature change does not necessarily mean that a small quantity of heat was transferred. A small change in temperature may be produced by a large quantity of heat in an object that has a very large heat capacity.

Now that you understand the concept of specific heat, you are ready to learn how a calorimeter is used to determine the quantity of heat transferred in a chemical reaction. A calorimeter, shown in Figure 12–12, consists of a well-insulated container filled with a known mass of water in which the reaction of interest is carried out. The temperature of the water is measured before the reaction takes place. This is called the initial temperature, T_i. The temperature of the water is recorded periodically during the course of the reaction so that the final temperature, T_f, can be easily determined.

Let's now determine the ΔH for the following reaction by working through typical sample data.

$$\text{NaOH} (s) \rightarrow \text{Na}^+ (aq) + \text{OH}^- (aq) \qquad \Delta H = ? \quad \textbf{(Eq. 13)}$$

In this reaction, solid sodium hydroxide, NaOH (s), is added to water and an aqueous solution of sodium hydroxide is produced.

Specific Heats of Some Substances

Substance	Specific Heat, J/g·C°
H_2O (l)	4.184
H_2O (s)	2.03
Al (s)	0.89
C (s)	0.71
Fe (s)	0.45
Hg (l)	0.14

Figure 12–11 *The specific heats of some familiar substances are listed in the table. How much heat must be added to 5 g of aluminum to raise its temperature by 2 Celsius degrees?*

The calorimeter in Figure 12–12 is filled with 75.0 grams of water at an initial temperature of 19.8°C. A 0.050-mole sample of solid NaOH is added, and the temperature increases to 26.7°C. What is the enthalpy change for this solution process?

Because the temperature of the water increased, you know that the reaction was exothermic, releasing heat to the water in the calorimeter. The heat lost in the reaction is the heat gained by the water. Scientists usually use q to denote heat measurements made in a calorimeter. Thus, we can say that the heat transferred in a reaction, q_{rxn}, is equal in magnitude but opposite in sign to the heat absorbed by the surroundings, q_{sur}.

$$q_{rxn} = -q_{sur} \qquad \textbf{(Eq. 14)}$$

You can determine the quantity of heat absorbed by the water, q_{sur}, from the mass of the water (m), its specific heat (C), and the temperature change ($T_f - T_i$).

$$q_{sur} = m \times C \times (T_f - T_i) \qquad \textbf{(Eq. 15)}$$

Substituting values for the terms on the right side of Equation 15, q_{sur} for the solution of NaOH (s) can be calculated.

$$q_{sur} = (75.0 \text{ g})(4.184 \text{ J/g} \cdot \text{C}°)(26.7°\text{C} - 19.8°\text{C})$$
$$= +2170 \text{ J} \qquad \textbf{(Eq. 16)}$$

The positive sign of q_{sur} indicates that the water absorbed 2170 joules, or 2.17 kilojoules, of heat from the reaction.

The heat that flowed into the water, q_{sur}, was lost from the reaction, q_{rxn}.

$$q_{rxn} = -q_{sur} = -2.17 \text{ kJ} \qquad \textbf{(Eq. 17)}$$

How is the enthalpy change, or the ΔH, to be determined from q_{rxn}? Recall that the heat transferred in a reaction performed at constant pressure is the ΔH for that reaction. However, ΔH for Equation 13 represents the heat transfer for 1 mole of NaOH (s). In this experiment, only 0.050 mole of NaOH (s) was used in the calorimeter. Therefore, the value of ΔH is proportionately greater.

$$\Delta H = \frac{-2.17 \text{ kJ}}{0.050 \text{ mol NaOH}} \times (1 \text{ mol NaOH})$$
$$= -43 \text{ kJ} \qquad \textbf{(Eq. 18)}$$

So Equation 13 can be rewritten as

$$\text{NaOH } (s) \rightarrow \text{Na}^+ (aq) + \text{OH}^- (aq) \qquad \Delta H = -43 \text{ kJ}$$
$$\textbf{(Eq. 19)}$$

The enthalpy change, -43 kilojoules, is negative as expected. Indeed, if the temperature of the water increases, you can conclude that the reaction is an exothermic one and that the sign of ΔH for the reaction is negative. Can you make a similar statement for the opposite situation?

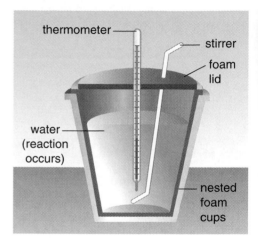

Figure 12–12 *In a simple foam-cup calorimeter, the thermometer measures the change in temperature of a measured mass of water as the reaction takes place. What is the function of the stirrer?*

When applying Hess's law, pay special attention to the units (calories, Calories, kilojoules, and so on). Because of the variety of units, the use of dimensional analysis is very important here.

CONSUMER TIP

Counting Calories

The energy value of food is measured in units called Calories. A Calorie (1 Calorie = 1000 calories) is the amount of heat needed to raise the temperature of 1 kg of water 1 C°. Carbohydrates, proteins, and fats are called macronutrients because they are needed in large quantities. Vitamins and minerals constitute micronutrients because they are required by the body in small quantities to help convert the macronutrients into energy and body tissue.

Carbohydrates and proteins both furnish 4 Calories per gram, and fats and oils provide 9 Calories per gram. The amount of energy each of these groups of substances delivers to the body is independent of the kind of food in which it occurs. So, 1 gram of carbohydrate provides 4 Calories whether it comes from honey, candy, or bread.

SAMPLE PROBLEM 3

When a 4.25-g sample of solid NH_4NO_3 dissolves in 60.0 g of water in a calorimeter, the temperature drops from 21.0°C to 16.9°C. Calculate ΔH for the solution process.

$$NH_4NO_3\,(s) \rightarrow NH_4^+\,(aq) + NO_3^-\,(aq) \qquad \Delta H = ?$$

STRATEGY	SOLUTION
1. Analyze	You must use the calorimetry data to calculate ΔH for the given reaction.
2. Plan	First, use Equation 15 to calculate q_{sur}, then use Equations 14 and 18 to calculate ΔH. You will need to convert grams of NH_4NO_3 to moles of NH_4NO_3.

3. Solve

$$q_{sur} = m \times C \times (T_f - T_i)$$
$$q_{sur} = (60.0\text{ g})(4.184\text{ J/g} \cdot \text{C}°)$$
$$\times (16.9°C - 21.0°C)$$
$$= -1.0 \times 10^3\text{ J}$$

q_{sur} is negative, as expected, based on the temperature drop of the water.

$$q_{rxn} = -q_{sur} = +1.0 \times 10^3\text{ J}$$

q_{rxn} represents the heat absorbed due to the reaction of 4.25 g NH_4NO_3.

$$4.25\text{ g }NH_4NO_3 \times \frac{1\text{ mol }NH_4NO_3}{80.0\text{ g }NH_4NO_3} = $$
$$0.0531\text{ mol }NH_4NO_3$$

Because 1 mol NH_4NO_3 dissolves in the balanced equation,

$$\Delta H = \frac{1.0 \times 10^3\text{ J}}{0.0531\text{ mol }NH_4NO_3}$$
$$\times 1\text{ mol }NH_4NO_3$$

$$\Delta H = +19\text{ kJ}$$

4. Evaluate   Because the temperature of the calorimeter dropped during the experiment, the reaction is endothermic and the value of ΔH must be positive.

Foods as Fuels

Fuels are chemical compounds that burn readily with the release of large amounts of heat energy. Gasoline, which is a mixture of several compounds of carbon and hydrogen, releases 48 kilojoules of heat per gram when burned in an automobile engine. But what about the fuel that drives you? The foods you eat are your body's fuel. They react to provide the energy required for all your body's activities.

Now that you have studied some aspects of thermochemistry, you can appreciate the role played by the combustion reactions that occur in your body. You probably give very little thought to food once the process of eating is finished. But it is the ultimate bond-breaking and bond-forming processes that foods such as carbohydrates and fats undergo that meet the energy needs of

Figure 12–13 *Like all machines, the engines in these race cars need fuel to power the cars around the race track. The food you eat constitutes the fuel to power your body's activities.*

How does your body's metabolism of starch and fiber, which consists of cellulose, differ?

Figure 12–14 Some animals, such as the black bear, hibernate in the winter. These animals store excess calories in the form of fat so that they have enough energy to get through the winter. Carbohydrates (top) and fats (bottom) are two groups of compounds that provide the human body with energy. What elements are present in carbohydrates and in fats?

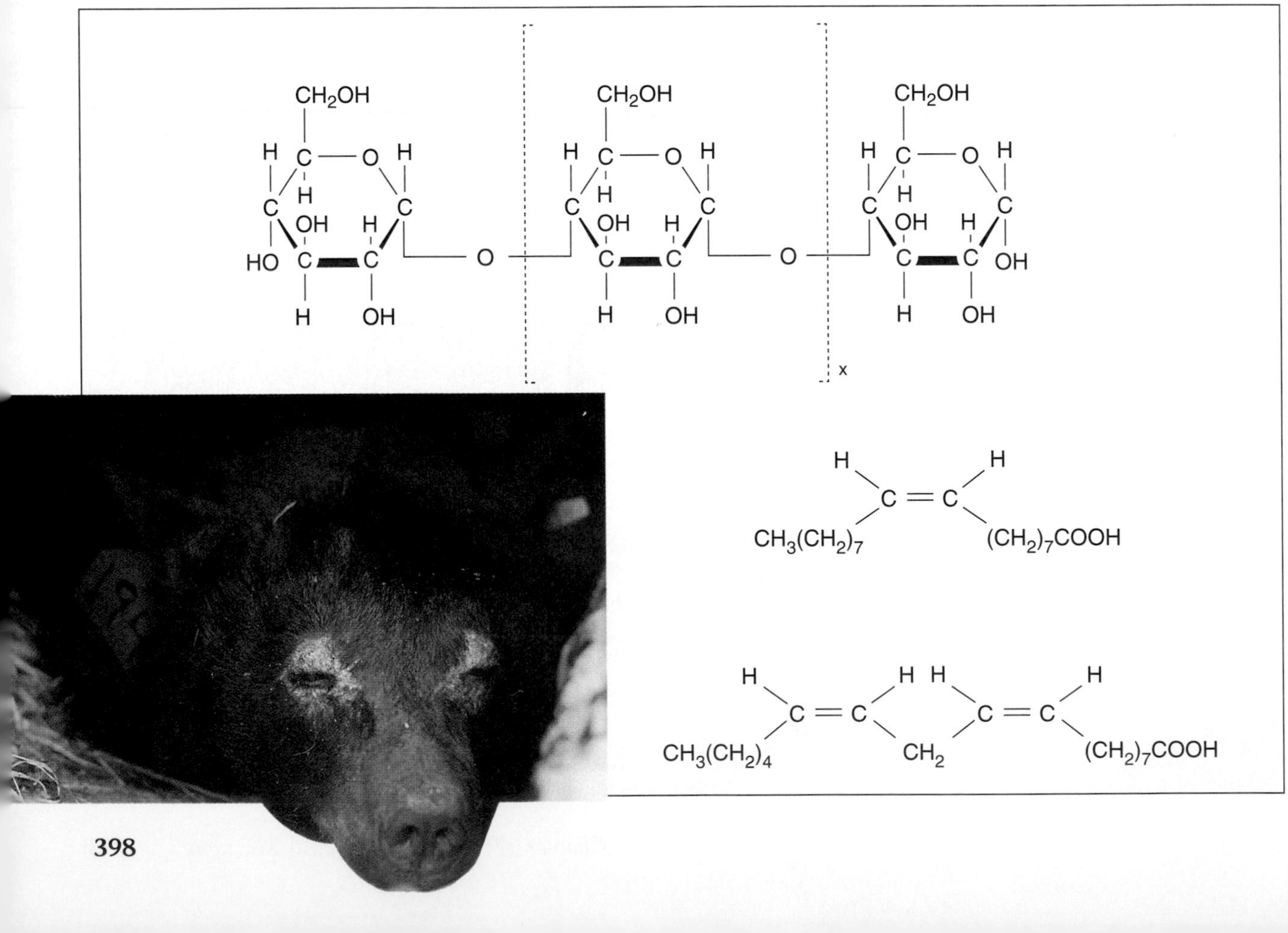

your body. Carbohydrates and fats are groups of compounds that contain the elements carbon, hydrogen, and oxygen. These compounds have high enthalpies. Their combustion products—typically CO_2 and H_2O—have relatively low enthalpies. For this reason, the combustion of carbohydrates, and especially fats, is an exothermic reaction. You will learn more about carbohydrates and fats in Chapter 27.

Sugars and starches are the most common carbohydrates. Through the process of digestion, the human body is able to break down sugars and starches into glucose ($C_6H_{12}O_6$). Cellulose, which is found in foods such as lettuce and celery, is also a carbohydrate. However, cellulose is made up of glucose molecules linked together in such a way that your body is unable to break them apart. Unlike sugars and starches, cellulose passes through your body without contributing any energy.

Glucose is the simple sugar that circulates in your bloodstream, which is why it is sometimes called blood sugar. Glucose reacts with oxygen in a complex series of steps, which can be summarized by the following overall reaction, to produce large quantities of energy.

$$C_6H_{12}O_6 \ (s) + 6 \, O_2 \ (g) \rightarrow 6 \, CO_2 \ (g) + 6 \, H_2O \ (l)$$

$$\Delta H^\circ = -2803 \text{ kJ} \quad \textbf{(Eq. 20)}$$

Calorie Content of Typical Foods and Their Exercise Equivalents for a 70-kg (154-pound) Person

Food (Portions)	Calories	Time (Minutes) Spent				
		Lying Down, Resting	Walking	Bicycle Riding	Swimming	Running
Apple (large)	101	78	19	12	9	5
Bacon (2 strips)	96	74	18	12	9	5
Carrot, raw	42	32	8	5	4	2
Chicken, fried ($\frac{1}{2}$ breast)	232	178	45	28	21	12
Egg, fried	110	85	21	13	10	6
Halibut steak ($\frac{1}{4}$ pound)	205	158	39	25	18	11
Hamburger sandwich	350	269	67	43	31	18
Malted milk shake	502	386	97	61	45	26
Milk (1 cup)	150	115	28	19	13	7
Orange juice (1 glass)	120	92	23	15	11	6
Pizza, cheese ($\frac{1}{8}$)	180	138	35	22	16	9
Potato chips (1 serving)	108	83	21	13	10	6
Soda (1 glass)	106	82	20	13	9	5
Tuna fish salad sandwich	278	214	53	34	25	14
Shrimp, fried (1 piece)	180	138	35	22	16	9

Figure 12–15 *In a food laboratory, a chemist carries out the combustion of foods in a bomb calorimeter to determine food values like the ones in the table. How many minutes would you have to spend walking to use up the calories in a hamburger sandwich?*

Perhaps you can now better understand why your body cells draw on their supply of glucose when energy is needed. On the average, carbohydrates supply 17 kJ/g (4 Cal/g) of energy. But eating too much carbohydrate is not necessarily healthful because it could result in a buildup of fat in the body. Why is this so? Unused carbohydrates are stored in the body as fat. On the average, fats supply 38 kJ/g (9 Cal/g) of energy. Thus, the body is able to store energy more efficiently as fat. In other words, the same amount of energy can be stored with a smaller mass gain. What is the significance of using an upper case C in Cal/g?

Carbohydrates and fats—as well as the whole foods that they are part of, such as apples, cheese, and bread—are reacted with oxygen in a laboratory calorimeter to determine their food values. Their exothermic combustion reactions produce CO_2, H_2O, and heat, which raises the temperature of the water in the calorimeter. From accurate measurements of masses of reactants and water, and temperature changes, ΔH of these combustion reactions is

Fatty Fuel

Unused carbohydrates as well as proteins are converted by the body into fat. This fat is deposited as tiny globules in the cells of adipose tissue, or the fatty tissue of the body.

Converting excess carbohydrates and proteins into body fat, and reconverting the fat into energy when we need it, is a very effective means of long-term energy storage. But just how effective is it?

Making Comparisons

- How much energy is stored in 1 pound of fat?
- How much energy is stored in 1 pound of carbohydrate or protein?
- If adipose tissue stores about 3500 Calories of energy per pound, what is the percent fat in adipose tissue?

easily determined. These values form the basis of food value tables such as those found in nutrition books. The table in Figure 12–15 on the previous page gives a list of some typical foods along with their calorie content. In addition, the table lists several activities and the amount of time that must be spent doing each in order to burn up the calories in that food.

12–4 Section Review

1. What is a calorimeter? How does it determine the heat transferred in a chemical reaction?
2. What is the difference between heat capacity and specific heat?
3. Fats are able to provide twice the energy (per gram) that carbohydrates do. Give an explanation for this fact.
4. **Critical Thinking—Making predictions** What error is introduced by including only the water in the calorimeter as the surroundings? Explain your answer.

12–5 What Is Heat?

Everyone has a commonsense notion of what heat is, but that does not make heat any easier to define. In this chapter, you have worked extensively with the concept of heat. You have examined endothermic and exothermic reactions. You have learned how heat can be measured in the laboratory using a calorimeter. And you know how scientists relate measured heats of reactions to the enthalpy changes between reactants and products. But after all is said and done, just what is heat?

The Caloric Theory

Early chemists, including Antoine Lavoisier, thought that heat was an invisible, weightless fluid that was capable of flowing from hotter objects to colder ones. They called this fluid caloric. These scientists believed that caloric filled the spaces between the atoms of a substance. It is easy to understand why the caloric theory was so appealing. After all, when you hold a cup of hot cocoa, you can feel the heat from the cocoa flow through the cup into your hand. Heat really does seem to act like a fluid!

Figure 12–16 *The American scientist Benjamin Thompson (inset), or as he is more widely known, Count Rumford, observed the heat produced due to friction as the drill bits used to bore cannons became very hot. Forty years later, an English scientist named James Joule used an apparatus such as the one shown here to measure the "mechanical equivalent of heat."*

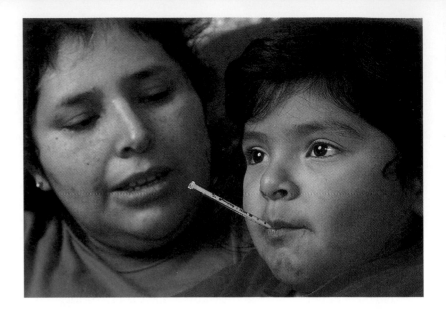

Figure 12–17 *When a thermometer is placed in contact with a child's body, kinetic energy is transferred to the mercury inside the thermometer. The mercury expands and rises in the thin capillary tube, which is calibrated to read the temperature in Fahrenheit or Celsius degrees. What is normal human body temperature?*

But the caloric theory cannot explain every effect of heat, especially the heat produced by friction. In 1798, American military adviser and amateur scientist Benjamin Thompson, also known as Count Rumford, observed that rubbing two pieces of metal together could produce an uninterrupted flow of heat for as long as the pieces were being rubbed. If heat was really a kind of fluid, the metal pieces should gradually produce less heat as their caloric was lost. Forty years after Count Rumford's experiments, James Joule showed that mechanical energy (such as that involved in friction) could be converted into an exactly equivalent amount of heat. This suggested that heat is a form of energy rather than an actual fluid. Experiments such as the ones performed by Count Rumford and others cast doubt on the validity of the caloric theory.

The Kinetic Theory

In place of the caloric theory, scientists in the nineteenth century suggested that heat results from the motion and vibration of particles of matter. This theory, extended over the years by the work of many scientists, is called the **kinetic theory** and is accepted today.

When you hold a cup of hot cocoa, fast-moving molecules in the liquid strike the walls of the cup, transferring kinetic energy to the cup. The extra energy makes the atoms in the cup vibrate faster. The cup is able to warm your hand because the vibrating atoms in the cup strike the surface of your skin, transferring some kinetic energy to your skin. What you feel as heat is a transfer of kinetic energy. **Heat is defined as the transfer of kinetic energy from a hotter object to a colder object.**

The kinetic theory successfully explains more than just heat effects in chemistry. In the next unit, you will examine further consequences of the kinetic theory as you study the properties of gases.

CONNECTION

The Greenhouse Effect

Do you know why flowers and vegetables are able to grow in a greenhouse even when the outside temperature is very cold? The glass or plastic used to build a greenhouse allows the visible rays of the sun to enter. Here the visible radiation is converted to infrared radiation, which the glass or plastic does not transmit. So the interior of a greenhouse warms up and is, in essence, a heat trap.

In a similar way, the Earth's atmosphere traps heat. The sun's visible and ultraviolet radiation reaches the Earth, where it is converted to heat. As infrared radiation, it is absorbed by the atmospheric gases, which keep the Earth substantially warmer than it would be without this effect, called the greenhouse effect.

One of the most important of the greenhouse gases is carbon dioxide. The delicate balance that maintained a steady level of CO_2 in the atmosphere is being increasingly disturbed by human acities such as the burning of fossil fuels for onorgy. Today the atmosphere holds over 27 percent more CO_2 than it did just a little over 100 years ago. Most scientists now believe that a doubling of atmospheric CO_2 will lead to a warmer Earth—warmer by about 2 to 4 Celsius degrees. Why should this matter? Some computer models predict that global warming by even a few degrees could cause polar ice to melt, which would raise the sea level and submerge coastal cities.

What can be done to slow down global warming? Reducing carbon dioxide levels by burning less fossil fuels (coal, oil, and natural gas) is an important step. This can be done by using alternative sources of energy such as solar, wind, and wave power. Conserving energy will also reduce the amount of carbon dioxide released into the atmosphere. It is also important to stop cutting down and burning forests because trees, like all green plants, use carbon dioxide to make glucose and oxygen in the process of photosynthesis. What are some things you can do in your home and in your neighborhood to help prevent global warming?

12–5 Section Review

1. How does the kinetic theory explain heat?
2. Describe the experiments that led scientists to the current concept of heat.
3. **Critical Thinking—Giving an example**   Give some examples of heat being produced by the conversion of one form of energy to another.

Laboratory Investigation

Determining Specific Heat

Problem

What is the specific heat of glass marbles?

Materials (per group)

5 to 6 glass marbles   Bunsen burner
laboratory balance   wire gauze
400-mL beaker   thermometer
ring stand with iron ring   calorimeter
test tube
test-tube tongs
graduated cylinder

Procedure

1. Prepare a hot-water bath by filling the beaker two-thirds full of water. Place the beaker on the ring stand and heat it with the Bunsen burner.
2. Using the laboratory balance, determine the mass of the glass marbles.
3. Place the marbles inside the test tube and place the test tube in the hot-water bath.
4. Measure out 200 mL of room temperature water and pour it into a clean, dry calorimeter.
5. Measure and record the temperature of the water.
6. To obtain the temperature of the glass marbles, place the thermometer inside the test tube when the water begins to boil. Continue heating the marbles in the hot-water bath until the temperature remains constant for 3 minutes. Record the temperature of the marbles.
7. Carefully remove the test tube from the hot-water bath using the test tube tongs. Quickly transfer the marbles to the calorimeter being careful not to splash any water in the calorimeter.
8. Place the thermometer in the calorimeter and record the temperature of the water and marbles every 30 seconds until the temperature remains constant for four consecutive readings.

Observations

Time (min)	Temperature (°C)
0	
0.5	
1.0	
1.5	
2.0	

1. What was the mass of the marbles?
2. How much water was added to the calorimeter? (Use the density of water to calculate mass from volume.)
3. What was the temperature of the marbles before they were added to the calorimeter? What was the change in temperature for the marbles?
4. What was the change in temperature for the water in the calorimeter?

Analysis and Conclusions

1. Did the water gain or lose energy? Did the marbles gain or lose energy after being transferred to the calorimeter?
2. Calculate the heat transferred by the water, q_{water}.
3. Calculate the heat transferred by the marbles, $q_{marbles}$.
4. Using the heat transferred by the marbles, calculate the specific heat of the marbles.
5. **On Your Own** With your teacher's permission, use the same process to determine the specific heat of another material such as lead or plastic.

STUDY GUIDE

Summarizing Key Concepts

12–1 Chemical Reactions That Involve Heat

- The study of the heat effects in chemical reactions is called thermochemistry.
- Reactions that release heat are called exothermic reactions. Reactions that absorb heat are called endothermic reactions.

12–2 Heat and Enthalpy Changes

- The heat absorbed or released during a chemical reaction at constant pressure is the enthalpy change (ΔH) for the reaction.
- ΔH° is the enthalpy change for a reaction in which both reactants and products are in their standard states.

12–3 Hess's Law

- Hess's law states that if a series of reactions are added together, the enthalpy change for the net reaction will be the sum of the enthalpy changes for the individual steps.

12–4 Calorimetry

- A calorimeter is a device used to determine the heat transferred in a reaction.
- Calorimetry helps determine the energy value of foods.

12–5 What Is Heat?

- Particles of matter have kinetic energy.
- Heat is the transfer of kinetic energy from a hotter object to a colder object.

Reviewing Key Terms

Define each term in a complete sentence.

12–1 Chemical Reactions That Involve Heat

thermochemistry
exothermic reaction
endothermic reaction

12–2 Heat and Enthalpy Changes

enthalpy
standard enthalpy change

12–4 Calorimetry

calorimetry
heat capacity
specific heat

12–5 What Is Heat?

kinetic theory

CHAPTER REVIEW

Content Review

Multiple Choice
Choose the letter of the answer that best completes each statement.

1. Early chemists thought that heat was a kind of
   (a) vapor.
   (b) solid.
   (c) fluid.
   (d) plasma.

2. The symbol for standard enthalpy change for a reaction is
   (a) H.
   (b) ΔH.
   (c) ΔH°.
   (d) ΔE°.

3. If the coefficients of a balanced equation are doubled, the enthalpy change for the reaction is
   (a) halved.
   (b) squared.
   (c) unchanged.
   (d) doubled.

4. The study of heat flow and heat measurement is called
   (a) thermodynamics.
   (b) calorimetry.
   (c) thermochemistry.
   (d) enthalpy.

5. Carbon's standard state is
   (a) diamond.
   (b) graphite.
   (c) coal.
   (d) charcoal.

6. A nutritional calorie is equal to
   (a) 1 calorie.
   (b) 1000 calories.
   (c) 4.184 J.
   (d) 1 fat calorie.

7. Extra energy is stored in your body as
   (a) proteins.
   (b) carbohydrates.
   (c) starches.
   (d) fats.

8. The prefix *exo-* in the word exothermic means
   (a) heat.
   (b) temperature.
   (c) inside.
   (d) outside.

9. The chemist who helped build one of the first calorimeters was
   (a) Hess.
   (b) Lavoisier.
   (c) Rumford.
   (d) Joule.

True or False
If the statement is true, write "true." If it is false, change the underlined word or words to make the statement true.

10. The study of <u>sound</u> effects in chemical processes is called thermochemisty.

11. All combustion reactions are classified as <u>endothermic</u> reactions.

12. The SI unit for both energy and heat is the <u>joule</u>.

13. In the equation $\Delta H = H_{products} - H_{reactants}$, the letter H stands for <u>heat</u>.

14. Under standard conditions, the most stable form of carbon is <u>diamond</u>.

15. <u>Hess's</u> law describes how to find the net enthalpy change for a series of chemical reactions.

16. The amount of heat needed to raise the temperature of a container of water from 14°C to 15°C is the <u>specific heat</u> of water.

17. In an exothermic reaction, the sign of ΔH is <u>positive</u>.

Concept Mapping
Complete the following concept map for Section 12–1. Refer to pages xviii–xix to construct a concept map for the entire chapter.

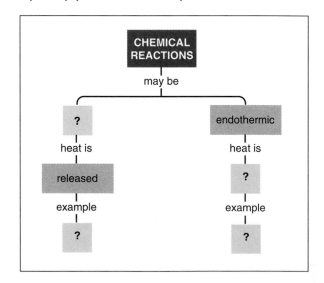

Concept Mastery

Discuss each of the following in a brief paragraph.

18. What is thermochemistry? How is it related to thermodynamics?
19. What is the difference between heat and enthalpy?
20. If the enthalpy of the products in a chemical reaction is less than the enthalpy of the reactants, is the reaction exothermic or endothermic? Explain.
21. What is meant by the standard conditions for a reaction?
22. How does a chemical reaction produce heat?
23. Describe the caloric and the kinetic theories of heat.
24. What is Hess's law of heat summation?
25. What is calorimetry? Describe how a calorimeter works.
26. What is the difference between heat capacity and specific heat?
27. **Tying it Together** How does the food you eat provide for the *energy* needs of

your body? What happens if you eat more food than your body needs for its daily energy requirements?

Critical Thinking and Problem Solving

Use the skills you have developed in this chapter to answer each of the following.

28. **Making comparisons** What is the difference between an exothermic reaction and an endothermic reaction? Give an example of each.
29. **Applying concepts** Explain the relationship between the breaking and formation of chemical bonds in a chemical reaction and the energy absorbed or released in the reaction.
30. **Making inferences** The combustion reaction of hydrogen gas with oxygen gas is highly exothermic. Is ΔH for this reaction positive or negative? Explain.

31. **Applying concepts** Your body gets most of its energy from glucose—a carbohydrate. But you can also obtain energy from proteins and fats. Explain.
32. **Making comparisons** How is the food you eat similar to the gasoline in a race car?
33. **Using the writing process** Imagine that you are a student in the early nineteenth century and you have just learned about the new kinetic theory. Write a letter to a friend in which you explain why you think the kinetic theory provides a better description of heat than the old caloric theory.

PROBLEM BANK

Group A

34. Which of the following processes are exothermic? Endothermic? *(Section 12–1)*

(a) $C_2H_4 \rightarrow 2\,C + 2\,H_2 + 52.3\ kJ$

(b) $B_2H_6 + 6\,H_2O \rightarrow$
$\qquad 2\,H_3BO_3 + 6\,H_2 + 493.4\ kJ$

(c) $2\,Fe + 3\,CO_2 + 26.8\ kJ \rightarrow$
$\qquad\qquad Fe_2O_3 + 3\,CO$

(d) $Br_2 + Cl_2 + 29.4\ kJ \rightarrow 2\,BrCl$

35. Which of the following processes are exothermic? Endothermic? *(Section 12–1)*

(a) $BCl_3 + 3\,H_2O \rightarrow H_3BO_3 + 3\,HCl$
$\qquad\qquad \Delta H = -112\ kJ$

(b) $2\,HgO \rightarrow 2\,Hg + O_2\ \Delta H = +181\ kJ$

(c) $S_2Cl_2 + CCl_4 \rightarrow CS_2 + 3\,Cl_2$
$\qquad\qquad \Delta H = +112\ kJ$

(d) $CaCO_3 + 2\,NH_3 \rightarrow CaCN_2 + 3\,H_2O$
$\qquad\qquad \Delta H = +90.\ kJ$

36. Draw an enthalpy diagram for the following reactions: *(Section 12–2)*

(a) $NH_4NO_3\ (s) \rightarrow NH_4^+\ (aq) +$
$\qquad\qquad NO_3^-\ (aq)\ \Delta H = +26\ kJ$

(b) $P_4 + 5\,O_2 \rightarrow P_4O_{10}\ \Delta H = -3010\ kJ$

(c) $Si + 2\,Cl_2 \rightarrow SiCl_4\ \Delta H = -657\ kJ$

(d) $2\,MnO_2 \rightarrow 2\,MnO + O_2$
$\qquad\qquad \Delta H = +264\ kJ$

37. Which of the following enthalpy diagrams represent exothermic reactions? Endothermic reactions? *(Section 12–2)*

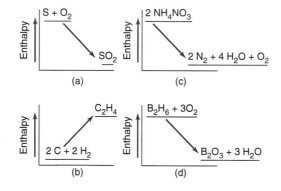

38. How much heat will be released if 6.0 g of carbon reacts with excess oxygen according to the equation below? *(Section 12–2)*

$C(s) + O_2\ (g) \rightarrow CO_2\ (g)\ \Delta H = -394\ kJ$

39. How much heat will be released if 9.75 g of aluminum reacts with excess ammonium nitrate (NH_4NO_3) according to the equation below? *(Section 12–2)*

$2\,Al\ (s) + 3\,NH_4NO_3\ (s) \rightarrow 3\,N_2\ (g) +$
$\qquad 6\,H_2O\ (g) + Al_2O_3\ (s)\ \Delta H = -2030\ kJ$

40. How much heat will be absorbed if 27.1 g of iodine (I_2) reacts with excess hydrogen according to the following equation? *(Section 12–2)*

$H_2\ (g) + I_2\ (g) \rightarrow 2\,HI\ (g)\ \Delta H = +26.5\ kJ$

41. How much heat is transferred when 0.5113 g of ammonia (NH_3) reacts with excess oxygen according to the following equation? *(Section 12–2)*

$4\,NH_3\ (g) + 5\,O_2\ (g) \rightarrow 4\,NO\ (g) +$
$\qquad 6\,H_2O\ (g)\quad \Delta H = -905.4\ kJ$

42. How much heat will be transferred when 0.50 mol of TiO_2 reacts with 1.60 mol of HCl according to the following equation?

$TiO_2\ (s) + 4\,HCl\ (g) \rightarrow$
$\qquad TiCl_4\ (l) + 2\,H_2O\ (g)\quad \Delta H = -67\ kJ$

How many moles of $TiCl_4$ will be produced? H_2O? *(Section 12–2)*

43. From the following enthalpy changes

$TiCl_4\ (l) + CO_2\ (g) \rightarrow$
$\qquad TiO_2\ (s) + CCl_4\ (g)\ \Delta H = +155\ kJ$

$TiCl_4\ (l) + 2\,Mg\ (s) \rightarrow$
$\qquad Ti\ (s) + 2\,MgCl_2\ (s)\ \Delta H = -478\ kJ$

calculate ΔH for the following reaction:

$TiO_2\ (s) + CCl_4\ (g) + 2\,Mg\ (s) \rightarrow$
$\qquad Ti\ (s) + CO_2\ (g) + 2\,MgCl_2\ (g)$
$\qquad\qquad$ *(Section 12–3)*

44. From the following enthalpy changes

$SOCl_2\ (g) + NiO\ (s) \rightarrow$
$\qquad SO_2\ (g) + NiCl_2\ (s)\ \Delta H = -150.\ kJ$

$SOCl_2\ (g) + H_2O\ (g) \rightarrow$
$\qquad SO_2\ (g) + 2\,HCl\ (g)\ \Delta H = -27\ kJ$

calculate ΔH for the following reaction:

$NiO\ (s) + 2\,HCl\ (g) \rightarrow$
$\qquad\qquad NiCl_2\ (s) + H_2O\ (g)$
$\qquad\qquad$ *(Section 12–3)*

45. The specific heat of water is 4.184 J/g • C°. How much heat is required to raise the temperature of 5.0 g of water by 3.0 C° ?
(Section 12–4)

46. A 21.0-g sample of water is cooled from 34.0°C to 28.0°C. How many joules of heat were removed from the water? (Specific heat of water: 4.184 J/g•C°) *(Section 12–4)*

47. An 18.7-g sample of platinum metal increases in temperature by 2.3 C° when 5.7 J of heat are added. What is the specific heat of platinum? *(Section 12–4)*

48. The specific heat of silver is 0.24 J/g • C°. How much heat must be added to a silver block of mass 86 g to raise its temperature by 9.0 C°? *(Section 12–4)*

Group B

49. How much heat will be transferred when 25.1 g of diborane (B_2H_6) reacts with 57.0 g of oxygen according to the following equation?

$$B_2H_6\,(g) + 3\,O_2\,(g) \rightarrow$$
$$B_2O_3\,(s) + 3\,H_2O \quad \Delta H = -1940 \text{ kJ}$$

50. How much heat is transferred when 8.00 g of nitrogen (N_2) reacts with 15.00 g of hydrogen (H_2) according to the following equation?

$$N_2\,(g) + 3\,I_2\,(g) \rightarrow 2\,NI_3\,(g)$$
$$\Delta H = +46.2 \text{ kJ}$$

51. From the following enthalpy changes

$$CaO\,(s) + CO_2\,(g) \rightarrow CaCO_3\,(s)$$
$$\Delta H = -178 \text{ kJ}$$
$$CaO\,(s) + H_2O\,(l) \rightarrow Ca(OH)_2\,(s)$$
$$\Delta H = -65 \text{ kJ}$$

calculate the enthalpy change for the following reaction:

$$Ca(OH)_2\,(s) + CO_2\,(g) \rightarrow$$
$$CaCO_3\,(s) + H_2O\,(l)$$

52. Given the following enthalpy changes

$$Cu_2O\,(s) + H_2O_2\,(l) \rightarrow$$
$$2\,CuO\,(s) + H_2O\,(l) \quad \Delta H = -239 \text{ kJ}$$
$$2\,H_2O_2\,(l) \rightarrow 2\,H_2O\,(l) + O_2\,(g)$$
$$\Delta H = -196 \text{ kJ}$$

calculate ΔH for the following reaction:

$$Cu_2O\,(s) + \tfrac{1}{2}O_2\,(g) \rightarrow 2\,CuO\,(s)$$

53. Teresa has performed a calorimetry experiment to determine ΔH for the following reaction:

$$CuSO_4\,(s) \rightarrow Cu^{2+}\,(aq) + SO_4^{\,2-}\,(aq)$$

She placed 0.800 g of $CuSO_4$ (s) in a calorimeter with 43.0 g of water at an initial temperature of 18.3°C. As the $CuSO_4$ (s) dissolved in the water, the temperature rose to 20.2°C. What value of ΔH can Teresa obtain from her data?

54. How much heat will be transferred when 0.54 mol sulfur reacts with 0.75 mol oxygen according to the following equation?

$$2\,S\,(s) + 3\,O_2\,(g) \rightarrow 2\,SO_3\,(g)$$
$$\Delta H = -790.\text{ kJ}$$

How many moles of SO_3 will be produced?

55. Given the following enthalpy changes

$$Fe_2O_3\,(s) + 3\,CO\,(g) \rightarrow$$
$$2\,Fe\,(s) + 3\,CO_2\,(g)\ \Delta H = -27 \text{ kJ}$$
$$C\,(s) + CO_2\,(g) \rightarrow 2\,CO\,(g)$$
$$\Delta H = +172 \text{ kJ}$$

calculate ΔH for the following reaction:

$$2\,Fe_2O_3 + 3\,C \rightarrow 4\,Fe + 3\,CO_2$$

56. Juan performed a calorimetry experiment to determine ΔH for the following reaction:

$$KOH\,(s) \rightarrow K^+\,(aq) + OH^-\,(aq)$$

His calorimeter contained 64.0 g of water at an initial temperature of 20.7°C. When he added 1.65 g of KOH (s) to the calorimeter, the temperature rose to 26.9°C. What value of ΔH can Juan obtain from his data?

57. Sunita performed a calorimetry experiment to determine ΔH for the following reaction:

$$KMnO_4\,(s) \rightarrow K^+\,(aq) + MnO_4^-\,(aq)$$

Her calorimeter contained 50.0 g of water at an initial temperature of 17.4°C. After adding 1.10 g of $KMnO_4$ (s), the temperature fell to 16.0°C. What value of ΔH can Sunita obtain from her data?

FROM SCHOOL TO WORK

Cristina de la Torre—Student

When Cristina de la Torre is busy designing her next ceramic piece, she doesn't really think about chemistry. But she knows that a lot of chemistry is involved in what she does. "First you start with a hard lump of clay that softens up as you work with it. Then you shape it and leave it exposed to the air to dry. When it's dry, it's ready to be fired in the kiln, where high temperatures make the piece rock hard."

Of course, the creative process doesn't always go smoothly. Pieces sometimes explode in the kiln, where air bubbles that are trapped in the clay expand in the heat. Even when a piece survives the kiln, there is still room for error in the glazing process. At moments like those, Cristina remembers something her chemistry teacher always said: "Chemistry is not just some guy in a lab coat mixing together a bunch of chemicals. It's everywhere."

Food Technologist

Food technologists who are involved in basic research study the structure and composition of food as well as the changes that take place during storage or processing. Biotechnology is a rapidly growing area of food technology. Food technologists who work in this area may be involved with gene splicing, plant breeding, and growing tissue cell cultures to produce enhanced food products.

Becoming a food technologist requires at least a bachelor's degree in food technology or some other area, such as chemistry, biology, or agriculture. Many food technologists have advanced degrees in specialized areas. High-school students who are interested in a career as a food technologist should concentrate on courses in chemistry, biology, physics, and mathematics.

To receive additional information, write to the Institute of Food Technologists, 221 North LaSalle Street, Suite 300, Chicago, IL 60601.

How to Use the Want Ads

Help-wanted ads are a good place to begin a job search. They list positions that are available and provide some idea of which fields are hiring people, what salaries are being offered, and what qualifications are necessary.

Want ads can be found in a variety of publications. Newspapers usually have a section listing job openings under the title of the position. Trade magazines, which are periodicals related to a specific field, also list job openings.

As you look through the want ads, be sure to check all the categories that apply to you. Answer ads that give specific information about the position and the company that placed the ad. Respond promptly with a neatly typed letter and make sure you include all the information requested in the ad.

Karen Robblee

From the Author

My interest in chemistry dates back to when I was 7 or 8 years old. My mother liked to cook, and I was often her helper. While I enjoyed eating the things she baked, I was more fascinated by the changes that occurred as she mixed ingredients together. One of my favorite activities was to randomly mix the items in our kitchen cabinet to see what kind of reaction I might produce.

Fortunately, my parents were more concerned with letting me satisfy my curiosity than with keeping a tidy kitchen. I made quite a mess with some of my "experiments" but was delighted to see the effect of reactions such as the one between vinegar and baking soda.

My interest in chemistry continued through high school, but my curiosity began to focus on "why" questions instead of "what if" questions. I began to see chemistry as a puzzle whose pieces fit into a fascinatingly organized pattern. One of the pleasures I have in teaching is observing the natural curiosity of students and watching them discover the answers to their questions.

I believe that questions are important, and I encourage my students to ask lots of them. In fact, I continue to learn through the questions of my students. They sometimes are curious about things I have not even considered. In helping my students to find answers, I increase my own depth of understanding. You should ask questions, too. Ask them of yourself, your teacher, your friends and family. One of the joys of science is in finding answers to satisfy your curiosity.

UNIT REVIEW

Concept Mastery

Discuss each of the following in a brief paragraph.

1. Explain the similarities and differences in the atomic mass of a substance and the molar mass of a substance.
2. What is stoichiometry and what information can it provide about a chemical reaction?
3. Describe how you would find the enthalpy change for a reaction from the mass of one of the products and ΔH.
4. Why is the mole the unit chemists use for calculating the amounts of substances or the energy changes involved in chemical reactions?
5. Explain the significance of standard enthalpies of change, $\Delta H°$. How are standard states defined?
6. Why might the actual energy change for a reaction be different from the predicted energy change?
7. How is the enthalpy change for a reaction related to the enthalpy of the reactants and products?
8. You know that the relative masses of reactants can limit the amount of products formed in a chemical reaction. Can the amount of energy available in the surroundings also affect the amount of products? Explain.
9. Describe how a calorimeter is used to find the enthalpy of a sample of food.
10. Your lab partner performs an experiment to find the enthalpy change for the combustion of sucrose. She finds the temperature change resulting from the combustion of 30. g $C_{12}H_{22}O_{11}$ in a bomb calorimeter. Describe the procedure she should follow to determine the enthalpy change for the combustion of 1 mole of sucrose.

Problem Bank

11. Given 4.84 mol NH_3 (*g*) (a) What is the mass of the sample? (b) What volume would this gas occupy at STP?
12. How many moles of carbon are found in 250.0 g $CaCO_3$?
13. Determine the mass of Li necessary to produce 43.6 g of LiOH according to the following equation:

    $$2\ Li + 2\ H_2O \rightarrow 2\ LiOH + H_2$$

14. Determine how many liters of H_2 and O_2 at STP are necessary to produce 2.68 g of H_2O.
15. Given the following equation:
    $$N_2\ (g) + 3\ Cl_2\ (g) \rightarrow 2NCl_3\ (g)$$
    $$\Delta H° = +\ 230.\ kJ$$
    (a) What mass of N_2 would absorb 96.5 kJ of heat as it reacts?
    (b) What volume of Cl_2 at STP would be required to react with the N_2 in part (a)?
16. If 3.89 g $Mg(OH)_2$ is added to a flask containing 1.78 g HCl, what mass of $MgCl_2$ will be produced?
17. Nitrogen dioxide is a component of air pollution that contributes to the production of acid rain. When NO_2 reacts with water vapor in the air, the products are nitric acid (HNO_3) and NO. If 74.5 g NO_2 is released into air that is saturated with water vapor, how many moles of HNO_3 will be produced as a result?
18. A 36.0-g piece of lead at a temperature of 154.5°C is added to a calorimeter containing 100.0 g of water at 24.2°C. The final temperature of the water is 25.6°C. What is the specific heat of lead?
19. The enthalpy change for the reaction

    $$2\ H_2\ (g) + O_2\ (g) \rightarrow 2\ H_2O\ (l)$$

    is -571.6 kJ. Determine the enthalpy change for the decomposition of 24.0 g H_2O (*l*).

20. The combustion of methane in a laboratory burner is represented by the following equation:

$$CH_4\ (g) + 2\ O_2\ (g) \rightarrow CO_2\ (g) + 2\ H_2O\ (l)$$

Given the following three thermochemical equations:

$$C\ (s) + 2\ H_2\ (g) \rightarrow CH_4\ (g)$$
$$\Delta H^\circ = -74.87\ kJ$$

$$C\ (s) + O_2\ (g) \rightarrow CO_2\ (g)$$
$$\Delta H^\circ = -393.5\ kJ$$

$$2\ H_2\ (g) + O_2\ (g) \rightarrow 2\ H_2O\ (l)$$
$$\Delta H^\circ = -571.6\ kJ$$

(a) Determine the molar heat of combustion of CH_4.
(b) Determine the enthalpy change when 6.4 g of methane burns.

21. Barium hydroxide reacts with ammonium chloride according to the following chemical equation:

$$Ba(OH)_2 + 2\ NH_4Cl \rightarrow BaCl_2\ (s) + 2\ NH_3\ (g) + 2\ H_2O\ (l)$$

If 16.7 g $Ba(OH)_2$ is combined with 8.8 g NH_4Cl

(a) What is the limiting reactant?
(b) What mass of $BaCl_2$ will be formed?
(c) Determine the standard enthalpy change of the reaction given the following thermochemical equations:

$$Ba\ (s) + O_2\ (g) + H_2\ (g) \rightarrow Ba(OH)_2\ (s)$$
$$\Delta H^\circ = -946.0\ kJ$$

$$N_2\ (g) + 4H_2\ (g) + Cl_2\ (g) \rightarrow 2\ NH_4Cl\ (s)$$
$$\Delta H^\circ = -628.8\ kJ$$

$$Ba\ (s) + Cl_2\ (g) \rightarrow BaCl_2\ (s)$$
$$\Delta H^\circ = -858.1\ kJ$$

$$N_2\ (g) + 3\ H_2\ (g) \rightarrow 2\ NH_3\ (g)$$
$$\Delta H^\circ = -92.22\ kJ$$

$$2\ H_2\ (g) + O_2\ (g) \rightarrow 2\ H_2O\ (l)$$
$$\Delta H^\circ = -571.6\ kJ$$

Performance-Based Task

What Is That Stuff?

How did the first chemist to perform a particular chemical reaction in the laboratory figure out what the products of the reaction were? For that matter, how can you predict and verify the products of a particular reaction—say, a decomposition reaction? Design an experiment to answer this question.

1. Start by obtaining safety goggles, a lab apron, a sample of copper(II) carbonate ($CuCO_3$), an evaporating dish, a hot plate, a stirring rod, and a balance.
2. Predict what the products will be if you decompose $CuCO_3$.
3. Carry out your experiment, making careful measurements of mass before and after the reaction. Record all your observations.
4. Write a balanced equation for this reaction. Explain how the number of moles of reactant and products in this reaction are related to the balanced equation for the reaction.

Going Further

5. Assume that the solid product of the reaction can be used as a pigment for making paint and that 100 g of pigment is needed to make 1 L of paint. Use your knowledge of the mole to calculate the amount of $CuCO_3$ you would need to produce enough pigment for 1 L of paint.
6. Using the information from a scientific supply catalog shown below, determine if it would be more cost effective to buy the $CuCO_3$ to make the pigment or to buy the pigment directly. Explain your reasoning.

copper(II) carbonate: 500 g \$14.20
pigment: 500 g \$17.60

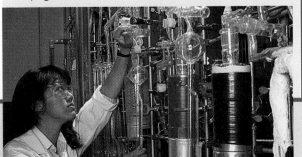

Unit 5 States of Matter

Imagine taking a cross-country train trip 100 years ago. As you sit in your plush seat, a shrill whistle drowns out the rhythmic clackety-clack of iron wheels on iron tracks. Specks of ashes and coal dust from the locomotive engine drift past your window.

Now let your imagination soar on a hot-air balloon ride. Drifting lazily with the wind, you look down on a miniature landscape of houses and roads, ponds and hills. With a blast from your propane burner, your balloon rises safely above some power lines.

It is the year 2010. As you step out into the bright sunshine, you smile. Today you can drive your solar-powered car to work instead of riding your bicycle. No one uses gasoline-powered vehicles anymore because they pollute the environment.

What do these three scenarios from the past, present, and future have to do with the states of matter? In some way, each activity is connected to the behavior of matter in its three fundamental states—gas, liquid, and solid. In Unit Five you will explore the behavior of matter and discover how this behavior is related to the forces that exist between the tiny particles of matter.

DISCOVERY LEARNING

1. Push an ordinary party balloon into an empty 2-liter plastic soft drink bottle. Stretch its mouthpiece over the opening of the bottle.

2. Blow into the balloon.

3. Blow up an identical balloon outside the soft drink bottle to serve as a comparison.

   ■ How big does the balloon in the soft drink bottle get?

   ■ How big does the balloon outside the soft drink bottle get?

   ■ How can you explain the difference?

Chapter

13 Gases

Imagine that you are the mountain climber in the adjacent photograph. You pause for a moment to appreciate the magnificent view beneath you and also use the opportunity to catch your breath. You are equipped with an oxygen mask to help you breathe because the air at high altitudes is very thin.

Air also becomes thinner, or less dense, when it is heated. This is what enables a hot-air balloon to rise. Like air, all gases become less dense when they are heated.

Gases also exhibit many other similar behaviors. In the pages that follow, you will discover how scientists developed a fairly simple model to explain gas behavior—a model that has evolved over several hundred years.

The air on top of a mountain is less dense than the air at sea level. It is also less dense inside a hot-air balloon. Density is just one of the properties common to air and all other gases.

Chem Journal

YOU AND YOUR WORLD

Imagine that you are taking a trip in a lighter-than-air craft. In your journal, describe what you might experience during your trip. What would your craft look like? Where would it go and what would you see? You might want to draw pictures as part of your description.

13–1 A Model to Explain Gas Behavior

Guide for Reading
- What is the kinetic-molecular theory of gases?
- What are some distinctive properties of gases?

You might not think so right away, but you already know a lot about gases. Air is a gas—actually a mixture of several gases. It surrounds you all the time. Air pumps up the tires of automobiles, serves as springs in trucks and buses, drives tools such as jackhammers and power wrenches, and provides soft cushioning in air mattresses when you go camping. Air is also a medium through which energy and matter are transported. You need air to hear your friends' voices, to listen to music, or to hear the surf crashing on a beach. You know how the fragrance of perfume or the unpleasant smell of a skunk spreads quickly through the air from its source to your nose!

Although you can feel the air all around you, you cannot see it because the gases in air are colorless. Unlike the gases in air, however, some gases have color. Chlorine gas is greenish yellow and nitrogen dioxide, one of the components of polluted air, is reddish brown. You can see the overall color of these gases but you cannot see the actual particles—atoms and molecules—that compose them. How then did scientists learn about gases?

Figure 13–1   These palm trees are being blown by the strong winds of a hurricane. The energy of the wind also carries a wind surfer on an adventurous and exhilarating ride! Wind is the result of the movement of air from an area of high pressure to an area of low pressure. What is pressure?

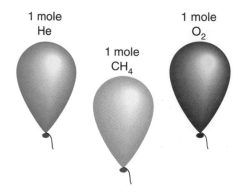

1 mole
He

1 mole
CH₄

1 mole
O₂

Figure 13–2 *Does it surprise you to know that 1 mole of each of these gases occupies 22.4 L at 0°C and 1 atm pressure?*

The Nature of Gases

Certain gas behaviors are well-known to all of us. For example, you know that gases can be compressed by exerting pressure on them. You know that unlike liquids and solids, gases will occupy the volume that they have available to them. How can you account for these and several other gas behaviors?

The systematic study of gases began about 300 years ago in an attempt to answer this question. Air was the first gas to be studied—and it was studied long before the discovery that it was not a single element or compound but actually a mixture of several elements and compounds. But this fact did not make the study of gas behavior more difficult. Instead, it led to a startling and important scientific discovery. Although air is a mixture of several different gases, its physical behavior is very much like that of a single gas! Chemists studying and observing different gases two centuries ago found that regardless of their chemical identity, all gases exhibit remarkably similar physical behavior. For example, 1 mole of helium, oxygen, or methane at 0° Celsius and 1 atmosphere pressure occupies a volume of almost exactly 22.4 liters.

You might find it interesting to follow the logical path scientists took from systematic observations of gas behavior to construction of a model that explains and accounts for that behavior. A scientific model helps us understand a phenomenon by making it less abstract and easier to visualize. A model is very useful in chemistry because the atoms, molecules, and other equally small particles that chemists deal with cannot be put under a microscope to be viewed directly. What do you think should be the first step in building a model for gases? You would be correct if you suggested listing some of the more important behaviors that all gases exhibit.

But before we can do this, we must first resolve a minor but important issue: How should we refer to the representative particles that make up gases? As you may recall from Chapter

Figure 13–3 *The representative particles of a gas may consist of one, two, or more atoms. Neon particles are monatomic, carbon dioxide particles are triatomic, and propane particles consist of 11 atoms each.*

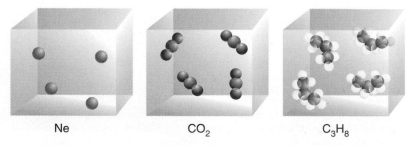

Ne CO_2 C_3H_8

7, most gases are made up of molecules—two or more atoms bonded together. You have already encountered many examples of such gases: N_2, O_2, CO_2, CH_4, and many others. There are some gases, however, that exist as single atoms. Do you remember which gases these are? Recall that the noble gases—He, Ne, Ar, Kr, Xe, and Rn—do not bond with any other atoms under ordinary conditions. Thus they are the only gases that are made up of single atoms. Do you recall another name for this group of gases?

In the following discussion, the number of atoms making up a representative gas particle does not make a difference. So when we say particles, we mean single atoms (He, Ne), diatomic molecules (N_2, O_2), or polyatomic molecules (CO_2, CH_4), depending on the identity of the gas. The number of atoms in a representative gas particle does not affect the physical behavior of the gas.

We are now ready to list the familiar behaviors, or the physical properties, of gases. The following physical properties are common to all gases:

1. Gases have mass. You can test this fact by weighing a basketball when it is empty and again when it is pumped up hard enough to bounce well. The mass of the basketball increases. This increase in mass is due to the air that you pumped in. The density of a gas—the mass per unit volume—is much less than the density of a liquid or a solid, however. So if you filled a basketball with a liquid such as water or a solid such as concrete, its mass would be much greater.

2. It is easy to compress gases. If you squeeze a gas, its volume can be reduced considerably. This behavior is quite unlike that of liquids and solids. And it is precisely the reason that air is used as a shock absorber in the form of safety air bags installed in automobiles.

3. Gases fill their containers completely. This property explains why nowhere around you is there an absence of air. When a balloon is filled with air, the air is distributed evenly throughout

Figure 13–4 These youngsters are having a lot of fun blowing soap bubbles. How can you make a very large soap bubble?

Figure 13–5 A few drops of bromine, an orange-brown liquid, are placed at the bottom of a test tube. After some time, orange bromine gas has moved partway up the test tube. After still more time, the bromine gas has moved even farther up the test tube. Do you think bromine diffuses slowly?

the balloon. You know that it does not concentrate in any one part of the balloon.

4. Different gases can move through each other quite rapidly. The movement of one substance through another is called **diffusion.** Thus we say that gases diffuse easily through each other. You are observing gas diffusion when you smell the enticing aroma of tandoori chicken as you walk up the steps to your house or when you get the first whiff of the unpleasant odor of a skunk while on a hiking trip.

5. Gases exert pressure. The concept of pressure may already be familiar to you. Perhaps you experienced the effects of changing air pressure when you rode in a rapidly ascending elevator. The "pop" that you might have felt in your ears was due to the sensitivity of your eardrums to changes in external air pressure. Or perhaps you observed gas pressure when you inflated balloons for a party. The pressure of the gas inside a balloon is responsible for the balloon keeping its shape.

6. The pressure of a gas depends on its temperature. The higher the temperature of a gas, the higher the pressure. The lower the temperature of a gas, the lower the pressure. Have you ever heard of automobile tire pressures getting dangerously high on hot summer days in the desert southwest? If so, you can now explain why. What do you think is the danger of a gas under high pressure? You may also have heard that motorists are advised to check their tire pressure as it gets cold in the winter. Why do you think this is so? As the weather gets cold, the air in the tires exerts a much lower pressure. This causes the automobile tires to flatten. What do you think might happen as a result? Do you know how tire pressure can be increased?

We have just listed six properties that all gases exhibit. How are these properties explained? **Gas properties are explained by a kinetic-molecular model that describes the behavior of the submicroscopic particles that make up a gas.** As we continue to follow the path scientists took in exploring gases, we will now construct this model, making sure that it is consistent with the listed properties.

The Kinetic-Molecular Theory

The kinetic-molecular model begins with the assumption that a gas consists of small particles that have mass. Keep in mind that for most gases these particles are molecules. For the noble gases, however, the particles are single atoms. You know that you cannot see the particles directly, so they must be very small. But you also know that an inflated basketball weighs more than a deflated basketball. Therefore, the particles must have mass.

Second, the particles in a gas must be separated from each other by relatively large distances. This assumption explains why gases can be so easily compressed. The space between the particles allows them to be pushed closer together. Liquids and solids

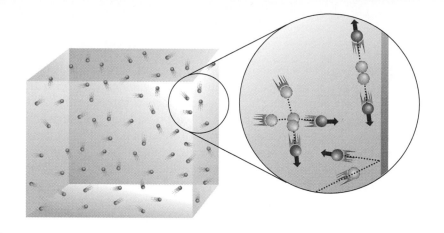

Figure 13–6 *Gas particles are in constant random motion, undergoing thousands of collisions with each other and with the walls of their container.*

do not compress easily. This indicates that their particles are packed much more tightly. The idea that gas particles are far apart is also consistent with the low densities of gases compared with the densities of liquids and solids.

Third, the particles of a gas must be in constant, rapid motion. Such motion easily explains why gases immediately fill their containers. These rapidly moving particles can also easily mix with each other so that a gas released at one end of a container quickly diffuses throughout the container.

Next, our model proposes that gases exert pressure because their particles frequently collide with the walls of the container in which they are held. Does this sound reasonable to you? If gas particles are in constant, rapid motion, you can expect that they will frequently collide with each other and with the walls of their container. Between collisions, the particles travel in straight lines.

You can better visualize this idea if you imagine a gas in a container as a room filled with hard rubber balls. Imagine these balls to be in rapid, random motion so that they collide with the walls of the room and also with each other. But there is one big difference between the rubber balls and the particles of gas. Every time a rubber ball collides with another ball or with the walls of the room, it slows down. Eventually, all the rubber balls will end up motionless on the floor. If gas particles behaved in the same way, the gas would soon become a liquid or possibly a solid. But you know that this does not happen. So the particles of a gas must collide with each other and with the container walls without slowing down.

Because gas particles keep colliding with each other and with the container walls without slowing down, the collisions of gas particles must be perfectly **elastic.** In a perfectly elastic collision, no energy of motion is lost. If you dropped a ball on the floor and it rebounded to exactly the same height from which it was dropped, you would say that the collision of the ball with the floor was perfectly elastic. Objects that you are familiar with have inelastic collisions. (You can prove this for yourself by actually dropping a small rubber ball on the floor and observing how high it rebounds.)

Figure 13–7 *In this diagram, you can see the difference between an elastic and an inelastic collision. The energy of motion remains unchanged during an elastic collision. What happens to the energy in an inelastic collision?*

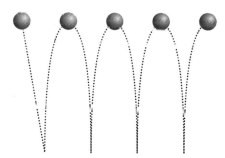

(a) elastic collisions with floor

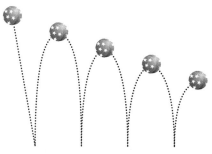

(b) inelastic collisions with floor

How do collisions account for gas pressure? Recall that pressure is force per unit area. When gas particles collide with the walls of their container, their impact exerts a force on the wall. That force exerted over that area of wall results in pressure. The fact that pressure increases when more gas is added to a nearly rigid container, such as a basketball, makes good sense. The added gas particles cause a larger number of wall collisions per unit area. The greater force exerted per unit area results in increased pressure.

Finally, our model must explain why gas pressure increases when temperature is increased. To do this, we will take a bold step and suggest that the temperature of a gas is simply a measure of the kinetic energy of the gas particles. You should recall from Chapter 2 that energy of motion is called kinetic energy. The kinetic energy (KE) of any object in motion is given by the equation $KE = mv^2/2$, where m is the mass of the object and v is its velocity. Our model states that the higher the temperature of the gas, the higher the kinetic energy of its particles. Because the mass of the gas particles does not change, the gas particles speed up as the temperature increases.

Why do you think a gas exerts a greater pressure when its particles are moving faster? The force with which gas particles impact the walls of their container is proportional to their velocity. So at higher velocities the collisions are more forceful. Thus a greater force is being exerted over the same area of wall. Because pressure is force per unit area, gas pressure increases. In addition, as gas particles move with greater velocities, they also collide more frequently with the walls of their container. Again the result is an increase in pressure. Can you now explain why the pressure exerted by a gas decreases when its temperature is lowered?

Let us pause for a moment and think about what we have accomplished. We started with six important physical properties of gases. We then developed step-by-step a model that explains these properties. We used only a few pages to present what

INTEGRATING
PHYSICS

Why does an object dropped on your toe from a height of 1 meter cause more pain than the same object dropped from a height of a few centimeters?

Figure 13–8 Rudolf Clausius (left), James Clerk Maxwell (center), and Ludwig Boltzmann (right) were three of the scientists whose work established the foundation for the kinetic-molecular theory of gases.

scientists actually took more than 100 years to develop. This model is called the **kinetic-molecular theory** of gases. It is now called a theory because the ideas stated have withstood the test of time, and more importantly, have been upheld by a great deal of further experimentation. This theory was primarily the work of three outstanding scientists: Rudolf Clausius (1822–1888), James Clerk Maxwell (1831–1879), and Ludwig Boltzmann (1844–1906).

Before we move on to a discussion of the quantitative measurement of gases, it might be helpful to summarize the kinetic-molecular theory and state it as a set of postulates. A scientific postulate is a statement assumed to be true unless proven otherwise. The postulates of the kinetic-molecular theory are as follows:

1. A gas consists of very small particles, each of which has a mass.

2. The distances separating gas particles are relatively large. Stated another way, the volume of the gas particles themselves is assumed to be zero because it is negligible compared with the total volume in which the gas is contained.

3. Gas particles are in constant, rapid, random motion.

4. Collisions of gas particles with each other or with the walls of the container are perfectly elastic.

5. The average kinetic energy of gas particles depends only on the temperature of the gas. Gas particles have higher kinetic energy at a higher temperature and lower kinetic energy at a lower temperature.

6. Gas particles exert no force on one another. In other words, attractive forces between gas particles are so weak that the model assumes them to be zero. We will take a closer look at this postulate in Section 13–4. For now, you need to understand that gas particles do not slow down and condense into a liquid because they exert only very weak attractive forces upon each other.

Figure 13–9 *The air at this mountain summit is very thin. Why?*

13–1 Section Review

1. State the postulates of the kinetic-molecular theory of gases.
2. List five properties of gases.
3. What do the words atoms, molecules, and particles mean in a discussion of gases? Give examples.
4. How can you prove that particles in a gas have mass?
5. How does the kinetic-molecular theory account for gas pressure?
6. **Critical Thinking—Making inferences** What evidence suggests that gas particles are in constant motion?

Guide for Reading

- What are the four gas variables and how are they expressed?
- How is gas pressure measured?

13–2 Measuring Gases

When a researcher takes a sample of matter for observation, she needs to know accurately the conditions under which it is being studied. Recall, for example, the water sample Joanie took from the swamp as described in Chapter 1. As part of her research, she probably recorded its source and volume, and measured its temperature. Experimental work in chemistry requires the measurement of quantities such as the volume, temperature, pressure, and the amount of a sample. These quantities are called variables. Some other variables that you might encounter later are concentration of solutions, pH of acids and bases, and radiation from a radioactive sample.

If the sample is a liquid or a solid, the relevant variables are typically the amount and temperature of the substance. Monitoring pressure is not very important for liquids and solids because their volume does not change appreciably due to a change in pressure. Does this idea sound familiar? It should, for it is simply a different way of stating the fact that liquids and solids cannot be easily compressed. Because gases are highly compressible, however, their volume depends on pressure as well as on temperature and the amount of the gas.

In order to describe a gas sample completely and then make predictions about its behavior under changed conditions, it is important to deal with the values of four variables—amount of gas, volume, temperature, and pressure.

AMOUNT OF GAS (n) You were introduced to the mole in Unit 4. The mole is the chemist's standard unit for specifying the amount of any sample of matter. So the quantity of gas in a given sample is expressed in terms of moles of gas. You have learned and practiced how to calculate the mass of a gas sample by using the molar mass of the gas. By using Avogadro's number, you can also relate the number of moles and the mass to the number of gas particles:

$$n = \frac{\text{mass}}{\text{molar mass}} = \frac{m\text{(g)}}{\mathcal{M}\text{ (g/mol)}} \qquad \textbf{(Eq. 1)}$$

VOLUME (V) A gas uniformly fills any container in which it is placed. Thus the volume of the gas is simply the volume of its container. The metric unit of volume, you will recall, is the liter (L). 1 L = 1000. cm^3. Metric prefixes may be used to modify the size of the unit as necessary.

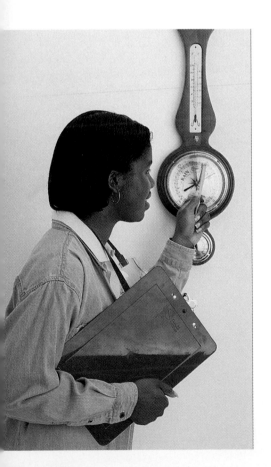

Figure 13–10 *Chemistry is an experimental science. All of the knowledge chemists have been able to acquire about the behavior of matter is based on careful observations and accurate measurements. This student is using a pressure-measuring device to record the pressure of the atmosphere.*

TEMPERATURE (*T*) Temperature of a gas is usually measured with a thermometer marked in degrees Celsius. However, all calculations involving gases should only be made after converting the Celsius temperature to Kelvin temperature. Do you remember that the Kelvin temperature scale has no negative temperatures? The significance of this fact and the Kelvin temperature scale will become apparent as you read further in this chapter. The Kelvin and Celsius temperatures are related by the following equation:

$$T(K) = T(°C) + 273 \qquad \textbf{(Eq. 2)}$$

PRESSURE (*P*) In the previous section you learned how collisions of gas particles with container walls result in gas pressure. Every time a particle collides with a wall, it exerts an outward push or force on the wall. This outward force spread over the area of the container is called pressure. The gases of the atmosphere also exert pressure on everything they are in contact with. Let's now consider how the pressure of the atmosphere is measured and expressed.

Atmospheric Pressure and the Barometer

Suppose you pump some air into a basketball. The moving particles in the air, mainly oxygen and nitrogen molecules, will collide with the inner surface of the basketball and push outward on it. But the ball does not expand to the point where it bursts, does it? Why not? Part of the reason is that the cover of the ball can resist some of the effect of the pressure of the air on the inside. But a major part of the reason is that the atmosphere, the air around us, exerts a pressure on the outside of the ball countering the pressure of the air on the inside. The strength of the pressure of the atmosphere can be demonstrated if you pump the air out of a can. With no air on the inside to balance the atmospheric pressure, the can is easily crushed. See Figure 13–11.

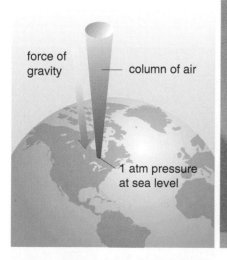

force of gravity — column of air

1 atm pressure at sea level

Figure 13–11 *The atmosphere exerts pressure on the surface of the Earth. Here you see a graphic demonstration of the pressure of the air all around you. With no air inside the can, the can is easily crushed by outside air pressure.*

Figure 13–12 *Using this table, what is the equivalent of 1 atmosphere of pressure in pounds per square inch?*

*I*NTEGRATING
*E*ARTH *S*CIENCE

How might you use atmospheric pressure to predict your local weather?

Figure 13–13 *Pressure measuring devices are used in weather prediction (center) and in the regulation of gas flow (right). What does the letter* h *in the simple mercury barometer (left) represent?*

The pressure exerted by the air in the atmosphere is called **atmospheric pressure.** Atmospheric pressure is a result of the fact that air has mass and is attracted by Earth's gravity. The mass of the air attracted by gravity produces a force. The force exerted on a unit area of the Earth's surface, say one square meter (m²), is atmospheric pressure. Pressure is calculated in units of force per unit area. The SI unit of force is the newton. The SI unit of pressure is the pascal. One newton of force per square meter of area is called one pascal (Pa). One thousand pascals is, of course, one kilopascal (kPa). Another unit of pressure is the atmosphere (atm). A standard atmosphere is close to the average atmospheric pressure at sea level. One atmosphere equals 101,325 Pa, or 101.3 kPa. See Figure 13–12.

Atmospheric pressure varies with altitude because the lower the altitude, the longer and heavier is the column of air above an area of the Earth. This principle is the basis for the operation of altimeters used in airplanes. An altimeter simply converts the atmospheric pressure reading to altitude. Atmospheric pressure also varies with the composition of the atmosphere. Water vapor is lighter than nitrogen and oxygen, the main gases of the atmosphere. Therefore, a higher water vapor content in the local atmosphere gives a lower atmospheric pressure. Conversely, a low atmospheric pressure indicates that the water vapor content is high and the chances of rain are great.

You can measure the pressure of the atmosphere with a **barometer,** such as the one shown in Figure 13–13. This barometer is a glass tube that is sealed at one end, filled with mercury, and then inverted into a reservoir of mercury. The mercury in the tube immediately seeks a height so that the pressure exerted on the surface of the mercury in the reservoir is exactly balanced by the pressure exerted by the mercury column. The height of the mercury column that will be balanced by a pressure of exactly 1 atmosphere is 760 millimeters (mm) at sea level. Pressures are often given in millimeters of mercury, which is written as mm Hg. Commonly used units of pressure are listed in Figure 13–12.

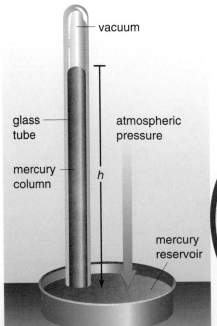

vacuum

glass tube

atmospheric pressure

mercury column

h

mercury reservoir

The column of mercury in a barometer is 745 mm above the mercury reservoir at the bottom. What is the atmospheric pressure in pascals?

STRATEGY	SOLUTION
1. Analyze	You are given the height of the mercury column in millimeters This is actually a measurement of the atmospheric pressure. However, it will be necessary to convert to units of pascals.
2. Plan	101,325 Pa equals 760 mm Hg. Set up the conversion factor to convert from mm Hg to Pa.
3. Solve 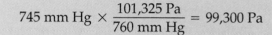	$745 \text{ mm Hg} \times \dfrac{101,325 \text{ Pa}}{760 \text{ mm Hg}} = 99,300 \text{ Pa}$
4. Evaluate	One standard atmosphere of pressure is very close to 100,000 Pa. The measured pressure in this experiment is a little less than one standard atmosphere and so the pressure in pascals is reasonable.

PRACTICE PROBLEMS

1. The air pressure inside the cabin of an airplane is 8.3 lb/in.^{2} What is this pressure in atmosphere units? *(Answer: 0.56 atm)*

2. Pressure is considered the most accurate measure of storm strength, with lower pressure indicating a stronger storm. One of the lowest recorded pressures in the Western Hemisphere is 88.86 kPa. How high a column of mercury would be balanced by this atmospheric pressure? *(Answer: 666.5 mm Hg)*

Enclosed Gases

If a gas is in an open container, some of the gas will escape through the opening and the pressure within the container will quickly be equal to the pressure of the atmosphere. This principle allows you to find the pressure in an open container simply by measuring the atmospheric pressure with a barometer.

If the container is closed, the pressure inside the container may be different from the atmospheric pressure. How, then, can the pressure be measured? An instrument called a **manometer** is used to measure the pressure in a closed container. A simple

pressure of
atmosphere

gas

(a)

pressure of
atmosphere

gas

(b)

Figure 13–14 *In the
diagram, a manometer registers
two different gas pressures.
Which manometer shows the
higher gas pressure?*

manometer such as the one shown in Figure 13–14 can be made
using a U-shaped glass tube filled with mercury. One end of the
tube opens into the container in which the gas pressure is to
be measured. The other end of the tube is open to the surrounding atmosphere.

Determining the pressure in the container will depend on
whether the levels of mercury on the two sides of the U-tube are
the same or different. If the levels of the mercury are the same
on both sides of the U-tube, the pressure of the gas in the container
is the same as the pressure of the atmosphere. If the level of
mercury is lower on the container side, the pressure in the container is higher than atmospheric pressure because the gas in the
container is pushing on the mercury harder than the atmosphere
is. See Figure 13–14. In this case, the difference between atmospheric pressure and the pressure in the container in units of
mm Hg is simply the difference between the heights of the two
mercury columns. To find the pressure of the gas in the container,
you must add the difference in the pressures to the atmospheric
pressure, which you have separately determined by using a
barometer.

If the pressure in the container is less than atmospheric pressure, the mercury level will be higher on the container side and
the difference in pressures must be subtracted from atmospheric
pressure to determine the pressure in the container.

SAMPLE PROBLEM   2

You have a closed container attached to a U-tube as in
Figure 13–14. The mercury in the open-ended side of the
tube is higher, and the difference between the heights of the
mercury columns is 27 mm. You have measured the atmospheric pressure with a barometer to be 755 mm Hg. What
is the pressure of the gas in the container in atmospheres?

STRATEGY	SOLUTION
1. Analyze	You are given the difference between the levels of mercury in the two columns of a U-tube manometer. You are told that the mercury in the open-ended side of the tube is higher, and you are asked to deter-mine the pressure of the gas. You are also given the atmospheric pressure in mm Hg. From the relative levels of mercury you know that the pressure of the gas is greater than the pressure of the atmo-sphere. In the end you will need to con-vert from mm Hg to atm.

2. Plan	The atmospheric pressure and the pressure in the container are related by the following equation:

pressure in container
= height difference
+ atmospheric pressure

3. Solve Substitute the values for height difference and atmospheric pressure into the equation:

pressure in container
= 27 mm Hg + 755 mm Hg

= 782 mm Hg

Using the conversion factor,
1 atm = 760 mm Hg,

$$782 \text{ mm Hg} \times \frac{1 \text{ atm}}{760 \text{ mm Hg}} = 1.03 \text{ atm}$$

4. Evaluate 27 mm Hg is a small difference in height compared to 760 mm Hg. This means the pressure of the gas in the container is only slightly more than 1 atm, so 1.03 atm is a reasonable answer.

PRACTICE PROBLEMS

3. A balloon is attached to an open-ended manometer. The mercury level in the manometer is 13 mm lower on the side attached to the balloon than on the side open to the atmosphere. The pressure of the atmosphere is measured to be 755 mm Hg in a separate measurement. What is the gas pressure in the balloon? *(Answer: 768 mm Hg)*

4. Suppose you have a gas container fitted with a manometer. You measure the height of the mercury on the side of the manometer open to the atmosphere. Then the atmospheric pressure drops and you measure the height of the mercury on the open side again. Will the level of the mercury on the open side have moved, and if so, in which direction? *(Answer: It will have moved upward.)*

STP

The behavior of a gas depends very strongly on the temperature and the pressure at which the gas is held. In the next section you will be looking closely at ways in which gases respond to changes in these variables. In order to make it easier to discuss the behavior of a gas, it is convenient to designate standard

Magic or Science?

The scene: The local county fair. A magician has just announced to a crowd of people at the fair that he can tell one gas apart from another just by feeling the gases. "You can't feel a gas," came a voice from the crowd. "Well," said the magician, "for the price of my show, which happens to be one dollar, I'll demonstrate that I can identify a gas by the way it feels. If I can do it successfully, I get to keep your money. But if I fail, you will get a refund. How's that?"

Their curiosity aroused, people quickly paid the money and within a very short time the magician's tent was full of eager spectators. They could not imagine how the magician would be able to tell two gases apart just by feel, without relying on color or odor. The magician stepped from behind a curtain holding two stoppered bottles. "Fill one bottle with xenon and the other with helium. Make sure you keep track of which gas is in which bottle."

A volunteer from the crowd filled the bottles from the compressed gas tanks that were conveniently secured to the stage. She identified each bottle with a secret mark and then gave the bottles to the magician.

The magician examined each bottle, took each stopper off briefly and stuck his finger into the bottles. "This is helium and this is xenon," he said. He was right! He performed the trick several times and never failed.

How did he do it? Consider the properties of gases that you know. Do these gases differ significantly from each other with respect to any one of these properties? Could the magician have used this difference in identifying the gases?

temperature and pressure, or **STP.** The temperature that is designated as standard temperature is the freezing point of water, 0°C or 273 K. Designated standard pressure is 1 atmosphere. Recall that 1 atm = 760 mm Hg = 101,325 Pa. STP is the condition under which various properties of gases, such as volume and density, are normally listed in handbooks used for reference.

13–2 Section Review

1. List the four gas variables. How is each expressed?
2. Explain how a mercury barometer works.
3. Explain how a manometer measures the pressure of an enclosed gas.
4. Define STP and explain its importance.
5. **Connection—Meteorology** Explain the significance of barometric pressure in weather forecasting.

13–3 The Gas Laws

Guide for Reading
- How do the gas laws relate the variables P, V, n, and T?

Studies of the behavior of gases played a major role in the development of the physical sciences in the seventeenth and eighteenth centuries. The kinetic-molecular theory of gases was a significant scientific achievement when it was first developed and occupies an important place in today's scientific framework. In Section 13–1 we developed the kinetic-molecular model to explain simple, familar gas behavior. In this section you will learn about the work of several brilliant scientists, which paved the way for our present understanding of the gaseous state. Robert Boyle and Jacques Charles among others experimented with different aspects of gas behavior and produced results quite impressive for their times. In the pages that follow you will study these results as the gas laws of Boyle, Charles, Avogadro, and Dalton. The gas laws are mathematical representations of the observed relationships among the four variables—pressure, volume, temperature, and quantity of a gas.

Boyle's Law: The Pressure-Volume Relationship

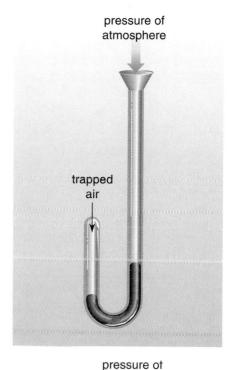

You are familiar with the use of air for its cushioning effect in tires, air mattresses and pillows, air-bag suspension systems for trucks and buses, and other applications. Gases can be used in this way because they can be compressed. This is because their particles are well separated from one other. Robert Boyle (1627–1691), an English chemist and physicist, was among the first to note this property of air. Boyle described the "spring of air" in a number of his writings.

Boyle's most famous experiment involved trapping a fixed amount of air, changing its pressure, and measuring its volume. His simple apparatus is pictured in Figure 13–15. It consists of a J-shaped tube with the short end closed off. Some air was trapped in the short end of the J-tube. The pressure on this air could be changed by altering the amount of mercury in the longer, open-ended side of the tube. The level of the mercury moved until the pressure exerted by the trapped air in the short column was equal to the pressure of the atmosphere plus the pressure of the additional mercury in the long column.

Boyle measured the volume of the air at different pressures, that is, with different amounts of mercury in the column. For

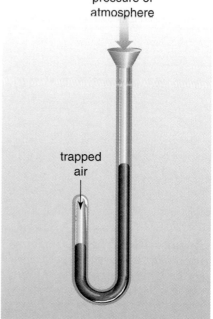

Figure 13–15 *The diagram shows a Boyle's law apparatus: A J-tube is used to determine the relationship between the pressure and volume of a gas. What happens to the volume of the trapped air as more mercury is added to the open tube (bottom)?*

Volumes of a Trapped Air Sample at Different Pressures and Constant Temperature

Trial	Pressure (atm)	Volume (cm³)
1	1.30	3.10
2	1.60	2.51
3	1.90	2.11
4	2.20	1.84

each series of measurements, the temperature was kept constant. Have you noticed that two of the four gas variables remain constant in this experiment? Which ones are they? A sample series of Boyle's pressure-volume data is given in Figure 13–16. Boyle wanted to answer the question: "Is there a relationship between the pressure and volume of a gas?"

Take a look at the values for pressure and volume in Figure 13–16. You will notice that as pressure increases, volume decreases. This suggests that one way that you can try to find a relationship between pressure and volume is to multiply the pressure times the volume for each trial and see if you get the same product. If you do this, the products of pressure times volume for the four trials are 4.03, 4.02, 4.01, and 4.05. Although these values are not identical, they are close. The differences between the products in this experiment are less than 1 percent of the products themselves. This is a very reasonable difference for the simple and somewhat inaccurate experimental apparatus used. Repeated trials of this and similar experiments by Boyle and many others have given consistent results that scientists have come to feel they can depend on. This kind of dependability leads to Boyle's observations being accepted as a law, which is known as Boyle's law. Boyle's law states: If the temperature of a given gas sample remains unchanged, the product of the pressure times the volume has a constant value. The mathematical statement of Boyle's law is

$$PV = k_1 \qquad \textbf{(Eq. 3)}$$

Figure 13–17 *Scuba diving opens up a fascinating underwater world. What must these divers know about gas pressure to ensure their safety?*

where P is the pressure of the gas, V is its volume, and k_1 is the constant. The value of the constant will depend on a number of things, including the units of P and V, the temperature, and the amount of gas in the sample. What can you say about the relationship between the pressure and the volume of a gas (constant n and T) if their product is a constant? If the gas is forced into a smaller volume, then its pressure will increase so that the product of the new pressure and volume still equals the constant k_1. Similarly, if the pressure of the gas is changed to a new, lower value, its volume must increase sufficiently so that the product of the new values of pressure and volume again equals k_1. Thus an equivalent statement of Boyle's law is as follows: **The pressure and volume of a sample of gas at constant temperature are inversely proportional to each other.**

Boyle's law allows you to calculate some quantities without having to measure them. For example, the mathematical statement of Boyle's law tells you that at the same temperature, the product of the pressure times the volume for a given gas sample is always the same. Suppose you perform two trials. For trial one, the pressure is P_1 and the volume is V_1. For trial two, they are P_2 and V_2. According to Boyle's law, $P_1V_1 = k_1$ and $P_2V_2 = k_1$. Therefore,

$$P_1V_1 = P_2V_2 \qquad \textbf{(Eq. 4)}$$

If three of the values in this equation are known, the fourth can be readily calculated.

SAMPLE PROBLEM 3

You have volunteered to decorate the gym with 300 helium balloons for a party. You find a store that will rent a 25-L helium tank filled with helium gas at a pressure of 30.0 atm. Each balloon, when filled, holds 2.5 L of helium at a pressure of 1.04 atm. Will one tank be enough to fill all of the balloons? Assume that the gas temperature does not change as the balloons are filled.

STRATEGY	SOLUTION
1. Analyze	In this problem pressure and volume are the variables. There is a fixed amount of helium, which means that n does not change. The problem states that the temperature also remains unchanged. A sketch can help you identify what information is given and focus on what must be calculated.

Scuba Diving

What does a scuba diver need to know about gas laws in order to enjoy diving without danger? As the underwater depth increases, the pressure increases. Due to the weight of water, the pressure exerted at a depth of 10 meters is 2 atmospheres. At 20 meters the pressure exerted is 3 atmospheres. Scuba equipment provides air at a pressure equal to the surrounding water pressure. This allows the diver's lungs to function at their normal volume although at a higher pressure. Suppose a diver rises to the surface very quickly and the pressure drops from 2 atmospheres to 1 atmosphere. According to Boyle's law the volume of the air in this diver's lungs would double. This sudden expansion of air can rupture the membranes of the diver's lungs. So scuba divers must remember to ascend slowly.

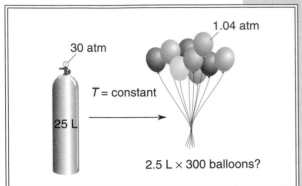

30 atm

1.04 atm

T = constant

25 L

2.5 L × 300 balloons?

2. Plan

Boyle's law states that the product of the pressure and volume remains constant as long as n and T are unchanged. Assign the symbols P_1 and V_1 to the pressure and volume of the tank and the symbol P_2 to the pressure of a balloon. According to Boyle's law, $P_1V_1 = P_2V_2$. You can calculate V_2, the total volume of all the balloons that the tank can fill. Because you know the volume of each balloon to be 2.5 L, you can then calculate the number of balloons that can be filled from the tank.

3. Solve

$$V_2 = \frac{P_1V_1}{P_2}$$

$$= \frac{(30 \text{ atm})(25 \text{ L})}{1.04 \text{ atm}}$$

$$= 720 \text{ L}$$

$$\text{number of balloons} = \frac{720 \text{ L}}{2.5 \text{ L/balloon}}$$

$$= 290 \text{ balloons}$$

4. Evaluate

The PV product of the tank is 750 atm-L. The PV product for each balloon is 2.6 atm-L. This indicates that fewer than 300 balloons can be filled with the helium in the tank. Another tank of helium would be required to fill all 300 balloons.

PRACTICE PROBLEMS

5. A partially inflated helium weather balloon contains 150 L of gas. The balloon's internal gas pressure is 1.0 atm when it is released. The research team wants to place a payload of measurement instruments at an altitude of 41 km, where the atmospheric pressure (and therefore the pressure inside the balloon) is only 0.4 atm. How large must the balloon be to accommodate the gas volume at 41 km, assuming the gas temperature does not change and the balloon does not leak? *(Answer: 375 L)*

6. A gas at a pressure of 608 mm Hg is held in a container with a volume of 545 cm^3. The volume of the container is then increased to 1065 cm^3 without a change in temperature. Calculate the new pressure of the gas. *(Answer: 311 mm Hg)*

Charles's Law: The Temperature-Volume Relationship

Just as Boyle determined the relationship between the pressure of a gas and its volume, Jacques Charles determined the relationship between the temperature and volume of a gas sample. An experimental apparatus for determining this relationship is shown in Figure 13–18. The gas sample is trapped in a cylinder with a movable piston. The temperature of the gas sample can be changed by immersing the cylinder in water baths at different temperatures. Remember, the piston must be free to move. When the cylinder is moved to a water bath at a different temperature, the gas sample will take on a new volume. The cylinder is calibrated so that the volume of the gas can be easily related to the position of the piston. Thus the experiment performed by Charles determined the relationship of the volume of a gas to its temperature while the pressure and the amount of gas were held constant.

The results for oxygen and carbon dioxide are shown in Figure 13–19 on the next page. What stands out immediately is that a plot of volume against temperature is a straight line of positive slope, which indicates that volume increases as temperature increases. In other words, the volume of a gas is directly proportional to its temperature. Although Charles was not able to achieve very low temperatures in his experiments, he was able to extend the straight line so that he could see what would happen to a gas if its temperature were to be made very low.

Figure 13–18 *A cylinder fitted with a movable piston is used to determine the relationship between the temperature and the volume of a gas. Which two variables are held constant in this setup?*

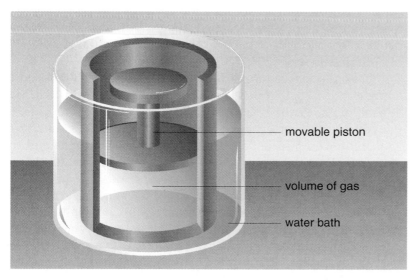

movable piston

volume of gas

water bath

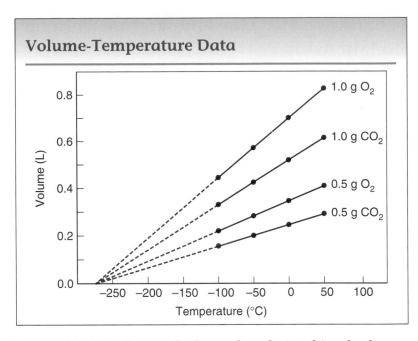

Figure 13–19 *The graph shows the relationship of volume versus temperature at constant pressure for O_2 and CO_2. What is the significance of extrapolating to zero volume?*

Volume and temperature data have been experimentally obtained for several different gases using various amounts of gas at different pressures. In each case the data approximate a straight line. What is most surprising is that extending each line to zero volume gives essentially the same result. There is a lower limit for temperature and the numerical value of this limit appears to be essentially the same for all gases. This absolute minimum in temperature occurs at $-273.15°C$. This temperature is called **absolute zero** because it is theoretically the lowest possible temperature that can be reached. Practically, absolute zero has never been reached, although temperatures within a millionth of a degree above $-273.15°C$ have been achieved!

These discoveries about temperature and gas volume led to a further idea. If a temperature scale is adopted that has its zero at absolute zero, the relationship between the temperature and the volume of a gas is simplified. A scale that has its minimum at absolute zero is called an absolute temperature scale, and the temperature on this scale is called the absolute temperature. Thus an absolute temperature scale can have only positive values. The Kelvin scale, which is calibrated in units called kelvins (K), is the SI temperature scale, as you learned in Chapter 1. Zero on the Kelvin scale coincides with absolute zero. Kelvins have the same magnitude as Celsius degrees. Thus, conversions between the Kelvin and the Celsius scales can be made using the equation that you first encountered in Chapter 2: $K = °C + 273$.

Figure 13-20 *Here you see a demonstration of Charles's law. In the photograph on the left, a balloon is submerged in a beaker of ice water. In the photograph on the right, the water in the beaker is heated with a Bunsen burner. What happens to the volume of the balloon as the water is heated?*

When Kelvin temperature is used, the volume of a gas and its temperature are very simply related by the following equation:

$$V = k_2 T \qquad \text{(Eq. 5)}$$

Here, k_2 is the Charles's law constant of proportionality for a given gas sample at a particular pressure. This is a mathematical expression of Charles's law. **Charles's law states that at constant pressure, the volume of a fixed amount of gas is directly proportional to its absolute temperature.** Charles's law can be modified to a convenient form by solving for k_2:

$$k_2 = \frac{V}{T} \qquad \text{(Eq. 6)}$$

In a sample with volume V_1 and temperature T_1, changing either volume or temperature converts these variables to V_2 and T_2. The ratio V/T in each case still equals k_2:

$$\frac{V_1}{T_1} = k_2 = \frac{V_2}{T_2} \qquad \text{(Eq. 7)}$$

Therefore,

$$V_1 T_2 = V_2 T_1 \qquad \text{(Eq. 8)}$$

SAMPLE PROBLEM 4

On a cool morning (10.0°C) a group of hot-air balloonists start filling their balloon with air, using a large fan. After the balloon's envelope is three-fourths filled, they turn on the propane burner to heat the air. At what Celsius temperature will the air completely fill the envelope to its maximum capacity of 1700. m^3? (You may assume that the pressure is constant and that no air escapes from the balloon while it is being heated.)

STRATEGY

SOLUTION

1. Analyze

This problem can be solved using Charles's law. Volume and temperature are variable and the amount of gas and its pressure remain constant.

2. Plan

Charles's law mathematically states $V_1T_2 = V_2T_1$. V_2 is the maximum balloon volume and V_1 is three fourths of V_2. The unknown value is T_2. Rearrange the equation to solve for T_2. Remember to convert the temperature T_1 to kelvins. You will need to convert the calculated Kelvin temperature T_2 back to Celsius as required.

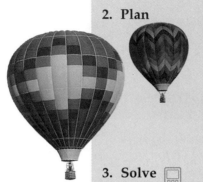

3. Solve

$$T_2 = \frac{V_2T_1}{V_1}$$

$$T_1 = 10.0°C + 273 = 283\ K$$

$$V_1 = \left(\tfrac{3}{4}\right) V_2 = \left(\tfrac{3}{4}\right) 1700.\ m^3 = 1275.\ m^3$$

$$T_2 = \frac{V_2T_1}{V_1} = \frac{(1700.\ m^3)(283\ K)}{(1275.\ m^3)} = 377\ K$$

$$T_2 = 377\ K - 273 = 104°C$$

4. Evaluate

The answer tells you that the balloon will inflate to its maximum capacity at a temperature higher than the boiling point of water. Notice also that a 33 percent increase in volume requires a 33 percent increase in the Kelvin temperature.

PRACTICE PROBLEMS

7. What will be the volume of a gas sample at 355 K if its volume at 273 K is 8.57 L? Assume that the pressure of the gas remains unchanged. *(Answer: 11.1 L)*

8. A gas can be used as a thermometer. If it is known that a sample of gas has a volume of 1.00 L at 255 K, what is the temperature if the volume of the same gas sample is changed to 0.45 L at constant pressure? *(Answer: 110 K)*

Avogadro's Law: The Amount-Volume Relationship

Early in the nineteenth century the Italian chemist Amedeo Avogadro proposed a very simple but profound hypothesis relating the volume of a gas to the number of gas particles. Although this hypothesis resolved many of the problems that puzzled scientists in those times, only decades later did the hypothesis gain acceptance. **Avogadro's law states that equal volumes of gases at the same temperature and pressure contain an equal number of particles.**

Avogadro's law contains two important points worth noting. First, it states that all gases show the same physical behavior. Second, the law tells you that a gas with a larger volume must consist of a greater number of particles. This is quite reasonable: As long as the pressure and temperature of a gas do not change, the only way to change the volume is by changing the number of gas particles.

Because n, the number of moles, is directly proportional to the number of particles, the relationship expressed by Avogadro's law can be written as

$$V = k_3 n \qquad \text{(Eq. 9)}$$

where n is the number of moles and k_3 is yet another proportionality constant—Avogadro's law constant. The volume of one mole of gas is called the **molar volume.** You might recall that the molar volume at STP (273 K and 1 atm) is 22.4 L.

Dalton's Law of Partial Pressures

The English chemist John Dalton (1766–1844) was among the first scientists to consider mixtures of gases even though he did not have the kinetic-molecular theory of gases available to help him formulate and develop his ideas. After experimenting with gases and gas mixtures, he proposed that the particles of different gases in a mixture act independently in exerting pressures upon the walls of the container. In other words, he concluded that each gas in a mixture exerts the same pressure that it would if it were present alone at the same temperature. The pressure exerted by each component of a mixture of gases is called the **partial pressure** of that component. **Dalton's law of partial pressures states that the sum of the partial pressures of all the components in a gas mixture is equal to the total pressure of the gas mixture.**

$$P_T = p_a + p_b + p_c + \cdots \qquad \text{(Eq. 10)}$$

In this equation, P_T is the total pressure of a gas mixture, p_a is the partial pressure of component a, p_b is the partial pressure of component b, and so on. Would you expect this law to be true if component gases chemically reacted with each other?

Figure 13–21 The total pressure of a mixture of gases is the sum of the partial pressures of the component gases. Can you explain this in terms of the kinetic-molecular theory of gases?

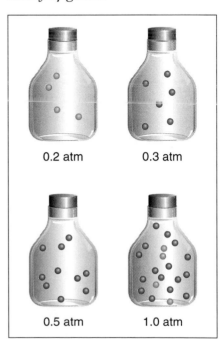

0.2 atm   0.3 atm

0.5 atm   1.0 atm

SAMPLE PROBLEM 5

What is the atmospheric pressure if the partial pressures of nitrogen, oxygen, and argon are 604.5 mm Hg, 162.8 mm Hg, and 0.5 mm Hg, respectively?

STRATEGY	SOLUTION
1. **Analyze**	You are given the partial pressures of nitrogen, oxygen, and argon and asked to calculate the atmospheric pressure.
2. **Plan**	You can assume that Dalton's law of partial pressures will give an answer that is close to the true value since all the important components in air have been accounted for. Thus, you can use the mathematical equation of Dalton's law.
3. **Solve**	Substitute the given partial pressure values in the equation

$$P_T = p_{N_2} + p_{O_2} + p_{Ar}$$

604.5 mm Hg + 162.8 mm Hg

+ 0.5 mm Hg = 767.8 mm Hg

| 4. **Evaluate** | The result is realistic since it gives a reasonable value for the atmospheric pressure. |

PRACTICE PROBLEMS

9. A person using an oxygen mask is breathing air with 33% O_2. What is the partial pressure of the O_2 when the air pressure in the mask is 110 kPa? *(Answer: 36 kPa)*

10. The gases carbon dioxide, oxygen, nitrogen, neon, and krypton are mixed in a container. All gases have the same partial pressure and the total pressure in the container is 33,500 Pa. What is the partial pressure of nitrogen? *(Answer: 6700 Pa)*

Figure 13–22 *An oxygen mask provides a higher partial pressure of oxygen than the surrounding atmosphere. Give instances where an oxygen mask is used.*

13–3 Section Review

1. State the laws of Boyle, Charles, Avogadro, and Dalton.

2. How does the kinetic-molecular theory account for Dalton's law? For Charles's law?

3. **Critical Thinking—Applying concepts**   Describe how you could construct a thermometer using the result of Charles's law. Such a thermometer is called a gas thermometer.

13–4 The Ideal Gas Law

The gas laws you have just learned—Boyle's law, Charles's law, and Avogadro's law—relate one of the four gas variables to another variable. You will find a summary of these laws in Figure 13–23. Notice that each of these three laws expresses a proportionality between two variables while the remaining two variables are held constant. A much more powerful equation can be derived by combining the proportionalities expressed by these laws. Doing so, we get the following equation:

$$P = R\frac{nT}{V} \qquad \textbf{(Eq. 11)}$$

where P is the gas pressure, n is the number of moles of gas, T is the Kelvin temperature, and V is the gas volume. R is a new proportionality constant that chemists know only too well. You will soon find out its numerical value and how to use it. Chemists prefer to write the above equation in a modified, equivalent form as follows:

$$PV = nRT \qquad \text{(Eq. 12)}$$

The Ideal Gas Equation

The equation $PV = nRT$, called the ideal gas equation, **describes the physical behavior of an ideal gas in terms of the pressure, volume, temperature, and the number of moles of gas.** By an **ideal gas** chemists mean a gas that is described by the kinetic-molecular theory postulates that you learned in Section 13–1. The ideal gas equation is a mathematical tool that is useful in dealing with ideal gases. Although no such ideal gas exists, the ideal gas equation can be used to describe the behavior of a **real gas.** All gases are real gases. Real gases behave like ideal gases under many ordinary conditions. Only at low temperatures and high pressures do real gases show significant nonideal behavior. You will learn more about this later on in this section. For now, let us assume that gases are close to ideal and the ideal gas equation applies.

Guide for Reading
- What is the ideal gas equation and how is it applied?
- What is a real gas?

Figure 13–23 *The table summarizes the four gas laws: Boyle's, Charles's, Avogadro's, and Dalton's.*

Gas Law Summary

Law	Statement	Equation	Constant
Boyle's	P inversely proportional to V	$PV = k_1$	T, n
Charles's	V directly proportional to T^*	$\frac{V}{T} = k_2$	P, n
Avogadro's	V directly proportional to n	$\frac{V}{n} = k_3$	P, T
Dalton's	P_T is sum of partial pressures of components	$P_T = P_a + P_b + P_c + \ldots$	T, V

* T = absolute temperature in kelvins

Value of Gas Constant in Various Units	
Numerical Value	**Units**
0.0821	atm-L/mol-K
8.314	Pa-m³/mol-K
8.314	J/mol-K

Figure 13–24 *The value of the gas constant* R *can be expressed in different units.*

The constant R in the ideal gas equation is called the **gas constant** (sometimes the universal gas constant). The numerical value of R depends upon its units. As you read earlier, 1.00 mole of gas at 273 K (0°C) and 1.00 atm (that is, at STP) occupies a volume of 22.4 L. If the ideal gas equation is rearranged to solve for R and these values for the appropriate variables are substituted, the numerical value of R can be determined as follows:

$$PV = nRT$$

$$R = \frac{PV}{nT} = \frac{(1.00 \text{ atm})(22.4 \text{ L})}{(1.00 \text{ mol})(273 \text{ K})} = 0.0821 \text{ atm-L/mol-K}$$

The numerical value of 0.0821 is only correct if the units are atm-L/mol-K, which is read as atmosphere liter per mole kelvin. Figure 13–24 lists the numerical values of R for various units of pressure and volume. Which R value should you use in solving problems? That will depend upon the pressure and volume units used in the problem. Remember also that the ideal gas equation will give correct volumes, pressures, and moles only if the absolute temperature is used. This means that the temperature must be expressed in kelvins and not in degrees Celsius.

MATH TIP

Notice that for the universal gas constant, *R*, the units in the numerator will always be those of energy (usually atm-L, J, or kJ), while in the denominator the unit will be mol-K.

SAMPLE PROBLEM 6

How many moles of a gas at 100.°C does it take to fill a 1.00-L flask to a pressure of 1.50 atm?

STRATEGY	SOLUTION
1. Analyze	This is a problem for the ideal gas equation, which can be rearranged to solve for n, the number of moles of gas. Values for the temperature, volume, and pressure are provided.
2. Plan	Rearrange the ideal gas equation to solve for the number of moles: $$PV = nRT$$ $$n = \frac{PV}{RT}$$ The temperature must be converted from degrees Celsius to kelvins.
3. Solve	Convert the temperature to kelvins and then substitute into the rearranged equation above. $$T(K) = 100.°C + 273 = 373 \text{ K}$$ $$n = \frac{PV}{RT}$$ $$= \frac{(1.50 \text{ atm})(1.00 \text{ L})}{(0.0821 \text{ atm-L/mol-K})(373 \text{ K})}$$ $$= 0.0490 \text{ mol}$$

4. Evaluate   All other units cancel to give the answer in the correct units of moles.

PRACTICE PROBLEMS

11. What is the volume occupied by 9.45 g of C_2H_2 at STP?
    (Answer: 8.15 L)

12. A camping stove uses a 5.0-L propane tank that holds 3.0 kg of liquid C_3H_8. How large a container would be needed to hold the same amount of propane as a gas at 25°C and a pressure of 3.0 atm?   *(Answer: 560 L)*

Ideal Gas Law and the Kinetic-Molecular Theory

You have just seen that the ideal gas law, $PV = nRT$, was obtained by combining results that were derived experimentally. This proves that under ordinary temperature and pressure conditions, gases behave ideally. Now it is appropriate to ask the following question: Can the ideal gas law be accounted for by the kinetic-molecular theory?

First, the ideal gas equation says that P increases as n increases (V and T remain constant). This is just what the kinetic-molecular model predicts. As more gas is added (n is increased), there will be many more collisions of gas particles per unit area of the container wall in a given amount of time. This will cause pressure to increase.

Second, the ideal gas equation says that P increases as T increases (n and V remain constant). Recall that this was the sixth gas property outlined in Section 13–1. As temperature increases, the gas particles move faster. This causes the gas particles to collide with the container wall with greater force, as well as to collide with the container wall more frequently. The result of both is an increase in gas pressure.

Third, the ideal gas equation says that P increases as V decreases (n and T remain constant). The same number of gas particles with the same average velocity are now confined to a smaller volume. This results in an increase in the number of collisions per unit area of the container wall. Therefore, the pressure increases.

Why is it important to show agreement between the ideal gas law and the kinetic-molecular theory? As we said before, the ideal gas law was obtained experimentally. The better the agreement between experiment and theory, the better that theory holds up. So far we have shown that the kinetic-molecular theory is holding up rather well!

CHEMISTRY IN ACTION

CONSUMER TIP

A Brighter Idea

Light is produced as an incandescent tungsten filament gets white hot when electricity passes through it. The most common, pear-shaped light bulbs are filled with the inert gas argon. Argon atoms prevent the evaporation of the tungsten filament as it heats to a temperature of 3000°C.

Krypton is much better than argon as a filler gas because the heavier krypton atoms move slower. Krypton-filled light bulbs burn brighter for the same amount of electricity flowing through them. Substituting krypton for argon also prolongs the life of a light bulb from 1000 hours to 3000 hours.

Why are we still using argon-filled light bulbs? Because krypton is much more expensive than argon!

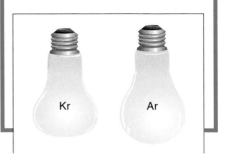

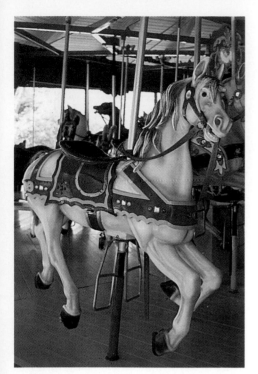

Figure 13–25 *The horses on this carousel may be moved up and down by mechanical, hydraulic, or pneumatic means. A pneumatic system is based on the properties of gases, such as compressibility.*

Deviations From Ideal Behavior

You have seen how the ideal gas equation can be used to make valuable calculations involving the gas variables that it relates. The ideal gas equation $PV = nRT$ is simple to use and accurately predicts gas behavior in many everyday situations. However, it is an approximation and does not describe the behavior of real gases exactly. For example, when you have a gas at very high pressure, the results given by this equation do not coincide with their experimentally measured values. At very high pressure, the calculated volume and the measured volume of a gas are significantly different. Such disagreement between calculated and measured values also occurs when a gas sample is at very low temperature. Why do gases not obey the ideal gas equation at high pressures and low temperatures?

To answer this question, let's visualize what happens to a gas as its pressure is increased and its temperature is decreased. An increase in pressure compresses the gas and the gas particles are forced closer together. As pressure is increased even more, compression becomes more and more difficult because the gas particles do have a volume of their own. As the volume of the particles themselves becomes a significant proportion of the total volume of a gas, the ideal gas law begins to fail. This is because the ideal gas law is based on the kinetic-molecular theory, which assumes that gas particles have no volume of their own.

A decrease in temperature takes away energy from the gas, and the gas particles slow down. Attractive forces between gas

Figure 13–26 *Compressing a gas in a cylinder with a movable piston illustrates the difference between a real gas and an ideal gas. At high compression (right), the volume of the actual gas particles becomes significant. How does this differ from the behavior of an ideal gas?*

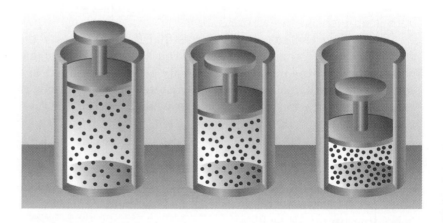

Figure 13–27 *In a real gas, attractive forces between gas particles become significant as the temperature is lowered. The pressure exerted by the gas is less because the impact with which the particles strike the walls of their container is less forceful due to the attractive forces between the particles.*

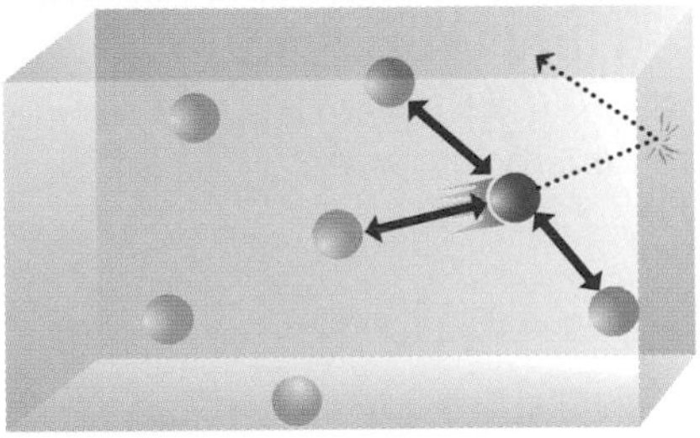

particles, which are negligibly small when the particles are moving fast, become significant as the particles slow down. Thus the ideal gas law also fails at very low temperatures because it is based on the assumption that gas particles exert no attractive forces upon one another.

Stating it another way, if the pressure is moderately low—a few atmospheres—gas particles are far enough apart so that the volume of the particles themselves can be assumed to be zero. If the temperature is moderately high—near room temperature—the movements of the gas particles is rapid enough so that the attractive forces between them can be assumed to be zero. Under such conditions, a real gas behaves as an ideal gas and its behavior is accurately described by the ideal gas equation. For gases such as oxygen and nitrogen, ideal behavior is approximated at temperatures around room temperature and pressures around normal atmospheric pressure.

In summary, the kinetic-molecular model makes two simplifying but false assumptions. Therefore it does not correspond exactly to real situations. The approximations are valid under most ordinary conditions, however, and the theory is very useful. Knowing what the limitations of the theory are and why they exist enables chemists to use it with appropriate modifications when necessary. Scientific progress depends upon many such simplifications of the real world.

13–4 Section Review

1. Write the ideal gas equation. Identify each variable, indicating the units that are commonly used.

2. Why does the value of the gas constant depend on its units?

3. Why must the temperature in the ideal gas equation be in kelvins?

4. What are the assumptions of the kinetic-molecular theory that are not valid for real gases?

5. **Theme Trace—Stability** Show that the laws of Boyle, Charles, and Avogadro are contained in the ideal gas equation.

13-5 How Gases Work

What happens to a helium-filled party balloon if you let go of the string? You probably know from experience that it will float up and away. Does a balloon that is filled with air from your lungs also behave this way? You probably know that it does not. Why do these two balloons behave differently? If you hypothesize that it is due to the difference in density between air and helium, you are correct. Just how do these densities differ?

Lifting Power of Gases

Because of their low density, some gases can be used to inflate lighter-than-air craft such as balloons and blimps. In order for a balloon to rise in air, it must weigh less than the air it is displacing. If the air is more dense than the balloon, the air will slide under the balloon and force it upward—just as water forces a submerged log upward. In order for a balloon to rise, it has to be filled with something that is not just a little lighter than air, but considerably lighter than air. The gas the balloon is filled with must be light enough to compensate for the material making up the balloon, hardware such as valves and fixtures, and the human passengers. As you know, none of these objects is remotely close to being lighter than air!

How can you identify such a gas? You need to look for one whose density is less than the density of air. The ideal gas equation can also be used to compare densities of different gases. **Because the density of a gas depends on its pressure, temperature, and molar mass—variables contained in the ideal gas equation—all of these variables can theoretically be adjusted to give low density.** However, if the pressure of the gas within a balloon were significantly less than that of the atmosphere, the balloon would be crushed. So practically, there are two ways to achieve a low density: by choosing a gas with a low molar mass or by heating the gas—usually air—inside the balloon.

Gases that have potential as lifting gases include ammonia (NH_3) and methane (CH_4). Ammonia is a corrosive gas that dissolves in water to produce a solution of ammonium hydroxide—the liquid used as a household cleaner. Methane is the primary constituent of natural gas, which is piped into homes for cooking and heating because it burns readily. It should be obvious to you, then, that neither is practical to use as a lifting gas in lighter-than-air craft.

Figure 13-28 *Here you see a radar balloon floating near the coast of Key West, Florida. Is the density of the gas in the balloon greater than or less than the density of air? How do you know?*

Figure 13–29 *In 1937, the passenger airship* Hindenburg *caught fire and crashed while trying to land at Lakehurst, New Jersey. How did this incident lead to the use of helium in modern dirigibles?*

The two principal lifting gases are hydrogen (H_2) and helium (He). Hydrogen, which can be prepared in a number of simple chemical reactions, has been readily available for more than 200 years. In fact, hydrogen was once the principal gas used for inflating lighter-than-air craft. However, hydrogen burns with incredible speed and gives off tremendous heat. This reaction might be familiar to you as the explosive reaction that drives a rocket engine. The flammability of hydrogen-filled, lighter-than-air craft was always a problem, the most notable result of which was the spectacular accidental explosion of the airship *Hindenburg* in 1937.

Interest in the development of lighter-than-air craft for military and commercial purposes has been and continues to be intense. Because of the dangers involved with the use of hydrogen, only helium is used today. Helium has less lifting power than hydrogen because its molar mass is twice that of hydrogen. Helium is also rare and expensive, occurring in the United States mainly in natural gas fields in Texas and adjoining regions. However, helium, the first member in the family of noble gases, has no tendency whatsoever to burn. This safety factor overrides all other considerations. So when you see that funny looking vehicle known as a blimp floating overhead, you are looking at an enormous bag of helium!

⟨ *Historical Perspective*

The Ozone Hole—Worse Before it Gets Better?

You have probably read news stories about an "ozone hole" in the Earth's atmosphere. Just what is the ozone hole and how does it affect life on our planet?

The Earth's atmosphere is made up of several gases, as you have just learned. The pressure, temperature, and composition of the atmosphere vary with altitude. Like a birthday cake, the atmosphere is divided into layers. The layer nearest the Earth, the troposphere, is the scene of nearly all life and human activity. The next layer, the stratosphere, is where ozone gas is found. Ozone (O_3) is a form of oxygen produced when a molecule of oxygen (O_2) combines with an atom of oxygen (O). Chemically, the properties of ozone are quite different from those of oxygen. In the stratosphere, ozone molecules absorb the major portion of the incoming ultraviolet (UV) radiation from the sun. Ultraviolet radiation, you will recall, is a high-energy form of electromagnetic radiation. Exposure to UV radiation is extremely hazardous to living things. It can cause cancer, blindness, mutations, and damage to crops on land as well as to life in the oceans.

In the 1970s, atmospheric data began to reveal that there might be a hole in the ozone layer. Over the past 20 years, more and more data have indicated the existence of a large hole over the South Pole during the winter months and a similar, but smaller, hole emerging over the North Pole. In addition, an overall thinning of the ozone layer seems to be occurring steadily.

Experiments have shown that a group of molecules called chlorofluorocarbons (CFCs) are involved in chemical reactions that break up the ozone molecules. CFCs are chlorine- and fluorine-substituted compounds of carbon

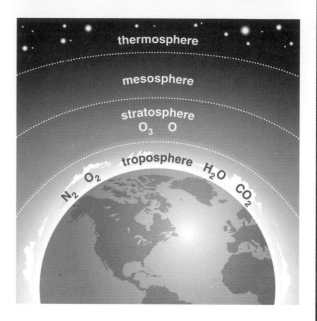

that have been extensively used as aerosol propellants, as refrigerants in freezers and air conditioners, and as solvents in industry.

If the amount of CFCs in the atmosphere is reduced significantly, the ozone layer can be recovered. To this end, the United States banned the use of CFCs as aerosol propellants in 1978 and the major industrial nations reached an agreement to end the use and production of CFCs by the year 2000. The chemical industry has come up with safer substitutes for the banned CFCs. But these substitutes are often more expensive than CFCs and the developing nations of the world may resist the use of more expensive substitutes just when they are trying to achieve rapid economic growth in their desire to catch up with the industrial world. Will we be able to reach a balance between economic progress and environmental responsibility?

The other method of lowering the density of a gas at a constant pressure is to raise its temperature. Hot-air balloons, which have been in use for more than 200 years, are currently very popular for recreational flights. A modern hot-air balloon is open at the bottom where it is fitted with a propane burner. The burner sends a stream of combustion products and heated air up into the bag of the balloon.

The advantages of a hot-air balloon are that the gas that inflates the balloon is much less expensive than helium and much safer than hydrogen. However, the lift available from hot air is relatively weak. So weak, in fact, that to achieve the same lift as that obtained from helium, the air inside the balloon would need to be heated to a temperature of 2146 K, or 1873°C. This temperature is higher than the melting point of most solids! Needless to say, this kind of density difference is not feasible in a hot-air balloon. But such a density difference is not necessary for the enjoyment of recreational hot-air ballooning because only light loads are involved.

Gas Effusion

Earlier in this chapter you read that diffusion is the process by which the particles of one substance move through another. Because of diffusion, a gas with an odor can be smelled at one end of a room when it has only recently been released at the other end. **Effusion,** a process closely related to diffusion, is the movement of atoms or molecules through a hole so tiny that they do not stream through but instead pass through one particle at a time. Experiments have shown that some gases effuse and diffuse faster than others. For example, hydrogen effuses faster than helium, which in turn effuses faster than oxygen. Do you see a pattern here? If you noticed that hydrogen particles are the lightest and oxygen particles are the heaviest, then you are right on target! Lighter gases effuse and diffuse faster than heavier gases because, at a given temperature, the particles of the lighter gas have greater speeds than the particles of the heavier gas.

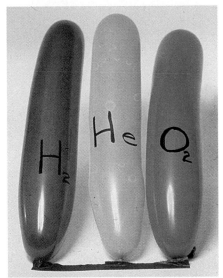

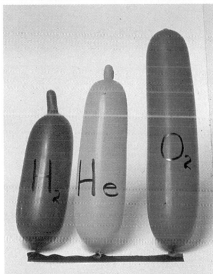

Figure 13–30 *The balloons in the photograph on the top are shown before effusion has taken place. The same balloons are shown in the photograph on the bottom after effusion. Which of the three gases effuses fastest? Slowest?*

13–5 Section Review

1. Explain how gas density is related to molar mass and temperature.
2. Describe two ways in which a balloon can get lift in air.
3. **Critical Thinking—Developing models** The density of a gas is given by the equation $d = P\mathcal{M}/RT$. Derive this from the ideal gas equation.

Testing Charles's Law

Problem

How does temperature affect the size (volume) of a balloon?

Suggested Materials (per group)

round balloon
Celsius thermometer
metric tape measure
permanent marker
ice
large container (washtub, bucket)

tripod
Bunsen burner
400-mL beaker
tongs

Suggested Procedure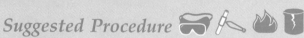

1. Devise an experiment to determine how temperature affects the size of a balloon.
2. Write down the steps of your experimental procedure. The drawing below may provide you with some help in writing your procedure.
3. Prepare a data table, similar to the one shown, to record all of your data.
4. Conduct your experiment after having your teacher approve your procedure and data table.
5. From your data, determine what effects ice and steam have on the volume of a balloon.

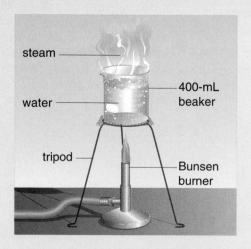

steam

water

400-mL beaker

tripod

Bunsen burner

Observations

1. How did the circumference of the balloon change as the temperature was increased?
2. Make a graph of your circumference versus temperature data.
3. How is the circumference of a balloon related to its temperature?

	Ice	Room	Steam
Temperature (°C)			
Temperature (K)			
Circumference (cm)			
Volume (cm³)			

Analysis and Conclusions

1. Calculate the volume of your balloon. First calculate the radius of your balloon from its circumference, then substitute this value of the radius in the formula for the volume of a sphere.
2. Draw a graph of volume versus Kelvin temperature.
3. What can you conclude about the relationship between the volume and temperature of a fixed amount of gas at constant temperature?
4. **On Your Own** Confirm the validity of Charles's law by comparing the size of a helium balloon at room temperature with its size in the freezer compartment of your refrigerator.

STUDY GUIDE

Summarizing Key Concepts

13–1 A Model to Explain Gas Behavior

- Gases do not have a definite shape or volume; they have low densities. They are easily compressed. Gases exert pressure.
- The behavior of gases is explained in terms of the kinetic-molecular theory.

13–2 Measuring Gases

- The physical behavior of all gases is adequately determined by measuring the values of four quantities: the amount of gas (n), volume (V), temperature (T), and pressure (P).
- The air around us exerts a pressure called atmospheric pressure.
- 0°C and 1 atm are designated as standard temperature and pressure (STP).

13–3 The Gas Laws

- Boyle's law states that the pressure and volume of a gas are inversely proportional to each other (constant T, n).
- Charles's law states that the volume of a gas is directly proportional to its absolute temperature (constant P, n).

- Avogadro's law states that at constant T and P, equal volumes of different gases contain the same number of particles.
- Dalton's law states that the pressure of a mixture of gases is the sum of the partial pressures of the component gases.

13–4 The Ideal Gas Law

- The gas laws are combined into the ideal gas equation, $PV = nRT$, which mathematically relates the four gas variables.
- Real gas particles do have volume and do exert forces upon each other. This results in real gas behavior that deviates substantially from ideal at relatively high pressures and low temperatures.

13–5 How Gases Work

- Gases with densities lower than the density of air can be used in lighter-than-air craft. Densities of gases increase with increasing molar mass and decrease with increasing temperature.
- Lighter gases effuse and diffuse faster than heavier gases.

Reviewing Key Terms

Define each term in a complete sentence.

13–1 A Model to Explain Gas Behavior

diffusion
elastic
kinetic-molecular theory

13–2 Measuring Gases

atmospheric pressure
barometer
manometer
STP

13–3 The Gas Laws

absolute zero
molar volume
partial pressure

13–4 The Ideal Gas Law

ideal gas
real gas
gas constant

13–5 How Gases Work

effusion

CHAPTER REVIEW

Content Review

Multiple Choice
Choose the letter of the answer that best completes each statement.

1. All gases
   (a) have high densities.
   (b) have no definite shape or volume.
   (c) are lighter than air.
   (d) exhibit similar chemical behavior.

2. According to the kinetic-molecular theory, gas particles
   (a) are spaced far apart.
   (b) are constantly moving.
   (c) have mass.
   (d) all of the above

3. Atmospheric pressure
   (a) is always 760 mm Hg.
   (b) can be measured by a barometer.
   (c) is greater on Mount Everest than at sea level.
   (d) exists because air is a mixture of gases.

4. Which of the following is not equivalent to the remaining three?
   (a) 100,000 Pa   (c) 1 atm
   (b) 760 mm Hg   (d) 101.3 kPa

5. The gas law that describes the relationship between volume and temperature is
   (a) Boyle's law.   (c) Avogadro's law.
   (b) Charles's law.   (d) Dalton's law.

6. Which of the following expresses an inverse proportionality?
   (a) As n increases, V increases.
   (b) As T decreases, P decreases.
   (c) As P increases, V decreases.
   (d) As n increases, P increases.

7. The density of a balloon will decrease if
   (a) more gas is added to the balloon.
   (b) a higher molar mass gas is substituted.
   (c) the temperature of the gas is increased.
   (d) none of the above

8. A real gas behaves most ideally at
   (a) high T and low P.
   (b) low P and high V.
   (c) low P and low T.
   (d) high P and high T.

True or False
If the statement is true, write "true." If it is false, change the underlined word or words to make the statement true.

9. All gases are <u>more</u> dense than their corresponding liquids.

10. All gases exhibit <u>the same</u> physical behavior.

11. The gas laws are based on <u>quantitative</u> measurements of gases.

12. According to the ideal gas equation, the volume of a gas is <u>inversely</u> proportional to the number of moles.

13. For a certain sample of gas particles, the average kinetic energy depends on <u>density</u>.

14. An increase in the temperature of a gas sample causes the gas to exert <u>greater</u> pressure.

Concept Mapping
Complete the following concept map for Section 13–1. Refer to pages xviii–xix to construct a concept map for the entire chapter.

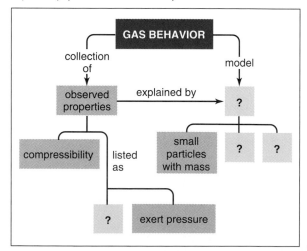

Concept Mastery

Discuss each of the following in a brief paragraph.

15. State Boyle's and Charles's laws in your own words and account for them in terms of the kinetic-molecular theory.

16. What is the significance of an absolute temperature scale?

17. State Dalton's law and explain the term partial pressure.

18. Why does a hot-air balloon not have a density advantage comparable to that of a helium balloon?

19. What are the two false assumptions of the kinetic-molecular theory of gases?

20. Elaborate on this statement: "The ideal gas equation is simply a combination of the laws of Boyle, Charles, and Avogadro."

21. A gas exerts pressure because its particles strike the surface of its container. Explain this using the kinetic-molecular theory.

22. Tying it Together Explain how the statement "Real gases behave ideally under most ordinary conditions of temperature and pressure" represents *stability* of gas behavior.

Critical Thinking and Problem Solving

Use the skills you have developed in this chapter to answer each of the following.

23. Making inferences You are given a container of 1 mole of helium gas (He), and an identical container of 1 mole of oxygen gas (O_2). Both gases are at STP. Determine whether the following statements are true or false.

(a) Both gas samples have the same number of particles (molecules).

(b) Both gas samples have the same number of atoms.

(c) Both gas samples have the same mass.

(d) Both gas samples have the same density

(e) Both gas samples have the same average kinetic energy.

(f) The particles of both gas samples have the same average speed.

(g) If there was an identical pinhole in both containers, both samples would effuse at the same rate.

(h) The actual volume occupied by the gas particles is the same for both gas samples.

(i) Both are ideal gases.

24. Drawing conclusions Why do the gases of the Earth's atmosphere not escape into the vacuum of outer space?

25. Applying concepts A certain gas is usually transported in a high-pressure cylinder. You have been asked to transport twice the original amount of gas. What are the different options you could consider and what might be the drawbacks of each?

26. Using the writing process Imagine that you are riding an oxygen molecule as it moves around near a mountain top. In a paragraph or two, describe what you see and experience as the oxygen molecule goes about its business.

PROBLEM BANK

Group A

27. Two containers have an equal number of moles of helium and hydrogen gases. Which container has the greater number of atoms? *(Section 13–1)*

28. What is the ratio of the average kinetic energies of hydrogen and helium at the same temperature? *(Section 13–1)*

29. The atmospheric pressure on a rainy day in Seattle is 99,100 Pa. How high will the mercury column in a barometer be on that day? *(Section 13–2)*

30. What is the pressure in Pa inside a container if the mercury level in the manometer arm attached to the container stands 18.5 mm higher than the mercury level in the manometer arm that is open to the atmosphere? The atmospheric pressure as determined with a barometer is 103,000 Pa. *(Section 13–2)*

31. A manometer is attached to a closed container of a gas. The other end of the manometer is open to the atmosphere. The levels of the mercury are the same on either side of the U-tube, and the atmospheric pressure is 766 mm Hg. Calculate the pressure of the gas in the container in Pa. *(Section 13–2)*

32. The mercury level on the container side of a manometer is 47 mm lower than the level on the open side. You have measured the atmospheric pressure using a barometer and it is 771 mm Hg. What is the pressure of the gas in the container in atm? In kPa? *(Section 13–2)*

33. A gas sample occupies a volume of 0.923 L at a temperature of 25°C. What is the Charles's law constant for this sample including units? *(Section 13–3)*

34. Two hot-air balloon envelopes are being inflated on a field. The envelope of balloon A is 1.25 times the volume of the envelope of balloon B. At the same temperature and pressure, which balloon will contain the larger mass of air after they are both in-flated to 75% of their capacity? *(Section 13–3)*

35. Suppose you are in the laboratory repeating Robert Boyle's experiment on the "spring of air." You have a J-tube that is open on the long end and sealed on the short end. Some air is trapped between the mercury and the sealed short end. For the first measurement, the height of the mercury on the long side of the J-tube is 10.4 cm higher than on the short side and the volume of the air is 9.40 mL. Then more mercury is added so that the level on the long side is 18.1 cm higher than on the short side. What is the volume of the trapped air now? The atmospheric pressure throughout the experiment reads 75.6 cm Hg. *(Section 13–3)*

36. A balloon has a volume of 1.75 L at a temperature of 25°C. What will be the volume of the balloon if you take it out into the winter cold air at −15°C? *(Section 13–3)*

37. A gas mixture contains hydrogen, helium, neon, and argon. The total pressure of the mixture is 93.6 kPa. The partial pressures of helium, neon, and argon are 15.4 kPa, 25.7 kPa, and 35.6 kPa, respectively. What is the pressure exerted by hydrogen? *(Section 13–3)*

38. Complete the following table for argon gas using the ideal gas law. *(Section 13–4)*

Pressure	748 mm Hg	—	1.21 atm
Volume	—	5.25 L	465 L
Temperature	200°C	373 K	—
Moles	—	0.0857	25.0
Mass	12.5 g	—	—

39. What is the volume of a 24.7 mol gas sample that exerts a pressure of 0.999 atm at a temperature of 305 K? *(Section 13–4)*

40. To what temperature would you have to heat a 1.90 mol sample of a gas at 1.05 atm pressure to get its volume up to 50.0 L? *(Section 13–4)*

41. What is the volume in liters of a sample of 100.0 g of O_2 (g) at 298 K and a pressure of 3.33 atm? *(Section 13–4)*

42. Which gas diffuses faster at the same pressure and temperature, CO_2 or CO? *(Section 13–5)*

Group B

43. Which sample contains the greater number of hydrogen atoms: 1.0 L of CH_4 or 1.0 L of H_2? Both are at STP.

44. A weather balloon at launch is partially inflated with 3.00×10^4 L of helium at STP. What will be the volume of helium at an altitude of 7 km, where the pressure is 0.41 atm and the temperature is −20°C?

45. How many kilograms of oxygen (O_2) are contained in an oxygen sample that occupies 505 L at 5.76 atm and 273 K?

46. How many liters of hydrogen will it take to react completely with 4.65 L of oxygen gas to produce water, provided that both gases are at the same temperature and pressure?

47. How many nitrogen molecules are contained in 1.00 L of nitrogen gas at 1.00 atm and 298 K? How many nitrogen atoms?

48. What are the partial pressures of the gases in air if the total pressure is 1.15 atm? (Hint: You know the percentages of the atmospheric gases in the air. The partial pressures must add up to the given total pressure.)

49. Every year thousands of tons of limestone, or calcium carbonate, are decomposed by heating into carbon dioxide (CO_2) and calcium oxide (CaO), or quicklime, according to the reaction,

$$CaCO_3 \ (s) \rightarrow CO_2 \ (g) + CaO \ (s)$$

How many liters of carbon dioxide at 1.03 atm and a temperature of 950.°C will be produced if 1.00 kg of calcium carbonate ($CaCO_3$) is decomposed?

50. If a round balloon has a radius of 10.0 cm at 273 K, what will the radius be at 373 K?

51. Scuba divers breathe a mixture containing 10% O_2, 10% N_2, and 80% He.
(a) What is the molar mass of this mixture?
(b) Calculate the density of this mixture using the equation $d = P\mathcal{M}/RT$ and compare it with the density of air ($\mathcal{M} = 29$ g/mol).

52. A bicycle tire is inflated to a pressure of 60 lb/in.^{2} at 12°C. What is the pressure in the tire if the tire gets heated to 32°C? You may assume that the volume of the tire does not change.

53. The N_2 gas inside a fire extinguisher is pressurized to 1345 kPa. What is the density of the N_2 at 25°C? How does this compare with the density of N_2 in the air you breathe?

54. Rank the following gases in order of increasing effusion rate: (a) C_2H_6 (b) SO_3 (c) O_3 (d) Xe (e) H_2

55. The balanced equation for the combustion of octane, one of the components of gasoline, is shown below:

$$2 \ C_8H_{18} \ (g) + 25 \ O_2 \ (g) \rightarrow$$
$$16 \ CO_2 \ (g) + 18 \ H_2O \ (g)$$

The volume of one cylinder of an automobile engine is 0.500 L. If the air intake is at 45°C and 1.0 atm pressure, calculate the grams of octane that the fuel injection system should send to the cylinder to completely react with the O_2 in the air. Assume that air is 20 percent oxygen.

14 Liquids and Solids

Have you ever been caught in the rain on a cold, wintry day? If the conditions were just right (or maybe just wrong), the rain turned to ice the instant it touched something solid. That something might have been the sidewalk, your ski parka, or the windshield of your car.

Freezing rain is caused by a warm layer of air on top of a cold layer. Drops of rain form high up in the warm layer. As they fall through the cold layer, they get colder—even colder than the temperature at which water normally freezes to ice. But the raindrops do not freeze until they strike a solid object.

As you might have already guessed, there is a connection between the temperature of a substance and the physical state in which it is found. In this chapter, you will learn more about this connection.

In winter, the Upper Geyser Basin in Yellowstone National Park provides a glimpse of water in its solid, liquid, and gaseous states. This pre-Columbian mask has existed in the solid state for centuries.

Chem Journal

YOU AND YOUR WORLD
Water, ice, and snow have been subjects of beautiful artistic works for centuries. Imagine a situation in which ice changes to water or water changes to ice. Draw a picture or write a poem that describes the image.

14–1 Condensed States of Matter

Guide for Reading
- How does the kinetic-molecular theory account for the physical properties of the condensed states?
- What are the three types of intermolecular forces of attraction?

What do steam rising from a tea kettle, water in a swimming pool, and ice on a frozen pond have in common? You are right if you said that they are all forms of the same compound—H_2O. Yet as you know, they have very different properties—properties that range from an easily compressible, freely moving gas to an almost incompressible, rigid solid. In the previous chapter, you studied the physical behavior of gases. Now you are going to learn about liquids and solids. Liquids and solids are collectively referred to as the **condensed states** of matter because substances in these states have substantially higher densities than they do in the gaseous state. In order to understand this and other properties of liquids and solids, you will again apply the ideas of the kinetic-molecular theory.

Figure 14–1 A water slide is a fun-filled way to cool off in summer. Because water is a liquid, it flows. As ice, it is used as the building material for this igloo in Alaska. In what other ways do liquids differ from solids?

Kinetic-Molecular Theory Applied to Liquids and Solids

You have already seen how gas behavior can be accounted for by the kinetic-molecular theory. That explanation was based on the assumption (valid under most ordinary conditions) that the attractive forces among gas particles are very weak. The average kinetic energy of the gas particles is large compared to these weak attractive forces. Thus gas particles act essentially independently of one another. In the kinetic-molecular theory, gases are treated as a collection of independent, widely separated, rapidly moving particles.

The kinetic-molecular theory can be applied to liquids and solids as well. In fact this theory is also called the kinetic-molecular theory of matter (including liquids, solids, and gases) and it provides a good framework for exploring the nature of the condensed states of matter. Figure 14–2 shows a comparison of the three states. You may find it helpful to refer to this diagram as you read the descriptions that follow.

As you can see in the diagram, the particles of a gas are far apart from each other, occupy their entire container, and are in rapid motion. By contrast, the particles of a liquid remain close together and do not occupy their entire container. They are, however, in constant motion. And like the particles of a gas, liquid particles also collide with each other and with the walls of their container. But because liquid particles, unlike gas particles, are close together, they can move only a short distance before a collision changes their direction of motion. You can imagine what this is like if you have ever tried to walk through a crowd of people. You can only take a few steps before you bump into someone! In a similar way, the particles of a liquid are crowded together. Although they can move freely and randomly, they can move only short distances. This type of movement allows liquids to flow and to take the shape of their container without filling it completely as gases do. It also explains why diffusion is much slower in liquids than it is in gases.

Figure 14–2 *The differences between the three states of matter are illustrated in this diagram. The representative particles can be atoms, ions, or molecules. Which state is least dense?*

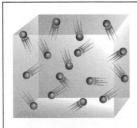

gas
total disorder; particles have freedom of motion; particles far apart from one another

liquid
disorder; particles are free to move relative to one another; particles close together

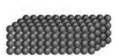

crystalline solid
ordered arrangement; particles can vibrate, but remain in fixed positions; particles close together

Physical Properties of the States of Matter

Gas	Liquid	Solid
1. highly compressible	only slightly compressible	only slightly compressible
2. low density	high density	high density
3. fills container completely	does not expand to fill container– has a definite volume	rigidly retains its volume
4. assumes the shape of the container it occupies	assumes the shape of the container it occupies	retains its own shape
5. rapid diffusion	slow diffusion	extremely slow diffusion; occurs only at surfaces
6. high expansion on heating	low expansion on heating	low expansion on heating

Figure 14–3 *The table lists the physical properties of the states of matter. In which state does matter retain its shape?*

The fact that the particles of a liquid are close together explains two other important properties of liquids—density and compressibility. Because the particles are crowded, the densities of liquids are much higher than the densities of gases. And because the particles are already close together, it is difficult to force them any closer. Thus liquids are not very compressible. All of these observations might lead you to conclude that the attractive forces between the particles of a liquid are substantially stronger than those between the particles of a gas—and you would be correct. Yet these forces are still not strong enough to hold the particles in fixed positions.

As you can see in Figure 14–2, a solid shows a more ordered arrangement of particles in which the particles are not free to move around. Their movement is limited to vibrations while they remain locked in their fixed positions in the solid. As you might expect, the attractive forces between the particles of a solid are stronger than those in gases and liquids. The particles cannot overcome these forces and move away from each other. Thus a solid has a fixed volume as well as a fixed shape. In other words, solids do not flow. Solids have high densities and are virtually incompressible. Can you now explain why diffusion in solids is practically nonexistent? A comparison of the physical properties of gases, liquids, and solids is shown in Figure 14–3.

You know from experience that water is a liquid when it flows from a faucet, a solid when it freezes in an ice-cube tray, and a gas when it rises from a steaming tea kettle. If you were asked what accounts for the different states of water, you would probably say temperature. And you would be correct. But what about the three substances in Figure 14–2? They are all at room

CHEM Exploration

Is It Crystal or Is It Clear?

Have you ever seen light-colored crystals form in a jar of honey? Usually this happens when a jar of honey is left sitting on a shelf for a long time. More and more crystals form until eventually the entire jar is filled with them. This "solid honey" spreads quite easily and tastes as good as the normal liquid form.

Suppose you wanted to make solid honey but didn't want to wait for weeks and weeks to get it. Can you think of a way to speed up the crystallizing process? Try this. Put a jar of honey in the freezer compartment of your refrigerator. The next day take the jar out to examine the honey. What does the honey look like? How does it spread on toast? What happens when you allow the honey to warm up? What kind of substance did you form in the jar when you cooled it? What is the basis of your conclusion?

Figure 14–4 *In winter, ice formed on airplane wings reduces the lift during takeoff. So airplanes need to be deiced prior to takeoff. How is this task accomplished?*

temperature, yet they are found in three different states. Some factor other than temperature must account for their difference in state. **According to the kinetic-molecular theory, the state of a substance at room temperature depends on the strength of the attractions between its particles.** Substances in which particles are held together by strong forces of attraction are solids at room temperature. Substances in which the attractive forces between particles are of moderate strength are typically liquids at room temperature. And substances in which the forces of attraction between particles are very weak are gases at room temperature.

Let's now return to the example of water. Recall from Chapter 13 that temperature is simply a measure of the average kinetic energy of the particles of a substance. At different temperatures, the particles, or molecules, of water have different amounts of kinetic energy. Below 0°C, water is a solid because the kinetic energy of the water molecules is too low to overcome the strong attraction between the molecules. Thus the molecules remain "bound" to their fixed positions. At temperatures above 0°C, however, the molecules have enough kinetic energy to "get away" from each other and flow. The molecules are no longer held together rigidly as ice, but move easily as a flowing liquid. Above a temperature of 100°C, the average kinetic energy of the molecules is so high that they can—and do—totally escape from each other to fill the entire space available to them. The same molecules now exist as a gas. Notice that we used the term molecule in place of the general term particle in talking about water. Water, like almost all other substances that are liquids at room temperature, consists of molecules. It is important to keep in mind that the temperatures of 0°C and 100°C apply only to changes of state in water. You will study changes of state in greater detail in Section 14–4.

Intermolecular Forces

You have just discovered the important connection between the strength of the attractive forces between particles of a substance and the state in which the substance exists. Your next step is to explore the nature of these forces. How do they arise? What does their strength depend on? How do they determine the physical properties of a substance?

Before we begin to answer these questions, it might be helpful to briefly review some important concepts about chemical bonding. Recall that atoms of elements bond in different ways to achieve a more stable arrangement of electrons. There are three categories of bonding, two of which you studied in Chapter 7. The three categories of bonding are ionic, metallic, and covalent bonding.

Ionic bonds involve the transfer of electrons and typically form between metallic and nonmetallic elements. This is because

Figure 14–5 *Stalactites (left) are an example of an ionic compound: calcium carbonate. The young girl (right) is adorned with Bedoya jewelry. Since ancient times, gold, a precious metal, has been used to make beautiful ornaments.*

a metallic element can achieve a more stable, noble gas electron configuration by losing one or more of its valence electrons. A nonmetallic element can achieve a noble gas electron configuration by gaining one or more electrons from the metal. A transfer of electrons results in the formation of oppositely charged ions that attract each other. This force of attraction is called an ionic bond. All ionic compounds are solids at room temperature. What does this tell you about the strength of attraction between oppositely charged ions?

Metallic bonds hold atoms together in a metallic substance. Atoms of metals achieve a more stable electron arrangement by sharing their valence electrons among themselves. Metallic bonds are the attractive forces between fixed positive ions and the moving valence electrons in a metal. Do you think metallic bonds are strong? You are right if you said yes. Are all metals solids at room temperature? Just about! One familiar exception is mercury, which is a liquid at room temperature. Two other metals, cesium and gallium, have melting points slightly above room temperature and therefore melt readily when warmed. The remaining metallic elements are quite comfortably solids at room temperature. We will discuss the properties of ionic and metallic solids later in this chapter.

You now know that all ionic substances and almost all metals are solids at room temperature. But what kinds of bonds hold gases and liquids together? Gases and liquids exhibit the second type of bonding that you studied in Chapter 7—covalent bonding. Strong covalent bonds form between nonmetallic elements as they share pairs of electrons to achieve a more stable, noble gas electron arrangement. Recall that covalently bonded atoms form units that are referred to as molecules. Molecular substances can be solids, liquids, or gases at room temperature. How is this possible? you might be wondering. Shouldn't molecular substances be solids at room temperature because of the strong

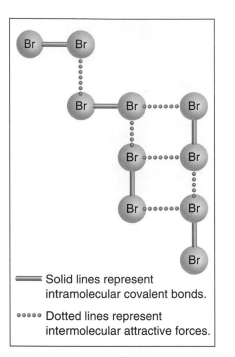

Solid lines represent
intramolecular covalent bonds.

••••• Dotted lines represent
intermolecular attractive forces.

Figure 14–6 *Bromine
molecules (Br₂) illustrate
the distinction between
intramolecular bonds and
intermolecular forces. Which of
the two represents the stronger
attractive force?*

Figure 14–7 *The table lists
the boiling points of the
liquefied noble gases. What is
the boiling point of helium in
kelvins?*

Boiling Points of the Noble Gases

Element	Boiling Point (°C)
He	−269.0
Ne	−246.0
Ar	−185.9
Kr	−152.9
Xe	−107.1
Rn	−67.0

covalent bonds between atoms? To answer these questions, it is necessary to make a very important distinction. Covalent bonds exist within the molecule, holding the atoms together in a specific geometrical shape. Covalent bonds constitute **intramolecular forces,** or forces that exist inside the molecule. (The prefix *intra-* means within or inside.) Whether a substance is a molecular solid, liquid, or gas at room temperature does not depend on the strength of intramolecular forces. Rather, it depends on how strongly the molecules of that substance attract each other. Think back to the example of the different states of water. In each case, we discussed the forces of attraction between the water molecules, not between the hydrogen and oxygen atoms in each molecule. The forces of attraction between neighboring molecules are called **intermolecular forces.** (The prefix *inter-* means between or among.)

Just how strong are intermolecular forces? Because molecular substances can be gases, liquids, or solids, intermolecular forces must span a wide range of strengths. Yet compared with the strengths of ionic, covalent, or even metallic bonds, intermolecular forces are substantially weaker. The energy associated with an intermolecular force is typically less than 15 percent of the energy associated with an ionic or a covalent bond. For example, it takes 463 kilojoules of energy to break a mole of O–H bonds in water molecules. But it takes only 6 kilojoules to melt a mole of ice into water and 41 kilojoules to convert a mole of water into steam. When ice melts or water changes into steam no intramolecular covalent bonds (O–H bonds) are broken. Only intermolecular forces are involved in changes of state. In other words, the H_2O molecules remain intact when ice changes to water and water changes to steam.

There are a number of different types of intermolecular forces. In the following pages we will discuss the nature of three such forces of attraction between molecules: dispersion forces, dipole-dipole forces, and hydrogen bonds.

DISPERSION FORCES The noble gases exist as single atoms and have very little tendency to form covalent bonds with other atoms because of their stable electron configurations. Yet, at sufficiently high pressures and low temperatures, these gases can be condensed to liquids. This means that some kind of weak force can hold these atoms close together in the liquid or solid state. What is the nature of such a force and how do chemists measure its strength?

When you heat water, its temperature increases until it boils at 100°C. At this temperature, the average kinetic energy of its molecules is sufficient to overcome the intermolecular forces holding them together. What do you think would happen if the intermolecular forces in water were even stronger than they are? Would water still boil at 100°C? The answer is no. Boiling would occur at a higher temperature because a higher average kinetic energy would be required to overcome a stronger intermolecular force. The boiling point of a liquid—the temperature at which a liquid boils—is thus a measure of the strength of the attractive forces between molecules in the liquid state. The stronger the attractive forces, the higher the boiling point.

Take a look at the boiling points of the liquefied noble gases shown in Figure 14–7. Do you see a trend as you go down the column of noble gases? The boiling point clearly increases with atomic size and mass. So the strength of the attractive force between noble gas atoms must also increase with atomic size and mass.

Now that you know how the strength of this attractive force is measured, you can turn your attention to its origin and nature. Each noble gas atom consists of an extremely "rigid," high-density nucleus surrounded by its extremely "soft," low-density electron cloud. The net, or overall, charge on the atom is zero because the number of electrons (negative) in the electron cloud equals the number of protons (positive) in the nucleus. In an isolated atom, the electron cloud is a perfectly symmetrical sphere. There is a positive charge on the nucleus and an equivalent negative charge evenly distributed over the electron cloud. There is no separation of charge because the centers of positive and negative charge coincide. Refer to Figure 14–8 to help you visualize this idea.

Figure 14–8 *A symmetrical, spherical atom has no separation of charge (a). The electrons are distributed uniformly around the nucleus. At any time, however, such an atom can lose its spherical shape and become a temporary dipole (b). A temporary dipole can distort the electron cloud of a symmetrical atom and induce a dipole in it (c).*

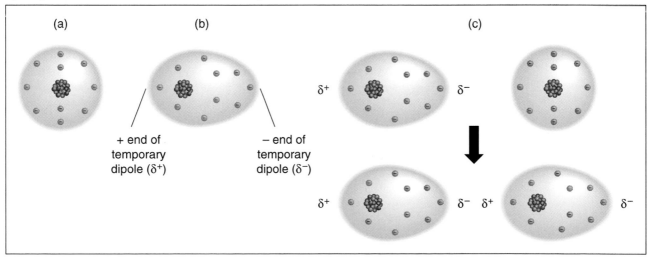

Liquid Crystals

Do you know what calculator display panels, watches, laptop computer screens, and this bug have in common? They all make use of the ability of liquid-crystalline substances to alter their appearance or color when an electric potential is applied or the temperature is changed.

A liquid-crystalline substance has a temperature range over which it can flow like a liquid. Yet its ordered molecular arrangement gives it some of the properties of a crystal. This order can be altered by applying an electric potential or by changing the temperature. Color changes occur because different molecular arrangements reflect different frequencies of light.

It is possible, however, for an atom to lose its spherical shape for short periods of time. This can result in a temporary dipole. Do you remember the definition of a dipole from Chapter 8? A dipole consists of a separation of the two opposite charges, + and −, by some distance. Figure 14–8 shows how the electrons in an atom can shift so as to concentrate on one side of the nucleus. As a result of such a shift, one end of the atom is relatively more positive than the opposite end, which becomes relatively more negative. In other words, the centers of positive and negative charges do not coincide. The atom now has a temporary dipole.

Such a temporary dipole on one atom can cause the formation of a temporary dipole on a neighboring atom. This happens because the negative end of the dipole repels electrons in an adjacent atom, causing them to shift position. A dipole is created in the adjacent atom. A dipole that is created by the presence of a neighboring dipole is called an **induced dipole.** In this manner temporary dipoles can be induced throughout a substance, as shown in Figure 14–8.

The very manner in which these dipoles are induced results in the negative end of the dipole of one atom being next to the positive end of another dipole. These unlike charges attract each other. Such a force of attraction between induced dipoles is called a **dispersion force.** Dispersion forces are present in all molecular substances.

In cases such as the noble gases, induced dipole dispersion forces are the only type of intermolecular forces that exist. You might ask why a force between individual noble gas atoms is called an intermolecular force. The answer is that by its origin, nature, and strength, it belongs to the category of intermolecular forces. This should not suggest, however, that noble gas atoms are molecules! To avoid confusion, think of the noble gases as monatomic molecules—molecules made up of just one atom.

The boiling points of the noble gases increase from helium to radon. This means that the dispersion forces become greater as the atoms become larger. Does this make sense? Yes, because the larger the electron cloud, the more easily it is distorted into a dipole. For this reason, larger atoms exert greater dispersion forces.

A similar trend can be seen among molecules. If the atoms in a molecule are large, relatively large temporary dipoles can be induced. If the atoms in a molecule are small, just the opposite is true. If the molecules themselves are very large, meaning that they consist of many atoms, the dispersion forces between them will also be correspondingly large. This is why dispersion forces increase with increasing molecular size and mass. For example, Br_2 has stronger dispersion forces than either H_2 or F_2. Would you expect Br_2 to have a higher or lower boiling point than H_2 or F_2?

DIPOLE-DIPOLE FORCES Dispersion forces depend on temporary dipoles induced in neighboring atoms. But as you may remember, some molecules have permanent dipoles. These molecules are called polar molecules. Polar molecules have a small positive charge at one end of the molecule and an equal negative charge at the other end. Attractions between opposite charges of neighboring permanent dipoles are called **dipole-dipole forces.**

A permanent dipole is a result of a covalent bond between two different atoms. Because the two atoms are not identical, there is a difference in their electronegativities. As a result, each atom acquires a partial charge. The more electronegative atom is said to have a partial negative charge. This charge is somewhere between 0 and -1. The other atom will have a partial positive charge equal in magnitude to the partial negative charge. These partial charges are shown by the lowercase Greek letter delta, δ^- or δ^+. The greater the difference in the electronegativities of the two atoms in the covalent bond, the greater the values of δ^- and δ^+, and the greater the dipole moment, or polarity, of the bond.

All diatomic molecules with polar bonds constitute permanent dipoles. What about the polarity of molecules with more than two atoms—also referred to as polyatomic molecules? These molecules can be polar or nonpolar depending on their geometric shape. For example, SO_2 is a polar molecule due to its angular shape, while CO_2 is nonpolar because it has a linear shape. The bonding and shape for both molecules are shown in Figure 14–9. The boiling point of SO_2 is $-10°C$ compared with $-78°C$ for CO_2. This indicates that the intermolecular forces are stronger between SO_2 molecules than between CO_2 molecules.

HYDROGEN BONDING A few molecular substances, such as HF and H_2O, have higher boiling points than can be accounted for either by dispersion forces or by dipole-dipole forces. The high boiling points of these substances indicate the presence of a stronger intermolecular force. What is the nature of this force?

The partial charges on atoms in a molecule are particularly large if one of the atoms in the covalent bond is hydrogen and the other atom is fluorine, oxygen, or nitrogen. This is because fluorine, oxygen, and nitrogen are the three most electronegative nonmetals, whereas hydrogen is one of the least electronegative nonmetals. Because of the large difference in electronegativities in the F–H, O–H, and N–H bonds, these bonds are very polar, giving rise to large δ^+ and δ^-. The large partial charges result in an extremely strong dipole-dipole force between the hydrogen atom of one molecule (δ^+) and the F, O, or N atom of another molecule (δ^-). This intermolecular force is so large that it is given a special name. It is called a **hydrogen bond.** See Figure 14–10 on page 466. In spite of its misleading name, a hydrogen bond is only a strong intermolecular force and not a covalent bond!

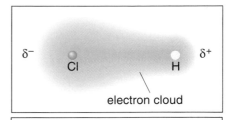

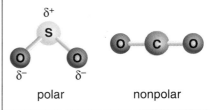

Figure 14–9 *The diagram on top shows diatomic HCl—a molecule with a permanent dipole. The chlorine atom attracts electrons more strongly and acquires a partial negative charge (δ^-). The hydrogen atom acquires a partial positive charge (δ^+). The diagram below compares two similar molecules: SO_2 and CO_2. Are the intermolecular forces stronger in SO_2 or CO_2?*

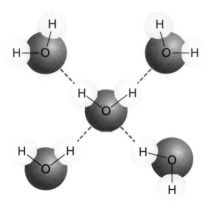

Figure 14–10 *The diagram shows hydrogen bonds between water molecules. The boiling points of several hydrogen compounds are plotted in the graph. Notice the abnormally high boiling points of H₂O, HF, and NH₃. What can you conclude about the intermolecular forces in CH₄?*

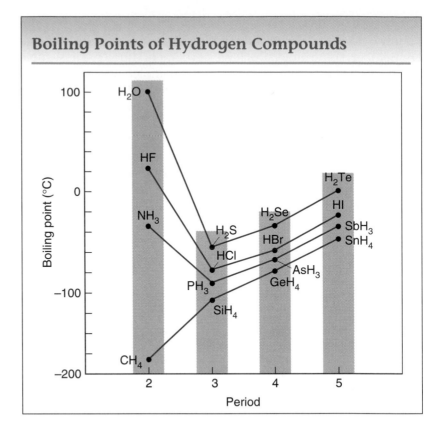

Boiling Points of Hydrogen Compounds

Of the liquids containing hydrogen bonds, water is by far the best known. The effect of hydrogen bonding on the boiling point of water can be seen by comparing the hydrogen compounds of the elements of Group 6A.

14–1 Section Review

1. Compare the physical properties of liquids and solids. How does the kinetic-molecular theory explain these properties?
2. Describe the three types of intermolecular forces.
3. Explain the difference between a chemical bond and an intermolecular force.
4. What is the difference between a temporary and a permanent dipole? Give an example of each.
5. Why does water have an unexpectedly high boiling point?
6. **Critical Thinking—Making comparisons**   Rank the intermolecular forces you learned about in this section in order from weakest to strongest.

14–2 Properties of Liquids

Guide for Reading

• Why do liquids have viscosity and surface tension?

• What are some of the unique properties of water?

Most of the substances that are liquids at room temperature and normal atmospheric pressure are made up of molecules. **The physical properties of liquids are determined mainly by the nature and strength of the intermolecular forces present between their molecules.** Now that you understand the origins of intermolecular forces of attraction, let's take a closer look at two properties of liquids.

Viscosity

Have you ever tried to pour honey or molasses? If so, you have observed the effect of **viscosity.** Viscosity is the "friction," or resistance to motion, that exists between the molecules of a liquid when they move past each other. The "slow as molasses" pouring rate of certain liquids compared with the ease of pouring other liquids is a result of high viscosity.

It is logical that the stronger the attraction between the molecules of a liquid, the greater its resistance to flow—and thus the greater its viscosity. So the viscosity of a liquid depends on its intermolecular forces. Because hydrogen bonds are such strong intermolecular forces, liquids with hydrogen bonds tend to have high viscosities. Water is strongly hydrogen bonded and has a relatively high viscosity. You might not believe this because water seems to flow very easily. But have you noticed how fast liquids such as alcohol and gasoline flow or how "runny" they are when compared with water? Molecules of alcohol and gasoline are substantially larger than molecules of water, so they have much stronger dispersion forces. But the strong hydrogen bonding in water gives it a viscosity that is much higher than that of alcohol or gasoline.

Glycerol is an example of a liquid with extremely high viscosity. This compound is a byproduct of the manufacture of soap and is used in cosmetics, medicine, and for manufacturing nitroglycerine. A molecule of glycerol has three O–H bonds. The O–H bonds are very polar and give rise to strong, extensive, intermolecular hydrogen bonds.

Viscosity increases as the temperature decreases. Perhaps you have heard the phrase "as slow as molasses in January." At lower temperatures, the speed of liquid molecules decreases, so they stay closer together. It becomes more difficult for molecules to overcome the attractive forces between them. They do not flow as easily and the viscosity of the liquid increases.

Figure 14–11 *If it was not for viscosity, pancake syrup would rapidly end up at the bottom of your plate, rather than atop your pancakes. The viscosity of motor oil must be carefully controlled to provide proper lubrication at a wide range of temperatures. Which oil is more viscous?*

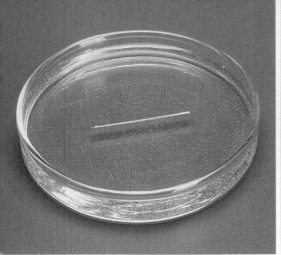

Figure 14–12 *No, this is not trick photography. The needle and the water strider are actually resting on the surface of the water without breaking through it. The property of liquids that makes this possible is called surface tension.*

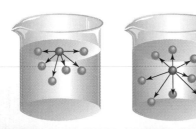

Surface Tension

Fill a beaker with water. Now try to place a sewing needle on the surface of the water so that it does not sink. You can succeed in doing this if you use a clean needle and very gently lower it onto the water's surface. Your common sense tells you that the needle should sink in water because its density is greater than the density of water. Why then does it float? In fact, the needle only rests on the surface of the water. It does not float!

Look at Figure 14–13. Molecules at the surface of the liquid experience attractive forces downward, toward the inside of the liquid, and sideways, along the surface of the liquid. This is unlike the uniformly distributed attractive forces that molecules in the center of the liquid experience. The imbalance of forces at the surface of a liquid results in a property called **surface tension.** The uneven forces make the surface behave as if it had a tight film stretched across it. Depending on the magnitude of the surface tension of the liquid, the film is able to support the weight of small objects such as a razor blade or a needle. Surface tension also explains an observation you may have made quite often—the "beading" of raindrops on the shiny surface of a car. Surface tension causes small quantities of a liquid to take on spherical shapes in order to minimize surface area.

As with viscosity, surface tension is greater in liquids with strong intermolecular forces of attraction. So glycerol, with its extensive hydrogen bonding, exhibits a very high surface tension and forms tight balls of liquid when present in small, droplike quantities. As you might expect, the surface tension of a liquid also increases when the temperature is lowered. Can you explain why?

Figure 14–13 *A molecule at the liquid's surface does not have equal forces acting on it from every direction as does a molecule in the liquid's center. Such an imbalance of forces results in surface tension. Surface tension causes these lovely dew drops to take on a nearly spherical shape. Why do you think the reflections in these dew drops are inverted?*

Water: Some Unusual Properties

Water is the most abundant substance on the Earth's surface. In addition to forming the oceans, water is found in the atmosphere and within the Earth's crust. Water makes up a large proportion of all of Earth's living plants and animals. It may surprise you to learn that you are about 60 percent water! The properties of water, which are unusual and unique, stem from the strong intermolecular hydrogen bonds that are formed between the polar water molecules. The consequences of these properties are significant for life on Earth. Let's see just how.

- The unexpectedly high boiling point of water is why it is a liquid at room temperature. Other hydrogen compounds, such as NH_3, H_2S, and HF, are corrosive gases at room temperature.
- Water can absorb or release relatively large quantities of heat without large changes in temperature. You should recall from Chapter 12 that the specific heat of a substance is the amount of heat required to raise the temperature of one gram of the substance by one Celsius degree. Water has an unusually high specific heat. This is why oceans and lakes exert a moderating influence on climate. Without the large bodies of water on its surface, the Earth would experience much larger temperature variations.
- The density of the solid form of water—ice—is less than the density of its liquid form. For most substances the solid form is more dense than the liquid form. Why does water exhibit this unusual behavior? Hydrogen bonding is even

Figure 14–14 *Seen from thousands of kilometers away, this fantastic view of Earth provides dramatic proof that water is the most abundant substance on the planet's surface.*

INTEGRATING
EARTH SCIENCE

Have you ever wondered what temperatures on Earth might be if there were no surface water?

Figure 14–15 *Ice has a more open structure than water because the hydrogen bonding is more extensive in ice than in water. This explains why ice is less dense than water. Are all solids less dense than their corresponding liquids? The hockey players are skating on a frozen pond. But is the pond solid ice all the way down?*

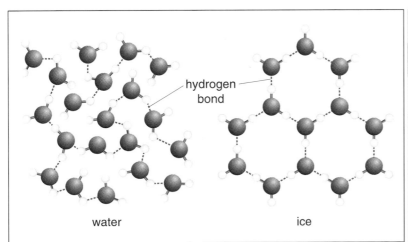

water   ice

Figure 14–16 *Capillary action is partially responsible for the movement of water up this giant California redwood tree.*

more extensive in ice than it is in liquid water. Figure 14–15 on page 469 shows the structures of H_2O in the liquid and the solid states. Ice has a more open structure because the hydrogen bonds keep other water molecules from getting inside the hexagonal ring structure. Thus there are fewer molecules packed in a given volume, giving ice its lower density.

Because of its lower density, ice floats on water and ponds and lakes freeze from the top down. Ice is also a good insulator—a substance that does not readily transmit heat energy. This keeps ponds and lakes from freezing completely in the winter, ensuring the survival of aquatic plant and animal life.

- Water has a relatively high surface tension. This property plays an important part in carrying water from the roots to the tops of the tallest trees by a phenomenon called capillary action.

- Water has a very high heat of vaporization. The heat of vaporization is the amount of heat required to convert a given amount of a liquid into gas. You will study this property in greater detail in Section 14–4. As you might expect, a high heat of vaporization results from strong intermolecular attractive forces. Have you experienced the cooling effect of perspiration? This effect is a direct consequence of water's high heat of vaporization.

- Perhaps you have heard water referred to as the universal solvent. A solvent is a substance (often a liquid) in which another substance dissolves. In the next chapter you will learn about solutions and the solution process. Solutions involving water are the most common and familiar solutions. For now you need to know that water is an excellent solvent because of the polar nature of its molecules.

14–2 Section Review

1. What determines the physical properties of liquids?

2. What are the similarities between viscosity and surface tension?

3. What is the relationship between temperature and viscosity? How is this relationship explained? Does it hold true for surface tension as well?

4. List some unique properties of water and account for them on the basis of its structure.

5. **Critical Thinking—Making predictions** When you drop a weight into a liquid, the weight drops very slowly. What would you predict about the magnitude of the surface tension of this liquid? Why?

14–3 The Nature of Solids

The most important feature of the solid state that differentiates it from the other two states (liquid and gas) is that each particle of a solid remains in a fixed location with respect to the surrounding particles. The intermolecular forces in liquids are strong enough to keep the molecules close to one another, yet allow the molecules to move randomly throughout the liquid. Particles in the solid state—which may be atoms, molecules, or ions—are not free to move away from each other. Instead, they remain packed together in an organized pattern. See Figure 14–2 on page 458. The only movements they can make are vibrations in the fixed positions that they occupy. Thus, the striking difference between the two condensed states of matter is that the particles in the solid state are highly ordered and remain in fixed positions, whereas the particles in the liquid state are disordered and freely moving.

The distances between particles are comparable for liquids and solids, however. Therefore, the densities of the liquid and solid forms of the same substance are not very different. Some examples of liquid and solid densities are given in Figure 14–17. For most substances, solid density is greater than liquid density. However, as you just read, water is an exception.

Crystalline Solids

Most solid substances are crystalline in nature. A solid in which the representative particles exist in a highly ordered, repeating pattern is called a **crystalline solid**. Snow consists of crystals. And you see small crystals every time you use sugar or salt. Almost all of the precious stones used in jewelry are crystals. And just about all of the metals are crystalline solids.

Figure 14–17 This table presents a comparison of the densities of some substances in their liquid and solid states.

Guide for Reading

- How are the properties of solids related to their bonding?
- How do crystalline solids differ from amorphous solids?

Figure 14–18 Although gemstones come in a variety of shapes, sizes, and colors, most of them have one thing in common—they are crystalline solids. What are some other examples of crystalline solids?

Densities of Some Substances in Their Liquid and Solid States

Substance	Density of liquid (g/cm³)	Density of solid (g/cm³)
Potassium	0.83	0.851
Lead	10.645	11.005
Hydrogen	0.07	0.076
Neon	1.204	1.0
Water	1.000	0.917

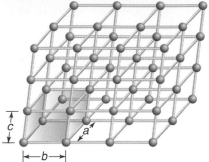

Figure 14–19 *Like Moroccan tile, crystals have definite patterns that are repeated throughout the structure of a crystalline solid. However, the pattern on the tile is two-dimensional, whereas that in a crystalline solid is three-dimensional.*

UNIT CELLS Because crystals have definite patterns that repeat themselves throughout, the structure of a crystalline solid can be described by choosing a small portion of the structure as a representative unit. Such a minimal, repeating unit is called a unit cell. A unit cell is usually chosen to be as small as possible while accurately representing the pattern found in the crystal. Figure 14–20 shows the unit cells of the seven principal crystal patterns.

CRYSTAL FORMATION AND WATER OF HYDRATION As you learned earlier in this chapter, water is a polar molecule with a relatively large permanent dipole. This is what makes it a good solvent for many ionic solids. Many of the chemical reactions of ionic substances occur in water. This can sometimes cause ionic crystals to include water molecules in their solid structure. A solid that includes H_2O units within its crystal structure is called a hydrate, and the H_2O units are called water of hydration. A common hydrate of copper sulfate is called copper sulfate pentahydrate, $CuSO_4 \cdot 5\ H_2O$. The chemical formula indicates that 5 moles of H_2O are present along with 1 mole of Cu^{2+} ions and 1 mole of SO_4^{2-} ions. If some blue crystals of copper sulfate

Figure 14–20 *The unit cells of the seven fundamental crystal lattice arrangements are shown. Gypsum (top) is an example of a monoclinic lattice structure. Rutile (bottom) is an example of a tetragonal lattice structure.*

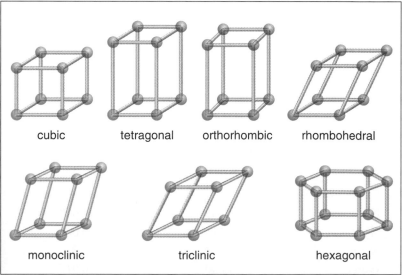

Figure 14-21 *A hydrate is a solid that contains units of water embedded in its lattice structure. When blue crystals of copper sulfate pentahydrate ($CuSO_4 \cdot 5\ H_2O$) are heated, they lose their water, leaving behind white crystals of the anhydrous ionic compound ($CuSO_4$).*

pentahydrate are heated, the water of hydration is driven off, leaving white crystals of the anhydrous ionic compound. What do you think the word anhydrous means?

Amorphous Solids

Some substances are rigid and appear solid but do not behave like crystalline solids. These substances are called **amorphous solids.** The word amorphous comes from a Greek word meaning without form. Some scientists object to these substances being called solids because they believe that only crystalline substances deserve that name. So these substances are occasionally referred to as supercooled liquids, which is often a more accurate description of their behavior and structure.

Glass, rubber, and several plastics are the most common amorphous materials. You can think of amorphous substances as liquids that have been cooled to such low temperatures that their viscosities have become very high. The viscosities are high enough to prevent liquid flow. The particles become trapped in the disordered arrangement that is characteristic of liquids. When an amorphous solid is heated, it gets softer and softer over a wide range of temperatures before it melts. Crystalline solids, on the other hand, show no such temperature range over which they soften. Heating simply leads to a sharp melting point at which the entire sample becomes a free-flowing liquid. Unlike crystalline solids, amorphous substances also lack any preferential planes or edges along which they might shatter when stress is applied.

Bonding in Solids

Earlier in this chapter you saw how several of the physical properties of liquids are explained in terms of the strength of intermolecular forces—forces that vary in their origin, as well as in their strength, from liquid to liquid. **The physical properties of solids, such as hardness, electrical conductivity, and melting point, depend on the kind of particles that make up the solid and on the strength of the attractive forces between them.**

Solids can be classified into four categories depending on the nature of the particles that make them up. These categories are metallic, molecular, ionic, and covalent-network. Figure 14–23 summarizes the properties of these four types of solids. You probably recognize the first three categories and are already familiar with some of their properties.

Figure 14-22 *The masterful work of a glassblower has crafted this handsome unicorn. A glassblower makes use of the amorphous properties of glass. How do amorphous solids differ from crystalline solids?*

Summary of Types of Crystalline Solids

Type of Solid	Type of Particles	Forces Between Particles	Properties	Examples
metallic	atoms	metallic bond	soft to hard, low to high melting point, excellent electrical and thermal conductivity, malleable, and ductile	all metallic elements— for example Al, Cu, Na, Ag, Fe
molecular	atoms or molecules	hydrogen bond, dipole-dipole, dispersion	soft, low to moderately high melting point, poor electrical and thermal conductivity	most organic compounds such as CH_4, $C_{12}H_{22}O_{11}$, as well as many inorganic compounds such as H_2O, CO_2, SO_3
ionic	positive and negative ions	electrostatic attractions	hard, brittle, high melting point, poor electrical and thermal conductivity	typical salts—for example NaCl, KBr, $MgSO_4$
covalent-network	atoms	covalent bonds	very hard, very high melting point, often poor thermal and electrical conductivity	diamond, C; graphite, C; silicon, Si; quartz, SiO_2

Figure 14–23 *This table summarizes the features of the different categories of solids.*

*I*NTEGRATING

*P*HYSICS

What is an electric current?

METALLIC SOLIDS Metals, which constitute more than three fourths of the elements in the periodic table, typically have a small number of valence electrons available for bonding. The principal feature of the metallic bond is the mobility of the valence electrons around positive metal ions. These ions remain fixed in their locations in a three-dimensional crystal array. An analogy that might help you visualize this arrangement is that the metal ions are engulfed in a "sea" of electrons washing through the entire crystal.

The particles in metallic solids are atoms, but the forces that bind these atoms together are the forces of attraction between the mobile valence electrons and the fixed positive metal ions. The strength of these forces can be moderate to very strong, depending on the metal.

Metals are typically good electrical conductors because their valence electrons are free to move. When opposite electric charges are placed at the ends of a metal wire, a current flows as electrons in the wire move away from the negatively charged end and toward the positively charged end. Metals are also good thermal conductors because the electrons can also transmit heat energy. Two other important properties of metals are malleability and ductility. Malleability is the ability to be pounded into thin sheets. Ductility is the ability to be drawn into wire. Because metals are malleable, thin foils of aluminum or silver can be easily made. Because metals are ductile, copper wire can be used in electrical circuits. When a piece of metal is forced to take a different shape,

it continues to hold together because the electrons can shift to bond the atoms in their new positions. If you attempt to pound sulfur, a nonmetallic molecular solid, into a new shape, it simply crumbles because the bonding cannot adapt to the new arrangement of atoms.

Figure 14–24 *Because metals are good conductors of heat, aluminum foil is used to wrap foods for grilling on a barbecue. Metals are valuable as construction materials because of their strength and flexibility.*

MOLECULAR SOLIDS The particles in molecular solids can be atoms or molecules. The forces that hold these particles together are the intermolecular forces we discussed in the first section of this chapter—dispersion forces, dipole-dipole forces, and hydrogen bonds.

Substances that consist of molecules are solids at room temperature if the forces between their molecules are strong. Such strong forces will occur if the molecules are so large that the dispersion forces are large, or if the molecules are so polar that large dipole-dipole forces, or even hydrogen bonds, arise. A combination of these factors will also result in strong intermolecular forces.

Molecular solids are relatively soft and have low melting points. This is because in order to melt a molecular substance, only the weaker intermolecular forces need to be overcome. And although the intramolecular covalent bonds within the molecules are strong, the intermolecular forces between the molecules are relatively weak. Molecular solids typically do not conduct heat and electricity well because there are no "free-moving" electrons or other charged particles.

Just as the strength of the intermolecular forces is related to the boiling point of a liquid, so it is related to the melting point of a solid. The melting point is the temperature at which a solid melts, or becomes a liquid. The stronger the intermolecular forces, the more kinetic energy the particles of a solid need to break away from their fixed positions. Thus, the stronger the intermolecular forces between the particles of a solid, the higher the temperature required to melt the solid.

Figure 14–25 *As these burning candles illustrate, molecular solids are relatively soft and have low melting points. What are some other examples of molecular solids?*

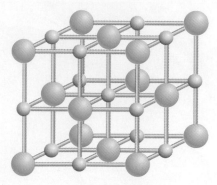

Figure 14–26 Sodium and chloride ions are arranged in an alternating pattern in crystals of sodium chloride. Are ionic solids good electrical conductors?

IONIC SOLIDS Ionic compounds such as sodium chloride (NaCl) consist of oppositely charged ions that attract each other. The forces of attraction are quite strong and extend throughout the crystal. What about the forces of repulsion between similarly charged ions? Look at Figure 14–26, which shows the structure of NaCl. Notice that the oppositely charged ions are close to each other, whereas the similarly charged ions are somewhat farther apart. This crystal arrangement, which maximizes attractions while simultaneously minimizing repulsions, gives the greatest stability.

Ionic solids tend to be hard and brittle, and have high melting points. These properties indicate that the ionic bonds that must be broken are quite strong. Ionic solids are also typically poor conductors of heat and electricity. Yet, interestingly, an ionic substance in its liquid state, which only exists at a high temperature, can conduct electricity! This is because ions are free to move about in the liquid state and can thus carry an electric current. Several types of batteries make use of the fact that in the form of a paste, positive and negative ions are carriers of electricity.

COVALENT-NETWORK SOLIDS In some solids, atoms are bonded to each other with strong covalent bonds without forming molecules. Instead, the covalent bonds form a network extending throughout the solid crystal. Such solids are called **covalent-network solids.** Covalent-network solids have high melting points, corresponding to the breaking of strong covalent bonds. See Figure 14–23 on page 474.

The diamond form of the element carbon is a prime example of a covalent-network solid. The structure of diamond is shown in Figure 14–27, along with the structure of another covalent-network solid, graphite. Both solids are naturally occurring forms

Figure 14–27 In diamond, each carbon is rigidly bonded to 4 other carbon atoms. This arrangement forms a three-dimensional network of covalent bonds, which accounts for the fact that diamond is the hardest natural substance. Graphite has planes of carbon atoms in which each carbon atom rigidly bonds to 3 other carbon atoms. The planes are held together by much weaker forces, accounting for the properties of graphite.

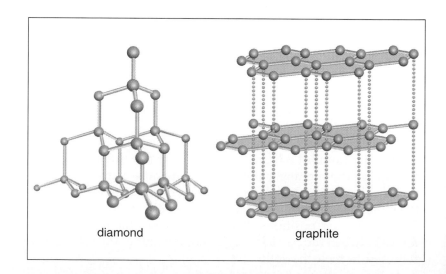

diamond   graphite

Semiconductor Technology

Back in the year 1952, the newspapers and radio reports were talking about a computer that was programmed to perform calculations rapidly. This computer was so large that it occupied an entire house. The computer was built with thousands of wires and devices called vacuum tubes, which processed small electric currents through hundreds of circuits. Today these calculations can be performed by a computer that can fit in your pocket. The electronics revolution that began more than 40 years ago has led to computers with tremendously enhanced capabilities. These high-performance computers are small, convenient, and getting more affordable every year.

What is the recent microelectronics revolution based on? The answer is a chip made of the semimetal silicon. (A chip in today's computer age is the familiar name for an integrated circuit.)

Unlike metals (which are very good electrical conductors) and nonmetals (which are very poor electrical conductors), semimetals are semiconductors. Silicon, the most familiar semiconductor, begins to conduct only after a certain voltage is applied, and then only moderately. However, it is possible to change the conductivity properties of silicon in a predictable way by adding a small number of atoms of elements like gallium (Ga) and arsenic (As).

The process of deliberately adding atoms of other elements (sometimes referred to as impurities) to a pure silicon or germanium crystal is known as doping. Doped semiconductors are at the heart of the modern electronics industry.

Do you know what diodes and transistors are? They are the essential components of all modern electronic devices. Thousands of diodes, transistors, and other circuit elements can fit on an integrated circuit, or chip, that measures only 1 centimeter on a side. This is accomplished by placing small amounts of impurities at specific locations in the tiny silicon crystal. Today, smaller and smaller chips are doing bigger jobs faster! An entire computer, called a microprocessor, is built on a tiny chip no larger than a millimeter or so in diameter!

A typical electrical pulse representing one "bit" of information usually consists of about 500,000 electrons. Two physicists have recently built a circuit that uses just 50 to 100 electrons as the basis for a single bit. This represents the latest effort in the race toward greater speed and smaller size. Is there a limit to this trend? Yes, scientists do see constraints and limits in all processes. We may be quite far from these limits in some areas of technology, but we have already approached them in others.

Figure 14–28 *These skis are an example of a graphite "composite." Graphite incorporated into the material of the skis makes the skis strong, flexible, and lightweight. Silicon, also a covalent-network solid, is at the heart of modern electronics. A silicon wafer with hundreds of electrical circuits is shown here.*

of carbon. You will learn more about carbon and its compounds in Chapter 25. However, the different structures of diamond and graphite produce different physical properties. In diamond, every carbon atom bonds to four other carbon atoms in a giant three-dimensional network of covalent bonds. This structure makes diamond one of the hardest substances known. Naturally formed diamonds are valued in the form of jewelry and synthetic diamonds play an important role in industry as cutting and grinding tools. The melting point of diamond is 3550°C!

In graphite, a carbon atom covalently bonds to three other carbon atoms in a planar arrangement. These planes or "sheets," are held together by dispersion forces that are significantly weaker than carbon-carbon bonds. The electrons found between successive planes are free to move, as are the valence electrons in metals. This makes graphite an electrical conductor, whereas diamond is not. The sheets that make up graphite can also slide past each other quite easily. This is why graphite, a black solid that is soft and slippery, is used in pencils.

14–3 Section Review

1. List the four types of solids. How do they differ in their bonding and properties?
2. Compare the properties of crystalline and amorphous solids.
3. **Critical Thinking—Drawing conclusions** Water is the best-known case of a substance that has a greater density in the liquid state than in the solid state. What conclusion can be made about the structure of water in the solid state?

14–4 Changes of State

In this and the previous chapter, you have learned a great deal about the nature and behavior of matter in its three familiar states: gases, liquids, and solids. From time to time, you have encountered references to processes that convert a substance from one physical state to another. The processes of freezing, melting, and boiling are collectively called changes of state. **A change of state, also called a phase change, is the conversion of a substance from one of the three physical states of matter to another. A change of state always involves a change in energy.**

Energy and Change of State

When a substance is converted from a solid to a liquid or from a liquid to a gas, the particles making up the substance (atoms, molecules, or ions) must overcome the attractive forces holding them together in the more condensed state. This pulling away against the forces of attraction is analogous to stretching a spring. As the spring gets stretched farther and farther, the potential energy of the spring becomes greater and greater. Similarly, as the atoms, molecules, or ions are pulled apart, their potential energy increases. Remember that potential energy is the energy due to position or configuration. Just as a stretched spring is in a high potential energy configuration compared with a relaxed spring, so the particles of a gas are in a high potential energy configuration compared with the particles of a liquid or

Guide for Reading
- What is involved in a change of state?
- What information is provided by heating curves and phase diagrams?

Figure 14–29 *As this boy unhappily discovered, ice cream melts. The process of melting is a change of state. This dry landscape in Australia reflects another change of state: evaporation!*

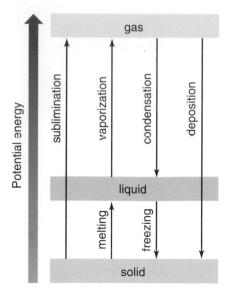

Figure 14–30 *The illustration shows the relative potential energy of the three states of matter. Which changes of state release energy?*

solid. A typical plot of potential energy as it varies with physical state is shown in Figure 14–30. For a given substance, the solid has the lowest potential energy and the gas has the highest. So a phase change from a state of lower potential energy to a state of higher potential energy requires energy. Energy must be added to the substance. On the other hand, a phase change from a state of higher potential energy to a state of lower potential energy releases energy. Do you remember the scientific term for a process that absorbs energy? Releases energy?

Vaporization and Condensation

The change of state from liquid to gas is called **vaporization.** The opposite change, from gas to liquid, is called **condensation.** You know that when you leave water in an open container, sooner or later it will disappear. The process by which molecules of a liquid escape from the surface of the liquid and enter the vapor (gas) phase is also called **evaporation.** Are the terms evaporation and vaporization different? The use of the term evaporation is generally limited to describing the escape of liquid molecules from the surface of a liquid. Vaporization is a broader term that includes evaporation as well as boiling. What about the difference between the terms gas and vapor? The word vapor is generally used when referring to the gaseous state of a substance that is normally a liquid or a solid at room temperature.

EVAPORATION Why do liquids evaporate? Once again we turn to the kinetic-molecular theory for an answer. An important statement of the kinetic-molecular theory is that temperature is a measure of the average kinetic energy of the particles of a substance. The average kinetic energy of gas as well as liquid particles depends on the temperature. At any given temperature,

Figure 14–31 *The distribution of kinetic energy among molecules of a liquid at two different temperatures is shown in this graph. E_{min} denotes the minimum energy required for evaporation. Evaporation occurs at a greater rate at the higher temperature because more molecules have energy greater than E_{min}. How is E_{min} related to intermolecular forces?*

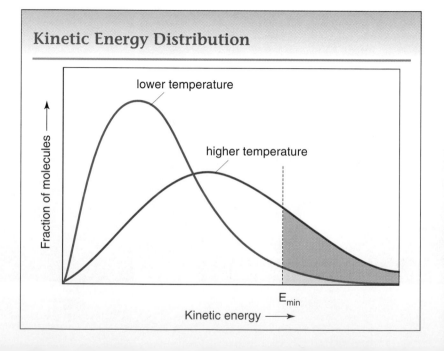

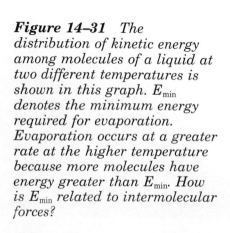

most liquid molecules have energies that are close to the average kinetic energy of molecules at that temperature. Some molecules, however, have energies less than average while others have energies greater than average. A plot of the fraction of molecules versus the kinetic energy they possess is shown in Figure 14–31.

A rapidly moving molecule near the surface of the liquid occasionally possesses enough energy to overcome the attractions of neighboring molecules and escape. Slower molecules simply stay in the liquid state. Because of the very large number of molecules and the wide range of their speeds, there are always some molecules with sufficient energy to evaporate, or escape from the liquid surface. Thus vapor will form above any liquid in a container that has some space above the liquid surface.

How do you think an increase in the liquid temperature affects evaporation? The rate of evaporation increases as temperature increases. Perhaps you know this to be true if you have seen that water left in a container disappears faster when it is warm than when it is cool.

Have you ever heard the word volatile used to describe a liquid? Do you know what it means? The original meaning is able to fly. Chemically, a volatile liquid is one that evaporates easily. It does so because its molecules do not exert strong attractive forces upon one another. Molecules are "able to fly" away from the surface of the liquid. Examples of volatile liquids include gasoline, paint thinner, alcohol, and dry-cleaning solvents. The word volatile often suggests "danger." This is because most volatile liquids are organic compounds that are also flammable. You will learn more about organic compounds in Chapters 25 and 26. The area around volatile liquids contains vapor that can easily catch fire. So extreme caution is required to keep flames or sparks away. This is why smoking is not permitted at a gas station or inside a dry-cleaning facility.

As evaporation proceeds, it is the molecules with the highest kinetic energies that escape into the gas phase. The molecules remaining behind are the ones with lower kinetic energies. Thus the average kinetic energy of the molecules in the liquid is decreased. This decrease in the average kinetic energy of the molecules in the liquid that remains is observed as a decrease in the liquid's temperature. This phenomenon is familiarly known as evaporative cooling. The cooling effect of a fan or the "wind chill" temperatures associated with weather forecasts are common examples of this phenomenon. A less common example is the fact that since long before refrigeration, people in hot climates such as India and Mexico have used porous clay vessels and pots to keep water and other liquids substantially cooler than the outside air temperatures. Evaporation occurs through the pores in the clay, leaving the "slower" or colder molecules behind. As the liquid cools, the insulating property of clay (a covalent-network solid) keeps the liquid from absorbing outside heat.

Figure 14–32 *During strenuous activity, the human body produces perspiration, which leaves the body through tiny openings in the skin called pores. As perspiration reaches the surface of the skin, it begins to evaporate, thus cooling the body. What is this phenomenon called?*

open container   closed container

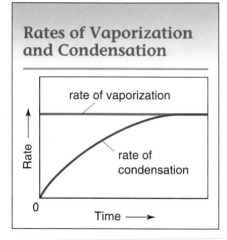

Rates of Vaporization and Condensation

rate of vaporization

Rate →

rate of condensation

0

Time →

Figure 14–33   In an open container, a liquid evaporates until none remains. Equilibrium cannot be established. In a sealed container, evaporation is soon followed by condensation until the two processes occur at equal rates, as shown by the graph. A dynamic equilibrium is established. What does the word dynamic refer to?

LIQUID-VAPOR EQUILIBRIUM   Evaporation occurs because molecules with high kinetic energies overcome the intermolecular attractions within the liquid. Molecules of vapor, however, can return to the liquid state merely by colliding with the liquid surface, as shown in Figure 14–33. Remember, the change of a gas to a liquid is the process of condensation. Condensation is essentially assured for any particle colliding with the liquid surface because the particle immediately becomes trapped by the intermolecular attractions of the liquid.

Imagine a covered container, half-filled with a liquid. Also imagine that the space above the liquid is initially empty. Vaporization will occur and the rate of vaporization will depend only on the temperature. This is because only the temperature determines how many molecules have sufficient kinetic energy to break through the liquid surface. Initially, there will be no condensation because there are no vapor molecules in the space above the liquid. But the rate of condensation will increase as the number of vapor molecules increases. This is because the rate of condensation depends only on the number of molecules in the vapor phase and is proportional to it.

Figure 14–33 also shows a plot of the rates of vaporization and condensation as time passes. The rate of vaporization, in number of molecules per minute, actually stays the same as long as the temperature is held constant. The rate of condensation, however, increases from its initial value of 0 molecules per minute until it reaches the rate of vaporization. Once the rates of vaporization and condensation are equal, both processes continue to occur at identical rates. This means that the number of molecules entering and leaving the vapor phase is the same. A state of dynamic equilibrium has been reached by this liquid-vapor system. A dynamic equilibrium exists when two opposing processes take place simultaneously at equal rates. The word dynamic refers to the changes continually occurring at the molecular level. The word equilibrium refers to the fact that there is no apparent change in measurable quantities pertaining to the system. For instance, if you could count the number of vapor molecules present in the space above the liquid, you would find that it no longer changes after equilibrium is reached. Equilibrium is a very important concept in all systems. You will study it in greater detail in Chapter 16.

EQUILIBRIUM VAPOR PRESSURE   As you just read, the number of molecules in the vapor phase remains constant after equilibrium has been reached at a particular temperature. These molecules exert a pressure called **equilibrium vapor pressure.** How do you think the value of the equilibrium vapor pressure will change if the temperature of the liquid-vapor system is changed? Figure 14–34 lists the values of equilibrium vapor pressure for water at various temperatures. The vapor pressure values increase steadily as the temperature increases, indicating that a greater number of vapor molecules are present at higher temperatures. For all liquids, the equilibrium vapor pressure increases as a function of temperature. Do you notice anything interesting about the highest temperature given in Figure 14–34 and the vapor pressure that corresponds to it?

BOILING POINT Have you ever watched a pot of water being heated on a stove? As you wait patiently for the water to boil, you see small bubbles begin to rise to the surface. Eventually, the bubbles get bigger and rise to the surface faster. At some point, the bubbles are rising fast and furiously. The water is finally boiling. What happened to the water as it got hotter and hotter and finally began to boil?

As the water is heated, bubbles of vapor are formed within it. The pressure of this vapor is the vapor pressure of water at that temperature. As long as this vapor pressure is less than the pressure of the atmosphere pushing down on the surface of the water, the bubbles of vapor simply collapse. However, as the water gets hotter, a temperature is eventually reached at which the vapor pressure of the water is equal to the atmospheric pressure. At this temperature, the bubbles of vapor do not collapse. They get bigger! More and more bubbles form and escape from the water as steam. You recognize this phenomenon as boiling. If you place a thermometer in the water as it begins to boil, you will see that the temperature is close to 100°C. Now look again at the last entry in Figure 14–34.

Figure 14–35 *Compare the appearance of the heated water in each beaker. What is the vapor pressure of water at 83°C?*

Vapor Pressure of Water at Several Temperatures	
Temperature (°C)	**Vapor Pressure of Water (mm Hg)**
0.0	4.58
10.0	9.21
20.0	17.54
30.0	31.81
40.0	55.3
50.0	92.5
60.0	149.4
70.0	233.7
80.0	355.1
90.0	525.8
100.0	760.0

Figure 14–34 *The equilibrium vapor pressure of water is listed for several temperatures. What pattern do you see?*

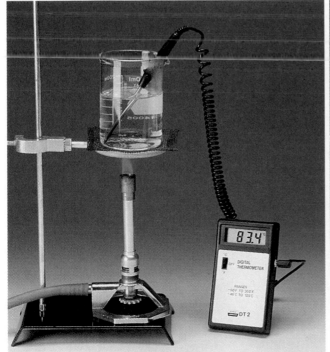
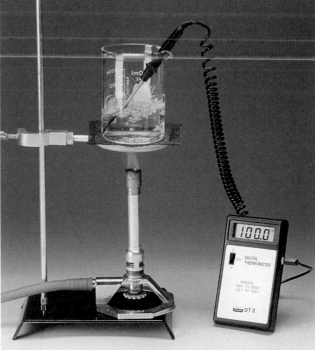

What's Cooking?

Do you think that where you live affects the way you cook vegetables? The variation of boiling point with atmospheric pressure is important to food preparation. Do you know why frozen peas boiled for 6 minutes atop Pikes Peak, Colorado (elevation 4300 meters) will be decidedly undercooked? Although water will begin to boil at 86°C, the amount of heat delivered to the frozen peas during the 6 minutes will be much less than needed to achieve satisfactory cooking.

Food manufacturers, well aware of this relationship between boiling and external pressure, provide cooking instructions for both normal and high-altitude conditions. Look for such cooking directions next time your meal includes frozen foods.

The temperature at which the vapor pressure of a liquid becomes equal to the atmospheric pressure is called its **boiling point**. Thus the boiling point of a liquid depends on the atmospheric pressure. The higher the atmospheric pressure, the higher the temperature needed for the vapor pressure to match the atmospheric pressure. Conversely, lowering the atmospheric pressure lowers the boiling point. This effect is dramatically evident at high altitudes where atmospheric pressure is considerably less than at sea level. It takes longer to cook a hard-boiled egg in Denver, the "mile-high city," because water boils at a lower temperature. By the same token, food in a pressure cooker cooks faster because the pressure inside is much higher than external atmospheric pressure and so water inside the cooker boils at a much higher temperature.

The standard pressure for measuring boiling points is 760 mm Hg, or exactly one standard atmosphere. A boiling point measured at this pressure is called a normal boiling point. What is the normal boiling point of water?

HEAT OF VAPORIZATION   As you learned earlier, the potential energy of a substance in the gas phase is greater than its potential energy in the liquid phase. Therefore, energy must be added to the liquid for vaporization to occur. Vaporization is an endothermic process. The most familiar way of providing the energy for vaporization is in the form of heat. The amount of heat necessary to vaporize a given amount of a liquid at its boiling point is called its **heat of vaporization.** The molar heat of vaporization of water is 40.7 kJ/mol. This means that to vaporize 1 mole (18 grams) of water, 40.7 kilojoules of energy must be supplied. This energy converts 1 mole of H_2O molecules in the liquid state to 1 mole of H_2O molecules in the vapor state at the same temperature and at 1 atmosphere pressure. Heat of vaporization can also be expressed in units of calories. The heat of vaporization of water is 540. cal/g. Does the term heat of vaporization sound familiar? It should, as it is the enthalpy change (or ΔH) for the process H_2O $(l) \rightarrow H_2O$ (g) you learned about in Chapter 12.

Although energy is added to the liquid, the energy does not increase the kinetic energy of the molecules. The temperature remains constant throughout the phase change. Liquids with strong intermolecular attractions have high heats of vaporization. A greater amount of energy is required to overcome the stronger attractive forces between the liquid molecules. Heats of vaporization of some common liquids are given in Figure 14–36.

Condensation is the exact opposite of vaporization. Therefore, the amount of heat released (ΔH) when 1 mole of a liquid condenses is numerically the same as the corresponding molar heat of vaporization. It simply bears the opposite sign. Is condensation endothermic or exothermic?

Heats of Vaporization and Fusion of Some Substances		
Substance	Heat of Vaporization (kJ/mol)	Heat of Fusion (kJ/mol)
Benzene, C_6H_6	44.3	9.84
Bromine, Br_2	29.5	10.8
Mercury, Hg	59.4	2.33
Methane, CH_4	9.2	0.84
Water, H_2O	40.7	6.00

Figure 14–36 *This table lists the heats of vaporization and the heats of fusion of some common substances.*

Freezing and Melting

Freezing liquid water to form a solid ice cube is the exact opposite of melting the ice cube. Freezing and melting involve smaller potential energy changes than vaporization and condensation because the particles are about the same distance apart in both the liquid and the solid states. The temperature at which the solid and liquid forms of a substance exist in equilibrium is called the **freezing point.** It is also called the melting point. Unlike boiling points, freezing points are not affected significantly by a change in external pressure.

The heat that is necessary to convert a given amount of a solid into a liquid is called its **heat of fusion.** This energy is required to separate the solid particles. It results in the higher potential energy of the liquid as compared with that of the solid. Again, as in the case of vaporization, this added energy does not increase the kinetic energy of the particles. The temperature of the sample remains fixed as long as the phase change continues and some amount of each phase is present. The magnitude of the heat of fusion also depends on the strength of the attractive forces between particles. Figure 14–36 also lists the molar heats of fusion of some substances.

Freezing is the exact opposite of melting. Therefore, the amount of heat released (ΔH) when a given amount of liquid freezes is numerically the same as the corresponding heat of fusion, but opposite in sign.

Sublimation and Deposition

Some solids, such as iodine and dry ice (solid carbon dioxide), vaporize without passing through the liquid state at normal atmospheric pressure. The conversion of a solid directly into a gas is called **sublimation.** The reverse transformation of a gas directly into a solid is called **deposition.**

Figure 14–37 *Normally, solids pass through the liquid state before they vaporize. However, some solids, such as dry ice (left) and iodine (right), change directly into a gas at normal atmospheric pressure. What is this process called?*

Solids exhibit vapor pressures just as liquids do, but solid vapor pressures tend to be generally much lower. Solids with high vapor pressures sublime relatively easily. What kinds of solids do you think these tend to be? Solids that do not have strong attractive forces between their particles sublime readily. Of the four categories of solids, molecular solids have the weakest forces between their particles. Therefore, it is in this category of solids that familiar examples of sublimation are found. The characteristic odor of naphthalene (moth balls), for example, is due to its ease of sublimation. Naphthalene is one of many organic compounds that sublime readily. Other fragrant organic compounds that have this property are used in solid air fresheners and deodorizers.

Sublimation and deposition play a role in weather conditions. Snow can disappear through sublimation even though the temperature stays below the freezing point. Snow itself is a result of deposition from water vapor.

The energies associated with sublimation and deposition are called the heat of sublimation and the heat of deposition. These enthalpy changes are equal to each other in magnitude, but opposite in sign. You might find it interesting to note that the heat of sublimation is closely related to the sum of the heats of fusion and vaporization. Can you explain why?

Heating Curves

The phase changes that we have discussed in this section are graphically illustrated in a plot called a **heating curve.** A heating curve is a plot of the temperature of a sample as a function of time. Temperature and time measurements are started on a solid sample below its melting point. Then heat is added at a slow and steady rate. This is continued until the sample has changed into a gas above the boiling point. A heating curve for water is shown in Figure 14–38. Refer to this diagram as you read the following description.

A The temperature of ice rises steadily as heat is absorbed by the solid sample. (Recall from Chapter 12 that the amount of heat absorbed is related to the specific heat of the substance in that state.) An increase in temperature corresponds to an increase in the average kinetic energy of the H_2O molecules.

B Ice is being converted to water at the melting point. Added heat constitutes the heat of fusion and increases the potential energy of water, which is greater than the potential energy of ice. Although heat is absorbed by the sample, the temperature remains constant throughout the phase change, indicating that there is no increase in the average kinetic energy of the molecules.

C Added heat now increases the temperature of the liquid. The average kinetic energy of the water molecules increases steadily until the boiling point is reached.

In a heating curve such as the one shown in Figure 14–38, the slope of each of the nonhorizontal portions of the curve reflects the specific heat of each phase (solid, liquid, or gas) of the substance.

At the horizontal portions of the curve (the plateaus), the kinetic energy (heat) being added does not go toward increasing the temperature of the sample, but rather toward accomplishing the phase change.

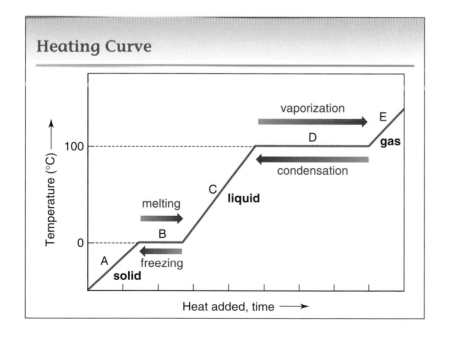

Heating Curve

Figure 14–38 *The three states of water and the changes from state to state are shown on this heating curve. A heating curve plots the temperature as a function of time. Why is the heating curve flat at segments B and D?*

D At the boiling point, the vapor pressure of the water equals the external atmospheric pressure. Added heat constitutes the heat of vaporization and is used to overcome intermolecular forces. The energy becomes the higher potential energy of the gas molecules. The temperature remains constant until the liquid has completely vaporized.

E The temperature of the steam increases steadily as the heat increases the kinetic energy of the gas molecules.

Phase Diagrams

You have seen that substances can exist as solids, liquids, or gases depending on the existing temperature and pressure. In addition, at certain temperatures and pressures, it is possible for two or more phases to be present simultaneously. This happens when the liquid and vapor phases are in equilibrium at the boiling point or when the solid and liquid phases are in equilibrium at the melting point. A diagram that relates the states of a substance to temperature and pressure is called a **phase diagram.** A typical phase diagram is shown in Figure 14–39.

Let's look at some of the details of the phase diagram. Three regions of the diagram are labeled solid, liquid, and gas. This means that only the labeled state can exist under the combinations of temperature and pressure represented by that region. Two phases exist in equilibrium along the three lines of the diagram, which represent the temperatures of sublimation, melting, and boiling as a function of pressure. The point of intersection of these lines near the center of the diagram is the only combination of pressure and temperature at which all three states can exist at equilibrium. This is called the triple point of the substance. What is the triple point of the substance shown in the diagram?

Figure 14–39   A phase diagram shows how the state exhibited by a substance depends on the pressure and the temperature. Where would you mark the normal boiling point of this substance?

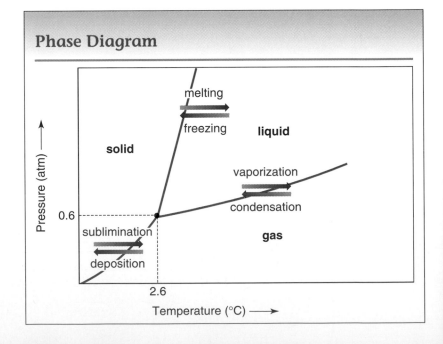

Phase Diagram

A Flood at the Library

Have you ever spilled a glass of milk on your homework? Perhaps you have had a box of juice break open in your book bag? Even if this has never happened to you, you have probably seen books damaged or even ruined when they got wet. Through the years there have been many cases of water spills, leaks, and floods that have damaged valuable books and documents.

Several years ago, a water main break at a library caused flooding in some of the lower stacks that housed several thousand rare and precious books. The wet books were immediately placed in a freezer at about $-25°C$. They were kept frozen until arrangements were made to transport them to a vacuum chamber. Here they were subjected to vacuum pumping at a pressure of 10^{-7} mm Hg while remaining at a temperature below $0°C$.

When this treatment was completed, the books came out quite dry and brittle. They were next put into a high-humidity environment so that they absorbed sufficient moisture to return to their pre-flood state. The entire process took six to eight weeks but the results were remarkable.

What would have happened to the books if they were left to dry out on their own? What was the principle behind the treatment that was used? (Hint: Take a look at the phase diagram of water.)

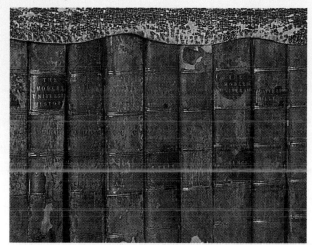

14–4 Section Review

1. What are the important characteristics of a change of state?

2. Explain how vaporization and condensation occur at the molecular level.

3. What is meant by dynamic equilibrium?

4. What is vapor pressure? How is it related to boiling?

5. What information do heating curves and phase diagrams provide?

6. **Theme Trace—Unity and Diversity**   Identify the changes of state that liquids and solids undergo. How are the changes alike? How are they different? What is the role of energy in a change of state?

Laboratory Investigation DESIGNING an EXPERIMENT

Determining the Heat of Fusion of Ice

Problem

How much energy is needed to melt a gram of ice at 0°C?

Suggested Materials (per group)

centigram balance
plastic foam coffee cup (calorimeter)
lab grade thermometer
supply of purified water at room
  temperature
supply of ice chips or cubes
plastic spoon

Suggested Procedure

1. Devise an experiment to determine how much energy is needed to melt a gram of ice at 0°C.
2. Write down the steps of your experimental procedure. The drawing of the calorimeter cup may provide you with some help in writing your procedure.

3. Prepare a data table to record all of your data.
4. Conduct your experiment after having your teacher approve your procedure and data table.
5. From your data, calculate the amount of energy needed to melt a gram of ice at 0°C.

Observations

1. What evidence do you have that the water molecules were losing energy?
2. Graph your temperature and time data.
3. Draw a dashed line to show how the graph would continue with further energy loss.

Analysis and Conclusions

1. Determine the original mass of the water in the cup, and the mass of ice that melted over the course of the experiment.
2. Calculate the energy lost by the original water in the calorimeter cup. One calorie of energy is given up by each gram of water decreasing its temperature by 1 C° (specific heat of water is 1.00 cal/g·C°).
3. Determine the heat of fusion of ice in calories of heat gained per gram of ice melted. Compare this with the accepted value of 80 cal/g and determine your percent error.
4. Convert your calculated heat of fusion of ice to units of kJ/mol and then compare with the value listed in Figure 14–36.
5. **On Your Own** You assumed that the energy lost by the water in the cup was responsible for melting the ice. What were other possible sources of energy for melting ice, and how are these sources minimized? Design an improved experimental setup that reduces the effect of "stray" energy.

STUDY GUIDE

Summarizing Key Concepts

14–1 Condensed States of Matter

- Substances with weak forces of attraction between their particles are gases at room temperature. Substances with moderate forces of attraction between their particles are liquids at room temperature. And substances with strong forces of attraction between their particles are solids at room temperature.
- The kinetic-molecular theory of matter explains the physical properties of liquids and solids.
- Intermolecular forces include dispersion forces, dipole-dipole forces, and hydrogen bonds.

14–2 Properties of Liquids

- Liquids possess the properties of viscosity and surface tension.
- Water exhibits unique properties because of extensive intermolecular hydrogen bonding.

14–3 The Nature of Solids

- Particles in a crystalline solid exist in a highly ordered, repeating pattern called a crystal.

- Particles in an amorphous solid are not arranged in an orderly manner.
- Properties of solids can be explained on the basis of the nature and strength of attractive forces between their particles. The four categories of solids are metallic, molecular, ionic, and covalent-network.

14–4 Changes of State

- A change of state, or the conversion of a substance from one physical state to another, always involves a change in energy. Melting, vaporization, and sublimation are endothermic processes. Freezing, condensation, and deposition are exothermic processes.
- Vapor in equilibrium with its liquid exerts a vapor pressure. A liquid boils when its vapor pressure is equal to the external atmospheric pressure.
- A heating curve is a plot of temperature versus time for phase changes.
- A phase diagram indicates the state or states of a given substance that exist under specific conditions of temperature and pressure.

Reviewing Key Terms

Define each term in a complete sentence.

14–1 Condensed States of Matter

condensed state
intramolecular force
intermolecular force
induced dipole
dispersion force
dipole-dipole force
hydrogen bond

14–2 Properties of Liquids

viscosity
surface tension

14–3 The Nature of Solids

crystalline solid
amorphous solid
covalent-network solid

14–4 Changes of State

vaporization
condensation
evaporation
equilibrium vapor pressure
boiling point
heat of vaporization
freezing point
heat of fusion
sublimation
deposition
heating curve
phase diagram

CHAPTER REVIEW

Content Review

Multiple Choice
Choose the letter of the answer that best completes each statement.

1. The state of matter in which particles are close to each other, but do not remain in fixed positions is
   (a) gas.　　　　　(c) solid.
   (b) liquid.　　　　(d) plasma.

2. Solids maintain a definite shape and volume because their particles
   (a) have no kinetic energy.
   (b) have weak attractive forces.
   (c) have strong attractive forces.
   (d) are ions.

3. Which of the following is an intermolecular force?
   (a) hydrogen bond　(c) ionic bond
   (b) covalent bond　(d) metallic bond

4. What kind of intermolecular force would be found between hydrogen (H_2) molecules?
   (a) covalent bond　(c) dipole-dipole
   (b) hydrogen bond　(d) dispersion

5. Viscosity
   (a) increases as temperature increases.
   (b) decreases as temperature increases.
   (c) does not depend on temperature.
   (d) does not vary from liquid to liquid.

6. Supercooled liquids are
   (a) crystalline.　　(c) ionic.
   (b) amorphous.　　(d) metallic.

7. Which solids conduct electricity?
   (a) ionic　　　　　(c) metallic
   (b) molecular　　　(d) all of these

8. Evaporation
   (a) occurs at the same rate for all liquids.
   (b) increases as temperature increases.
   (c) is in equilibrium with condensation.
   (d) is the same as boiling.

9. The flat part of a heating curve indicates
   (a) solid state.　(c) gaseous state.
   (b) liquid state.　(d) constant temperature.

True or False
If the statement is true, write "true." If it is false, change the underlined word or words to make the statement true.

10. The solid state is characterized by the <u>weakest</u> interparticle forces of attraction.

11. Dispersion and dipole-dipole forces are <u>intermolecular</u> attractive forces.

12. The average kinetic energy of particles of a liquid and a solid at the same temperature is <u>the same</u>.

13. Viscosity and surface tension are <u>greater</u> for liquids with stronger intermolecular attractive forces.

14. An <u>amorphous</u> solid has a highly ordered, repeating arrangement of particles.

15. <u>Ionic substances</u> exist as gases, liquids, or solids at room temperature.

16. The process of <u>deposition</u> converts a gas into a solid.

17. Points along a line on a phase diagram represent a <u>three-phase</u> equilibrium.

Concept Mapping
Complete the following concept map for Section 14–1. Refer to pages xviii–xix to construct a concept map for the entire chapter.

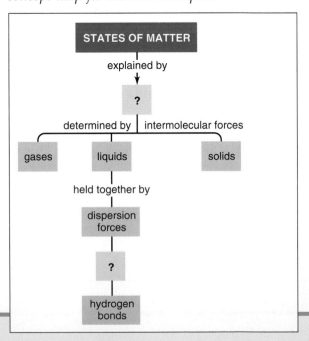

Concept Mastery

Discuss each of the following in a brief paragraph.

18. How does diffusion vary from gas to liquid to solid? Can you explain these differences using the kinetic-molecular theory?
19. Identify the similarities and the differences between liquids and solids.
20. Define and give an example of each of the following types of intermolecular forces: (a) dispersion force, (b) dipole-dipole force, (c) hydrogen bond.
21. Why does the viscosity of a liquid increase when temperature is lowered?
22. What are crystalline solids and how do they differ from amorphous substances?
23. List some unique properties of water.

24. What are the principal differences in structure between a covalent-network solid and a molecular solid? How do their properties differ from each other?
25. Explain the difference between evaporation and boiling.
26. You have a sample of vapor at a certain high temperature. Describe what would happen as you slowly cool this sample and monitor its temperature.
27. **Tying it Together** Describe how *unity and diversity* are exhibited by (a) the states of matter, (b) bonding in solids, (c) phase changes.

Critical Thinking and Problem Solving

Use the skills you have developed in this chapter to answer each of the following.

28. **Classifying** Identify the type of attractive forces that must be overcome to (a) vaporize diamond (b) melt ice (c) vaporize liquid nitrogen (N_2) (d) melt NaCl
29. **Applying concepts** Why does the boiling point of a liquid vary significantly with pressure, whereas the melting point of a solid does not?
30. **Drawing conclusions** A researcher in a laboratory tells you that she has a sample of water boiling vigorously. Its temperature is holding steady at 120°C. Explain.
31. **Interpreting diagrams** Answer the following questions by referring to the CO_2 phase diagram at right.
    (a) Describe the changes that take place when a sample of solid CO_2 is heated at a pressure of 1 atm, starting at a temperature of −100°C.
    (b) How can you get a sample of liquid CO_2?
    (c) What is the significance of the pressure 5.11 atm?

32. **Developing hypotheses** Why is the heat of fusion of a substance usually much smaller than the heat of vaporization?
33. **Making comparisons** What type of a solid would each of the following substances form? (a) HI (b) Xe (c) Si (d) $CaBr_2$ (e) Ag (f) C_5H_{12} (You might have to cool some of them down substantially to get them to solidify!)
34. **Using the writing process** Suppose that the density of ice were not less than the density of water. Write a short essay describing life in such a world.

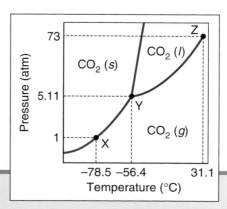

FROM SCHOOL TO WORK

Kevin Powers—Student

Kevin Powers is a senior at Clarkstown South High School in West Nyack, New York. He is an Eagle Scout who enjoys playing and watching all sports.

Kevin works in a gas station in his spare time. He has observed that gas stations help to protect our environment by disposing of waste motor oil and used batteries. Kevin can appreciate this because last year in chemistry class he learned the importance of conserving our energy and mineral resources and protecting our environment.

Laboratory work was Kevin's favorite part of chemistry. Chemical concepts became "real" when there was a "hands-on" approach to learning. He cautions new chemistry students to be aware of safety considerations, however. "Wear those goggles and aprons," he says. Kevin looks forward to more chemistry courses as he plans a career in sports medicine.

Weather Observer

Accurate weather reports depend on weather observers located at observation stations around the country. Weather observers take hourly measurements of wind speed and direction, air pressure, temperature, and relative humidity. They then transmit this information to centers where weather forecasts are prepared. Some of the qualities a weather observer should have include a keen intelligence and curiosity.

To become a weather observer, a Bachelor's degree with a major in meteorology is necessary, although a degree in a related science is acceptable. The United States National Weather Service is the main employer of weather observers. Airlines, weather consulting firms, and colleges and universities also employ weather observers.

If you are interested in obtaining more information, write to the American Meteorological Society, 45 Beacon Street, Boston, MA 02108.

How to Find a Summer Job

Various summer jobs are available to high school students. Your local newspaper probably lists summer job openings that are specifically meant for students in a separate section of the classified ads.

Local and state governments often provide summer work programs for students. Contact your local government to find out if such programs are available in your area. Many companies and local businesses also hire students to work part-time or full-time during the summer. Your school or community library may have a list of such employers. Because it will take time to find a summer job, it is important to begin looking for one before you are actually ready to start working.

From the Author

Probably like many chemists, I was first attracted to the field of chemistry by the chemical reactions: the smoke and the explosions, the dramatic color changes, and the smells—pleasant and unpleasant. And then there was this wonderful array of elements in the periodic table: some familiar, like iron and sulfur, and some mysterious, like beryllium and cadmium. I would say to myself, "I wonder what germanium looks like," or "What would happen if I put some rubidium in water?" (I had already learned that sodium reacts violently with water.) It was partly to find the answers to these questions that I made my career choice.

This unit on gases, liquids, and solids is a little more subtle. You aren't changing one substance into another, and you don't see any smoke, hear any explosions, or observe any color changes. The fascination here is that these topics are so close to home. They include phenomena involved in pumping up a basketball, using a ceiling fan to drive warm air down from the top of a room, bending a metal paper clip, boiling an egg at a high altitude, and cooling a drink with ice cubes. And there are many, many more examples all around us. I'm sure that you can think of several more.

It took me a little longer to learn to appreciate this kind of chemistry—the states of matter and the changes that these states can undergo. The enjoyment I derive in studying these topics comes from being able to understand and appreciate things that happen around me all the time. I hope that you have found such an appreciation too.

UNIT REVIEW

Concept Mastery

Discuss each of the following in a brief paragraph.

1. Describe the kinetic-molecular theory for solids, liquids, and gases.
2. How does the kinetic-molecular theory help explain the differences between solids, liquids, and gases?
3. Explain why a gas exerts a pressure on its container.
4. How did Boyle's observations on the pressures and volumes of gases become a scientific law?
5. Name the three types of forces that exist between molecules of liquids. Describe the origin of each.
6. What is an ideal gas?
7. Give an example of a substance in which the representative particles are atoms and an example of a substance in which they are molecules.
8. What is kinetic energy? How do you increase the kinetic energy of a gas?
9. Suppose you constructed a barometer using water rather than mercury as the fluid in the tube. Would you need a longer tube or a shorter tube for the water barometer? Explain your reasoning.
10. Why does a liquid have surface tension?
11. How does the melting point of a substance depend on the nature of bonding that is found in the substance?
12. Describe evaporation. How is evaporation explained by the kinetic-molecular theory?
13. How did the volume-temperature data obtained by Charles lead to the concept of absolute zero?
14. Explain viscosity. What can you conclude about the attractive forces between molecules of a highly viscous liquid?
15. Explain why ice floats on water. Would you expect solid mercury to float on liquid mercury at its melting point? Why or why not?
16. How can effusion be used to separate a mixture of two gases?

Problem Bank

17. What is the pressure in pascals if a force of 25.5 N acts on a square with a length of 0.00750 m per side?
18. What is the atmospheric pressure in kilopascals if the mercury column in the barometer is 775 mm high?
19. A container filled with a gas is attached to an open-ended manometer. The mercury in the manometer is 13.5 mm higher on the open-ended side. The atmospheric pressure has been determined using a barometer and has been found to be 765.2 mm Hg. What is the pressure of the gas in the container?
20. A mixture of oxygen gas (O_2) and dinitrogen monoxide (N_2O) has a total pressure of 103 kPa. The partial pressure of dinitrogen monoxide is 78.3 kPa. What is the partial pressure of oxygen?
21. A gas has a volume of 3.50 L at a pressure of 1.05 atm. What is its volume if its pressure is raised to 4.56 atm?
22. Physical properties of several substances are tabulated below. Classify each of the following into one of the four categories of solids: ionic, metallic, molecular, and covalent-network.

	Melting Point (°C)	Boiling Point (°C)	Electrical conductivity	
			Solid	Liquid
$MgCl_2$	708	1412	no	yes
Sc	1541	2831	yes	yes
PBr_3	−40	173	no	no
Ag	960.8	1950	yes	yes
OF_2	−223.8	−144.8	no	no
Ge	937	2830	poor	poor
Ar	−189.3	−185.6	no	no
CH_3OH	−93.9	65.15	no	no

23. Can you base an absolute temperature scale on the Fahrenheit degree rather than the Celsius degree? Draw a diagram to illustrate your answer.

24. Identify each of the following statements as true or false. Explain your answer in each case. (Assume constant pressure.)
    (a) If a gas sample is cooled from 1000°C to 200°C, its volume will decrease by a factor of 5.
    (b) If a gas sample is heated from 0°C to 273°C, its volume will double.
    (c) Two moles of gas are added to a 4-mole gas sample at a constant temperature. The volume will decrease by 50 percent.

25. You are told that a helium-filled balloon needs to displace at least 7×10^4 L of air. You then fill the balloon with helium to this volume at ground level where the pressure is 750 mm Hg and the temperature is 20°C. The balloon is allowed to rise to an altitude of 2 km where the pressure is only 620 mm Hg and the temperature is −30°C. Will the balloon still displace at least 7×10^4 L of air?

26. Chloroform is an organic liquid commonly found in a chemistry laboratory. It is fairly volatile. The density of the vapor at a pressure of 220 mm Hg and 25°C is 1.42 g/L. Calculate the molar mass of chloroform.

27. The pressure gauges on two nitrogen tanks of equal volume show identical readings. One tank is indoors at a temperature of 22°C. The other tank is outdoors at a temperature of −7°C. Which tank contains the greater mass of nitrogen?

Performance-Based Task

How Does Temperature Affect a Cartesian Diver?

What is a Cartesian diver? How does it work?

1. Graduate a test tube by placing a strip of transparent tape down the side of the tube and marking the levels of different volumes of water. Assemble the Cartesian diver setup shown below using the test tube, a stopper, and a graduated cylinder filled with water.

2. Add water to the test tube until the top of the stopper is nearly even with the surface of the water in the graduated cylinder. You may want to experiment with the amount of water in the test tube to see how it affects the buoyancy of the diver. Hereafter, the inverted test tube constitutes the Cartesian diver. You will need to tie a string to the stopper to retrieve your test tube.

3. Write a hypothesis and describe what you expect to be the effect of temperature change on the buoyancy of your diver.

4. Design an experiment to test your hypothesis. You may use a large beaker of water at different temperatures. Use appropriate safety cautions. With your teacher's permission, conduct the experiment and then write your conclusions.

Going Further

5. Explain the difference between the buoyancy of a hot-air balloon and that of a submarine.

6. Form and test a hypothesis about another way to affect the Cartesian diver.

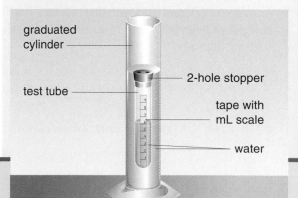

graduated cylinder

2-hole stopper

test tube

tape with mL scale

water

6 Chemical Equilibrium

Imagine that you are taking a leisurely stroll through the country-side. Can you picture a more idyllic scene than a quiet farm on the shore of a placid lake? Just the place to stop for a picnic. But wait. What about that power plant looming in the background? Might some of the materials discharged by the power plant have a harmful effect on the quality of the lake water? For that matter, how might fertilizers, pesticides, and other materials used on the farm affect the water quality?

One way to answer these questions is to find out what types of substances are dissolved in the water. A lake, like other bodies of water, is essentially one large solution. You are already familiar with lots of other solutions, from a frosty pitcher of lemonade to the blood coursing through your body. In this unit, you will learn about the nature of solutions and how they are formed. You will also be introduced to an important concept called chemical equilibrium, which has applications in many areas of chemistry.

DISCOVERY LEARNING

1. Fill a plastic foam cup half full with water and half full with crushed ice.

2. Place a thermometer into the cup and observe the temperature of the ice-water mixture.

3. Add two or three spoonfuls of salt to the ice-water mixture and stir. Observe the temperature of the mixture after adding the salt.

   - How did the temperature of the ice-water mixture after adding salt compare with the temperature before adding the salt?

   - How can you explain your observations?

Chapter
15 *Solutions*

Picture a warm, sunny day in beautiful Venice, Italy. All sorts of boats—gondolas, speed boats, and water taxis—can be seen moving through the winding canals. Tourists stroll along the picturesque waterways or dine at colorful outdoor cafes.

The salt water that makes up the "streets" of Venice is one example of the many forms of matter known as solutions. In this chapter, you will learn what a solution is, how to describe different types of solutions, and how different solutions are formed. And you will learn to recognize many solutions that you encounter every day—from the vinegar in your salad dressing to the air you breathe.

Gondolas float on a saltwater solution along the liquid "streets" in Venice, Italy. An eagle, meanwhile, soars majestically through a solution of air in the skies above Alaska.

Chem Journal

YOU AND YOUR WORLD

A cold, refreshing glass of water from your kitchen faucet is just about crystal clear. Look through it from any direction and you will see right through the other side of the glass. It's just pure H_2O, right? Not necessarily. A number of substances are found naturally in drinking water and others are routinely added to make it safer for you to drink. And occasionally, other substances that are not so safe may find their way into your drinking water as well. In your journal, use your imagination to write a poem or story describing the water you drink every day.

15–1 The Nature of Solutions

Guide for Reading

- What is a solution?

What do the following have in common: the air you breathe, the water in the oceans, the fluids in your body, and the brass in a button? Although they may sound totally unrelated, all of these examples describe mixtures. Recall from Chapter 2 that a mixture is a blend of two or more pure substances that are not chemically combined. Very few of the materials you encounter every day are pure substances. Instead, most are either heterogeneous mixtures or homogeneous mixtures. A pile of pennies and nickels, for example, is a heterogeneous mixture, which is characterized by visibly different parts. Lemonade from a mix is a homogeneous mixture. A homogeneous mixture does not have parts that can be distinguished from one another. As hard as you might try, you cannot see the individual particles of sugar, lemon juice, or water in lemonade. Unlike the coins, lemonade is a **solution.** Air, ocean water, some body fluids, and brass are also solutions. **A solution is a homogeneous mixture of two or more substances in a single physical state.** Examples of solutions are all around you.

Figure 15–1 *This talented musician is making music with a French horn, which consists of a metal tube. The French horn is made of a solution of zinc in copper known as brass. Can you name other items made of brass?*

Properties of Solutions

Despite their differences, all solutions share several important properties. First, the particles in a solution are very small. In fact, they are atoms, molecules, or ions, which is why you cannot see them. Second, the particles in a solution are evenly distributed, or intermingled uniformly on a molecular level. Thus, a small sample of one part of a solution will be the same as a sample from any other part of the solution. For example, a spoonful from any part of a pitcher of lemonade will taste equally sweet. Third, the particles in a solution will not separate no matter how long the solution is allowed to stand under constant conditions. Once a pitcher of lemonade is made, it will remain lemonade. You do not have to worry about returning to the refrigerator to find that the sugar has separated from the water. If you pour the lemonade through filter paper, the sugar, lemon juice, and water will pass through together.

In a solution, one substance is usually considered to be dissolved, or broken down, in another. The substance that is dissolved is called the **solute.** The substance that does the dissolving is called the **solvent.** For example, salt is the solute and water is the solvent in a solution of seawater. Not every substance dissolves in every other substance. A substance that dissolves in another substance is said to be **soluble** in that substance. Soluble means capable of being dissolved. Salt and sugar are soluble in water. A substance that does not dissolve in another is said to be **insoluble.** Mercury and oil are insoluble in water.

The solute and solvent are usually easy to differentiate. If a substance in a solution was originally in a different physical state (solid, liquid, or gas), that substance is the solute. For instance, when solid sugar is added to liquid water to make liquid lemonade, you know that sugar is the solute and water is the solvent. If there is no change in state, the solvent is normally the substance present in the greatest amount. Occasionally the terms solute and solvent have little meaning when describing a solution. For example, there is not much point in trying to differentiate between the solute and solvent in a solution that is 50 percent ethyl alcohol and 50 percent water. What is the solvent when food coloring is used to color water?

Types of Solutions

There are several different possible combinations of solute and solvent according to physical state. They are listed in Figure 15–3. It is useful, however, to categorize solutions according to the physical state of the solution: solid solutions, gaseous solutions, and liquid solutions.

SOLID SOLUTIONS   You may not think of solids when you hear the word solution, but if you wear sterling silver or gold jewelry, you are wearing solid solutions. Sterling silver contains

Figure 15–2 *Some vitamins, such as A, D, E, and K, are soluble in fat. Others, such as vitamins B_2 and B_{12}, are soluble in water. Which type of vitamins do you think accumulate in the body and which type are eliminated in urine?*

Types of Solutions

Solute	Solvent	Example
Gas	Gas	Air (oxygen in nitrogen)
Gas	Liquid	Seltzer (carbon dioxide in water)
Liquid	Liquid	Antifreeze (ethylene glycol in water)
Solid	Liquid	Ocean water (salt in water)
Gas	Solid	Charcoal filter (poisonous gases in carbon)
Liquid	Solid	Dental filling (mercury in silver)
Solid	Solid	Sterling silver (copper in silver)

Figure 15–3 *Solutions can be observed in each of the three different physical states. Notice how solutes in one physical state can dissolve in solvents in another physical state or in the same physical state. Which type of solutions do you think are most common?*

small amounts of copper in solution with silver. Gold jewelry is actually a solid solution of gold and copper.

The most common solid solutions contain two or more metals and are called **alloys.** Alloys are formed by melting the component metals, mixing them together, and then allowing them to cool. Alloys are extremely useful because the properties of an alloy are often quite different from the properties of the component metals. By properly choosing the proportions of each metal in the alloy, many desirable properties can be obtained. For example, alloys can be designed to have greater strength, greater resistance to corrosion, and higher melting points than the pure elements from which they are made. The table in Figure 15–4 lists several useful alloys.

GASEOUS SOLUTIONS The air we breathe is an example of a solution in the gaseous state. Molecules in a gas are far apart and in constant motion. When two or more gases are mixed, the molecules quickly become uniformly intermingled. If gases placed in the same container do not react with each other, they will mix to form a solution. So actually, all mixtures of gases are solutions.

Figure 15–4 *Many common materials are actually alloys. The steel being poured in a steel mill (bottom right) will become a hard metal composed of iron alloyed with other metals and carbon. The melted solder (top right) is a metal alloy used for joining or patching metal parts.*

Types of Alloys

Alloy	Components	Uses
Babbitt	tin, antimony, copper	bearings
Bell metal	copper, tin	bells
Coinage bronze	copper, tin, zinc	coins
16 karat gold	gold, copper, silver	jewelry
Sterling	silver, copper	jewelry, flatware
Nichrome	nickel, iron, chromium, manganese	heating elements

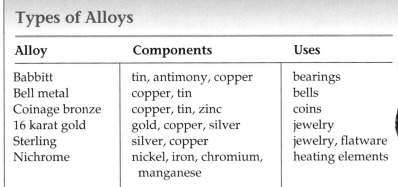

A Fishy Situation

Your neighbor has gone on vacation for a week and has asked you to take care of her aquarium. The aquarium is filled with water and contains a few fishes and plants. Unfortunately, your neighbor forgot to tell you whether the water is fresh water or salt water and you need to know before adding any more water. You cannot analyze the water by smell and you certainly do not want to taste the water! Devise a method of determining which type of water is in the aquarium using only materials available in the kitchen.

Figure 15–5 A substance called muriatic acid is used to increase the acidity of swimming pools. Muriatic acid is produced by dissolving hydrogen chloride gas in water. What is the state of the solute, solvent, and solution?

The molecules in a gas are so far apart that more gas particles can be added to change the composition of the solution. For example, when water vapor is added to the air, the humidity goes up. Unfortunately, pollutants including sulfur dioxide (SO_2) and nitrogen oxides, such as nitrogen dioxide (NO_2), are also readily added to the air.

The properties of a gaseous solution depend on the properties of its components. For example, air has the properties of both nitrogen and oxygen. The oxygen is available for combustion reactions and for respiration. The nitrogen serves the important role of "diluting" the oxygen. Did you ever think that there could be too much oxygen in the air? In fact, pure oxygen is toxic to people and animals, and if it were the only gas present in air, fires would rage out of control all over the Earth. Other minor components in air, such as argon and neon, have little effect on the properties of the solution.

LIQUID SOLUTIONS Oxygen from the air dissolves in the water of ponds, lakes, and oceans, and this dissolved oxygen is the lifeline for the fishes and other animals that live under the water's surface. The gills of a fish are just a gas exchange system by which oxygen dissolved in the water is transferred across a thin membrane so that it can dissolve in the fish's blood. Oxygen dissolved in water is an example of a liquid solution.

Liquid solutions are probably the most familiar to you and you will find them to be the most common examples as you read this chapter. In liquid solutions, the solvent and the solution are liquids. The solute may be a gas, a liquid, or a solid. Sugar dissolved in water is a solid dissolved in a liquid. Vinegar, which is acetic acid dissolved in water, and antifreeze, which is ethylene glycol dissolved in water, are examples of liquids dissolved in liquids. Soft drinks, which are solutions of carbon dioxide in water, and household ammonia, which is gaseous NH_3 dissolved in water, are examples of gases dissolved in liquids.

Unlike gases, which can easily accommodate another gaseous component, there are limits to the amounts of most liquid solutes that will dissolve in liquid solvents. Some pairs of liquids can mix in any amount. These are said to be **miscible** in all proportions. Water and ethanol are miscible in any proportions and can form a complete range of solutions from pure water to pure alcohol. Liquids that cannot mix in any proportions are said to be **immiscible.** Oil and water are immiscible.

AQUEOUS SOLUTIONS Water dissolves a large number of solutes and its solutions are particularly important to life and industry. Solutions with water as the solvent are given a special name. They are called **aqueous solutions.** The word aqueous comes from the Latin *aqueus*, meaning of, like, or containing water. You were introduced to the notation for aqueous solutions (*aq*) in Chapter 9 when you learned about chemical reactions. Now you can understand why the notation is used. And because water can dissolve so many substances, it is often called the "universal solvent."

Substances that dissolve in water are classified according to whether they yield ions or molecules in solution. When an ionic compound dissolves, the positive and negative ions separate from each other and become surrounded by water molecules. These solute ions are free to move, making it possible for an electric current to pass through the solution. A substance that dissolves in water to form a solution that conducts an electric current is called an electrolyte. Sodium chloride is an electrolyte, as is any soluble ionic compound. By contrast, a solution containing neutral solute molecules does not conduct an electric current because no charged particles are available. A substance that dissolves in water to give a solution that does not conduct an electric current is called a nonelectrolyte. Sugar is an example of a nonelectrolyte.

Figure 15–6 *This lovable fellow, known as a turkey vulture, is responsible for cleaning up decaying carcasses in the wild. Strong gastric juices in their stomachs enable these birds to make a meal out of rancid meat that might kill another animal that dared eat the same food. Gastric juices in these birds and in other species are actually aqueous solutions. What is an aqueous solution?*

15–1 Section Review

1. What is a solution? Describe its properties.
2. What are the two parts of a solution? How can you differentiate between them?
3. How are solutions grouped by physical state?
4. **Theme Trace—Unity and Diversity** Explain how the different types of solutions are alike and how they are different.

Guide for Reading
- How is the concentration of a solution described?
- How does a saturated solution differ from a supersaturated solution?

Figure 15–7 *Tree sap gathered from maple trees is carefully boiled to become the concentrated solution you pour on your pancakes or waffles. What is a concentrated solution?*

15–2 Concentration of Solutions

What could be more refreshing on a hot summer day than a glass of ice-cold lemonade? But suppose your glass of lemonade is too sweet. You could say that the solution of water, lemon juice, and sugar is too concentrated. A concentrated solution contains a large amount of solute for the amount of solvent. Pancake syrup is a concentrated solution of sugar in water. Battery acid is a concentrated solution of sulfuric acid (H_2SO_4) in water. Liquid drain cleaners are usually concentrated solutions of sodium hydroxide (NaOH) in water. A concentrated solution can be diluted by adding more solvent. So you could add water to your lemonade to make it less sweet. Solutions that have a relatively small amount of solute for the amount of solvent are said to be dilute.

You can easily determine if your lemonade needs more water, lemon juice, or sugar by simply tasting it. But a qualitative evaluation of the amount of solute in a solution is not adequate for all situations. Chemists often need to specify precisely how concentrated or dilute a solution is. The measurement that describes the solution in this way is the **concentration** of the solution. **The concentration of a solution is the amount of solute in a given amount of solvent or solution.** In Chapter 10, we discussed the concept of the mole as it applies to the mass of a substance or the volume of a gas. The mole is also used to express the concentration of a solution. The most commonly used measurements of concentration are molarity, molality, and mole fraction.

Molarity

Perhaps the most common expression of solution concentration is **molarity (M).** The molarity of a solution is defined as the number of moles of solute dissolved in each liter of solution.

$$\text{molarity} = \frac{\text{moles of solute}}{\text{liters of solution}} \qquad \text{(Eq. 1)}$$

To see how molarity is used, consider a household cleaner that is a solution of caustic sodium hydroxide (NaOH). If a manufacturer prepares a solution from 10.0 grams of NaOH dissolved in enough solvent to make 0.100 liter of solution, what is the molarity of the cleaner? The molarity equation includes the number of moles of solute and the number of liters of solution. You know the mass of the solute and the number of liters of solution. Recall from Chapter 10 that you can find the number of moles of a substance given its mass and molar mass. You can complete the calculation in one step as follows:

$$\frac{10.0\,\text{g NaOH}}{0.100\,\text{L solution}} \times \frac{1\,\text{mol NaOH}}{40.0\,\text{g NaOH}} = 2.50\,\text{mol NaOH}/1\,\text{L solution}$$

$$= 2.50\,M\,\text{NaOH} \qquad \textbf{(Eq. 2)}$$

A volumetric flask is the best container for making a solution of a precise molarity. A balance is used to obtain the desired number of moles of solute, which is then added to the flask. Solvent is added to the flask until the solution reaches the desired volume. The number of moles of solute, the volume of the solution, and therefore the molarity will then be known with great precision. See Figure 15–8 on page 508.

SAMPLE PROBLEM 1

What is the molarity of a solution formed by mixing 10.0 g H_2SO_4 with enough water to make 100.0 mL of solution?

STRATEGY	SOLUTION
1. **Analyze**	You are given the mass of the solute and the volume of the solution. You are asked to calculate the molarity of the solution.
2. **Plan**	To calculate molarity, you need to convert the mass of the solute to moles using molar mass, and the volume of the solution to liters. The resulting information can be used in the molarity equation.

3. **Solve**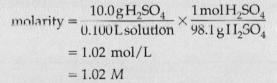

$$\text{molarity} = \frac{10.0\,\text{g H}_2\text{SO}_4}{0.100\,\text{L solution}} \times \frac{1\,\text{mol H}_2\text{SO}_4}{98.1\,\text{g H}_2\text{SO}_4}$$

$$= 1.02\,\text{mol/L}$$

$$= 1.02\,M$$

4. **Evaluate**   The units of the answer make sense because the answer describes the concentration of the solution in terms of moles of solute per liter of solution.

PRACTICE PROBLEMS

1. Vinegar is a solution of acetic acid. What is the molarity of the solution produced when 125 g of acetic acid ($C_2H_4O_2$) is dissolved in sufficient water to prepare 1.50 L of solution? *(Answer: 1.39 M)*

2. How many grams of bromine are needed to prepare 0.500 L of a 0.0100 M solution of bromine in water? *(Answer: 0.799 g)*

CONSUMER TIP

An Expensive Lesson

You go to the store to buy fruit juice. One brand is half the price of another. You think, what a great deal! But do not stock up just yet. Whenever you buy a product that is in solution—chlorine bleach, liquid cleaners, liquid laundry detergents, vinegar, vanilla extract, and fruit drinks, to name just a few—you should know the concentration. In many cases, less expensive brands have lower concentrations of ingredients. You might actually end up paying more for the active ingredient in the bargain brand. Because manufacturers are not usually required to provide information about concentration on the package, it is not always easy to evaluate products. About the most you can do is look for the concentration and be aware that it can vary considerably in similar products. If a cheaper brand seems to be doing a poor job, it is probably because of a low concentration of the active ingredient. It might be time to look for a new brand.

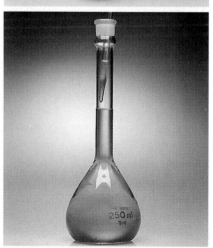

Figure 15–8 *To prepare a 0.250 M solution of potassium chromate (K_2CrO_4), add 12.1 g of the solid to a clean, dry 250.0-mL volumetric flask (top). Add less than 250.0 mL of water to the flask, and then gently shake to dissolve the solid (center). Add water to the flask drop by drop until the meniscus reaches the 250.0-mL calibration mark (bottom).*

Molality

Another measure of concentration is called **molality (*m*).** The molality of a solution is the number of moles of solute dissolved in each kilogram of solvent.

$$\text{molality} = \frac{\text{moles of solute}}{\text{kilograms of solvent}} \qquad \textbf{(Eq. 3)}$$

Consider an example in which 18.0 grams of $C_6H_{12}O_6$ (180. g/mol) is dissolved in 1 kilogram of water. What is the molality of the resulting solution? To find the answer, you must again convert the given mass of solute to moles using molar mass. The resulting equation is

$$\frac{18.0\,\text{g}\,C_6H_{12}O_6}{1\,\text{kg}\,H_2O} \times \frac{1\,\text{mol}\,C_6H_{12}O_6}{180.\,\text{g}\,C_6H_{12}O_6} = 0.100\,\text{mol}\,C_6H_{12}O_6/\text{kg}\,H_2O$$

$$= 0.100\,m \qquad \textbf{(Eq. 4)}$$

Molality is defined in terms of the mass of solvent, whereas molarity is defined in terms of the volume of solution. A 3.0 *m* solution contains 3.0 moles of solute for every kilogram of solvent. A 3.0 *M* solution contains 3.0 moles of solute for every liter of solution. In addition, molality is independent of temperature, whereas molarity is not.

SAMPLE PROBLEM 2

Chlorine is often added to water in swimming pools and to drinking water to keep the water clear and free of living organisms. What is the molality of a solution made up of 16.1 g of chlorine in 5000. g of water?

STRATEGY	SOLUTION
1. Analyze	You are given the mass of the solute and solvent and are asked to determine the molality.
2. Plan	The molality is the number of moles of solute divided by the mass of the solvent in kilograms. You must be sure to convert the mass of the solute to moles and the mass of the solvent to kilograms.

3. Solve

$$\text{molality} = \frac{\text{mol solute}}{\text{kg solvent}}$$

$$= \frac{16.1 \text{ g Cl}_2}{5.00 \text{ kg H}_2\text{O}} \times \frac{1 \text{ mol Cl}_2}{70.9 \text{ g Cl}_2}$$

$$= 0.0454 \text{ mol Cl}_2/\text{kg H}_2\text{O}$$

$$= 0.0454 \text{ } m$$

4. Evaluate   The answer makes sense because it gives the concentration of the solution in terms of the number of moles of the solute for each kilogram of the solvent.

PRACTICE PROBLEMS

3. What is the molality of a solution containing 125 g of iodine and 750. g of carbon tetrachloride (CCl_4)?   *(Answer: 0.657m)*

4. What is the molality of a solid solution containing 1.576 g of iron and 0.0021 g of lead?   *(Answer: 0.0064m)*

Mole Fraction

A third measure of concentration involves **mole fractions** (*X*). The mole fraction is the number of moles of one component divided by the total number of moles in the solution. The component can be either solute or solvent.

$$\text{mole fraction} = \frac{\text{moles of component}}{\text{total moles of solution}} \quad \text{(Eq. 5)}$$

The symbol *X* is commonly used for mole fraction with a subscript to indicate which component of the solution is being solved for. So the equation to find the mole fraction of the solute can be written as

$$X_{\text{solute}} = \frac{\text{moles of solute}}{\text{total moles of solution}} \quad \text{(Eq. 6)}$$

The equation to find the mole fraction of the solvent is written as

$$X_{\text{solvent}} = \frac{\text{moles of solvent}}{\text{total moles of solution}} \quad \text{(Eq. 7)}$$

Mole fraction has no units because moles appear in the numerator and in the denominator and thus cancel out.

The sum of the mole fractions for the solute and solvent must add up to 1.

$$X_{\text{solute}} + X_{\text{solvent}} = \frac{\text{moles of solute}}{\text{total moles of solution}} +$$

$$\frac{\text{moles of solvent}}{\text{total moles of solution}}$$

$$= 1 \quad \text{(Eq. 8)}$$

CONSUMER TIP

All That Glitters Is Not Gold

For most people, gold has a certain allure. Search through humanity's cultural heritage and you will find thousands of gold artifacts. Why has gold been so valued over the centuries? Gold has several valuable qualities, but one of its most characteristic properties is the fact that it is malleable. This means that it can be hammered into different shapes. Although this property might have been useful to ancient artisans, it is not particularly helpful in rings or other jewelry that can easily be bent out of shape. For this reason, most modern gold jewelry is an alloy made of gold mixed with copper and silver. The copper and silver give the gold added strength. Gold jewelry is rated by its purity. Pure gold is 24 karat, which is impractical for most jewelry. Instead, jewelry in the United States is predominantly made of 14 karat gold. In 14 karat gold, a little more than 58 percent of the piece is gold. The other 42 percent consists of other metals. Jewelry made of 14 karat gold has a slightly different color than 24 karat gold. The additional metals account for the difference in color.

Making Rock Candy

1. Boil 0.25 L of water. CAUTION: Be sure to follow all safety precautions when boiling water.
2. Add sugar to the water until no more sugar will dissolve. Pour the sugar solution into a glass.
3. Tie a washer to one end of a piece of string. Tie the other end of the string to a pencil.
4. Place the pencil across the top of the glass so that the string and washer hang down into the sugar solution. Do not let the washer touch the bottom of the glass.
5. Allow the solution to cool. After several days, observe the string. What formed on the string? Explain your observations in terms of saturation.

MATH
TIP

You can always check your answers in mole-fraction problems by adding all the mole fractions. If you have calculated correctly, the sum of the fractions will equal 1.

SAMPLE PROBLEM 3

What is the mole fraction of sulfur dioxide (SO_2) in an industrial exhaust gas containing 128.0 g of sulfur dioxide dissolved in every 1500. g of carbon dioxide?

STRATEGY	SOLUTION
1. Analyze	You are given the mass of solute relative to the mass of the solvent. You are asked to find the mole fraction of solute.
2. Plan	The mole fraction calculation requires that you first determine the number of moles of each of the components in the solution. The molar mass will enable you to convert from mass to moles.
3. Solve	Find the number of moles of each component:

$$\text{mol } SO_2 = 128.0 \text{ g } SO_2 \times \frac{1 \text{ mol } SO_2}{64.04 \text{ g } SO_2}$$

$$= 1.999 \text{ mol } SO_2$$

$$\text{mol } CO_2 = 1500. \text{ g } CO_2 \times \frac{1 \text{ mol } CO_2}{43.99 \text{ g } CO_2}$$

$$= 34.09 \text{ mol } CO_2$$

Find the mole fraction of SO_2.

$$X_{SO_2} = \frac{\text{moles of } SO_2}{\text{total moles of solution}}$$

$$= \frac{1.999 \text{ mol } SO_2}{1.999 \text{ mol } SO_2 + 34.09 \text{ mol } CO_2}$$

$$= 0.05539$$

4. Evaluate — The answer makes sense. The mole value of sulfur dioxide is a small fraction of the mole value of carbon dioxide. If you further calculate the mole fraction of carbon dioxide, you can show that the mole fraction of sulfur dioxide plus the mole fraction of carbon dioxide equal 1.

PRACTICE PROBLEMS

5. A gas mixture contains 50.4 g of dinitrogen monoxide (N_2O) and 65.2 g of oxygen gas. What is the mole fraction of dinitrogen monoxide? *(Answer: 0.360)*

6. A gas mixture contains the following gases with the mole fractions indicated: N_2 (0.450), O_2 (0.334), CO_2 (0.023), SO_2 (0.017), and N_2O_4 (0.120). The mixture also contains the gas argon. What is the mole fraction of argon? *(Answer: 0.056)*

Saturation

Now that you know how to measure the concentration of a solution, perhaps you can answer this question: Do you think there is any limit to how concentrated a solution can be? For example, will all the sugar you add to a cup of tea dissolve no matter how much sugar you add? Perhaps your experience has taught you that the answer is no. While you can add as much sugar as you like, it will not all dissolve in the water. Instead, some will sink to the bottom of the cup.

There is usually a limit to the amount of solute that can be dissolved in a solvent. A solution is called **saturated** when no more solute can be dissolved in it. **A solution is saturated if it contains as much solute as can possibly be dissolved under the existing conditions of temperature and pressure.** When more solute is added to a saturated solution, it will not dissolve.

Saturated does not mean the same thing as concentrated. There are some combinations of solute and solvent for which only a tiny amount of solute will dissolve. In these cases, a solution can be saturated without being concentrated. On the other hand, as with ammonia gas dissolved in water, so much solute can be dissolved in a solvent that a highly concentrated solution still might not be saturated.

A solution that has less than the maximum amount of solute that can be dissolved is called an **unsaturated** solution. A solution that contains a greater amount of solute than that needed to form a saturated solution is said to be **supersaturated.** Supersaturated solutions are very unstable solutions, meaning that they do not remain supersaturated for long. Instead, under proper conditions some of the solute particles will escape from the solution and reform the pure solute.

If you have ever eaten rock candy, you have enjoyed the benefits of a supersaturated solution. Rock candy is made by suspending a small sugar crystal in a supersaturated sugar solution. The small crystal grows into a large rock of sugar as excess solute particles escape from the supersaturated solution.

Figure 15–9 *When a single crystal of sodium acetate ($NaC_2H_3O_2$) is added to a supersaturated solution of sodium acetate in water, the excess solute crystallizes out of the solution.*

15–2 Section Review

1. Define the concentration of a solution. Describe three methods of measuring concentration.

2. What is a saturated solution? An unsaturated solution? A supersaturated solution?

3. **Connection—Economics** When too many restaurants open in the same neighborhood, you may hear someone say that the market for restaurants is saturated. Explain what is meant by the statement and relate it to saturated solutions.

Guide for Reading

- What is solubility?
- What factors affect the rate of dissolving?

15–3 The Formation of Solutions

If you have ever tried to rinse a greasy stain out of your favorite shirt, you know that water alone cannot remove the stain. Instead, some soap is necessary to dissolve the grease. Some substances dissolve in a solvent, and others do not. Sodium chloride is highly soluble in water, but gasoline is not. Gasoline mixes readily with benzene (C_6H_6), but sodium chloride does not. To understand why such differences occur, you need to know how a solution forms.

How a Solution Forms

Let's consider the formation of a solution of sodium chloride in water. Sodium chloride is an ionic compound made up of Na^+ and Cl^- ions. Sodium chloride dissolves in water because the water molecules have a sufficient attraction for the Na^+ and Cl^- ions—enough to overcome the attraction of these two ions for one another in the crystal. Just as intermolecular forces hold particles together in a pure substance, intermolecular forces also operate between solute and solvent particles in a solution. The only difference is that in a solution, the forces are among unlike particles.

The process of dissolving takes place at the surface of the solid. Water molecules orient themselves on the surface of the NaCl crystal so that they can separate, or dissociate, the ions and pull them into solution. Once separated from their crystal, the Na^+ and Cl^- ions are surrounded by water molecules as shown in Figure 15–10. The interaction between solute and solvent particles is called **solvation.** The interaction is called **hydration** when the solvent is water. Similar principles operate in dissolving a molecular compound, such as sugar, in water.

In a solution, solute and solvent particles are intermingled. This means that the water molecules must also separate from one another to make room for the solute particles. Thus the formation of a solution of NaCl in water involves the breaking of attractions among solute particles, the breaking of attractions among solvent particles, and the formation of attractions between solute and solvent particles.

Anytime that attractions are broken, energy is required. So the separation of solute particles from one another and of solvent particles from one another are both endothermic (energy absorbing) processes. The formation of attractions between solute and solvent particles is an exothermic (energy releasing) process. Whether energy, in the form of heat, is absorbed or given off in

Figure 15–10 *When sodium chloride is placed in water, molecules of water pull sodium and chloride ions into solution. The water molecules orient themselves so that the oxygen ends are closest to the sodium ion and the hydrogen ends are closest to the chloride ion. The ions then become surrounded in the solution.*

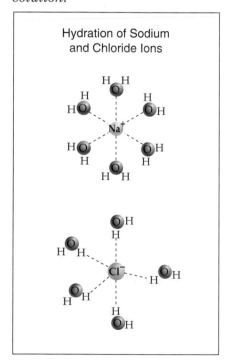

Hydration of Sodium and Chloride Ions

the overall process of solution formation depends on the balance between the two processes. If breaking attractions requires more energy than is released in forming attractions, heat will be absorbed in the overall process. If breaking attractions requires less energy than is released in forming attractions, heat will be given off in the overall process.

When sodium hydroxide (NaOH) is added to water, the resulting solution gets quite warm. The overall process of solution formation is exothermic. In contrast, dissolving ammonium nitrate (NH_4NO_3) in water is an endothermic process. If you have ever used an instant cold pack to reduce swelling caused by an injury, you may even have taken advantage of this fact. The effect of an instant cold pack is equivalent to melting a great deal of ice. The cold pack works because when the pack is hit the breaking of attractions in forming this solution absorbs more energy than is released during the formation of attractions between solute and solvent particles. The heat is absorbed from outside the cold pack, thereby cooling the injured area to which the pack is applied. In a similar but opposite process, a supersaturated solution of $Na_2S_2O_3$ is used to make instant heat packs. When the pack is squeezed, a crystal of $Na_2S_2O_3$ is released from a small compartment in the pack. The crystal causes excess solute to come out of solution. The process during which the crystal pulls particles out of solution is exothermic. The released heat is what makes the pack useful. The heat pack can be recycled by placing it in boiling water to redissolve the $Na_2S_2O_3$.

Solubility

You now know how a solution forms, and why some solution processes are endothermic and others are exothermic. But we must still answer the question about why some substances are soluble and others are not. And we must also explore why different solutes dissolve to different extents in the same solvent. Whether or not a solute will dissolve in a solvent and the extent to which it will dissolve depend on the **solubility** of the solute. **The solubility is the amount of a solute that will dissolve in a specific solvent under given conditions.** Thus the solubility of a substance is the amount of solute required to form a saturated solution. Solubilities must be determined experimentally and are usually expressed in grams of solute per 100 grams of solvent at a specified temperature and pressure.

A number of factors influence solubility. These factors give chemists considerable guidance about how to choose conditions so as to achieve the desired solubility. The extent to which one substance dissolves in another depends on the nature of the solute and solvent, the temperature, and the pressure (for gases).

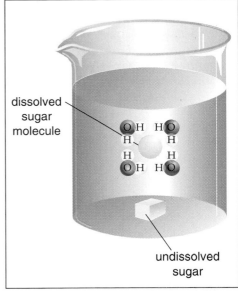

Figure 15–11 *The process by which molecular substances dissolve is similar to that by which ionic substances dissolve. Solute particles at the surface are pulled into solution and surrounded by solvent particles. The photograph shows a sugar cube being pulled through water. Notice how the sugar particles are being dissolved near the surface of the cube.*

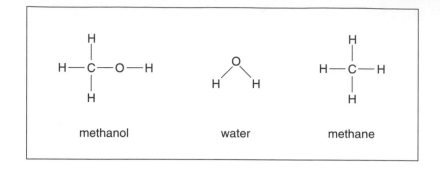

Figure 15–12 *The illustration shows the structure of methanol, water, and methane. Notice that both methanol and water have O—H bonds, while methane does not. Do you think that methanol or methane is more likely to be soluble in water?*

NATURE OF SOLUTE AND SOLVENT As you may recall from earlier chapters, polar covalent bonds are the result of a difference in electronegativity between two bonded atoms. Thus a polar bond in a molecule creates areas of partial positive and partial negative charge. In a water molecule, for example, the more electronegative oxygen atom has a partial negative charge and the two hydrogen atoms have a partial positive charge. The separation of charge is called a dipole. A liquid made up of polar molecules is called a polar solvent. Water is the most common polar solvent. Nonpolar molecules have bonded atoms with comparable electronegativities. A liquid made up of nonpolar molecules is called a nonpolar solvent. Common nonpolar solvents are carbon tetrachloride (CCl_4) and hexane (C_6H_{14}).

When two substances are similar, they can dissolve in each other. Polar solutes tend to dissolve in polar solvents. Nonpolar solutes tend to dissolve in nonpolar solvents. Let's consider an example. Suppose the solvent is water and the two solutes under consideration are methane (CH_4) and methanol (CH_3OH). One of the most significant features of a water molecule is the acute angle (105°) between the two polar O—H bonds. Because the angle is not 180°, water molecules are polar. The same structural feature, the polar O—H bond, appears in a methanol molecule. Water and methanol are structurally similar and can be mixed in all proportions to form solutions. Methane on the other hand has no O—H bonds, is nonpolar, and shares no structural features with water. So the solubility of methane in water is close to zero.

Visit our Web site at
http://www.phschool.com
to support your
study of chemistry.

Figure 15–13 *The table lists several polar and nonpolar substances. How is this list important when applying the "like dissolves like" rule?*

Some Polar and Nonpolar Substances

Polar	Nonpolar
water (H_2O)	hexane (C_6H_{14})
alcohols	heptane (C_7H_{16})
methyl alcohol (CH_3OH)	octane (C_8H_{18})
ethyl alcohol (C_2H_5OH)	carbon tetrachloride (CCl_4)
isopropyl alcohol (C_3H_7OH)	In general, greases,
acetone (C_3H_6O)	petroleum oils, vegetable oils,
acetic acid ($HC_2H_3O_2$)	waxes, tars, gasoline
formic acid ($HCHO_2$)	

Like Dissolves Like Rule for a Solid in a Liquid		
Solute	**Polar Solvent**	**Nonpolar Solvent**
polar	soluble	insoluble
nonpolar	insoluble	soluble
ionic	soluble	insoluble

Figure 15–14 *You can use this table to predict whether or not a particular solute will be soluble in a given solvent. In which type of solvent is a nonpolar solute soluble?*

The principle that similar substances dissolve in each other is usually expressed as the "like dissolves like" rule. According to this rule, two liquids dissolve in each other because their molecules are alike in polarity. Grease on your hands does not come off with water because grease is a nonpolar compound and water is a polar solvent. Turpentine, however, can dissolve grease because turpentine is a nonpolar solvent. Figure 15–13 lists several polar and nonpolar substances.

Ionic compounds are made up of charged ions. In this way, they are similar to polar compounds. In general, ionic compounds are more soluble in a polar solvent than in a nonpolar solvent. For example, table salt dissolves readily in the polar solvent water but does not dissolve readily in the nonpolar solvent gasoline. Many ionic compounds, however, are only slightly soluble in water.

Some compounds contain both polar and nonpolar components, yet exhibit properties more like one component than the other. Cholesterol ($C_{27}H_{26}O$) is such a compound. It is considered nonpolar. Cholesterol is insoluble in water and soluble in nonpolar solvents. In the human body, cholesterol is deposited in fat tissue, which is nonpolar, rather than being dissolved in water and flushed from the body.

TEMPERATURE Open a bottle of a carbonated beverage right after you take it out of the refrigerator and you probably will not notice anything special. But open that same bottle after letting it sit on your kitchen table and you may make a very different observation. Most likely, the beverage will foam up and out of the bottle because the carbon dioxide gas escapes from the solution. Eventually, a carbonated beverage will go flat as it warms. The reason is that the carbon dioxide in the beverage is more soluble at colder temperatures. As the beverage warms, the carbon dioxide is forced out of the liquid solution.

Solutions of gases in liquids are greatly affected by changes in temperature. As the temperature increases, the kinetic energy of the solute gas becomes greater. The gas particles acquire more of a tendency to escape from the solvent. Thus, as the temperature increases, the solubility of a gas in a liquid decreases. Have you

Figure 15–15 *Pour oil into a beaker of water and the oil will form a layer that floats on the water. You can see from this illustration that oil and water molecules are very different. Oil and water are immiscible because oil molecules are nonpolar and water molecules are polar.*

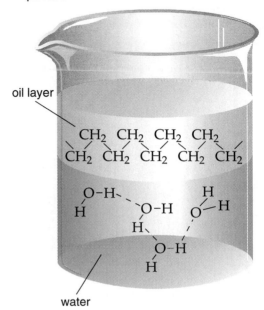

Cleaning Up Your Act

Spill an oily salad dressing on your favorite shirt and no amount of water will get it out. Instead, you might need to take the shirt to the dry cleaner. What can the dry cleaner do that you cannot? When a garment is dry cleaned, it is not (as you might assume from the name) cleaned without getting wet. The difference is that the garment is not washed in water. The dry cleaner uses a nonpolar cleaning solvent to remove the oily stain.

You are probably already familiar with the different characteristics of oil and water, and you know that they do not mix. Oil and water separate into layers. In fact, if oil is spilled in water, the oil will spread out in a layer so thin that it creates brightly colored patterns on the surface of the water.

ever noticed that as a glass of cold tap water is warmed, bubbles of air form on the inside of the glass? The decreased solubility of oxygen in water as temperature increases is one of the effects of thermal pollution in lakes and streams. Fish and other organisms die because there is less dissolved oxygen in the water.

The effect of temperature changes on the solubility of solids in liquids is very different from that of gases. You know that if you add sugar to a hot beverage, the solubility of sugar decreases as the beverage cools. Although a few compounds are exceptions, in general the solubility of a solid solute increases as the temperature increases. Figure 15–17 shows the solubility of a number of solid substances in water as a function of temperature.

The relationship between solubility and temperature depends on the energy change during solution formation for a particular set of solutes and solvents. If the temperature drops when the solute and solvent are mixed, raising the temperature will increase the solubility. If the temperature stays the same when they are mixed, the solubility will not be affected significantly by changing the temperature in either direction. And if the temperature rises when the solute and solvent are mixed, raising the temperature will decrease the solubility.

The fact that solubility changes with temperature is the key to preparing supersaturated solutions. In order to prepare a supersaturated solution, it is necessary to choose a solute and solvent for which the solubility depends on temperature. Look again at Figure 15–17. You can see that the solubilities of sodium nitrate ($NaNO_3$), potassium nitrate (KNO_3) and potassium chlorate ($KClO_3$) all increase greatly as temperature increases. All of these compounds are candidates for supersaturation. To prepare a su-

Figure 15–16 *The solubility of a gas decreases as temperature increases, as indicated by the negative slope of each line on the graph. Why is this true?*

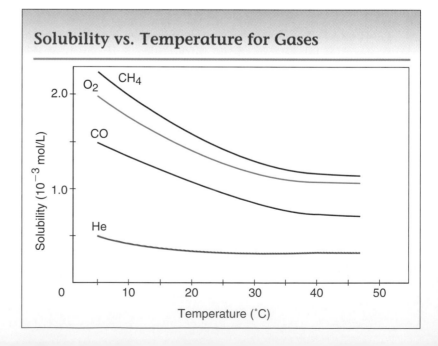

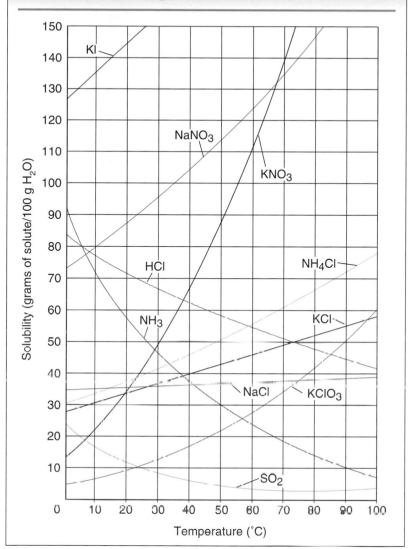

Solubility vs. Temperature for Solids

KI

NaNO₃

KNO₃

HCl

NH₄Cl

NH₃

KCl

NaCl

KClO₃

SO₂

Solubility (grams of solute/100 g H₂O)

Temperature (°C)

Figure 15–17 *Unlike gases, the solubility of most solids dissolved in water increases with increasing temperature. As you can see in this graph, temperature affects the solubility of different substances in different ways.*

persaturated solution, the solution must be heated and then excess solute added. If the solution is then cooled slowly, the extra solute will stay in the solution. Shaking or disturbing a supersaturated solution or adding a tiny crystal of the solid solute can destroy the supersaturation and cause the excess solid solute to crystallize, leaving a saturated solution.

PRESSURE While the solubilities of solids and liquids are not appreciably affected by pressure, the solubility of a gas in a liquid is strongly influenced by pressure. When pressure is increased, the rate at which gas molecules strike the surface to enter the solution is increased. The solubility of a gas in any solvent is increased as the pressure of the gas over the solvent increases. In 1803, the English chemist William Henry (1774–1836) conducted experiments on the solubility of gases in liquids. He found that the solubility of a gas was proportional to the

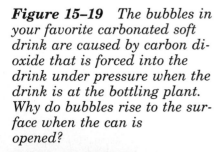

Figure 15–18 *This scuba diver must remember to surface slowly. Otherwise, the nitrogen that dissolved in her blood under the increased pressures of the ocean depths will bubble out of her blood too quickly. If this occurs, she must enter a decompression chamber in which the pressure is decreased slowly to prevent the bends.*

Figure 15–19 *The bubbles in your favorite carbonated soft drink are caused by carbon dioxide that is forced into the drink under pressure when the drink is at the bottling plant. Why do bubbles rise to the surface when the can is opened?*

partial pressure of the gas above the liquid. This is known as Henry's law.

Bottlers use the effect of pressure on solubility in producing carbonated beverages. These are bottled under a carbon dioxide pressure slightly greater than 1 atmosphere. When the bottles are opened, the partial pressure of carbon dioxide above the solution is decreased. With the pressure of carbon dioxide reduced, the solubility of the gas drops and bubbles of carbon dioxide can be seen escaping throughout the liquid. If the bottle cap is left off for an extended period of time, essentially all of the dissolved carbon dioxide will escape.

Factors Affecting the Rate of Dissolving

You know that sugar will dissolve in water, but what do you know about the speed, or rate, at which it dissolves? Do you think a sugar cube would dissolve faster than a spoonful of granulated sugar? And would either form of sugar dissolve faster in hot water than in cold water? To answer these questions, you need to know about the factors that affect the rate at which a solid solute dissolves. **The rate at which a solid solute dissolves in a solution depends on three factors: surface area, stirring, and temperature.** Different solutes dissolve in solvents at varying rates depending on these conditions. The rate at which a solute dissolves is unrelated to its solubility. Whether a solute dissolves quickly or slowly does not alter or depend upon its solubility.

SURFACE AREA The dissolving of a solid solute takes place at the surface of the solid. Solvent particles pull particles from the surface of the solute into the solution. Because dissolving occurs at the surface of the solute, it can be speeded up by increasing the surface area. Thus the greater the surface area, the faster the solid can be dissolved. One method of increasing the surface area is to grind the solid into smaller and smaller particles. The more finely divided the substance, the greater the surface area per unit mass and the more quickly it will dissolve. Powdered sugar dissolves faster in water than granulated sugar, which dissolves faster than cubed sugar.

Figure 15–20 *Hard candies are essentially solid pieces of sugar with added flavoring and coloring. Because of their relatively small surface area, hard candies dissolve much more slowly than the same mass of granulated sugar. Would you want a candy to dissolve quickly?*

STIRRING If you make iced tea or lemonade from a mix, you probably stir the mix into the water. Stirring is a technique that is frequently used to speed up the solution process. The reason that stirring increases the rate of dissolving goes back to the fact that dissolving occurs at the surface of the solid. Dissolved solute tends to build up in the solvent close to the solid, causing the dissolving process to slow down. Stirring sweeps the heavy concentration of dissolved solute away from the surface of the undissolved solute and makes fresh solvent available to continue the solution process. Thus, the effect of stirring is similar to that of grinding a solid into small pieces—contact between the solvent and the solute surface is increased.

TEMPERATURE If you add powdered chocolate to cold milk, it dissolves slowly. But if you add it to warm milk, the chocolate dissolves quickly to make a tasty cup of hot chocolate. Raising the temperature of a solvent increases the rate at which a solute dissolves. This is because as temperature increases, solvent particles move faster. When solvent particles move faster, more particles come into contact with the solute. In addition, the solvent particles have more energy to remove particles from the solid solute.

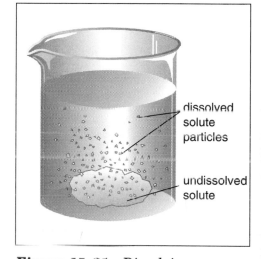

dissolved solute particles

undissolved solute

Figure 15–21 *Dissolving occurs at the surface of a solid. The dissolved solute particles are most concentrated in the solution immediately surrounding the solid. What can you do to increase the rate at which a solid dissolves?*

15–3 Section Review

1. What is solubility?
2. How does a solution form? What is the role of energy in this process?
3. List and describe three factors that affect the solubility of a substance.
4. Explain how the rate at which a solute dissolves can be increased.
5. **Critical Thinking—Making inferences** In terms of the kinetic-molecular theory, explain why the solubility of gases in liquids generally decreases with increasing temperature.

15–4 Colligative Properties

Some physical properties of liquid solutions differ from those of the pure solvent. A property that depends on the concentration of solute particles but is independent of their nature is called a **colligative property.** Colligative means "depending upon the collection." Colligative properties depend upon the collective effect of the solute particles and not their chemical identity. **Four colligative properties are vapor pressure reduction, boiling point elevation, freezing point depression, and osmotic pressure.**

Vapor Pressure Reduction

In Chapter 14 we discussed the vapor pressure of a liquid. Vapor pressure arises because some molecules of a pure liquid leave the liquid surface and enter the gaseous state (vaporization). At the same time, molecules from the gaseous state return to the liquid (condensation). When the rate at which these two processes occur becomes equal, the processes are said to be in equilibrium. The gas pressure resulting from the vapor molecules over the liquid is the vapor pressure. Experiments show that the vapor pressure of a solvent containing a nonvolatile solute is lower than the vapor pressure of the pure solvent. Nonvolatile means that a substance has no tendency to vaporize or sublime under existing conditions. Sugar is a nonvolatile substance.

When the nonvolatile solute is added to a pure solvent, the solute molecules take up space at the surface of the liquid as shown in Figure 15–22. This prevents some solvent molecules from leaving the liquid. Meanwhile, there is no change in the rate at which molecules in the gas state return to the liquid. Thus there is a shift in the movement of molecules from the gaseous state to the liquid state. Because more molecules leave the gas than enter it, the pressure of the gas is reduced. This is known as **vapor pressure reduction.** Because the reduction in vapor pressure does not depend on the identity of the solute involved, vapor pressure reduction is a colligative property.

Figure 15–22 *In a pure liquid solvent, numerous solvent particles come into contact with the surface. A fraction of those particles escape the liquid state and enter the gaseous state. When nonvolatile solute particles are added to the solvent, they take up space at the surface. Because fewer solvent particles come into contact with the surface, fewer leave the solution. How does this affect the vapor pressure?*

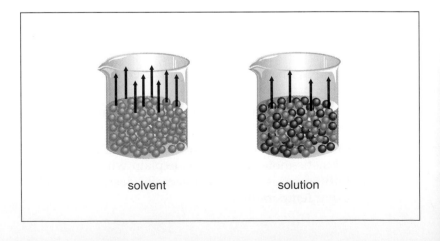

solvent   solution

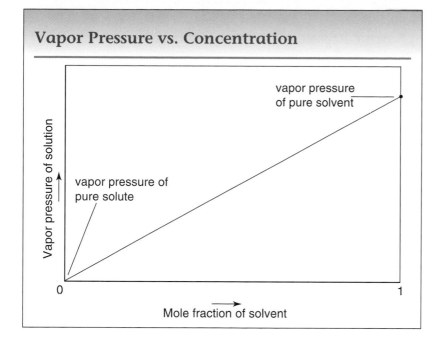

Vapor Pressure vs. Concentration

Vapor pressure of solution

vapor pressure
of pure solvent

vapor pressure of
pure solute

0

1

Mole fraction of solvent

Figure 15–23 The vapor pressure of a solution increases as the mole fraction of the solvent increases. Notice that the vapor pressure is greatest when the solvent is pure. As you look from right to left on the graph, more solute is added and vapor pressure is reduced.

The extent to which a nonvolatile solute lowers the vapor pressure is proportional to its concentration. Doubling the concentration of solute doubles its effect. Detailed studies of the vapor pressures of solutions were carried out by Francois-Marie Raoult (1830–1901). The fact that the magnitude of the vapor-pressure reduction is proportional to solute concentration is known as Raoult's law.

Boiling Point Elevation

Have you ever seen an overheated car with steam rising from the engine pulled over to the side of the road? When the water in a car's engine boils, the engine can be damaged. Antifreeze is added to the water in a car's cooling system to protect against such damage. But how does antifreeze work? Antifreeze raises the boiling point of the water in the engine. The boiling point of a substance is the temperature at which the vapor pressure of a liquid is equal to the external pressure on its surface—in this case, atmospheric pressure. Because the addition of a nonvolatile solute reduces the vapor pressure of the solution, a higher temperature is necessary to get the vapor pressure of the solution up to atmospheric pressure so that the solution boils. The amount by which the boiling temperature is raised is the **boiling point elevation,** another colligative property of solutions. Figure 15–24 on page 522 shows the changes created by the solute. Antifreeze, usually ethylene glycol, is a solute added to water to raise the temperature at which it boils.

The boiling point elevation (ΔT_b) is the difference between the boiling point of the solution and the boiling point of the pure solvent. It is directly proportional to the number of solute particles per mole of solvent particles. Molality expresses the number of moles of solute per kilogram of solvent, which in

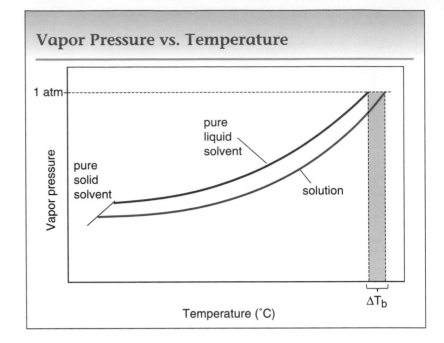

Vapor Pressure vs. Temperature

Figure 15–24 *According to the graph, the vapor pressure of a solution is lower than that of the pure solvent at all temperatures when the total pressure is held constant at 1 atm. Thus the solution must be at a higher temperature than the pure solvent in order to boil at the same pressure. What is this phenomenon called?*

turn represents a fixed number of moles of solvent. Thus ΔT_b is proportional to molality.

$$\Delta T_b = K_b m \qquad \text{(Eq.11)}$$

K_b is a constant called the molal boiling point elevation constant. The value K_b depends on the solvent. Each solvent has its own value of K_b as shown by Figure 15–25.

Elevating the boiling point of a solution has other familiar applications. For example, when candy is made, a common procedure is to add a lot of sugar and a little flavoring to water and then boil the solution. As the water slowly boils away, the concentration of sugar in the water increases. Because vapor pressure lowering is proportional to the increase in concentration, the vapor pressure is reduced. As the vapor pressure is reduced, the boiling point goes up. A candy thermometer is used to determine the temperature of the boiling solution. When this temperature is sufficiently high, the solution is judged to be concentrated enough to be taken to the next step in the candy recipe. In a similar fashion, sugar maple sap, a very dilute sugar solution, is concentrated by boiling and the temperature is monitored to determine when the product is sufficiently concentrated to be called maple syrup.

Figure 15–25 *Each solvent has its own molal boiling point elevation constant. The constants for several solvents are given. Which solvent has the highest constant? The lowest?*

Molal Boiling Point Elevation Constants

Solvent	K_b (C°/m)
acetic acid ($C_2H_4O_2$)	2.93
benzene (C_6H_6)	2.67
carbon tetrachloride (CCl_4)	5.02
chloroform ($CHCl_3$)	3.85
ethanol (C_2H_6O)	1.20
water (H_2O)	0.52

SAMPLE PROBLEM 4

Water with sugar added to it will boil at a higher temperature than pure water. By how much will the boiling point of water be elevated if 100. g of sucrose ($C_{12}H_{22}O_{11}$) is added to 500. g of water? For water, K_b is 0.52 C°/m.

STRATEGY	SOLUTION
1. Analyze	You are given the mass of the solute and solvent and are asked to determine the boiling point elevation.
2. Plan	To calculate boiling point elevation, you need to know the molality of the solution. The molality times the molal boiling point elevation constant will yield the change in temperature.
3. Solve	Calculate the molality of the solution, making sure to convert from mass to moles.

$$\text{molality} = \frac{\text{mol solute}}{\text{kg solution}}$$

$$= \frac{100.\text{ g C}_{12}\text{H}_{22}\text{O}_{11}}{0.500\text{ kg H}_2\text{O}}$$

$$\times \frac{1\text{ mol C}_{12}\text{H}_{22}\text{O}_{11}}{342.3\text{ g C}_{12}\text{H}_{22}\text{O}_{11}}$$

$$= 0.584\text{ mol/kg}$$

$$= 0.584\ m$$

Determine ΔT_b.

$$\Delta T_b = K_b m$$

$$= 0.52\text{ C°}/m \times 0.584\ m$$

$$= 0.30\text{ C°}$$

4. Evaluate   The answer makes sense because a small value of K_b results in a small ΔT_b. The boiling point of the solution would be 0.30 C° higher than the boiling point of pure water. Thus the boiling point of the solution would be 100.30°C.

PRACTICE PROBLEMS

7. What is the boiling point elevation when 12.0 g of iodine is dissolved in 100. g of carbon tetrachloride (CCl_4)? K_b for carbon tetrachloride is 5.02 C°/m.   *(Answer: 2.37 C°)*

8. How many grams of sucrose would have to be added to 0.500 kg of water to elevate the boiling point by 5.0 C°? *(Answer: 1600 g)*

Figure 15–26 *Several colligative properties of solutions are illustrated on this graph. Notice that the greater the concentration of solute particles, the lower the vapor pressure and freezing point and the higher the boiling point of the solution. Why does the 2X solution have the highest boiling point and the lowest freezing point?*

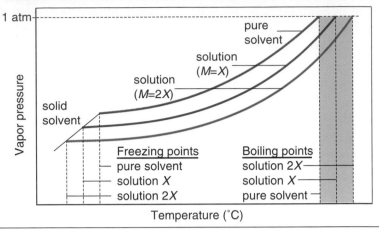

Vapor Pressure Reduction, Boiling Point Elevation, Freezing Point Depression

Figure 15–27 *This contraption actually produces deliciously smooth ice cream. You can see that the central canister is surrounded by a mixture of ice and salt, which serves to lower the freezing point of the ice cream mixture inside the canister. What colligative property does this ice-cream maker employ?*

Freezing Point Depression

You probably know that putting rock salt on wintry roads melts the ice and snow. But do you know why? When the rock salt solute, NaCl, dissolves in water, it lowers the freezing point of the water several degrees. The water, which normally freezes to ice at 0°C, will remain a liquid through lower temperatures. Thus it might not freeze until the temperature drops as low as −10°C. This colligative property, which describes the ability of a dissolved solute to lower the freezing point of its solution, is known as **freezing point depression.** The freezing point of a substance is the temperature at which the vapor pressures of the solid and liquid phases are the same. If the solute is nonvolatile, the vapor pressure of the solution is reduced in proportion to the mole fraction of the solute. This means that the temperature at which the solution and solid phase have the same vapor pressure is reduced. Figure 15–26 shows the relationship among vapor pressure reduction, boiling point elevation, and freezing point depression.

The depression of the freezing point of water by salt is so important that it was once believed that a mixture of salt and ice created the lowest temperature that could be reached by humans. In fact, Gabriel Fahrenheit, a pioneer in the study of temperature, used depressed freezing points for the low points of his thermometers. The zero point of the Fahrenheit temperature scale that was named after him was originally set at the lowest temperature that he could reach using an ice-salt mixture.

Like boiling point elevation, the decrease in the freezing point (ΔT_f) is directly proportional to the molality of the solute. The relationship of molality to the change in freezing point is given by the equation

$$\Delta T_f = K_f m \qquad \text{(Eq. 12)}$$

The molal freezing point depression constant (K_f) is the specific effect of a solute on a given solvent. Figure 15–28 on page 526 gives the constants for several different solvents.

SAMPLE PROBLEM 5

While antifreeze protects a car from freezing (as its name implies), it also protects it from overheating. Calculate the freezing point depression of a solution of 100. g of ethylene glycol ($C_2H_6O_2$) antifreeze in 0.500 kg of water. K_f for water is 1.86 C°/m.

STRATEGY	SOLUTION
1. Analyze	You are given the mass of the solute and solvent and are asked to find the freezing point depression of the solution.
2. Plan	The freezing point depression can be calculated from the molal freezing point depression constant and the molality of the solute. You must use molar mass to find the molality.
3. Solve	Calculate the molality, converting the mass of solute to the number of moles.

$$\text{molality} = \frac{\text{mol solute}}{\text{kg solution}}$$

$$= \frac{100.\text{ g } C_2H_6O_2}{0.500 \text{ kg } H_2O}$$

$$\times \frac{1 \text{ mol } C_2H_6O_2}{62.0 \text{ g } C_2H_6O_2}$$

$$= 3.23 \text{ mol/kg}$$

$$= 3.23 \, m$$

Calculate the freezing point depression.

$$\Delta T_f = K_f m$$

$$= 1.86 \text{ C°}/m \times 3.23 \, m$$

$$= 6.01 \text{ C°}$$

4. Evaluate	The answer makes sense because the addition of antifreeze lowers the freezing point of water by 6.01 C°.

PRACTICE PROBLEMS

9. How many kilograms of ethylene glycol would have to be added to 16.0 kg of water to depress the freezing point to -30.0°C? *(Answer: 16.0 kg $C_2H_6O_2$)*

10. What is the freezing point depression when 153 g of bromine is added to 1000. g of benzene? *(Answer: 4.90 C°)*

Figure 15–28 Each solvent
has its own molal freezing
point depression constant. This
table lists the constants for several solvents. Which solvent has
the highest constant? The
lowest?

Molal Freezing Point Depression Constants

Solvent	K_f (C°/m)
acetic acid ($C_2H_4O_2$)	3.90
benzene (C_6H_6)	5.12
naphthalene ($C_{10}H_8$)	7.00
chloroform ($CHCl_3$)	4.68
camphor ($C_{10}H_{16}O$)	40.0
water (H_2O)	1.86

INTEGRATING BIOLOGY

Do you know why people who
are dehydrated are given
isotonic solutions intravenously?

CHEM Exploration

Solutions and Spuds

1. Obtain a medium-sized
potato.
2. Make a small hole in the potato with the end of a potato
peeler. Use the potato peeler
to partially hollow out the inside
of the potato. CAUTION: Be
sure to follow all appropriate
safety procedures when using
sharp instruments.
3. Fill the hole you made with
table salt.
4. Observe what happens to
the potato over the next one or
two days.
5. Describe what happened to
the potato. Explain your observations in terms of osmosis.

Osmotic Pressure

Certain materials are semipermeable. This means that they
allow some particles to pass through, but not others. A semipermeable membrane may permit the passage of small solvent molecules, such as water, but not larger solute molecules or ions. If
such a membrane is placed between two solutions of different
concentration, solvent molecules will move in both directions
through the membrane while solute particles will remain on one
side of the membrane or the other. The result is a net flow of
solvent molecules from the less concentrated solution to the more
concentrated solution. This process is called **osmosis.**

Figure 15–29 shows two solutions separated by a semipermeable membrane. Solvent moves through the membrane from right
to left. As a result, the liquid levels in the two sides of the tube
become uneven. Eventually, the pressure difference resulting
from the uneven heights becomes so large that the net flow of
solvent ceases. The pressure required to prevent osmosis is
known as the **osmotic pressure (π)** of the solution. Osmotic
pressure is another colligative property of solutions. Osmotic
pressure can also exist between a pure solvent and a solution.

What do you think happens when two solutions with identical osmotic pressure are separated by a semipermeable membrane? The answer is that no osmosis occurs. The solutions are
said to be isotonic. Fluids administered intravenously to people
needing replacement of body fluids must be isotonic with body
fluids because the membranes of red blood cells are semipermeable. If one solution has a lower osmotic pressure than another,
it is said to be hypotonic. Placing cells in a hypotonic solution
would cause water to move into the cells, eventually causing the
cells to burst. If one solution has a higher osmotic pressure than
another, it is said to be hypertonic. Placing cells in a hypertonic
solution would cause water to leave the cells. This causes the
cells to shrivel and die.

You can identify many examples of osmosis in your daily
life. For example, did you ever notice that when you eat a lot of
salty foods you tend to become bloated? This is because the salty
solutions in your body fluids are more concentrated than usual.
Your cells then tend to absorb water from surrounding solutions.
And think about a pickle. Pickles are cucumbers that have been

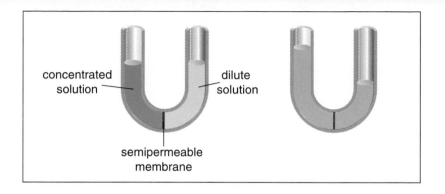

Figure 15–29 *The tube on the left shows a concentrated solution and a dilute solution separated by a semipermeable membrane. Only solvent particles can travel through the membrane. In which direction do solvent particles travel? Why?*

soaked in a brine, or salt solution. The cucumber loses water through osmosis and shrivels into a pickle. Other foods can be preserved by treating their surfaces with a solute that forms a solution with a greater osmotic pressure than the fluids in the food. Bacteria on the food tend to shrivel and die as a result. This is why salt can be used to preserve meat and sugar can be used to preserve fruit. The movement of water from soil into plant roots and then into the upper portions of the plant is also due in part to osmosis.

Determining Molar Mass

Now that you know about the colligative properties of solutions, how can you apply them? The colligative properties of solutions provide a useful means of experimentally determining the molar mass of an unknown substance. Because the molar mass is used in some way to determine the extent of any of the four colligative properties, any of the properties can be used to determine molar mass. For example, you may discover that a compound raises the boiling point of water significantly, yet you might not know what the compound is. You can work backward from the boiling point elevation to determine the molar mass of the unknown substance.

Let's consider an example. Suppose a 10.0-gram sample of an unknown compound is dissolved in 0.100 kilogram of water. The boiling point of the solution is elevated to 0.433 C° above the normal boiling point of pure water. What is the molar mass of the unknown sample? Always start with the given information. You know the boiling point elevation and you can look up the molal boiling point constant. The only unknown remaining in the boiling point elevation equation is molality, which you can calculate. First rewrite the equation so that you can solve for molality.

$$\Delta T_b = K_b m$$

$$m = \frac{\Delta T_b}{K_b}$$

$$= \frac{0.433 \text{ C}°}{0.52 \text{ C}°/m}$$

$$= 0.83 \ m$$

$$= 0.83 \text{ mol/kg} \qquad \textbf{(Eq. 13)}$$

Figure 15–30 *A cell containing a lower concentration of a solute than the surrounding fluid will lose solvent particles to the surrounding fluid. The loss causes the cell to shrivel. A cell containing a higher concentration of a solute than the surrounding fluid, however, will take in solvent particles. This gain causes the cell to swell. What is this process called?*

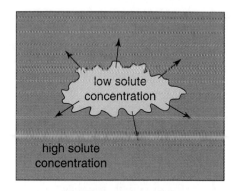

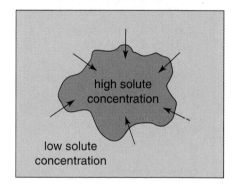

Olfactory Offerings

The mouthwatering aroma of baking bread is unmistakable. So too is the scent of a newly mowed lawn, salty ocean air, smoke from a fire, and the interior of a brand new car. You can probably recall each of these smells from memory. And specific odors—such as cookies baking—may trigger powerful memories.

The sense of smell is particularly interesting because it operates differently than the other four senses—sight, hearing, touch, taste. Unlike other kinds of sensory information, odors are routed directly to the area of the brain that controls emotion, creativity, and memory. It is for this reason that smells come laden with feelings, recollections, and ideas. And it is this phenomenon that manufacturers rely on when they attempt to capture moods and emotions in perfumes.

How do perfumes mimic natural odors? The answer has to do with the solubility of certain oils found in plants. These oils, known as essential oils, give flowers their scents and spices their flavors. Creating a perfume depends on being able to remove these oils from plants. Your first impulse might be to soak flower petals in water to remove the fragrant oils, but remember that oils are not soluble in water. They are, however, soluble in warm fat. The Egyptians were among the first to capture the fragrance of flowers by soaking flower petals in warm liquid fat. Gradually, the essential oils dissolve in the fat until the fat becomes saturated with the oils.

When the fat is saturated, it is cooled and mixed with ethyl alcohol. The fat forms a separate liquid layer, which floats on the alcohol. The essential oils are even more soluble in alcohol than in fat. So the oils leave the fat and dissolve in the alcohol layer. When the alcohol is evaporated, a concentrated mixture of fragrant oils is left behind.

Many improvements have been made in this process over the years. The modern process involves running a liquid solvent, such as petroleum ether, through flower petals placed on perforated trays in a sealed vat. The essential oils dissolve in the solvent and are carried away. The solution is then mixed with alcohol. Because some flowers contain several different oils, each with its own solubility, a series of different solvents must be passed through the petals to capture all of the fragrances. Similar processes are used for essential oils from other sources, such as citrus oils from fruits or musk oils from certain deer.

Once the essential oils are isolated, they can be chemically analyzed. And when the chemical compounds in an essential oil have been identified, chemists can make them synthetically in the laboratory. In fact, most of the fragrances used today are synthetic. Synthetic materials tend to be more uniform and stable than those found naturally.

Our lives would be very different without the many odors we encounter each day. Take a moment to appreciate them, both the pleasant odors and the not so pleasant ones. And be thankful that chemists have learned how to use their knowledge of solutions to enhance our lives with a wide variety of fragrant products, such as soaps, powders, and air fresheners.

Molality is the number of moles per kilogram of solvent. Now you know the molality and you also know the number of kilograms of solvent. The only unknown remaining in the molality equation is the number of moles of solute. Rewrite the equation and solve for this unknown.

$$m = \frac{\text{mol solute}}{\text{kg solvent}}$$

$$\text{mol solute} = m \times \text{kg solvent}$$

$$= 0.83 \text{ mol/kg} \times 0.100 \text{ kg}$$

$$= 0.083 \text{ mol} \qquad \textbf{(Eq. 14)}$$

Finally, think about what the number of moles of solute tells you. The number of moles of a substance is the mass of the sample divided by the molar mass of the substance. And that is what you are looking for—molar mass. So write an equation to solve for molar mass.

$$\text{mol solute} = \frac{\text{mass solute}}{\text{molar mass of solute}}$$

$$\text{molar mass} = \frac{\text{mass solute}}{\text{mol solute}} \qquad \textbf{(Eq. 15)}$$

You were given the mass of the solute, and you calculated the number of moles of solute, so you can solve for molar mass.

$$\text{molar mass} = \frac{10. \text{ g}}{0.083 \text{ mol}}$$

$$- 120 \text{ g/mol} \qquad \textbf{(Eq. 16)}$$

Any of the four colligative properties can be used to determine the molar mass of an unknown substance in this fashion. Although it may seem a little confusing at first, just work each problem through slowly and logically, and you should arrive at the correct answer!

Molality will remain constant with changes in temperature because it is based on mass (mol solute/*mass* solvent). Molarity is based on volume (mol solute/*volume* solution), which increases with increasing temperature because of thermal expansion. In very exact laboratory work, molarities are always specified at 25°C.

15–4 Section Review

1. What are four colligative properties of solutions? What characteristics do colligative properties of solutions share?

2. Describe the property of vapor pressure reduction.

3. Compare and contrast boiling point elevation and freezing point depression.

4. Describe the colligative property of osmotic pressure.

5. **Connection—You and Your World**   Give examples of the applications of each of the four colligative properties.

Laboratory Investigation | DESIGNING an EXPERIMENT

Preparing Solutions

Problem

What factors affect the rate of solution?

Suggested Materials (per group)

balance
mortar and pestle
Bunsen burner
ring stand and ring
wire gauze
four 400-mL beakers
100-mL graduated cylinder
copper sulfate pentahydrate crystals
   ($CuSO_4 \cdot 5 H_2O$)
glass stirring rod
scoopula

Suggested Procedure

1. Devise an experiment to determine how the factors of temperature, surface area, and stirring affect the rate at which the compound $CuSO_4 \cdot 5H_2O$ dissolves.
2. Write down the steps of your experimental procedure, dividing them into a set of steps for each factor to be tested. Be sure to specify what you will use as a control to compare your results with. Also think about what factors you will hold constant in your experiment in order to make your data easier to compare.
3. Prepare a data table, similar to the one shown, to record all your data.
4. Conduct your experiment after having your teacher approve your procedure and data table.

Observations

Beaker	Conditions	Time		Length of Time to Dissolve
		Crystals Added	Crystals Dissolved	
1				
2				
3				
4				

1. What effect does heating the solvent have on dissolving time?
2. What effect does crushing the solute have on dissolving time?
3. How does stirring affect the dissolving time?

Analysis and Conclusions

1. Which conditions caused the crystals to dissolve fastest?
2. Why is Beaker 2 included in this investigation?
3. What is the effect on the movement of the particles when the mixture is heated? What other condition created the same effect on the movement of the particles?
4. **On Your Own**   Try combining two or more of the conditions in this experiment to find the combination that results in the fastest rate of dissolving the solute in the solvent.

STUDY GUIDE

Summarizing Key Concepts

15–1 The Nature of Solutions

- Homogeneous mixtures of two or more substances in a single physical state are called solutions.
- A solution is made up of a solute, which is dissolved, and a solvent, which does the dissolving.
- A substance is soluble if it dissolves in another substance. If it does not dissolve in that substance, it is said to be insoluble.
- Liquid solutions in which the solvent is water are called aqueous solutions.

15–2 Concentration of Solutions

- The amount of solute in a given amount of solvent is the concentration of the solution.
- Concentration can be measured by molarity, molality, and mole fraction.
- A saturated solution contains all the dissolved solute that it can hold. A solution that contains less than the maximum amount is unsaturated, and a solution that is forced to hold more than the maximum amount is supersaturated.

15–3 The Formation of Solutions

- The process by which solvent particles pull solute particles into solution and surround them is known as solvation. When solvation occurs in water, the process is called hydration.
- The extent to which a solute will dissolve in a solvent is its solubility.
- Solubility depends upon the nature of solute and solvent. Like solvents dissolve like solutes. Solubility also depends on the temperature and pressure of the solution.
- The rate at which a solute dissolves can be increased by increasing the surface area of the solute, stirring the solvent, or increasing the temperature of the solution.

15–4 Colligative Properties

- Colligative properties depend on the concentration of solute in solvent and not upon the identity of the solute.
- Four colligative properties are vapor pressure reduction, boiling point elevation, freezing point depression, and osmotic pressure.

Reviewing Key Terms

Define each term in a complete sentence.

15–1 The Nature of Solutions

solution
solute
solvent
soluble
insoluble
alloy
miscible
immiscible
aqueous solution

15–2 Concentration of Solutions

concentration
molarity

molality
mole fraction
saturated
unsaturated
supersaturated

15–3 The Formation of Solutions

solvation
hydration
solubility

15–4 Colligative Properties

colligative property
vapor pressure reduction
boiling point elevation
freezing point depression
osmosis
osmotic pressure

CHAPTER REVIEW

Content Review

Multiple Choice
Choose the letter of the answer that best completes each statement.

1. The process by which dissolved solute particles become surrounded by solvent particles is
   (a) crystallization.   (c) molarity.
   (b) solvation.   (d) osmosis.

2. Which of the following is not an alloy?
   (a) zinc   (c) brass
   (b) sterling silver   (d) stainless steel

3. A solution containing the maximum amount of dissolved solute is
   (a) concentrated.   (c) dilute.
   (b) unsaturated.   (d) saturated.

4. The molarity of a 0.50-L solution containing 9.0 g NaCl in water is
   (a) 18 *M*.   (c) 0.31 *M*.
   (b) 0.055 *M*.   (d) 114 *M*.

5. The number of moles of solute divided by the number of kilograms of solvent is
   (a) molarity.   (c) mole fraction.
   (b) molality.   (d) solubility.

6. The solubility of a gas dissolved in a liquid is not affected by the
   (a) nature of the solute and solvent.
   (b) rate at which the gas dissolves.
   (c) temperature.
   (d) pressure.

7. Which of the following would increase the rate at which a solid dissolves in a liquid?
   (a) lowering the temperature of the solvent
   (b) grinding the solid into smaller pieces
   (c) placing the solution in an opaque jar
   (d) supersaturating the solution

8. Which involves a colligative property?
   (a) heating a solvent
   (b) allowing a carbonated beverage to warm to room temperature
   (c) adding salt to the water in which pasta is being cooked
   (d) pouring a concentrated solution into a dilute solution

True or False
If the statement is true, write "true." If it is false, change the underlined word or words to make the statement true.

9. A solution is a <u>heterogeneous</u> mixture of substances.

10. In a solution, the <u>solute</u> is the substance that does the dissolving.

11. A substance that dissolves in another is said to be <u>soluble.</u>

12. <u>Solvation</u> involving the solvent water is called hydration.

13. An unstable solution containing more than the maximum amount of dissolved solute is a <u>saturated</u> solution.

14. The amount of solute in a given amount of solvent is the <u>solubility</u> of the solution.

15. The number of moles of solute per liter of solution is <u>molarity</u>.

16. The <u>mole fractions</u> of each component in a solution must add up to 1.

Concept Mapping
Complete the following concept map for Section 15–2. Refer to pages xviii–xix to construct a concept map for the entire chapter.

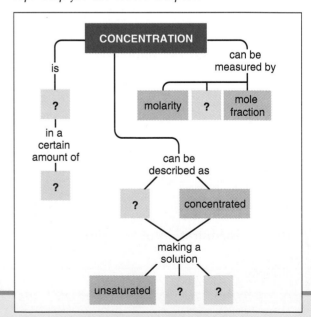

Concept Mastery

Discuss each of the following in a brief paragraph.

17. Give an example of a solution. Explain why it is a solution and how it is formed.
18. What are the two parts of a solution? How can you differentiate between them?
19. Identify seven different types of solutions according to physical state. Then explain how they can be divided into three main categories.
20. An oil and vinegar salad dressing separates into layers. Explain why this happens in terms of the "like dissolves like" rule.
21. List three methods of measuring the concentration of a solution. Write and explain the equation used for each method.

22. Both heat packs and cold packs are useful applications of solutions. Explain the role of energy in solutions in both of these products.
23. What factors affect the rate at which a solute dissolves in a solvent?
24. What factors affect the solubility of a specific substance?
25. What is a colligative property? Describe four colligative properties of solutions.
26. **Tying it Together** Compare molarity and molality in terms of *unity and diversity*. How are they alike and how are they different?

Critical Thinking and Problem Solving

Use the skills you have developed in this chapter to answer each of the following.

27. **Designing experiments** Describe an experiment to show that sugar-water is a solution rather than a pure substance.
28. **Applying concepts** Explain what happens as potassium chloride (KCl) dissolves in water.
29. **Drawing conclusions** Alloys such as brass and steel must be prepared in the liquid (molten) state. Why must such solid solutions be prepared in this way?
30. **Evaluating statements** A classmate states that milk is a solution. Provide an argument explaining why you agree or disagree with your classmate.
31. **Interpreting diagrams** Assume that the solute and solvent is the same in each beaker. Which solution has the highest concentration? The lowest concentration? If solutions a and b were separated by a semipermeable membrane, what would happen? What about solutions b and c?
32. **Applying concepts** Which will have a greater boiling point elevation: 3.00 g $Ca(NO_3)_2$ in 60.0 g of water or 6.00 g $Ca(NO_3)_2$ in 30.0 g of water?

33. **Applying concepts** Which will have a smaller freezing point depression: 100.0 g of methanol (CH_3OH) in 500.0 g of water or 200.0 g of methanol in 250.0 g of water?
34. **Making comparisons** Explain the difference among saturated, unsaturated, and supersaturated solutions.
35. **Using the writing process** Salt is effective for removing ice from roads. However, it is equally effective at corroding cars and killing roadside trees. Write a short essay stating the arguments for and against using salt on roads.

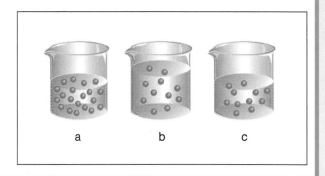

Chapter
16
Chemical Equilibrium

Imagine you are watching a football game. The quarterback steps back with the ball poised to throw to an open receiver. He throws a rocketing spiral. But the pass is incomplete! Now it is fourth down—time to punt the ball. Several players from both teams head for the sidelines while an equal number of different players run onto the field.

In football, each team can have only a certain number of players on the field for each play. Different players come and go, but the total number of players on the field remains the same. You can think of players leaving and entering the field as opposing processes that occur at the same rate. Such a condition is known as equilibrium. In this chapter, you will learn about equilibrium in chemistry.

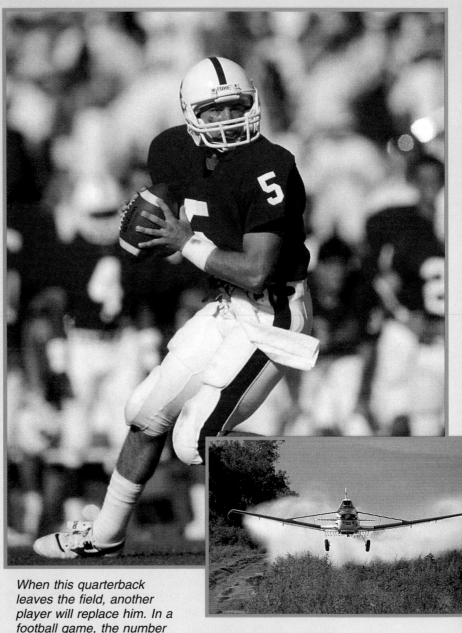

When this quarterback leaves the field, another player will replace him. In a football game, the number of players on the field does not change—it is in equilibrium. Understanding chemical equilibrium led to increased production of many products, such as fertilizer (inset).

Chem Journal

YOU AND YOUR WORLD
Sometimes in life, two processes occur in opposite directions. It is somewhat similar to walking in the wrong direction on a moving walkway. The result is that you do not move at all. Write a description or draw an illustration of something that is gained and lost at about the same rate. Indicate what would happen if either process speeded up or slowed down.

16–1 The Concept of Equilibrium

Guide for Reading
- What is a reversible reaction?
- How is chemical equilibrium characterized?

Ride an elevator in a tall building and chances are you will encounter a wide variety of people. The elevator might serve 20 or 30 floors, carrying hundreds of busy people to their various destinations. Yet the number of people the elevator can carry at any one time is limited. Assuming the elevator is full, the number of people able to get on at any floor is limited by the number of people who get off the elevator. Suppose three people get on and three people get off the elevator at every floor. While the particular people in the elevator change, the total number of people in the elevator does not. The situation in the elevator could be described as being in a state of equilibrium, just as in the football game you read about at the beginning of the chapter. Equilibrium exists when two opposing processes occur at the same rate. Even though changes are occurring, there is no overall, or net, change.

Equilibria (the plural of equilibrium) can also be observed in chemistry. In fact, you have already studied some examples of equilibrium. In Chapter 14, you learned that when a liquid is

Figure 16–1 *Suppose 10 people enter this elevator in the lobby. At every stop on the ride up, three people get in and three others get off. How many people are in the elevator when it reaches the top floor?*

placed in a closed container, some molecules leave the liquid state and enter the gaseous state, forming a vapor above the liquid. At the same time, some molecules in the gaseous state strike the surface of the liquid and return to the liquid state. These are opposing processes. When the rate at which molecules escape from the liquid equals the rate at which molecules return to the liquid, a state of equilibrium is achieved.

Similarly, in Chapter 15 you learned that when a solid solute is added to a liquid solvent, solute particles are pulled into solution. At the same time, some solute particles escape the solution and regenerate the solid. These are opposing processes. Eventually, the rate at which solute particles leave the solid equals the rate at which solute particles leave the liquid. This is a state of equilibrium, and it occurs when a solution is saturated.

INTEGRATING
ENVIRONMENTAL SCIENCE

Do you know why smog is brown in color?

Reversible Reactions

The football game, the elevator, vaporization, and saturated solutions all describe physical processes that oppose each other. Chemical processes can also operate in opposing directions. Consider an example in which nitrogen dioxide gas (NO_2) produced in automobile exhaust is converted into dinitrogen tetroxide gas (N_2O_4). Both substances are major contributors to air pollution in the form of smog, which exists in many cities. Although N_2O_4 is colorless, NO_2 is brown in color and is responsible for giving smog its characteristic brown tint. The equation that describes the reaction between these two substances is shown below.

$$2\,NO_2\,(g) \;\rightarrow\; N_2O_4\,(g)$$
$$\text{brown} \qquad\quad \text{colorless}$$

(Eq. 1)

When NO_2 is placed in an evacuated, sealed glass container, the initial dark brown color decreases in intensity as the NO_2 is converted to colorless N_2O_4. You might expect that as the reaction proceeds, the brown gas will eventually be completely changed into the colorless gas. This is not the case, however. Instead, the intensity of the brown color decreases but eventually becomes constant, indicating that the concentrations of the reactant and product are no longer changing.

Why isn't all of the brown NO_2 consumed in the reaction to form colorless N_2O_4? After all, in computing stoichiometry problems, we always assumed that chemical reactions proceeded until one of the reactants was entirely consumed. In other words, the reactions proceeded to completion. While this is the case in many reactions, some chemical reactions stop short of completion—sometimes far short. Why is this true? The reason is that some reactions are **reversible reactions,** in which the products take part in a separate reaction to reform the reactants. **A chemical reaction in which the products can regenerate the original reactants is called a reversible reaction.** In theory, all chemical

Figure 16–2 *This brown smog over the city of Los Angeles is the result of several chemical reactions that produce pollutants. One such reaction involves the production of dinitrogen tetroxide from nitrogen dioxide gas.*

reactions are reversible reactions. However, while some reactions are reversible on their own, others are only reversible under restricted conditions. And still other reactions cannot even be forced to reverse under any conditions because chemists have not yet discovered how to reverse them.

The reaction involving the conversion of NO_2 to N_2O_4 is an example of a reversible reaction. This means that just as NO_2 forms N_2O_4 in one direction, N_2O_4 forms NO_2 in the opposite direction. Rather than using the single arrow with which you have become familiar, the standard convention for writing a reversible reaction is to use two half-arrows to show that the reaction can proceed in either direction. The equation for the reversible reaction between NO_2 and N_2O_4 is shown below.

$$2\,NO_2\,(g) \rightleftharpoons N_2O_4\,(g) \qquad \textbf{(Eq. 2)}$$

The reaction in which NO_2 forms N_2O_4 is called the forward reaction. The reaction in which N_2O_4 forms NO_2 is called the reverse reaction. The two reactions are opposite processes.

Chemical Equilibrium

As you will learn in Chapter 22, different chemical reactions occur at different speeds, or rates. The reaction in which dynamite explodes, for example, takes place in a fraction of a second while the reaction in which metal rusts may take several years. The rate of a reaction, or the reaction rate, depends on the concentration of the substances in the reaction, the temperature at which the reaction takes place, and (for gases) the pressure at which the reaction takes place. You will learn more about reaction rates later on in this textbook. For now it is important for you to know that, in general, reaction rate is proportional to concentration. Reaction rates tend to be faster when the concentration of the reactants increases.

When substances enter into a reaction, the concentration of the reactants decreases as the reactants are converted into products. In turn, the concentration of the products increases. In the reaction involving NO_2 and N_2O_4, for example, the concentration of NO_2 decreases and the concentration of N_2O_4 increases as NO_2 is converted into N_2O_4. Once N_2O_4 is formed, the reverse reaction begins. In this reaction, the concentration of N_2O_4 decreases and the concentration of NO_2 increases as N_2O_4 is converted to NO_2. Each of the two reactions proceeds at its own rate. Because the concentration of each substance changes, the rate of each reaction changes throughout the reaction. The rate of the forward reaction decreases from its original rate as the concentration of NO_2 decreases. And the rate of the reverse reaction increases from zero as the concentration of N_2O_4 increases. Eventually, the reaction reaches a stage known as **chemical equilibrium** at which the rate of the forward reaction is equal to the rate of the reverse

Figure 16–3 *These adventurous sky divers tumble freely and gracefully through the air. Their downward velocity depends upon the relationship between the downward pull of gravity and the upward resistance of the air through which they travel. When the downward pull becomes equal to the upward resistance, their velocity no longer increases. At this point, they float to the ground at a constant velocity. What are the two opposing processes?*

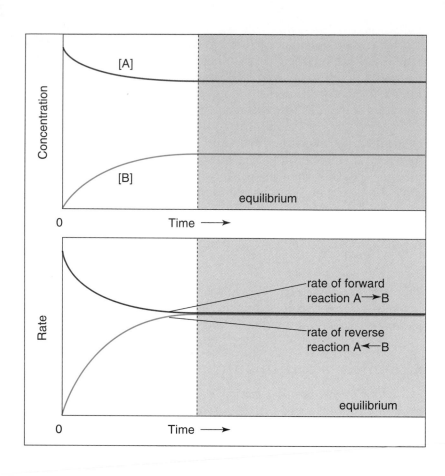

Figure 16–4 The top graph shows the concentration of A decreasing to a constant level and the concentration of B increasing to a constant level as a reversible reaction proceeds. The bottom graph shows what happens to reaction rates as concentrations change. The rate of the forward reaction decreases to a constant rate while the rate of the reverse reaction increases to the same constant rate. At what point are the concentrations of reactants and products constant and the rates of the forward and reverse reactions equal?

reaction. In other words, NO_2 is being consumed by the forward reaction at exactly the same rate as it is being produced by the reverse reaction. Thus its concentration becomes constant. The same is true for N_2O_4. **Chemical equilibrium is the state in which the concentrations of reactants and products remain constant with time because the rate at which they are formed in each reaction equals the rate at which they are consumed in the opposite reaction.** Chemical equilibrium, like other examples of equilibrium, occurs when opposing reactions are proceeding at equal rates. Any chemical reaction carried out in a closed container will eventually reach equilibrium.

Figure 16–4 shows the equilibrium state for a reversible reaction in which compound A is converted into compound B. It is a reversible reaction much like the reaction between NO_2 and N_2O_4. To denote the concentration of each substance, chemists

Figure 16–5 The Lions Gate Bridge in Vancouver enables thousands of people to travel back and forth to their various destinations all day. If the same number of people travel each way, the total number of people on each side of the bridge remains constant.

Ups and Downs Down Under

Visit the beautiful continent of Australia and you will discover a cute and fuzzy problem—rabbits. Years ago, there were no rabbits at all in Australia. To fill the void, people eventually brought rabbits onto the continent. It may have seemed like a good idea at the time, but all too soon the flaw in the plan was evident. Within a relatively short time, the rabbit population "exploded" out of control. They infested the countryside and devoured much of the natural vegetation. They have been a problem ever since.

Why did rabbits become such a problem in Australia when they live without incident in other parts of the world? The answer has to do with the balance, or equilibrium, that exists among animal populations in nature. This equilibrium is based on the relationship between predators and prey.

Just about every species serves as food for some other species. For example, a hawk might eat a harvest mouse, which ate a grasshopper, which ate a snail. While the average number of animals in a particular population is generally constant over time, the actual number changes in a continuous cycle. The population increases and decreases away from the equilibrium value. At one part of the cycle, the prey population grows so large that prey are numerous and easy to find. With such a large and available food supply to feast upon, the number of predators swells. As predators become numerous, they eat more prey than are born. As a result, the prey population shrinks. But as the prey population shrinks, predators begin to starve. So the predator population drops too. When only a few predators are left, the prey population expands once again and the whole cycle repeats itself.

The problem with rabbits in Australia is that rabbits were not indigenous, or native, to the land and therefore had no natural predators. Without predators to complete the predator-prey cycle, the rabbit population was able to expand beyond some equilibrium level.

The relationship between predators and prey may be violent, but it serves to keep their populations in check.

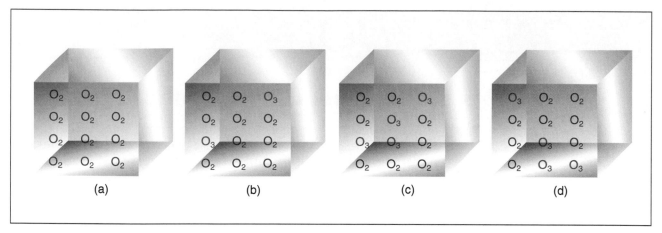

(a)   (b)   (c)   (d)

Figure 16–6 *In the atmosphere, oxygen molecules form ozone molecules in a reversible reaction. Although the actual mechanism is much more complicated, the illustration simplifies the dynamic equilibrium attained by the reaction. Box (a) shows the reaction beginning with only oxygen molecules. As time goes on, some oxygen molecules are converted to ozone molecules as shown in box (b). By box (c), the reaction has reached equilibrium. Although oxygen is still converted to ozone and vice versa, the concentration of each substance remains constant. This is an example of dynamic equilibrium.*

use square brackets around the formula. Thus the concentration of substance A is [A], and the concentration of substance B is [B]. As A reacts to form B, [A] decreases and [B] increases as shown at the top of Figure 16–4. As [A] decreases, the rate of the forward reaction decreases as shown at the bottom of Figure 16–4. Similarly, as [B] increases, the rate of the reverse reaction increases. Eventually, the reaction reaches equilibrium, at which point the forward reaction and the reverse reaction are proceeding at the same rate, and the concentrations of A and B are kept constant.

It is important for you to recognize that reaching equilibrium does not mean that the reaction has come to a stop. Quite the contrary. Like the different people entering and leaving the elevator while the total number of people remains constant, chemical equilibrium is a dynamic, or changing, process. Compound A is converted into compound B and compound B is converted into compound A, but both processes occur at the same rate. So the net change in concentration is zero. For this reason, chemical equilibrium is said to be a dynamic equilibrium. Figure 16–6 shows the dynamic equilibrium that exists in the reversible reaction between oxygen and ozone, which is an important reaction in the atmosphere.

16–1 Section Review

1. What constitutes a reversible reaction?
2. Describe what it means when a reaction is in a state of chemical equilibrium.
3. How do the rates of the forward and reverse reactions change throughout a reaction?
4. **Connection—You and Your World** Relate the concept of equilibrium to a game of tug-of-war.

16–2 The Law of Chemical Equilibrium

Guide for Reading
- What is an equilibrium constant and what does it indicate?
- How are reaction quotients related to equilibrium constants?

So far you have learned that a reversible reaction achieves a state of equilibrium when the rate of the forward reaction is equal to the rate of the reverse reaction. You have also learned that the rate of a reaction depends upon the concentration of the reactants and products in the reaction. The development of the concept of equilibrium was empirical, or based on experiment. This means that it depended upon chemists' ability to measure certain quantities related to a chemical reaction. One of these measurable quantities is the concentration of reactants and products.

The Equilibrium Constant

In 1864, after observing many chemical reactions, two Norwegian chemists, Cato Maximillian Guldberg (1836–1902) and Peter Waage (1833–1900), formulated a general expression describing the equilibrium condition. They proposed the **law of mass action,** which expresses the relative concentrations of reactants and products at equilibrium in terms of a quantity called the **equilibrium constant.** Consider a reaction described by the general equation

$$aA + bB \rightleftharpoons cC + dD \qquad \textbf{(Eq. 3)}$$

In this equation, a, b, c, and d are the coefficients for substances A, B, C, and D. The **equilibrium expression** for this reaction is

$$K_{eq} = \frac{[C]^c[D]^d}{[A]^a[B]^b} \qquad \textbf{(Eq. 4)}$$

where K_{eq} is the equilibrium constant. Thus the equilibrium constant is equal to the ratio of the product concentrations (raised to powers indicated by the coefficients) to the reactant concentrations (raised to powers indicated by the coefficients). Remember that square brackets denote concentration. The concentrations of the products of the forward reaction are found in the numerator, and the concentrations of the reactants of the forward reaction are found in the denominator.

Guldberg and Waage observed that this ratio is always a constant value for a given reaction regardless of initial concentrations. When the concentrations of the reactants and products are measured at equilibrium and inserted into the equilibrium expression, the result is a constant (at a given temperature). Every reversible reaction obeys this relationship and has a specific K_{eq},

Three Equilibrium Positions for the Reaction $2\,NO_2 \rightleftharpoons N_2O_4$

Experiment	Initial $[NO_2]$ (M)	Initial $[N_2O_4]$ (M)	Equilibrium $[NO_2]$ (M)	Equilibrium $[N_2O_4]$ (M)	K_{eq}
1	0.0200	0.0	0.0172	0.00140	4.73
2	0.0300	0.0	0.0243	0.00280	4.74
3	0.0	0.0200	0.0310	0.00452	4.70

Figure 16–7 *Each of the three experiments shown started with specific initial concentrations of both NO_2 and N_2O_4. Once the reactions reached equilibrium, the concentration of each substance was measured. How was the equilibrium constant calculated?*

or equilibrium constant. This observation is called the **law of chemical equilibrium.** According to the law of chemical equilibrium, every reversible reaction proceeds to an equilibrium state that has a specific ratio of the concentrations of reactants and products expressed by K_{eq}.

Let's return to our example in which NO_2 is converted into N_2O_4 in a reversible reaction: $2\,NO_2 \rightleftharpoons N_2O_4$. The equilibrium expression for this reaction is

$$K_{eq} = \frac{[N_2O_4]}{[NO_2]^2} \qquad \textbf{(Eq. 5)}$$

The equilibrium constant is equal to the concentration of N_2O_4 divided by the concentration of NO_2 raised to a power of 2, as indicated by its coefficient in the balanced chemical equation.

To determine the numerical value of K_{eq} and verify that it is constant regardless of the starting concentrations of NO_2 and N_2O_4, experiments must be performed in which different concentrations of NO_2 and N_2O_4 are added to several sealed tubes. After the reaction in each tube reaches equilibrium, the final concentration of each substance is determined. Figure 16–7 lists the data for a particular experiment. The concentrations of the gases are measured in units of molarity. K_{eq} is found by inserting the equilibrium concentrations—not the initial concentrations—into the equilibrium expression. For example, for the first set of data

$$K_{eq} = \frac{0.00140}{(0.0172)^2}$$

$$= 4.73 \qquad \textbf{(Eq. 6)}$$

Molarity units are customarily omitted from the equilibrium constant. You can see from the table that the value of the equilibrium constant does not depend on the initial concentrations of the reactants and products. Regardless of the initial concentrations, each reaction will establish equilibrium, and that equilibrium can be described by the same equilibrium constant. Furthermore, you can see that the equilibrium state can be attained beginning with either NO_2, as in the first two experiments, or N_2O_4, as in the third experiment. Thus the equilibrium state can be reached from either direction—the forward reaction or the reverse reaction. Each set of equilibrium concentrations is called an **equilibrium position.** Figure 16–7 shows three different equilibrium positions that arise as a result of the initial concentrations. Thus the equilibrium position depends upon the initial concentrations, but the equilibrium constant does not. There are an infinite number of equilibrium positions, but there is only one equilibrium constant.

SAMPLE PROBLEM 1

What is the equilibrium expression for this reaction?

$$2\,CO\,(g) + O_2\,(g) \rightleftharpoons 2\,CO_2\,(g)$$

STRATEGY	SOLUTION
1. Analyze	You are given a reversible reaction and asked to determine the equilibrium expression.
2. Plan	The equilibrium expression is the ratio of the product concentration to the reactant concentration. Each concentration is raised to a power as indicated by its coefficient in the equation. Thus [CO] and [CO_2] will each be raised to a power of 2.
3. Solve	$K_{eq} = \dfrac{[CO_2]^2}{[CO]^2[O_2]}$
4. Evaluate	As it should, the expression shows the concentration of the product of the forward reaction in the numerator and the concentrations of the reactants of the forward reaction in the denominator. The exponents, which are based on the coefficients, have been correctly included.

You may wonder why K_{eq} is written with no units. Because molarities (M) are raised to powers in the equilibrium equation, the constant can have many different units, such as M, M^2, $1/M$, or no units at all. Each reaction has a unique equilibrium constant. Therefore, the units of a constant do not matter, because it will be applied only to that reaction.

PRACTICE PROBLEMS

1. Write the equilibrium expression for the reaction

$$2\,SO_2\,(g) + O_2\,(g) \rightleftharpoons 2\,SO_3\,(g)$$

$$\left(\text{Answer: } K_{eq} = \dfrac{[SO_3]^2}{[SO_2]^2[O_2]}\right)$$

2. Write the equilibrium expression for the reaction

$$CO\,(g) + 3\,H_2\,(g) \rightleftharpoons CH_4\,(g) + H_2O\,(g)$$

$$\left(\text{Answer: } K_{eq} = \dfrac{[CH_4][H_2O]}{[CO][H_2]^3}\right)$$

While the equilibrium constant does not tell you anything about the time it takes to reach equilibrium, it does provide important information about the mixture of reactants and products at equilibrium. **The equilibrium constant is a measure of the extent to which a reaction proceeds to completion.** The magnitude of the equilibrium constant for different reactions varies over a tremendous range, from very small to very large.

A shorthand notation for showing that the equilibrium constant is much greater than 1 is $K_{eq} \gg 1$. The symbol $\gg$ is read as "significantly greater than" or "very much greater than." (The symbol $>$ means greater than.) If the equilibrium constant is very large, the numerator of the equilibrium expression must be much larger than the denominator. In other words, the equilibrium concentration of the products must be much greater than that of the reactants. At equilibrium, then, this reaction system consists mainly of products and is therefore considered to proceed to completion. In this case, chemists say that equilibrium "lies to the right," toward the product side.

A very small value for the equilibrium constant, $K_{eq} \ll 1$, indicates that the denominator of the equilibrium expression must be much larger than the numerator. At equilibrium this reaction system contains mostly reactants and almost no products. This reaction barely gets going! Equilibrium in this case "lies to the left," toward the reactant side. In the intermediate situation, when the equilibrium constant is about equal to 1 ($K_{eq} \approx 1$), considerable concentrations of both reactants and products are usually present at equilibrium.

Homogeneous and Heterogeneous Equilibria

The equilibrium expression correctly describes the equilibrium behavior of all chemical reaction systems. So far, the examples we have discussed have involved only gases. Equilibrium conditions for reactions in which all the reactants and products are in the same state are called **homogeneous equilibria.** As you know, however, many reactions involve substances that are in different states. Equilibrium conditions for reactions that involve substances in more than one state are called **heterogeneous equilibria.** As an example of a heterogeneous equilibrium, consider the reaction described by the equation below.

$$NH_4Cl\,(s) \rightleftharpoons NH_3\,(g) + HCl\,(g) \qquad \textbf{(Eq. 7)}$$

As before, the first step in analyzing the equilibrium condition for this reaction is to determine the equilibrium constant. This presents a bit of a problem, however. The concentrations we have been using were the concentrations of gases in units of molarity. How do chemists express the concentration of a solid substance? The concentration of a pure substance—liquid or solid—is its density divided by its molar mass. The density of a pure liquid or solid is essentially constant and changes very little with temperature. Thus the concentration of a pure solid or liquid does not change during a reaction, regardless of how much pure solid or liquid is present. Because these constants are effectively incorporated into the equilibrium constant, the concentrations of pure solids and liquids can be left out of the equilibrium expression.

Now we can determine the equilibrium expression for the reaction. Because ammonium chloride (NH_4Cl) is a pure solid, it is excluded from the expression. Thus the equilibrium expression for the reaction is

$$K_{eq} = [NH_3][HCl] \qquad \textbf{(Eq. 8)}$$

Do not think that because they do not appear in the equilibrium expression, pure solids and liquids have nothing to do with equilibrium. These substances are just as important as the other substances in a reaction and are necessary for establishing equilibrium. However, their concentrations do not change substantially and so are by convention included in the equilibrium constant.

SAMPLE PROBLEM 2

What is the equilibrium expression for this reaction?

$$C\,(s) + H_2O\,(g) \rightleftharpoons CO\,(g) + H_2\,(g)$$

STRATEGY	SOLUTION
1. Analyze	You are asked to find the equilibrium expression for a reversible reaction.
2. Plan	The equilibrium expression is the ratio of the product concentrations to the reactant concentrations. However, one reactant (carbon) is a pure solid and is thus not part of the equilibrium expression.
3. Solve	$K_{eq} = \dfrac{[CO][H_2]}{[H_2O]}$
4. Evaluate	The answer shows the concentrations of the products in the numerator and the concentration of a reactant in the denominator. The concentration of carbon is essentially a constant and does not appear in the answer.

PRACTICE PROBLEMS

3. Write the equilibrium expression for the following reaction: $NH_4NO_3\,(s) \rightleftharpoons N_2O\,(g) + 2\,H_2O\,(g)$. (Answer: $K_{eq} = [N_2O][H_2O]^2$)

4. Write the equilibrium expression for the following reaction: $ZnCO_3\,(s) \rightleftharpoons ZnO\,(s) + CO_2\,(g)$. (Answer: $K_{eq} = [CO_2]$)

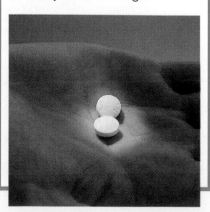
The Reaction Quotient

When the reactants and products of a chemical reaction are mixed, it is not always obvious if the mixture has or has not reached equilibrium. And if the mixture is not at equilibrium, it is useful to know the direction in which the system will shift to reach equilibrium. **The reaction quotient (Q) is used to determine if a reaction is at equilibrium.** The **reaction quotient** is calculated much like the equilibrium constant except that the concentrations that exist at the time the measurement is taken, not the equilibrium concentrations, are inserted into the equilibrium expression.

Let's consider the synthesis of ammonia from nitrogen and hydrogen at 472°C.

$$N_2 (g) + 3 H_2 (g) \rightleftharpoons 2 NH_3 (g) \qquad \textbf{(Eq. 9)}$$

The equilibrium constant for this reaction at this temperature is 0.105. Suppose you are running this reaction and want to find out if it is at equilibrium. You measure the concentrations and find that $[NH_3] = 0.15\ M$, $[N_2] = 0.0020\ M$, and $[H_2] = 0.10\ M$. The reaction quotient is calculated by substituting these concentrations into the equilibrium expression.

$$K_{eq} = \frac{[NH_3]^2}{[N_2][H_2]^3}$$

$$Q = \frac{(0.15)^2}{(0.0020)(0.10)^3}$$

$$= 1.1 \times 10^4 \qquad \textbf{(Eq. 10)}$$

The reaction is not at equilibrium because Q does not equal K_{eq}. If the reaction was at equilibrium, Q would equal K_{eq} because the reaction quotient is simply the equilibrium expression using concentrations at a given time.

The question now is, if the system is not at equilibrium, in which direction will it proceed to reach equilibrium? The answer depends upon the relationship between Q and K_{eq}. The following statements summarize the relationship:

- If Q is less than K_{eq} ($Q < K_{eq}$), the denominator of the reaction quotient expression is too large and the numerator is too small. This means that at the time of measurement there is too much of the reactants and too little of the products. The reaction will consume reactants and form products to reach equilibrium. Thus the reaction will proceed to the right, in the direction of the products.
- If Q is greater than K_{eq} ($Q > K_{eq}$), the denominator of the reaction quotient expression is too small and the numerator is too large. This means that at the time of measurement there is too much of the products and too little of the reactants. For the system to reach equilibrium, reactants must be formed and products must be consumed. The reaction will proceed to the left, in the direction of the reactants.
- If Q is equal to K_{eq} ($Q = K_{eq}$), the system is at equilibrium and no shift in direction will occur.

Consider this reaction:

$$COCl_2 \, (g) \rightleftharpoons CO \, (g) + Cl_2 \, (g) \quad K_{eq} = 170$$

If the concentrations of CO and Cl_2 are each 0.15 M and the concentration of $COCl_2$ is 1.1×10^{-3} M, is the reaction at equilibrium? If not, in which direction will it proceed?

STRATEGY	SOLUTION
1. Analyze	To determine if a reaction is in equilibrium, you need to calculate the reaction quotient (Q) and compare it to the equilibrium constant (K_{eq}).
2. Plan	Q is calculated much like K_{eq}. Use the concentrations that the problem provides.
3. Solve	$Q = \dfrac{[CO][Cl_2]}{[COCl_2]} = \dfrac{(0.15)(0.15)}{1.1 \times 10^{-3}} = 20.$
	$Q < K_{eq}$, thus the reaction is not at equilibrium and proceeds to the right.
4. Evaluate	The concentration of the reactant is much smaller than the concentration of either product. K_{eq} is very large, however, so it is reasonable that the reaction proceeds to the right.

PRACTICE PROBLEMS

5. A vial contains 0.150 M NO_2 and 0.300 M N_2O_4. Calculate Q for the reaction 2 NO_2 $(g) \rightleftharpoons N_2O_4$ (g) *(Answer: 13.3)*

6. At 448°C, K_{eq} = 50.5 for the reaction H_2 $(g) + I_2$ $(g) \rightleftharpoons$ 2 HI (g). Find Q and predict how the reaction proceeds if $[H_2]$ = 0.150 M, $[I_2]$ = 0.175 M, and $[HI]$ = 0.950 M
   (Answer: 34.4, to the right.)

16–2 Section Review

1. Define the term equilibrium constant. How is it related to the law of chemical equilibrium?

2. What can you conclude from the magnitude of the equilibrium constant? Why?

3. Describe a reaction quotient. How can it be used to determine if a reaction is at equilibrium?

4. **Critical Thinking—Making inferences** For the reaction A + C $\rightleftharpoons$ B, K_{eq} = 0.025. What is the equilibrium constant for the reverse reaction?

Guide for Reading
- What is Le Chatelier's principle?
- How does the Haber process utilize Le Chatelier's principle?

16-3 Le Chatelier's Principle

Imagine this scene: A daring tightrope walker balances precariously on a thin wire high above Niagara Falls. The smallest gust of wind could cause the tightrope walker to lose his balance and plunge into the raging torrent below! Luckily, he is able to maintain his balance by adjusting the long pole he carries. In a similar way, a chemical reaction at equilibrium can be disturbed and shifted away from equilibrium. Instead of a gust of wind, the factors that alter chemical equilibria are concentrations of reactants and products, pressure, and temperature.

You can qualitatively predict the effects of changes in concentrations, pressure, and temperature using a principle developed by Henri Louis Le Chatelier (leh-SHAHT-lee-ay). Le Chatelier (1850–1936) was trained in France as a mining engineer. Upon graduation, he joined the faculty of the mining school as a professor of chemistry. Le Chatelier began studying flames in hopes of preventing mine explosions. His work eventually led him to establish **Le Chatelier's principle** in 1888. **Le Chatelier's principle states that if a change in conditions is imposed on a system at equilibrium, the equilibrium position will shift in the direction that tends to reduce that change in conditions.** In other words, a reaction system will shift in the forward or reverse direction to "undo," or compensate for, the altering factor.

Historical Perspective ➤

Changes in Concentration

For any equilibrium system, the reaction can be shifted forward or backward by changing the concentration of a reactant or product. If more of a particular substance is added to a reaction at equilibrium, the concentration of that substance increases. The reaction will return to equilibrium by consuming some of the added substance. Conversely, if a substance is removed, its concentration decreases. The reaction will return to equilibrium by producing more of the substance that was removed.

Figure 16–8 *Both the graceful child and the daring high-wire artist are relying upon their ability to balance themselves and regain their equilibrium at all costs. Chemical reactions, too, can regain their equilibrium once lost. What factors alter chemical equilibria?*

Let's return to the smog reaction as an example. Assume that the reaction in which NO_2 is converted to N_2O_4 is at equilibrium and that more NO_2 is injected into the mixture. According to Le Chatelier's principle, the reaction will run in the direction that will partially counter the disturbance—that is, the direction that will consume the excess NO_2. This will be accomplished if the reaction runs to the right, using up some of the reactant (NO_2) and producing some more of the product (N_2O_4). See Figure 16–9. If more N_2O_4 is added to the system instead, the reaction will run to the left, consuming the excess N_2O_4 and producing NO_2. Note, however, that only the equilibrium position shifts. The equilibrium constant does not. What will happen if either substance is removed from the mixture?

If you find Le Chatelier's principle confusing at first, it may help you to understand the shift in terms of the reaction quotient. You know that when the reaction is at equilibrium, the reaction quotient is equal to K_{eq}. The reaction quotient for this reaction, in which N_2O_4 is formed from NO_2, is

$$Q = \frac{[N_2O_4]}{[NO_2]^2} \qquad \textbf{(Eq. 11)}$$

If extra NO_2 is injected into the reaction system, the value of $[NO_2]$ increases, raising the value of the denominator of the expression. A larger denominator results in a lower value of Q. Thus Q will become less than K_{eq}. Recall what happens when $Q < K_{eq}$. In order to return to equilibrium, the reaction will shift to the right. Adding N_2O_4 to the system results in a larger numerator, making $Q > K_{eq}$. In this case, the reaction will shift to the left in order to reach equilibrium. Removing either substance will have the opposite effect. The changes can be summarized as follows: Adding a substance to a system at equilibrium drives the system to consume that substance. Removing a substance from a system at equilibrium drives the system to produce more of that substance.

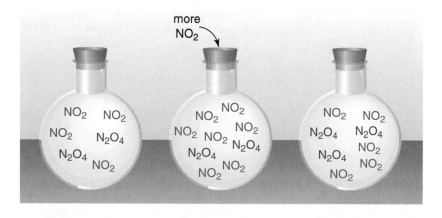

more
NO_2

NO_2 NO_2
NO_2 N_2O_4
N_2O_4 NO_2

NO_2 NO_2
NO_2 NO_2
NO_2 NO_2 N_2O_4
N_2O_4
NO_2 NO_2

NO_2 NO_2
N_2O_4 N_2O_4
N_2O_4 NO_2
NO_2

Figure 16–9 *Once the reaction between NO_2 and N_2O_4 reaches equilibrium, any change in the concentrations of either substance will create a mixture that is not at equilibrium. The reaction will then proceed in the direction that restores equilibrium. How are the equilibrium position and the equilibrium constant affected by such changes?*

Changes in Pressure

For some gaseous equilibrium systems, the reaction can be shifted forward or backward by changing the pressure. One way of changing the pressure of a system is by changing the volume of the container. If the total pressure of a system is increased, the system will shift to reduce that pressure by proceeding in the direction that produces fewer molecules.

Imagine that the reaction involving NO_2 and N_2O_4 is at equilibrium in a container with a moveable piston. The pressure is increased by moving the piston and reducing the volume, as shown in Figure 16–10. In which direction will the reaction run as a result of this disturbance? Look again at the equation.

$$2\,NO_2\,(g) \rightleftharpoons N_2O_4\,(g) \qquad \textbf{(Eq. 12)}$$

In this reaction, 2 moles of NO_2 produce 1 mole of N_2O_4. Because half as many moles are produced in the forward reaction, the reaction will respond to increased pressure by shifting to the right, producing more N_2O_4. As with changes in concentration, the reaction shifts to change the equilibrium position, not the equilibrium constant.

Figure 16–10 Both the photographs and illustrations show how the equilibrium between NO_2 and N_2O_4 changes with pressure. Increase the pressure (top middle, bottom middle), and the volume shrinks, altering the concentrations of both gases and changing the color to dark brown. To restore equilibrium, the reaction shifts to produce fewer molecules, which means it makes more N_2O_4 (top right, bottom right). How can you tell that equilibrium has been restored?

What if the following reaction is at equilibrium and is then disturbed by an increase in pressure?

$$NH_4Cl\,(s) \rightleftharpoons NH_3\,(g) + HCl\,(g) \qquad \textbf{(Eq. 13)}$$

In this case, 0 moles of gas on the left produce 2 moles of gas on the right. The reaction will run from right to left in order to reduce the number of moles of gas produced.

Let's look at one last example. Consider the following reaction. What will happen if the pressure is increased?

$$H_2\,(g) + Cl_2\,(g) \rightleftharpoons 2\,HCl\,(g) \qquad \textbf{(Eq. 14)}$$

Here there are 2 moles of gas on each side of the equation. A shift in either direction will not reduce the pressure. As a result, the increase in pressure has no effect on the equilibrium situation. An equilibrium reaction that has the same number of moles of gas on both sides of the equation will not be affected by changes in pressure.

Effect of Changing Temperature

As you know by now in your study of chemistry, temperature is extremely important in many chemical systems, including chemical equilibrium. In fact, the value of the equilibrium constant for a particular reaction depends on temperature. Increasing the temperature causes some chemical reactions to proceed more completely to products, increasing the value of the equilibrium constant. But increasing the temperature causes other chemical reactions to proceed less completely, lowering the value of the equilibrium constant. By understanding how temperature changes affect equilibrium, you can predict how specific reactions will respond to such changes.

Consider the reaction in which hydrogen and iodine join to form hydrogen iodide.

$$H_2\,(g) + I_2\,(g) \rightleftharpoons 2\,HI\,(g) + heat \qquad \textbf{(Eq. 15)}$$

The equilibrium constant for this reaction is 54.5 at 400°C and 45.9 at 490°C. Recall that the equilibrium constant is a measure of the extent to which a reaction proceeds. You can thus conclude that raising the temperature causes this reaction to proceed less completely to products. Lowering the temperature would produce a higher yield of HI.

To use Le Chatelier's principle to understand the effect of temperature on equilibrium, you must first know if the reaction gives off heat or absorbs heat. The reaction in Equation 15 gives off heat and is therefore exothermic. (Recall that an endothermic reaction must absorb heat in order to proceed.) In a reversible reaction, if the forward reaction is exothermic, the reverse reaction is endothermic. Thus when heat is added to the system, the reaction tends to reestablish equilibrium by consuming that additional heat through the reverse (endothermic) reaction. It

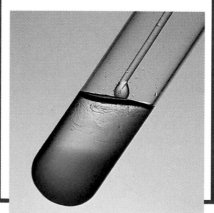

Figure 16–11 These tubes contain a mixture of NO_2 and N_2O_4. When the mixture is heated (left), the clear N_2O_4 is partly converted to brown NO_2. But when the same mixture is frozen (right), it is almost colorless.

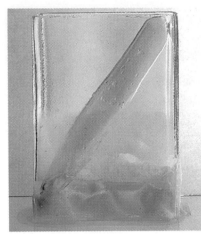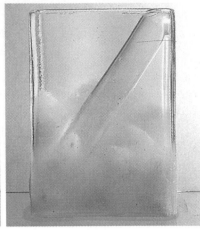

may help you to view heat as a component of the reaction. Because heat appears on the right side of this equation, the addition of heat will cause the reaction to run to the left. Figure 16–11 shows the changes that occur to the smog reaction when the temperature is raised.

For an endothermic reaction, the responses will be the reverse of an exothermic reaction.

$$\text{heat} + NH_4Cl\,(s) \rightleftharpoons NH_3\,(g) + HCl\,(g) \quad \textbf{(Eq. 16)}$$

For this reaction, raising the temperature will drive the reaction in the forward direction and lowering the temperature will drive it in the reverse direction.

Unlike changing concentration or pressure, changing temperature causes a reaction to reestablish equilibrium by effectively changing the value of the equilibrium constant. The first two factors (concentration and pressure) affect only the equilibrium position. Temperature is the only factor that affects the value of the equilibrium constant.

The Haber Process

Throughout your study of chemistry, you will encounter numerous examples of the essential role science plays in your life. Yet even so, you may sometimes feel that a particular topic has no useful applications. Chemical equilibrium might be such a topic. In reality, this perception is far from the truth. Without realizing it, you depend upon chemical equilibrium for many of the fruits and vegetables you eat each day. Surprised? You will see the connection shortly. It involves nitrogen-containing compounds that are essential to both fertilizers and explosives. How can two such diverse products be related? Let's find out.

Although nitrogen gas is very common, making up about 78 percent of air, usable nitrogen compounds are not readily available. Breaking the strong triple bond between the nitrogen atoms in nitrogen gas and bonding them to other atoms requires a tremendous amount of energy. Thus, the nitrogen in naturally

Sprouting Beans

1. Obtain several bean seeds, such as lima beans, and a small amount of nitrogen-based fertilizer.
2. Fill two disposable cups or small planting pots with soil. Plant two or three seeds in each cup or pot.
3. Label one cup "Plain" and the other "Fertilized." Add a small amount of fertilizer to the soil of the plant in the "Fertilized" cup.
4. Place both plants in the same location so that they get the same amount of sunlight and water each plant regularly. After several weeks, observe the two plants. Do you see any differences between them?
5. On Your Own Repeat the experiment with two other types of plants.

Making the Most of It

Carla the chemistry student has landed her first job working for a manufacturer of methanol. Methanol—CH_3OH—is prepared from CO (*g*) and H_2 (*g*). The more methanol that is produced, the greater the company's profits, so Carla's first challenge is to set the reaction conditions to make as much CH_3OH as possible. What should she do? Are there any experiments she should perform in order to determine the conditions? What conclusions can she draw from each experiment?

occurring minerals was more commonly used to produce nitrogen compounds than was nitrogen from air. The most important natural source of nitrogen is sodium nitrate ($NaNO_3$), also known as Chile saltpeter because most deposits are located in Chile.

At the start of World War I, Germany was dependent on sodium nitrate deposits in Chile for the nitrogen-containing compounds needed to make explosives. During the war, however, the allied blockade of South America cut off this supply. Seeking to free Germany from dependence on Chile saltpeter, a German chemist named Fritz Haber (1868–1934) examined the direct combination reaction between nitrogen and hydrogen, a reaction that forms ammonia.

> < *Historical Perspective*

$$N_2\,(g) + 3\,H_2\,(g) \rightleftharpoons 2\,NH_3\,(g) + \text{heat} \quad \textbf{(Eq. 17)}$$

Although in theory this reaction should produce ammonia, it had never been used for this purpose. On its own, the reaction reached equilibrium long before any sizable amount of ammonia was produced. Haber and his team studied the reaction in hopes of maximizing the equilibrium yield of ammonia. Special equipment had to be developed to reach the pressures and temperatures Haber needed. A practical system was finally achieved, which enabled Germany to continue production of explosives regardless of the blockade. The **Haber process,** as it was called, is believed to have prolonged the war by several years.

In addition to the Haber process, Haber developed the use of chlorine as a poison-gas weapon. In 1918, notwithstanding much controversy and criticism, he was awarded the Nobel Prize for Chemistry. The ultimate irony was that in 1933, despite his work for Germany, Haber was expelled from the country because he was Jewish.

Visit our Web site at
http://www.phschool.com
to support your
study of chemistry.

None for Me, I'll Make My Own

Some crops are actually able to "fertilize" their own soil. Members of the bean family have this ability. The fertilizing activity takes place in lumpy structures, called nodules, that grow on their roots as shown in the photograph. These nodules contain certain types of bacteria that are able to remove nitrogen gas from the air and convert it into ammonia. The ammonia is absorbed and used by the plant as a source of nitrogen to make proteins.

Farmers often dust bean seeds with bacteria to make sure they will grow in the nodules that form on the roots. When you compare the bacteria's ability to break the bonds of nitrogen molecules and form ammonia with the high temperature and pressure requirements of the Haber process, you can see that these tiny bacteria living in the roots of bean plants certainly are amazing organisms.

Haber was able to substantially increase the ammonia yield by analyzing its equilibrium mixture. The equilibrium expression for this reaction is

$$K_{eq} = \frac{[NH_3]^2}{[N_2][H_2]^3} \qquad \textbf{(Eq. 18)}$$

As you know, the equilibrium mixture of N_2, H_2, and NH_3 depends upon the initial concentration of each component. In their studies of ammonia synthesis, Haber and his co-workers determined the equilibrium constant for this reaction by starting with various mixtures of the three components and allowing them to reach equilibrium at a specific temperature and pressure. They then shifted the equilibrium to produce the maximum amount of ammonia.

The first method of shifting the equilibrium is to change the concentration of one or more of the components. For example, consider what happens when ammonia is removed from the reaction container. The reaction shifts to the right to produce more ammonia and restore equilibrium. In the Haber process, ammonia is continuously removed so that the reaction continuously shifts to the right to produce more ammonia.

The second method of shifting the equilibrium is to change the pressure at which the reaction occurs. Look again at the reaction in Equation 17. There are 4 moles of gas on the left and 2 moles on the right. One way to force the reaction to the right is to increase the pressure, which shifts the reaction to the side with fewer moles. And in fact, the Haber process requires high pressures.

The third and final method of shifting the equilibrium is to change the temperature at which the reaction occurs. The forward reaction in the synthesis of ammonia is exothermic. What would happen if the temperature was increased? Increasing the temperature of an exothermic reaction causes the reaction to shift in the reverse direction—toward the production of less ammonia. Yet the Haber process occurs at high temperatures. How can this be so? The reason is that at lower temperatures, the reaction proceeds too slowly to be practical. Increasing the temperature increases the rate of the reaction, but decreases the yield of ammonia. To compensate for this, even higher pressures are necessary to favor the production of ammonia.

Today, more than 300 Haber ammonia plants are in operation around the world. Rather than providing nitrogen exclusively for explosives, ammonia is produced for use in home cleaning products and, more importantly, in fertilizers. Plant growth requires a substantial supply of nitrogen in the soil. Just as is true of explosives, the triple bonds in nitrogen gas must be broken before the nitrogen can be used by plants.

Figure 16–12 To help Germany produce more explosives for World War I, Fritz Haber (left) developed a practical method of synthesizing ammonia. Today, ammonia from the Haber process is used to make fertilizer. Are you surprised that war-time research led to an increase in our supply of fruits and vegetables (right)?

Amazingly enough, certain plant roots can convert nitrogen in the soil into a usable form in a process known as nitrogen fixation. And they can do this without the tremendous pressures and high temperatures needed in the laboratory! The quantity of food produced in the world today, however, is far greater than the amount that could be produced if we relied solely on naturally available nitrogen in the soil and the efforts of plant roots. Instead, ammonia is added to soil in the form of fertilizer.

INTEGRATING

BIOLOGY

Would you believe that tiny bacteria can do essentially the same job as complex and expensive factories?

16–3 Section Review

1. State Le Chatelier's principle.

2. Predict the direction of the shift in the equilibrium position of this reaction when (a) CO is added, (b) As_4 is removed, and (c) pressure is increased.

$$As_4O_6 (s) + 6 C (s) \rightleftharpoons As_4 (g) + 6 CO (g)$$

3. With added heat, calcium carbonate decomposes to form calcium oxide and carbon dioxide. In which direction will the equilibrium shift if the temperature of the reaction is lowered? Explain.

4. What is the Haber process? Why is an understanding of chemical equilibrium essential to the industrial production of ammonia?

5. **Theme Trace—Patterns of Change**   Summarize how changes in concentration, pressure, and temperature affect reversible reactions at equilibrium.

Laboratory Investigation

Establishing Equilibrium

Problem

How can you determine when a system is at equilibrium?

Materials (per group)

2 25-mL graduated cylinders
2 drinking straws with different diameters
food coloring
graph paper
paper and pencil

Procedure

1. Label one graduated cylinder "Reactants" and the other "Products." Label one straw "Forward" and the other "Reverse."
2. Add a few drops of food coloring to the reactant cylinder. Then fill the cylinder with water to the 25.0-mL mark.
3. Place the forward straw into the reactant cylinder. Place the reverse straw in the empty product cylinder.
4. Put your finger over the top of the forward straw. Transfer the colored water in the straw to the product cylinder.
5. Now put your finger over the reverse straw and transfer colored liquid from the product cylinder to the reactant cylinder.
6. Record the volume of each cylinder in a data table similar to the one shown. Each time you transfer liquid from the reactant cylinder to the product cylinder and back from the product cylinder to the reactant cylinder constitutes one transfer.
7. Repeat Steps 4, 5, and 6 until the volumes in the cylinders remain constant for at least 5 readings.
8. Repeat the entire experiment, but this time begin with 25.0 mL of colored water in the product cylinder and nothing in the reactant cylinder. Use the same straws for the forward and reverse reactions.

Observations

	Volume	
Transfer	Reactant Cylinder (mL)	Product Cylinder (mL)
1		
2		
3		

1. Did you use the larger straw for the forward or reverse reaction?
2. At equilibrium, was there a greater volume of products or reactants?
3. What was the effect on equilibrium volumes when you started with no reactants and 25.0 mL of products?
4. Graph your results for both experiments by plotting the transfer number on the x-axis and the volumes for both reactants and products on the y-axis.

Analysis and Conclusions

1. Was equilibrium established in both experiments? If so, what can you conclude?
2. What variable determined whether there was a greater volume of reactants or products at equilibrium?
3. Why could this system be called a dynamic equilibrium?
4. **On Your Own**   Repeat this experiment starting with a portion of the 25.0 mL of colored water in one cylinder and the remaining amount in the other cylinder.

STUDY GUIDE

Summarizing Key Concepts

16–1 The Concept of Equilibrium

- Reversible reactions are chemical reactions in which the products can reform the original reactants.
- A reversible reaction reaches chemical equilibrium when the rate of the forward reaction is equal to the rate of the reverse reaction.

16–2 The Law of Chemical Equilibrium

- The law of mass action expresses the ratio of concentrations of reactants and products of a reversible reaction in terms of the equilibrium constant, which is found by an equilibrium expression.
- The law of chemical equilibrium states that every reaction that reaches equilibrium has a specific equilibrium constant, which indicates the extent of the reaction.
- The equilibrium position relates to the equilibrium concentrations of the components of a reaction and depends upon the initial concentrations.
- Pure solids and liquids involved in heterogeneous equilibria do not appear in the equilibrium expression.

- The reaction quotient (Q) is found by inserting the concentrations of reactants and products at a given point into the equilibrium expression. If $Q = K_{eq}$, the reaction is at equilibrium. If $Q > K_{eq}$, the reaction will proceed to the left. If $Q < K_{eq}$, the reaction will proceed to the right.

16–3 Le Chatelier's Principle

- According to Le Chatelier's principle, a system that is disturbed from equilibrium will shift in order to reduce the disturbance. Factors that disturb a system at equilibrium are changes in the concentrations of reactants and products, changes in pressure, or changes in temperature.
- The Haber process is an industrial process through which ammonia is synthesized. The process depends upon Le Chatelier's principle to maximize the yield of ammonia.

Reviewing Key Terms

Define each term in a complete sentence.

16–1 The Concept of Equilibrium

reversible reaction
chemical equilibrium

16–2 The Law of Chemical Equilibrium

law of mass action
equilibrium constant
equilibrium expression
law of chemical equilibrium

equilibrium position
homogeneous equilibria
heterogeneous equilibria
reaction quotient

16–3 Le Chatelier's Principle

Le Chatelier's principle
Haber process

CHAPTER REVIEW

Content Review

Multiple Choice
Choose the letter of the answer that best completes each statement.

1. The equilibrium expression for the reaction $H_2 (g) + I_2 (g) \rightleftharpoons 2 HI (g)$ is
   (a) $\dfrac{[2 \, HI]}{[H_2][I_2]}.$
   (b) $\dfrac{[H_2][I_2]}{[2 \, HI]}.$
   (c) $\dfrac{[H_2][I_2]}{[HI]^2}.$
   (d) $\dfrac{[HI]^2}{[H_2][I_2]}.$

2. If the equilibrium constant is very large,
   (a) it still is less than 1.
   (b) more products than reactants exist at equilibrium.
   (c) more reactants than products exist at equilibrium.
   (d) the reaction barely gets going.

3. $SnO_2 (s) + 2 CO (g) \rightleftharpoons Sn (s) + 2 CO_2 (g)$ K_{eq} for this reaction is
   (a) $\dfrac{[Sn][CO_2]^2}{[SnO_2][CO]^2}.$
   (b) $\dfrac{[CO_2]^2}{[CO]^2}.$
   (c) $\dfrac{[SnO_2][CO]^2}{[Sn][CO_2]^2}.$
   (d) $\dfrac{[CO]^2}{[CO_2]^2}.$

4. At equilibrium,
   (a) $K_{eq} = Q.$
   (b) $K_{eq} > 1.$
   (c) $K_{eq} = 1.$
   (d) $K_{eq} < 1.$

5. Which change will increase the production of water vapor in this reaction: $2 H_2S (g) + 3 O_2 (g) \rightleftharpoons 2 H_2O (g) + 2 SO_2 (g)$?
   (a) adding SO_2
   (b) removing H_2S
   (c) removing O_2
   (d) removing SO_2

6. Which reaction will produce more products when the pressure is increased?
   (a) $P_4 (s) + 6 Cl_2 (g) \rightleftharpoons 4 PCl_3 (l)$
   (b) $PCl_3 (g) + 3 NH_3 (g) \rightleftharpoons P(NH_2)_3 (g) + 3 HCl (g)$
   (c) $4 HCl (g) + O_2 (g) \rightleftharpoons 2 H_2O (g) + 2 Cl_2 (g)$
   (d) $2 H_2O_2 (l) \rightleftharpoons 2 H_2O (l) + O_2 (g)$

7. The equilibrium constant changes with
   (a) volume.
   (b) pressure.
   (c) temperature.
   (d) Q.

8. In a sealed container, the reaction $CH_4 (g) + H_2O (g) \rightleftharpoons CO (g) + 3 H_2 (g)$ will produce additional hydrogen gas if
   (a) carbon monoxide is added.
   (b) water vapor is removed.
   (c) the volume is decreased.
   (d) the volume is increased.

True or False
If the statement is true, write "true." If it is false, change the underlined word or words to make the statement true.

9. K_{eq} does <u>depend</u> on the initial concentrations of reactants and products.
10. For a reaction that has mostly reactants at equilibrium, $K_{eq} \underline{\geq 1}$.
11. At equilibrium, the <u>rates</u> of the forward and reverse reactions are equal.
12. Pure liquids and solids <u>should be</u> included in the equilibrium expression.
13. To determine if a reaction is at equilibrium, compare the <u>reaction quotient</u> with the equilibrium constant.
14. The Haber process results in the production of <u>ammonia</u>.

Concept Mapping
Complete the following concept map for Section 16–2. Refer to pages xviii–xix to construct a concept map for the entire chapter.

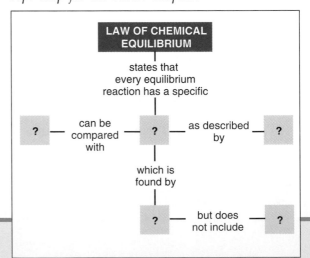

Concept Mastery

Discuss each of the following in a brief paragraph.

15. Explain how reversible reactions are related to chemical equilibrium.
16. What is the law of mass action? Why is it significant?
17. Write a general form of the equilibrium expression for the reaction described by the following equation: $eA + fB \rightleftharpoons gC + hD$, in which A, B, C, and D are all gases.
18. Which reaction is favored in each of the following cases—forward or reverse? Explain your answers.
    (a) $K_{eq} = 1$ (b) $K_{eq} >> 1$ (c) $K_{eq} << 1$
19. Do changes in concentration, pressure, and temperature affect systems at equilibrium? Use examples in your answer.

20. Explain how the reaction quotient can be used to determine whether or not a reaction is at equilibrium and, if not, in what direction it will proceed.
21. What is Le Chatelier's principle and why is it important?
22. Describe the Haber process and its relationship to chemical equilibrium.
23. **Tying it Together** The concentrations of reactants and products follow definite *patterns of change*. Explain how the concentrations of A, B, C, and D change from the beginning of the reaction to equilibrium in the reaction described by the following equation:
$$A + B \rightleftharpoons C + D.$$

Critical Thinking and Problem Solving

Use the skills you have developed in this chapter to answer each of the following.

24. **Applying concepts** Indicate whether each of the following reactions is homogeneous or heterogeneous. Then write the equilibrium expression for each.
    (a) $N_2O_5(g) \rightleftharpoons NO_2(g) + NO_3(g)$
    (b) $H_2(g) + FeO(s) \rightleftharpoons H_2O(g) + Fe(s)$
    (c) $2SO_2(g) + O_2(g) \rightleftharpoons 2SO_3(g)$
    (d) $2H_2O(g) \rightleftharpoons O_2(g) + 2H_2(g)$
25. **Making comparisons** Compare and contrast the equilibrium constant and the reaction quotient for a reaction.
26. **Evaluating statements** A classmate concludes that reactions with large equilibrium constants are extremely fast. Explain whether the statement is true or false.
27. **Interpreting data** The table below shows data from two experiments with the reaction $H_2(g) + I_2(g) \rightleftharpoons 2HI(g)$ at 425°C. What is the equilibrium constant for this reaction? What phenomenon does the data indicate?

28. **Making predictions** Predict whether each change would favor the forward or reverse reaction in the following reaction at equilibrium: $2HI(g) \rightleftharpoons H_2(g) + I_2(g)$.
    (a) adding HI   (c) removing I_2
    (b) adding H_2 (d) removing HI.
29. **Making predictions** At equilibrium, what effect would decreasing the pressure have on this reaction: $2NO(g) + O_2(g) \rightleftharpoons 2NO_2(g)$? Explain your answer.
30. **Using the writing process** Nitrogen-containing fertilizers can increase crop yield tremendously. However, these fertilizers can enter the runoff water and be carried to nearby lakes. There, they cause the algae population to grow out of control, eventually killing the fish in the lake. Therefore, some people suggest that these fertilizers should be banned. Write an essay in which you debate the pros and cons of using fertilizers.

Experiment	Initial Concentration (*M*)			Equilibrium Concentration (*M*)		
	[H_2]	[I_2]	[HI]	[H_2]	[I_2]	[HI]
1	1.000	1.000	0.0	0.212	0.212	1.576
2	0.0	0.0	1.000	0.106	0.106	0.788

Solubility and Precipitation

Your group is wriggling through a passage that is not much wider in some spots than your body. The limestone under your fingers is slick with mud, and your breath condenses in the cold air illuminated by the light on your helmet.

Your destination is near. When you reach the end of the passage, the awesome sight takes your breath away. Amazingly, it was water and the minerals dissolved in that water that created this unbelievable spectacle over thousands of years. The cavern was formed by fresh rainwater that dissolved limestone rock. After evaporating, that water deposited the limestone in the various formations you see. In this chapter, you will learn about the processes that made all this possible—the formation of aqueous solutions of ionic solids and the reformation of ionic solids from aqueous solutions.

Both the splendor of a limestone cavern and the activity of an adventurous tyke depend upon ions formed in aqueous solutions.

Chem Journal

YOU AND YOUR WORLD

Describe in your journal whatever thoughts come to mind when you hear the word precipitation. Write a short story involving your perception of precipitation. Did your perception change after reading this chapter?

17–1 Solubility Equilibria

Guide for Reading
- How are dissolution and precipitation alike and different?
- What is a solubility product?

If you have ever had a cavity in your tooth drilled, you have already had a painful lesson about the solubility of solid substances. Tooth enamel is a solid that is soluble in substances that form when food lodges between your teeth. Unfortunately for you, tooth enamel dissolves to form cavities. Fluoride prevents cavities because, when it dissolves, it reacts with a mineral found in tooth enamel to form compounds that are less soluble than the untreated enamel. Many chemical phenomena involve the dissolving of solids such as tooth enamel. The previous chapters introduced the concept of solubility and a general explanation of how solids dissolve. In this chapter you will discover that if the solid is an ionic compound placed in water, it forms an aqueous solution with specific and important characteristics. You have also studied chemical equilibrium and can now consider the equilibrium associated with ionic solids dissolving in water to form aqueous solutions.

Figure 17–1 *Many solids, such as soap, dissolve in water. The dissolving of ionic solids in water is a very important chemical process. One particular ionic solid—NaCl—stretches as far as the eye can see in this photograph of Bonneville Salt Flats in Utah.*

Dissolution and Precipitation

Ionic substances have characteristic lattice structures made up of ions. Although the ions exhibit positive charge and negative charge, the overall structure is neutral because the positive charges are exactly balanced by the negative charges. In solution, these ions separate from each other. As you learned in Chapter 15, when an ionic solid such as AgCl dissolves in water, the positive ends of water molecules are attracted to the Cl^- ions, and the negative ends are attracted to the Ag^+ ions. The attraction is strong enough to draw the ions away from the crystal surface and into solution. The actual separation of ions that occurs when an ionic compound dissolves is called dissociation. As ions move into the solution surrounded by a shell of water molecules, other ions are exposed and attracted away from the crystal. In this manner, the crystal continues to dissolve and ions become uniformly distributed in the solution. **The process in which an ionic solid dissolves in a polar liquid is called dissolution.** The **dissolution** of AgCl (s) increases the concentrations of both Ag^+ and Cl^- ions in solution.

Just as you did with chemical reactions, you can write an equation to show the dissolution of an ionic solid placed in water. The equation for AgCl (s) is shown below.

$$AgCl\ (s) \rightarrow Ag^+\ (aq) + Cl^-\ (aq) \qquad \textbf{(Eq. 1)}$$

Recall that the symbol (aq) denotes an aqueous solution. Only dissociated substances are written as ions in equations. Gases and pure liquids or solids are represented by complete formulas even when in aqueous solutions.

If an Ag^+ ion or a Cl^- ion collides with the surface of AgCl (s), the ion may lose its shell of water molecules and rejoin the

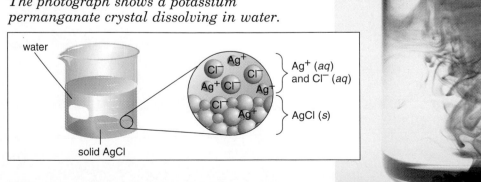

Figure 17–2 *When AgCl (s) is placed in water, Ag^+ and Cl^- ions are pulled from the surface of the solid into solution. Gradually, ions become uniformly distributed throughout the solution. The photograph shows a potassium permanganate crystal dissolving in water.*

solid state. At that spot on the surface of the solid, a local imbalance of electric charge is created. An oppositely charged ion in the solution is then quickly attracted to the spot. When the second ion collides with the solid and sheds its water molecules, electrical neutrality is restored and both ions regenerate part of the solid. **The process in which ions leave a solution and regenerate an ionic solid is called precipitation.** Dissolution and **precipitation** are opposite processes. The solid formed during precipitation is known as the precipitate. The precipitation of AgCl (s) lowers the concentration of Ag^+ and Cl^- ions in the solution. The equation showing the precipitation of ions from a solution is the reverse of the dissolution equation. Notice the direction of the arrow in the equation below.

$$AgCl\ (s) \leftarrow Ag^+\ (aq) + Cl^-\ (aq) \qquad \textbf{(Eq. 2)}$$

When an ionic solid such as AgCl (s) is placed in pure water, dissolution begins. Over time, the concentrations of Ag^+ ions and Cl^- ions increase as more ions escape from the solid state and enter the solution. Recall that every substance has its own solubility, which is the maximum quantity of that substance that will dissolve in a given solvent. Because 1 Ag^+ ion and 1 Cl^- ion enter solution for each formula unit of AgCl (s) that dissolves, the concentrations of Ag^+ and Cl^- ions entering the solution depend on the solubility of AgCl. At some point, no additional AgCl (s) can dissolve because the solution is saturated with ions. Although ions continue to dissolve into solution, other ions begin to precipitate out of solution. When dissolution and precipitation are occurring at the same rate, $[Ag^+]$ and $[Cl^-]$ have constant values. The solution is said to have attained **solubility equilibrium** because the saturated solution of ions and the remaining solid are in chemical equilibrium.

As with earlier reactions, a solubility equilibrium equation can be written to incorporate both dissolution and precipitation. Two arrows, pointing in opposite directions, are used to indicate a reversible reaction. The solubility equilibrium equation for silver chloride is

$$AgCl\ (s) \rightleftharpoons Ag^+\ (aq) + Cl^-\ (aq) \qquad \textbf{(Eq. 3)}$$

How would you write the equations for the dissolution of sodium chloride and calcium chloride in water? The equations are shown below.

$$NaCl\ (s) \rightarrow Na^+\ (aq) + Cl^-\ (aq) \qquad \textbf{(Eq. 4)}$$

$$CaCl_2\ (s) \rightarrow Ca^{2+}\ (aq) + 2\ Cl^-\ (aq) \qquad \textbf{(Eq. 5)}$$

Notice that there is a coefficient in Equation 5. Ionic solids must be broken up into their constituent ions according to their chemical formulas. Once you know which ions are formed, you must balance the equation as always. When an equation containing ions is balanced, both sides are electrically neutral. The 2+ charge on the calcium ion would not be balanced by a single negative

Figure 17–3 *When potassium iodide is poured into lead(II) nitrate, a beautiful yellow precipitate is formed. What is a precipitate?*

Figure 17–4 *A solute is at equilibrium with its dissolved ions when the rate at which ions are pulled into solution equals the rate at which they leave the solution to regenerate the solid. How can you describe the concentrations of ions at equilibrium?*

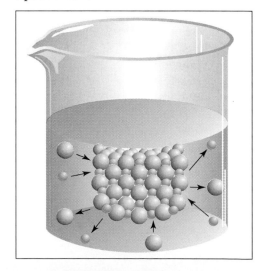

charge on the chloride ion. It is, however, balanced by the negative charges of 2 chloride ions.

You can use an equation to determine how many ions are produced by each formula unit. One formula unit of AgCl produces 2 ions in solution—1 Ag^+ ion and 1 Cl^- ion. Similarly, 1 formula unit of NaCl produces 2 ions in solution. What are they? One formula unit of calcium chloride, however, produces 3 ions in solution—1 Ca^{2+} ion and 2 Cl^- ions. How many ions will 1 formula unit of Bi_2S_3 (s) produce in solution? How would you write the solubility equilibrium equation for Bi_2S_3 (s)?

The Solubility Product

Much like the compounds you studied earlier, ionic compounds have different degrees of solubility. In fact, much of the knowledge chemists have about aqueous solutions of ionic substances came from experiments with solids that were believed to be insoluble in water. The experiments proved that even seemingly insoluble solids are actually slightly, or sparingly, soluble in aqueous solutions. Silver chloride, for example, is sparingly soluble as opposed to sodium chloride, which is highly soluble.

Recall the law of mass action from Chapter 16, which states that the concentrations of reactants and products at equilibrium are always related to a constant as described by the equilibrium expression. Solubility equilibria can also be described by equilibrium expressions. As an example, let's return to AgCl.

$$AgCl\ (s) \rightleftharpoons Ag^+\ (aq) + Cl^-\ (aq) \qquad \text{(Eq. 6)}$$

The equilibrium expression for this reaction would show the concentrations of the products, which in this case are ions, in the numerator. The concentration of the reactant, which in this case is the ionic solid, appears in the denominator. All concentrations are raised to the coefficient indicated in the balanced equation. In this case, the coefficient for each entity is 1.

$$K_{eq} = \frac{[Ag^+][Cl^-]}{[AgCl]} \qquad \text{(Eq. 7)}$$

However, AgCl is a pure solid. Recall that concentrations of pure liquids and solids are considered constant. Thus the concentration of silver chloride is a constant and becomes part of the equilibrium constant. The equilibrium expression then becomes

$$K_{sp} = [Ag^+][Cl^-] \qquad \text{(Eq. 8)}$$

Notice that the subscript of the equilibrium constant has changed. The constant K_{sp} is called the solubility product constant, or simply the **solubility product,** because it incorporates the constant value of the solid in solution. The solubility product expression is used for aqueous solutions of dissociated ions.

Figure 17–5 *When ionic solids dissolve in the water supply, ions become part of our drinking water. The U.S. Health Service provides this list of acceptable concentrations of ions in drinking water.*

Maximum Concentration of Ions in Drinking Water

Contaminating Ions	Maximum Concentration (mg/liter)
arsenic	0.05
barium	1.00
cadmium	0.01
chloride	250
chromium	0.05
copper	1.00
cyanide	0.20
fluoride	2.00
iron	0.30
lead	0.05
manganese	0.05
nitrate	45
organics	0.20
selenium	0.01
silver	0.05
sulfate	250
zinc	5.00
total dissolved solids	500

SAMPLE PROBLEM 1

Write the expression for the solubility product for $Fe(OH)_3$. The equation for the solubility equilibrium is $Fe(OH)_3\ (s) \rightleftharpoons Fe^{3+}\ (aq) + 3\ OH^-\ (aq)$.

STRATEGY	SOLUTION
1. Analyze	You are given the equation and are asked to determine the solubility product expression for the reaction.
2. Plan	The solubility product is equal to the product of the concentrations of ions raised to the power of their coefficients in the balanced equation.
3. Solve	$K_{sp} = [Fe^{3+}][OH^-]^3$
4. Evaluate	The answer relates the concentrations of ions to a constant. The concentration of the solid reactant is essentially constant and is not part of the expression.

PRACTICE PROBLEMS

1. Write the expression for the solubility product constant for Ag_2CrO_4. The equation is $Ag_2CrO_4\ (s) \rightleftharpoons 2\ Ag^+\ (aq) + CrO_4^{2-}\ (aq)$ *(Answer: $K_{sp} = [Ag^+]^2[CrO_4^{2-}]$)*

2. Write the expression for the solubility product constant for $PbI_2\ (s)$. *(Answer: $K_{sp} = [Pb^{2+}][I^-]^2$)*

Finding and Using Solubility Products

The value of K_{sp} for a substance is calculated from the concentrations of ions at equilibrium. As an example, consider a particular experiment in which $AgCl\ (s)$ is added to pure water and allowed to come to equilibrium with a solution of its ions at 25°C. At equilibrium, $[Ag^+] = 1.3 \times 10^{-5}\ M$ and $[Cl^-] = 1.3 \times 10^{-5}\ M$. Inserting these values into the solubility product expression yields the value of K_{sp}.

$$K_{sp} = [Ag^+][Cl^-]$$
$$= (1.3 \times 10^{-5})(1.3 \times 10^{-5})$$
$$= 1.7 \times 10^{-10} \qquad \textbf{(Eq. 9)}$$

Following the usual practice for writing equilibrium constants, no units are assigned to the value of K_{sp}.

It is important to differentiate between the solubility of a given solid and its solubility product. The solubility is the amount that can dissolve in a given solvent. Solubility is an equilibrium

YOU AND YOUR WORLD

Getting on Your Nerves

Did you know that a nerve impulse is a flow of electrical charges along the membrane of a nerve cell? The flow is due to the movement of ions across the membrane.

In a nerve cell, certain proteins pump Na^+ ions out of the cell and K^+ ions into the cell. The K^+ ions leak back out of the cell more easily than Na^+ ions leak back in. The net result is that more positive ions leave the cell than enter it, creating a region of positive charge outside the cell and negative charge inside the cell. Nerve impulses, such as those created when you touch a hot stove, cause changes in the relationship between these ions. Those changes travel along the nervous system like a falling row of dominoes until the message reaches your brain telling you to move your hand.

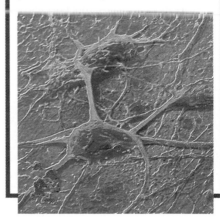

position and has an infinite number of possible values at a given temperature depending on what other solutes are present in the solution. The solubility product, on the other hand, is an equilibrium constant and has only one value for a given solid at a given temperature.

Figure 17–6 shows the values of K_{sp} for a number of substances at 25°C. As you read in Chapter 16, the magnitude of the constant gives you important information about the reaction. A small value of K_{sp} indicates that a substance is not very soluble in water. Does the value of K_{sp} for AgCl support the fact that it is considered to be a sparingly soluble solid?

Figure 17–6 *Each sparingly soluble ionic compound is described by a specific solubility constant. How does this constant relate to the concentrations of ions at equilibrium?*

K_{sp} Values at 25°C for Common Ionic Solids

Ionic Solid	K_{sp} (at 25°C)	Ionic Solid	K_{sp} (at 25°C)	Ionic Solid	K_{sp} (at 25°C)
Fluorides		Chromates			
BaF_2	1.7×10^{-6}	$SrCrO_4$	3.6×10^{-5}	$Zn(OH)_2$	4.5×10^{-17}
MgF_2	6.4×10^{-9}	$BaCrO_4$	2.0×10^{-10}	$Cu(OH)_2$	1.6×10^{-19}
PbF_2	4×10^{-8}	Ag_2CrO_4	9.0×10^{-12}	$Sn(OH)_2$	3×10^{-27}
SrF_2	7.9×10^{-10}	$PbCrO_4$	2×10^{-14}	$Cr(OH)_3$	6.7×10^{-31}
CaF_2	4.0×10^{-11}			$Al(OH)_3$	2×10^{-32}
		Carbonates		$Fe(OH)_3$	4×10^{-38}
Chlorides		$NiCO_3$	6.6×10^{-9}		
$PbCl_2$	1.6×10^{-5}	$CaCO_3$	8.7×10^{-9}		
$AgCl$	1.6×10^{-10}	$BaCO_3$	8.1×10^{-9}	Sulfides	
		$CuCO_3$	2.5×10^{-10}	MnS	5×10^{-14}
Bromides		$ZnCO_3$	1.5×10^{-11}	FeS	3.7×10^{-19}
$PbBr_2$	4.6×10^{-6}	$FeCO_3$	2.1×10^{-11}	NiS	3×10^{-21}
$AgBr$	5.0×10^{-13}	Ag_2CO_3	8.1×10^{-12}	ZnS	2.5×10^{-22}
		$PbCO_3$	7.4×10^{-14}	SnS	1×10^{-28}
Iodides		$MgCO_3$	4×10^{-5}	PbS	7×10^{-29}
PbI_2	1.4×10^{-8}			CuS	6.3×10^{-36}
AgI	1.5×10^{-16}			Ag_2S	1.6×10^{-49}
		Hydroxides			
		$Ba(OH)_2$	5.0×10^{-3}		
Sulfates		$Ca(OH)_2$	1.3×10^{-6}	Phosphates	
$CaSO_4$	2.4×10^{-5}	$AgOH$	2.0×10^{-8}	Ag_3PO_4	1.8×10^{-18}
Ag_2SO_4	1.2×10^{-5}	$Mg(OH)_2$	8.9×10^{-12}	$Sr_3(PO_4)_2$	1×10^{-31}
$SrSO_4$	3.2×10^{-7}	$Pb(OH)_2$	1.2×10^{-15}	$Ca_3(PO_4)_2$	2×10^{-29}
$PbSO_4$	1.3×10^{-8}	$Fe(OH)_2$	1.8×10^{-15}	$Ba_3(PO_4)_2$	1×10^{-23}
$BaSO_4$	1.1×10^{-10}	$Ni(OH)_2$	1.6×10^{-16}	$Pb_3(PO_4)_2$	1×10^{-54}

SAMPLE PROBLEM 2

At 25°C, the concentration of Pb^{2+} ions in a saturated solution of PbF_2 is 1.9×10^{-3} M. What is the value of K_{sp} for PbF_2?

STRATEGY	SOLUTION
1. Analyze	You are asked to find the value of the solubility product for an ionic compound.
2. Plan	You must first write the equation for the solubility equilibrium and the solubility product expression. Then you can insert the concentration of ions into the expression to find the value K_{sp}.

3. Solve

The solubility equilibrium equation is

$$PbF_2 \ (s) \rightleftharpoons Pb^{2+} \ (aq) + 2 \ F^- \ (aq)$$

The solubility product expression is:

$$K_{sp} = [Pb^{2+}][F^-]^2$$

You know $[Pb^{2+}]$. You also know from the equation that 2 F^- ions are produced for every Pb^{2+} ion. So $[F^-]$ is twice as great as $[Pb^{2+}]$. Thus,

$$[Pb^{2+}] = 1.9 \times 10^{-3} \, M$$
$$[F^-] \quad = 2[Pb^{2+}] = 3.8 \times 10^{-3} \, M$$
$$K_{sp} \quad = (1.9 \times 10^{-3})(3.8 \times 10^{-3})^2$$
$$= 2.7 \times 10^{-8}$$

4. Evaluate

Because at equilibrium the concentration of Pb^{2+} ions is small, you would expect K_{sp} to be small and it is.

PRACTICE PROBLEMS

3. A sample of $Cd(OH)_2$ (s) is added to pure water and allowed to come to equilibrium at 25°C. The concentration of Cd^{2+} is 1.7×10^{-5} M at equilibrium. What is the value of K_{sp} for $Cd(OH)_2$? *(Answer: 2.0×10^{-14})*

4. A sample of $Ce(OH)_3$ (s) is added to pure water and allowed to come to equilibrium at 25°C. The concentration of Ce^{3+} is 5.2×10^{-6} M at equilibrium. What is the value of K_{sp} for $Ce(OH)^3$? *(Answer: 2.0×10^{-20})*

CONSUMER TIP

Keeping an "Ion" Your Pearly Whites

Chances are that fluoride has been added to the water you drink and the toothpaste you use to brush your teeth. Although this has been true for many years, it was not always the case. Back in the 1930s, several dentists working for the U.S. Public Health Service noticed that in certain communities throughout the country, children had significantly fewer cavities. After a great deal of research, they found that the only factor common to all of the communities was a naturally high concentration of fluoride ions in the water.

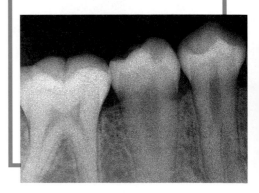

Raindrops Keep Falling on My Head

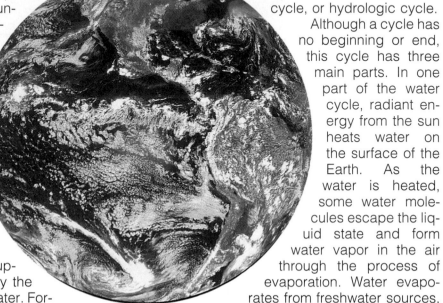

The blue appearance of the Earth when viewed from space results from the planet's bountiful supply of water. Unfortunately, most of the Earth's water is in the form of undrinkable salt water in the oceans. The remaining amount is fresh water, but some of that water is frozen in the ice caps and in glaciers. That leaves a small supply of fresh water in rivers, streams, ponds, lakes, and marshes.

With such a limited supply, you might wonder why the Earth does not run out of water. Fortunately for us, the supply of fresh water is continuously being renewed in nature. The process by which fresh water is "recycled" is called the water cycle, or hydrologic cycle. Although a cycle has no beginning or end, this cycle has three main parts. In one part of the water cycle, radiant energy from the sun heats water on the surface of the Earth. As the water is heated, some water molecules escape the liquid state and form water vapor in the air through the process of evaporation. Water evaporates from freshwater sources, the soil, the oceans, and even from plants. No matter what the source, water vapor consists only of fresh water. Salt and other substances are left behind during evaporation.

In the next part of the cycle, the air containing the water vapor rises from the Earth's surface. As it rises, the air cools. Because cool air cannot hold as much water vapor as warm air, the water vapor undergoes condensation during which it forms droplets. The tiny droplets of water remain suspended in air and form clouds.

In the last part of the cycle, the water droplets become too numerous and too heavy to remain in the air. At this point, droplets join together and fall to the Earth in the form of rain, snow, sleet, or hail. This process is known as precipitation. Fifteen trillion liters of fresh water fall on the United States every day in some form of precipitation. Once on the ground, the water is eventually heated by the sun, and the cycle repeats itself.

So far you have used the equilibrium concentrations of ions in a saturated solution of a substance to calculate the value of K_{sp}. As you learned in Chapter 16, the reverse process is also possible—you can use the value of K_{sp} to predict the equilibrium concentrations of ions in a saturated solution. Suppose, for example, that a sample of $CaSO_4$ (s) is placed in pure water at 25°C and stirred. What will be the concentrations of Ca^{2+} and SO_4^{2-} in the solution at equilibrium? As always, you should begin by writing the solubility equilibrium and using it to determine the solubility product expression.

$$CaSO_4 \ (s) \rightleftharpoons Ca^{2+} \ (aq) + SO_4^{2-} \ (aq) \quad \textbf{(Eq. 10)}$$
$$K_{sp} = [Ca^{2+}][SO_4^{2-}] \quad \textbf{(Eq. 11)}$$

From the balanced equation, you know that equal numbers of calcium ions and sulfate ions are produced when calcium sulfate dissolves. Therefore the concentration of Ca^{2+} is equal to the concentration of SO_4^{2-}. Thus you can simplify Equation 11 by representing both concentrations with a single variable, x.

$$K_{sp} = x \times x = x^2 \quad \textbf{(Eq. 12)}$$

According to Figure 17–6, K_{sp} for calcium sulfate at this temperature is 2.4×10^{-5}. By substituting this number into the equation, you can solve for x.

$$2.4 \times 10^{-5} = x^2$$
$$\sqrt{2.4 \times 10^{-5}} = x \quad \textbf{(Eq. 13)}$$
$$4.9 \times 10^{-3} \ M = x$$

Because you set the concentrations of both ions equal to x, you know that $[Ca^{2+}]$ and $[SO_4^{2-}]$ each equals $4.9 \times 10^{-3} \ M$. Notice that you had to include the concentration unit mol/L or M in the final answer. Although the solubility equilibrium constant is not written with a unit, the concentrations are.

Whenever possible, let x be the concentration of an ion that occurs once in the formula. Then you can let other ions be integer multiples of x. For example, when calculating K_{sp} for $Al(OH)_3$, let $x = [Al^{3+}]$. Because there are three OH^- ions for each Al^{3+} ion, you could write the equation $K_{sp} = x(3x)^3 = 27x^4$.

SAMPLE PROBLEM 3

What will be the equilibrium concentrations of the dissolved ions in a saturated solution of $Mg(OH)_2$ at 25°C? ($K_{sp} = 8.9 \times 10^{-12}$)

STRATEGY	SOLUTION
1. Analyze	You are asked to find the concentrations of the ions produced by the dissolution of magnesium hydroxide at equilibrium.
2. Plan	First, write the equation for the solubility equilibrium and then find the solubility product expression. Use the given K_{sp} to determine the unknown concentrations.

3. Solve The solubility equilibrium equation and solubility product expression are

$$Mg(OH)_2 \ (s) \rightleftharpoons Mg^{2+} \ (aq) + 2\,OH^- \ (aq)$$
$$K_{sp} = [Mg^{2+}][OH^-]^2$$

From the equation, you know that 2 OH^- ions are produced for every Mg^{2+} ion. So, if you set $[Mg^{2+}]$ equal to x, $[OH^-]$ will equal $2x$.

$$K_{sp} = x\,(2x)^2$$
$$= 4x^3$$

Insert the given value of K_{sp}.

$$8.9 \times 10^{-12} = 4x^3$$
$$2.225 \times 10^{-12} = x^3$$
$$\sqrt[3]{2.225 \times 10^{-12}} = x$$
$$1.3 \times 10^{-4} = x$$
$$[Mg^{2+}] = 1.3 \times 10^{-4} \ M$$
$$[OH^-] = 2[Mg^{2+}] = 2.6 \times 10^{-4} \ M$$

4. Evaluate The equilibrium concentrations are small values, which is consistent with the small value of K_{sp}.

PRACTICE PROBLEMS

5. What are the equilibrium concentrations of Ca^{2+} and F^- in a saturated solution of CaF_2? ($K_{sp} = 3.9 \times 10^{-11}$) *(Answer: $[Ca^{2+}] = 2.1 \times 10^{-4}$ and $[F^-] = 4.3 \times 10^{-4}$)*

6. Calculate the number of moles of $BaCrO_4$ that must dissolve to produce 1.00 L of a saturated solution at 25°C. ($K_{sp} = 2.0 \times 10^{-10}$) *(Answer: 1.4×10^{-5})*

17–1 Section Review

1. Explain how dissolution and precipitation are related in an aqueous solution of an ionic solid.

2. Define solubility equilibrium.

3. What is the solubility equilibrium equation and the solubility product for the reaction that occurs when $Cu(IO_3)_2 \ (s)$ is placed in pure water?

4. **Theme Trace—Stability** What is the significance of the fact that the solubility product for a given compound is always the same? How does this differ from the equilibrium position for a given solution?

17–2 Precipitates

If you have ever seen an X-ray image or had one taken, you know that X-rays allow doctors to make observations about bones and other internal parts without invading the body. X-rays are a form of electromagnetic radiation similar to light. Just as light can be reflected and absorbed, so too can X-rays. The usefulness of X-ray images comes from the fact that X-rays reflect off hard structures, such as bones, and are absorbed by softer structures, such as tissue. Sometimes, however, doctors can use chemical compounds to increase the usefulness of X-rays. For example, barium sulfate is sometimes used to improve the clarity of X-ray images of the gastrointestinal tract, which is predominantly tissue. The Ba^{2+} ion is actually quite toxic to the human body. However, because barium sulfate is essentially insoluble, the compound releases very few Ba^{2+} ions in the body. As a result, the ingestion of the compound is safe.

Although the barium sulfate is very insoluble in water, other ionic compounds, such as table salt, are quite soluble. How can you predict which compounds form precipitates?

Predicting the Formation of a Precipitate

Imagine a theater accidentally selling too many tickets for a popular show. After some confusion, it will be clear that there are not enough seats for all the customers with tickets. Some customers will have to leave the theater. (And presumably get their money back!) The theater situation can be likened to an aqueous solution in which there are more dissolved ions than the solvent can hold. When this happens, some ions will have to precipitate out of the solution. Recall that a solution containing more particles, in this case dissolved ions, than it can hold is a supersaturated solution. A supersaturated solution is an unstable, nonequilibrium state achieved by manipulating conditions such as temperature. Thus a precipitate will form in a supersaturated solution.

How do you know if a solution is supersaturated? The answer is that you can use the value of K_{sp} for the dissolved substance and the existing concentrations of ions. Just as you did in Chapter 16, you can insert the actual concentrations measured at a given point into the equilibrium expression and compare the resulting value with K_{sp}. The answer will be the reaction quotient, Q, which is called the **ion product** in this case. **The ion product can be compared with the solubility product to determine if an aqueous solution of ions is supersaturated and will form a precipitate.** If the value of Q is greater than K_{sp}, the numerator of the expression is too large relative to the value of the denominator. Thus the concentration of ions is too high and the solution is supersaturated. To attain equilibrium, ions must precipitate from

Guide for Reading

- How can you predict when a precipitate will form in solution?
- What is a precipitation reaction?
- How is a net ionic equation written?

INTEGRATING

PHYSICS

Do you know what X-rays are and how they are used to produce an image?

Figure 17–7 *A precipitate of barium chromate forms when potassium chromate is poured into barium nitrate. Do ions leave or enter a solution to form a precipitate?*

Let It Snow
1. Pour 5 teaspoons of boric acid crystals into a small jar. CAUTION: Be careful when using acid.
2. Fill the jar to the very top with water and tightly screw its lid on.
3. Gently shake the jar to mix the crystals with the water. Then set the jar aside and allow it to stand undisturbed for several minutes.
4. Describe and explain your observations.

the solution, lowering the concentrations of the ions to their equilibrium values. If the value of Q is less than K_{sp}, the numerator of the expression is too small relative to the value of the denominator. The compound will continue to dissolve until ion concentrations reach equilibrium levels.

As an example, suppose 0.010 mol of $PbCl_2$ (s) is dissolved in 150. mL of hot water, and the solution is cooled slowly to 25°C. The volume of the final solution is 150. mL. Is the solution supersaturated? Begin by writing the balanced equation for the dissolution of $PbCl_2$ (s) and the solubility product expression.

$$PbCl_2\ (s) \rightleftharpoons Pb^{2+}\ (aq) + 2\ Cl^-\ (aq) \qquad \textbf{(Eq. 14)}$$

$$K_{sp} = [Pb^{2+}][Cl^-]^2 \qquad \textbf{(Eq. 15)}$$

The equation shows that each mole of $PbCl_2$ (s) will produce 1 mole of Pb^{2+} and 2 moles of Cl^- in solution. So 0.010 mole $PbCl_2$ (s) will produce 0.010 mole of Pb^{2+} and twice as much, or 0.020 mole, Cl^- in the solution. The concentration of each ion is then the number of moles divided by the number of liters of solution.

$$[Pb^{2+}] = \frac{0.010\ \text{mol}\ Pb^{2+}}{150.\ \text{mL}} \times \frac{1000\ \text{mL}}{1\ \text{L}} \qquad \textbf{(Eq. 16)}$$

$$= 0.067\ \text{mol/L}$$

$$[Cl^-] = \frac{0.020\ \text{mol}\ Cl^-}{150.\ \text{mL}} \times \frac{1000\ \text{mL}}{1\ \text{L}} \qquad \textbf{(Eq. 17)}$$

$$= 0.13\ \text{mol/L}$$

The next step is to insert the concentrations into the solubility product expression.

$$K_{sp} = [Pb^{2+}][Cl^-]^2$$
$$Q = (0.067\ M)(0.13\ M)^2$$
$$= 1.1 \times 10^{-3} \qquad \textbf{(Eq. 18)}$$

The solubility product for $PbCl_2$ is 1.6×10^{-5}. Thus Q is greater than K_{sp}, so the solution is supersaturated. To attain equilibrium, $PbCl_2$ (s) must precipitate from the solution. How would you describe the solution if K_{sp} was equal to Q?

Precipitation Reactions

So far we have been discussing single solid substances added to pure water to form aqueous solutions. But what happens when two different aqueous solutions are mixed? Figure 17–8 shows a clear aqueous solution of potassium iodide (KI) being mixed with a clear aqueous solution of lead(II) nitrate ($Pb(NO_3)_2$). At once, a precipitate of lead(II) iodide (PbI_2) appears. **A reaction** in which two solutions are mixed and a precipitate forms is called a precipitation reaction. As with other reactions, **precipitation reactions** are described by balanced equations. The equation representing this particular reaction is shown below.

$$2 \text{ KI } (aq) + \text{Pb(NO}_3)_2 \ (aq) \rightarrow \text{PbI}_2 \ (s) + 2 \text{ KNO}_3 \ (aq) \quad \textbf{(Eq. 19)}$$

On the left side of the equation you can see the original solutions. And on the right side of the equation is the solid precipitate and the remaining solution.

When the formula for an ionic compound is written followed by (aq), it is actually being described as a solution of its ions. Thus when two solutions are mixed, two sets of ions are being mixed. The final solution contains all of the ions from each of the individual solutions. The precipitate that forms must be a combination of those ions. Consider an example in which a solution of $AgNO_3$ is mixed with a solution of KBr. You know that an aqueous solution of $AgNO_3$ contains Ag^+ and NO_3^- ions and an aqueous solution of KBr contains K^+ and Br^- ions. Thus the combined solution contains Ag^+, NO_3^-, K^+, and Br^-. Ions can combine only if they form an electrically neutral compound. The possible compounds in this mixture are $AgNO_3$, KBr, AgBr, and KNO_3. The first two possibilities are the original reactants so you can disregard them. That leaves just two possibilities for the precipitate. The precipitate that forms in this reaction is a combination of the silver and bromide ions, AgBr (s), as shown in the equation below.

$$AgNO_3 \ (aq) + \text{KBr} \ (aq) \rightarrow \text{AgBr} \ (s) + \text{KNO}_3 \ (aq) \qquad \textbf{(Eq. 20)}$$

Which two ions combined to form the precipitate?

You may be wondering how to determine which product is the precipitate. Do not be discouraged if you are a little confused because predicting the identity of the precipitate is no simple task. In reality, in many cases even chemists can make only educated guesses based on the probable products and the known characteristics of each. The actual identity of the products must be confirmed experimentally. There is, however, some guiding information that you can use to make such predictions. Predicting the identity of the solid product in a precipitation reaction requires a knowledge of the solubilities of common ionic substances. A list of solubility rules is provided in Figure 17–9 on page 574. The list classifies a large number of ionic compounds as either soluble or sparingly soluble in water. Recall that sparingly soluble substances dissolve so slightly in water that a small concentration of ions saturates the solution. You will find that the terms sparingly soluble and insoluble are often used interchangeably. The solubility rules classify a substance as sparingly soluble if 0.01 mole or less dissolves in a liter of water. Dissociating into ions only slightly in solution, a sparingly soluble substance will

Figure 17–8 *A yellow precipitate of PbI_2 forms as a clear solution of $Pb(NO_3)_2$ is poured from a burette into a clear solution of KI. What is this type of reaction called?*

usually precipitate in a precipitation reaction. Most of the concepts we have been discussing apply only to sparingly soluble substances. The solubility product principle cannot be applied to solutions of moderately soluble or very soluble substances.

Now let's return to the example in Equation 20. You can see from the solubility rules that a compound containing NO_3^- is soluble and will therefore dissolve in water. And compounds containing Ag^+ are generally insoluble in water. Thus KNO_3 must dissociate into ions in solution while $AgBr$ must be the insoluble precipitate.

Do you notice anything interesting about Equation 20? (Hint: The ions switch partners.) The equation describes a double-replacement reaction. A precipitation reaction is an example of a double-replacement reaction in which the positive and negative ions of the reactants exchange partners like dancers at a square dance. Figure 17–10 shows this rearrangement. When you were first introduced to double-replacement reactions in Chapter 9, you learned that not all combinations of compounds take part in double-replacement reactions. And you were told that you would find out why this is true later on. Well, the time has come

Figure 17–9 *The solubility rules can be used to predict whether a product of a precipitation reaction will be a solid or will remain as dissolved ions in solution. According to the rules, will $BaSO_4$ form a precipitate in a precipitation reaction?*

Solubility Rules for Ionic Compounds

Compounds containing the following ions are generally *soluble* in water:
1. alkali metal ions and ammonium ions, Li^+, Na^+, K^+, NH_4^+
2. acetate ion, $C_2H_3O_2^-$
3. nitrate ion, NO_3^-
4. halide ions (X), Cl^-, Br^-, I^-, (AgX, Hg_2X_2, and PbX_2 are insoluble exceptions)
5. sulfate ion, SO_4^{2-} ($SrSO_4$, $BaSO_4$, and $PbSO_4$ are insoluble exceptions)

Compounds containing the following ions are generally *insoluble* in water:
6. carbonate ion, CO_3^{2-} (see rule 1 exceptions, which are soluble)
7. chromate ion, CrO_4^{2-} (see rule 1 exceptions, which are soluble)
8. phosphate ion, PO_4^{3-} (see rule 1 exceptions, which are soluble)
9. sulfide ion, S^{2-} (CaS, SrS, BaS, and rule 1 exceptions are soluble)
10. hydroxide ion, OH^- [$Ca(OH)_2$, $Sr(OH)_2$, $Ba(OH)_2$, and rule 1 exceptions are soluble]

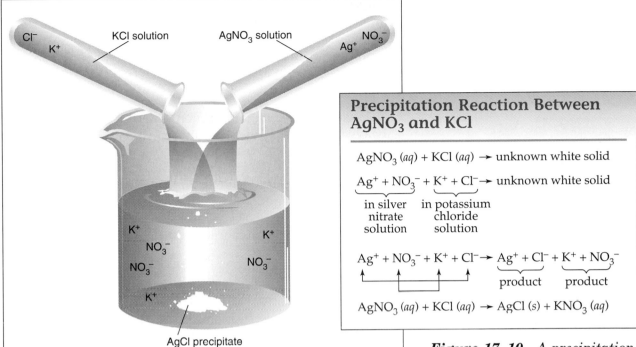

Precipitation Reaction Between AgNO₃ and KCl

$AgNO_3 \, (aq) + KCl \, (aq) \rightarrow$ unknown white solid

$\underbrace{Ag^+ + NO_3^-}_{\substack{\text{in silver} \\ \text{nitrate} \\ \text{solution}}} + \underbrace{K^+ + Cl^-}_{\substack{\text{in potassium} \\ \text{chloride} \\ \text{solution}}} \rightarrow$ unknown white solid

$Ag^+ + NO_3^- + K^+ + Cl^- \rightarrow \underbrace{Ag^+ + Cl^-}_{\text{product}} + \underbrace{K^+ + NO_3^-}_{\text{product}}$

$AgNO_3 \, (aq) + KCl \, (aq) \rightarrow AgCl \, (s) + KNO_3 \, (aq)$

Figure 17–10 *A precipitation reaction may occur when two solutions of ionic substances are mixed. The result is that the ions of the reactants switch partners and the final solution contains two new products. One product is insoluble and forms a precipitate. The other is soluble and exists as dissolved ions in solution.*

for you to learn what drives such reactions to completion. A double-replacement reaction requires a driving force to push the reaction to completion. Without a driving force, there is no reason for the reactants to exchange partners. One of the fundamental principles according to which a reaction proceeds is as follows: If the products have less energy and are therefore more stable than the reactants, the reaction tends to proceed to completion. (You will learn more about these driving forces in Chapter 23.) In an aqueous solution, an insoluble substance is more stable as a solid than as dissociated ions in solution. An insoluble substance formed in solution is a precipitate. Thus the driving force in a double-replacement reaction is the formation of a precipitate. Other common driving forces in double-replacement reactions are the formation of water and the formation of a gas.

Because sparingly soluble substances precipitate in a double-replacement reaction, you can use the solubility rules to predict whether a particular double-replacement reaction is likely to proceed. For example, if a solution of $Cu(NO_3)_2$ is mixed with a solution of NaOH under normal laboratory conditions, will a precipitate form? We can answer this question by first writing the double-replacement reaction.

$$Cu(NO_3)_2 \, (aq) + 2 \, NaOH \, (aq) \rightarrow Cu(OH)_2 \underline{\quad} + 2 \, NaNO_3 \underline{\quad}$$
(Eq. 21)

According to the solubility rules, all hydroxides are sparingly soluble except those of the Group 1A elements, $Ba(OH)_2$ and

Figure 17–11 *A precipitate of Cu(OH)₂ is formed when a solution of ammonium hydroxide is mixed with a solution of copper sulfate. Can you tell that a precipitation reaction has taken place by looking at the photograph?*

$Ca(OH)_2$. Therefore, $Cu(OH)_2$ is sparingly soluble. When $Cu(NO_3)_2$ is mixed with NaOH, $Cu(OH)_2$ (s) will precipitate. On the other hand, sodium nitrate is soluble in water. Thus, the complete equation for the precipitation reaction is

$$Cu(NO_3)_2 \text{ (aq)} + 2\,NaOH \text{ (aq)} \rightarrow Cu(OH)_2 \text{ (s)} + 2\,NaNO_3 \text{ (aq)}$$
(Eq. 22)

Even if a precipitation reaction can proceed, it still does not always proceed. Whether or not a precipitate actually forms in a double-replacement reaction depends upon the concentrations of the dissolved ions after the solutions are mixed. If the final solution is too dilute, no precipitate can form and the double replacement does not occur. Only if the ion product exceeds the solubility product will a precipitate form. And precipitation will continue until the ion concentrations decrease to the equilibrium levels.

You can use the solubility product to predict whether a precipitation reaction will take place. For example, will AgBr (s) precipitate if 20. mL of 0.010 M $AgNO_3$ and 20. mL of 3.0×10^{-4} M KBr are mixed? Assume the final volume of the solution is 40. mL. The K_{sp} for AgBr is 5.0×10^{-13}. As always, begin by writing the solubility equilibrium equation and solubility product expression for the expected precipitate, silver bromide.

$$AgBr \text{ (s)} \rightleftharpoons Ag^+ \text{ (aq)} + Br^- \text{ (aq)} \qquad \textbf{(Eq. 23)}$$

$$K_{sp} = [Ag^+][Br^-] \qquad \textbf{(Eq. 24)}$$

Because the formation of AgBr (s) depends upon Ag^+ and Br^- precipitating out of solution once the solution is saturated, you need to determine the concentration of each ion in the final solution.

There are several pieces of information you must recognize from the example. First, both $AgNO_3$ and KBr produce 2 ions in solution. The concentration of each ion in solution is directly related to the concentration of the original compound. Thus 3.0×10^{-4} M KBr produces 3.0×10^{-4} M K^+ and 3.0×10^{-4} M Br^-. Then the solution is diluted to twice its volume, from 20. milliliters to 40. milliliters. If the volume of the original solution containing $AgNO_3$ is doubled without changing the number of ions in solution, the concentration of silver ions must be cut in half, to 0.0050 M. Similarly, the concentrations of bromide ions is also reduced by half, to 1.5×10^{-4} M. Inserting these values in the solubility product expression gives you the value of Q.

$$Q = (0.0050)(1.5 \times 10^{-4}) \qquad \textbf{(Eq. 25)}$$
$$= 7.5 \times 10^{-7}$$

Because Q is greater than K_{sp} for AgBr, a precipitate forms in the solution.

SAMPLE PROBLEM 4

A solution is prepared by dissolving 1.5×10^{-3} mol of silver acetate $(AgC_2H_3O_2)$ in 50. mL of hot water. Silver acetate dissolves according to the equation $AgC_2H_3O_2$ $(s) \rightleftharpoons Ag^+$ $(aq) + C_2H_3O_2^-$ (aq). Will a precipitate form if the solution is cooled to 25°C? Assume that a negligible change in volume occurs during the operations. $(K_{sp} = 2.3 \times 10^{-3})$

STRATEGY	SOLUTION
1. Analyze	You are given the equation and the solubility equilibrium constant, and are asked to determine if a precipitate will form when a solution of silver acetate is cooled to room temperature.
2. Plan	You must first calculate the concentrations of ions dissolved in the solution. Then you can insert the concentrations into the solubility product expression to find Q. The relationship between Q and K_{sp} will indicate the answer.
3. Solve	One mole of silver ions and 1 mole of acetate ions are produced for each mole of silver acetate that dissolves. Therefore,

$$[Ag^+] = \frac{1.5 \times 10^{-3} \text{ mol } Ag^+}{50. \text{ mL}} \times \frac{1000 \text{ mL}}{1 \text{ L}}$$

$$= 0.030 \ M$$

Thus, $[C_2H_3O_2^-] = 0.030 \ M$

Then,

$$Q = [Ag^+][C_2H_3O_2^-]$$

$$= (0.030)(0.030)$$

$$= 9.0 \times 10^{-4}$$

Because Q is not greater than K_{sp}, the solution is less than saturated and a precipitate will not form.

| **4. Evaluate** | Calculating the value of Q and comparing it to K_{sp} determines whether a solution is unsaturated, saturated, or whether a precipitate will form. In this case, Q is less than K_{sp}, so the solution is unsaturated. |

Figure 17–12 *Sodium hydroxide is slowly poured into ferric sulfate to form a dark-colored precipitate of ferric hydroxide. Will the precipitate form if the solution is not saturated with ions?*

PRACTICE PROBLEMS

7. A solution is prepared by dissolving 0.030 mol of potassium perchlorate ($KClO_4$) in 75. mL of hot water. $KClO_4$ dissolves according to the equation $KClO_4$ $(s) \rightarrow K^+$ (aq) + ClO_4^- (aq). Will a precipitate form if the solution is cooled to 25°C? Assume that a negligible change in volume occurs during the operations. ($K_{sp} = 8.9 \times 10^{-3}$) *(Answer: yes)*

8. A solution is prepared by dissolving 1.40 g of silver sulfate (Ag_2SO_4) in 100. mL of hot water. Will a precipitate form if the solution is cooled to 25°C? Assume that a negligible change in volume occurs during the operations. ($K_{sp} = 1.2 \times 10^{-5}$) *(Answer: yes)*

Net Ionic Equations

The equations used to describe precipitation reactions have been formula equations, which show the reactants and products of the reaction. Equation 22 for example, is a formula equation describing the precipitation of $Cu(OH)_2$ (s) from a mixture of $Cu(NO_3)_2$ and NaOH. But formula equations do not give a true picture of what is occurring in solution because, as you know, the soluble ionic compounds actually dissociate into ions. A clearer picture is formed when you write an equation in which all the soluble ionic compounds are shown as dissociated ions in solution. An equation that shows all soluble ionic substances as ions is called a **complete ionic equation**. A complete ionic equation is found by writing each original solution as the sum of its constituent ions. Complete ionic equations are balanced just like any other chemical equations. In this example, you know that $Cu(NO_3)_2$ forms Cu^{2+} and NO_3^- ions in solution and NaOH forms Na^+ and OH^- ions in solution. Thus the complete ionic equation is

$$Cu^{2+} (aq) + 2\, NO_3^- (aq) + 2\, Na^+ (aq) + 2\, OH^- (aq) \rightarrow$$

$$Cu(OH)_2 (s) + 2\, Na^+ (aq) + 2\, NO_3^- (aq) \qquad \textbf{(Eq. 26)}$$

Notice that the total charge on each side of the equation is zero. Though the equation is rather cumbersome, it illustrates an important point: Only the hydroxide ions and the copper(II) ions undergo a chemical change. The sodium ions and nitrate ions are unchanged in the reaction. Ions that do not take part in a chemical reaction and are found in solution both before and after the reaction are called **spectator ions** because they "watch" while their more reactive partners undergo a chemical change. If we

Figure 17–13 *A white precipitate of silver chloride forms when silver nitrate and potassium chloride are mixed. Which ions are present in the final solution but are not part of the net ionic equation?*

remove the spectator ions from the complete ionic equations, a much simpler equation called the **net ionic equation** results.

$$Cu^{2+} \ (aq) + 2 \ OH^- \ (aq) \rightarrow Cu(OH)_2 \ (s) \quad \textbf{(Eq. 27)}$$

A net ionic equation includes only those compounds and ions that undergo a chemical change in a reaction in an aqueous solution. Net ionic equations are frequently used to describe precipitation reactions.

17–2 Section Review

1. Explain how the solubility product and the ion product can be used to predict whether a precipitate will form when an ionic solid is dissolved in water.

2. What type of reaction is a precipitation reaction? Describe what happens to the ions during a precipitation reaction.

3. What are solubility rules and how can they be used to predict the identity of the precipitate in a reaction?

4. Differentiate between a complete ionic equation and a net ionic equation. What are spectator ions? In which type of equations are they included?

5. **Critical Thinking—Drawing conclusions** Explain how the solubility product can be used to predict if a precipitate will form when two aqueous solutions are mixed.

17–3 The Common-ion Effect

Calcium sulfate is sparingly soluble in water. At equilibrium, a small amount of calcium sulfate will dissolve in pure water, producing calcium ions and sulfate ions. The equation for the solubility equilibrium is

$$CaSO_4 \ (s) \rightleftharpoons Ca^{2+} \ (aq) + SO_4^{2-} \ (aq) \quad \textbf{(Eq. 28)}$$

Suppose sodium sulfate (Na_2SO_4) is added to a saturated solution of calcium sulfate. What will happen to the solubility equilibrium for $CaSO_4$? To answer the question, let's think about what is happening. As the Na_2SO_4 dissolves, Na^+ and SO_4^{2-} ions are added to the solution. Because both solutes form sulfate ions, the sulfate ion is called a common ion. While the sodium ions are just being introduced into the solution, the sulfate ions are added to the sulfate ions already present in solution from the calcium sulfate. Thus the concentration of sulfate ions is increased beyond the equilibrium level. As you learned in Chapter 16, Le Chatelier's principle predicts that if the concentration of a substance in a reaction at equilibrium is changed, the reaction will proceed in the direction that minimizes the change. The same is true for aqueous solutions.

In accordance with Le Chatelier's principle, this solution will return to equilibrium by removing some sulfate ions. This is accomplished by precipitating additional $CaSO_4$.

$$CaSO_4 \ (s) \leftarrow Ca^{2+} \ (aq) + SO_4^{2-} \ (aq) \quad \textbf{(Eq. 29)}$$

Notice that this process also removes Ca^{2+} ions from solution. Thus, increasing the concentration of SO_4^{2-} ions has the effect of decreasing the concentration of Ca^{2+} ions. This phenomenon in which the addition of an ion common to two solutes brings about precipitation is called the **common-ion effect.** After equilibrium is restored, the concentrations of sulfate ions and calcium ions are smaller than before. Thus the equilibrium position has shifted. **The common-ion effect is a shift in equilibrium that occurs because the concentration of an ion that is part of the equilibrium is changed.**

Let's examine one more example of the common-ion effect. Like calcium sulfate, silver chloride (AgCl) is only slightly soluble in water.

$$AgCl \ (s) \rightleftharpoons Ag^+ \ (aq) + Cl^- \ (aq) \quad \textbf{(Eq. 30)}$$

Suppose you add AgCl to water and stir until no more will dissolve. You then remove any undissolved solid by filtration, leaving behind a clear solution of AgCl. What will happen to the concentration of Ag^+ and Cl^- ions if you add sodium chloride to the solution? The answer is that the concentration of Cl^-—the common ion—will increase, causing the equilibrium to shift

Problem Solving — *Chemistry at Work*

Resolving a "Hard" Problem

The water supply to Secinia's house consists of hard water. Hard water is water that contains a high concentration of certain ions, usually Ca^{2+}. The problem with hard water is that these ions react with soap to form insoluble compounds that you recognize as soap scum. When soap precipitates out of solution in this way, not only is it unavailable for cleaning, but it also leaves deposits on clothes, skin, and hair.

A local company installed a system that softens the water by removing the calcium ions. The problem seemed to be solved—that is until Secinia's father went for his annual physical examination. He is on a low sodium diet and although his eating habits had not changed, his blood pressure had risen in response to increased sodium.

- Use this information to infer how the water was softened at Secinia's house.

to the left. As a result, more AgCl will precipitate out of solution. As the equilibrium shifts, the concentration of Ag^{+} ions will decrease.

There is one more result of the common-ion effect. Suppose the same calcium sulfate solute is added to water already containing sulfate ions. The result is that in order to establish equilibrium, less $CaSO_4$ dissolves. Thus the common-ion effect can be stated in another way: The presence of a common ion lowers the solubility of a sparingly soluble substance.

17–3 Section Review

1. Explain the common-ion effect in your own words.
2. **Critical Thinking—Making comparisons** The solubility product of Ag_2CrO_4 is 9.0×10^{-12}. Explain the difference between the equilibrium position attained when silver chromate is added to pure water and when it is added to $0.100\ M$ $AgNO_3$.

Laboratory Investigation

Finding a Solubility Product

Problem

What is the solubility product constant of lime water (calcium hydroxide)?

Materials (per group)

thermometer
24-well chem plate
plastic transfer pipet
toothpick
3 250-mL beakers
distilled water
saturated solution of calcium hydroxide
0.1 M HCl
0.5% phenolphthalein solution

Procedure

1. Determine the temperature of the saturated calcium hydroxide solution. Fill a transfer pipet with distilled water and then squeeze dry. Partially fill the pipet with a few drops of the stock solution of saturated calcium hydroxide. Swirl and expel in a waste beaker.
2. Fill the pipet with the stock solution of saturated calcium hydroxide and carefully transfer 50 drops to each of three wells in a 24-well chem plate. Discard the unused calcium hydroxide in the waste beaker. Wash the pipet with distilled water and squeeze dry. Repeat several times to wash the pipet thoroughly.
3. Add two drops of 0.5% phenolphthalein to each well and stir with a clean toothpick.
4. Fill the plastic transfer pipet with 0.1 M HCl. CAUTION: Be careful when handling acids. Swirl and expel in a waste beaker. Fill the pipet with the 0.1 M HCl.
5. Add the acid to the first well dropwise with continuous stirring. Count the number of

drops it takes for the pink color to disappear. Record the number of drops required to reach this endpoint.
6. Repeat step 5 for wells two and three.
7. Check your data. All three titrations should agree within two drops of each other. If they do not, repeat the titration.
8. Clean the plastic transfer pipet and the 24-well chem plate with running water and rinse with distilled water. Return the waste beakers to your teacher. Wash your hands.

Observations

	Trial 1	Trial 2	Trial 3
Drops of HCl used			

1. Write the net ionic equation that represents solid calcium hydroxide dissolving in water.
2. Calculate the average number of drops of HCl used.
3. Calculate the molarity of the OH^- ion by using the formula $M_a \times V_a = M_b \times V_b$.
4. Determine the molarity of the calcium ion.

Analysis and Conclusions

1. Calculate the molarity of a saturated $Ca(OH)_2$ solution.
2. Write the solubility equilibrium expression for the dissociation of calcium hydroxide.
3. Calculate the K_{sp} of calcium hydroxide.
4. Explain how a solution of calcium hydroxide can be saturated but dilute.
5. Predict whether calcium hydroxide is more or less soluble in 0.1 M NaOH than in water.
6. **On Your Own** With your teacher's permission, design and perform a procedure to determine the effect of temperature on the value of K_{sp}.

STUDY GUIDE

Summarizing Key Concepts

17–1 Solubility Equilibria

- When an ionic solid is placed in water, attractions between the polar water molecules and the ions of the solid cause the solid to dissociate. The ions spread throughout the solution during dissolution. At the same time, ions in the solution collide with the remaining ionic solid and become part of it during precipitation. Dissolution and precipitation are reverse processes.

- A solution attains solubility with undissolved solute when dissolution and precipitation occur at the same rate. The ion concentrations in solution are constant at equilibrium.

- The solubility product of a solution at equilibrium with undissolved solute is equal to the concentrations of its constituent ions each raised to the power indicated by the coefficient in the balanced equation.

17–2 Precipitates

- A solution will form a precipitate if the ion concentrations at a given point are greater than the concentrations at equilibrium. Such a solution is supersaturated. The formation of a precipitate can be predicted by comparing K_{sp}, which relates the equilibrium concentrations, to the ion product (Q), which relates the actual ion concentrations. If $Q > K_{sp}$, a precipitate will form. If $Q = K_{sp}$, the solution is saturated. And if $Q < K_{sp}$, the solute will continue to dissolve.

- A precipitation reaction occurs when two aqueous solutions are mixed to form a precipitate. Precipitation reactions are double-replacement reactions in which ions exchange partners. The formation of a precipitate drives a double-replacement reaction toward completion.

- Precipitation reactions can be described by equations that show all the ions that enter into and result from the reaction. Spectator ions remain unchanged before and after the reaction. An equation that includes only those compounds and ions that undergo a chemical change and excludes spectator ions is called a net ionic equation.

17–3 The Common-ion Effect

- An ion that is contained in more than one solute in a solution is called a common ion. According to the common-ion effect, any change in the concentration of an ion involved in a solubility equilibrium will shift the equilibrium position of the solution. Similarly, the solubility of an ionic solid added to a solution already containing a concentration of common ions is decreased.

Reviewing Key Terms

Define each term in a complete sentence.

17–1 Solubility Equilibria

dissolution
precipitation
solubility equilibrium
solubility product

17–2 Precipitates

ion product
precipitation reaction
complete ionic equation
spectator ion
net ionic equation

17–3 The Common-ion Effect

common-ion effect

CHAPTER REVIEW

Content Review

Multiple Choice
Choose the letter of the answer that best completes each statement.

1. When solubility equilibrium is attained, the
   (a) concentrations of ions are equal.
   (b) solution is saturated.
   (c) solution is concentrated.
   (d) ion product is smaller than the solubility product.

2. The solubility expression for an aqueous solution of $Mg(OH)_2$ (s) is
   (a) $Mg(OH)_2$ $(s) \rightleftharpoons Mg^+$ $(aq) + OH^-$ (aq).
   (b) $Mg(OH)_2$ $(s) \rightleftharpoons 2\ Mg^+$ $(aq) + OH^{2-}$ (aq).
   (c) $Mg(OH)_2$ $(s) \rightleftharpoons Mg^{2+}$ $(aq) + 2\ OH^-$ (aq).
   (d) $Mg(OH)_2$ $(s) \rightleftharpoons Mg^{2+}$ $(aq) + OH^-$ (aq).

3. The solubility product for the reaction Ag_2CrO_4 $(s) \rightleftharpoons 2\ Ag^+$ $(aq) + CrO_4^{2-}$ (aq) is
   (a) $[Ag^+][CrO_4^-]^2$
   (b) $[2\ Ag^+][CrO_4^{2-}]$
   (c) $[Ag^+][CrO_4^{2-}]$
   (d) $[Ag^+]^2[CrO_4^{2-}]$

4. The dissolution of an ionic solid is described by $AB \rightarrow A^+ + B^-$. If the solubility of AB is 0.0427 M, K_{sp} is

   (a) 0.0427
   (b) 4.6×10^{-3}
   (c) 1.82×10^{-3}
   (d) 3.3×10^{-6}

5. A precipitation reaction is a
   (a) synthesis reaction.
   (b) decomposition reaction.
   (c) single-replacement reaction.
   (d) double-replacement reaction.

6. In a solution of $BaCO_3$ (s), the equilibrium concentration of CO_3^{2-} is 1.1×10^{-4} M. If the K_{sp} is 8.1×10^{-9}, the solution is
   (a) unsaturated.   (c) supersatured.
   (b) at equilibrium.   (d) saturated.

7. When an aqueous solution of Ag_2CrO_4 is mixed with an aqueous solution of $AgNO_3$, the common ion is
   (a) CrO_4^{2-}.   (c) NO_3^-.
   (b) Ag^{2+}.   (d) Ag^+.

8. An antacid tablet consisting primarily of sparingly soluble $Al(OH)_3$ is in a saturated solution. The solubility reaction will be shifted to the left by the addition of
   (a) $AlCl_3$.   (c) Na_3PO_4.
   (b) $NaCl$.   (d) $Al(OH)_3$.

True or False
If the statement is true, write "true." If it is false, change the underlined word or words to make the statement true.

9. The process by which ions join to reform the solid is called <u>dissolution</u>.

10. Solubility equilibrium is attained when the rates of dissolution and <u>dissociation</u> are equal.

11. At equilibrium with undissolved solid, an aqueous solution is <u>saturated</u>.

12. When an aqueous solution of $PbBr_2$ ($K_{sp} = 4.6 \times 10^{-6}$) is saturated at 25°C, the concentration of Br^- is <u>0.010 M</u>.

13. <u>Spectator</u> ions remain unchanged after a precipitation reaction.

Concept Mapping
Complete the following concept map for Section 17–1. Refer to pages xviii–xix to construct a concept map for the entire chapter.

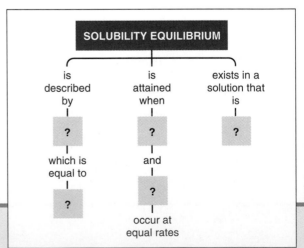

Concept Mastery

Discuss each of the following in a brief paragraph.

14. Explain the process by which an ionic compound attains equilibrium in an aqueous solution.
15. Describe how you would go about writing an equation describing the dissolution of $Ba_3(PO_4)_2$.
16. How does the common-ion effect alter the solubility of an ionic solid?
17. What force drives a reversible reaction in aqueous solution to completion? Explain.
18. Define the terms complete ionic equation, spectator ion, and net ionic equation.

19. What is a solubility product and what information does it provide about an aqueous solution of an ionic solid?
20. Describe how you write an equation to solve for K_{sp} for an aqueous solution of $SrSO_4$. How can you solve for K_{sp} if you know the solubility of a given solute?
21. **Tying it Together** The solubility product for an ionic solid is a *stable* value. The ion product, however, varies. Explain the relationship between the solubility product and the ion product.

Critical Thinking and Problem Solving

Use the skills you have developed in this chapter to answer each of the following.

22. **Applying concepts** The solubility of compound AB is 8.45×10^{-6} M. If the compound dissolves according to the following equation, AB $(s) \rightarrow A^{2+}$ $(aq) + B^{2-}$ (aq), what is K_{sp}?
23. **Applying concepts** The K_{sp} of X_2Y is 6.83×10^{-19}. Use the following equation to determine the equilibrium concentrations of ions: $X_2Y \rightarrow 2 X^+ + Y^{2-}$.
24. **Interpreting data** Use the solubility rules to determine whether or not the following are soluble or insoluble: (a) Na_2SO_4 (b) $HgCl_2$ (c) $Zn_3(PO_4)_2$ (d) $Al(NO_3)_3$ (e) PbS (f) $MgCO_3$.
25. **Drawing conclusions** Determine whether a precipitate will form when 70.0 mL of a 0.0040 M $Ca(NO_3)_2$ solution is mixed with 30.0 mL of a 0.010 M Na_2SO_4 solution at 25°C.
26. **Making inferences** A local group believes that a lake is polluted with lead ions (Pb^{2+}). The company accused of polluting the lake is denying any such pollution. How could you test for the ions?
27. **Developing hypotheses** A solution contains Cu^+ and Pb^{2+} ions. If I^- ions are slowly added to the solution, which solid do you think will precipitate first, PbI_2 or CuI?

28. **Making predictions** Teeth and bones are composed mainly of calcium phosphate, $Ca_3(PO_4)_2$ (s). Predict the direction of the reaction if the following changes are made to a saturated aqueous solution of calcium phosphate: (a) $[Ca^{2+}]$ is decreased; (b) $[Ca^{2+}]$ is increased; (c) $[PO_4^{3-}]$ is decreased; (d) $[PO_4^{3-}]$ is increased; (e) $Ca(NO_3)_2$ is added; (f) KNO_3 is added.
29. **Using the writing process** More than 2000 years ago, the Romans constructed elaborate public water systems using lead pipes. Unfortunately, because lead slowly dissolves in water, drinking water transported through lead pipes contains Pb^{2+} ions. Since that time, it has been found that lead is harmful to humans and has been shown to decrease learning ability in children. Studies suggest that lead ions may have played a role in the fall of the Roman Empire. Research the effects of lead on humans. Write a magazine article describing the hazards of lead. Include modern sources of lead, the role it may have played in ancient history, and the role it plays today.

PROBLEM BANK

Group A

30. Write a balanced chemical equation for the dissolution of each of the following compounds:
(a) Ag_2CO_3 (b) $PbSO_4$ (c) $Ni(OH)_2$
(d) $Sr_3(PO_4)_2$ *(Section 17–1)*

31. What is the expression for the solubility product for each of the following compounds? (a) MnS (b) $Cr(OH)_3$ (c) Ag_3PO_4
(d) Bi_2S_3 *(Section 17–1)*

32. Is the solubility product expression written correctly for each compound below? If not, write the correct expression.

(a) MgF_2: $K_{sp} = [Mg^{2+}][F^{2-}]$

(b) $NiCO_3$: $K_{sp} = \dfrac{[Ni^{2+}][CO_3^{2-}]}{[NiCO_3]}$

(c) $Cu_3(PO_4)_2$: $K_{sp} = [Cu^{2+}]^3[PO_4^{3-}]^2$

(d) Ag_2SO_4: $K_{sp} = [Ag^+]^2[S^{2-}][O^{2-}]^4$
(Section 17–1)

33. A sample of $Ba(OH)_2$ (s) is added to pure water and allowed to come to equilibrium at 25°C. The concentration of Ba^{2+} is 0.108 M. What is the value of K_{sp}? *(Section 17–1)*

34. A sample of Ag_2SO_4 (s) is added to pure water and allowed to come to equilibrium at 25°C. The concentration of Ag^+ is 0.029 M. What is the value of K_{sp}? *(Section 17–1)*

35. What will be the equilibrium concentration of Ag^+ and I^- in a saturated solution of AgI? ($K_{sp} = 1.5 \times 10^{-16}$) *(Section 17–1)*

36. What will be the equilibrium concentrations of Pb^{2+} and SO_4^{2-} in a saturated solution of $PbSO_4$? ($K_{sp} = 1.3 \times 10^{-8}$)
(Section 17–1)

37. What will be the equilibrium concentrations of Ca^{2+} and OH^- in a saturated solution of $Ca(OH)_2$? ($K_{sp} = 1.3 \times 10^{-6}$)
(Section 17–1)

38. What will be the equilibrium concentrations of Ni^{2+} and OH^- in a saturated solution of $Ni(OH)_2$? ($K_{sp} = 1.6 \times 10^{-16}$)
(Section 17–1)

39. Calculate the number of moles of AgBr that must dissolve to produce 0.750 L of a saturated solution at 25°C? ($K_{sp} = 5.0 \times 10^{-13}$) *(Section 17–1)*

40. Calculate the number of moles of $Zn(OH)_2$ that must dissolve to produce 0.125 L of a saturated solution at 25°C. ($K_{sp} = 4.5 \times 10^{-17}$) *(Section 17–1)*

41. Use the solubility rules to fill in the state of the products of the following double-replacement reactions. Example:
LiBr (aq) + $AgNO_3$ (aq) →
        $LiNO_3$___ + AgBr___

LiBr (aq) + $AgNO_3$ (aq) →
        $LiNO_3$ (aq) + AgBr (s)

(a) Na_2SO_4 (aq) + $Ba(NO_3)_2$ (aq) →
        $BaSO_4$___ + 2 $NaNO_3$___

(b) $FeCl_2$ (aq) + 2 NaOH (aq) →
        2 NaCl___ + $Fe(OH)_2$___

(c) $CaCl_2$ (aq) + K_2S (aq) →
        CaS___ + 2 KCl___

(d) Li_2CO_3 (aq) + $CaCl_2$ (aq) →
        $CaCO_3$___ + 2 LiCl___ *(Section 17–2)*

42. Should a precipitate of AgCl form if 10.0 mL of 1.0×10^{-4} M $AgNO_3$ is mixed with 10.0 mL of 2.0×10^{-6} M NaCl? (For AgCl, $K_{sp} = 1.7 \times 10^{-10}$) *(Section 17–2)*

43. At a given time after Bi_2S_3 begins dissolving, the concentrations of ions in solution are $[Bi^{3+}] = 1.5 \times 10^{-12}$ M
$[S^{2-}] = 2.6 \times 10^{-13}$ M
Is the solute at equilibrium with the dissolved ions? ($K_{sp} = 1.1 \times 10^{-73}$) *(Section 17–2)*

44. Write the net ionic equation corresponding to the precipitation reaction that occurs. *(Section 17–2)*
(a) Na^+ (aq) + Cl^- (aq) + Ag^+ (aq) + NO_3^- (aq) → AgCl (s) + Na^+ (aq) + NO_3^- (aq)

(b) 2 NH_4^+ (aq) + CO_3^{2-} (aq) + Ca^{2+} (aq) + 2 Cl^- (aq) → $CaCO_3$ (s) + 2 NH_4^+ (aq) + 2 Cl^- (aq)

(c) Pb^{2+} (aq) + 2 NO_3^- (aq) + 2 H^+
(aq) + 2 Br^- (aq) → $PbBr_2$ (s) +
2 NO_3^- (aq) + 2 H^+ (aq)

(d) Fe^{2+} (aq) + 2 Cl^- (aq) + 2 K^+
(aq) + S^{2-} (aq) → FeS (s) +
2 Cl^- (aq) + 2 K^+ (aq)

45. How is the solubility of $NiCO_3$ affected by the addition of (a) Na_2CO_3 (b) $NiCl_2$ (c) KCl (d) HNO_3? *(Section 17–3)*

46. A solution of $PbBr_2$ contains solid $PbBr_2$ in equilibrium with dissolved Pb^{2+} and Br^-. Which of the following disturbs the equilibrium when added to the solution by providing a common ion? *(Section 17–3)*
(a) KOH (b) $NaCl$ (c) $Pb(NO_3)_2$ (d) H_2S
(e) $Ca(NO_3)_2$

Group B

47. Write the solubility product expression for the following slightly soluble ionic compounds in aqueous solution:
(a) Sb_2S_3 (s) ⇌ 2 Sb^{3+} (aq) + 3 S^{2-} (aq)
(b) AuI_3 (s) ⇌ Au^{3+} (aq) + 3 I^- (aq)
(c) $MnCO_3$ (s) ⇌ Mn^{2+} (aq) + CO_3^{2-} (aq)

48. A sample of $AgBr$ (s) is added to pure water and allowed to come to equilibrium at 25°C. The concentration of Ag^+ is 7.1×10^{-7} M. What is the value of K_{sp}?

49. A sample of $SrSO_4$ (s) is added to pure water and allowed to come to equilibrium at 25°C. The concentration of Sr^{2+} is 8.7×10^{-4} M. What is the value of K_{sp}?

50. What will be the equilibrium concentrations of Ba^{2+} and SO_4^{2-} in a saturated solution of $BaSO_4$? (K_{sp} = 1.1×10^{-10})

51. What will be the equilibrium concentrations of Sr^{2+} and F^- in a saturated solution of SrF_2? (K_{sp} = 7.9×10^{-10})

52. A solution is prepared by dissolving 1.6 g of $SrCrO_4$ in 100. mL of hot water. $SrCrO_4$ dissolves according to the equation

$$SrCrO_4 \rightarrow Sr^{2+} + CrO_4^{2-}$$

Should a precipitate form if the solution is cooled to 25°C? Assume that a negligible

change in volume occurs during the process. (K_{sp} = 3.6×10^{-5})

53. A solution is prepared by dissolving 2.75 g of K_2PtCl_6 in 100. mL of hot water. K_2PtCl_6 dissolves according to the equation

$$K_2PtCl_6 \rightarrow 2\ K^+ + PtCl_6^{2-}$$

Should a precipitate form if the solution is cooled to 25°C? Assume that a negligible change in volume occurs during the process. (K_{sp} = 1.4×10^{-6})

54. A solution is prepared by dissolving 9.2×10^{-4} mol of $PbCl_2$ in 100. mL of hot water. Should a precipitate form if the solution is cooled to 25°C? Assume that a negligible change in volume occurs during the process. (K_{sp} = 1.6×10^{-5})

55. Does $PbCrO_4$ (s) form if 5.0 mL of 3.0×10^{-4} M $Pb(NO_3)_2$ is mixed with 5.0 mL of 3.0×10^{-4} M Na_2CrO_4? (For $PbCrO_4$, K_{sp} = 2×10^{-14})

56. Should a precipitate of $PbCl_2$ form if 5.0 mL of 0.02 M KCl is mixed with 5.0 mL of 0.02 M $Pb(NO_3)_2$? (For $PbCl_2$, K_{sp} = 1.6×10^{-5})

57. If a 40. mL of 6.0×10^{-4} M $BaCl_2$ is mixed with 30. mL of 4.0×10^{-15} M Na_2SO_4, will $BaSO_4$ precipitate? (K_{sp} = 1.1×10^{-10})

58. If 2.5 mL of 0.30 M $AgNO_3$ is mixed with 7.5 mL of 0.015 M Na_2SO_4, should a precipitate of Ag_2SO_4 form? (K_{sp} = 1.2×10^{-5})

59. Calcium phosphate ($Ca_3(PO_4)_2$) is the main component of teeth and bones. It dissolves to form calcium ions and phosphate ions. In what direction will the equilibrium shift in response to each of the following?
(a) increase $[Ca^{2+}]$
(b) decrease $[Ca^{2+}]$
(c) increase $[PO_4^{3-}]$
(d) decrease $[PO_4^{3-}]$
(e) addition of $Ca(NO_3)_2$ (s)
(f) addition of solid KNO_3 (s)

FROM SCHOOL TO WORK

Ryan Whitacre—Student

Chemistry came alive for Ryan Whitacre of Flint, Michigan, one summer when the swimming pool he managed turned an unattractive shade of green. "The pool is in a rural area surrounded by corn fields," Ryan explained. "Somehow the chemical fertilizers used on the fields found their way into the pool and reacted with the normally crystal-clear water. It was so bad that you couldn't even see the bottom of the pool's deep end." To clean up the mess, other chemicals were added to the pool to precipitate out the fertilizer chemicals. "Then we just vacuumed up the precipitate," recalled Ryan.

Now in college and studying international affairs, Ryan sees how environmental issues such as global warming and acid rain can strain relationships among nations. He advises chemistry students to "stick it out and you will find chemical applications in the most unlikely places."

Soil Conservation Technician

Soil conservation technicians work closely with landowners to establish and maintain good land use practices. Soil conservation technicians may take soil samples and examine specific areas to determine conservation needs. Many soil conservation technicians help oversee the hundreds of millions of acres of public lands or are involved in the construction of dams and agricultural irrigation projects.

In addition to their practical skills and knowledge, soil conservation technicians should also have a love for the outdoors and a respect and appreciation for all natural resources. Educational requirements include high-school courses in biology, algebra, and English, followed by two years of post-high-school training.

If you are interested in additional information, write to the American Society of Agronomy, 677 South Segoe Road, Madison, WI 53711.

How to Select Companies to Contact

When searching for a job, you will probably want to send your résumé to a large number of companies. Unless you have specific employers in mind, you may find it rather confusing to choose those companies. However, there are publications in your school or community library that will be of help to you. These publications list major employers—either alphabetically, by industry, or by geographical location. They also give a brief description of the company and list the major positions or careers that are available at that company. Two such publications are *The National Job Bank* and *Dun's Employment Opportunity Directory*.

Doug Brown

From the Author

Chemical equilibrium is a topic in which I couldn't see the forest for the trees for a long time. To me equilibrium was just a maze of unrelated facts and mainly a way for my high school teacher and even my early chemistry professors to assign me lots of difficult problems. So I calculated the partial pressure of NO_2 in a reaction mixture and determined the concentration of Ag^+ ions in a saturated solution of silver chloride. By practicing on many problems like these, I learned how to work my problem assignments and do all right on my tests.

However, I didn't really know what equilibrium was, and I didn't realize that the problems on vapor pressure, gas reactions, solubility, and acid-base reactions were actually very closely related. Eventually it came to me, and I appreciated how it all tied together: In chemistry, essentially all processes or reactions can go in both directions, at least to a small extent.

The wonderful symmetry of nature is displayed in every reaction system that is not at equilibrium. Since the forward and reverse reactions are going at different rates, there are changing amounts of reactants and products. The effect of this change is to adjust the rates of these opposite reactions so that they come closer and closer to being equal until finally equilibrium is reached. The whole universe is governed by this principle and will eventually be at equilibrium although, mercifully, this will not happen for a very long time!

UNIT REVIEW

Concept Mastery

Discuss each of the following in a brief paragraph.

1. What is a solution? How can you test to see if a mixture actually is a solution?
2. In a solution, what is the difference between the solute and the solvent? Give an example.
3. In a solution is it always obvious which is the solute and which is the solvent? Explain your answer.
4. What is solvation?
5. Is the solution process always endothermic or always exothermic? Explain.
6. What is solubility?
7. Give some examples of the kinds of solutes that will dissolve in water but not in gasoline.
8. In what kind of solvent-solute system is the solubility strongly affected by pressure?
9. What would you do to get a solid solute to dissolve in a liquid solvent as quickly as possible?
10. In your own words explain the difference between the terms concentrated and saturated. Use specific examples.

11. What is a colligative property?
12. How can you tell if a reaction is at equilibrium?
13. Under what conditions is the equilibrium constant K_{eq} actually constant?
14. How is the reaction quotient Q different from the equilibrium constant K_{eq}?
15. How can you use Le Chatelier's principle to predict what effect changing the pressure will have on a reaction?
16. How does a decrease in temperature affect the equilibrium position of a reaction?
17. Suppose you know that two ions form a precipitate. If you are given the concentration of ions in a solution, how can you predict if precipitation will actually occur?
18. What is meant by the common-ion effect? Give an example.

Problem Bank

19. What is the molarity of a water solution that contains 10.0 g NaCl in a total volume of 750. mL of solution?
20. What mass of I_2 (s) would be necessary to form a 0.550 m solution in 450. g of dichloromethane (CCl_2H_2)?
21. What is the mole fraction of each component of solder that contains 50.0% tin and 50.0% lead by mass?
22. What will be the freezing point of a solution containing 100. g of H_2O and 35.0 g of the nondissociated solute glucose ($C_6H_{12}O_6$)? The normal freezing or melting point of water is 0°C and the molal freezing point depression constant of water is -1.86 C°/m.
23. The following reaction has an equilibrium constant of 160.

$$2\ NO_2\ (g) \rightleftharpoons 2\ NO\ (g) + O_2\ (g)$$

What will be the reaction quotient and in which direction will the reaction proceed if the partial pressure of NO_2 is 5.0×10^{-4} atm, the partial pressure of NO is 0.080 atm, and that of O_2 is 0.020 atm?

24. In an aqueous solution in equilibrium with AgCl, the concentration of Ag^+ (aq) is 1.3×10^{-4} M and the concentration of Cl^- (aq) is 2.2×10^{-6} M. What is the solubility product of AgCl?

25. How many moles of FeS (s) will dissolve in water to form 1.00 L of solution? K_{sp} for FeS is 3.7×10^{-19}.

26. If the concentration of Ba^{2+} (aq) in an equilibrium solution of BaF_2 is 2.5×10^{-2} M, what is the concentration of F^- (aq)? K_{sp} for BaF_2 is 1.7×10^{-6}.

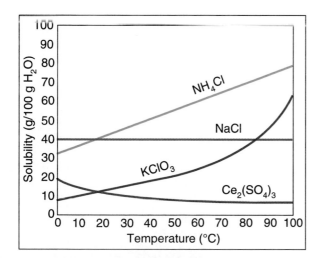

Performance-Based Task

How Do Changes in Temperature Affect Solubility?

You know that when you prepare a solution, the process of dissolving is accompanied by changes in energy. Do changes in temperature cause changes in solubility? Formulate a hypothesis to answer the question.

1. Start by obtaining the following: graduated cylinder, 2 beakers, thermometer, plastic foam cup, 2 test tubes, stopper to fit test tube, test-tube rack, balance, hot plate, ice, and potassium nitrate (KNO_3).

2. Measure the heat of solution of KNO_3. Record the temperature of 100 ml of water. Add 5 g KNO_3 and stir. Record the lowest temperature reached. Calculate the energy change in kilojoules per mole.

3. Prepare a saturated solution of KNO_3. Place 5 g KNO_3 in a test tube and add 10 mL of water. Stopper the test tube and shake for 1 to 2 minutes. Decant the saturated solution into a second test tube.

4. Place the test tube in an ice-water bath. Record your observations every 30 seconds for 2 minutes. Then place the test tube in a hot-water bath. Repeat your observations. Did your observations support your hypothesis?

Going Further

5. When added to water, some chemicals cause the temperature to rise. Following a similar experimental procedure, predict what would happen if you prepared a saturated solution and changed its temperature. Explain.

6. Based on the solubility curves for several compounds shown in the graph, can you choose the most effective compound to use in a cold pack? Explain.

591

 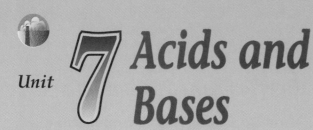 **7** ## Acids and Bases

The colorful flowers in this gorgeous garden in Giverny, France, did not spring into existence fully grown! A lot of patience and hard work went into planning, planting, and maintaining such a living work of art. Just as much patience and hard work are poured into hundreds of community gardens in cities and towns all across the country. Whether in a lavish formal garden, a small vegetable patch in a vacant lot, or even a simple window box—most plants require specific conditions to grow and thrive.

One of the conditions necessary for plants to grow properly is correct soil pH. What is pH? As you will learn in this unit, pH refers to how acidic or basic a substance is. Some plants grow well in acidic soil, whereas others will grow only in basic soil. You are probably already familiar with the terms acid and base because they are commonly used in areas other than chemistry. In the chapters that follow, however, you will learn the chemical definition of acids and bases. You will also learn how to measure pH, in case you want to test some soil for planting!

DISCOVERY LEARNING

1. Obtain two clear plastic cups. Place a few drops of household ammonia in one cup and a few drops of vinegar in the second cup.

2. Add a drop of grape juice to each cup. Observe what happens to the color of the grape juice in each cup.

3. Now add ammonia drop by drop to the cup with the vinegar. Observe what happens to the color of the grape juice as you add the ammonia.

   - What happened to the color of the grape juice in ammonia? In vinegar?

   - What happened to the color of the grape juice when you added ammonia to the vinegar?

   - How can you explain your observations?

Chapter 18
Acids, Bases, and Salts

You would not want to be spit upon by a giant petrel. This seabird, pictured on the right, regurgitates partly digested food and spits it at would-be antagonists. You may find such behavior disgusting, but for the petrel it is an effective defense. Why? One reason is that the spit includes a strong acid from the petrel's stomach. Strong acids burn the skin of most animals—including humans.

Acids are very common compounds. Although some have the sting and destructive power of stomach acid, others are much milder—such as the acid in your favorite carbonated beverage. In this chapter you will study acids and two related classes of compounds, bases and salts. As you explore these topics, you might even discover a good defense for a petrel attack!

The giant petrel—also called the "stinker" bird—spits stomach acid at its enemies. To neutralize excess acid in your stomach, you might take an antacid tablet (inset).

Chem Journal

YOU AND YOUR WORLD

What images does the word acid conjure up in your mind? Have you ever used or had contact with an acid? Do you think acids are dangerous? Respond to these and any other questions you may have about acids. When you complete this chapter, review your journal entry and see if your thoughts about acids have changed.

18–1 Defining Acids and Bases

Guide for Reading

- What is the Brønsted-Lowry definition of acids and bases?
- What are some common properties of acids and bases?

Do you recognize the animals shown in Figure 18–1? Although you might not be familiar with a specific breed, you probably recognize a dog or cat when you see one. But can you come up with a good definition for a dog or a cat? And exactly why are these animals so different?

As this example shows, defining and understanding even the simplest things in our lives is not always an easy task. This also is true in chemistry. As early as the seventeenth century, chemists recognized two important classes of compounds, which they called **acids** and **bases.** As you will see, recognizing acids and bases is easy, but defining and understanding them takes a little more effort. Over time, as chemists gained a better understanding of acid-base behavior, they have broadened the original definition of acids and bases.

Figure 18–1 *Recognizing cats and dogs is easy, but understanding and defining these animals takes more effort. Chemists face a similar dilemma in their studies of two important classes of compounds: acids and bases.*

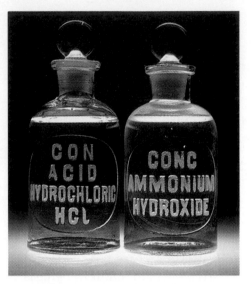

Figure 18–2 *Without the labels on the bottles, could you tell which liquid is the acid and which is the base? Although many acids and bases look the same as pure water, other features distinguish them.*

Properties of Acids and Bases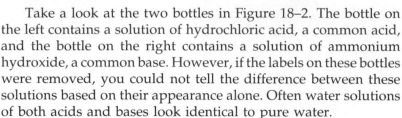

Take a look at the two bottles in Figure 18–2. The bottle on the left contains a solution of hydrochloric acid, a common acid, and the bottle on the right contains a solution of ammonium hydroxide, a common base. However, if the labels on these bottles were removed, you could not tell the difference between these solutions based on their appearance alone. Often water solutions of both acids and bases look identical to pure water.

Appearance in water, however, is one of the few properties that hydrochloric acid and ammonium hydroxide have in common. As you will discover, there are several differences among acidic solutions, basic solutions, and solutions—like pure water—that have the properties of neither an acid nor a base. Let's examine some of the properties of acids and bases.

TASTE The word acid comes from the Latin word *acidus*, meaning sour or tart. When an acid is dissolved in water, the solution tastes sour. You taste such solutions every day in the food you eat. Foods that contain acids include citrus fruits, such as oranges and grapefruit, which contain citric acid; yogurt and sour milk, which contain lactic acid; carbonated beverages, which contain carbonic acid; and vinegar, which contains acetic acid.

Water solutions of bases, on the other hand, have a characteristic bitter taste. If you have ever put soap or soapy water in your mouth (either accidentally or on purpose), then you are acquainted with the bitter taste of bases.

In the laboratory, however, taste is a property that you should never test. *Never eat or drink in the laboratory, and never taste any laboratory chemical.* Although some laboratory chemicals are harmless, others are dangerous and toxic.

Figure 18–3 *Acids give a tart taste to many foods and beverages, including fruit drinks and sodas (left). Basic solutions, such as soapy water (right), feel smooth and slippery.*

TOUCH On normal skin, most dilute acids feel like water. But you feel a different sensation if an acid contacts broken or injured skin. If you have ever eaten a grapefruit or orange when you had a sore in your mouth, then you know the sharp sting that an acid can give.

Mild basic solutions do not sting—except in your eyes. Everywhere else on your body, basic solutions feel smooth, soothing, and slippery. One very common basic solution—soapy water—is an excellent example of this smooth, slippery feel.

Again, remember that many laboratory chemicals are dangerous and toxic. *Do not touch any laboratory chemical or place it on your skin or clothing.* If you accidentally spill any chemical in the laboratory, alert your teacher and clean up the spilled chemical immediately.

REACTIONS WITH METALS Acids react vigorously with many metals, including magnesium, zinc, iron, and aluminum. Bases, however, do not react with most metals.

Figure 18–4 shows the reaction between hydrochloric acid and a ribbon of magnesium, which produces a gas. This gas can be collected in a beaker and tested with a burning splint. The result is a "popping" noise, which indicates that the gas is hydrogen (H_2). Acids react with magnesium or with the other metals listed above to produce hydrogen gas. As you will discover as you read on, this reaction provides a key to understanding an acid's chemical properties.

ELECTRICAL CONDUCTIVITY Pure water is an extremely poor conductor of electricity. However, a solution of hydrochloric acid conducts electricity quite well, as does a solution of sodium hydroxide, a base.

Both acids and bases are examples of electrolytes. As you learned in Chapter 15, an electrolyte is a substance that ionizes when it dissolves in water. A solution that contains electrolytes conducts electricity.

INDICATORS An acid-base **indicator** is a substance that turns one color in an acidic solution and another color in a basic solution. One of the most common acid-base indicators is litmus, a kind of dye that comes from a species of lichen. (You may have seen lichens growing on rocks or on an old sidewalk.)

You are probably familiar with litmus in the form of litmus paper, which is litmus coated onto small paper strips. An acid turns litmus paper from blue to red, and a base turns litmus from red to blue.

Placing a drop of an unknown solution onto a strip of litmus paper is a quick, easy way to determine whether the solution is acidic or basic. Such a procedure is called a litmus test. Although the term litmus test has a specific meaning in chemistry, in other contexts it has come to mean any simple test or question that reveals an important characteristic. In politics, if a voter supports

Figure 18–4 *This magnesium ribbon is reacting with hydrochloric acid. What gas does this reaction produce? How can you prove the identity of this gas?*

*I*NTEGRATING

*B*IOLOGY

Where can you find lichens?

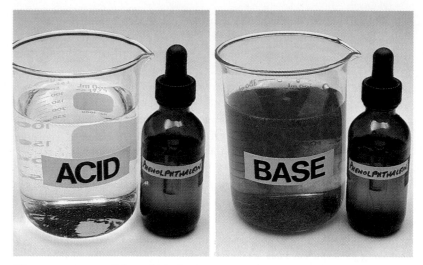

Figure 18–5 *Phenolphthalein is an acid-base indicator, a substance that has different colors in acidic and basic solutions. Can you name another common indicator?*

or rejects a candidate based on the candidate's stand on a single issue, then that voter is said to be applying a litmus test.

Aside from litmus, popular indicators include phenolphthalein, methyl red, and thymol blue. Each of these indicators changes color at different levels of acidity or basicity.

NEUTRALIZATION Mix together an acid and a base, and they quickly react with each other. If the proper amounts of acid and base are used, the result is a solution that has none of the distinctive properties of an acid or a base. In other words, the properties of both the acid and the base have been neutralized, or destroyed. For this reason, the reaction between an acid and a base is called an acid-base **neutralization reaction.** In such a reaction, the acid neutralizes the base and the base neutralizes the acid.

What happens in an acid-base neutralization reaction? You will be better able to answer this question after you have completed this chapter. But as a rule, one of the products that forms in this reaction is an ionic compound—one of the types of compounds that you studied in Chapter 7. An ionic compound that forms from an acid-base neutralization reaction is called a **salt.** The characteristics of salts are more varied than those of acids and bases. In general, salts are crystalline compounds that have high melting points. Many salts ionize and dissolve in water, which makes them good electrolytes, or conductors of electricity. Outside of your chemistry studies, you probably use the word salt as the name of a specific compound: sodium chloride, or ordinary table salt. But for chemists, a salt can be any number of ionic compounds.

The Arrhenius Definition

By using the information you have just learned, you could readily identify acids and bases in the laboratory. For example, if an unknown compound reacts readily with a strip of magnesium, dissolves in water to form a solution that conducts electricity, and turns litmus paper from blue to red, then you can conclude that the compound is an acid. What results would you expect if the unknown compound was a base?

To truly understand the properties of acids and bases, however, you need to study them at the molecular level. The properties of acids and bases—like other compounds—come from the structure and composition of their molecules.

Over the years, chemists have proposed several definitions of acids and bases. The first successful definition came in 1884 from Swedish chemist Svante Arrhenius (ah-RAY-nee-uhs) (1859–1927). Arrhenius suggested that acids and bases could be understood in terms of the ions they release when they dissolve in water. He proposed the following definitions:

- An acid is a substance that dissociates in water to produce hydrogen ions (H^+).
- A base is a substance that dissociates in water to produce hydroxide ions (OH^-).

Acids that fit the Arrhenius definition—or Arrhenius acids, for short—include hydrochloric acid (HCl), nitric acid (HNO_3), sulfuric acid (H_2SO_4), and other acids listed on the left side of Figure 18–6. Each of these compounds dissociates in water to produce an H^+ cation and a characteristic anion. Notice that the formulas for these acids each begin with H. This emphasizes that acids are sources of H^+ ions. Can you suggest an Arrhenius acid that is not listed in Figure 18–6? What ions does this acid produce in water?

Bases that fit the Arrhenius definition—or Arrhenius bases—include the compounds listed on the right side of Figure 18–6. Each Arrhenius base produces a hydroxide anion (OH^-) and a characteristic cation when dissolved in water. Can you suggest

Common Arrhenius Acids and Bases

Name	Formula	Name	Formula
hydrochloric acid	HCl	sodium hydroxide	NaOH
nitric acid	HNO_3	potassium hydroxide	KOH
acetic acid	$HC_2H_3O_2$	magnesium hydroxide	$Mg(OH)_2$
sulfuric acid	H_2SO_4	calcium hydroxide	$Ca(OH)_2$
carbonic acid	H_2CO_3	barium hydroxide	$Ba(OH)_2$
phosphoric acid	H_3PO_4		

Figure 18–6 *This table lists some common Arrhenius acids and bases. What do the acids have in common? What do the bases have in common?*

another base that fits the Arrhenius definition? What ions does it produce in water?

By applying the Arrhenius definition and using the above examples, you can explain many of the properties of acids and bases that you learned earlier in this section. First, when dissolved in water, both acids and bases are electrolytes because they form ions. The sour taste of a water solution of an acid comes from the dissolved hydrogen ions, and the slippery feel of a water solution of a base comes in part from the dissolved hydroxide ions. Furthermore, the Arrhenius definition offers a simple explanation for why acids and bases neutralize each other: An H^+ ion and an OH^- ion combine to form a molecule of water.

$$H^+ (aq) + OH^- (aq) \rightarrow H_2O (l) \qquad \textbf{(Eq. 1)}$$

For example, consider the neutralization reaction between hydrochloric acid (HCl) and sodium hydroxide (NaOH):

$$\underset{\text{acid}}{HCl (aq)} + \underset{\text{base}}{NaOH (aq)} \rightarrow \underset{\text{water}}{H_2O (l)} + \underset{\text{salt}}{NaCl (aq)} \qquad \textbf{(Eq. 2)}$$

Perhaps you recognize this reaction as a double-replacement reaction—a type of reaction that you studied in Chapter 9. Notice that the acid and base combine to form two products, neither of which have the properties of an acid or a base. This fact agrees with the definition of neutralization. In addition, one of the products in this reaction is sodium chloride—a salt. As you learned earlier, an acid-base neutralization reaction always produces an ionic compound called a salt. In all acid-base neutralization reactions, including the one described in Equation 2, the salt produced is formed from the cation of the base and the anion of the acid. Because so many cations and anions can be a part of acids and bases, a salt is sometimes defined as an ionic compound formed from any cation other than H^+ and any anion other than OH^- or O^{2-}.

With Arrhenius acids and bases, an acid-base neutralization reaction always produces water and a salt. What products would you expect from the neutralization reaction between nitric acid (HNO_3) and potassium hydroxide (KOH)? Between hydroiodic acid (HI) and calcium hydroxide ($Ca(OH)_2$)?

Another kind of reaction—the reaction between an acid and a metal—can also be understood in terms of the Arrhenius definition. Remember that acids and most metals react to produce hydrogen gas. According to the Arrhenius definition, an acid is simply a source of hydrogen ions. Thus the reaction between an acid and a metal such as magnesium follows this form:

$$\underset{\text{metal}}{Mg (s)} + \underset{\substack{\text{hydrogen} \\ \text{ion}}}{2 H^+ (aq)} \rightarrow \underset{\substack{\text{metal} \\ \text{ion}}}{Mg^{2+} (aq)} + \underset{\substack{\text{hydrogen} \\ \text{gas}}}{H_2 (g)} \qquad \textbf{(Eq. 3)}$$

This reaction is an example of an oxidation-reduction reaction. You will learn more about this category of reactions in Chapter 20.

The Brønsted-Lowry Definition

Although the Arrhenius definition of acids and bases is useful, it is limited in several ways. First, it restricts acids and bases to water solutions. As illustrated in Figure 18–7, similar reactions occur in the gas phase and in solvents other than water. Second, it oversimplifies what happens when acids dissolve in water. In an acid such as HCl, the hydrogen atom forms a covalent bond—not an ionic bond—with the chlorine atom. The Arrhenius definition of an acid does not explain why this bond breaks, as it must to produce an H^+ ion. Third, the Arrhenius definition of a base does not include certain compounds that have the characteristic properties of bases. For example, ammonia (NH_3) has the properties of a base, but it might not be recognized as a base if we use the Arrhenius definition. Can you explain why not?

To overcome the limitations of the Arrhenius definition, chemists needed to define acids and bases in a more general way. In 1923, Danish chemist Johannes Brønsted (1879–1947) and English chemist Thomas Lowry (1874–1936) independently proposed the following definition:

- **An acid is any substance that can donate H^+ ions.**
- **A base is any substance that can accept H^+ ions.**

The Brønsted-Lowry definition expands the Arrhenius definition in two important ways. First, it defines acids and bases independently of how they behave in water. And second, it focuses solely on H^+ ions. (Indeed, OH^- ions are not even a part of the Brønsted-Lowry definition of a base!) According to the Brønsted-Lowry definition, a base is any compound that accepts H^+ ions. As you will discover, such bases include a wide range of compounds, including several that are excluded from the Arrhenius definition.

At this point in our discussion, we need to ask a simple but important question: What is an H^+ ion? As you should know from your chemistry studies thus far, an H^+ ion is a hydrogen atom that has lost one of its electrons. But a hydrogen atom is the smallest possible atom: A nucleus of 1 proton surrounded by 1 electron. Therefore, aside from the rare isotopes of hydrogen, an H^+ ion is simply a proton!

For this reason, the Brønsted-Lowry definition of acids and bases is often presented in terms of protons. A Brønsted-Lowry acid is a proton donor, and a Brønsted-Lowry base is a proton acceptor. The fact that an H^+ ion is a proton lends itself to other definitions as well. For example, an acid that can donate only one H^+ ion per molecule is called a monoprotic acid. Acids such as HCl, HNO_3, and $HC_2H_3O_2$ are examples of monoprotic acids. Acids such as H_2SO_4 or H_2CO_3, each of which can donate two H^+ ions per molecule, are examples of diprotic acids. An acid such as H_3PO_4, which can donate three H^+ ions per molecule, is a triprotic acid.

Figure 18–7 *Arrhenius acids and bases must be water solutions. But NH_4OH, a base, and HCl, an acid, can react in the gaseous state, as indicated by the cloud in this photograph. Whose definition expanded Arrhenius' definition of acids and bases?*

Figure 18–8 *This sea slug produces sulfuric acid (H_2SO_4) to defend itself from predators. Why is sulfuric acid described as a diprotic acid?*

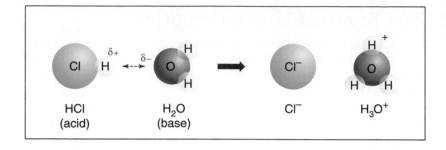

HCl (acid)   H₂O (base)   Cl⁻   H₃O⁺

The Hydronium Ion

Throughout this chapter, we have discussed H^+ ions as if they dissolved in water like any other ion. However, because an H^+ ion is simply a proton, it is strongly attracted to the electrons of surrounding water molecules. Essentially, this interaction forms an H_3O^+ ion:

$$H^+ + H_2O \rightarrow H_3O^+ \qquad \textbf{(Eq. 4)}$$

The H_3O^+ ion is called a **hydronium ion.** While chemists often use the term H^+ (*aq*) for simplicity and convenience, it is more accurate to use the hydronium ion, H_3O^+ (*aq*)—the complex an H^+ ion forms with water.

So, from the Brønsted-Lowry perspective, an acid such as HCl does not simply dissociate in water to form H^+ and Cl^- ions. Rather, a molecule of HCl transfers an H^+ ion to a water molecule to form H_3O^+ ions and Cl^- ions:

$$HCl\ (g) + H_2O\ (l) \rightarrow H_3O^+\ (aq) + Cl^-\ (aq) \ \textbf{(Eq. 5)}$$

By applying the Brønsted-Lowry definition to this reaction, you can identify not only an acid but a base as well. The HCl donates, or gives away, an H^+ ion, so it is the Brønsted-Lowry acid. And the H_2O accepts the H^+ ion, so it is the Brønsted-Lowry base. This reaction is illustrated with three-dimensional models in Figure 18–9.

From the Brønsted-Lowry perspective, whenever one compound in a reaction acts as an acid—or donates an H^+ ion—another compound acts as a base—or receives an H^+ ion. However, we still describe the water solution of HCl as acidic. The dissolved H^+ ion—or H_3O^+ ion—gives a water solution the characteristic properties of an acid.

The Brønsted-Lowry perspective also explains why water solutions of ammonia (NH_3) are basic. When an ammonia molecule comes in contact with a water molecule, it accepts an H^+ ion from the water molecule. Considering this reaction only, the chemical equation is

$$NH_3\ (g) + H_2O\ (l) \rightarrow NH_4^+\ (aq) + OH^-\ (aq) \ \textbf{(Eq. 6)}$$

In this reaction, ammonia (NH_3) is the H^+ acceptor, so it is the Brønsted-Lowry base. Water (H_2O) is the H^+ donor, so it is the

Brønsted-Lowry acid. This reaction is represented with three-dimensional models in Figure 18–10. The water solution of ammonia has the characteristic properties of basic solutions because it contains OH^- ions.

Notice that a molecule of water acts as a Brønsted-Lowry base in Equation 5 but as a Brønsted-Lowry acid in Equation 6. A substance such as water that can act as either an acid or a base, depending on the circumstances, is described as **amphoteric** (am-fuh-TAIR-ihk). You can determine whether water acts as a Brønsted-Lowry acid or base by examining the specific reaction it undergoes.

Conjugate Acid-Base Pairs

Equation 3 indicates that the reaction between ammonia and water proceeds in one direction only. However, this reaction can also proceed in the reverse direction. Therefore, the reaction is more accurately represented with two half arrows:

$$NH_3 \,(g) + H_2O \,(l) \rightleftharpoons NH_4^+ \,(aq) + OH^- \,(aq) \quad \textbf{(Eq. 7)}$$

Remember that by the Brønsted-Lowry definition, an acid donates an H^+ ion and a base receives an H^+ ion. So, as this reaction proceeds from left to right, H_2O is the acid and NH_3 is the base. However, moving from right to left, OH^- is the base and NH_4^+ is the acid. Notice that the base in the forward reaction—NH_3—gains a hydrogen ion to become the acid in the reverse reaction—NH_4^+. Similarly, the acid in the forward reaction—H_2O—loses a hydrogen ion to become the base in the reverse reaction—OH^-.

As the previous example demonstrates, the difference between an acid and a base can be as simple as the difference of one H^+ ion. To emphasize this difference, chemists use the terms **conjugate acid** and **conjugate base.** (The word conjugate means joined together, or coupled.) When an acid loses an H^+ ion, it becomes its conjugate base. For example, hydrochloric acid (HCl) loses an H^+ ion to become its conjugate base, Cl^-. And the conjugate base of water (H_2O) is the hydroxide ion, OH^-. Likewise, when a base gains an H^+ ion, it becomes its conjugate acid. For example, an ammonia molecule (NH_3) gains an H^+ ion to become its conjugate acid, NH_4^+. And the conjugate acid of OH^- is H_2O.

A pair of compounds that differ by only one H^+ ion—such as H_2O and OH^- or NH_3 and NH_4^+—is called a conjugate acid-base pair.

$$\underset{\text{base}}{NH_3 \,(g)} + \underset{\text{acid}}{H_2O \,(l)} \rightleftharpoons \underset{\text{conjugate acid}}{NH_4^+ \,(aq)} + \underset{\text{conjugate base}}{OH^- \,(aq)} \quad \textbf{(Eq. 8)}$$

Figure 18–11 lists several Brønsted-Lowry acids and their conjugate bases. You will learn more about conjugate acid-base pairs in the next section.

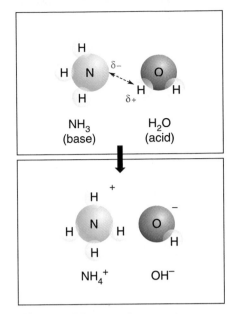

Figure 18–10 *Ammonia* (NH_3) *is a Brønsted-Lowry base because it accepts an H^+ ion from water, producing an OH^- ion. Why is water the Brønsted-Lowry acid in this reaction?*

Several Conjugate Acid-Base Pairs

Acid		Base
HCl		Cl^-
H_2SO_4		HSO_4^-
H_3O^+		H_2O
HSO_4^-	gain H^+	SO_4^{2-}
$HC_2H_3O_2$	lose H^+	$C_2H_3O_2^-$
NH_4^+		NH_3
HCO_3^-		CO_3^{2-}
H_2O		OH^-

Figure 18–11 *When an acid loses an H^+ ion, it becomes its conjugate base. And when a base gains an H^+ ion, it becomes its conjugate acid. What is the conjugate acid of ammonia (NH_3)?*

The Pop of Soda

You may call a certain class of fizzy drinks soda, pop, or even the combined name: soda pop. These drinks come in a variety of flavors, they can contain either sugars or artificial sweeteners, and many brands are more popular—and more expensive—than others. But what they all have in common is carbon dioxide gas. Indeed, a more formal name for soda is the term carbonated beverage. Carbon dioxide gives these drinks both their bubbles and their acidic, tart taste.

The history of carbonated beverages goes back to the 1700s, when chemists and others tried to re-create the effervescence of certain natural waters—what we now call mineral water. English chemist Joseph Priestley (1733–1804) identified the gas in these waters as carbon dioxide, or "fixed air" as it was called at the time. Priestley also devised a method of producing carbonated water. Other scientists have revised and improved this method, and bottled carbonated water eventually was produced and sold throughout Europe.

One way to produce carbonated water is to combine sulfuric acid with an excess amount of marble dust, which contains calcium carbonate. In 1891, the magazine *Harper's Weekly* reported that soda water was being produced from leftover marble chips from the building of St. Patrick's Cathedral in New York City. (Although this was done with no reported ill effects a century ago, we do not recommend that you make beverages from sulfuric acid and marble today!)

18–1 Section Review

1. What is the Brønsted-Lowry definition of an acid? Of a base?

2. Identify five properties of an acid and five properties of a base.

3. State the Arrhenius definition of acids and bases. Explain why ammonia is classified as a base under the Brønsted-Lowry definition but might not be under the Arrhenius definition.

4. **Connection—You and Your World**   Milk of magnesia is a suspension of magnesium hydroxide in water. A small dose of it effectively neutralizes excess stomach acid, which is mostly hydrochloric acid. Write an equation for this neutralization reaction.

18–2 Determining the Strengths of Acids and Bases

Vinegar, an ingredient in salad dressings and other foods, is an acidic solution. Typically, vinegar consists of 1 M acetic acid ($HC_2H_3O_2$) in water. Spilling vinegar on your skin or clothing is not a great cause for concern (except perhaps for the cleaning bill). However, if you should spill a 1 M solution of hydrochloric acid (HCl), you could face some serious consequences. A 1 M solution of hydrochloric acid will burn your skin and "eat" holes in your clothing. If you should ever spill any acid or base in the laboratory, you should wash it away immediately and alert your instructor.

Why does hydrochloric acid behave so differently from acetic acid? The simple answer is that hydrochloric acid is stronger than acetic acid. But all by itself, this answer does not explain too much. Let's examine the strengths of acids and bases more closely.

Strong and Weak Acids

A strong acid, such as hydrochloric acid, readily transfers H^+ ions to water to form H_3O^+ ions. If you placed 1 mole of HCl in a liter of water, nearly all of the HCl molecules would dissociate into ions, forming a solution of 1 M H_3O^+ ions and 1 M Cl^- ions. Because strong acids react completely to form ions, they are strong electrolytes. In contrast, a weak acid, such as

Guide for Reading

- What do dissociation constants indicate about an acid or a base?
- How can you use experimental data to compute a dissociation constant?

Figure 18–12 *Certain weak acids give soda and other beverages their tart taste. Sulfuric acid, which is a strong acid, can be dangerous—if not lethal—if swallowed. Remember never to taste or touch any chemical in the laboratory!*

Figure 18–13 *Dissolve a strong acid in water, and almost all of it dissociates into ions. Dissolve a weak acid in water, however, and only some of it dissociates. Which ions are found in a solution of nitric acid (HNO₃)? In a solution of acetic acid (HC₂H₃O₂)?*

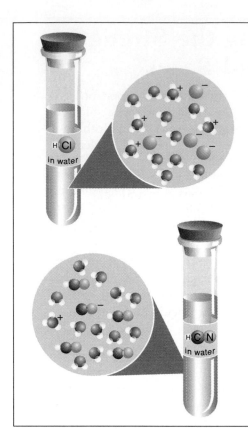

Common Strong Acids

hydrochloric acid (HCl)
hydrobromic acid (HBr)
hydroiodic acid (HI)
nitric acid (HNO_3)
sulfuric acid (H_2SO_4)
perchloric acid ($HClO_4$)

Common Weak Acids

acetic acid ($HC_2H_3O_2$)
hydrocyanic acid (HCN)
nitrous acid (HNO_2)
hydrofluoric acid (HF)
hypochlorous acid (HClO)
hydrogen carbonate ion (HCO_3^-)

acetic acid ($HC_2H_3O_2$), does not readily transfer H^+ ions to water. If you placed 1 mole of acetic acid in a liter of water, only 0.4 percent of the acetic acid molecules would form H_3O^+ and $C_2H_3O_2^-$ ions. This means that 99.6 percent of the acetic acid in a water solution remains un-ionized, or that 99.6 percent of the $HC_2H_3O_2$ molecules do not dissociate. For this reason, weak acids are poor electrolytes.

 One way to signify the difference between a strong acid and a weak acid is by using either a single arrow or a double arrow in the equations for their reactions with water. Because the dissociation of HCl in water is essentially complete, we use a single arrow in the equation for its reaction with water:

$$HCl\ (aq) + H_2O\ (l) \rightarrow H_3O^+\ (aq) + Cl^-\ (aq) \textbf{ (Eq. 9)}$$

To show that the reaction of acetic acid and water is incomplete, or that it comes to an equilibrium, we use two half arrows:

$$HC_2H_3O_2\ (aq) + H_2O\ (l) \rightleftharpoons H_3O^+\ (aq) + C_2H_3O_2^-\ (aq)$$
$$\textbf{(Eq. 10)}$$

Figure 18–13 illustrates how strong and weak acids react with water, and it lists several common examples of each kind of acid. What equation describes the reaction of hydrocyanic acid (HCN) and water? In a water solution of this acid, would you expect to find more HCN molecules or CN^- ions?

Strong and Weak Bases

The substances that have the strongest affinity for H^+ ions are called strong bases. The OH^- ion is a strong base, and so we consider compounds such as NaOH or $Ca(OH)_2$, which readily yield OH^- ions when they dissolve in water, to be strong bases as well. Do you think that strong bases are good electrolytes? Why or why not?

The most widely used commercial base is calcium oxide (CaO), which is often called lime. But don't mistake this base for the green, lemon-shaped fruit of the same name! Rather, this kind of lime is a white, slimy substance that is used to make cement and mortar, as shown in Figure 18–14.

Calcium oxide is a very strong base because the oxide ion (O^{2-}) strongly attracts H^+ ions—even more so than the OH^- ion attracts them. When CaO is dissolved in water, the O^{2-} ion reacts completely with water to form OH^- ions:

$$O^{2-} (aq) + H_2O (l) \rightarrow 2\ OH^- (aq) \qquad \textbf{(Eq. 11)}$$

Because the reaction is complete, we use a single arrow in the equation. Can you identify the Brønsted-Lowry acid and base in this reaction?

Other compounds and ions react only partially with water to form OH^- ions. These compounds or ions are called weak bases. The most common weak bases are ammonia (NH_3) and certain polyatomic ions with negative charges, such as the carbonate ion (CO_3^{2-}) and phosphate ion (PO_4^{3-}). For example, carbonate ions in water reach equilibrium with HCO_3^- and OH^- ions, as signified by the half arrows in the equation for the reaction:

$$CO_3^{2-} (aq) + H_2O (l) \rightleftharpoons HCO_3^- (aq) + OH^- (aq) \qquad \textbf{(Eq. 12)}$$

Figure 18–14 includes lists of several common strong bases and weak bases.

Figure 18–14 *Mortar and cement contain a strong base, calcium oxide (CaO), also known as lime. Rocket fuel often contains hydrazine (H_2NNH_2), a weak base. Which kind of base—strong or weak—reacts to completion with water?*

Four Weak Bases

ammonia (NH_3)
hydrazine (H_2NNH_2)
carbonate ion (CO_3^{2-})
phosphate ion (PO_4^{3-})

Four Strong Bases

calcium oxide (CaO)
sodium hydroxide (NaOH)
potassium hydroxide (KOH)
calcium hydroxide ($Ca(OH)_2$)

Strength of Conjugate Acid-Base Pairs

Take a look at Figure 18–15, which lists several acids and their conjugate bases, as well as the relative strengths of each. Do you see a pattern in these data? There is an inverse relationship between the strengths of conjugate acid-base pairs. The stronger the acid, the weaker its conjugate base. And the stronger the base, the weaker its conjugate acid.

This pattern is not a coincidence. In fact, it makes a good deal of sense when you consider the definitions you have learned in this chapter. For example, consider the dissociation of the hydrogen carbonate ion (HCO_3^-) in water.

$$\underset{\text{acid}}{HCO_3^-} \ (aq) + H_2O \ (l) \rightleftharpoons H_3O^+ \ (aq) + \underset{\substack{\text{conjugate}\\\text{base}}}{CO_3^{2-}} \ (aq) \quad \textbf{(Eq. 13)}$$

As Figure 18–15 indicates, the hydrogen carbonate ion is a relatively weak acid. This means that the reaction described by Equation 13 proceeds mainly from right to left. (That is, very few of the HCO_3^- ions dissociate in water to form H_3O^+ and CO_3^{2-} ions.) This also means that the reverse reaction is very likely to occur: Carbonate ions (CO_3^{2-}) are very likely to gain H^+ ions from H_3O^+ and become HCO_3^- ions. In other words, because HCO_3^- is a relatively weak acid, CO_3^{2-} is a relatively strong base.

Consider a second example, the reaction of the cyanide ion (CN^-) in water:

$$CN^- \ (aq) + H_2O \ (l) \rightleftharpoons HCN \ (aq) + OH^- \ (aq) \quad \textbf{(Eq. 14)}$$

What is the conjugate acid of the cyanide ion? The cyanide ion is a slightly stronger base than the fluoride ion (F^-). Is its conjugate acid stronger or weaker than the conjugate acid of the fluoride ion?

Figure 18–15 *The stronger the acid, the weaker its conjugate base. And the stronger the base, the weaker its conjugate acid. What is the weakest acid listed in the table? What is the strongest base?*

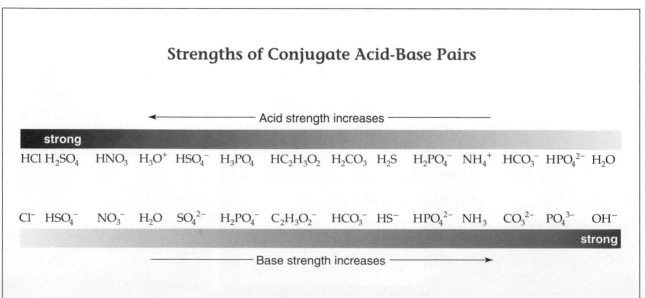

Strengths of Conjugate Acid-Base Pairs

← Acid strength increases ─────────

strong

HCl H_2SO_4 HNO_3 H_3O^+ HSO_4^- H_3PO_4 $HC_2H_3O_2$ H_2CO_3 H_2S $H_2PO_4^-$ NH_4^+ HCO_3^- HPO_4^{2-} H_2O

Cl^- HSO_4^- NO_3^- H_2O SO_4^{2-} $H_2PO_4^-$ $C_2H_3O_2^-$ HCO_3^- HS^- HPO_4^{2-} NH_3 CO_3^{2-} PO_4^{3-} OH^-

strong

───── Base strength increases ─────→

The Acid Dissociation Constant

So far, we have discussed the strength of acids in qualitative terms only. Is there a way to quantify the strength of an acid? The answer is yes, although it takes a few steps to explain. To begin, consider a generic weak acid that we will call HA, where H is a hydrogen atom and A is the rest of the acid molecule. Because HA is a weak acid, it partially dissociates in water, as indicated by the two half-arrows in this equation:

$$HA\ (aq) + H_2O\ (l) \rightleftharpoons H_3O^+\ (aq) + A^-\ (aq) \qquad \textbf{(Eq. 15)}$$

As you learned in Chapter 16, when the products and reactants of a reaction reach equilibrium, a certain ratio of their concentrations always has the same value. This ratio is called the equilibrium constant, or K_{eq}. For the reaction between HA and water, the equilibrium constant is

$$K_{eq} = \frac{[H_3O^+][A^-]}{[HA][H_2O]}$$

However, remember that for dilute solutions, the concentration of H_2O is essentially constant. (For a 1 M solution of a typical weak acid, only 0.007 percent of the H_2O molecules react.) To separate the constants from the variables, chemists typically move the concentration of H_2O to the left side of the equation, which gives

$$K_{eq}\ [H_2O] = \frac{[H_3O^+][A^-]}{[HA]}$$

The product of any two constants is another constant. Thus, the product of K_{eq} and $[H_2O]$ equals a constant, which is called the **acid dissociation constant**, or K_a. For any acid,

$$K_a = \frac{[H_3O^+][A^-]}{[HA]} \qquad \textbf{(Eq. 16)}$$

What does the acid dissociation constant indicate? Remember what you learned about equilibrium constants in Chapter 16: The greater the equilibrium constant, the further the reaction runs to completion. For acids, this means that the larger the K_a, the more the acid reacts with water to produce H_3O^+ ions. **The acid dissociation constant, K_a, is a measure of the strength of an acid.** In other words, the greater the K_a, the stronger the acid. Every acid has a characteristic K_a, many of which are listed in Figure 18–17 on the next page.

Figure 18–16 *Lemons and other citrus fruits contain citric acid, a weak acid. Would you predict the K_a for citric acid to be less than 1 or greater than 1?*

Figure 18–17 *The K_a for a weak acid is always less than 1, which indicates that a weak acid only partly dissociates in water. Of the acids listed in this table, which is the strongest? Which is the weakest?*

Dissociation Constants of Several Weak Acids

Name	Formula	K_a
hydrogen sulfate ion	HSO_4^-	1.2×10^{-2}
hydrofluoric acid	HF	6.8×10^{-4}
formic acid	HCO_2H	1.8×10^{-4}
benzoic acid	$HC_7H_6O_2$	6.5×10^{-5}
acetic acid	$HC_2H_3O_2$	1.8×10^{-5}
carbonic acid	H_2CO_3	4.5×10^{-7}
hypochlorous acid	$HClO$	3.0×10^{-8}
hydrogen carbonate ion	HCO_3^-	5.6×10^{-11}

As you look at Figure 18–17, notice that all the weak acids listed have K_a values less than 1. Remember that when a reaction proceeds only minimally to the right side, or the product side, of an equation, the K_{eq} is less than 1. Similarly, when an acid dissociates only slightly in water, its K_a is less than 1. The K_a for acetic acid ($HC_2H_3O_2$) is only 1.8×10^{-5}.

$$K_a = \frac{[H_3O^+][C_2H_3O_2^-]}{[HC_2H_3O_2]} = 1.8 \times 10^{-5} \qquad \textbf{(Eq. 17)}$$

For acetic acid, the low K_a means that only a small fraction of acetic acid molecules ionize in water. This also agrees with the definition of weak acids that you learned earlier in this section.

For diprotic and triprotic acids, each dissociation takes place in a separate step, which means that each dissociation has its own K_a. For example, consider the dissociation of carbonic acid, a diprotic acid which has the formula H_2CO_3. It dissociates in two steps:

Step 1: $H_2CO_3\ (aq) + H_2O\ (l) \rightleftharpoons H_3O^+\ (aq) + HCO_3^-\ (aq)$

$$K_{a_1} = \frac{[H_3O^+][HCO_3^-]}{[H_2CO_3]} = 4.5 \times 10^{-7} \qquad \textbf{(Eq. 18)}$$

Step 2: $HCO_3^-\ (aq) + H_2O\ (l) \rightleftharpoons H_3O^+\ (aq) + CO_3^{2-}\ (aq)$

$$K_{a_2} = \frac{[H_3O^+][CO_3^{2-}]}{[HCO_3^-]} = 5.6 \times 10^{-11} \qquad \textbf{(Eq. 19)}$$

Notice that both dissociation constants for carbonic acid are small—even smaller than the dissociation constant for acetic acid—and that the second K_a for carbonic acid is smaller than the first. If you placed a sample of carbonic acid in water, would a large or small fraction of it dissociate? Would it yield more HCO_3^- ions or CO_3^{2-} ions?

MATH TIP

The greater the ionization of the acid, the greater the concentration of the product ions in solution. Therefore, as the degree of ionization increases, the value of K_a also increases. Look at the K_a expression for the strong acid, HCl.

$$K_a = \frac{[H_3O^+][Cl^-]}{[HCl]}$$

But in dilute solution, the concentration of unionized HCl is practically zero. Therefore, the value of K_a would approach infinity.

Dissociation Constants of Several Weak Bases

Name	Formula	K_b
phosphate ion	PO_4^{3-}	2.4×10^{-2}
methylamine	CH_3NH_2	4.4×10^{-4}
carbonate ion	CO_3^{2-}	1.8×10^{-4}
ammonia	NH_3	1.8×10^{-5}
hydrogen carbonate ion	HCO_3^-	2.2×10^{-8}
fluoride ion	F^-	1.5×10^{-11}

The Base Dissociation Constant

Like the acid dissociation constant, the **base dissociation constant,** or K_b, is derived from the equilibrium constant for a reaction with water. For a generic base, B, this reaction is

$$B \ (aq) + H_2O \ (l) \rightleftharpoons HB^+ \ (aq) + OH^- \ (aq) \quad \textbf{(Eq. 20)}$$

The K_b for this reaction is the same as the equilibrium constant, without including the concentration of water:

$$K_b = \frac{[HB^+][OH^-]}{[B]} \qquad \textbf{(Eq. 21)}$$

Figure 18–18 *Egg whites are weakly basic. In fact, like other basic solutions, egg whites can be used as a cleaning solution! Of the bases listed in the table, which is the strongest? Which is the weakest?*

The stronger the base, the larger the concentration of hydroxide ions in the solution. And the larger the $[OH^-]$, the larger the K_b. **The base dissociation constant, K_b, is a measure of the strength of a base.** Figure 18–18 lists the dissociation constants of several bases. For example, the value listed for CH_3NH_2 is a measure of its ability to accept an H^+ ion from H_2O, forming an OH^- ion:

$$CH_3NH_2 \ (aq) + H_2O \ (l) \rightleftharpoons CH_3NH_3^+ \ (aq) + OH^- \ (aq)$$

$$K_b = \frac{[CH_3NH_3^+][OH^-]}{[CH_3NH_2]} = 4.4 \times 10^{-4} \quad \textbf{(Eq. 22)}$$

Just like a weak acid, the dissociation constant of a weak base is less than 1. When CH_3NH_2 is placed in water, does a large or a small amount of it ionize? Is a relatively large or small number of OH^- ions produced?

Calculating Dissociation Constants

The dissociation constants listed in Figures 18–17 and 18–18 were calculated from experimental data. From the definitions of K_a and K_b (see Equations 16 and 21), you might think that a chemist would need to measure the concentrations of three separate compounds or ions to calculate a dissociation constant. However, a dissociation constant can be calculated with far less information. To see just how little information is needed, try the following Sample Problem:

Acetylsalicylic acid, better known as aspirin, is a weak monoprotic acid. A chemist mixes 0.1000 mole of aspirin in 1.00 liter of water. When the solution reaches equilibrium, she measures the concentration of H_3O^+ to be 0.0057 M. Calculate the K_a for aspirin.

STRATEGY	SOLUTION
1. Analyze	The problem asks for the K_a of aspirin, but provides only the concentration of H_3O^+. It must be possible to calculate the other concentrations that are needed to find K_a.
2. Plan	Let HA represent acetylsalicylic acid. In water, HA dissociates to form a hydronium ion and an anion:

$$HA + H_2O \rightleftharpoons H_3O^+ + A^-$$

The dissociation constant is

$$K_a = \frac{[H_3O^+][A^-]}{[HA]}$$

3. Solve From the stoichiometry, the reaction produces an A^- ion for each H_3O^+ ion. Therefore, the concentrations of H_3O^+ and A^- must be equal. The equilibrium concentration of HA equals its initial concentration minus the amount that ionizes. So the equilibrium concentration of aspirin, or [HA], is 0.1000 M − 0.0057 M = 0.0943 M. These data are summarized in the table below. Notice that the numbers in the "Change" row are in a 1:1:1 ratio, the same as the stoichiometry of the reaction.

	HA	**+**	**H₂O**	**⇌**	**H₃O⁺**	**+**	**A⁻**
Initial	0.1000 M				0		0
Change	−0.0057 M				+0.0057 M		+0.0057 M
Equilibrium	0.0943 M				0.0057 M		0.0057 M

To find K_a, substitute the equilibrium concentrations of HA, H_3O^+, and A^- into the general equation and solve:

$$K_a = \frac{[H_3O^+][A^-]}{[HA]} = \frac{(0.0057)(0.0057)}{0.0943}$$

$$= 3.4 \times 10^{-4}$$

4. Evaluate The value of K_a is less than 1, which is correct for a weak acid such as aspirin.

Acid-Base Properties of Salts

Salts are strong electrolytes. When they dissolve in water, they dissociate into their component cations and anions. In many cases, these ions are weak Brønsted-Lowry acids or bases. The reactions of ions from salts to form H_3O^+ or OH^- ions are called **salt hydrolysis reactions.**

It is possible to predict whether a salt hydrolysis reaction produces an acidic solution (containing H_3O^+ ions) or a basic solution (containing OH^- ions). One simple way is to consider the acid and base from which the salt is formed. There are four possibilities.

Figure 18-19   Sodium chloride (NaCl) is also known as table salt—or just salt, for short (left). But NaCl is only one of many kinds of salt. Seawater contains several different salts (right). Are all salt solutions neutral? ❶

SALTS OF STRONG ACIDS AND STRONG BASES Solutions of these salts are neither acidic nor basic; they are neutral. For example, the neutralization reaction between NaOH and HCl produces the salt NaCl. A water solution of NaCl is neither acidic nor basic.

$$\underset{\substack{\text{strong}\\\text{base}}}{NaOH\ (aq)}\ +\ \underset{\substack{\text{strong}\\\text{acid}}}{HCl\ (aq)}\ \rightarrow\ \underset{\text{neutral}}{NaCl\ (aq)}\ +\ H_2O\ (l) \qquad \textbf{(Eq. 23)}$$

SALTS OF STRONG ACIDS AND WEAK BASES Solutions of these salts are acidic. For example, NH_4Cl is a salt formed by the neutralization reaction between NH_3 and HCl. Its water solutions are slightly acidic:

$$\underset{\substack{\text{weak}\\\text{base}}}{NH_3\ (aq)}\ +\ \underset{\substack{\text{strong}\\\text{acid}}}{HCl\ (aq)}\ \rightarrow\ \underset{\text{slightly acidic}}{NH_4Cl\ (aq)} \qquad \textbf{(Eq. 24)}$$

The solution is acidic because the NH_4^+ ion is a Brønsted-Lowry acid and donates H^+ ions to water:

$$NH_4^+\ (aq)\ +\ H_2O\ (l)\ \rightleftharpoons\ NH_3\ (aq)\ +\ H_3O^+\ (aq) \qquad \textbf{(Eq. 25)}$$
$$K_a = 5.6 \times 10^{-10}$$

The chloride (Cl^-) ion, being the conjugate base of a strong acid (HCl), has virtually no affinity for H^+ ions. It is merely a spectator ion in the solution.

SALTS OF WEAK ACIDS AND STRONG BASES Solutions of these salts are basic. For example, Na_2CO_3 is a salt formed by the neutralization reaction between NaOH and H_2CO_3. Its water solutions are basic:

$$2\ \underset{\substack{\text{strong}\\\text{base}}}{NaOH\ (aq)}\ +\ \underset{\substack{\text{weak}\\\text{acid}}}{H_2CO_3\ (aq)}\ \rightarrow\ \underset{\text{slightly basic}}{Na_2CO_3\ (aq)}\ +\ 2\ H_2O\ (l)$$
$$\textbf{(Eq. 26)}$$

The solution is basic because the CO_3^{2-} ion is a weak Brønsted-Lowry base and accepts H^+ ions from water:

$$CO_3^{2-}\ (aq)\ +\ H_2O\ (l)\ \rightleftharpoons\ HCO_3^-\ (aq)\ +\ OH^-\ (aq)$$
$$K_b = 1.8 \times 10^{-4} \qquad \textbf{(Eq. 27)}$$

The Na^+ ion is merely a spectator ion in the reaction.

SALTS OF WEAK ACIDS AND WEAK BASES Aqueous solutions of these salts can be acidic, basic, or neutral, depending on the relative strengths of the acids and bases from which the salt is formed. In this case, both the cation and the anion react with water. Predicting the behavior of these salts is beyond the scope of this chapter.

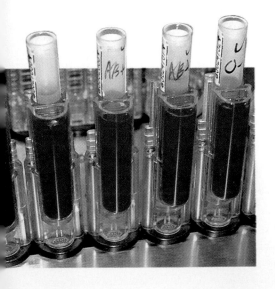

Figure 18–20 *A variety of salts help to keep blood slightly basic. You will learn more about blood in Chapter 19.*

Problem Solving — Chemistry at Work

Old News That's Good News!

Like other inexpensive kinds of paper, newspaper contains certain aluminum salts that help to prevent ink from soaking into the paper and blurring. However, water from the air can react with these salts, forming acidic solutions. Eventually, these acids cause the paper to disintegrate.

At the library one afternoon, you discover an old journal called *Grocery Store Chemistry*. In it, you discover a procedure for preserving newspaper clippings. Unfortunately, the name of the key ingredient is too smudged to read! Here are the steps of the procedure.

1. Dissolve 1 tablespoon of ▨▨▨ ▨▨ ▨▨▨▨▨ in a quart of seltzer water. Let stand overnight.

2. Pour the mixture into a large pan. Soak the newspaper clippings for 1 hour. Remove and let the excess water drip off.

3. Place the clippings on a towel. Do not move them until they are completely dry.

Designing Experiments

1. The diagram below lists the relative acidity and basicity of several products from the grocery store. Which is most likely the smudged ingredient in the journal's procedure? Explain your answer.

2. Design an experiment to prove your answer to Question 1. What is the control in your experiment? What are the variables?

3. Acid-free paper is made with calcium carbonate instead of aluminum salts. Do you think that the journal's procedure would help acid-free paper last longer? Explain your answer.

Going Further With your teacher's permission, perform the experiment you designed. Do you think you correctly identified the procedure's missing ingredient? Can you suggest ways to improve the procedure?

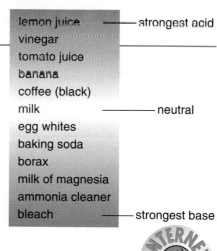

lemon juice ——— strongest acid
vinegar
tomato juice
banana
coffee (black)
milk ——————— neutral
egg whites
baking soda
borax
milk of magnesia
ammonia cleaner
bleach ——————— strongest base

18–2 Section Review

1. What does the acid dissociation constant indicate about an acid? What does the base dissociation constant indicate about a base?

2. Explain the relationship between the strengths of an acid and its conjugate base, and of a base and its conjugate acid.

3. Identify the four kinds of salts discussed in this section. State whether they form acidic, basic, or neutral solutions in water.

4. **Critical Thinking—Interpreting data** Harriet dissolves 1.0 mole of a weak monoprotic acid in 2.0 liters of water. She measures the concentration of H_3O^+ ions to be 3.4×10^{-2} M. What is the K_a of the acid?

Visit our Web site at
http://www.phschool.com
to support your
study of chemistry.

Guide for Reading

- What is an acidic hydrogen?
- What structural feature is a part of most bases?
- How are acids named?

18–3 Naming and Identifying Acids and Bases

Take a look at the three structural formulas shown in Figure 18–21. One is an acid, one is a base, and one has the properties of neither an acid nor a base. Can you correctly label these structures? If not, try again when you have completed this section. As you will discover, the structures of most acids have certain common features, as do the structures of many bases.

Acids

Remember the Brønsted-Lowry definition of an acid: An acid is a substance that can donate an H^+ ion. In a molecule of an acid, a hydrogen atom that can be donated is called an **acidic hydrogen.** A molecule of hydrochloric acid (HCl) contains 1 acidic hydrogen, and a molecule of sulfuric acid (H_2SO_4) contains 2 acidic hydrogens. But not all hydrogen atoms are acidic hydrogens. In a molecule of acetic acid ($HC_2H_3O_2$), for example, only 1 of the molecule's 4 hydrogen atoms is acidic.

Why are some hydrogen atoms acidic and others are not? The reasons are often complex, but we can make one general observation: **As a rule, an acidic hydrogen already has a slight positive charge while it is still a part of a molecule.** This statement is another way of saying that an acidic hydrogen is on the positive end of a polar covalent bond. Thus, acidic hydrogens are usually bonded to very electronegative elements, such as oxygen, nitrogen, and members of the halogen family.

For example, consider the hydrogen atom in hydrochloric acid (HCl), shown in Figure 18–22. In HCl, the hydrogen atom already has a slight positive charge from the polar bond it forms with the chlorine atom. As a result, this bond can break readily in water, forming H_3O^+ and Cl^- ions.

On the other hand, hydrogen atoms that are a part of nonpolar bonds are much less likely to form H^+ ions. For example, consider a molecule of methane (CH_4), also shown in Figure 18–22. As you learned in Chapter 7, carbon and hydrogen have approximately equal electronegativity, and so the bonds in methane are nonpolar and the atoms do not have partial charges. As a result, a methane molecule is unlikely to dissociate and form H^+ ions. In fact, as a very general rule, a hydrogen atom bonded to a carbon atom is not an acidic hydrogen.

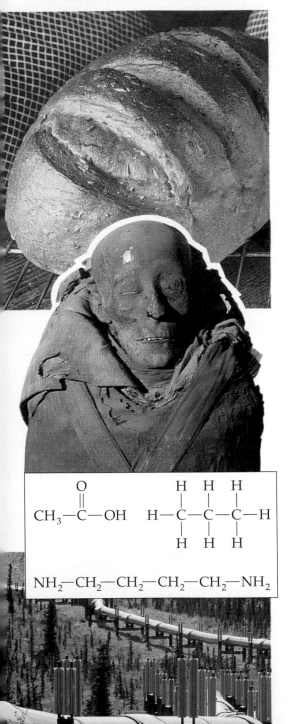

Figure 18–21 *Acids give sourdough bread its sour taste (top). Bases are responsible for the smell of decaying organic matter—a decay being prevented in this mummy (middle). Neutral compounds, such as propane, form the petroleum that the Alaskan pipeline carries (bottom). Match each structural formula with the correct photograph.*

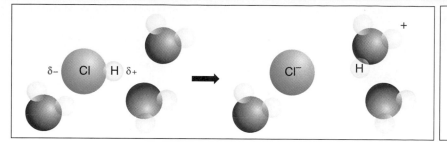
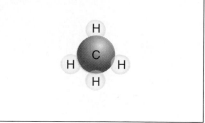

Chemists have identified thousands of acids. Most fall into three categories based on their composition and structure. These categories are binary acids, oxy acids, and carboxylic acids.

BINARY ACIDS Molecules of these acids contain hydrogen and one other element. Usually, the other element is from Group 6A or Group 7A. One of the strongest binary acids is hydrochloric acid (HCl), which the stomach produces as part of the digestive process. Commercially, HCl is sold as muriatic acid and is used to clean tile and bricks. Other strong binary acids are HBr and HI. Weak binary acids include HF, H_2S, and H_2Se.

OXY ACIDS These acids contain hydrogen, oxygen, and one other element. One oxy acid, sulfuric acid (H_2SO_4), is sometimes called the "King of Chemicals": More than 20 million tons of H_2SO_4 is used in the United States each year. Sulfuric acid is used to make dyes, paints, explosives, and other products. It is also called battery acid because it is used in the lead storage batteries of automobiles. Other important oxy acids include nitric acid (HNO_3) and phosphoric acid (H_3PO_4), both of which are used to make fertilizers.

The acidic hydrogens of oxy acids are attached to oxygen atoms. The common strong oxy acids are H_2SO_4, HNO_3, and $HClO_4$. Most other oxy acids are weak acids.

CARBOXYLIC ACIDS These acids are organic acids, or acids that include the carbon atom. (The word organic comes from organism. The chemistry of living organisms is in many ways the chemistry of carbon.) You will learn more about these acids and other organic molecules in Chapter 26.

Most carboxylic acids are weak. Their name comes from a group of atoms called a carboxyl group ($-COOH$). A carboxylic acid can donate the hydrogen atom in its carboxyl group to form a relatively stable anion called a carboxylate ion.

One common carboxylic acid is acetic acid ($HC_2H_3O_2$), which is found in vinegar. The structure of acetic acid is shown below:

$$H-\overset{\overset{\displaystyle H}{|}}{\underset{\underset{\displaystyle H}{|}}{C}}-\overset{\overset{\displaystyle \ddot{O}:}{||}}{C}-\ddot{\underset{}{O}}-H$$

A molecule of acetic acid contains only one acidic hydrogen. Can you identify it?

Figure 18–22 The hydrogen atom in hydrochloric acid (HCl) is part of a polar covalent bond, giving it a partial positive charge. As a result it is an acidic hydrogen, which means it can readily break away from the molecule (left). On the other hand, each hydrogen in methane (CH_4) is part of a nonpolar covalent bond (right). None of the hydrogen atoms in methane are acidic.

Figure 18–23 Carboxylic acids include acetic acid, which is found in vinegar, and lactic acid, which causes the achy feel of overworked muscles.

Figure 18–24 Caffeine, an amine, is the ingredient in coffee that keeps you awake. Although caffeine is a weak base, other ingredients make black coffee slightly acidic.

Bases

What makes a compound basic? **A Brønsted-Lowry base always contains an unshared pair of electrons.** For example, a molecule of ammonia (NH_3) has an unshared pair of electrons on the nitrogen atom. With this unshared pair, an ammonia molecule attracts and bonds with an H^+ ion. Most Brønsted-Lowry bases fall into two categories: anions and amines.

ANIONS Because of their negative charges and available electron pairs, many anions function as bases. Recall that the stronger an acid, the weaker its conjugate base. Because HCl, HBr, HI, HNO_3, H_2SO_4, and $HClO_4$ are strong acids, the anions that are their conjugate bases (Cl^-, Br^-, I^-, NO_3^-, HSO_4^-, and ClO_4^-) are extremely weak bases—so weak that they exhibit few, if any, of the characteristics of bases. Other anions, however, are stronger bases. For example, as you learned earlier in this chapter, O^{2-} ions and OH^- ions are very strong bases, and certain polyatomic anions, such as PO_4^{3-} and CO_3^{2-}, are weakly or moderately basic.

Earlier in this chapter, you learned that compounds such as NaOH and $Ca(OH)_2$ are strong bases. However, from a strict interpretation of the Brønsted-Lowry definition, the bases are not the compounds themselves but the OH^- ions that they yield in water.

AMINES These compounds are related to ammonia. All amines contain a nitrogen atom that has an unshared pair of electrons, which makes amines weakly basic. Methylamine (CH_3NH_2) is one example of an amine:

$$\begin{array}{ccccc} & & H & & H \\ & & | & & | \\ H & - & C & - & \overset{..}{N} & - & H \\ & & | & & \\ & & H & & \end{array}$$

Many drugs, such as the caffeine found in coffee and cola drinks, are amines. Other amines are noteworthy for very different reasons. The decomposition of dead organisms can produce a variety of foul-smelling amines, including putrescine ($H_2N(CH_2)_4NH_2$) and cadaverine ($H_2N(CH_2)_5NH_2$). (Your instructor is not likely to let you work with these compounds in the laboratory!)

Naming Acids and Bases

Chemists name compounds—including acids and bases—using a logical system of roots, prefixes, and suffixes. From Chapter 7, you already know how to name most bases. The compound NaOH, for example, is sodium hydroxide, and $Ca(OH)_2$ is calcium hydroxide. Other bases are common anions. For example, CO_3^{2-} is the carbonate ion, and PO_4^{3-} is the phosphate ion. Many bases are listed and named in Figure 18–14.

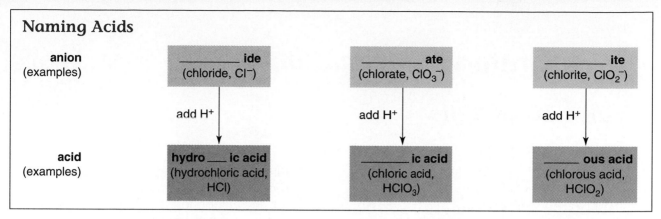

Naming Acids

anion (examples)	_____ ide (chloride, Cl⁻)	_____ ate (chlorate, ClO₃⁻)	_____ ite (chlorite, ClO₂⁻)
	add H⁺	add H⁺	add H⁺
acid (examples)	hydro ___ ic acid (hydrochloric acid, HCl)	_____ ic acid (chloric acid, HClO₃)	_____ ous acid (chlorous acid, HClO₂)

Figure 18–25 *This diagram summarizes the rules for naming acids. What is the name of H₃PO₄, the acid formed from the phosphate ion? Of HNO₂, the acid formed from the nitrite ion?*

However, you need to learn a few more rules to name the common acids. Typically, the name of an acid comes from the name of the anion it produces when it dissociates. To name an acid, here are three general rules:

1. If the name of an anion ends in *-ide*, the name of the acid that produces it includes the name of the anion, a *hydro-* prefix, and an *-ic* ending. For example, the Cl⁻ ion is the chlor*ide* ion. The acid that produces the chloride ion is HCl, which is named *hydro*chlor*ic* acid. All binary acids are named this way.

2. If the name of an anion ends in *-ate*, the name of the acid that produces this anion has no prefix and an *-ic* ending. For example, the NO₃⁻ ion is the nitr*ate* ion. The acid that produces this anion is HNO₃, and its name is nitr*ic* acid. Many acids, including all carboxylic acids, are named this way.

3. If the name of an anion ends in *-ite*, the name of the acid that produces this anion has no prefix and an *-ous* ending. For example, the SO₃²⁻ ion is the sulf*ite* ion. The acid that produces this anion is H₂SO₃, and its name is sulfur*ous* acid. The names of all oxy acids include either *-ous* or *-ic* endings.

These rules are summarized in Figure 18–25.

18–3 Section Review

1. What is an acidic hydrogen?

2. What structural feature do Brønsted-Lowry bases have in common?

3. **Theme Trace—Unity and Diversity** Below is the structural formula for a molecule of glycine:

$$H-\underset{\underset{H}{|}}{\overset{\overset{H}{|}}{N}}-\underset{\underset{H}{|}}{\overset{\overset{H}{|}}{C}}-\overset{\overset{\ddot{O}:}{\|}}{C}-\ddot{O}-H$$

Would you expect that glycine has the characteristics of an acid? Of a base? Explain your answer.

Laboratory Investigation

Hydrolysis of Salts

Problem

What are the acid-base properties of salts?

Materials

assorted salts: NH_4Cl, KNO_3, $NaC_2H_3O_2$,
Na_2CO_3, $ZnCl_2$, Na_3PO_4, $NaCl$
8 small dishes, or an 8-well microplate
red litmus paper
blue litmus paper
toothpicks
water
labels

Procedure

1. Prepare a data table similar to the one shown.
2. Add 2 to 3 mL of water to each dish. Label the dishes from 1 to 8.
3. Add a small sample of a different salt to the first seven dishes. Record the name of each salt in the appropriate box of the data table. Do not add any salt to Dish 8.
4. Stir each salt solution with a clean toothpick until the salt dissolves completely. Use a different toothpick for each dish.

5. Place a drop from each dish onto a strip of red litmus paper. Observe the litmus paper for any color changes. Record your observations in the data table.
6. Repeat Step 5 using blue litmus paper.

Analysis and Conclusions

1. For each salt, identify its water solution as acidic, basic, or neutral.
2. Select a salt that forms an acidic solution in water and a salt that forms a basic solution in water. For each, write an equation for the reaction between the salt and water. In which reaction does water act as an acid? In which reaction does water act as a base?
3. Describe the rules for predicting whether a salt will form an acidic, basic, or neutral solution in water. Did your results confirm or challenge these rules?
4. What is the purpose of Dish 8 in this experiment?
5. **On Your Own**   With your teacher's or parent's permission, repeat this experiment using several common salts, such as table salt, tenderizing salt for meat, road salt, or epsom salts.

Dish	Salt	Color Change of Red Litmus	Blue Litmus	Dish	Salt	Color Change of Red Litmus	Blue Litmus
1				5			
2				6			
3				7			
4				8			

STUDY GUIDE

Summarizing Key Concepts

18–1 Defining Acids and Bases

- Acids taste tart or sour, react with metals to produce hydrogen gas, and turn litmus paper red. Bases taste bitter, feel slippery, and turn litmus paper blue. Both acids and bases are electrolytes. An acid and base will neutralize each other's properties.

- According to the Arrhenius definition, an acid dissociates to produce H^+ ions in water and a base dissociates to produce OH^- ions in water. An acid and base can combine to form water.

- Brønsted and Lowry defined an acid as an H^+ ion donor and a base as an H^+ ion acceptor. An H^+ ion is the same as a proton, and combines with a water molecule to form H_3O^+, or a hydronium ion.

- An acid that loses an H^+ ion becomes its conjugate base. A base that accepts an H^+ ion becomes its conjugate acid.

18–2 Determining the Strengths of Acids and Bases

- The strength of an acid or base reflects how completely it ionizes in water. The stronger the acid, the weaker its conjugate base. The stronger the base, the weaker its conjugate acid.

- Both the acid dissociation constant (K_a) and the base dissociation constant (K_b) are derived from the equilibrium constant (K_{eq}). K_a reflects the strength of an acid and K_b reflects the strength of a base.

- You can calculate the K_a for an acid from its original concentration and the concentration of H_3O^+ ions at equilibrium.

18–3 Naming and Identifying Acids and Bases

- An acidic hydrogen can leave a molecule as an H^+ ion. Typically, an acidic hydrogen is part of a polar covalent bond.

- Binary acids, such as HCl, contain a hydrogen atom bonded to one other element. Oxyacids, such as H_2SO_4, contain hydrogen atoms bonded to oxygen atoms. Carboxylic acids are organic acids. They contain the carboxyl group ($-COOH$).

- Bases typically contain an unshared pair of electrons. The two important categories of bases are the common anions, such as OH^- and CO_3^{2-}, and the amines, which are related to ammonia.

- Like other compounds, acids and bases are named using a system of roots, prefixes, and suffixes.

Reviewing Key Terms

Define each term in a complete sentence.

18–1 Defining Acids and Bases

acid
base
indicator
neutralization reaction
salt
hydronium ion
amphoteric
conjugate acid
conjugate base

18–2 Determining the Strengths of Acids and Bases

acid dissociation constant
base dissociation constant
salt hydrolysis reaction

18–3 Naming and Identifying Acids and Bases

acidic hydrogen

CHAPTER REVIEW

Content Review

Multiple Choice
Choose the letter of the answer that best completes each statement.

1. An acid
   (a) tastes salty. (c) tastes bitter.
   (b) feels slippery. (d) is an electrolyte.
2. By the Arrhenius definition, a base
   (a) produces an H^+ ion in water.
   (b) reacts with a metal to produce H_2.
   (c) feels slippery on skin.
   (d) produces an OH^- ion in water.
3. An H^+ ion in water is more accurately described as a(an):
   (a) hydroxide ion. (c) oxy acid.
   (b) hydronium ion. (d) binary acid.
4. A substance that can act as an acid or a base is
   (a) a conjugate acid. (c) amphoteric.
   (b) a conjugate base. (d) methane.
5. A strong acid in a water solution is
   (a) completely ionized.
   (b) partially ionized.
   (c) not ionized.
   (d) a good source of hydroxide ions.
6. The K_a of a weak acid
   (a) is called the reaction constant.
   (b) is less than 1.
   (c) equals the K_b of the conjugate base.
   (d) is larger than the K_a of a strong acid.
7. The reaction of a strong acid and weak base in water produces
   (a) a slightly acidic salt solution.
   (b) a slightly basic salt solution.
   (c) a neutral salt solution.
   (d) pure water.
8. Typically, an acidic hydrogen is found in a
   (a) bond to a carbon atom.
   (b) nonpolar covalent bond.
   (c) polar covalent bond.
   (d) bond to another hydrogen atom.
9. Sulfuric acid (H_2SO_4) is an example of a(an)
   (a) binary acid (c) oxy acid.
   (b) carboxylic acid (d) weak acid.
10. The acid with the formula HI is
    (a) iodine acid. (c) iodate acid.
    (b) iodite acid. (d) hydroiodic acid.

True or False
If the statement is true, write "true." If it is false, change the underlined word or words to make the statement true.

11. To identify an acid or base in the laboratory, you <u>should</u> taste or touch it.
12. An acid and base destroy each others' properties in a(an) <u>conjugate</u> reaction.
13. Ammonia is an example of a <u>weak acid</u>.
14. A strong base has a <u>strong</u> conjugate acid.
15. Disregarding the rare isotopes of hydrogen, an H^+ ion is a <u>proton</u>.
16. An acid with a K_a of 2.4×10^{-5} is a <u>strong</u> acid.
17. An acid reacts with certain metals to produce <u>carbon dioxide</u> gas.
18. Sulfuric acid (H_2SO_4) is an example of a <u>monoprotic</u> acid because of the number of its acidic hydrogens.

Concept Mapping
Complete the following concept map for Section 18–1. Refer to pages xviii–xix to construct a concept map for the entire chapter.

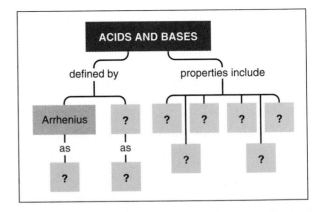

Concept Mastery

Discuss each of the following in a brief paragraph.

19. Discuss at least four different properties that distinguish acids and bases.

20. In what ways is the Brønsted-Lowry definition of acids and bases an improvement on the Arrhenius definition?

21. What kind of salt solution is produced when a strong acid reacts with a strong base? When a strong acid reacts with a weak base? When a weak acid reacts with a strong base?

22. Explain the relationship between the strengths of an acid and its conjugate base.

23. Why are strong acids and bases good electrolytes?

24. A student dissolves 1.0 mole of acid HA in 1.0 liter of water. She measures the concentration of H_3O^+ ions to be 10^{-3} M. Is this enough information to compute the K_a of the acid? Explain.

25. The molecular formula for butane is C_4H_{10}. Do you think that butane has the properties of an acid? Explain.

26. **Tying it Together** Discuss the *unity and diversity* among acids and bases. By the Brønsted-Lowry definition, what do acids have in common? What do bases have in common? Why can the same compound act as an acid or base under different circumstances?

Critical Thinking and Problem Solving

Use the skills you have developed in this chapter to answer each of the following.

27. **Applying concepts** Consider the compound with the following structure:

$$H-\overset{..}{\underset{..}{O}}-\overset{\overset{..}{\overset{\displaystyle \ddot{O}}{\|}}}{C}-\overset{\overset{..}{\overset{\displaystyle \ddot{O}}{\|}}}{C}-\overset{..}{\underset{..}{O}}-H$$

Do you think this compound is an acid, a base, or neither an acid nor a base? Explain your answer.

28. **Making inferences** A chemistry teacher dissolves 0.10 mole of acetic acid in 1.0 liter of water, measures the concentration of H_3O^+, and calculates the K_a. She then repeats these steps, but substitutes twice as much acetic acid. Will she calculate the same K_a? Explain.

29. **Classifying** Identify the following as either a strong acid, a strong base, a weak acid, a weak base, or neither an acid nor a base:
(a) $Mg(OH)_2$ (c) HNO_3 (e) H_2CO_3
(b) CH_4 (d) NH_3 (f) NH_4^+

30. **Evaluating experiments** Three beakers each contain a 0.10 M solution of a differ-

ent acid. When 2.0 grams of magnesium is added to each beaker, the solutions yield the same volume of hydrogen gas. Can you conclude that the strength of each acid solution is the same? Explain your answer.

31. **Making predictions** A student combines a 0.1 M solution of an acid with a 0.1 M solution of a base. Will the product be a neutral solution? Explain.

32. **Making comparisons** Both calcium hydroxide ($Ca(OH)_2$) and sodium hydroxide (NaOH) are strong bases. Compare a 1.0 M solution of $Ca(OH)_2$ with a 2.0 M solution of NaOH. Which solution contains a higher concentration of OH^- ions? Explain your answer.

33. **Using the writing process** Write a short story, poem, or play that includes someone being attacked by a giant petrel. Suggest possible defenses, including a way to neutralize the acid from the petrel's stomach.

Chapter 19

Reactions of Acids and Bases

Hydrangeas, the plants shown in this photograph, respond in an interesting way to acids and bases in soil. When grown in acidic soil, hydrangeas produce blue flowers. And in basic soil, they produce red flowers.

You can think of hydrangeas as an acid-base indicator for soil, just as litmus and other substances are acid-base indicators for solutions. But how do chemists accurately measure the acidity of a solution? You will learn the answer to this question and other questions about acids and bases as you study this chapter.

Hydrangeas produce blue flowers when grown in acidic soil and red flowers when grown in basic soil. Litmus paper, however, changes color in the opposite way. Litmus turns red in acidic solutions and blue in basic solutions.

Chem Journal

YOU AND YOUR WORLD

In your journal, describe some devices that are indicators. A weather vane, for example, indicates wind direction, and the speedometer of a car indicates speed. Do these devices have anything in common? Which of these devices have you encountered or used?

19–1 The Self-ionization of Water and pH

Guide for Reading
- What are the ion concentrations in pure water?
- What is the pH scale?

Suppose you had a few drops of pure water. If you could individually inspect every molecule in these drops, would you expect to find only molecules of H_2O? Do you think you would find anything else?

From your knowledge of chemistry so far, you might think that a drop of pure water consists entirely of molecules of H_2O. But even the purest water always contains small quantities of two important ions: H_3O^+ ions and OH^- ions. To understand why this is so, you need to understand an important reaction that we will discuss in this section.

The Self-ionization of Water

As you learned in Chapter 18, water is amphoteric, which means it can act either as an acid or a base. As an acid, a water molecule gives up an H^+ ion to become an OH^- ion. And as a base, it accepts an H^+ ion to become an H_3O^+ ion. You already have studied several reactions in which water behaves in one of these two different ways. But one example you have yet to

Figure 19–1   In even the purest sample of water, would you expect to find only molecules of H_2O? What ions are always present in water?

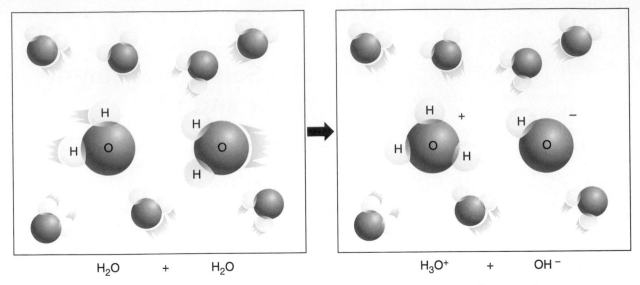

H_2O + H_2O $\qquad$ H_3O^+ + OH^-

Figure 19–2 *In the self-ionization of water, 1 water molecule transfers a hydrogen atom to another water molecule, forming an OH^- ion and an H_3O^+ ion. At 25°C, what is the concentration of these ions in pure water?*

encounter is the **self-ionization** of water. In this reaction, 1 water molecule transfers an H^+ ion to a second water molecule, forming an H_3O^+ ion and an OH^- ion. In other words, water acts as both and acid and a base in the same reaction:

$$H_2O \ (l) + H_2O \ (l) \rightleftharpoons H_3O^+ \ (aq) + OH^- \ (aq) \quad \textbf{(Eq. 1)}$$

As indicated by the long and short arrows, the self-ionization of water proceeds only minimally to the product side of the reaction. In fact, in a 1.0-liter sample of pure water at 25°C, only slightly above room temperature, this reaction produces only 1.0×10^{-7} mole of both H_3O^+ ions and OH^- ions. **In pure water at 25°C, both H_3O^+ ions and OH^- ions are found at concentrations of 1.0×10^{-7} M.** A concentration of 1.0×10^{-7} M—or 1 ten-millionth of a mole per liter—is very small. Nevertheless, this concentration is both important and significant.

To better understand the self-ionization of water, first take a look at its equilibrium constant. Remember that the equilibrium constant equals the concentrations of the products at equilibrium divided by the concentration of the reactants:

$$K_{eq} = \frac{[H_3O^+][OH^-]}{[H_2O]^2} \quad \textbf{(Eq. 2)}$$

However, in both pure water and in dilute solutions at constant temperature, the concentration of H_2O is constant. For this reason, chemists typically multiply both sides of Equation 2 by $[H_2O]^2$, which gives

$$K_{eq} \times [H_2O]^2 = [H_3O^+][OH^-] \quad \textbf{(Eq. 3)}$$

The left side of this equation is called the **ion-product constant** for water, and is abbreviated with the symbol K_W. In pure water at 25°C, K_W equals 1.0×10^{-14}.

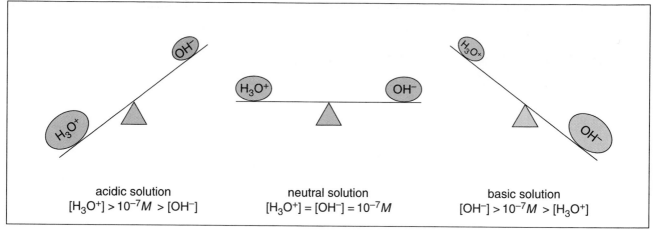

acidic solution	neutral solution	basic solution
$[H_3O^+] > 10^{-7}M > [OH^-]$	$[H_3O^+] = [OH^-] = 10^{-7}M$	$[OH^-] > 10^{-7}M > [H_3O^+]$

Figure 19–3 *You can pretend that H_3O^+ ions and OH^- ions are on a seesaw, with the fulcrum at 10^{-7} M. The ion more concentrated than 10^{-7} M determines the acidity or basicity of the solution.*

$$K_W = [H_3O^+][OH^-]$$
$$= (1.0 \times 10^{-7})(1.0 \times 10^{-7})$$
$$= 1.0 \times 10^{-14} \qquad \text{(Eq. 4)}$$

K_W is useful because it applies not only to pure water, but to every water solution at 25°C, even a solution in which the concentrations of H_3O^+ ions and OH^- ions are not equal. For example, suppose you measure the concentration of H_3O^+ ions in an acid solution to be 1.0×10^{-2} M. Because K_W is always 1.0×10^{-14}, you can use K_W to calculate the concentration of OH^- ions in the solution. As shown below, this concentration is 1.0×10^{-12} M.

$$[H_3O^+][OH^-] = K_W$$
$$(1.0 \times 10^{-2})[OH^-] = (1.0 \times 10^{-14})$$
$$[OH^-] = \frac{1.0 \times 10^{-14}}{1.0 \times 10^{-2}}$$
$$[OH^-] = 1.0 \times 10^{-12} \qquad \text{(Eq. 5)}$$

The self-ionization of water means that acidic, basic, and neutral solutions are slightly more complicated than you might have thought them to be. An acidic solution contains not only H_3O^+ ions, but also a small number of OH^- ions. A basic solution contains not only OH^- ions, but also a small number of H_3O^+ ions. And in all solutions at 25°C, the product of the concentrations of H_3O^+ ions and OH^- ions equals 1.0×10^{-14}.

These facts are summarized for you in Figure 19–3. Notice that a key number is 1.0×10^{-7}, which is the concentration of both H_3O^+ ions and OH^- ions in pure water. If a solution has a concentration of H_3O^+ ions greater than 1.0×10^{-7} M, the solution is acidic. If a solution has a concentration of OH^- ions greater than 1.0×10^{-7} M, the solution is basic. And if the concentrations of both H_3O^+ ions and OH^- ions equal 1.0×10^{-7} M, the solution is neutral.

CONSUMER TIP

Cleaning Acid Spills

One way to neutralize an acid spill is with baking soda, or sodium bicarbonate ($NaHCO_3$). Baking soda is often used to clean battery acid off the terminals of automobile batteries, thus protecting the terminals from the corrosive effects of the acid.

When baking soda reacts with a strong acid, it releases bubbles of CO_2 gas. To completely neutralize an acid, baking soda should be added until the bubbling stops.

MATH TIP

Notice that an H_3O^+ concentration of 1×10^0 is not 14 times a concentration of 1×10^{-14}, but rather a factor of 10^{14}, which is 100 trillion. Chemists have simplified this scheme in order to avoid such unwieldy numbers by adopting the pH scale. It is a simple linear scale from 0 to 14, but it is important to remember that each unit on that scale represents a tenfold change in the concentration of H_3O^+.

SAMPLE PROBLEM 1

If the concentration of H_3O^+ in blood is 4.0×10^{-8} M, is blood acidic, basic, or neutral? What is the concentration of OH^- ions in blood?

STRATEGY	SOLUTION
1. **Analyze**	The problem centers on the relationship between $[H_3O^+]$ and $[OH^-]$ and the definitions of acidic, basic, and neutral solutions.
2. **Plan**	Compare $[H_3O^+]$ in blood with $[H_3O^+]$ in pure water, which is 1.0×10^{-7} M. Use the definition of K_W, given in Equation 4, to calculate $[OH^-]$ in blood.
3. **Solve**	Blood is slightly basic because 4.0×10^{-8} M is slightly less than 1.0×10^{-7} M. From the definition of K_W:

$$[H_3O^+][OH^-] = K_W$$

$$[H_3O^+][OH^-] = 1.0 \times 10^{-14}$$

$$(4.0 \times 10^{-8}) \times [OH^-] = 1.0 \times 10^{-14}$$

Solving for $[OH^-]$:

$$[OH^-] = \frac{1.0 \times 10^{-14}}{4.0 \times 10^{-8}}$$

$$[OH^-] = 2.5 \times 10^{-7} M$$

4. Evaluate The calculated value of $[OH^-]$ is greater than 1.0×10^{-7}, as expected for a basic solution.

PRACTICE PROBLEMS

1. What is the concentration of OH^- ions in chocolate milk if $[H_3O^+] = 4.5 \times 10^{-7}$ M? Is chocolate milk acidic, basic, or neutral? *(Answer: $[OH^-] = 2.2 \times 10^{-8}$ M; slightly acidic)*

2. What is the concentration of H_3O^+ ions in black coffee if $[OH^-] = 1.3 \times 10^{-9}$ M. Is black coffee acidic, basic, or neutral? *(Answer: $[H_3O^+] = 7.7 \times 10^{-6}$ M; slightly acidic)*

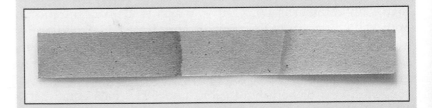

The pH Scale

For most solutions, the molar concentration of H_3O^+ ions is a very small number. Even in strongly acidic solutions, such as the hydrochloric acid solution produced in your stomach, the concentration of H_3O^+ ions is only about 0.01 mole per liter, or 1×10^{-2} M. In pure water, the concentration of H_3O^+ ions is 10^{-7} M. And in a strong basic solution, the concentration of H_3O^+ ions may be as low as 10^{-12} M or 10^{-13} M.

In 1909, Danish biochemist Søren Sørensen proposed a more compact way to express the concentrations of H_3O^+ ions. His scale is based on logarithms and is known as the **pH** scale. The pH of a solution is -1 times the base 10 logarithm of the H_3O^+ concentration in moles per liter:

$$pH = -\log[H_3O^+] \qquad \text{(Eq. 6)}$$

A number's base 10 logarithm is its exponent when 10 is the base. For example, 10,000 is the same as 10^4, so log(10,000) is 4. The number 0.001 is the same as 10^{-3}, so log(0.001) is -3. Most numbers are not whole number powers of 10, so you need a log table or a scientific calculator to compute most logarithms accurately. However, you can estimate a number's logarithm by comparing it to nearby numbers that have simpler logarithms. For example, the number 6.3×10^8 is between 10^8 and 10^9, so its logarithm is between 8 and 9. (The actual logarithm is 8.80) The number 1.4×10^{-7} is a little greater than 10^{-7}, so its logarithm is a little greater than -7. (The actual logarithm is -6.85.) Can you estimate the logarithm of 3.2×10^5? Of 1.1×10^{-3}?

Figure 19–4 shows the pH for several concentrations of H_3O^+ ions and lists the pH for several common substances. Notice that the smaller the pH, the more acidic the solution. For example, a solution in which the concentraion of H_3O^+ ions is 10^{-1} M—a strongly acidic solution—has a pH of 1. A solution in which the concentration of H_3O^+ ions is 10^{-7} M—a neutral solution—has a pH of 7. What is the pH of a solution in which the concentration of H_3O^+ ions is 10^{-13} M? Is this solution acidic, basic, or neutral?

Because the pH scale is a logarithmic scale, each one-unit change in pH represents a 10-fold change in the concentration of H_3O^+ ions. For example, saying that the pH of a solution drops from 4 to 3 is another way of saying that its concentration of H_3O^+ ions increases by a factor of 10—from 10^{-4} M to 10^{-3} M. If the pH of a solution increases from 8 to 10, how does its concentration of H_3O^+ ions change? Is the solution becoming more acidic or more basic?

In calculating pH, you must be careful with significant digits. For any logarithm, the number of digits after the decimal point should equal the number of significant digits in the original number. For example, consider the logarithm of 8.7×10^{-4}. Your calculator will probably provide a logarithm with lots of digits

	pH	$[H_3O^+]$
	0	10^0 M
0.1 M HCl	1	10^{-1} M
lemon juice	2	10^{-2} M
	3	10^{-3} M
	4	10^{-4} M
banana		
coffee	5	10^{-5} M
	6	10^{-6} M
saliva		
pure water	7	10^{-7} M
blood		
	8	10^{-8} M
	9	10^{-9} M
borax		
	10	10^{-10} M
limewater	11	10^{-11} M
	12	10^{-12} M
bleach		
	13	10^{-13} M
1.0 M NaOH	14	10^{-14} M

Figure 19–4 *For whole numbers, converting pH to $[H_3O^+]$ is easy. When the pH is 12, what is $[H_3O^+]$? When $[H_3O^+]$ is 10^{-4} M, what is the pH?*

CHEMISTRY IN ACTION

Are Two Scales Better Than One?

Different scales can express the same quantity. For example, both 1.0 mile and 1.6 kilometers describe the same distance, just as 70°F and 21°C describe the same temperature. In chemistry, both the pH scale and molarity are used to describe the concentration of H_3O^+ ions in a solution. Can you think of other examples of two scales that express the same quantity?

after the decimal point, a logarithm such as -3.0604807. However, 8.7×10^{-4} has only two significant figures, so its logarithm should be rounded off at the second digit past the decimal point.

$$-\log(8.7 \times 10^{-4}) = 3.06 \qquad \textbf{(Eq. 7)}$$

Confused? Understanding logarithms and the pH scale takes practice. Try solving the following problems.

SAMPLE PROBLEM   2

In one brand of vegetable juice, the concentration of H_3O^+ ions is 7.3×10^{-5} M. What is the pH of the juice?

STRATEGY	SOLUTION
1. **Analyze**	You are given the concentration of H_3O^+ ions and asked to find the pH. The pH scale is another way to describe the concentration of H_3O^+ ions in a solution.
2. **Plan**	Use the formula for pH: $$pH = -\log[H_3O^+].$$ Remember to include the correct number of significant digits.
3. **Solve**	Substituting the concentration of H_3O^+ ions into the above equation gives: $$pH = -\log(7.3 \times 10^{-5}\ M)$$ Using a scientific calculator, the log is -4.1366771. Because $[H_3O^+]$ is given with 2 significant digits, the logarithm should be rounded off to the second digit after the decimal. Therefore, $$pH = -(-4.14)$$ $$pH = 4.14$$
4. **Evaluate**	The concentration of H_3O^+ is between 10^{-5} and 10^{-4}, so it makes sense that the pH is between 5 and 4.

PRACTICE PROBLEMS

3. Normal rainwater has a pH near 6. In rainwater that falls close to a coal-burning power plant, the concentration of H_3O^+ ions is 6.23×10^{-4} M. What is the pH? Is this more or less acidic than normal rainwater? *(Answer: pH = 3.206. The rainwater is more acidic than normal.)*

4. In household bleach, the concentration of OH^- ions is 5.0×10^{-2} M. What is the pH? *(Answer: pH = 12.70)*

CONNECTION

Acid Rain

While normal rain has a pH near 6, in some places the pH of rainwater has been measured as low as 3.5. Rainwater with a pH below 5.6 is defined as acid rain—a growing environmental problem in the United States, Canada, and elsewhere. Scientists have identified both the causes and effects of acid rain. But as you will discover, solving an environmental problem is not always as easy as understanding it.

The principal cause of acid rain is coal-burning electrical power plants. Coal consists mainly of carbon, but it also contains small quantities of sulfur. When coal is burned, the sulfur reacts with oxygen to form sulfur dioxide (SO_2) and sulfur trioxide (SO_3). Both compounds react with water in the atmosphere to form oxy acids of sulfur:

$$SO_2 \ (g) + H_2O \ (l) \rightarrow H_2SO_3 \ (aq)$$
$$SO_3 \ (g) + H_2O \ (l) \rightarrow H_2SO_4 \ (aq)$$

Another source of acid comes from the nitrogen gas (N_2) in the atmosphere. At high temperatures, nitrogen combines with oxygen to form nitrogen dioxide (NO_2). Nitrogen dioxide reacts with water to form both nitric acid and nitrous acid:

$$2\,NO_2 \ (g) + H_2O \ (l) \rightarrow HNO_3 \ (aq) + HNO_2 \ (aq)$$

Any combustion reaction that produces high temperatures can trigger the formation of NO_2. Thus, automobile engines are an important contributor to acid rain.

Acid rain harms both living and nonliving things in a variety of ways. For example, acid rain damages metals and many stone building materials. Limestone and marble, for example, contain calcium carbonate—or calcite—which reacts readily with acids. Acid rain also washes nutrients out of the soil, damages the bark and leaves of trees, and harms the fine root

hairs of many plants, which plants need to absorb water. In addition, acid rain eventually finds its way into rivers and lakes. When the pH of a river or a lake falls below 4.5, few aquatic species of any kind can survive.

One way to reduce acid rain is to reduce the production of sulfur dioxide, sulfur trioxide, and other nonmetal oxides. In one procedure, powdered limestone ($CaCO_3$) is injected into the furnace of a power plant, where it reacts with sulfur dioxide to form carbon dioxide and a solid, calcium sulfite ($CaSO_3$). The calcium sulfite is later collected and removed. But this procedure is costly, and at best is only a partial solution.

The surest way to stop acid rain would be to stop burning all fossil fuels! But people depend on coal and other fossil fuels for electricity. And the number of automobiles in many cities increases year after year. How do you think we should prevent acid rain?

Figure 19–5 *Indicators change color over characteristic pH ranges. These vials contain the indicator methyl red, which changes from red to yellow between a pH of 5 and 7.*

Common Indicators

	pH Range for Color Change							
	0	2	4	6	8	10	12	14
methyl violet	yellow	violet						
thymol blue		red	yellow		yellow	blue		
methyl orange		red	yellow					
methyl red			red	yellow				
litmus			red		blue			
bromthymol blue			yellow		blue			
phenolphthalein					colorless	pink		
alizarin yellow R					yellow	red		

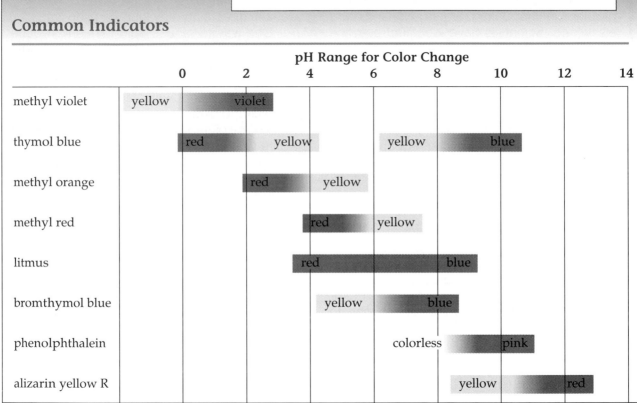

Figure 19–6 *Indicators change color over characteristic pH ranges, as indicated in the table. If both methyl red and bromthymol blue are colored yellow in the same solution, what is the solution's pH?*

Figure 19–7 *The pH meter on the left uses special electrodes to measure a solution's pH. Is the solution in the photograph acidic, basic, or neutral?*

Measuring pH

There are two common ways to measure the pH of a solution. The simplest way is to use an acid-base indicator. Indicators are weak acids or bases that undergo a color change when they gain or lose an H^+ ion. From Chapter 18 you should be familiar with one common indicator: litmus. In an acidic solution, litmus gains H^+ ions and turns red; in a basic solution, litmus loses H^+ ions and turns blue. Other indicators are illustrated in Figure 19–6.

Litmus and other indicators can be explained by one simple equation. Using HIn to represent the acid form of the indicator and In^- to represent the base form, this equation is

$$HIn\ (aq) + H_2O\ (l) \rightleftharpoons H_3O^+\ (aq) + In^-\ (aq)\ \textbf{(Eq. 8)}$$

Adding acid, which adds H_3O^+ ions to the solution, shifts the equilibrium to the left, increasing [HIn]. For litmus, HIn is colored red. Adding base, which removes H_3O^+ ions, shifts the equilibrium to the right, increasing $[In^-]$. For litmus, In^- is colored blue. Each indicator has a different equilibrium constant for Equation 8, which means that each has a different pH range over which it changes color. For example, litmus is red below pH 4.8, blue above pH 7.8, and has intermediate colors in the pH values in between. Other indicators have different pH ranges, as illustrated in Figure 19–6.

One way to pinpoint a solution's pH is to test it with a combination of indicators that takes advantage of the different pH ranges over which different indicators change color. Chemists often use strips of paper coated with such a combination of indicators. Place a drop of a solution on this paper, and the paper will turn a color that indicates the pH. A second, much more accurate way to measure pH is to use a device called a pH meter, such as the one pictured in Figure 19–7. A pH meter uses a special electrode that is sensitive to H_3O^+ ions.

19–1 Section Review

1. Describe the self-ionization of water. At what concentrations are H_3O^+ and OH^- ions found in pure water?

2. What is the pH scale? What does this scale measure?

3. If you know the concentration of H_3O^+ ions in a solution, can you calculate the concentration of OH^- ions? Explain.

4. Describe two ways of measuring the pH of a solution.

5. **Connection—You and Your World**   A solution of baking soda in water has a pH of 8.40. What are the concentrations of H_3O^+ and OH^- ions in this solution? Is this solution basic, acidic, or neutral?

Visit our Web site at
http://www.phschool.com
to support your
study of chemistry.

19–2 Buffers

In many solutions—including solutions found in living things—the pH must be controlled within very narrow limits. For example, the human body must maintain the pH of blood between 7.35 and 7.45. A pH outside this range causes many ill effects and can lead to death.

One way to control the pH of a solution is with a **buffer,** which typically is a mixture of acids and bases. **A buffer is a mixture that is able to release or absorb H^+ ions, keeping a solution's pH constant.** Most common buffers are mixtures of weak acids and their conjugate bases. For example, a solution of acetic acid ($HC_2H_3O_2$) and its conjugate base—the acetate ion ($C_2H_3O_2^-$)—acts as a buffer. So does a solution of ammonium ions (NH_4^+) and the ion's conjugate base, ammonia (NH_3).

To understand how buffers work, consider a buffer solution of acetic acid and the acetate ion, as illustrated in Figure 19–9. When H_3O^+ ions are added to this solution, they react with the acetate ion, the basic component of the buffer.

$$H_3O^+ \ (aq) \ + \ C_2H_3O_2^- \ (aq) \rightarrow H_2O \ (l) \ + \ HC_2H_3O_2 \ (aq)$$
$$\textbf{(Eq. 9)}$$

As the single arrow indicates, this reaction proceeds nearly to completion from left to right. Because acetate ions so readily accept H^+ ions, few of the added H_3O^+ ions remain in the solution. Therefore, the solution's pH changes only slightly.

When OH^- ions are added to the solution, they react with the acidic component of the buffer, the acetic acid:

$$OH^- \ (aq) \ + \ HC_2H_3O_2 \ (aq) \rightarrow H_2O \ (l) \ + \ C_2H_3O_2^- \ (aq)$$
$$\textbf{(Eq. 10)}$$

Like the buffer's reaction with H_3O^+, this reaction with OH^- proceeds nearly to completion from left to right. As a result, few of the additional OH^- ions remain in the solution, and the solution's pH changes only slightly.

All buffers have a limited capacity to neutralize added H_3O^+ ions or OH^- ions. For the buffer described above, adding H_3O^+ ions will eventually exhaust the supply of acetate ions. Similarly, adding OH^- ions will eventually exhaust the supply of acetic acid. The amount of acid or base that a buffer can neutralize is called the **buffer capacity.** If you add H_3O^+ ions or OH^- ions beyond the buffer capacity, the ions will remain in the solution, changing the pH. As a general rule, the greater the concentration of buffer in the solution, the greater the buffer capacity. Most buffer solutions contain roughly equal concentrations of acid and its conjugate base, which means the buffer has an equal capacity to neutralize either H_3O^+ ions or OH^- ions.

Figure 19–8 *Humans need the pH of their blood to fall between 7.35 and 7.45. A system of buffers helps to maintain blood pH.*

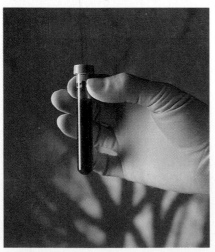

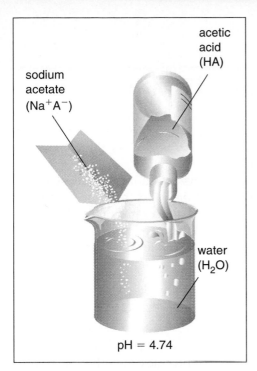

Figure 19–9 *One buffer is a mixture of a weak acid (HA) and its conjugate base (A⁻). Add acid, and the additional H⁺ ions bond to the A⁻ ions (top right). Add base, and the additional OH⁻ ions take hydrogen atoms away from the HA molecules (bottom right). A buffer of acetic acid and the acetate anion keeps the pH near 4.74.*

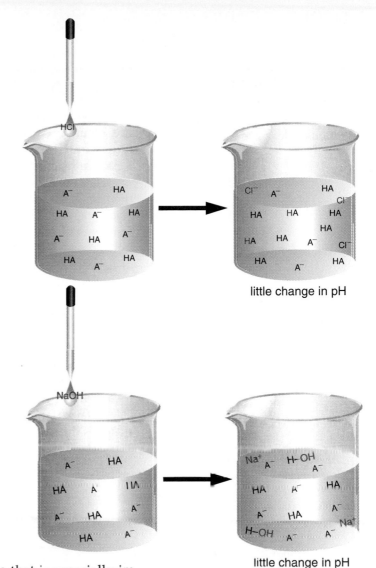

In the human body, one buffer system that is especially important is the carbonic acid and bicarbonate buffer (H_2CO_3 and HCO_3^-). In the blood, the ratio of carbonic acid to bicarbonate is about 1:20. As a result, this buffer has a much greater capacity for neutralizing acids than for neutralizing bases. This difference is appropriate, however, because excess acid is a much more common problem in the blood than is excess base.

INTEGRATING

BIOLOGY

What is one way that pH is controlled in the blood?

19–2 Section Review

1. What is a buffer?
2. Describe how buffers work.
3. **Theme Trace—Stability** A buffer of equal amounts of acetic acid and the acetate ion stabilizes a solution at a pH near 4.7. Derive this pH value from the K_a of acetic acid, which is 1.8×10^{-5}. (Hint: See Equation 17 in Chapter 18.)

Guide for Reading

- What is an acid-base titration?
- Why are indicators used in titrations? How are they chosen?

Figure 19–10 *Vinegar is used in salad dressings and other foods. How can you determine the concentration of acetic acid in vinegar?*

19–3 Acid-Base Titration

Vinegar, which is used in salad dressings and other foods, is a solution of acetic acid ($HC_2H_3O_2$) and water. But just how concentrated is the acetic acid in vinegar? Is there a way to measure its concentration?

The answers to these questions are more complicated than they may first appear. You may think that the concentration of acid in a solution is the same as the concentration of H_3O^+ ions. But remember that weak acids, such as acetic acid, only partially ionize in water. This is indicated by the low K_{eq} for the reaction of acetic acid and water:

$$HC_2H_3O_2\ (aq)\ +\ H_2O\ (l)\ \rightleftharpoons\ H_3O^+\ (aq)\ +\ C_2H_3O_2^-\ (aq)$$

$$K_{eq} = 1.8 \times 10^{-5} \qquad \textbf{(Eq. 11)}$$

As the low K_{eq} indicates, the bulk of the acetic acid in a water solution remains as un-ionized molecules. In other words, for weak acids, measuring the pH of a solution is not the same as measuring the acid's concentration.

In fact, the concentration of a weak acid or a weak base in water is difficult—if not impossible—to measure directly. However, the concentration can be calculated from the results of a clever procedure called an **acid-base titration.** You will learn how to perform this procedure in this section.

Performing a Titration

The most convenient way to quantify the amount of acetic acid in vinegar—or of an acid or a base in any solution—is with a procedure called an acid-base titration, or just titration, for short. **An acid-base titration is a carefully controlled neutralization reaction.** A titration on an acetic acid solution is illustrated for you in Figure 19–11.

To run a titration on a solution of unknown concentration of an acid or a base, you need a second solution called a **standard solution.** A standard solution contains an acid or a base in a known concentration. If the unknown solution is an acid, the standard solution always contains a strong base. And if the unknown solution is a base, the standard solution always contains a strong acid. In the titration illustrated in Figure 19–11, the unknown solution is an acid, so the standard solution is of a strong base, sodium hydroxide (NaOH).

Chemists typically use one additional substance in a titration: an acid-base indicator. As you learned earlier, an indicator is a substance that changes color at a certain pH value. The indicator phenolphthalein is used in the titration illustrated in Figure 19–11. Phenolphthalein is clear in acidic solutions and pink in basic solutions. It changes color over a pH range of 8 to 10.

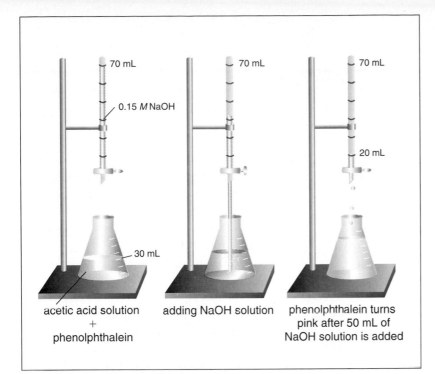

Figure 19–11 *At the beginning of this titration, the acetic acid solution and indicator are in the flask and the standard solution of 0.15 M NaOH is in a tall burette (left). The standard solution is allowed to fall into the flask and react with the acetic acid (middle) until the indicator changes color (right). What volume of standard solution was added?*

To run a titration, the standard solution is slowly added to the unknown solution. As the two solutions mix, the acid in one solution neutralizes the base in the other solution, a reaction that runs nearly to completion. For the titration illustrated in Figure 19–11, the reaction between acetic acid and sodium hydroxide is described by this equation:

$$HC_2H_3O_2 \ (aq) \ + \ NaOH \ (aq) \rightarrow H_2O \ (l) \ + \ NaC_2H_3O_2 \ (aq)$$

acid   base   water   salt

$$K_{eq} = 1.8 \times 10^9 \qquad \textbf{(Eq. 12)}$$

Eventually, enough standard solution is added to neutralize all the acid or base in the unknown solution. The point at which this occurs is called the **equivalence point.** For the titration illustrated in Figure 19–11, the equivalence point was reached in the illustration on the right, after 50 milliliters of NaOH was added to the acetic acid. Notice that the solution in this illustration has a different color than in the other illustrations. The color change came from the phenolphthalein.

The point at which the indicator changes color is called the **end point** of the titration. If the indicator is chosen correctly, the end point is very close to the equivalence point. Therefore, at approximately the end point of a titration, the total number of moles H^+ ions donated by the acid equals the total number of moles of H^+ ions accepted by the base. And for Arrhenius acids and bases, the following equation holds true:

total moles of H^+ ions   =   total moles of OH^- ions
from the acid (at end point)   from the base (at end point)

(Eq. 13)

As you will see, this equation is the key to calculating the concentration of an acid or base using the data from a titration.

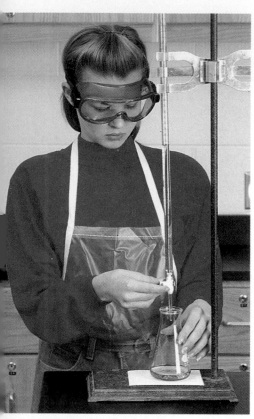

Figure 19–12 *This chemistry student is performing an acid-base titration. Whenever you work with chemicals in the laboratory, remember to take proper safety precautions.*

SAMPLE PROBLEM 3

What is the concentration of the acetic acid solution illustrated in Figure 19–11?

STRATEGY	SOLUTION
1. Analyze	At the equivalence point of a titration, the added base has completely neutralized the acid. Figure 19–11 shows that 50. mL of 0.15 M NaOH neutralized 30. mL of the acetic acid solution.
2. Plan	To solve this problem, use Equation 13:

$$\text{total moles H}^+ = \text{total moles OH}^-$$
$$\text{(at end point)}$$

3. Solve   For both OH^- and H^+, the total number of moles equals the concentration times the volume. The concentration of H^+ is unknown.

$$\text{total moles OH}^- = 50.\text{ mL} \times 0.15 \text{ mol/L}$$
$$\text{total moles H}^+ = 30.\text{ mL} \times [\text{H}^+]$$

Now set these expressions equal to each other and solve for $[H^+]$:

$$30.\text{ mL} \times [\text{H}^+] = 50.\text{ mL} \times 0.15 \text{ mol/L}$$

$$[\text{H}^+] = \frac{50.\text{ mL} \times 0.15 \text{ mol/L}}{30.\text{ mL}}$$

$$[\text{H}^+] = 0.25 \text{ mol/L}$$

Because acetic acid yields one H^+ ion per molecule, the concentration of acetic acid is also 0.25 mole per liter, or 0.25 M.

4. Evaluate   50. mL of NaOH solution neutralized a smaller volume—30. mL—of the acetic acid solution. Therefore, it makes sense that the acetic acid solution is more concentrated than the NaOH solution.

PRACTICE PROBLEMS

5. Solutions of sodium hydroxide (NaOH) are used to unclog drains. A 43.0-mL volume of NaOH was titrated with 32.0 mL of 0.100 M HCl. What is the molarity of the sodium hydroxide solution?   *(Answer: 0.0744 M)*

6. A volume of 25. mL of 0.120 M H_2SO_4 neutralizes 40. mL of an NaOH solution. What is the concentration of the NaOH solution? (Hint: Remember that H_2SO_4 yields two H^+ ions per molecule of acid.)   *(Answer: 0.15 M)*

Figure 19–13 *Many acid-base indicators are dyes from common plants, such as beets. Litmus is extracted from certain species of lichen, and the juice from red cabbage changes from deep purple to green with increasing pH.*

Choosing the Proper Indicator

As you just learned, the color change of an indicator during a titration should indicate the equivalence point. So how do you choose the correct indicator? The answer depends on the strengths of the acid and base involved in the titration. Let's take a look at three important combinations of acids and bases for titrations.

TITRATION OF A STRONG ACID WITH A STRONG BASE Consider a titration between HCl, a strong acid, and NaOH, a strong base. The reaction between these two compounds is described by the following equation:

$$NaOH\ (aq)\ +\ HCl\ (aq)\ \rightarrow\ H_2O\ (l)\ +\ NaCl\ (aq)$$

(Eq. 14)

At the equivalence point of the titration, equal amounts of NaOH and HCl have reacted—there is no excess of either reagent. Therefore, the solution at the equivalence point is merely a water solution of NaCl. And as you learned in Chapter 18, the salts of strong acids and strong bases form neutral water solutions. So, in the titration of a strong acid and a strong base, the solution at the equivalence point has a pH of 7.

To accurately identify the equivalence point—as well as to keep track of the overall progress of the acid-base reaction—

Titration Data

NaOH added (mL)	pH
0.00	1.00
10.00	1.37
20.00	1.95
22.00	2.19
24.00	2.70
25.00	7.00
26.00	11.30
28.00	11.75
30.00	11.96
40.00	12.36
50.00	12.52

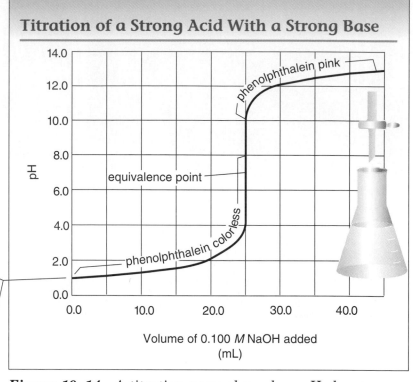

25 mL

HCl solution

Figure 19–14 *A titration curve shows how pH changes as the standard solution is added to the flask. Why is the equivalence point found at a pH of 7? What is the concentration of the HCl solution?*

chemists monitor pH throughout the titration. These pH data are typically presented in a graph, which is called a **titration curve.** Figure 19–14 shows the titration curve for the titration of HCl with NaOH. At the beginning of the titration, the solution consists of hydrochloric acid in water, so the pH is low. Then, as NaOH is added, the pH slowly begins to climb. Eventually, just enough base is added to neutralize the acid, and the equivalence point is reached at a pH of 7.

When titrating a strong acid with a strong base, the indicator should change color at a pH of 7. But as you can see in the graph in Figure 19–14, the slope of the titration curve is very steep near pH 7, which indicates that the equivalence point comes at an extremely precise stage of the titration. For the titration of a strong acid with a strong base, the pH increases from 4 to 10 with only a few drops of standard solution.

For this reason, a successful indicator can have a wide range of values for the pH at which it changes color. For the titration of a strong acid and a strong base, any indicator that changes color in the range of about 3.5 to 10.5 would work. This is why phenolphthalein, which changes color at a pH around 9, is an acceptable indicator for a titration of HCl and NaOH.

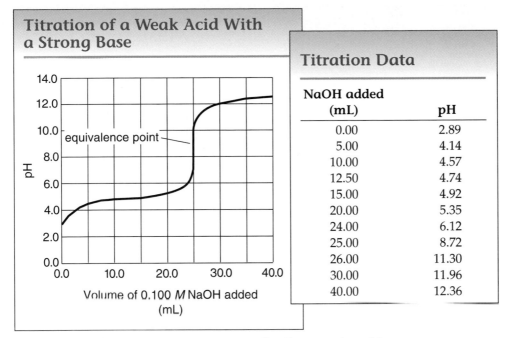

Titration of a Weak Acid With a Strong Base

pH vs. Volume of 0.100 M NaOH added (mL)

equivalence point

Titration Data

NaOH added (mL)	pH
0.00	2.89
5.00	4.14
10.00	4.57
12.50	4.74
15.00	4.92
20.00	5.35
24.00	6.12
25.00	8.72
26.00	11.30
30.00	11.96
40.00	12.36

Figure 19–15 *In this titration, 30 mL of an acetic acid solution was titrated with 0.100 M NaOH. Why is the equivalence point found at a basic pH? What is the concentration of the acetic acid solution?*

TITRATION OF A WEAK ACID WITH A STRONG BASE The graph in Figure 19–15 is the titration curve for the titration of acetic acid ($HC_2H_3O_2$) and sodium hydroxide (NaOH). The reaction between these compounds produces water and a salt, sodium acetate ($NaC_2H_3O_2$):

$$NaOH\ (aq)\ +\ HC_2H_3O_2\ (aq)\ \rightarrow\ H_2O\ (l)\ +\ NaC_2H_3O_2\ (aq)$$
(Eq. 15)

As you learned in Chapter 18, the salts of weak acids and strong bases are basic. Thus, for this titration, the equivalence point should come at a basic pH—a pH greater than 7.

The titration curve for a weak acid and a strong base is similar to the graph in Figure 19–14, the curve for the titration of a strong acid and strong base. But the two curves differ in two important ways. First, notice that the pH at the beginning of each titration is different. This is because a weak acid only slightly ionizes in water, producing relatively few H_3O^+ ions, whereas a strong acid completely ionizes in water. Second, notice that the vertical portions of the two curves are different. The vertical portion for a weak acid-strong base titration covers a shorter range than for a strong acid-strong base titration. This means that for the titration of a weak acid with a strong base, the choice of indicator is limited to a smaller pH range. Would phenolphthalein be an appropriate indicator for the titration of acetic acid and sodium hydroxide?

Titration Data	
HCl added (mL)	pH
0.00	11.24
10.00	9.91
20.00	9.47
30.00	8.93
40.00	8.61
45.00	8.30
47.00	7.92
48.00	7.70
49.00	7.47
50.00	5.85
51.00	3.34

Titration of a Weak Base With a Strong Acid

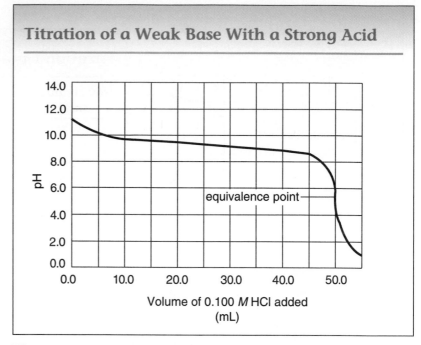

Figure 19–16 *In this titration, 40 mL of an ammonia solution was titrated with 0.100 M HCl. What is the concentration of the ammonia solution? Why does this titration curve have a downward slope?*

TITRATION OF A WEAK BASE WITH A STRONG ACID The graph in Figure 19–16 is the titration curve for the titration of ammonia (NH_3) with hydrochloric acid (HCl). Notice that unlike the titration curves you have studied so far, this curve has a downward slope. The pH of this titration starts out high because the unknown solution—the ammonia—is basic. And the pH drops because the standard solution—the hydrochloric acid—is acidic.

The reaction between NH_3 and HCl produces NH_4Cl:

$$NH_3\ (aq)\ +\ HCl\ (aq) \rightarrow NH_4Cl\ (aq) \qquad \textbf{(Eq. 16)}$$

The salts of weak bases and strong acids are acidic. So for this titration, the equivalence point should come at a pH below 7. Where is the equivalence point in the graph in Figure 19–16?

Like the titration curve for a weak acid and a strong base, the titration curve for a weak base and a strong acid has a relatively small vertical portion around its equivalence point. From the list of indicators in Figure 19–6, can you suggest a good indicator for the titration of ammonia with hydrochloric acid? Why would phenolphthalein not be a good indicator for this titration?

Problem Solving   *Chemistry at Work*

Save Fern Hill Lake!

Fern Hill Lake has a low pH, presumably the result of acid rain. The lake is about 3 kilometers long, 2.5 kilometers across, and has an average depth of 8 meters. Its pH is 4.1. Someone in your community proposes that calcium hydroxide ($Ca(OH)_2$) be added to the lake to increase the pH to 6.5, a more favorable level.

- About how many grams of $Ca(OH)_2$ should be added to the lake to accomplish this task?
- What approximations must you make in your calculations? How reasonable do you think your approximations are?
- Is adding $Ca(OH)_2$ a long-term solution to the problem of acid rain?

19–3 Section Review

1. What is an acid-base titration?

2. What do indicators do in a titration? Describe how to choose an appropriate indicator.

3. Describe the difference between the equivalence point and the end point of a titration.

4. Oxalic acid is a poisonous, colorless acid used in dyes and bleaches. In an acid-base titration, 36.0 mL of 2.00 M NaOH completely neutralize 25.0 mL of 1.44 M oxalic acid. From these data, is oxalic acid a monoprotic, diprotic, or triprotic acid? Explain.

5. **Critical Thinking—Applying a concept** Draw a titration curve for the titration of a strong base with a standard solution of a strong acid. Label the equivalence point on your graph. Would phenolphthalein be a good indicator for this titration? Explain.

Laboratory Investigation

Amount of CaCO₃ in Eggshells

Problem

What is the percentage of calcium carbonate in an eggshell?

Materials (*per group*)

small pieces of dried eggshell
   with membrane removed
mortar and pestle
10-mL graduated cylinder
250-mL Erlenmeyer flask
glass stirring rod
balance with precision of ±0.01 g
filter paper   3.0 *M* HCl
funnel   50-mL beaker

Procedure

1. Grind about one fourth of an eggshell into very small pieces using the mortar and pestle.
2. Measure the mass of a piece of filter paper. Record the mass in a data table similar to the one shown.
3. Add approximately 0.20 g of eggshell to the filter paper on the balance. Measure the exact mass of the paper and eggshell. Record this mass in your data table.
4. Place the eggshell into the beaker.
5. Measure 5.0 mL of 3.0 *M* HCl in the graduated cylinder. Add the acid to the beaker.
6. Record any signs that a chemical reaction is taking place. Stir the eggshell and acid periodically to increase the rate of the reaction. Allow the acid to react with the eggshell until there are no more signs of reaction.
7. Fold the filter paper and place it into a funnel. Place the funnel on an Erlenmeyer flask to collect the filtrate.

8. Carefully pour the remaining eggshell and acid through the filter paper and funnel, being careful to transfer all the shell onto the paper. Rinse the eggshell and filter paper with water.
9. Allow the filter paper and shell to dry completely. Find the final mass of the unreacted eggshell and filter paper. Record this mass in your data table.

Observations

Mass of filter paper alone	
Mass of filter paper and eggshell before reaction	
Mass of filter paper and eggshell after reaction	

1. What signs indicated that a chemical reaction was occurring?
2. What was the mass of the eggshell alone before reacting?
3. What was the mass of the eggshell alone after reacting?
4. What was the change in the mass of the eggshell?

Analysis and Conclusions

1. Write the balanced chemical equation for the reaction between the acid and the calcium carbonate in the eggshell.
2. What gas was produced in this reaction?
3. Calculate the percentage of the eggshell that was calcium carbonate.
4. **On Your Own** With your teacher's permission, repeat this experiment using pieces of seashell. How does the percentage of CaCO₃ in eggshell compare with the percentage in seashell?

644

STUDY GUIDE

Summarizing Key Concepts

19–1 The Self-ionization of Water and pH

- Water undergoes a self-ionization reaction, in which 2 H_2O molecules form an H_3O^+ ion and an OH^- ion. In pure water at 25°C, this reaction produces 1.0×10^{-7} M concentrations of both ions.

- At 25°C, the product of the molar concentrations of H_3O^+ ions and OH^- ions in water equals 1.0×10^{-14}. This number is called the ion-product constant for water, or K_w.

- The pH of a solution is -1 times the logarithm of the concentration of H_3O^+ ions. The pH is less than 7 in acidic solutions, equal to 7 in neutral solutions, and greater than 7 in basic solutions.

- pH can be measured either with indicators, such as litmus, or with an electric device called a pH meter.

19–2 Buffers

- A buffer is a mixture that is able to release or absorb H^+ ions, keeping the pH of a solution constant. Most buffers are mixtures of weak acids and their conjugate bases.

- The amount of acid or base a buffer can neutralize is called the buffer capacity. In general, the greater the concentration of buffer, the greater the buffer capacity.

19–3 Acid-Base Titration

- An acid-base titration is used to calculate the concentration of acid or base in a solution. An acid-base titration is a carefully controlled neutralization reaction.

- The equivalence point is reached when the standard solution has completely neutralized the acid or base in the unknown solution. The equivalence point should be near the end point, which is reached when the indicator changes color.

- At the end point, the number of moles of H^+ ions donated by the acid equals the number of moles of H^+ ions accepted by the base. For Arrhenius bases, this means that the number of moles of H^+ from the acid equals the number of moles of OH^- from the base. These facts can be used to calculate the concentration of the unknown solution.

- The proper indicator for a titration depends on the strengths of the acid and base being used. The indicator may change color over a wide range of pH, a range that corresponds to the steep region of the titration curve around the equivalence point.

Reviewing Key Terms

Define each term in a complete sentence.

19–1 The Self-ionization of Water and pH

self-ionization
ion-product constant
pH

19–2 Buffers

buffer
buffer capacity

19–3 Acid-Base Titration

acid-base titration
standard solution
equivalence point
end point
titration curve

CHAPTER REVIEW

Content Review

Multiple Choice
Choose the letter of the answer that best completes each statement.

1. In pure water at 25°C, $[OH^-]$ equals
   (a) 1.0×10^{-12} M. (c) 1.0×10^{-7} M.
   (b) 1.0×10^{-6} M. (d) 0 M.

2. An acidic solution may have a pH of
   (a) 3. (c) 7.
   (b) 8. (d) 14.

3. The product of $[H_3O^+]$ and $[OH^-]$ in water
   (a) is K_W, the ion-product constant.
   (b) increases with pH.
   (c) decreases with pH.
   (d) is greater than 1.

4. If the pH drops from 3 to 2, $[H_3O^+]$ changes by a factor of
   (a) 10. (c) 1/10.
   (b) 100. (d) 3/2.

5. Phenolphthalein is used as a(an)
   (a) base. (c) standard solution.
   (b) indicator. (d) buffer.

6. To stabilize a solution's pH, add a(an)
   (a) buffer. (c) indicator.
   (b) weak acid. (d) standard solution.

7. In a titration of a weak base, the standard solution should be a(an)
   (a) strong acid. (c) strong base.
   (b) weak base. (d) indicator.

8. The end point of a titration indicates the
   (a) acid point. (c) base point.
   (b) equivalence point. (d) buffer region.

9. In a titration curve, the vertical axis is a scale for
   (a) pH. (c) volume of base added.
   (b) K_W. (d) volume of indicator.

10. A good buffer could be a mixture of
    (a) ammonia and NaOH.
    (b) acetic acid and HCl.
    (c) acetic acid and sodium acetate.
    (d) a strong acid and a strong base.

True or False
If the statement is true, write "true." If it is false, change the underlined word or words to make the statement true.

11. Two water molecules may react to produce 2 H_3O^+ ions.

12. pH indicates $\underline{[H_2O]}$ in a solution.

13. A pH of 3 indicates a(an) <u>basic</u> solution.

14. Adding OH^- ions to a buffer solution <u>raises</u> the pH at first, then <u>lowers</u> it.

15. Blood uses a buffer of bicarbonate ions and <u>carbonic acid</u>.

16. In the titration of a strong acid and a <u>weak base</u>, the equivalence point is reached at pH 7.

17. In the titration of a weak acid and a strong base, the equivalence point is reached at a pH <u>less than</u> 7.

18. If the pH is 5, $[H_3O^+]$ is equal to $\underline{10^5}$.

19. A neutral solution has a pH of <u>0</u>.

Concept Mapping
Complete the following concept map for Section 19–1. Refer to pages xviii–xix to construct a concept map for the entire chapter.

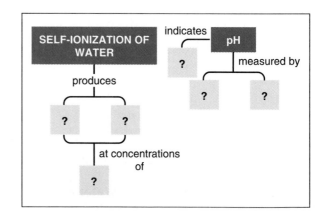

Concept Mastery

Discuss each of the following in a brief paragraph.

20. Does pure water contain only H_2O molecules? Explain.

21. If you know $[H_3O^+]$ in a water solution, how can you calculate $[OH^-]$?

22. Your calculator provides the number -1.2898826 for the logarithm of the number 5.13×10^{-2}. What is the correct logarithm? Explain.

23. Chemists often measure pH with strips of paper coated with a combination of acid-base indicators. Why is a combination of indicators better than a single indicator?

24. Give an example of a buffer solution. Explain how the buffer reacts with added H_3O^+ ions and with added OH^- ions.

25. Phenolphthalein and methyl red change color over different pH ranges, but both can be used in the titration of a stong base with a strong acid. Explain why.

26. In the titration of a weak acid with a strong base, why is the equivalence point reached at a pH greater than 7?

27. Draw the titration curve for the titration of a weak acid with a strong base. Label the equivalence point and suggest an appropriate indicator.

28. Draw the titration curve for the titration of a weak base with a strong acid. Label the equivalence point and suggest an appropriate indicator.

29. Tying it Together Why do buffers have only a limited capacity to *stabilize* the pH of a solution?

Critical Thinking and Problem Solving

Use the skills you have developed in this chapter to answer each of the following.

30. Drawing conclusions Amy wants to add a tiny amount of a strong acid to a solution that contains a buffer. Can she be sure that the pH of the solution will not change? Explain.

31. Applying concepts A value called pOH is defined by this equation:

$$pOH = -\log[OH^-]$$

What is the pOH when the pH is 4? When the pH is 9? When the pH is 3.2? (Hint: Refer to Figure 19–3.)

32. Interpreting data 18.5 mL of 0.100 *M* H_2SO_4 neutralized 40.0 mL of an ammonia solution. What is the concentration of the ammonia solution? (Hint: Remember that H_2SO_4 yields 2 H^+ ions per molecule of acid.)

33. Interpreting data In a titration, 34.0 mL of 1.50 *M* NaOH neutralized 52.0 mL of an ammonium chloride (NH_4Cl) solution. What is the concentration of the NH_4Cl?

34. Evaluating experiments Greg wants to find the concentration of NaCl in a neutral salt solution. He decides to run a titration using HCl on a standard solution. Will this procedure work? Explain.

35. Using the writing process On the Planet Kusanovich, the inhabitants have a blood pH close to 2. Describe what difficulties a Kusanovichian might have if she visited Earth. What liquids could she drink? What liquids might be deadly? Answer these questions in a short story, play, poem, or essay.

PROBLEM BANK

Group A

36. At 37°C, which is normal body temperature, $K_w = 2.4 \times 10^{-14}$. Calculate $[H_3O^+]$ and $[OH^-]$ in a neutral solution at this temperature. *(Section 19–1)*

37. At 50°C, $K_w = 5.47 \times 10^{-14}$. Calculate $[H_3O^+]$ and $[OH^-]$ in a neutral solution at this temperature. *(Section 19–1)*

38. Calculate $[OH^-]$ for the following water solutions, then state whether the solution is acidic or basic. *(Section 19–1)*

(a) $[H_3O^+] = 1.0\ M$
(b) $[H_3O^+] = 4.2 \times 10^{-9}\ M$
(c) $[OH^-]$ is twice as great as $[H_3O^+]$.

39. Calculate $[H_3O^+]$ for the following water solutions, then state whether the solution is acidic or basic. *(Section 19–1)*

(a) $[OH^-] = 1.4 \times 10^{-6}\ M$
(b) $[OH^-] = 5.8 \times 10^{-10}\ M$
(c) $[H_3O^+]$ is 10 times $[OH^-]$

40. Find the pH for the following solutions: *(Section 19–1)*

(a) $[H_3O^+] = 1.0 \times 10^{-5}\ M$
(b) $[H_3O^+] = 4.50 \times 10^{-4}\ M$
(c) $[OH^-] = 1.0 \times 10^{-3}\ M$
(d) $[OH^-] = 7.84 \times 10^{-6}\ M$

41. Calculate $[H_3O^+]$ for the solutions with the following pH values: *(Section 19–1)*

(a) 4.00   (b) 5.52   (c) 2.896   (d) 7.850

42. Calculate $[OH^-]$ for the solutions with the following pH values: *(Section 19–1)*

(a) 8.00   (b) 9.50   (c) 3.22   (d) 12.662

43. What is $[H_3O^+]$ in a 0.002 M solution of HCl? What is the pH of this solution? *(Section 19–1)*

44. What is $[H_3O^+]$ in a 0.002 M solution of NaOH? What is the pH of this solution? *(Section 19–1)*

45. After some acid is added to a neutral solution, $[H_3O^+]$ increases by a factor of 1000. What is the pH of the new solution? *(Section 19–1)*

46. After some base is added to a neutral solution, $[OH^-]$ increases by a factor of 50. What is the new pH? *(Section 19–1)*

47. A buffer solution is formed from acetic acid ($HC_2H_3O_2$) and the acetate ion ($C_2H_3O_2^-$). *(Section 19–2)*

(a) Write the equation for the reaction that occurs when an acid is added to this solution.
(b) Write the equation for the reaction that occurs when a base is added to this solution.
(c) In both (a) and (b), does the pH change? Explain.

48. Explain why a mixture of HCl and NaCl functions poorly as a buffer. *(Section 19–2)*

49. In a titration of 40.0 mL of an acetic acid solution, the end point is reached when 35.0 mL of 1.00 M NaOH is added. Calculate the concentration of the acetic acid solution. *(Section 19–3).*

50. In a titration of 45 mL of an acetic acid solution, the end point is reached when 35.0 mL of 0.100 M $Ba(OH)_2$ is added. Calculate the concentration of the acetic acid solution. *(Section 19–3)*

51. It requires 50 mL of 0.150 M NaOH to completely neutralize 30 mL of a 0.125 M solution of malonic acid. Is malonic acid a monoprotic, diprotic, or triprotic acid? *(Section 19–3)*

52. It requires 15 mL of 1.10 M NaOH to completely neutralize 22 mL of a 0.25 M solution of citric acid. Is citric acid a monoprotic, diprotic, or triprotic acid? *(Section 19–3)*

53. Which of the following indicators works best for the titration of cyanic acid (HCNO, $K_a = 3.5 \times 10^{-4}$) with a strong base? Explain your answer.

Indicator	pH Range for Color Change
phenolphthalein	8 to 10
methyl red	5 to 6
methyl violet	0 to 2

Group B

54. A 0.010 M solution of aspirin, a weak monoprotic acid, has a pH of 3.3. What is the K_a of aspirin?

55. A 0.513 M solution of a weak base has a pH of 11.4. What is the K_b of the base?

56. Describe a solution that has a pH of 0. Describe a solution that has a pH of -1.

57. In the same way that pH expresses acidity, pOH can be used to express basicity. The pOH is defined as $-\log[OH^-]$. Calculate the pOH for the following solutions:
(a) $[OH^-] = 5.0 \times 10^{-5}\ M$
(b) $[H_3O^+] = 2.0 \times 10^{-9}\ M$
(c) pH = 4.55
(d) pH = 8.09

58. Sometimes K_a and K_b values are reported as pK_a or pK_b. In these terms, the letter p symbolizes the negative logarithm, just as in pH and pOH. Calculate the following values:
(a) pK_a, when $K_a = 5.0 \times 10^{-6}$
(b) pK_b, when $K_b = 2.5 \times 10^{-7}$
(c) K_a, when $pK_a = 8.22$
(d) K_b, when $pK_b = 4.37$

59. Pure water is added to 25.0 mL of a 1.00 M HCl solution. The new solution has a volume of 2.00 L. What is the pH of the new solution?

60. How many grams of NaOH must be added to 0.250 L of water to form a solution of pH = 10.0?

61. A 1.00 L water solution contains 8.50 g of $Ba(OH)_2$. What is the concentration of OH^- ions in the solution? What is the pH of the solution?

62. In most effective buffer solutions, the concentration of the acid equals the concentration of the conjugate base. For such a solution, show that $[H_3O^+]$ equals the K_a of the acid.

63. A titration was performed on 40.0 mL of a solution of aniline. The following data were recorded:

Volume of 0.100 M HCl Added (mL)	pH
0	11.5
10.0	10.0
20.0	9.4
30.0	9.3
40.0	8.8
45.0	7.9
48.0	6.6
50.0	5.2
51.0	2.3
52.0	1.9

(a) Use these data to sketch a titration curve. Label the equivalence point.
(b) Is aniline an acid or a base? Is it strong or weak? Explain
(c) Why did the pH change only slightly between 20 and 30 mL of added HCl solution?
(d) What is the concentration of the aniline solution?

FROM SCHOOL TO WORK

Ben Osborne—Student

Ben Osborne of Los Angeles, California, sees chemistry in action every day in his work at the Food from the 'Hood program. "Students at my high school started Food from the 'Hood in October of 1992, a few months after the Los Angeles riots," Ben explains. "We grow totally organic produce right in our own neighborhood and sell it at local farmers' markets." Food from the 'Hood also produces an all-natural salad dressing that is sold in stores all over southern California.

Food from the 'Hood teaches students a lot about business ownership, responsibility, and science. Says Ben, "We make our own compost. Take a banana peel and two weeks later, it's fertilizer. We also use only natural substances to fend off insects. Pepper really seems to keep the bugs away. And when we have a problem to solve, like figuring out the conditions needed to grow a new crop, we follow the logic of the scientific method." Call it learning by growing!

Textile Manufacturing Technician

Textile manufacturing technicians may work in textile mills or factories, although many are employed by chemical companies that produce synthetic fibers. In textile mills, textile manufacturing technicians may be involved in the dyeing and bleaching of unfinished fabrics. Many textile manufacturing technicians who work for chemical companies tend the complex machines that produce synthetic fibers through chemical processes. Other textile manufacturing technicians work in laboratories.

Most jobs as textile manufacturing technicians require at least a high-school diploma plus some technical training. High-school courses in shop, mechanical drawing, and chemistry can be helpful.

For more information write to the American Textile Manufacturers Institute, 1801 K Street, NW, Suite 900, Washington, DC 20006.

How to Write a Résumé

A résumé is a short summary of your background and accomplishments. Whether or not you will be granted an interview is dependent upon how you present yourself in your résumé. Your résumé, therefore, must highlight your skills.

Your résumé must first include your name, address, and telephone number. Your high school and the major courses you took as well as your past employers and the positions you held should be listed next. You can also include any personal accomplishments such as awards or scholarships. Any organizations to which you belong that might be of importance to an employer should be added.

Your résumé must be neatly typed without errors. If possible, your résumé should not exceed one page.

H. Eugene Le May, Jr

From the Author

We started this textbook by saying that chemistry can be fun. By now you've also discovered that it requires work. Many people think that fun and work are totally separate and mutually exclusive from each other. It's often that way, but it doesn't have to be. I hope that you have discovered that work can also be fun. It's fun to learn new things. It's also fun to face challenges and discover that you can overcome them. Self-confidence comes by facing challenges and mastering them through hard work and persistence. That's what equips you to face life's challenges when you leave school. Unfortunately, it's a lesson that some of your classmates may have to learn later the hard way. Effort is the path to success. There are really no shortcuts to anywhere worth going in life.

UNIT REVIEW

Concept Mastery

Discuss each of the following in a brief paragraph.

1. Describe the properties of water solutions of (a) acids (b) bases.

2. How does the Brønsted-Lowry definition of acids and bases differ from the Arrhenius definition? Include at least two examples in your answer.

3. Give an example of an acid-base neutralization reaction. Label the acid, base, and salt in your reaction.

4. Explain how a strong acid differs from a weak acid.

5. For a generic weak acid with the formula HA, define the acid dissociation constant (K_a) in terms of equilibrium concentrations. What does K_a indicate about the strength of an acid?

6. How does the strength of an acid relate to the strength of its conjugate base?

7. Define the term salt hydrolysis. Give examples of acidic, basic, and neutral salt solutions.

8. Explain why acetic acid ($HC_2H_3O_2$) is only a monoprotic acid, even though 4 hydrogen atoms are in an acetic acid molecule.

9. Outline the rules for naming acids.

10. Does pure water contain only molecules of H_2O? Explain.

11. Write the equation that defines pH. How does pH indicate whether a solution is acidic, basic, or neutral?

12. Describe two ways of measuring the pH of a solution.

13. Give an example of a buffer. Describe how buffers react when an acid or a base is added to a solution.

14. What is an acid-base titration? What purpose does this procedure serve?

15. What is an indicator? Explain how an indicator is selected for a titration.

16. Is the end point of a titration the same as the equivalence point? Explain.

Problem Bank

17. Write the names and chemical formulas for (a) three strong oxy acids (b) three strong binary acids.

18. Identify two conjugate acid-base pairs in each of the following equations:
    (a) $H_2PO_4^- + NH_3 \rightleftharpoons HPO_4^{2-} + NH_4^+$
    (b) $CO_3^{2-} + H_2O \rightleftharpoons HCO_3^- + OH^-$

19. For each of the following salts, predict whether its aqueous solution is acidic, basic, or neutral:
    (a) KI   (b) NH_4NO_3 (c) $KClO$
    (d) $CaCl_2$ (e) $Fe(NO_3)_3$ (f) $NaC_2H_3O_2$

20. At 40°C, the ion product for water is 3.8×10^{-14}. Calculate the concentrations of ions in water at this temperature.

21. The $[OH^-]$ in a solution is found to be 5×10^{-10} M. Is this solution acidic, basic, or neutral?

22. Calculate the pH for solutions in which
    (a) $[H_3O^+] = 1.0 \times 10^{-3}$
    (b) $[H_3O^+] = 8.35 \times 10^{-8}$
    (c) $[OH^-] = 4.5 \times 10^{-6}$
    (d) $[H_3O^+] = [OH^-]$

23. Calculate the pH for the following solutions of strong acids or strong bases:
    (a) 0.015 M nitric acid (HNO_3)
    (b) 0.030 M sodium hydroxide (NaOH)
    (c) 0.015 M sulfuric acid (H_2SO_4)

24. In a 0.200 M solution of benzoic acid ($HC_7H_5O_2$), the $[H_3O^+]$ is measured to be 3.6×10^{-3} M. Calculate the K_a for benzoic acid.

25. In a 0.100 M solution of a weak monoprotic acid, the pH is measured to be 3.8. Find the K_a of this acid.

26. Water is added to an unknown weak base to form a 0.015 M solution. The pH is measured to be 11.2. Calculate the K_b for this base.

27. The K_a for formic acid ($HCHO_2$) is 1.8×10^{-4}. Calculate the concentrations of H_3O^+, CHO_2^-, and $HCHO_2$ in a 0.10 M solution of formic acid.

28. The K_b for ammonia is 1.8×10^{-5}. Calculate the pH of a 0.020 M solution of ammonia.

29. Ascorbic acid ($HC_6H_7O_6$) has a K_a of 8.0×10^{-5}. Calculate the pH of a 0.100 M solution of ascorbic acid.

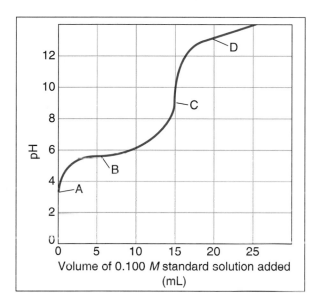

Volume of 0.100 M standard solution added (mL)

30. This graph shows the titration curve for 40 mL of an unknown solution.
  (a) Is the standard solution a strong acid or a strong base?
  (b) Is the unknown solution an acid or a base? Is it strong or weak?
  (c) In the graph, which letter labels the equivalence point?
  (d) From the data provided, can the concentration of the unknown solution be calculated? Explain.

31. In the titration of 50 mL of an ammonia solution, the end point was reached when 28 mL of 0.100 M HCl was added. Calculate the concentration of the ammonia solution.

32. 64.0 mL of acetic acid was neutralized by 16.0 mL of 0.075 M Ca(OH)$_2$. Calculate the concentration of the acetic acid.

33. What volume of 0.150 M H$_3$PO$_4$ neutralizes 40.0 mL of 0.277 M Ca(OH)$_2$?

Performance-Based Task

Does Buffered Aspirin Really Reduce Stomach Irritation?

Has this ever happened to you? You have a pounding headache, but you're reluctant to take aspirin because regular aspirin might irritate your stomach. Buffered aspirin might be a better choice because it contains buffering compounds that neutralize stomach acid. Do these buffering compounds really affect the pH of stomach acid? Perform an experiment to answer this question.

1. Begin by obtaining safety goggles, a lab apron, three flasks, a mortar and pestle, buffered aspirin tablets and regular aspirin tablets, universal indicator, pH color chart, distilled water, a 10-mL graduated cylinder, and 0.5 M HCl.

2. Add 100 mL of distilled water and 20 drops of universal indicator to each flask.

3. Grind one regular aspirin tablet to a fine powder and add the powder to Flask 1. Do the same with the buffered aspirin tablet and add the powder to Flask 2. Do not add anything else to Flask 3.

4. Predict what will happen if you add HCl dropwise to the flasks. Carry out your experiment and make careful observations of the color of the solutions in each flask. Did your observations support your prediction?

Going Further

5. Find the number of drops of HCl needed to make 1 mL.

6. Compare the volumes of HCl added to Flasks 2 and 3. Calculate the number of moles of HCl that were absorbed by the buffering compounds.

7. Some products, such as shampoos, are advertised as "pH balanced." Formulate a hypothesis and design an experiment to determine if "pH balanced" means that the product contains buffering compounds.

Unit 8 Redox Chemistry

Do you notice anything unusual about the accompanying photograph? This type of photograph is called a test strip. A test strip is a section of printing paper with several different exposures made from the same negative. The test strip shows a series of gradations from light to dark, which represent the different exposure times. Making a test strip helps a photographer to choose the exposure that looks best for a particular photograph. A test strip is just one of many techniques available to photographers in developing a print from a negative.

As you may know—especially if you are an amateur photographer—photography involves a lot of chemistry. Each step in the process of developing a print from a negative requires different chemicals, such as developers, stop baths, and fixers. Photographers must know which chemicals to use and how to control the chemical reactions necessary to produce the effects they want.

In this unit, you will learn about the reactions involved in redox chemistry. Redox chemistry is important in photography, as well as in many other applications from batteries to electroplating.

DISCOVERY LEARNING

1. Stack several pieces of copper and several pieces of zinc of the same size one on top of the other, alternating the copper and zinc.

2. Insert a piece of blotting paper that has been soaked in salt water in between each copper and zinc pair.

3. Wrap a length of insulated copper wire about 50 times around a magnetic compass.

4. Touch one of the bare ends of the copper wire to the piece of copper on one end of the stack and the other end to the piece of zinc on the opposite end of the stack.

   - What happens to the compass needle?
   - How can you explain your observations?

Chapter
20 Oxidation and Reduction

Did you know that lightning, often dramatic and breathtaking, is the result of huge surges of electrons from one thundercloud to another thundercloud or to the Earth? Perhaps you are wondering what electron surges have to do with the topic of this chapter. The transfer, or movement, of electrons between atoms of reactants is the central idea governing numerous chemical reactions—reactions that give rise to the field of electrochemistry. These chemical reactions are called oxidation-reduction reactions and are the subject of this chapter.

The terms oxidation and reduction may sound unfamiliar to you. Yet you see the results of these processes often in your daily life: the destruction of metal structures and monuments, the combustion of fuels, and the processing of photographic film.

What do the eerie lightning bolts over the midwestern plains and the corroded green surface of the copper Statue of Liberty have in common? Both phenomena are accompanied by a movement, or transfer, of electrons.

Chem Journal

YOU AND YOUR WORLD

Have you ever watched a storm with severe lightning and thunder? Were you impressed, overwhelmed, or perhaps intimidated by the sheer power of the storm? Describe your feelings as you witness the fury of a thunderstorm. Do phenomena become less intimidating after you learn about them?

20–1 Oxidation-Reduction Reactions

Guide for Reading
- What are oxidation and reduction?
- What are oxidation numbers?

You may think you know nothing about oxidation-reduction reactions, but you may be surprised to find how many of the familiar reactions that are going on around you at this very moment involve oxidation-reduction. Have you ever powered a radio, calculator, or CD player with batteries or captured images on film and later printed them for a memorable permanent record? If so, you already have some experience with reactions that involve oxidation and reduction. Here are two other familiar examples: The gas burner of a stove and the combustion engine in an automobile operate because of oxidation and reduction reactions. Even the food you eat gets subjected to oxidation and reduction reactions during metabolism, thus making the food's stored energy available for your use.

Oxidation and Reduction

Today the words oxidation and reduction have several definitions. Originally, however, **oxidation** was used to describe reactions in which oxygen was added to a reactant. For example, the

Figure 20–1 *Did you know that the chemical reactions that are the basis of photography are oxidation-reduction reactions?*

Figure 20–2 *As the iron in these anchor chains combines with oxygen to produce rust, it is oxidized. Similarly, methane gas released at an oil refinery combines with oxygen and is oxidized. What was the original definition of oxidation?*

Figure 20–3 *In a blast furnace, iron oxide in iron ore is converted to free iron metal. Is the iron ore oxidized or reduced?*

formation of rust is an oxidation reaction in which iron metal reacts with oxygen in the presence of water to form rust, or iron oxide.

$$4 \text{ Fe } (s) + 3 \text{ O}_2 (g) \rightarrow 2 \text{ Fe}_2\text{O}_3 (s) \qquad \textbf{(Eq. 1)}$$

Similarly, when methane gas (CH_4) burns, it combines with oxygen to form carbon dioxide and water.

$$\text{CH}_4 (g) + 2 \text{ O}_2 (g) \rightarrow \text{CO}_2 (g) + 2 \text{ H}_2\text{O} (l) \qquad \textbf{(Eq. 2)}$$

The term **reduction** at first meant the removal of oxygen from a compound. For example, the Fe_2O_3 in iron ore can be reduced to obtain iron metal. You may remember that this is normally accomplished inside a blast furnace by heating the iron oxide in the presence of carbon.

$$2 \text{ Fe}_2\text{O}_3 (l) + 3 \text{ C } (s) \rightarrow 4 \text{ Fe } (l) + 3 \text{ CO}_2 (g) \qquad \textbf{(Eq. 3)}$$

The term reduction comes from the fact that the free metal has a lower mass than its oxide compound. Thus there is a decrease, or reduction, in the mass of the iron-containing material as the oxygen is removed.

The words oxidation and reduction are still used to describe the addition or removal of oxygen. But chemists today use the terms in a much broader way. The broader definitions arise from the fact that oxygen is very electronegative and tends to gain electrons when it reacts with other substances. For example, the reaction of magnesium with oxygen produces MgO, an ionic compound containing Mg^{2+} ions.

$$2 \text{ Mg } (s) + \text{O}_2 (g) \rightarrow 2 \text{ MgO } (s) \qquad \textbf{(Eq. 4)}$$

You should remember from Chapter 7 that in going from Mg to Mg^{2+}, a magnesium atom loses 2 electrons. Similar analyses of other oxidation reactions reveal that substances that are oxidized lose electrons. On the other hand, substances that are reduced gain electrons. Thus it is convenient to define oxidation and reduction in terms of the movements of electrons.

- **Oxidation is the process by which a substance loses one or more electrons.**
- **Reduction is the process by which a substance gains one or more electrons.**

You can use the expression OIL RIG to help you remember these definitions: OIL = **O**xidation **I**s **L**oss of electrons; RIG = **R**eduction **I**s **G**ain of electrons. Or perhaps you can devise your own device for remembering the definitions.

By defining oxidation and reduction in terms of electrons lost and gained, reactions similar to but not involving oxygen can also be classified as oxidation and reduction processes. For example, the reaction of magnesium metal with chlorine is quite similar to the reaction of magnesium with oxygen.

$$Mg\ (s)\ +\ Cl_2\ (g) \rightarrow 2\ MgCl_2\ (s) \qquad \textbf{(Eq. 5)}$$

In both cases, the reaction produces an ionic compound containing Mg^{2+} ions. Using the definition of oxidation as loss of electrons, chemists say that magnesium is oxidized and that chlorine oxidizes magnesium. Thus free metals are oxidized as they lose electrons to form positive ions in compounds. What is the name of the process that converts positive metal ions in compounds into the free metal atoms?

Oxidation and reduction always occur together. If electrons are lost by one substance, they do not merely disappear. Instead, they are gained by another substance. When Mg reacts with Cl_2, the Cl_2 gains the electrons, forming two Cl^- ions. Thus Mg is oxidized and Cl_2 is reduced. Because oxidation and reduction occur together, reactions in which electrons are transferred between reactants are called **oxidation-reduction reactions,** or simply **redox reactions.**

Figure 20–4 *Oxidation and reduction follow the pattern of "one person's loss is another person's gain."*

Visit our Web site at
http://www.phschool.com
to support your
study of chemistry.

Figure 20–5 *The tiny bubbles seen here are due to oxygen gas produced by a green plant submerged in water. Chlorophyll molecules make use of light energy to oxidize water to O_2 gas.*

Oxidation Number

Many redox reactions can be quite complex. It is not always easy to identify the chemical species that is being oxidized or reduced. Even after the oxidized and reduced species are identified, balancing the complex equations by the simple techniques you have learned so far may prove to be nearly impossible. Fortunately, chemists have devised a system that helps to solve both of these problems. This system is based on the concept of oxidation numbers.

The **oxidation number** of an atom in a substance is equal to the charge that the atom would have if the electrons in each bond belonged to the more electronegative atom. It is important for you to understand that oxidation numbers are not actual charges. They are, however, a very convenient bookkeeping system used to help keep track of electrons. Although oxidation numbers can be determined by examining the bonding in a substance, it is more convenient to obtain them by using the following rules:

1. The oxidation number of an atom in an uncombined element is zero.
2. The oxidation number of any monatomic ion equals its ionic charge.
3. In compounds, the oxidation number of many elements corresponds to the element's position in the periodic table:
   a. Elements in Group 1A are always $+1$.
   b. Elements in Group 2A are always $+2$.
   c. Aluminum is always $+3$.
   d. Fluorine is always -1.
   e. Hydrogen has an oxidation number of $+1$ when combined with nonmetals.
   f. Oxygen has an oxidation number of -2 in most compounds and ions.
4. The oxidation numbers of elements in compounds are written per atom.
5. The algebraic sum of the individual oxidation numbers of all the atoms in the formula for a compound is zero.
6. The algebraic sum of the individual oxidation numbers of all the atoms in the formula for a polyatomic ion is equal to the charge of the ion.

Notice that oxidation numbers are written with the charge ($+$ or $-$) followed by the number, whereas actual ionic charges are written with the number followed by the charge. For example, the ionic charges of magnesium and chloride ions in the compound $MgCl_2$ are $2+$ and $1-$ respectively. Their oxidation numbers, however, are $+2$ and -1. All these rules will begin to make more sense once you have had an opportunity to apply them. Follow the process of assigning oxidation numbers that is illustrated in Sample Problem 1, and then apply the rules to the compounds in the Practice Problems that follow.

SAMPLE PROBLEM   1

What is the oxidation number of each element in potassium dichromate ($K_2Cr_2O_7$)?

STRATEGY	SOLUTION
1. Analyze	You are given the chemical formula for a compound and asked to determine the oxidation number of each of its elements.
2. Plan	You can solve this problem by applying the rules for oxidation numbers: oxidation numbers of elements in compounds are written per atom and the sum of the individual oxidation numbers must equal zero.
3. Solve	According to the rules for oxidation numbers, K (Group 1A) is $+1$ and O is -2. You can now determine the oxidation number of Cr because the sum of the individual oxidation numbers of all the elements in the compound taken per atom must equal zero. Let x equal the oxidation number of Cr:

$$2(+1) + 2x + 7(-2) = 0$$
$$+2 + 2x - 14 = 0$$
$$2x = +12$$
$$x = +6$$

4. Evaluate	Checking that the individual oxidation numbers of the elements in the compound add to zero validates your answer. A less elaborate way of assigning oxidation numbers is to write them above the formula:

$$\overset{+1}{K}_2\overset{x}{Cr}_2\overset{-2}{O}_7$$

It is easy to see that when $x = +6$, the oxidation numbers taken per atom add up to zero.

PRACTICE PROBLEMS

1. What is the oxidation number of an atom of each element in (a) SO_2 (b) $Al(NO_3)_3$? *(Answer: (a) $S = +4$, $O = -2$ (b) $Al = +3$, $N = +5$, $O = -2$)*

2. Although the oxidation number of O is usually -2 in its compounds, there are compounds called peroxides in which it is -1. What is the oxidation number of O in the following compounds: (a) Al_2O_3 (b) BaO_2 (c) H_2O_2 (d) Li_2O? *(Answer: (a) -2 (b) -1 (c) -1 (d) -2)*

Figure 20–6 *The oxidation number of chromium can vary from compound to compound, resulting in chromium compounds with strikingly different colors. What is chromium's oxidation number in the blue solution of $CrCl_2$?*

The year is 1969. The giant *Saturn* 5 rocket rises from the launch pad, carrying the first astronauts to the moon. The 111-meter tall rocket was the most powerful launch vehicle ever built in the United States. With the help of a rocket propellant the 2.7-million-kilogram *Saturn* 5 rocket lifted off the launch pad.

Rocket propellants are combinations of oxidizing and reducing agents. These redox reactions are strongly exothermic and produce thrust due to the rapid formation and expansion of large amounts of gases.

Now we can address the question of how changes in oxidation number are related to oxidation and reduction. When an atom loses an electron (oxidation), it becomes more positive and its oxidation number increases. When an atom gains an electron (reduction), it becomes more negative and its oxidation number decreases. In any oxidation-reduction reaction, at least one atom must increase in oxidation number and another must decrease in oxidation number. Thus oxidation and reduction can also be defined in terms of changes in oxidation number:

- Oxidation is said to occur when the oxidation number of an atom increases.
- Reduction is said to occur when the oxidation number of an atom decreases.

You now have three ways to identify oxidation and reduction: loss and gain of oxygen; loss and gain of electrons; and changes in oxidation numbers. These three definitions are summarized in the table in Figure 20–7.

Figure 20–7 *Various definitions of oxidation and reduction are summarized in this table. Which process results in an increase in oxidation number?*

Ways to Identify Oxidation and Reduction

Basis	Oxidation	Reduction
oxygen	gain of oxygen	loss of oxygen
electrons	loss of electrons	gain of electrons
oxidation number	increase in oxidation number	decrease in oxidation number

Oxidizing and Reducing Agents

In any oxidation-reduction reaction, chemists are often more interested in what is happening to one reactant than to the others. For example, in the reaction between magnesium and oxygen to form magnesium oxide (MgO), a chemist may be primarily interested in what is happening to the magnesium. From this perspective, it can be said that the magnesium is oxidized, and that oxygen causes the oxidation. Because oxygen causes the oxidation of magnesium, oxygen can be called the oxidizing agent. On the other hand, if the focus were on oxygen, it is just as correct to say that oxygen is reduced, and because magnesium causes the reduction, magnesium is the reducing agent.

An **oxidizing agent** causes the oxidation of another substance by accepting electrons from that substance. Thus the oxidizing agent contains the atom that shows a decrease in oxidation number. In other words, the oxidizing agent is itself reduced. In an analogous way, a **reducing agent** causes reduction by providing electrons to another substance. Thus the reducing agent contains the atom that shows an increase in oxidation number. In other words, the substance that is oxidized is the reducing agent. The substance that is reduced is the oxidizing agent.

This terminology can easily cause confusion unless you pause for a moment to think about what is happening in the reaction. One analogy that may help you is that a travel agent is not the person who takes the trip but the person who arranges the trip for someone else. Similarly, an oxidizing agent does not undergo oxidation, but rather causes another substance to be oxidized.

What characteristics do you think a substance should have in order to be a strong oxidizing agent? Recall that an oxidizing agent accepts electrons. So, many strong oxidizing agents contain an atom with a high electronegativity, such as F, O, or Cl. Electrons are also easily accepted by high positive charges. Thus many strong oxidizing agents contain an atom with a high positive oxidation number such as $+5$, $+6$, or $+7$.

What are some common oxidizing agents? The table in Figure 20–9 lists a few. Oxygen (both as O_2 and as ozone, O_3) and the halogens (F_2, Cl_2, Br_2, and I_2) are always oxidizing agents in their

oxidizing agent   reducing agent

Figure 20–8 *The species that enables oxidation to occur by being reduced is the oxidizing agent. The species that enables reduction to occur by being oxidized is the reducing agent.*

Figure 20–9 *Notice that electronegative nonmetals are listed as oxidizing agents, and metals and hydrocarbons are listed as reducing agents. Why is the element carbon a reducing agent?*

Some Common Oxidizing and Reducing Agents

Oxidizing Agent	Reaction Product	Reducing Agent	Reaction Product
O_2	O^{2-}, H_2O, or CO_2	H_2	H^+ or H_2O
F_2, Cl_2, Br_2, I_2	F^-, Cl^-, Br^-, I^-	metals	metal ions
HNO_3	NO and NO_2	C	CO_2
$Cr_2O_7^{2-}$	Cr^{3+}	hydrocarbons	CO_2 and H_2O
MnO_4^-	Mn^{2+}		

Living Systems and Redox Reactions

In all living systems, the energy-capturing reactions (photosynthesis) and the energy-releasing reactions (cellular respiration) are redox reactions. In photosynthesis, the reduction of carbon dioxide to form glucose stores chemical energy in the bonds of glucose. In cellular respiration, the complete oxidation of glucose releases energy. This energy is what enables you to run, walk, play, or sit quietly reading your chemistry textbook.

reactions with metals and most nonmetals. Chlorine is widely used as an oxidizing agent to purify drinking water, swimming pools, and even sewage. In this role, the Cl_2 kills bacteria by literally oxidizing them to death.

What characteristics should you look for in a reducing agent, a substance that is a source of electrons? You should recall that active metals have low electronegativities and tend to give up their valence electrons rather easily. Thus common reducing agents include active free metals such as Na, K, Mg, Al, Zn, and Fe. Other reducing agents include substances that burn readily, forming strong bonds with oxygen. These include hydrogen, carbon, and combustible compounds composed of hydrogen and carbon, such as methane (CH_4), which is the principal component of natural gas.

SAMPLE PROBLEM 2

Use changes in oxidation numbers to identify which element is oxidized and which is reduced in the following reaction:

$$Cu + 2\ AgNO_3 \rightarrow Cu(NO_3)_2 + 2\ Ag$$

Also identify the oxidizing agent and the reducing agent.

STRATEGY	SOLUTION
1. Analyze	You are given a chemical equation and asked to assign oxidation numbers to each element in order to determine which element is oxidized and which element is reduced.
2. Plan	First assign oxidation numbers to each element. Then use the definitions of oxidation and reduction in terms of oxidation numbers: Oxidation is accompanied by an increase in oxidation number; reduction is accompanied by a decrease in oxidation number. Finally, identify the oxidizing agent and the reducing agent.
3. Solve	In order to assign an oxidation number to Ag in $AgNO_3$, recall that the nitrate group has a charge of $1-$. Thus, $AgNO_3$ must contain Ag as the Ag^+ ion. The oxidation number of each element in the equation is

$$\overset{0}{Cu} + 2\overset{+1\ +5\ -2}{AgNO_3} \rightarrow \overset{+2\ +5\ -2}{Cu(NO_3)} + 2\overset{0}{Ag}$$

Remember that uncombined elements always have an oxidation number equal to zero, so reactant Cu and product Ag have oxidation numbers of 0. The oxidation number of Cu increases from 0 to +2. Thus, Cu is oxidized in this reaction. The oxidation number of Ag^+ decreases from +1 to 0. Thus Ag^+ is reduced. Ag^+ caused the oxidation of Cu and is the oxidizing agent; Cu caused the reduction of Ag^+ and is the reducing agent.

4. Evaluate   Any time a free metal is converted to a compound, it is oxidized. This observation agrees with your conclusion that Cu is oxidized. Any time a metal compound is changed to the free metal, it is reduced. This observation agrees with your conclusion that Ag^+ is reduced.

PRACTICE PROBLEMS

3. Identify the oxidizing agent and the reducing agent in the following reaction:

$$3\ H_2S + 2\ HNO_3 \rightarrow 3\ S + 2\ NO + 4\ H_2O$$

(Answer: Oxidizing agent is HNO_3; reducing agent is H_2S.)

4. Identify the element that is oxidized and the element that is reduced in the following reaction:

$$K_2Cr_2O_7 + 14\ HI \rightarrow 2\ CrI_3 + 2\ KI + 3\ I_2 + 7\ H_2O$$

(Answer: I is oxidized; Cr is reduced.)

20–1 Section Review

1. Define oxidation and reduction.

2. Compare oxidation and reduction. Why must they occur simultaneously?

3. How are oxidation numbers different from ionic charges?

4. **Critical Thinking—Making predictions**   Where in the periodic table do you think strong oxidizing agents are found? Strong reducing agents? Explain.

20–2 Types of Redox Reactions

In Chapter 9, you learned about four kinds of chemical reactions: direct combination, or synthesis, reactions, decomposition reactions, single-replacement reactions, and double-replacement reactions. Almost without exception, reactions belonging to the first three categories are redox reactions. Let's examine these reactions again—this time from the perspective of what you have learned in this chapter.

Direct Combination and Decomposition Reactions

As you learned in Chapter 9, in a direct combination, or synthesis, reaction, two or more substances combine to form a single, more complex compound. Synthesis reactions in which elements combine to form compounds are oxidation-reduction reactions. For example, the combustion of sulfur to form sulfur dioxide and the reaction between aluminum metal and bromine are both redox reactions, as you can see from the assigned oxidation numbers.

$$\overset{0}{S}(s) + \overset{0}{O_2}(g) \rightarrow \overset{+4\ -2}{SO_2}(g) \qquad \textbf{(Eq. 6)}$$

$$2\ \overset{0}{Al}(s) + 3\ \overset{0}{Br_2}(l) \rightarrow 2\ \overset{+3\ -1}{AlBr_3}(s) \qquad \textbf{(Eq. 7)}$$

The decomposition of a compound into its component elements also involves oxidation-reduction. For example, when mercury(II) oxide is heated, it decomposes into mercury metal and oxygen gas.

$$2\ \overset{+2\ -2}{HgO}(s) \rightarrow 2\ \overset{0}{Hg}(l) + \overset{0}{O_2}(g) \qquad \textbf{(Eq. 8)}$$

Figure 20–10 *The combination of the elements aluminum and bromine (left) occurs vigorously, and the heat released causes some of the bromine liquid to vaporize. Beads of mercury along with invisible oxygen gas are produced (right) when the red compound HgO is heated. Which reaction is a redox reaction?*

Notice that in both combination and decomposition reactions, free elements are on one side of the equation and a compound is on the other. Because the oxidation number of uncombined elements is always zero, it is easy to see how these reactions are always redox reactions.

Single-Replacement Reactions

In a single-replacement reaction, a free element becomes an ion, and an ion becomes a free element. All reactions of this kind are oxidation-reduction reactions. Among the most common and important of these reactions are those in which one metal replaces another. For example, when copper metal is placed in a solution of silver nitrate, a blue solution of copper nitrate is produced along with metallic silver. This reaction is summarized by the following chemical equation.

$$Cu \ (s) \ + \ 2 \ AgNO_3 \ (aq) \rightarrow Cu(NO_3)_2 \ (aq) \ + \ 2 \ Ag \ (s) \quad \textbf{(Eq. 9)}$$

The net-ionic equation for this reaction reveals even more clearly that Cu is oxidized (to Cu^{2+}) and Ag^+ is reduced (to Ag).

$$Cu \ (s) \ + \ 2 \ Ag^+ \ (aq) \rightarrow Cu^{2+} \ (aq) \ + \ 2 \ Ag \ (s) \quad \textbf{(Eq. 10)}$$

What do you suppose will happen if you place silver metal in a solution of copper nitrate? Do you think the reverse chemical reaction will occur? The answer is no. The fact that this reaction occurs from left to right as written but not from right to left suggests that copper loses its valence electrons more readily than silver. Thus when Cu atoms are in contact with Ag^+ ions, the Cu atoms lose electrons to become Cu^{2+} ions. However, when silver atoms are in contact with Cu^{2+} ions, they do nothing.

Chemical equations for a great many single-replacement reactions can be written, but not all of the reactions actually occur. For example, copper will not replace magnesium ions from magnesium compounds, even though an equation can be written for such a reaction. The reason for this is that metals have different reactivities as seen by their tendency to give up electrons and become oxidized. The relative reactivity of metals is reflected in their relative abilities to replace one another from their compounds. **An activity series of metals is a listing that ranks metals according to their relative reactivity.** The **activity series,** shown in the table in Figure 20–12, lists metals in order of decreasing reactivity. Those metals that are oxidized most readily are on the top of the list, and those that are oxidized least readily are on the bottom. A metal can replace only those metals below it in the activity series. For example, notice that Cu is above Ag but below Mg. Thus Cu reacts with Ag^+, replacing Ag^+ from its compounds, but Cu does not react with Mg^{2+}.

$$Cu \ (s) \ + \ Mg^{2+} \ (aq) \rightarrow No \ Reaction \quad \textbf{(Eq. 11)}$$

Figure 20–11 *When copper metal is placed in a solution of silver nitrate, crystals of silver deposit onto the copper. Why does the solution turn blue?*

Figure 20–12 *The activity series ranks metals by their ease of oxidation. A metal that is easily oxidized becomes an ion that is not so easily reduced. Why is hydrogen, a nonmetal, listed in a table of the activity series of metals?*

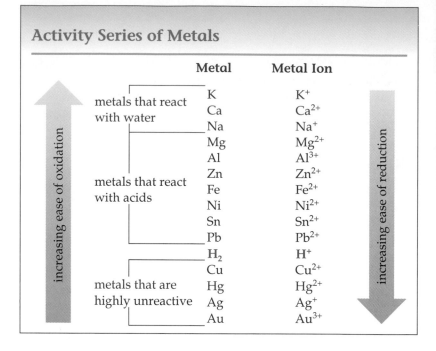

Activity Series of Metals

increasing ease of oxidation →

Metal	Metal Ion	
metals that react with water	K	K^+
	Ca	Ca^{2+}
	Na	Na^+
	Mg	Mg^{2+}
	Al	Al^{3+}
metals that react with acids	Zn	Zn^{2+}
	Fe	Fe^{2+}
	Ni	Ni^{2+}
	Sn	Sn^{2+}
	Pb	Pb^{2+}
	H_2	H^+
	Cu	Cu^{2+}
metals that are highly unreactive	Hg	Hg^{2+}
	Ag	Ag^+
	Au	Au^{3+}

increasing ease of reduction ↓

The activity series shown in Figure 20–12 divides metals into three groups. Those metals at the top are so reactive that they replace hydrogen from water, as illustrated by the behavior of sodium metal:

$$2 \text{ Na } (s) + 2 \text{ H}_2\text{O } (l) \rightarrow 2 \text{ NaOH } (aq) + \text{H}_2 (g) \quad \textbf{(Eq. 12)}$$

The metals in this group are the reactive metals of Groups 1A and 2A in the periodic table. Because they are oxidized so readily, they are very strong reducing agents.

In the middle of the activity series are metals that are able to replace hydrogen from acids but not from water. In other words, they are oxidized by acids, which are stronger oxidizing

Figure 20–13 *The reactivity of the metals magnesium, zinc, and copper can be compared by observing their reaction in dilute hydrochloric acid. Can you identify which test tube contains which metal?*

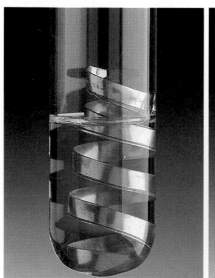

Solution to Tarnish

A mail-order catalog advertises a tarnish re-mover for silver that consists of a decorated bar made of magnesium metal. (Silver tarnish is mainly Ag_2S.) The catalog claims that you can remove silver tarnish by simply placing the bar and the tarnished silver in a plastic pan with water and detergent. Your friend's mother is planning to buy the product.

As an eager chemistry student, can you decide if this product has any merit? Are there any simple tests that you could do before the product is purchased?

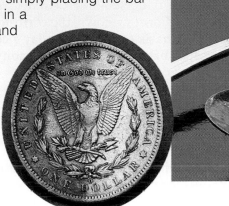

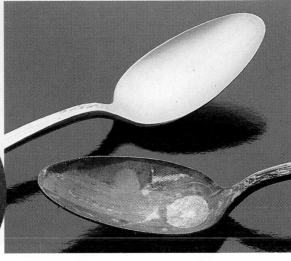

agents than water. For example, zinc reacts readily with sulfuric acid to form zinc sulfate and hydrogen gas:

$$Zn\ (s)\ +\ H_2SO_4\ (aq) \rightarrow ZnSO_4\ (aq)\ +\ H_2\ (g)\ \textbf{(Eq. 13)}$$

These metals are listed above hydrogen in the activity series. Why is hydrogen, a nonmetal, listed in the activity series of metals, you may wonder. It is listed there to serve as a standard against which metals can be effectively compared.

The metals at the bottom of the list are very resistant to oxidation. They are very stable as metals and do not replace hydrogen from water or acids. These metals include the coinage metals copper, silver, and gold.

20–2 Section Review

1. Describe a way of comparing the reactivity of metals.

2. Explain why all direct combination and decomposition reactions are oxidation-reduction reactions.

3. **Critical Thinking—Making inferences** Is a metal that is close to the top of the activity series a stronger or a weaker reducing agent than one found close to the bottom? Explain your answer.

Figure 20-14 Redox reactions are the source of electrical energy in batteries of various shapes and sizes.

*I*NTEGRATING
*E*NVIRONMENTAL *S*CIENCE

Why is the corrosion of structural metals such as iron undesirable?

Figure 20-15 The formation of rust results in the pitting of iron metal. These pits weaken the metal, making it unable to perform the task it was designed to perform.

20-3 Applications of Redox Reactions

As you learned earlier, examples of oxidation and reduction reactions are abundant in the world around you. The corrosion of metals, which is an oxidation reaction, is undesirable because it changes the free metal into its oxidized form. This oxidized form has properties completely different from those of the free metal. An understanding of redox reactions provides methods to prevent, or slow down, the corrosion process. **Redox reactions form the basis of many of today's conveniences such as fuels, bleaches, batteries, and photography.** Let's now examine some of these applications.

Preventing Corrosion

Corrosion is the oxidation of a metal caused by a reaction between the metal and some substance in its environment. The most familiar example of corrosion is the rusting of iron, which occurs when iron is oxidized by oxygen in the presence of water. Through a series of reactions, the iron is eventually converted into red-brown iron oxide (Fe_2O_3), which you know as rust. This process takes place quite readily, and is accelerated by the presence of acids and salts. Corrosion poses a problem because it results in the loss of the structural strength of the metal. About 20 percent of the annual production of iron and steel in the United States goes toward replacing corroded materials.

Corrosion can be prevented by coating the metal with oil, paint, plastic, or another metal. These surface coatings prevent oxygen, water, and other substances from coming into direct

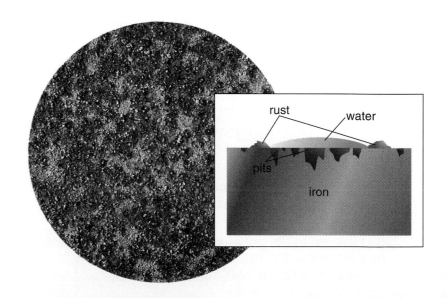

contact with the metal. Corrosion is also prevented by electro-chemical processes that are based on the fact that when two metals are in contact, the metal that is more readily oxidized will corrode in preference to the other metal. Thus a piece of an expendable metal such as magnesium can be attached to iron to prevent the iron from corroding. When oxygen and moisture attack the iron, electrons flow from the magnesium to the iron, causing the magnesium to corrode in preference to the iron. Why is magnesium a good choice for this kind of protection?

Bleaching

Bleaches are chemical substances that are used to eliminate unwanted color from fabrics and other materials. Color is caused by the movement of electrons between different energy levels of the atoms of the material. Consequently, the color of a material can often be eliminated by removing these electrons by the process of oxidation. Thus bleaches are oxidizing agents, and just about any oxidizing agent can serve as a bleach. It may not be practical to use some oxidizing agents as bleaches, however, because these oxidizing agents may be toxic, harmful to the fabric, or undesirable for other reasons. Three of the most common commercial and household bleaches are chlorine (Cl_2), hypochlorite ion (ClO^-), and hydrogen peroxide (H_2O_2). NaClO is the active compound in common liquid household bleaches. Solid chlorine bleaches contain $Ca(ClO)_2$. In both compounds, the hypochlorite ion is the oxidizing agent that causes bleaching.

Hydrogen peroxide is a good oxidizing agent. One of the common household uses for H_2O_2 is as a mild antiseptic. It kills bacteria by oxidizing them. The fizzing that occurs when H_2O_2 is poured on a cut is caused by the decomposition of H_2O_2 into O_2 and H_2O, which is catalyzed by enzymes in blood. Nonchlorine bleaching powders contain sodium perborate ($NaBO_3$), which slowly liberates hydrogen peroxide when dissolved in water.

Figure 20–16 *Applying a thin coating of an oxide (top) or a paint (bottom) are two ways of protecting a metal surface from contact with air and moisture. Can you think of other ways?*

Figure 20–17 *Which of these teenagers is wearing bleached jeans? Color, the result of loosely bound electrons, can be effectively eliminated by treating the colored object with an oxidizing agent. What does the oxidizing agent do?*

671

Figure 20–18 *An explosion of TNT is initiated by the detonation of another explosive: mercury fulminate.*

Fuels and Explosives

Fuels release energy as they are oxidized. Common fuels such as gasoline, kerosene, and natural gas contain compounds composed largely of carbon and hydrogen. Once ignited, they are readily oxidized by oxygen in air, forming CO_2 and H_2O.

Explosives contain both oxidizing and reducing agents, often within the same compound. For example, nitroglycerin ($C_3H_5(NO_3)_3$) contains C and H atoms that are oxidized to form CO_2 and H_2O, as well as N atoms that are reduced to form N_2. The C and H atoms are the reducing agents and the NO_3 groups are the oxidizing agents. When suitably activated, a highly exothermic redox reaction occurs in which large amounts of gaseous products form. The rapid formation and expansion of the gas creates the shock wave that accompanies the detonation of an explosive. Nitroglycerin, which can be activated merely by shaking, decomposes as follows:

$$4\,C_3H_5(NO_3)_3\,(l) \rightarrow 6\,N_2\,(g) + 12\,CO_2\,(g) + 10\,H_2O\,(g) + O_2\,(g)$$
(Eq. 14)

Notice that all of the products, including H_2O, are gases.

Photography

Photography involves the capturing of a light image on a light-sensitive medium and the processing of the image to make a permanent record. These processes are based on the redox reactions of silver halides. The film behind the camera lens is an emulsion of silver bromide (AgBr) deposited onto a plastic backing. The silver bromide grains in the emulsion are light sensitive. A single light photon can activate a grain by initially oxidizing a bromide ion and subsequently reducing a silver ion:

$$\overset{-1}{Br^-} \rightarrow \overset{0}{Br} + e^- \qquad \text{(oxidation)} \qquad \textbf{(Eq. 15)}$$

$$\overset{+1}{Ag^+} + e^- \rightarrow \overset{0}{Ag} \qquad \text{(reduction)} \qquad \textbf{(Eq. 16)}$$

The activated grains represent the captured image, although at this stage you would not be able to "see" the image on the film. At the film processing laboratory, the remaining Ag^+ ions in the activated grains are first converted to free silver (Ag) by a reducing agent. Next, the unreacted AgBr in the nonactivated grains is removed by an appropriate solution process. At this stage you would be able to recognize the film as a negative. The final step in film processing involves the printing of the negative onto photographic paper. This process also involves redox reactions analogous to the ones involved in the development of the film.

It is, therefore, no surprise that carefully controlled redox reactions in the developing as well as printing stages are the key to the production of high-quality pictures.

Figure 20–19 *The chemical processes that convert exposed film into photographs are redox reactions. Redox reactions are also what enabled the film to capture the image in the first place. Why does this photograph have a red tint?*

CONNECTION

Corrosion—An Unwanted Oxidation-Reduction Reaction

It is the first day of spring. While looking out the window of your room, you notice that the change in season has brought changes to that small patch of land you call the backyard. Once blanketed by snow, the lawn now shows signs of life with the appearance of blades of green grass. Everything looks so new and alive. But wait. What is that object against the fence in the corner of the yard? Oh no, it's the shovel you forgot to clean off and put away after the last snowfall. Even from this distance, you can see that the shovel is covered with rust.

Although rusting may not pose a serious problem to you, it does pose a serious economic problem to industries that use iron and steel. In the United States alone, corrosion destroys more than $70 billion worth of equipment annually. Corrosion is the reaction of a metal with substances in the environment. The rusting of iron, a familiar type of corrosion, is a complex chemical reaction that involves both oxygen and moisture.

What are some solutions to the problem of corrosion? One way to prevent corrosion is to apply protective coatings such as paint, grease, oil, or some corrosion-resistant metal such as chromium, which shields the metal from the air and water. Linings made of plastic, rubber, or ceramics are also very effective against corrosion.

Another way to prevent corrosion is called cathodic protection. This process involves placing iron or steel in contact with a metal that is more easily oxidized. If corrosion occurs, the iron or steel is protected from oxidation because the other metal reacts instead. Zinc and magnesium are two metals that are often used to provide cathodic protection.

In the continuing effort to fight corrosion, research scientists in the area of materials science have also come up with new alloys of iron that are more corrosion resistant.

So the next time you use anything that is made of metal, such as a garden tool or a kitchen utensil, remember that it should be thoroughly cleaned and dried before you put it away. As a further precaution against corrosion, you may want to apply some oil or paint to areas where the metal is exposed.

20–3 Section Review

1. List some everyday applications of oxidation-reduction reactions.

2. What specific measures can be taken to prevent the destruction of iron due to corrosion?

3. Explain what a bleach is and how it works.

4. **Connection—Pyrotechnics**   Many redox reactions are the basis of today's fuels and explosives. Identify two important requirements for a redox reaction to be used in the production of fireworks.

Guide for Reading

- What is the main principle used to balance redox equations?

20–4 Balancing Redox Equations

A balanced equation that accurately represents the chemical reaction of interest is essential to chemists. On the basis of such balanced equations, chemists and chemical engineers make quantitative predictions and evaluations about the reaction process. In Chapter 9 you learned some general principles to use in balancing chemical equations. However, many redox equations are difficult to balance by the methods of inspection or trial and error that you have used until now. If you do not believe this, try balancing the following equation, which is only moderately complex.

$$S\ (s)\ +\ HNO_3\ (aq)\ \rightarrow\ SO_2\ (g)\ +\ NO\ (g)\ +\ H_2O\ (l) \quad \textbf{(Eq. 17)}$$

Not as easy as it looks, is it? In order to balance this equation and others like it, you need to use a systematic approach. And oxidation numbers are at the root of such an approach. You will now learn to apply your knowledge of oxidation numbers to balancing redox equations. **The fundamental principle in balancing redox equations is that the number of electrons lost in an oxidation process (increase in oxidation number) must equal the number of electrons gained in the reduction process (decrease in oxidation number).**

Although we will use Equation 17 as a model, the following steps can be used to balance any redox equation.

1. Assign oxidation numbers to all atoms in the equation, writing them above the chemical symbol for each element.

$$\overset{0}{S}\ (s)\ +\ \overset{+1\ +5\ -2}{H\,NO_3}\ (aq)\ \rightarrow\ \overset{+4\ -2}{SO_2}\ (g)\ +\ \overset{+2\ -2}{NO}\ (g)\ +\ \overset{+1\ -2}{H_2O}\ (l)$$
$$\textbf{(Eq. 18)}$$

Notice, again, that the oxidation number is written per atom. For example, although there are 3 O atoms in HNO_3, only the oxidation state of a single O atom, -2, is shown.

2. Identify the element oxidized and the element reduced, and determine the change in oxidation number of each.
    In this reaction, sulfur changes from 0 to $+4$, a change of $+4$ (oxidation). Nitrogen changes from $+5$ to $+2$, a change of -3 (reduction).

3. Connect the atoms that change oxidation numbers by using a bracket, and write the change in oxidation number at the midpoint of each bracket:

Figure 20–20 *A fascinating effect of the redox reaction that takes place in the body of a firefly is the production of light.*

$$\overset{+4}{\underset{-3}{\text{S}\,(s)\;+\;\overset{0\quad +1+5-2}{\text{H}\,\text{NO}_3\,(aq)}\;\rightarrow\;\overset{+4-2}{\text{SO}_2\,(g)}\;+\;\overset{+2\;-2}{\text{NO}\,(g)}\;+\;\overset{+1\;-2}{\text{H}_2\text{O}\,(l)}}}$$

(Eq. 19)

4. Choose coefficients that make the total increase in oxidation number equal the total decrease in oxidation number.

   In this example, you will need to multiply the increase by 3 and the decrease by 4. This will make the change in oxidation number for the oxidation and the reduction each equal to 12. This step should seem reasonable to you because it is a direct consequence of the fact that oxidation and reduction occur together and in precisely equal amounts.

$$3\,\text{S}\,(s)\;+\;4\,\text{H}\,\text{NO}_3\,(aq)\;\rightarrow\;\text{SO}_2\,(g)$$
$$+\;\text{NO}\,(g)\;+\;\text{H}_2\text{O}\,(l)$$

with annotations $3(+4) = +12$ and $4(-3) = -12$

(Eq. 20)

5. Balance the remaining elements by inspection, and then check the final equation.

   The coefficients of SO_2 and NO will be 3 and 4, respectively, to balance the S and the N.

$$3\,\text{S}\,(s)\;+\;4\,\text{H}\,\text{NO}_3\,(aq)\;\rightarrow\;3\,\text{SO}_2\,(g)$$
$$+\;4\,\text{NO}\,(g)\;+\;\text{H}_2\text{O}\,(l)$$

with annotations $3(+4) = +12$ and $4(-3) = -12$

(Eq. 21)

You now need only to balance H and O. Balancing H gives a coefficient of 2 for the product H_2O. This gives a total of 12 O atoms on the products side and a total of 12 O atoms on the reactants side.

$$3\,\text{S}\,(s)\;+\;4\,\text{H}\,\text{NO}_3\,(aq)\;\rightarrow\;3\,\text{SO}_2\,(g)$$
$$+\;4\,\text{NO}\,(g)\;+\;2\,\text{H}_2\text{O}\,(l)$$

with annotations $3(+4) = +12$ and $4(-3) = -12$

(Eq. 22)

Sometimes a reaction that occurs in an acidic water solution can be balanced by adding H_2O and H^+ to either side of the equation as necessary. In such cases, you should add H_2O to the side of the equation that needs O atoms and H^+ to the side that needs H atoms.

In an acidic water solution, the perchlorate ion (ClO_4^-) reacts with the iodide ion (I^-) to form the chloride ion (Cl^-) and iodine (I_2). Write a balanced chemical equation for this reaction.

STRATEGY	SOLUTION
1. Analyze	You are given the main reactants and products for a redox reaction in an acidic solution and asked to write a balanced chemical equation.
2. Plan	Follow the steps for balancing a redox equation. Then add H^+ and H_2O as needed to balance the H and O atoms because the reaction occurs in an acidic solution.
3. Solve	Assign oxidation numbers to all atoms in the equation.

$$\overset{+7\,-2}{ClO_4^-} + \overset{-1}{I^-} \rightarrow \overset{-1}{Cl^-} + \overset{0}{I_2}$$

Identify the elements oxidized and reduced. Chlorine is reduced with a change in oxidation number of -8 ($+7$ to -1). Iodine is oxidized with a change in oxidation number of $+1$ (-1 to 0). Connect these atoms with brackets and choose coefficients that make the total increase in oxidation number equal to the total decrease in oxidation number.

$$\overset{8\,(+1)\,=\,+8}{\overset{+7\,-2}{ClO_4^-} + 8\,\overset{-1}{I^-} \rightarrow \overset{-1}{Cl} + \overset{0}{I_2}}$$
$$1\,(-8) = -8$$

Now balance the Cl and I atoms.

$$\overset{8\,(+1)\,=\,+8}{\overset{+7\,-2}{ClO_4^-} + 8\,\overset{-1}{I^-} \rightarrow \overset{-1}{Cl^-} + 4\,\overset{0}{I_2}}$$
$$1\,(-8) = -8$$

To balance the O atoms you will need to add 4 H_2O to the right side of the equation.

$$\overset{8\,(+1)\,=\,+8}{\overset{+7\,-2}{ClO_4^-} + 8\,\overset{-1}{I^-} \rightarrow \overset{-1}{Cl^-} + 4\,\overset{0}{I_2} + 4\,H_2O}$$
$$1\,(-8) = -8$$

MATH TIP

If a reaction occurs in acid solution, do not be afraid to add H^+ ions and H_2O molecules as needed. Make sure, however, that you have completely accounted for changes in oxidation numbers first.

You can now balance the H atoms by adding $8H^+$ to the left side of the equation. The final balanced equation is:

$$ClO_4^- + 8I^- + 8H^+ \rightarrow Cl^- + 4I_2 + 4H_2O$$

4. Evaluate   Check to make sure that each element as well as the overall charge are balanced. There are 8 I, 1 Cl, 4 O, and 8 H on each side of the equation. In addition, the net charge for the reactants is $1-$ (8 H^+ and 8 I^- give a net charge of 0), the same as that for the products.

PRACTICE PROBLEMS

5. Balance the following equation and identify the element oxidized and the oxidizing agent.
$NaI\ (s) + H_2SO_4\ (aq) \rightarrow H_2S\ (g) + I_2\ (s) + Na_2SO_4\ (aq) + H_2O\ (l)$ *(Answer: 8 NaI (s) + 5 H_2SO_4 (aq) → H_2S (g) + 4 I_2 (s) + 4 Na_2SO_4 (aq) + 4 H_2O (l). The element oxidized is I and the oxidizing agent is H_2SO_4. Notice, however, that not all the H_2SO_4 is reduced; some is used to make Na_2SO_4.)*

6. Balance the chemical equation for the reaction that occurs when permanganate ions (MnO_4^-) react with chloride ions (Cl^-) to form manganese ions (Mn^{2+}) and chlorine gas (Cl_2). The reaction occurs in an acidic solution. *(Answer: 2 MnO_4^- + 10 Cl^- + 16 H^+ → 2 Mn^{2+} + 5 Cl_2 + 8 H_2O)*

Just as you can use H^+ and H_2O to balance reactions in acidic solutions, you can use OH^- and H_2O to balance reactions in basic solutions. You probably remember that in basic aqueous solutions the concentration of OH^- ions exceeds the concentration of H^+ ions. Thus, when reactions occur in basic solutions, OH^- is used instead of H^+ to balance the equation. However, this can often be more cumbersome than dealing with acidic solutions because both OH^- and H_2O contain H and O atoms. Therefore you will not be asked to balance a redox equation in a basic solution. But feel free to ask your teacher if you would like a challenge!

20-4 Section Review

1. Explain the main principle used to balance complex redox equations.

2. Can an element undergo oxidation as well as reduction in the same reaction? Explain your answer.

3. **Theme Trace—Stability**   Why must the total charge on either side of a balanced equation be the same? What law does this represent?

Laboratory Investigation

Changes During Redox Reactions

Problem

What changes occur during redox reactions?

Materials (per group)

24 well-reaction plates
micropipettes containing the following
   solutions:
   1.0 *M* HCl
   1.0 *M* $Cu(NO_3)_2$
   1.0 *M* $Zn(NO_3)_2$
small pieces of Mg, Cu, Zn

Procedure

1. Place 10 to 12 drops of HCl into each of the wells of three well-reaction plates. Add one piece of Mg to one of the wells, Cu to a second well, and Zn to a third well. Record your observations in a data table similar to the one shown.
2. Place 10 to 12 drops of $Cu(NO_3)_2$ in a clean well. Add a piece of Zn to the well. After 5 minutes, record your observations in the data table.

3. Place 10 to 12 drops of $Zn(NO_3)_2$ in a clean well. Add a piece of Cu to the well. After 5 minutes, record your observations in the data table.
4. Following your teacher's instructions, discard all solutions and clean all well-reaction plates.

Observations

1. Which metal did not react with HCl?
2. Which metal did not react in steps 2 and 3?

Analysis and Conclusions

1. What is the name of the gas produced by the reactions in Step 1? Write a half reaction for one of the reactions in Step 1.
2. Based on the reactions in Steps 2 and 3, which is more easily reduced, Cu or Zn?
3. **On Your Own**   With your teacher's permission, try reacting Cu with $AgNO_3$ and Ag with $Cu(NO_3)_2$ to determine which metal is more easily reduced.

Reactants	Observations	Substance Oxidized	Substance Reduced
HCl + Mg			
HCl + Cu			
HCl + Zn			
$Cu(NO_3)_2$ + Zn			
$Zn(NO_3)_2$ + Cu			

STUDY GUIDE

Summarizing Key Concepts

20–1 Oxidation-Reduction Reactions

- The loss of electrons by a substance is oxidation, and the gain of electrons by a substance is reduction.
- The oxidation number of an atom represents the charge that the atom would have if the electrons in each bond belonged entirely to the more electronegative atom.
- The reduced substance is the oxidizing agent, and the oxidized substance is the reducing agent.

20–2 Types of Redox Reactions

- Direct combination, decomposition, and single-replacement reactions are redox reactions.
- The activity series of metals is a relative listing of the reactivity of metals.

20–3 Applications of Redox Reactions

- Corrosion, a redox process, can be prevented by the use of protective coatings such as paint and oil. The use of a metal that is more active than iron is another simple way to retard corrosion.

- Bleaches are oxidizing agents that eliminate unwanted color by removing the loosely bound electrons that cause color.
- All combustion reactions such as those of fuels and explosives are redox reactions.
- Photography makes use of the light-initiated reduction of silver ions (present in the film grains) to silver atoms.

20–4 Balancing Redox Equations

- Oxidation numbers can be used to balance complex redox equations by ensuring that the total increase in oxidation number equals the total decrease in oxidation number.

Reviewing Key Terms

Define each term in a complete sentence.

20–1 Oxidation-Reduction Reactions

oxidation
reduction
oxidation-reduction reaction
redox reaction
oxidation number

oxidizing agent
reducing agent

20–2 Types of Redox Reactions

activity series

CHAPTER REVIEW

Content Review

Multiple Choice
Choose the letter of the answer that best completes each statement.

1. Oxidation is
   (a) a gain of electrons.
   (b) an increase in oxidation number.
   (c) a decrease in oxidation number.
   (d) removal of oxygen.

2. The oxidation number of sodium in a compound is
   (a) 0.   (c) $+1$.
   (b) $+2$.   (d) -1.

3. In a direct combination reaction,
   (a) elements are oxidized.
   (b) elements are reduced.
   (c) no change occurs.
   (d) an element is oxidized while another is reduced.

4. If zinc is less reactive than magnesium,
   (a) magnesium can replace zinc ions from zinc compounds.
   (b) zinc can replace magnesium ions from magnesium compounds.
   (c) magnesium is lower than zinc in the activity series of metals.
   (d) zinc is a stronger reducing agent than magnesium.

5. A reducing agent
   (a) is an acid.
   (b) can act as a bleach.
   (c) can be oxygen gas.
   (d) always gives up electrons.

6. Bleaches are
   (a) sources of electrons
   (b) reducing agents.
   (c) oxidizing agents.
   (d) oxidized as they react.

7. When a light photon hits the silver bromide in a grain of a photographic film,
   (a) bromide ions are produced.
   (b) silver ions are reduced.
   (c) silver ions are oxidized.
   (d) bromide ions are reduced.

8. To balance a redox equation, you must
   (a) equalize the increase and decrease in oxidation numbers.
   (b) add H_2O to both sides of the equation.
   (c) add H^+ and OH^- to opposite sides of the equation.
   (d) make sure that the ionic charge on both sides of the equation is 0.

True or False
If the statement is true, write "true." If it is false, change the underlined word or words to make the statement true.

9. All decomposition reactions are <u>redox</u> reactions.

10. A reducing agent causes <u>oxidation</u> to occur.

11. An <u>increase</u> in oxidation number indicates reduction.

12. The rusting of an iron object can be prevented by attaching a <u>less</u> reactive metal to the object.

13. Bleaches work by <u>releasing electrons to</u> colored fabrics.

Concept Mapping
Complete the following concept map for Section 20–1. Refer to pages xviii–xix to construct a concept map for the entire chapter.

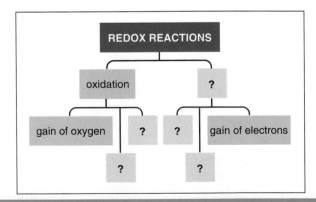

Concept Mastery

Discuss each of the following in a brief paragraph.

14. Is it possible for oxidation to occur without reduction? Explain.

15. Which of the following are redox reactions?

(a) $Ba(NO_3)_2$ (aq) + H_2SO_4 (aq) → $BaSO_4$ (s) + 2 HNO_3 (aq)

(b) NH_4NO_2 (s) → N_2 (g) + 2 H_2O (g)

(c) CuO (s) + H_2 (g) → Cu (s) + H_2O (l)

16. What is common about the oxidation numbers of the elements in the following molecules: H_2, P_4, S_8, C_{60}?

17. Compare direct combination reactions with decomposition reactions.

18. Explain the use of the activity series of metals. Give examples.

19. Describe some common applications of redox reactions.

20. Determine the oxidation number for phosphorus in each of the following compounds. (a) $AlPO_4$ (b) H_3PO_2 (c) $H_4P_2O_7$ (d) Na_2HPO_3. Show how you arrived at each answer.

21. Tying it Together   Identify what is common in the *patterns of change* described by the three definitions of oxidation and reduction that are presented in this chapter.

Critical Thinking and Problem Solving

Use the skills you have developed in this chapter to answer each of the following.

22. Applying concepts   Nitrogen forms several oxides. Write the chemical formula for the oxide in which nitrogen has an oxidation number of (a) +1 (b) +2 (c) +3 (d) +4 (e) +5.

23. Drawing conclusions   The highest positive oxidation number that chlorine can exhibit in any compound is +7, whereas its most negative oxidation number is −1. Write the electron configuration of chlorine and explain why these are the limiting oxidation numbers for chlorine.

24. Applying concepts   Indicate whether the following species could possibly function as reducing agents: (a) Mg^{2+} (b) Ca (c) H_2. Explain your reasoning.

25. Making comparisons   Referring to Figure 20–12, indicate which of the following is the stronger oxidizing agent: (a) magnesium or tin (b) lead or mercury.

26. Making predictions   Using the activity series, predict which of the following reactions occur and write their balanced chemical equations.

(a) Cu (s) + HCl (aq) →

(b) Ni (s) + $AgNO_3$ (aq) →

(c) Al (s) + $FeSO_4$ (aq) →

27. Applying concepts   Balance the following redox equations:

(a) Al (s) + $NaOH$ (aq) + H_2O (l) → $NaAl(OH)_4$ (aq) + H_2 (g)

(b) PbO_2 (s) + HI (aq) → I_2 (s) + PbI_2 (aq) + H_2O (l)

28. Applying concepts   Complete and balance each of the following equations occuring in acidic aqueous solutions.

(a) Br_2 (aq) + $S_2O_3^{2-}$ (aq) → Br^- (aq) + SO_4^{2-} (aq)

(b) Sn^{2+} (aq) + IO_3^- (aq) → Sn^{4+} (aq) + I_2 (s)

29. Using the writing process   In addition to the processes of oxidation and reduction, what are some other pairs of opposites? Write about these opposites, making sure to include a description of the situation in which they are found.

Chapter
21 Electrochemistry

How can you tell if a motorcycle or an automobile is a well-preserved antique? Perhaps you recognize the classic designs and shapes of the 1940s and the 1950s. But more likely, you will be clued in by the abundant presence of shiny chrome. The thin layer of chromium, applied to metal parts by an electrochemical process, protects the metal beneath from being oxidized by the environment. Undoubtedly, the dazzle it lends to the motorcycle is a definite plus!

Applications of electrochemistry such as electroplating are the subject of this chapter. Electrochemistry is the coupling of redox reactions with the flow of electricity. In some applications, electricity is produced by redox reactions and in others, electricity causes redox reactions to occur.

An electric eel has specialized electrical organs that it uses for defense and to stun its prey. Chromium electroplating is generously used for protection as well as decoration on a motorcycle.

Chem Journal

YOU AND YOUR WORLD

Make a list of the batteries you use in and around your home. Identify them by their size, voltage, and the chemical ingredients if possible. After you complete your study of the chapter, indicate if any of the batteries on your list are examples of the batteries discussed in the chapter.

21-1 Electrochemical Cells

Guide for Reading

- What are electrochemical cells?

In Chapter 20 you studied an important class of chemical reactions called redox reactions. As you learned, redox, or oxidation-reduction, reactions are defined in terms of the loss and gain of electrons. Indeed, you studied several examples of such reactions in which one substance gave up its electrons to another substance. Do you remember how oxidation and reduction are defined?

Perhaps you know that the transfer, or movement, of electrons is the very basis of electricity. Electric energy is transported through matter in the form of an electric current. In earlier chapters you learned that metals, in general, are good electrical conductors because of the ease of movement of their loosely held valence electrons. An electric current can also be carried by the movement of positive and negative ions, as in solutions and molten salts. You may recall that substances that release or produce ions when dissolved in water are called electrolytes. It is the presence of ions in water that makes water dangerous around electrical equipment.

Figure 21-1 *Power lines consist of metal wires that transport electrical energy in the form of an electric current. At a game arcade, electrical energy tapped from an electrical outlet operates a variety of games, providing fun and entertainment.*

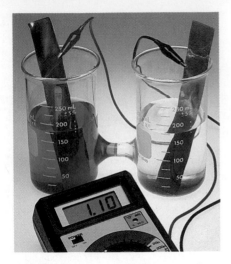

Figure 21–2 *A redox reaction between zinc and copper produces electrical energy in an electrochemical cell. What type of an electrochemical cell is shown?*

Because redox reactions involve a transfer of electrons, electricity plays a significant role in their application. For example, zinc, being more reactive than copper, gives up its valence electrons to copper ions when placed in a solution of copper sulfate. This reaction can be conducted in an **electrochemical cell,** where the transfer of electrons from Zn to Cu^{2+} occurs through a metal wire, generating an electric current. **Devices that use redox reactions to either produce or use electricity are called electrochemical cells.**

Electrons enter and exit electrochemical cells with the help of **electrodes.** Electrodes are made of electrical conductors such as metals or graphite, and they provide the surfaces on which oxidation and reduction occur. The sites of oxidation and reduction are separated so that oxidation occurs at one electrode and reduction occurs at the other electrode. Why is this necessary?

There are two types of electrochemical cells, those that produce electricity and those that use electricity. Those that produce electricity as the result of spontaneous redox reactions are called **voltaic cells.** A battery consists of one or more voltaic cells. For example, a common flashlight battery consists of a single voltaic cell that generates 1.5 volts, whereas a 12-volt automobile battery consists of six voltaic cells that each generate 2 volts. Voltaic cells make use of spontaneous redox reactions that release energy. When a flashlight is turned on, a spontaneous redox reaction takes place in the flashlight battery generating a flow of electrons through the lightbulb. The word spontaneous has a precise meaning when used in this context, and you will learn more about it when you read Chapter 23. For now, it is sufficient for you to

Figure 21–3 *The filament in a flashlight bulb glows due to redox chemical reactions that generate a flow of electrons. How many volts does this flashlight require to operate?*

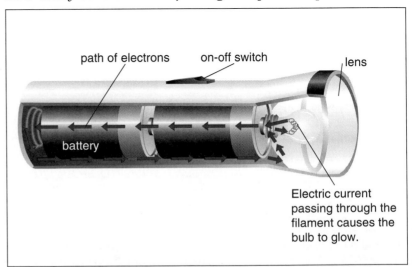

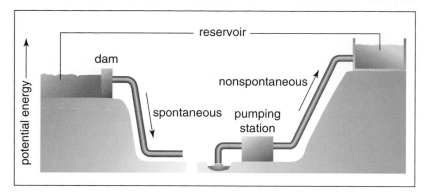

Figure 21–4 *A dam regulates the spontaneous downhill flow of water. How does water get from a low elevation to a high elevation?*

understand that a spontaneous reaction can occur on its own and releases energy as it proceeds. The reverse of a spontaneous reaction (a nonspontaneous reaction) cannot take place on its own, and requires an input of energy for it to occur.

Electrochemical cells can also be used to drive redox reactions that do not occur of their own accord. Electrochemical cells in which electrical energy drives nonspontaneous redox reactions are called **electrolytic cells.** Electrolytic cells are used to plate precious metals onto jewelry, to purify metals, and to obtain active metals from their compounds. For example, both aluminum and magnesium metals are obtained from their compounds using electrolytic cells.

In many ways, the flow of water serves as a useful analogy to describe the flow of electricity in electrochemical processes. Water flows spontaneously downhill. This process can be harnessed in a hydroelectric plant to produce electricity. In a similar way, the spontaneous flow of electrons from a higher energy state to a lower energy state causes voltaic cells to produce electricity. On the other hand, a source of electrical energy must be used to drive nonspontaneous redox reactions to higher energy in an electrolytic cell. This process is analogous to the uphill transport of water. Because water does not naturally flow uphill, energy is required to pump water to a higher elevation, which represents a state of greater potential energy.

Metals From Ores

Have you wondered how we manage to have metals such as sodium, aluminum, chromium, and iron when in nature they always occur in the form of their compounds?

For most metals, and certainly for the active metals, oxidation by loss of their valence electrons is a spontaneous process. This is why these metals corrode and end up in the environment as the metal oxides, sulfides, nitrates, carbonates, and so forth.

Producing the free, uncombined metal from its compound is the reverse, nonspontaneous process—one that requires an input of energy.

Electrolysis is one way to supply this energy in order to produce a free metal. The very active sodium metal is produced in the Down's electrolytic cell. Aluminum is produced by the Hall-Heroult electrolytic process. Copper, cadmium, and gallium are other metals that can be electrolyzed from aqueous solutions of their salts.

21–1 Section Review

1. Describe the features of an electrochemical cell.

2. Explain the fundamental difference between voltaic cells and electrolytic cells.

3. **Connection—Physics** Compare an electric current in a metallic conductor and in an electrolyte.

Guide for Reading

- What are cell potentials?
- What factors determine the potential of a voltaic cell?

21–2 Voltaic Cells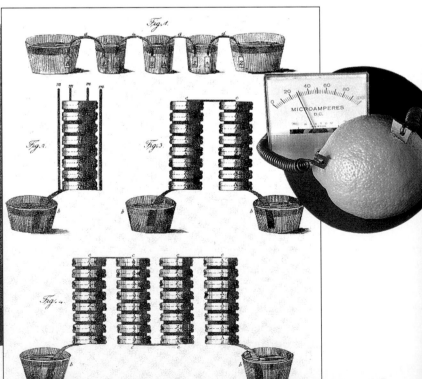

In the late eighteenth century, Italian physician Luigi Galvani made an important observation while dissecting frogs. He noticed that the frog legs twitched when brought in contact with a pair of different metals, such as the iron and copper scalpels he was using. The frog legs also twitched when lightning struck near a wire connected to them. These observations stimulated the curiosity of a fellow countryman, Alessandro Volta, who concluded that the contact between two metals in the presence of moisture produces electricity.

In 1800, Volta successfully built the first battery, a device consisting of alternating disks of dissimilar metals separated by pieces of leather that had been soaked in salt water. Volta discovered that any two metals and any electrolyte could be used to produce electricity. Indeed, if you stick two metals, such as zinc and copper, into a lemon, and connect them with a wire, the assembly will produce an electric current. An electric current is also produced if you have metal dental fillings, and you bite down on a piece of aluminum foil. In fact, you then have a voltaic cell in your mouth. The result is a very unpleasant shock as electrons move from the aluminum to your fillings and from the fillings to the nerve endings in your teeth.

Although any redox reaction can, in principle, serve as the basis for a voltaic cell, some reactions are more easily adapted

Figure 21–5 *Serendipity—combined with Alessandro Volta's curious and prepared mind—made possible the conceptual leap from twitching frog legs to modern batteries. The early drawing shows sketches of Volta's alternating zinc and copper discs. What did Volta use to separate the dissimilar metal discs? In what way is the setup using a lemon similar to Volta's device?*

to this purpose than others. By studying voltaic cells utilizing different redox reactions, a wide variety of convenient and reasonably inexpensive batteries have been developed.

Voltaic Cell Setup

All voltaic cells operate in a similar fashion and share certain common features. We will use the spontaneous redox reaction between zinc metal and a solution of copper sulfate to illustrate the main ideas.

$$Zn\ (s)\ +\ CuSO_4\ (aq)\ \rightarrow\ ZnSO_4\ (aq)\ +\ Cu\ (s) \qquad \textbf{(Eq. 1)}$$

When a strip of zinc metal is placed in a solution of copper sulfate, as shown in Figure 21–6, the Zn is "eaten away" and a coating of Cu is formed. At the same time, the blue color of the solution due to Cu^{2+} ions disappears as the Cu^{2+} ions are reduced to Cu and replaced in solution by the colorless Zn^{2+} ions. In this redox reaction, zinc metal is oxidized and copper ions are reduced.

oxidation: $\quad Zn\ (s) \rightarrow Zn^{2+}\ (aq)\ +\ 2e^- \qquad \textbf{(Eq. 2)}$

reduction: $\quad Cu^{2+}\ (aq)\ +\ 2e^- \rightarrow Cu\ (s) \qquad \textbf{(Eq. 3)}$

In the simple setup shown in Figure 21–6, the electron transfer between Zn atoms and Cu^{2+} ions is direct. When a Cu^{2+} ion collides with the surface of the Zn strip, 2 electrons are transferred directly from the Zn to the Cu^{2+}, forming Zn^{2+} and Cu. The condition that makes a voltaic cell possible is indirect electron transfer.

Figure 21–6 *When a strip of zinc is immersed in a solution of copper sulfate, a direct transfer of electrons takes place between copper ions and zinc atoms. Can you write an ionic equation for this reaction?*

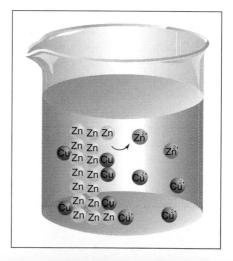

Figure 21–7 *The familiar zinc-copper redox reaction generates an electric current in a voltaic cell. What is the purpose of the salt bridge?*

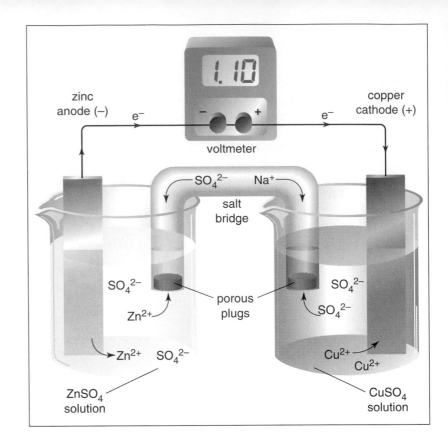

In order to eliminate direct electron transfer and permit only indirect electron transfer, the Zn strip and the Cu^{2+} ions must be placed in separate compartments. Figure 21–7 illustrates one way to separate the reactants, placing a Zn strip and an aqueous solution of $ZnSO_4$ in one container and a Cu strip and an aqueous solution of $CuSO_4$ in another. In essence, the cell reaction is split into two half reactions, one for the oxidation of Zn and one for the reduction of Cu^{2+}. A voltaic cell can be visualized as consisting of two **half-cells,** one corresponding to the oxidation half reaction and one corresponding to the reduction half reaction. As the Zn is oxidized in one half-cell, the electrons that are given up pass through the wire to the copper electrode that is located in the other half-cell. These electrons become available to reduce the Cu^{2+} ions that are in contact with that electrode.

The electrode at which oxidation occurs is called the **anode.** In the zinc-copper cell, the zinc electrode is the anode because zinc is oxidized as the cell operates. The electrode at which reduction occurs is called the **cathode.** The copper electrode is the cathode in this voltaic cell.

As you know, all batteries are marked with + and − signs indicating the positive and negative electrodes. The negative electrode of a battery, or a voltaic cell, is the anode because that is where the negatively charged electrons are released. These electrons move spontaneously from the negative electrode (the anode) to the positive electrode (the cathode). In a zinc-copper cell, the zinc electrode, the anode, is the negative electrode and the copper electrode, the cathode, is the positive electrode.

An important feature of the voltaic cell illustrated in Figure 21–7 is the tube connecting the two half-cells. This tube, called a **salt bridge,** contains an electrolyte solution. The salt bridge allows ions to move from one compartment to another but prevents the solutions from mixing totally. Other devices such as a porous clay barrier between solutions can be used in place of the salt bridge to allow the flow of ions between half-cells. The movement of ions between half-cells keeps the number of positive and negative ions equal in each half-cell and is essential to complete the electrical circuit. Without this flow of ions within the cell, charge will begin to accumulate in each half-cell. As a result, the flow of electrons between electrodes will cease almost instantaneously.

INTEGRATING
PHYSICS

Why must ions be able to flow from one half-cell to another for a voltaic cell to produce electricity?

Cell Potential

Just as a ball spontaneously rolls downhill, electrons move spontaneously from a higher energy state to a lower energy state. When two different metal electrodes are placed in an electrolyte solution, electrons move from the electrode with higher electrical potential energy to the electrode with lower electrical potential energy. The difference in the electrical potential energy of the electrodes "drives" electrons from the anode to the cathode in a voltaic cell. The energy released as electrons move from one electrode to the other can be used to do work, such as winding a cassette tape, starting a car, or running a computer.

The ability of a cell reaction to move electrons through a wire from one electrode of a voltaic cell to another is described by a quantity called the electrical potential of the cell or merely the cell potential. As you might expect, the **cell potential** represents the difference in the electrical potential energy between the two electrodes of the cell. Because cell potential is measured in units of volts (V), it is often referred to as **cell voltage.** You can measure the voltage of a cell by connecting one terminal of a

Figure 21–8 *An electric current is the flow of electrons from a state of higher electrical potential energy to a state of lower electrical potential energy. Electrical appliances utilize the energy released to perform work.*

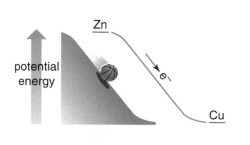

voltmeter to one electrode and the other terminal to the other electrode. The voltage of a cell represents the force with which each electron is "pushed" as it moves from one electrode to the other. It is a measure of the cell's ability to drive an electric current through a wire and thereby do work. The role of voltage in electrical circuits is analogous to that of water pressure in water pipes. Just as a higher water pressure moves water more forcefully through a given pipe, a higher voltage gives electrons a greater amount of energy. The cell is able to perform more work.

In the zinc-copper cell, electrons in the zinc electrode have a higher electrical potential energy than electrons in the copper electrode. Thus the electrons move spontaneously from Zn to Cu when a path (a wire) is provided between them. The voltage of the zinc-copper cell is about 1 volt. The exact voltage depends on the temperature and concentrations of ions in the solution. The voltage of any voltaic cell is always a positive number. What do you think a negative cell voltage would mean?

Standard Cell Potential

As you have just read, the magnitude of the cell potential represents the driving force of the redox reaction. The cell potential can also be related to the energy released as the cell reaction proceeds, and to the electrical work that the cell can perform. Therefore electrochemists are interested in knowing the exact voltages for various reactions.

The magnitude of a voltaic cell's potential depends largely on the nature of the cell reaction itself. It also depends on the ion concentration in solution, the pressure of any gases involved, and the reaction temperature. In order to compare the potentials of different voltaic cells, a set of standard conditions has been defined for electrochemical measurements. In a cell reaction at standard-state conditions, the concentration of solutions is 1 M, and the partial pressure of gases is 1 atmosphere. Although standard-state measurements can be made at any temperature, they are usually made at 25°C. You may remember that standard conditions were discussed in Chapter 12. The voltage of a zinc-copper cell at 25°C is +1.10 volts under standard-state conditions (that is, when the concentration of both zinc ions and copper ions is 1 M).

Standard Electrode Potentials

Each electrode of a voltaic cell makes a characteristic contribution to the cell potential. Thus, the cell potential, designated by E_{cell}, can be considered to be the sum of the contributions from the oxidation reaction at the anode, $E_{oxidation}$, and the reduction reaction at the cathode, $E_{reduction}$.

$$E_{cell} = E_{oxidation} + E_{reduction} \qquad \textbf{(Eq. 4)}$$

These contributions are called **electrode potentials.** To more specifically indicate the type of half reaction occurring at each electrode, the electrode potential for a reduction half reaction is commonly called a **reduction potential.** In a similar way, the electrode potential for an oxidation half reaction is called an **oxidation potential.**

When a cell is operated under standard-state conditions, the cell potential and electrode potentials are called standard cell potentials and standard electrode potentials, respectively. The standard-state conditions are indicated by a superscript o.

$$E^o_{cell} = E^o_{ox} + E^o_{red} \qquad \text{(Eq. 5)}$$

Unfortunately, the electrode potentials due to isolated oxidation and reduction half reactions cannot be directly measured. Only the difference between two electrode potentials can be measured. However, a set of relative electrode potentials has been determined instead. Relative electrode potentials are obtained by measuring cell voltages obtained by combining different half-cells with the same reference half-cell electrode. The reference electrode that chemists have chosen is the standard hydrogen electrode. The standard hydrogen electrode reaction is the reduction of H^+ to form H_2. This reduction reaction is assigned a standard reduction potential of exactly zero.

$$2\,H^+\,(aq,\,1\,M)\,+\,2e^-\,\rightarrow H_2\,(g,\,1\,atm) \qquad E^o = 0.00\,V \quad \text{(Eq. 6)}$$

The standard hydrogen electrode, shown in Figure 21–9, consists of a platinum electrode immersed in an acidic solution with $[H^+\,(aq)] = 1.00\,M$. Hydrogen gas at a pressure of 1 atmosphere is bubbled over the electrode surface through a glass envelope.

Figure 21–10 on page 692 shows a voltaic cell consisting of a standard hydrogen electrode as one half-cell and a strip of zinc immersed in 1.0 M Zn^{2+} solution as the other half-cell. A voltmeter indicates a cell voltage equal to 0.76 V. Thus $E^o_{cell} = +0.76\,V$. As the cell operates, zinc is oxidized, and reduction occurs at the standard hydrogen electrode. The standard oxidation potential for the zinc electrode can be calculated from Equation 5.

$$E^o_{cell} = E^o_{ox} + E^o_{red}$$

$$0.76\,V = E^o_{ox} + 0.00\,V$$

$$0.76\,V = E^o_{ox} \qquad \text{(Eq. 7)}$$

Thus the standard oxidation potential for zinc is determined to be 0.76 V. This information can be stated by writing the half reaction for the oxidation of zinc and its associated standard oxidation potential.

$$Zn\,(s)\,\rightarrow Zn^{2+}\,(aq)\,+\,2e^- \qquad E^o_{ox} = +0.76\,V \quad \text{(Eq. 8)}$$

Figure 21–9 *The standard hydrogen electrode is assigned a standard electrode potential of 0.00 V. Why?*

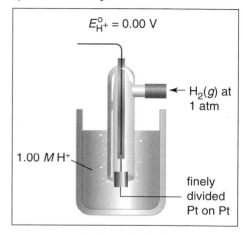

$E^o_{H^+} = 0.00\,V$

← $H_2(g)$ at 1 atm

1.00 M H^+

finely divided Pt on Pt

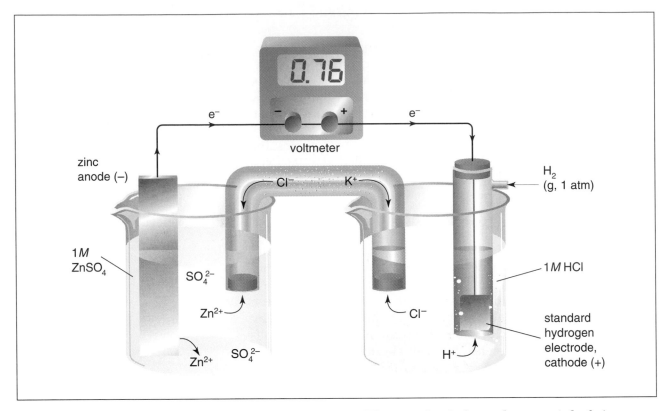

Figure 21–10 *The standard electrode potential of zinc can be found by measuring the potential of a voltaic cell consisting of a zinc electrode as one half-cell and the standard hydrogen electrode as the other half-cell. Is the voltage of 0.76 V E_{ox}^o or E_{red}^o?*

Equation 7 may also be reversed. If you are interested in the reduction of Zn^{2+} to form Zn, the standard reduction potential is equal in magnitude but opposite in sign to the standard oxidation potential.

$$Zn^{2+} (aq) + 2e^- \rightarrow Zn (s) \qquad E_{red}^o = -0.76 \text{ V} \quad \textbf{(Eq. 9)}$$

Standard oxidation and standard reduction potentials for other half reactions can be determined in a similar way. The table in Figure 21–11 lists the standard reduction potentials for a variety of different substances. You will generally find tables listing only reduction potentials. This is because, as you have just seen, oxidation potentials are easily obtained from reduction potentials by reversing the sign. Standard electrode potentials are useful in a variety of ways, two of which are illustrated next.

DETERMINING EASE OF OXIDATION AND REDUCTION
The more positive the standard reduction potential of a molecule or ion, the more readily that species is reduced. The more negative the standard reduction potential, the harder the species is to reduce. Thus, of the substances listed in Figure 21–11, F_2, the species at the top of the table, is reduced most readily

Standard Reduction Potentials

(Ionic Concentrations 1 M Water at 298 K and 101.3 kPa)

Half Reaction	E° (volts)
$F_2(g) + 2e^- \longrightarrow 2\,F^-$	+2.87
$8\,H^+ + MnO_4^- + 5e^- \longrightarrow Mn^{2+} + 4\,H_2O$	+1.51
$Au^{3+} + 3e^- \longrightarrow Au\,(s)$	+1.50
$Cl_2(g) + 2e^- \longrightarrow 2\,Cl^-$	+1.36
$14\,H^+ + Cr_2O_7^{2-} + 6e^- \longrightarrow 2\,Cr^{3+} + 7\,H_2O$	+1.23
$4\,H^+ + O_2(g) + 4e^- \longrightarrow 2\,H_2O$	+1.23
$4\,H^+ + MnO_2(s) + 2e^- \longrightarrow Mn^{2+} + 2\,H_2O$	+1.22
$Br_2(l) + 2e^- \longrightarrow 2\,Br^-$	+1.09
$Hg^{2+} + 2e^- \longrightarrow Hg\,(l)$	+0.85
$Ag^+ + e^- \longrightarrow Ag\,(s)$	+0.80
$Hg_2^{2+} + 2e^- \longrightarrow 2\,Hg\,(l)$	+0.80
$Fe^{3+} + e^- \longrightarrow Fe^{2+}$	+0.77
$I_2(s) + 2e^- \longrightarrow 2\,I^-$	+0.54
$Cu^+ + e^- \longrightarrow Cu\,(s)$	+0.52
$Cu^{2+} + 2e^- \longrightarrow Cu\,(s)$	+0.34
$4\,H^+ + SO_4^{2-} + 2e^- \longrightarrow SO_2\,(aq) + 2\,H_2O$	+0.17
$Sn^{4+} + 2e^- \longrightarrow Sn^{2+}$	+0.15
$2\,H^+ + 2e^- \longrightarrow H_2(g)$	0.00
$Pb^{2+} + 2e^- \longrightarrow Pb\,(s)$	−0.13
$Sn^{2+} + 2e^- \longrightarrow Sn\,(s)$	−0.14
$Ni^{2+} + 2e^- \longrightarrow Ni\,(s)$	−0.26
$Co^{2+} + 2e^- \longrightarrow Co\,(s)$	−0.28
$Fe^{2+} + 2e^- \longrightarrow Fe\,(s)$	−0.45
$Cr^{3+} + 3e^- \longrightarrow Cr\,(s)$	−0.74
$Zn^{2+} + 2e^- \longrightarrow Zn\,(s)$	−0.76
$2\,H_2O + 2e^- \longrightarrow 2\,OH^- + H_2(g)$	−0.83
$Mn^{2+} + 2e^- \longrightarrow Mn\,(s)$	−1.19
$Al^{3+} + 3e^- \longrightarrow Al\,(s)$	−1.66
$Mg^{2+} + 2e^- \longrightarrow Mg\,(s)$	−2.37
$Na^+ + e^- \longrightarrow Na\,(s)$	−2.71
$Ca^{2+} + 2e^- \longrightarrow Ca\,(s)$	−2.87
$Sr^{2+} + 2e^- \longrightarrow Sr\,(s)$	−2.89
$Ba^{2+} + 2e^- \longrightarrow Ba\,(s)$	−2.91
$Cs^+ + e^- \longrightarrow Cs\,(s)$	−2.92
$K^+ + e^- \longrightarrow K\,(s)$	−2.93
$Rb^+ + e^- \longrightarrow Rb\,(s)$	−2.98
$Li^+ + e^- \longrightarrow Li\,(s)$	−3.04

Figure 21–11 *The table provides a listing of the standard reduction potentials for several common half reactions.*

Observe signs carefully when working with reduction potentials. If a half-reaction proceeds in the direction of oxidation, the sign of the half-cell voltage must be reversed.

Visit our Web site at
http://www.phschool.com
to support your
study of chemistry.

$(E^{\text{o}}_{\text{red}} = +2.87 \text{ V})$. The species at the bottom of the table, the Li^+ ion, is reduced with great difficulty $(E^{\text{o}}_{\text{red}} = -3.05 \text{ V})$.

Notice that the reduction of H^+ is near the middle of the table in Figure 21–11, and has a value of 0.00 V because it has been defined as the reference half reaction. A positive value for a standard reduction potential of a molecule or ion indicates that it is easier to reduce than H^+. On the other hand, a negative value indicates that the species is more difficult to reduce compared to H^+.

If you want to compare the ease with which different ions and molecules are oxidized, you must reverse the half reactions in Figure 21–11 and change the signs of the electrode potentials. For example, reversing the half reactions for the reduction of Li^+ and F_2 yields

$$Li \ (s) \rightarrow Li^+ \ (aq) + e^- \qquad E^{\text{o}}_{\text{ox}} = +3.05 \text{ V} \quad \textbf{(Eq. 10)}$$

$$2 \ F^- \ (aq) \rightarrow F_2 \ (g) + 2e^- \qquad E^{\text{o}}_{\text{ox}} = -2.87 \text{ V} \quad \textbf{(Eq. 11)}$$

Notice that the standard oxidation potential for the oxidation of Li ($+3.05$ V) is far more positive than that for F^- (-2.87 V). This comparison indicates that Li is far easier to oxidize than F^-.

CALCULATING CELL POTENTIALS   Equation 5 indicates that standard oxidation potentials and standard reduction potentials can be used to calculate a standard cell potential. The following Sample Problem outlines the procedure for determining a standard cell potential from standard electrode potentials.

SAMPLE PROBLEM   1

Calculate the voltage produced under standard conditions by a voltaic cell composed of a silver electrode in a Ag^+ solution in one half-cell and an aluminum electrode in an Al^{3+} solution in the other half-cell.

STRATEGY	SOLUTION
1. Analyze	Each half-cell of the voltaic cell has a metal electrode in contact with a solution containing ions of that metal. From the contents of the half-cells, you are asked to calculate the standard cell potential.
2. Plan	The standard cell potential depends on the standard electrode potentials for the half reactions in each half-cell. You can use Figure 21–11 to obtain standard reduction potentials.

$$Ag^+ \ (aq) + e^- \rightarrow Ag \ (s) \quad E^{\text{o}}_{\text{red}} = +0.80 \text{ V}$$

$$Al^{3+} \ (aq) + 3e^- \rightarrow Al \ (s) \quad E^{\text{o}}_{\text{red}} = -1.66 \text{ V}$$

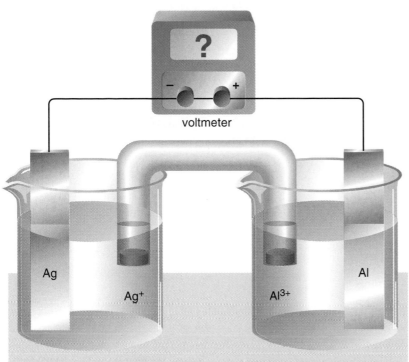

voltmeter

Because Ag^+ has the more positive reduction potential, it undergoes reduction in the cell. Thus, Ag^+ is reduced at the cathode. Therefore Al must be oxidized at the anode.

The standard cell potential is the sum of the standard reduction potential for Ag^+ plus the standard oxidation potential for Al. The half reaction for the oxidation of Al is obtained by reversing the half reaction for reduction, and the oxidation potential is obtained by changing the sign of the reduction potential.

3. Solve

$$Al\,(s) \rightarrow Al^{3+}\,(aq) + 3e^- \quad E^o_{ox} = 1.66\ V$$

$$E^o_{cell} = E^o_{ox} + E^o_{red}$$

$$= +1.66\ V + 0.80\ V$$

$$= +2.46\ V$$

4. Evaluate

The Ag^+ is reduced more readily than Al^{3+} and therefore undergoes reduction in the cell. The Al undergoes oxidation more readily than Ag and therefore undergoes oxidation. The voltage is positive, as required for a voltaic cell.

The table of standard reduction potentials in Figure 21–11 may remind you of the activity series of metals discussed earlier in Chapter 20. Recall that any metal in the series chemically reacts with a compound of any metal below it in the series, displacing the lower metal from its compound. This simple, but important principle can now be understood in terms of standard reduction potentials. As you can see, nickel is found above silver in the activity series (page 668). Therefore, nickel is expected to displace silver according to the redox reaction

$$Ni (s) + 2 Ag^+ (aq) \rightarrow Ni^{2+} (aq) + 2 Ag \quad \textbf{(Eq. 12)}$$

The standard cell potential for this equation can easily be obtained in a manner similar to that illustrated in Sample Problem 1. You should get $E^\circ = 1.06$ V for Equation 12.

21–2 Section Review

1. What is meant by the cell potential of a voltaic cell? What factors determine its magnitude?

2. Can you measure the half-cell potential of an isolated half-cell? Explain your answer.

3. Would a voltaic cell work equally well if a copper wire were used in place of a salt bridge? Explain.

4. What are standard oxidation and reduction potentials? How are they related?

5. **Theme Trace—Energy** How are standard electrode potentials indicative of the energy required to carry out a nonspontaneous process or the energy obtained from a spontaneous process?

21–3 Common Batteries

You are probably already aware of the tremendous variety of batteries available in stores today. Small batteries are used in flashlights, toys, portable radios, and tools. Even smaller ones are found in pacemakers and watches. And then there are the large batteries used to start automobiles. Batteries come in different sizes, shapes, and brands. Batteries are also based on different redox reactions. Some batteries can be recharged while others cannot. **Batteries that can be recharged use an outside power source to reverse electrode reactions. Those that cannot be recharged use redox reactions that cannot be easily reversed.** When the initial reactants are used up, nonrechargeable batteries must be discarded.

In this section, you will learn about four common kinds of batteries, two that cannot be recharged—the common dry cell and the alkaline dry cell—and two that can be recharged—the lead storage battery and the nickel-cadmium battery. In addition, you will discover that a fuel cell is a kind of voltaic cell that uses a continuous supply of a conventional fuel like hydrogen or methane to generate electricity.

The Common Dry Cell

A voltaic cell in which the electrolyte is a paste is called a dry cell. The common dry cell, sometimes referred to as a flashlight battery, consists of a zinc container filled with a thick paste of zinc chloride ($ZnCl_2$), manganese(IV) oxide (MnO_2), ammonium chloride (NH_4Cl), and water. The zinc is separated from the other chemicals by a liner of porous paper that acts as the salt bridge. A graphite rod is placed in the center of the paste. Graphite is an electrical conductor and serves as an inexpensive electrode. A cross section of the common dry cell is shown in Figure 21–13.

When a flashlight operated by a dry cell is switched on, electrons flow from the negative electrode through the bulb to the positive electrode. This flow of electrons is possible because zinc is oxidized in the battery, and MnO_2 is reduced. The chemical reactions that occur are

oxidation: $Zn\ (s) \rightarrow Zn^{2+}\ (aq)\ +\ 2e^-$ **(Eq. 13)**

reduction: $2\ MnO_2\ (s)\ +\ 2\ NH_4^+\ (aq)\ +\ 2e^- \rightarrow$
$Mn_2O_3\ (s)\ +\ 2\ NH_3\ (aq)\ +\ H_2O\ (l)$ **(Eq. 14)**

One of the primary advantages of the common dry cell is its low cost. However, it has a number of disadvantages. First, it is not rechargeable. If the battery is placed in a charger, the added electrical energy causes the decomposition of H_2O rather than the reversal of the reactions that occur during discharge. Second, if current is drawn rapidly from the cell, the voltage drops from

Guide for Reading
• How do rechargeable and nonrechargeable batteries differ?
• How does a lead storage battery operate?

Figure 21–12   *Batteries are convenient because they provide a direct and often mobile source of electrical energy. What battery-operated devices do you use on a typical day?*

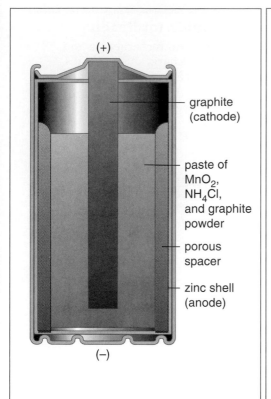

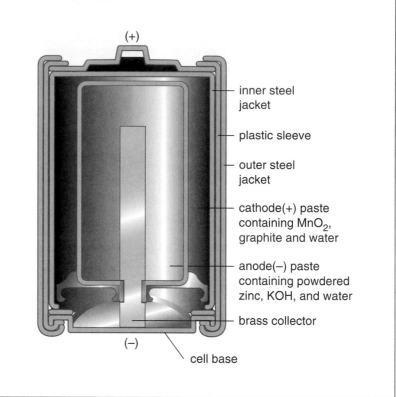

graphite
(cathode)

paste of
MnO$_2$,
NH$_4$Cl,
and graphite
powder

porous
spacer

zinc shell
(anode)

inner steel
jacket

plastic sleeve

outer steel
jacket

cathode(+) paste
containing MnO$_2$,
graphite and water

anode(−) paste
containing powdered
zinc, KOH, and water

brass collector

cell base

Figure 21–13 *A cross section of a common dry cell (left) is compared with that of an alkaline dry cell (right). What differences do you notice?*

its normal value of about 1.5 V, as reactants close to the cathode are depleted. Third, the zinc reacts directly with the slightly acidic ammonium ions, causing the cell to run down even when current is not being drawn. Thus, common dry cells have a poor shelf life. Because the rates of almost all chemical reactions decrease with decreasing temperature, the shelf life of dry cells can be increased by storing them in a refrigerator prior to use.

The Alkaline Dry Cell

The alkaline dry cell is a modification of the ordinary dry cell. In an alkaline cell, KOH replaces NH$_4$Cl in the paste, giving rise to slightly different reactions at the electrodes.

oxidation: $Zn\ (s)\ +\ 2\ OH^-\ (aq) \rightarrow ZnO\ (s)\ +\ H_2O\ (l)\ +2e^-$
(Eq. 15)

reduction: $2\ MnO_2\ (s)\ +\ H_2O\ (l)\ +\ 2e^- \rightarrow Mn_2O_3\ (s)\ +\ 2\ OH^-$
(Eq. 16)

In addition, the design of the alkaline dry cell is more elaborate than that of the ordinary dry cell. For example, as illustrated in Figure 21–13, powdered zinc is used in the paste that surrounds the anode. This paste is separated by a porous paper or fabric barrier from the paste that contains the MnO_2. The MnO_2 paste is in contact with the cathode.

The alkaline cell has several advantages over the common dry cell. It has a longer shelf life because zinc does not react as readily with the alkaline KOH as it does with the acidic NH_4Cl. It also maintains a steady voltage of about 1.5 V under high current loads, and it generates about 50 percent more total energy than a common dry cell of the same size. One disadvantage of the alkaline cell is its higher cost, largely because of its more complicated construction.

Lead Storage Battery

The familiar automobile battery is the best known example of a rechargeable battery. This battery is also known as the lead storage battery because its electrodes are composed of alternating sheets of lead and lead dioxide. The electrolyte in the battery is sulfuric acid, commonly called battery acid. During discharge, the lead is oxidized and therefore serves as the anode. In the presence of sulfate ions from the electrolyte, the oxidation of the lead produces lead(II) sulfate ($PbSO_4$). The cathode consists of lead dioxide (PbO_2), also immersed in the sulfuric acid. During discharge, the PbO_2 is reduced in the presence of the sulfuric acid and also produces $PbSO_4$.

Figure 21–14 *Three lead-lead oxide voltaic cells connected together form a 6-V lead storage battery. Why do you think it is called a storage battery?*

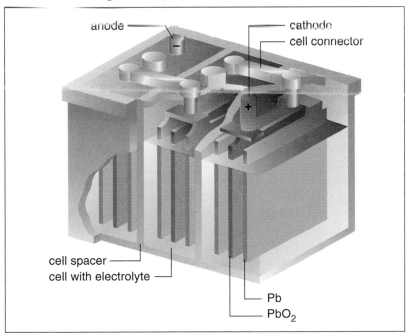

anode
cathode
cell connector
cell spacer
cell with electrolyte
Pb
PbO_2

Are Electric Cars Pollution Free?

There is increasing global concern over the environmental pollution caused by vehicle emissions. You probably already know that the combustion engines in automobiles and trucks release nitrogen oxides and carbon monoxide, as well as unburned hydrocarbon fuel, which is referred to as voc's, or volatile organic compounds.

One of the initiatives undertaken to reduce the amount of these pollutants in the environment is to promote the use of electric cars. California, always a leader in taking steps to protect the environment, will require that by 2003, 10 percent of all cars and light trucks sold in California must be pollution free. It means that these vehicles must produce zero emissions, giving off no nitrogen oxides, carbon monoxide, or voc's.

To meet these standards, automobile companies have developed and begun selling electric cars. They are working hard to develop less expensive electric cars with lighter, longer lasting batteries.

1. Identify ways in which electricity can be produced for powering electric cars.
2. For each of these ways, list pollution problems that could arise.
3. Compare these with the pollution problems caused by today's cars.
4. What do you think are the advantages and disadvantages in the use of electric cars?

Feel free to go to your local library for the research to address this task.

oxidation: $Pb\ (s)\ +\ SO_4^{2-}\ (aq) \rightarrow PbSO_4\ (s)\ +\ 2e^-$

(Eq. 17)

reduction: $PbO_2\ (s)\ +\ 4\ H^+\ (aq)\ +\ SO_4^{2-}\ (aq)\ +\ 2e^- \rightarrow$

$PbSO_4\ (s)\ +\ 2\ H_2O\ (l)$ **(Eq. 18)**

The sheets of Pb and PbO_2 in the battery are separated from each other by porous spacers. To increase the electrical current, each cell contains several sheets of lead that are connected to form the anode and several sheets of lead dioxide that are connected to form the cathode. Each cell generates a voltage of 2 volts. Thus, a 12-volt battery consists of six voltaic cells.

The lead sulfate formed at the anode and cathode during discharge is insoluble and adheres to the electrode surfaces. This makes it possible to reverse the reactions when the battery is recharged. To recharge a lead storage battery, a source of direct electrical current is used to reverse the electrode reaction and regenerate the original reactants.

$$Pb\,(s) + PbO_2\,(s) + 4\,H^+\,(aq) + 2\,SO_4^{2-}\,(aq) \underset{\text{charge}}{\overset{\text{discharge}}{\rightleftharpoons}}$$

$$2\,PbSO_4\,(s) + 2\,H_2O\,(l) \quad \textbf{(Eq. 19)}$$

A lead storage battery can usually be recharged thousands of times. Both mechanical jarring as a car travels over rough roads and the recharging process itself eventually cause the $PbSO_4$ to become dislodged from the electrodes. As this happens, recharging becomes ineffective. When Pb is lost from the anode, it ends up between the electrodes, introducing an internal short circuit, causing the battery to go "dead" and not accept a charge.

The lead storage battery is relatively simple, inexpensive, and reliable. Its major drawback is its mass. A typical battery contains about 15 to 20 kilograms of lead. Lead storage batteries must also be disposed of properly because of the toxicity of lead and its compounds.

Nickel-Cadmium Battery

Nickel-cadmium (nicad) batteries are popular rechargeable voltaic cells. These batteries are widely used in cordless appliances and tools. The anode is composed of cadmium. During discharge, the cadmium is oxidized, forming Cd^{2+}, which reacts with OH^- ions to form $Cd(OH)_2$. The cathode reaction involves the reduction of NiO_2, which is present in the paste. Like the lead

Figure 21–15 *Rechargeable batteries are environmentally friendly because they are not discarded after a single use. Do you think they contribute to pollution in other ways?*

What Do We Do With Toxic Metals?

Batteries have many uses. The small button battery powers a wristwatch. The large lead storage battery provides the power to start an automobile engine. A lithium battery provides the energy to run a pacemaker. Other batteries operate flashlights, toys, tape recorders, and portable radios and tools. During power failures, batteries even provide an emergency supply of electricity for telephones, fire alarms, and to hospitals.

Batteries contain electrodes and electrolytes, which consist of different kinds of chemically active materials. These materials include compounds of toxic metals such as lead, cadmium, and mercury. The use of metals is not limited to batteries. Lead is used as a shield to block radiation. Cadmium is used in the manufacture of plastics and pigments. Mercury is added to paints to prevent mildew.

Although these metals are useful, they pose an environmental health problem. Some of these metals are toxic, and their toxicity is a function of the structure of their atoms. Often the metals are toxic because of their ability to disrupt the normal function of body chemicals such as enzymes. For this reason, some metals as well as their compounds pose a threat to the environment and to humans.

The problems that were associated with hazardous wastes were relatively unknown decades ago. Today, hundred of millions of kilograms of hazardous waste, which includes the category of toxic metals, are produced each year around the world. It is estimated that in the United States alone two thirds of our hazardous wastes are disposed of in wells, pits, ponds, lagoons, and landfills. Another one fifth is discharged directly into rivers and streams. Only a small percent of hazardous wastes is recycled or detoxified.

Have you heard of the three R's for protecting the environment: Reduce, Reuse, and Recycle? What do these words mean to you? Can you offer any other solutions to this problem? What can you, as a consumer, do to decrease the production of hazardous wastes?

storage battery, the products formed in the electrode reactions are insoluble and adhere to the electrode surfaces, thus permitting recharging.

oxidation: $Cd\ (s)\ +\ 2\ OH^-\ (aq) \rightarrow Cd(OH)_2\ (s)\ +\ 2e^-$ **(Eq. 20)**

reduction: $NiO_2\ (s)\ +\ 2\ H_2O\ (l)\ +\ 2e^- \rightarrow$
$Ni(OH)_2\ (s)\ +\ 2\ OH^-\ (aq)$ **(Eq. 21)**

overall reaction: $Cd\ (s)\ +\ NiO_2\ (s)\ +\ 2\ H_2O\ (l) \rightarrow$
$Cd(OH)_2\ (s)\ +\ Ni(OH)_2\ (s)$ **(Eq. 22)**

The nicad battery is lightweight and produces a constant voltage during discharge. However, it suffers somewhat from discharge "memory." If it is discharged only partially and then recharged, it develops the tendency to need recharging after only a short use. The batteries are most effective if totally discharged before recharging. These batteries must also be disposed of properly because of the toxicity of cadmium and its compounds.

Fuel Cells

A fuel cell is a voltaic cell in which a fuel is continuously supplied from an external reservoir to the cell. Because the fuel is supplied continuously, fuel cells do not run down like ordinary batteries. Furthermore, fuel cells are very efficient—about 90 percent—at converting chemical energy into electrical energy. The most common fuel cell is the hydrogen-oxygen fuel cell, which is used in the space shuttle.

oxidation: $2\,H_2\,(g)\ +\ 4\,OH^-\,(aq) \rightarrow 4\,H_2O\,(l)\ +\ 4e^-$ **(Eq. 23)**

reduction: $O_2\,(g)\ +\ 2\,H_2O\,(l)\ +\ 4e^- \rightarrow 4\,OH^-\,(aq)$ **(Eq. 24)**

overall reaction: $2\,H_2\,(g)\ +\ O_2\,(g) \rightarrow 2\,H_2O\,(l)$ **(Eq. 25)**

The net reaction in this fuel cell is simply the oxidation of H_2 to produce water. A stream of hydrogen flows into the anode compartment of the cell, where it is oxidized. A stream of oxygen is directed into the cathode compartment, where it is reduced. The cell contains concentrated KOH, which supplies OH^- ions that participate in the electrode reactions.

A hydrogen-oxygen fuel cell supplies all the electrical needs of the space shuttle. On a 7-day mission, the shuttle consumes

Figure 21–16   Apollo 13 *was launched on a journey to the moon on April 11, 1970. Unfortunately, the landing never took place. Only two days into the trip, an oxygen tank supplying the ship's fuel cells exploded. With power from their fuel cells dwindling, the astronauts were forced to do some creative problem solving to get back to Earth safely!*

What hazard is posed by the improper disposal of batteries?

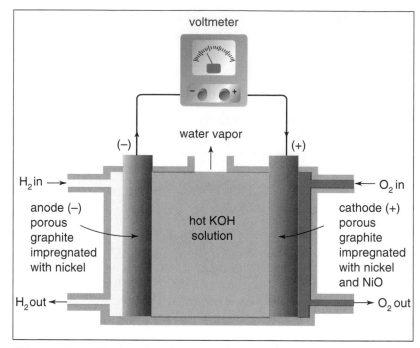

Figure 21–17 *Fuel cells provide an efficient method to convert chemical energy into electrical energy. What is the efficiency of typical fuel cells?*

over 700 kilograms of hydrogen and generates over 700 liters of water, which is subsequently used for drinking. A power plant in New York City uses hydrogen-oxygen fuel cells to quickly provide the extra electrical power needed when power demands suddenly peak.

21–3 Section Review

1. What is the difference between rechargeable and nonrechargeable batteries?
2. Describe the reactions that occur in the common dry cell and the alkaline dry cell. How do the two types of cells differ?
3. Explain how a lead storage battery operates. How is it made rechargeable?
4. Compare a fuel cell with other voltaic cells.
5. **Connection—Environmental Science** Discuss the environmental impact of the use of metals such as lead and cadmium in the consumer products of today's society.

21–4 Electrolytic Cells

The previous section discussed various examples of spontaneous redox reactions that were a source of electrical energy. In this section you will learn about the reverse process—one in which electrical energy is applied to cause nonspontaneous redox reactions to occur. **The process by which electricity in an electrolytic cell is used to bring about a nonspontaneous chemical change is called electrolysis.** An electrolytic cell consists of a source of direct electrical current that is connected to the electrodes, which are immersed in the reactants. Inert electrodes are often used because they do not participate in the redox reactions themselves, but merely serve as surfaces on which the redox reactions take place. As in a voltaic cell, electrons flow from the anode, which is the site of oxidation, to the cathode, which is the site of reduction. However, the electrons are "pushed" through the circuit by the external source of electrical energy.

There are a number of important applications of electrolysis reactions, including preparation of active metals like sodium and aluminum, purification of metals, and electroplating. The reactions that occur during the charging of rechargeable batteries such as a lead storage battery or a nickel-cadmium battery are also electrolysis reactions.

Electrolysis of Molten Sodium Chloride

The decomposition of molten sodium chloride into sodium and chlorine is a simple example of a nonspontaneous reaction that can be accomplished by electrolysis. First the NaCl is heated above its melting point (801°C). In the molten state, the Na^+ and Cl^- ions of NaCl are mobile. The external source of electricity pushes electrons into the cathode. The Na^+ ions pick up electrons at this electron-rich electrode and are reduced. At the same time, the external source of electricity pulls electrons from the anode. The Cl^- ions lose electrons when they collide with this electron-deficient electrode. Thus, the half reactions and overall reaction are as follows:

oxidation: $2\,Cl^-\,(l) \rightarrow Cl_2\,(g) + 2e^-$ **(Eq. 26)**

reduction: $2\,Na^+\,(l) + 2e^- \rightarrow 2\,Na\,(l)$ **(Eq. 27)**

overall reaction: $2\,NaCl\,(l) \rightarrow 2\,Na\,(l) + Cl_2\,(g)$ **(Eq. 28)**

The electrolysis of molten NaCl is the most practical means for obtaining metallic Na. The use of chemical reducing agents is impractical because of sodium's extremely high reactivity. The electrolytic cell in which NaCl is electrolyzed commercially is called the Down's cell and is shown in Figure 21–18. The design

Guide for Reading
- What is electrolysis?
- What are some applications of electrolysis?

CHEMISTRY IN ACTION

CONSUMER TIP

A Jump Start

During the charging of an automobile battery, some H^+ ions in the battery acid are converted to H_2 gas and a little water is converted to O_2 gas. As a result, a mixture of hydrogen and oxygen gases forms at the top of the battery. If an electrical spark occurs, it will ignite the mixture, which can cause the battery to explode. So, if you ever use jumper cables to start a car, be sure to follow the directions carefully. By connecting and disconnecting the cables in the proper order, you can avoid sparks and start your car safely.

Figure 21–18 *Molten sodium chloride electrolyzed in a commercial Down's cell yields Na (l) and Cl₂ (g). Why must the NaCl be molten?*

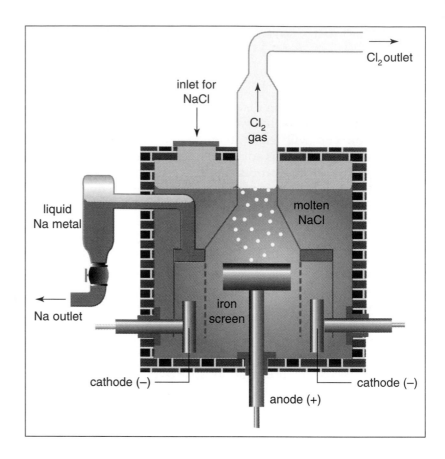

allows for NaCl to be added to the cell as necessary. Notice that the Na and Cl_2 formed are kept well separated. Why do you think this is done?

Electrolysis of Water

When inert electrodes are placed in water and the electrodes are connected to an electric power supply, the water is slowly electrolyzed, forming H_2 at the anode and O_2 at the cathode. Adding a small amount of an electrolyte such as Na_2SO_4 or H_2SO_4 to the water increases the current flow through the solution and increases the rate of the electrolysis reaction. If an acid-base indicator is added to the solution, the formation of OH^- ions is detected around the cathode and the formation of H^+ ions is detected around the anode. The half reactions and overall cell reaction are

oxidation: $2\,H_2O\,(l) \rightarrow 4\,H^+\,(aq) + O_2\,(g) + 4e^-$ **(Eq. 29)**

reduction: $4\,H_2O\,(l) + 4e^- \rightarrow 2\,H_2\,(g) + 4\,OH^-\,(aq)$ **(Eq. 30)**

overall reaction: $6\,H_2O\,(l) \rightarrow 2\,H_2\,(g) + O_2\,(g) + 4\,H^+\,(aq) +$

$4\,OH^-\,(aq)$ **(Eq. 31)**

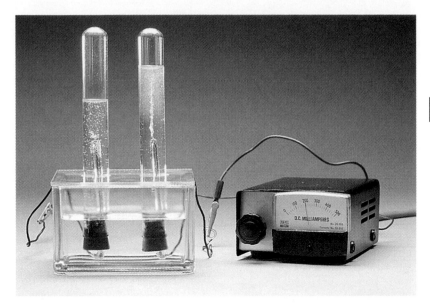

Figure 21–19 *Electrical energy passed through water by means of two inert electrodes decomposes water into the elements hydrogen and oxygen. Which test tube contains hydrogen gas and which contains oxygen gas? How can you tell?*

The OH^- ions and H^+ ions migrate through the solution and neutralize each other, forming H_2O:

$$4\,H^+\,(aq) + 4\,OH^-\,(aq) \rightarrow 4\,H_2O\,(l) \qquad \textbf{(Eq. 32)}$$

Thus, eliminating 4 H^+ and 4 OH^- from the reactants and 4 H_2O from the products of the overall cell reaction gives the net reaction for the electrolysis process:

$$2\,H_2O\,(l) \rightarrow 2\,H_2\,(g) + O_2\,(g) \qquad \textbf{(Eq. 33)}$$

The electrolysis of water is not a commercially important source of either O_2 or H_2. Oxygen can be obtained much less expensively from air. Hydrogen can be obtained chemically from hydrocarbons as well as by electrolysis of aqueous salt solutions. The main source of very pure H_2 is the electrolysis of concentrated aqueous NaCl solutions, known as brine.

Electrolysis of Aqueous Sodium Chloride

An aqueous solution of NaCl contains Na^+ and Cl^- ions along with H_2O molecules. When a moderately concentrated aqueous solution of NaCl is electrolyzed using inert electrodes, chlorine gas forms at the anode and hydrogen gas forms at the cathode. It is apparent that Cl^- is oxidized to Cl_2, and that H_2O must be the source of H_2. Why do you think sodium ions were not reduced as was the case in the electrolysis of molten sodium chloride? The half reactions and overall reaction for this electrolysis are

Figure 21-20 *Electrolysis of saturated salt solutions is at the center of the chloralkali industry. What are the products of this industry?*

oxidation: $2\,Cl^-\,(l) \rightarrow Cl_2\,(g) + 2e^-$ **(Eq. 34)**

reduction: $2\,H_2O\,(l) + 2e^- \rightarrow H_2\,(g) + 2\,OH^-\,(aq)$ **(Eq. 35)**

overall reaction: $2\,Cl^-\,(aq) + 2\,H_2O\,(l) \rightarrow Cl_2\,(g) + H_2\,(g)$
$$+ 2\,OH^-\,(aq) \quad \textbf{(Eq. 36)}$$

The spectator ion, Na^+, is present in association with reactant Cl^- and with product OH^-.

$2\,NaCl\,(aq) + 2\,H_2O\,(l) \rightarrow Cl_2\,(g) + H_2\,(g) + 2\,NaOH\,(aq)$

(Eq. 37)

The electrolysis of brine is commercially important. It is the primary way in which hydrogen, chlorine, and sodium hydroxide are produced industrially. This electrolysis is much less expensive than the electrolysis of molten NaCl because it is not necessary to heat the solution to 801°C.

Electroplating

The use of electrolysis to deposit a thin coating of metal on an object is called **electroplating.** The thin coating protects the metal underneath from corrosion and is often decorative as well. For example, table utensils may be plated with silver, and jewelry is often plated with gold or silver. A "tin" can is actually a steel can with a thin coating of tin.

In order to electroplate an object, the object is made the cathode of an electrolytic cell, as shown in Figure 21–21. The plating metal constitutes the anode of the cell. For example, to put a coat of silver on a spoon, the spoon is made the cathode

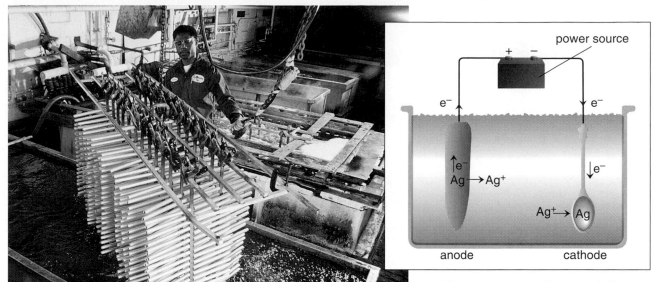

Figure 21-21 *By carefully controlling the voltage applied, a thin coating of a metal can be deposited onto an object such as a spoon or the rods in the photograph. What are some commonly used electroplating metals?*

and a bar of silver is made the anode in an electrolytic cell. When a power source is turned on, silver is oxidized at the anode:

oxidation: $Ag \ (s) \rightarrow Ag^+ \ (aq) \ + \ e^-$ **(Eq. 38)**

The resulting silver ions then migrate through the solution to the cathode where they are reduced, forming a silver plate on the spoon.

reduction: $Ag^+ \ (aq) \ + \ e^- \rightarrow Ag \ (s)$ **(Eq. 39)**

During this process, the voltage applied to the cell is controlled at a value low enough to prevent the oxidation or reduction of water at the electrodes.

21–4 Section Review

1. Explain what is meant by electrolysis and describe how it takes place in an electrolytic cell.

2. How does the electrolysis of molten sodium chloride differ from the electrolysis of aqueous sodium chloride? Why?

3. Describe the electrolysis of water. Why is some sulfuric acid added to the water?

4. **Critical Thinking—Applying concepts**   If you carry out the electrolysis of pure water, the electrolysis proceeds very slowly, producing oxygen at the anode. If you add a moderate amount of table salt to the solution, the electrolysis proceeds much faster and produces chlorine at the anode. Explain how the increased rate and the production of a different product are related to each other.

Experimenting With Voltaic Cells

Problem

How can you construct and compare voltaic cells?

Suggested Materials (per group)

voltmeter
4 plastic drinking cups
strips of the following metals:
   magnesium
   copper
   zinc
   lead
   aluminum
   iron
5 wire leads with alligator clips
electrolyte solutions:
   sports drink
   club soda
   cola
   salt water solution

Suggested Procedure

1. Devise an experiment to construct and compare several voltaic cells.
2. Write down the steps of your experimental procedure. The drawing may provide you with some help in writing your procedure. Try to make at least four different cells using different combinations of metals and electrolytes.

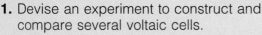
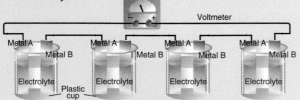

3. Prepare a data table similar to the one shown to record your data.
4. Conduct your experiment after having your teacher approve your procedure and data table.
5. From your data, determine the voltaic cell with the highest voltage.

Observations

Cell Number	Metal A	Metal B	Electrolyte	Voltmeter Reading
1				
2				
3				
4				
5				

Analysis and Conclusions

1. What metal combinations produced the highest voltage? The lowest voltage?
2. Use a table of reduction potentials as a reference. For each cell that you constructed, do you notice any relationship between relative locations of the two metals in the table and the voltmeter reading?
3. For each cell that you constructed, use the table of reduction potentials to write the two half reactions and calculate the cell potential. How do your voltmeter readings compare to this value? Give reasons for the differences.
4. Write the net ionic equation for each of your cells.
5. Identify the anode and cathode for each battery.
6. Compare your data with that of others in your class. Identify the metal combination that produces the highest voltage. What electrolyte worked the best?
7. Describe what takes place at the electrodes and in the electrolyte in a voltaic cell.
8. Predict which would make a better cell—one with copper and zinc electrodes or one with copper and iron? Explain your answers.
9. **On Your Own** Test these two cells. Do your results support your predictions?

STUDY GUIDE

Summarizing Key Concepts

21–1 Electrochemical Cells

- Devices in which redox reactions produce or use electricity are called electrochemical cells.
- Spontaneous redox reactions produce electricity in voltaic cells. External electrical energy drives nonspontaneous redox reactions in electrolytic cells.

21–2 Voltaic Cells

- A voltaic cell consists of an anode, where oxidation takes place, and a cathode, where reduction takes place.
- A voltaic cell's potential is the sum of the oxidation and reduction electrode potentials.
- Standard electrode potentials represent the tendency of that half reaction to occur and are based on a comparison with the standard hydrogen electrode potential of 0.00 V.

21–3 Common Batteries

- A dry cell is a voltaic cell in which the electrolyte is a paste.

- The alkaline dry cell lasts longer than a common dry cell and maintains a steady voltage of 1.5 V due to a modified redox reaction.
- The lead storage battery and the nickel-cadmium battery are examples of rechargeable voltaic cells.
- A fuel cell is a voltaic cell in which a continuous fuel supply reacts to generate electricity.

21–4 Electrolytic Cells

- Electrolytic cells use electricity to drive nonspontaneous redox reactions such as the production of active metals from their compounds and the recharging of discharged batteries.
- The electrolysis of molten sodium chloride produces the elements sodium and chlorine, while the electrolysis of aqueous sodium chloride produces hydrogen, chlorine, and sodium hydroxide.
- Electroplating is the depositing of a thin coating of a metal on an object by the application of an electric current.

Reviewing Key Terms

Define each term in a complete sentence.

21–1 Electrochemical Cells

electrochemical cell
electrode
voltaic cell
electrolytic cell

21–2 Voltaic Cells

half-cell
anode
cathode
salt bridge
cell potential
cell voltage
electrode potential
reduction potential
oxidation potential

21–4 Electrolytic Cells

electroplating

CHAPTER REVIEW

Content Review

Multiple Choice

Choose the letter of the answer that best completes each statement.

1. The process by which electricity is used to bring about a chemical change is called
   (a) corrosion.   (c) electrolysis.
   (b) voltage.   (d) oxidation.

2. In a chemical cell composed of two half-cells, ions are allowed to flow from one half-cell to the other by means of
   (a) electrodes.   (c) a voltmeter.
   (b) a wire.   (d) a salt bridge.

3. According to the table of standard reduction potentials, which of the following metals is most easily oxidized?
   (a) Cu   (c) Ba
   (b) Ag   (d) Sn

4. Which is the most readily reduced?
   (a) $Ag^+ + e^- \rightarrow Ag\,(s)$ $E° =$ 0.80 V
   (b) $Cl_2\,(g) + 2e^- \rightarrow 2\,Cl^-$ $E° =$ 1.36 V
   (c) $F_2\,(g) + 2e^- \rightarrow 2\,F^-$ $E° =$ 2.87 V
   (d) $Pb^{2+} + 2e^- \rightarrow Pb(s)$ $E° = -0.13$ V

5. The first battery was developed by
   (a) Galvani.   (c) Volta.
   (b) Franklin.   (d) Haber.

6. In the reaction for a nickel-cadmium battery, $2\,Ni(OH)_3 + Cd \rightarrow 2\,Ni(OH)_2 + Cd(OH)_2$, which species is oxidized during the discharge of the battery?
   (a) Ni^{3+} (c) Cd
   (b) Ni^{2+} (d) Cd^{2+}

7. According to Figure 21–11, which is the strongest reducing agent?
   (a) Li (s)   (c) $F_2\,(g)$
   (b) Na (s)   (d) $Br_2\,(l)$

8. Which of the following is not produced by the electrolysis of aqueous NaCl?
   (a) Na   (c) NaOH
   (b) Cl_2 (d) H_2

9. In a voltaic cell, reduction occurs at the
   (a) anode.   (c) salt bridge.
   (b) electrolyte.   (d) cathode.

True or False

If the statement is true, write "true." If it is false, change the underlined word or words to make the statement true.

10. Oxidation always occurs at the <u>cathode</u>.
11. A <u>voltmeter</u> allows ions to move between half-cells.
12. The lead storage battery is an example of a <u>rechargeable</u> battery.
13. A <u>half-cell</u> is the part of an electrochemical cell in which oxidation or reduction occurs.
14. The process by which an electric current is used to deposit a layer of metal on an object is known as <u>corrosion</u>.
15. A voltaic cell in which the electrolyte is a paste is called a <u>wet cell</u>.
16. An electrochemical cell that uses electrical energy to drive nonspontaneous redox reactions is called a <u>voltaic cell</u>.
17. In the electrolysis of water, hydrogen gas forms at the <u>cathode</u>.

Concept Mapping

Complete the following concept map for Section 21–1. Refer to pages xviii–xix to construct a concept map for the entire chapter.

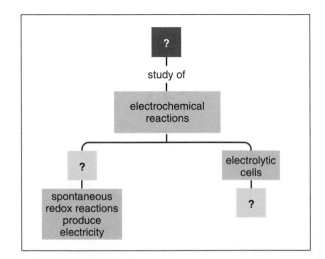

Concept Mastery

Discuss each of the following in a brief paragraph.

18. What is the difference between a voltaic cell and an electrolytic cell?

19. The mercury battery, a kind of voltaic cell used to make miniature batteries for hearing aids and electric watches, uses the following half reactions to generate energy:

$$HgO\ (s) + H_2O\ (l) + 2e^- \rightarrow$$
$$Hg\ (l) + 2\,OH^-\ (aq)$$

$$Zn\ (s) + 2\,OH^-\ (aq) \rightarrow$$
$$Zn(OH)_2\ (s) + 2e^-$$

Which half reaction occurs at the anode and which occurs at the cathode? What is the overall cell reaction?

20. Given a table of standard electrode potentials, how do you determine (a) the standard reduction potential for a given half-cell? (b) the standard oxidation potential for a given half-cell? (c) the voltage for the voltaic cell?

21. Describe the composition of the anode, the cathode, and the electrolyte in a lead storage battery.

22. A student makes a voltaic cell that is based on the following spontaneous redox reaction between magnesium and chromium:

$$3\,Mg\ (s) + 2\,Cr^{3+}\ (aq) \rightarrow$$
$$3\,Mg^{2+}\ (aq) + 2\,Cr\ (s)$$

(a) Sketch the cell, label all components, and indicate direction of electron flow. (b) Write the two half-cell reactions. (c) Calculate the standard cell potential for the voltaic cell.

23. Describe the operation of a hydrogen-oxygen fuel cell.

24. Tying it Together Explain how the table of standard reduction potentials can yield information about the *energy* input or output of a redox reaction.

Critical Thinking and Problem Solving

Use the skills you have developed in this chapter to answer each of the following.

25. Applying concepts What, if anything, would you expect to observe if you put (a) a strip of silver in a solution of magnesium sulfate? (b) a strip of magnesium in a solution of silver nitrate? Explain.

26. Making comparisons (a) Which of the following has the greater tendency to lose an electron, Zn or Cl^-? (b) Which of the following is the stronger oxidizing agent, H^+ or I_2? (c) Which of the following is the stronger reducing agent, Li or F_2?

27. Applying concepts What voltage would you expect to obtain from the following voltaic cells? (a) One whose electrodes are lead and silver in contact with 1.0 M solutions of their cations. (b) One containing an iron electrode in contact with 1.0 M $Fe(NO_3)_2$ and a magnesium electrode in contact with 1.0 M $MgCl_2$.

28. Using the writing process Describe in your own words how you would set up an electrolytic cell to deposit copper onto a pair of baby shoes.

FROM SCHOOL TO WORK

Miwa Linehan—Student

Until Miwa Linehan of Littleton, Colorado, took a chemistry course, she did not know that the sciences could be highly mathematical subjects. "I have always been very good at math. So when I took chemistry, I was happy to find new ways to put my analytical skills to use." Miwa remembers one particular lab in which she was given an unknown chemical and asked to figure out what it was. "You had to conduct different tests on your unknown and compare the results with those for known chemicals. It was like a big puzzle. To solve it, you had to draw upon quantitative skills, observational skills, and analytical skills. It felt great when I finally figured it out."

Miwa hopes to learn more chemistry in college, where she plans to study electrical engineering. "Chemistry changes the way you look at the world. Waiting for water to boil while camping in the mountains is more interesting than before. Soap isn't just soap anymore."

Photographer

Professional photographers fall into two categories: freelance and staff. Photographers are employed by the media (newspapers, magazines, television), stock houses (photographic rental libraries), museums, and photo studios. Many corporations, industries, and even some hospitals also employ staff photographers. After gaining experience as a staff photographer, many photographers choose to pursue a freelance career.

Experience as a staff photographer for a high-school yearbook or campus newspaper, a summer or part-time job in a camera shop, processing lab, or photo studio, or work as a photographer's apprentice all provide a good background for a career in photography. You should also assemble both a black-and-white and a color portfolio.

To receive additional information write to the American Society of Magazine Photographers, 419 Park Avenue South, New York, NY 10016.

How to Write a Cover Letter

When you contact an employer through the mail, you should write a cover letter to introduce yourself. You must realize that the person receiving your letter probably reads many letters like yours every day. Therefore, your cover letter must be impressive, organized, and brief. Your letter must be an original, not a copy, typed without errors.

It is best to begin your letter with a statement explaining the kind of position you are seeking. The second paragraph is usually used to sum up your qualifications for the position. The third paragraph is used to close the letter and ask for an interview at a convenient time.

H. Eugene LeMay, Jr.

From the Author

As I finished the last chapter, I was reminded of a time not too long ago when a friend asked me how an alkaline battery worked. To be honest, I didn't know, so I started looking for information in the library. At the same time, I took one of these batteries into my garage and cut it in half with a saw. Through these two kinds of efforts, I was able to gain a good understanding of the construction and operation of the battery.

I recount this story to you because I want you to know that there is much about chemistry that I don't know. I have a good education, but getting an education doesn't mean that you merely stuff your brain full of facts. Don't get me wrong—there's nothing wrong with facts. It is important to learn facts, but that is not the ultimate goal. The goal of education is to teach us how to learn—to help us develop self-discipline, motivation, curiosity, problem-solving skills, and a general awareness of what is known and what is yet unknown. Learning is a life-long endeavor. Education is a journey—not a destination.

I also want you to be aware of the fact that the borders of chemistry are constantly expanding, with new discoveries being made every day. Honestly, I have a hard time trying to keep up with even the parts of it that are most interesting to me. The many concepts and facts in this book are a testimony to how far we have come in our understanding of chemistry. Still, many important problems remain to be solved. Maybe you will be the one to solve some of them.

UNIT REVIEW

Concept Mastery

Discuss each of the following in a brief paragraph.

1. Considering oxidation in terms of electron transfer, explain why substances that combine with oxygen are oxidized.

2. Using the electron configuration of nitrogen, explain why the maximum positive oxidation number of this element is $+5$ and its minimum oxidation number is -3.

3. Explain how oxidation numbers can be used to identify the oxidizing agent in a redox equation.

4. Explain why Na^+ cannot be oxidized.

5. Explain why Cl^- cannot be reduced.

6. Sketch the standard hydrogen electrode and explain how it is used to determine reduction potentials.

7. Briefly describe how you would determine the standard reduction potential of Ag^+.

8. (a) Where in a table of standard reduction potentials are the best oxidizing agents found: top left, top right, bottom left, or bottom right? (b) Where are the best reducing agents found?

9. (a) How does the oxidation number of oxygen in a peroxide differ from that in a normal oxide? (b) Which of the following compounds are peroxides: K_2O_2, BaO, Al_2O_3, CaO_2?

10. In a voltaic cell, what charge is assigned to the anode? What kind of reaction occurs at the anode?

11. (a) What metal makes up the outer casing of a common flashlight battery? (b) What is the function of that metal? (c) What element is used for the central electrode in the battery? (d) What compounds other than water make up the bulk of the battery's interior?

12. What advantages does the alkaline dry cell have over the ordinary dry cell? What disadvantages does it have?

13. How do fuel cells differ from ordinary batteries?

14. What happens to the electrical energy consumed in the electrolysis of an aqueous solution of NaCl? Could we get this energy back? How?

15. When a lead storage battery is discharged, the electrolyte in the cells has a lower density than that in fully charged cells. The difference is due to the consumption of the dense sulfuric acid in the cells during discharge. Could a discharged battery be recharged by replacing the electrolyte with sulfuric acid? Explain.

Problem Bank

16. Assign oxidation numbers to every atom in each of the following: (a) H_2CO_3 (b) $FeCl_2$ (c) $PbSO_4$ (d) Cr_2S_3.

17. Which of the following reactions are redox reactions?

   (a) $N_2O_5 (g) + H_2O (l) \rightarrow 2\ HNO_3 (aq)$

   (b) $4\ NH_3 (g) + 5\ O_2 (g) \rightarrow 4\ NO (g) + 6\ H_2O (g)$

   (c) $NaOH (aq) + HCl (aq) \rightarrow NaCl (aq) + H_2O (l)$

   (d) $ClO^- (aq) + I_2 (s) \rightarrow Cl^- (aq) + IO_3^- (aq)$

18. What are the oxidation numbers of H and O in water? Which element in the compound H_2O can undergo oxidation? Write a balanced half reaction for the oxidation of water.

19. Balance each of the following equations:

   (a) $Cr(OH)_2 (s) \rightarrow Cr_2O_3 (s) + H_2 (g) + H_2O (l)$

   (b) $H_2S (g) + SO_2 (g) \rightarrow S (s) + H_2O (l)$

   (c) $BrO_3^- (aq) + HAsO_3^{2-} (aq) + H^+ (aq) \rightarrow Br^- (aq) + H_3AsO_4 (aq)$

20. Identify the oxidizing agent and the reducing agent in each equation in item 19.

21. When solid KI reacts with concentrated sulfuric acid, the products are I_2, H_2S, K_2SO_4, and H_2O. (a) Write a balanced equation for this reaction. (b) How many grams of H_2S are produced when 5.00 g of KI reacts with sulfuric acid?

22. (a) Sketch a voltaic cell based on the following reaction: $Mg\ (s)\ +\ Cu^{2+}\ (aq)\ \rightarrow$ $Mg^{2+}\ (aq)\ +\ Cu\ (s)$. (b) Label the anode and the cathode in your cell. (c) Indicate the direction of electron flow through the external circuit. (d) What is the voltage of the cell when operated under standard conditions?

23. A nickel rod in a 1.00 M $NiSO_4$ solution is connected to a copper rod in a 1.00 M $CuSO_4$ solution in order to generate electricity. (a) Which electrode serves as the cathode? (b) Write half reactions to show what happens at each electrode. (c) Which electrode serves as the negative terminal of the cell? (d) Indicate the direction of electron flow through the external circuit. (e) What is the standard potential of the cell?

24. Using the information in Figure 21–11, predict whether H^+ (aq) is capable of oxidizing Fe.

25. The Sn^{2+} ion has a higher (more positive) standard reduction potential than Mn^{2+}. (a) Which ion is more easily reduced to the metal? (b) Which metal is more easily oxidized?

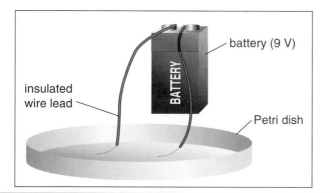

insulated wire lead

battery (9 V)

BATTERY

Petri dish

Performance-Based Task

How Does Electricity Cause a Chemical Reaction?

Oxidation-reduction, or redox, reactions occur when one substance loses electrons while another substance gains electrons. How can a battery be used to cause a redox reaction? Design an experiment to answer this question. You can use two indicators to identify the products of the redox reaction. Phenolphthalein turns from colorless to blue in the presence of a base. Starch solution turns blue-black in the presence of iodine.

1. Set up the equipment as shown in the diagram. Add equal parts of 0.1 M potassium iodide solution and starch solution to the Petri dish to just cover the bottom. Add 3 to 4 drops of phenolphthalein solution and stir. Record the color of the solution.
2. Attach wire leads to the battery as shown in the diagram. Leave about 1 cm of wire exposed at the end of each lead.
3. Predict what will happen if you put the wire leads into the solution one at a time. Predict what will happen if you put both wire leads into the solution at the same time. Now test your predictions. Record your observations.
4. Did the results of your experiment support your predictions? Write the oxidation half reaction, the reduction half reaction, and the complete balanced equation for the reaction. Indicate which product was formed at each wire lead. Was the reaction spontaneous or nonspontaneous? Explain.

Going Further

5. Predict what would happen if the wire leads were kept in the solution for an extended period of time. Explain.
6. In this experiment, the reaction required an input of energy. This means that the reverse reaction should release energy. Design a battery that would use the reverse reaction.

9 Kinetics and Thermodynamics

Sirens wailing, fire trucks speed to the scene of an early morning blaze. Firefighters know that a delay of a few minutes—or even seconds—can result in a fire raging out of control. Burning is a special type of chemical reaction called a combustion reaction. The swiftly moving flames of a combustion reaction are capable of spreading quickly and burning a building to the ground in a matter of minutes. But some combustion reactions, such as the gradual decomposition of a dead log on a forest floor, take place at a slow, steady rate. What conditions determine if a chemical reaction will proceed quickly, slowly, or not at all? You will learn the answer in this unit.

The chapters that follow deal with the topics of kinetics and thermodynamics. You should be at least partially familiar with these terms already. Together, kinetics and thermodynamics describe the rate at which a chemical reaction occurs, as well as the energy changes that accompany a chemical reaction.

DISCOVERY LEARNING

1. Fill two clear plastic cups with water.

2. Crush an antacid tablet into a fine powder.

3. Pour the powdered tablet into one of the cups. At the same time, drop a whole tablet into the second cup.

4. Observe the reaction between the antacid and water in each cup.

   - In which cup was the reaction rate faster? How can you tell?

   - How can you explain your observations?

Rates of Reaction

An explosion is a chemical reaction that gives off a tremendous amount of heat and produces a large volume of gas. One of the most important characteristics of an explosive reaction is its speed. Imagine the same reaction occurring over the course of an hour. Such a slow reaction certainly would not raze a building or fracture a rock ledge. In order to produce the necessary shock, the whole reaction has to take place in a fraction of a second.

The rate at which any reaction proceeds is an important characteristic of that reaction. In this chapter you will discover how to measure the rate of a chemical reaction and how that rate depends on activities at the molecular level.

A quick blast and this stunt van is consumed in flames. The chemical reaction that caused this explosion was almost instantaneous. Equally significant but slower reactions take place within the body of this adorable bobcat kitten.

Chem Journal

YOU AND YOUR WORLD
Think about some of the chemical reactions you encounter every day. Write a fictional story about a day in which those chemical reactions suddenly proceed at different speeds. For example, it might take hours for an egg to cook or minutes for your bicycle to rust. Be sure to consider the wide variety of chemical reactions that affect your life.

22–1 Chemical Kinetics

Guide for Reading
- How is the rate of a reaction described?
- What are reaction mechanisms and how do they differ from chemical equations?
- What is a rate law?

You return to your locker only to find the sandwich you left in there yesterday reeking of spoiled mayonnaise. What happened? After all, you have left sandwiches in the refrigerator at home for longer periods of time without any problems. The spoiling of food involves chemical reactions. The question is why does this reaction proceed slowly in the refrigerator yet rapidly in a warm locker? The speed with which chemical reactions occur depends on the external conditions. Just as it is important to know which substances are formed from a given set of reactants, it is equally important to know how rapidly chemical reactions occur and to understand the factors that control their speeds. Knowing the speed of some chemical reactions—the spoiling of food, the rusting of steel, the setting of dental fillings, and the burning of fuel, for example—is important. The area of chemistry concerned with the speed at which reactions occur is called **chemical kinetics.**

Figure 22–1   Oxygen and ozone in the air react with rubber tires, making them dry and brittle. Fortunately, these chemical reactions occur so slowly that the tires usually become worn from use and are replaced before they become dangerously damaged. Why is the speed of this reaction important?

Figure 22–2 *Racers strain to cover just a few more meters to the finish line in this exciting race. This racer's rate is measured by the distance from the starting line to the finish line divided by the time it took her to finish. How else could her rate be measured?*

Reaction Rates

The speed, or rate, of any event is measured by the amount of change that occurs in a given interval of time. A car, for example, might travel at a rate of 60 kilometers per hour and a dolphin might swim at a rate of 4 meters per second. But rates do not relate to changes in distance only. Almost any event can be described by a rate. The rate at which you read a book might be 1 page per minute, the population in a particular town might grow at a rate of 50 people per year, and the rate at which a shop repairs bicycles might be 9 bicycles per week.

If a rate measures a change over time, by what, then, do you measure the rate at which a chemical reaction takes place? To answer this question, you must stop a moment and consider what occurs during a chemical reaction. During a chemical reaction, reactants are changed into products. As you might expect, such changes do not occur instantaneously. Instead, chemical reactions occur over some time interval. That time interval might be as long as the hundreds of years it takes some hazardous wastes to decompose or as brief as the seconds during which an explosion occurs. Nonetheless, the chemical changes in a chemical reaction do not occur all at once. Throughout the time during which a chemical reaction is occurring, some portion of reactants is being changed into products. At any time during the reaction, some amount of reactants exists and some amount of products exists. Only after the reaction is complete are all the reactants converted into products.

It makes sense, then, to measure the rate of a chemical reaction, or the **reaction rate,** as the rate at which reactants disappear and products appear. The amount of reactants and products is better described as the concentration of reactants and products. Recall that concentration is the quantity of a substance in a given volume. **The reaction rate is the change in concentration of reactants and products in a certain amount of time.** Because concentration is expressed by molarity, the unit used to measure reaction rates is usually molarity per second (M/s).

Unlike the amounts of substances you calculated stoichiometrically, the rate of a reaction cannot be calculated from the balanced chemical equation. Instead, it must be determined experimentally. The rate of reaction can be found by measuring the concentration of a reactant or product at various times throughout the reaction. For example, consider the reaction that occurs when nitrogen dioxide decomposes into nitrogen monoxide and oxygen.

$$2\ NO_2 \rightarrow 2\ NO + O_2 \qquad \textbf{(Eq. 1)}$$

Suppose a chemist begins with 0.1000 M of NO_2 and measures the concentration every 5 seconds. Figure 22–3 shows the recorded data. In this case, the average rate of reaction is equal to the decrease in the concentration of NO_2 divided by the time in which that change occurs.

average rate of reaction

$$= \frac{\text{concentration of } NO_2 \text{ at } t_1 - \text{concentration of } NO_2 \text{ at } t_2}{t_2 - t_1}$$

(Eq. 2)

The initial time at which the concentration is measured is t_1 and the final time is t_2. Because the concentration of reactants decreases with time, subtracting $[NO_2]$ at t_1 from $[NO_2]$ at t_2 would produce a negative number. For this reason, $[NO_2]$ at t_2 is subtracted from $[NO_2]$ at t_1 to make the rate positive.

Determining the reaction rate is not limited to measuring the concentration of reactants, however. It can be determined by measuring changes in products as well. For example, because NO is a product of the reaction, its concentration increases with time and can also be used to determine the reaction rate. Thus the reaction rate equation could also be

average rate of reaction

$$= \frac{\text{concentration of } NO \text{ at } t_2 - \text{concentration of } NO \text{ at } t_1}{t_2 - t_1}$$

(Eq. 3)

This equation would yield a positive number because the product is gradually appearing. What other equations could be used to describe the rate of this reaction?

The general rate equation for any chemical reaction can be written in a similar fashion:

$$\text{average rate of reaction} = \frac{\text{change in concentration}}{\text{change in time}}$$

(Eq. 4)

The Greek letter delta (Δ), which means "change in," is often used to denote change. Square brackets are used to denote concentration. Thus the rate equation can be rewritten as

$$\text{average rate of reaction} = \frac{\Delta[\text{reactant or product}]}{\Delta\text{time}}$$

(Eq. 5)

Any time you see a capital Greek delta, Δ, before a quantity it almost always means "change in" that quantity. The change in a quantity is calculated as (its value at the end $-$ its value at the beginning). For example, suppose the odometer of your car reads 42,305 miles at the beginning of a trip and 43,122 miles at the end. If you let the odometer reading (mileage) equal m, the distance you drove is equal to $\Delta m = (m_{end} - m_{beginning}) = 43,122$ miles $-$ 42,305 miles $=$ 817 miles. Note that if a quantity decreases in value, the change in the quantity is negative. Suppose you start the week with \$392 in your savings account and a week later you have \$210 in the account. The change in the value of your account is $\Delta d = (d_{end} - d_{beginning}) = $210 - $392 = -$182$.

Time (s)	$[NO_2]$ (M)	Average Rate (M/s)
0	0.040	1.8×10^{-3}
5.0	0.031	1.2×10^{-3}
10.0	0.025	8.0×10^{-4}
15.0	0.021	6.0×10^{-4}
20.0	0.018	

Figure 22–3 The table shows how the concentration of the reactant NO_2 changes with time. The speed at which NO_2 disappears is the rate of the reaction. How is the rate calculated from the data?

Reaction rates usually change throughout a chemical reaction. For this reason, the time interval between the two measurements must be small and the rate found is an average. A reaction rate for any particular point during a reaction can be determined using mathematical calculations that are unnecessary for this discussion.

Reaction Mechanisms

In order to understand why the reaction rate cannot be determined from the balanced chemical equation, it is essential to understand what actually occurs during a chemical reaction. Although a balanced equation indicates the substances present at the beginning and end of a chemical reaction, it does not indicate the actual details of the reaction. The rearrangement of atoms that takes place during a chemical reaction is often a complicated process. Despite a relatively straightforward chemical equation, a chemical reaction does not necessarily occur in one step. More often, a chemical reaction occurs as the result of several steps made up of simple chemical reactions. **A series of steps that leads from reactants to products is called a reaction mechanism.** A detailed **reaction mechanism** describes the order in which bonds break and atoms rearrange throughout the course of a chemical reaction. Some reactions have very simple mechanisms, but others have multistep mechanisms that can be quite complex.

When you create a chemical reaction in the laboratory or even at home, you observe only the overall, or net, chemical change. For example, when you pour vinegar onto baking soda you see a foamy froth of bubbles. And when you make pancakes, you see a liquid batter become your breakfast. But you have no way to see what is happening at the molecular level. For some reactions, chemists have been able to devise experiments that reveal the sequence of steps in a reaction mechanism. Each individual reaction step, or **elementary step,** is usually a simple process.

Let's look at an example to make this concept a little clearer. Consider the following reaction:

$$2 \text{ NO } (g) \ + \ \text{F}_2 \ (g) \rightarrow 2 \text{ NOF } (g) \qquad \textbf{(Eq. 6)}$$

Although the reaction seems simple from the equation—2 molecules of NO react with 1 molecule of F_2—this is not the case. Chemists have found that rather than proceeding in one step, this reaction involves two elementary steps. In the first step, 1 molecule of NO reacts with 1 molecule of F_2 to produce NOF_2.

HF (aq) + CN$^-$ $(aq) \longrightarrow$
$\qquad\qquad$ F$^-$ (aq) + HCN (aq)

Rate of reaction
$\qquad$ = rate of decrease in [HF]
$\qquad$ = rate of decrease in [CN$^-$]
$\qquad$ = rate of increase in [F$^-$]
$\qquad$ = rate of increase in [HCN]

Figure 22–4 *This reaction can be described in terms of the disappearance of either of the reactants or the appearance of either of the products. Thus the number of ways of describing the rate of a reaction depends upon the number of reactants and products in the reaction.*

$$\text{Step 1:} \quad NO\ (g)\ +\ F_2\ (g) \rightarrow NOF_2\ (g) \quad \textbf{(Eq. 7)}$$

The product of this first step then becomes a reactant in the second elementary step. In the second step, NOF_2 reacts with the remaining molecule of NO.

$$\text{Step 2:} \quad NOF_2\ (g)\ +\ NO\ (g) \rightarrow 2\ NOF\ (g) \quad \textbf{(Eq. 8)}$$

If you write an equation that shows all the reactants and products from both the elementary steps, you will see that the sum of the two equations gives the general equation for the reaction.

$$NO\ (g)\ +\ F_2\ (g)\ +\ \cancel{NOF_2\ (g)}\ +\ NO\ (g) \rightarrow$$
$$\cancel{NOF_2\ (g)}\ +\ 2\ NOF\ (g) \quad \textbf{(Eq. 9)}$$

$$2\ NO\ (g)\ +\ F_2\ (g) \rightarrow 2\ NOF\ (g) \quad \textbf{(Eq. 10)}$$

The elementary steps in a multistep reaction mechanism must always add to give the chemical equation of the overall process. Notice that NOF_2 does not appear as either a reactant or product in the overall equation. This is because, although it is produced in the first elementary step, it is consumed in the second. Substances that are produced in one step of a reaction but consumed in a later step are called **intermediate products,** or intermediates. Multistep reaction mechanisms always involve one or more intermediate products.

Reaction mechanisms begin to explain why the rate of a chemical reaction must be found experimentally and cannot be determined from a chemical equation—a chemical equation does not indicate the elementary steps. Each elementary step proceeds at its own rate. One step might proceed quickly while another might proceed slowly. The rate of the overall reaction is limited by the rate of the slowest elementary step. For this reason, the slowest elementary step is called the **rate-determining step.** Thus the rate of the net reaction is dependent on the rates of the elementary steps, especially the rate-determining one.

Determining a reaction mechanism is often a difficult task requiring a great deal of skill, experience, and intuition. Simply proposing a mechanism that adds up to the net equation is not enough. Several mechanisms might be possible for a single reaction. Because it is, often easier to prove what does not happen than to determine exactly what does, chemists study reaction mechanisms by analyzing proposed mechanisms through experimentation. At this point in your study of chemistry, you might have jumped to the conclusion that because chemistry is so exact, the mechanisms for all reactions are already known. But this is not the case. Sometimes you need to remind yourself that science is not simply a set of facts. It is a changing body of knowledge that grows in response to simple questioning.

Figure 22–5 *Although the brilliant explosion of ammonium nitrate appears to be a straightforward reaction, it actually occurs through a number of elementary steps.*

Nitrogen dioxide and carbon monoxide gases react to form nitrogen monoxide and carbon dioxide. The equation that describes this reaction is $NO_2\ (g) + CO\ (g) \rightarrow NO\ (g) + CO_2\ (g)$. Experiments show that $NO_3\ (g)$ appears to be an intermediate product for this reaction. Propose a mechanism for this reaction.

STRATEGY	SOLUTION
1. Analyze	You are given the net equation as well as an intermediate product. You must use this information to determine a logical reaction mechanism.
2. Plan	The reaction cannot proceed by a one-step mechanism since there is an intermediate. The simplest mechanism that produces an intermediate product would be a two-step mechanism.
3. Solve	The first step will form the intermediate product from only NO_2 because there is no carbon atom in the intermediate product. In the second step, the intermediate product will react with CO to produce the final product.

Step 1:
$$NO_2\ (g) + NO_2\ (g) \rightarrow NO_3\ (g) + NO\ (g)$$

Step 2:
$$NO_3\ (g) + CO\ (g) \rightarrow NO_2\ (g) + CO_2\ (g)$$

4. Evaluate   When the two reactions are added together, the overall equation is left

$$NO_2(g) + \cancel{NO_2(g)} + \cancel{NO_3(g)} + CO(g) \rightarrow$$
$$\cancel{NO_3(g)} + NO\ (g) + \cancel{NO_2(g)} + CO_2\ (g)$$

PRACTICE PROBLEMS

1. Dinitrogen monoxide gas (N_2O) decomposes to nitrogen and oxygen gases. The intermediate product O (g) is believed to take part in the mechanism. Propose a two-step mechanism consistent with this intermediate product. *(Answer: Step 1: $N_2O\ (g) \rightarrow N_2\ (g) + O\ (g)$ Step 2: $N_2O\ (g) + O\ (g) \rightarrow N_2\ (g) + O_2\ (g)$)*

2. The decomposition of nitrogen dioxide into oxygen gas and nitrogen monoxide takes place without an intermediate product. Propose a mechanism for this reaction. *(Answer: One-step mechanism: $2\ NO_2 \rightarrow O_2\ (g) + 2\ NO\ (g)$)*

Rate Laws

The experimental data used to evaluate proposed reaction mechanisms depend upon the reaction rate and how that rate is influenced by changes in the concentration of the reactants. The effect of concentration on the rate of reaction is described using a **rate law.** A rate law is an equation that can be used to calculate the reaction rate for any given concentration of reactants. Recall that earlier you saw how the reaction rate was calculated from data for a particular concentration of a reactant or product. Those data were found by allowing a known concentration of reactant to take part in a reaction and then observing changes in that concentration (or the concentration of other substances in the reaction) throughout the reaction. The rate law, on the other hand, gives chemists a tool to determine the rate for different concentrations of reactants. The rate law can be determined by keeping the concentrations of all but one reactant constant while measuring the reaction rate for various concentrations of that reactant. The process is repeated for each reactant.

We can write the reaction rate as an equation. The rate equation is

$$\text{rate} = k[A]^x[B]^y \qquad \text{(Eq. 11)}$$

[A] and [B] represent the molar concentrations of reactants A and B in moles/liter (M). The exponents x and y are the powers of the concentrations of the reactants. In all cases, x and y must be determined experimentally. The proportionality constant, k, is called a rate constant, which has a fixed value for a reaction at a particular temperature. It, too, must be determined experimentally. The rate equation is not limited to only two reactants. The equation could be expanded to include all related reactants. How would the general rate law be written for a reaction involving reactants A, B, and C?

The actual form of the rate law varies from reaction to reaction. As an example, consider the reaction of nitrogen dioxide, which is released in automobile exhaust, with ozone (O_3) in the lower atmosphere.

$$NO_2\,(g) + O_3\,(g) \rightarrow NO_3\,(g) + O_2\,(g) \qquad \textbf{(Eq. 12)}$$

Experiments have shown that the rate law for this reaction is

$$\text{rate} = k[NO_2][O_3] \qquad \textbf{(Eq. 13)}$$

In this reaction, the rate is directly proportional to the concentrations of both NO_2 and O_3. Suppose the initial concentration of each reactant is 1.00 M. If the concentration of either reactant is doubled to 2.00 M, the rate increases by a factor of 2. Similarly, if the concentration of either reactant is multiplied by 5 to 5.00 M, the rate is increased by a factor of 5. By how much would the rate increase if the concentration of ozone is multiplied by 10?

The reaction between nitrogen monoxide and oxygen is described by a different rate law. The equation for this reaction and the rate law are shown below.

$$2\ NO\ (g)\ +\ O_2\ (g) \rightarrow 2\ NO_2\ (g) \qquad \textbf{(Eq. 14)}$$

$$\text{rate}\ =\ k[NO]^2[O_2] \qquad \textbf{(Eq. 15)}$$

Notice that the concentration of NO is squared. So in this case, if the concentration of NO is multiplied by 5, the rate increases by a factor of 25 (5^2). However, the concentration of O_2 is directly proportional to the rate. So if the concentration of O_2 is multiplied by 5, the rate increases only by a factor of 5. By how much would the rate increase if the concentration of both reactants is multiplied by 2?

You might mistakenly think that the exponents in the rate law come from the coefficients in the balanced equation. However, this is not the case. Do not forget that most reactions occur through a series of elementary steps. Thus you cannot determine the impact of the concentration of a reactant merely from the balanced equation. It must be determined experimentally. For example, you might assume that in the following reaction, the concentration of the reactant will have an exponent of 2 to match its coefficient.

$$2\ N_2O_5\ (g) \rightarrow 4\ NO_2\ (g)\ +\ O_2\ (g) \qquad \textbf{(Eq. 16)}$$

However, the rate law for this reaction has been found by experiment to be

$$\text{rate}\ =\ k[N_2O_5] \qquad \textbf{(Eq. 17)}$$

One important point to note is that not necessarily all reactants appear in the rate law. If changing the concentration of a particular reactant does not change the rate, that reactant does not appear in the rate law. Consider the reaction in which nitrogen dioxide reacts with carbon monoxide as shown in the following equation.

$$NO_2\ (g)\ +\ CO\ (g) \rightarrow NO\ (g)\ +\ CO_2\ (g) \qquad \textbf{(Eq. 18)}$$

The rate law for this reaction is

$$\text{rate}\ =\ k[NO_2]^2 \qquad \textbf{(Eq. 19)}$$

Because changes in the concentration of carbon monoxide do not affect the reaction rate, [CO] does not appear in the rate law for this reaction.

You may be wondering why you have not seen how to evaluate a proposed reaction mechanism when you know the rate law for the reaction. The reason is that the analysis of the data and mechanisms involves a bit more detail that is unnecessarily complex at this point. For now, it is enough that you recognize the relationships among reaction rate, reaction mechanisms, and rate laws.

What's Up With the Ozone Layer?

Ozone is a molecule consisting of 3 atoms of oxygen (O_3). In the Earth's lower atmosphere, ozone is considered to be harmful because it is unhealthy to breathe and is involved in reactions that create the harmful pollutants in smog. In the upper atmosphere, however, ozone serves an essential function by protecting the Earth's living systems from the dangerous ultraviolet rays of the sun.

Ozone is formed in the upper atmosphere when an oxygen molecule is split into 2 oxygen atoms by the sun's intense radiation.

$$O_2\,(g) \rightarrow 2\,O\,(g)$$

The freed oxygen atoms then attach to remaining oxygen molecules to form ozone.

$$O\,(g) + O_2\,(g) \rightarrow O_3\,(g)$$

Under natural conditions, ozone is destroyed when another oxygen atom reacts with the ozone molecule to form 2 oxygen molecules.

$$O_3\,(g) + O\,(g) \rightarrow 2\,O_2\,(g)$$

For many years, the reactions that result in the production and destruction of ozone were occurring at the same rate so that the overall ozone level remained stable. In recent decades, however, chlorine atoms have been introduced into the atmosphere. Chlorine acts as a catalyst, greatly increasing the rate at which ozone is destroyed by oxygen atoms. Because the rate of the reaction that produces ozone has remained the same, the level of ozone in the atmosphere has decreased.

Where does the chlorine come from and how does it act as a catalyst? Chlorine atoms in the atmosphere come from compounds containing Cl, F, and C called chlorofluorocarbons (CFCs). Once released, CFCs drift toward the upper atmosphere, protected from decomposition by their high stability. It is estimated that several million tons of CFCs are present in the atmosphere.

In the upper atmosphere, CFCs absorb a tremendous amount of energy from the sun. This energy breaks the bond holding chlorine onto the molecule. The released chlorine atom reacts rapidly with ozone to form chlorine monoxide (ClO) and an oxygen molecule.

$$O_3\,(g) + Cl\,(g) \rightarrow ClO\,(g) + O_2\,(g)$$

The chlorine monoxide molecule can then react with the oxygen atoms, which would otherwise destroy ozone in a much slower reaction, to regenerate the chlorine atom.

$$ClO\,(g) + O\,(g) \rightarrow$$
$$Cl\,(g) + O_2\,(g)$$

The net result of these reactions is the conversion of ozone into O_2. Notice that chlorine is consumed in the first step, but regenerated in the second step. This is how chlorine functions as a catalyst. It is then available to take part in additional ozone-destroying reactions. It has been estimated that each chlorine atom can destroy about 100,000 molecules of ozone before it is itself destroyed in another reaction!

Several countries have begun to ban or phase out the use of CFCs. But change is slow and expensive. New products are appearing that do not contain CFCs, but unfortunately many existing products still contain the harmful substances.

MATH TIP

Keep in mind that there is no way to determine the rate law of a reaction except by actually carrying out the reaction and making concentration measurements. Your main responsibility here is to interpret a rate law and be able to say how a reaction rate changes as the concentrations of one or more reactants change. This change depends on the powers to which the concentrations are raised in the rate law. Suppose you have a reaction involving reactants X and Y and the concentrations of both reactants are doubled. Look at the effect of that change with some different rate laws. Start out by allowing the concentrations, [X] and [Y], to be equal to one and then two when doubled.

1. rate $= k[X] = k[1] = 1k$
   new rate $= k[2] = 2k$
2. rate $= k[X][Y] = k[1][1] = 1k$
   new rate $= k[2][2] = 4k$
3. rate $= k[Y]^2 = k[1]^2 = 1k$
   new rate $= k[2]^2 = 4k$
4. rate $= k[X]^2[Y] = k[1]^2[1] = 1k$
   new rate $= k[2]^2[2] = 8k$

SAMPLE PROBLEM 2

The rate law for the reaction in which nitrogen monoxide reacts with oxygen to produce nitrogen dioxide was shown to be

$$\text{rate} = k[NO]^2[O_2]$$

Suppose you measure the rate of the reaction with the concentration of each reactant at 1.00 M. What will happen to the reaction rate if the concentration of NO is doubled? What will happen to the reaction rate if the concentration of O_2 is doubled instead?

STRATEGY	SOLUTION
1. Analyze	Although the exact rate has not been provided, the given law indicates the relationship of each component to the reaction rate. You need to use this rate law to determine the effect on the rate each change will have.
2. Plan	The rate law shows that while the concentration of oxygen is directly related to the rate of reaction, the square of the concentration of nitrogen monoxide is related to the rate. This information can be used to determine the answer to the problem.
3. Solve	Initially, the concentration of NO is 1.00 M. Thus its value in the rate law is

$$[NO]^2 = [1.00]^2 = 1.00$$

If [NO] is doubled, its concentration will go from 1.00 M to 2.00 M.

$$[NO]^2 = [2.00]^2 = 4.00$$

Therefore, if the NO concentration is doubled, the reaction rate will increase by a factor of 4.00.

Initially the concentration of O_2 is 1.00 M. Thus its value in the rate law is

$$[O_2] = [1.00] = 1.00$$

After [O_2] is doubled, its concentration will go from 1.00 M to 2.00 M.

$$[O_2] = [2.00] = 2.00$$

Therefore if the O_2 concentration is doubled, the reaction rate will increase by a factor of 2.

4. Evaluate The rate law shows that in this reaction the rate is more responsive to changes in the concentration of NO.

PRACTICE PROBLEMS

3. The chemical equation and the rate law for the decomposition of hydrogen iodide are shown. What will be the effect on the reaction rate if the concentration of HI is raised from 1.00 M to 4.00 M? 2 HI $(g) \rightarrow H_2 (g) + I_2 (g)$ rate = $k[HI]^2$ *(Answer: Will increase by a factor of 16.0)*

4. What will happen to the reaction rate in the decomposition of hydrogen iodide in Practice Problem 3 if the concentration of HI is initially 1.00 M and is then reduced to 0.333 M? *(Answer: Will be reduced by a factor of 0.111)*

Figure 22–6 *As this spectacular photograph illustrates, fine wires of steel wool burn rapidly in pure oxygen.*

22–1 Section Review

1. How is the rate of reaction defined?

2. Explain what it means for a chemical reaction to have a multistep reaction mechanism.

3. What is a rate law for a chemical reaction and how is it determined?

4. **Critical Thinking—Applying concepts** Describe the reaction rate for the following equation in three different ways: $H_2 (g) + Cl_2 (g) \rightarrow 2$ HCl (g). How do you think the rate of consumption of H_2 is related to the rate of production of HCl?

- How does collision theory explain chemical reactions?
- Why is the activation energy of a reaction important?
- What is an activated complex?

22–2 The Reaction Process

It turns out that chemical reactions are more complex than they seem from their balanced chemical equations. Why is it that reactions occur through reaction mechanisms rather than exactly as they appear in the balanced chemical equation? To answer this question, we need to probe a little deeper into chemical reactions at the molecular level.

Collision Theory

If asked what simple condition is necessary for a chemical reaction to occur, you might say reactants coming together. On the molecular level, combining two substances means forcing their particles to hit, or collide with, one another. **Chemists have proposed a theoretical model, known as collision theory, which states that molecules must collide in order to react.** The basis for **collision theory** is the assumption that in order for a molecule, atom, or ion to react it is necessary that it collide either with another molecule, atom, or ion or with a wall of the container. These collisions can involve one particle and a container wall or two particles colliding with each other. A few reactions involve three-body collisions, but these are rare since they occur only when three particles are at precisely the same location at precisely the same time. No cases of four-body collisions are known.

Collision theory helps to explain why chemical reactions proceed through reaction mechanisms. Most chemical equations show three or more particles on the reactant side of the equation. Think back to Equation 6, for example. According to the equation, 2 molecules of NO would have to collide with 1 molecule of F_2. This means that three particles would have to be at exactly the same place at exactly the same time under the right conditions. Yet according to collision theory, it is unlikely that many collisions involve more than two particles. Instead, the reaction proceeds through two elementary steps, each of which involves a collision between only two particles.

The only question remaining, then, is what does collision theory have to do with reaction rates? As you will see, collision theory has a lot to do with reaction rates. If there were no collisions among the particles of reactants, there would be no reaction. However, there can also be billions of collisions and still no reaction. This is because not all collisions are effective in leading to the production of products. A collision is an **effective collision** if it leads to the formation of products. A collision that does not lead to the formation of products is an **ineffective collision.** If every collision led to a reaction, all chemical reactions would have rates hundreds of times faster than they actually are. For example, in a mixture of H_2 and I_2 at ordinary temperatures and

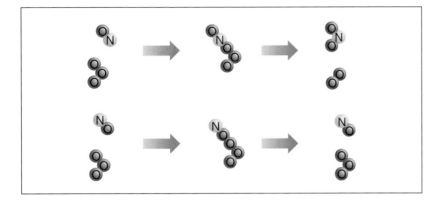

pressures, each molecule undergoes about 10^{10} collisions per second. If every collision resulted in the formation of HI, the reaction would be over in a fraction of a second. Instead, at room temperature, the reaction proceeds quite slowly because in reality only about 1 in every 10^{13} collisions is effective.

So what determines whether or not a collision is effective? There are two general factors that determine the effectiveness of a collision—the orientation and energy of the colliding particles. For a reaction to occur, the particles must be oriented in a favorable position that allows the bonds to break and atoms to rearrange. Otherwise, the colliding molecules simply bounce off one another. See Figure 22–7. Some collision orientations can lead to reaction, while others do not. Not all collisions in which the particles are in suitable orientations lead to reactions. The colliding particles must also have sufficient energy so that bonds are broken and new bonds formed. The energy involved in chemical reactions is discussed in the next several paragraphs.

Energy in Chemical Reactions

Collision theory maintains that particles must collide at the proper orientation and with sufficient energy in order to react. But what does sufficient energy mean and where does the energy come from? According to collision theory, energy is required to break the bonds that hold reactants together. The energy for this purpose must be present in the reacting particles before a collision.

POTENTIAL AND KINETIC ENERGY Recall from earlier chapters that there are two types of energy—potential energy and kinetic energy. Potential energy is stored energy. The gasoline used to fuel a car, the food you eat, and a chandelier hanging from the ceiling all have potential energy. Kinetic energy is energy of motion. An athlete running in a marathon, a butterfly darting from one flower to the next, and a soccer ball flying through the air all have kinetic energy. The total amount of energy in a system is conserved. This means that no energy is

Figure 22–8 *This athlete's flexed bow has increased potential energy. Once released, its potential energy will be converted to kinetic energy as the arrow speeds through the air toward its target.*

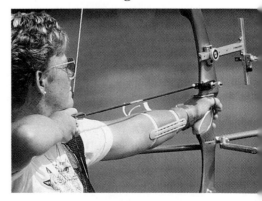

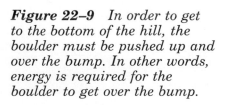
lost. Rather, one form of energy can be converted to another. If, for example, the chain holding the chandelier is cut, the chandelier will crash to the floor. As it falls, the chandelier loses potential energy but gains kinetic energy as one type of energy is converted to the other.

Particles of matter, like any objects, can have potential and kinetic energy. According to collision theory, the energy required to break bonds among reactant particles comes from the kinetic energy of the reactant particles. During a collision, kinetic energy is converted into potential energy as the reactant particles are deformed, bonds are broken, and atoms are rearranged. The amount of kinetic energy of a particle is dependent upon its mass and velocity. (Velocity is speed in a given direction.) The more massive the particle or the faster its speed, the greater its kinetic energy.

ACTIVATION ENERGY In 1888, Swedish chemist Svante Arrhenius (1859–1927) suggested that particles must possess a certain minimum amount of kinetic energy in order to react. The situation is often likened to that of a boulder being pushed up and over a bump before rolling down a hill as shown in Figure 22–9. Even though the boulder will be more stable at the bottom of the hill, it needs a push to get up and over the bump first. Similarly, even though the bonding is more stable in the product than in the reactants, energy is required to force the reactants up and over an energy bump, or barrier.

Energy diagrams are used to show the changes in energy that occur during a chemical reaction. A typical energy diagram is shown in Figure 22–10. Does this energy diagram look at all familiar to you? While you have never seen this particular type of diagram, you have seen a diagram to which it is closely related—the diagrams in Chapter 12 that were used to show the energy changes that take place during endothermic and exothermic reactions. Those diagrams used horizontal lines to show the energy of reactants and products, and thus the change between them. This new diagram also shows the energy of reactants and products, but unlike the earlier diagrams, this diagram shows the energy at every point throughout the reaction pathway. The

Figure 22–9 In order to get to the bottom of the hill, the boulder must be pushed up and over the bump. In other words, energy is required for the boulder to get over the bump.

Energy Diagram

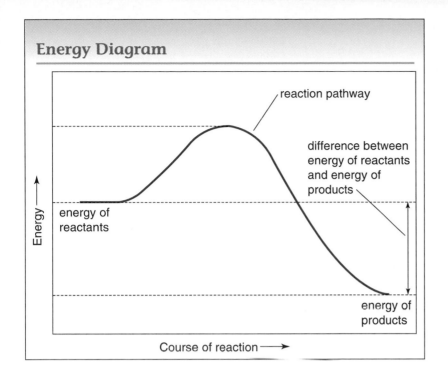

reaction pathway

difference between energy of reactants and energy of products

energy of reactants

energy of products

Energy

Course of reaction →

Figure 22–10 An energy diagram shows how energy (y-axis) changes throughout the course of a chemical reaction (x-axis). Notice that the energy level of the reactants must first be increased before it can be lowered to that of the products. How is this diagram similar to that of the boulder and the hill?

energy diagrams of an endothermic reaction and exothermic reaction are shown in Figure 22–11.

Notice that the shape of the energy diagram in Figure 22–10 is similar to the shape of the hill in Figure 22–9. Here you can see that the energy of the reactants must be raised to the top of the energy barrier before it can drop to a lower level. The difference between the energy at the peak and the energy of the reactants is called the **activation energy**. The activation energy is the energy needed to start the reaction. When particles collide with sufficient energy—at least equal to the activation energy—existing bonds may be disrupted and new bonds can form.

Figure 22–11 In an endothermic reaction the energy of the product is greater than that of the reactants. In an exothermic reaction the energy of the products is lower than that of the reactants. In each reaction, however, energy is required to lift the reactants up and over some energy barrier.

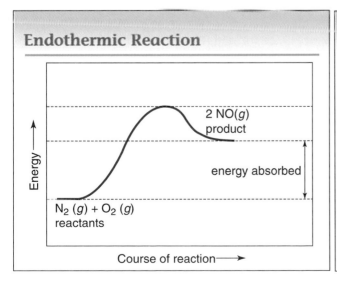

Endothermic Reaction

2 NO(g) product

energy absorbed

N_2 (g) + O_2 (g) reactants

Energy

Course of reaction →

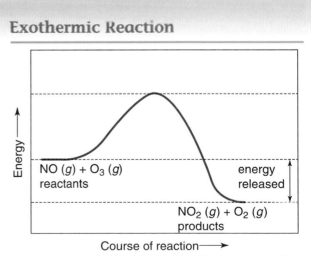

Exothermic Reaction

NO (g) + O_3 (g) reactants

energy released

NO_2 (g) + O_2 (g) products

Energy

Course of reaction →

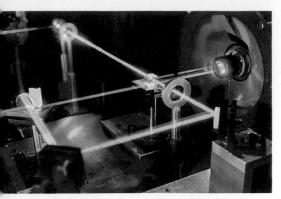

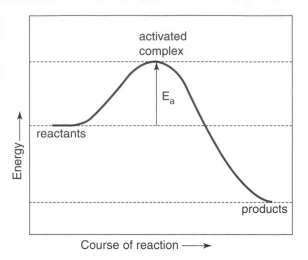

Figure 22–12 *When reactants collide at the proper angle with energy equal to the activation energy* (E_a)*, they undergo a transition state in which they form an activated complex. Scientists attempt to analyze the transition state by shining high-speed lasers at specific points during a chemical reaction. Where along the energy diagram does the activated complex exist?*

ACTIVATED COMPLEX There is an extremely brief interval of bond disruption and bond formation known as a **transition state.** During the transition state, the reactants form a short-lived complex that is neither reactant nor product, but has partial bonding characteristics of both. This transitional structure is called an **activated complex.** The activated complex exists along the reaction pathway at the point where the energy is greatest—at the peak indicated by the activation energy. Now the activation energy becomes even more significant. **The activation energy, E_a, is the energy required to achieve the transition state and form the activated complex.** Because of the short lifetime of an activated complex, chemists cannot isolate one for study. However, they are experimenting with lasers to analyze the transition state.

Have you ever bumped into any object so that it teeters precariously? You're not sure if it is going to fall over or simply settle back into place. Eventually, it does one or the other. This is somewhat similar to the situation for the activated complex. Just as you imparted energy to the object when you bumped into it, the activated complex is energized by the particle collision. Because of its high energy, it is extremely unstable and will quickly break up. Once formed, the activated complex can break up in one of two ways: It may reform the original bonds and separate back into the reactant particles or it may form new bonds and separate into products. At this point, the formation of products and the formation of reactants are equally probable.

Before going on, we want to make sure that you do not confuse the unstable activated complex with the relatively stable intermediate products of the elementary steps of a reaction mechanism. The activated complex, unlike intermediate products, is a very short-lived molecular complex in which bonds are in the process of being broken and formed. Intermediate products, on the other hand, are chemical substances produced in one part of a reaction and consumed in another. Each elementary step of a reaction mechanism requires its own activation energy in order to proceed, will produce its own activated complex, and may produce intermediate products.

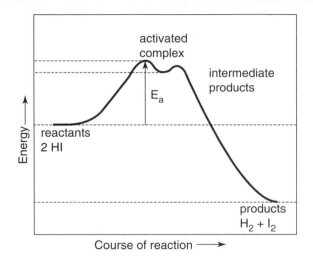

Figure 22–13 Only after the transition state is achieved and the activated complex is formed can intermediate products be produced. The intermediate products then become reactants in another reaction that must also achieve a transition state determined by the activation energy for this second reaction. Which reaction has a lower activation energy?

Tying Up Loose Ends

Now we can finally answer one of the questions posed at the beginning of the chapter: Why do different reactions occur at different rates? The answer involves energy. Reactant particles must not only collide at the proper orientation, but they must also acquire enough energy to overcome the activation energy barrier in order to be converted into products. Only a small fraction of reactant particles has sufficient energy to overcome the barrier at any given time during the reaction. Thus all reactant particles cannot surmount the energy barrier at once. As the reaction proceeds, however, more and more reactant particles achieve sufficient energy as they move and collide. The reaction rate, then, is the rate at which reactant particles move over the energy barrier. Every reaction has its own activation energy. Reaction rate is directly related to activation energy. The higher the activation energy, the smaller the fraction of collisions with sufficient energy, and the slower the reaction rate.

22–2 Section Review

1. What is collision theory and how does it relate to reaction rates?

2. What is activation energy? How is it related to collision theory?

3. What is an activated complex and at what point during a chemical reaction is it produced?

4. Can a chemical reaction involve more than one activated complex?

5. **Theme Trace—Energy** Collision theory is dependent upon the role of energy in chemical reactions. Explain how energy is involved in and changes throughout a chemical reaction.

CHEM
Activity

Chemistry in a Box

1. Obtain a cereal box (empty or full).
2. Stand the box in an upright position.
3. Tap the box so that it teeters and almost falls.
4. Now tap the box so that it falls over.
5. What is the most stable position for the box? How do you know?
6. Repeat Step 4 so that the box falls to its most stable position in two steps rather than one.
7. Relate what happened in this activity to reaction mechanisms and the role of energy in chemical reactions.

Guide for Reading

- What factors affect the rate at which a reaction proceeds?

22–3 Factors Affecting Reaction Rates

Now you know that the rate of a reaction depends upon the rate of effective collisions, which in turn depends upon the orientation and energy of the reactant particles as well as the activation energy barrier for the reaction. This explains how the rates of different chemical reactions can vary widely. However, the same exact reaction can proceed at different rates under varied conditions. The spoiling of the sandwich you read about at the beginning of the chapter proceeded slowly in the refrigerator yet rapidly in a warm locker. There are several factors that affect the rates of reactions by altering the frequency, orientation, or energy levels at which particles collide. It is important to know what these factors are since it is often desirable to speed up a useful chemical reaction or slow down an unwanted reaction. **There are five general factors that affect the rate of a reaction: nature of reactants, temperature, concentration, surface area, and catalysts.** The effect of each factor can be understood in terms of collision theory.

Nature of the Reactants

The rate of a reaction depends on the particular reactants and the complexity of the bonds that have to be broken and formed in order for the reaction to proceed. Reactions in which there are only slight rearrangements of atoms are usually rapid at room temperature. For example, hydrogen and oxgyen react to form water in an explosive reaction compressed into one ear-splitting moment, as demonstrated during the tragic explosion of the *Hindenburg.* The reaction of hydrogen gas with oxygen gas to produce water involves simple bonds. The H–H and O–O bonds in the hydrogen and oxygen molecules must be broken and then two bonds between H and O must be formed to yield the H–O–H molecule.

In reactions in which there are many covalent bonds to be broken, the reaction usually takes place slowly at room temperature. For example, the reactions that cause the hardening of a type of cement known as portland cement are very slow. The cement will continue to harden for weeks after it has been poured. The hardening of portland cement involves the formation of a complex three-dimensional structure including bonds between alternating silicon and oxygen atoms that make it a strong and durable material. This very complicated structure can be formed only 1 atom at a time.

The state of a reactant in a chemical reaction can also have a considerable effect on reaction rate. A reaction in which the reactants are in different states is said to be a **heterogeneous**

Figure 22–14 *When a clear solution of potassium iodide is added to a clear solution of lead nitrate, a yellow cloud of precipitate immediately forms. The formation of the product is almost instantaneous because the bonding situation is very simple.*

Figure 22–15 *The flask shows the reaction in which carbon dioxide gas is added to calcium oxide solution to produce calcium carbonate. The iron nail that has been dropped into a solution of sulfuric acid is quickly dissolving. Are these reactions heterogeneous or homogeneous?*

reaction. A reaction in which all the reactants are in the same state is said to be a **homogeneous reaction.** A reaction between two gases is likely to proceed more quickly than a reaction between two liquids and certainly much more quickly than a reaction between two solids. According to the kinetic theory of matter, the particles in gases are moving more freely than those in liquids, which are moving more freely than those in solids. Since the frequency at which particles collide and the amount of energy they possess increase with increasing motion, you should expect reaction rates to be fastest among gases and slowest among solids.

Temperature

Food spoils faster at room temperature than when it is refrigerated. Cake batter will cook only when it is heated. Plants grow more rapidly in warm weather than in cold. These and many other reactions occur more rapidly with increased temperatures. Temperature obviously has a profound effect on reaction rate. Why?

The reason for the effect of temperature on reaction rate goes back to collision theory. In Chapter 13, we talked about the effect of temperature on molecular speed: the higher the temperature, the faster the average speed of a group of molecules. The faster the molecules are moving, the more frequently they will collide. But there is more to it than this. Effective collisions depend on the colliding particles having sufficient kinetic energy to surmount the activation energy barrier. Increasing the temperature

Figure 22–16 *These glowing green sticks are called cyalume sticks. As you can see, cyalume sticks shine in warm water but not in cold water because the higher temperature increases the rate of the reaction in the stick.*

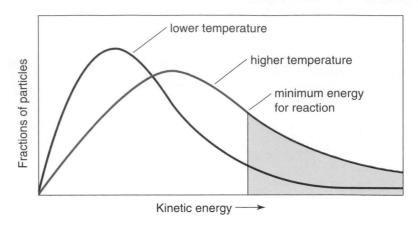

Figure 22–17 *The red line shows that at a lower temperature, more of the reactant particles have low amounts of kinetic energy. As the temperature is increased, the blue line shows that more of the reactant particles have a higher kinetic energy. If the vertical line shows the amount of kinetic energy necessary for reaction, how does increasing the temperature affect a reaction?*

always increases the speed of a particle. Remember that the kinetic energy is proportional to the square of the speed. Thus increasing the temperature increases the kinetic energy of each particle. Increasing the temperature increases the fraction of particles that collide with sufficient kinetic energy to form the activated complex. So the effect of increasing the temperature is twofold: It increases the frequency of collisions and also the fraction of the collisions that have sufficient energy to be effective.

The standard rule of thumb that all chemists keep in mind is a $10\,C°$ increase in temperature approximately doubles or triples the reaction rate. The actual amount must be determined experimentally. Think about the consequences of this phenomenon!

Concentration

The rate of a reaction was defined as the change in concentration over time, so obviously concentration has a major impact on the rate. Now you can see why. An increase in reaction rate caused by an increase in concentration can be explained by collision theory. An increase in concentration means that there are more particles within a given volume and thus smaller spaces between the reacting particles. With less distance to travel between collisions, more collisions will take place during any given unit of time. Thus, an increase in concentration increases the frequency of the collisions. The situation might be likened to that of a room filled with people. If there are only a few people, you can walk through the room easily without bumping into another person. But if the room is very crowded, you will bump into several people as you make your way through. The more crowded the room, the more difficult it will be to walk across the room without bumping into someone.

Figure 22–18 *Automobiles pollute the air with oxides of nitrogen. In air, nitrogen and oxygen are essentially unreactive. But at the high temperatures and pressures inside an automobile engine, the two gases react quickly.*

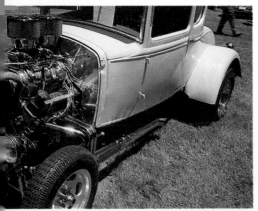

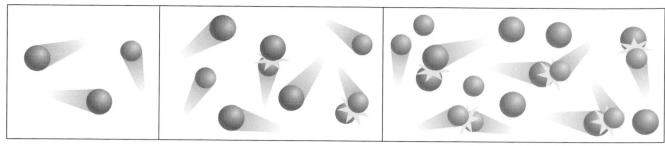

Surface Area

Which do you think would burn faster: a lump of coal or many small pieces of coal? You are correct if you said the small pieces. When the coal is broken up, more oxygen particles can collide with coal particles each second. This example shows that the larger the surface area of a reactant, the greater the number of particles that are exposed for reaction. In other words, the larger surface area increases the frequency at which particles collide. If particles collide more often, the chances for effective collisions increase.

Increasing the surface area of a solid per unit mass or volume is normally accomplished by choosing a very finely divided reactant or grinding it into a fine powder. Sometimes finely ground substances can produce dangerous results. Flour mills have been known to explode when a large amount of flour suspended in the air is accidentally ignited by a spark. Many medicines are produced in the form of a fine powder or small crystals. Why might this be done?

Figure 22–19   When particles of matter are spread out, the probability that they will collide is low. But as the concentration of particles increases, the particles tend to collide more and more frequently. An increased number of collisions results in a greater number of effective collisions and thus a faster reaction.

Catalysts

A sample of sugar exposed to oxygen in the air can last for centuries. In your body, however, sugar exposed to oxygen is consumed in a few seconds. What accounts for this difference?

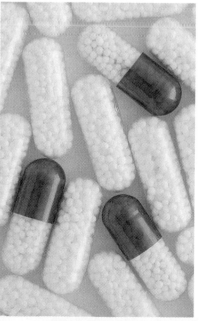

Figure 22–20   The photograph on the left shows a fine powder consisting of the spores of primitive plants called lycopodium, or common club moss. When thrown into the air, the exposed surface area of the spores is so great that they ignite explosively if a spark or flame is present. The photograph on the right shows several medicine capsules. Rather than being incorporated into a solid pill that will react slowly, the medicine is divided into many small beads to increase the overall reaction rate in the body.

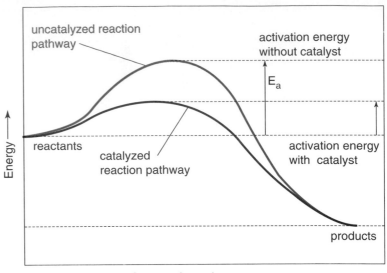

Figure 22–21 A catalyst creates a different pathway for the reactants to take. The alternate pathway has a lower activation energy.

Get the Lead Out

Perhaps you have heard "knocks" in a car's engine or seen advertisements for gasoline that prevents "knocking." What causes knocking? If gas burns too rapidly in the engine, the piston receives a single hard smash rather than a smooth push. The result is a knocking sound and a reduction in engine efficiency.

For over half a century, gasoline included tetraethyl lead ($Pb(C_2H_5)_4$) which inhibited, or slowed, gasoline's combustion. In recent years, however, the health and environmental hazards posed by lead, a toxic metal, have become known. In addition, lead was found to deactivate the catalysts in catalytic converters. For these reasons, the use of lead in gasolines has been greatly reduced. Other additives, usually compounds of hydrogen and oxygen, continue to be used to slow the burning reaction.

The answer is the action of **catalysts.** A catalyst is a substance that increases the rate of the reaction without itself being used up in the reaction. Catalysts in the body, such as those involved in breaking down sugar, are called enzymes. Enzymes increase the speed of reactions essential to life that would otherwise be hopelessly slow.

A catalyst does not appear in the overall chemical equation as either a reactant or a product because the reaction mechanism of a catalyzed reaction involves one step in which the catalyst is consumed and one step in which it is regenerated. Catalysts exist before a reaction occurs and can be recovered and reused after the reaction is complete. This is the opposite of intermediate products, which are produced in one step of a mechanism and consumed in another.

The explanation of how catalysts work once again goes back to collision theory. Catalysts act in one or more steps of a reaction by lowering the activation energy. Thus a catalyst creates a different pathway from reactants to products—one that requires less energy. Figure 22–21 shows how a catalyst changes the energy diagram of a reaction. With the lower activation energy, more collisions will have sufficient energy to pass over the energy barrier. The reaction is faster simply because a greater fraction of collisions is effective at any given point.

A well-known example of a catalyst is in the catalytic converters of automobiles. Automobile exhaust may contain toxic carbon monoxide and nitrogen oxides. Even the best-designed engines cannot reduce these pollutants to acceptable levels. It is therefore necessary to remove them from the exhaust gases before they leave the exhaust system. This is accomplished by a catalytic converter, which mixes the pollutants with extra air and then passes them over a catalyst made of specially prepared rhodium and platinum metals. The catalyst accelerates the reaction of

Seeing the Bottom

After being used for about a year without being scoured, a metal tea kettle has developed a considerable buildup of a solid on its inside bottom surface. The substance is calcium carbonate ($CaCO_3$), which can be dissolved by an acid. Using only apparatus and materials available inside the kitchen, how would you most rapidly remove the deposit on the inside of the kettle?

The photograph shows thick deposits of lime scale on the electrical elements of a kettle. The lime consists mostly of calcium carbonate that precipitated out of treated tap water after the water was boiled.

carbon monoxide with oxygen in the air, converting it to nontoxic carbon dioxide. It also increases the rate at which nitrogen oxides are broken down into their elements.

It is not desirable to speed up all chemical reactions. Rather, slowing down some reactions is very important. Substances that slow the rate of a reaction are called **inhibitors.** For example, inhibitors slow the rate of spoilage and increase the shelf-life of many food products. Unlike catalysts, inhibitors cannot work by providing an alternate pathway with a higher activation barrier. If this were the case, the reaction would simply continue at the lower route. Instead, inhibitors work by either removing catalysts or by causing the reaction to take other routes that produce side products and do not lead to the ordinary products.

INTEGRATING
ENVIRONMENTAL SCIENCE

How do you think a car's catalytic converter works?

22–3 Section Review

1. List five factors that affect the rate at which a reaction proceeds. Explain each one in terms of collision theory.

2. Why will a mixture of hydrogen gas and chlorine gas react faster when the volume they occupy is decreased?

3. **Connection—Biology** Enzymes, which are natural catalysts, are used in almost every chemical reaction within the body. Does the body have to continuously produce enzymes? Why or why not?

Laboratory Investigation

Observing Changes in Reaction Rate

Problem

How does concentration affect reaction rate?

Materials (per group)

3 graduated cylinders
5 125-mL beakers, labeled 1–5
0.20 M $Na_2S_2O_3$
2.0 M HCl
distilled water
sheet of white paper
black marking pen
timer or stopwatch

Procedure

1. Use graduated cylinders to measure and add 0.20 M $Na_2S_2O_3$ and distilled water to the beakers as described below:

Beaker	1	2	3	4	5
$Na_2S_2O_3$	10.0 mL	20.0 mL	30.0 mL	40.0 mL	50.0 mL
Water	40.0 mL	30.0 mL	20.0 mL	10.0 mL	0.0 mL

2. On a sheet of paper, use the marking pen to write the letter X small enough so that it can be covered by a beaker.
3. Place Beaker 1 on the X. Use the remaining graduated cylinder to add 5.0 mL of 2.0 M HCl to the beaker. Be careful to use proper safety precautions when working with acid.
4. Record the time at which the HCl is added. Immediately give the beaker one gentle swirl and place it back on the X. Look through the solution at the X and record the time at which the X is no longer visible.
5. Repeat Steps 3 and 4 for the remaining beakers.

Observations

Beaker	Volume of $Na_2S_2O_3$ (mL)	Volume of Water (mL)	Volume of HCl (mL)	Reaction Time (s)
1				
2				
3				
4				
5				

1. What visible indication is there that a chemical reaction is occurring?
2. How is the concentration of $Na_2S_2O_3$ affected by the volume of distilled water?
3. What happens to the reaction time as the volume of $Na_2S_2O_3$ increases relative to the volume of distilled water?
4. Prepare a graph of time versus volume of $Na_2S_2O_3$ by plotting time along the x-axis and volume along the y-axis.

Analysis and Conclusions

1. How did the concentration of $Na_2S_2O_3$ affect the rate of the reaction?
2. Does your graph support your conclusion for Question 1? Explain.
3. In this investigation, what are the variables? What is the control?
4. Based on your data, what do you think might be the rate law for this reaction?
5. **On Your Own** With your teacher's permission, repeat this experiment keeping the concentration of $Na_2S_2O_3$ constant and varying the concentration of HCl.

STUDY GUIDE

Summarizing Key Concepts

22–1 Chemical Kinetics

- The rate of a reaction is a measure of how quickly reactants turn into products.
- Most chemical reactions proceed through a series of simple reactions, or elementary steps. The series of steps is called the reaction mechanism.
- Substances that are produced in one elementary step and consumed in another are called intermediate products.
- A rate law for a chemical reaction describes the relationship between the concentrations of the reactants and the reaction rate.

22–2 The Reaction Process

- Collision theory is based on the assumption that particles must collide at the proper orientation and with sufficient energy in order to react. Collisions that lead to the development of products are effective collisions, while those that do not are ineffective collisions.
- Potential energy is stored energy, and kinetic energy is energy of motion. Like any objects, particles of matter can have potential and kinetic energy.
- Energy diagrams are used to analyze the changes in energy that occur during a chemical reaction.
- The energy of the reactants in any reaction must be raised up over an energy barrier.

Activation energy is the energy required to initiate a reaction and force the reactants to form an activated complex. The activated complex is located at the peak of the energy diagram for a reaction.

22–3 Factors Affecting Reaction Rates

- Several factors affect the rate at which a chemical reaction proceeds: the nature of the reactants, the temperature at which the reaction occurs, the surface area of reactants exposed to each other, the concentration of the reactants present, and the presence of catalysts.
- Every factor that affects reaction rate can be understood relative to collision theory. The nature of the reactants determines the orientation of collisions and the amount of energy required to break bonds and form new ones. The higher the temperature at which a reaction occurs, the faster the particles will move. This results in a higher frequency of collisions as well as a higher kinetic energy among the particles. The higher the concentration of reactants, the greater the frequency of collisions among their particles. The greater the surface area of the reactants, the greater the frequency of collisions. Catalysts lower the activation energy required for a reaction to occur.

Reviewing Key Terms

Define each term in a complete sentence.

22–1 Chemical Kinetics

chemical kinetics
reaction rate
reaction mechanism
elementary step
intermediate product
rate-determining step
rate law

22–2 The Reaction Process

collision theory
effective collision
ineffective collision
activation energy
transition state
activated complex

22–3 Factors Affecting Reaction Rates

heterogeneous reaction
homogeneous reaction
catalyst
inhibitor

CHAPTER REVIEW

Content Review

Multiple Choice
Choose the letter of the answer that best completes each statement.

1. A change in concentration over time is the
   (a) reaction rate.
   (b) transition state.
   (c) activated complex.
   (d) intermediate product.

2. In a proposed reaction mechanism,
   Step 1: $NO\ (g) + NO\ (g) \rightarrow N_2O_2\ (g)$
   Step 2: $N_2O_2\ (g) + H_2\ (g) \rightarrow$
   $\qquad\qquad\qquad N_2O\ (g) + H_2O\ (g).$
   The intermediate product is
   (a) $NO\ (g)$.   (c) $N_2O_2\ (g)$.
   (b) $H_2\ (g)$.   (d) $N_2O\ (g)$.

3. According to collision theory, the rate of a reaction does not depend on
   (a) frequency of collisions.
   (b) energy of collisions.
   (c) direction of collisions.
   (d) orientation of colliding particles.

4. The activation energy of a reaction is the amount of energy necessary to form the
   (a) products.   (c) reaction mechanism.
   (b) catalyst.   (d) activated complex.

5. Which is a homogeneous reaction?
   (a) $2\ Na\ (s) + 2\ H_2O\ (l) \rightarrow$
   $\qquad\qquad 2\ NaOH\ (aq) + H_2\ (g)$
   (b) $N_2\ (g) + 3\ H_2\ (g) \rightarrow 2\ NH_3\ (g)$
   (c) $CaO\ (s) + H_2O\ (l) \rightarrow Ca(OH)_2\ (s)$
   (d) $2\ Mg\ (s) + O_2\ (g) \rightarrow 2\ MgO\ (s)$

6. The rate of a particular reaction doubles for each 10 C° increase in temperature. If the reaction takes 200 seconds to be completed at 30°C, at 70°C it will require
   (a) 12.5 seconds.   (c) 100 seconds.
   (b) 1000 seconds.   (d) 160 seconds.

7. For a particular reaction, rate $= k[A]^2[B]$. If the concentration of reactant A is tripled, the rate is increased by a factor of
   (a) 3.   (c) 6.
   (b) 4.   (d) 9.

8. The rate of a chemical reaction can be increased by
   (a) decreasing the concentration of the reactants.
   (b) increasing the surface area of the reactants.
   (c) removing a catalyst.
   (d) decreasing the reaction temperature.

9. Catalysts
   (a) slow the rate of a reaction.
   (b) increase the energy of the reactant particles.
   (c) lower the activation energy barrier.
   (d) are used up in reactions.

True or False
If the statement is true, write "true." If it is false, change the underlined word or words to make the statement true.

10. The study of the rates of chemical reactions is called <u>kinetics</u>.

11. The steps of a reaction mechanism are called <u>intermediates</u>.

12. <u>All</u> reactions proceed through a multistep reaction mechanism.

13. <u>Collision theory</u> is used to explain why various factors affect the reaction rate.

14. An increase in the speed of a particle increases its <u>potential energy</u>.

15. An <u>activated complex</u> is a short-lived complex produced from an effective collision.

Concept Mapping

Complete the following concept map for Section 22–1. Refer to pages xviii–xix to construct a concept map for the entire chapter.

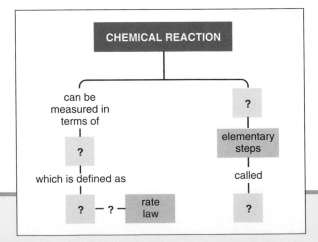

Concept Mastery

Discuss each of the following in a brief paragraph.

16. What is chemical kinetics and why is it important? Give examples in your answer.

17. Use collision theory to explain why most reactions probably occur through multi-step reaction mechanisms.

18. What is an intermediate product and what can it tell you about the path of a chemical reaction?

19. Describe collision theory. Discuss the difference between an effective and an ineffective collision.

20. How are each of the following related to the rate of a reaction? (a) frequency of collisions, (b) kinetic energy of collisions, and (c) orientation of colliding particles.

21. How is activation energy affected by a catalyst? Distinguish between a catalyst and an inhibitor.

22. Write the general form of a rate law. Make sure you define the various components of the equation.

23. Can a rate law ever be written from a chemical equation?

24. **Tying it Together** Some of the factors that affect reaction rates involve changes in *energy*. Name five factors that affect reaction rate and explain how they are related to collision theory and which factors involve energy.

Critical Thinking and Problem Solving

Use the skills you have developed in this chapter to answer each of the following.

25. **Making inferences** For each of these reactions, indicate how the rate of disappearance of each reactant is related to the appearance of each product:
(a) $H_2O_2 (g) \rightarrow H_2 (g) + O_2 (g)$
(b) $CO (g) + 2 H_2 (g) \rightarrow CH_3OH (g)$

26. **Making judgments** Determine whether or not the proposed mechanism is possible for the reaction described by the following equation:
$H_2 (g) + 2 ICl (g) \rightarrow 2 HCl (g) + I_2 (g)$.
If it is a possible reaction mechanism, do you know for sure that this is the actual mechanism? Explain.
Step 1: $H_2 (g) + ICl (g) \rightarrow$
$HI (g) + HCl (g)$
Step 2: $HI (g) + ICl (g) \rightarrow HCl (g) + I_2 (g)$

27. **Interpreting diagrams** Compare the energy content of the products of a reaction with that of the reactants when the reaction is endothermic and when it is exothermic. Draw and label a diagram to support your answer.

28. **Drawing conclusions** Two reactions have identical values for activation energy. Will they necessarily have the same rate constant if run at the same temperature?

29. **Making predictions** Hydrochloric acid reacts with zinc to produce zinc chloride and hydrogen. Will the hydrogen be given off more slowly when the acid is made more dilute? Explain.

30. **Using the writing process** As more and more landfills reach maximum capacity, garbage is becoming a major threat to the environment. Research and write a summary of a waste disposal issue. Include an explanation of some of the chemical reactions that must occur to break down the waste, the rates at which they occur, and the obstacles that inhibit them. Propose as many solutions to the problem as you can.

Chapter

23 Thermodynamics

The gently rolling Berkshire Hills of Massachusetts were once rocky and craggy and higher than they are today. As a result of the processes of weathering and erosion, the Berkshires were worn down by elements such as wind and rain into their present shape. In nature's endless drive toward disorder, much of the matter that makes up these hills has been scattered into an increasingly disordered state. These hills will continue to diminish until maximum disorder is reached, and they are no longer any higher than the surrounding terrain.

Just why does nature favor disorder? In this chapter, you will learn the answer to this question.

Just as the toss of dice favors disorder, so, too, does the gradual erosion of the Berkshires in Massachusetts. The once rocky and craggy mountains have become the gently rolling hills you see here because of the universal drive toward disorder.

Chem Journal

YOU AND YOUR WORLD

Imagine that you could travel a few hundred years into the future and visit your favorite vacation spot— perhaps a sandy beach or a mountain canyon. In your journal, describe the changes that have occurred there and your reaction to them.

23–1 Spontaneous Processes

Guide for Reading

- What is a spontaneous process?

You have studied many chemical reactions since you were first introduced to them in Chapter 9. So now would be a good time to review just what you have learned. Let's do this with the help of a particular reaction—the familiar chemical reaction of the rusting of iron. A word equation for this chemical reaction is, Iron reacts with atmospheric oxygen to produce a solid compound called iron(III) oxide. You can represent this reaction with a balanced equation that includes the enthalpy change, ΔH°, for the reaction.

$$4\,Fe\,(s) + 3\,O_2\,(g) \rightarrow 2\,Fe_2O_3\,(s) \qquad \Delta H^\circ = -1644\text{ kJ} \quad \textbf{(Eq. 1)}$$

You also know that from such a thermochemical equation you can relate the amounts of reactants and products as well as the accompanying heat transferred.

What other information about this reaction is of interest and value? To chemists, there are three fundamental questions that must be answered in order to understand a reaction completely. Such an understanding is essential in accurately predicting and controlling the reaction.

Figure 23–1   Although the process of sky diving is not a chemical change, it, too, occurs at a characteristic rate and ceases upon reaching equilibrium, factors of importance to sky divers.

Figure 23–2 *In what way is the rusting of iron equipment on a seashore similar to the downward fall of the sky divers in Figure 23–1?*

One of these questions is, How rapidly does iron turn into rust? You explored the answer to this question in Chapter 22. There you learned that the rate of a reaction depends primarily on the reaction's activation energy. You also discovered the role played by factors such as temperature, surface area, and catalysts in controlling a reaction rate. Fortunately for us, the rusting of iron is a relatively slow process!

Another question chemists strive to answer is, Will all the iron exposed to the atmosphere be converted to rust, or will the reaction come to a stop before this happens? You should recognize this question as an equilibrium problem. Reactions may proceed to completion, or they may proceed to a state in which there is a mixture of reactants and products. The equilibrium situation for a reaction is described by its equilibrium constant, which you studied in Chapter 16. And as you will remember, the greater the magnitude of the equilibrium constant, the greater the proportion of products found at equilibrium. What, then, is the difference between a reaction with an equilibrium constant greater than 1 and a reaction with an equilibrium constant substantially less than 1?

Figure 23–3 *These photographs of a white-water river and urban water tanks depict the movement of water from one location to another. The water in the river flows down spontaneously. How does water flow up into the rooftop water tanks?*

In the first case where the equilibrium constant is much greater than 1 (this is written as $K_{eq} \gg 1$), the reaction has a significant tendency to proceed to form products. In the second case where the equilibrium constant is much less than 1 ($K_{eq} \ll 1$), reactants are favored. So, for $K_{eq} \ll 1$, the reverse reaction has the greater tendency to occur. Thus some reactions yield products just as written, whereas others must be reversed in order to represent the formation of products.

If you are beginning to get the idea that there is an inherent direction in which a given reaction has a tendency to proceed, you are absolutely correct. Thinking back to the rusting of iron, you know from experience that a pile of brand new nails left outside will definitely rust. And you can also be sure that a rusty nail will not turn back into a shiny new one, no matter how long you wait!

The rusting of iron is an example of a **spontaneous chemical reaction.** There are many examples of spontaneous occurrences in nature. The melting of an ice cube left on the kitchen counter is a spontaneous physical change. The flow of a river from its origin in the mountains to where it joins the ocean is a spontaneous process. **A spontaneous process is one that proceeds on its own, without any outside intervention.** Can you think of other examples?

It is easy to confuse the word spontaneous with the words instantaneous or explosive. The word instantaneous indicates the speed, or rate, of a process. A spontaneous process may be so rapid that it is instantaneous, or so slow that products are not detected even after thousands of years. The word explosive indicates a rapid, exothermic reaction. Although all explosive reactions are spontaneous, most spontaneous reactions are not explosive.

Now think about one of the examples of a spontaneous process we just mentioned. What can you conclude about its reverse? The reverse of a spontaneous process cannot occur on its own. However, processes such as producing iron from rust or freezing water into an ice cube can be made to occur by an expenditure of energy. And although a river will never flow back up to its origin in the mountains, water can be carried against gravity by an expenditure of energy. In Unit 8 dealing with redox reactions and their applications, you discovered how spontaneous redox reactions are the basis of portable electrical energy—batteries. You also learned that electrical energy supplied from the outside enables nonspontaneous processes to take place in electrochemical cells.

The spontaneous direction of a given reaction is in some ways the first question chemists must answer. Once the spontaneous direction is established, questions regarding the extent of a reaction (how far toward products it will proceed) and its speed (how fast it will get there) become significant. In the pages that follow, you will come to understand and appreciate the criteria

Figure 23–4 *Applications of spontaneous chemical reactions are the source of battery power and locomotive power. Spontaneous processes also created this magnificent arch in the red rock of the Arches National Monument Park in Utah.*

that determine the spontaneous direction of any given process—be it a chemical or a physical one. The spontaneous direction of a given reaction and the extent to which the reaction will proceed (K_{eq}) are a part of the subject of thermodynamics. Reaction rates, however, are not. Thermodynamics provides no information about the speed of a reaction.

Thermodynamics is an important area of study for chemists, physicists, and engineers because it is the study of the heat and work effects that accompany all changes in matter. The applications of thermodynamics are all around you—applications such as generating electricity at power plants, heating and cooling your home, producing and consuming food, and even the changing face of the Earth.

23–1 Section Review

1. What is meant by a spontaneous process?

2. What are two questions answered by thermodynamics?

3. **Critical Thinking—Developing hypotheses** The reverse of a spontaneous process can be made to occur by the expenditure of energy. What might this indicate about a spontaneous process?

23–2 Enthalpy

Have you ever played with a "wind-up" toy? If so, you know that the unwinding of the toy's spring is a spontaneous physical process. It proceeds on its own, and its reverse process (the "winding up" action) requires an expenditure of energy. This process, as well as the action of a river flowing downhill to sea level, can be explained in terms of minimizing potential energy. Both processes are driven by a tendency to reach a state of minimum potential energy. Because low potential energy represents a stable situation, it is logical to hypothesize that a reaction in which products have lower energy than reactants will be spontaneous. How do products come to have less energy than reactants? This question should remind you of what you learned about enthalpy in Chapter 12. Because that may have been some time ago, it would be useful to review energy and enthalpy changes.

Revisiting Enthalpy

The enthalpy of a substance, for all practical purposes, represents the energy of the substance. (Recall from Chapter 12 that, strictly speaking, the enthalpy of a substance is numerically slightly greater than its energy.) Thus the difference in enthalpies of products and reactants approximately represents the difference in their energies. The following points summarize what you learned about enthalpy changes in Chapter 12.

- The enthalpy of products (H_p) minus the enthalpy of reactants (H_r) is called the ΔH for the reaction. This difference corresponds to the heat transferred in that reaction under constant pressure.
- The ΔH for an exothermic reaction is negative and the ΔH for an endothermic reaction is positive.

Guide for Reading

- What is the connection between a spontaneous process and its enthalpy change?

Figure 23–5 *Does one of the situations illustrated here strike you as being absurd? Of course it does because you know that a ball cannot chase a person up a hill. The important point made here is that a ball rolls downhill on its own (spontaneous) whereas the reverse process (nonspontaneous) does not.*

Figure 23–6 *Here you see the enthalpy diagram for an exothermic reaction. What does the activation energy for a reaction represent?*

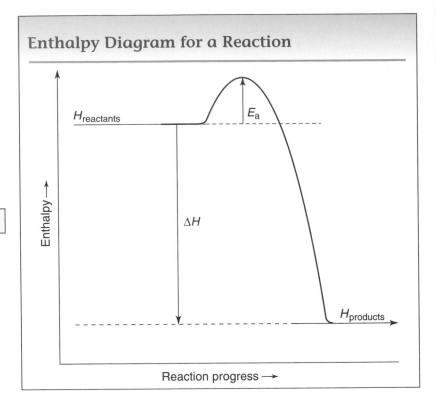

Enthalpy Diagram for a Reaction

$H_{reactants}$

E_a

Enthalpy →

ΔH

$H_{products}$

Reaction progress →

What's an R-value?

If you have ever used a Thermos™ bottle you probably already know the importance of insulation. Insulation is a way of preventing or at least dramatically slowing down the spontaneous transfer of heat from a warmer object to a cooler object. In buildings, insulation is placed in areas, such as the exterior walls, where the greatest heat loss occurs.

Materials that are used as insulation are designated by an R-value, indicating the material's resistance to the flow of heat. Materials with high R-values are the best insulators. Insulation with an adequate R-value can greatly reduce the amount of fuel needed to heat or cool a building.

- $\Delta H°$, the standard enthalpy change, is the heat transferred in the reaction with reactants and products in their standard states. Thus the pressure involved is 1 atmosphere, and the temperature, by convention, is 25°C.
- The enthalpy change for a reaction is directly proportional to the amount of reactants and products involved.
- The enthalpy change for a net reaction (sum of two or more reactions) is the sum of the enthalpy changes for the summed reactions. This is simply the principle of conservation of energy stated as Hess's law.

Enthalpy and Spontaneity

Exothermic reactions release heat. Thus products of this type of reaction contain less enthalpy than reactants. An exothermic reaction can be visualized as one in which reactants "roll down a potential energy hill" to become products at the bottom of the hill. Using this model, you would probably predict that all exothermic reactions are spontaneous, as their final state corresponds to a lower energy than their initial state. By the reverse logic, you would also predict that all endothermic reactions are nonspontaneous, because product enthalpies are greater than reactant enthalpies. This could be visualized as "rolling up the potential energy hill."

As a matter of fact, most exothermic reactions are spontaneous—especially those in which large amounts of heat are released.

Figure 23–7 *The combustion of propane gas and the spectacular reaction between sodium and chlorine to form sodium chloride are examples of spontaneous exothermic reactions. What is the sign of ΔH for these reactions?*

Did you notice the sign of ΔH for the rusting of iron? Yes, it is negative, indicating that this spontaneous process is exothermic. What about reactions such as the combustion of propane or the formation of sodium chloride from sodium and chlorine? Both of these reactions are strongly exothermic and spontaneous.

$$C_3H_8 \text{ } (g) + 5 \text{ } O_2 \text{ } (g) \rightarrow 3 \text{ } CO_2 \text{ } (g) + 4 \text{ } H_2O \text{ } (g)$$

$$\Delta H^\circ = -2043 \text{ kJ} \quad \textbf{(Eq. 2)}$$

$$2 \text{ Na}(s) + Cl_2 \text{ } (g) \rightarrow 2 \text{ NaCl } (s) \quad \Delta H^\circ = -822 \text{ kJ} \quad \textbf{(Eq. 3)}$$

But are all spontaneous processes exothermic? What about the melting of an ice cube? You know that a change of state from a solid to a liquid is an endothermic process.

$$H_2O \text{ } (s) \rightarrow H_2O \text{ } (l) \quad \Delta H^\circ = +6.01 \text{ kJ} \quad \textbf{(Eq. 4)}$$

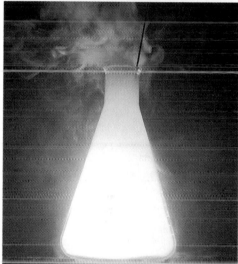

Why, then, does an ice cube melt on its own? (But it does not melt if you put it back in the freezer, where the temperature is below 0°C, does it?) Similarly, what about the endothermic reaction that is used in cold packs? Ammonium nitrate dissolves in water spontaneously, and the temperature of the solution drops. **Although most spontaneous processes are exothermic, some are endothermic.**

If exothermic reactions lead to lower energy products and endothermic reactions lead to higher energy products, how can both exothermic reactions and endothermic reactions be spontaneous? Is there something wrong with our lower energy (enthalpy) model for predicting a reaction's spontaneous direction? As you are about to find out, enthalpy is only part of the picture. To complete the picture you will need to learn about entropy, a fundamental concept in thermodynamics.

23–2 Section Review

1. Is the enthalpy change for a reaction a good indicator of its spontaneity? Explain why or why not.

2. How are enthalpy changes of reactions determined?

3. What happens to the sign of ΔH when an equation is reversed?

4. **Critical Thinking—Giving an example** Give two examples of exothermic processes that are not spontaneous.

Guide for Reading

- What is entropy?
- How does entropy help to determine the spontaneous direction of a reaction?

Figure 23–8 *The entropy of the gaseous, liquid, and solid states of matter is compared on the basis of the arrangement of the particles—atoms, molecules, or ions—in these states. Which state of matter has the lowest entropy? The highest?*

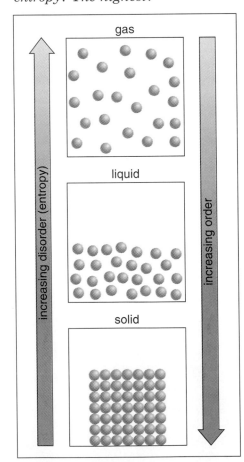

23–3 Entropy

As ice melts into water, molecules of H_2O arranged in an ordered crystalline pattern as solid ice become more disordered as liquid water. When ammonium nitrate dissolves in water, the ordered arrangement of the ammonium and nitrate ions in the solid state is replaced by the disordered arrangement of the hydrated ions in solution. These two examples illustrate the important concept that in all spontaneous endothermic reactions the products are more disordered than the reactants. Disorder is an important driving force in spontaneous processes. To provide a means of comparing the disorder in various substances and situations, the thermodynamic concept of **entropy** was invented. **Entropy is a quantitative measure of the disorder, or randomness, in the substances involved in a reaction.** Entropy is given the symbol S. The greater the disorder, the larger the value of S.

Refer to the comparison of the three states of matter in Figure 23–8. Disorder is greatest in gases and least in solids. Liquids are moderately disordered. Therefore, the entropy of a gas is greater than the entropy of a liquid, and the entropy of a liquid is greater than the entropy of a solid.

A comparison of the disorder present in the products with the disorder present in the reactants is a fundamental factor in predicting the direction of a spontaneous process. Such a comparison is made by examining the entropy change for a reaction, ΔS.

Entropy Changes

When a reaction occurs, there is usually an accompanying change in entropy. In a manner analogous to the definition of ΔH, the entropy of products minus the entropy of reactants is defined as the entropy change for a reaction.

$$\Delta S = S_{products} - S_{reactants} \qquad \textbf{(Eq. 5)}$$

However, unlike ΔH, which can be obtained by measuring the heat transferred in a reaction, ΔS of a reaction cannot be directly measured. But because it is possible to determine the actual entropy S for many substances, ΔS can be calculated from these values using Equation 5. Although the numerical values of S and ΔS are important and useful, we will limit our discussion of entropy to the sign (negative or positive) of ΔS. This will serve you just as well in understanding the significance of entropy in spontaneous processes.

When $S_{products} > S_{reactants}$, the change in entropy, ΔS, is positive. In such reactions, entropy increases and the products have more disorder than the reactants. The melting of ice fits this description because there is more disorder in water than there is in ice. Similarly, the change of water into steam also has a

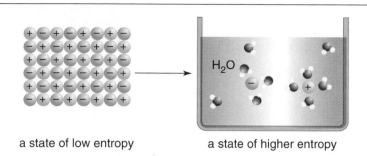

a state of low entropy   a state of higher entropy

Figure 23–9 *The endothermic reaction between ammonium nitrate and water absorbs heat from the surroundings, which consists of the flask and the water between the flask and the wood block. The water freezes and causes the wood block to stick to the flask. What factor makes this endothermic solution reaction spontaneous?*

positive ΔS because $S_{H_2O(g)} > S_{H_2O(l)}$. For the condensation of steam and the freezing of water, $S_{products} < S_{reactants}$. For these processes, ΔS is negative.

What about the entropy change when solid ammonium nitrate dissolves in water? Can you visualize the increase in entropy as the ammonium and nitrate ions break loose and become free to move about in the aqueous solution?

The following list will help you predict the sign of ΔS for several simple physical and chemical changes. Entropy increases when

1. gases are formed from liquids and solids.

$$CO_2 \ (s) \ \rightarrow \ CO_2 \ (g) \qquad \Delta S > 0$$
$$H_2O \ (l) \ \rightarrow \ H_2O \ (g) \qquad \Delta S > 0$$

2. solutions are formed from liquids and solids.

$$NaCl \ (s) \ \rightarrow \ Na^+ \ (aq) + Cl^- \ (aq) \qquad \Delta S > 0$$

3. there are more molecules of gas as products than there are as reactants.

$$2 \ NH_3 \ (g) \ \rightarrow \ N_2 \ (g) + 3 \ H_2 \ (g) \qquad \Delta S > 0$$
$$NH_4Cl \ (s) \ \rightarrow \ NH_3 \ (g) + HCl \ (g) \qquad \Delta S > 0$$

4. the temperature of a substance is increased.

$$H_2O \ (l, \ 25°C) \ \rightarrow \ H_2O \ (l, \ 50°C) \qquad \Delta S > 0$$

Figure 23–10 *Entropy increases when a solid such as dry ice changes into a gas (top). Does entropy increase or decrease when ammonia gas reacts with hydrogen chloride gas to form solid ammonium chloride (bottom)?*

Figure 23–11 *Only one arrangement of the puzzle pieces leads to the completed puzzle, whereas thousands of arrangements are possible for a disordered state of the puzzle. For this reason, states of greater disorder, or entropy, are more probable. What is the symbol for entropy?*

Figure 23–12 *In any spontaneous process, including the flight of a swarm of butterflies or the wearing away of the Egyptian pyramids, entropy increases.*

The Entropy Criterion

You are now ready to discover how the entropy change for a reaction, $\Delta S_{reaction}$, helps determine its spontaneous direction. **A very important law of thermodynamics states that in any spontaneous process, the overall entropy of the universe always increases.** This law, the result of years of scientific observations and experimentation, is something that you may already know or find easy to believe, based on your experience. There is a strong tendency for things to become more disordered. You know what happens to an orderly pile of leaves in your backyard, to a swarm of bees emerging from a hive, and to the gases leaving a car's tailpipe. Even the great pyramids in Egypt are very slowly reverting to the fine sand of the desert.

Did you notice that the thermodynamic law refers to the overall entropy change of the universe and not to the entropy change for the reaction under consideration? This is an important distinction, as you will see. The change in the entropy of the universe as the reaction takes place is the sum of the entropy change for the reaction itself plus the entropy change for the surroundings.

$$\Delta S_{universe} = \Delta S_{reaction} + \Delta S_{surroundings} \qquad \textbf{(Eq. 6)}$$

Problem Solving *Chemistry at Work*

Fifty-two Pickup

Entropy is defined as a measure of the disorder, or randomness, of a particular state. Processes that produce a more disordered final state are more likely to occur. Do you know why? The following activity may suggest an answer.

1. Obtain a newly opened deck of playing cards.
2. Without shuffling the cards, spread them out on a table in front of you.
3. Observe the order in which the cards are placed.
4. Shuffle the deck and then spread the cards out in front of you again. Observe the order of the cards.
5. Repeat Step 4 ten more times.

Developing Models

• After shuffling the cards, were you able to reproduce the order of the cards in the newly opened deck?
• How likely is it that after shuffling a deck of cards, the cards would fall in the same order as a newly opened deck?

• Did you notice order, or pockets of order, in any of the ten trials? Describe the nature of this order and compare it with the newly opened deck.
• Why are states with high disorder more likely to occur?
• Define entropy in terms of the number of arrangements leading to a particular final state.

A reaction is spontaneous when $\Delta S_{universe}$ is positive, that is, when the sum on the right side of Equation 6 is greater than zero. You have learned how to predict the sign of $\Delta S_{reaction}$ for some simple reactions. How does the entropy of the surroundings change as a result of the reaction? The entropy of the surroundings increases or decreases because of the heat transferred by the reaction. An exothermic reaction (ΔH negative) heats up the surroundings, thereby increasing the entropy of the surroundings ($\Delta S_{surroundings}$ positive). An endothermic reaction (ΔH positive) cools the surroundings, thereby decreasing the entropy of the surroundings ($\Delta S_{surroundings}$ negative). Thus the sign of $\Delta S_{surroundings}$ is the opposite of the sign of the ΔH for the reaction.

If all these positive and negative signs are becoming confusing, look at the table in Figure 23–13 on page 760. The table summarizes the four possible combinations of the signs of ΔS and ΔH.

When a reaction has a positive entropy change and is exothermic (Case 1), the reaction is definitely spontaneous. The entropy of the universe certainly increases because $\Delta S_{reaction}$ and $\Delta S_{surroundings}$ are both positive. You can now understand

MATH TIP

Keeping signs straight in thermodynamics can be a confusing matter. A quantity has a *positive* value whenever the quantity *increases* during a reaction. If the disorder of products is greater than the disorder of reactants, entropy has increased and ΔS has a positive value. A reaction gives off energy when the energy value of the products is less than the energy value of reactants. Therefore, matter decreases in enthalpy during an exothermic reaction, and ΔH is negative.

Entropy Change for Reaction and Surroundings

Case	Reaction	$\Delta S_{reaction}$	$\Delta H_{reaction}$	$\Delta S_{surroundings}$	$\Delta S_{reaction}$ + $\Delta S_{surroundings}$	Spontaneous Reaction?
1	exothermic, entropy increase	+	–	+	+	yes
2	endothermic, entropy increase	+	+	–	+ or –	depends
3	exothermic, entropy decrease	–	–	+	+ or –	depends
4	endothermic, entropy decrease	–	+	–	–	no

Figure 23–13 *This table shows how the signs of the enthalpy change (ΔH) and the entropy change (ΔS) determine a reaction's spontaneity. Which case is definitely spontaneous?*

why entropy and enthalpy are often referred to as the driving forces of chemical reactions. For Case 1, they are both favorable. In Case 4, the reaction has a negative entropy change and is endothermic. The entropy and enthalpy factors are unfavorable for such a reaction and the reaction is not spontaneous. It is, however, spontaneous in the reverse direction.

What about Cases 2 and 3? They represent reactions in which one of the two driving forces is favorable. Now you can understand why ice melts at room temperature and ammonium nitrate dissolves in water although both processes are endothermic (Case 2). In both examples, the entropy of the surroundings decreases because the reaction absorbs heat from the surroundings. But in both reactions, the entropy of the products is greater than the entropy of the reactants. This entropy increase is greater than the entropy decrease of the surroundings, so the entropy of the universe increases. In general, to predict the spontaneous direction of a reaction represented by Cases 2 and 3, it is necessary to use numerical values of ΔS and ΔH so that a comparison of the driving forces can be made. Such a numerical comparison of the ΔS and ΔH factors is accomplished by introducing the concept of free energy, which is the topic of the next section.

Observing Entropy

1. Obtain 3 beakers. Place ice water in one beaker, warm water in the second beaker, and water that is at room temperature in the third beaker.
2. Put 3 drops of red food coloring in each beaker.
3. Observe what happens in the beakers.

How is entropy influenced by temperature?

23–3 Section Review

1. Explain the concept of entropy.
2. An endothermic reaction has a positive entropy change. Is the reaction spontaneous? Explain.
3. Explain how the entropy change of the surroundings is related to the enthalpy change of the reaction.
4. **Theme Trace—Patterns of Change** Why is an increase in disorder a natural outcome?

23-4 Gibbs Free Energy

You have learned that the spontaneity of a reaction depends upon two factors: entropy and enthalpy. As you just read, when these two factors oppose each other, the spontaneous direction depends on which factor is larger. The American mathematician J. Willard Gibbs (1839–1903) proposed a thermodynamic concept to simultaneously incorporate the concepts of entropy and enthalpy. He called this concept free energy. It is now called **Gibbs free energy** in his honor and is given the symbol G.

The change in Gibbs free energy, ΔG, for a reaction occurring at constant temperature is given by Equation 7.

$$\Delta G = \Delta H - T\Delta S \qquad \textbf{(Eq. 7)}$$

The change in Gibbs free energy (ΔG) equals the enthalpy change (ΔH) for the reaction minus the product of the absolute temperature and the reaction's entropy change ($T\Delta S$). Just how is the free energy change used to determine the spontaneous direction of a reaction? What other useful information does it provide? We will now explore the answers to these questions.

Free Energy and Spontaneity

Look at Case 1 in the table in Figure 23–13 again. This reaction is definitely spontaneous because both driving forces are favorable. What is the sign of the free energy change in this case? You are correct if you said negative. (This is because ΔH is negative and ΔS is positive.) There are three simple rules that relate the spontaneity of a reaction to the sign of its free energy change at constant temperature and pressure. Knowing these rules will help you predict reaction spontaneity.

- If ΔG is negative, the reaction is spontaneous and can proceed on its own.
- If ΔG is positive, the reaction is not spontaneous and requires a sustained input of energy to make it occur.
- If ΔG is zero, the reaction is at equilibrium.

Let's take a closer look at Equation 7 to understand the significance of temperature. When a reaction is exothermic and its products are more disordered than its reactants (Case 1), ΔG is always negative. Such a reaction is spontaneous at all temperatures. When a reaction is endothermic and its products are more ordered than its reactants (Case 4), ΔG is always positive. Such a reaction is nonspontaneous at all temperatures.

For reactions that belong to Case 2 or Case 3, spontaneity can depend on temperature. The enthalpy and entropy changes (ΔH and ΔS) for the melting of ice (Case 2) are both positive. When you apply this information to Equation 7,

Guide for Reading
- What is the free energy criterion for a spontaneous process?

Figure 23-14 *J. Willard Gibbs was the first recipient of a Ph.D. in science from an American university (Yale, 1863). Gibbs is credited with much of the development of the field of chemical thermodynamics. What is Gibbs free energy?*

Figure 23–15 *This table provides a summary of the free energy change and reaction spontaneity for the four cases listed in Figure 23–13.*

$$\Delta G = \Delta H - T\Delta S$$
$$ (+) (+)$$

(Eq. 8)

you can see that below a particular temperature, ΔG will be positive and the reaction will be nonspontaneous. Above that temperature, ΔG will be negative and the reaction will be spontaneous. For the melting of ice, this temperature is clearly its melting point, or 273 K. The opposite logic holds true for reactions described by Case 3. The table in Figure 23–15 provides a summary of the spontaneity characteristics of the four cases.

Just as ΔH° is the enthalpy change for a reaction at standard conditions, ΔG° is the Gibbs free energy change for a reaction at standard conditions. Entropy values for substances can be found and used to calculate ΔS°. Equation 8 can be used to make calculations of ΔG. Although such calculations are beyond the scope of this textbook, it is important for you to understand the concept and significance of Gibbs free energy change.

Gibbs free energy change plays a significant role in determining the equilibrium constant for a reaction. You know that a reaction is spontaneous when its ΔG is negative. In fact, the more negative the ΔG, the greater the driving force of the reaction. Therefore, when ΔG° is large and negative ($\Delta G^{\circ} << 0$), products are heavily favored ($K_{eq} >> 1$). When ΔG° is large and positive ($\Delta G^{\circ} >> 0$), reactants are heavily favored ($K_{eq} << 1$).

Figure 23–16 *Based on this table, what is the sign of the free energy change for a reaction in which products are heavily favored?*

ΔG° and Equilibrium

ΔG°	Reaction	K_{eq}
+	nonspontaneous	<< 1
–	spontaneous	>> 1
0	at equilibrium	= 1

CHEMISTRY IN ACTION

CONSUMER TIP

Efficiency of Light Bulbs

Which is more energy efficient—a fluorescent bulb or an incandescent bulb? A fluorescent bulb uses only about one fifth as much electricity as an incandescent bulb uses to produce the same amount of light. And because fluorescent bulbs produce only one fifth as much heat for the same amount of light, they are sometimes called "cool" lights. Fluorescent bulbs also last much longer than incandescent bulbs.

Free Energy and Work

A spontaneous reaction is defined as one that can proceed on its own. On the other hand, a nonspontaneous reaction cannot proceed on its own but can be made to occur by a sustained input of energy. Because energy is defined as the capacity to do work, it is also true that work must be performed to make a nonspontaneous reaction occur. Does this mean that a spontaneous reaction can do work as it occurs? Yes, it does.

Spontaneous reactions release free energy (ΔG negative) that can perform work. For example, when charcoal is burned in a barbecue grill, the free energy released heats up the surroundings. But when coal is burned at a power plant, the free energy released is harnessed to drive a generator to produce electricity. Depending upon the manner and setup in which the reaction occurs, different amounts of work can be obtained from a spontaneous reaction. However, this work can never exceed the magnitude of ΔG for the reaction. (Note that the units used for enthalpy and free energy are the same as the units used for energy and work.) In essence, the free energy change, ΔG, represents the maximum work that a spontaneous process can perform. This explains the origin of the name free energy. Free refers to the portion of the total energy change of a spontaneous process that is "free" to do useful work. The remainder is unavailable because it is "lost" to the environment to meet the criterion that the entropy of the universe must increase. This is an important consequence of the entropy criterion because it tells us that, although the total energy of the universe is constant, the energy is continually dispersed so that it is not as useful for doing work.

*I*NTEGRATING
ENVIRONMENTAL **S**CIENCE

What is the essence of the energy crisis?

Figure 23–17 *Spontaneous reactions release free energy that can do work. The free energy released during the combustion of charcoal cooks hamburgers on a barbecue grill, and the free energy released by the movement of water to a state of lower potential energy can be harnessed to produce electricity.*

Too Hot to Handle

You probably would not even be aware of an increase of 2 to 3 C° in the temperature of your local swimming pond. But such a slight temperature change could prove disastrous to other living things. Trout eggs, for example, take approximately $5\frac{1}{2}$ months to hatch in cool water (3°C), but will hatch in only a month at 12°C. And they will not hatch at all if temperatures reach 15°C.

What can cause the temperature of the water in streams, lakes, and rivers to increase? Water has a very high heat capacity, allowing it to absorb large quantities of heat with relatively small changes in temperature. This property of water is used by industry to dispose of the huge amounts of waste heat produced at each stage of manufacturing. Waste heat is a consequence of the fact that the entropy of the universe always increases in a spontaneous process. And all energy conversions "lose," or waste, some energy during the conversion.

The biggest producers of waste heat are electric power plants in general, and nuclear plants in particular. Because the typical efficiency of power plants is about 30 percent, two thirds of the energy of the fuel ultimately escapes into the environment. The easiest way to do this is for a power plant to take in water from a nearby source, run it over coils so that heat is transferred to the water, and release the hot water back into the source. The result is called thermal pollution.

A rise in water temperature of just a few degrees can "cook" oxygen out of the water, disrupting the breeding habitats of fish and killing off plant life. Because temperature helps regulate spawning and reproduction for many species of fish, higher temperatures can disrupt the hatching of fish eggs. Increased water temperature also provides a better environment for the growth of blue-green bacteria than for the growth of many types of algae (a source of food for fish). This population explosion of blue-green bacteria is often accompanied by significant levels of toxins that are produced by the bacteria. As a result, aquatic life, including fish, is killed.

In response to these undesirable effects, the Federal Government has established regulations to reduce and control thermal pollution. For example, an increase of no more than 0.35 C° in the temperature of river water is permitted after it is mixed with the hot water discharge. To meet this requirement, power plants usually use cooling towers or cooling ponds to dissipate the waste heat into the atmosphere. These methods are not the most ecologically sensible ways to reduce thermal pollution, however. One sure way to protect the environment is to start at the beginning and adopt technologies and practices that conserve energy.

How do you feel about this idea? Do you think that cutting back on energy consumption will help preserve the quality of the environment? Can you suggest any other solutions to the problem of thermal pollution?

Figure 23–18 *In order to heat and cool large areas such as the inside of this sports arena, a great deal of energy must be expended. Can you identify one way to increase the efficiency of heating and cooling systems?*

By the reverse logic, ΔG for a nonspontaneous reaction is the minimum amount of work that must be performed by an external source to make the reaction occur. In practice, even more work is required because of factors such as friction. This is the origin of the concept of efficiency. The efficiency of a process compares the actual work (or energy) output to the theoretical maximum and the actual work (or energy) input to the theoretical minimum. In physics, efficiency is expressed as a percentage and can never be greater than 100 percent. In fact, there is no machine—not even the most efficient one—that has an efficiency of 100 percent.

23–4 Section Review

1. What is the sign of ΔG for a spontaneous process? Why?

2. How is the equilibrium constant for a reaction related to its free energy change?

3. What must be true if a process that is endothermic and is accompanied by an entropy decrease is found to be taking place?

4. **Connection—Environmental Science** "Energy is neither created nor destroyed." If so, why should you conserve energy? Why must society seek alternative energy sources?

Laboratory Investigation

Evaluating Enthalpy and Entropy in Spontaneous Reactions

Problem

How do enthalpy and entropy affect the spontaneity of reactions?

Materials (per group)

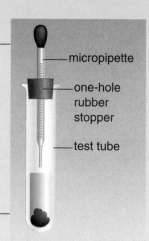

thermometer
small test tube
one-hole rubber stopper
   to fit a test tube
micropipette
1.0 M HCl
magnesium turnings
Bunsen burner
rubber bulb

— micropipette

— one-hole rubber stopper

— test tube

Procedure

Part A

1. Insert a micropipette topped with a rubber bulb into the one-hole rubber stopper. Cut the end of the micropipette so that it extends halfway into the test tube when the stopper is inserted.
2. Pour 4 to 5 mL of 1.0 M HCl into the test tube. Add a few pieces of magnesium turnings. Squeeze as much air out of the rubber bulb as you can and then tightly insert the stopper with the micropipette into the test tube.
3. Note the change in temperature of the reaction in the test tube. Record the sign of ΔH in a data table similar to the one shown.

Part B

1. When the micropipette in Part A has filled with gas, light the Bunsen burner.
2. Remove the stopper from the test tube. Carefully point the end of the micropipette toward the flame of the Bunsen burner and quickly squeeze the rubber bulb of the micropipette so that the gas is released into the flame.
3. Record the sign of ΔH in the data table.

Observations

1. Based on an increase or decrease in entropy of each reaction, indicate the sign for ΔS in the appropriate place in the data table.
2. Based on the spontaneity of each reaction, indicate the sign for ΔG in the appropriate place in the data table.

Analysis and Conclusions

1. What is the relationship among the three variables examined in the investigation (ΔH, ΔS, and ΔG)?
2. Based on your observations for the signs of ΔH, ΔS, and ΔG for each of the reactions, predict the temperature conditions at which each would be nonspontaneous.
3. **On Your Own**   Add a row to your data table for the solution of ammonium nitrate in water. Base your conclusions on Figure 23–9 on page 757.

Part	Balanced Equation	Sign of ΔH	Sign of ΔS	Sign of ΔG
A	Mg (s) + 2 HCl (aq) → Mg^{2+} (aq) + 2 Cl$^-$ (aq) + H$_2$ (g)			
B	2 H$_2$ (g) + O$_2$ (g) → 2 H$_2$O (g)			

STUDY GUIDE

Summarizing Key Concepts

23–1 Spontaneous Processes

- A spontaneous process is one that proceeds on its own without any outside intervention.

23–2 Enthalpy

- The enthalpy of a substance is a measure of its total energy, and enthalpy changes represent the heat transferred in chemical and physical processes.
- Most exothermic reactions are spontaneous.

23–3 Entropy

- Entropy is a measure of the disorder present in a given substance or system.

- Gases have the highest entropy, solids have the lowest entropy, and liquids have moderate entropy.
- In any spontaneous process, the entropy of the universe always increases.

23–4 Gibbs Free Energy

- Gibbs free energy always decreases in a spontaneous process.
- The change in the Gibbs free energy is the maximum work that a spontaneous process can perform. It is also the minimum work required to carry out a nonspontaneous process.

Reviewing Key Terms

Define each term in a complete sentence.

23–1 Spontaneous Processes

spontaneous chemical reaction

23–3 Entropy

entropy

23–4 Gibbs Free Energy

Gibbs free energy

CHAPTER REVIEW

Content Review

Multiple Choice
Choose the letter of the answer that best completes each statement.

1. A spontaneous process is one that
   (a) is instantaneous.
   (b) can proceed on its own.
   (c) releases heat.
   (d) has a positive ΔS.

2. When the enthalpy of the products is greater than the enthalpy of the reactants, the reaction
   (a) releases heat.   (c) is spontaneous.
   (b) absorbs heat.   (d) can do work.

3. The entropy of a substance or system is a measure of its
   (a) disorder.   (c) free energy.
   (b) work capacity. (d) temperature.

4. The entropy change for a reaction is
   (a) $\Delta G - \Delta H$.
   (b) usually zero.
   (c) $S_{products} - S_{reactants}$.
   (d) $S_{reactants} - S_{products}$.

5. The Gibbs free energy change is equal to
   (a) $\Delta H - T\Delta S$.   (c) $\Delta G - T\Delta S$.
   (b) $\Delta H - S\Delta T$.   (d) $\Delta H + T\Delta S$.

6. The entropy of the universe always increases when
   (a) $\Delta S_{reaction}$ is > 0.
   (b) $\Delta H_{reaction}$ is < 0.
   (c) $\Delta S_{reaction}$ is > 0 and $\Delta H_{reaction}$ is < 0.
   (d) $\Delta S_{reaction}$ is < 0 and $\Delta H_{reaction}$ is > 0.

7. Thermodynamics does not deal with
   (a) rates of reactions.
   (b) equilibrium.
   (c) spontaneity.
   (d) work and heat effects.

8. In all spontaneous processes
   (a) enthalpy decreases.
   (b) free energy increases.
   (c) useful work can be performed.
   (d) $S_{universe}$ decreases.

True or False
If the statement is true, write "true." If it is false, change the underlined word or words to make the statement true.

9. The sign of ΔH for an endothermic process is <u>negative</u>.

10. <u>Energy and enthalpy</u> are the two driving forces of chemical and physical reactions.

11. The entropy change for the evaporation of a liquid is <u>positive</u>.

12. An endothermic reaction in which the entropy change is negative <u>is spontaneous</u>.

13. $\Delta S_{surroundings}$ depends on $\underline{\Delta S_{reaction}}$.

14. The spontaneity of a reaction with opposing enthalpy and entropy factors depends on <u>atmospheric pressure</u>.

15. When $\Delta G° >> 1$, $\underline{K_{eq} >> 1}$.

16. The work performed by a spontaneous reaction is always <u>more</u> than the ΔG for the reaction.

Concept Mapping
Complete the following concept map for Section 23–4. Refer to pages xviii–xix to construct a concept map for the entire chapter.

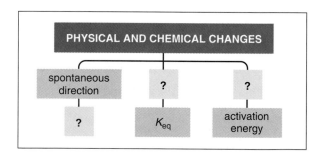

768

Concept Mastery

Discuss each of the following in a brief paragraph.

17. What is a spontaneous reaction?

18. Define entropy. Give two examples of changes that show an entropy increase.

19. Describe the relationship between the spontaneity of a reaction and its ΔH, ΔS, and ΔG.

20. Explain the significance of free energy.

21. When a reaction has a positive enthalpy change as well as a positive entropy change, the reaction spontaneity depends on temperature. Explain why.

22. Predict the sign of ΔS for the following transformations:
(a) $CO_2\ (s) \rightarrow CO_2\ (g)$
(b) $NaCl\ (l) \rightarrow NaCl\ (s)$
(c) $Hg\ (l) \rightarrow Hg\ (g)$

23. For the following reactions, predict the sign of ΔS from the nature of the reaction. Then predict if the reaction is spontaneous, not spontaneous, or dependent on the values of ΔS, ΔH, and temperature.
(a) $CaCO_3\ (s) \rightarrow CaO\ (s) + CO_2\ (g)$
(endothermic)
(b) $2\ NF_3\ (l) \rightarrow N_2\ (g) + 3\ F_2\ (g)$
(exothermic)
(c) $2\ XeO_3\ (s) \rightarrow 2\ Xe\ (g) + 3\ O_2\ (g)$
(exothermic)

24. Tying it Together State the entropy criterion for a spontaneous reaction. Explain how this criterion is reflected in the *patterns of change* in the enthalpy and the entropy of the reaction.

Critical Thinking and Problem Solving

Use the skills you have developed in this chapter to answer each of the following.

25. Making inferences Predict the sign of ΔH in each of the following reactions:
(a) $NH_3\ (g) + HCl\ (g) \rightarrow NH_4Cl\ (s)$
(spontaneous)
(b) $Fe\ (s) + Cu^{2+}\ (aq) \rightarrow$
$Fe^{2+}\ (aq) + Cu\ (s)$ (spontaneous)
(c) $Cl_2\ (g) + 2\ Na\ (s) \rightarrow 2\ NaCl\ (s)$
(spontaneous)

26. Applying concepts What is the sign of ΔS for each of the following processes?
(a) A football stadium empties after a game.
(b) A baby develops into an adult.
(c) Paper, plastics, and aluminum are separated and recycled.

27. Using the writing process You have learned that in all spontaneous processes, the entropy of the universe always increases. What do you think this means for the future of Earth as well as for the future of the universe? Write a short essay in which you describe your predictions. You might like to include what you think happens to the total energy of the universe over time.

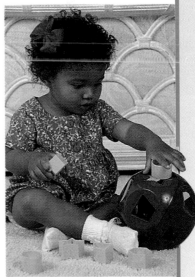

FROM SCHOOL TO WORK

David Emanuel—Student

While David Emanuel of Stratham, New Hampshire, was taking chemistry in high school, he was also training to become a volunteer firefighter through a program sponsored by the Boy Scouts of America. "Chemistry was very relevant to everything I was learning about firefighting. I even wrote a report for my chemistry course on the four classes of fire extinguishers, and how they break down the chemical reactions in different types of fires."

Now that he is in college, David continues to work as both a firefighter and an emergency medical technician. David's knowledge of chemistry comes into play at many different points—from identifying the material that is burning, to knowing how to contain the fire, to guarding against possible environmental catastrophes. For David, fighting fires is truly "chemistry in action."

Chemical Engineer

Chemical engineers are responsible for turning basic chemical research into practical applications. Many chemical engineers work in the energy industry. Chemical engineers may design and operate oil refineries, supervise oil and natural gas drilling operations, and design specialized equipment for industrial applications.

High-school students interested in pursuing a career as a chemical engineer should concentrate on courses in chemistry, physics, and mathematics. Courses in English are also helpful, since the ability to write clearly is an asset in preparing engineering reports. Although a college degree is usually sufficient for a starting job in chemical engineering, a Master of Science degree is required for any advanced engineering positions.

To receive additional information write to the American Petroleum Institute, 1220 L Street, NW, Washington, DC 20005.

How to Prepare for a Job Interview

A job interview gives you a chance to meet an employer and express your qualifications for a job. The interview is a deciding factor in whether or not you get the job.

You should first find out about the company at which you are having the interview. Information on the history, structure, and financial status of different companies can be found at your local library.

Before the interview, you might want to call to confirm the date and time of the interview. You should dress neatly and properly for any job interview, and you should take along any information that might be requested, such as a résumé. Be prepared to answer questions about yourself, your goals, your background, and why you want to work for that particular company.

From the Author

If you feel a little overwhelmed after your first experience with rates of chemical reactions and chemical thermodynamics, you feel exactly as I did when I was in your situation. You probably also feel exactly as every other chemist felt when he or she first studied these topics. Two things are true of the study of reaction rates or chemical kinetics and thermodynamics: They are terribly important, but they are also pretty difficult.

These topics seem difficult because they require us to think in new and unusual ways. Concepts like rate laws and free energy are developed from theory, but they are useful because they help us to predict and understand reality. The free energy change, ΔG, may seem artificial and contrary to ordinary intuition. However, the free energy change tells us a great deal about chemical reactions.

Besides tending to overwhelm new chemistry students, chemical kinetics and chemical thermodynamics are overwhelming in the power they give us for understanding our environment and our universe. They represent a one-two punch for understanding what can, or will, happen. Thermodynamics tells us what can happen and kinetics tells us how fast it will happen. These ideas come somewhat slowly to all of us, and repeated exposure to them is usually the most effective long-range plan. But understanding does come and if you continue to pursue these topics, you will find yourself thinking about everything—even subway crowds or football games—in kinetic and themodynamic terms.

UNIT REVIEW

Concept Mastery

Discuss each of the following in a brief paragraph.

1. How is the rate of a reaction defined?
2. Does every molecular collision lead to a reaction? Why or why not?
3. What are the effects of surface area, temperature, and concentration on reaction rate?
4. What is the relationship between the rate constant of a reaction and the actual rate of the reaction?
5. What is the effect on the rate of a reaction of changing the concentration or partial pressure of a substance in the reaction that does not appear in the rate law?
6. What is the difference between an activated complex and an intermediate in a reaction?
7. Explain how the potential energy of two particles changes during a collision that leads to products.
8. What is a catalyst? How does a catalyst increase the rate of a reaction?
9. Are enthalpy and energy the same? Explain your answer.
10. Why is the concept of enthalpy so useful in chemistry?
11. Compare enthalpy change with standard enthalpy change of a reaction.
12. What is the relationship between the value of the enthalpy change of vaporization and the value of the enthalpy change of condensation for a substance?
13. What does Hess's law say about the value of the enthalpy change for the reaction that results from adding two chemical equations together?
14. What is a spontaneous reaction?
15. What is the relationship between the enthalpy change of a reaction and its spontaneous direction?
16. What are possible low and high entropy situations for 25 books in an otherwise empty room?
17. What is the relationship between the entropy change of a reaction and its spontaneous direction?
18. Give two examples of reactions that are favored by entropy.
19. What is the relationship between the free energy change of a reaction and its spontaneous direction?

Problem Bank

20. The rate law for the reaction $NO\ (g) + O_3\ (g) \rightarrow NO_2\ (g) + O_2\ (g)$ is rate $= k[NO][O_3]$. What will be the effect on the reaction rate if the partial pressure of $NO\ (g)$ is doubled? What will be the effect if the partial pressure of $O_2\ (g)$ is tripled?

21. The hydroxide ion reacts with the $H_2PO_2^-$ ion according to the following equation:
$$OH^-\ (aq) + H_2PO_2^-\ (aq) \rightarrow$$
$$HPO_2^-\ (aq) + H_2\ (g)$$
The rate law for this reaction is rate $= k[OH^-]^2[H_2PO_2^-]$. What will be the change in the reaction rate if the $H_2PO_2^-$ (aq) ion concentration is doubled? What will be the effect if the hydroxide ion concentration is tripled?

22. When the following reaction is performed, 890 kJ of heat escapes from the system for every mole of methane (CH_4) that reacts.
$$CH_4\ (g) + 2\,O_2\ (g) \rightarrow CO_2\ (g) + 2\,H_2O\ (l)$$
What is the enthalpy change, ΔH, for the reaction?

23. The enthalpy change of the following reaction is -185 kJ.
$$H_2\ (g) + Cl_2\ (g) \rightarrow 2\,HCl\ (g)$$
What is the enthalpy change for the following reaction:
$$6\,HCl\ (g) \rightarrow 3\,H_2\ (g) + 3\,Cl_2\ (g)$$

24. Combine the following two reactions so that O_2 (g) cancels out and calculate the overall enthalpy change.

$$C\ (s) + O_2\ (g) \rightarrow CO_2\ (g)$$
$$\Delta H = -393\ \text{kJ}$$
$$2\ N_2O\ (g) \rightarrow 2\ N_2\ (g) + O_2\ (g)$$
$$\Delta H = -164\ \text{kJ}$$

25. Combine the first two equations to find the enthalpy change of the third equation.

(1) $S\ (s) + O_2\ (g) \rightarrow SO_2\ (g)$
$$\Delta H = -297\ \text{kJ}$$
(2) $2\ S\ (s) + 3\ O_2\ (g) \rightarrow 2\ SO_3\ (l)$
$$\Delta H = -790.\ \text{kJ}$$
(3) $2\ SO_2\ (g) + O_2\ (g) \rightarrow 2\ SO_3\ (l)$

26. What is the sign of the entropy change for the following reaction, which is the principal process taking place when mortar hardens?

$$Ca(OH)_2\ (s) + CO_2\ (g) \rightarrow$$
$$CaCO_3\ (s) + H_2O\ (l)$$

27. What data do you need to determine whether the following reaction is spontaneous or not?

$$4\ Fe\ (s) + 3\ O_2\ (g) \rightarrow 2\ Fe_2O_3\ (s)$$

28. Predict whether each of the following reactions would be spontaneous or nonspontaneous under standard conditions or if it is impossible to tell with the data given.

(a) $2\ KClO_3\ (s) + 3\ C\ (s) \rightarrow$
$$3\ CO_2\ (g) + 2\ KCl\ (s)$$
exothermic
(b) $2\ NO\ (g) + O_2\ (g) \rightarrow 2\ NO_2\ (g)$
exothermic
(c) $H_2\ (g) + Zn(ClO_3)_2\ (s) \rightarrow$
$$2\ HClO_3\ (l) + Zn\ (s)$$
endothermic

29. What is the sign of the standard free energy change for the following reaction? Is the reaction spontaneous?

$$2\ HI\ (g) + F_2\ (g) \rightarrow 2\ HF\ (g) + I_2\ (s)$$
$$\Delta H^\circ = -595.16\ \text{kJ}$$

Performance-Based Task

How Does Surface Area Affect Reaction Rate?

You know that the rate of reaction is affected by several factors, including surface area, concentration, and the presence of a catalyst. You can test the effects of one of these factors—surface area—using hydrogen peroxide and a potato.

1. Start by placing a piece of transparent tape around the bottom of a test tube. Make a mark on the tape about 1.5 cm from the bottom of the test tube.

2. Cut the potato into small pieces about 1.5 cm × 0.5 cm × 0.5 cm. Fill a plastic cup half full of water. Fill the test tube with hydrogen peroxide.

3. Working with a partner to act as timer, carefully drop one piece of potato into the test tube. Quickly stopper the test tube with a two-hole stopper. Hold your finger over the stopper and invert the test tube into the cup of water. Record the time it takes for gas to accumulate in the test tube up to the 1.5-cm mark.

4. What effect will adding two or more pieces of potato to the test tube have on the rate of the reaction? Repeat the experiment to test your prediction.

Going Further

5. Prepare a graph of your data by plotting the number of pieces of potato on the x-axis vs. time on the y-axis. Does your graph support your prediction?

6. Design an experiment to prove or disprove the following statement: "Catalysts are not used up in a reaction."

Unit 10 Chemistry and Our World

Hidden away in twisting canyons and inaccessible ledges, mysterious rock carvings are all that now remain of civilizations that once flourished in the southwestern United States. Today, archaeologists study these carvings—called petroglyphs—in an effort to learn whatever they can about the vanished people who made them. One of the most important pieces of information they are seeking is just how long ago the carvings and other remaining artifacts were made. For how many hundreds or thousands of years have they remained hidden? And when did the people who left this legacy behind first appear on this continent?

The key to pinpointing the age of ancient human remains and artifacts is the element carbon—specifically the isotope called carbon-14. In this unit, you will learn why scientists are able to use carbon-14 for this purpose. You will also learn why, of all the elements in the periodic table, carbon plays a unique role in the chemistry of our living world.

DISCOVERY LEARNING

1. Fill two clear plastic cups with water.

2. Add a drop of food coloring to each cup.

3. Add a small amount of activated charcoal or carbon to one of the cups.

4. Cover both cups and let them stand overnight.

   ■ What did you observe?

   ■ How can you explain your observations?

   ■ Based on your observations, can you explain what activated charcoal or carbon might be used for?

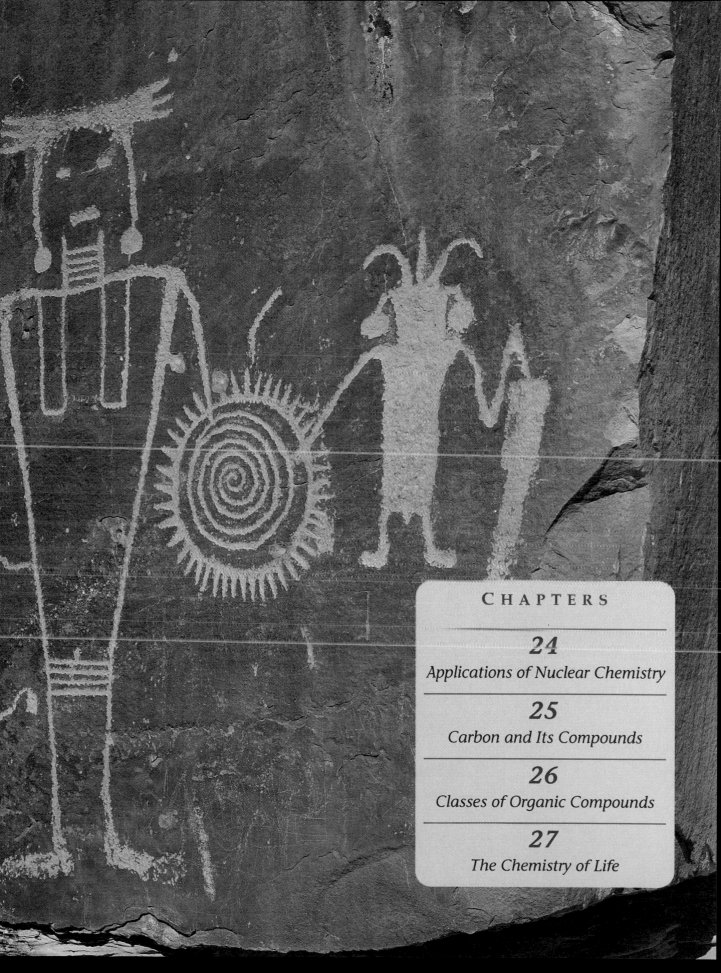

Chapter
24

Applications of Nuclear Chemistry

The explosion of an atomic bomb is spectacular, and it is terrifying. The detonation of the first nuclear device in the southwestern United States in 1945 signaled a huge and abrupt increase in the amounts of energy available to the human race. It ushered us into a new age that offered the possibilities of large-scale destruction and the serious effects and nagging worries of exposure to radioactivity. It also offered incredible possibilities of improved health, inexpensive energy, and a better way of life.

In this chapter you will explore the applications of nuclear reactions and the problems and benefits brought about by their application. You will begin by reviewing the nature of radioactivity and nuclear reactions.

A mushroom cloud—the frightening symbol of our entry into the nuclear age—rises over the Nevada desert. A more benign aspect of nuclear energy is represented by the pottery figure from Ecuador, which can be accurately dated to 400 BC by means of radiocarbon dating.

Chem Journal

YOU AND YOUR WORLD
One of the longest and most intense debates in recent times has been the controversy over nuclear power. You have probably read or heard lively debates about the advantages and disadvantages of nuclear power. In your journal, write an essay explaining your position on the nuclear power issue. Explain your position thoroughly, giving all of your reasons. Remember, if you are still undecided on this issue, that is also a position. Return to your journal after you finish this chapter. Has your position changed?

24–1 Radioisotopes

Guide for Reading
- What is the half-life of a radioactive element?
- What is a nuclear bombardment reaction?

As you learned in Chapter 3, the atoms of most of the elements that you are familiar with are tremendously stable. You can hold in your hands a piece of limestone in which the calcium, carbon, and oxygen atoms are more than 1.8×10^9 years old—the age of the solid crust of the Earth. In many cases these stable atoms may have been "recycled" several times. A carbon atom in a starch molecule that is part of your breakfast cereal may have been exhaled as carbon dioxide by Cleopatra in 50 BC. A nitrogen atom that was in the body of the first amphibian to crawl out of the ocean onto the land may now be a part of the family cat! As you can see, stable atoms may be around for a long, long time.

However, as you also read in Chapter 3, some atoms are not stable. Actually, it is their nuclei that are not stable. An unstable nucleus decays, or emits radiation, to change into a different nucleus. A sample of the element francium, the last element in Group 1A, will have almost completely decayed into radium after only one or two hours.

Although most carbon atoms are stable and date back to before the formation of the Earth's crust, some carbon atoms are

Figure 24–1 Most of the carbon you are familiar with, such as the coal that is mined from the Earth, is stable. That is, it does not decay into other elements. A form of carbon called carbon-14, however, is unstable. This unstable isotope is radioactive. What is another name for a radioactive isotope?

If you would like to examine half-lives in mathematical terms, the fraction of a radio-isotope remaining after n half-lives is given by:
fraction remaining $= (1/2)^n$.
So, the mass in grams remaining, m_{final}, is given by
$m_{final} = m_{initial} \times (1/2)^n$. The same calculation can be applied to molar quantities.

Figure 24–2 *The photograph shows a tin-mining operation in Malaysia. Although most naturally occurring tin is stable—nonradioactive—a small percentage is unstable. What is the name of this radioactive isotope of tin?*

unstable and will decay into nitrogen atoms. The stable and unstable carbon atoms are isotopes of each other. Recall that isotopes are atoms of the same element with the same number of protons but different numbers of neutrons.

Radioisotopes

What kinds of changes take place in the nucleus of an unstable atom when it decays? All nuclear decay is accompanied by the emission of radiation, which is called radioactivity. As you should recall from Chapter 3, radioactivity was first observed in 1896 by Henri Becquerel. Becquerel had stored some photographic film in the same drawer as a sample of uranium ore with only a piece of black paper separating them. When the film was developed, it showed signs of exposure even though it had been kept in the dark. Radiation from the uranium had passed through the black paper and produced an image on the film.

The decay of unstable isotopes is a spontaneous process that takes place all the time. All elements have one or more isotopes that are unstable and that decay to produce other elements. These isotopes may be natural or they may be artificial. Many elements have at least one radioactive isotope, or **radioisotope,** that occurs naturally. Several elements, such as fluorine, do not. The only natural isotope of fluorine is fluorine-19, which is stable. However, unstable isotopes of fluorine can be produced artificially in a nuclear bombardment reaction. You will learn more about nuclear bombardment reactions later in this section.

Half-life

The element rubidium (Rb) has two naturally occurring isotopes. As it is found naturally, rubidium consists of 72.15 percent rubidium-85 and 27.85 percent rubidium-87. The ^{85}Rb isotope is perfectly stable, but ^{87}Rb is radioactive, giving off a beta particle and decaying to strontium-87:

$$^{87}_{37}\text{Rb} \rightarrow\ ^{87}_{38}\text{Sr} +\ ^{0}_{-1}\beta \qquad \textbf{(Eq. 1)}$$

Tin (Sn) also has a naturally occurring radioactive isotope, tin-124. This isotope accounts for 6.01 percent of naturally occurring tin and decays to produce beta particles and antimony-124.

Rubidium-87 and tin-124 are examples of natural radioactive isotopes. The radioactive fraction of any natural sample of either of these two metals is continuously decaying into another element and beta particles. Are either of these metals dangerous to your health? (You probably will not encounter much rubidium, but tin is a commonly used metal.) The answer is that these metals are not dangerous and the reason involves the **half-life** of each element. **The half-life of a radioactive isotope is the time it takes for one half of a sample of that isotope to decay.**

The half-life of rubidium-87 is 6×10^{10} (60 billion) years. This means that in 60 billion years, one half of the ^{87}Rb in a particular

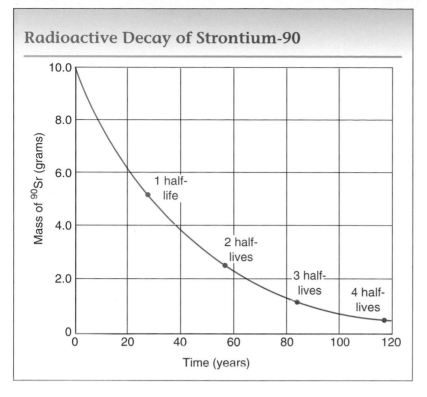

Radioactive Decay of Strontium-90

Mass of ^{90}Sr (grams) vs *Time (years)*

1 half-life

2 half-lives

3 half-lives

4 half-lives

Figure 24–3 *The graph shows the decay of a 10.0-gram sample of radioactive strontium-90. The half-life of strontium-90 is 28.8 years.*

sample would be gone. Suppose you started with a sample containing 1.000 gram of ^{87}Rb. In 60 billion years, 0.500 gram would be left. After another 60 billion years, half of that amount, or 0.250 gram, would be left, and in yet another 60 billion years only 0.125 gram would be left. This process would continue as the amount of ^{87}Rb remaining slowly got smaller and smaller. Of course, 60 billion years is older than the current age of the universe, which is estimated to be about 15 billion years old!

Of course, the more slowly an isotope decays, the more slowly the alpha, beta, or gamma radiation that accompanies radioactive decay is produced. Normally, one particle is emitted every time the nucleus of an atom decays. If ^{87}Rb is decaying so slowly that it takes 6×10^{10} years for just half of it to change, the emission of beta particles must be very slow. And ^{124}Sn with a half-life of 1.7×10^{17} years is decaying and producing beta particles even more slowly. As a result, these isotopes are not dangerous to living things. The half-lives of some common radioisotopes are listed in Figure 24–4.

INTEGRATING

EARTH SCIENCE

Do you know what the age of the universe is?

Figure 24–4 *The table lists the half-lives of several naturally occurring and artificial radioisotopes. What is the half-life of potassium-40?*

Some Radioactive Isotopes, Their Half-lives, and Type of Decay

	Isotope	Half-life (years)	Type of Decay
Natural radioisotopes	uranium-238	4.5×10^9	alpha
	uranium-235	7.1×10^8	alpha
	thorium-232	1.4×10^{10}	alpha
	potassium-40	1.3×10^9	beta
	carbon-14	5730	beta
Artificial radioisotopes	plutonium-239	24,000	alpha
	cesium-137	30	beta
	strontium-90	28.8	beta
	iodine-131	0.022	beta

CHEMISTRY IN ACTION

CONSUMER TIP

Isotopes All Around

There may be more radioisotopes around you than you might think. Starters for fluorescent lamps and electrical appliances use radioisotopes such as promethium-147, krypton-85, and thorium-232 for fast and efficient operation. Some antistatic devices use polonium-210 to ionize the air and prevent discharges of static electricity. Most smoke detectors use americium-241, which has a half-life of 475 years although the useful life of the product is about 10 years. The use of these and other radioisotopes in consumer products is not a hazard unless the product is broken or not disposed of properly.

SAMPLE PROBLEM 1

The half-life of mercury-195 is 31 hours. If you start with a sample of 5.00 g of pure mercury-195, how much of it will still be present after 93 hours?

STRATEGY

SOLUTION

1. Analyze

You know that one half of the sample is changed for each half-life that passes. Therefore, you can calculate the amount of sample that is unchanged based on the half-life, the amount of time that has passed, and the initial mass.

2. Plan

You must first calculate the number of half-lives that will have passed in 93 hours. Then divide the mass of the sample in half for each half-life that has passed. The result will give you the total amount of the sample that remains unchanged after 93 hours.

3. Solve

After 93 hours, three half-lives will have passed ($93 \div 31 = 3$). Therefore, the initial mass of 5.00 g will have been divided in half three times.

$$\frac{5.00 \text{ g}}{2} = 2.50 \text{ g} \qquad \frac{2.50 \text{ g}}{2} = 1.25 \text{ g}$$

$$\frac{1.25 \text{ g}}{2} = 0.625 \text{ g}$$

After 93 hours, or three half-lives, 0.625 g of mercury-195 will be present in the sample.

4. Evaluate

The answer is reasonable because it indicates that a small (but nonzero) amount of the original sample still remains unchanged after 93 hours, or three half-lives.

PRACTICE PROBLEMS

1. Gold-191 has a half-life of 12.4 hours. What mass of this isotope would remain after 49.6 hours if you started with a 7.50-mg sample of pure ^{191}Au? *(Answer: 0.469 mg)*

2. A sample of iodine-126 with an original mass of 15.000 mg loses 13.125 mg of the original mass of the isotope in 39 days. What is the half-life of iodine-126? *(Answer: 13 days)*

Radiocarbon Dating ^{14}C

One of the best known radioactive isotopes is carbon-14, which decays to produce nitrogen-14 and beta particles. The half-life of carbon-14 is 5730 years. Carbon-14 is produced in the Earth's atmosphere by the action of cosmic rays on ordinary atmospheric nitrogen (nitrogen-14). (Cosmic rays are streams of high-energy charged particles from outer space that collide with atoms in the Earth's upper atmosphere.)

New atoms of carbon-14 are produced at the same rate that the isotope decays. Scientists assume that the production of carbon-14 has been essentially constant for a long time. After being produced by the cosmic rays, the carbon-14 is then oxidized in the atmosphere to form $^{14}CO_2$, which mixes with the $^{12}CO_2$ already present in the atmosphere. As a result, the atmosphere always contains a fixed ratio of $^{14}CO_2$ to $^{12}CO_2$.

What makes carbon-14 such an important isotope? The answer is in the way in which carbon dioxide is used by plants and animals. Carbon dioxide is an essential part of the process of photosynthesis in plants. Photosynthesis is the process by which green plants use the sun's energy to convert carbon dioxide and water into sugars and starches. The sugars and starches, in turn, are food for animals that eat the plants and exhale carbon dioxide. Because this cycle exposes plants and animals to a constant source of carbon-14, the amount of this isotope in living plants and animals is constant. The emission of beta particles is likewise constant as the isotope decays.

The incorporation of carbon-14 into plant or animal tissue stops once the organism dies. The emission of beta particles will then drop as the carbon-14 decays. After 5730 years the rate of beta emission will have dropped to one half the rate in living organisms; after 11,460 years the rate will have dropped to one quarter, and so forth. By determining the rate of beta emission from plant and animal remains or products—such as wooden objects, textiles, and leather—scientists can estimate the age of these objects. Such estimates are accurate up to about 7000 years and give a reasonable approximation up to 30,000 years. (After this length of time, the rate of beta emission is too slow to be measured reliably.)

Nuclear Bombardment Reactions

As you have learned, an unstable nucleus is radioactive, which means that it undergoes a spontaneous nuclear reaction to become more stable. Do you think that a stable, nonradioactive nucleus can ever become unstable? The answer is yes. One way to make a stable nucleus unstable is with a **nuclear bombardment reaction.** In a nuclear bombardment reaction, an atom is bombarded with a stream of particles such as alpha particles. When a few of these particles strike their target—the atom's nucleus—particle and nucleus combine to form a new nucleus.

INTEGRATING

BIOLOGY

What is the process of photosynthesis?

Figure 24–5   The Dead Sea Scrolls have been accurately dated using radiocarbon dating. Bristlecone pine trees may reach ages of up to 2000 years. Could radiocarbon dating be used to determine the age of a bristlecone pine? Explain.

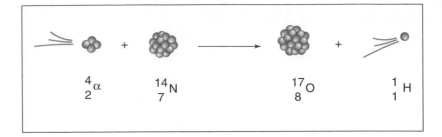

Figure 24–6 *The diagram illustrates a nuclear bombardment reaction in which an alpha particle strikes a nitrogen-14 nucleus, producing an oxygen-17 nucleus and a proton (hydrogen-1).*

Ernest Rutherford was the first scientist to identify a nuclear bombardment reaction. In 1919, he observed that when a high-speed alpha particle strikes a nitrogen-14 nucleus, oxygen-17 and hydrogen-1 are produced:

$$^{4}_{2}\alpha + ^{14}_{7}\text{N} \rightarrow ^{17}_{8}\text{O} + ^{1}_{1}\text{H} \qquad \textbf{(Eq. 2)}$$

Just as in equations for radioactive decay, both the mass numbers and the atomic numbers balance on each side of the arrow in equations for nuclear bombardment reactions.

Using alpha particles to transform one element into another is typically not an easy task. Remember that both a nucleus and an alpha particle carry a positive charge. Ordinarily, an alpha particle would be deflected away from a nucleus because like charges repel each other. For an alpha particle to overcome this force of repulsion and physically collide with a nucleus, it must have a great deal of kinetic energy. In other words, for a successful nuclear bombardment reaction to take place, an alpha particle must be moving extremely fast.

Scientists have developed a variety of devices to accelerate alpha particles and other particles to the speeds needed to collide with a nucleus. These devices, sometimes called "atom smashers," are more formally called particle accelerators. There are many kinds of particle accelerators, which go by such names as cyclotron, synchotron, bevatron, and linac (short for linear

Figure 24–7 *Particles are accelerated to very high energies by circulating them through a huge ring at the Fermi National Accelerator Laboratory in Illinois (left). At the Stanford Linear Accelerator Center in California (right), particles are accelerated down a series of long tubes.*

What's the Half-life?

Having successfully completed all of your chemistry courses, you have found a part-time job as a radiation technician. Part of your job involves analyzing samples of soil contaminated by radioactive waste. One day you are asked to measure the half-life of a radioisotope that decays very quickly. Its half-life appears to be about 25 minutes. Unfortunately, your equipment can only measure a decay rate of one disintegration every 2 or 3 seconds.

Designing Experiments

1. How would you design an experiment to determine the half-life of this radioisotope?
2. How could you check your results?

---

accelerator). Although different in many ways, they all use the same basic strategy to accelerate particles.

A linear particle accelerator is essentially a long series of metal tubes, each connected to a voltage supply that can give the tubes a positive or negative charge. To accelerate positively charged particles, the first tube is given a negative charge and the particles are aimed into it. As the particles pass through the first tube, the tube's charge is changed to positive and the second tube is made negative. Thus the particles accelerate as they are repelled from the first tube and attracted into the second. The process continues through subsequent tubes. After the particles pass through the last tube, they smash into the target nuclei at close to the speed of light (3×10^8 meters per second).

Not all nuclear bombardment reactions require particles to be accelerated to such high speeds. In 1934, Enrico Fermi (1901–1954) reasoned that because neutrons are neutral, they would not need to be accelerated to collide with a nucleus. By bombarding atoms with neutrons, scientists have created more than 1500 artificial radioactive isotopes. For example, a neutron bombardment reaction turns molybdenum-98 into radioactive technecium-99, an isotope that physicians use to detect brain tumors and to examine other human body organs. Here is the nuclear equation for the production of technecium-99:

$$\,^{1}_{0}\text{n} + \,^{98}_{42}\text{Mo} \rightarrow \,^{99}_{43}\text{Tc} + \,^{0}_{-1}\text{e} \qquad \textbf{(Eq. 3)}$$

Visit our Web site at
http://www.phschool.com
to support your
study of chemistry.

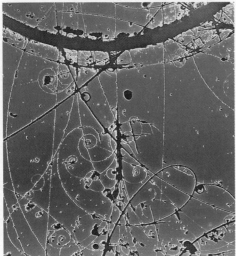

Figure 24–8 *Enrico Fermi, a pioneer in the study of the atomic nucleus, first suggested using neutrons in nuclear bombardment reactions. This colorful bubble chamber photograph records the tracks of particles produced as a result of a nuclear bombardment reaction.*

Notice that the neutron in this equation is represented as $_0^1$n. You can think of a neutron as having atomic number 0 (because it has no protons) and mass number 1 (0 protons + 1 neutron). Also notice that the reaction produces an electron ($_{-1}^0$e). This electron is a byproduct of changes in the nucleus. Most nuclear bombardment reactions produce such particles as byproducts. You can predict the identity of these particles by balancing the mass numbers and atomic numbers in the nuclear equation for the reaction.

SAMPLE PROBLEM   2

The neutron bombardment of calcium-40 produces potassium-40 and possibly another particle as a byproduct. Write the nuclear equation for this reaction.

STRATEGY	SOLUTION
1. Analyze	You know that when calcium-40 is bombarded with neutrons, potassium-40 and possibly another particle are produced. You are asked to write the nuclear equation for this reaction. If a particle is formed as a byproduct, it will have a nonzero mass number and atomic number, which you can find by balancing the mass numbers and atomic numbers on each side of the equation.
2. Plan	Write the symbols for calcium-40 and the neutron on the left side of the equation. Write the symbols for potassium-40 and the unknown particle on the right side of the equation. You already know the mass numbers of calcium-40 and potassium-40. You can find their atomic numbers in the periodic table. The symbol for a neutron is $_0^1$n.
3. Solve	According to the periodic table, the atomic number of calcium is 20 and the atomic number of potassium is 19. You now have enough information to write a preliminary nuclear equation:

$$_{20}^{40}\text{Ca} + _0^1\text{n} \rightarrow _{19}^{40}\text{K} + _Z^M\text{X}$$

where $^M_Z X$ represents the unknown particle. To identify this particle, first balance the mass numbers on each side of the equation: $40 + 1 = 40 + 1$, so the mass number of the particle is 1. Then balance the atomic numbers: $20 + 0 = 19 + 1$ so the atomic number of the particle is also 1. This means that the unknown particle is a hydrogen-1 nucleus. The complete nuclear equation is

$$^{40}_{20}Ca + ^1_0n \rightarrow ^{40}_{19}K + ^1_1H$$

4. Evaluate Make sure that the particles on the left side of the equation are the ones that are colliding and those on the right are the ones that are produced in the reaction. Check to see that the mass numbers and atomic numbers on each side of the equation balance. Be sure that you have correctly identified the particle based on its mass number and atomic number.

PRACTICE PROBLEMS

3. Write the nuclear equation for the neutron bombardment of gold-197 to produce gold-198. *(Answer:* $^1_0n + ^{197}_{79}Au \rightarrow ^{198}_{79}Au)$

4. A hydrogen-2 nucleus is accelerated and strikes a helium-3 nucleus, producing helium-4. Write the nuclear equation for this reaction. What other particle does the reaction produce? *(Answer:* $^2_1H + ^3_2He \rightarrow ^4_2He + ^1_1H$. *The other particle is a hydrogen-1 nucleus.)*

24–1 Section Review

1. What is meant by the half-life of a radioactive element?

2. What is a nuclear bombardment reaction? Give an example.

3. Why is the method of radiocarbon dating unreliable for materials much more than 30,000 years old?

4. **Theme Trace—Stability** Why does the percentage of carbon-14 in an organism remain constant while the organism is alive and then decrease after the organism dies?

Guide for Reading
- How does radiation affect living things?
- What are some beneficial applications of radioisotopes?

24–2 Biological Effects of Radiation

As you have learned, most of the elements that you encounter every day are not radioactive. Only a few elements are naturally radioactive, which is fortunate because radiation is harmful to living things. The extent of damage depends on the amount and type of radiation that the organism is exposed to.

Let's review the characteristics of the three types of natural radiation that were summarized in Chapter 3. Alpha particles are usually not a hazard to humans since they are easily stopped, even by clothing. Beta particles are more penetrating and can pass through clothing and damage the skin. Gamma rays are similar to X-rays and are extremely penetrating. Heavy lead shielding is needed to stop gamma rays, which can penetrate deep into the body causing serious tissue damage and even death.

Units of Radiation

The SI unit of radioactivity is the becquerel, named after Henri Becquerel. A more widely used unit of radioactivity is the **curie** (Ci) named after Pierre and Marie Curie, the discoverers of radium. One curie of radiation is equal to the number of nuclear disintegrations per second from 1 gram of radium. The radiation produced may be alpha particles, beta particles, or gamma rays. This measure of radioactivity takes no account of the level of damage caused by the radiation. Exposure to 1 curie of alpha particles could be almost harmless whereas exposure to the same amount of gamma rays would be devastating.

The unit most often used to measure radiation exposure in humans is the **rem** (short for roentgen equivalent for man), named after Wilhelm Roentgen, the discoverer of X-rays. The rem includes both the amount of energy transferred by the radiation and the sensitivity of the body to that type of radiation. Thus a dose of 150 rem would cause the same amount of damage no matter what kind of radiation is involved or what part of the body is exposed. Very high doses of radiation—well above 1000

Figure 24–9 *The table lists the properties of alpha, beta, and gamma radiation. Which type of radiation is the most penetrating?*

Properties of Alpha, Beta, and Gamma Radiation

Property	Type of Radiation		
	α	β	γ
charge	2+	1-	0
relative penetrating power	1	100	1000
nature of radiation	$_2^4$He nuclei	electrons	electromagnetic energy

rem—are always fatal and doses below 1000 rem may eventually be fatal. Doses below 150 rem are generally not fatal but can cause serious tissue damage.

Measuring Radiation Doses

A **dosimeter** (doh-SIHM-uh-ter) measures the total amount of radiation that a person has received. Most dosimeters take advantage of the fact that photographic film is sensitive to radiation. (Remember how Becquerel first discovered natural radiation.) The film is covered by a layer of material such as paper or plastic that prevents light from reaching the film but allows the radiation to pass through. A badge-type dosimeter is commonly worn by people who might be exposed to radiation, such as nuclear power plant workers. After use, the film is slipped out of the dosimeter and developed. The extent of darkening on the developed film can be translated into a measure of the total amount of radiation actually received by the person.

Effects of Radiation on Living Tissue

How does radiation damage living tissue? Highly penetrating radiation, particularly gamma radiation, follows an essentially straight path through living tissue. The radiation has enough energy to strip electrons from molecules, forming ions through the process of ionization. (For this reason, this radiation is called ionizing radiation.)

These ions—and high-energy fragments of molecules called free radicals also formed by ionizing radiation—are so reactive that they easily disrupt living cells. This can lead to the destruction of tissues, particularly those in which cells multiply rapidly, such as blood-forming tissues and lymph nodes. Leukemia, which is characterized by excessive growth of white blood cells and swollen lymph nodes, is probably the most common cancer caused by radiation. Ironically, both Marie Curie and her daughter Irene died of leukemia, probably as a result of long exposure to radiation.

Types of Radiation Damage

There are two ways in which radiation may damage an organism. **Radiation damage may affect an organism directly or it may affect the organism's offspring.** Damage to the organism that received the radiation directly is called somatic damage. Somatic damage affects only body cells. Burns and rashes on the skin, cataracts in the eyes, and a wide range of cancers are examples of somatic damage.

An organism that is exposed to radiation may also experience damage to the cells of its reproductive organs. Damage that affects reproductive cells is called genetic damage. Genetic damage may result in the birth of deformed offspring.

Figure 24–10 Workers at a nuclear-waste storage facility must wear protective clothing to minimize their exposure to potentially harmful radiation.

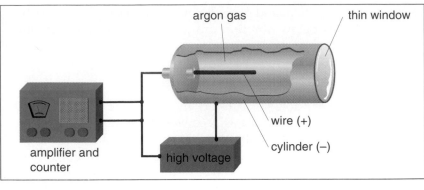

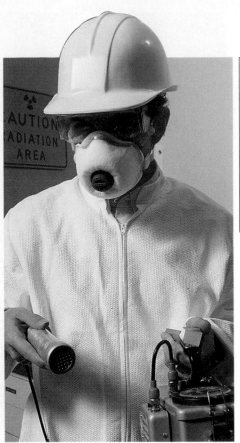

Figure 24–11 *A Geiger counter is an instrument used to detect radiation. The diagram shows the basic parts of a Geiger counter.*

*I*NTEGRATING

*B*IOLOGY

Why is iodine-131 used to monitor thyroid function?

Detection of Radiation

Because of the dangers posed by radiation, it is crucial to be able to detect radiation in the environment. Early radiation detectors used a screen coated with zinc sulfide (ZnS), which gives off a green flash whenever an alpha particle, a beta particle, or a gamma ray strikes it. The flashes can be counted to determine the intensity and direction of the radiation. Modern instruments called scintillation counters automatically detect the flashes of light and then relay this data to a computer.

The **Geiger counter,** which depends on the ionizing ability of radiation, is the most common instrument for detecting radiation. A Geiger counter, illustrated in Figure 24–11, consists of a hollow cylinder with a wire in the center. The wire is given a positive charge and the cylinder a negative charge. Both ends of the cylinder are blocked but one end has a very thin window through which radiation can easily pass. An alpha particle, a beta particle, or a gamma ray passing through this window will ionize the gas within the cylinder. The positive ions produced will be attracted to the negatively charged cylinder and the negative ions will be attracted to the positively charged wire. When the ions strike the charged cylinder and wire, they create an electric pulse, which can be amplified to give an audible "click." This electric pulse can be directed to a recorder or data processor.

Beneficial Uses of Radioisotopes

In spite of the hazards of radiation, radioisotopes have many beneficial applications in medicine, agriculture, and industry.

RADIOTRACERS Radiotracers—sometimes referred to as radioactive labels—are used to follow a specific substance as it moves through a natural system. Normally, a very small amount of a compound containing a radioactive isotope is introduced into the system to be studied. The radiotracer will be carried along with the other materials in the system and can be followed using a Geiger counter. In this way, the movement of materials within the system can be charted.

Figure 24–12 *In 1977, Rosalyn Yalow received the Nobel Prize for the development of a technique called radioimmunoassay, which is a sensitive method of using radiotracers in the human body. Here you see a nuclear scan of a human thyroid using the radiotracer iodine-131.*

Iodine-131 is a beta emitter with a half-life of 8.1 days. Thyroid function can be tested with this isotope because the thyroid is the only part of the body that takes up iodine. A small amount of radioactive iodine-131 is added to ordinary nonradioactive iodide and is then administered to the patient. The movement of the iodine, which is determined by tracking the iodine-131 radiotracer, gives valuable information on thyroid function.

There are many other examples of radiotracers. Barium sulfate ($BaSO_4$), which is insoluble in water, containing radioactive barium-140 is used to follow the movement of silt in rivers. Compounds containing radioactive phosphorus-32 have been used to study the uptake of nutrients by plants. Cobalt-58 is being used to trace the body's ability to absorb vitamin B_{12}, which contains cobalt.

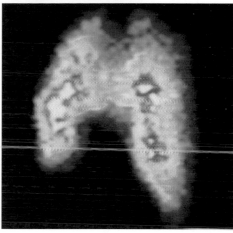

CANCER TREATMENT   Cancer is a disease in which abnormal cells in the body are produced at a rate far beyond the rate for normal cells. The mass of cancerous tissue resulting from this runaway growth is called a tumor. Cancer is particularly suitable for radiation therapy because the fast-growing cancer cells are more susceptible to high-energy radiation such as gamma rays than are the healthy cells. This is slightly confusing since the same radiation can also cause cancer in healthy cells. Clearly, the choice of which radioactive isotope to use and how to administer it is crucial to ensuring that the therapy will do more good than harm. In most cases, the radioactive source must be implanted in the appropriate organ.

Thyroid cancer can be treated with iodine-131 because, as you read earlier, almost all the iodine in the body is taken up by the thyroid. Iridium-192 is used to treat some cancers. Small "seeds" with iridium-192 at the center have a platinum metal coating to ensure that the radioactive iridium will not escape

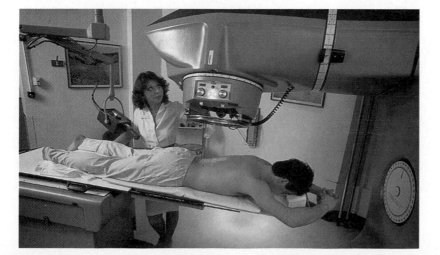

Figure 24–13 *The man in the photograph is undergoing radiotherapy for cancer of the spine using cobalt-60. The cobalt-60 source delivers a high-energy dose of radiation to a localized area.*

and spread throughout the body. In addition, the platinum coating stops the alpha and beta particles emitted by the iridium, allowing only the therapeutic gamma rays to escape.

Instead of implanting the radiation source, external sources of radiation may also be used. Cobalt-60, which produces a beam of gamma rays that is applied to the cancerous tissue, is an example of a radioactive source that is used externally.

Because fast-growing cells are particularly susceptible to high-energy radiation, naturally fast-growing cells within the body are subject to damage during radiation therapy. The growth of hair and maintenance of the stomach lining both involve fast-growing cells. For this reason, loss of hair and stomach problems, such as nausea, are common during radiation therapy.

FOOD PRESERVATION   The ability of radiation to damage organisms has been used to preserve certain foods, particularly sensitive fruits such as strawberries. The strawberries are exposed to a cobalt-60 source of gamma rays. Most of the microorganisms on the strawberries, such as molds and bacteria that are the principal causes of spoilage, are killed by the radiation. As a result, radiation greatly extends the shelf life of the strawberries. Figure 24–14 shows a comparison between strawberries that have been treated with gamma rays and those that have not.

We have mentioned only a few of the current applications of radioisotopes in this section. Undoubtedly, the potential for future beneficial applications exists.

Figure 24–14   *The strawberries on the left, which were treated with gamma rays, remain fresh even after several days on a store shelf. The strawberries on the right, which were not treated with gamma rays, have developed a thick growth of mold.*

INTEGRATING
BIOLOGY

Why do cancer patients often lose their hair during radiation treatment?

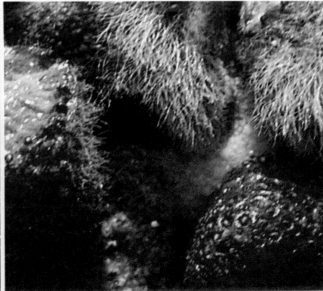

Radon—The Hidden Hazard

The granite bedrock under much of the United States contains small amounts of uranium-238. This is a naturally occurring radioactive isotope with a half-life of more than a billion years. Uranium-238 slowly decays in a decay series that finally terminates in lead-206, a stable isotope of lead. One of the steps along the way is radon-222, an isotope of the noble gas that is extremely radioactive, with a half-life of minutes.

The danger of exposure to radon is considerable to anyone living in a community that is built on granite bedrock. Radon gas can seep into the basement of a house through holes or cracks in the foundation. But the danger does not come from the radon gas itself. The half-life of radon-222 is so short that when it is breathed into the lungs, some of it will decay before it is exhaled. As radon decays, however, the decay products combine with tiny dust particles in the air and stick to the lung tissue. Radiation from the decay products of radon-222 is suspected of playing a significant role in causing lung cancer.

To protect against the danger of radon, the Environmental Protection Agency (EPA) rec-

ommends that all homes be tested for radon levels, which should not exceed 4 picocuries per liter of air. The health risks from high levels of radon can be lessened by installing a ventilation system to lower the level of radon in the air.

24–2 Section Review

1. What are two ways in which radiation may damage organisms?

2. Give three examples of the beneficial applications of radioisotopes.

3. How does a badge-type dosimeter work?

4. **Connection—You and Your World** Considering the varying applications of radioisotopes, do you think the benefits outweigh the risks involved in their use? Give examples to support your opinion.

Guide for Reading

- What is the difference between nuclear fission and nuclear fusion?
- How is energy produced in a nuclear reactor?

24–3 Harnessing the Nucleus

The energy produced by the decay of radioactive atoms is enormous. As a very rough approximation, an ordinary chemical reaction will liberate a little less than 50 kilojoules of energy per gram of reactant. In contrast, the decay of a radioactive isotope will liberate energy in the range of 10^6 kilojoules per gram of isotope! Clearly there is a huge source of energy here.

For most applications, however, radioactive decay reactions are not good candidates for power sources. These reactions cannot be controlled and the rate of energy output is not constant. An isotope with a short half-life gives off a lot of energy, but only for a short time. An isotope with a long half-life provides energy for a long time, but its rate of energy output is low. And as half-life after half-life passes, the energy output of any radioactive isotope becomes less and less.

It seems that a different kind of nuclear reaction is necessary to make an effective energy source. There are two possibilities. In addition to radioactive decay and nuclear bombardment reactions, two other categories of nuclear reactions are **nuclear fission** and **nuclear fusion.**

Nuclear Fission

In the late 1930s, the largest known nucleus was the nucleus of a uranium atom, which has 92 protons. In the hope of making a larger nucleus, Enrico Fermi and his colleagues bombarded uranium with neutrons. Fermi thought that a nuclear bombardment reaction would produce a heavier isotope of uranium, which would then decay into an atom with more protons. Fermi was indeed correct. Uranium-238 can absorb a neutron to form uranium-239, which decays to neptunium-239:

$$\,_0^1\text{n} + \,_{92}^{238}\text{U} \rightarrow \,_{92}^{239}\text{U} \rightarrow \,_{93}^{239}\text{Np} + \,_{-1}^{0}\text{e} \qquad \textbf{(Eq. 4)}$$

In 1938, German scientists Otto Hahn (1879–1968) and Fritz Strassman (1902–1980) attempted to repeat Fermi's experiment. To their dismay, they discovered barium among their products. At first they thought that barium might be an impurity. But barium is not a particularly common element and they had no idea how barium had found its way into their experiment.

Historical Perspective ➤

Hahn wrote a letter about this puzzle to his former colleague, Lise Meitner (1878–1968). Meitner was living in Sweden, where she had emigrated to escape German anti-Semitism. It was Meitner who grasped the significance of barium among the products. She came to the bold conclusion that a uranium nucleus had split during the reaction, producing a barium nucleus as one

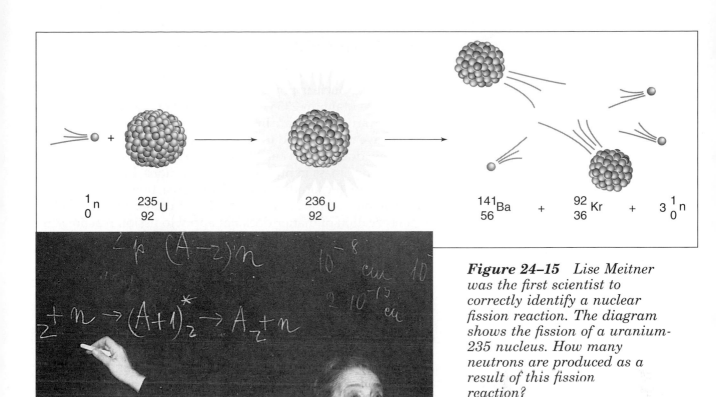

$$\begin{array}{ccccccc} {}^{1}_{0}n & {}^{235}_{92}U & & {}^{236}_{92}U & & {}^{141}_{56}Ba & + & {}^{92}_{36}Kr & + & 3\,{}^{1}_{0}n \end{array}$$

Figure 24–15 *Lise Meitner was the first scientist to correctly identify a nuclear fission reaction. The diagram shows the fission of a uranium-235 nucleus. How many neutrons are produced as a result of this fission reaction?*

of its products. She also recognized that the nuclei produced in this reaction would violently repel each other because of their large positive charges, which meant that a single uranium atom was a source of tremendous energy.

Meitner's ideas proved to be correct. Later investigations showed that neutron bombardment could split one of uranium's less abundant isotopes, uranium-235, into two smaller nuclei, one of which is a barium nucleus. Here is the nuclear equation for this reaction:

$$\text{(Eq. 5)} \qquad {}^{1}_{0}n + {}^{235}_{92}U \rightarrow {}^{236}_{92}U \rightarrow {}^{141}_{56}Ba + {}^{92}_{36}Kr + 3\,{}^{1}_{0}n$$

Figure 24–15 illustrates this reaction, which Meitner called a nuclear fission reaction, or fission for short. **In a nuclear fission reaction, a large nucleus is split into two smaller nuclei of approximately equal mass.** When a uranium-235 nucleus undergoes a fission reaction, it may form isotopes other than barium-141 and krypton-92.

When you are checking nuclear equations for correct mass and charge balance, do not forget to apply a coefficient to the mass and charge of the particle. In Equation 5, notice the mass balance is correct only when 3 neutrons are accounted for.

$$236 = 141 + 92 + 3(1)$$

Energy and "Missing" Mass

Today, fission reactions are used to provide what is commonly called nuclear power. In a nuclear reactor, the fission of 4.5 grams of uranium-235 will satisfy the average person's energy needs for an entire year. In comparison, about 15 tons of coal would have to be burned to provide the same amount of energy.

Where does all this energy come from? The answer involves the "missing" mass in nuclear fission reactions. Intriguingly, the total mass of the products in a fission reaction is slightly less than the mass of the starting materials. In other words, the law of conservation of matter does not apply to fission reactions! So what happens to the missing mass? The answer is that the missing mass is converted into energy. The amount of energy released can be calculated from a famous equation derived by Albert Einstein:

$$E = mc^2 \qquad \text{(Eq. 6)}$$

In this equation, E is the amount of energy released, m is the mass lost in the reaction, and c is the speed of light (3×10^8 meters per second). Even though the lost mass is very small, when it is multiplied by c^2 (9×10^{16} m^2/s^2), the resulting value for the energy released is immense.

There is another important feature of fission reactions. If you look again at Equation 5, you will see that the reaction produces more neutrons than it absorbs. This means that one fission reaction produces enough neutrons to start three more fission reactions, each of which in turn produces the neutrons needed to start three more reactions, and so on, in a series of fission reactions. This continuous series of fission reactions is called a **nuclear chain reaction**. A chain reaction is illustrated in Figure 24–16. Once started, a nuclear chain reaction can escalate rapidly. An atomic bomb is designed to produce a "runaway" chain reaction, creating an incredibly powerful explosion.

Figure 24–16 *The diagram illustrates a nuclear chain reaction. The explosion of an atomic bomb is the result of a runaway chain reaction. The photograph shows an atomic bomb explosion in the Bikini Islands—one of a series of tests conducted by the United States in the 1940s.*

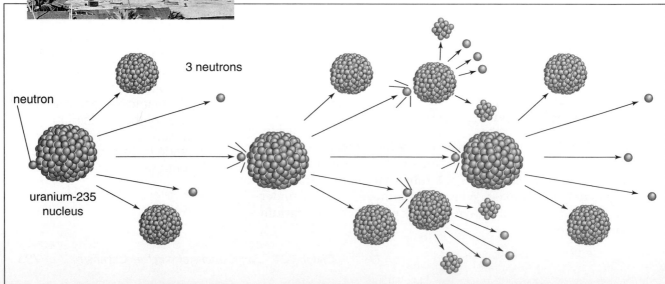

neutron

uranium-235 nucleus

3 neutrons

Nuclear Reactors

Could a nuclear power plant ever explode like an atomic bomb, you might be wondering? The answer is no, it cannot. The fuel rods in a nuclear reactor contain too little uranium-235 to sustain a runaway chain reaction. Reactors are further regulated by control rods that absorb neutrons and thus regulate the speed of the nuclear chain reaction. Figure 24–17 illustrates the major parts of a typical nuclear reactor.

Most of the concern about nuclear power plants is with the highly radioactive waste materials that are formed as a result of the fission process. However, several incidents at nuclear power plants have raised questions about the basic safety of these plants.

In 1979, the cooling system of the reactor at Three Mile Island, Pennsylvania, lost water due to operator error. As a result, heat generated in the fuel rods by the decay of radioactive isotopes could not be dissipated, raising concern that the melting point of the fuel would be reached and a "meltdown" would occur. Fortunately, coolant water was restored and the meltdown was prevented.

The reactor in Chernobyl, Ukraine, used graphite as a moderator to slow down neutrons. Although it is normally very difficult to ignite, once graphite is burning it can reach very high temperatures and is extremely difficult to extinguish. In 1986, excessive heat within the Chernobyl reactor, again a result of operator error, ignited the graphite and the fire that resulted burned for days. Many firefighters later died as a result of exposure to radiation. The reactor was completely destroyed, allowing tremendous amounts of radiation to be released into the atmosphere and carried on the winds to many parts of Europe. Thousands of fatal cancers in humans exposed to the radiation are eventually expected as a result of the Chernobyl accident.

Figure 24–17 *Here you see a schematic diagram of a nuclear power plant. The core of a nuclear reactor is shown in the photograph.*

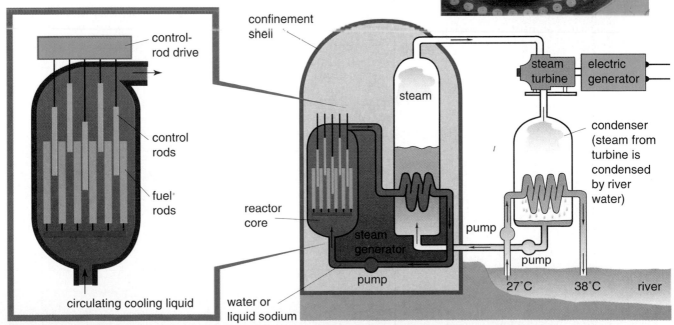

Nuclear Waste Disposal

As a nuclear reactor operates, radioactive fission products build up in the fuel rods as the fissionable material is used up. About one fourth of all the fuel rods must be replaced every year, representing several hundred tons of highly radioactive material to dispose of. Disposal of this radioactive waste is a major problem. Burial appears to be the best solution to the problem, but there is no agreement as to where the radioactive wastes can be safely buried. A reprocessing program, in which the uranium fuel left in the rods is extracted for reuse, leaving only the fission products in the rods for disposal, might be a desirable alternative. Until a substantially risk-free method of nuclear waste disposal can be found, however, it seems that nuclear power will remain a controversial source of energy for our rapidly growing population.

Nuclear Fusion

If nuclear fission is a questionable source of energy for the future, might nuclear fusion be an acceptable alternative? **In a nuclear fusion reaction, two small nuclei join to form a large nucleus.** For example, consider the fusion reaction in which two isotopes of hydrogen combine to form helium:

$$^{2}_{1}\text{H} + ^{3}_{1}\text{H} \rightarrow ^{4}_{2}\text{He} + ^{1}_{0}\text{n} \qquad \textbf{(Eq. 7)}$$

Like a fission reaction, a fusion reaction converts some of the mass of the original nuclei into energy—a great deal of energy. Unfortunately, fusion reactions are difficult to produce and control. In order for 2 atoms to fuse, their nuclei must come together. That goal is strongly resisted, first by the repulsion of the atom's negatively charged electron clouds and then by the repulsion between the positively charged nuclei.

Stripping off the electrons at very high temperatures solves the first problem. The resulting "sea" of bare nuclei is called a

Figure 24–18 *The diagram illustrates the fusion reaction between two isotopes of hydrogen—deuterium ($^{2}_{1}H$) and tritium ($^{3}_{1}H$)—to produce a helium nucleus and a neutron.*

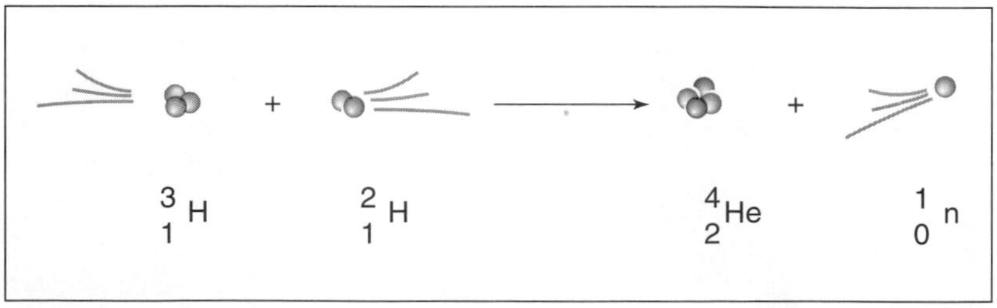

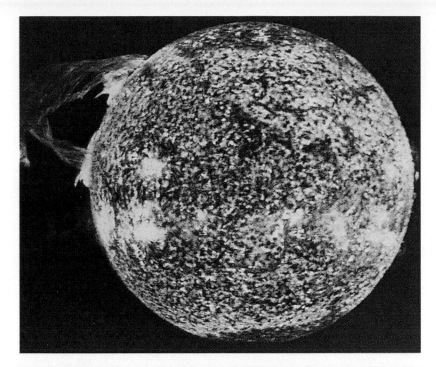

Figure 24–19 *This spectacular photograph of the sun provides only an inkling of the titanic energy generated by thermonuclear fusion reactions.*

plasma. (You may remember that we introduced the term plasma in Chapter 2 as one of the basic forms of matter.) These bare nuclei must then be forced together to allow a fusion reaction to take place. If 2 nuclei are to overcome the force of repulsion so that they can combine in a fusion reaction, they must be moving very fast. To reach the speeds required, the nuclei must be heated to an extremely high temperature—about 40 million kelvins! Because of these high temperatures, nuclear fusion reactions are often called thermonuclear reactions. (The prefix *thermo-* means heat.) Thermonuclear reactions are responsible for the energy produced by the sun and other stars. Thermonuclear reactions are also the source of the destructive power of a hydrogen bomb.

Fusion Research

In the future, fusion reactions may be an important source of energy. A fusion reaction using hydrogen—an abundant element—as fuel would release more energy per gram of fuel than does a fission reaction. Furthermore, the products of a fusion reaction are not radioactive. However, the controlled use of fusion is still in the experimental stage because the high temperatures required are hard to achieve and maintain. Several research groups are attempting to produce a sustained and controlled fusion reaction.

Whether or not fusion will ever be made commercially practical remains to be seen. Huge barriers need to be surmounted. As you just learned, the temperature needed to cause the fusion of hydrogen-2 (deuterium) and hydrogen-3 (tritium) is calculated to be about 40 million kelvins. No material can withstand such high temperatures. Therefore the hot plasma must be confined

Domino Effect

Arrange 15 dominoes to form a triangle. Place 1 domino in the first row, 2 in the second row, 3 in the third row, and so forth. Knock over the first domino so that it falls backward. What happens to the other dominoes? How is this model similar to what happens in a nuclear chain reaction?

Figure 24–20 Scientists are exploring nuclear fusion using magnetic confinement as well as lasers. Here you see the Tokamak Fusion Test Reactor at Princeton University in New Jersey (top) and the target chamber of Nova, the world's most powerful laser at Lawrence Livermore National Laboratory in California (bottom).

without touching any material surface. A tokamak is a device that creates a plasma and then uses a magnetic field to hold the plasma in a doughnut-shaped chamber called a magnetic bottle. Temperatures of 3 million kelvins have been reached in tokamaks. This is still not hot enough, however, and much research remains to be done. An alternative method using lasers as a source of heat is considered promising.

The energy needed to initiate nuclear fusion can be produced by means of a very powerful laser. The hydrogen isotopes are sealed in a tiny glass bead about 0.1 millimeter in diameter. The laser then fires a tremendous blast of energy at the bead almost instantaneously—within about 10^{-9} second, or 1 nanosecond. The resulting conditions of temperature and pressure inside the bead are comparable to the conditions created in a magnetic confinement fusion reactor.

The Cold Fusion Controversy

The excitement surrounding the quest for almost limitless energy has occasionally resulted in hasty reporting of results and intense controversies. The most striking demonstration of this is "cold fusion." In 1989, Stanley Pons and Martin Fleishman, two chemists working at the University of Utah, reported a nuclear fusion reaction that could be performed under ordinary laboratory conditions.

Pons and Fleishman's "cold fusion" reaction was very simple—basically the electrolysis of water to yield hydrogen and oxygen. The water they used, however, was not ordinary H_2O. Instead, Pons and Fleishman used deuterium oxide, or heavy water (^2H_2O). In addition, the reaction used palladium as the cathode, the electrode at which deuterium gas would be liberated. Two pieces of evidence were reported to support the occurrence of cold fusion: Much more heat was liberated than was possible by the ordinary chemical reaction, and helium, an impossible product of the ordinary reaction, was detected.

The Utah chemists proposed that before the deuterium atoms could combine to form deuterium gas, they were absorbed into the palladium cathode. The deuterium atoms were packed so tightly within the palladium that they reportedly underwent a fusion reaction as follows:

$$^2_1H + {}^2_1H \rightarrow {}^4_2He \qquad \textbf{(Eq. 8)}$$

The chemists claimed that the extra energy detected in the reaction was the energy given off in the fusion reaction and the helium detected was the product of the reaction shown in Equation 8.

The announcement of cold fusion caused a massive furor, not only among scientists but also among politicians and ordinary citizens. Enormous amounts of money were appropriated for additional cold fusion research. As more and more negative results have been reported, however, the dream of using cold fusion as a source of cheap, unlimited energy has receded.

24–3 Section Review

1. What is the difference between a nuclear fission reaction and a nuclear fusion reaction?

2. What is the source of energy in a nuclear reactor?

3. What are some of the problems involved in using fusion as a source of energy?

4. **Critical Thinking—Making comparisons** Which kind of isotopes are more dangerous in nuclear waste, isotopes with short half-lives or isotopes with long half-lives? Explain.

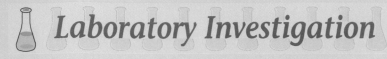

Laboratory Investigation

A Penny for Your Neutron: A Model of Half-life

Problem

How can you make a model of beta decay?

Materials (per group)

100 pennies
paper or plastic cup
graph paper

Procedure

1. Work in groups of three. Designate one classmate to be the coordinator, one to be the "Geiger counter," and one to be the recorder.
2. Place 100 pennies into a paper or plastic cup. The pennies will represent carbon-14 nuclei.
3. Have the coordinator shake the cup of pennies and carefully empty them onto a flat surface. Have the counter separate the pennies that are heads up from those that are tails up. The heads represent carbon-14 nuclei that have decayed and the tails represent unchanged carbon-14 nuclei. This step represents one half-life. Have the recorder record the number of carbon-14 nuclei remaining after one half-life in a data table similar to the one shown.
4. Return the unchanged carbon-14 nuclei (tails) to the cup. Repeat Step 3 five more times.

Observations

1. How many carbon-14 nuclei were left after one half-life? After six half-lives?
2. Draw a graph of the number of remaining carbon-14 nuclei vs. half-life.

Half-lives	Remaining Carbon-14 Nuclei
1	
2	
3	
4	
5	
6	

Analysis and Conclusions

1. Does this model of beta decay correctly represent the rate of decay of a radioactive substance? Explain.
2. Do you think that after more half-lives you would eventually have no carbon-14 nuclei remaining? Does your answer suggest why scientists use half-life to describe radioactive decay? Explain.
3. Radioactive carbon-14 has a half-life of 5730 years. Suppose a piece of wood has a decay rate of 15 disintegrations per minute. How many years would it take for the rate to decrease to 4 disintegrations per minute?
4. **On Your Own** Extend your data table and graph by repeating Step 3 several more times to collect data for additional half-lives. If time permits, repeat the entire investigation using different numbers of pennies.

STUDY GUIDE

Summarizing Key Concepts

24–1 Radioisotopes

- Many elements have at least one naturally occurring radioactive isotope, or radio-isotope.
- The half-life of a radioisotope is the time it takes for one half of a sample of that isotope to decay.
- Carbon-14 is a common radioisotope that is used in radiocarbon dating to estimate the age of plant and animal remains or products.
- In a nuclear bombardment reaction, an atom's nucleus is bombarded with a stream of particles and changed into a different nucleus.

24–2 Biological Effects of Radiation

- Radiation is harmful to living things. Highly penetrating radiation damages living tissue by ionizing molecules in the tissue.
- Radiation damage may affect an organism's body cells directly (somatic damage) or it may affect an organism's reproductive cells and thus the organism's offspring (genetic damage).
- In spite of the hazards of radiation, radioisotopes have many beneficial applications. They are useful in medicine as radiotracers and in cancer treatment, as well as in food preservation.

24–3 Harnessing the Nucleus

- Two types of nuclear reactions that are effective energy sources are nuclear fission and nuclear fusion.
- In a nuclear fission reaction, a large nucleus is split into two smaller nuclei, releasing energy in the process.
- The extra neutrons produced in a nuclear fission reaction are able to start a continuous series of fission reactions called a nuclear chain reaction.
- In a nuclear fusion reaction, two small nuclei combine to form a larger nucleus, releasing energy in the process

Reviewing Key Terms

Define each term in a complete sentence.

24–1 Radioisotopes
radioisotope
half-life
nuclear bombardment
   reaction

24–2 Biological Effects of Radiation
curie
rem
dosimeter
Geiger counter

24–3 Harnessing the Nucleus
nuclear fission
nuclear fusion
nuclear chain reaction
plasma

CHAPTER REVIEW

Content Review

Multiple Choice
Choose the letter of the answer that best completes each statement.

1. The first scientist to observe natural radio-activity was
   (a) Ernest Rutherford.
   (b) Wilhelm Roentgen.
   (c) Marie Curie.
   (d) Henri Becquerel.
2. The three types of radiation emitted when a radioisotope decays are called alpha, beta, and
   (a) delta.   (c) neutron.
   (b) gamma.   (d) X-ray.
3. The first scientist to identify a nuclear bombardment reaction was
   (a) Ernest Rutherford.
   (b) Wilhelm Roentgen.
   (c) Marie Curie.
   (d) Henri Becquerel.
4. Isotopes that are used as radiotracers include all of the following except
   (a) iodine-131.   (c) cobalt-58.
   (b) barium-140.   (d) carbon-14.
5. The unit of radiation that is equal to the number of particles produced per second by 1 gram of radium is the
   (a) rem.   (c) becquerel.
   (b) roentgen.   (d) curie.
6. A tokamak is a device that confines the plasma required for nuclear fusion by means of a
   (a) magnetic field.
   (b) high-powered laser.
   (c) lead plate.
   (d) glass container.
7. The radioisotope that is used to treat cancer as well as to preserve food is
   (a) iridium-192.   (c) barium-140.
   (b) iodine-131.   (d) cobalt-60.

True or False
If the statement is true, write "true." If it is false, change the underlined word or words to make the statement true.

8. Most of the elements you are familiar with are <u>unstable</u>.
9. The radioisotope commonly used for radiocarbon dating is <u>carbon-12</u>.
10. The particles used to bombard a nucleus in a nuclear bombardment reaction are neutrons and <u>beta</u> particles.
11. The most penetrating form of radiation consists of <u>gamma rays</u>.
12. Damage caused by radiation to an organism's reproductive cells is called <u>somatic</u> damage.
13. The bombardment of a uranium-235 nucleus with neutrons is an example of a nuclear <u>fusion</u> reaction.
14. The amount of radiation a nuclear power plant worker has been exposed to can be measured with an instrument called a <u>Geiger counter</u>.

Concept Mapping
Complete the following concept map for Section 24–1. Refer to pages xviii–xix to construct a concept map for the entire chapter.

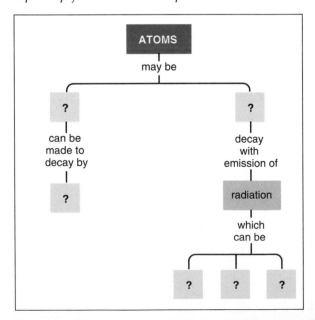

Concept Mastery

Discuss each of the following in a brief paragraph.

15. The half-life of carbon-14 is 5730 years. What does this statement mean?

16. Compare the penetrating power of alpha particles, beta particles, and gamma rays. Which is the most dangerous to humans?

17. Why is it difficult for alpha particles to collide with a nucleus in a nuclear bombardment reaction? How do scientists overcome this difficulty?

18. What is the difference between the curie and the rem as units of radiation?

19. What is the principle behind the use of a dosimeter to measure radiation?

20. What is a nuclear chain reaction?

21. Tying it Together What is the cause of the *stability* in the ratio of carbon-14 to carbon-12 in the atmosphere?

Critical Thinking and Problem Solving

Use the skills you have developed in this chapter to answer each of the following.

22. Making predictions (a) What particle is emitted when polonium-214 decays to lead-210? (b) Rubidium-87 very rapidly converts to strontium-87. What particle is emitted in the process? (c) Predict the likely mode of decay of uranium-227 and write the nuclear equation for this reaction.

23. Applying concepts (a) Write the nuclear equation for the decay of germanium-71 with the emission of beta particles. (b) Radon-217 decays with the emission of alpha particles. Write the nuclear equation for this reaction.

24. Making predictions (a) Indium-115 has a half-life of 4.5 hours. If you start with a 12.0-mg sample of indium-115, how much will remain after 13.5 hours? (b) How much of a 3.50-mg sample of nickel-63 will remain after 368 years? The half-life of nickel-63 is 92 years.

25. Interpreting data A 7.500-mg sample of chromium-55 is analyzed after 14.0 min and found to contain 0.469 mg of chromium-55. What is the half-life of chromium-55?

26. Making inferences Some of the sun's energy is produced by the following fusion reaction:

$$^1_1H + ^1_1H + ^1_1H + ^1_1H \rightarrow ^4_2He + 2\,^0_1e$$

(^0_1e is a positron, or a positive electron). This reaction requires temperatures of 10^6 to 10^7 kelvins. Why are such high temperatures needed?

27. Using the writing process Pretend that you are Lise Meitner. Write a letter in reply to Otto Hahn, explaining why you think that the fission of a uranium-235 nucleus would explain the results of his nuclear bombardment reaction. Include the nuclear equation for the fission reaction in your reply.

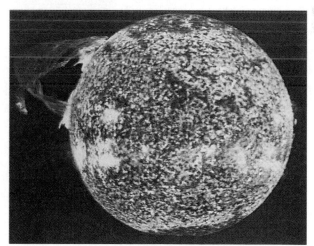

Chapter 25 Carbon and Its Compounds

Peer into the lush greenery of a tropical rain forest. The towering, slender trees crowd out your view of the sky. Perhaps a snake is hissing ominously as it slithers toward its prey. And if you listen carefully, you may hear drops of water as they cascade from leaf to leaf on their journey to the forest floor.

Yet beyond all that you can see and hear, there is much more to be found in a rain forest. Buried deep in the ground, high above in the atmosphere, and inside every cell of every plant, animal, or other living organism, you can find atoms of carbon. Without carbon, life in a rain forest—or anyplace else—would not be possible.

Carbon and its compounds make up the grand structures and diverse forms of life that you see in a rain forest—or anyplace else on Earth. The sparkling diamonds shown in the inset are made entirely of carbon atoms.

Chem Journal

YOU AND YOUR WORLD
Which substances contain carbon and which do not? The answers might surprise you! Pick a room in your house and list at least 20 objects that can be found there. In your journal, label each object either as one that you think contains carbon atoms or as one that you think does not. When you finish the chapter, review your journal entry and see if you would label any of the objects differently.

25–1 The Element Carbon

Guide for Reading
- What characteristics of carbon give it its unique bonding properties?
- How are the allotropes of carbon alike and how are they different?

If asked, you might not consider carbon to be an especially important or interesting element. You probably do not think of carbon as a rare or valuable commodity, as you do such elements as gold, silver, or uranium. However, first opinions are often wrong.

While elemental carbon can be as soft and shapeless as soot, in another form it can be crystalline, hard, and valuable. And carbon's properties allow it to form an almost infinite variety of compounds, many of which are essential to life on Earth. In fact, carbon may be more important to life than any other element you can name. Why? Because carbon atoms form the "backbone" of almost every molecule that living organisms use or make, from the simplest sugars to the most complex proteins and DNA. As you read on in this chapter, you will discover that carbon is truly a unique and amazing element.

Figure 25–1 *Carbon's properties allow it to be a part of an unusually wide variety of compounds. Carbon is found everywhere—from a butterfly's wings to the charcoal in a barbeque. Carbon is also found in gases such as methane, which is produced by rotting plant matter in swamps.*

Figure 25–2 *Tightly packed carbon atoms make diamond the hardest natural substance on Earth. Diamond-tipped cutters are used to etch hard surfaces.*

Figure 25–3 *The carbon atoms in graphite are bound in layers. The "lead" in lead pencils is actually graphite mixed with clay.*

Allotropes of Carbon

Elemental carbon can exist in many different **allotropes.** Allotropes are forms of the same element that have different bonding patterns or arrangements. Several of carbon's allotropes are discussed in the following paragraphs, and some examples of allotropes are shown in the accompanying photographs. As you will discover, the allotropes of elemental carbon cover a wide range of properties and characteristics.

DIAMOND One allotrope of carbon is **diamond.** In diamond, every carbon atom is bonded to four other carbon atoms in a tetrahedral pattern, which is shown in Figure 25–2. The covalent bonds between carbon atoms in diamond are extremely strong, and the arrangement and symmetry of these bonds make diamond unusually strong and hard. In fact, diamond is the hardest natural substance known on Earth.

Diamond is used for a wide variety of purposes, from the centerpieces of precious ornaments and jewelry to the tips of drills used to cut through metal. Recently, diamond films have been used to coat metal surfaces, making them more resistant to wear. In what industries do you think such films might be useful?

GRAPHITE An abundant, soft allotrope of carbon is called **graphite.** In graphite, carbon atoms are arranged in sheets or layers, as shown in Figure 25–3. These layers are held together by weak attractive forces, illustrated by the light vertical lines in the figure.

Graphite's structure makes it a very useful writing material. The so-called "lead" in a lead pencil is actually powdered graphite mixed with clay. When you use a pencil, the pressure you apply causes one sheet of carbon atoms to slide from the pencil onto the paper. The layered structure of a piece of graphite also gives it good lubricating properties. You may have seen a graphite spray used to make a key slide more easily into a lock.

AMORPHOUS CARBON Unlike the other carbon allotropes, the atoms in **amorphous carbon** have no predictable arrangement. Amorphous carbon is usually produced when carbon compounds decompose. Examples of amorphous carbon include charcoal, soot, and two compounds with which you may be less familiar: bone black and coke. Bone black comes from the decomposition of animal bones and is used as a pigment and in refining sugars. Coke comes from the decomposition of coal. It can be converted to graphite and used in dry cell batteries.

FULLERENES The most recently discovered allotropes of carbon are **fullerenes.** As shown in Figure 25–4, fullerenes are globe-shaped, cagelike arrangements of carbon atoms. Because they resemble the structure of a geodesic dome, fullerenes were

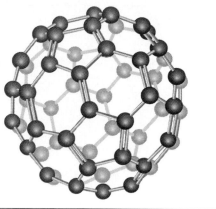

Figure 25–4 Fullerenes are named in honor of R. Buckminster Fuller, who designed the geodesic dome shown on the left. In what ways is the structure of a geodesic dome similar to the structure of a fullerene? In what ways is it different?

named in honor of the American engineer R. Buckminster "Bucky" Fuller (1895–1983), who is famous for his geodesic dome designs. Fullerenes are also called carbon balls or "Buckyballs" because they resemble tiny soccer balls.

A 60-carbon fullerene is found in the soot produced by burning certain carbon-containing compounds. To date, researchers are looking for other fullerenes with different shapes and numbers of carbon atoms, and they are investigating the properties and possible uses of fullerenes and their compounds. At Emory University in Atlanta, Georgia, one research team has found a fullerene that attacks an enzyme found in the virus that causes AIDS.

As you learned in Chapter 7, carbon forms four bonds to satisfy the octet rule. What makes these allotropes different from one another is how their carbon bonds are arranged. The carbon in diamond is bonded in a compact, three-dimensional arrangement; the carbon in graphite is bonded in layers; amorphous carbon has a random bonding pattern; and fullerenes exist as individual, ball-shaped units. How does the carbon arrangement of each allotrope relate to its physical properties?

Unique Bonding of Carbon

Why can carbon form so many different bonds and bonding patterns? To find the answer, the first place to look is the periodic table.

The periodic table tells you that carbon is a relatively small atom, with only six electrons in two principal energy levels. Carbon is also in Group 4 of the periodic table, which means that it has four valence electrons, or half the number of a full level. **Carbon's half-filled valence level and relatively small size give it its unique bonding properties.** Carbon's position in the periodic table may seem ordinary enough, but in fact that position is the key to understanding carbon's special qualities.

Figure 25–5 Carbon's unique properties come from its small size and 4 valence electrons. How many bonds does a carbon atom typically form?

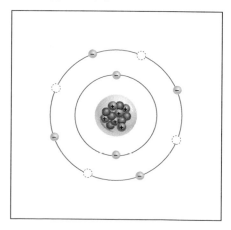

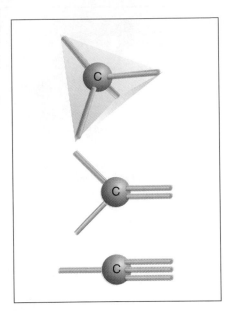

Figure 25–6 *A carbon atom typically forms four bonds. By forming single, double, or triple bonds, a carbon atom can form bonds with 4, 3, or 2 other atoms. Can you describe each shape shown in this figure?*

*I*NTEGRATING
*B*IOLOGY

What is DNA? Why is it important?

Figure 25–7 *Carbon's unique properties allow it to form long, stable chains of atoms, chains which are a part of DNA, proteins, and other molecules of living organisms. Atoms other than carbon may be found attached to the chain or included in the chain itself.*

First, remember the octet rule, which says that an atom is most stable when it has a full outer level of electrons. A carbon atom needs four more electrons to satisfy the octet rule. Therefore, carbon atoms form exactly four covalent bonds with other atoms. As shown in Figure 25–6, these bonds may take the form of four single bonds, two double bonds, a double bond and two single bonds, or a triple bond and one single bond. Carbon is one of the few elements that forms four bonds, and the only element that bonds in such a variety of combinations.

A carbon atom's relatively small size is the other characteristic that gives it its unique properties. A carbon atom's electrons fill only two principal energy levels, so its valence electrons are relatively close to the nucleus. This closeness allows carbon to form short, strong covalent bonds. In addition, a carbon atom is small enough to share one, two, or three pairs of electrons with other atoms. However, carbon atoms differ from other small atoms because carbon does not typically exist as a diatomic molecule. Chlorine exists as Cl_2, oxygen exists as O_2, but carbon is not stable as C_2. Why not? You learned the reason in Chapter 7: Only under exceptional circumstances can atoms share four pairs of electrons in a chemical bond. A pair of carbon atoms would need to share four pairs of electrons to form a stable C_2 molecule.

Instead of forming diatomic molecules, carbon atoms typically form long chains, as shown in Figure 25–7. The bonds in these chains are short, strong, and covalent, which makes the chains very stable. Carbon is one of the few elements that can successfully form such long chains of atoms.

Long chains of carbon atoms provide the framework for an enormous variety of compounds, including most of the molecules that living organisms make or use. In fact, many of life's important molecules have carbon chains that are incredibly long. For example, a single strand of human DNA can have a chain of well over a million atoms! DNA is the molecule that stores and encodes genetic traits—it is the molecule that makes you who you are. Other important molecules with long chains of carbon atoms are proteins and carbohydrates. Proteins are used as enzymes to build and repair parts of the body, and they are important components of muscles, skin, and other organs. Carbohydrates include starches and sugars, and they make up nearly 80 percent of plant matter. Most of the food you eat is carbohydrate in one form or another.

$$-C=C-C-C=C-C\equiv C-C=C-C-C=C-C\equiv C-$$

Figure 25–8 *Each of these teenagers has a unique form of DNA, the molecule that codes for all of our physical traits. What other carbon-containing substances do you see in these photographs?*

When you study the structures of DNA, proteins, and carbo-hydrates in Chapter 27, you will discover that elements other than carbon are a part of each molecule's long chain of atoms. However, carbon is always the chain's most common element. Take away the carbon, and these compounds would collapse into a countless number of tinier, simpler molecules. It is hard to imagine life without carbon.

25–1 Section Review

1. What characteristics of the carbon atom give it its unique bonding properties?
2. What do the different allotropes of carbon have in common? What are some of their differences?
3. Why can carbon form long chains of atoms? Why do other elements not form long chains?
4. Name three types of important molecules that contain long chains of carbon.
5. **Critical Thinking—Applying concepts** Some researchers have suggested that fullerenes may be useful as lubricants in microscopic machines. Explain why fullerenes might make good lubricants.

Guide for Reading

- What are the characteristics of an organic compound?
- How are natural and synthetic organic compounds different?

Structural Formula for Urea

Figure 25–9 *Friedrich Wöhler completed medical school before he turned his full attention to chemistry. Wöhler surprised himself and his colleagues when he synthesized urea, which they had believed could only come from the metabolism of a living organism. The structure of urea is shown in the inset.*

25–2 Carbon Compounds

In the time it takes to read a single sentence, organisms across the Earth are carrying out an amazingly large number of chemical reactions, almost all of which involve carbon and its compounds. And organisms perform these carbon reactions with a speed, accuracy, and efficiency that any professional chemist would envy. For this reason, the scientists of centuries ago concluded that living organisms were endowed with special, almost magical chemical properties. These scientists thought that the chemistry of life was fundamentally different from the chemistry they performed in their laboratories.

Today, we know much more about the carbon compounds of living organisms, and scientists view carbon chemistry very differently than their predecessors viewed it. Even so, many of the observations and conclusions made hundreds of years ago remain valid today.

Organic Chemistry

In the early 1800s, chemists proposed what they called a "vitalist theory." They thought that a "vital" force—some special force created only in living organisms—was necessary to produce the carbon compounds found in nature. According to this theory, a compound produced in an organism was one that could not be synthesized in a laboratory. From the word organism, the compounds of life were classified as organic. Organic compounds were thought to have different properties and obey different laws than other compounds, which were called inorganic.

In 1828, German chemist Friedrich Wöhler (1800–1882) raised a challenge to this idea when he synthesized urea in his laboratory. Urea is a carbon compound produced in humans and other animals, and it is the principal component of urine. Wöhler was amazed when he realized that he had synthesized a "vital" compound, one thought to come only from the metabolism of a living being. He exclaimed to a colleague, "I tell you that I can make urea without the use of kidneys: either man or dog." You may not find Wöhler's discovery to be that impressive, but it was quite a revelation in its day.

Wöhler's laboratory synthesis of urea helped to convince the scientists of the era to abandon the vitalist theory. These scientists decided that the compounds of a living organism did not depend on some mysterious, invisible force. Instead, they concluded that life's compounds were unique simply because they contained the element carbon. This conclusion helped to define a new branch of chemistry: **organic chemistry,** the study of the thousands of carbon-containing compounds. **As a general rule, an organic molecule is one that contains carbon and organic chemistry is**

Characteristics of Typical Organic and Inorganic Compounds

Property	Organic	Inorganic
Solubility in water	insoluble	soluble
Melting point	low	high
Boiling point	low	high
Decomposition	occurs easily when heated	requires very high temperatures
Reaction with O_2	combustion (produces CO_2 + H_2O)	no combustion

Figure 25–10 *This table shows some of the general differences between organic and inorganic compounds.*

the study of carbon compounds. Organic molecules range from methane, a type of natural gas and a byproduct of digestion in humans and other animals, to sucrose, better known as table sugar, to the most complex molecule of DNA, the molecule that codes the development of every cell in your body. Organic molecules include not only the carbon compounds made in living organisms, but carbon compounds made anywhere else. The chlorofluorocarbons are a class of organic compounds that are not made by living organisms. These compounds are made of carbon, fluorine, and hydrogen, and are used in the cooling systems of refrigerators.

At this point in your study of chemistry, it will probably come as no surprise to learn that there are some exceptions to the general definition of an organic molecule. Not all carbon-containing compounds are classified as organic. Inorganic carbon compounds include the oxides of carbon (such as carbon dioxide) and compounds that contain the carbonate ion (such as potassium carbonate). These compounds have physical and chemical properties that are more closely related to inorganic than to organic molecules. However, the vast majority of compounds that contain carbon are classified as organic. Consult Figure 25–10 to compare the properties of organic and inorganic compounds.

Natural and Synthetic Organic Compounds

Of all the organic compounds found in nature, how many would you guess could be synthesized in a laboratory? In principle, the answer is all of them! To date, the organic compounds that are found in nature and have been produced in a laboratory range from urea, the compound Friedrich Wöhler synthesized, to a long list of human vitamins, drugs, and hormones. One such compound is thyroxine, a hormone normally produced in the thyroid gland. Doctors prescribe synthetically produced thyroxine for patients with malfunctioning thyroid glands, and for those who have had cancerous thyroid glands removed surgically.

Figure 25–11 *This woman has a goiter, an enlarged thyroid gland that expands the neck. The goiter could be removed surgically, and the woman could take synthetically produced thyroid hormone that is identical to natural thyroid hormone.*

Figure 25–12 *The synthetic compound DDT was once used to kill insects and other pests. Unfortunately, it became concentrated in other animals, including the eagle that laid the damaged eggs shown on the right. But synthetic chemistry has had far more successes than failures. The spacesuit shown on the left is made of a synthetic fabric called Kevlar™.*

Does the idea of synthetic thyroxin bother you? Actually, a synthetic hormone—or any other synthetic organic compound—is exactly the same as its naturally produced counterpart. A compound's identity comes from the atoms that compose it and the way these atoms are bonded. Whether the bonds were assembled in a laboratory or in a human body does not make the molecule any different.

Not surprisingly, chemists have also synthesized a wide variety of organic compounds not found in nature. These compounds include plastics, synthetic fibers, refrigerants, and pharmaceuticals. Some of these synthetic compounds have proved more powerful or dangerous than their inventors had intended. The synthetic insecticide DDT is still causing damage to the environment some 20 years after its use was banned. But synthetic chemistry has produced far more successes than failures. The polymer Kevlar™ is light and flexible, yet stronger than steel. Kevlar™ is used in space suits, bulletproof vests, and other products.

25–2 Section Review

1. What is an organic molecule?
2. How are organic and inorganic compounds different?
3. Why are some carbon compounds categorized as inorganic?
4. What is the difference between natural and synthetic organic compounds?
5. **Critical Thinking—Making judgments** To many consumers, "organic farming" means safer, more nutritious foods. What judgments are they making about natural and synthetically produced fertilizers or pesticides? Can you think of a better term than "organically grown" to describe produce that has not been treated with synthetically made chemicals?

25–3 Hydrocarbons

Have you ever noticed a sign at a service station advertising high-octane gasoline? Gasoline with a high octane rating burns smoothly and is an efficient fuel. Octane is also one example of a **hydrocarbon,** an important class of organic molecules. **Hydrocarbons are organic molecules that contain only carbon and hydrogen.** Like octane, most hydrocarbons make excellent fuels. They react readily with oxygen to produce carbon dioxide and water, releasing energy and light in the process.

Aside from their practical uses, hydrocarbons serve as excellent introductions to other classes of organic molecules. When you learn the properties, structures, and geometries of hydrocarbons, you learn principles that apply to a host of other carbon compounds. Carbon and hydrogen are only two elements, but you will be amazed at how diverse and interesting their combinations can be.

Properties of Hydrocarbons C

Hydrocarbons contain only two kinds of bonds, carbon-carbon bonds and carbon-hydrogen bonds. To understand the nature of these bonds, you need to examine the electronegativities of carbon and hydrogen. The electronegativity of carbon is 2.5 and the electronegativity of hydrogen is 2.1, which is a difference of only 0.4. As you learned in Chapter 7, this small electronegativity difference means that a carbon-hydrogen bond is nonpolar. Thus, the combination of carbon-carbon and carbon-hydrogen bonds makes hydrocarbons very nonpolar molecules, or molecules without positive and negative ends.

Being nonpolar gives hydrocarbons many important properties. Hydrocarbons are poor conductors of electricity, have a low

Guide for Reading

- How can carbon and hydrogen atoms combine to form thousands of different compounds?
- What are the important properties of hydrocarbons?

Figure 25–13 Hydrocarbon fuels are valuable enough to make offshore drilling profitable. Compare the elaborate ocean-based station shown at left to the simpler, land-based pump shown at right.

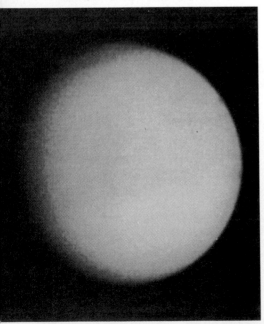

density, have low boiling points and melting points, and they do not dissolve in water. (Have you heard the expression "Oil and water don't mix"? An oil can be any liquid mixture of hydrocarbons.)

Hydrocarbons typically are found deep beneath the Earth's surface. If hydrocarbons could be more commonly found elsewhere, then gasoline, natural gas, and other hydrocarbon fuels might not cost as much as they do! Why are hydrocarbons so rare and difficult to obtain? In part, the answer is because carbon reacts readily with oxygen and nitrogen. Here on Earth, oxygen and nitrogen are very common in the atmosphere. So, it is not surprising that the carbon compounds on the Earth's surface typically contain one or the other of these elements, if not both. Even the carbon in the air is bonded to oxygen, in the form of carbon dioxide. To find hydrocarbons—compounds that contain only carbon and hydrogen—you need to look far away from the oxygen and nitrogen supplies in the atmosphere.

Most of the Earth's hydrocarbons exist in deposits of natural gas and petroleum. Natural gas is mostly the hydrocarbon methane, and petroleum is a complex mixture of several hydrocarbons. Both natural gas and petroleum were formed from the compressed, decomposed remains of ancient plants and animals, and so they are called **fossil fuels.** (Fossils are the remains or traces of long-dead organisms.) The Earth contains only a limited supply of all fossil fuels, and so they should be conserved and used wisely.

You may find it interesting to learn that hydrocarbons are much more common on other planets than they are on Earth. For example, methane gas is a significant part of the atmospheres of Jupiter and Saturn. Do you think you would want a methane atmosphere here on Earth? It definitely would make the planet a very different place!

INTEGRATING
EARTH SCIENCE

Where on Earth do you find hydrocarbons?

Figure 25–14 *The atmosphere of Titan, the largest of Saturn's moons, is rich in methane gas and other hydrocarbons. This photograph of Titan was transmitted by Voyager II, a NASA space probe to the outer edge of the solar system.*

Hydrocarbon Structures and Formulas

How many different hydrocarbons are possible? Organic chemists have isolated thousands! Such a large number is possible because of the bonding versatility of the carbon atom. **The carbon atoms in a hydrocarbon can form single, double, or triple bonds, and can make straight chains, branched chains, or rings.** These different bonds and bond patterns allow carbon and hydrogen to form a great variety of compounds.

There are several ways to represent a hydrocarbon. The simplest of these ways is with a **molecular formula.** As you read in Chapter 7, a molecular formula tells you the names and numbers of a compound's atoms. However, it provides no information about the atoms' arrangement. For example, the molecular formula C_4H_8 tells you that the molecule is a hydrocarbon with 4 carbon atoms and 8 hydrogen atoms. But there are several ways in which these atoms can combine to form a molecule. The formula C_4H_8 represents any of these molecules.

A more descriptive way to represent an organic molecule is with its **structural formula.** Here is the structural formula for one arrangement of C_4H_8:

structural formula

$$\begin{array}{ccccc} & H & H & H & \\ & | & | & | & \\ H\!-\!C\!-\!&C\!-\!&C\!=\!&C\!-\!H \\ & | & | & & | \\ & H & H & & H \end{array}$$

This formula tells you that a double bond connects the 2 carbon atoms at one end of the molecule. The other carbon atoms are connected with single bonds.

Because structural formulas provide excellent ways to describe and visualize the bonds in an organic molecule, they are often the formula of choice. However, they do have drawbacks. Remember that structural formulas are only two-dimensional representations; real organic molecules exist in three dimensions. As you look at the structural formula in the example, you may be tempted to think that the molecule is planar (or flat) and that all the bond angles are 90°. In fact, as you learned in Chapter 8, the actual molecule is three-dimensional, and the bond angles are all greater than 90°.

Structural formulas can also be complex and unwieldy, especially for large organic molecules. For this reason, chemists often use a **condensed structural formula.** A condensed structural formula is similar to a structural formula, but it does not include all the dashes that represent the bonds. The condensed structural formula below includes dashes for the carbon-carbon bonds, but not the carbon-hydrogen bonds.

condensed structural formula $CH_3\!-\!CH_2\!-\!CH\!=\!CH_2$

This condensed structural formula represents the same arrangement of C_4H_8 that was discussed previously. For complex molecules, a condensed structural formula may be easier to interpret.

25–3 Section Review

1. Why can carbon and hydrogen form so many hydrocarbons?

2. Where are hydrocarbons commonly found?

3. Are hydrocarbons polar or nonpolar molecules? Explain.

4. **Critical Thinking—Making comparisons**   Compare the advantages and disadvantages of structural and condensed structural formulas. Which formula do you think is more useful? Why?

Guide for Reading

- What is an alkane?
- What are conformations and structural isomers?
- What are the different classes of unsaturated hydrocarbons?

25–4 Saturated and Unsaturated Hydrocarbons

You probably use methane gas as a burner fuel in your chemistry lab. At home you might find propane used in a gas grill or butane in a pocket lighter. You also find octane in the gasoline that runs your family's car or your school bus. These hydrocarbons—methane, propane, butane, and octane, along with many other compounds—all belong to the **alkane** family of hydrocarbons. An alkane is a hydrocarbon with only single bonds. As you will discover in this section, alkanes can come in many different sizes, shapes, and lengths—but they all contain only single bonds between carbon atoms.

Alkanes

Look again at the names of the alkanes you just read. Do you notice something similar about them? You are right if you said that the names of these compounds all end in the suffix *-ane*. An alkane's IUPAC name always ends in this suffix. The root part of an alkane's name tells you how many carbon atoms it has. For example, *meth-* means 1 carbon atom, *eth-* means 2 carbon atoms, *prop-* means 3 carbon atoms, and *but-* means 4 carbon atoms. Can you guess how many carbon atoms are in a molecule of octane? Figure 25–15 lists the root words for chains of 1 to 10 carbon atoms. Now is a good time to become familiar with these root words.

When an alkane's carbon-carbon bonds can be connected with a single line, the alkane is called a straight-chain alkane. Figure 25–16 shows the straight-chain alkanes that have between 1 and 5 carbon atoms. As you look at them, do you notice any pattern in how they are assembled? With the exception of methane, each straight-chain alkane has two $-CH_3$ groups, one at each end of the molecule, and different numbers of $-CH_2-$ groups in between. You can think of these alkanes as a series—from ethane, to propane, to butane, to pentane—with each alkane having one more $-CH_2-$ group in its interior than the alkane that precedes it.

This pattern in alkanes gives rise to an important mathematical principle. If an alkane contains n number of carbon atoms, it will also contain $2n + 2$ number of hydrogen atoms. The number $2n + 2$ comes from counting 2 hydrogen atoms on each carbon atom, plus one extra hydrogen for each of the 2 end carbon atoms. So, an alkane that has 3 carbon atoms also has $2 \times 3 + 2 = 8$ hydrogen atoms. An alkane that has 4 carbon atoms has $2 \times 4 + 2 = 10$ hydrogen atoms.

Another way of expressing this principle is with a **general formula.** A general formula uses variables as subscripts instead

Hydrocarbon Prefixes

Number of Carbon Atoms	Root Word
1	meth-
2	eth-
3	prop-
4	but-
5	pent-
6	hex-
7	hept-
8	oct-
9	non-
10	dec-

Figure 25–15 *The attractive blue flame indicates that this stove runs on natural gas, which consists mostly of methane. How many carbon atoms are in a molecule of methane? How many are in a molecule of butane?*

of numbers, but otherwise is similar to a molecular formula. The general formula for alkanes is C_nH_{2n+2}. With this formula, you can determine an alkane's molecular formula from its number of carbon atoms. For example, butane has 4 carbon atoms, so its molecular formula is C_4H_{10}. What is the molecular formula of heptane? Of octane? Of the alkane that contains 22 carbon atoms?

The mathematics of carbon and hydrogen bonding gives rise to one other important principle for alkanes. Look again at the alkanes shown in Figure 25–16. Do you think it is possible to add more hydrogen atoms onto the carbon atoms in any of these molecules? The answer is no. Try as you might, you cannot assemble a hydrocarbon with 3 carbon atoms and more than 8 hydrogen atoms, or with 5 carbon atoms and more than 12 hydrogen atoms. Because alkanes contain only single bonds, alkanes always contain the greatest possible number of hydrogen atoms for their number of carbon atoms. Hydrocarbons do not exist with formulas such as C_3H_{10} and C_5H_{14}.

To emphasize this principle, alkanes are often described as **saturated hydrocarbons.** The word saturated means filled to capacity, and saturated hydrocarbons have carbon skeletons that are filled to capacity with hydrogen atoms. You may have come across the term saturated fats in a health or nutrition class. Saturated fats, which you should try to minimize in your diet, contain long hydrocarbon chains that have only single bonds.

Branched Alkanes

So far you have seen only straight-chain alkanes. But the carbon chain in an alkane can also be branched, as shown in Figure 25–17. Alkanes with branched carbon chains are called **branched alkanes.** As you can see in Figure 25–17, the carbon-carbon bonds in branched alkanes cannot be connected with a straight line. Notice that branched alkanes contain at least 1 **branch carbon,** which is a carbon atom that is bonded to more than 2 other carbon atoms. A good way to recognize a branched alkane is to look for at least 1 branch carbon in the structural formula.

Notice that branching does not make an alkane unsaturated. Branched alkanes are still saturated hydrocarbons, and their general formula is C_nH_{2n+2}. In general, branched and straight-chain alkanes have similar chemical and physical properties. However, branched alkanes do have lower boiling and melting points than their straight-chain counterparts.

To find the IUPAC name for a branched alkane, first identify its longest continuous chain of carbon atoms, which is called the **parent chain.** Next, identify the shorter chains that make up the branches and specify their locations. The name of a branched alkane is the combination of the names of its parts.

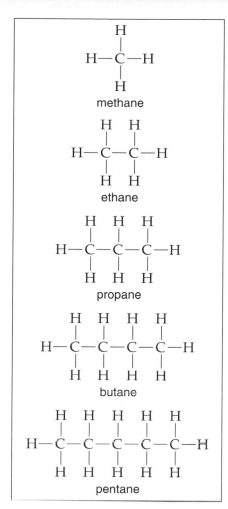

Figure 25–16 *After ethane, each straight-chain alkane has one more –CH₂ group than the alkane that precedes it. The general formula for alkanes is C_nH_{2n+2}.*

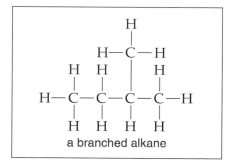

Figure 25–17 *Where is the branch carbon in this branched alkane?*

Dangerous Marcy

Your neighbor, Dangerous Marcy, has invited you into her garage. As you look around, you notice a shelf of glass jars, each containing liquids of various colors. Some of the jars are tightly sealed, others are left open. You ask Dangerous Marcy what she keeps in the jars, and she tells you that most of them contain different hydrocarbons. She says that she has jars for kerosene, gasoline, heating oil, turpentine (a paint thinner and cleaner that contains hydrocarbons), and the oil she uses to lubricate her bicycle. She says that other jars contain nonhydrocarbon liquids, such as beverages left over from a picnic. You notice that none of the jars have labels.

Designing Experiments

1. Do you think that your neighbor deserves her nickname, "Dangerous"? Use what you know about hydrocarbons to explain your answer.

2. Design a series of experiments to determine whether each jar contains a hydrocarbon or nonhydrocarbon liquid. What safety precautions would you need to follow?

3. Some of the jars contain a mixture of more than one hydrocarbon. Design an experiment to determine which jars contain mixtures, and which contain pure substances.

Visit our Web site at
http://www.phschool.com
to support your
study of chemistry.

For an example, here is how to name the following branched alkane:

$$CH_3-\underset{\underset{H}{|}}{\overset{\overset{CH_3}{|}}{C}}-CH_2-CH_2-CH_3$$

To begin, count the number of carbons in the longest continuous carbon chain, or parent chain. Here, the longest carbon chain is 5 atoms, so the parent chain is pentane. Next, number the parent chain's carbon atoms from end to end, starting with the end that is closer to a branch carbon. The branch carbon in the example is closer to the left end, so the carbon on the left side of the diagram is carbon number 1, and the carbon to its right (the branch carbon) is carbon number 2. The next steps are to count the number of carbon atoms in the branch chain, find the root word for that number, and add the suffix -*yl* to that root word. The branch chain in the example contains 1 carbon atom and the root word for 1 carbon is *meth,* so this is a methyl branch (*meth*-plus -*yl*.) Put together these parts—the number of the branch carbon, the name of the branch, and the name of the parent chain—and you produce the compound's IUPAC name, which is 2-methylpentane.

Confused? Naming even the simplest branched alkanes takes practice. Try the following sample problems.

SAMPLE PROBLEM   1

Give the IUPAC name for this alkane:

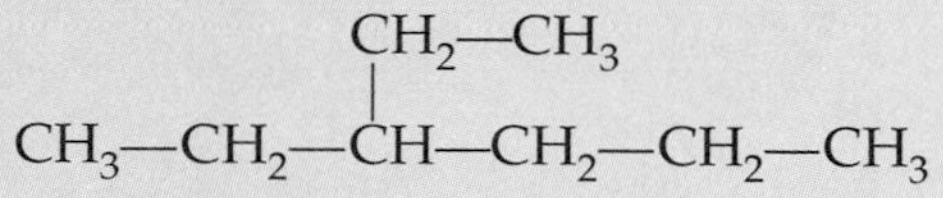

$$CH_2—CH_3$$
$$CH_3—CH_2—CH—CH_2—CH_2—CH_3$$

STRATEGY	SOLUTION
1. **Analyze**	The molecule is an alkane because it is a hydrocarbon with only single bonds. It has a branch on a middle carbon.
2. **Plan**	Identify the roots and suffixes for the parent and branch chains, and identify the number of the branch carbon. Remember that carbon 1 of the parent chain is at the end closest to the branch.
3. **Solve**	The parent chain has 6 carbon atoms, so it is hexane. The branch carbon is the third carbon atom from the left, or carbon number 3. The branch chain has 2 carbon atoms, and the prefix for a 2-carbon chain is *ethyl-*. Combine the prefixes, suffix, and root to form the name 3-ethylhexane.
4. **Evaluate**	The name correctly identifies a 6-carbon parent chain (hexane) with one 2-carbon branch (*ethyl-*) on carbon 3.

PRACTICE PROBLEMS

1. Give the IUPAC names for the following molecules:

   (a)
   $$CH_3$$
   $$CH_3—CH—CH_2—CH_3$$

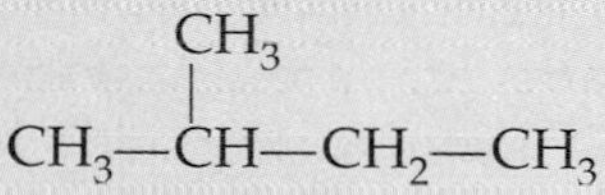

   (b)
   $$CH_2—CH_3$$
   $$CH_3—CH_2—CH_2—CH—CH_2—CH_3$$

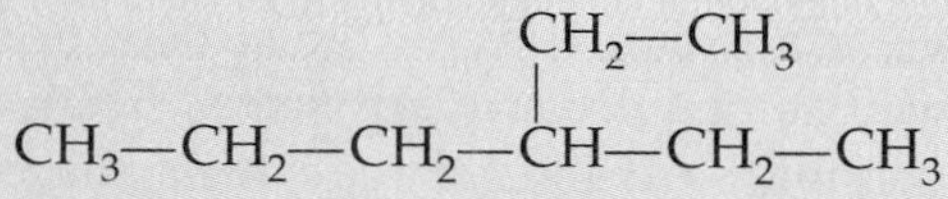

   (c)
   $$CH_2—CH_3$$
   $$CH_3—CH_2—CH_2—CH—CH_2—CH_2—CH_2—CH_3$$

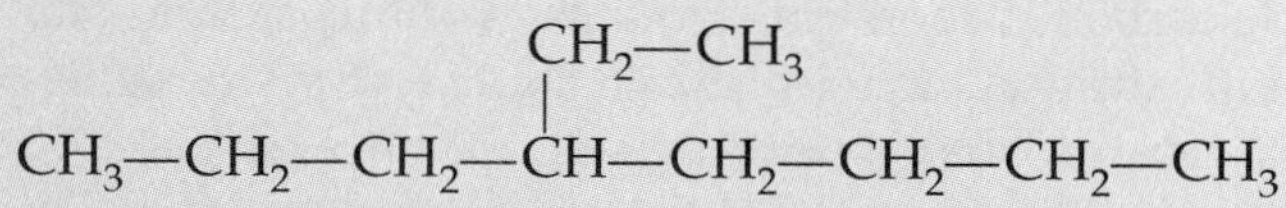

   (Answer: 2-methylbutane, 3-ethylhexane, 4-ethyloctane)

2. Write condensed structural formulas for
   (a) 2-methylpentane   (b) 3-ethylheptane

   $$CH_3$$
   (Answer: $CH_3—CH—CH_2—CH_2—CH_3$

   $$CH_2—CH_3$$
   $$CH_3—CH_2—CH—CH_2—CH_2—CH_2—CH_3$$

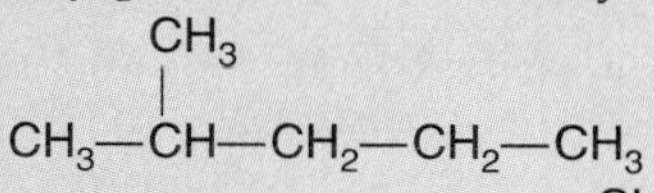

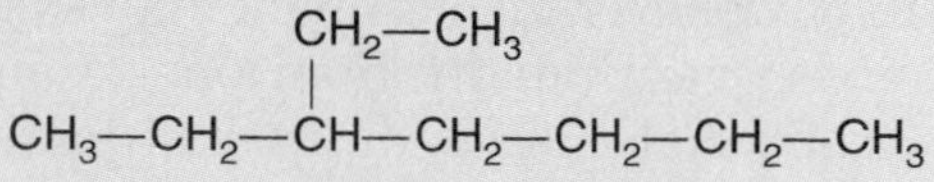

Finding the longest chain in a branched hydrocarbon molecule is sometimes tricky. Look at the following carbon skeleton, for example.

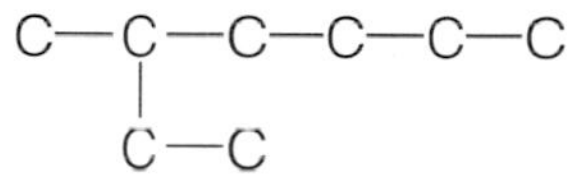

$$C—C—C—C—C—C$$
$$C—C$$

Its correct name is 3-methyl heptane.

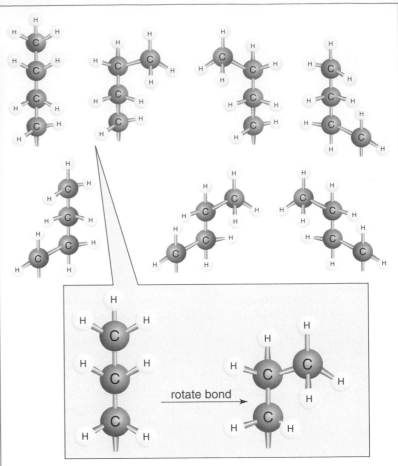

Figure 25–18 *Just like the dancers in the photograph, alkanes are in constant motion. An alkane's carbon-carbon bonds can rotate easily, changing the alkane from one conformation to another. The inset shows how the alkane on the left can be rotated to produce a different conformation.*

Conformations and Structural Isomers

In a structural formula, an alkane's atoms and bonds are shown in one position only. As a result, you may be tempted to think of alkanes as rigid and inflexible molecules. However, the truth is just the opposite. Alkanes are in constant motion! Although the bonds do not break, they are constantly rotating—and each rotation changes the atoms' positions in space. A butyl group, for example, can exist in any of the structures shown in Figure 25–18, as well as in a great many more.

How is this possible? Alkanes change their shape when a single carbon-carbon bond rotates about its axis, as shown in the inset illustration in Figure 25–18. Notice that when this particular bond rotates, the two hydrogen atoms and one $-CH_3$ group change their position about the central carbon atom. This rotation is the difference between the first two structures shown in the main illustration of Figure 25–18. Rotating different combinations of carbon-carbon bonds creates each of the other structures.

When two structures differ only by one or more bond rotations, they are said to be **conformations** of each other. Figure 25–18 shows several conformations of a butyl group. Conformations convert very rapidly from one to another. If you imagine an organic molecule as the star of an animated cartoon, then its

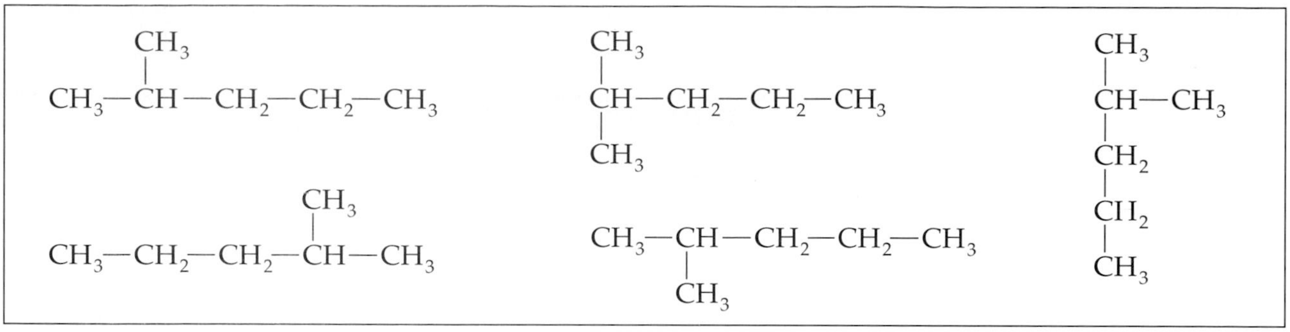

CH₃—CH(CH₃)—CH₂—CH₂—CH₃ structures (Figure 25-19)

$$CH_3-\overset{\overset{\displaystyle CH_3}{|}}{CH}-CH_2-CH_2-CH_3$$

$$\overset{\overset{\displaystyle CH_3}{|}}{CH}-CH_2-CH_2-CH_3$$
$$|$$
$$CH_3$$

$$\overset{\overset{\displaystyle CH_3}{|}}{CH}-CH_3$$
$$|$$
$$CH_2$$
$$|$$
$$CH_2$$
$$|$$
$$CH_3$$

$$CH_3-CH_2-CH_2-\overset{\overset{\displaystyle CH_3}{|}}{CH}-CH_3$$

$$CH_3-\overset{}{CH}-CH_2-CH_2-CH_3$$
$$|$$
$$CH_3$$

conformations are what you would see in each frame or cell of the film.

Now that you know about conformations, look again at the last set of practice problems. Practice Problem 2(a) asked you to write the condensed structural formula for 2-methylpentane. Do you think that only one answer is possible for this problem? You are correct if you said no. Figure 25–19 shows five different condensed structural formulas, each of which equally represents 2-methylpentane. These structures represent different conformations or simply different perspectives on the same conformation. Your answer to Practice Problem 2(a) could have been any of these structural formulas—or a host of others. To be correct, all that a structural formula needs to show is the proper sequence of atoms and bonds.

Now take a close look at the three structures in Figure 25–20. Are they conformations of each other? You are correct if you said they are not. No combination of bond rotations will convert any one of these structures into any of the others. The first structure represents a straight-chain alkane, pentane; the second represents a branched alkane, 2-methylbutane; and the third represents a double-branched molecule called 2,2-dimethylpropane. However, these molecules do have one thing in common. They each contain 5 carbon atoms and 12 hydrogen atoms, which gives each the molecular formula C_5H_{12}.

The molecules represented in Figure 25–20 are examples of **structural isomers.** The word isomer comes from the Greek roots *iso-*, meaning same, and *mer-*, meaning part. Structural isomers have the same molecular formula, but their atoms bond in different orders. In Figure 25–20, the structural isomers of pentane have been arranged from the least branched to the most branched. For alkanes, structural isomers take the form of different branching patterns.

As you might imagine, alkanes with more than 5 carbon atoms can have larger numbers of structural isomers. Hexane is one of 5 structural isomers, octane is one of 18, and decane is one of 75. The molecule eicosane, the 20-carbon alkane, is one of exactly 366,319 different structural isomers. (Your teacher is not likely to make you list them all!)

The following problems will give you practice writing and identifying structural isomers. You might discover that these problems are both challenging and enjoyable!

Figure 25–19 *These structural formulas may look different, but each represents the same compound: 2-methylpentane.*

Figure 25–20 *These three molecules have the same molecular formula, C_5H_{12}, but in each the atoms are bonded in different orders. So, they are structural isomers of each other.*

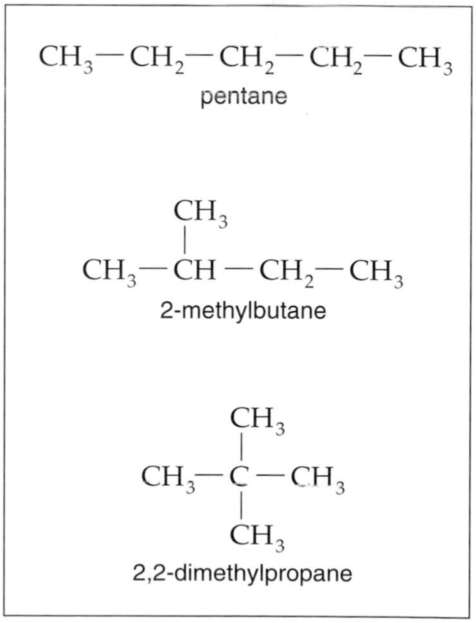

$$CH_3-CH_2-CH_2-CH_2-CH_3$$
pentane

$$CH_3-\overset{\overset{\displaystyle CH_3}{|}}{CH}-CH_2-CH_3$$
2-methylbutane

$$CH_3-\overset{\overset{\displaystyle CH_3}{|}}{\underset{\underset{\displaystyle CH_3}{|}}{C}}-CH_3$$
2,2-dimethylpropane

Draw formulas for three structural isomers of hexane.

STRATEGY	SOLUTION
1. Analyze	Hexane has the molecular formula C_6H_{14}. All of its structural isomers will have the same molecular formula, but different branching patterns.
2. Plan	A structural isomer of hexane could have a parent chain of pentane with a methyl chain as a branch. Other isomers could have a butane parent chain with two methyl chains as branches.

3. Solve

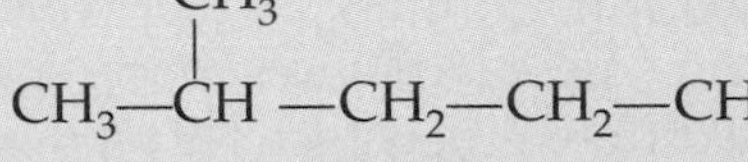

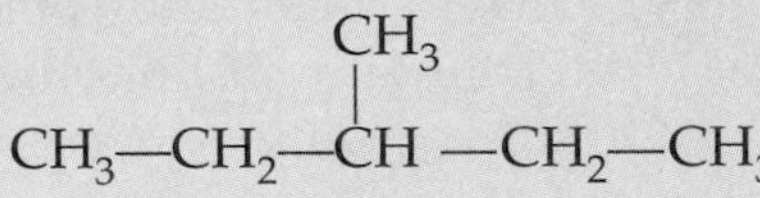

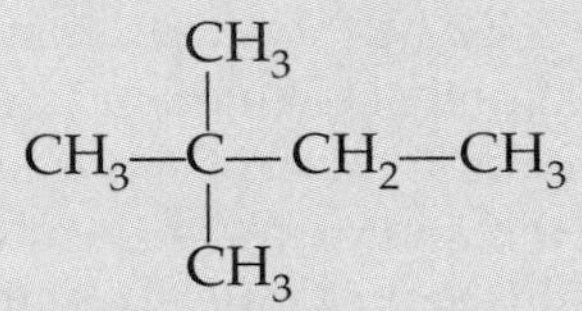

$$CH_3-\overset{\overset{\displaystyle CH_3}{|}}{CH}-CH_2-CH_2-CH_3$$

$$CH_3-CH_2-\overset{\overset{\displaystyle CH_3}{|}}{CH}-CH_2-CH_3$$

$$CH_3-\overset{\overset{\displaystyle CH_3}{|}}{\underset{\underset{\displaystyle CH_3}{|}}{C}}-CH_2-CH_3$$

(One other structural isomer exists.)

4. Evaluate   Check that each structural isomer has 6 carbon atoms and 14 hydrogen atoms. No two answers should be either conformations of each other or the same molecule.

PRACTICE PROBLEMS

3. Draw formulas for four structural isomers of heptane. Name the isomers that have only one branch.

Answer:

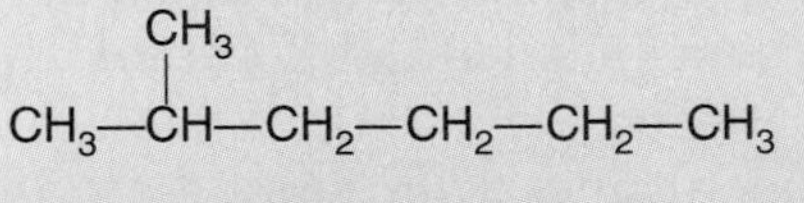

$$CH_3-\overset{\overset{\displaystyle CH_3}{|}}{CH}-CH_2-CH_2-CH_2-CH_3 \quad \text{(2-methylhexane),}$$

$$CH_3-CH_2-\overset{\overset{\displaystyle CH_3}{|}}{CH}-CH_2-CH_2-CH_3 \quad \text{(3-methylhexane),}$$

$$CH_3-\overset{\overset{\displaystyle CH_3}{|}}{CH}-\overset{\overset{\displaystyle CH_3}{|}}{CH}-CH_2-CH_3 \qquad CH_3-\overset{\overset{\displaystyle CH_3}{|}}{CH}-CH_2-\overset{\overset{\displaystyle CH_3}{|}}{CH}-CH_3$$

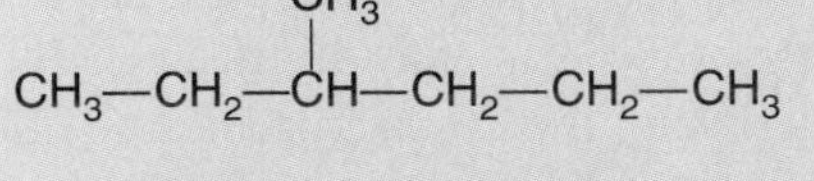

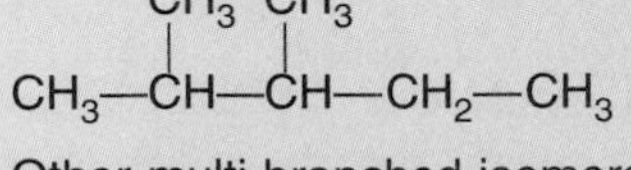

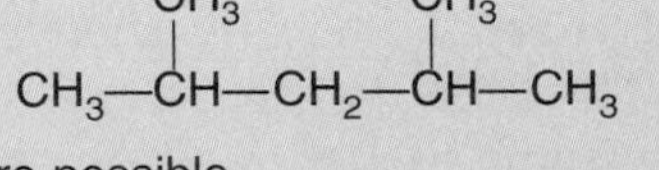

Other multi-branched isomers are possible.

4. The molecule 3-ethylhexane is a structural isomer of which straight-chain alkane? *(Answer: octane)*

Petroleum—More Than Just Fuel

Petroleum, or crude oil, is a mixture of many hydrocarbons and other compounds. Petroleum is not very useful in its crude form, so oil refineries use a process called fractional distillation to separate its components. First, the petroleum is boiled and its vapors are allowed to rise up a tall tower. The tower is warm on the bottom and cool on top, so products with different boiling points condense at different levels. Heavier hydrocarbons condense at lower temperatures, so they are collected at lower levels of the tower. Lighter hydrocarbons, such as propane and butane, condense at higher temperatures, so they are collected at higher levels. The figure at the right outlines the fractional distillation process and identifies some of the products it separates.

The larger hydrocarbons, which have limited commercial use, are further refined in a process called cracking. In cracking, heat is used to break some of the carbon-carbon bonds, forming a mixture of smaller hydrocarbons. Cracking also can convert straight-chain alkanes into branched alkanes, which are more suitable for automobile fuel.

How important are petroleum products? The most common of these products, gasoline, powers nearly every automobile on the road today. Other petroleum products include jet fuel for airplanes, diesel fuel for trucks and locomotives, kerosene, heating oil, and the oil and grease used for lubrication. Few would argue that without petroleum, modern life would rapidly grind to a halt.

But one petroleum-based product may have more uses than all of the other products put together. Petroleum provides the raw materials for plastics. You can see plastics almost everywhere and used for almost every purpose. Plastics are made into countertops, paints, water bottles, insulation, artificial limbs,

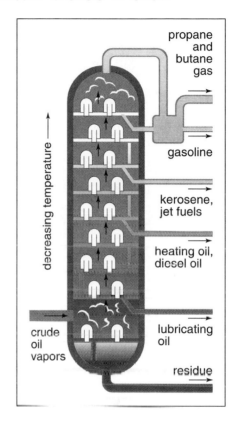

adhesive bandages, credit cards, garden hoses—even kitchen sinks! Plastics are used so widely and in so many products that it is difficult to imagine our lives without them.

The next time you see an oil refinery, stop for a moment and think about the incredible variety of petroleum products. You might also want to think about the best way to use petroleum in the future. The world contains only limited petroleum reserves. Is it wise to consume petroleum products in automobiles and airplanes? Or should all petroleum be saved for making plastics? The decision is one that all of us face in the years ahead.

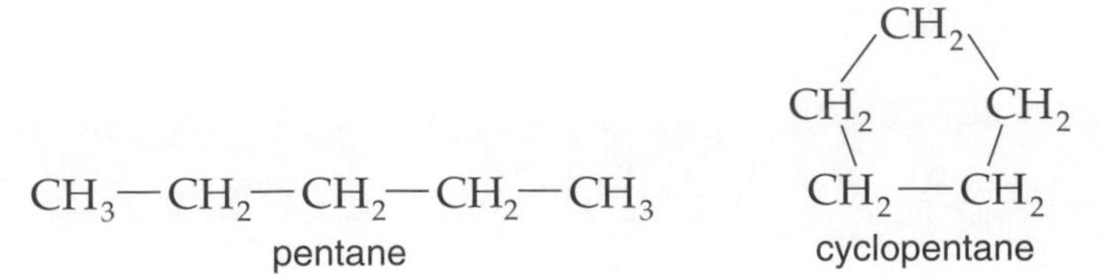

Figure 25–21 *Pentane is a straight-chain alkane, and cyclopentane is a cycloalkane. Are pentane and cyclopentane structural isomers?*

CH₃—CH₂—CH₂—CH₂—CH₃
pentane

cyclopentane

Cycloalkanes

Both straight-chain and branched hydrocarbons have open chains of carbon atoms. Open chains have at least 2 "end" carbon atoms, or carbon atoms that are bonded to only 1 other carbon atom. Carbon's versatility, however, allows it to form closed chains, or rings. The carbon atoms in a closed chain form a circle, in which each carbon atom is bonded to at least 2 other carbon atoms. Hydrocarbons that contain a carbon ring are called **cyclic hydrocarbons.** In theory, any number of carbon atoms greater than 3 can form a cyclic hydrocarbon. However, cyclic hydrocarbons that have more than 9 or 10 carbon atoms in a single ring are usually unstable.

The cyclic hydrocarbons with only single bonds are called **cycloalkanes.** In Figure 25–21 you see a cycloalkane with 5 carbon atoms. To give it its IUPAC name, first find the root word for the number of carbon atoms in its ring, then add the suffix *-ane* and the prefix *cyclo-*. This molecule is named cyclopentane.

Do you think that the general formula for cycloalkanes is the same as the general formula for open-chain alkanes? The answer is no! Cycloalkanes have the general formula C_nH_{2n}, which is 2 hydrogen atoms fewer than you find in open-chain alkanes. To explain this difference, compare the structures of pentane and cyclopentane shown in Figure 25–21. Notice that both molecules contain 5 carbon atoms. The difference is that pentane has two –CH₃ groups, one at each end of the molecule, whereas cyclopentane has –CH₂– groups only. Because cyclopentane consists of five –CH₂– groups, you can think of its molecular formula as "5 times" a –CH₂– group, or C_5H_{10}. What is the molecular formula for cyclohexane? For cyclooctane?

Like open-chain alkanes, cycloalkanes exist in different conformations. The most interesting and important of these conformations is the chair conformation of cyclohexane, which is shown in Figure 25–22. Notice that the chair conformation is not a planar structure, but one that exists in three dimensions. The chair conformation is stable because all of its bond angles are close to 109.5°, the angle that allows the maximum separation of four single bonds around a carbon atom.

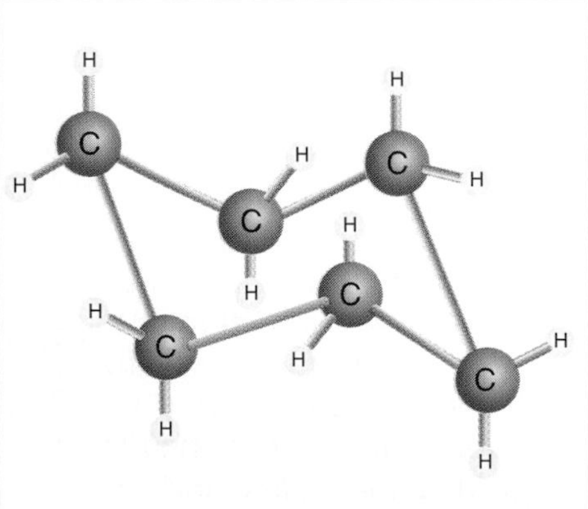

Cyclohexane's chair conformation is important because it is seen in a wide variety of other organic molecules. Glucose, a simple sugar that is the building block of most carbohydrates, also has a ring that is most stable in the chair conformation. Other compounds with such rings include cholesterol and the steroid hormones. You will learn more about all of these compounds in Chapter 27.

Figure 25–22 *Cyclohexane, C_6H_{12}, is most stable in the chair conformation, shown above. What bond angles would you expect to find in this conformation?*

Unsaturated Hydrocarbons

As you have learned, alkanes that are filled to capacity with hydrogen atoms are called saturated hydrocarbons. So it should not surprise you to learn that **unsaturated hydrocarbons** are the class of hydrocarbons that are not filled to capacity with hydrogen atoms. **Unsaturated hydrocarbons contain at least one double or triple bond between carbon atoms.** Figure 25–23 shows the structure of ethene, a very simple unsaturated hydrocarbon. More complicated ones exist in longer chains, branched chains, or rings.

Ethene is an example of an **alkene.** Alkenes are unsaturated hydrocarbons that contain at least one double bond. The names of molecules in the alkene family end in the suffix -*ene.* The alkene that has 3 carbon atoms, 2 of them joined by a double bond, is named propene. Do you see a similarity between the names of alkanes and alkenes? The names differ by only one letter—an "e" instead of an "a"! For this reason, it is important to read a hydrocarbon's name carefully.

Hydrocarbons with a triple bond are members of the **alkyne** family. The names of molecules in the alkyne family end in the suffix -*yne.* The smallest alkyne has 2 carbon atoms joined by a triple bond, and its name is ethyne. What is the name of the alkyne that contains 3 carbon atoms?

The table in Figure 25–24 shows the structures of alkenes, alkynes, and their corresponding alkanes. Select any row of the table and look across it. Do you see a mathematical pattern as you progress from alkane to alkene to alkyne? In each row, the hydrocarbons lose 2 hydrogen atoms with every additional bond between carbon atoms. For example, compare the molecular formulas for propane, propene, and propyne: The formulas progress from C_3H_8 to C_3H_6 to C_3H_4. If you compare the molecular formulas of any trio of alkane, alkene, and alkyne that have the same number of carbon atoms, you will find that each hydrocarbon has 2 fewer hydrogen atoms than its predecessor.

You can use this pattern to find the general formulas for alkenes and alkynes. Remember from the previous section that the general formula for an alkane is C_nH_{2n+2}. The general formula for alkenes is C_nH_{2n} because alkenes have 2 fewer hydrogen atoms than alkanes. The general formula for alkynes is C_nH_{2n-2}

Figure 25–23 *These apples produce ethene gas, which helps them to ripen. Ethene's structural formula is shown in the inset. What is the molecular formula for ethene?*

Figure 25–24 *Choose any row of this table and look across it from left to right. How many hydrogen atoms are lost with each additional carbon-carbon bond?*

Hydrocarbon Structures

Root \ Suffix	-*ane*	-*ene*	-*yne*
eth-	CH_3-CH_3	$CH_2{=}CH_2$	$CH{\equiv}CH$
prop-	$CH_3-CH_2-CH_3$	$CH_2{=}CH-CH_3$	$CH{\equiv}C-CH_3$
but-	$CH_3-CH_2-CH_2-CH_3$	$CH_3-CH{=}CH-CH_3$	$CH_3-C{\equiv}C-CH_3$

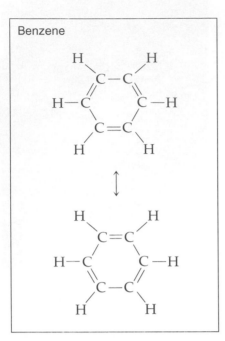

Benzene

Figure 25–25 *A molecule of benzene contains 6 carbon atoms in a ring. However, neither structure shown here accurately describes this ring. The actual carbon-carbon bonds in a benzene ring are a hybrid, or a kind of combination, of a single bond and a double bond.*

because alkynes have 4 fewer hydrogen atoms than alkanes. You can use these general formulas to compute a specific hydrocarbon's molecular formula. An alkene with 4 carbon atoms has the molecular formula C_4H_8. What would be the molecular formula of an alkene with 6 carbon atoms? Of an alkyne with 5 carbon atoms?

Benzene

Just like saturated hydrocarbons, unsaturated hydrocarbons can be found in cyclic form. There are cycloalkenes, cycloalkynes, and cyclic hydrocarbons that contain more than one double or triple bond. However, one unsaturated cyclic hydrocarbon is especially common and stable. This compound is called **benzene.** The structure of benzene is illustrated in Figure 25–25. Benzene is a cyclic arrangement of 6 carbon atoms and 6 hydrogen atoms.

One reason why benzene is stable is because it has two resonance structures, which Figure 25–25 also shows you. Resonance structures are different bonding arrangements for the same molecule. However, neither of benzene's resonance structures accurately describes its bonds. Benzene does not exist as a molecule with alternating single and double bonds between its carbon atoms. The actual benzene molecule is a hybrid, or combination, of its two resonance forms.

While benzene exists as an individual molecule, its characteristic ring is usually found as a part of larger molecules. Many of these compounds have distinctive odors, and for this reason they are often called **aromatic compounds.** Some foods whose distinctive aromas come from aromatic compounds include cloves, vanilla beans, and almonds. Other compounds that contain rings similar to benzene's ring include nucleic acids, which are key parts of DNA, and several vitamins, hormones, and pharmaceuticals.

25–4 Section Review

1. What is an alkane?
2. What are the conformations of a molecule? What are its structural isomers?
3. Name three classes of unsaturated hydrocarbons. Give one molecule as an example for each class.
4. What is a general formula? How does a general formula help you to categorize different hydrocarbons?
5. **Theme Trace—Unity and Diversity** Compare the molecules cyclohexane and benzene. Why do they have different shapes?

25–5 Polymers

Do you know what fabrics you are wearing today? Whether they are natural fibers (like cotton or silk) or synthetic fibers (like rayon or nylon), you are wearing **polymers,** an important class of organic compounds. **Polymers are very large organic compounds made of repeating units.** The term polymer comes from two Greek roots, *poly* meaning many and *mer* meaning part. The repeating units in a polymer are called **monomers.** (*Mono* means one in Greek.) You can compare a polymer to a long string of beads and a monomer to an individual bead.

Almost all living organisms make and use different polymers. Plants use glucose as a monomer to form the polymers starch, an important food source, and cellulose, an important structural compound in plants and the principal component of paper. These glucose polymers are only one type of natural polymer. Different amino acids link together to form proteins, which are also polymers. Depending on the sequence of amino acids, the protein might be the hair on your head, a muscle in your arm, or an enzyme that helps you to digest food.

One of the first completely synthetic polymers was nylon, invented by American chemist Wallace Carothers (1896–1937). Carothers synthesized nylon in the 1930s, and one of its earliest uses was to make women's hosiery. In World War II, nylon's strength and lightness made it an ideal material for parachutes. Since the war, numerous other uses have been found for nylon, as illustrated in Figure 25–26.

Guide for Reading

- What are polymers?
- What are the two principal ways of making polymers?
- Why is it important to recycle plastics?

Figure 25–26 *These objects are made of nylon, one of the first synthetic polymers. For which products was nylon originally used?*

Spare Tires

What happens to old automobile tires? The answer often is "not much." Today's tires are made from synthetic rubbers, which typically are synthetic hydrocarbon polymers. These polymers are designed to be strong, durable, airtight, and resistant to extremes in temperature. But while such qualities help the tires on the road, they make tires all the more difficult to dispose of. Used tires often end up piled on top of each other in dumps or landfills.

Call an auto junkyard or rubbish removal company and ask what they do with old tires. Find out if your community is trying any novel ways to use, destroy, or recycle tires.

Other synthetic polymers have a wide variety of different properties and uses. Polyethylene is a lightweight, inexpensive polymer used to make such items as trash bags and plastic containers. Polyvinyl chloride is used as plastic wrap because it can be made into a thin film that adheres well to itself. Polymethyl methacrylate is a polymer valued for its transparency and resistance to shattering. It is used as a substitute for glass. Another well-known polymer is Teflon™, which is used as a nonstick finish on metal cookware.

The two principal methods of synthesizing polymers are addition polymerization and condensation polymerization. Addition polymerization begins with an unsaturated monomer that contains a double bond. In a catalyzed reaction, the double bond of one monomer breaks. Then one of its carbon atoms forms a single bond to a carbon atom on an adjacent monomer. This new, single bond breaks the second monomer's double bond, which induces it to unite with a third monomer. The third monomer unites with a fourth, and on and on the reaction continues. This chain reaction is outlined in Figure 25–27. Addition polymerization can proceed almost indefinitely, uniting thousands and thousands of monomers into a single, enormous molecule.

Polyethylene is one polymer formed by the addition polymerization method. The monomer of polyethylene is ethene ($CH_2{=}CH_2$), which under the right circumstances will form a chain of thousands of $-CH_2-$ groups, each united by a single bond to the next. Polyvinyl chloride, polystyrene, and Teflon™ are other polymers formed by addition polymerization.

Figure 25–27 *An ethene monomer can undergo an addition polymerization reaction to form polyethylene, which is used to make trash bags and other products.*

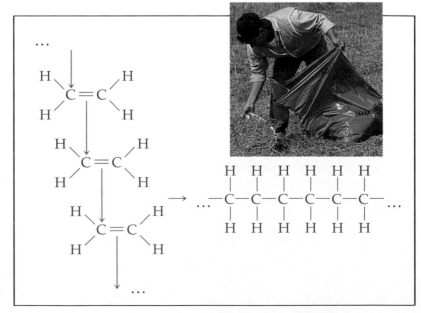

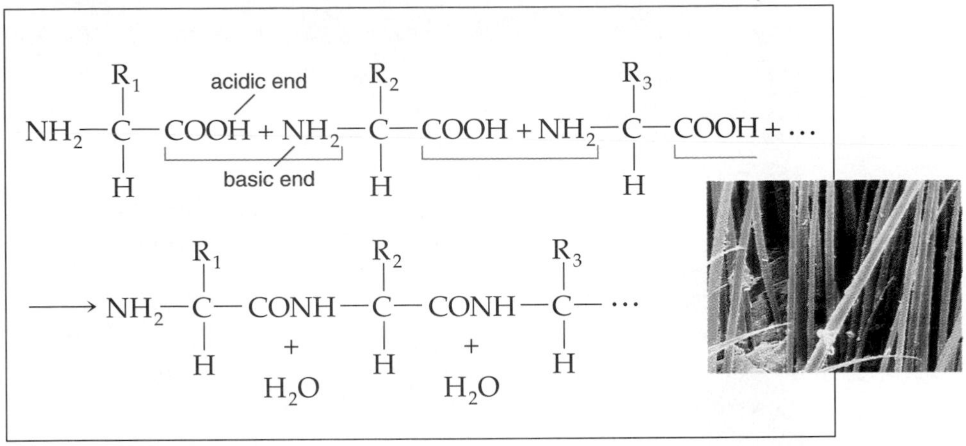

Figure 25–28 *Amino acids can combine at their acidic and basic ends, an example of condensation polymerization. The product of this reaction is a protein, an important class of compounds. Proteins are found in hair (inset) and elsewhere in the body.*

In condensation polymerization, monomers combine more slowly and in a manner that is easier to regulate. A protein is one example of a polymer formed by condensation polymerization. The monomers of proteins are amino acids, which are molecules with both acidic and basic ends. The acidic end of one amino acid combines with the basic end of the next amino acid, releasing a molecule of water in the process. All of the important polymers in living organisms, including DNA, proteins, and the complex carbohydrates, are made by condensation polymerization. Nylon is a synthetic polymer made by this method.

Recycling

When you hear the word recycling, what comes to mind? Perhaps you think of a recycling program in your community. Since the 1970s and 1980s, communities throughout the United States have been recycling aluminum cans, glass bottles, newspapers, and plastics. Recycling these products is important because we otherwise could exhaust the raw materials from which these products are made.

For the same reason, the carbon compounds of living organisms also need to be recycled. Natural processes have been recycling carbon compounds for billions of years, and life would grind to a halt if these processes did not exist. Over a given stretch of time, a carbon atom may find itself first in a carbon dioxide molecule in the atmosphere, then taken up by a plant and assembled into glucose, and then eaten and metabolized by an animal, which returns it to carbon dioxide again. Other carbon cycles exist, some of which rely on tiny bacteria and fungi to break

Figure 25–29 *Old plastic bottles can be recycled into new plastics. One of the first steps is to grind them into small nodules, such as those shown in the inset.*

INTEGRATING
ENVIRONMENTAL **S**CIENCE

What is the difference between biodegradable and nonbio-degradable substances?

down complex carbon molecules. A general rule to remember is that no naturally made compound is ever a recycling "dead end." If living organisms produce a certain complex compound, then a process exists to return the elements of that compound to simpler forms.

Many synthetic carbon compounds, including some polymers, fit well into nature's carbon cycle. These compounds are said to be **biodegradable,** from *bio-* meaning life, and *degradable* meaning able to be broken down. Biodegradable compounds are ones that will naturally decompose over time. But other synthetic polymers, including most plastics, are **nonbiodegradable.** Nature provides only very slow ways of decomposing nonbiodegradable compounds. A plastic milk jug, a plastic garbage bag, a disposable diaper: Each of these products can easily outlast the lives of the persons who purchased them, as well as the lives of their children, grandchildren, and great-grandchildren!

The best way to limit the world's supply of nonbiodegradable plastics is to use them wisely and to recycle them whenever possible. More and more plastics should be recycled in the future as technology improves and the need for recycling grows. Is there a program in your community to recycle plastics? If so, does your family or school participate?

Chemists are also exploring ways to make plastics more biodegradable. One strategy is to take an otherwise nonbiodegradable plastic and interweave it with natural, biodegradable compounds. The next time you are at the grocery store, look at the labels on products that are made of plastic or that come in plastic containers. See if any manufacturers claim that their plastic is biodegradable or friendly to the environment in some way. Do you think that such claims are true, or are you skeptical? Can you think of a way to test these claims?

Carbon atoms have a fantastic ability to combine in countless combinations, many of which are important—or even essential—in our daily lives. Some of these compounds, like fossil fuels, can be used but not replaced. Others, like some plastics, are difficult for natural processes to disassemble. For these compounds to be available for future generations, we must learn to use them carefully and wisely.

25–5 Section Review

1. What are polymers?
2. Why is it important to recycle plastics?
3. What are addition polymerization and condensation polymerization reactions?
4. **Connection—Biology** Suppose that geneticists develop a strain of bacteria that breaks down polyethylene, an otherwise nonbiodegradable plastic. How would such bacteria be useful? Do you foresee any dangers from these new bacteria?

Laboratory Investigation

Molecular Models of Hydrocarbons

Problem

What different shapes can hydrocarbons have?

Materials (per group)

> 11 small balls made of modeling clay:
>   3 balls to represent carbon atoms
>   (usually black)
>   8 balls to represent hydrogen (usually
>   light yellow)
> one box of multicolored toothpicks
> ruler   protractor
> sheet of paper

Procedure

Part A: Methane (CH_4)

1. Select four toothpicks of different colors. These toothpicks represent methane's four carbon-hydrogen bonds. Select one ball to represent a carbon atom.
2. Stick one end of each toothpick into the ball. The ends should touch each other at the ball's center. The other ends of the toothpicks should be as far apart as possible.

3. Measure the distance between the far ends of two toothpicks. Record this distance in an appropriate data table.
4. On a sheet of paper, draw a straight line of the same length that you recorded in Step 3. Choose two extra toothpicks from the box and arrange them to form a triangle, with the straight line as the third side. Use the protractor to measure the angle between the two toothpicks. This angle is the same as the bond angle in your model. Record this bond angle in your data table.

5. Repeat Steps 3 and 4 for each of the six bond angles in your model.
6. To complete the model, place a ball for hydrogen at the end of each toothpick.

Part B: Ethene (C_2H_4)

1. Select six toothpicks, two balls to represent carbon atoms, and four balls to represent hydrogen atoms. Build a model of ethene. Use one toothpick for a single bond and two toothpicks for a double bond.
2. Use the protractor to measure each bond angle in your model. Record these bond angles in an appropriate data table.

Part C: Cyclic hydrocarbons

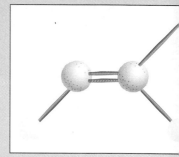

1. Remove two balls that represent hydrogen atoms from the top side of your model of ethene. Remove one toothpick. With two other groups, build a model of benzene.

2. Remove two balls that represent hydrogen atoms from your model of methane. Do not remove the toothpicks or change their positions. With five other groups, build a model of cyclohexane. (NOTE: In this model, a single bond may be represented by two toothpicks.)

Analysis and Conclusions

1. In an actual methane molecule, would you expect the six bond angles to be different or the same? What angles would you expect for the bonds in ethene? Explain.
2. Compare the bond angles in your models to those in actual molecules.
3. Discuss the differences between the structures of cyclohexane and benzene.
4. **On Your Own** Use balls and toothpicks to make other hydrocarbon models. Display your models in the classroom.

STUDY GUIDE

Summarizing Key Concepts

25–1 The Element Carbon

- Elemental carbon exists in different forms, or allotropes, including diamond, graphite, amorphous carbon, and fullerenes.
- Carbon atoms form strong covalent bonds because they have a half-filled valence level and the bonding electrons are close to the nucleus. Carbon forms long, stable chains because it cannot stably exist as a diatomic molecule.

25–2 Carbon Compounds

- Generally, a molecule that contains carbon is an organic molecule. Carbon compounds classified as inorganic include oxides of carbon and compounds of the carbonate ion.
- A molecule's identity comes from its sequence of atoms and bonds, not the site where the molecule was assembled.

25–3 Hydrocarbons

- Hydrocarbons consist of carbon and hydrogen only. They can exist in straight chains, branched chains, or rings, and may include single, double, and triple bonds. Hydrocarbons are nonpolar molecules.

25–4 Saturated and Unsaturated Hydrocarbons

- Alkanes, or saturated hydrocarbons, contain only single bonds. Their names end in the suffix -ane.
- Alkanes exist in many conformations because single bonds can freely rotate about their axis. Structural isomers of alkanes take the form of different branching patterns.
- Unsaturated hydrocarbons contain at least one multiple bond. Alkenes contain a double bond and alkynes contain a triple bond.
- Benzene is an unusually stable cyclic hydrocarbon. Its carbon-carbon bonds are a hybrid between single and double bonds.

25–5 Polymers

- Polymers are large organic molecules made by joining small units, or monomers.
- Biodegradable compounds recycle naturally. Most plastics are nonbiodegradable.

Reviewing Key Terms

Define each term in a complete sentence.

25–1 The Element Carbon

allotrope
diamond
graphite
amorphous carbon
fullerene

25–2 Carbon Compounds

organic chemistry

25–3 Hydrocarbons

hydrocarbon
fossil fuel

molecular formula
structural formula
condensed structural formula

25–4 Saturated and Unsaturated Hydrocarbons

alkane
general formula
saturated hydrocarbon
branched alkane
branch carbon
parent chain
conformation

structural isomer
cyclic hydrocarbon
cycloalkane
unsaturated hydrocarbon
alkene
alkyne
benzene
aromatic compound

25–5 Polymers

polymer
monomer
biodegradable
nonbiodegradable

CHAPTER REVIEW

Content Review

Multiple Choice

Choose the letter of the answer that best completes each statement.

1. Carbon is unique in part because it can
   (a) form covalent bonds.
   (b) become a metal.
   (c) bond with other nonmetals.
   (d) form long chains of atoms.
2. Which of the following is not an allotrope of carbon?
   (a) graphite   (c) lead
   (b) fullerene   (d) diamond
3. Vitamin C made in a laboratory is
   (a) chemically identical to the Vitamin C in oranges.
   (b) inferior to natural compounds.
   (c) dangerous to consume.
   (d) weaker than natural Vitamin C.
4. Which is not an organic compound?
   (a) C_8H_{18} (c) CO_2
   (b) $C_6H_{12}O_6$ (d) CH_2O
5. Which of the following formulas represents an alkane?
   (a) C_3H_6 (c) C_5H_{10}
   (b) C_8H_{14} (d) C_6H_{14}

6. C_6H_{12} could represent a(an)
   (a) alkane.   (c) alkene.
   (b) alkyne.   (d) benzene.
7. A saturated hydrocarbon always has
   (a) only single bonds.
   (b) at least one double or triple bond.
   (c) a ring.
   (d) more carbon atoms than hydrogen atoms.
8. A 6-carbon hydrocarbon that has two resonance structures is
   (a) hexane.   (c) cyclane.
   (b) hexene.   (d) benzene.
9. Structural isomers have the same
   (a) molecular formula.
   (b) structural formula.
   (c) condensed structural formula.
   (d) electron dot formula.
10. Polymers are formed by joining individual units called
    (a) plastics.   (c) monomers.
    (b) carbon.   (d) minimers.

True or False

If the statement is true, write "true." If it is false, change the underlined word or words to make the statement true.

11. The general formula for an <u>alkane</u> is C_nH_{2n}.
12. <u>Hydrocarbons</u> contain only the elements carbon and hydrogen.
13. The hardest form of carbon is <u>graphite</u>.
14. Hydrocarbons are <u>soluble</u> in water.
15. <u>Cyclooctane</u> has the formula C_8H_{16}.
16. Compounds with the same molecular formulas but different structural formulas are called <u>structural isomers</u>.
17. Two <u>structural isomers</u> differ by rotated single bonds.
18. Proteins are made by <u>monomerization</u>.
19. Propyne is a(an) <u>saturated</u> hydrocarbon.
20. Most plastics are <u>biodegradable</u>.

Concept Mapping

Complete the following concept map for Section 25–3. Refer to pages xviii–xix to construct a concept map for the entire chapter.

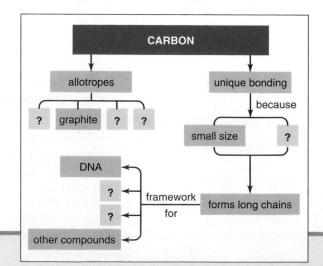

Concept Mastery

Discuss each of the following in a brief paragraph.

21. Describe the different allotropes of carbon.
22. Why did early chemists believe that carbon compounds contained a vital force?
23. Why is carbon more successful than other elements at forming long chains of atoms?
24. Describe the different chemical and physical properties of organic and inorganic compounds.
25. Draw structural formulas for 2-methylpentane and 3-methylpentane.

26. Why are hydrocarbons typically found beneath the Earth's surface?
27. Describe two methods of assembling monomers into polymers.
28. **Tying it Together** In terms of *unity and diversity*, the molecular formula C_4H_6 could represent an alkyne, a cycloalkene, or a hydrocarbon with two double bonds. Write condensed structural formulas for each. Which do you think is the least stable, and why?

Critical Thinking and Problem Solving

Use the skills you have developed in this chapter to answer each of the following.

29. **Applying concepts** An organic chemistry student tries to synthesize an allotrope of carbon in which 6 carbon atoms form a single ring. The molecular formula for this compound would be C_6. The student is unsuccessful. Why?
30. **Making comparisons** Silicon, which is in the same group as carbon, is a more abundant element than carbon. Why does carbon form so many different compounds and silicon does not?
31. **Making predictions** Alkadienes are hydrocarbons with two double bonds. Draw the structural formula of the alkadiene with the molecular formula C_3H_4. Predict the bond angle around the central carbon atom.

32. **Applying concepts** Some people who take vitamin supplements insist on vitamins that were extracted from plant products. What assumptions are these individuals making?
33. **Making judgments** Fossil fuels are a nonrenewable energy source. Should governments impose mandatory rationing or recycling programs to conserve fossil fuels? Give reasons for your answer.
34. **Using the writing process** Think about all the synthetic materials you use every day. Write a story about being suddenly transported into a society whose only organic compounds were made naturally. How would your life change?

Classes of Organic Compounds

Step into your favorite ice cream parlor and smell that isobutyl formate. Mmmm! And what about the pentyl ethanoate? Or would you prefer a scoop of octyl ethanoate sherbet!

Sound a little strange? While the names may be unfamiliar to you, the scents and tastes are probably not. Isobutyl formate, for example, is responsible for raspberry flavor. Pentyl ethanoate is banana-flavored, and octyl ethanoate provides orange flavor.

In this chapter you will learn about nine important classes of organic compounds. As you will see, these compounds have tremendously varied properties—from the sweet taste of vanilla to the putrid odor of rotting fish.

Organic compounds are everywhere—from your favorite desserts to some not-so-fresh fish.

Chem Journal

YOU AND YOUR WORLD

Open your medicine cabinet and read the lists of ingredients on the product labels you find there. In your journal, record the names of at least ten different ingredients and the products that contain them. For any ingredients you recognize, describe some of their properties or uses. When you finish this chapter, review your journal entry and see if you better understand any of these ingredients.

26–1 Halocarbons, Alcohols, and Ethers

Guide for Reading
- What are hydrocarbon derivatives?
- How are halocarbons, alcohols, and ethers similar and different?

From the shampoo you use to wash your hair to the food you eat, you are surrounded by organic compounds. In Chapter 25, you found out that there are millions of different organic compounds. Many of these compounds are hydrocarbons, consisting of only carbon and hydrogen. The vast majority of organic compounds, however, contain elements in addition to carbon

Figure 26–1 *Hydrocarbon derivatives are all around you. They fill your medicine cabinet in the form of aspirin, cosmetics, throat lozenges, hair spray, and cologne, and they make many ordinary tasks easier. What is a hydrocarbon derivative?*

and hydrogen. Organic compounds such as these are often called **hydrocarbon derivatives** because they can be derived from basic hydrocarbons. **Hydrocarbon derivatives are molecules that contain carbon and hydrogen atoms, as do hydrocarbons, but contain additional atoms or groups of atoms.**

If you find the huge number and variety of organic compounds staggering, you are not alone. In the nineteenth century, as organic compounds were rapidly being discovered, chemists also found the information awesome. As more compounds were identified and their properties recorded, the subject became overwhelming. The data were so intimidating that German chemist Friedrich Wöhler remarked that organic chemistry seemed a "dreadful endless jungle."

Fortunately, however, chemists began to realize that while there are millions of organic compounds, they could group them into a small number of classes. This grouping is based on the presence of structural features called **functional groups.** A functional group is an atom or group of atoms that has a characteristic chemical behavior. Because different functional groups give rise to different types of reactions, the properties of a hydrocarbon derivative depend upon its functional group. Hydrocarbon derivatives are grouped into classes according to their functional group. The classes of hydrocarbon derivatives are halocarbons, alcohols, ethers, aldehydes, ketones, carboxylic acids, esters, amines, and amides. Due to their common structural feature, all compounds in a given class have similar properties and are described by the same general formula. You will be introduced to each of these classes of compounds in this chapter. Let's start with halocarbons.

Halocarbons

You know that hydrocarbons are made up of carbon and hydrogen atoms. In certain reactions, hydrogen atoms in a hydrocarbon can be replaced by other atoms. If the replacement atom is an element from the halogen family, an organic compound known as a **halocarbon** is formed. **In a halocarbon, one or more of the hydrogen atoms of a hydrocarbon have been replaced by atoms from the halogen family.** The general formula for a halocarbon is R—X, where R symbolizes the hydrocarbon portion of the molecule, and X represents the halogen atom. The X could stand for fluorine, chlorine, bromine, or iodine. To what group of the periodic table do these elements belong? The halogen atom in a halocarbon is the functional group in this class of compounds.

Figure 26–2 The Teflon™ coating that allows these scrumptious scrambled eggs to slide from the pan to your plate is a halocarbon. What is the general formula for a halocarbon?

NAMING HALOCARBONS Just as the physical structure of a halocarbon is different from that of the hydrocarbon from which it was formed, so too is its name. Do not be alarmed, however, because you will find that you use what you have already learned about naming hydrocarbons to name hydrocarbon derivatives. To name a halocarbon according to the IUPAC system, you first name the hydrocarbon portion of the molecule as usual, then add a prefix to indicate the presence of halogen atoms.

As an example, consider the compound with the structural formula shown below.

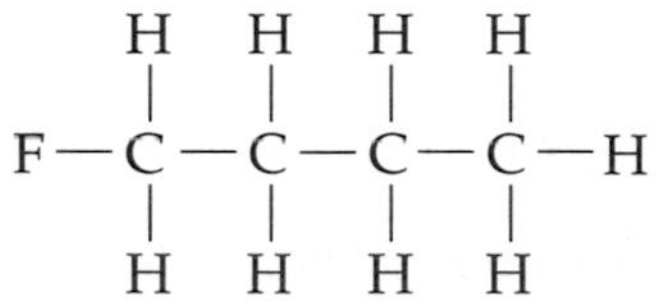

$$\begin{array}{ccccccccc}
 & H & & H & & H & & H & \\
 & | & & | & & | & & | & \\
F - & C & - & C & - & C & - & C & - H \\
 & | & & | & & | & & | & \\
 & H & & H & & H & & H & \\
\end{array}$$

This is a hydrocarbon that has had the hydrogen atom on the end replaced by a fluorine atom. The first step in naming this compound is naming the hydrocarbon portion. This molecule has 4 carbon atoms in the parent chain, so its root name is *but-*. It contains all single bonds, so its suffix is *-ane*. Thus the hydrocarbon portion is butane. To indicate that the molecule contains a halogen atom, the halogen is named as a prefix much as branch chains are named. The halogen prefix contains the root name of the halogen element plus the suffix *-o*, which in this case is *fluoro-*. The last step in naming the compound is to designate the location of the halogen atom. The fluorine atom is bonded to the first carbon atom, so the molecule is called 1-fluorobutane. Remember to count carbon atoms from the end that gives the smallest prefix.

If 2 halogen atoms had been present in the compound, the prefix *di-* would have been used to indicate both atoms, and the locations of each would have been included in the name. For example, the name 2,2-dichlorobutane indicates that 2 chlorine atoms are present in a halocarbon consisting of 4 carbon atoms. Both chlorine atoms are located on the second carbon atom in the chain. If two different halogen atoms are present in the halocarbon, both are included in the name.

One other note about naming halocarbons: As with other compounds there are IUPAC names and common names. You may occasionally see common names for some halocarbons. In fact, you are already familiar with some of these names. Some common names are formed by identifying the alkyl group attached to the halocarbon. The compound mentioned earlier, 1-fluorobutane, would commonly be called butyl fluoride.

Name this halocarbon:

$$\begin{array}{ccccccccccc} & & F & & H & & F & & H & & H \\ & & | & & | & & | & & | & & | \\ Cl & - & C & - & C & - & C & - & C & - & C & - H \\ & & | & & | & & | & & | & & | \\ & & H & & H & & H & & H & & H \end{array}$$

STRATEGY	SOLUTION
1. Analyze	You are asked to name a halocarbon that includes atoms of fluorine and chlorine.
2. Plan	First determine the root name of the parent chain. Then form the prefixes by adding the suffix -*o* to the root names of the halogen atoms. Use numbers to indicate the locations of the halogen atoms.
3. Solve	The parent hydrocarbon is pentane because it has 5 carbon atoms in the parent chain and all single bonds. The compound has 2 fluorine atoms: one at carbon 1 and one at carbon 3, so the name has the prefix 1,3-difluoro. The chlorine atom at carbon 1 is denoted by the prefix 1-chloro. Placing the prefixes in alphabetical order gives 1-chloro-1,3-difluoropentane.
4. Evaluate	Check your answer by reconstructing the structural formula from the name. Pentane implies 5 carbon atoms; 1-chloro means a chlorine atom on the first carbon atom; 1,3-difluoro means 2 fluorine atoms, 1 on the first carbon atom and 1 on the third.

PRACTICE PROBLEMS

1. Name the following halocarbon:

$$\begin{array}{ccccccccc} & & H & & H & & H & & Br \\ & & | & & | & & | & & | \\ H & - & C & - & C & - & C & - & C & - Br \\ & & | & & | & & | & & | \\ & & H & & H & & H & & H \end{array}$$

(Answer: 1,1-dibromobutane)

2. Draw the structural formula for 1,1-difluoro-3-bromopentane.

$$\text{(Answer: }\begin{array}{ccccccccccc} & F & & H & & H & & H & & H \\ & | & & | & & | & & | & & | \\ F - & C & - & C & - & C & - & C & - & C & - H \\ & | & & | & & | & & | & & | \\ & H & & H & & Br & & H & & H \end{array}\text{)}$$

PROPERTIES OF HALOCARBONS Halocarbon molecules may have polar regions, but they are primarily nonpolar. As such, halocarbons have physical properties similar to those of alkanes. They have low boiling points and are insoluble in water but soluble in hydrocarbon solvents.

By now in your study of chemistry you have encountered the topic of chlorofluorocarbons (CFCs) more than once. Now you can understand CFCs from another perspective because they are an example of halocarbons that contain atoms of chlorine and fluorine. Recall that CFCs have been used as aerosol propellants and refrigerant gases. Because CFCs are involved in the depletion of the ozone layer, carbon dioxide is now employed in most aerosol cans and CFCs are gradually being replaced by hydrofluorocarbons (HFCs) in many new refrigeration and air-conditioning units.

Halocarbons are also used as industrial and household solvents. For example, the halocarbon tetrachloromethane (commonly known as carbon tetrachloride) was once widely used for dry cleaning and spot removal. Due to its toxicity and carcinogenic effect, however, other solvents, such as dichloromethane (commonly known as methylene chloride), are currently used in dry cleaning. Halocarbons are also found in many pesticides, including DDT and chlordane. In 1972, the U.S. Environmental Protection Agency banned DDT because of its threat to wildlife (and humans).

Aside from these industrial applications, one of the most important uses for halocarbons is as intermediates in the synthesis of other classes of organic compounds. Because it is relatively easy to substitute a halogen atom into a hydrocarbon molecule, a halocarbon can be formed and then the halogen atom can be replaced with other functional groups.

Alcohols

Just as halogen atoms can be substituted into a hydrocarbon, so can other atoms or groups of atoms. For example, an –OH group—called a **hydroxyl group**—might replace one or more hydrogen atoms. **In an alcohol, one or more hydrogen atoms of a hydrocarbon are replaced by a hydroxyl group.** The general formula for an **alcohol** is R—OH, where R represents the hydrocarbon portion, and OH represents the hydroxyl group. The hydroxyl group is the functional group of an alcohol.

Alcohols are further divided into groups based upon the position of the hydroxyl group. Alcohols can be classified as primary, secondary, or tertiary. Figure 26–4 shows the structures of three different types of alcohols. Primary alcohols have hydroxyl groups attached to a carbon atom that is attached to only 1 other carbon atom. In other words, in primary alcohols the hydroxyl group is on the end of the chain. Secondary alcohols

INTEGRATING
ENVIRONMENTAL SCIENCE

Do you know why the pesticide DDT was banned in 1972?

Figure 26–3 When this man finishes shaving, he may reach for his favorite after-shave. The alcohol in most after-shave lotions is responsible for a cooling, but sometimes stinging, sensation. What is the general formula for an alcohol?

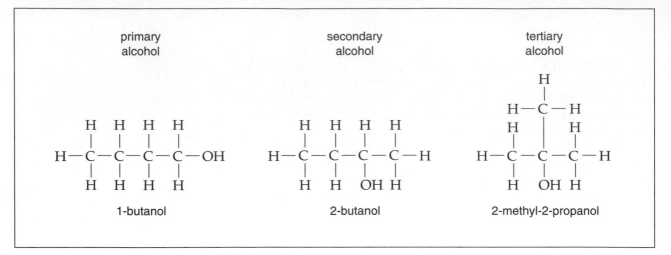

Figure 26–4 *Notice the position of the hydroxyl group on each of the alcohols. How would you describe the three different types of alcohols?*

have the hydroxyl group attached to a carbon atom that is attached to 2 other carbon atoms. So, in secondary alcohols, the hydroxyl group is on a carbon atom in the interior of the chain. Tertiary alcohols have their hydroxyl groups attached to a carbon atom that is attached to 3 other carbon atoms. Thus, in tertiary alcohols, the hydroxyl group is not only attached to a carbon atom in the interior of the chain, but an alkyl group is also branched from the same carbon atom.

NAMING ALCOHOLS   There are many different alcohols, and each one is named for the hydrocarbon that bears the hydroxyl group. In naming an alcohol according to the IUPAC system, the suffix *-ol* is added to the root of the hydrocarbon name. The alcohol containing only 1 carbon atom, for example, is methanol. Its structure is shown below.

$$\begin{array}{c} H \\ | \\ H-C-OH \\ | \\ H \end{array}$$

Again, you may encounter the common name, which for alcohols is found by identifying the alkyl group and adding the word alcohol. The common name for methanol is methyl alcohol. This alcohol also has another name. It is sometimes called wood alcohol because it was originally produced by heating wood chips in the absence of air. Ingestion of even small amounts of methanol can dissolve the sheath surrounding the optic nerve and cause blindness. Ingesting larger amounts of methanol can be lethal.

What is the name of the compound shown below?

$$\begin{array}{cc} H & H \\ | & | \\ H-C-C-OH \\ | & | \\ H & H \end{array}$$

What Can it Be?

In the chemistry lab, Raphael accidentally mixed a halocarbon with a base. He identified one of the products as a salt. What was the other product? Use condensed structural formulas to show a reaction that supports your answer.

Hint: When a base reacts with a halocarbon, the hydroxyl group of the base can replace the halogen atom in the halocarbon.

The hydroxyl group is attached to a 2-carbon chain, or ethyl group. Thus the name of the compound is ethanol. The common name for this compound is ethyl alcohol. Ethanol is sometimes called grain alcohol because it is produced from the fermentation of carbohydrates found in various grains, such as corn, rye, and barley. Ethanol is found in beer, wine, and other alcoholic beverages. Because it burns in an internal combustion engine, ethanol is also blended with gasoline to give a mixture called gasohol that is 10 percent ethanol.

When a hydroxyl group is added to a longer hydrocarbon chain, several structural isomers may form. To identify a particular isomer, the name of the compound includes a number prefix to designate the location of the hydroxyl group on the parent chain. The compound shown below is called 2-propanol because the parent hydrocarbon is propane, and the hydroxyl group is located on the second carbon atom.

$$
\begin{array}{ccccc}
& H & H & H & \\
& | & | & | & \\
H - & C & - C & - C & - H \\
& | & | & | & \\
& H & OH & H &
\end{array}
$$

You probably have this alcohol in your bathroom at home. It is used as rubbing alcohol and for sterilizing medical instruments.

Do not think that you always need a full structural formula to name an alcohol or other class of organic compound. You can also use a condensed structural formula. For example, what is the name of the compound represented by the condensed structural formula $CH_3CH(OH)CH_3$? Although the condensed structural formula can be a little intimidating at first, the naming process is the same as before. The parent chain contains 3 carbon atoms and thus has the root *propan-*. The suffix must indicate the alcohol, making it propanol. The hydroxyl group is on the second carbon atom, so a 2- is used to designate the location. The name is 2-propanol, which is exactly the compound you named from its structural formula above!

Visit our Web site at
http://www.phschool.com
to support your
study of chemistry.

SAMPLE PROBLEM 2

What is the name of the compound with the following condensed structural formula:

$$CH_3CH_2CH(OH)CH_3$$

STRATEGY	SOLUTION
1. Analyze	You are given the condensed structural formula and are asked to name the compound.
2. Plan	You must first recognize that this compound is an alcohol because it contains a hydroxyl group attached to a carbon atom. You must determine the root name of the parent chain and add a suffix to indicate an alcohol. The final step will be to indicate the location of the hydroxyl group.
3. Solve	This is a 4-carbon chain, so the root name is *butan-*. In the name of an alcohol, the suffix is *-ol,* so the name becomes butanol. Because the hydroxyl group is located on the second carbon atom, a 2 is used to indicate the position. The name is 2-butanol.
4. Evaluate	Your answer makes sense because it indicates a compound with 4 carbon atoms and a hydroxyl group attached to the second carbon atom. This is a secondary alcohol because the hydroxyl group is bonded to a carbon atom that is attached to 2 other carbon atoms.

PRACTICE PROBLEMS

3. What is the name and type of the alcohol described by this condensed structural formula:

$$CH_3CH_2CH(OH)CH_2CH_2CH_3$$

(Answer: 3-hexanol; secondary)

4. Draw a structural formula for 1-octanol. What type of alcohol is it?   *(Answer: structural formula below; primary)*

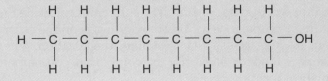

PROPERTIES OF ALCOHOLS Do you recognize anything special about hydroxyl groups? A hydroxyl group is part of a water molecule. It makes sense then that the physical properties of alcohols and water are generally similar. The hydroxyl group imparts polar properties to alcohols. Small alcohols are polar because the hydrocarbon portions are not large enough to confer nonpolar properties. Similarly, alcohols with up to 4 carbon atoms are soluble in water because the polarity of the hydroxyl group is more significant than the nonpolar hydrocarbon portion of the molecule. But as more carbon atoms are added to an alcohol, its polarity decreases. Therefore, an alcohol with a longer hydrocarbon portion is less soluble in water than one with a shorter hydrocarbon portion.

Like water, alcohols can form hydrogen bonds between oxygen and hydrogen atoms in separate molecules. Therefore, they have stronger intermolecular forces than the corresponding hydrocarbon. For this reason, alcohols have much higher boiling points than do the hydrocarbons from which they are formed.

So far, all the alcohols we have discussed have contained a single hydroxyl group. Alcohols, however, are not limited to having only one hydroxyl group. But one difference that occurs when more than one hydroxyl group is present is that the alcohol is given a special name. An alcohol with two hydroxyl groups is called a diol and an alcohol with three hydroxyl groups is called a triol.

Figure 26–5 *One important diol is ethylene glycol, which you know as automotive antifreeze. An important triol is glycerol, which is sometimes used in hand creams, soaps, and cosmetics.*

ethylene glycol
(1, 2-ethanediol)

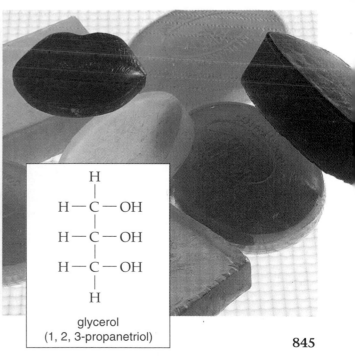

glycerol
(1, 2, 3-propanetriol)

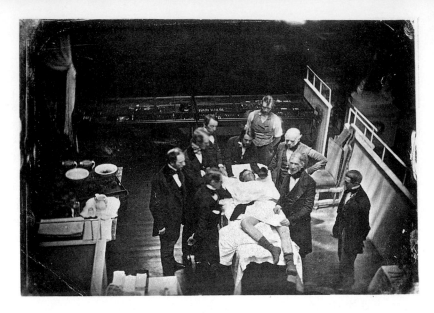

Figure 26–6 *In the nineteenth century, surgeons used ethers to anesthetize patients. Ethers can cause nausea and other side effects, however, so doctors today use other anesthetics. What is the general formula for ethers?*

Ethers

Alcohols are not the only class of organic compounds that contain oxygen. A class of organic compounds known as **ethers** also contain oxygen. In ethers, however, the oxygen is not part of a hydroxyl group. Instead, two hydrocarbon groups are bonded to the same oxygen atom. **An ether molecule contains an oxygen atom that is bonded to two carbon atoms.** The general formula for an ether is R—O—R′, where R and R′ are hydrocarbon chains. The prime symbol (′) is used to show that the hydrocarbon chains may be the same or different. The functional group on an ether molecule is —O—.

NAMING ETHERS The IUPAC name for an ether gives the suffix *-oxy* to the smaller hydrocarbon chain bonded to the central oxygen atom. The remainder of the molecule is named just as a hydrocarbon is named. For example, let's name the compound with the condensed structural formula $CH_3CH_2OCH_2CH_2CH_3$. The first step is to identify the two hydrocarbon chains: one on either side of the oxygen atom. One hydrocarbon chain contains 2 carbon atoms and the other hydrocarbon chain contains 3 carbon atoms. The smaller chain is thus the one with 2 carbon atoms. So the root is *eth-* and the suffix is *-oxy*, or ethoxy. The name of the remaining hydrocarbon, which contain 3 single-bonded carbon atoms, is propane. The name of the whole compound, then, is ethoxypropane.

Fortunately, most ethers are named in a simpler manner and are described by their common names. To identify the common name of an ether, locate the central oxygen atom and simply call the molecule an ether. The hydrocarbon chains that are attached to the oxygen are then named just as you would name a branch chain, using the *-yl* suffix for each. Therefore, ethoxypropane ($CH_3CH_2OCH_2CH_2CH_3$) could be called ethyl propyl ether, because the hydrocarbon portions of the ether contain 2 carbon atoms (ethyl) and 3 carbon atoms (propyl).

SAMPLE PROBLEM 3

Give the IUPAC name and the common name for the ether with the following condensed structural formula:

$$CH_3CH_2CH_2—O—CH_2CH_2CH_2CH_3.$$

STRATEGY	SOLUTION
1. Analyze	You are given the formula for an ether and are asked to give its name according to IUPAC rules and according to the rules for common names.
2. Plan	There is a 3-carbon chain on one side of the oxygen atom and a 4-carbon chain on the other side. You can find the IUPAC name by adding the suffix *-oxy* to the root name of the smaller hydrocarbon chain and adding this name to the name of the remaining hydrocarbon. The common name is found by calling the molecule an ether and using a *-yl* suffix for both hydrocarbon portions of the molecule.
3. Solve	According to the IUPAC system, the 3-carbon group is given the name propoxy because it is the smaller group. The larger hydrocarbon group is called butane. The IUPAC name for the ether is propoxybutane. The common name is propyl butyl ether.
4. Evaluate	Both names make sense because they indicate a molecule containing 7 carbon atoms as indicated in the given formula.

PRACTICE PROBLEMS

5. What are the IUPAC name and the common name for $CH_3OCH_2CH_2CH_2CH_2CH_3$? *(Answer: methoxypentane; methyl pentyl ether)*

6. An ether has the IUPAC name ethoxyethane. What is its common name? *(Answer: diethyl ether)*

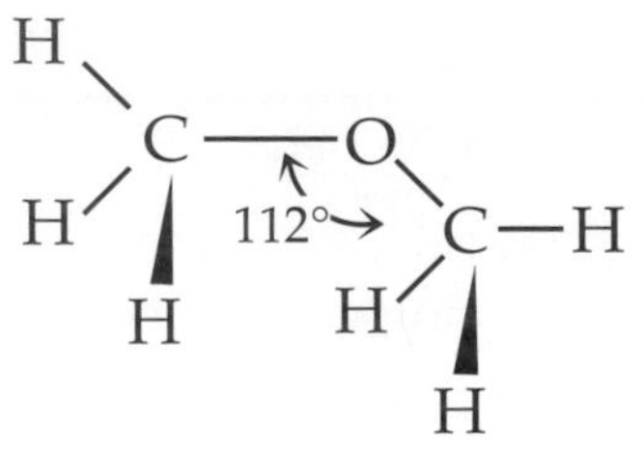

Figure 26–7 *This diagram illustrates the molecular shape of dimethyl ether (CH₃OCH₃). Why does the oxygen atom in this molecule have a partial negative charge?*

PROPERTIES OF ETHERS The properties of ethers result from the presence of the oxygen atom. Because oxygen is more electronegative than either carbon or hydrogen and because of the molecule's shape, the oxygen atom in an ether molecule creates a slightly polar region. Small ethers are soluble in water due to this polarity. Larger ether molecules, however, have longer nonpolar hydrocarbon portions that decrease the polarity, making them less soluble in water.

Recall from Chapter 14 that one of the conditions for hydrogen bonding is that a hydrogen atom be bonded to a highly electronegative element such as oxygen. In an ether molecule, however, hydrogen is bonded only to carbon atoms, which are not highly electronegative. Thus, ethers do not form hydrogen bonds. For this reason, ethers have boiling points that are lower than the corresponding alcohols, but higher than the corresponding hydrocarbons.

Various ethers have applications both inside and outside the chemistry laboratory. One such ether, diethyl ether, is a common solvent for organic compounds. Other ethers were used as surgical anesthetics in hospitals during the nineteenth century. A third ether, one of the methyl butyl ethers, has been used in gasoline to reduce pollution and improve engine efficiency.

26–1 Section Review

1. Explain what hydrocarbon derivatives are and how they are divided into classes according to their functional groups.

2. Compare and contrast the structures of halocarbons, alcohols, and ethers.

3. Discuss the polarity, solubility, and boiling points of halocarbons, alcohols, and ethers.

4. Explain how halocarbons, alcohols, and ethers are named.

5. **Critical Thinking—Making inferences** One method of synthesizing ethers is by removing a water molecule from two primary alcohols. Use structural formulas to propose an equation for the synthesis of diethyl ether.

26–2 Aldehydes and Ketones

You have seen that an oxygen atom can be located between 2 other atoms in a hydrocarbon to form an alcohol or an ether. An oxygen atom can also be attached to a single carbon atom by a double covalent bond (C=O). Such an arrangement is called a **carbonyl** (KAHR-buh-nihl) **group.** A carbonyl group is the functional group of the next two classes of organic compounds: aldehydes and ketones.

The exact nature of compounds containing a carbonyl group depends upon the location of the group on the parent hydrocarbon chain. If one of the remaining bonds of the carbonyl group carbon is attached to a hydrogen atom, an **aldehyde** is formed. **An aldehyde molecule has a carbonyl group at the end of a hydrocarbon chain.** The general formula for an aldehyde is R—CHO. One bond of the carbonyl group carbon atom is attached to a hydrogen atom and the remaining bond may be to either a second hydrogen atom or an alkyl group.

When both bonds of the carbonyl group carbon are attached to carbon atoms, a **ketone** is formed. **A ketone molecule has a carbonyl group on the interior of a hydrocarbon chain.** Ketones have the general formula R—COR'. As with ethers, R and R' may be the same or different hydrocarbon groups. Figure 26–8 shows the basic structure of a carbonyl group, an aldehyde, and a ketone.

NAMING ALDEHYDES AND KETONES Naming an aldehyde according to the IUPAC system requires that you add the suffix -*al* to the root name of the parent hydrocarbon to identify the molecule as an aldehyde. With this in mind, how would you name CH_3CHO? (Its structural formula is shown in red in Figure 26–8.) The compound is an aldehyde because the carbon atom of the carbonyl group is bonded to a hydrogen atom. Two carbon atoms indicate the stem *ethan-*, so the aldehyde suffix makes the name ethanal. Why is it not necessary to use a number prefix when naming an aldehyde? The answer is that an aldehyde always has the carbonyl group on the first carbon atom.

The name of a ketone according to the IUPAC system is also formed from the root of the hydrocarbon. In this case, however, the suffix is -*one*. Let's name the structure shown in blue in Figure 26–8. This compound is a ketone because it contains a carbonyl group in the interior of the hydrocarbon. The stem is *pentan-* due to the 5 carbon atoms, so the IUPAC name is 3-pentanone.

Because the carbonyl group can be located on any interior carbon, the name of the ketone must also include the number of the carbonyl carbon in the parent chain. How would you name a 7-carbon ketone that has the carbonyl group on the second carbon atom?

Guide for Reading
- What are the characteristics of aldehydes and ketones?
- How are aldehydes and ketones named?

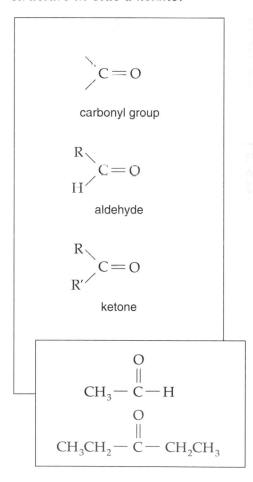

Figure 26–8 *Both aldehydes and ketones contain a carbonyl group. Why is the structure in red an aldehyde? Why is the structure in blue a ketone?*

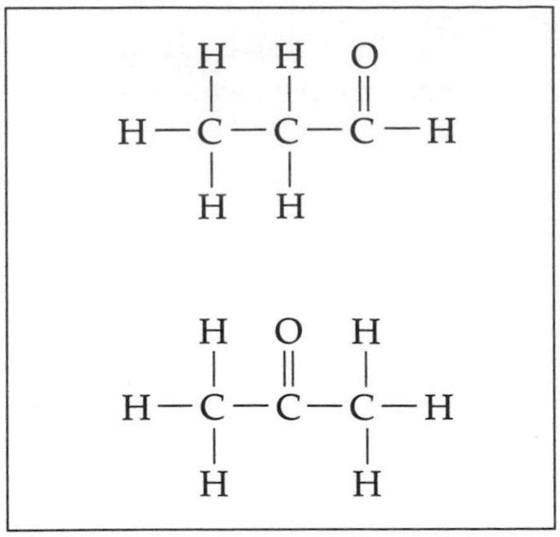

The molecular structures shown:

First molecule:
```
     H   H   O
     |   |   ||
 H — C — C — C — H
     |   |
     H   H
```

Second molecule:
```
     H   O   H
     |   ||   |
 H — C — C — C — H
     |       |
     H       H
```

SAMPLE PROBLEM 4

What are the names of the molecules shown at the left?

STRATEGY	SOLUTION

1. Analyze   You are given structural formulas for two molecules containing a carbonyl group and are asked to name each.

2. Plan   You must first recognize the carbonyl groups, their locations, and the atoms to which they are bonded. You can use this information and what you know about naming aldehydes and ketones to name the compounds.

3. Solve   Both compounds have the root *propan-* due to the 3 carbon atoms. The first molecule is an aldehyde because the carbonyl group is on a terminal carbon atom. To name an aldehyde, add the suffix *-al* to the root. The name of this aldehyde is propanal.

The second molecule is a ketone because the carbonyl group is located on a central atom. To name a ketone, add the suffix *-one* to the root and use a number to indicate the location of the carbonyl group. The name of this ketone is 2-propanone because the carbonyl group is on carbon 2.

4. Evaluate   These molecules both have a carbonyl group. The location of the carbonyl group determines whether the compound is an aldehyde or a ketone.

PRACTICE PROBLEMS

7. Name the molecule shown.

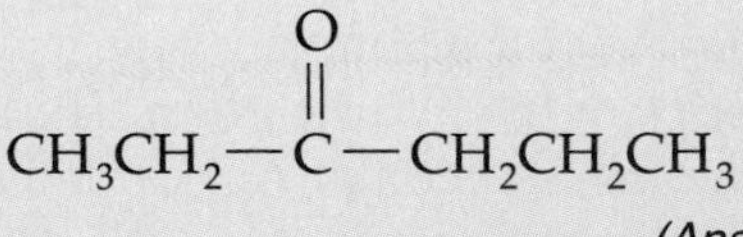

$$CH_3CH_2 - \overset{\overset{\textstyle O}{\|}}{C} - CH_2CH_2CH_3$$

(Answer: 3-hexanone)

8. Write the structural formula for 4-octanone.

(Answer: $CH_3CH_2CH_2 - \overset{\overset{\textstyle O}{\|}}{C} - CH_2CH_2CH_2CH_3$ *)*

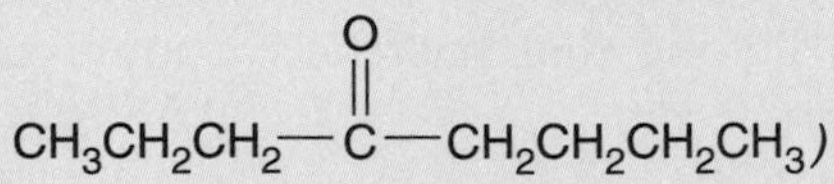

PROPERTIES OF ALDEHYDES AND KETONES The carbonyl group of aldehydes and ketones causes these molecules to be more polar than hydrocarbons. Therefore, these molecules have stronger intermolecular attractions and higher melting and boiling points than the corresponding hydrocarbons. However, aldehydes and ketones do not form hydrogen bonds as alcohols do, which causes them to have lower melting and boiling points than alcohols. Remember that hydrogen atoms must be bonded to one of the more electronegative elements to form hydrogen bonds. In aldehydes and ketones, hydrogen atoms are bonded to carbon atoms, which are not highly electronegative.

The simplest aldehyde, methanal (HCOH), has the common name formaldehyde. It is one of the 25 most important industrial chemicals. About 3 billion kilograms of formaldehyde are produced each year. Most of the formaldehyde is used to make polymers. An aqueous solution of formaldehyde was used in the past to preserve biological specimens. Because it has been identified as a carcinogen, however, formaldehyde has been replaced by other preservatives.

The simplest ketone is propanone (CH_3COCH_3), also called acetone. Acetone is one of the top 50 industrial chemicals. About 1 billion kilograms of acetone are produced each year. Acetone is a common solvent, and is the primary component in fingernail polish remover. Although acetone has a polar region due to the carbonyl group, it also has a nonpolar nature due to the hydrocarbon portion of the molecule. The nonpolar region makes it possible for acetone to remove nail polish, which is insoluble in water. Acetone is a volatile liquid and its vapor is quite flammable.

Many aldehydes and ketones have appealing tastes and fragrant odors. As such, they are frequently used as flavorings in food and candy and as fragrances in inhalants and perfumes. The vanilla flavoring in the ice cream you read about at the beginning of the chapter and the cinnamon you might find in your hot chocolate are natural aldehydes.

26–2 Section Review

1. What are aldehydes and ketones?
2. Define the term carbonyl group and explain how you can differentiate between an aldehyde and a ketone by analyzing the carbonyl group in the structural formula.
3. What suffixes are used to identify aldehydes and ketones?
4. **Critical Thinking—Making inferences** Describe how an aldehyde might be synthesized from a primary alcohol and a ketone from a secondary alcohol.

CONSUMER TIP

The Good and the Bad

If you have ever felt your heart racing in response to a near accident, you have experienced one of the effects of a ketone called cortisone. Cortisone is produced by the adrenal glands and is released into the body in response to fear, excitement, or surprise. Because cortisone also acts to inhibit responses from the immune system, it is sometimes used to treat severe allergic reactions and diseases such as multiple sclerosis and rheumatoid arthritis. And you may be aware of the fact that cortisone is sometimes used to treat an inflamed shoulder or knee. Chemists have created several forms of cortisone and similar compounds.

Unfortunately, as with all drugs, cortisone has some serious side effects. Because it breaks down connective tissue, long-term use of cortisone can lead to osteoporosis. In the digestive system, cortisone can increase the production of stomach acids while decreasing the synthesis of the mucus that coats the stomach. The result may be a gastric ulcer. In addition, long-term use of cortisone might cause the body to stop producing it naturally.

Guide for Reading

- What are the characteristics of carboxylic acids and esters?
- How are carboxylic acids and esters named?

26–3 Carboxylic Acids and Esters

The next two classes of organic compounds have functional groups that include 2 oxygen atoms bonded to the same carbon atom. One of the oxygen atoms is connected by a single bond whereas the other oxygen atom is connected by a double bond. This structure is present in two important classes of compounds: carboxylic acid and esters. You will learn about both of these classes in this section.

Carboxylic Acids

Take a look at the carbon atom in the middle of the structural formula shown in Figure 26–9. This carbon atom is connected to a hydroxyl group with a single bond and to an oxygen atom with a double bond. Together, this structure of one carbon atom, two oxygen atoms, and one hydrogen atom is called a **carboxyl group,** and is abbreviated —COOH.

As you learned in Chapter 18, the hydrogen atom in a carboxyl group is an acidic hydrogen. For this reason, the hydrocarbon derivatives that contain a carboxyl group act as acids. They are called **carboxylic** (kahr-bahk-SIHL-ihk) **acids,** a name derived from their characteristic carboxyl group. **Carboxylic acids are identified by the presence of a carboxyl group.** The general formula for a carboxylic acid is R—COOH, which shows a carboxyl group attached to a hydrocarbon group. Carboxylic acids are also called organic acids.

In naming carboxylic acids, the suffix *-oic* and the word acid are added to the root name of the parent chain. Thus, a simple 6-carbon carboxylic acid is called hexanoic acid. In addition to

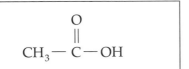

Figure 26–9 *This is a condensed structural formula for acetic acid, the principal ingredient in vinegar. As you learned in Unit 7, only one of the four hydrogen atoms in this molecule is an acidic hydrogen. Can you identify it?*

Figure 26–10 *If you have ever eaten any of the foods on this list, you have eaten a carboxylic acid. What is the functional group of a carboxylic acid?*

Selected Foods That Contain Carboxylic Acids

Food	Acid	Formula
vinegar	acetic	CH_3COOH
citrus fruits	citric	$HOC(CH_2COOH)_2COOH$
rhubarb	oxalic	$HOOCCOOH$
raspberries	benzoic	C_6H_5COOH
citrus fruits, tomatoes	ascorbic	$C_6H_8O_6$
tea	tannic	$C_{76}H_{52}O_{46}$
green apples	maleic	$HOOCCH = CHCOOH$

their IUPAC names, many carboxylic acids have common names based on their properties or the materials from which they have been extracted. The carboxylic acids with long hydrocarbon chains that were first extracted from animal fats are called fatty acids. The formula for a carboxylic acid shows —COOH at the end. Whenever you see this functional group, you should recognize the compound as a carboxylic acid.

The carboxyl end of a carboxylic acid is an electron-rich site because both of the oxygen atoms contain unshared electron pairs. This part of the molecule is very polar, making carboxylic acids far more soluble in water than their corresponding hydrocarbons. Also, because carboxylic acids have a polar —COOH group, they are capable of forming intermolecular hydrogen bonds. They are similar to the alcohols in that they have higher boiling points than hydrocarbons of comparable molecular mass.

The simplest carboxylic acid is formic acid (HCOOH), or methanoic acid. Formic acid was first extracted from ants. Its name, therefore, is derived from the Latin *formica*, meaning ant. If you have ever felt the sting of a bite from a red ant, you can blame formic acid for your discomfort. You have probably eaten another carboxylic acid—acetic acid (CH_3COOH), or ethanoic acid. Acetic acid was first isolated from vinegar, and its name is derived from the Latin *acetum*, meaning sour. Acetic acid gives vinegar its sour taste. Acetic acid is used for manufacturing other chemicals and for preparing foods such as pickles, mayonnaise, and salad dressing. Figure 26–10 lists several carboxylic acids found in foods.

Figure 26–11 *Milk collected from cows on a dairy farm is quickly processed while it is fresh. When milk sours, a carboxylic acid called lactic acid is formed.*

SAMPLE PROBLEM 5

Name the organic acid with the condensed structural formula $CH_3(CH_2)_2COOH$.

STRATEGY	SOLUTION
1. Analyze	You are given the condensed structural formula of a molecule with 4 carbon atoms and a carboxyl group, and are asked to name the molecule.
2. Plan	The root name of the molecule is based on the number of carbon atoms in the parent chain. Its suffix is based on the presence of the carboxyl group, which makes the compound a carboxylic acid.
3. Solve	Because the molecule has 4 carbon atoms in a straight chain with all single bonds, it has the root name *butan-*. Make sure that you recognize that there are 2 CH_2 groups. The suffix of a carboxylic acid is *-oic*. The name of the molecule is, therefore, butanoic acid.
4. Evaluate	Because of the carboxyl group, this compound is a carboxylic acid. This compound, also called butyric acid, gives rancid butter its pungent odor.

PRACTICE PROBLEMS

9. Name the carboxylic acid with the condensed structural formula $CH_3(CH_2)_4COOH$.   *(Answer: hexanoic acid)*

10. Write the condensed structural formula for ethanoic acid.   *(Answer: CH_3COOH)*

Esters

You now know that carboxylic acids are hydrocarbon derivatives that contain a carboxyl group. And a carboxyl group is a functional group that contains a carbonyl group and a hydroxyl group. If the hydrogen atom in the hydroxyl group is replaced by a hydrocarbon group, a different class of organic compounds known as **esters** is formed. **An ester is similar to a carboxylic acid, but has a hydrocarbon group in place of the hydrogen atom of the carboxyl group.** The general formula for an ester is R—COOR' because the carbonyl group is attached to an —OR' group.

$$R - \overset{\overset{\displaystyle O}{\displaystyle \|}}{C} - OR'$$

An ester can be formed from a reaction between a carboxylic acid and an alcohol. For this reason, esters are named for the alcohol and acid from which they are produced. The name of the alcohol is given first, with the suffix changed to -yl. Then the name of the acid is given, with the suffix changed to -oate. An ester made from ethanol and propanoic acid, for example, would be called ethyl propanoate.

You will also occasionally see the common name of an ester, which is found by writing the name of the alcohol from which it was derived and adding the suffix -ate to the stem of the carboxylic acid from which it was derived. Thus the common name for an ester formed from propyl alcohol and formic acid is propyl formate.

Esters are polar molecules, but they do not form hydrogen bonds with each other. Therefore, the boiling points of esters are lower than the boiling points of alcohols or acids with similar molar masses. Esters have distinctive odors that vary depending

Figure 26–12 *The synthesis of soap is one of the oldest known chemical reactions. The process, which is known as saponification, is a reaction in which a base is used to break the bond between the acid and the alcohol portions of an ester. Soap molecules contain a nonpolar hydrocarbon end and a highly polar carboxylate end.*

Figure 26–13 *The scent and flavor of an ester varies, depending upon the alcohol and carboxylic acid that joined to form it. Do you recognize some of these flavors from the ice cream parlor discussed at the beginning of the chapter?*

Selected Esters and Their Fragrances

Alcohol	Acid	Ester	Fragrance
ethanol	butanoic acid	ethyl butanoate	pineapple
pentanol	ethanoic acid	pentyl ethanoate	banana
octanol	ethanoic acid	octyl ethanoate	orange
methanol	salicylic acid	methyl salicylate	wintergreen
methanol	butanoic acid	methyl butanoate	apple

INTEGRATING
BIOLOGY

Which organic compounds are responsible for many of the artificial flavors and odors used in food products?

on the alcohol and acid used to synthesize the ester. The table in Figure 26–13 lists familiar odors and the esters that are responsible for them. Esters typically have fruity odors, creating the aroma of bananas and the fragrance of pineapples.

SAMPLE PROBLEM 6

What is the name of the ester derived from the reaction between methanol and butyric acid?

STRATEGY	SOLUTION
1. **Analyze**	You are given the name of the acid and the alcohol that combined to form an ester. You are asked to name the ester.
2. **Plan**	To determine the name of the ester, you must place the appropriate suffixes on the stems of the carboxylic acid and alcohol.
3. **Solve**	The stem of the alcohol is *meth-*, so it becomes methyl in the ester's name. The stem of the acid is *butan-*, so it becomes butanoate in the ester's name. The ester is, therefore, called methyl butanoate.
4. **Evaluate**	To name an ester, you must identify the acid and the alcohol that were used to synthesize the ester. The name of the ester should indicate those original substances, which it does.

PRACTICE PROBLEMS

11. Name the ester formed from acetic acid (CH_3COOH) and ethyl alcohol   *(Answer: ethyl ethanoate)*

12. Write a condensed structural formula for ethyl hexanoate.   *(Answer: $CH_3(CH_2)_4COOCH_2CH_3$)*

CONNECTION

Knockout

If you have ever been given a shot to dull the pain from a dental filling, stitches, or even surgery, you are probably thankful that anesthetics were developed. The term anesthesia is derived from the Greek word meaning "lack of feeling." All anesthetics work by blocking the pathway of pain signals to the brain.

Now imagine undergoing surgery without the aid of an anesthetic. You might find the idea utterly absurd, but less than 150 years ago anesthetics simply did not exist. Of course, people still required surgery, especially in times of war. However, surgery was performed without any anesthetic. Instead, strong people were employed to hold a patient down as the surgeon operated. Occasionally, ice was used to freeze the surgical area on the body and often surgeons resorted to forcing their patients to drink alcohol until they became unconscious.

An anesthetic was used for the first time on March 30, 1842 in Jefferson, Georgia when Dr. Crawford Long removed a tumor from the neck of a patient named James Venable. The anesthetic was ethoxyethane, or diethyl ether. Oddly enough, people at the time feared the new anesthetic almost as much as they feared pain. So even after its first use, wide use of anesthetics did not begin until 1846 when a doctor named William Morton publicly demonstrated the extraction of a tooth under the use of ether in Boston. Ether is an extremely safe anesthetic because a much smaller amount is needed to anesthetize than would be lethal. Also, it has little effect on blood pressure or respiration. However, it is highly flammable and posed a new threat in the operating room. For this reason it is rarely used today.

In the time since then, numerous other anesthetics have come in and out of common use. Novocain, which contains an amine, has been used for dental procedures. Chloroform, the halocarbon trichloromethane, has been used for general anesthesia, including as a relief for women during childbirth. And aspirin, an ester, is used to relieve minor pain. As some anesthetics are found to have negative side effects, they are replaced by more appropriate compounds. In the future, even better anesthetics may be developed. But for now, relax in knowing that if the need ever arises, safe anesthetics exist to ease your pain.

26–3 Section Review

1. What are the characteristics of carboxylic acids and esters?

2. What is a carboxyl group? What class of compound contains this group?

3. How are carboxylic acids and esters named?

4. **Theme Trace—Unity and Diversity** Compare and contrast carboxylic acids and esters. Take into account functional groups, names, polarity, and examples of each.

Guide for Reading

- What is the difference between an amine and an amide?
- How are amines and amides named?

26–4 Amines and Amides

You have seen several classes of organic compounds that are produced when oxygen or halogens combine with a hydrocarbon. Other classes of organic compounds include nitrogen in their functional groups. These classes are the **amines** and **amides.**

Amines

You know that an ammonia molecule is made up of 1 nitrogen atom and 3 hydrogen atoms. Sometimes, 1 of the hydrogen atoms is replaced by an alkyl group. The result is an alkyl group attached to 1 nitrogen atom that is also bonded to 2 hydrogen atoms ($-NH_2$). The $-NH_2$ group is known as an amino group. **An amine is an organic compound containing an amino group attached to a hydrocarbon chain.** The general formula for a simple amine is $R-NH_2$ where the amino group is the functional group.

More than 1 hydrogen atom in the ammonia group can be replaced. Like alcohols, amines can be distinguished as primary, secondary, or tertiary, depending on how many organic groups are attached to the nitrogen atom. A secondary amine has the general formula $R-NHR'$, and a tertiary amine has the general formula $R-NR'R''$.

Amines are named by adding the suffix *-amine* to the root name of the hydrocarbon. Thus $CH_3CH_2NH_2$ is ethanamine because the hydrocarbon is ethane. The common name for amines is given by naming the hydrocarbon chain as a branch chain before adding the suffix *-amine*. Ethanamine is more commonly known as ethylamine.

Figure 26–14 *Many suntan lotions contain PABA, which is an amine that prevents ultraviolet light from reaching the skin. What is an amine?*

SAMPLE PROBLEM 7

Name the compound $CH_3CH_2CH_2CH_2NH_2$.

STRATEGY	SOLUTION
1. Analyze	You are given the formula for a compound containing an amino group and are asked to name the compound.
2. Plan	You know that the compound is an amine because of the amino group. Its name is based on the name of the hydrocarbon portion. Determine this name and add the suffix *-amine*.
3. Solve	The molecule contains 4 carbon atoms in the parent chain, so its root name is butane. Because it contains an amino group, the final *-e* is replaced by *-amine*. The name is 1-butanamine.
4. Evaluate	The name indicates an amine of 4 carbon atoms. It is a primary amine because only 1 carbon atom is bonded to the amino group. Its common name is 1-butylamine.

PRACTICE PROBLEMS

13. Find the name of the following compound:
    $CH_3CH_2CH_2CH_2CH_2NH_2$.   *(Answer: pentanamine)*

14. Write the condensed structural formula for propanamine.   *(Answer: $CH_3CH_2CH_2NH_2$)*

The amino group is polar, but not as polar as the hydroxyl group of an alcohol. Therefore, the boiling points of amines are higher than the boiling point of their corresponding hydrocarbon, but lower than that of the corresponding alcohol. Amines are weak bases because the unshared electron pair on the nitrogen atom attracts hydrogen ions in solution.

There are many biologically important compounds that contain amino groups, including the amino acids that link together to form proteins in your body. Amino groups are found in DNA, in several important vitamins, and in the anesthetic drug, Novocain. They are the basis of many addictive compounds, such as nicotine, cocaine, and amphetamines. You will learn more about the role of amines in your body when you read Chapter 27. Other amines are responsible for some familiar, though often unpleasant, odors. The amine commonly known as cadaverine is produced by bacteria on decaying organisms. These amines, known as ptomaines, are also formed by bacteria on meat and fish and can cause food poisoning.

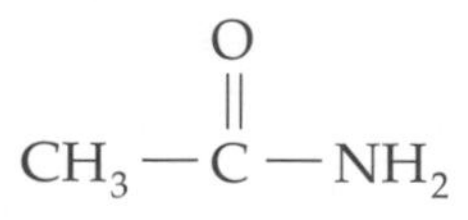

O
‖
$CH_3 — C — NH_2$

ethanamide

Figure 26–15 *In an amide, the carbon atom at the end of a hydrocarbon chain is attached to an oxygen atom by a double bond and to an amino group by a single bond.*

Amides

When amines react with carboxylic acids, a new class of organic compound, the amides, is formed. **An amide is an organic compound that contains an amino group attached to the carbon atom of a carbonyl group.** The general formula for an amide is $R—CONH_2$.

Amides are named by adding the suffix -*amide* to the root name of the hydrocarbon. The parent chain of the hydrocarbon depends upon the carboxylic acid from which the amide is derived. For example, the amide derived from ethanoic acid is CH_3CONH_2. It is called ethanamide and is shown in Figure 26–15. What is the name of $CH_3CH_2CH_2CONH_2$? The answer is butanamide.

Like amines, amides are important biological molecules. An amide bond, called a peptide bond, links amino acids together to form proteins. An amide functional group is also found in synthetic polyamide fibers such as nylon.

SAMPLE PROBLEM 8

Name the following amide: $CH_3CH_2CONH_2$.

STRATEGY	SOLUTION
1. Analyze	You are given the condensed structural formula for a compound and are asked to determine its name.
2. Plan	The compound contains 3 carbon atoms. One of the carbon atoms is part of a carbonyl group and has an amino group attached to it. The compound is, therefore, an amide. You can determine the name of the amide only after determining the name of the acid from which it is derived, or the parent chain.
3. Solve	Because the compound has 3 carbon atoms in its parent chain with all single bonds between carbon atoms, it is an amide of propane. The name of the compound is propanamide.
4. Evaluate	The name indicates an amide containing 3 carbon atoms as it should.

PRACTICE PROBLEMS

15. What is the name of CH_3CONH_2? *(Answer: ethanamide)*

16. Propose a condensed structural formula for pentanamide. *(Answer: $CH_3(CH_2)_3CONH_2$)*

Classes of Organic Compounds

Class of Compound	Functional Group	General Formula	Example
halocarbon	$-F, -Cl, -Br,$ $-I$	$R-X$	CH_3Cl chloromethane
alcohol	$-OH$	$R-OH$	$CH_3CH_2CH_2OH$ 1-propanol
ether	$-O-$	$R-O-R'$	$CH_3OCH_2CH_3$ methoxyethane
aldehyde	$\overset{\displaystyle O}{\overset{\|}{-C-}}$	$R-\overset{\displaystyle O}{\overset{\|}{C}}-H$	$CH_3CH_2\overset{\displaystyle O}{\overset{\|}{C}}H$ propanal
ketone	$\overset{\displaystyle O}{\overset{\|}{-C-}}$	$R-\overset{\displaystyle O}{\overset{\|}{C}}-R'$	$CH_3\overset{\displaystyle O}{\overset{\|}{C}}CH_3$ propanone
carboxylic acid	$\overset{\displaystyle O}{\overset{\|}{-C}}-OH$	$R-\overset{\displaystyle O}{\overset{\|}{C}}-OH$	$CH_3CH_2\overset{\displaystyle O}{\overset{\|}{C}}OH$ propanoic acid
ester	$\overset{\displaystyle O}{\overset{\|}{-C}}-O-$	$R-\overset{\displaystyle O}{\overset{\|}{C}}-OR'$	$CH_3\overset{\displaystyle O}{\overset{\|}{C}}OCH_3$ methylethanoate
amine	$-NH_2$	$R-NH_2$	$CH_3CH_2CH_2NH_2$ propanamine
amide	$\overset{\displaystyle O}{\overset{\|}{-C}}-NH_2$	$R-\overset{\displaystyle O}{\overset{\|}{C}}-NH_2$	$CH_3CH_2\overset{\displaystyle O}{\overset{\|}{C}}NH_2$ propanamide

Figure 26–16 *The nine classes of organic compounds you have read about are summarized in this table. Notice how the functional group and general formula for each class is different.*

26–4 Section Review

1. What is an amine? An amide?
2. What is an amino group?
3. How are amines and amides named?
4. **Connection—Biology** In an amino acid, a central carbon atom is bonded to an amino group, a carboxyl group, a hydrogen atom, and one other functional group that differs among the amino acids and is responsible for their different properties. What is the general formula for an amino acid? Do amino acids have the properties of an acid? Of a base? Explain.

Laboratory Investigation

Ester Synthesis

Problem

What fragrances are produced when esters are formed from combinations of different alcohols with different carboxylic acids?

Materials (*per group*)

test tube
600-mL beaker
hot plate
graduated cylinder
stirring rod
test-tube tongs
5.0 mL of one of the following alcohols:
   methanol, ethanol, amyl alcohol, octanol
5.0 mL of one of the following carboxylic
   acids: ethanoic, salicylic, butyric
(Caution: Butyric acid has an unpleasant
   odor; use under the fume hood.)
1.0 mL of 6.0 M H_2SO_4

Procedure

1. Fill the beaker half full with water, then heat on the hot plate.
2. Pour 5.0 mL of one of the carboxylic acids into the test tube.
3. Add 5.0 mL of one of the alcohols to the test tube.
4. Add 1.0 mL of 6.0 M H_2SO_4 to the test tube and stir with a stirring rod. CAUTION: H_2SO_4 is corrosive.
5. Heat the test tube in the hot-water bath until the mixture is hot, but not boiling.
6. Remove the test tube from the hot-water bath using test-tube tongs. Carefully waft the fumes from the test tube to detect the odor of the ester you produced.

Observations

Record the identity of the alcohol and acid you used and the fragrance of the ester produced in a data table similar to the one shown.

Alcohol	Carboxylic Acid	Fragrance

Analysis and Conclusions

1. Using structural formulas, write a balanced equation for the reaction that produced an ester. Name the ester produced.
2. Describe how the reaction between a carboxylic acid and an alcohol accounts for the general formula of an ester.
3. What are some uses for synthetically produced esters?
4. **On Your Own** With your teacher's permission, repeat the investigation using other combinations of acids and alcohols.

STUDY GUIDE

Summarizing Key Concepts

26–1 Halocarbons, Alcohols, and Ethers

- Organic compounds containing elements in addition to carbon and hydrogen are called hydrocarbon derivatives.
- The huge number of hydrocarbon derivatives is broken down into classes, 9 of which are halocarbons, alcohols, ethers, aldehydes, ketones, carboxylic acids, esters, amines, and amides.
- Each class of organic compounds is differentiated by its functional group. A general formula is used to describe the compounds in each class.
- In a halocarbon, one or more of the hydrogen atoms of a hydrocarbon is replaced by a halogen atom.
- In an alcohol, one or more of the hydrogen atoms of a hydrocarbon is replaced by a hydroxyl group.
- A compound consisting of two hydrocarbon chains attached to the same oxygen atom is called an ether.

26–2 Aldehydes and Ketones

- A carbon atom attached to an oxygen atom by a double bond is called a carbonyl group.

- An aldehyde contains a carbonyl group located at the end of a carbon chain.
- A ketone contains a carbonyl group located within the interior of a carbon chain.

26–3 Carboxylic Acids and Esters

- When a carbonyl group and a hydroxyl group combine, the result is a carboxyl group. In a carboxyl group, a carbon atom is attached to an oxygen atom by a double bond and to a hydroxyl group by a single bond.
- A carboxylic acid, or organic acid, contains a carboxyl group.
- When the hydrogen atom in the carboxyl group of an organic acid is replaced by a hydrocarbon chain, the compound is known as an ester.

26–4 Amines and Amides

- A hydrocarbon chain attached to an amino group is called an amine.
- When an amino group is attached to the carbon atom of a carbonyl group, the compound is called an amide.

Reviewing Key Terms

Define each term in a complete sentence.

26–1 Halocarbons, Alcohols, and Ethers

hydrocarbon derivative
functional group
halocarbon
hydroxyl group
alcohol
ether

26–2 Aldehydes and Ketones

carbonyl group
aldehyde
ketone

26–3 Carboxylic Acids and Esters

carboxyl group
carboxylic acid
ester

26–4 Amines and Amides

amine
amide

CHAPTER REVIEW

Content Review

Multiple Choice
Choose the letter of the answer that best completes each statement.

1. Halocarbons are organic compounds that include atoms from Group
   (a) 3A. (b) 2A. (c) 6A. (d) 7A.

2. The general formula for an alcohol is
   (a) RX. (b) ROR'. (c) RCOOH. (d) ROH.

3. Two classes of organic compound that contain nitrogen are
   (a) alcohols and ethers.
   (b) esters and carboxylic acids.
   (c) amines and amides.
   (d) aldehydes and ketones.

4. Esters are synthesized by combining an
   (a) alcohol and an ether.
   (b) amine and a carboxylic acid.
   (c) alcohol and a carboxylic acid.
   (d) aldehyde and an ether.

5. All of the following include a carbonyl group except
   (a) ethers.   (c) esters.
   (b) aldehydes.   (d) ketones.

6. The most polar organic molecules are
   (a) amines.   (c) carboxylic acids.
   (b) alcohols.   (d) ethers.

7. The IUPAC name for ethyl butyl ether is
   (a) ethoxybutane.   (c) butylethoxate.
   (b) ethylbutyrate. (d) butyric ethoxide.

8. The difference between the structures of aldehydes and ketones is the
   (a) type of functional group.
   (b) kind of atoms in the molecules.
   (c) placement of the functional group in the molecule.
   (d) ability to form hydrogen bonds.

9. Which does not contain oxygen?
   (a) halocarbons   (c) esters
   (b) ethers   (d) ketones

10. The condensed structural formula CH_3CH_2COH signifies a(an)
    (a) alcohol.   (c) ketone.
    (b) aldehyde.   (d) carboxylic acid.

True or False
If the statement is true, write "true." If it is false, change the underlined word or words to make the statement true.

11. The names of organic compounds are based on the name of the corresponding <u>hydrocarbons</u>.

12. Chlorofluorocarbons are classified as <u>alcohols</u>.

13. The process used to make soap is called <u>saponification</u>.

14. An alcohol contains a <u>hydroxyl</u> group.

15. The functional group of an aldehyde is a <u>carboxyl</u> group.

16. The compound with the formula $CH_3(CH_2)_2COH$ is named <u>butanone</u>.

17. The general formula for an <u>amide</u> is RNH_2.

18. The main ingredient in natural gas is <u>aldehyde</u>.

19. The synthesis of an ester results from the reaction between an alcohol and <u>an ether</u>.

Concept Mapping
Complete the following concept map for Section 26–1. Refer to pages xviii–xix to construct a concept map for the entire chapter.

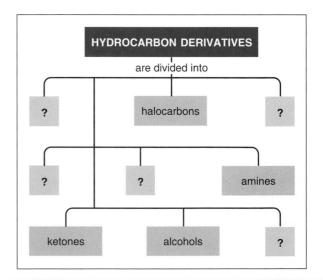

Concept Mastery

Discuss each of the following in a brief paragraph.

20. Explain what a halocarbon is. Discuss some of the uses and problems associated with halocarbons.

21. Structural isomers of the formula $C_nH_{2n+2}O$ can be either alcohols or ethers. Explain why the formulas for these two classes of compounds can be the same while their properties are different.

22. Why do alcohols have a higher boiling point than ethers with the same number of carbon atoms?

23. Carboxylic acids and alcohols are the most water-soluble organic compounds. Explain how the structures of these two classes of compounds give them increased solubility in water.

24. A carboxyl group is found on organic acids and an amino group is found on organic bases. Describe the reaction you would expect between an organic acid and an organic base.

25. Discuss the similarities and differences between aldehydes and ketones.

26. Based on the types of bonds in carboxylic acids, explain why they are acids.

27. When discussing the classes of organic compounds, amines can be grouped with amides as they are in this chapter. Sometimes, however, amines are grouped with ethers and aldehydes. Give a rationale for this alternative grouping.

28. Use Figure 26–16 to divide the classes of organic compounds into two major groups. Draw a concept map to show the arrangement and explain your reasoning.

29. Tying it Together Consider the *unity and diversity* of organic compounds. The nine classes of organic compounds are all similar because they are hydrocarbon derivatives, yet they differ according to their functional groups. Discuss these similarities and differences.

Critical Thinking and Problem Solving

Use the skills you have developed in this chapter to answer each of the following.

30. Making comparisons Why are alcohols with 1 to 4 carbon atoms soluble in water while ethers with the same molecular formula are not?

31. Drawing conclusions Sam's pen leaked on his favorite shirt. His sister Harriet told him that soaking the stain in hair spray would remove it, but they had no hair spray. They did have some fingernail polish remover containing acetone and they had some soda water. Which would better remove the stain? Explain.

32. Making comparisons Compounds that contain a metal and an –OH group are bases, but organic acids also contain an –OH group. Why do bases release an OH^- ion in solution, but a carboxylic acid retains the oxygen atom, giving up an H^+ ion in solution?

33. Making predictions Arrange the following compounds from lowest to highest boiling points: (a) 1-pentanol (b) pentanoic acid (c) methylbutyl ether (d) 2-pentanone (e) pentanal.

34. Applying concepts Write structural formulas for the following: (a) 3-bromohexane (b) 3-methyl-3-hexanol (c) methoxypentane (d) 2-methylpropanal.

35. Using the writing process Ethanol is the alcohol in alcoholic beverages. Ethanol is toxic, and consuming it in excess causes depression and confusion, and can lead to death. Should consumers be warned about the toxic effects of ethanol? What are some current measures to encourage consumers to limit alcohol consumption?

Chapter 27

The Chemistry of Life

How often do you take time to marvel at the wonders of the living world? Looking out over the plains of Africa, you can see that there is an amazing variety of plants and animals on planet Earth.

Most forms of life on our planet owe their existence to the energy that radiates from the sun and to the chemical processes that convert that energy into living matter.

As you have read each chapter in this textbook, you have learned how important chemistry is in your daily life. In fact, your life would not be possible without chemistry. In this chapter you will examine the chemical compounds and reactions that are the basis of all life.

A watering hole on the African plains attracts a variety of wildlife. All animals ultimately rely on plants, such as these sunflowers, as a source of energy.

Chem Journal

YOU AND YOUR WORLD

Green plants are capable of producing their own food through the process of photosynthesis. Have you ever wondered how your life might be different if you were able to carry out photosynthesis? In your journal, describe a typical day in your life if everything else remained the same but you were capable of photosynthesis.

27–1 Chemistry and Living Things

Guide for Reading
- What is photosynthesis?
- What is biochemistry?
- Why is the sun the ultimate energy source for life?

The sun has long been a source of awe and wonder to humans. Ancient civilizations worshiped the sun because it provided warmth and light. The ancient Egyptians honored the sun god Ra in their pyramids, the sloping sides of which represented the sun's rays shining through a break in the clouds.

As a trip to the beach will prove, many people still "worship" the sun, despite the potentially harmful effects of the sun's ultraviolet radiation. The sun is also a powerful source of energy that we can tap into through the use of solar collectors and photovoltaic cells. There is no doubt that humans appreciate the sun and would like to harness its energy. However, our attempts to utilize the energy of the sun have not approached the efficiency of plants in that endeavor.

Figure 27–1   The sun is the primary source of energy for most kinds of living things on Earth. Unlike plants, humans cannot use solar energy directly. Instead, humans build huge solar energy facilities like the one in the photograph to obtain energy from the sun.

The Sun: The Ultimate Source of Energy

Life exists on Earth largely because of the ability of plants to capture and use radiant energy from the sun to synthesize glucose from carbon dioxide and water. **The process by which light energy is used to synthesize organic products from inorganic reactants is called photosynthesis.** Humans, like other animals, are not capable of **photosynthesis** and must obtain energy by breaking down the chemicals stored in plants and other animals. In other words, the energy required by our cells comes from the potential energy stored in the chemical bonds of plant and animal tissue. That stored energy is the result of the ability of photosynthetic plants to convert radiant energy into chemical energy.

The product of photosynthesis is the simple sugar glucose, which can be decomposed by plant and animal metabolism. (Metabolism refers to all the chemical reactions that take place in the body.) Energy is released when the chemical bonds in glucose are broken. This energy can then be used to fuel other reactions, such as tissue repair, muscle contractions, and transmission of messages along the nerves.

Biologically Important Compounds

The study of the chemistry that occurs in living organisms is called biochemistry. Most of the compounds formed and used by living organisms can be classified into four categories: carbohydrates, lipids, proteins, and nucleic acids. All of these important compounds, or biomolecules, are organic molecules containing carbon, hydrogen, and oxygen. Many biomolecules also contain other elements, such as nitrogen, phosphorus, and sulfur. In this chapter, we will discuss the characteristics of the four major classes of biomolecules and also look briefly at the chemistry of vitamins. But first let's examine how energy is transferred in biochemical reactions.

Figure 27–2 All animals are parts of complex food chains. Some rely on plants for their food whereas others rely on animals that may, in turn, have eaten plants.

Energy Changes in Biochemical Reactions

You have just read about the role of glucose in storing energy that is released when cells need it. How is the energy from glucose converted into a form that can be used by the cells?

If you burned a mole of glucose in the laboratory, the reaction would produce light and a significant amount of heat. In fact, 1 mole of glucose releases 161 kilojoules of heat when it is burned. If you burned glucose in your body in a single step, it would be difficult to capture the energy from its chemical bonds for useful work, not to mention what would happen to your body temperature! To use the chemical energy stored in glucose, you must be able to break those bonds in a more controlled manner. You must also have a way to capture the chemical energy of glucose in a form that can be used by your cells.

The controlled burning, or combustion, of glucose that occurs in your body is called **cellular respiration.** The process of cellular respiration consists of a series of reactions that rearrange atoms and break bonds so that the potential energy stored in these bonds can be captured. A small amount of the chemical energy is released as heat, which helps you to maintain a stable body temperature. Most of the energy from glucose, however, is captured in other chemical bonds and can be used by cells in biochemical reactions. You will learn how this energy is transferred between compounds later in this section.

Photosynthesis and Cellular Respiration

As you learned earlier, only plants are capable of synthesizing glucose through photosynthesis. The balanced equation for photosynthesis is

$$6\ CO_2\ +\ 6\ H_2O \rightarrow C_6H_{12}O_6\ +\ 6\ O_2 \qquad \textbf{(Eq. 1)}$$

When plants and animals need the energy stored in glucose, cellular respiration releases that energy. The net reaction for cellular respiration is

$$C_6H_{12}O_6\ +\ 6\ O_2 \rightarrow 6\ CO_2\ +\ 6\ H_2O \qquad \textbf{(Eq. 2)}$$

Notice that photosynthesis and respiration are reverse reactions. The oxygen you inhale is a product of photosynthesis and a necessary reactant for cellular respiration. Likewise, the carbon dioxide and water vapor you exhale as the waste products of cellular respiration are reactants in photosynthesis.

Energy Transfer Molecules

Some biochemical reactions release energy while other reactions require energy. There must, therefore, be a mechanism for transferring the energy from one type of reaction to the other. The molecule that performs this function is adenosine triphosphate (ATP).

Figure 27–3 *Like all green plants, apple trees make their own food through the process of photosynthesis. A gymnast obtains the energy he needs by "burning" food in his body cells. What is this process called?*

ATP stores chemical energy in its phosphate bonds. The energy released by biochemical reactions is used directly to add an extra phosphate group to adenosine diphosphate (ADP). ADP plus phosphate becomes ATP. The high-energy ATP molecule is available for use in reactions that require energy. The phosphate bond is broken, releasing the energy needed for the reaction. In the process, ATP is converted back into ADP and phosphate. ADP and ATP molecules are recycled thousands of times to capture and release the energy needed for metabolism.

27–1 Section Review

1. How is the sun's radiant energy converted into chemical energy? What is this process called?

2. What is biochemistry?

3. List the four major classes of biomolecules.

4. In the process of cellular respiration, the combustion of glucose occurs in a number of controlled steps. Predict the consequences to organisms if the combustion of glucose occurred in a single step within the cells of the organism.

5. **Connection—Biology** A food chain traces the path of energy transfer from one organism to another. Describe a food chain that shows how the energy derived by a bear eating a salmon originally came from the sun.

870

27–2 Carbohydrates

Guide for Reading
- What are carbohydrates?
- What is the general formula for a carbohydrate?

One of the most important functions of biomolecules is to store energy that can be released when it is needed by the cells. Glucose and other molecules that serve this function belong to a class of compounds called **carbohydrates.** Carbohydrates are the most abundant class of biomolecules. **Carbohydrates are formed from aldehydes or ketones that contain numerous hydroxyl groups.** Most carbohydrates in plants are support tissue called cellulose or energy-storing molecules called starches.

The name carbohydrate, which indicates that the compound contains hydrated carbon atoms, comes from the general formula for this class of compounds. Although the number of carbon atoms can vary, the ratio of carbon to hydrogen to oxygen atoms in a simple carbohydrate is 1:2:1. **The general formula for a simple carbohydrate is $C_nH_{2n}O_n$.** Notice that for every carbon atom in the formula there are 2 hydrogen atoms and 1 oxygen atom.

Structure of Glucose

Glucose can have a straight-chain or a ring structure. The straight-chain form, however, makes up only 0.02 percent of all glucose molecules. Glucose molecules form a ring when an oxygen atom on carbon 1 bonds to the carbon 5 atom near the opposite end of the molecule, as shown in Figure 27–4.

Glucose actually has two possible ring structures, which differ only at carbon 1. The two forms are called the alpha and beta forms of glucose. The glucose molecule can convert between

Figure 27–4 *The diagram shows the structural formulas for the sugars glucose, galactose, and fructose.*

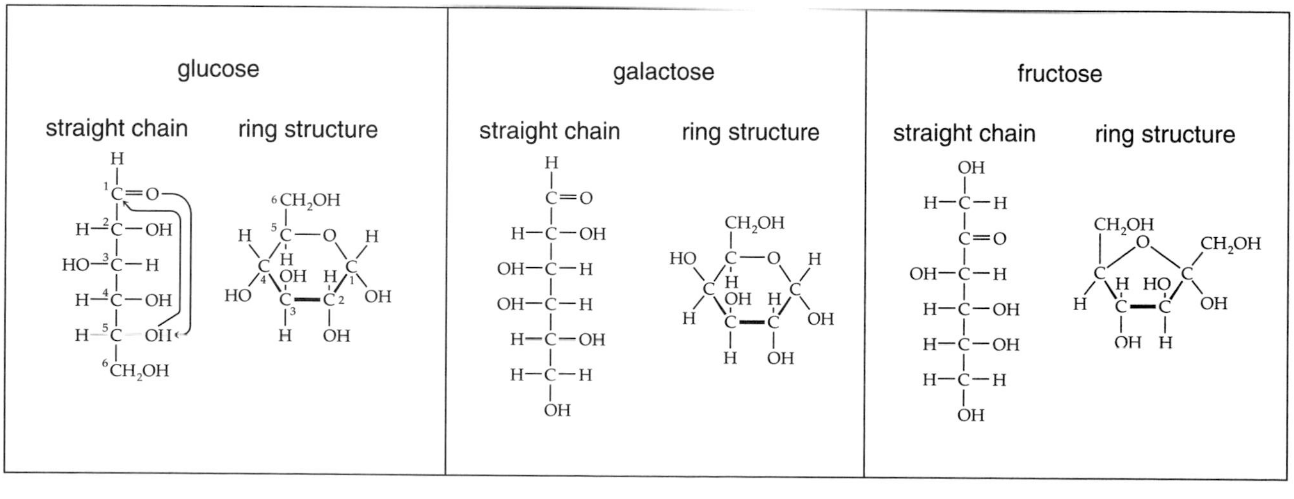

glucose	galactose	fructose
straight chain ring structure	straight chain ring structure	straight chain ring structure

Figure 27–5

α-glucose   β-glucose

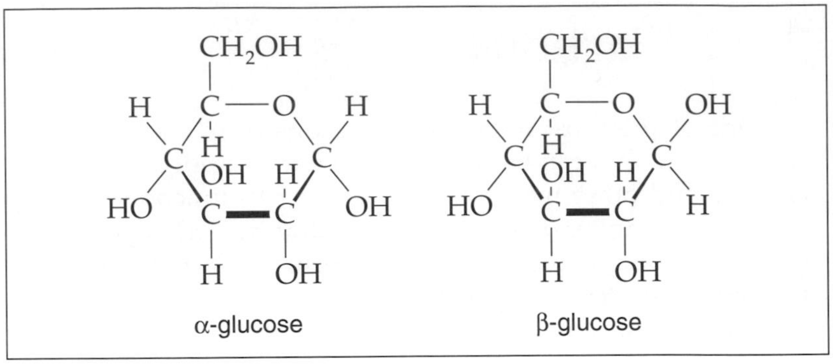

these two forms by opening and reclosing the ring structure. If the hydroxyl (—OH) group on carbon 1 is below the plane of the ring, the molecule is α-glucose. If it is above the plane of the ring, the molecule is β-glucose. Figure 27–5 illustrates the alpha and beta forms of glucose. Although the structures are often shown as planar molecules, recall from Chapter 25 that glucose is most stable in the three-dimensional chair conformation.

Glucose has the formula $C_6H_{12}O_6$, as do all of its isomers, the most common of which are galactose and fructose. The three isomers differ from one another in how the hydroxyl groups are arranged in the ring. Glucose and galactose have rings containing 6 atoms, whereas fructose has only 5 atoms in the ring. Figure 27–4 illustrates the straight-chain and ring structures of glucose, fructose, and galactose. Your body is able to distinguish the slight differences among these molecules. Even though these molecules have similar structures, your body uses them in very different ways.

Monosaccharides

Carbohydrates are classified according to the size of the molecule. Simple carbohydrates that cannot be broken down into

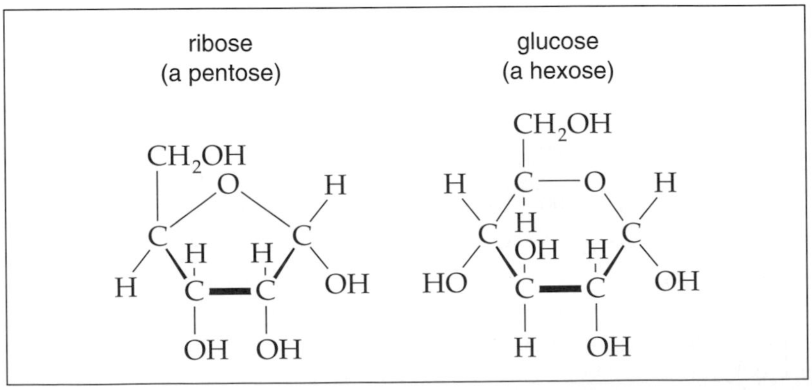

Figure 27–6 *Ribose (a pentose) is a 5-carbon sugar. Glucose (a hexose) is a 6-carbon sugar.*

ribose
(a pentose)

glucose
(a hexose)

Figure 27–7 *Although the fruits in this market in Cameroon, Africa, may be unfamiliar to you, they all contain fructose—just as apples, pears, and other more common fruits do. What is another name for fructose?*

smaller units are called **monosaccharides.** (The prefix *mono-* means one.) A monosaccharide with 5 carbon atoms is called a **pentose.** The most important pentose is deoxyribose, which is part of the structure of the nucleic acid DNA. We will discuss nucleic acids later in this chapter.

A monosaccharide with 6 carbon atoms is called a **hexose.** The most important hexose is glucose, which is the starting material for cellular respiration and the primary energy source for cellular metabolism. Fructose is another important hexose that is found in fresh fruits and is often called fruit sugar.

After you eat, all carbohydrates are converted into monosaccharides by your digestive system. These monosaccharides are then absorbed by the circulatory system and carried to your body cells.

Disaccharides

Glucose is an essential nutrient, but you generally do not eat pure glucose. Instead, you consume glucose in more complex forms. When two monosaccharides combine chemically, the product is a **disaccharide.** (The prefix *di-* means two.) The synthesis of a disaccharide involves the removal of the hydroxyl group from one monosaccharide and a hydrogen atom from another monosaccharide to form a molecule of water. A new bond forms between the two monosaccharide rings, producing a disaccharide. The process by which two smaller molecules join to form a larger molecule, producing water as a byproduct, is known as **dehydration synthesis.**

Several disaccharides are common in your diet. Sucrose is the chemical name for table sugar. It is the disaccharide formed by combining 1 glucose molecule with 1 fructose molecule. Figure 27–8 on the following page illustrates how sucrose is formed by dehydration synthesis. Sucrose is also called cane sugar or beet sugar because it is prepared commercially from sugar cane or sugar beets.

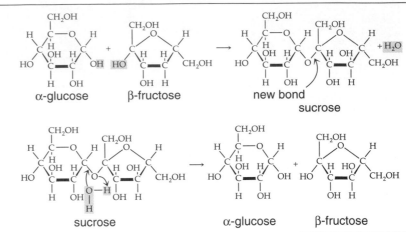

Figure 27–8 *Sucrose is also called cane sugar because it is obtained from sugar cane. Two molecules of glucose combine to form one molecule of sucrose through dehydration synthesis. What is the other product formed as a result of this reaction?*

INTEGRATING

BIOLOGY

Do you know why you often feel thirsty after you eat chocolate or other sweets?

When you digest sucrose, the bond between the two monosaccharides is broken and fructose is rearranged to form another glucose molecule. Both glucose molecules are used by your cells to provide energy for metabolic reactions. The decomposition of sucrose into glucose and fructose requires the addition of a water molecule and is, therefore, called a **hydrolysis** reaction. Figure 27–8 shows how a water molecule is introduced to break the bond between glucose and fructose.

Notice that the hydrolysis of a disaccharide is the reverse of the dehydration synthesis by which a disaccharide molecule is formed. This may help explain why you feel thirsty when you eat sweets: Your body craves the water necessary to break down the sucrose.

Lactose, another disaccharide, is present in milk and is sometimes called milk sugar. Lactose is made when a bond forms between 1 glucose molecule and 1 galactose molecule. A specific enzyme is necessary to help break the bond between the two monosaccharides when lactose is digested.

People who cannot digest milk products are called "lactose intolerant" because they do not produce the enzyme necessary to break the bond between glucose and galactose. As disaccharides, lactose molecules are too large to be absorbed into the circulatory system. Instead, they continue through the digestive system, where they are eventually broken down by bacteria in the large intestine. These bacteria digest the monosaccharides, producing carbon dioxide gas in the process. As a result, a common symptom of lactose intolerance is a buildup of intestinal gas along with a bloated feeling.

Figure 27–9 *Here you see one stage in the production of cheese. What is the name of the disaccharide found in cheese and other milk products?*

Polysaccharides

When many monosaccharides are joined together by dehydration synthesis, the polymer that is formed is referred to as a **polysaccharide.** (The prefix *poly-* means many.) Polysaccharides are also called complex carbohydrates. Common polysaccharides are starch, glycogen, and cellulose. All three of these polysaccharides are produced by joining glucose monomers. However, there are some dramatic differences in the chemistry of these three common polysaccharides.

Figure 27–10 *The diagram shows the structure of two carbohydrates: starch and cellulose. Perhaps this exhausted runner should have eaten more carbohydrates before running the New York City Marathon! Why are complex carbohydrates good sources of stored energy?*

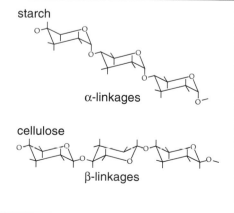

starch

α-linkages

cellulose

β-linkages

Like other polysaccharides, starch is a complex carbohydrate. The glucose units in starch are all alpha isomers that are joined to form a straight-chain polymer. The decomposition of starch is a hydrolysis reaction, which requires a water molecule to provide a hydrogen atom and a hydroxyl group to the site where the bond is broken. The glucose units can be separated from one another with the help of enzymes in your digestive system.

Once a glucose molecule is separated from the rest of the starch polymer, it can be absorbed and used as fuel by your cells. Because it takes time for glucose to be separated from the polysaccharide, glucose is released to the cells gradually. As a result the glucose from starch reaches muscle cells over a period of time, providing energy as it is needed. For this reason, athletes often eat meals rich in complex carbohydrates before an athletic event.

If your body absorbs more glucose than it needs at one time, the excess glucose is stored until it is needed. Some of the glucose is converted to fat for long-term storage, and some is converted to another polysaccharide, glycogen, in your liver and muscle tissue. Glycogen is a polysaccharide that is similar to starch because it also is composed of α-glucose units. It differs from starch in that glycogen is a branched polysaccharide that is made by animals, whereas starch is a straight-chain polysaccharide made only by plants.

Cellulose is another polysaccharide made by plants. In fact, cellulose accounts for more than 50 percent of the organic material on Earth! The structure of cellulose is similar to starch in that it is made up only of glucose units. The glucose units in cellulose, however, are isomers of the glucose molecules found in starch, and are joined in a slightly different pattern—β-glucose units. This small difference in bonding makes a tremendous difference in the properties of cellulose.

Animals have the necessary enzyme to break the bonds between glucose units in starch, but they do not have an enzyme to break the bonds in cellulose. As a result, animals can digest starch and use the energy of its chemical bonds, but they cannot digest cellulose. This is why you eat a sandwich made with two slices of bread rather than two sheets of paper! Some animals, such as cows, have bacteria in their digestive system that can supply the missing enzyme. These bacteria break the bonds between glucose units in cellulose, allowing the cows to digest the cellulose.

27–2 Section Review

1. What is a carbohydrate? What is the general formula for a simple carbohydrate?

2. Explain the differences in the structures of monosaccharides, disaccharides, and polysaccharides.

3. What kind of reaction is used to make a polysaccharide from monosaccharides? To break down a polysaccharide into monosaccharides?

4. **Connection—You and Your World** Potato chips and celery are both made up of molecules that are polysaccharides, or polymers of glucose. Which would be a better snack for a person on a diet? Explain.

INTEGRATING
BIOLOGY

Why do you think marathon runners eat a meal rich in carbohydrates the day before a race?

CHEM
Exploration

Iodine Test for Starch

Simple chemical tests can identify the types of molecules in foods. Starch can be identified by its reaction with an iodine solution. Iodine solution has a reddish-brown color. A positive test for starch will change the color to blue-black.

1. Place small samples of the foods to be tested in the well of a spot plate.

2. Add one drop of iodine solution to each food to be tested.

3. Record the observed color of the iodine on the foods you tested.

• Which foods contain starch? Which do not?

Guide for Reading
- What are lipids?
- How are fats, oils, and waxes different?

27–3 Lipids

Carbohydrates are important in providing "instant" energy for cells, but members of another class of molecules called **lipids** have the job of storing energy for later use. **Lipids are molecules composed of carbon, oxygen, and hydrogen that are insoluble in water.** Fats, oils, and waxes are the three major types of lipids.

Chemical Composition of Lipids

The glucose in your blood will supply your energy needs for only 15 minutes, so your body must constantly replenish the supply of glucose in the blood. This is where lipids come in. Lipids serve as energy reserves by storing more potential energy in their chemical bonds. Lipid molecules contain carbon, hydrogen, and oxygen, but have a much smaller percentage of oxygen than is found in carbohydrates. Because lipid molecules are composed primarily of long hydrocarbon chains, lipids are highly insoluble in water. Lipids are formed in an esterification reaction between an alcohol and one or more long-chain carboxylic acids. Recall from Chapter 26 that in an esterification reaction an organic acid combines with an alcohol to form an ester. When glycerol is the alcohol, the resulting lipid is called a **triglyceride.**

Triglycerides

Triglycerides are formed in a dehydration reaction in which the hydroxyl groups of three long-chain carboxylic acids—also called fatty acids—combine with the hydroxyl hydrogens from glycerol, producing 3 molecules of water. The remaining molecules are joined in three ester linkages to form a triglyceride. Figure 27–12 shows the structure of a triglyceride.

Figure 27–12 *Triglycerides are formed from glycerol and fatty acids. What is a triglyceride?*

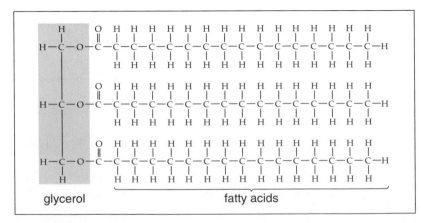

glycerol   fatty acids

The two types of triglycerides are fats and oils. The difference between fats and oils is based on the presence of saturated or unsaturated fatty acids. In general, **fats** are triglycerides that are solid at room temperature and contain saturated fatty acids. Recall from Chapter 25 that saturated hydrocarbons contain all single bonds. Fats are produced only by animals. Animal fats include lard and butter. Triglycerides that are liquid at room temperature and contain unsaturated fatty acids are called **oils.** Unsaturated fatty acids contain one or more double bonds. Most oils—for example, vegetable oils such as corn oil and olive oil—are produced by plants.

Sometimes a product is more desirable as a solid than as a liquid. For example, would you rather spread margarine on a piece of toast or pour oil on it? Margarine is more acceptable to consumers when it is a solid because it looks more like butter. Although margarine is made from vegetable oils that are liquid at room temperature, the oils can be processed to form solid margarine. How is this done?

Manufacturers use a process called **hydrogenation** to add hydrogen atoms to unsaturated lipid molecules at the sites of the double bonds. When hydrogen atoms are added to double bonds, new bonds are formed and the molecules become saturated. After the vegetable oil has been hydrogenated, it has the chemical structure of a fat and is solid at room temperature.

Other Lipids

Lipids that include an alcohol other than glycerol are called **waxes.** Both the alcohol and the acid that make up the wax molecule have long hydrocarbon chains. Waxes are produced by both plants and animals and have similar functions in both types of organisms. Waxes serve as a waterproofing material and as a protective coating on skin, hair, and leaves.

Figure 27–13 *Most oils, such as olive oil, are obtained from plants. What are the differences between fats and oils?*

YOU AND YOUR WORLD

Controlling Cholesterol

Cholesterol has been proven to cause heart problems for many people. You probably know that you should avoid eating foods that contain too much cholesterol. But did you know that your body manufactures it own cholesterol, and that even young people with healthy eating habits may have high cholesterol levels? Having your cholesterol level checked is a good idea, particularly if you have a family history that includes circulatory or cholesterol problems.

Figure 27–14 *What do these ducks and this plant have in common? Both rely on a waxy coating as a form of waterproofing for their feathers and leaves, respectively.*

Figure 27–15 *The diagram on the top shows phospholipids as part of the double layer that forms the cell membrane. The structural diagram represents cholesterol, a member of the important class of lipids called steroids.*

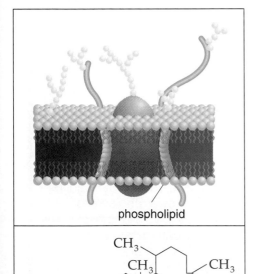

More complex lipids include important molecules such as phospholipids and steroids. **Phospholipids** are the major structural components of cell membranes, forming a double layer that protects the cell's contents from its environment.

Steroids are a class of lipids whose molecules are composed of several fused rings of atoms. Steroids are not derived from fatty acids. Cholesterol, the most important steroid in animals, is synthesized by animals, but not by plants. Animals are able to use cholesterol to synthesize other steroids, such as cortisone, testosterone, and estrogen. Cortisone, a hormone produced by the adrenal glands, controls carbohydrate metabolism. Testosterone is a male sex hormone and estrogen is a female sex hormone. Although cholesterol is an essential lipid for humans, excessive levels of cholesterol in the blood can lead to deposits in the arteries of the heart. These arterial deposits are a leading cause of heart disease.

27–3 Section Review

1. What is a lipid?
2. Describe the differences among fats, oils, and waxes.
3. Explain how waxes, phospholipids, and steroids are different from triglycerides.
4. **Critical Thinking—Making predictions** Carbohydrates and lipids are composed of the same chemical elements, but in different proportions. Both are used as energy sources for cell metabolism. Based on their functions, predict which type of molecule has the higher calorie content per gram. Explain the reasons for your answer.

27–4 Proteins

You have a greater assortment of **proteins** in your body than any other type of compound. Proteins serve a variety of functions, both in the structure and the metabolism of your body. Structural proteins include those found in hair, muscle, and connective tissue. The enzymes that catalyze metabolic reactions and molecules such as hemoglobin that transport vital nutrients are also proteins. In this section, you will examine the structure of proteins and learn how the structure of a particular protein determines its function. Let's begin by examining the molecules that comprise proteins: amino acids.

Amino Acids

Proteins are polymers that are made up of hundreds of amino acid monomers. Proteins are made from 20 different amino acids that can be joined in any sequence. These amino acids all have the same basic structure, but vary in one side chain. Figure 27–17 on the following page shows the structures of selected amino acids. The central carbon atom of each amino acid is bonded to both an amino group (—NH$_2$) and a carboxyl group (—COOH). The central carbon is also bonded to an R group that is different in each of the 20 natural amino acids.

Amino acids are amphoteric molecules. Recall from Chapter 18 that amphoteric compounds can act as either an acid or a base. An amino acid acts as a base at the amino end of the molecule and as an acid at the carboxyl end. Within every protein

Guide for Reading
- What are proteins?
- How are models used to explain enzyme function?

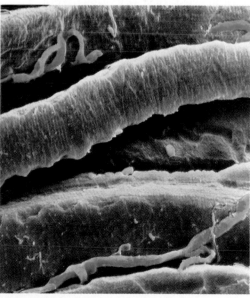

Figure 27–16 Human hair (left) and muscle fiber (right) are both composed of structural proteins. How are proteins formed?

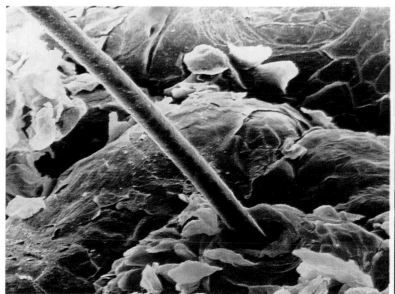

Figure 27–17 *The table lists the names and structures of several common amino acids. Which groups of atoms are found in all amino acids?*

Some Amino Acids and Their Structures

Name	Structure
glycine	 $H_2N-\overset{\overset{\displaystyle H}{\mid}}{\underset{\underset{\displaystyle H}{\mid}}{C}}-\overset{\overset{\displaystyle O}{\parallel}}{C}OH$
alanine	$H_2N-\overset{\overset{\displaystyle H}{\mid}}{\underset{\underset{\displaystyle CH_3}{\mid}}{C}}-\overset{\overset{\displaystyle O}{\parallel}}{C}OH$
valine	$H_2N-C-COH$ with CH and $CH_3\ CH_3$
leucine	$H_2N-C-COH$ with CH_2, CH, $CH_3\ CH_3$
phenylalanine	$H_2N-C-COH$ with CH_2 and phenyl ring
cysteine	$H_2N-C-COH$ with CH_2, SH
aspartic acid	$H_2N-C-COH$ with CH_2, COH, O

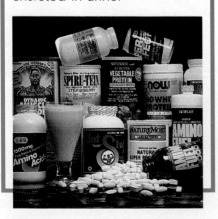
molecule, there are numerous sites for hydrogen bonding between the amino acids. The location of these sites is crucial in determining the overall structure of the protein.

The particular arrangement of the amino acid monomers determines the function of the protein. Long protein molecules bend and twist to create unique three-dimensional geometries. The three-dimensional shape of a protein depends on the attractive and repulsive forces among different portions of the molecule. If only one of the hundreds of amino acids in a protein is incorrect, the protein may have a slightly different shape and will not be able to carry out its function. Such a loss of function in only one type of protein can lead to severe health problems.

At the top, a chemical diagram:

peptide bond

$$H-N-C-C-\boxed{OH} + \boxed{H}-N-C-C-OH \rightarrow H-N-C-C-N-C-C-OH + \boxed{H}-\boxed{OH}$$

with H, O, H, R₁ / H, O, H, R₂ labels on the amino acids.

Figure 27–18 *The diagram shows the formation of a peptide bond between two amino acids.*

Peptide Bonds

Proteins are synthesized in the body by dehydration synthesis. The amino end of one amino acid forms an amide bond with the carboxyl end of another amino acid. A molecule of water is the byproduct of the reaction. Biochemists call the amide bond between amino acids a **peptide bond.** When two amino acids are joined, the resulting molecule is called a **dipeptide.** When several amino acids are joined, the product is a polypeptide, or protein.

Primary, Secondary, and Tertiary Structure

Proteins are macromolecules with complex structures. Because there are so many attractive and repulsive forces among different parts of the protein molecule, its structure must be described on different levels. The **primary structure** of a protein is the sequence of amino acids in the molecule. The primary structure describes the chemical composition and the molecular mass of the protein, but it does not describe the shape of the protein nor the intermolecular forces within the molecule.

The **secondary structure** of a protein describes how the sequence of amino acids folds back on itself. Usually the secondary

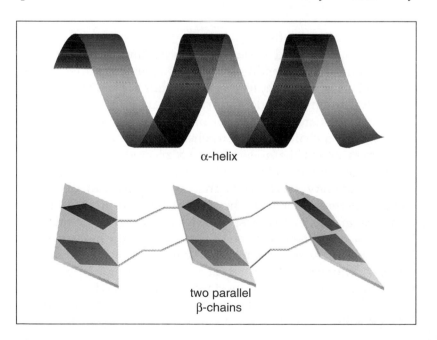

α-helix

two parallel
β-chains

Figure 27–19 *Here you see two possible secondary structures for a protein: the twisted, or alpha-helix, form (top) and the pleated, or beta-chain, form (bottom).*

One Size Fits All?

Michelle bought two new sweaters, one made of cotton and one made of wool. After she had worn the sweaters to school a few times, she decided to wash them together. She washed both sweaters in cool water so they would not shrink, then put the sweaters into the clothes drier. After 40 minutes, Michelle checked to see if the sweaters were dry. To her disappointment, she discovered that the wool sweater had shrunk. The cotton sweater, however, had remained the same size.

Michelle could not understand why one sweater would shrink if the other one did not, since she had washed and dried the two sweaters under identical conditions. She asks you if you know why the wool sweater shrank.

Drawing Conclusions

1. The fibers in cotton come from a plant, whereas wool is a protein that comes from an animal. What type of biochemical molecule would you expect cotton to be made of?

2. Recall that there are two types of secondary structures in proteins. What is the secondary structure of the protein in wool? How does that structure compare with the other type of secondary structure?

3. What probably happened to the wool fibers to cause the shrinkage?

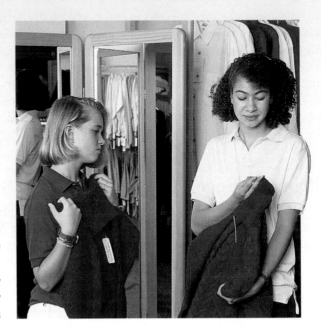

---

structure is in the form of a tightly twisted chain (called an α-helix) or a pleated sheet (called a β-chain). Changes in the environment can sometimes cause a β-chain to contract into an α-helix formation. Hair, feathers, and nails are composed of proteins whose amino acids are arranged in an α-helix structure. Silk and wool are composed of proteins whose amino acids are arranged in β-chains. Other proteins may have a helical structure in some parts of the molecule and a pleated structure in other regions of the molecule.

The **tertiary structure** of the protein refers to the way in which the entire molecule bends and folds to produce a three-dimensional shape that is specific to that protein. The numerous intermolecular forces between amino acids in the molecule determine this tertiary structure. Some covalent bonds also form between sulfur atoms in different parts of the molecule. Tertiary structure is particularly important in enzymes, where the shape of the molecule helps to determine the biological function of the protein.

Denaturation

The tertiary structure of a protein depends primarily on intermolecular forces, not on covalent bonds. Recall from Chapter 14 that intermolecular forces are weak attractive forces between different molecules or between different groups in the same molecule. These intermolecular forces are easily disrupted by changes in the protein's environment. For this reason, the shape of a protein molecule can be altered by changing such factors as temperature and pH.

Most proteins maintain their shape within a narrow pH range and at low or moderate temperatures. If the temperature or pH is not within this range, the protein goes through a process called **denaturation.** Denaturation is an unfolding of the protein so that it is no longer in its "natural" shape. No chemical bonds are broken during denaturation, but the secondary and tertiary structures of the molecule undergo some changes.

You observe the denaturation of proteins when egg whites are cooked. The protein of the egg (ovalbumin) is colorless in its folded tertiary structure. When the egg is exposed to higher temperatures, the protein is denatured, causing the ovalbumin to turn white and become more solid. You can also denature the proteins in egg white by pouring an acid over the egg. The change that occurs will resemble the changes in cooking an egg. Figure 27–20 illustrates the changes that occur when proteins in egg white are denatured.

Figure 27–20   When you cook an egg, the protein in the egg changes from colorless to white, mirroring changes in the structure of the protein. What is this process called?

Functions of Proteins

Proteins have a number of different functions. One of those functions is as structural material in the body. Collagen and elastin are structural proteins found in tendons and ligaments. Keratin is a protein that is the major component of hair and nails.

Actin and myosin are proteins that give muscle tissue its strength and ability to contract. Other proteins, such as insulin, act as hormones and regulate some aspect of metabolism. Proteins can also be involved in defending the body. Antibodies attack disease-causing microbes, and blood-clotting proteins prevent foreign organisms from entering wounds.

Enzymes

Enzymes are the most specialized type of proteins. There are thousands of different enzymes, each of which has a very specific function. Enzymes are biological catalysts. Their job is to speed up the many biological reactions that are necessary for life. Without enzymes, living things could not have evolved into such complex organisms.

The tertiary structure of an enzyme is crucial for its effectiveness as a catalyst. Each enzyme has an active site that has the right shape for the molecule it is designed to catalyze. The molecule that is catalyzed by an enzyme is called the substrate.

You will find it easier to understand the function of enzymes in terms of models. One model for the mechanism of an enzyme is called the lock and key model. This model compares the enzyme to a lock and the substrate to a key. The "key" must fit exactly into the "lock" for the system to operate. Just as the wrong key will not open a locked door, the wrong substrate will not be catalyzed by an enzyme. Figure 27–21(a) illustrates the lock and key model for enzyme function.

Enzyme activity can also be described by the induced fit model. This model describes an enzyme as having one shape when it does not have a substrate bound to it and another shape when the substrate attaches. According to the induced fit model, the binding of the substrate to the active site causes the enzyme to change its shape to fit the substrate. To better understand this model, think of a hand slipping into a glove. Once the reaction has been catalyzed, the products leave the active site and the enzyme returns to its original shape. Figure 27–21(b) shows how an enzyme functions according to the induced fit model.

Figure 27–21 *Here you see two models of enzyme function: the lock and key model (left) and the induced fit model (right).*

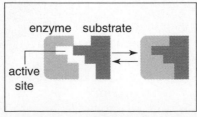

(a)

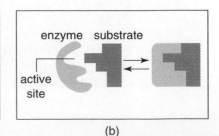

(b)

Vitamins

The importance of **vitamins** has been recognized for more than 200 years. Vitamins are molecules that are essential to maintaining good health. They are required in small amounts in the diet. Some vitamins act as coenzymes, or enzyme "helpers." Because vitamins are not as specific as enzymes, each vitamin helps to catalyze a number of different reactions.

Although vitamins are not required in large amounts in the diet, a deficiency of one or more vitamins can lead to serious nutritional disorders. For example, scurvy is a nutritional disorder that is caused by an absence of vitamin C in the diet. The symptoms of scurvy include swollen gums, loose teeth, bruising, and painful joints. This disorder was particularly common among sailors until it was discovered that the juice of citrus fruits could prevent or cure scurvy. Because British sailors carried limes with them to prevent scurvy, they were known as "limeys."

Vitamins are divided into two classes based on their solubility. All of the B vitamins and vitamin C are water-soluble. Vitamins A, D, E, and K are fat-soluble. Water-soluble vitamins are not stored in the body, so they must be included in your daily diet. Fat-soluble vitamins, which are stored in fatty tissues, do not have to be consumed daily. There is a danger of vitamin toxicity, in fact, if high doses of these vitamins are ingested and stored in the body.

Figure 27–22 *Dorothy Crowfoot-Hodgkin and Linus Pauling both received the Nobel Prize in Chemistry for their research on vitamins.*

◁ *Historical Perspective*

27–4 Section Review

1. What is a protein?
2. Identify and describe two models to explain enzyme function.
3. **Theme Trace—Form and Function** Some genetic diseases are caused by the substitution of one incorrect amino acid in a protein. Explain why one incorrect amino acid at the active site of an enzyme could alter its ability to act as a catalyst in a reaction.

Guide for Reading

- What are nucleic acids?
- What is the structure and function of DNA?
- What is the structure and function of RNA?

27–5 Nucleic Acids

In previous sections, you learned that glucose is made by plants in the process of photosynthesis and that more complex carbohydrates can be made using glucose molecules as a starting point. Lipids contain the same elements as carbohydrates, but in different ratios.

Proteins, however, are very complex molecules that contain nitrogen and sulfur atoms in addition to the carbon, hydrogen, and oxygen atoms in carbohydrates. The synthesis of proteins by living organisms is a complicated process that is orchestrated by another class of biomolecules: **nucleic acids.** In this section, you will learn about the structure of nucleic acids and how nucleic acids direct the synthesis of proteins. What are nucleic acids? **Nucleic acids are the biological molecules that code for hereditary traits by controlling the production of proteins.**

Nucleotides

The class of compounds called nucleic acids includes **DNA (deoxyribonucleic acid)** and **RNA (ribonucleic acid).** Both DNA and RNA are polymers made up of monomers called **nucleotides.** Each nucleotide unit consists of three parts: a nitrogen-containing base, a five-carbon sugar, and a phosphate group.

The nucleotides in DNA and RNA differ in the nitrogen-containing bases they contain. The four different bases in DNA are adenine, guanine, cytosine, and thymine. Three of the bases in RNA are the same as in DNA. They are adenine, cytosine, and guanine. The fourth base in RNA is uracil. Figure 27–24 shows the structural formulas of all five bases.

Figure 27–23 *Every nucleotide is made up of a nitrogen-containing base, a five-carbon sugar, and a phosphate group. What is a nucleotide?*

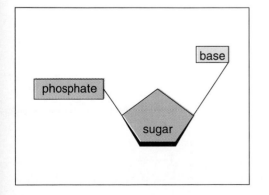

Figure 27–24 *Here you see the structures of the bases that make up DNA and RNA. Which base is found only in RNA?*

Genetic Engineering

Genetic engineering is no longer the stuff of science fiction. Genetically engineered foods are now in our grocery stores, and genetically altered DNA is being tested as treatment for certain diseases. What is genetic engineering? Should you be concerned about the use (or possible misuse) of genetic engineering techniques?

Genetic engineering is a process in which the DNA of a host organism is split and a new gene is inserted. The host organisms are usually bacteria such as *E. coli* that reproduce at a rapid rate. The new gene is the DNA sequence that codes for a desired protein such as human insulin. When the new gene is inserted into the host DNA, the host organisms produce the desired protein. When the host cells reproduce, their offspring also produce the desired protein. If the protein is insulin, for example, it can then be collected and used to treat diabetic patients whose bodies cannot manufacture insulin.

In agriculture, genetic engineering has been used to produce fruits that are resistant to frost, tomatoes that have a longer ripening period, and other produce that can be stored or transported more easily. The result is a decrease in spoilage and the availability of seasonal produce year-round.

Some plants have been genetically engineered to make them more resistant to insects. One example of this application is the insertion of a modified bacterial gene into cotton plants. The new gene causes the plants to produce a protein that is harmful to the cotton bollworm. As a result, farmers can cut down on the use of insecticides to protect their crops.

The potential for this new technology is limitless, but many people are alarmed by the potential for misuse or the possibility of mistakes. Suppose, for example, that genetically altered oil-eating bacteria—which can be used to clean up oil spills—were to escape and contaminate an oil well?

Another concern is the moral question of whether or not humans have the right to alter human genes. If it is acceptable to alter genes to cure disease, is it also acceptable to alter genes to make people stronger, taller, or more intelligent? In his novel, *Brave New World*, Aldous Huxley explored some of the moral dilemmas that may face us as genetic engineering technology becomes more refined. What is your opinion about genetic engineering?

Ribose is the five-carbon sugar in both DNA and RNA. In DNA, however, one of the hydroxyl groups (–OH) in the ribose molecule has been replaced with a hydrogen atom, giving it the name deoxyribose (meaning without oxygen).

Structure and Function of DNA

Deoxyribonucleic acid, or DNA, is the biomolecule responsible for carrying hereditary information from old cells to new ones and from one generation to another. The very slight differences in DNA account for the physical uniqueness of every individual. The larger differences in DNA determine whether an organism is a plant, an animal, or a bacterium. When organisms reproduce, the DNA from the parent organisms is copied and passed on to the offspring. This is why tomato seeds produce new tomato plants and why children resemble their parents.

In 1953, the team of James Watson and Francis Crick proposed the double helix structure of DNA. Using X-ray diffraction patterns, Watson and Crick were able to infer the structure of the DNA molecule, one of the most important scientific discoveries of the twentieth century. The term double helix refers to the fact that the DNA molecule is made of two long chains of nucleotides that are twisted around each other in a helical shape. Figure 27–25 shows the double helix structure of DNA.

Each of the strands in the double helix is composed of nucleotides attached by covalent bonds. The two strands are aligned in an antiparallel arrangement (facing in opposite directions). These antiparallel strands are attracted to each other by numerous

Figure 27–25 *The top photograph shows a computerized, color-coded model of DNA. James Watson and Francis Crick discovered the structure of the DNA molecule. Much of their work was based on the X-ray diffraction photographs taken by Rosalind Franklin, which revealed DNA's double-helix structure.*

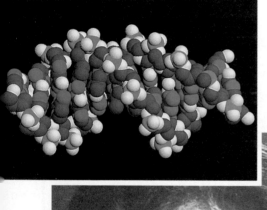

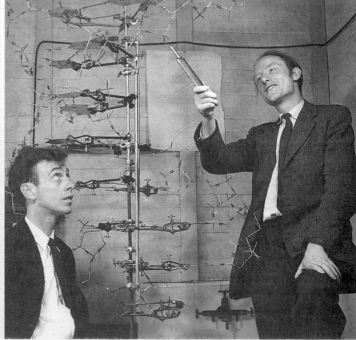

intermolecular hydrogen bonds. The intermolecular hydrogen bonds cause the double strand to twist into a helical shape.

DNA functions as a template, or pattern, to code for the sequence of amino acids in proteins. A single DNA molecule contains the code for the synthesis of many different proteins. A **gene** is the sequence of DNA nucleotides that codes for the synthesis of a single protein.

Structure and Function of RNA

There are three types of RNA, or ribonucleic acid. Each of the three is similar in structure, and all are involved in protein synthesis. The differences lie in the role of each type of RNA in assisting the process of protein synthesis.

All types of RNA are composed of a single strand of nucleotides. These RNA molecules are much shorter than DNA. Whereas DNA is found only within the nucleus of the cell, RNA is found outside the nucleus. RNA carries the code stored by DNA out of the nucleus, where it can be used in protein synthesis.

The code carried by RNA is made up of a series of three nucleotides, called triplets. Each triplet codes for one amino acid to be incorporated into the protein being synthesized. One type of RNA, called messenger RNA, carries the sequence of triplets for the synthesis of a specific protein. A second type of RNA, called transfer RNA, attaches to the correct amino acids, carries them to the site of protein synthesis, and then arranges them in the proper order. The third type of RNA, called ribosomal RNA, assists in the process of protein synthesis.

27–5 Section Review

1. What are nucleic acids?
2. Compare DNA and RNA in terms of their structure and function.
3. What are the three parts that make up the structure of a nucleotide?
4. **Critical Thinking—Making predictions** The synthesis of new DNA and RNA molecules involves a number of enzymes that check the molecules to ensure that there are no mistakes in the order of nucleotides. If these enzymes did not check the new DNA and RNA molecules, what are some of the possible short-term and long-term consequences?

YOU AND YOUR WORLD

DNA Fingerprinting

Blood typing has been used for many years to narrow the range of suspects in various crimes. Unfortunately, large segments of the population have the same blood type, so this alone cannot determine a person's guilt. A more recent forensic technique has been developed that enables law enforcement officials to positively identify criminals based on any type of tissue or body fluid left at the scene of the crime. This technique was first developed by Alec Jeffreys at Leicester University in England. Jeffreys discovered that some segments of human DNA were as individual as a person's fingerprints. These segments could be isolated and matched to a known sample, just as a set of known fingerprints can be matched to those at a crime scene. The process was, therefore, called DNA fingerprinting. This method of identifying criminals is commonly used today, although there is still some question as to the admissibility of DNA evidence in court.

Laboratory Investigation DESIGNING an EXPERIMENT

Identifying Proteins in Foods

Problem

How can you identify foods that contain protein?

Suggested Materials (per group)

1 24-well reaction plate
plastic pipet
wood toothpick
Biuret reagent
protein solution
food samples

Suggested Procedure

1. Devise an experiment to detect the presence of protein in 5 different food samples. It may help you to know that Biuret reagent indicates the presence of protein by turning purple.
2. Write down the steps of your experimental procedure.
3. Prepare a data table similar to the one shown to record all of your data.
4. Conduct your experiment after having your teacher approve your procedure and data table. Be sure to include a control.
5. From your data, determine which of your food samples contain protein.

Observations

Sample	Observations
1	
2	
3	
4	
5	
Control	

Analysis and Conclusions

1. Describe a positive Biuret test for the presence of protein.
2. What was the control in your experiment? What was its purpose?
3. How did you determine what a positive test for protein should look like?
4. Which of the foods you tested contained protein?
5. What functional groups in proteins are the probable sites of reaction with the Biuret reagent? (*Hint:* Which functional groups are present in proteins but are not present in carbohydrates or fats?)
6. Is it necessary for you to blend your food samples before testing?
7. Predict the effect of testing the following foods with the Biuret reagent: sugar, salt, banana, raw egg white, cooked egg white, unroasted peanuts, roasted peanuts. Give reasons for your predictions.
8. **On Your Own**   Test the foods listed in item 7. Do your results support your predictions?

STUDY GUIDE

Summarizing Key Concepts

27–1 Chemistry and Living Things
- Biochemistry is the study of the chemical processes that occur in living organisms.
- In the process of photosynthesis, plants use the radiant energy from the sun to convert carbon dioxide and water into glucose.
- Cellular respiration is the process used by cells to release the energy stored in the bonds of glucose molecules.

27–2 Carbohydrates
- Carbohydrates are molecules made from aldehydes and ketones containing numerous hydroxyl groups.
- Simple carbohydrates, or monosaccharides, are composed of a single ring.
- Disaccharides consist of two monosaccharides that are chemically combined.
- Polysaccharides are polymers containing numerous monosaccharide monomers.

27–3 Lipids
- Lipids are water-insoluble molecules that are composed of carbon, hydrogen, and oxygen.

- Fats and oils are triglycerides that are combinations of glycerol and three fatty acids.
- Waxes are lipids that are combinations of a long-chain alcohol and a fatty acid.

27–4 Proteins
- Proteins are polymers of amino acids. Proteins are found as structural materials in hair, nails, and connective tissue.
- Enzymes are proteins that act as biological catalysts.
- Vitamins A, D, E, and K are fat-soluble. Vitamin C and the B vitamins are water-soluble.

27–5 Nucleic Acids
- Deoxyribonucleic acid (DNA) and ribonucleic acid (RNA) are nucleic acids. Both DNA and RNA are polymers that are made up of nucleotides.
- Nucleotides are molecules that are composed of three parts: a five-carbon sugar, a nitrogen-containing base, and a phosphate group.

Reviewing Key Terms

Define each term in a complete sentence.

27–1 Chemistry and Living Things
photosynthesis
cellular respiration

27–2 Carbohydrates
carbohydrate
monosaccharide
pentose
hexose
disaccharide
dehydration synthesis
hydrolysis
polysaccharide

27–3 Lipids
lipid
triglyceride
fat
oil
hydrogenation
wax
phospholipid
steroid

27–4 Proteins
protein
peptide bond
dipeptide

primary structure
secondary structure
tertiary structure
denaturation
enzyme
vitamin

27–5 Nucleic Acids
nucleic acid
DNA (deoxyribonucleic acid)
RNA (ribonucleic acid)
nucleotide
gene

CHAPTER REVIEW

Content Review

Multiple Choice
Choose the letter of the answer that best completes each statement.

1. In the process of photosynthesis, which type of energy conversion do plants carry out?
   - (a) chemical to mechanical
   - (b) heat to light
   - (c) radiant to chemical
   - (d) electrical to chemical

2. The study of chemical reactions that occur in living organisms is called
   - (a) biochemistry.
   - (b) organic chemistry.
   - (c) analytical chemistry.
   - (d) inorganic chemistry.

3. All of the following are carbohydrates except
   - (a) glucose.
   - (b) starch.
   - (c) amino acids.
   - (d) cellulose.

4. A disaccharide is formed by combining two monosaccharides in a process called
   - (a) hydrolysis.
   - (b) peptide bonding.
   - (c) saccharide bonding.
   - (d) dehydration synthesis.

5. Which of the following biomolecules contain only the elements carbon, hydrogen, and oxygen?
   - (a) carbohydrates and lipids
   - (b) lipids and proteins
   - (c) proteins and nucleic acids
   - (d) nucleic acids and carbohydrates

6. All of the following are lipids except
   - (a) triglycerides.
   - (b) glycogen.
   - (c) waxes.
   - (d) steroids.

7. The structural units of proteins are
   - (a) glucose.
   - (b) amino acids.
   - (c) nucleic acids.
   - (d) enzymes.

8. The process by which a protein loses its natural shape is called
   - (a) hydrolysis.
   - (b) synthesis.
   - (c) polymerization.
   - (d) denaturation.

9. DNA is a type of
   - (a) protein.
   - (b) amino acid.
   - (c) nucleic acid.
   - (d) enzyme.

True or False
If the statement is true, write "true." If it is false, change the underlined word or words to make the statement true.

10. The energy required by most living organisms comes originally from <u>plants</u>.
11. Starch and glycogen are both examples of <u>polysaccharides</u>.
12. If a lipid contains fatty acids with all single bonds, then it is a(an) <u>saturated</u> fat.
13. The type of nucleic acid that consists of a double helix is <u>RNA</u>.
14. Enzymes are a type of <u>nucleic acid</u>.
15. When glucose is metabolized by cells, the energy in its chemical bonds is stored in <u>ATP</u>.
16. Vitamins A, D, E, and K are <u>fat</u> soluble.
17. Glucose is broken down in cells by a process called <u>cellular respiration</u>.

Concept Mapping
Complete the following concept map for Section 27–5. Refer to pages xviii–xix to construct a concept map for the entire chapter.

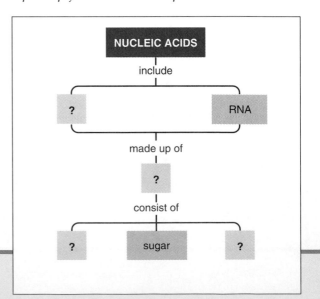

Concept Mastery

Discuss each of the following in a brief paragraph.

18. Explain why photosynthesis might be considered the most important chemical process on Earth.

19. Describe the differences among monosaccharides, disaccharides, and polysaccharides. Give examples of each type of carbohydrate.

20. Compare the structures of cellulose and starch, and explain why animals can digest one but not the other.

21. Describe the similarities and differences in fats and oils.

22. Explain how waxes, phospholipids, and steroids are different from oils and fats.

23. Describe how amino acids join to form a peptide bond.

24. Describe the primary, secondary, and tertiary structure of proteins.

25. Explain how enzymes affect substrate molecules according to the lock and key and induced fit models of enzyme behavior.

26. Describe the similarities and differences in DNA and RNA.

27. Explain the role of vitamins in biochemical reactions.

28. **Tying it Together** Describe how the *form*, or structure, of ATP and ADP are related to their *function* of transferring energy in biochemical reactions.

Critical Thinking and Problem Solving

Use the skills you have developed in this chapter to answer each of the following.

29. **Applying concepts** Humans are able to digest starch, but cannot digest cellulose despite the fact that both of these polysaccharides are made up of glucose monomers. Based on what you have learned about enzymes, explain why we cannot digest cellulose.

30. **Making inferences** Why is the three-dimensional structure of an enzyme critical to its function?

31. **Interpreting data** Nutritional chemists have found that burning 1 gram of fat releases twice the amount of heat energy as burning 1 gram of starch. Based on this information, which type of biomolecule would cause a person to gain more weight?

32. **Designing experiments** Early scientists believed that plants grew by extracting all their nutrients from the soil. Design an experiment that would test this hypothesis.

33. **Using the writing process** Sickle cell anemia and cystic fibrosis are two diseases that are caused by the insertion of a single incorrect amino acid in one type of protein. Research one of these genetic diseases and write a report describing it. How can even a tiny change in the structure of DNA affect the proteins that a cell produces?

FROM SCHOOL TO WORK

Maya Mehta—Student

Before Maya Mehta of Danville, Illinois, took a chemistry course, she didn't really understand how relevant chemistry was to many of the activities she enjoys. "I've always loved to cook," says Maya, "but I never thought about the chemical reactions and changes that occur." Maya was also surprised to find out how much chemistry is involved in the production of such everyday products as shampoos and cosmetics.

Maya hopes to pursue her interests in chemistry and human anatomy in college, where she plans to study premedical sciences. From her experiences working for a physician over the summer, Maya knows how large a role chemistry plays in treating patients. "When you take X-rays or pour a cast, that's chemistry. When you prescribe medications, give inoculations, or recommend changes in a patient's diet, it's all related to chemistry."

Nuclear Medicine Technologist

Nuclear medicine technologists work closely with nuclear medicine physicians and other professionals in the field of nuclear medicine. Nuclear medicine technologists may prepare and administer radioactive drugs to patients. They may use radiation detection devices to trace radionuclides through a patient's body, provide therapy, or perform diagnostic procedures.

High-school students interested in this field should take courses in chemistry, mathematics, physics, and human biology, followed by a two-year Associate or four-year Bachelor of Science or Arts degree in nuclear medicine technology. In addition, a one-year professional curriculum includes studies in patient care, nuclear physics, health physics, and biochemistry.

For more information, write to the Society of Nuclear Medicine—Technologist Section, 136 Madison Avenue, New York, NY 10016.

How to Follow Up on a Job Interview

After you have had a job interview, you may have to wait several weeks to hear the results. During that period, however, you should send a letter to the interviewer thanking him or her for the time and consideration. You can also call the person to show your interest in working for that company and to provide any additional information that might be needed.

If you do not get the job that you interviewed for, ask the interviewer for comments or suggestions on how to improve your interviewing skills. Most employers are willing to discuss the interview with you and explain their impressions so that you can be better prepared for your next interview.

Karen Robblee

From the Author

It is easy to take for granted the chemistry that occurs in and around us: breakfast digesting, plants growing, or a bottle of aspirin available to ease a headache. But when chemistry produces major changes in your life, you begin truly to appreciate its importance. Several years ago, the availability of new chemical compounds made a dramatic difference in my life. At a fairly young age, I had become severely crippled by the damage caused by rheumatoid arthritis. Fifty years earlier, I would have been confined to a wheelchair in constant pain. However, thanks to chemists and biomedical engineers, it was possible to have a damaged knee replaced by one made of a synthetic compound.

It was interesting to hear my doctor explain the composition of my new knee. It had to be made of a material that was strong but that would not react with all the other substances in my body. Likewise, the compound that would be used to cement the new knee to the bones in my leg had to be made of a substance that would last a long time, but would not react with bones or body fluids. The materials used for parts of the knee and the cement to hold it in place are polymers, like the ones you read about in this unit.

My new knee works fine and is pain-free. Besides providing mobility and relief from pain, this experience gave me a more personal appreciation of the importance of chemical compounds and their properties.

UNIT REVIEW

Concept Mastery

Discuss each of the following in a brief paragraph.

1. What are the differences between fission and fusion reactions?
2. Why is gamma radiation considered more dangerous than alpha or beta radiation?
3. A rem is a unit that measures the exposure of living things to radiation. What chemical changes could occur in biomolecules because of exposure to radiation?
4. In which type of biomolecule would exposure to radiation cause the most serious damage to an organism? Explain your answer.
5. Why is carbon essential for life?
6. Are all organic compounds biomolecules? Explain your answer.
7. Carbon-14 dating is used to determine the age of organic material. Explain why carbon isotopes are used rather than nitrogen isotopes, which are also present in organic matter.
8. What functional groups are present in a straight-chain glucose molecule? What groups are present when glucose is in its ring form?
9. One type of nylon is made by reacting adipic acid ($HOOC(CH_2)_4COOH$) with hexamethyldiamine ($H_2N(CH_2)_6NH_2$). The nylon has the following structure:

$$\left[\overset{O}{\overset{\|}{C}}(CH_2)_4 \overset{O}{\overset{\|}{C}}NH(CH_2)_6NH \right]_n$$

Compare and contrast the structure of the nylon molecule with the structure of a protein molecule.

10. The hydrocarbons found in petroleum are the products of the decay of organic matter. What type of chemical reactions might have converted carbohydrates, lipids, and proteins into hydrocarbons?

11. Explain why organic compounds with a carboxyl group (–COOH) are acids, but organic compounds with hydroxyl groups (–OH) are not bases.
12. Explain how the polarity of organic molecules directly affects the functions of the molecules. Give examples in your answer.

Problem Bank

13. You learned in Chapter 27 that natural polymers such as proteins and complex carbohydrates are made by dehydration synthesis. What is the term that refers to the same type of reaction used to produce synthetic polymers?
14. Name four classes of organic compounds and give an example of a biomolecule that belongs to each of the four classes you name.
15. Phenol is an alcohol derived from the hydrocarbon benzene. The structure of phenol is

What would be the name of this compound if it were considered as an alcohol of benzene?

16. Balance the following nuclear reactions:

(a) $^{232}_{90}Th \rightarrow ^{228}_{88}Ra + ?$
(b) $^{214}_{82}Pb \rightarrow ^{214}_{83}Bi + ?$
(c) $^{214}_{83}Bi \rightarrow ? + ^{0}_{-1}\beta$
(d) $^{214}_{84}Po \rightarrow ? + ^{4}_{2}He$

17. Identify the following compounds as organic or inorganic. Then name each compound.

(a) CO_2 (b) C_2H_6 (c) CH_3COOH
(d) $CaCO_3$ (e) $CH_3CH_2NH_2$

18. Identify the following hydrocarbons as alkanes, alkenes, or alkynes.

(a) C_6H_{10} (b) C_8H_{18} (c) C_4H_8
(d) $C_{20}H_{42}$ (e) C_7H_{14}

19. Write structural formulas for the following compounds:

(a) 2-pentene
(b) 1-butanol
(c) methanoic acid
(d) ethylpentyl ether
(e) propanal
(f) 3-octyne
(g) ethanamine
(h) propylethanoate
(i) methoxybutane
(j) 3-heptanone

Which of these compounds belong to the same class of compounds?

20. Write the structural formula for the dipeptide formed when the carboxyl end of cysteine bonds to the amino end of valine.

21. Write the net chemical reaction for cellular respiration. How does this reaction compare with the chemical reaction for photosynthesis?

22. Identify the following vitamins as water-soluble or fat-soluble.

(a) A (b) B_2 (c) C (d) D (e) E
(f) B_{12} (g) K

23. The structural formula for riboflavin (vitamin B_2) is shown below. Identify the functional groups in riboflavin.

Performance-Based Task

How Does an Enzyme Aid Digestion?

Imagine a pharmacist has just recommended a commercially available enzyme because you experience difficulty digesting certain foods. How does this enzyme aid digestion? Design an experiment to answer the question.

1. Start by obtaining Beano, glucose test tape, bean extract, egg white, table sugar, glucose, a spot plate, a dropper/pipette, and tap water.
2. State a hypothesis and develop a procedure for testing it.
3. Carry out your experiment. Make and record observations in order to determine the types of nutrients present both before and after the treatment with Beano.
4. Produce extracts of other nutrient sources and perform tests to see how these are affected by the enzyme.

Going Further

5. Do you think your results would be different if you changed the temperature of the nutrient solutions or enzyme? Explain.
6. How would your results differ if you changed other properties of the nutrient solutions, such as pH or concentration?

PRACTICE PROBLEMS

Chapter 1 Chemistry and You

Section 1-1

1. What is chemistry? Give three examples of questions that a chemist might try to answer.

2. Give three examples of ways that chemistry relates to other sciences.

Section 1-2

The following paragraph applies to Problems 3 and 4.

Carmen accidentally scattered a handful of nails on her porch. After a week, she observed that some of the nails became rusty, while others did not. The rusty nails tended to be closer to an open window. During the week, it had been windy and rainy.

3. Think of a question based on Carmen's observations. Propose a hypothesis to answer this question.

4. Design an experiment to test the hypothesis you proposed. Identify the variable and the experimental control.

Section 1-3

5. Identify the safety rules that John violates in the following paragraph:

John runs to the lab bench, carrying chemicals from the supply cabinet. As he snacks on potato chips, he mixes the chemicals into a beaker. He accidentally spills some of the chemicals, so he moves to a new lab bench. There, he holds the beaker over an open flame. When the bell rings, he runs out of the lab to his next class.

Section 1-4

6. Change the following measurements into meters:
   a. 1 kilometer b. 2 millimeters
   c. 8 nanometers d. 4 decimeters.

7. A sheet of plastic is 20 cm long, 40 cm wide, and 0.20 cm thick. Calculate the volume of the plastic in cubic centimeters.

Section 1-5

8. A chemist states that the mass of an iron sample is 62.51 ± 0.02 grams. What range of mass does the iron sample have?

9. Compare a precise measurement with an accurate measurement.

Section 1-6

10. Round off the following numbers to the third significant digit: a. 13.88 b. 0.1021 c. 6.0991 d. 18,070 e. 0.004 555 0 f. 0.004 051 99

11. A box has dimensions 2.75 m $\times$ 130. m $\times$ 0.880 m. Calculate the volume of the box. Express your answer with the correct number of significant digits.

12. Write the following numbers in scientific notation:
    a. 840 b. 0.006 c. 1,206,000
    d. 0.008 126 e. 0.93
    f. 0.000 000 002 103

13. A metal bar has a mass of 348 grams and a volume of 54 cm^3. What is the density of the metal bar in grams per cm^3?

14. Aluminum has a density of 2.7 g/cm^3. What volume of aluminum has a mass of 60. grams?

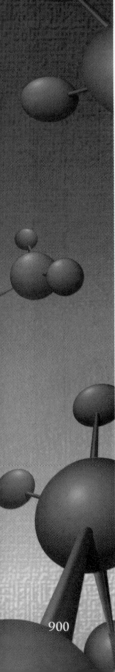

PRACTICE PROBLEMS

Section 1-7

15. A car uses gasoline at a rate of 22 miles per gallon. What is its rate in kilometers per liter (km/L)?

16. The length of a wave of green light is 580 nanometers (1 nanometer = 10^{-9} m). How many waves of green light could fit through a slit that is 2.0 centimeters wide?

17. A large block of an unidentified substance measures 7.2 feet by 9.2 feet by 2.5 feet. Its mass is 5230 kg. What is the density of the block in terms of g/cm^3?

Chapter 2 — *Energy and Matter*

Section 2-1

1. A food label states that the food contains 134 Calories per serving. Convert this figure to both calories and Joules.

2. Convert 84.9 kJ into calories and Calories.

3. A test tube containing 6.0 grams of water is raised from 10°C to 25°C. How much heat (in calories) has the water gained?

4. A supply of water at 22°C is heated with a source that transfers energy to the water at a rate of 42 calories per minute. After 12 minutes, the temperature of the water is 40°C. Assuming that no energy was lost to the surroundings, what is the mass of the water?

Section 2-2

5. The temperature inside a boiler increased by 36 K. How much did it increase in degrees Celsius?

6. Today's temperature is 17°C. What is the temperature in degrees Kelvin?

Section 2-3

7. Identify the following changes in matter as physical changes or chemical changes. Explain your reasoning.
   a. Adding milk and fruit to a bowl of cereal.
   b. Frying an egg.
   c. Boiling water.
   d. Tearing a cotton T-shirt into small pieces.
   e. Dissolving sugar in a glass of water.

8. An iron nail has a mass of 2.5 grams. Over time, the nail rusts. The rusty nail has a mass of 2.8 grams. Does this result contradict the law of conservation of matter? Explain.

Section 2-4

9. Magnesium oxide (MgO) is 60% magnesium and 40% oxygen by mass. If 50 grams of magnesium oxide are submitted to electrolysis, how many grams of magnesium and oxygen are produced?

10. Water contains 88.9% oxygen and 11.1% hydrogen by mass. An unidentified compound is submitted to electrolysis, and produces 44.2 grams of oxygen and 2.76 grams of hydrogen. Could the unidentified compound be water? Explain.

901

PRACTICE PROBLEMS

Section 2-5

11. Classify the following materials as pure substances, homogeneous mixtures, or heterogeneous mixtures:
a. ammonia (NH_3)
b. a cinnamon-raisin bagel
c. a blue crayon (without the wrapper)
d. a blue crayon (with the wrapper)
e. radon (Rn)
f. soda pop

12. Ethanol and water form a homogeneous mixture. Ethanol boils at 80°C and water boils at 100°C. Describe a procedure for separating the two components of an ethanol and water mixture.

13. Hydrogen gas and oxygen gas combine to form water, releasing a great deal of energy in the process. Do you expect the same amount of energy to be released when the reverse reaction occurs (i.e., when water separates into hydrogen and oxygen)?

Chapter 3 — *Atomic Structure*

Section 3-1

1. In a chemical reaction, 23.0 grams of sodium metal combines with chlorine gas to form 58.5 grams of sodium chloride. How much chlorine gas was used by this reaction?

2. Carbon dioxide is a common gas. A sample of carbon dioxide contains 27% carbon and 73% oxygen by mass. How much carbon and oxygen are contained in 36 grams of carbon dioxide?

3. Imagine that you had a tool that let you clearly examine individual atoms. With this tool, how could you distinguish an element from a compound? The work of which scientist helps you answer this question?

Section 3-2

4. Millikan calculated the mass of an electron to be 9.11×10^{-28} gram, and the charge of a single electron to be 1.60×10^{-19} C. How many electrons make up 1 C of charge? What is the mass of electrons that make up 1 C of charge?

5. Millikan's experiment relied on a series of oil droplets that carried negative charges. He calculated that the charge on every oil droplet was a multiple of 1.60×10^{-19} C.

Is this conclusive proof that 1.60×10^{-19} C is the charge of a single electron?

Section 3-3

6. A chart states that the mass of a proton or neutron is approximately 1 amu, and the mass of an electron is essentially 0 amu. If this chart is accurate, do electrons have no mass? Explain your answer.

7. The radius of an aluminum atom is 1.43×10^{-10} meter. When placed end to end, how many aluminum atoms would make a length of 1.00 cm?

8. Compare the electrons in a carbon atom ($^{12}_{6}C$), a nitrogen ion with a charge of $1+$ ($^{14}_{7}N^+$), and a boron ion with a charge of $1-$ ($^{11}_{5}B^-$).

9. How many protons, neutrons, and electrons are found in the following atoms?
a. $^{7}_{3}Li$ c. $^{45}_{21}Sc$
b. $^{29}_{14}Si$ d. $^{223}_{87}Fr$

10. Write the chemical symbols for the atoms or ions specified by the following combinations of particles.
a. 8 protons, 9 neutrons, 10 electrons
b. 12 protons, 12 neutrons, 12 electrons
c. 49 protons, 65 neutrons, 52 electrons
d. 100 protons, 157 neutrons, 99 electrons

11. In a laboratory setting, the mass of a single silicon atom is measured to be 4.81×10^{-23} gram. In a collection of 10^{23} silicon atoms, is the mass necessarily 4.81 grams? Explain your answer.

Section 3-4

Use the following answers for Problems 12 through 15. Each represents the composition of a nucleus.

  a. 30 protons and 39 neutrons
  b. 31 protons and 31 neutrons
  c. 31 protons and 39 neutrons
  d. 31 protons and 47 neutrons
  e. 32 protons and 48 neutrons

12. How many protons and neutrons are in an atom of gallium-70 ($^{70}_{31}$Ga)?

13. Gallium-69 ($^{69}_{31}$Ga) and gallium-70 ($^{70}_{31}$Ga) are stable isotopes. Of the five nuclei listed, which two are the most stable? Explain your answer.

14. Of the five nuclei listed, which two are most likely to emit beta radiation? Explain your answer.

15. Fill in the missing components of the following nuclear reactions. Consult the periodic table as necessary.
  a. $^{20}_{9}\text{F} \rightarrow$ _____ $+ \, ^{20}_{10}\text{Ne}$
  b. $^{93}_{42}\text{Mo} \rightarrow$ _____ $+ \, ^{89}_{40}\text{Zr}$
  c. $^{48}_{23}\text{V} \rightarrow \, ^{4}_{2}\alpha +$ _____
  d. $^{68}_{30}\text{Zn} \rightarrow \, ^{0}_{-1}\beta +$ _____

Chapter 4 — *Electron Configurations*

Section 4-1

1. Which has the higher frequency—dim purple light ($\lambda = 400$ nm) or bright red light ($\lambda = 700$ nm)?

2. Which has the higher amplitude—dim purple light ($\lambda = 400$ nm) or bright red light ($\lambda - 700$ nm)?

3. What is the frequency of monochromatic light of wavelength 485 nm? (The speed of light is 3.00×10^8 m/s.)

Section 4-2

4. Which has more energy—dim purple light ($\lambda = 400$ nm) or bright red light ($\lambda = 700$ nm)? How does the work of Max Planck explain the answer to this question?

5. An unidentified source of electromagnetic radiation produces waves with frequency 1.25×10^{19}/s. What kind of radiation is this? How dangerous is the energy? What is the energy of a photon of this radiation? (Planck's constant $= 6.63 \times 10^{-34}$ J-s.)

Section 4-3

6. Sodium produces an intense yellow color when it is burned. Is this light part of a continuous spectrum or a line spectrum? Explain your answer.

7. Explain why the line spectrum of hydrogen includes light of several different wavelengths, even though a hydrogen atom has only one electron.

8. Why are scientists not able to show that electrons move about the nucleus of an atom in well-defined orbitals?

Section 4-4

Match the following answer choices to Problems 9 through 14. An answer may be used once, more than once, or not at all.

  a. 1s   b. 2s   c. 2d   d. 3s
  e. 3d   f. 4s   g. 4p   h. 4d

9. This sublevel contains dumbbell-shaped orbitals for electrons in the fourth principal energy level.

PRACTICE PROBLEMS

10. This sublevel contains the orbital for electrons of the lowest energy.

11. Among the answer choices, this sublevel contains the largest spherical orbital.

12. Both of these sublevels can contain a maximum of 10 electrons each.

13. This sublevel contains exactly 3 orbitals, which can hold a total of 6 electrons.

14. No sublevel exists with this designation.

Section 4-5

15. Write the orbital diagram for the ground state electron configuration for each of the following atoms.
  a. beryllium (4 electrons)
  b. oxygen (8 electrons)
  c. sodium (11 electrons)

16. For each of the following electron configurations, identify the configuration as a ground state, an excited state, or a state that does not exist. For the configurations that do exist, identify the element.
  a. $1s^2\ 2s^2\ 2p^6\ 3s^2\ 3p^6$
  b. $1s^2\ 2s^2\ 2p^6\ 3s^1\ 3p^1$
  c. $1s^2\ 2s^2\ 2p^6\ 3s^2\ 3p^6\ 4s^3\ 3d^8$
  d. $1s^2\ 2s^2\ 2p^6\ 2d^{10}\ 3s^2$

17. Write the ground state electron configurations for the following elements:
  a. hydrogen (1 electron)
  b. lithium (3 electrons)
  c. nitrogen (7 electrons)
  d. aluminum (13 electrons)

Chapter 5

The Periodic Table

Section 5-1

Use the following table to answer Problems 1 through 3. Elements A, B, and C represent one of Dobereiner's triads.

Element	Atomic mass (amu)	Properties
A	6.9	highly reactive metal
B	—	highly reactive metal
C	39.1	highly reactive metal

1. Predict the atomic mass of Element B.

2. What is Newlands's law of octaves? According to this law, what can be inferred about the relationship between elements A, B, and C and the other elements?

3. Using the periodic table, identify elements A, B, and C.

Section 5-2

4. Most groups of elements contain metals only. Which groups contain metals, semimetals, and nonmetals?

5. How do the inner transition metals properly fit into the rest of the table? (The inner transition metals are the 28 elements placed below the rest of the table.)

6. Element 118 has not yet been discovered or created. If it did exist, of which group of the periodic table would it be a member?

7. Identify the elements that have the following electron configurations:
  a. [He] $2s^2\ 2p^3$
  b. [Ne] $3s^2\ 3p^3$
  c. [Ne] $3s^2\ 3p^4$
  d. [Kr] $5s^2\ 4d^2$
  e. [Xe] $6s^2\ 4f^9$

PRACTICE PROBLEMS

Section 5-3

8. Why is an H^+ ion smaller than any other ion with a 1+ charge?

9. The following ions all have the same number of electrons: N^{3-}, O^{2-}, and F^-. Of the three ions, explain why N^{3-} is the largest and F^- is the smallest.

Use the following diagram to answer Problems 10 through 14. The diagram represents four squares of the periodic table. The element symbols have been changed.

37 **Aa**	38 **Bb**
55 **Cc**	56 **Dd**

10. An atom from which element has the larger radius—Aa or Bb? Explain your answer.

11. Predict which element has the larger ionization energy—Bb or Dd? Explain your answer.

12. For most periodic trends, is it easier to compare elements Aa and Dd, or elements Bb and Cc? Explain your answer.

13. Which is greater, the ionization energy of a lithium atom or the electron affinity of a lithium ion (Li^+)? Explain your answer.

14. Unidentified element X has low 1st and 2nd ionization energies, but a very high 3rd ionization energy. What can be concluded about element X?

15. An unidentified element releases a great deal of energy when an electron is added to it, but requires energy to add a second electron. It has an unusually high electronegativity and has the smallest atomic radius in its family. Name this element.

Chapter 6 — *Groups of Elements*

Section 6-1

1. Compare the alkali metals with familiar metals such as iron, copper, and silver.

2. What is an alloy? Why are alloys used in products much more often than metals in their elemental form?

3. Suppose you have a sample of an alkali metal and a sample of an alkaline earth metal. You do not know which sample is which, nor do you know the identity of either metal. To determine most easily which sample is the alkali metal and which is the alkaline earth metal, should you investigate their chemical properties or their physical properties? Explain your answer.

Section 6-2

4. Some elements are more abundant on Earth than others. Is abundance a periodic trend? Explain your answer.

5. Why is chromium used as a protective coat over other metals?

6. Why are copper, silver, and gold ideal for making coins?

7. Calcium is a member of Group 2A. Its electron configuration is [Ar] $4s^2$. Cobalt, a transition metal, has the electron configuration [Ar] $4s^2\ 3d^7$. From this information alone, can you predict the ions formed by calcium and cobalt? Explain your answer.

Section 6-3

8. Why is it difficult to separate a mixture of lanthanide elements?

9. Which are more common in nature—the lanthanides or the actinides? Explain.

Section 6-4

10. Compare and contrast the halogens and the alkali metals.

PRACTICE PROBLEMS

11. When a sample of sodium metal needs to be stored for a long period of time, it is often stored in a vacuum container. Why would storing sodium in an argon-filled container be an acceptable alternative?

12. Why do you suspect that argon was not discovered until 1894, years after many less-abundant elements had been discovered?

Section 6-5

13. In the periodic table, why is the square for hydrogen typically separated slightly from the elements in Group 1A?

14. The Earth today has significantly less hydrogen than it did billions of years ago. Describe a process that is depleting the Earth's hydrogen.

Chapter 7 — Chemical Formulas and Bonding

Section 7-1

1. Barium (Ba) has the electron configuration of [Xe] $6s^2$. Draw the Lewis dot diagram for barium.

2. Using Lewis dot diagrams, show the reaction of one magnesium atom and two chlorine atoms forming magnesium chloride.

3. Name the following cations: a. H^+, b. Ca^{2+}, c. Cu^{2+}, d. Cu^+, e. Mn^{3+}, f. Mn^{4+}, g. Os^{4+}, h. NH_4^+.

4. Name the following anions: a. Cl^-, b. OH^-, c. HCO_3^-, d. SO_4^{2-}, e. P^{3-}, f. PO_4^{3-}, g. CO_3^{2-}.

5. Write the empirical formula for each of the following ionic compounds: a. calcium iodide, b. iron (II) oxide, c. iron (III) oxide, d. magnesium nitrate, e. potassium hydroxide.

Section 7-2

6. Ethane has the molecular formula C_2H_6. Draw the structural formula for ethane, using Lewis dot structures.

7. Identify the bonds (single, double, or triple covalent) in molecular chlorine (Cl_2), molecular oxygen (O_2), and molecular nitrogen (N_2). Explain how the octet rule is satisfied in each molecule.

8. Some of the following formulas signify a stable chemical compound, while others do not. For each legitimate formula, identify whether it signifies an ionic compound or a molecular compound. For the other formulas, explain why no stable compound exists with that formula, or why that formula makes no sense.
a. C_2H_4, b. K_2Mg, c. Li_2S, d. KO_2, e. H_3, f. CO^2, g. NH_4NO_3.

Use the following molecules to answer Problems 9 through 11.
a. chloromethane (CH_3Cl)
b. carbon dioxide (CO_2)
c. nitrogen tribromide (NBr_3)
d. formic acid (HCO_2H)

9. Draw Lewis structures for each of the molecules.

10. For each molecule, label each bond in the molecule as nonpolar covalent, polar covalent, or ionic.

11. For each molecule, identify the atoms with the unshared pairs of electrons.

12. Rank the following bonds in order of least polar to most polar:
a. Na—F, b. C—H, c. Ca—O, d. S—S, e. B—Cl.

Section 7-3

13. Name the following ionic compounds:
a. $Co(OH)_2$, b. Li_2SO_4, c. $Ba_3(PO_4)_2$, d. $NiCl_3$, e. $Sn(CO_3)_2$.

14. Name the following hydrated compounds:
a. $MnO_2 \cdot 3\ H_2O$, b. $Ca_3(PO_4)_2 \cdot 2\ H_2O$,
c. $SrSO_4 \cdot 8\ H_2O$.

15. Name the following molecular compounds:
a. CBr_4, b. OF_2, c. SCl_6, d. N_2O_4, e. O_3.

16. Name the following acids:
a. HCl, b. H_2CO_3, c. HNO_3, d. H_3PO_4.

17. Name the following compounds:
a. NaN_3, b. PCl_3, c. NH_3, d. Al_2O_3, e. HF.

Chapter 8 — *Molecular Shape*

Section 8-1

1. Compare a ball-and-stick model of a molecule to an actual molecule.

The following structural formula applies to Problems 2 through 4.

$$H-\overset{\displaystyle\overset{H}{\overset{|}{}}}{\underset{\displaystyle\underset{H}{\underset{|}{}}}{C}}-\overset{..}{\underset{..}{O}}-H$$

Methanol

2. In what ways does the structural formula accurately represent a molecule of methanol? In what ways is it inaccurate?

3. What is the hybridization of the carbon atom in methanol? Of the oxygen atom?

4. Draw a ball-and-stick model for methanol.

The following molecules apply to Problems 5 through 9.

a. HCN   b. PBr_3 c. BF_3 d. CCl_4

5. Identify the molecular shapes and bond angles of each molecule.

6. Molecules b. and c. both contain a central atom bonded to three other atoms. Explain why their molecular shapes are different.

7. Does molecule b. have the same shape as ammonia (NH_3)? Explain your answer.

8. Does molecule d. have the same shape as chloromethane (CH_3Cl)? Explain your answer.

9. For each molecule, identify the hybrid orbitals of the central atom.

10. Rank the following bonds from shortest to longest. Explain your reasoning.
a. C—C   b. Cl—Cl   c. C—Cl

11. Rank the following bonds from shortest to longest. Explain your reasoning.
a. O—H   b. O=O   c. S=S

Section 8-2

12. In each of the following molecules, describe the polarity of the bonds and the polarity of the molecule:
a. CH_4 b. CH_3Cl c. $CHCl_3$ d. CCl_4

13. In each of the following molecules, describe the polarity of the bonds and the polarity of the molecule:
a. NH_3 b. BF_3 c. Br_2 d. HCN

14. Carbon dioxide (CO_2) can be reacted with hydrogen atoms to form a compound called formic acid. The structure of formic acid is shown below.

$$H-\overset{\displaystyle\overset{O}{\|}}{C}-OH$$

Explain why carbon dioxide is a nonpolar molecule, while formic acid is a polar molecule.

PRACTICE PROBLEMS

Chapter 9

Chemical Reactions and Equations

Section 9-1

Events a, b, c, d, and e apply to Problems 1 and 2.

    a. Over several years, the iron in a chain-link fence reacts with the oxygen in the air, forming rust.

    b. In a high-pressure chamber, nitrogen gas and hydrogen gas combine to form ammonia gas.

    c. A glass of water is left outside on a cold day, and the water freezes.

    d. The pieces of a jigsaw puzzle are snapped together to form a completed puzzle.

    e. The pieces of a jigsaw puzzle are thrown into a fireplace and burned!

1. Which events describe chemical reactions? Explain your answer.

2. For the events that describe chemical reactions, identify the reactants and products.

Section 9-2

3. Compare the expressions $3 O_2$ and $2 O_3$.

Problems 4 through 6 apply to the following sentence:

    Liquid butane (C_4H_{10}) combines with oxygen gas to form carbon dioxide and water vapor.

4. Write the formula equation for the reaction described in the sentence.

5. Write the balanced chemical equation for the reaction.

6. Write the complete chemical equation for the reaction.

7. Potassium metal and bromine liquid combine to form potassium bromide. Write the balanced chemical equation for this reaction.

8. Calcium metal and chlorine gas react to form calcium chloride. Write the balanced chemical equation for this reaction.

9. Manganese (VII) oxide decomposes to form manganese metal and oxygen gas. Write the balanced chemical equation for this reaction.

10. Aqueous sulfuric acid and sodium hydroxide react to form sodium sulfate and water. Write the complete chemical equation for this reaction.

11. Balance the following chemical equation:

$$I_2 + Cl_2 + H_2O \rightarrow HIO_3 + HCl$$

Section 9-3

Use the following choices to answer Problems 12 through 14.

    a. $2 Al + 3 O_2 \rightarrow Al_2O_3$
    b. $3 Mg + 2 Fe(OH)_3 \rightarrow$
                        $3 Mg(OH)_2 + 2 Fe$
    c. $Ag_2SO_4 + CaCl_2 \rightarrow 2 AgCl + CaSO_4$
    d. $H_2O_2 \rightarrow H_2 + O_2$
    e. $2 CH_3OH + 3 O_2 \rightarrow 2 CO_2 + 4 H_2O$

12. Classify each reaction as a direct combination, decomposition, single-displacement, or double-displacement.

13. Classify reactions a. and d. when they are read backwards (from right to left).

14. In reaction b., suppose that magnesium (Mg) was replaced with gold (Au). Gold is one of the lowest metals on the activity series. Will reaction b. still occur? Explain.

15. In an aqueous solution, sodium iodide reacts with lead (II) nitrate in a double-displacement reaction. The reaction produces a solid product that is identified as lead (II) iodide. Write the complete chemical equation for this reaction.

Use the following paragraph to answer Problems 16 and 17.

Aluminum metal is placed in acetic acid (CH_3CO_2H). A reaction produces hydrogen gas. From radiolabeling, it is determined that the hydrogen gas comes from the hydrogen atoms in the hydroxide (—OH) group of acetic acid.

16. Write the complete chemical equation for the reaction.

17. Classify this reaction as a direct combination, decomposition, single-replacement, double-replacement, or none of these. Explain your answer.

Chapter 10 — *The Mole*

Throughout Chapter 10, use the atomic mass values listed in Figure 10-2 on page 312.

Section 10-1

1. How many atoms are found in exactly 12 grams of carbon-12? Describe the significance of this value.

2. Calculate the formula mass and molar mass of methane (CH_4).

3. Calculate the molar mass of magnesium hydroxide ($Mg(OH)_2$).

Problems 4 through 6 discuss boron trichloride (BCl_3).

4. Calculate the formula mass and molar mass of boron trichloride.

5. What is the ratio of the mass of chlorine to the mass of boron in this compound?

6. A sample of 8.0 grams of boron reacts with excess chlorine gas to form boron trichloride. What is the mass of the chlorine in the product? What is the total mass of the product?

7. Calculate the molar mass of copper (I) oxide and copper (II) oxide.

8. What is the ratio of the mass of copper to the mass of oxygen in copper (I) oxide? In copper (II) oxide?

9. How many atoms of hydrogen, sulfur, and oxygen are found in 1 mole of sulfuric acid (H_2SO_4)?

10. How many moles of hydrogen ions and sulfate ions are contained in 2.65 moles of sulfuric acid (H_2SO_4)?

Section 10-2

11. What is the mass of 2.77 moles of calcium chloride ($CaCl_2$)?

12. What is the mass of 2.58 moles of mercury (II) nitrate ($Hg(NO_3)_2$)?

13. Calculate the number of moles of potassium hydroxide (KOH) found in 100. grams.

14. How many lithium ions and carbonate ions are found in 3.4 moles of lithium carbonate (Li_2CO_3)?

15. A sample of iron (III) oxide (Fe_2O_3) contains 3.61×10^{24} formula units. How many moles of iron (III) oxide are in this sample? How many moles of iron ions are in the sample?

16. A 5.00-liter tank is filled with ammonia gas (NH_3) at STP. What is the mass of the ammonia in the tank?

Section 10-3

17. What is the percentage of carbon and chlorine in carbon tetrachloride (CCl_4)?

18. What is the percentage of carbon, hydrogen, and oxygen in acetone (C_3H_6O)?

PRACTICE PROBLEMS

Problems 19 through 21 use the following information:

A sample of a nitrogen-oxygen compound is found to contain 30.4% nitrogen and 69.6% oxygen.

19. How many grams of nitrogen and oxygen are found in a 8.50-gram sample of the compound?

20. What is the empirical formula for this compound?

21. Could the molecular formula for the compound be N_2O_4? Explain your answer.

22. Decomposing a 10.8-gram sample of a compound produces 5.6 g iron, 4.9 g oxygen, and 0.3 g hydrogen. What is the empirical formula of this compound?

23. A compound has molar mass of 60 g/mol. When a sample is decomposed, it produces 3.90 g carbon, 4.55 g nitrogen, and 1.30 g hydrogen. What is the molecular formula for this compound?

Chapter 11

The Mathematics of Chemical Equations

Section 11-1

Use the following reaction to answer Problems 1 through 3.

Aluminum metal and chlorine gas combine to form aluminum chloride.

1. To calculate stoichiometry problems on this reaction, what is the first step you need to do?

2. How many moles of aluminum will react with 9.0 moles of chlorine gas?

3. Suppose you want to produce 15.0 moles of aluminum chloride. Assuming the reaction goes to completion, how many moles of aluminum and chlorine should you use?

Use the following chemical equation to answer Problems 4 and 5.

$$I_2 + 5\,Cl_2 + 6\,H_2O \rightarrow 2\,HIO_3 + 10\,HCl$$

4. Wendy reacts 3.5 moles of iodine with excess chlorine and water. Assuming the reaction runs to completion, how many moles of iodic acid (HIO_3) and hydrochloric acid (HCl) will be produced?

5. Norman adds iodine and chlorine to a beaker of water. After the reaction runs to completion, he determines that 2.4 moles of hydrochloric acid (HCl) were produced. How many moles of each reactant participated in the reaction?

Section 11-2

Use the following equation to answer Problems 6 and 7.

$$2\,K + Cl_2 \rightarrow 2\,KCl$$

6. Ruth has 78.0 grams of potassium and excess chlorine gas. How many moles of potassium chloride (KCl) could she produce? How many grams of KCl is this?

7. Larry has 78.0 grams of chlorine gas and excess potassium metal. How many moles of potassium chloride (KCl) could he produce? How many grams of KCl is this?

Use the following equation to answer Problems 8 and 9.

$$3\,NO_2\,(g) + H_2O\,(l) \rightarrow 2\,HNO_3\,(aq) + NO\,(g)$$

8. Regina reacts 92 grams of nitrogen dioxide with excess water. How many grams of nitric acid and nitrogen monoxide are produced? Assume the reaction goes to completion.

9. In Darren's reaction, 7.50 grams of nitrogen monoxide are produced. How many grams of nitrogen dioxide participated in the reaction?

Use the following unbalanced formula equation to answer Problems 10 and 11.

$$BCl_3 + P_4 + H_2 \rightarrow BP + HCl$$

10. LaKeesha reacts 12.8 grams of boron trichloride (BCl_3) with excess phosphorus and hydrogen. Assuming the reaction goes to completion, how many grams of boron phosphide (BP) and hydrochloric acid (HCl) are produced?

11. Diane wants to produce 7.5 grams of boron phosphide (BP). How many grams of each reactant does she need, assuming the reaction goes to completion?

12. If 43 grams of calcium carbonate participate in the reaction shown below, how many grams of calcium oxide are produced? What volume of carbon dioxide is produced at STP?

$$CaCO_3 \, (s) \rightarrow CaO \, (s) + CO_2 \, (g)$$

13. According to the equation shown below, how many liters of oxygen gas at STP can react with 8.9 grams of iron? How many grams of iron (II) oxide would be formed?

$$4 \, Fe \, (s) + 3 \, O_2 \, (g) \rightarrow 2 \, Fe_2O_3 \, (s)$$

Use the following unbalanced formula equation to answer Problems 14 and 15.

$$C_6H_{14} \, (l) + O_2 \, (g) \rightarrow CO_2 \, (g) + H_2O \, (g)$$

14. How many liters of oxygen gas at STP are needed to react with 11.0 grams of hexane (C_6H_{14})? How many liters of carbon dioxide and water vapor are produced?

15. Compare the total volume of the reactant gases to the total volume of the product gases. Should these volumes equal each other? Explain your answer.

Section 11-3

Problems 16 through 18 refer to the following equation:

$$2 \, HCl + Ba(OH)_2 \rightarrow BaCl_2 + 2 \, H_2O$$

16. Mary concludes that because of the stoichiometry of the reaction, barium hydroxide ($Ba(OH)_2$) is always the limiting reagent. Is her argument correct or incorrect? Explain your answer.

17. Greg reacts 5.0 moles of hydrochloric acid (HCl) with 1.5 moles of barium hydroxide ($Ba(OH)_2$). Which reagent is the limiting reagent, and which is in excess? If the reaction runs to completion, how many moles of barium chloride ($BaCl_2$) will be produced?

18. Paula reacts 36.5 grams of hydrochloric acid (HCl) with 85.6 grams of barium hydroxide ($Ba(OH)_2$). Which reagent is the limiting reagent, and which is in excess? If the reaction runs to completion, how many grams of barium chloride ($BaCl_2$) will be produced?

Use the following equation to answer Problems 19 through 22.

$$3 \, FeO + 2 \, Al \rightarrow Al_2O_3 + 3 \, Fe$$

19. Sylvia reacts 5.3 moles of iron (II) oxide (FeO) with 3.2 moles of aluminum. Which is the limiting reagent? Assuming the reaction goes to completion, how many moles of each product are formed?

20. Ted reacts 250. grams of iron (II) oxide (FeO) with 67.0 grams of aluminum (Al). Which is the limiting reagent? Assuming the reaction goes to completion, how many moles of each product are formed?

21. In Ted's reaction (see Problem 20), the reactants have a total mass of 317 grams. However, this is not the total mass of the products. Account for the difference.

22. In Ted's reaction (see Problem 20), the actual yield of iron (Fe) is 137.0 grams. Calculate the percent yield of iron in the reaction.

Chapter 12

Heat in Chemical Reactions

Section 12-1

Use the following reaction to answer Problems 1, 2, and 3.

$$C_5H_{12}\,(l) + 8\,O_2\,(g) \rightarrow 5\,CO_2\,(g) + 6\,H_2O\,(g)$$

1. Predict whether this reaction is endothermic or exothermic. Explain your answer.

2. Which bonds are broken in this reaction? Which bonds are formed?

3. Describe how breaking and making bonds accounts for the energy change in this reaction.

4. Tin metal can react with chlorine gas to produce tin (IV) chloride. In the process, 511.3 kilojoules of heat are released for every 1 mole of tin. Is this reaction exothermic or endothermic? Write the balanced chemical equation for this reaction, and include the heat change in the equation.

Section 12-2

Use the following equation for Problems 5 and 6.

$$C\,(graphite) + O_2\,(g) \rightarrow CO_2\,(g)$$
$$\Delta H° = -393.5\text{ kJ}$$

5. How much heat is transferred when 8.03 grams of graphite are combusted with oxygen? Is the heat absorbed or released?

6. When performing this reaction on a graphite sample, a chemist measures a heat transfer of 1,530 kJ. How many grams of graphite combined with oxygen?

Use the following equation for Problems 7 and 8.

$$2\,FeCl_2\,(aq) + Cl_2\,(g) \rightarrow 2\,FeCl_3\,(aq)$$
$$\Delta H° = -125\text{ kJ}$$

7. How much energy is transferred when 80.0 grams of $FeCl_2$ combines with excess chlorine gas to form $FeCl_3$? Assume the reaction runs to completion. Is the energy released or absorbed?

8. How much energy is transferred when 80.0 grams of Cl_2 combines with excess $FeCl_2$ to form $FeCl_3$? Assume the reaction runs to completion. Is the energy released or absorbed?

Section 12-3

9. If a reaction has $\Delta H° = 250$ kJ, can you conclude that the reverse reaction has $\Delta H° = -250$ kJ? Explain your answer.

10. Use the data below to calculate the change in enthalpy when carbon dioxide gas (CO_2) decomposes into carbon monoxide gas (CO) and oxygen gas (O_2).

$$C\,(s) + O_2\,(g) \rightarrow CO_2\,(g)$$
$$\Delta H° = -393.5\text{ kJ}$$

$$2\,C\,(s) + O_2\,(g) \rightarrow 2\,CO\,(g)$$
$$\Delta H° = -221.0\text{ kJ}$$

11. $2\,As\,(s) + O_2\,(g) \rightarrow 2\,AsO\,(s)$
$$\Delta H° = 140.0\text{ kJ}$$

$$4\,As\,(s) + 3\,O_2\,(g) \rightarrow 2\,As_2O_3\,(s)$$
$$\Delta H° = -1587.6\text{ kJ}$$

Using the above data, calculate the change in enthalpy for the following reaction:

$$4\,AsO\,(s) + O_2\,(g) \rightarrow 2\,As_2O_3\,(s)$$

Section 12-4

12. The specific heat of aluminum is 0.89 $J/g \cdot °C$. How much heat is required to raise the temperature of 16 grams of aluminum from 25°C to 75°C?

13. When 198 Joules of heat are added to 5.0 grams of methane gas at $-10°C$, the temperature of the methane gas rises to 8°C. Calculate the specific heat of methane gas.

14. When 89.5 Joules of heat are added to a 15.7-gram sample of graphite, its temperature rises from 21.15°C to 29.13°C. Calculate the specific heat of graphite.

15. How much heat is transferred when 67.5 grams of methane gas (CH_4) is combined with excess oxygen gas in the following reaction?

$$CH_4 (g) + 2 O_2 (g) \rightarrow CO_2 (g) + 2 H_2O (g)$$
$$\Delta H° = -891 \text{ kJ}$$

16. How much heat is transferred when 18.2 grams of sulfur dioxide (SO_2) is combined with excess oxygen gas in the following reaction?

$$2 SO_2 (g) + O_2 (g) \rightarrow 2 SO_3 (g)$$
$$\Delta H° = -196 \text{ kJ}$$

17. In an insulated container, 95 grams of water at 20°C are mixed with 55 grams of water at 88°C. Assuming no heat is lost to the surroundings, calculate the final temperature of the mixture. (HINT: The heat gained by the cooler water must equal the heat lost by the warmer water.)

18. A 5.0-gram iron sample is heated to a temperature of 103°C, then dropped into 50. grams of water. The initial temperature of the water is 20°C. Assuming no heat is lost to the surroundings, what is the final temperature of the iron and water mixture?

Section 12-5

19. Use the kinetic theory to explain why a glass of warm milk becomes cooler when you put it in the refrigerator.

20. Why are calories and Joules different units that measure the same property?

Chapter 13

Gases

Section 13-1

1. A closed container of concentrated nitrogen gas is placed in one corner of a sealed room. A closed container of concentrated argon gas is placed in another corner. At the same instant, the containers are opened. Describe what happens to the gases.

2. A sample of carbon dioxide gas has a volume of 35 mL at STP. According to the kinetic-molecular theory of gases, how much of the volume is filled by the gas particles themselves? Explain your answer.

Section 13-2

3. The pressure of a gas is 892 torr. Convert this value to mm Hg, atmospheres, and Pascals.

4. The temperature of a gas is 35°C. What is the temperature in Kelvin?

Section 13-3

5. The gas in a 20.0-mL container has a pressure of 2.77 atmospheres. When the gas is transferred to a 34.0-mL container at the same temperature, what is the new pressure of the gas?

6. A piston is a closed container with a movable top. (Assume the top moves freely.) The gas inside a 42.5-mL piston has a temperature of 21.0°C. If the temperature is raised to 60.0°C, what is the new volume of the gas?

7. At STP, what is the volume of 2.9 moles of carbon dioxide gas?

8. A container filled with oxygen, nitrogen, and carbon dioxide gases is kept at 1 atmosphere of pressure. If the pressure of oxygen in the container is 0.56 atm, and the pressure of nitrogen gas is 0.23 atm, what is the pressure of the carbon dioxide gas?

9. An elastic container is inflated to a volume of 18.0 liters at a pressure of 1.26 atm. The container then expands to a new volume at a pressure of 1.05 atm. What is the new volume?

10. A 55-L container has a freely movable top, and is originally at 20°C. How high must the temperature be raised to increase the volume to 65 liters?

11. A 28.5-L tank of helium gas is kept at 42.0 atm. How many large balloons will the tank fill? Assume each balloon has a volume of 3.20 liters at a pressure of 1.10 atm, and that the tank and balloons are kept at the same temperature.

12. Suppose the pressure is tripled on a 27-liter sample of methane. Assuming constant temperature, what is the new volume of the methane?

13. Suppose the temperature of a gas is raised from 12°C to 112°C at constant pressure. By what factor does its volume increase?

Section 13-4

14. A sample of gas fills a 60-liter container at 298 K and 1.2 atm of pressure. How many moles of gas are in the container?

15. A 0.050-mole sample of gas fills a 1200-mL container at −34°C. What is the pressure of the gas?

16. A closed kettle with a volume of 15 m³ contains 130 moles of nitrogen gas, 78 moles of argon gas, and 48 moles of carbon dioxide gas. The temperature of the gases is 450 K. What is the pressure in Pascals? What is the partial pressure of each gas?

17. Carbonic acid provides the "fizz" in carbonated beverages. Carbonic acid is made by combining carbon dioxide and water. The equation for this reaction is:

$$H_2O \ (l) + CO_2(g) \rightarrow H_2CO_3 \ (aq)$$

If carbon dioxide is kept in 35-liter canisters at a pressure of 2.8 atm and a temperature of 20°C, how many grams of carbonic acid can be made from one canister of carbon dioxide? Assume the reaction goes to completion.

Section 13-5

For Problems 18 through 20, use the equation $d = PM/RT$, where d is density and M is molar mass.

18. Calculate the density of hydrogen gas (H_2) at a temperature of 20°C and a pressure of 1.0 atmospheres.

19. How hot must helium gas be for it to have a density of 0.15 g/L? Assume a pressure of 1.0 atmosphere.

20. At what pressure will oxygen gas have a density of 1.00 g/L at 0°C?

Chapter **14**

Liquids and Solids

Section 14-1

1. Compare the intermolecular forces in methane (CH_4) and ethane (CH_3CH_3). Explain why ethane has the higher boiling point.

2. Compare the intermolecular forces in methane (CH_4) and chloromethane (CH_3Cl). Explain why chloromethane has the higher boiling point.

3. Compare the intermolecular forces in methane (CH_4), ammonia (NH_3), and water (H_2O). Explain why water has the highest boiling point and methane the lowest.

Section 14-2

4. Ethylamine ($CH_3CH_2NH_2$), ethanol (CH_3CH_2OH), and glycerol ($CH_2(OH)$ $CH(OH)$ CH_2OH) are all liquids at room temperature. Predict which liquid has the lowest viscosity and which has the highest. Explain your prediction.

5. Describe the intermolecular forces on the surface of a liquid. What phenomenon does this description explain?

Section 14-3

6. Cobalt (II) chloride hexahydrate ($CoCl_2 \cdot 6\ H_2O$) has a reddish color. A chemistry student pours a few grams of this compound onto a spoon, then heats it over an open flame. Gradually, the compound takes on a lavender color. Explain what occurred.

7. Why does solid sodium chloride conduct electricity in the liquid state, but not the solid state?

8. Describe the carbon-carbon bonds in the diamond form of elemental carbon. Use this description to explain the physical properties of diamond.

9. Why do ionic solids typically have high melting points, while molecular solids typically have low melting points?

Section 14-4

10. Use the concept of vapor pressure to explain why water boils at 100°C at a pressure of 1 atmosphere (760 mm Hg).

11. The heat of fusion of ice is 6.00 kJ/mol. Express this concept in terms of ΔH and a complete chemical equation.

12. The heat of vaporization of methane is 9.2 kJ/mol. From this information, can you calculate the heat of condensation? Can you calculate the heat of fusion? Explain.

13. The water vapor in a closed container has a temperature of 120°C. Gradually, the temperature is lowered to 20°C. Draw a heating curve for this process.

14. The triple point for carbon dioxide occurs at -57°C and approximately 5 atmospheres of pressure. Could you find liquid carbon dioxide at pressures below 5 atmospheres? Explain your answer.

Chapter 15 Solutions

Section 15-1

1. A typical carbonated beverage is a solution of water, carbon dioxide, sugar, and other substances. Identify the solvent and two solutes in a carbonated beverage.

2. One beaker contains a solution of salt and water, another contains a solution of sugar and water. Devise a procedure to determine which solution is which. Your procedure may not involve tasting the solutions.

Section 15-2

3. A 35.0-mL solution is prepared from 2.60 grams of NaCl and a sufficient amount of water. Calculate the molarity of the solution.

4. Mr. Daingen has a supply of 0.50 M KOH. How many grams of KOH are contained in 2.4 liters of this solution?

5. Lionel has a supply of 1.25 M H_2SO_4. For a chemical reaction, he needs 36 grams of

PRACTICE PROBLEMS

H_2SO_4. How many liters of the solution should he use?

6. A solution is prepared from 16 grams of acetic acid (CH_3CO_2H) and 1450 grams of water. Calculate the solution's molality.

7. Mohammed is studying a 3.66-m solution of sodium iodide (NaI). If the solution contains 350 grams of water, how many grams of sodium iodide are present?

8. LaGail has 45.0 grams of potassium acetate (KCH_3CO_2). To make a 0.50-m solution, how much water should she add?

9. A solution is made from 45 grams of nitrogen gas (N_2) and 40 grams of argon. Calculate the mole fraction of each component of the mixture.

10. A gas mixture contains 88 grams of oxygen gas (O_2), 88 grams of nitrogen gas (N_2), and 12 grams of nitrogen dioxide gas (NO_2). Calculate the mole fraction of each component of the mixture.

11. A gas solution is 41% carbon dioxide (CO_2), 41% water vapor (H_2O), and 18% methane gas (CH_4). The mixture contains a total of 19 moles. Determine the mass of each component of the solution.

12. Audrey is given 50. mL of 1.25 M KOH. To it she adds 125 mL of water. What is the concentration of the KOH solution?

13. Lai mixes 30. mL of 1.20 M HNO_3, 40. mL of 0.50 M HNO_3, and 30. mL of water. What is the concentration of the solution?

14. Wally has a stock solution of 2.8 M NaCl. He would like a supply of 0.70 M NaCl. How many liters of water should he add to 12. Liters of the stock solution?

Section 15-3

15. Fiona has a solution of ammonia gas and water at room temperature. She wants to liberate ammonia gas from the solution. How could she accomplish this?

16. Of potassium nitrate (KNO_3), hydrochloric acid (HCl), and sodium chloride (NaCl), which is the best candidate for forming a supersaturated solution? Explain.

17. The "fizz" in a carbonated beverage comes from dissolved carbon dioxide gas. Explain why a carbonated beverage gradually loses dissolved carbon dioxide once the container is opened.

Section 15-4

18. Water normally freezes at 0°C and boils at 100°C. Describe the changes in boiling and freezing point when sugar is added.

19. A sample of 0.59 moles of sucrose is added to 1.20 kilograms of water. Calculate the boiling point of the solution. (K_b for water is 0.52C°/m)

20. A sample of 140. grams of glucose ($C_6H_{12}O_6$) is added to 650. grams of water. Calculate the freezing point of the solution. (K_f for water is 1.86C°/m)

21. How many grams of glucose ($C_6H_{12}O_6$) should be added to 2.50 kg of water so that the freezing point of the solution is -1.50°C? (K_f for water is 1.86C°/m)

22. A sample of an unidentified molecular substance is dissolved in water. The boiling point of the solution is 101.37°C. What is the molality of the solution? (K_b for water is 0.52C°/m)

23. A chemist is trying to identify a certain solvent. He dissolves 29.0 grams of chloroform ($CHCl_3$) in 800. grams of the solvent, and calculates that its freezing point is lowered by 2.13°C. What is the K_f of the solvent?

24. Why will drinking seawater actually cause you to lose body water?

Chemical Equilibrium

Chapter 16

Section 16-1

Use the following to answer Problems 1 through 4.

In a reversible reaction, molecular oxygen (O_2) converts to ozone (O_3).

1. Write the complete chemical equation for the reaction.

2. A collection of ozone molecules are placed in a sealed box. According to the reaction, what will happen in the box over time?

3. According to the information provided, can you tell whether molecular oxygen or ozone is more prevalent at equilibrium? Explain your answer.

4. Suppose that you have the power to select and label individual oxygen atoms. When the reaction is at equilibrium, you decide to label 2 oxygen atoms that are bonded together in a molecule of O_2. After a few hours, are the 2 oxygen atoms necessarily still a part of the same molecule? Explain.

Section 16-2

Use the following reaction to answer Problems 5 and 6:

$$2\ NaHCO_3\ (s) \rightleftharpoons$$
$$Na_2CO_3\ (s)\ +\ CO_2\ (g)\ +\ H_2O\ (g)$$

5. Write the equilibrium expression for the reaction.

6. Is this reaction in homogeneous equilibrium or heterogeneous equilibrium? Explain your answer.

7. Compare the equilibrium constants for a forward reaction and a reverse reaction.

Use the following reaction for Problems 8 through 11:

$$CO_2\ (g)\ +\ H_2\ (g)\ \rightleftharpoons\ CO\ (g)\ +\ H_2O\ (g)$$
$$\text{at } 1727°C,\ K_{eq}\ =\ 4.40$$

8. Write the equilibrium expression for this reaction.

9. Which is greater at equilibrium at 1727°C—the concentration of the products or the concentration of the reactants? How do you know this information?

10. The reaction is carried out in a closed vessel at 1727°C. The concentrations of the reaction components are [CO] = 0.45 M, [H_2O] = 0.66 M, [H_2] = 0.10 M, and [CO_2] = 0.88 M. Calculate the reaction quotient, Q. Is the reaction at equilibrium? If not, in which direction will it proceed?

11. Assume the reaction is at equilibrium at 1727°C, and the following concentrations were measured: [CO] = 0.90 M, [H_2O] = 0.90 M, [H_2] = 0.53 M. What is the concentration of carbon dioxide?

Use the following reaction to answer Problems 12 through 14.

$$CO\ (g)\ +\ 2\ H_2\ (g)\ \rightleftharpoons\ CH_3OH\ (g)$$
$$\text{at } 430°C,\ K_{eq}\ =\ 290$$

12. Write the equilibrium expression for this reaction.

13. The reaction was carried out at 430°C. After a period of time, the concentrations of the components of the reaction were measured at [CO] = 0.250 M, [H_2] = 0.250 M, and [CH_3OH] = 4.53 M. Calculate the reaction quotient, Q. Is the reaction at equilibrium? If not, in which direction will it proceed? Explain.

14. Howard fills a reaction vessel with methanol gas (CH_3OH) only. He then raises the temperature to 430°C and waits for equilibrium. Juwan performs the same procedure, but replaces methanol with a mixture of hydrogen gas (H_2) and carbon monoxide (CO). Will the two reaction

vessels reach the same equilibrium position? Does the equilibrium constant apply to both vessels? Explain.

Section 16-3

Use the following paragraph and equation to answer Problems 15 and 16.

A chamber at 670°C and 1 atm of pressure contains three gases: phosphorous pentachloride (PCl_5), phosphorous trichloride (PCl_3), and chlorine (Cl_2). The reaction among these three gases is described by the following equation:

$$PCl_5\ (g) \rightleftharpoons PCl_3\ (g) + Cl_2\ (g)$$
$$\text{at } 670°C, K_{eq} = 0.076$$

15. Suppose the pressure of the chamber is raised from 1 atm to 1.5 atm. Use LeChatelier's principle to explain how the concentrations of the gases will change.

16. Suppose the temperature of the chamber is lowered from 670°C to 470°C. From the information provided, can you determine

how the contents of the chamber will change? If not, what further information do you need?

Use the following paragraph and equation to answer Problems 17 and 18.

Lionel places sulfur dioxide, sulfur trioxide, and oxygen gases into a reaction chamber at 1.50 atm of pressure and a high temperature. These compounds react with each other according to the following equation:

$$2\ SO_2\ (g) + O_2\ (g) \rightleftharpoons 2\ SO_3\ (g)$$
$$\Delta H° = -196\ kJ$$

17. Assume the pressure of the chamber is raised from 1.50 atm to 2.00 atm. From the information provided, how will the reagents change? Explain your answer.

18. Assume the temperature of the chamber is raised by 50°C. From the information provided, predict the effect of the temperature change. Explain your answer.

Chapter 17 Solubility and Precipitation

Section 17-1

1. Write the complete chemical equation for the precipitation reaction that produces $Fe(OH)_3\ (s)$.

2. The solubility product (K_{sp}) at 25°C for $Fe(OH)_3$ is 4×10^{-38}. Use this value to describe the extent to which $Fe(OH)_3$ dissolves in water at 25°C.

3. Write the solubility equilibrium equation for silver hydroxide ($AgOH$).

4. A sample of water is saturated with silver hydroxide. The concentration of both the silver and hydroxide ions is measured to be $1.4 \times 10^{-4}\ M$. Calculate the solubility product for silver hydroxide.

5. What are the equilibrium concentrations of copper (II) ion and sulfide ion when copper (II) sulfide (CuS) forms a saturated water solution at 25°C? ($K_{sp} = 6.3 \times 10^{-36}$)

6. What are the concentrations of the ions in a saturated solution of zinc hydroxide ($Zn(OH)_2$) at 25°C? ($K_{sp} = 4.5 \times 10^{-17}$)

7. What are the concentrations of the ions in a saturated solution of aluminum hydroxide ($Al(OH)_3$) at 25°C? ($K_{sp} = 2.0 \times 10^{-32}$)

Section 17-2

8. Albert dissolves some silver iodide (AgI) in hot water. The silver iodide dissociates

completely into ions. Albert measures $[Ag^+]$ to be 1.4×10^{-8} M. What further information does he need to predict whether silver iodide will precipitate from the solution once it cools to 25°C? Does he need to measure the concentration of iodide ions?

Use the following information to answer Problems 9 and 10:

The solubility product (K_{sp}) at 25°C for strontium chromate ($SrCrO_4$) is 3.6×10^{-5}.

9. Lucy completely dissolves 0.050 moles of strontium chromate in 2.5 liters of very hot water. She then lets the water cool to 25°C. Calculate the ion product. Will there be a precipitate? Explain your answer.

10. Ed completely dissolves 3.0×10^{-3} moles of strontium chromate in 850. mL of very hot water. He then lets the water cool to 25°C. Calculate the ion product. Will there be a precipitate? Explain your answer.

Use the following information to answer Problems 11 and 12.

Equal amounts of 1.00 M K_2CrO_4 and 2.50 M $AgNO_3$ are mixed at 25°C.

11. Explain why a precipitate forms in the mixture. Identify the precipitate.

12. Write the chemical equation that describes the reaction that occurs in the mixture.

13. Reggie mixes 82. mL of 4.0×10^{-4} M lead acetate ($AgC_2H_3O_2$) and 18. mL of 1.0×10^{-4} M sodium chloride (NaCl). Will a precipitate form? Explain your answer. (NOTE: K_{sp} for AgCl is 1.6×10^{-10})

Section 17-3

Use the following paragraph to answer Problems 14 through 16.

Bob stirs 2.0×10^{-8} moles of silver iodide (AgI) into 2000 mL of water at 25°C. The next day, he adds 1.4×10^{-8} moles of sodium iodide (NaI) to the solution. The solubility product (K_{sp}) for AgI is 1.5×10^{-16}.

14. Before Bob added the sodium iodide, was all of the silver iodide dissociated into the solution? Explain.

15. After Bob adds the sodium iodide, will any substance precipitate? If so, identify this substance. Explain.

16. Later, Bob adds more NaI, and significant quantities of AgI precipitate. Explain why this occurs.

Chapter 18 — Acids, Bases, and Salts

Section 18-1

1. Give one example of an Arrhenius acid and an Arrhenius base. Write the equation for the reaction between these two compounds.

2. Write the chemical equation for the reaction between zinc (Zn) and hydrochloric acid (HCl).

3. Write a reaction that demonstrates the definition of Bronsted-Lowry acids and bases. Identify the acid and base in your example.

4. The carbonate ion (CO_3^{2-}) acts as a Brønsted-Lowry base. What is the conjugate acid of the carbonate ion? Write a chemical equation that includes both the carbonate ion and its conjugate acid.

PRACTICE PROBLEMS

Section 18-2

Problems 5 and 6 refer to hydrochloric acid (HCl) and acetic acid ($HC_2H_3O_2$).

5. Compare the ways in which hydrochloric acid (HCl) and acetic acid ($HC_2H_3O_2$) dissolve in water.

6. Which is the stronger base—the chloride ion (Cl^-) or the acetate ion ($C_2H_3O_2^-$)? Explain your answer.

Use the following reactions to answer Problems 7 through 9.

a. PO_4^{3-} (aq) + H_2O (l) $\rightleftharpoons$
$$HPO_4^{2-} \text{ (aq)} + OH^- \text{ (aq)}$$

b. HPO_4^{2-} (aq) + H_2O (l) $\rightleftharpoons$
$$PO_4^{3-} \text{ (aq)} + H_3O^+ \text{ (aq)}$$

7. Identify the conjugate acid-base pairs in both reactions.

8. What property of water do reactions a. and b. demonstrate?

9. Write the equation for a reaction in which HPO_4^{2-} acts as a base, and water acts as an acid.

Problems 10 through 12 refer to boric acid (H_3BO_3), a weak acid.

10. Write the chemical equation for the dissociation of boric acid in water (losing one proton only). Then, write the expression for the dissociation constant.

11. Adelle dissolves 0.025 moles of boric acid in 460 mL of water. She then measures $[H_3O^+]$ to be 6.3×10^{-6} M. Using this information, calculate the dissociation constant (K_a) for the first proton of boric acid. (NOTE: Assume only the first proton dissociates from boric acid.)

12. Jack dissolves 1.96 moles of boric acid in 2.40 L of water. He then measures $[H_3O^+]$ to be 2.44×10^{-5} M. Using this information, calculate the dissociation constant (K_a) for the first proton of boric acid. (NOTE: Assume only the first proton dissociates from boric acid.)

Problems 13 and 14 refer to pyridine (C_5H_5N), a weak base.

13. Write the chemical equation for the reaction of pyridine and water. Then, write the expression for the dissociation constant (K_b).

14. Ursula dissolves 0.0250 moles of pyridine in 420. mL of water. She then measures $[OH^-]$ to be 1.03×10^{-5} M. Using this information, calculate the dissociation constant (K_b) for pyridine.

Use the following information to answer Problems 15 and 16.

The dissociation constant (K_a) for formic acid (HCO_2H) is 1.8×10^{-4}.

15. Write the chemical equation for the dissociation of formic acid in water, and write the expression for the dissociation constant.

16. Reggie places 0.35 mole of formic acid in 1.0 liter of water. Calculate $[H_3O^+]$. (Assume that the amount of formic acid that dissociates does not significantly change its initial concentration.)

17. Write the chemical equation for the reaction of methyl amine (CH_3NH_2) and nitric acid (HNO_3) in water. Is the product solution slightly acidic, slightly basic, or neutral? Explain.

Section 18-3

18. Name the acids with the following formulas:
a. H_2CO_3 b. $HClO_2$ c. HI   d. HNO_3

19. Name the bases with the following formulas:
a. $Mg(OH)_2$ b. CO_3^{2-} c. PO_4^{3-} d. NH_3

20. Rank the compounds listed below from the most basic to the least basic. Explain your answer.
CaO   NaI Na_2CO_3

PRACTICE PROBLEMS

Reactions of Acids and Bases

Chapter 19

Section 19-1

1. The concentration of H_3O^+ ions in a water solution at 25°C is 3.8×10^{-4} M. Calculate the concentration of OH^- ions in this solution. Is this an acidic, basic, or neutral solution? Explain your answer.

2. The concentration of OH^- ions in a water solution at 25°C is 1.8×10^{-2} M. Calculate the concentration of H_3O^+ ions in this solution. Is this an acidic, basic, or neutral solution? Explain your answer.

3. Calculate the pH of a solution in which $[H_3O^+] = 7.5 \times 10^{-4}$ M.

4. Calculate the pH of a solution in which $[OH^-] = 2.5 \times 10^{-8}$ M.

5. The pH of a water solution is 2.0. Calculate $[H_3O^+]$ and $[OH^-]$.

6. The pH of a water solution is 11.34. Calculate $[H_3O^+]$ and $[OH^-]$.

7. The dissociation constant (K_a) for formic acid (HCO_2H) is 1.8×10^{-4}. In a 1.50 M solution of formic acid, what is the pH?

8. In a 0.45 M solution of a monoprotic weak acid (HA), the pH is measured to be 4.25. Calculate the dissociation constant (K_a) for the acid.

Section 19-2

9. A buffer solution contains 1.0 M carbonic acid (H_2CO_3) and 1.0 M hydrogen carbonate ion (HCO_3^-). The solution has a pH of 4.74. Suppose that the concentration of both H_2CO_3 and HCO_3^- is raised to 2.0 M. Will the pH of the solution change? In what ways does the buffer solution change?

10. A buffer solution of volume 2.0 L is prepared with 1.5 moles of hydrogen carbonate ion (HCO_3^-) and 1.5 moles of its conjugate base (CO_3^{2-}). Calculate the pH of the buffer solution. (K_a for HCO_3^- is 5.6×10^{-11})

11. A buffer solution contains equal concentrations of formic acid (HCO_2H) and its conjugate base (CO_2H^-). The pH of the solution is 3.74. Use this information to calculate K_a for formic acid.

Section 19-3

Use the following paragraph to answer Problems 12 through 14.

A titration was performed on 45 mL of a solution of hypochlorous acid (HClO), a weak acid. The standard solution used was 0.50 M NaOH, and the indicator was phenolphthalein. When 82 mL of the standard solution was added, the solution turned from clear to a pale pink color.

12. Calculate the concentration of the hypochlorous acid (HClO) solution.

13. Like phenolphthalein, methyl orange is an acid-base indicator. Methyl orange changes from red to yellow around a pH of 4. Could methyl orange have successfully been used as an indicator in this titration? Explain.

14. Draw the general shape of the titration curve. Label the equivalence point.

Use the following information to answer Problems 15 through 17.

A titration was performed on 20. mL of a solution of methyl amine (CH_3NH_2), a weak base. The standard solution used was 1.20 M HNO_3. Instead of a chemical indicator, an electric pH meter was used. The equivalence point of the titration came when 35 mL of acid was added.

15. Calculate the concentration of methyl amine.

16. Draw the general shape of the titration curve. Label the equivalence point.

17. Would phenolphthalein have been a good indicator for this titration? Explain your answer.

Use the following information to answer Problems 18 through 20.

A titration was performed on 25 mL of a solution of sodium hydroxide (NaOH), a strong base. The standard solution used was 0.60 *M* H_2SO_4. Instead of a chemical indicator, an electric pH meter was used.

The equivalence point of the titration came when 9.0 mL of acid was added.

18. Calculate the concentration of the sodium hydroxide solution.

19. Draw the general shape of the titration curve. Label the equivalence point.

20. Phenolphthalein changes color at a basic pH, while methyl orange changes color at an acidic pH. Explain why either of these indicators could have been used in this titration.

Chapter

20 *Oxidation and Reduction*

Section 20-1

Reactions a., b., and c. apply to Problems 1 through 4.

  a. $H_2\ (g)\ +\ I_2\ (g)\ \rightarrow\ 2\ HI\ (g)$
  b. $HCl\ (aq)\ +\ NaOH\ (aq)\ \rightarrow$
                  $NaCl\ (aq)\ +\ H_2O\ (l)$
  c. $2\ CuO\ (s)\ +\ C\ (s)\ \rightarrow\ CO_2\ (g)\ +\ 2\ Cu\ (s)$

1. Which of the above reactions is an oxidation-reduction? Explain why oxidation-reduction does not occur in the other reaction(s).

2. In the oxidation-reduction reaction(s), identify the elements that are oxidized, and how their oxidation state changes.

3. In the oxidation-reduction reaction(s), identify the elements that are reduced, and how their oxidation state changes.

4. In the oxidation-reduction reaction(s), identify the oxidizing agents and the reducing agents.

5. Calculate the oxidation state of each element in the following compounds:
a. HNO_3 b. $KMnO_4$ c. H_2SO_4

6. Calculate the oxidation state of each element in the following polyatomic anions: a. $(CO_3)^{2-}$ b. $(PO_4)^{3-}$ c. $(CN)^-$

Use the following reaction to answer Problems 7 through 9.

   $4\ AsO\ (g)\ +\ O_2\ (g)\ \rightarrow\ 2\ As_2O_3\ (s)$

7. Is the oxidation state of oxygen the same in each compound? Explain.

8. Calculate the change in oxidation state of the arsenic and oxygen atoms in this reaction. Identify which is oxidized and which is reduced.

9. Identify the oxidizing agent and the reducing agent in this reaction.

Use the following reaction to answer Problems 10 and 11.

   $NH_4Cl\ (aq)\ +\ KNO_3\ (aq)\ \rightarrow$
             $N_2O\ (aq)\ +\ 2\ H_2O\ (l)\ +\ KCl\ (aq)$

10. Identify the elements that are being oxidized and reduced in the reaction. Calculate the changes in oxidation state for these elements.

11. Identify the oxidizing agent and the reducing agent in this reaction.

Section 20-2

12. For the following reactions, predict whether the reaction will proceed as written. For those reactions that do not proceed, predict if the reverse reaction will occur. Explain your reasoning.

a. $2 Na (s) + 2 H_2O (l) \rightarrow$
$2 NaOH (aq) + H_2 (g)$

b. $Pb (s) + MgCl_2 (aq) \rightarrow$
$PbCl_2 (aq) + Mg (s)$

c. $2 Al (s) + 3 Ag_2SO_4 (aq) \rightarrow$
$Al_2(SO_4)_3 (aq) + 6 Ag (s)$

13. For the following reactions, predict whether or not the reaction will proceed as written. Explain your reasoning.

a. $Fe (s) + CH_4 (g) \rightarrow FeCH_2 (aq) + H_2 (g)$

b. $2 NaCl (aq) + 2 HNO_3 (aq) \rightarrow$
$2 NaNO_3 (aq) + H_2 (g) + Cl_2 (g)$

c. $2 Al (s) + 6 H_2O (l) \rightarrow$
$2 Al(OH)_3 (aq) + 3 H_2 (g)$

Section 20-3

14. Why does a magnesium coat prevent iron from corroding?

15. Why do bleaches remove bright colors from clothing?

16. Suppose you tried to drive an ordinary car on the moon. Would it run? Explain your answer.

Section 20-4

17. Write the balanced equation for the reaction between iron and oxygen, producing iron (III) oxide. Identify the elements being oxidized and reduced.

18. Write the balanced chemical reaction for the reaction below. Identify the atoms being oxidized and reduced.

$Cl_2O_5 + CO \rightarrow Cl_2 + CO_2$

19. Write the balanced chemical reaction for the reaction below. Identify the atoms being oxidized and reduced.

$H_2SO_4 + NaBr \rightarrow$
$Na_2SO_4 + Br_2 + SO_2 + H_2O$

Chapter 21 Electrochemistry

Section 21-1

1. Which of the following solutions conducts electricity best—pure water, 1.0 M glucose, or 1.0 M NaCl? Explain your answer.

2. Susie wants to use an electrochemical cell to create sodium metal (Na) from a supply of sodium ions (Na$^+$). Should she use a voltaic cell or an electrolytic cell? Explain your answer.

3. What is an electrode? Describe the purpose of electrodes in an electrochemical cell.

Section 21-2

Problems 4 through 12 refer to the following paragraph and data. For each question, briefly explain how you determined your answer.

An electrochemical cell is set up with a lead (Pb) electrode in one half-cell and a

nickel (Ni) electrode in the other half-cell. Surrounding the lead electrode is a bath of 1.0 M PbSO$_4$, and surrounding the nickel electrode is a bath of 1.0 M NiSO$_4$. A salt bridge connects the two half-cells, and a wire connects the two electrodes.

Standard reduction potentials:

$Pb^{2+} + 2 e^- \rightarrow Pb (s)$ $E° = -0.13 V$
$Ni^{2+} + 2 e^- \rightarrow Ni (s)$ $E° = -0.26 V$

4. Is this electrochemical cell a voltaic cell or an electrolytic cell?

5. Which metal—lead or nickel—is more easily reduced?

6. Does oxidation or reduction occur at the lead electrode? Does oxidation or reduction occur at the nickel electrode?

7. Which of the two electrodes is the anode? Which is the cathode?

PRACTICE PROBLEMS

8. Which electrode is positive? Which is negative?

9. Write the equations for the two half-reactions, and calculate E°_{cell}.

10. Draw a model of the electrochemical cell. Label the anode and cathode and show the reactions that occur at each. Indicate the movement of electrons across the wire.

11. Describe the changes in the electrochemical cell over time. Will the electrochemical cell run without end?

12. As the electrochemical cell runs, what chemical changes do the sulfate ions $(SO_4)^{2-}$ undergo?

Use the following paragraph to answer Problems 13 and 14.

A voltaic cell is made with a copper (Cu) electrode in 1.0 M $CuCl_2$, and a zinc (Zn) electrode in 1.0 M $ZnCl_2$. The standard reduction potentials are as follows:

$Cu^{2+} + 2\,e^- \rightarrow Cu\ (s)$ $E^{\circ} = +0.34$ V
$Zn^{2+} + 2\,e^- \rightarrow Zn\ (s)$ $E^{\circ} = -0.76$ V

13. Write the equations for the reactions that occur at the anode and cathode, and calculate E°_{cell}.

14. Draw a picture of the electrochemical cell. Label the cathode and electrode, and show the reactions that occur there. Show the direction of the electrons across the wire.

Use the following information to answer Problems 15 and 16.

A voltmeter is attached to a voltaic cell, and it reads 0.48 V. In one half-cell, cobalt ions (Co^{2+}) in a standard solution are depositing as cobalt metal on an electrode. In the other electrode is a zinc electrode in a standard solution.

Standard reduction potential:

$Zn^{2+} + 2\,e^- \rightarrow Zn\ (s)$ $E^{\circ} = -0.76$ V

15. Identify the cathode and anode in this electrochemical cell. Explain how you determined your answer.

16. Calculate the standard reduction potential for the reaction $Co^{2+} + 2\,e^- \rightarrow Co\ (s)$.

Section 21-3

17. List three disadvantages of common dry cell batteries.

Use the following paragraph to answer Problems 18 and 19.

Lead storage batteries rely on lead in three forms: Pb, $PbSO_4$, and PbO_2. When the battery discharges, lead is the only element that changes oxidation state.

18. Calculate the oxidation state of lead in each of the three forms.

19. When a lead storage battery discharges, the concentration of which form of lead increases? Which form decreases? Explain your answer.

Section 21-4

20. List three applications of electrolysis.

21. Why does adding a small amount of acid or base help speed up the electrolysis of water?

Chapter 22 *Rates of Reaction*

Section 22-1

1. Assume that both reactions A and B are reversible. The equilibrium constant (K_{eq}) for reaction A is 4.3×10^2; for reaction B it is 1.4×10^{14}. From this information, can you determine which reaction proceeds at the faster rate? Explain your answer.

2. From the information provided below, can

PRACTICE PROBLEMS

you calculate the rate of formation of methanol (CH_3OH) from carbon monoxide and hydrogen gas? Explain.

$$CO\ (g) + 2\ H_2\ (g) \rightleftharpoons CH_3OH\ (g)$$
$$\text{at } 430\ °C,\ K_{eq} = 290$$

Use the following data to answer Problems 3 through 5.

The following reactions represent a proposed reaction mechanism for the formation of triphenyl methanol ($C(C_6H_5)_3OH$) from triphenyl chloride ($C(C_6H_5)_3Cl$).

Step 1.
$$C(C_6H_5)_3Cl \rightarrow C(C_6H_5)_3^+ + Cl^-$$
$$\text{rate: slow}$$

Step 2.
$$C(C_6H_5)_3^+ + OH^- \rightarrow C(C_6H_5)_3OH$$
$$\text{rate: fast}$$

3. Write the equation for the net reaction.

4. What are the intermediate product(s) of the net reaction? Explain your answer.

5. Which step is the rate-determining step? Explain your answer.

Use the following information to answer Problems 6 through 8.

$$CO\ (g) + NO_2\ (g) \rightarrow CO_2\ (g) + NO\ (g)$$
$$\text{rate of formation of } CO_2 = k\ [NO_2]^2$$

Initial concentrations of CO and NO_2 in four trials of an experiment at 20°C.

Trial	[CO] (*M*)	[NO₂] (*M*)
1	0.50	0.50
2	1.00	0.50
3	1.00	1.00
4	1.50	1.50

6. Compare the rates at which CO_2 initially forms in each of the four trials.

7. In another trial of this reaction, the initial rate of formation of CO_2 is 25 times greater than in trial 1. What concentrations of the reagents would produce such a result?

8. In another trial of this reaction, the rate of formation of CO_2 is one fourth the rate in trial 1. What concentrations of the reagents would produce such a result?

Section 22-2

9. When a molecule of gas A collides with a molecule of gas B, the collision may result in the formation of gas C. Describe the factors that influence whether this result will occur.

10. In the reaction below, identify the activated complex. Which component of the reaction is the least stable? Which lasts the shortest amount of time during the course of the reaction? Which is represented by the highest portion of the energy diagram curve?

$$CH_3Cl + OH^- \rightarrow [OH—CH_3—Cl] \rightarrow$$
$$CH_3OH + Cl^-$$

Section 22-3

11. Suppose you want to burn a large log in your fireplace. Why will chopping the log into pieces make the log burn faster? Will burning the chopped log provide more heat than the whole log? Explain.

12. Reaction A is exothermic, with a change in enthalpy of −35 kJ/mol. When a catalyst is added to the reaction, will the change in enthalpy increase, decrease, or stay the same? Explain.

13. Do inhibitors work by providing a reaction with an alternate pathway of higher activation energy? Explain why or why not.

PRACTICE PROBLEMS

Chapter 23 — Thermodynamics

Section 23-1

Use the following answer choices for Problems 1 and 2.

  a. A lump of sugar slowly dissolves in a pitcher of water.

  b. A mixture of red and blue marbles separates into all red marbles and all blue marbles.

  c. Sodium chloride reacts to form sodium metal and chlorine gas.

  d. Water falls from a high place to a lower place.

  e. Water freezes on a hot summer day.

1. Which of the choices are spontaneous processes? Which are nonspontaneous?

2. Of the nonspontaneous reactions, which could be made to occur? In general, what needs to be done to make a nonspontaneous reaction proceed?

3. List three examples of nonspontaneous processes that occur in nature.

Section 23-2

4. Describe the difference between a positive ΔH and a negative ΔH.

Use the following data to answer Problems 5 and 6.

$$C_3H_8 \ (g) \ + \ 5 \ O_2 \ (g) \ \rightarrow$$
$$3 \ CO_2 \ (g) \ + \ 4 \ H_2O \ (g)$$
$$\Delta H° \ = \ -2043 \ kJ$$

5. Stu, a chemistry student, reacts 88 grams of propane gas (C_3H_8) with excess oxygen gas, yielding carbon dioxide and water vapor. He measures a heat change of slightly over 4000 kJ, which is nearly double the value of $\Delta H°$ for the reaction. Did Stu necessarily mismeasure the heat change, or otherwise introduce a significant error to his experiment? Explain.

6. Propane (C_3H_8) exists as a liquid at low temperatures. For the combustion of liquid propane, does $\Delta H°$ equal -2043 kJ? Explain.

Section 23-3

Use the following choices to answer Problems 7 and 8.

  a. An ice sculpture melts into a large puddle of water.

  b. A drop of green food coloring diffuses through cookie dough.

  c. The cards in a used deck are arranged in order from aces to kings.

  d. One end of a block of steel becomes hotter, while the other end of the block becomes colder.

  e. A grocery store clerk arranges 80 cans of beans into a pyramid.

7. Identify which processes demonstrate an increase in entropy, and which demonstrate a decrease in entropy.

8. Which processes require energy input for them to occur? Which processes do not require energy input for them to occur? Explain how entropy relates to your answer.

9. Describe three examples from nature of entropy increasing.

Section 23-4

Use the following reaction and paragraph to answer Problems 10 through 13.

$$CH_3CH_2OH \ (l) \ + \ 3 \ O_2 \ (g) \ \rightarrow$$
$$2 \ CO_2 \ (g) \ + \ 3 \ H_2O \ (g)$$

A novice chemistry student is researching the reaction shown above. From a reference source, he discovers that the change in enthalpy for the reaction is 1235 kJ/mol and the change in entropy is 0.22 kJ/mol · K. However, he neglects to record the signs (positive or negative) for these two values.

10. Does ΔH equal $+1235$ kJ/mol or -1235 kJ/mol? Explain.

11. Does ΔS equal $+0.22$ kJ/mol $\cdot$ K or -0.22 kJ/mol $\cdot$ K? Explain.

12. Calculate the change in Gibbs free energy (ΔG) for this reaction at 25°C. What information does ΔG provide? (Hint: When calculating Gibbs free energy, use degrees Kelvin.)

13. Will the sign of ΔG change when this reaction is conducted at different temperatures? Explain the significance of your answer.

Use the following reaction and data to answer Problems 14 through 17.

$$NH_4Cl\ (s) \rightarrow NH_3\ (g) + HCl\ (g)$$
$$\Delta H = +176 \text{ kJ/mol},$$
$$\Delta G = +98 \text{ kJ/mol at } 0°C$$

14. Is the reaction spontaneous at 0°C? Explain.

15. At 0°C, could the reaction be used to melt ice cubes? Explain.

16. Calculate the change in enthalpy for this reaction.

17. Could the sign of ΔG change at different temperatures? Explain the significance of your answer.

Chapter 24 *Applications of Nuclear Chemistry*

Section 24-1

1. The half-life of cesium-137 is 30 years. From a 64-microgram sample of cesium-137, how much cesium-137 would be left after 90 years? After 120 years?

2. The half-life of plutonium-239 is 2.4×10^4 years. From a 0.19-gram sample of plutonium-239, how much is left after 1.2×10^5 years?

3. The half-life of strontium-90 is 28.8 years. How many years would it take a 120-microgram sample of strontium-90 to be reduced to 7.5 micrograms of strontium-90?

4. Fill in the missing blanks from the following equation, which describes a nuclear bombardment reaction:

$$^{14}_{7}N + ^{4}_{2}He \rightarrow [\underline{\quad}] \rightarrow ^{17}_{8}O + \overline{\underline{\quad}}$$

5. Fill in the missing blanks from the following equation.

$$^{252}_{98}Cf + \overline{\ }_{5}B \rightarrow ^{258}_{103}Lr + 4\ \overline{\ }n$$

Use the following equations to answer Problems 6 through 10. (Note: $\underline{\quad}X$ is the same in both equations.)

Reaction 1: $^{238}_{92}U + ^{2}_{1}H \rightarrow \underline{\quad}X + 2\,^{1}_{0}n$

Reaction 2: $\underline{\quad}X \rightarrow \underline{\quad}Y + _{-1}^{0}e$

6. Fill in the missing blanks in these equations, and determine the identity of elements X and Y.

7. Is Reaction 1 an example of nuclear bombardment, nuclear fission, nuclear fusion, or none of these reaction types?

8. Is Reaction 2 an example of nuclear fission, nuclear fusion, alpha radiation, beta radiation, gamma radiation, or none of these reaction types?

9. Reaction 2 produces electrons. Is Reaction 2 an example of an oxidation reaction? Explain why or why not.

10. Would you expect further nuclear reactions to occur to the new element produced in Reaction 2? Why or why not?

PRACTICE PROBLEMS

Section 24-2

11. Compare the penetrating power of alpha, beta, and gamma radiation.

12. Why is injecting small amounts of iodine-131 an excellent way to determine thyroid function, with very little harm to the patient?

13. Why is gamma radiation used to treat some cancers? Why is it an imperfect treatment?

Section 24-3

Use the following equation to answer Problems 14 through 17.

$$^{235}_{92}U + ^{1}_{0}n \rightarrow ^{89}_{37}Rb + \underline{\quad}X + 3\,^{0}_{-1}e + 3\,^{1}_{0}n$$

14. Fill in the blanks and determine the identity of element X.

15. Why are neutrons included among both the products and the reactants in this equation?

16. Does the conservation of mass apply to this equation? Explain why or why not.

17. Describe the significance of the equation $E = mc^2$. Describe an application of the equation.

Use the following equation to answer Problems 18 and 19.

$$^{4}_{2}He + ^{9}_{4}Be \rightarrow ^{12}_{6}C + ^{1}_{0}n$$

18. Is this reaction an example of a nuclear bombardment, nuclear fission, nuclear fusion, alpha decay, beta decay, or gamma decay? Explain your answer.

19. Suppose you put helium and beryllium atoms in a high-pressure reaction chamber. Do you expect that carbon atoms would be produced? Why or why not?

 Chapter 25

Carbon and Its Compounds

Section 25-1

1. Why is C_2 not a stable molecule?

2. Why would oxygen or nitrogen atoms not be stable in the atomic arrangement found in a diamond?

3. Carbon can make single, double, and triple bonds with other atoms. Give an example of a carbon molecule for each of these bond types.

Section 25-2

4. Compare the urea (NH_2CONH_2) that Friedrich Wohler synthesized in his laboratory with the urea found in living things.

5. Are all carbon-containing compounds classified as organic compounds? Explain.

Section 25-3

6. Why are hydrocarbons typically found underneath the Earth's surface, and not on the surface or in the atmosphere?

7. What information does the molecular formula C_6H_{12} provide? What information does it not provide?

8. Draw two structural formulas for the molecular formula C_5H_{12}.

9. Draw two structural formulas for the molecular formula C_6H_{12}.

Section 25-4

10. Suppose a carbon molecule has 15 carbon atoms. How many hydrogen atoms would it have if it were a straight-chain alkane? If it were a branched alkane? If it were a cycloalkane?

11. Mary is studying a hydrocarbon. She proposes that the formula for the hydrocarbon is C_5H_{14}. Is Mary's proposed formula valid? Explain.

12. Your friend describes three hydrocarbons, which he names 2-methylpentane, 3-methylpentane, and 4-methylpentane. Draw structural formulas for each of these names. Are these three different compounds? Explain.

13. A novice chemistry student describes a compound he calls 1-ethylpropane. Draw a structural formula for this compound. What is the correct name for the compound?

14. A hydrocarbon has the formula C_5H_8. Could its molecules have only single bonds? Could it have one double bond, and otherwise only single bonds? Could it

have a triple bond? Draw a structural formula for this compound, and name the molecule you drew.

15. A hydrocarbon has one double bond, and all its other bonds are single bonds. It has 8 hydrogen atoms. Draw a structural formula for a molecule that fits these criteria. Classify the compound as an alkane, cycloalkane, alkene, or alkyne.

Section 25-5

16. Hydrocarbons can be used as fuels, or they can be made into plastics. In the future, which do you think will be the best use of hydrocarbons?

17. In your own words, describe the importance of recycling.

18. Why are fungi and bacteria important organisms for all living things?

Chapter 26 **Classes of Organic Compounds**

Section 26-1

1. Classify each of the following organic compounds as a halocarbon, alcohol, or ether.
   a. CH_3—$CHBr$—CH_2—CH_3
   b. CH_3—$CH(OH)$—CH_3
   c. $CH(CH_3)_2$—O—$CH(CH_3)_2$

2. Draw the structural formula for the pentane derivative in which a hydrogen on the third carbon has been substituted for an iodine atom. Name this compound.

3. Draw the structural formula for a cyclopentane derivative in which 2 chlorine atoms have substituted for hydrogen atoms on 2 adjacent carbon atoms. Name this compound.

4. How many isomers are there with the molecular formula C_2H_5Cl? Draw structural formulas and name each isomer.

Use the following structural formulas to answer Problems 5 and 6.

   a. CH_3—CH_2—CH_2—CH_2OH
   b. CH_3—$CH(CH_3)$—CH_2OH
   c. CH_3—$CHOH$—CH_3
   d. $C(CH_3)_3OH$

5. Classify each alcohol as a primary, secondary, or tertiary alcohol.

6. Name each compound.

7. Draw structural formulas for all the ethers with the molecular formula $C_4H_{10}O$. Name each of these compounds.

8. Give an example of an ether and an alcohol that are structural isomers. Name each compound.

9. Which has the higher boiling point—a three-carbon ether or a three-carbon alcohol? Explain your answer.

PRACTICE PROBLEMS

Section 26-2

The following condensed structural formulas apply to Problems 10 and 11.

Hint: To expand a condensed structural formula, remember that each carbon atom forms four bonds. For example, the "CO" group represents a carbonyl group ($C=O$).

a. $CH_3-CH_2-CO-CH_2-CH_3$
b. $CH_3-CH_2-CH_2-CO-CH_3$
c. $CH_3-CH_2-CH_2-COH$
d. $CH_3-CH_2-CH_2-CH_2OH$

10. Classify each of these compounds as a ketone, aldehyde, or another class of organic compound.

11. Name the ketones and aldehydes represented in this list.

Use the following paragraph to answer Problems 12 and 13.

In a procedure called ozonolysis, alkenes are broken apart by ozone (O_3). When the procedure is complete, a carbon atom that was a part of a carbon-carbon double bond becomes part of a carbonyl group instead.

A chemistry professor performs ozonolysis on 2-methyl, 2-butene ($CH_3-C(CH_3)=CH-CH_3$)

12. Draw structural formulas for the two products of the ozonolysis reaction.

13. Name the two products of the reaction.

Section 26-3

Use the following equation to answer Problems 14 and 15.

$CH_3-CH_2-CH_2-COOH +$
$\qquad\qquad CH_3-CH_2OH \rightarrow$
$CH_3-CH_2-CH_2-COOCH_2-CH_3 + H_2O$

14. Name each of the compounds in this reaction.

15. Imagine you are conducting this reaction in the laboratory. Describe a simple way

to determine if the reaction is proceeding properly.

16. According to the Bronsted-Lowry definition, an acid is a hydrogen ion donor. In acetic acid (CH_3-COOH), which of the four hydrogen atoms is acidic?

Section 26-4

17. Like alcohols, amines are classified as primary, secondary, and tertiary amines. Draw structural formulas for amines that are examples of each of these classes.

Use the following structural formulas to answer Problems 18 and 19.

a. CH_3NH_2
b. CH_3OH
c. CH_3CH_3

18. Name each of these compounds.

19. Rank these compounds from lowest boiling point to highest boiling point. Explain how you determined the ranking.

20. An amide can form when a carboxylic acid undergoes a dehydration synthesis with an amine. Using structural formulas, write the equation that shows the synthesis reaction between propanoic acid and ethylamine, forming an amide.

21. A carboxylic acid can undergo a self-reaction to form a compound called an anhydride, which has two carbonyl groups separated by an oxygen atom. The reaction that produces an anhydride is a dehydration synthesis, because water is eliminated as two carboxylic acid molecules combine. Write the chemical equation for the dehydration synthesis of acetic anhydride from two acetic acid molecules.

Chapter 27 *The Chemistry of Life*

Section 27-1

1. Would the production of glucose from carbon dioxide and water be possible without an influx of energy? Explain your answer.

2. Compare ATP to a rechargeable battery.

3. Many environmentalists argue that the large-scale destruction of rain forests could damage living things all over the Earth. Discuss the logic behind their argument.

Section 27-2

4. Why can α-glucose and β-glucose readily convert to one another?

5. Animals are not able to produce all the enzymes necessary to digest cellulose. Why are cows able to digest grass, which is mostly cellulose?

6. Compare the amount of energy contained in equal masses of glycogen and starch.

7. In its ring form, is glucose a planar or 3-dimensional molecule? Explain.

Section 27-3

8. In ancient times, people used animal fats as fuel for lamps and torches. Why are fats good fuels?

9. Waxes serve as a waterproof covering for leaves and skin. Why do waxes repel water?

10. Compare the ratio of carbon, oxygen, and hydrogen atoms in lipids and carbohydrates.

Section 27-4

11. Describe the structural features that all amino acids have in common. What structural features differ among the amino acids?

12. In an acidic solution (such as at pH 2), the amino group of an amino acid acts as a base and gains a hydrogen ion from the solution. Draw the structure of glycine at pH 2. What is the net charge on glycine at this pH?

13. In a basic solution (such as at pH 11), the carboxylic acid group of an amino acid acts as an acid and loses a hydrogen ion to the solution. Draw the structure of glycine at pH 11. What is the net charge on glycine at this pH?

14. Using structural formulas, write the chemical equation for the dehydration synthesis of two amino acids into a dipeptide. What functional group does the reaction create?

15. Organisms assemble proteins one amino acid at a time. Why can the substitution or elimination of even a single amino acid significantly change the usefulness of the protein?

16. Why do you need to take in vitamin C regularly, but you can remain healthy without daily taking in vitamin A or vitamin D?

Section 27-5

17. DNA is made of only four nucleotides, yet it codes for 20 different amino acids. How is this possible?

18. Suppose you wanted to follow the path of a DNA molecule and the path of a protein molecule. Which elements in each would you label with radioactive isotopes? (Hint: Think of elements present in DNA or proteins, but not both.)

19. Among DNA, messenger-RNA, ribosomal-RNA, and transfer-RNA, which binds amino acids and joins them together?

One of the first lessons a chemist learns is that working in the laboratory can be an exciting experience. But the laboratory can also be quite dangerous if proper safety rules are not followed at all times. To prepare yourself for a safe year in the laboratory, read over the following safety rules. Then read them a second time. Make sure you understand each rule. If you do not, ask your teacher to explain any rules you are unsure of.

General Safety Rules

1. Read all directions for an experiment several times. Follow the directions exactly as they are written. If you are in doubt about any part of the experiment, ask your teacher for assistance.

2. Never perform activities that are not authorized by your teacher. Obtain permission before "experimenting" on your own.

3. Never handle any equipment unless you have specific permission.

4. Take extreme care not to spill any material in the laboratory. If a spill occurs, immediately ask your teacher about the proper cleanup procedure. Never simply pour chemicals or other substances into the sink or trash container.

5. Never eat in the laboratory.

6. Wash your hands before and after each experiment.

Dress Code

7. Many materials in the laboratory can cause eye injury. To protect yourself from possible injury, wear safety goggles whenever you are working with chemicals, burners, or any substance that might get into your eyes. Never wear contact lenses in the laboratory.

8. Wear a laboratory apron or coat whenever you are working with chemicals or heated substances.

9. Tie back long hair to keep it away from any chemicals, burners and candles, or other laboratory equipment.

10. Remove or tie back any article of clothing or jewelry that can hang down and touch chemicals and flames.

First Aid

11. Immediately report all accidents, no matter how minor, to your teacher.

12. Learn what to do in case of specific accidents, such as getting acid in your eyes or on your skin. (Rinse acids from your body with lots of water.)

13. Become aware of the location of the first-aid kit. But your teacher should administer any required first aid due to injury. Or your teacher may send you to the school nurse or call a physician.

14. Know where and how to report an accident or fire. Find out the location of the fire extinguisher, phone, and fire alarm. Keep a list of important phone numbers—such as the fire department and the school nurse—near the phone. Immediately report any fires to your teacher.

Heating and Fire Safely

15. Never use a heat source, such as a candle or burner, without wearing safety goggles.

16. Never heat a chemical you are not instructed to heat. A chemical that is harmless at room temperature may be dangerous when heated.

17. Maintain a clean work area and keep all materials away from flames.

18. Never reach across a flame.

19. Make sure you know how to light a Bunsen burner. (Your teacher will demonstrate the proper procedure for lighting a burner.) If the flame leaps out of a burner toward you, immediately turn off the gas. Do not touch the burner. It may be hot. And never leave a lighted burner unattended!

20. When heating a test tube, always point it away from you and others. Chemicals can splash or boil out of a heated test tube.

21. Never heat a liquid in a closed container. The expanding gases produced may blow the container apart, injuring you or others.

22. Before picking up a container that has been heated, first hold the back of your hand near it. If you can feel the heat on the back of your hand, the container may be too hot to handle. Use a clamp or tongs when handling hot containers.

Using Chemicals Safely

23. Never mix chemicals for the "fun of it." You might produce a dangerous, possibly explosive substance.

24. Never touch, taste, or smell a chemical unless you are instructed by your teacher to do so. Many chemicals are poisonous. If you are instructed to note the odor in an experiment, gently wave your hand over the opening of the container and direct the fumes toward your nose. Do not inhale the fumes directly from the container.

25. Use only those chemicals needed in the experiment. Keep all lids closed when a chemical is not being used. Notify your teacher whenever chemicals are spilled.

26. Dispose of all chemicals as instructed by your teacher. To avoid contamination, never return chemicals to their original containers.

27. Be extra careful when working with acids or bases: Pour such chemicals over the sink, not over your workbench.

28. When diluting an acid, pour the acid into water. Never pour water into an acid.

29. Immediately rinse with water any acids that get on your skin or clothing. Then notify your teacher of any acid spill.

Using Glassware Safely

30. Never force glass tubing into a rubber stopper. A turning motion and lubricant will be helpful when inserting glass tubing into rubber stoppers or rubber tubing. Your teacher will demonstrate the proper way to insert glass tubing.

31. Never heat glassware that is not thoroughly dry. Use a wire screen to protect glassware from any flame.

32. Keep in mind that hot glassware will not appear hot. Never pick up glassware without first checking to see if it is hot. See #22.

33. If you are instructed to cut glass tubing, fire-polish the ends immediately to remove sharp edges.

34. Never use broken or chipped glassware. If glassware breaks, notify your teacher and dispose of the glassware in the proper trash container.

35. Never eat or drink from laboratory glassware. Thoroughly clean glassware before putting it away.

Using Sharp Instruments

36. Handle scalpels or razor blades with extreme care. Never cut material toward you; cut away from you.

37. Immediately notify your teacher if you cut your skin when working in the laboratory.

End-of-Experiment Rules

38. After an experiment has been completed, clean up your work area and return all equipment to its proper place.

39. Wash your hands after every experiment.

40. Turn off all burners before leaving the laboratory. Check that the gas line leading to the burner is off as well.

The laboratory balance is an important tool in scientific investigations. You can use the balance to determine the mass of materials that you study or experiment with in the laboratory.

Different kinds of balances are used in the laboratory. One kind of balance is the double-pan balance. Another kind of balance is the triple-beam balance. The balance that you may use in your chemistry class is probably similar to one of the balances illustrated in this Appendix. To use the balance properly, you should learn the name, function, and location of each part of the balance you are using.

The Double-Pan Balance

The double-pan balance shown has two beams. Some double-pan balances have only one beam. The beams are calibrated, or marked, in grams. The upper beam is divided into ten major units of 1 gram each. Each of these units is further divided into units of 1/10 of a gram. The lower beam is divided into twenty units, and each unit is equal to 10 grams. The lower beam can be used to find the masses of objects up to 200 grams. Each beam has a rider that is moved to the right along the beam. The rider indicates the number of grams needed to balance the object in the left pan.

Before using the balance, you should be sure that the pans are empty and both riders are pointing to zero. The balance should be on a flat, level surface. The pointer should be at the zero point. If your pointer does not read zero, slowly turn the adjustment knob so that the pointer does read zero.

The following procedure can be used to find the mass of an object with a double-pan balance:

1. Place the object whose mass is to be determined on the left pan.

2. Move the rider on the lower beam to the 10-gram notch.

3. If the pointer moves to the right of the zero point on the scale, the object has a mass less than 10 grams. Return the rider on the lower beam to zero. Slowly move the rider on the upper beam

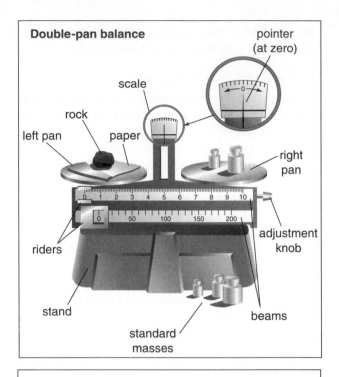

Double-pan balance

pointer (at zero)

scale

rock

left pan   paper

right pan

0 1 2 3 4 5 6 7 8 9 10
0   50   100   150   200

riders

adjustment knob

stand

beams

standard masses

Parts of a Double-Pan Balance and Their Functions

Pointer Indicator used to determine when the mass being measured is balanced by the riders or masses of the balance

Scale Series of marks along which the pointer moves

Zero Point Center line of the scale to which the pointer moves when the mass being measured is balanced by the riders or masses of the balance

Adjustment Knob Knob used to set the balance at the zero point when the riders are all on zero and no masses are on either pan

Left Pan Platform on which an object whose mass is to be determined is placed

Right Pan Platform on which standard masses are placed

Beams Horizontal strips of metal on which marks, or graduations, appear that indicate grams or parts of grams

Riders Devices that are moved along the beams and used to balance the object being measured and to determine its mass

Stand Support for the balance

until the pointer is at zero. The reading on the beam is the mass of the object.

4. If the pointer did not move to the right of the zero, move the rider on the lower beam notch by notch until the pointer does move to the right. Move the rider back one notch. Then move the rider on the upper beam until the pointer is at zero. The sum of the readings on both beams is the mass of the object.

5. If the two riders are moved completely to the right side of the beams and the pointer remains to the left of the zero point, the object has a mass greater than the balance can measure.

The total mass that most double-pan balances can measure is 210 grams. If an object has a mass greater than 210 grams, return the riders to the zero point.

The following procedure can be used to find the mass of an object greater than 210 grams:

1. Place the standard masses on the right pan one at a time, starting with the largest, until the pointer remains to the right of the zero point.

2. Remove one of the large standard masses and replace it with a smaller one. Continue replacing the standard masses with smaller ones until the pointer remains to the left of the zero point. When the pointer remains to the left of the zero point, the mass of the object on the left pan is greater than the total mass of the standard masses on the right pan.

3. Move the rider on the lower beam and then the rider on the upper beam until the pointer stops at the zero point on the scale. The mass of the object is equal to the sum of the readings on the beams plus the mass of the standard masses.

The Triple-Beam Balance

The triple-beam balance is a single-pan balance with three beams calibrated in grams. The back, or 100-gram, beam is divided into ten units of 10 grams each. The middle, or 500-gram, beam is divided into five units of 100 grams each. The front, or 10-gram, beam is divided into ten major units of 1 gram each. Each of these units is further divided into units of 1/10 of a gram. What is the largest mass you could find with a triple-beam balance?

The following procedure can be used to find the mass of an object with a triple-beam balance:

1. Place the object on the pan.

2. Move the rider on the middle beam notch by notch until the horizontal pointer drops below zero. Move the rider back one notch.

3. Move the rider on the back beam notch by notch until the pointer again drops below zero. Move the rider back one notch.

4. Slowly slide the rider along the front beam until the pointer stops at the zero point.

5. The mass of the object is equal to the sum of the readings on the three beams.

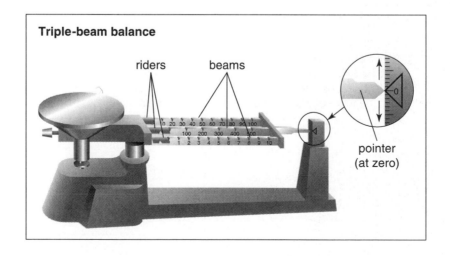

Triple-beam balance

riders   beams

pointer
(at zero)

APPENDIX C The Use of SI and Non-SI Units in Chemistry

Throughout your study of chemistry, you have encountered and will continue to encounter numerous properties of matter that are quantitative, or measurable. When a number is used to represent a measured quantity, the units of that quantity must always be specified. The units used for scientific measurements are those of the metric system, which is based on units of ten. Computations using metric units are relatively simple compared with those of the English system.

Metric-English Equivalents

1 km = 0.62 mi	1 kg = 2.2 lb	3.744 L = 1 gal
1 m = 39.37 in.	907.185 kg = 1 ton	1 L = 1.06 qt
1 m = 1.0963 yd	28.3 g = 1 oz	250 mL = 1 c
1 cm = 0.39370 in.	453.59 g = 1 lb	°C = 5/9 × (°F − 32)
101,325 Pa = 1 atm	4.184 J = 1 cal	

Within the metric system, more than one unit can be used to describe the same property. Different scientists, therefore, might use different units to measure the same quantity, making communication difficult. This problem was solved by an international agreement among scientists to use only certain metric units. This subgroup of preferred metric units is known as SI units (from the French *Système International d'Unités*). There are seven fundamental SI units from which all other necessary units can be derived. The seven base units, the physical quantities they measure, and the abbreviation for each is shown below.

SI Base Units

Physical Quantity	Name of Unit	Abbreviation
mass	kilogram	kg
length	meter	m
time	second	s
electric current	ampere	A
temperature	kelvin	K
luminous intensity	candela	cd
amount of a substance	mole	mol

Prefixes are used to describe SI measurements and to convert among them.

The Prefixes Used with SI Units			
Prefix	Symbol	Meaning	Scientific Notation
exa-	E	1,000,000,000,000,000,000	10^{18}
peta-	P	1,000,000,000,000,000	10^{15}
tera-	T	1,000,000,000,000	10^{12}
giga-	G	1,000,000,000	10^{9}
mega-	M	1,000,000	10^{6}
kilo-	k	1,000	10^{3}
hecto-	h	100	10^{2}
deka-	da	10	10^{1}
—	—	1	10^{0}
deci-	d	0.1	10^{-1}
centi-	c	0.01	10^{-2}
milli-	m	0.001	10^{-3}
micro-	μ	0.000 001	10^{-6}
nano-	n	0.000 000 001	10^{-9}
pico-	p	0.000 000 000 001	10^{-12}
femto-	f	0.000 000 000 000 001	10^{-15}
atto-	a	0.000 000 000 000 000 001	10^{-18}

As with any change, switching from one system of measurement units to another comes about slowly. So although non-SI units are being phased out, there are still some that are commonly used by scientists. You have encountered most of these non-SI units in this textbook as well as in your daily life. When you see or use these units, you must recognize that they are not SI units and are not as universally understandable as their SI counterparts. And someday, these non-SI units may be uncommon as well.

Common Non-SI Units		
Physical Quantity	Non-SI Unit	SI Unit
volume	liter, L	cubic meter, m^3
pressure	atmosphere, atm	pascal, Pa
	millimeters of mercury, mm Hg	
temperature	Celsius degree, C°	kelvin, K
heat energy	calorie, cal	joule, J

Throughout your study of chemistry, you will need to analyze or perform mathematical calculations. This refresher is designed to review those mathematical topics that may trouble you. You may wish to study this material before working on problems presented in the textbook. In addition, you may wish to refer to the folder in the Teaching Resources to review the operation of the scientific calculator and the graphing calculator.

FRACTIONS

Addition and Subtraction

To add or subtract fractions that have the same denominator, add or subtract the numerators, then write the sum or difference over the denominator. Express the answer in lowest terms.

Examples

$$\frac{3}{10} + \frac{1}{10} = \frac{3+1}{10} = \frac{4}{10} = \frac{2}{5}$$

$$\frac{5}{7} - \frac{2}{7} = \frac{5-2}{7} = \frac{3}{7}$$

To add or subtract fractions with different denominators, find the least common denominator. Write an equivalent fraction for each fraction using the least common denominator. Then add or subtract the numerators. Write the sum or difference over the denominator and express the answer in lowest terms.

Examples

$$\frac{1}{3} + \frac{3}{5} = \frac{5}{15} + \frac{9}{15} = \frac{5+9}{15} = \frac{14}{15}$$

$$\frac{7}{8} - \frac{1}{4} = \frac{7}{8} - \frac{2}{8} = \frac{7-2}{8} = \frac{5}{8}$$

Multiplication

To multiply two or more fractions, multiply the numerators to obtain the numerator of the product. Then multiply the denominators to obtain the denominator of the product. Whenever possible, divide any numerator and denominator by their greatest common factor before multiplying. Express the answer in lowest terms.

Examples

$$\frac{3}{5} \times \frac{2}{7} = \frac{3 \times 2}{5 \times 7} = \frac{6}{35}$$

$$\frac{1}{\overset{}{\underset{2}{4}}} \times \frac{\overset{3}{6}}{9} = \frac{1 \times 3}{2 \times 9} = \frac{3}{18} = \frac{1}{6}$$

Division

To divide one fraction by another, invert the divisor and then multiply the two fractions. Express the answer in lowest terms.

Examples

$$\frac{2}{5} \div \frac{3}{4} = \frac{2}{5} \times \frac{4}{3} = \frac{2 \times 4}{5 \times 3} = \frac{8}{15}$$

$$\frac{9}{16} \div \frac{5}{8} = \frac{9}{\underset{2}{16}} \times \frac{\overset{1}{8}}{5} = \frac{9 \times 1}{2 \times 5} = \frac{9}{10}$$

PERCENTS AND DECIMALS

To convert a percent to a decimal, write the number without the percent sign and move the decimal point two places to the left. Always add a zero before the decimal.

Examples

38% = 0.38
74% = 0.74
13.92% = 0.1392

When you know a decimal value of 100, you can convert the decimal to a percent by moving the decimal point two places to the right and adding a percent sign.

Examples

0.12 = 12%
0.46 = 46%
0.8215 = 82.15%

RATIOS AND PROPORTIONS

A ratio compares two numbers. A ratio is often written as a fraction in which the number being compared is the numerator and the number to which it is being compared is the denominator. The fraction is then expressed in lowest terms. A ratio may also be written with a colon.

Examples

Ratio of 3 to 4

$$3 \text{ to } 4 \text{ or } \frac{3}{4} \text{ or } 3:4$$

Ratio of 10 to 5

$$10 \text{ to } 5 \text{ or } \frac{10}{5} = \frac{2}{1} \text{ or } 2:1$$

A proportion is a mathematical sentence that states that two ratios are equivalent. To write a proportion, place an equal sign between the two equivalent ratios.

Examples

The ratio of 6 to 9 is the same as the ratio of 8 to 12.

$$\frac{6}{9} = \frac{8}{12}$$

The ratio of 2 to 4 is the same as the ratio of 7 to 14.

$$\frac{2}{4} = \frac{7}{14}$$

You can set up a proportion to determine an unknown quantity. Use X to represent the unknown.

Examples

What number is in the same ratio with 15 as 3 is with 9?

$$\frac{3}{9} = \frac{X}{15}$$

Two out of five students have blue notebooks. If the same ratio exists in a class of twenty students, how many students have blue notebooks?

$$\frac{2}{5} = \frac{X}{20}$$

To find the value of the unknown number in a proportion, cross multiply then divide both sides of the equal sign by the number that precedes X.

Examples

$$\frac{3}{9} \bowtie \frac{X}{15}$$
$$3 \times 15 = 9 \times X$$
$$45 = 9X$$
$$5 = X$$

$$\frac{2}{5} \bowtie \frac{X}{20}$$
$$2 \times 20 = 5 \times X$$
$$40 = 5X$$
$$8 = X$$

EQUATIONS AND FORMULAS

An equation is a mathematical sentence that contains a variable and an equal sign. An equation expresses a relationship between two or more quantities. A formula is a special kind of equation. A formula shows relationships between quantities that are always true. To solve for a quantity in an equation or formula, substitute the known values. Be sure to include units.

Example

Find the mass of a sample of aluminum with a volume of 5.00 cm^3 and a density of 2.70 g/cm^3.

$$\text{density} = \frac{\text{mass}}{\text{volume}}$$

$$2.70 \text{ g/cm}^3 = \frac{\text{mass}}{5 \text{ cm}^3}$$

$$5.00 \text{ cm}^3 \times 2.70 \text{ g/cm}^3 = \text{mass}$$

$$13.5 \text{ g} = \text{mass}$$

SCIENTIFIC NOTATION

You have learned that scientific notation is used to express a very large or a very small number. To express a number that is greater than 1, you can group the powers of ten together. One method of determining the correct scientific notation is to move the decimal point to the left until it is located to the right of the first nonzero number. The number of places the decimal was moved becomes the positive exponent of 10 in the notation.

Examples

2,500,000 be expressed as $2.5 \times 10^6 = 2.5 \times 10 \times 10 \times 10 \times 10 \times 10 \times 10$

18,930,000 can be expressed as
$1.893 \times 10^7 = 1.893 \times 10 \times 10 \times 10 \times 10 \times 10 \times 10 \times 10$

To express a number smaller than 1 in scientific notation, move the decimal point to the right until it is located to the right of the first nonzero number. Count the number of places the decimal point was moved and write this number as the negative exponent of 10.

Examples

0.000056 can be written as 5.6×10^{-5}

$$= \frac{5.6}{10 \times 10 \times 10 \times 10 \times 10}$$

0.0027 can be written as 2.7×10^{-3}

$$= \frac{2.7}{10 \times 10 \times 10}$$

To add or subtract numbers in scientific notation, the exponents of the numbers must be the same. If they are different, you must rewrite one number to make them the same. Rewrite the answer so that only one number is to the left of the decimal point.

Examples

Add 3.2×10^3 and 5.1×10^2.

$$\begin{array}{r} 32 \times 10^2 \\ +\,5.1 \times 10^2 \\ \hline 37.1 \times 10^2 \end{array} \rightarrow 3.7 \times 10^3$$

Subtract 5.4×10^7 from 6.8×10^8.

$$\begin{array}{r} 68 \times 10^7 \\ -\,5.4 \times 10^7 \\ \hline 62.6 \times 10^7 \end{array} \rightarrow 6.3 \times 10^8$$

To multiply or divide numbers in scientific notation, the exponents must be added or subtracted.

Examples

Find the product of 1.2×10^3 and 3.4×10^4.
$$(1.2 \times 10^3)(3.4 \times 10^4) = (4.08 \times 10^{3+4})$$
$$= 4.1 \times 10^7$$

Divide 5.0×10^9 by 2.5×10^6.
$$(5.0 \times 10^9) \div (2.5 \times 10^6) = (2.0 \times 10^{9-6})$$
$$= 2.0 \times 10^3$$

GRAPHING

It is often useful to make a graph of the results of a scientific experiment. There are several different types of graphs depending upon the type of data you are presenting—line graphs, bar graphs, and pie graphs. Line graphs will probably be used most often.

You will find graphing most convenient when the form of a graph is a straight line. For example,

suppose you have twenty small balls that each have a mass of 10 grams. Each time you add one ball to a container, the total mass increases by 10 grams. If you plot the number of balls on the *x*-axis and the total mass of the balls on the *y*-axis, the result will be a straight-line graph. The total mass increases 10 times as fast as the number of balls.

You plot the data by drawing a point on the intercept identified by the *x* and *y* values. For example, the total mass of the balls after you add the fourth ball is 40 grams. The intercept that identifies these values is (4 balls, 40 grams) or simply (4, 40). Count over to 4 on the *x*-axis and straight up to 40 on the *y*-axis. Repeat this procedure for all your data.

The equation for a straight line can be described as

$$y = mx + b$$

where m is the slope of the line and b is the point at which the line intersects the *y*-axis when the value on the *x*-axis is set to zero. The function $y = 2x + 4$ is plotted below.

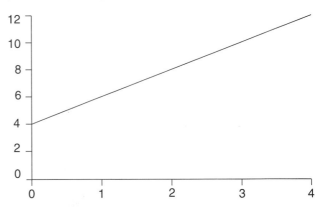

For this graph, the slope is 2 and the line intersects the *y*-axis at 4. In this example, the value of the *y* intercept increases twice as quickly as that of the *x* intercept.

Other data may result in graphs that are not straight lines. For these, you plot the data in a similar manner. However, you cannot predict additional intercepts on the graph from the line equation.

APPENDIX E *Important Formulas, Equations, and Constants*

Density (*d*)

$$\text{density} = \frac{\text{mass}}{\text{volume}} \qquad d = \frac{m}{V}$$

Percent Error

$$\text{percent error} = \frac{\text{measured value} - \text{accepted value}}{\text{accepted value}} \times 100\%$$

Percent Yield

$$\text{percent yield} = \frac{\text{actual yield}}{\text{expected yield}} \times 100\%$$

Percentage Composition

$$\text{percentage composition by mass} = \frac{\text{mass of element}}{\text{mass of compound}} \times 100\%$$

Planck's Equation

$E = h\nu$

where h is Planck's constant, E is energy, and ν is frequency

Kinetic Energy (KE)

$$\text{kinetic energy} = \frac{\text{mass} \times \text{velocity}^2}{2}$$

$$\text{KE} = \frac{mv^2}{2}$$

Gravitational Potential Energy (GPE)

gravitational potential energy = mass × acceleration due to gravity × height

$\text{GPE} = mgh$

Amount of Gas (*n*) in a Sample

$$n = \frac{\text{mass}}{\text{molar mass}} = \frac{m \text{ (g)}}{M \text{ (g/mol)}}$$

Boyle's Law

$P_1 V_1 = P_2 V_2$

Charles's Law

$V_1 T_2 = V_2 T_1$

Avogadro's Law

$V = k_3 n$

where k_3 is Avogadro's law constant and n is the number of moles

Dalton's Law of Partial Pressures

$P_T = p_a + p_b + p_c + \cdots$

Ideal Gas Law

$PV = nRT$

Molarity (*M*)

$$\text{molarity} = \frac{\text{moles of solute}}{\text{liters of solution}}$$

Molality (*m*)

$$\text{molality} = \frac{\text{moles of solute}}{\text{kilograms of solvent}}$$

Mole Fraction (*χ*)

$$\text{mole fraction} = \frac{\text{moles of solute or solvent}}{\text{total moles of solution}}$$

Boiling Point Elevation

$\Delta T_b = K_b m$

where K_b is the molal boiling point elevation constant

Freezing Point Depression

$\Delta T_f = K_f m$

where K_f is the molal boiling point elevation constant

Rate of Reaction

$\text{rate} = k[A]^x[B]^y$

where $[A]$ and $[B]$ are molar concentrations of reactants and k is a rate constant

Entropy Change

$\Delta S = S_{\text{products}} - S_{\text{reactants}}$

Gibbs Free Energy

$\Delta G = \Delta H - T\Delta S$

Avogadro's number	6.02×10^{23}
Speed of light in a vacuum	3.00×10^8 m/s
Atomic mass unit (amu)	1.66054×10^{-27} kg
Charge of an electron	1.60×10^{-19} C
Mass of an electron	9.11×10^{-31} kg
	5.486×10^{-4} amu
Mass of a proton	1.0073 amu
	1.6726×10^{-27} kg
Mass of a neutron	1.0087 amu
	1.6749×10^{-27} kg
Planck's constant (*h*)	6.6262×10^{-34} J-s
Gas constant (*R*)	0.08206 atm-L/mol-K
	8.314 Pa-m³/mol-K
	8.314 J/mol-K
Molar volume of a gas at STP	22.4 L

APPENDIX F   *The Chemical Elements*

THE CHEMICAL ELEMENTS WITH THEIR SYMBOLS, ATOMIC NUMBERS, AND ATOMIC MASSES

Element	Symbol	Atomic Number	Atomic Mass	Element	Symbol	Atomic Number	Atomic Mass
Actinium	Ac	89	227.0278	Molybdenum	Mo	42	95.94
Aluminum	Al	13	26.98154	Neodymium	Nd	60	144.24
Americium	Am	95	(243)[a]	Neon	Ne	10	20.1797
Antimony	Sb	51	121.157	Neptunium	Np	93	237.048
Argon	Ar	18	39.948	Nickel	Ni	28	58.69
Arsenic	As	33	74.9216	Niobium	Nb	41	92.9064
Astatine	At	85	(210)	Nitrogen	N	7	14.0067
Barium	Ba	56	137.33	Nobelium	No	102	(259)
Berkelium	Bk	97	(247)	Osmium	Os	76	190.2
Beryllium	Be	4	9.01218	Oxygen	O	8	15.9994
Bismuth	Bi	83	208.9804	Palladium	Pd	46	106.42
Bohrium	Bh	107	(262)	Phosphorus	P	15	30.97376
Boron	B	5	10.81	Platinum	Pt	78	195.08
Bromine	Br	35	79.904	Plutonium	Pu	94	(244)
Cadmium	Cd	48	112.41	Polonium	Po	84	(209)
Calcium	Ca	20	40.078	Potassium	K	19	39.0983
Californium	Cf	98	(251)	Praseodymium	Pr	59	140.9077
Carbon	C	6	12.011	Promethium	Pm	61	(145)
Cerium	Ce	58	140.12	Protactinium	Pa	91	231.0359
Cesium	Cs	55	132.9054	Radium	Ra	88	226.0254
Chlorine	Cl	17	35.453	Radon	Rn	86	(222)
Chromium	Cr	24	51.996	Rhenium	Re	75	186.207
Cobalt	Co	27	58.9332	Rhodium	Rh	45	102.9055
Copper	Cu	29	63.546	Rubidium	Rb	37	85.4678
Curium	Cm	96	(247)	Ruthenium	Ru	44	101.07
Dubnium	Db	105	(262)	Rutherfordium	Rf	104	(261)
Dysprosium	Dy	66	162.50	Samarium	Sm	62	150.36
Einsteinium	Es	99	(252)	Scandium	Sc	21	44.9559
Erbium	Er	68	167.26	Seaborgium[b]	Sg	106	(263)
Europium	Eu	63	151.96	Selenium	Se	34	78.96
Fermium	Fm	100	(257)	Silicon	Si	14	28.0855
Fluorine	F	9	18.998403	Silver	Ag	47	107.8682
Francium	Fr	87	(223)	Sodium	Na	11	22.98977
Gadolinium	Gd	64	157.25	Strontium	Sr	38	87.62
Gallium	Ga	31	69.72	Sulfur	S	16	32.066
Germanium	Ge	32	72.61	Tantalum	Ta	73	180.9479
Gold	Au	79	196.9665	Technetium	Tc	43	(98)
Hafnium	Hf	72	178.49	Tellurium	Te	52	127.60
Hassium	Hs	108	(265)	Terbium	Tb	65	158.9254
Helium	He	2	4.00260	Thallium	Tl	81	204.383
Holmium	Ho	67	164.9304	Thorium	Th	90	232.0381
Hydrogen	H	1	1.00794	Thulium	Tm	69	168.9342
Indium	In	49	114.82	Tin	Sn	50	118.710
Iodine	I	53	126.9045	Titanium	Ti	22	47.88
Iridium	Ir	77	192.22	Tungsten	W	74	183.85
Iron	Fe	26	55.847	Ununbium	Uub	112	(277)
Krypton	Kr	36	83.80	Ununnilium	Uun	110	(269)
Lanthanum	La	57	138.9055	Unununium	Uuu	111	(272)
Lawrencium	Lr	103	(260)	Uranium	U	92	238.0289
Lead	Pb	82	207.2	Vanadium	V	23	50.9415
Lithium	Li	3	6.941	Xenon	Xe	54	131.29
Lutetium	Lu	71	174.967	Ytterbium	Yb	70	173.04
Magnesium	Mg	12	24.305	Yttrium	Y	39	88.9059
Manganese	Mn	25	54.9380	Zinc	Zn	30	65.39
Meitnerium	Mt	109	(266)	Zirconium	Zr	40	91.224
Mendelevium	Md	101	(258)				
Mercury	Hg	80	200.59				

[a] Approximate values for radioactive elements are listed in parentheses.
[b] The official name and symbol have not been agreed to.

APPENDIX G Answers to Selected Problem Bank Questions

UNIT 1 THE NATURE OF CHEMISTRY
CHAPTER 1 Chemistry and You

Group A
39. 2.0 g/cm^3
43. (a) 1.348 milligrams (b) 3.56 kilonewtons (c) 0.0529 seconds (d) 0.081 watts

Group B
50. 16.0 g/cm^3; ring is not solid gold
52. density = 160 cars/km; rate = 42 cars/min
54. 17 cm^3
56. (a) 10.42 mm (b) 5.83×10^2 m^3 (c) 0.253 atm (d) 1.8×10^6 in. (e) 9.7×10^6 ms (f) impossible conversion

UNIT 3 INTERACTIONS OF MATTER
CHAPTER 9 Chemical Reactions and Equations

Group A
31. (a) Reactants: manganese and sulfuric acid. Products: manganese(II) sulfate and hydrogen
  (b) Reactant: silver chlorate. Products: silver chloride and oxygen
  (c) Reactants: chromium and oxygen. Product: chromium(III) oxide
33. (a) $NaOH + HCl \rightarrow H_2O + NaCl$
  (b) $2 Li + 2 H_2O \rightarrow 2 LiOH + H_2$
35. (a) $4 Li + O_2 \rightarrow 2 Li_2O$
  (b) $6 Ag + N_2 \rightarrow 2 Ag_3N$
37. (a) $2 Al + 3 Fe(NO_3)_2 \rightarrow 2 Al(NO_3)_3 + 3 Fe$
  (b) $2 K + 2 H_2O \rightarrow 2 KOH + H_2$
39. (a) $2 NH_3 \rightarrow N_2 + 3 H_2$; decomposition
  (b) $3 Ba(C_2H_3O_2)_2 + 2 Na_3PO_4 \rightarrow Ba_3(PO_4)_2 + 6 NaC_2H_3O_2$; double-replacement
  (c) $Zn + 2 HCl \rightarrow ZnCl_2 + H_2$; single-replacement
  (d) $2 Hg + O_2 \rightarrow 2 HgO$; direct combination
41. (a) single-replacement reaction
  (b) decomposition reaction
  (c) double-replacement reaction
  (d) direct combination reaction

43. (a) $2 K_3PO_4 + 3BaCl_2 \rightarrow 6 KCl + Ba_3(PO_4)_2$
  (b) $Ca + 2 H_2O \rightarrow Ca(OH)_2 + H_2$
  (c) $2 Al + 3 Cl_2 \rightarrow 2 AlCl_3$

Group B
44. (a) Reactants: copper and fluorine. Product: copper(II) fluoride.
  (b) Reactant: mercury oxide. Products: oxygen and mercury.
46. (a) $Mg + Cl_2 \rightarrow MgCl_2$
  (b) $SO_2 + H_2O \rightarrow H_2SO_3$
48. (a) $2 Cl_2 + 2 Na_2O \rightarrow O_2 + 4 NaCl$
  (b) $PbCl_2 + Ni \rightarrow NiCl_2 + Pb$
50. $C_3H_8 + 5 O_2 \rightarrow 3 CO_2 + 4 H_2O$

UNIT 4 STOICHIOMETRY
CHAPTER 10 The Mole

Group A
31. (a) atom (b) formula unit (c) molecule (d) atom (e) molecule (f) atom (g) formula unit (h) formula unit
33. (a) 3.76 mol H_2O (b) 3.570 mol $Ca(OH)_2$ (c) 0.956 mol SO_3 (d) 2.694 mol $NaNO_3$
35. (a) 28.2 g O_2 (b) 162 g $CaCO_3$ (c) 285 g CF_4 (d) 19 g $BaCl_2$
37. (a) 9.0×10^{23} molecules CH_4 (b) 6.98×10^{22} molecules NO_2 (c) 7.95×10^{23} molecules F_2 (d) 5.5×10^{23} molecules H_2
39. (a) 0.0444 mol Mg (b) 0.540 mol $FeSO_4$ (c) 1.54 mol O_2 (d) 13.6 mol NH_3
41. (a) 3.73 mol CO_2 (b) 0.705 mol NH_3 (c) 2.46 mol He (d) 1.54 mol H_2
43. (a) 40.0% Ca, 12.0% C, 48.0% O
  (b) 80.0 g Ca
45. (a) $C_7H_5N_3O_6$ (b) $C_7H_5N_3O_6$

Group B
46. (a) 7.8×10^{23} formula units $Mg(OH)_2$ (b) 8.88×10^{23} molecules H_2 (c) 6.97×10^{23} atoms Ag (d) 3.62×10^{22} molecules PCl_3
48. 1.67×10^{21} molecules $C_9H_8O_4$
50. 4.8×10^{27} gas particles
52. 470 mol C; 2.8×10^{26} atoms C
54. (a) C_3H_6O (b) $C_6H_{12}O_2$

CHAPTER 11 The Mathematics of Chemical Equations

Group A
29. 3 mol Cu
31. 12 mol H_2O
33. (a) Mass of both reactants and products equals 117.69 g (b) Mass of both reactants and products equals 326.2 g
35. 3.1 mol O_2
37. 226 g FeS
39. 182 g MgO
41. 8.8 L CO_2
43. 125 mL O_2
45. 4.5×10^{24} molecules H_2SO_4
49. 86.2%

Group B
50. $Mg(OH)_2$ is the more effective antacid. Each gram of this antacid neutralizes 0.0343 mol HCl.
52. 960 g Ca
54. 31.00 g Al
56. 373 L O_2
58. (a) 2.64 g Cu (b) 95.1%

CHAPTER 12 Heat in Chemical Reactions

Group A
35. Exothermic: a
Endothermic: b, c, d
37. Exothermic: a, c, d
Endothermic: b
39. −367 kJ
41. −6.795 kJ
43. −633 kJ
45. 63 J
48. 186 J

Group B
50. 13.2 kJ
52. −141 kJ
54. −200 kJ; 0.50
56. −56 kJ

UNIT 5 STATES OF MATTER

CHAPTER 13 Gases

Group A
27. More atoms will be present in the container of hydrogen gas because hydrogen gas ex-ists as diatomic molecules rather than single atoms as in helium gas.
29. 743 mm Hg
31. 102,000 Pa
33. 3.10×10^{-3} L/K
35. 8.63 mL
37. 16.9 kPa
39. 619 L
41. 23.0 L
42. CO has a faster rate of diffusion.

Group B
44. 6.8×10^4 L
46. 9.30 L H_2
48. $P_{N_2} = 0.90$ atm; $P_{O_2} = 0.24$ atm; $P_{Ar} = 0.012$ atm
50. 11.1 cm
52. 64 lb/in.^{2}
54. Slowest to fastest: d, b, c, a, e

UNIT 6 CHEMICAL EQUILIBRIUM

CHAPTER 17 Solubility and Precipitation

Group A
31. (a) $[Mn^{2+}][S^{2-}]$ (b) $[Cr^{3+}][OH^-]^3$ (c) $[Ag^+]^3[PO_4^{3-}]$ (d) $[Bi^{3+}]^2[S^{2-}]^3$
33. 5.04×10^{-3}
35. $[Ag^+] = [I^-] = 1.2 \times 10^{-8}$ M
37. $[Ca^{2+}] = 6.9 \times 10^{-3}$ M
$[OH^-] = 1.4 \times 10^{-2}$ M
39. 5.3×10^{-7} mol AgBr
41. (a) $BaSO_4$ (s) + 2 $NaNO_3$ (aq) (b) 2 NaCl (aq) + $Fe(OH)_2$ (s) (c) CaS (aq) + 2 KCl (aq) (d) $CaCO_3$ (s) + 2 LiC (aq)
43. $Q = 4.0 \times 10^{-62}$. The solution is not at equilibrium.
46. (c)

Group B
48. 5.0×10^{-13}
50. $[Ba^{2+}] = [SO_4^{2-}] = 1.0 \times 10^{-5}$
52. $Q = 6.1 \times 10^{-3}$. A precipitate will form.
54. $Q = 3.0 \times 10^{-6}$. A precipitate will not form.
56. $Q = 1 \times 10^{-6}$. A precipitate will not form.
58. $Q = 6.2 \times 10^{-5}$. A precipitate will form.

CHAPTER 19 Reactions of Acids and Bases

Group A

37. $[H_3O^+] = [OH^-] = 2.34 \times 10^{-7}$ *M*

39. (a) $[H_3O^+] = 7.1 \times 10^{-9}$ *M*; basic
(b) $[H_3O^+] = 1.7 \times 10^{-5}$ *M*; acidic
(c) $[H_3O^+] = 3.2 \times 10^{-7}$ *M*; acidic

41. (a) $[H_3O^+] = 1.0 \times 10^{-4}$ *M*
(b) $[H_3O^+] = 3.0 \times 10^{-6}$ *M* (c) $[H_3O^+] = 1.27 \times 10^{-3}$ *M* $[H_3O^+] = 1.41 \times 10^{-8}$ *M*

43. .002; 2.7

45. 4

47. (a) H_3O^+ (*aq*) + $C_2H_3O_2^-$ (*aq*) → H_2O (*l*) + $HC_2H_3O_2$ (*aq*) (b) OH^- (*aq*) + $HC_2H_3O_2$ (*aq*) → H_2O (*l*) + $C_2H_3O_2^-$ (*aq*) (c) Buffer solutions absorb a limited amount of H_3O^+ ions and OH^- ions, so the pH does not change.

49. 0.875 *M*

51. diprotic acid

53. Cyanic acid is a weak acid. In the titration of a weak acid with a strong base, the equivalence point falls in a basic pH range. Therefore, phenolphthalein is the best of the three indicators for this titration. Only phenolphthalein changes color over a basic pH range.

Group B

54. 2.5×10^{-5}

56. Answers will vary. Students should suggest that a solution with a pH of 0 contains a concentration of 1 *M* of H_3O^+ ions and 10^{-14} *M* of OH^- ions. A solution with a pH of -1 contains a concentration of 10 *M* of H_3O^+ ions and 10^{-15} *M* of OH^- ions.

58. (a) 4.30 (b) 6.60 (c) 6.0×10^{-9} (d) 1.3×10^{-5}

60. 1×10^{-3} g

Glossary

abbreviated electron configuration: shorthand notation describing the distribution of electrons among the energy levels of an atom

absolute zero: theoretically lowest temperature that can be reached, $-273.15°C$ or 0 K

accepted value: standard value for a measurement

accuracy: indication of how close a measurement is to its accepted value

acid: according to the Brønsted-Lowry definition, compound that donates a proton, or H_3O^+ ion

acid-base titration: procedure used to determine the acidity or basicity of a solution by adding a controlled amount of a solution of known concentration to a measured amount of a solution of unknown concentration

acid dissociation constant (K_a): constant that indicates the strength of an acid; derived from the equilibrium constant (K_{eq}) for the acid's dissociation in water

acidic hydrogen: hydrogen atom that an acid may lose as an H_3O^+ ion

activated complex: transitional structure that exhibits properties of both the reactants and the products of a chemical reaction, which is produced by an effective collision of particles

activation energy: difference between the energy of an activated complex and the energy of the reactants of a chemical reaction; energy with which particles must collide in order to react

activity series: list of elements organized according to the ease with which they undergo certain chemical reactions

actual yield: amount of product obtained from a chemical reaction

alcohol: hydrocarbon derivative in which one or more hydrogen atoms has been replaced by a hydroxyl group (R—OH)

aldehyde: hydrocarbon derivative in which a carbonyl group is located on the end of a hydrocarbon chain (R—CHO)

alkali metal: element in Group 1A of the periodic table (lithium, sodium, potassium, rubidium, cesium, and francium)

alkaline earth metal: element in Group 2A of the periodic table (beryllium, magnesium, calcium, strontium, barium, and radium)

alkane: hydrocarbon molecule with only single bonds

alkene: unsaturated hydrocarbon that contains at least one double bond

alkyne: unsaturated hydrocarbon that contains at least one triple bond

allotrope: form of an element that has a bonding pattern or arrangement different from other forms of the same element

alloy: solid solution in which the atoms of two or more metals are uniformly mixed

amide: hydrocarbon derivative containing an amino group attached to the carbon atom of a carbonyl group (R—CONH—R')

amine: hydrocarbon derivative in which an amino group is attached to a hydrocarbon chain (R—NH₂)

amorphous carbon: allotrope of carbon in which the atoms have no predictable arrangement

amorphous solid: solid in which the arrangement of the representative particles lacks a regular, repeating pattern

amphoteric: description of any substance that can react as either an acid or a base

amplitude: height of a wave measured from its origin to its crest

anhydrous substance: substance that is without water; often produced by removing the water from a hydrate

anion (AN-igh-ahn): negative ion

anode: electrode at which oxidation occurs

aqueous solution: solution in which the solvent is water

aromatic compound: organic compound that typically contains the characteristic benzene ring

atmospheric pressure: pressure exerted by the weight of air in the atmosphere

atom: smallest particle of an element that retains the chemical identity of the element; made up of negatively charged electrons, positively charged protons, and uncharged neutrons

atomic mass: weighted average of the masses of the existing isotopes of an element

atomic mass unit (amu): unit by which the mass of an atom or atomic particle is expressed; unit of mass equal to 1/1 the mass of a carbon-12 atom

atomic number: number of protons in the nucleus of an atom

atomic radius: distance between the center of the nucleus of an atom and the outermost electrons

atomic theory of matter: theory proposed by John Dalton stating that elements are composed of atoms, all atoms of a given element are identical but different from atoms of other elements, atoms are neither created nor destroyed in a chemical reaction, and a given compound always has the same relative numbers and kinds of atoms

Avogadro's number: number of representative particles in one mole; equal to 6.02×10^{23}

balanced chemical equation: chemical equation that uses coefficients to show that the number of atoms of each element that enters into a reaction is equal to the number of atoms of that same element produced during the reaction; shows that the mass of the reactants is equal to the mass of the products as described by the law of conservation of matter

ball-and-stick model: three-dimensional physical model of molecular shape in which a ball represents an atom, straight sticks represent single bonds, and curved springs represent multiple bonds

barometer: instrument used to measure atmospheric pressure

base: according to the Brønsted-Lowry definition, compound that accepts a proton, or H_3O^+ ion

base dissociation constant (K_b): constant that indicates the strength of a base; derived from the equilibrium constant (K_{eq}) for the base's dissociation in water

base unit: one of seven units used in the International System of Units, including the meter, kilogram, second, mole, kelvin, ampere, and candela

benzene: C_6H_6; stable cyclic hydrocarbon that exists as a hybrid of two resonance forms

binary ionic compound: ionic compound consisting of two elements

biodegradable: ability of a compound to decompose naturally over time

boiling point: temperature at which the vapor pressure of a liquid becomes equal to atmospheric pressure

boiling point elevation: colligative property in which the boiling point of a solvent is raised when a nonvolatile solute is dissolved in the solvent; directly related to the concentration of a solution

bond angle: geometric angle between two adjacent bonds in a molecule

branch carbon: carbon atom that is bonded to more than two other carbon atoms in a hydrocarbon

branched alkane: alkane molecule with at least one branch carbon

buffer: solution in which adding small amounts of acid or base does not markedly change the pH

buffer capacity: amount of acid or base that a buffer can neutralize

calorimetry: measurement of the amount of heat released or absorbed during a chemical reaction

carbohydrate: organic compound containing carbon, hydrogen, and oxygen in a 1:2:1 ratio; human body's main source of energy

carbonyl (KAHR-buh-nihl) group (—CO): carbon atom double-bonded to an oxygen atom

carboxyl group (—COOH): combination of a carbonyl group and a hydroxyl group

carboxylic (kahr-bahk-SIHL-ihk) acid: hydrocarbon derivative containing a carboxyl group attached to the end of a hydrocarbon chain (R—COOH)

catalyst: substance that increases the rate of a chemical reaction by lowering the activation energy without being chemically changed by the reaction

cathode: electrode at which reduction occurs

cathode ray: stream of electrons emitted by a negatively charged electrode and attracted by a positively charged electrode

cathode ray tube: evacuated glass tube in which a stream of electrons emitted by a cathode strikes a fluorescent material, causing it to glow

cation (KAT-igh-ahn): positive ion

cell potential: difference in the electrical potential energy between the two electrodes of a voltaic cell

cellular respiration: series of reactions in which glucose is oxidized to form carbon dioxide, water, and energy

cell voltage: description of cell potential, which is often measured in volts

chemical change: process by which the composition and properties of a substance change, thus altering the identity of the substance and producing a new substance

chemical equation: condensed statement that uses chemical formulas and identifies the reactants and products in a chemical reaction

chemical equilibrium: dynamic state in which the concentrations of reactants and products involved in a reversible reaction remain constant with time because the rates of the forward and reverse reactions are equal

chemical kinetics: area of chemistry concerned with the speed, or rate, at which chemical reactions proceed

chemical property: characteristic of a substance that cannot be observed without altering the identity of the substance

chemical reaction: process in which one or more substances are converted into new substances with different physical and chemical properties

chemistry: study of the composition and properties of substances, and the changes that such substances can undergo

coefficient: whole number that precedes a reactant or product symbol or formula in a chemical equation and indicates the relative number of representative particles involved in the reaction

colligative property: property of a solution that depends upon the concentration of the solute, but not its identity

collision theory: theory that suggests an explanation of chemical reactions based upon the collisions of particles and the orientation and energy with which they collide

common-ion effect: shift in solubility equilibrium that occurs when the concentration of an ion that is part of the equilibrium is changed

complete ionic equation: chemical equation that shows all soluble substances in a precipitation reaction as ions regardless of whether or not they participate in the reaction

compound: substance that contains two or more elements chemically combined in a fixed proportion

concentration: amount of solute dissolved in a given amount of solvent

conclusion: judgment or opinion formed as a result of analyzing experimental data

condensation: change of state from gas to liquid

condensed states: liquid and solid states of matter; states in which a substance has a substantially higher density than in the gaseous state

condensed structural formula: condensed version of a structural formula that does not include dashes to represent all the bonds in a molecule

conformation: structure of an organic molecule that differs from another structure by only one or more bond rotations

conjugate acid: acid formed when a Brønsted-Lowry base gains a proton

conjugate base: base formed when a Brønsted-Lowry acid loses a proton

conversion factor: fraction having a value of 1 that is written from a unit equality and is used to change a measurement from one unit to another

corrosion: gradual wearing away of a metal, as by rusting or by the action of chemicals

covalent bond: chemical bond resulting from the sharing of electrons between two bonding atoms

covalent-network solid: solid in which strong covalent bonds form a network extending throughout the solid

crystalline solid: solid in which the representative particles are in a highly ordered, repeating pattern called a crystal

curie: unit used in measuring radioactivity; equal to 3.7×10^{10} nuclear disintegrations per second

cyclic hydrocarbon: hydrocarbon with a carbon ring

cycloalkane: cyclic hydrocarbon with only single bonds

decomposition reaction: chemical reaction in which a single complex compound is broken down into two or more products; general form is $AB \rightarrow A + B$

dehydration synthesis: process by which two molecules are joined by removing a molecule of water

denaturation: process by which proteins are destroyed by breaking up their three-dimensional structure

density: mass of an object divided by its volume; can be used to identify a substance

deposition: conversion of a gas directly into a solid without first becoming a liquid

derived unit: unit in the International System of Units that results from a combination of base units

diamond: allotrope of carbon in which every carbon atom is bonded to four other carbon atoms in a tetrahedral pattern

diffusion: movement of one substance through another

dimensional analysis: technique for converting between units by using the numerical relationship between the units

dipeptide: molecule that can be hydrolyzed to form two amino acids

dipole: molecule in which the centers of positive and negative charge are not the same

dipole-dipole force: intermolecular force of attraction between neighboring permanent dipoles that is created when the dipoles line up so that the positive and negative ends are close to each other

direct combination reaction: chemical reaction in which two or more simple reactants join to form a single, more complex product; general form is $A + B \rightarrow AB$; also known as a synthesis reaction

disaccharide: compound composed of two monosaccharides; double sugar

dispersion force: intermolecular force of attraction between induced dipoles

dissolution: process in which an ionic solid dissolves in a polar liquid

DNA (deoxyribonucleic acid): nucleic acid that stores and transmits genetic information by coding for the production of proteins

dosimeter: device for measuring the total absorbed dose from exposure to ionizing radiation

double covalent bond: chemical bond resulting from the sharing of two electron pairs between two atoms

double-replacement reaction: chemical reaction in which atoms or ions from two different compounds replace each other; general form is $AX + BY \rightarrow AY + BX$

effective collision: collision between particles that leads to the formation of products

effusion: movement of atoms or molecules through an opening so tiny that they pass through one particle at a time into an evacuated chamber

elastic: ability of a substance or object to readily spring back to its original size or shape after being squeezed, hit, or subjected to similar disturbances

electrochemical cell: device that uses redox reactions to either produce or use electricity

electrode: substance through which electrons enter or exit electrochemical cells; made of metal and provides surface on which oxidation and reduction can occur

electrode potential: contribution to the overall cell potential by each electrode of a voltaic cell

electrolytic cell: electrochemical cell in which electrical energy drives nonspontaneous redox reactions

electromagnetic radiation: form of energy consisting of waves made up of oscillating electric and magnetic fields at right angles to each other

electron: negatively charged particle within an atom; has mass at rest of 0.00055 amu

electron affinity: energy change that occurs when an atom gains an electron

electron configuration: distribution of electrons among the orbitals of an atom

electron density: concentration of electrons in an electron cloud of an atom

electronegativity: property of an element that indicates how strongly an atom of that element attracts electrons in a chemical bond

element: substance that cannot be separated into simpler substances by a chemical change; simplest type of pure substance

elementary step: individual reaction in an overall reaction mechanism

empirical formula: chemical formula that gives the simplest whole-number ratio of atoms of elements in a compound

endothermic reaction: process that absorbs heat

end point: point in a titration at which an indicator changes color to show that equivalent quantities of acid and base have reacted

energy: capacity to do work or transfer heat

enthalpy (H): heat content of a system at constant pressure

entropy (S): quantitative measure of the disorder or randomness of a system

enzyme: protein molecule that acts as a catalyst

equilibrium constant: constant that relates the concentration of reactants and products of a reversible reaction (each raised to the power indicated by its coefficient in the balanced chemical equation) at equilibrium; indicates the extent to which a reversible reaction proceeds

equilibrium position: set of concentrations of reactants and products of a reversible reaction at equilibrium; varies according to initial concentrations

equilibrium vapor pressure: pressure exerted by a vapor in equilibrium with its liquid; point at which the number of molecules in the vapor state remains constant

equivalence point: point at which there are equal quantities of hydronium ions and hydroxide ions

ester: hydrocarbon derivative containing a carboxyl group in which the hydrogen atom is replaced by a hydrocarbon group (R—COOR')

ether: hydrocarbon derivative in which an oxygen atom is positioned between two carbon atoms in a hydrocarbon chain (R—O—R')

evaporation: process by which molecules of a liquid escape from the surface of the liquid and enter the gaseous, or vapor, state

excited state: energy level attained by an electron that absorbs additional energy and jumps from its normal level to a higher energy level

exothermic reaction: process that releases heat

expected yield: amount of product that should be produced by a chemical reaction according to stoichiometric calculations

experiment: carefully devised procedure for making observations and gathering data

experimental control: factor that remains constant during an experiment and is compared with the variable

family: vertical column of the periodic table that contains elements with similar electron configurations; also known as a group

fat: triglyceride that is solid at room temperature and that contains mainly saturated fatty acids

formula mass: sum of the atomic masses of all atoms in a compound as represented in a chemical formula; measured in atomic mass units

fossil fuel: fuel consisting of compressed, decomposed remains of ancient plants and animals; typically made of hydrocarbons

freezing point: temperature at which the solid and liquid form of a substance exist in equilibrium

freezing point depression: colligative property in which the freezing point of a solvent is lowered when a nonvolatile solute is dissolved in the solvent; freezing point depression is directly related to the concentration of a solution

frequency: number of waves that pass a certain point in a given amount of time

fullerene: allotrope of carbon in which the carbon atoms are arranged in a globe-shaped, cagelike arrangement that resembles the structure of a geodesic dome

functional group: atom or group of atoms that gives characteristic chemical properties to a class of organic compounds

gas: state in which matter has no definite shape or volume

gas constant (R): universal constant represented by R in the ideal gas equation ($PV = nRT$); equal to 0.08206 atm-L/mol-K, or 8.314 J/mol-K

Geiger counter: device that can be used to detect and measure radioactivity

gene: sequence of bases on a DNA chain where the genetic instructions for making a specific protein are encoded

general formula: formula that represents a large class of compounds and uses variables, rather than numbers, as subscripts

geometric isomer: isomer that has the same sequence of atoms and bonds as another molecule, but a different orientation in space; also called stereoisomer

Gibbs free energy (G): energy equal to the energy change for a reaction minus the product of its entropy change times the absolute temperature ($\Delta G = \Delta H - T\Delta S$)

graphite: allotrope of carbon in which carbon atoms are arranged in sheets or layers

ground state: lowest energy level of electrons in an atom

group: vertical column of the periodic table that contains elements with similar electron configurations; also known as a family

Haber process: chemical process that utilizes Le Chatelier's principle to produce ammonia commercially from nitrogen gas and hydrogen gas

half-cell: container in which a half reaction of a redox reaction occurs

half-life: length of time required for half of a given sample of a radioisotope to decay

halocarbon: hydrocarbon derivative in which one or more hydrogen atoms has been replaced by an atom of a halogen element (R—X)

halogen: reactive, nonmetallic element in Group 7A of the periodic table (fluorine, chlorine, bromine, iodine, and astatine)

heat capacity: amount of heat energy needed to raise the temperature of a given sample of matter by 1 C°

heating curve: plot of the temperature of a sample as a function of time

heat of fusion: heat necessary to convert a given amount of a solid into a liquid

heat of vaporization: amount of heat necessary to vaporize a given amount of liquid

heterogeneous equilibrium: equilibrium condition for a reaction in which all the reactants and products are in two or more different states

heterogeneous mixture: mixture in which the particles are not uniformly intermingled and that therefore has visibly different parts

heterogeneous reaction: reaction in which the reactants and products are in different states

hexose: monosaccharide, or simple sugar, containing six carbon atoms

homogeneous equilibrium: equilibrium condition for a reaction in which all the reactants and products are in the same state

homogeneous mixture: mixture made up of uniformly intermingled particles that therefore does not contain visibly different parts

homogeneous reaction: reaction in which all the reactants and products are in the same state

hybrid orbital: orbital of electrons in a bond, which is a combination of the shapes and properties of the original atomic orbitals

hydrate: substance combined chemically with water in a definite ratio

hydration: process in which water molecules pull solute particles into solution and form a sphere around them

hydrocarbon: organic molecule containing only carbon and hydrogen

hydrocarbon derivative: organic molecule made up of hydrogen and carbon as well as additional atoms or groups of atoms; described by a general formula that indicates functional groups

hydrogenation: addition of a hydrogen molecule to a double or triple bond

hydrogen bond: strong intermolecular force between the hydrogen atom of one molecule and a highly electronegative atom of another molecule, such as fluorine, oxygen, or nitrogen

hydrolysis: reaction in which water is added to a reactant, breaking the reactant into two product molecules

hydronium ion (H_3O^+): ion formed by the addition of a proton to a water molecule; accounts for the properties of acids

hydroxyl group (—OH): combination of an oxygen atom and a hydrogen atom; functional group of alcohols

hypothesis: proposed, but unproved, explanation of observed facts

ideal gas: theoretical gas described perfectly by the kinetic-molecular theory of gases

immiscible: inability of a liquid to form a solution with another liquid in all proportions

indicator: substance that changes color at certain pH values and can therefore be used to roughly determine whether a sample is an acid or a base

induced dipole: dipole created by the presence of a neighboring dipole

ineffective collision: collision between particles that does not lead to the formation of products

inhibitor: substance that decreases the rate of a chemical reaction

insoluble: inability of a substance to dissolve in another substance

intermediate product: substance produced in one step of a reaction mechanism and consumed in another

intermolecular force: relatively weak force of attraction that exists between neighboring molecules

International System of Units (SI): system of units that is an extension of the metric system; includes seven base units to measure length, mass, time, temperature, electric current, light intensity, and amount of a substance

intramolecular force: force of attraction that exists within a molecule to hold it together

ion (IGH-ahn): atom or group of atoms that has a positive or negative charge because it has lost or gained electrons

ionic bond: chemical bond resulting from the transfer of electrons from one bonding atom to another

ionic compound: compound of positive and negative ions combined so that the charges are neutralized; formed from a metal and a nonmetal

ionization energy: energy required to remove the most loosely held electron from an atom

ion product: calculation determined by inserting concentrations at a given point in a reaction into the solubility product expression; value can be compared with the solubility product to determine whether or not a solution will form a precipitate

ion-product constant (K_w): for water, equal to $[H_3O^+][OH^-]$ = 1.0×10^{-14} at 25°C

isotope: atom that has the same number of protons as another atom, but that has a different number of neutrons

joule (J): basic unit of energy in the International System of Units; equal to 1 newton-meter

Kelvin scale: SI temperature scale with a zero point of absolute zero

ketone: hydrocarbon derivative in which a carbonyl group is located within a hydrocarbon chain (R—COR')

kinetic energy (KE): energy of motion; equal to $\frac{1}{2} mv^2$

kinetic-molecular theory: model that explains the physical properties of gases based on the submicroscopic behavior of gas particles; in mathematical form, it yields the ideal gas equation

kinetic theory: theory that explains the properties of matter in terms of the particles of matter always being in motion

law of chemical equilibrium: natural law that states that every reversible reaction proceeds to an equilibrium state that can be described by a specific equilibrium constant

law of conservation of energy: natural law describing the fact that energy is neither created nor destroyed in any process

law of conservation of matter: natural law describing the fact that matter is neither created nor destroyed in any process

law of constant composition: natural law describing the fact that a given compound always contains the same elements in the same proportions

law of mass action: natural law that states that the relative concentrations of reactants and products at equilibrium can be expressed in terms of the equilibrium constant (K_{eq})

Le Chatelier's principle: principle that states that a reversible reaction at equilibrium will shift to offset a stress, or change in conditions, imposed on the system

Lewis structure: type of structural formula that uses dots or dashes to indicate bonds

limiting reactant: reactant that is completely used up in a chemical reaction and that therefore determines the maximum amount of product that can be formed

line spectrum: spectrum that contains only certain wavelengths

lipid: organic compound with oily or waxy properties; includes fats, waxes, phospholipids, and steroids

liquid: state in which matter does not hold a definite shape but occupies a definite volume

manometer: instrument used to measure the pressure of a gas in a closed container

mass: quantity of matter in an object

mass-mass problem: stoichiometric problem in which the mass of one substance is determined from the mass of another substance in the reaction; solved by using the molar ratio indicated by the balanced chemical equation

mass number: sum of the number of protons and neutrons in the nucleus of a given atom

mass-volume problem: stoichiometric problem in which the volume of one substance is determined from the mass of another substance in the reaction; solved by using the molar ratio of the two substances as indicated by the balanced chemical equation

matter: anything that has mass and volume

matter wave: term used to describe the wavelike behavior of particles

metal: element that typically has a high melting point, is ductile, malleable, shiny, and a good conductor of heat and electricity; found on the left side of the periodic table

metric prefix: syllable or group of syllables attached to the beginning of a metric unit in order to make the unit larger or smaller

metric system: decimal system of measurement used internationally; basic units in this system are the meter for length, liter for volume, gram for mass, and Celsius degree for temperature

miscible: ability of a liquid to form a solution with another liquid in all proportions

mixture: blend of two or more pure substances that are not chemically combined

molality (m): concentration of a solution determined by the number of moles of solute per kilogram of solvent

molarity (M): concentration of a solution determined by the number of moles of solute per liter of solution

molar mass: mass in grams of one mole of a substance

molar volume: volume of one mole of an ideal gas at standard conditions (1 atm, 0°C); equal to 22.4 L

mole: quantity of a substance that has a mass in grams numerically equal to its formula mass; equal to 6.02×10^{23} representative particles

molecular formula: chemical formula that indicates the numbers of each atom in a molecular compound

molecular substance: substance that has atoms held together by covalent bonds

molecule: neutral group of atoms united by covalent bonds

mole fraction (X): concentration of a solution determined by the number of moles of a given solute divided by the total number of moles of solution

mole-mole problem: stoichiometric problem in which the number of moles of one substance is determined from the number of moles of another substance in the reaction; solved by using the molar ratio indicated by the balanced chemical equation

monatomic ion: ion formed from a single atom

monomer: small molecule that joins with other similar molecules to make a polymer; repeating unit of a polymer

monosaccharide: monomer of a carbohydrate; simple sugar

natural law: description of a phenomenon that has been repeatedly and uniformly observed in nature

net ionic equation: chemical equation that shows only those compounds and ions that undergo a chemical change in an aqueous solution

neutralization reaction: chemical reaction between an acid and a base that destroys the distinctive properties of both; produces water and a salt

neutron: neutral particle within the nucleus of an atom; has a mass of 1.00867 amu

noble gas: inactive element in Group 8A of the periodic table (helium, neon, argon, krypton, xenon, and radon)

noble gas inner core: group of electrons in an atom's inner, filled energy levels; configured much like electrons in a noble gas

nonbiodegradable: inability of a compound to decompose naturally over time

nonmetal: element that has a low melting point and a dull surface, breaks easily, is a poor conductor of heat and electricity, and tends to gain electrons in a chemical reaction

nonpolar: description of a bond that has an even distribution of charge due to an equal sharing of bonding electrons

nuclear bombardment reaction: reaction in which a high-speed nuclear particle collides with a nucleus to produce a different nucleus

nuclear chain reaction: series of fission reactions in which the products of one fission reaction initiate further fission reactions

nuclear equation: equation that describes the changes that occur during radioactive decay; chemical symbols are written with the atomic number to the lower left and the mass number to the upper left

nuclear fission: splitting of an atomic nucleus into two smaller nuclei of approximately equal mass

nuclear fusion: joining of two atomic nuclei of smaller mass to form a single nucleus of greater mass

nuclear reaction: process that changes the composition of the nucleus of an atom

nucleic acid: polymer made up of nucleotides

nucleotide: monomer of a nucleic acid that is made up of a 5-carbon sugar, a phosphate group, and a nitrogen base

nucleus: concentrated core of an atom, which contains protons and neutrons

observation: fact that is noticed either qualitatively or quantitatively, usually as an early part of the scientific method

octet rule: rule that states that atoms tend to gain, lose, or share electrons so that each atom has a full outermost energy level, which is typically 8 electrons (an octet)

oil: triglyceride that is solid at room temperature and that contains mainly unsaturated fatty acids

orbital: term used to describe the probability of finding electrons in certain regions of an atom

orbital diagram: representation of an atom in which arrows in boxes are used to show the electron configuration of an atom

organic chemistry: study of organic compounds, which in general are compounds containing carbon

osmosis: flow of solvent particles from a dilute solution to a concentrated solution across a semipermeable membrane

osmotic pressure: pressure required to prevent osmosis; arises when the flow of solvent particles from a dilute solution to a concentrated solution across a semipermeable membrane results in uneven heights of the solutions on either side of the membrane

oxidation: reaction in which the atoms or ions of an element lose one or more electrons and thus attain a more positive oxidation state (higher oxidation number)

oxidation number: number assigned to the atoms in a molecule that shows the general distribution of electrons among bonded atoms; equal to the charge in ionic compounds and the charge assigned the atom according to electronegativity rules for covalent compounds; algebraic sum of oxidation numbers in a molecule is zero

oxidation potential: electrode potential for an oxidation half reaction

oxidation-reduction reaction: chemical process in which elements undergo a change in oxidation number; redox reaction

oxidizing agent: substance that gains electrons or attains a more negative oxidation state (lower oxidation number) during an oxidation-reduction reaction

parent chain: longest continuous chain of carbon atoms in an organic molecule

partial pressure: pressure exerted by each component gas in a mixture of gases

pentose: monosaccharide, or simple sugar, containing five carbon atoms

peptide bond: covalent bond joining two amino acids in a protein

percentage composition: mass of each element in a compound relative to the total mass of the compound; found by dividing the mass of the element by the mass of the compound and multiplying the quotient by 100 percent

percent error: relative error as determined by finding the difference between an accepted value and a measured value, dividing the result by the accepted value, and multiplying the quotient by 100 percent

percent yield: actual yield divided by expected yield times 100 percent

period: horizontal row of elements in the periodic table

periodic law: natural law that states that the physical and chemical properties of the elements are periodic functions of their atomic numbers

periodic table: arrangement of the elements in order of their atomic numbers so that elements with similar electron configurations are located in the same column

periodic trend: property of the elements that can be predicted from the arrangement of the periodic table

pH: value equal to $-\log[H_3O^+]$; for acidic solutions, pH is below 7, for basic solutions pH is above 7, and for neutral solutions, pH is equal to 7

phase diagram: plot of the state of a sample as a function of temperature and pressure

phospholipid: lipid made up of an alcohol, fatty acids, and a phosphate group

photoelectric effect: phenomenon in which light can be used to knock electrons out of a metal; can be explained only in terms of the particle nature of radiant energy

photon: quantum of electromagnetic energy

photosynthesis: process in which green plants use energy from the sun to produce glucose from carbon dioxide and water

physical change: process by which a substance undergoes a change that does not alter its identity

physical property: characteristic of a substance that can be observed without altering the identity of the substance

Planck's constant (h): constant value used to relate the frequency of an electromagnetic wave to its energy; described as h in the equation $E = h\nu$, where $h = 6.6262 \times 10^{-34}$ J-s

plasma: state of matter at extremely high temperature in which atoms are highly ionized

polar: description of a bond that has an uneven distribution of charge due to an unequal sharing of bonding electrons

polyatomic ion: charged group of covalently bonded atoms

polymer: large organic molecule consisting of small repeating units called monomers

polysaccharide: polymer formed when three or more monosaccharides join together; complex carbohydrate

potential energy (PE): stored energy or energy of position

precipitation: process in which ions leave a solution and regenerate an ionic solid

precipitation reaction: chemical reaction in which a precipitate forms when two aqueous solutions of ions are mixed

precision: measure of the agreement between the numerical values of two or more measurements that have been made using the same method; when the same value results from repeated measurements, the measurements are said to have high precision regardless of how close they are to the accepted value for the measurement

primary structure: sequence of amino acids in the polypeptide chain of a protein

principal energy level: one of a limited number of energy levels in an atom

product: substance formed during a chemical reaction

protein: polymer made up of amino acid monomers

proton: positively charged particle within the nucleus of an atom; has a mass of 1.00720 amu

pure substance: substance made of one kind of material with a unique set of chemical and physical properties

quantum: discrete bit of energy; smallest unit of radiant energy that can be absorbed or emitted

quantum-mechanical model: model that explains the properties of atoms by treating the electron as a wave and by quantizing its energy

quantum number: number assigned to each orbit of an electron in an atom

question: something that is asked in order to gain knowledge, usually in response to an observation

radioactive decay: spontaneous breakdown of an unstable atomic nucleus, during which alpha particles, beta particles, and gamma rays may be emitted

radioactivity: spontaneous emission of radiation from an atom

radioisotope: isotope that is radioactive, or emits radiation; commonly used in medicine and industry

rate-determining step: slowest elementary step in a reaction mechanism

rate law: expression that relates the rate of a reaction to the concentrations of substances involved in the reaction

reactant: substance that enters into a chemical reaction

reaction mechanism: sequence of steps by which an overall chemical change occurs

reaction quotient (Q): calculation determined by inserting the concentrations of reactants and products of a reversible reaction at a given point into the equilibrium constant expression; can be compared with the equilibrium constant to determine if a reaction is at equilibrium

reaction rate: change in the concentration of reactants and products per unit time as a reaction proceeds

real gas: gas that behaves like an ideal gas under ordinary conditions, but behaves differently at low temperatures and high pressures; all gases are real gases

redox reaction: chemical process in which elements undergo a change in oxidation number; oxidation-reduction reaction

reducing agent: substance that loses electrons or attains a more positive oxidation state (higher oxidation number) during an oxidation-reduction reaction

reduction: reaction in which the atoms or ions of an element gain one or more electrons and thus attain a more negative oxidation state (lower oxidation number)

reduction potential: electrode potential for a reduction half reaction

rem: unit used to measure the biological damage caused by ionizing radiation

reversible reaction: chemical reaction in which the products can react to form the original products

RNA (ribonucleic acid): nucleic acid made of a single chain of nucleotides that acts as a messenger between DNA and the ribosome, and that carries out the process by which proteins are made from amino acids

salt: ionic compound formed from the anion of an acid and cation of a base; typically a crystalline compound with a high melting point

salt bridge: tube that contains an electrolyte solution and connects the two solutions of a voltaic cell; allows ions to move from one compartment to another without mixing the solutions

salt hydrolysis reaction: chemical reaction between water and the ions of a dissolved salt; may produce an acidic, basic, or neutral solution

saturated: description of a solution that contains as much dissolved solute as it can under existing conditions

saturated hydrocarbon: carbon chain that is filled to capacity with hydrogen atoms; an alkane or cycloalkane

scientific method: orderly and systematic approach to gathering information in order to answer questions about the world; involves making an observation, asking a question, proposing a hypothesis, performing an experiment, drawing a conclusion, and developing or altering a theory

secondary structure: localized arrangement of atoms in the backbone of the polypeptide chain of a protein

self-ionization: chemical reaction in which two molecules of the same substance, usually water, react to produce ions

semimetal: element that does not have metallic properties; found on the right side of the periodic table

significant digit: digit in a measurement that is certain, plus one digit that is an estimate

single covalent bond: chemical bond resulting from the sharing of an electron pair between two atoms

single-replacement reaction: chemical reaction in which an uncombined element replaces an element that is part of a compound; general form is $A + BX \rightarrow AX + B$

solid: state in which matter holds a definite shape and volume

solubility: amount of solute that dissolves in a given amount of solvent at a given temperature to form a saturated solution

solubility equilibrium: condition that exists when the rate at which an ionic solid dissolves in a solution is equal to the rate at which ions leave the solution to regenerate the solid

solubility product (K_{sp}): equilibrium constant for a solution of a sparingly soluble ionic compound; equal to the product of the concentrations of ions in solution, each raised to the powers indicated by their coefficients in the balanced equation

solubility rules: list of rules that classifies ionic compounds as soluble or sparingly soluble in water according to the ions present

soluble: ability of a substance to dissolve in another substance

solute: substance that is dissolved in a solvent to form a solution

solution: homogeneous mixture of two or more substances in a single physical state

solvation: process in which solvent particles pull solute particles into solution and form a sphere around them; called hydration if the solvent is water

solvent: substance that does the dissolving in a solution

specific heat: amount of heat energy required to raise the temperature of 1 g of a substance by 1 C°

spectator ion: ion that does not participate in a chemical reaction and is present before and after the reaction

speed of light: speed at which light waves travel; equal to 3.00×10^8 meters per second in a vacuum

spontaneous chemical reaction: process that proceeds on its own, without any outside intervention

standard enthalpy change ($H°$): change in enthalpy for a reaction that yields products in their standard states from reactants that are also in their standard states

standard solution: reactant of known concentration used in acid-base titration

stereoisomer: isomer that has the same sequence of atoms and bonds as another molecule, but a different orientation in space; also called geometric isomer

steroid: lipid with a skeleton structure consisting of four carbon rings

stoichiometry (stoi-kee-AHM-uh-tree): study of quantitative relationships that can be derived from chemical formulas and equations

STP: standard temperature and pressure; designated as 0°C or 273 K and 1 atmosphere

strong nuclear force: attractive force among the particles in the nucleus of an atom; in a stable atom, it overcomes the force of repulsion among protons

structural formula: formula that indicates how the atoms in a molecule are bonded to each other

structural isomer: molecule that has the same molecular formula as another molecule, but that has atoms bonded in a different order

sublevel: division of a principal energy level in an atom

sublimation: conversion of a solid directly into a gas, without first becoming a liquid

supersaturated: description of a solution that contains more dissolved solute than a saturated solution; excess solute will precipitate out of a supersaturated solution, leaving a crystallized solid and a saturated solution

surface tension: imbalance of attractive forces at the surface of a liquid that causes the surface to behave as if it had a thin film across it; resistance of a liquid to an increase in its surface area

tertiary structure: three-dimensional structure of the entire polypeptide chain of a protein

theory: logical and time-tested explanation of a phenomenon that occurs in the natural world

thermochemistry: study of the changes in heat energy that accompany chemical reactions and physical changes

titration curve: graph that shows how pH changes in a titration; center of steep, vertical region indicates the equivalence point

transition state: extremely brief interval of bond disruption and formation, during which the activated complex exists

triglyceride: ester of glycerol and three fatty acids; general term for fats and oils

triple covalent bond: chemical bond resulting from the sharing of three electron pairs between two atoms

uncertainty principle: principle that states that either the position or the momentum of a moving particle can be measured and known exactly, but that both measurements cannot be known at the same time; significant only for subatomic particles

unit cell: representative group that is repeated throughout a crystal structure

unit equality: equation that shows the numerical relationship between two units

unsaturated: description of a solution that contains less dissolved solute than it can under existing conditions

unsaturated hydrocarbon: hydrocarbon molecule that is not filled to capacity with hydrogen atoms; contains multiple bonds between carbon atoms

unshared pair: pair of electrons that is not involved in bonding but instead is held exclusively by one atom

valence electron: electron in the outermost energy level of an atom; for most atoms, it is available to be gained, lost, or shared in the formation of chemical bonds

valence-shell electron pair repulsion theory (VSEPR): theory that explains that in small molecules, valence electrons are arranged as far apart from each other as possible; can be used to predict the shapes of molecules; known as VSEPR theory

vaporization: change of state from liquid to gas

vapor pressure reduction: colligative property in which the pressure of the vapor over a solvent is reduced when a nonvolatile solute is dissolved in the solvent; vapor pressure reduction is directly related to the concentration of a solution

variable: factor being tested in an experiment

viscosity: resistance to motion that exists between the molecules of a liquid when they move past each other

visible spectrum: portion of the electromagnetic spectrum that can be seen with the unaided eye; includes red, orange, yellow, green, blue, indigo, and violet light

vitamin: complex molecule that cannot be synthesized by the body but that is needed by the body in small amounts

voltaic cell: electrochemical cell that produces electricity

volume: amount of space that an object occupies

volume-volume problem: stoichiometric problem in which the volume of one substance is determined from the volume of another substance in the reaction; solved by using the molar ratio of the two substances as indicated by the balanced chemical equation

wavelength: distance between two successive similar points on a wave

wax: ester of a long-chain fatty acid and a long-chain alcohol

954

Index

A

Abbreviated electron configurations, 164, 170
Absolute temperature, 436
Absolute temperature scale, 436
Absolute zero, 62, *63*, 64, 436
Accelerators, particle, 782–783
Accepted value, 24
Accuracy of measurement, 24, 48
Acetic acid, 605, 606, 610, 617, 853
    molal boiling point elevation constant for, *522*
    molal freezing point depression constant for, *526*
    structural formula of, 265
    in vinegar, 636
Acetone, 851
Acetylsalicylic acid (aspirin), 546, 612, 857
Acid-base indicators, 597–598, *624*, *632*, *633*. *See also* Acid-base titration
Acid-base pairs, conjugate, 603–604, 608
Acid-base properties of salts, 613–614, 620
Acid-base titration, 636–643
    acid-base indicator in, 363, 636, 639–642
    of strong acid with strong base, 639–640
    of weak acid with strong base, 641
    of weak base with strong acid, 642
    performing, 636–639
Acid dissociation constant (K_a), 609–611
Acid-free paper, 614
Acidic hydrogen, 616–617
Acid rain, 631
Acids, 594–649. *See also* DNA (deoxyribonucleic acid)
    amino, 859, 881–882
    binary, 617
    buffers and, 634–635
    carboxylic, 617, 852–854, 855
    cleaning spilled, 627
    defining, 248, 595–604
        Arrhenius definition, 599–600, 601
        Brønsted-Lowry definition, 601–603
    hydronium ion and, 602–603
    naming, 248–249, 618–619
    nucleic, 888–891
    oxy, 617
    pH, 629–633
    properties of, 596–598
    self-ionization of water, 625–628
    in stomach, 600
    strong and weak, 605–606, 610
        salts of, 614
        titration of, 639–643
Actin, 886
Actinides, 202, 203
Activated complex, 736–737
Activation energy, 734–735, 736
Activity series, 294, *295*, 667–669

Actual yield, 371
Addition, significant digits in, 28–29
Addition polymerization, 828
Adenine, 888
Adenosine diphosphate (ADP), 870
Adenosine triphosphate (ATP), 869–870
Affinity, electron, 181–183
Air, properties of, 504
Air bags, automobile, 358–359
Airplanes, deicing, *460*
Alabaster, *196*
Alanine, *882*
Alchemists, *200*
Alcohols, 841–845
    classification of, 841–842
    naming, 842–844
    properties of, 845
Aldehydes, 849–851. *See also* Carbohydrates
    naming, 849–850
    properties of, 851
Algae, blue-green, 764
Alkali metals, 168, 191–194
    properties of, 192–193
    sources and uses of, 193–194
Alkaline dry cell, 698–699
Alkaline earth metals, 168, 194–196
    properties of, 194–195
    sources and uses of, 195–196
Alkanes, 816–824
    branched, 817–819
    conformations and structural isomers of, 820–823
    cycloalkanes, 824
    straight-chain, 816–817
Alkenes, 825
Alkynes, 825
Allotropes of carbon, 806–807
Alloys, 195, 196, 503
    chromium, 197
    of copper, 199, 200
Alpha decay, 115
Alpha particles, 100–102, 114, 786
Alpha radiation, 100, 112, 114
Alpha-scattering experiment, 100–102
-al suffix, 849
Altimeter, 426
Altitude, atmospheric pressure and, 426
Aluminum, *168*, 204
Aluminum nitrate, 234
Aluminum oxide, 204–205, 233
American system of labeling, 165
Amides, 860
-amide suffix, 860
Amines, 618, 858–859
-amine suffix, *858*
Amino acids, 859, 881–882
Ammonia, 207, 213, 240, 601
    atoms in molecule of, 318
    ball-and-stick model for, 256
    as Brønsted-Lowry base, 603
    Lewis structure for, 238

    potential as lifting gas, 446
    pyramidal shape of, 259–260
    structural formula for, 256
    synthesis of, 361–362, 546, 553, 554, *555*
Ammonium nitrate, *725*, 755, 757
    decomposition of, 350–351
Amorphous carbon, 806
Amorphous solids, 473
Amount-volume relationship of gas, 439
Amphoteric compounds, 881
Amplitude of wave, 126
Analogies for states of matter, 66–67
Analysis, problem-solving strategy and, 43
Anesthesia, 857
-ane suffix, 839
Anhydrous substances, defined, 246
Anions, 226, 618
    monatomic, 232
Anode, 97, 688
Anthocyanin pigments, 290
Antibodies, 886
Antifreeze, 521
Antimony, *207*
Apollo 13, *703*
Aqueous solutions, 289, 505, 571–573
Archaeology, preserving artifacts in, 4
Area, derived SI unit for, 19
Argon, 211–212, 228
Argon-filled light bulbs, 443
Aristotle, 92
Aromatic compounds, 826
Arrhenius, Svante, 599, 734
Arrhenius definition of acids and bases, 599–600, 601
Arsenic, 207
Art, cleaning priceless, 6
Artificial sweeteners, 387
Aspartame, 387
Aspartic acid, *882*
Aspdin, Joseph, 370
Aspirin (acetylsalicylic acid), 546, 612, 857
Astatine, 209, 210
-ate suffix, 855
Atlantic-Pacific rule, *26*, 27, 30
Atmosphere, layers of, 448
Atmosphere (atm), 426
Atmospheric pressure, 425–427
    boiling point and, 484
Atocha (ship), 707
Atom(s)
    defined, 92
    early models of, 91
    electron configuration of, 147–153
    mass of, 110–111
    moles and, 317
    nuclear, 100–102
    "plum-pudding" model of, 101, *102*
    quantum-mechanical model of, 141
    spherical, *463*
Atomic bomb, 776

C

Cabbage, as acid-base indicator, 598
Cadaverine, 859
Calcium, 172, 194, *195*
Calcium carbonate, 196, 743
  decomposition of, 293
  in eggshells, 644
  reaction between hydrochloric acid
    and, 295
Calcium fluoride, 233
Calcium hydroxyapatite, 207
Calcium nitrate, 234
Calcium oxide, 607
  balancing chemical equation for,
    285–286
  chemical equations for, 282–283
  direct combination reaction forming,
    291
Calcium sulfate, 580, 581
Calculations
  density in, 35–37
  significant digits in, 28–30
Caloric theory, 401–402
Calorie (Cal), 57
calorie (cal), 57, 58
Calorimeter, 57, 394–395
Calorimetry, 393–400
  defined, 393
  foods as fuels, 397–400
  heat and temperature, 393–397
Camphor, *526*
Cancellation of units, 39–40
Cancer
  radioisotopes to treat, 789–790
  skin, 150
Candy, hard, *519*
Candy thermometer, 62
Cane sugar, 873–874
Capillary action, 470
Car battery, 699–701, 705
Carbohydrates, 808, 871–877. *See also*
  Glucose
  disaccharides, 873–874
  exothermic reactions of, 398–400
  monosaccharides, 872–873
  polysaccharides, 875–877
Carbon, 205–206, 804–807
  allotropes of, 806–807
  atomic number of, 149
  atoms of, 777–778
  bonding properties of, 807–809
  branch, 817
  electron configuration of, *148*, 149–150
  electronegativity of, 813
  isotopes of, *110*
Carbon-12, 110
Carbon-14, 777, 781
Carbon-14 dating (carbon dating), 118,
  781
Carbonated beverages, 518, 604
Carbon compounds, 810–835. *See also*
  Hydrocarbons; Hydrocarbon derivatives
  natural and synthetic, 811–812
  organic chemistry and, 810–811
Carbon cycle, 364
Carbon dioxide, 205–206, 246
  greenhouse effect and, 403

linear shape of, 257
polarity of, 268
to smother fire, *359*
temperature-volume relationship for,
  435, *436*
Carbon group (Group 4A), 205–206
Carbonic acid, *351*
Carbonic acid buffer, 635
Carbon monoxide, 205, *206*
Carbon tetrachloride, 246, *522*, 841
Carbonyl group, 849, 851, 855
Carboxyl group, 852, 855
Carboxylic acids, 617, 852–854, 855
Carotenoid pigments, 290
Carothers, Wallace, 827
Cars. *See* Automobiles
Catalysts, 741–743
Cathode, 97, 688
Cathode ray, 97–98
Cathode ray tube (CRT), 97, *98*
Cathodic protection, 673
Cations, 226, 231
"Cause-and-effect" statement, hypothesis
  as, 9
Cells, electrochemical. *See* Electrochemical
  cells
Cellular respiration, 869
Cellulose, 398, 871, 877
Cell voltage, 689–690
Celsius, Anders, 61
Celsius degree (C°), 19
Celsius scale, 61, 62
  conversion between Kelvin and, 62,
    63, 425, 436
Cement, 370
Centi- prefix, *20*
Central science, chemistry as, 4–5
Cerium, 202
Cesium, 191, *192*, 461
CFCs (chlorofluorocarbons), 210, 448, 729,
  839, 841
β-Chain, *883*, 884
Chain reaction, nuclear, 794
Changes in matter, 68–71, 79
Changes in state, 67, *68*
Charles, Jacques, 431, 435
Charles's law, 435–438, *441*, 450
Chemical bonds. *See* Bond(s); Covalent
  bond(s); Ionic bond(s)
Chemical changes, 68–71
Chemical equations. *See* Equations,
  chemical
Chemical kinetics. *See* Reaction rates
Chemical measurements, 311–322
  atomic mass, 110–111, 161, 164, 312, 321
  Avogadro's number, 319, 325, 326
  formula mass, 312
  molar mass, 320–321, 324, 527–529
  mole, 313–319, 506
    atoms and, 317
    defined, 313–316
    formula units and, 318–319
    molecules and, 317–318
  mole conversions, 323–331
    mass and moles, 323–326
    moles and gases, 329–331
    multistep conversions, 328–329
    particles and moles, 326–327

Chemical potential energy (chemical
  energy), 56, 79, 733–734
Chemical properties, 68
Chemical reactions. *See* Reaction(s)
Chemical symbols, 106, 108–109
Chemical wastes, disposal of, 15,
  796
Chemiluminescent reaction, *381*
Chemistry
  as central science, 4–5
  defined, 3
  examples of uses of, 3–4
  reasons for studying, 5–6
Chemists, types of, 5
Chernobyl, 795
Chile saltpeter, 553
Chlorine, 209, 210–211, 294, 553, 664, 729
  electron configuration of, 228
  isotopes of, *110*
Chlorofluorocarbons (CFCs), 210, 448,
  729, 839, 841
Chloroform, *522*, *526*, 857
Chlorophyll, 290
Cholesterol, 879, 880
Chromatography, 78
Chromium, 153, 197, *198*
Citric acid, 248, 369, 609
Clausius, Rudolf, *422*, 423
Clothing, safety, 16
Club moss, *741*
Coal, 59
Cobalt, 197
Cobalt-60, 790
Cobalt(II) chloride hexahydrate, 551
Coefficients in balanced chemical
  equation, 285 287, 318–349
Coinage metals, 197, 199–200
Coke, 806
Cold fusion, 799
Cold packs, 389
Collagen, 886
Colligative properties of solutions,
  520–529
  boiling point elevation, 521–523, *524*
  freezing point depression, 524–526
  molar mass determination using,
    527–529
  osmotic pressure, 526–527
  vapor pressure reduction, 520–521,
    524
Collision theory, 732–733, 742
Combustion reactions, 296, 382, 386
Common dry cell, 697–698
Common-ion effect, 580–581
Complete ionic equation, 578
Complex carbohydrates, 875–877
Compound(s), 75–76
  aromatic, 826
  biodegradable, 830
  biologically important. *See*
    Biomolecules
  distinguishing between elements and,
    76
  formulas for, 75–76
  ionic, 226–227
  naming, 244–249
  nonbiodegradable, 830
  percent composition of, 332–334

E

Credits

Photo Research: Natalie Goldstein
Acknowledgments: Keirsten Wallace and Julie DeWitt

XX-1 Richard Megna/Fundamental Photographs **02** (top) Richard Hutchings **03** ©P. Parrot/Sygma **04** Breck P. Kent **05** (bottom) Andre Dallant/The Image Bank; (top left) Brad Markel/Liaison International; (top right) Julie Houck/West Light **06** ©G. Giansanti/Sygma **07** (left) Gregory Heisler/The Image Bank; (right) ©Mark Marten/Photo Researchers, Inc. **09** (top to bottom) 1994, Steve Gravano/Lightwave **11** (top to bottom) Richard Megna/Fundamental Photographs **13** (bottom) David Young Wolff/Tony Stone Images'; (top) ©Stephen F. Rose/Rainbow **14** ©Bruce Roberts/Photo Researchers, Inc. **17** (left) ©Hank Morgan/Rainbow; (right) Al Teilemans/Duomo Photography, Inc. **18** NASA/Liaison International **20** (bottom) Wolfgang Kaehler; (top) Martti Kainulainen/Woodfin Camp & Associates **22** ©Robin Lawrence/Photo Researchers, Inc. **23** ©Photo Researchers, Inc. **25** Wolfgang Kaehler **31** (left) ©NIBSC/Science Photo Library/Photo Researchers, Inc.; (right) Lionel Isy-Schwart/The Image Bank **32** Lionel Isy-Schwart/The Image Bank **35** Ken Karp Photography **37** Mark C. Brunett/Stock, Boston **47** Mike Yamashita/Woodfin Camp & Associates **54** (bottom) ©Allsport/Simon Bruty; (top) ©Allsport/David Leah **55** (bottom) Grant V. Faint/The Image Bank; (top) ©NASA/Science Photo Library/Photo Researchers, Inc. **56** Breck P. Kent **57** The Bettmann Archive **59** Mitchell Layton/Stock, Boston **60** (left) Guido Alberto Rossi/The Image Bank; (right) ©T.J. Florian/Rainbow **61** ©Syd Greenberg/Photo Researchers, Inc. **62** David W. Hamilton/The Image Bank **64** Dan Winters/© 1993 The Walt Disney Co. Reprinted with permission of *Discover* Magazine **65** (center) Lynn M. Stone/The Image Bank; (left) George Hall/Woodfin Camp & Associates; (right) Wolfgang Kaehler **68** (bottom) Tom Hanson/Liaison International; (top left) Lightwave; (top right and top center) Richard Megna/Fundamental Photographs **69** (bottom left) Stuart Dee/The Image Bank; (bottom right) Paul Silverman/Fundamental Photographs; (center) Michael Abramson/Woodfin Camp & Associates; (top left) ©Joseph Nettis/Photo Researchers, Inc.; (top right) Wolfgang Kaehler **70** Stephen Frisch/Stock, Boston **72** (bottom) The Bettmann Archive; (top) William Johnson/Stock, Boston **75** Richard Megna/Fundamental Photographs **76** Ken Kay/Fundamental Photographs **77** Breck P. Kent **78** (left) Chip Clark/National Museum of Natural History; (right) Michael Dalton/Fundamental Photographs **79** Richard Megna/Fundamental Photographs **83** Kimmo Raisanen/Lehtikuva Oy/Woodfin Camp & Associates **84** (left) Courtesy of Connie Werner; (right) Robert Frerck/Odyssey Productions/Chicago **85** (bottom left) Jerry Markatos; (bottom right) Courtesy of Karen Robblee; (top left) Courtesy of H. Eugene LeMay, Jr.; (top right) Courtesy of Herbert Beall **86** Lawrence Migdale/Stock, Boston **87** ©Dan McCoy/Rainbow **89** ©Milton Heiberg/Photo Researchers, Inc. **90** (bottom) ©Patrice Loiez, Cern/Science Photo Library/Photo Researchers, Inc.; (top) The Bettmann Archive **91** ©Dan McCoy/Rainbow **92** (bottom) Robert M. Friedman/Frozen Images; (top) The Granger Collection, New York **93** ©IBM/Account Phototake/Phototake NYC **94** (bottom) ©Darwin Dale/Photo Researchers, Inc.; (top left) ©NIH/Science Source/Photo Researchers, Inc.; (top right) NASA **95** Garry Gay/The Image Bank **96** (left) Bill Brown/Liaison International; (right) Culver Pictures, Inc. **97** (bottom) Robert Mathena/Fundamental Photographs; (top) ©Hank Morgan/Rainbow **99** (left) Paul Silverman/Fundamental Photographs; (right) ©Science Photo Library/Photo Researchers, Inc. **101** (bottom) Charlie Stebbings/Good Housekeeping/The National Magazine CO; (top) ©Dan McCoy/Rainbow **102** ©David Nunuk/Science Photo Library/Photo Researchers, Inc. **105** (bottom) ©John Walsh/Science Photo Library/Photo Researchers, Inc.; (top left) A. Kaye/DRK Photo; (top right) Timothy Eagan/Woodfin Camp & Associates **110** Wolfgang Kaehler **114** Michael Dalton/Fundamental Photographs **115** Karen Kasmauski/Woodfin Camp & Associates **118** ©Will & Deni McIntyre/Photo Researchers, Inc. **119** Mike Yamashita/Woodfin Camp & Associates **125** ©D. Zirinsky/Photo Researchers, Inc. **127** (bottom) Chuck O'Rear/Woodfin Camp & Associates; (top left) ©Dan McCoy/Rainbow; (top right) ©Andrew McClenaghan/Science Photo Library/Photo Researchers, Inc. **128** Tom Bean/DRK Photo **129** (bottom) ©Scott Camazine/Photo Researchers, Inc.; (top) ©Alfred Pasieka/Peter Arnold, Inc. **130** (left) Paul Silverman/Fundamental Photographs; (right) D. Cavagnaro/DRK Photo **131** The Bettmann Archive **132** Eddie Hironaka/The Image Bank **133** NASA **134** Richard Nowitz/Phototake NYC **135** (left to right) Yoav Levy/Phototake **136** (bottom) ©Rich Treptow/Photo Researchers, Inc.; (top) ©Wabash Instrument Corp./Fundamental Photographs **138** (bottom left and center) Education Development Center, Inc.; (bottom right) ©David Scharf/Peter Arnold, Inc.; (top) AIP Emilio Segre/Visual Archives **140** (bottom) ©Sam C. Pierson, Jr./Photo Researchers, Inc.; (top) Stephen J. Kraseman/DRK Photo **146** Romilly Lokyer/The Image Bank **147** ©NASA/Peter Arnold, Inc. **150** ©Rafael Macia/Photo Researchers, Inc. **151** (top to bottom) Grace Davies/Omni-Photo Communications, Inc. **152** (left) Michael Dalton/Fundamental Photographs; (right) G.V. Faint/The Image Bank **158** (left) 1986, Pat O'Hara/DRK Photo; (right) ©A. & F. Michler/Peter Arnold, Inc. **159** Garry Gay/The Image Bank **160** (left) Robert Frerck/Odyssey Productions/Chicago; (right) Tom Carroll/Phototake NYC **161** (left) The Granger Collection, New York; (right) ©Novosti/Science Photo Library/Photo Researchers, Inc. **163** ©Science Photo Library/Photo Researchers, Inc. **168** (left) David Weintraub/Stock, Boston; (right) John Coletti/Stock, Boston **169** (center) Richard Megna/Fundamental Photographs; (left) ©Gregory G. Dimijian/Photo Researchers, Inc.; (right) Maria Faglienti/The Image Bank **172** Yoav Levy/Phototake **174** (bottom) 1988,Tom Bean/DRK Photo; (center) Walter Bibikow/The Image Bank; (top) ©Bill Binzen/Rainbow **179** ©A. & F. Michler/Peter Arnold, Inc. **190** (bottom) Place/The Image Bank; (top) ©Dan McCoy/Rainbow **191** (left to right) Richard Megna/ Fundamental Photographs **192** (bottom) Stephen Frisch/Stock, Boston; (top) Chip Clark/ National Museum of Natural History **193** (bottom) John Coletti/Stock, Boston; (top) ©Earth Satellite Corporation/ Science Photo Library/Photo Researchers, Inc. **194** (right) *The New Knowledge*, R.K. Duncan, *The Mineral Kingdom*; (left) Chip Clark/ National Museum of Natural History **195** ©Chris Priest/Science Photo Library/Photo Researchers, Inc. **196** (left) Michael Jacobs/Woodfin Camp & Associates; (right) ©Susan Leavines/Science Source/Photo Researchers, Inc. **198** (bottom left) Jeff Smith/The Image Bank; (bottom right) Alan Becker/The Image Bank; (center) The Science Museum/Science & Society Picture Library; (left center) Robert Kristofik/The Image Bank; (top left) ©IFA/Peter Arnold, Inc.; (top right) ©Porterfield/Chickering/Photo Researchers, Inc. **199** ©CNRI/SPL/Photo Researchers, Inc. **200** (bottom) The Bettmann Archive; (top) The Granger Collection, New York **201** The Image Bank **202** ©Alexander Tsiaras/Photo Researchers, Inc. **203** ©J&L Weber/Peter Arnold, Inc. **204** (bottom left) Steve Dunwell/The Image Bank; (center) Princehorn/Bettman; (right) UPI/Bettman; (top left) Jon Love/The Image Bank **205** ©Schaffer/Hill/Peter Arnold, Inc. **206** (bottom left) ©David Muench 1994; (bottom right) Jake Rais/The Image Bank; (top) Ken Cooper/The Image Bank **207** (bottom) Gerd Ludwig/Woodfin Camp & Associates; (center) Huhn Inc./The Image Bank; (top) ©Dr. Jeremy Burgess/Science Photo Library/Photo Researchers, Inc. **208** (left) T.A. Wiewandt/ DRK Photo; (right) Marty Cordano/ DRK Photo **209** ©Bill Pierce/Rainbow **210** (top) Ted Russell/The Image Bank; (bottom) Mel Di Giacomo/The Image Bank **211** (bottom) Argonne National Laboratory; (top) Robert Brenner/PhotoEdit **212** ©Bruno P. Zehnder/Peter Arnold, Inc.; **213** Michael Heller/Black Star **217** Richard Megna/ Fundamental Photographs **218** (left) Courtesy of Vikram Goghari; (right) Chuck Fisherman/The Image Bank **219** Courtesy of H. Eugene LeMay, Jr. **221** Barbara Campbell/Liaison International **223** ©Dan McCoy/Rainbow **224** (bottom) Sobel/Klonsky/The Image Bank; (top) D. Cavagnaro/DRK Photo **225** Mark C. Burnett/Stock, Boston **226** Chip Clark/National Museum of Natural History **227** (bottom left to right) Donald Clegg & Roxy Wilson; (top) Chip Clark/National Museum of Natural History **229** ©Katrina Thomas/Photo Researchers, Inc. **230** ACME/Bettman **233** (bottom) Derrik Murray/The Image Bank; (top) The Bettman Archive **235** (bottom) H. Wendler/The Image Bank; (top) ©David Muench 1994 **236** 1989, Falken Verlag Gmbh/ English translation,1990, Sterling Publishing Co., Inc. **237** (left) John W. Banagan/The Image Bank; (right) Spencer Grant/Stock, Boston **238** Cary Wolinsky/Stock, Boston **239** Don Klumpp/The Image Bank **244** Steve Dunwell/The Image Bank **245** Diana Gongora/Fundamental Photographs **246** Stephen Frisch/Stock, Boston **247** (bottom) ©Jack Fields/Photo Researchers, Inc.; (top) Kennan Ward/ DRK Photo **248** (center) Larry Dale Gordon/The Image Bank; (left) Denny Tillman/The Image Bank; (right) ©Dr. R.K.F. Schiller/Photo Researchers, Inc. **253** Chip Clark/National Museum of Natural History **254** (bottom) Curtis Willocks/The Image Bank; (top) Frozen Images **255** Cleo Photography/PhotoEdit **256** Jack Parsons/Omni-Photo Communications, Inc. **257** Ellis Herwig/Stock, Boston **258** ©Dan McCoy/Rainbow **259** Merril Wood/The Image Bank **261** ©Dan McCoy/Rainbow **264** Kristen Brochmann/Fundamental Photographs **265** ©Hans Reinhard/Photo Researchers, Inc. **266** (bottom left to right) Richard Megna/Fundamental Photographs; (top) Tony Freeman/PhotoEdit **267** Runk/Schoenberger/Grant Heilman Photography **269** (bottom) The Bettmann Archive; (top) ©Richard Weiss/Peter Arnold, Inc. **271** (bottom left) ©Ed Reschke/Peter Arnold, Inc.; (bottom right) ©Dean Hulse/Rainbow; (center) Robert Frerck/Odyssey Productions/Chicago; (top left) Lawrence Migdale; (top right) David Brownell/The Image Bank **278** (bottom) David Madison/Duomo Photography, Inc.; (top) ©1993, Kelvin Aitken/Peter Arnold, Inc. **279** (bottom) Owen Franklin/Stock, Boston; (top) Richard Megna/Fundamental Photographs **280** Visuals Unlimited **281** Joe Devenney/The Image Bank **283** (bottom) Steve Allen/The Image Bank; (top left to right and center) Richard Megna/Fundamental Photographs **284** ©Leonard Lessin/Peter Arnold, Inc. **285** (bottom) ©Bob Daemmrich; (top) Dr. E.R. Degginger **286** Wolfgang Kaehler **290** Stephen J. Krasemann/DRK Photo **291** Yoav Levy/Phototake **292** Paul Silverman/Fundamental Photographs **293** (bottom) ©Leonard Lessin/Peter Arnold, Inc.; (center) Duomo Photography, Inc.; (top) C. J. Allen/Stock, Boston **294** (bottom left to right) Peticolas/Megna/Fundamental Photographs; (top) Tom Bochsler Photography Ltd. **296** Wolfgang Kaehler **303** Richard Megna/ Fundamental Photographs **304** (left) Courtesy of Natalie Clemons; (right) Dennis Brack/Black Star **305** Jerry Markatos **306** 1989 by Falken Verlag Gmbh, English translation, 1990 by Sterling Publishing Co., Inc. **309** Rentmeester/The Image Bank **310** (bottom) Stacy Pick/Stock, Boston; (top) Leonard Lee Rue/DRK Photo **311** (bottom) Frank Siteman/Stock, Boston; (center) Paul Barton/The Stock Market ; (top) Jeffrey Muir Hamilton/Stock, Boston **315** (left) Frans Lanting/Minden Pictures; (right) Michael Fogden/DRK Photo **316** Ken O'Donoghue **317** (bottom) Steve Satushek/The Image Bank; (top) Roy Morsch/The Stock Market **319** Coco McCoy/Rainbow **320** ULF. E. Wallin/The Image Bank **321** Roger Du Buisson/The Stock Market **323** (bottom left) Lars Ternblad/The Image Bank; (bottom right) Patti McConville/The Image Bank; (top) Frank Siteman/Stock, Boston **324** Doug Cheeseman/Peter Arnold, Inc. **325** (center) James King Holes/OCMS/Science Photo Library/Photo Researchers, Inc.; (left and right) The Bettmann Archive **328** Harry Przekop/Medical Images, Inc. **330** Richard Megna/Fundamental Photographs **333** (bottom) Richard Megna/Fundamental Photographs; (center) Roy Morsch/The Stock Market; (top) Jim Brandenburg/Minden Pictures, Inc. **337** (bottom left) Charles Mahaux/The Image Bank; (bottom right)

ers, Inc. **731** Chip Clark/National Museum of Natural History **733** William R. Sallaz/Duomo Photography, Inc. **736** ©Hank Morgan/ VHSID Lab/ECE Dept. at U. MA. Amherst/ Science Source/Photo Researchers, Inc. **738** Richard Megna/Fundamental Photographs **739** (left to right) Chip Clark/National Museum of Natural History **740** (bottom) ©Coco McCoy/Rainbow; (top) Richard Megna/ Fundamental Photographs **741** (left) Dr. E.R. Degginger; (right) Hans Wolf/The Image Bank **742** Francoise Sauze/ The Image Bank **743** ©Francoise Sauze/Photo Researchers, Inc. **748** (bottom) Richard Megna/Fundamental Photographs; (top) Larry Ulrich/DRK Photo **749** ©Keith Kent /Peter Arnold, Inc. **750** (bottom left) ©Philippe Blondel/Photo Researchers, Inc.; (bottom right) Al Satterwhite/The Image Bank; (top) Diane Schiumo/Fundamental Photographs **751** Harald Sund/The Image Bank **752** (bottom) ©Blair Seitz/Photo Researchers, Inc.; (top left) Jan Cobb/The Image Bank; (top right) Jake Rajs/The Image Bank **754** Brownell/The Image Bank **755** (bottom) Yoav Levy/Phototake NYC; (top) Richard Megna/Fundamental Photographs **757** (bottom) Richard Megna/Fundamental Photographs; (center) ©Matt Meadows/Peter Arnold, Inc.; (top) ©Charles D. Winters/ Photo Researchers, Inc. **758** (bottom left) Peter Menzel/ Stock, Boston; (bottom right) Robert Frerck/Woodfin Camp & Associates; (top left) David Young-Wolff/Photo-Edit; (top right) David Young-Wolff/PhotoEdit **759** Murray Alcosser/The Image Bank **761** ©Science Photo Library/ Photo Researchers, Inc. **763** (bottom left) Antonio Rosario/The Image Bank; (bottom right) Terrace Moore/ Woodfin Camp & Associates; (top) Alvis Upitis/The Image Bank **764** ©Simon Fraser/Science Photo Library/ Photo Researchers, Inc. **765** (bottom) ©Chris Rogers/ Rainbow; (top) William R. Sallaz/Duomo Photography, Inc. **769** Myrleen Ferguson/PhotoEdit **770** (left) Courtesy of David Emanuel; (right) Gary Gladstone/The Image Bank **771** Courtesy of Herbert Beall **772** ©Charles D. Winters/Photo Researchers, Inc. **775** ©1989, Jeff Gnass/ The Stock Market **776** (bottom) ©Walter H. Hodge/Peter Arnold, Inc.; (top) Naval Historical Foundation Photo Service **777** Ovak Arslanian/Liaison International **778**

Editorial Services Support: Louise B. Capuano

Michael Salas/The Image Bank **780** Garry Gay/The Image Bank **781** (bottom) Lawrence Migdale/Stock, Boston; (top) Douglas Burrows/Liaison International **782** (left) Fermilab Visual Media Services; (right) Stanford Linear Accelerator Center/US Department of Energy **783** S. Morgan/F S.P./Liaison International **784** (bottom) ©Science Photo Library/Photo Researchers, Inc.; (top) ©Mark Marten/Los Alamos National Laboratory/Photo Researchers, Inc. **785** Richard Megna/Fundamental Photographs **787** Richard Falco/Black Star **788** Alvis Upitis/The Image Bank **789** (bottom) ©Martin/ Dohrn/ Science Photo Library/Photo Researchers, Inc.; (center) 1994/SIU Biomed Comm./Custom Medical Stock Photo; (top) UPI/Bettmann **790** (left) Cliff Feulner/The Image Bank; (right) Mark C. Burnett/Stock, Boston **791** Melchior Digiacomo/The Image Bank **793** UPI/Bettmann Newsphotos **794** The Bettmann Archive **795** ©Catherine Pouedras/Science Photo Library/Photo Researchers, Inc. **797** NASA **798** (bottom) ©LLNL/Science Source/ Photo Researchers, Inc.; (top) Princeton University/ Princeton Plasma Physics Lab **803** NASA **804** (bottom) John P. Endress/The Stock Market; (top) D. Cavagnaro/ DRK Photo **805** (bottom) Stephen Frisch/Stock, Boston; (center) D. Cavagnaro/DRK Photo; (top) Jose Azel/ Woodfin Camp & Associates **806** (bottom) Richard Megna/Fundamental Photographs; (top) Leonard Lessin/Peter Arnold, Inc. **807** Robert Fried/Stock, Boston **809** (left) Douglas Faulkner/Photo Researchers, Inc.; (right) The Image Bank **810** The Bettmann Archive **811** ©John Paul Kay/Peter Arnold, Inc. **812** (left) NASA/The Stock Market; (right) Dan Budnik/Woodfin Camp & Associates **813** (left to right) John Blaustein/Woodfin Camp & Associates **814** NASA **816** Garry Gay/The Image Bank **820** Ellis Herwig/Stock, Boston **825** D. Cavagnaro/DRK Photo **827** (center) Christensen/Liaison International; (left and right) Jeffry W. Myers/Stock, Boston **828** (left) Glenn McLaughlin/The Stock Market; (right) Bob Daemmrich/Stock, Boston **829** Professor P. Motta/Department of Anatomy/University "La Sapienza"/Photo Researchers, Inc. **830** (bottom) Stock, Boston; (top) Hank Morgan/ Photo Researchers, Inc. **831** American Plastics Council

835 D. Cavagnaro/DRK Photo **836** (bottom) Williamson/ Edwards Concepts/The Image Bank; (top) Murray Photography/The Image Bank **837** (left to right) ©Coco McCoy/Rainbow **838** ©Coco McCoy/Rainbow **841** 1993, Yellow Dog Prod./The Image Bank **845** (left) ©Dan McCoy/Rainbow; (right) ©Coco McCoy/Rainbow **846** The Bettmann Archive **853** Michal Heron/Woodfin Camp & Associates **854** Roy Morsch/The Stock Market **855** The Granger Collection, New York **858** (left) Lester Sloan/ Woodfin Camp & Associates; (right) Flip Chalfant/The Image Bank **866** (bottom) Frans Lanting/Minden Pictures, Inc.; (top) Snowdon/Hoyer/Woodfin Camp & Associates **867** (bottom) ©Hank Morgan/Rainbow; (top) Larry Ulrich/DRK Photo **868** (left) John Cancalosi/DRK Photo; (right) Michio Hoshino/Minden Pictures, Inc. **870** (left) William R. Sallaz/Duomo Photography, Inc.; (right) Michael Melford/The Image Bank **873** Wendy Stone/Odyssey Productions/Chicago **874** ©Porterfield-Chickering/ Photo Researchers, Inc.; **875** (bottom) ©Andy Levin/ Photo Researchers, Inc.; (top) James Wilson/Woodfin Camp & Associates **876** (bottom) ©James H. Robinson/ Photo Researchers, Inc.; (top) Benn Mitchell/The Image Bank **879** (left) Piergiorgio Sclarandis/Black Star; (right) Christian Vioujard/Liaison International **880** (left) Stephen J. Krasemann/DRK Photo; (right) Lewis Kemper/ DRK Photo **881** (left to right) ©Prof. P. Motta/Dept. of Anatomy/University "La Sapienza," Rome/Science Photo Library/Photo Researchers, Inc. **882** ©Charles D. Winters/Photo Researchers, Inc. **884** ©Dan McCoy/Rainbow **885** (left) Henry Wolf/The Image Bank; (right) Stephen Marks/The Image Bank **887** (left to right) The Bettmann Archive **889** (bottom) Gary Wagner/Stock, Boston; (top) Sepp Seitz/Woodfin Camp & Associates **890** (bottom left) ©CSHI Archives/Peter Arnold, Inc.; (bottom right) ©A. Barrington Brown/Photo Researchers, Inc.; (top) ©Ken Edward/Science Source/Photo Researchers, Inc. **891** Richard Norwitz/Phototake NYC **895** ©G.I. Bernard/ Animals Animals **896** (left) Courtesy of Maya Mehta; (right) ©Larry Mulvehill/Rainbow **897** Courtesy of Karen Robblee **899** ©Will & Deni McIntyre/Science Source/ Photo Researchers, Inc.

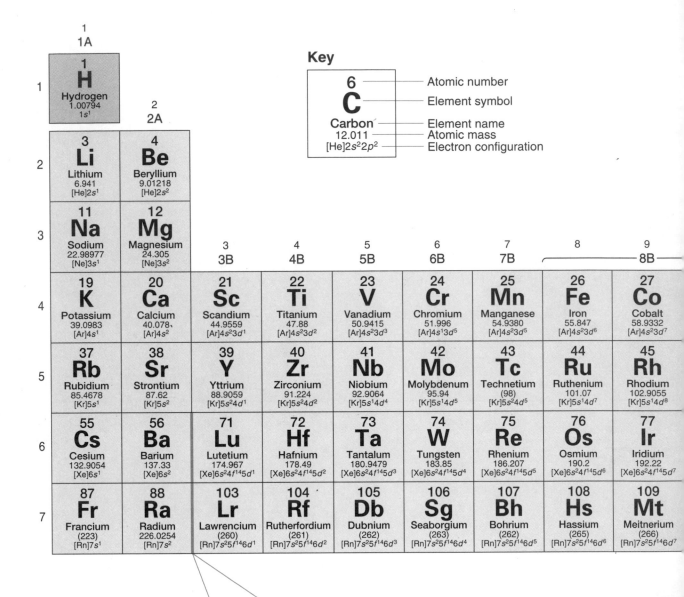

1								
1A								

Key

6	——— Atomic number
C	——— Element symbol
Carbon	——— Element name
12.011	——— Atomic mass
[He]$2s^2 2p^2$	——— Electron configuration

1	**1** **H** Hydrogen 1.00794 $1s^1$								

		2 **2A**							

2	**3** **Li** Lithium 6.941 [He]$2s^1$	**4** **Be** Beryllium 9.01218 [He]$2s^2$							

| 3 | **11**
Na
Sodium
22.98977
[Ne]$3s^1$ | **12**
Mg
Magnesium
24.305
[Ne]$3s^2$ | **3**
3B | **4**
4B | **5**
5B | **6**
6B | **7**
7B | **8** | **9**
8B |

| 4 | **19**
K
Potassium
39.0983
[Ar]$4s^1$ | **20**
Ca
Calcium
40.078,
[Ar]$4s^2$ | **21**
Sc
Scandium
44.9559
[Ar]$4s^2 3d^1$ | **22**
Ti
Titanium
47.88
[Ar]$4s^2 3d^2$ | **23**
V
Vanadium
50.9415
[Ar]$4s^2 3d^3$ | **24**
Cr
Chromium
51.996
[Ar]$4s^1 3d^5$ | **25**
Mn
Manganese
54.9380
[Ar]$4s^2 3d^5$ | **26**
Fe
Iron
55.847
[Ar]$4s^2 3d^6$ | **27**
Co
Cobalt
58.9332
[Ar]$4s^2 3d^7$ |

| 5 | **37**
Rb
Rubidium
85.4678
[Kr]$5s^1$ | **38**
Sr
Strontium
87.62
[Kr]$5s^2$ | **39**
Y
Yttrium
88.9059
[Kr]$5s^2 4d^1$ | **40**
Zr
Zirconium
91.224
[Kr]$5s^2 4d^2$ | **41**
Nb
Niobium
92.9064
[Kr]$5s^1 4d^4$ | **42**
Mo
Molybdenum
95.94
[Kr]$5s^1 4d^5$ | **43**
Tc
Technetium
(98)
[Kr]$5s^2 4d^5$ | **44**
Ru
Ruthenium
101.07
[Kr]$5s^1 4d^7$ | **45**
Rh
Rhodium
102.9055
[Kr]$5s^1 4d^8$ |

| 6 | **55**
Cs
Cesium
132.9054
[Xe]$6s^1$ | **56**
Ba
Barium
137.33
[Xe]$6s^2$ | **71**
Lu
Lutetium
174.967
[Xe]$6s^2 4f^{14} 5d^1$ | **72**
Hf
Hafnium
178.49
[Xe]$6s^2 4f^{14} 5d^2$ | **73**
Ta
Tantalum
180.9479
[Xe]$6s^2 4f^{14} 5d^3$ | **74**
W
Tungsten
183.85
[Xe]$6s^2 4f^{14} 5d^4$ | **75**
Re
Rhenium
186.207
[Xe]$6s^2 4f^{14} 5d^5$ | **76**
Os
Osmium
190.2
[Xe]$6s^2 4f^{14} 5d^6$ | **77**
Ir
Iridium
192.22
[Xe]$6s^2 4f^{14} 5d^7$ |

| 7 | **87**
Fr
Francium
(223)
[Rn]$7s^1$ | **88**
Ra
Radium
226.0254
[Rn]$7s^2$ | **103**
Lr
Lawrencium
(260)
[Rn]$7s^2 5f^{14} 6d^1$ | **104**
Rf
Rutherfordium
(261)
[Rn]$7s^2 5f^{14} 6d^2$ | **105**
Db
Dubnium
(262)
[Rn]$7s^2 5f^{14} 6d^3$ | **106**
Sg
Seaborgium
(263)
[Rn]$7s^2 5f^{14} 6d^4$ | **107**
Bh
Bohrium
(262)
[Rn]$7s^2 5f^{14} 6d^5$ | **108**
Hs
Hassium
(265)
[Rn]$7s^2 5f^{14} 6d^6$ | **109**
Mt
Meitnerium
(266)
[Rn]$7s^2 5f^{14} 6d^7$ |

57 **La** Lanthanum 138.9055 [Xe]$6s^2 5d^1$	**58** **Ce** Cerium 140.12 [Xe]$6s^2 4f^1 5d^1$	**59** **Pr** Praseodymium 140.9077 [Xe]$6s^2 4f^3$	**60** **Nd** Neodymium 144.24 [Xe]$6s^2 4f^4$	**61** **Pm** Promethium (145) [Xe]$6s^2 4f^5$	**62** **Sm** Samarium 150.36 [Xe]$6s^2 4f^6$
89 **Ac** Actinium 227.0278 [Rn]$7s^2 6d^1$	**90** **Th** Thorium 232.0381 [Rn]$7s^2 6d^2$	**91** **Pa** Protactinium 231.0359 [Rn]$7s^2 5f^2 6d^1$	**92** **U** Uranium 238.0289 [Rn]$7s^2 5f^3 6d^1$	**93** **Np** Neptunium 237.048 [Rn]$7s^2 5f^4 6d^1$	**94** **Pu** Plutonium (244) [Rn]$7s^2 5f^6$